Political and Historical Encyclopedia of Women

Translated by

Richard Dubois
Marjolin de Jaeger
Amy Jacobs
Marijke Rijsberman
Merle Shore
Jennifer Terni
Gwen Wells

With invaluable editorial assistance from Elizabeth Nishiura.

Translation Editor

Gwen Wells

POLITICAL
AND
HISTORICAL
ENCYCLOPEDIA
OF
WOMEN

Christine Fauré

EDITOR

Routledge
An Imprint of the Taylor and Francis Group
New York and London

Published in 2003 by
Routledge
An Imprint of the Taylor and Francis Group
29 West 35th Street
New York, NY 10001

Published in Great Britain by
Routledge
An Imprint of the Taylor and Francis Group
11 New Fetter Lane
London EC4P 4EE

Originally published as *Encyclopédie Politique et Historique des Femmes*, edited by Christine Fauré
(Paris: Presses Universitaires de France, 1997), ISBN 2 13 048316 X.
© Presses Universitaires de France, 1997 & 1998

Published with the participation of the *Ministère français chargé de la Culture—Centre National du Livre* (French Ministry of Culture—National Book Center).

10 9 8 7 6 5 4 3 2 1

Library of Congress Cataloging-in-Publication Data

Encyclopédie politique et historique des femmes. English.
   Political and historical encyclopedia of women / edited by Christine Fauré; translated by Richard Dubois . . . [et al.].
      p. cm.
Originally published: Encyclopédie politique et historique des femmes.
Paris: Presses Universitaires de France, 1997.
   ISBN 1-57958-237-0
   1. Women in politics—Europe. 2. Women in politics—North America.
3. Women legislators—Europe. 4. Women legislators—North America. 5.
Women's rights—Europe—History. 6. Women's rights—North
America—History. I. Fauré, Christine. II. Title.
   HQ1236.5.E85E52 2003
   320'. 082—dc21

2003004538

Printed in the United States of America on acid-free paper.

dedicated to the memory of Maximilien Rubel

TABLE OF CONTENTS

ACKNOWLEDGMENTS

A number of individuals and institutions made essential contributions to this volume. For the preparation of the French edition, Christine Fauré wishes to thank the Service des Catalogues de la Salle des Imprimés at the Bibliothèque Nationale in Paris, in particular Marie-Louise Aubert, librarian, Albert Obrier, conservator, Jean-Louis Pailhès, head conservator, and Raymond-Josué Seckel, general conservator. She is also grateful to Florence Assouline, a journalist and specialist in women's issues in the Arab world, Liliane Kandel, a researcher at the Centre National de Recherche Scientifique (Centre d'Enseignement, de Documentation et de Recherche pour les Études Féministes, or CEDREF, at the Université Paris VII-Denis Diderot), and Danièle Voldman, director of research at the Centre National de Recherche Scientifique (Institut d'Histoire du Temps Présent). Additionally, she is indebted to Jochen Becker, professor of art history at the University of Utrecht, Rémi Gossez, historian, Pierre Laurens, professor of Latin literature of the Middle Ages and the Renaissance at the Sorbonne, Thomas Lennon, professor of philosophy at the University of Western Ontario, Eluggero Pii, professor of political doctrine at the University of Florence, Georges Saro, assistant professor of Italian at the Université Paris III-Sorbonne Nouvelle, and Patrick Thierry, professor of philosophy at the Institut Universitaire de Formation des Maîtres in Versailles.

The editors of the English-language edition, in turn, gratefully acknowledge the generosity and significant contributions of time, energy, and vital information from Christine Fauré, Gilbert Klajnman, and individual authors. Their help has been indispensable.

INTRODUCTION

The idea of the international work on women in politics and history has become urgent and necessary in the wake of the current redefinition of the concepts of event and action. Indeed, such a redefinition seems to be inseparable from an attempt to locate, describe, and appreciate women's part in the overall movement of transformation that has marked our Western society.

What, then, should we consider as an event? Is there any correspondence between the great events whose inaugural significance is generally recognized, and a documented mobilization of women? Can it be justly said that the subjective and expressive dimension of the actions undertaken by women, outside the sphere of institutional power, helps to enrich our understanding of events? It is such questions that the authors of the articles in this volume have endeavored to resolve, bringing to bear their convictions and experience as well as their scholarship.

Why an Encyclopedia?

The encyclopedic genre comes to the fore at moments of discovery, when the novelty of a situation, its effects undeniable in all spheres, necessitates a reassessment. Hence the idea of a "sequence of human knowledge," of "genealogy and descent" set forth in the *Encyclopédie* of Diderot and d'Alembert, which took up the concept of origin established at the start of the 16th century by way of the Greek word *encyclios*, meaning circle: the poet Joachim du Bellay referred to the encyclopedia as a "round of learning."

On this occasion, however, the novelty does not concern technical or economic knowledge, but rather the political condition of women. The control of female fertility, implemented from the 1960s throughout the industrialized world, revolutionized women's position in society, helping to extend the idea of individual responsibility to all realms of life. The political effects of this change remain incalculable. They find expression in enthusiastic assent, but also in repudiations. The latter can sometimes be marked by a violence that runs counter to the general permissiveness of our way of life, since the transformation of the political role of women is not simply a consequence of one more private moral code, but involves the global future of our society, prompting constant readjustments of our democratic practices. The transformation of women's role thus concerns the whole political class of the industrialized nations and extends well beyond the scope of the interests expressed by the scientific community. As a sign of its importance and contemporary relevance, this issue now inspires conferences on a global scale and with an ever-growing audience.

A pioneering, albeit somewhat narcissistic, notion of an intrinsically inventive feminine nature prevailed over the last two decades of the 20th century, giving rise to a knowledge limited to the study of specifics. The imperious demand for meaning, now audible from every quarter, regarding women's place within the contemporary political system necessitates a will for synthesis and the bringing into play of a multidisciplinary perspective that includes anthropology, ethnology, history, philosophy, political science, and sociology. This will for synthesis, within the confines of existing work, does not aim to offer the illusion of covering an unlimited historical continuum. "An encyclopedia is not a collection of facts," as Raymond Queneau wrote in 1956 in his introduction to the Pléiade edition of Diderot and d'Alembert's *Encyclopédie*. The multidisciplinary approach sets out to reinforce this original purpose by endowing new subjects with a political dimension. Three subject areas will permit a simultaneously historical and thematic approach to the articles:

On the Threshold of Modernity: Are Women Capable of Governing?
The Age of Revolutions
Struggles for Democracy

The Event

In France, the notion of the event is little favored by the social sciences, and has long since been abandoned not only by historians but also by sociologists. The cathartic virtues of crisis, as understood by Edgar Morin at the beginning of the 1970s, no longer have an intellectual hold. In the work of Alain Touraine especially, the notion of the event now inspires nothing beyond a consideration of how to manage the troublesome encounters between rationalization and individual and collective freedoms: sociologists' farewells to revolution have come thick and fast. In parallel to this, the event has taken on a negative connotation with the development of psychoanalysis: trauma, the event that acts as a screen to hide the deeper meanings of our existence from us, and that for our own well-being we must surmount by an active effort of memory.

In history it is well known that the French school of *Les Annales*, in the tradition of Voltaire's *Essai sur les moeurs*, set itself up in opposition to the history of battles, society gossip, royal marriages, and plots. We may recall, for example, Marc Bloch's writings on agricultural systems, in which he posited that the "elongated or irregular" shapes of fields, and the "high cut, low cut" techniques represented an almost diagnostic difference of mentality. Nonetheless, the aim was synthetic history, human history, a refusal to carve mankind up into separate functions. That goal was not achieved, and the promised reconciliation between political man and economic man did not materialize; the first issues of the journal *Les Annales* after the war could be mistaken for a general history of prices. The original outlook underwent shifts, but the search for a lasting axiomatics capable of bridging the different mentalities continued in the least suitable fields. That approach also had discernible effects upon the new area of interest known as "women's history," of which the first texts appeared in France around the period 1976–1978, in the wake of the women's liberation movements.

How then did this project of a women's history take shape, stemming as it did directly from a political movement? What intellectual and scientific trajectory did it follow? The temporary abandonment of traditional political institutions in favor of alternative modes of expression led to a revalorization of personal life. The broadening of historians' field of study, such that from now on everything that concerned the individual, and that individual's senses and intimate life, could be considered as a subject for history, coincided with increasing interest in the "private sphere." Meanwhile, these historians of private life sought to capture the intrinsically volatile nature of their material, the fragmentation of everyday attitudes, by adapting a time-tested method to their new requirements: that of the large sample, drawn this time not so much from the economic as from the cultural order, and often focused on certain modes of writing, such as polite literature or the development of the private journal. The events that, inescapably, ran through this history and were conversely characterized by an intensification of public life, acted as a foil to the much-vaunted privatization of existence, which the bourgeois 19th century had taken as its ideal.

To appeal to readers, the uncovering of the secrets of private life through family rituals and the symbolic organization of domestic space has relied on the sense of transgression that historians' indiscretion inevitably aroused. Birth, eating, work, love, childbearing, and death were the key activities around which the idea of a women's history was formed. This history, taking shape through numerous texts, found in the timelessness of these activities a justification for ignoring political events, which were held to be insignificant to the majority of women.

The authors collected in the present volume firmly resist this tendency to skirt around the revolutions and conflicts which decisively marked the democratization of Western culture: the English revolutions, the French Revolution, the American Revolution, the 18th-century upheavals in the Netherlands (the territory of present-day Belgium), the Greek war of independence, the European uprisings of 1848, the Paris Commune, the Russian Revolution, and the German revolution. Assessing women's participation in these events is a way of expressing the extent to which the political changes and the disruption those events necessarily wrought upon everyday life are part of the human condition. Why should women be excluded from this?

Nevertheless, it is not a matter of fetishizing events by regarding them as unique and exemplary, or of refusing to question their inevitable polysemy, the phenomena that crystallize around any great upheaval as if to multiply its power.

The rehabilitation of the notion of the event in the contemporary period has been hailed as an essentially trivial occurrence that has been amplified in the context of mass media and information networks. The opposition between, on the one hand, a world that gave rise to a proliferation of events and, on the other, a traditional society living in a universe of repetition owed its extraordinary success as a concept to the verbal wizardry of Claude Lévi-Strauss, who distinguished "cold societies, or societies which produce little disorder, and hot societies," or societies that are conflictual and differentiated. The step from that opposition to the belief that Western societies of the past—and even those of the present in their least developed enclaves, rural societies—can be considered examples of these so-called cold societies, was one that has often been taken, by treating such societies as belonging to the world of ritual, and by removing women from history, with its turmoil and its innovations.

The second objective fulfilled by this publication concerns the ways in which women have set about appropriating public space. The introduction, to some extent, of a diachronic and comparative approach in the study of societies has proven inadequate to counter the reduction (so frequent where the condition of women is concerned) of public life to a space located outside the home. Can activities that are often the responsibility of women in rural societies, such as doing the collective laundry around the washing-place, fetching water from the spring, and going to market, be seen as a feminine way of appropriating public space?

Investment in the public sphere is not limited to activities carried out under the general gaze, but is rather defined by the exercise of a power whose aim is to criticize, by means of collective gatherings (demonstrations, for example) and control of the political authorities. It is clear that the complacency that has characterized the description of the cultural practices performed by women, their distinctive character often emphasized by structural analysis, has been tantamount to denying them any kind of access to politics.

At a time when it is generally accepted within anthropology that there is no society in the world, however remote, that is beyond the reach of the global order or its economic effects and political developments, the refusal to integrate women into the general movement of society seems like a scientific anachronism. This refusal amounts to a recognition of only those forms of behavior that conform to the rules, be they economic, familial, or religious. The study of the definitions that still encumber the condition of the vast majority of women, according to their geographical location and their social group, is relatively straightforward, because it is based on codified material, but in the final analysis it deals only in archetypes.

The existence of any social rule implies the possibility of conflicts, exceptions, and forms of resistance, ranging from the delayed obedience common in past societies to more open or declared opposition. Established powers, notably religious and political authorities, have never been able to avoid the occasional eruption of strategies of refusal that any individual might adopt, even in the grip of extreme circumstances such as slavery. But the individual is not only the key text for an understanding of how private moralities are formed. In the context of the development of collective norms, the individual remains the main indicator of the margins within which society as a whole permits action. Why should masculine domination be more effective and durable than any other form of domination? Must we believe, with the sociologist Pierre Bourdieu, that "the cultural unconscious has no history," that in the collective mythologies of the Kabyle mountain people and the primacy of masculinity in our Western societies there is the same symbolic violence expressing itself in speech and affecting our bodies and customs? If so, the persistence of millenarian mentalities would forever haunt our unconscious and organize our lives through the institution of a triumphant phallocentrism. By exposing the great founding texts of our political tradition to the blazing light of criticism, we hope to combat this presumption that masculine domination is timeless.

The acknowledgement that women have a capacity for freedom, as an individual or collective potentiality, occurred very early on in history, in the context of controversies such as the 16th century *querelle des femmes*. Perhaps women's freedom was all too often an object of confusion and doubt, but it was at least a concern of theoreticians such as Luther, Calvin, Bodin, Hobbes, Filmer, Locke, Montesquieu, Rousseau, Fourier, Marx, Engels, and John Stuart Mill. The political importance of women's place in society is thus anything but contemporary discovery derived from current events.

Action

The actions taken by women in the political field must be studied in the context of a general chronology of events. Even if such actions appear in hindsight to be the exceptional acts of a minority, they rarely exceed the possibilities of the society considered as a whole. Exceptional women do exist, but they generally correspond to the fulfillment of one ideal of their time among others. To thus relativize the exaggeration that often characterizes the discourse of exclusion is not to deny indisputable instances of rejection, but to understand the power relations in which these marginalizations of a part of the population came to be accepted by society. In this connection it should be recognized that the expression "half the human race," used very early on in literature to champion the feminine condition, was already a weapon of war, a sort of magnification of a "generic" state of exclusion that universal male suffrage only underscored. Nevertheless, this exclusion did not affect every political situation experienced by women. It has therefore seemed advisable, so as to avoid anachronism and confusion, to question the limits of what was and was not to be tolerated, as these limits were experienced in the relations between the sexes through their various twists and turns.

Historical interpretation remains arbitrary in its selectiveness, and dependent upon the convictions of the historian. The admission of subjectivity represents real progress over the neutrality claimed by the partisans of scientific positivism. Furthermore, it allows us to envisage the possibilities of a relationship between events, based on the conceptual work of the historian and the protagonists' understanding of their own actions. That said, this volume does not aim to establish a forced coincidence between historical processes and the construction of a collective actor. The links between the causes and effects of an event and the dynamic of collective action remain problematic and aleatory. Sometimes the mobilization of women did not have the effect of uniting their hopes and strengths with political movements whose aim was the seizure of power—the Paris Commune is one example. And when women do mobilize, a means must still be found to describe those actions which appear to be disparate and ephemeral initiatives, and whose rallying power is relatively weak.

Collective action by women is constantly compared with social movements that demand the reform of the industrial world: the workers' movement, the unions, and more recently the ecological movement. However, such comparisons are inappropriate. The actions by women are above all a kind of protest: they take irregular and highly individual forms, and are atomized within society as a whole. They represent an intermediate stage between strictly individual and collective action, detached from the regular patterns of both social and economic life. At the moments of greatest intensity in women's legal integration into democratic norms—their struggles for civil rights and rights of suffrage—alliances with existing parties or even the creation of specific organizations have never lent these actions a continuity and force comparable to those carried out elsewhere by political lobbies and unions, in spite of a desire to be seen as comparable, often loudly insisted on by the women themselves.

Faced with the need to identify these actions, to rescue them from the political invisibility to which historiography has consigned them, it is vital to consider the female subject's position with regard to her own act: whether she chooses to be anonymous, whether she gives her name or status, whether or not her intervention proves successful, whether she invokes established entities, and if so, which ones. The identification of documents is a perennial difficulty in scientific work. Uncertainty over attributions often affects analysis of these revolutionary periods, at precisely the moments when the "nameless," the anonymous crowd, those whose families or talents provide them with no mark of distinction, find a voice. Moreover, when one comes to consider the condition of women the problem grows ten times worse, as anonymous texts proliferate. They represent a way of expressing oneself without marking oneself out to the community to which one belongs, an evasion, a maneuver, a strategy to foil censorship and repression, and, more recently, a desire to question the transmission of the father's or husband's name, to belong to a mass, to form a group. Depending on the period, all kinds of reasons are advanced to explain the persistent phenomenon of anonymity, which is at times complicated by the fact that some of the feminine signatures that we do have are apocryphal, and are actually disguises for men.

Nevertheless, to be capable of action is first of all to project oneself through an act performed in one's own name, through protest, complaint, denunciation, demands, petitions—a whole range of acts that invest in the public space in an exceptional way, emanating from a subject who is sometimes impelled by very distinctive feelings and who chooses the best form to express her desire for intervention. Is the act of petitioning, which falls within the operations of democratic government, comparable to a letter of public denunciation published in a newspaper? In spite of the diversity of contexts, the common denominator of these actions remains an established relationship between the speaker and her imagined audience, public opinion. The effectiveness of the message is as much a matter of its content and its internal logic as of its social significance.

In activities that strongly implicate the self, the distinctive signs of individual identity—names, signatures—take center stage, and for this reason they are ruled out by "long-range" history, which, not content with denying the primacy of the event, also, according to the philosopher Jacques Rancière's critique, rejects the primacy of "proper names," in the name both of democracy and the "scientificity" of the large sample. However, any linguistic act that offers access to the subject's inner experience becomes a historical object for anyone who claims to deal with the history of women, which is in fact a history of domination. So, if we start from those acts which entail a representation of the self, what generally appears enigmatic and hard to explain may begin to make sense: modes of behavior ranging from compliance to refusal and open conflict, located at the borders of the private and the public, in a neglected margin of social life—which is nonetheless the key to understanding its upheavals.

The subjectivization of political events is not some emotional supplement that chatters away soothingly in our imagination, like the women's words that are supposed to bring a sensitive touch to an economic and social history that no longer dare to speak its name. Rather, this subjectivization is a fundamental part of a history which, going well beyond dates and battles, extends its field of research to encompass the whole of society's political expressions, all the signs of its democratization, and the passage from one system of hierarchy to another.

It would nevertheless be reductive to envisage this pairing of event and action in terms of the protagonists' complete awareness, irrespective of whether they are dominating or dominated. There is as much unconscious motivation in the strategies of evasion political powers adopt with regard to the condition of women as there is in harsh exclusionary decisions political powers make in response to specific circumstances. The casual, even accidental nature of some acts of protest that subsequently became symbolic is not to be underestimated either, if we are to make a break with the classical dramaturgy of the relations between the sexes—that of Antigone and her tyrant.

To express the invisible nature of the limits which feminine ambition comes up against today, the emblematic metaphor of the "glass ceiling" is now much used: it cannot be seen, but it is a barrier that prevents women from rising up. The *Political and Historical Encyclopedia of Women* sets out to make visible the boundaries that limit the political condition of women.

CHRISTINE FAURÉ

ON THE THRESHOLD OF MODERNITY

Are Women Capable of Governing?

THE SALIC LAW

SARAH HANLEY

DURING THE LATER MEDIEVAL era marked by growing national consciousness and construction of a polity, or public realm (12th through 15th centuries), and through the modern period of nascent state formation (16th through 18th centuries), the governance of France was circumscribed by two successive juridical frameworks, with the earlier one excluding women from rule in the French kingdom and the later one defining governing power as a male right. As the basis for the first framework, a French Salic law ordinance (from the Salic Law Code *Pactus Legis Salicae*, sixth through ninth centuries), was retrieved in 1358, and revived and debated in the 15th century. A forged version of it was transmitted in the 1530s as a French public, or fundamental, law founding a kingdom wherein women were excluded from rule. When the forgery of the Salic law was discovered by legal scholars in the mid-16th century, that first framework collapsed. It was followed by a French law canon, which was formulated from the mid-16th century through the 1650s and then maintained through the 18th century as a body of French law (civil and public) upholding a monarchic state wherein the male right to rule, modeled on the marital regime, was sanctioned in the household (in the person of the husband) and in the state (in the person of the king). Reflection upon the history of these successive legal systems—the French Salic law, legitimating female exclusion from rule, and the later French law canon prescribing the male right to rule—allows historians to assess a cultural process that configured political identity, moving from the establishment of a right to govern a kingdom, or *chose publique* (public realm), to the emergence of a modern monarchic state.

The uneven odyssey of the alleged Salic law presents an interesting historical trajectory, given its weak reintroduction to France in 1358, its debated validity between 1400 and the 1480s, its tempered success as a printed text from the 1480s to the 1540s, and its awkward collapse during the mid-16th century, when jurists adept at the new French method of historical research (the *mos gallicus*) discovered and revealed the forgery perpetrated in the 15th century. Chroniclers, jurists, politicians, and encyclopedists have held that the ancient Salic law juridically established the exclusion of women from rule in the kingdom of France. The case is quite the contrary. At the time of the earliest writing of the Salic law, no distinction existed between private lands and a public realm, since the latter concept did not yet exist. The Franco-Germanic Salic Law Code, civil and penal laws rendered in a Merovingian redaction, *Pactus Legis Salicae* (c. 507–511), then a Carolingian one with added titles, *Lex Salica Karolina* (802–803), did not contain an ordinance excluding women from succession to the realm in any kingdom of Europe and certainly not in the kingdom of France. As a result, when the Salic ordinance was recovered in 1358 (after a hiatus of almost five centuries) and then featured in a political debate over female exclusion from rule during the 15th century, its texts would not sustain the alleged exclusion of women. A Carolingian text of the Salic ordinance (Title 62, *De alode*, Article 6) stipulates: "De terra vero Salica nulla portio hereditatis mulieri veniat, sed ad virilem sexum tota terrae hereditas perveniat" (Indeed, concerning Salic land, no part of the inheritance may pass to a woman but all the inheritance of land passes to the virile sex). However, this ordinance was just one of the laws that regulated the inheritance of allodial lands (essentially family farms) in early centuries, and it was mediated, even contradicted, by other ordinances in *De alode*, and also by ordinances in other titles of the Salic law code. On the whole, Salic ordinances permitted women to inherit family lands, sometimes favored transmission through female lines, allowed other lands held in grant from rulers to pass (in the absence of males) to females, and made no reference either to succession in a public realm, or any European kingdom whatsoever, or to the exclusion of women and their sons from rule.

That said, the Salic laws did not extend to the whole Frankish kingdom or beyond the frontiers of Gaul. By the year 1000 they remained only in northern France and gradually meshed through usage with concurrent Roman laws and later feudal laws. During the 12th century, there emerged in northern France the *coutumiers* (customary laws) of that region, which were collected by jurists during the 13th and 14th centuries. Compiled and printed by kings in 1454, 1494, and 1509, customary laws were treated as "French common laws" that transcended regional differences and were cited in legal decisions. Redacted in the *Coutume de Paris* (1510, revised 1580), the *coutumiers* elicited learned commentaries over the next two centuries. Once again, in these later centuries beholden to French customary laws and some feudal laws, women inherited all types of lands, including duchies, fiefs, and apanages, and some women who did not directly inherit passed inheritance rights to successors (as was the case in the Paris region). As a result, when advocates of Salic law revived the ancient Salic ordinance and attempted in the 15th century to transform it from a particular law of the Salian Franks (treating family inheritance) into a national public law of the French kingdom (regulating succession to the royal domain), they met with contextual and textual obstacles that inspired a long debate. The routes taken in the protracted political debate over female exclusion throughout the 15th century and into 16th raise an important historical question: how can we account for the way the text of the Salic ordinance (*De alode*, Article 6), which did not exclude women from succession to the crown, was repeatedly interpolated, manipulated, and forged, in order to invent fraudulent juridical and constitutional grounds for female exclusion from rule in France?

In the 15th century, political debate over the possibility of female rule featured three groups: advocates of the Salic law, proponents of French custom, and an exponent of historical precedent. At least four writers were responsible for the recovery and fraudulent rendition of the Salic law, which was treated as a fundamental law of the French kingdom validating the strict exclusion of women from rule: Richard Lescot in the 1350s, Jean de Montreuil in the early 15th century, Jean Juvénal des Ursins (II) in the 1430s and 1440s, and an anonymous author in the 1460s. At least two jurists—Jean de Terrerouge around the 1420s and Noël de Fribois in the 1450s—proposed an alternative, "biological" reading of a French custom, which was considered a fundamental law, in order to exclude women from power. For these jurists, male right and female exclusion were grounded in a law of nature that was independent of Salic law. Along with kings in office at the time, one opposition writer—Christine de Pisan in 1405—acknowledged no law or custom strictly excluding women from rule and marshaled historical precedents to support the legitimacy of women called to rule (as exemplified by female rulers throughout history). Despite high hopes, Salic law advocates found no juridical support for female exclusion from succession in the text of *De alode*, Article 6, and the shock of that failure led some authors down the road of subterfuge, forgery, and fraud.

The Salic Law and Juridical Precedents, 1350–1430: Richard Lescot and Jean de Montreuil

Having discovered a Carolingian version of the Salic law in the archives of his abbey of Saint-Denis, the historiographer and monk Richard Lescot (1329–58) was the first author to engage in subterfuge. He composed a Latin tract, *Genealogia Aliquorum Regum Francie* (1358; Genealogy of the Kings of France), that established a link between succession by male lineage to the throne of France and the Salic law. Lescot appended to his genealogy of French kings a short commentary that names and identifies a Salic law promulgated by the first King Clovis and the emperors Charlemagne and Louis, a law that thus far had been only the subject of a few rumors. However, he did not

provide readers with a text of the law in question. That subterfuge gave rise to the misleading impression that the record of male rule observed in his genealogy resulted from subscription to an ancient Salic law deemed a fundamental law of the kingdom. This pattern—in which an author designates his own treatise (rather than the text of the Salic law) as the primary source legitimating the exclusion of women from rule—continued throughout the 15th century. In the meantime, however, Lescot's tract was either unknown or ignored for the rest of the century in which he wrote it, even though some authors were attempting to legitimate an uneasy political past.

In 1317 an Assembly of Notables had approved the direct exclusion of a Capetian royal daughter, Jeanne de France, the sole surviving descendant of Louis X. She was pressured into renouncing her succession rights in favor of her uncles, who became Philippe V (Philippe le Long) and Charles IV. In 1328 an Assembly of Notables had approved the strict exclusion of another Capetian royal daughter, Isabelle de France, who became queen consort of England upon her marriage to Edward II in 1308. Isabelle was the only living descendant of Philippe IV and sister of the deceased Charles IV, when her young son, Edward III, who became king of England in 1327, was denied in favor of a male cousin, Philippe VI de Valois (1294–1350). At the time, however, the notables offered no grounds in law, or even in reason, for such momentous decisions. When it was necessary later to validate those political decisions—especially after Charles de Navarre (son of Jeanne) asserted his right to the throne in 1349, a claim he did not renounce until 1350—retroactive justifications were advanced. From around 1340 onward, various advocates of strict female exclusion, including Pope Benedict XII (1340) and the Italian jurist Baldus de Ubaldis (1377), had invoked as grounds the vague notion of a custom supposedly excluding women and their sons. In the 1350s Lescot invoked a Salic law against the claim of Charles de Navarre but failed to attract attention. During royal sessions held in the Parlement of Paris, kings promulgated ordinances in 1375, 1392, and 1407 that regulated succession to the throne: the crown was transmitted from the father-king to the eldest son-dauphin, regardless of age. The ordinance of 26 December 1407 designated that system of male succession somewhat obliquely as a "right of nature," but none of the ordinances cited either a French custom or a Salic law that excluded royal daughters and their sons from succession to the crown. The royal ordinances thus indicate that in official circles the Salic law had no standing toward the end of the 14th and beginning of the 15th century, and that the succession of royal daughters, or sons through them, remained a possibility in the absence of royal sons. Not so thereafter. In some quarters by the early 15th century, definitive juridical validation was sought for female exclusion at almost any cost.

The prelate, politician, diplomat, secretary of finance for Charles VI, provost of Lille, and humanist writer, Jean de Montreuil (d. 1418), was determined to give female political exclusion more than the status of custom, which was susceptible to change over time. Rather, he intended to give the principle historical and juridical origins issued by alleging an ancient Salic law; in this way, the principle of female exclusion could be deemed a founding law of the French kingdom. While sporadic anti-English propaganda may have contributed to his stance against the succession of women, Montreuil actually was provoked to make his case by an unusual challenge to female exclusion that arose within royal circles. In fact, Montreuil resurrected the Salic ordinance, along with rote pronouncements defaming women, in a frantic attempt to refute the powerful arguments made by Christine de Pisan, who condemned the alliance underway between the moral defamation of women and female political exclusion and sought to legitimize rule by women. In his treatise *A Toute la chevalerie* (1409–13; The Complete Chivalry), Montreuil claims to have read a copy of the Salic ordinance excluding women. However, the Latin fragment he cites from the ordinance in question contains an interpolation not found in the original text: the crucial phrase "in the realm": "Mulier vero *in regno* nullum habeat portionem"(Indeed no part *in the realm* may pass to a woman). Moreover, he insists without any proof that Charlemagne also excluded the sons of excluded women. As falsified by this interpolation and commentary, this Salic ordinance permitted the exclusion of women and their sons from succession to the throne of France, and hence from the power to rule in the kingdom. Almost immediately, however, the author undermined the accomplishments of his forgery. In all the three versions of his *Traité contre les Anglais* (1413, 1415, 1416; Treatise against the English), Montreuil replaces this forged fragment with a Latin extract from the Salic ordinance. Although missing the first clause, the rest of that extract, which makes no reference to "the realm," is correct: "Nulla portio hereditatis mulieri veniat sed ad virilem sexum tota terra perveniat" (No part of the inheritance may pass to a woman but all the inheritance of land goes to the virile sex).

However, as soon as he supplied the correct version of the Salic law, Montreuil covered his textual loss (the phrase "in the realm") by attaching to the cited excerpt his own definitive legal opinion that this law "exclut et forclot femmes de tout en tout de pouvoir succeder à la couronne de France" (excludes and prevents women from any and all power to succeed to the crown of France). That is, he chose to maintain the substance of the falsification he had just corrected. As Richard Lescot had done, Jean de Montreuil employed the authorial technique of citing his own treatises, not the text of a Salic ordinance, as the primary source for establishing the Salic law as a fundamental law of the French kingdom. Nevertheless, once the correct text had been reproduced, it became obvious that the Salic law, related to family inheritance of land, did not prohibit women from monarchic rule in any realm and certainly not in the kingdom of France. Here Montreuil made important choices: to privilege forgery over philological integrity and his own legal opinion over the text of the Salic ordinance. Others after him would do the same.

How are we to explain this behavior on the part of intelligent men active in public affairs? Given the serious legal doubts introduced by textual evidence in hand, what sustained their unequivocal certainty that women were legally excluded from rule in the French kingdom? This query invites careful investigation into the decisive stance taken on female political exclusion by eminent figures in political circles who inspired national consciousness and defined political identity in the public realm, or body politic. It may be argued that juridical reasoning did not lead to the opinions that females were to be excluded; rather, the sources in vogue were authoritative moral ones. The case can be made that writers, jurists, and politicians who advocated either a French custom or a Salic law to justify the exclusion of women from rule were indebted primarily to the weighty moral dicta of the ubiquitous discourse positing female inferiority, which readily supported the case against women rulers, whereas weak juridical reasoning constantly undermined that case. Defamatory pronouncements alleging female inferiority in body and mind, which were familiar in medieval culture and became more intense in the 14th and 15th centuries, removed women (as generic Woman) from the mainstream of humanity. The moral intent of these claims—denying full human capacity and individual identity to women by relegating them to the generic, ostensibly inferior category of Woman— appeared in key cultural venues: clerical, theological, literary, philosophical, and juridical.

Early on the literary phenomenon called humanism, which resuscitated Greek and Roman writings, including works of Aristotle and Ovid, stimulated the defamatory impulse and crowned the discourse of female inferiority with the imprimatur of the ancient world. Aristotelian metaphysical-biological views of woman as defective man, passive in reproduction (because of her lack of seed), and inferior in body and mind (*The Generation of Animals*, II.3, IV.5), were appropriated, reshaped, and recited by theologians framing morality and by jurists framing a polity. Ovid's literary lessons, moral views reducing inferior woman to animal prey stalked and captured by men (*The Art of Love*, I), were adopted and recited in an almost litanic manner in other influential works. Such intellectual conceits attracted medieval writers who promoted binary views of human capacity: male *or* female, mind *or* matter, genius *or* nature. Among the more notable of these writers was Jean de Meun, whose continuation of the *Roman de la Rose* (1275–80; The Romance of the Rose), a work slandering women, was popular for centuries. Two other important authors were Matheolus, who was influenced by Jean de Meun and addressed prominent politicians and jurists in his *Lamentations* (Latin 1298; French translation, Jehan Le Fèvre, 1370); and Jean de Montreuil, who publicly defended Jean de Meun. Humanist moral pronouncements on female inferiority augmented the terms of the discourse defaming women precisely at the time a French custom was deployed and forgeries of the Salic law were being fabricated to legitimize the exclusion of women, as women, from rule in the kingdom. As a fount of knowledge about women, the repetitively intoned defamatory discourse—erudite and wise, vulgar and sometimes deranged— constituted a powerful moral force in medieval culture but did not completely evade criticism.

Human Nature and Historical Precedent (1400–1440): Christine de Pisan

Daughter of a royal official, widow of a notary and secretary of Charles VI, mother of a son and daughter, and a prolific writer, Christine de Pisan (c. 1364–c. 1431) was present at the courts of Charles V and Charles VI and was still writing during the early reign of Charles VII. An active author from 1390, she was at home in the royal entourage, the law courts, archives, and libraries; she understood the moral intent and the political implications of female defamation and attempted to open a debate on the problem. Just a few years before Jean de Montreuil produced the forged Salic law fragment excluding women from rule, Christine de Pisan wrote and disseminated in political circles her treatise written in French, *Le livre de la cité des dames* (1405; *The Book of the City of Ladies*), which recorded examples of female rulers throughout history and proved the legitimacy of their reigns. In this political treatise, which recognizes no custom or law—certainly no Salic law—excluding women from public affairs, Christine attacks the monstrous alliance through which the defamation of women was connected to their exclusion from governance. She denounces the defamatory impulse articulated by ancient and medieval writers, while defending the intellectual capacity of women and their right to govern. The malicious slander of women as a category and the trumpeting of female inferiority are unworthy of learned and honorable men: "Like a gushing fountain, a series of authorities," "philosophers, poets, moralists," appear to speak "from one and the same mouth," concurring "that the behavior of women is inclined to and full of every vice"; in effect, such denigrate and demean women whose perfections are in fact legion (I.1, I.2). Women should know, she warns, that the worst attacks against them are caused by sex-based jealousy born of male imperfections. For example, Aristotle's malice toward women was motivated by his physical deformities and unattractiveness (I.14, I.2, I.9, I.8). Similarly, Ovid's promiscuity and consequent castration spurred his anger toward women (I.9, II.54, III.19). If learned men—such as the famous writer Jean de Meun, purveyor of "badly colored lies" (I.2); the mediocre writer Matheolus, "an impotent old man filled with desire"(I.1, I.8, I.2, II.19); and a contemporary writer, Jean de Montreuil, who praised Jean de Meun's slanderous work (I.8, I.9, I.10, II.54)—really sought truth, they would distinguish fact from fiction and commend the admirable "natural behavior and character of women." Instead, they maliciously turn "the entire feminine sex" into "monstrosities in nature" (I.1). Challenging the prevailing moral opinion, Christine de Pisan criticizes the defamers. She unmasks the male writers who cast themselves as "authorities" on woman and nature as purveyors of falsehoods, men who lack critical faculties, authors whose supposed expertise issues not from intellectual strength of mind but from individual sexual weakness of body, and hence mind. That condemnation sets the tone for her discussion of women and politics.

Christine de Pisan supports her defense of the right of women to govern by turning to history. She refuses the reduction of individual women to generic Woman and offers historical evidence of women active in politics, past and present, named and placed in legend and life. She denies sex-based distinctions in the human capacity for learning and governing and declares that "a woman with a mind is fit for all tasks" when properly educated. She highlights compelling examples of women abroad and at home who have demonstrated a "natural disposition for politics and government" (I.11). As legend teaches, women rulers such as Semiramis, queen of the Assyrians (I.15, I.2), and Dido, founder of Carthage (I.46, I.3, II.54), have built, ruled, and defended empires and cities with political astuteness, military might, and spiritual merit. History shows that queens, including Frédégunde, Clothilde, Jeanne, Blanche, and the contemporary Isabelle of Bavaria (I.13, I.23, II.35, II.68), have served admirably as consorts, rulers, and regents in the kingdom. And noble women in France, wives and widows, have governed vast principalities—for example, the late duchesse d'Anjou, who

quelled a revolt against her rule in Provence (I.13), and the "good and wise ruler" Anne de Bourbon, then comtesse de La Marche (I.13). From such examples, Christine de Pisan draws a formidable conclusion: women are capable of attaining knowledge of the art of governance, and they have ruled, do rule, and may rule in empires, cities, and states. On the heels of this aggressive argument, she calls for an end to the vicious slander against women uncritically intoned by men over centuries. She indicts as "public defamers" philosophers and writers who lie, such as Aristotle, who holds that nature created woman imperfect, man perfect; and Ovid, who reduces women to the rank of animals to be captured. She also indicts nobles, knights, and clerics who slander women, such as Jean de Meun, Matheolus, and, by association, Jean de Montreuil: "From now on let them keep their mouths shut," she declares (I.38). Christine de Pisan thus challenges the union she observes between morality and politics, the first demeaning women in order to facilitate the second's exclusion of them from governance. Launched publicly in her treatises, that challenge provoked reactions from opponents.

Before she wrote *The Book of the City of Ladies*, Christine de Pisan composed a poem, *L'épistre au dieu d'Amours* (1399; Epistle to the God of Love), which accused Ovid and Jean de Meun of popularizing moral dicta against women. From 1401 to 1402, moreover, she began to move her arguments from literary quarters to public arenas, including the political circle of Queen Isabelle of Bavaria, who was regent during periods when King Charles VI was incapacitated. Circulating from 1405 among notable political elites, Christine de Pisan's *Book of the City of Ladies* and other writings publicly challenged authors who employed female defamation to justify political claims forbidding rule to women. Yet some authors either did not find the denigration of women worthy of debate, or did not wish to dilute a case made for the political exclusion of women that depended on defamation. In this milieu of juridical doubt and moral certainty, the peculiar actions of Jean de Montreuil are instructive.

Perhaps made anxious by the king's demonstrated incapacity for rule, as well as by pending discussions about delegating power to a queen regent, Montreuil responded angrily to Christine de Pisan's views, first in letters, then in treatises. From 1401 through 1404, he denounced "that woman Christine" for daring to criticize writings of the University of Paris's great teacher, Jean de Meun, and for committing the unforgivable act of taking her writings to the public. As Christine de Pisan's works moved from literary to political circles, including the entourage of Queen Isabelle, who became regent in 1408, Montreuil composed *A toute la chevalerie*. In that treatise he introduced the forged fragment of the Salic ordinance excluding women from rule and he further claimed that their sons were excluded as well. Although Montreuil replaced that forgery in the various versions of his *Traité* (1413, 1415, 1416) with a correct version of the Salic ordinance, he managed to retain the substance of the forgery by attaching in two versions (1413, 1416) his spurious legal opinion that the Salic law absolutely prevented rule by women. These actions suggest that when juridical evidence for female exclusion was put to the test and collapsed, subscription to defamatory moral pronouncements kept the false political claim afloat. Imbued with the discourse defaming women and its moral affirmation of female inferiority, Montreuil's treatises established critical transmission routes in the 15th century for fraudulent versions of a Salic ordinance purportedly excluding women (as Woman) from rule in France. Prior to that, however, he had been the object of virulent attacks by Christine de Pisan, who reproached him for defending the perverse slander found in Jean de Meun's *Roman de la Rose*, and who indicted both authors as public slanderers who "dare to defame and blame an entire sex without exception." Confronted by this heated criticism, Montreuil resorted to slander, characterizing Christine de Pisan as a courtesan. By 1404, however, he had lost this quarrel in an embarrassing denouement, and from 1405 to 1409, he resolved to counter Christine de Pisan's influential writings, particularly the arguments in *The Book of the City of Ladies,* a work he addressed in content but did not acknowledge by title or author.

Montreuil's hostile reaction to *The Book of the City of Ladies*— a hostility symptomatic of that work's popular reception—is recorded in two versions of his *Traité* (1413 and 1416), written in French for public consumption and intended to refute Christine de Pisan's arguments validating rule by women. In his treatise, he alternately ignores, derides, and contests her historical examples of women exercising the power to rule, and he makes his own case through transcendent arguments drawn from morals and the law. Defying Christine's call for public defamers of women to keep their mouths shut, he recites the rote moral injunctions confirming that women are inferior in body and mind, and hence unfit for governance. He rejects her bold redefinition of human capacity as unbiased by nature, which contradicts Aristotelian notions; her claim that women and men acquire fitness for public functions (political, judicial, military, or religious) through status and proper education; and her insistence that women may be called to exercise public functions. On the contrary, he characterizes service to the state as a uniquely male endeavor. As a last resort, he attempts to establish the foundation for female exclusion in law, first by presenting a forged version of the Salic ordinance in his *Traité* (1409, 1413), then by publishing a correct version manipulated by his own commentary to exclude women (1413, 1416). These falsified versions of the Salic ordinance represented Montreuil's last hope for defeating the powerful moral and political arguments developed by Christine de Pisan in *The Book of the City of Ladies* to justify rule by women. Reacting to her work, Montreuil ultimately depended on the moral persuasion of defamation and the juridical deceit of a forged Salic law to make his political case.

Placed in a broad cultural context marked by the important political debate over the exclusion of women from rule in the kingdom of France, Christine de Pisan's political stance cannot be cast as an antihumanist or merely moralist literary view taken by a woman against supposedly courageous humanist writers defying convention. On the contrary, her political treatise is progressive, powerful, free of perverse moral defamation, and rationally argued by a woman with two aims: to cast shame upon authors, past and present, who have defamed women; and to defeat efforts by some contemporaries to legitimate the exclusion of women from rule based on those perverse moral convictions. In this affair, Christine de Pisan was the critical political thinker, Jean de Montreuil and his cohorts the moralists. With his views unsubstantiated by Salic law, it was not juridical reasoning that sustained Montreuil's commitment to female political exclusion, it was his moral certainty, which in turn issued from his uncritical thinking about female inferiority. Other men would make

similar judgments also grounded in moral certainty, not in law. In the meantime, after his death in 1418, Montreuil's version of the Salic law, which had not been sanctioned by kings or others in official circles, was generally ignored for a couple of decades as proponents of French custom came forth.

French Customary Law and the Law of Nature, 1420–1460: Jean de Terrerouge, Jean Juvénal des Ursins, and Noël de Fribois

Taking another route, proponents of French custom offered alternative means for according female exclusion from rule the status of fundamental law. From 1418 through the 1450s, political events directed attention to a constitutional problem that the Salic ordinance, even when fabricated, did not address: must the son succeed the father to the throne of France? This question was posed when Charles VI attempted to dismiss his eldest son, the dauphin Charles (later Charles VII), from succession by a personal testament made in favor of the English king, Henry V, who was the son of the French king's daughter and the nephew of the dauphin Charles. The resulting political crises pitting Armagnacs against the English and their Burgundian allies were set in motion not by a French royal daughter, or her son, seeking succession to the crown in the absence of royal sons, but by the will of a father and incumbent king who wished to bypass his son-dauphin. In effect, that shocking act of the king, removing his own son from succession in favor of his grandson through his daughter, negated all the rationales for female exclusion: the alleged French custom and spurious Salic law on female exclusion, as well as the French royal ordinances of 1375 to 1407 that regulated male succession to the crown, from king to dauphin, when a son survived, as in this case. In a treatise written against the Burgundian rebels and titled *Contra rebelles suorum regum* (1420; Against the Rebels of the Kingdom), the lawyer Jean de Terrerouge addressed the problem. For him royal succession was not just an abstract custom observed over time in the French kingdom; it was a fundamental law instituted by the "the Three Estates and the whole civil and mystical body of the realm." That fundamental law, moreover, applied to the royal domain, which was an inalienable *chose publique* (public realm) governed by a succession of kings, not personal property that a sovereign could bequeath by testament. In this view, fundamental law mandated succession in the male line; therefore, a reigning king could not exclude a dauphin. Admittedly relying on an Aristotelian notion, Terrerouge established grounds for a French law of male succession without any reference to a Salic law.

Terrerouge adapted to politics an Aristotelian biological concept holding that man and woman, respectively, exercise superior and inferior roles in the process of human reproduction. For Aristotle, nature endows man with active reproductive seed essential to the propagation of the species but furnishes woman only with inert matter to contribute. Terrerouge begins by appropriating this Aristotelian biological concept, which in his treatise is called *naturalis causa filiationis* (natural filiation), but is better understood as natural male generation in reproduction.

Then he invents a corresponding French succession law, which he terms *successio simplex* (simple succession); this law can be understood as male political succession in the kingdom. Consequently, a perfect principle of continuity, biological and political, bound father to son, king to dauphin, whereas an imperfect principle of discontinuity left mother and son, queen and dauphin, unbound. The philosophical detour taken by Terrerouge, which was based on borrowed biological arguments, sheds light on what was meant in the royal ordinance of 1407 (which he cited) by the reference to male succession, father to son, as a "right of nature." Attributing natural biological superiority—a right of nature—to active male seed, and natural biological inferiority—a default of nature—to lack of seed, Terrerouge advanced a French public law of succession based on a male principle regulating both reproduction and succession. At this point, Salic law, which he may or may not have known, was redundant and might have disappeared, as it had after 1358 and after 1418, especially in the face of continuing doubts about the ordinance.

Crowned at Reims in 1429, Charles VII was greatly indebted to Joan of Arc, whose heroic military and political deeds were applauded immediately by Christine de Pisan in *Le Ditié de Jehanne d'Arc* (1429; The Story of Joan of Arc), a poem praising the woman who had saved France. In the same era, from around the 1430s into the 1440s, royal officials in the court of Charles VII discovered and read the ancient Salic law code, "the book of the Salic law, or law of the French," from which they transcribed the Salic ordinance in Latin and translated it into French. They decided, however, to abandon proposed scholarly work on the Salic law code. The men who read these documents and reported findings to the king must have faced the fact that neither *De alode*, Article 6, nor other ordinances in that code would sustain the juridical exclusion of women from rule in the French kingdom. Yet despite apparent doubts, another advocate of the Salic law reintroduced the ordinance into the ongoing debate over female exclusion from rule. Thenceforth, the Salic law owed its repute to a familiar combination of forces: the discourse defaming women that induced moral certainty and the juridical evidence forged to conform to that certainty.

Archbishop of Reims, historian, and jurist, Jean (II) Juvénal des Ursins (1388–1473) held the posts of *maître des requêtes* (master of petitions) and *avocat général* (general counselor) of the king in the Parlement of Paris. By 1431 he was a peer of France, and by 1445 he was the brother of the chancellor. His actions in the 1430s and 1440s attest to the anxiety induced by the inability of French jurists to legitimate female exclusion by reference to an extant text of the Salic law. His concerns cannot be explained merely by reference to the events of his times, such as the weak and sporadically voiced English claims to the French throne—rather, his exclusionary project (like those of Richard Lescot, Jean de Montreuil, and Jean de Terrerouge) reflects the broad cultural influence of the defamatory discourse, past and present, that proclaimed women inferior. Challenged and harshly criticized by Christine de Pisan as a cultural web woven by repeated lies, the moral dicta defaming women continued to influence political behavior even after her death and the departure of the English. In a treatise written in French but titled in Latin, *Audite celi que loquor* (1435; Listen to Heaven of Which

I Speak), Juvénal des Ursins begins by repeating negative moral pronouncements about women and refutations of Christine de Pisan's arguments, and he produces the falsified version of the Salic ordinance, which contains the interpolated phrase "in the realm," found earlier in the work of Jean de Montreuil. In another French treatise, *Tres crestien, tres hault, tres puissant roy* (1446; Most Christian, Most Exalted, All-Powerful King), he attempts to legitimate both the forged and the correct versions of the Salic ordinance, insisting, as had Montreuil, that the Salic law was a fundamental law that absolutely excluded women from the throne of France and that Charlemagne modified that law to exclude their sons as well. After reprinting the Salic ordinance *De alode*, Article 6, he adds his own explanation, which geographically equates the "Salic land" in the ordinance and the "kingdom of France," and which biologically equates the "virile sex" of the ordinance with male rulers in the French kingdom. Juvénal des Ursins thus continued to invoke a fraudulent Salic law despite textual and historical evidence to the contrary. That contrary evidence included both the correct and the forged copies of the Salic ordinance, available from 1413 and again in the 1430s and 1440s, which he cited; the historical arguments of Christine de Pisan, circulating from 1405, that validated female rule, which he countered; the alternative argument, silent on the Salic law, offered by Jean de Terrerouge in the 1420s, which he adapted to support the Salic law; and the kings' silence on female exclusion, as shown in royal ordinances from 1375 to 1407, and sustained long after. Like Richard Lescot and Jean de Montreuil, Jean Juvénal des Ursins adopted an authorial strategy whereby the primary source he cited was his own interpretation upholding the validity of the Salic law, not the correct text of the actual ordinance. In the face of forgery and fraud, however, these maneuvers failed to allay widespread persistent doubts.

The pressing political problem posed in the 1420s by the exclusion of a male successor resurfaced during the 1440s and 1450s when Charles VII quarreled with his son, the future Louis XI, who took part in a factional revolt, the Praguerie (1440), which was soon quelled by the king. This situation may have prompted a jurist who had experienced both crises and had read a correct extant copy of the Salic law to elaborate a new argument based on French custom. Jurist, historian, diplomat, notary, and secretary for Charles VII from 1425 to 1444, and royal councilor from 1452 to 1459, Noël de Fribois wrote a treatise entitled *Abrégé des chroniques de France* (1459; Brief Chronicles of France) in which he examined arguments in favor of the Salic law but defended a more ancient French custom already accorded the status of fundamental law. According to Fribois, it is preferable for men, rather than for women, to succeed to the kingdom; and he adds that if women do not succeed, neither do their sons. Realizing that texts from Roman law, Salic law, canon law, feudal law, or French customary law would not support the strict exclusion of women and their sons from rule, he looks for the origins of that precept. He argues that the French custom excluding women and their sons from rule, which follows "other reasons of divine and human law," originated not in an ordinance sometimes "called Salic law," but in a more ancient juridical Roman principle, the *Lex Voconia* (169 B.C.E.). Adopted under the first pagan king Pharamond (5th century), the Salian Franks turned this Roman principle of female exclusion into a custom; later, the first Christian French king, Clovis, affirmed the principle in the Salic law code and the emperor Charlemagne confirmed it. That is why, Fribois correctly notes, the French never alleged a Salic law during the 1328 debates with the English over succession. Finally, he offers new grounds to explain why that ancient French custom, founded in nature, became a French law of succession.

Fribois turns to Aristotelian biology, as Terrerouge had done, and appropriates, in effect, the idea of male biological superiority, which is given by nature and based on male reproduction in which the virile seed is transmitted from man to man, from generation to generation. Then he transposes that notion to politics: applying the same principle to French succession, he holds a king must adhere to "the nature of his own generation" and exclude from the throne all issue from "another generation or propagation"—that is, those engendered by a different source of male seed. Fribois gives his own French version of the Latin Salic ordinance, but at the end he adds words that modify its meaning: "Aucune porcion d'eritaige ne viengne . . . la femme, mais tout l'eritaige de la terre viengne au sexe virile, c'est a entendre d'omme" (No part of the inheritance may pass to a woman but all the inheritance of land goes to the virile sex, which means man). Shifting the focus of the argument, this passage emphasizes the biologically grounded male right to succeed, rather than female exclusion.

When Fribois added his own phrase to the Salic ordinance—emphasizing that the term "virile sex" "means man"—he signaled man (with seed) who propagates, in opposition to woman (lacking seed) who does not; therefore, he read into that ordinance Aristotelian notions of perfect male-to-male replication in reproduction. Furthermore, when he denied the right of succession to one born "outside of" his "own generation," he confirmed as well the natural and inviolable relationship between male-to-male continuity in reproduction and male-to-male continuity in succession to the throne. His reasoning became clear when he recalled the decision made in 1328 to deny the claim of a son to succeed through his mother. As he explained, Edward III, son of Isabelle de France and grandson of the French king Philippe IV, could not succeed to the French crown in 1328 because his progenitor, the source of his generation, was the seed of his father, Edward II, not the seed of his maternal grandfather, Philippe IV, which could not be transmitted through Edward III's mother, Isabelle. Moving beyond suggestions of Baldus, whom he cited, and insinuations found in Terrerouge's work, Fribois posited a grand structural homology between the laws of nature, which governed the body of the king, and the laws of the kingdom, which regulated the body politic of France. According to him, the exclusion of women and the succession of men were natural and irrevocable principles reflected in ancient French custom and in all law—natural, Roman, canon, and French—including Salic law, which justly recognized the privileges of the "virile sex," that is, man. Fribois believed that this structural homology provided irrefutable grounds for his main argument that French custom, as grounded in nature and observed in history, commanded male succession to rule. It allowed him, in addition, to insist that this French custom of male right, resting on foundations universally recognized and incontestable, had been transformed into a fundamental law of the kingdom.

From the 1460s through the mid-16th century, however, the Salic law was revived and figured once again in this political debate.

French Salic Law and the Fundamental Law of the Kingdom, 1460–1550: The "Grand Traité"

As king from 1461, Louis XI faced political troubles and skirmishes with the Ligue du Bien Publique (1465–68; League for the Public Good). However, those difficulties arose from the wrath of noble councilors removed from the governing circle, not from female claims to the crown or the threat of a king to exclude his male successor. Nevertheless, the exclusion of women from rule, which was the object of a crusade unconnected to specific political crises, aroused unprecedented fervor around this time. A vigorous defender of the Salic law attempted to bury once and for all the arguments of those who doubted or criticized the authority of the ordinance. This anonymous author of a treatise written in French, *Grand traité de la loy salique* (c. 1464; Great Treatise on the Salic Law), set forth a full moral, historical, and juridical rationale for adopting the Salic law as a fundamental law. Contrary to Fribois, the anonymous writer holds that neither the laws of the Holy Roman Empire nor French custom determine succession to the crown of France; rather, he argues, succession is regulated by the "French Salic law," which is a fundamental law of the kingdom, not a private law determining inheritance of particulars. In contrast to Fribois, he repeats the incorrect assertion that the Salic law had refuted English claims to the crown in 1328. As a legal guardian of the kingdom on many occasions, he concludes, the Salic law is justly held to be "la première loy des François" (the first law of the French). This author then presents a falsified replica of the Salic ordinance. He begins by citing correctly the Latin version of the ordinance *De alode*, Article 6; then he inserts into the middle of that citation his own invented passage (shown here in italics), also rendered in Latin:

> Nulla portio haereditatis de terra Salicqua mulieri veniat, *quod est interpretandum de regali dominio, quod a nullo dependet, nec alicui subiicitur ad doctrinam aliarum terrarum quae in alodio dividitur*, sed ad virile sexum tota haereditas perveniat
>
> [No part of Salic land may pass as an inheritance to a woman, *which* [Salic land] *is to be interpreted as the royal domain that is neither dependent on nor subject to anyone according to the principle covering other allodial land that is divided*, but all the inheritance goes to the virile sex.]

Produced by flagrant forgery, this "French Salic law" covered all the objections raised in this debate up to this time.

The author of the *Grand traité* triumphed over adversaries and brought this debate over female exclusion to an end by vanquishing juridical doubts, thanks to fabricated evidence, and by establishing moral certainty, thanks to female defamation. Contrary to the original text, his grossly forged ordinance excluded women from succession to the "royal domain," hence from governance of the kingdom, and privileged male succession that transmitted the crown from king to dauphin. The ordinance, as fabricated, identified "Salic land" as the "royal domain" and distinguished the royal domain from "allodial land," which was subject to different laws; and it also declared "Salic land" (or the royal domain) "inalienable," or indivisible, in contrast to allodial land, which could be subject to division. To this interpretation of Salic law, the author of the *Grand traité* adds stock defamatory assertions about the physical, intellectual, and moral inferiority of women and emphasizes the universally catastrophic consequences of female rule over the course of history. Adopting the familiar authorial pattern, he defends the Salic law as a fundamental law of the kingdom not by offering readers a proper text of the ordinance but by alleging his own interpolated and forged rendition. Known later under the title of *Loy salique, premiere loy des françois* (The Salic Law: First Law of the French), this work was influential; circulating widely in manuscript from the 1460s into the 1480s and published in five editions between 1488 and 1556, this treatise legitimating "French Salic law" reached a wide audience.

From 1476 to 1498, elaborate tableaux vivants set up for royal entries into French cities featured the theme of male succession. The tableau marking Charles VIII's coronation in 1483 depicted the mythical Pharamond, surrounded by his councilors, promulgating the Salic law; thus, all viewers, the king and the people, took in a new national history lesson featuring a founding law of the kingdom, the Salic law justly excluding women from rule. Commenting on the *Grand traité* in 1500, 1507, and 1517, jurists such as Guillaume Benedicti, Claude de Seyssel, and Jean Pyrrhus d'Angleberme insisted on the juridical and historical validity of the Salic law. Seeking to settle quarrels with emperor Charles V over national sovereignty and the integrity of the royal domain, François I convoked in the Parlement of Paris the first named *Lit de Justice* assemblies, two in 1526, another in 1537, which were officially designated as constitutional assemblies (as opposed to ordinary royal sessions held there). In speeches given by the president, Jean (II) de Selve, in the *Lit de Justice* assembly of 1527, and by the councilor Jacques Cappel, in that of 1537, the Salic law and the law of inalienability together achieved the status of fundamental laws of the kingdom. Nonetheless, this propagandizing did not prevent other jurists of the mid-16th century from discovering and publicizing the Salic law forgeries committed during the 15th century.

The Law of Male Succession and the Law of Nature, 1550–1650: Jurists, Historians, and Jean Bodin

During the middle decades of the 16th century, scholars trained in the new French method research (*mos gallicus*) gave priority to French documentary sources, in contrast to practitioners of the earlier method (*mos italicus*), who had focused on Roman antecedents. Searching in the archives for documents recording the French past, legal humanists and historians such as the eminent philologist, Jean du Tillet, bishop of Saint-Brieuc (d. 1572), found authentic Carolingian copies of the Salic law code and published scholarly editions of them. As a result, they discovered

and exposed the way the Salic ordinance had been falsified and interpolated. The efforts made by these jurists and historians to extricate the French monarchy from the trap of juridical fraud reopened the political debate concerning the validity of the Salic law. The recent and contemporary presence of women on certain thrones of Europe, however, distinguished this debate from that of the 15th century through the 1460s. Reigning in Castille from 1474, Isabella had passed her kingdom to her daughter, Joan, crowned queen of Castille in 1504. In turn, Joan had transmitted her rights to the crown in 1516 to her son, Charles I of Spain, who was soon elected emperor of the Holy Roman Empire as Charles V in 1519. In 1542 Mary Stuart came to the throne in Scotland, and in 1553 Mary Tudor reigned in England. As for Elizabeth Tudor, she came to reign without a prince consort from 1558 to 1603 and demonstrated the capacity of women to rule so well that she may have inspired Shakespeare's humorous treatment of the Salic law in his play *Henry V* (Act I, scene 2), destined for a popular audience.

Although the French scholars who exposed the Salic law as a forgery could have reevaluated the paradoxical precept of strict female exclusion at this time, they preferred to develop instead a companion precept validating the male right to govern. Jurists and historians thus defined the French kingdom as a political body that incorporated the king and the kingdom, as expressed in the political maxim, "The king is the husband of the kingdom," which was extended to include male successors, the dauphins, who were called "the natural children of the king and also children of the public realm." They also posited, as had Fribois, the existence of a French law of male succession in which male right was a law of nature long before the appearance of any problematic Salic law.

Active around 1540, Charles de Grassaille declared that the principle of excluding women from the throne, whatever its source, had been observed up to his time in France. In his view, the naturally superior aptitude of men for governance was clearly demonstrated in the French custom privileging male succession. Charles Dumoulin (d. 1566) made the same point: whatever the exact juridical origins of the Salic ordinance, the principle it posed was sanctioned by the law of nature, which required monarchies to be ruled by men (as was the case in France). A reputed scholar, François Pithou (d. 1596) published annotated editions of Salic law. Armed with those scholarly editions, jurists and historians, such as the eminent Étienne Pasquier (d. 1615), denounced the patently ridiculous etymologies of the word "Salic" invented by authors who wished to prove the Salic law was a French law applied in French lands. This was the problematic approach, in fact, of Guillaume Postel (d. 1581), who falsely claimed the word "Gallic" originally employed in the ordinance was later misread as "Salic." Refusing to recognize any political connection between a Salic law and the exclusion of women from rule in the kingdom of France, Bernard Girard Du Haillan popularized in his works that same view for a larger audience in the 1580s. Louis Charondas Le Caron (d. 1616) noted that ancient Frankish historians never mentioned a Salic law in connection with succession to the crown; he pointed out that the ordinance was falsified in past centuries and concluded that male succession to the throne in France rested on the law of nature, which alone rendered princes capable of ruling. François Hotman (d. 1590) delivered a scathing denunciation of the forged Salic ordinance and demonstrated it was a private law applicable to the allodial lands of particular persons, not a public law concerning the royal domain of France. He later grounded male succession in nature, in the fact that men are the source of generative seed—a rationale that echoed the biological view expressed in 1420 by Jean de Terrerouge, whose treatise Hotman appended to his own. Nonetheless, a flagrant contradiction was soon apparent: a political practice, rule by women, was considered legal and conformed to the law of nature in Spain, Scotland, and England but was deemed illegal and unnatural in France. The efforts that might have been made in France to resolve that contradiction were derailed by political concerns.

During the 1570s, religious wars fueled a succession crisis over an imminent change of dynasty: the last Valois ruler, Henry III, would be replaced by the first Bourbon, the future Henry IV. In reaction to this crisis, Jean Bodin (d. 1596), a political theorist conversant with comparative methods of history, defended a unique French law that extricated the principle of male succession from the reach of a defective Salic law. In *Les six livres de la République* (1576; *Six Bookes of a Commonweale*), Bodin begins by registering ambivalent thoughts about the Salic law but then elects to present in its place a law of male succession that is specifically French. Declaring the Salic law to be an inviolable fundamental law of the French kingdom (I.8), and citing the ordinance, he insists that in 1328 Phillip V had invoked it in order to exclude women and their sons from the French throne. Anticipating scholarly criticism of such disputed opinions, he then attempts to buttress his assertions. Bodin holds that even if there had been no Salic law, the more ancient Roman *Lex Voconia* would have upheld female exclusion anyway (VI.5). Setting aside both the Salic law and the Roman law, he replaces them with a French law securely anchoring male succession in dictates of nature. According to the law of nature, he affirms, the male is superior to the female; consequently, French law commands men to govern in order to maintain a stable monarchy, and it forbids women from governing in order to avoid an unstable gynecocracy (VI.5). He explains at the outset that the adherence of the French monarchy to a law of nature dictating strict male succession is expressed in a French precept adopted from time immemorial, "le roi ne meurt jamais" (the king never dies). According to this precept, he explains, the instant a king dies, "le plus proche masle de son estoc est saisi du royaume et en possession d'iceluy au paravant qu'il soit couronné" (the nearest male from his stock is seized by the kingdom, and is in possession of it before he is crowned [I.8]). Bodin actually invented this maxim that the king never dies, which encapsulates a biological notion of male continuity, from king to king, reminiscent of Terreroge in 1420 and Fribois in 1458. Bodin also drew a logical political corollary: the kingdom never dies. Embodied in a succession of kings, the French kingdom is endowed with the political power, issued from seminal force, to "seize" male successors and thus assure its own immortality. This explanation of the male right to rule was validated by royal ordinances that gave priority to nature, not to the Salic law. By his edict of December 1576, Henry III created, in effect, a special category of successors identified by their link to a common progenitor, the "princes of the blood," distinguished not only from other princes "by virtue of their degree of consanguinity" but also, implicitly, from princesses of the blood, who were not mentioned. Rejecting claims to the French throne made by the Spanish infanta Isabella, granddaughter of Henry II, a 28 June 1593 decision of the Parlement of Paris excluding the establishment of a foreign prince or princess, written by Jean Le Maistre, defined the monarch who reigns in accord with "the Salic law and other fundamental laws" as "a king and natural prince." Although covering both bases—female exclusion and male right—that definition drew attention to the most fundamental of all laws, the French law of male succession, or male right, beholden to the law of nature.

During the 17th century, jurists replaced the Salic law excluding women with the stronger law of male succession confirming male right. Bypassing the Salic law, Charles Loyseau around 1600 spoke of the French system of succession as one beholden to "law and nature" and recognized in the princes of the blood the male right to rule as denoted by the maxim, "the king never dies." Pierre Dupuy (d. 1651) ridiculed the fraudulent Salic law and its supposed relation to royal succession, arguing that French law and the law of nature conjointly commanded that rule must be exercised by men, thereby conforming to the celebrated maxim of the king's immortality. Adopted in political circles, that famous maxim signified biological and political continuity, a series of kings who embodied the French kingdom and thus guaranteed its political immortality as a kingdom that never dies. Finally, Chancellor Cardin Le Bret (d. 1655) justified the principle of female exclusion expressed by the Salic law, regardless of that principle's origins, but placed greater emphasis on the principle of male right. He rejected gynecocracy on the basis of the inferior nature of female rule, while reaffirming the virtues of monarchy as founded on the superiority of male rule exercised not only in the state but also in the family: "the law of nature having created the woman imperfect . . . has placed her under the power of the man . . . [and] . . . wishes the woman to recognize [male right] and to render obedience to her husband as to her head and to her king." By evoking male authority through a politicized marital analogy establishing husband and king as rulers in parallel units, family and state, Cardin Le Bret demonstrated the influence of the French law canon, civil laws and public laws propagated by jurists and kings from the 1530s to the 1650s, which modeled the modern monarchic state on the juridical principles of the marital regime. Toward the later 17th century, when the Salic law was nothing more than an antiquarian myth, the law of nature sustaining biological differences continued to validate male governance in family and state. Throughout the 18th century, jurists such as Robert Joseph Pothier (d. 1772) employed not the Salic law but the law of nature and familiar analogies between the political and marital regimes to defend the male right to govern in both state and family. As they specified that succession in the French monarchy must proceed from "male to male," the jurists who wrote the new constitution of 1791 stood on that foundation offered them by the law of nature; and those who adopted many of Pothier's juridical rubrics for use in the Napoleonic Civil Code of 1803 declared, in effect, that the male right to govern was founded in natural law. During the 19th century, the political imagination of some historians was captured by the law of nature on which the male right to rule rested: thus, Jules Michelet attributed the continuity of the French state and the preservation of French national identity to the tradition that had judiciously preserved male governance for so many centuries.

Bibliography

Sources

Aristotle, *The Generation of Animals*, translated by A. L. Peck, Cambridge, Massachusetts: Harvard University Press, 1943

Brisson, Barnabé, *Le code du roy Henry III, roy de France et de Pologne*, Paris: P. L'Huillier, 1610

Bodin, Jean, "Les six livres de la République," Paris, J. du Puys, 1576, as *The Six Bookes of a Commonweale*, translated by Richard Knolles, facsimile reprint of the English translation of 1606, edited with an introduction by Kenneth Douglas McRae, Cambridge, Massachusetts: Harvard University Press, 1962

Cardin Le Bret, *De la souveraineté du Roy*, Paris: J. C. Quesnel, 1630

Christine de Pisan, "Le livre de la Cité des dames," 1405, as *The Book of the City of Ladies*, translated by Earl Jeffrey Richards, New York: Persea Books, 1982

Eckhardt, Karl August, editor, *Pactus legis Salicae, Monumenta Germaniae historica: Legum sectio I: Legum nationum germanicorum*, vol. 4, Hanover: Hahn, 1962–69

Grand traité de la loy Salique (1464), in Claude de Seyssel, *La grande monarchie de France composée par Messire Claude de Seyssel, adressant au roi Françoys premier la loy salicque première loy des François*, Paris: Galiot du Pré, 1541

Guillaume de Lorris and Jean de Meun, "Le Roman de la Rose," 1236–1280, as *The Romance of the Rose*, translated by Charles Dahlberg, 3rd edition, Princeton, New Jersey: Princeton University Press, 1995

Jean de Montreuil, *A toute la chevalerie* (c. 1409–1413), in *Opera: L'oeuvre historique et polémique*, edited by Ezio Ornato, Nicole Grévy, and Gilbert Ouy, Turin, Italy: G. Giappichelli, 1975

Jean de Montreuil, *Traité contre les Anglais* (c. 1413, 1415, 1416), in *Opera: L'oeuvre historique et polémique*, edited by Ezio Ornato, Nicole Grévy, and Gilbert Ouy, Turin, Italy: G. Giappichelli, 1975

Jean Juvénal des Ursins, *Audite celi que loquor* (1436), in *Écrits Politiques de Jean Juvénal des Ursins*, edited by Peter S. Lewis, vol. 1, Paris: Librairie C. Klincksieck, 1978

Jean Juvénal des Ursins, *Tres crestien, tres hault, tres puissant roy* (1446), in *Écrits Politiques de Jean Juvénal des Ursins*, edited by Peter S. Lewis, vol. 2, Paris: Librairie C. Klincksieck, 1985

Lescot, Richard, *Genealogia aliquorum regum Francie per quam apparet quantum attinere potest regi Francie rex Navarre* (1358), in *Chronique de Richard Lescot, Religieux de Saint-Denis (1328–1344) suivie de la continuation de cette chronique (1344–1364)*, edited by Jean Lemoine, Paris: Librairie Renouard, 1896

Matheolus [Mahieu], *Les Lamentions de Matheolus*, vol.1, translated by Jehan Le Fèvre de Resson, edited by A. G. Van Hamel, Paris: Émile Bouillon, 1892

Ovid, *The Art of Love*, translated by Rolfe Humphries, Bloomington: Indiana University Press, 1957

Postel, Guillaume, *La loy salique, livret de la première humaine vérité, là où sont en brief les origines et auctoritez de la loy gallique nommée communément salicque*, Paris: Nivelle, 1552

Reference Works

Albistur, Maïté, and Daniel Armogathe, *Histoire du féminisme française du Moyen Age à nos jours*, 2 vols., Paris: Éditions des femmes, 1977

Barbey, Jean, Frédéric Bluche, and Stéphane Rials, editors, *Lois fondamentales et succession de France*, Paris: Diffusion-Université-Culture, 1984

Beaune, Colette, *Naissance de la nation France*, Paris: Gallimard, 1985–93; as *The Birth of an Ideology: Myths and Symbols of Nation in Late-Medieval France*, translated by Susan Ross Huston, Berkeley: University of California Press, 1991

Chénon, Émile, *Histoire générale du droit français public et privé des origines à 1815*, Paris: Société Anonyme du Recueil Sirey, 1926

Daly, Kathleen, and Ralph E. Giesey, "Noël de Fribois et la loi salique," *Bibliothéque de l'École des Chartes* 151 (1993)

Drew, Katherine, *The Laws of the Salian Franks*, Philadelphia: University of Pennsylvania Press, 1991

Giesey, Ralph E., "The Juristic Basis of Dynastic Right to the French Throne," *Transactions of the American Philosophical Society*, new series, vol. 51 (1961)

Hanley, Sarah, *Les droits des femmes et la loi salique*, Paris: Indigo and Cité-Femmes, 1994

Hanley, Sarah, "Engendering the State: Family Formation and State Building in Early Modern France," *French Historical Studies* 16, no. 1 (1989)

Hanley, Sarah, "Identity Politics and Rulership in France: Female Political Place and the Fraudulent Salic Law in Christine de Pisan and Jean de Montreuil," in *Changing Identities in Early Modern France*, edited by Michael Wolfe, Durham, North Carolina: Duke University Press, 1997

Hanley, Sarah, *The Lit de Justice of the Kings of France: Constitutional Ideology in Legend, Ritual, and Discourse*, Princeton, New Jersey: Princeton University Press, 1983

Hanley, Sarah, "Mapping Rulership in the French Body Politic: Political Identity, Public Law, and the King's One Body," *Historical Reflections/Reflexions Historiques* 23, no. 2 (1997)

Hanley, Sarah, "The Monarchic State in Early Modern France: Marital Regime Government and Male Right," in *Politics, Ideology and the Law in Early Modern Europe*, edited by Adrianna E. Bakos, Rochester, New York: University of Rochester Press, 1994

Hanley, Sarah, "Social Sites of Political Practice in France: Law, Civil Rights, and the Separation of Powers in Household and State Government," *American Historical Review* 102, no. 1 (1997)

Hicks, Eric, editor, *Le débat sur "Le Roman de la Rose,"* Paris: Honoré Champion, 1977

Kelley, Donald R., *Foundations of Modern Historical Scholarship: Language, Law, and History in the French Renaissance*, New York, New York: Columbia University Press, 1970

Lazard, Madeleine, *Images littéraires de la femme*, Paris: Presses Universitaires de France, 1985

Lewis, Peter S., "War Propaganda and Historiography," in *Transactions of the Royal Historical Society*, series 5, vol.15 (1965)

Olivier-Martin, François, *Histoire de la coutume de la prévôté et vicomté de Paris*, 2 vols., Paris: E. Leroux, 1922–30

Pinet, Marie-Josephe, *Christine de Pisan (1364–1430): Étude biographique et littéraire*, Paris: Honoré Champion, 1927

Potter, John, "The Development and Significance of the Salic Law of the French," *English Historical Review* 52 (1937)

Solterer, Helen, *The Master and Minerva: Disputing Women in French Medieval Culture*, Berkeley: University of California Press, 1995

Viollet, Paul, "Comment les femmes ont été exclues en France de la succession à la Couronne," *Mémoires de l'Académie des Inscriptions et Belles-Lettres* 34, no.2 (1895)

Wemple, Suzanne Fonay, *Women in Frankish Society: Marriage and the Cloister, 500–900*, Philadelphia: University of Pennsylvania Press, 1981

Wood, Charles T., *The French Apanages and the Capetian Monarchy, 1224–1328*, Cambridge, Massachusetts: Harvard University Press, 1966

FEMALE SOVEREIGNTY AND THE SUBORDINATION OF WOMEN IN THE WORKS OF MARTIN LUTHER, JEAN CALVIN, AND JEAN BODIN

CLAUDIA OPITZ

THE 16TH CENTURY IS generally seen as an era of upheaval and renewal, notably in the intellectual realm. Philosophical, theological, and scholastic traditions were rejected as the result of intensive reading and consideration of texts and ideas from antiquity. This movement produced a new image of humanity and the world. In the social realm, too, the 16th century represented a clear break with the past: the Reformation shattered the notion of the unity of the Christian West that had previously dominated. The premodern state established new political structures and new ways of exercising power.

Did this general upheaval include a transformation of the relationship between the sexes? In 1976, the American Renaissance scholar Joan Kelly posed the question in provocative terms in her frequently quoted essay, "Did Women Have a Renaissance?" (see Kelly). She responded in the negative, although she did not dispute that during the period in question, at least with regard to love and marriage, new concepts and values were generated that diverged from medieval traditions, and that the image of women changed accordingly. New forms of dependency and constraint were reinforced by new cultural norms of femininity that, according to Kelly, drove women—especially women of the nobility—back into a position of inferiority to men, as compared to the high status of courtly ladies of the Middle Ages.

This conclusion holds true in particular in the political realm. With the emergence of impersonal bureaucratized relationships, the women of the Italian Renaissance had far fewer opportunities to exercise power than they had had in the feudal territorial states of the high and late Middle Ages. Kelly recalls, however, that the situation at court had also changed for the men of the nobility: they, too, were subjected to a loss of power, which led to a certain equality between men and women in the area of cultural life.

To be sure, no unequivocal answer can be offered to the question of the transformation of women's position in the society and culture of the Renaissance, especially if one takes into account other social strata besides the court. Focusing in particular on the lower social classes, the German historian Heide Wunder has described a long-term process of change from the high Middle Ages onward, during the course of which the feudal relationship between production and servitude was dismantled and replaced by commodity production and waged labor (see Wunder). But this process also had ambiguous consequences for the relationship between the sexes and the position of women. Wunder notes that "the emancipation of the couple in marriage and work" would undoubtedly have been inconceivable without the participation of wives. But social and cultural traditions continued to encourage and demand the subordination of women, or at least the dominance of men, so considerable tension persisted between a symbolic order and legal system based on the inequality of the sexes, on the one hand, and more egalitarian economic relations, on the other.

This diagnosis also holds true for the upper classes—the nobility and the urban patriciate—which, in the beginning of the modern era, firmly controlled access to power. Extreme tensions and contradictions in the premodern relationship between the sexes bring us back to the long-lasting European debate on the place, value, and significance of women in society and history, a debate that is known in France as the *querelle des femmes* (quarrel over the status of women). One of the major focal points in this debate was women's ability and opportunity to exercise power and occupy the throne.

The "Querelle des Femmes" and Women's Exercise of Power in the 16th Century

The *querelle des femmes* was sparked by the writings of Christine de Pisan (c. 1365–1430), the first woman of letters in France—"the first in this insufferable line of women authors" as Gustave Lanson phrased it in *Histoire de la littérature française* (1892; History of French Literature). She joined the discussion that erudite men had maintained for centuries on the subject of women, marriage, and divine Providence. In this debate, called the *querelle du "Roman de la rose"* (quarrel of *The Romance of the Rose*) and taking place around 1400–02, Christine de Pisan disputed the passages defaming women in the literary works of antiquity and the Middle Ages, such as those of Ovid and the 13th-century poet Jean de Meun, author of *Le Roman de la Rose* (*The Romance of the Rose*).

In *Le livre de la cité des dames* (1405; *The Book of the City of Ladies*), Christine de Pisan continued her critique and made it into a defense of women. She argued that women were every bit as gifted with reason as men, that they were capable of accomplishing feats of valor and good deeds, and that there were a great many "famous women" whose abilities and virtues had been praised for centuries. Princesses, queens, and, above all, women warriors, such as the legendary Amazons or Queen Semiramis, acted as defenders and protectors of her allegorical "city of ladies," which was inhabited by the Virgin Mary and her cohort of female saints.

In writing this text, Christine de Pisan's intention was not to change the social situation of the women of her time, much less to obtain the right of political speech for them. However, in her *Livre des trois vertus* (1405; *The Treasure of the City of Ladies; or, The Book of the Three Virtues*), a pedagogical text meant for women and described at the time as "a book of etiquette," she did emphasize the important political responsibilities held by princesses, ladies at the court, and women of the landowning nobility. She insisted that girls of the nobility be given a suitable education and preparation for the duties they would have to fulfill.

Writers at court, in particular, took up Christine de Pisan's arguments and claims throughout the following decades. These authors, like Boccaccio (1313–75) in his *De claris mulieribus* (1361–62, first and second edition; *Famous Women*), saw the enumeration of virtues and vices of famous women as a means to offer women and princesses a humanist education. More radically, early in the 16th century the humanist Cornelius Agrippa of Nettesheim (1486–1535) took up Christine de Pisan's ideas in favor of women in one of his early works, *De nobilitate et praecellentia foeminei sexus* (c. 1506; *Female Pre-eminence: or, The Dignity and Excellency of That Sex, above the Male*), a work that overturned the traditional gendered hierarchy of values. As Christine de Pisan had done, Agrippa casts a positive light on the story of the creation, notably on Eve, but he adds an homage to Mary, the "mother of God," and ends by giving historical examples taken from ancient myths, the Bible, and biblical his-

tory to prove that women are or could be capable of accomplishing great deeds as virtuous and meaningful as those of men. He concludes with a bitter indictment of the arbitrary power and arrogance of men and of a legal system that clearly favored them:

> That this Sex are not *incapable* of, nor were in the primitive and more innocent Ages of the World, *debarr'd* from managing the most arduous or difficult affairs, till the *tyranny* of Men usurpt the dispose of all business, and *unjust* Law, *foolish Customes*, and an *ill mode* of education, *retrencht* their liberties. For now a Woman (as if she were only the *passtime* of Mens idle hours, or a thing made meerly for *trifling* Courtiers to throw away their *non-sensical* Complements on) is from her *Cradle* kept at home; as incapable of any nobler employment, suffered only to *knit*, *spin*, or practise the little curiosities of the *Needle*. And when she arrives at riper years, is delivered to the tyranny of a *jealous-pated* Husband, or cloistered up in a Nunnery; all publick *Offices* are denied them; implead, or sue at Law in the own Names, though never so prudent, they must not; no Jurisdiction they can exercise; nor make any *Contract* that is valid without their Husbands license; and several other hard *Impositions* they have laid on them.
>
> By which unworthy, *partial* means, they are forc'd to give place to Men, and like wretched *Captives* overcome in War, submit to their *insulting Conquerors*, not out of any natural or divine reason, or necessity, but only by the prevalency of *Custome, Education, Chance*, or some tyrannical occasion: yet might Womens excellent good natures possibly perswade them calmly to undergo this *servitude*, did not the male-usurpers adde *shame* and *reproach* to their tyranny. [emphases original]

An erudite jurist and physician, Agrippa knew whereof he spoke. From the end of the 15th century, and notably with the extensive dissemination of the *Malleus maleficarum* (1491; *The Malleus Maleficarum of Heinrich Kramer and James Sprenger*), by the Dominican inquisitors Heinrich Institoris and Jacques Sprenger, there was an intense focus on combating heresy, an evil typically represented in the guise of a woman: women were deemed particularly prone to heresy, and that image began to spread, particularly into the realm of jurisprudence. The acceptance of Roman law seems in many ways also to have contributed to the degradation of women's legal status relative to the old *coutumes* (customary laws). In France, for example, legal reforms provided an opportunity for standardizing customary law but also, under the influence of humanist jurists such as André Tiraqueau and Charles Dumoulin, for erasing the egalitarian aspirations of certain customs. The legal incapacity of married women was incorporated into most of the reformed customary laws.

It was therefore hardly surprising that Agrippa's appeals found no echo among scholars and jurists. On the contrary, these groups—although doubtless in a rather joking manner—began to speculate as to "whether women were human beings." Of course, the invectives and debates were directed less against the female sex than against rival methodological schools or principles. And although the arguments invariably ended with the affirmation that women were indeed human beings, it was very rarely concluded that women could compete with men in education, training, or the dignities associated with public office. Even Erasmus of Rotterdam, prudent and critical where tradition was concerned, reveals a certain anxiety about educated women in his *Familiarium Colloquiorum Formulae* (1518; *All the Familiar Colloques of Desiderius Erasmus . . . concerning Men, Manners and Things*) when he has the learned Magdalie pronounce, at the end of her argument with an uncultivated and highly prejudiced abbot, a threat in the form of a joke that mocks women's intellectual ambitions:

> in old times Princes and Emperors were as eminent for learning as for their Governments: and after all, it is not so great a rarity as you think it. There are both in Spain and Italy not a few women that are able to vye with the men and there are the Morites in England and the Bilibald dukes and Blaureticks in Germany. So that unless you take care of yourselves it will come to pass that we shall be divinity-professors in the schools and preach in the churches and take possession of your Mitres. ("The Abbott and the Learned Woman")

Those women who were educated to the same extent as the erudite men of their era and who wished to play a public role were not considered to be the ideal product of a humanist education. Instead, they were seen as repellant.

Luther and Calvin on the Question of Female Power

The resolutely "pro-women" positions of Agrippa continued to be an exception and had very few practical consequences throughout the 16th century. We find a much more conventional image of women in the writings of those who, in the course of the following decades, determined or influenced intellectual, religious, and political developments in Europe. As part of a generally increased concern with secular life, certain reformers undertook a reassessment of marriage and sexual life, and this examination transformed the conception of ideal femininity. Henceforth, in contrast to the virginal and celibate nun, a new ideal was upheld—that of the "mother of the family" and the undoubtedly virtuous but not ascetic spouse who ran a household, brought children into the world, and educated them to the greater honor of God.

Alice Zimmerli-Witschi has interpreted this phenomenon as a "domestication" of women under Protestantism (see Zimmerli-Witschi). On the contrary, however, it seems that the idealization and fixation of women's roles as wives and mothers entailed a revalorization of their public status. In Martin Luther's reform theory, the home assumed both religious and political importance. The household consisted of the "father of the family" (*Hausvater*), his "wife, child, male and female servants, his livestock, and his food"—the essence resided in the fact of "living as a family and keeping house" through the conjugal relationship. Domestic functions were described by concepts that came from the political world, and domestic obligations were associated with public positions (*Ämter*). The "father of the family" and the "mother of the family" formed an "authority" and exercised a "government," a sovereignty over all the other members of the household. The home constituted a microcosm, in principle capable of providing for all individual needs, and in which all social functions and authoritative acts were put into practice.

The state, the *politia*, was composed of different homes and essentially had to serve to supervise the practice of domestic government and maintain the functioning of the family community. This was to be done in a manner identical to that of the "fathers of the family" and the "mothers of the family," who governed the home and who were charged with assuring its order and smooth operation. As for parents who raised their children badly, they were considered to be more harmful "than Turks or Tartars" and the authorities should "punish them physically on each occasion or exile them from the world," as Luther affirms in his foreword to *The Christian Economy* by Justus Menius (1529). In "domestic government" the wife was given a true "right of coregency." To be sure, the wife generally remained subordinate to her husband and only in exceptional cases could she run the "domestic government" in her own name. Nevertheless, in the analogy between home and state, she shared the "governmental power" over children and household staff.

These ideas and plans of Luther's have until now not been studied in terms of their bearing on the German Protestant nobility or on the political culture of the citizens of the reformed cities, although it has been established that, in Germany as in France, women were integrated into political life, at least in their role as guardians of minor children. In the homes of Protestant pastors, this kind of female "coregency" seems to have been very widespread. It may be assumed, then, that the pastor's wife, with the dynamic role she played in the economic, social, and intellectual life of her community, became an efficient model in both everyday life and public life. According to Luther's ideas, women too—whether married or single—were called upon to participate in the common vocation of believers: "[A]ll baptized women are in a spiritual sense the sisters of all baptized men. They have in common the sacrament, the Spirit, faith, and spiritual gifts and blessings, by reason of which they are more closely related in Spirit than through the outward act of sponsorship" ("The Persons Related by Consanguinity and Affinity Who Are Forbidden to Marry According to the Scriptures, Leviticus 18" [1522]). However, in numerous passages of his texts, Luther tempers this emancipating idea, an idea that had come forth from theological logic but appeared to be literally subversive. In his 1521 text "Vom Missbrauch der Messe" ("The Misuse of the Mass"), he limits women's access to the priesthood by arguing that they are endowed with inferior intellectual gifts—and by invoking Saint Paul:

> Now, however, the papists quote to us the saying of Paul (I Cor. 14 [:34]): "The women should keep silence in the church; it is not becoming for a woman to preach. A woman is not permitted to preach, but she should be subordinate and obedient." They argue from this that preaching cannot be common to all Christians because women are excluded. My answer to this is that one also does not permit the dumb to preach, or those who are otherwise handicapped or incompetent. Although everyone has the right to preach, one should not use any person for this task, nor should anyone undertake it, unless he is better fitted than the others . . . The person who wishes to preach needs to have a good voice, good eloquence, a good memory and other natural gifts; whoever does not have these should properly keep still and let somebody else speak. Thus Paul forbids women to preach in the

congregation where men are present who are skilled in speaking, so that respect and discipline may be maintained; because it is much more fitting and proper for a man to speak, a man is also more skilled at it.

Paul did not forbid this out of his own devices, but appealed to the law, which says that women are to be subject [Gen. 3:16]. From the law Paul was certain that the Spirit was not contradicting Himself by now elevating the women above the men after He had formerly subjected them to the men; but rather, being mindful of His former institution, He was arousing the men to preach, as long as there is no lack of men . . . Therefore order, discipline, and respect demand that women keep silent when men speak; but if no man were to preach, then it would be necessary for the women to preach.

In his *Tischreden* (1566; *Table Talk*), Luther describes man as the sun, compared to whom woman represents the moon and thus is the weaker, more passive, and more dependent creature; furthermore, he most particularly expresses himself—in a disdainful or negative manner—on female rationality and on the attempts made by women to be educated or appear intelligent. To conclude, this discourse allows Luther to justify his affirmation that God did not intend for women to be in the government of the church or of the state, for to this end one needs the highest reason.

> [While] they certainly don't lack words, they [women] do lack the right understanding of the thing—and yet they talk. Therefore, when they speak of public questions, it is confused and inappropriate . . . . hence it is clear that woman is made for the household, man however for public life, for the business of war and law. (*Table Talk*, S.290)

For a woman to engage in public affairs was not only a breach of order, it was almost an act of effrontery. According to Luther's ideas, women may preach and baptize only in cases of emergency, when there are no men present to do so. He envisions that if the authorities refused to accept and propagate the intellectual patrimony of the Reform, "they will have to listen to women and allow children to speak." As for the rest, for Luther, women's subordination to their husbands' power remains unlimited:

> To Women,
>   You wives, be subject to your husbands as to the Lord, as Sarah was obedient to Abraham, calling him lord, whose daughters you have become when you do good, and do not be frightened away by any fear [I Peter 3]. (*Enchiridion: Small Catechism for Common Pastors and Preachers*)

All women, as "daughters of Eve," are subject to male control, a control that can be tempered only by the requirement for love and community between spouses. This requirement runs contrary to Luther's theology, which normally emphasizes that man and woman were both created in the image of God, and which insists on the guarantee of "rebirth" through baptism, which also was equal for men and women, making every christened person a member of the church by the same right.

A "right to resistance" was no more legitimate or imaginable in domestic relations and marriage than it was with regard to political authority. In difficult cases, divorce could in theory bring relief, but Luther wanted divorce to be restricted to cases of impotence, malicious desertion, or adultery. He did not consider mere "incompatibility" between spouses a reason for divorce—and he stringently exhorted believers to forgive and remain in the marriage, despite problems, rather than to seek a divorce. Lutheran divorce law—and divorce practices in Lutheran territories have shown this clearly throughout the following centuries—did not allow for tempering the situation of unhappily married couples. Thus, in his text *Vom ehelichen Leben* (1522; The Estate of Marriage), Luther states:

> Now if one of the parties were endowed with Christian fortitude and could endure the other's ill behavior, that would doubtless be a wonderfully blessed cross and a right way to heaven . . . Here the proverb applies: "He who wants a fire must endure the smoke."

Like Luther, Jean Calvin was against celibacy and Catholicism's traditional depreciation of the "secular world," of which marriage and the home were an important part. For Calvin, religious order and secular order were closely linked. In his *Institutio Christianae religionis* (1536; *Institutes of the Christian Religion*)—which was continually revised and expanded until 1669, after his death—he presents his ideas about the forms of "twofold government," one meant to ensure eternal salvation of the "inner man," the other to establish civil justice. In his view, "Christ's spiritual Kingdom and the civil jurisdiction" were without a doubt "things completely distinct," but they were closely linked, for both of them have the same master, who is Christ: "all worldly principalities are like the figure and image of the kingdom of our Lord Jesus Christ" (*Sermons on the First Epistle to Timothy XI, Corpus Reformatorum*, vols. 81–83).

For believers, this implied that the soul's salvation was fundamentally dependent on their exemplary conduct as citizens of the state; for Calvin even more strongly than for Luther, spiritual freedom was the freedom of being obedient and submitting to worldly and religious order, an order that was good because it was just. Within such an intellectual framework, it seems there would be no place for a new definition of the role of women in either church or state. But here again, a nuanced reading of the texts, such as that undertaken by the historian Jane Dempsey Douglass, shows that Calvin, within the framework of his critique of theological tradition, thoroughly challenged traditional female submission with respect to faith, the church, and the secular world (see Douglass). His ideas were not totally unrelated to the *querelle des femmes*. Following the example of the other reformers, Calvin was not content with mere equality of the sexes with regard to the soul's salvation and the promise of divine redemption—an idea that already had a long tradition in the Catholic Church and that had never been seriously cast into doubt. His reflection on women's participation in religious life was far more systematic than that of Luther. In the course of his work, he discovered that among the early Christians, women (generally older widows) had participated as deaconesses in community life, not to mention the prophetic and apostolic roles played by biblical women such as Sarah, Rachel, Mary Magdalene, or even Mary.

Like Luther, Calvin did not use these discoveries as the basis for demands for equal or more extensive participation of women in "public" religious life. As for secular power, he believed that despite the astonishing and commendable activities of some female characters in the Old Testament, such as Ruth or Judith, there was no reason to legitimize women's power in this world. Saint Paul's words about women having to remain silent in the community weighed too heavily upon his mind—notwithstanding the reservations he expressed elsewhere concerning the Pauline writings, particularly the Epistles to the Corinthians.

Debates on Gynecocracy in England

In the texts cited above, the question of women's ability to exercise power was more a theoretical problem, used within the framework of the *querelle des femmes* in order to bring about an ethical and moral revalorization of the female sex. In contrast, in England around the middle of the 16th century, the problem was posed in an altogether concrete manner when Edward VI died prematurely in 1553 without leaving a male descendent; all his close relatives, all pretenders to the throne were female. From 1544 on, Mary and Elizabeth Tudor—the daughters of Henry VIII by his first two wives—had been legally recognized as potential heirs to the throne, because the sickly constitution of Edward was public knowledge and the country feared another quarrel over succession such as the "War of the Roses" (1450–85), in which two branches of the Plantagenet family, York and Lancaster, had claimed the throne. Since England, unlike France, had neither the law of primogeniture nor the Salic law, succession to the throne had long depended on decisions of Parliament. After the equally premature death of Mary I, the succession was entrusted to Elizabeth I, who was to become a highly esteemed and universally recognized ruler. This succession took place in a most official manner and was supported by a relatively broad political consensus. However, the origins of the two queens, both women being the issue of marriages that were subsequently annulled, their sex, and the fact that no woman before Mary I had come to the throne despite a long dynastic tradition, were all conditions likely to provoke trouble or resistance from the political and religious adversaries of the royal house and of Parliament. In the same period, the throne of Scotland was also occupied by women: the regent Marie de Guise and her daughter Mary Stuart, the future queen. This only increased the discomposure and debate among contemporary Englishmen, all the more so because religious and political factions were forming, some of them loyal to the governing princess, others extremely hostile. In fact, the vast flow of works critical of women in power in the course of the second half of the 16th century was strongly linked to the religious affiliation and the political position of their authors. The polemic against Mary Tudor and Mary Stuart was led primarily by the Protestants, because the Catholic sympathies of both queens were well known. Conversely, Elizabeth I—and with her the notion of gynecocracy in general—were attacked and slandered above all by those who represented the Catholic camp.

The respective arguments of both sides, however, were astoundingly similar. Christopher Goodman and John Knox, for example, each upheld the rather conservative argument that God had made woman submissive to man and that a woman should therefore have no authority whatsoever over men. Meanwhile, those who supported the "power of women" stated that a woman was perfectly capable of ruling over men provided that she could conduct herself in a masculine way. Generally speaking, it was argued that a governing princess was an exception to the rule

of the subordination and inferiority of women in the same way that Mary, Mother of God, was seen as an exceptional case for her sex and was elevated to a level high above women in general.

One of the first attacks against women's power in this context was the work of Thomas Becon, an English Protestant living in exile. Written in 1554, "An Humble Suplicacioun unto God for Restoring of his Holye Woorde unto the Churche of England," was directed against Mary I, who had just been crowned. Becon claimed that female power had obviously been inflicted upon England by God—against his own laws—because of the strengthening of the "Papists." Historic examples, in Becon's view, had shown that women rulers are invariably perfidious, weak, even guilty of idolatry, and thus bring misfortune upon their people.

During the same period, beginning in Calvinist Geneva, other Protestants rose up against the English sovereign and against female rulers in general. Among these voices was Anthony Gilby, whose *Admonition to England and Scotland to Call Them to Repentance*, published in Geneva in 1558, was written in the same spirit. Gilby's text was an addendum to the *Appellation of John Knox against the Unjust Sentences Pronounced by the False Bishops and the False Clergy of Scotland*. These Protestant detractors also included Christopher Goodman, with a text more clearly related to political theory, *How Superior Powers Ought to be Obeyed of Their Subjects and Wherein They May Lawfully by Gods Worde Be Disobeyed and Resisted*, also published in Geneva in 1558. Goodman's attacks on Mary I were more a denunciation of tyranny than a reproach that Mary did not belong to the appropriate sex for governing—although he, like his reform ally, judged that Mary wanted to reintroduce Catholicism to England. In Goodman's view, Mary deserved to die because she had betrayed God; and the fact that, by her reign, she had gone against God's law mandating that women were to be subjects and never hold power was merely an aggravating circumstance.

The most memorable and most virulent Protestant polemic against women holding power was Knox's *The First Blast of the Trumpet against the Monstrous Regiment of Women*, also published in 1558. Knox attacked three female regents, to whom he erroneously attributed a religious alliance at the same time: Mary Tudor, Marie de Guise, and Catherine de Médicis, the French regent. Knox was firmly convinced that a woman in charge of political government was a transgression not only of divine law but also of the laws of nature. In order to prove his point, he first invokes Aristotle and confirms that the weakest can in no case whatsoever govern the strongest. He argues that the idea applies in two ways—not only in terms of physical weakness but also, and above all, in terms of woman's intellectual weakness, since she is, by nature, not made to govern. The reformer concedes that there had been examples in the past of the exact opposite. Although these exceptions to the rule of natural law must have been due to divine will, or they would not have been possible, an overturning of natural laws still could not be deduced from them. A woman's regency or government was and remained illegitimate.

Knox also appeals to the Holy Scriptures and theological tradition to sustain his criticism: according to Genesis, Eve incarnated only the weakest, "inferior or female" image of the divine, as opposed to the "superior or male image" of Adam. This made the reprehensible but essential role of Eve in original sin both possible and obvious. The resulting subordination of Eve to

Adam made any exercise of power by a woman a rebellion against divine will. Thus, women's sovereignty was "monstrous" and must be put to an end immediately.

Many Englishmen—essentially the Protestants—shared Knox's sentiments, at least when these were applied to the government of Mary I. The situation changed, however, when Elizabeth I, known for her Protestant sympathies, came to the throne in 1558. Henceforth, even Calvin, in a letter addressed to Sir William Cecil, secretary to the queen of England (letter 3036, March 1559), explained his position on the diplomatically delicate question of government by women:

— To Sir William Cecil, Secretary to the Queen of England,

I have learned from the messenger to whom I had entrusted the task of bringing my *Commentary on Isaiah* to Her Most Serene Highness that Her Majesty did not much appreciate my gesture, annoyed as she was with me because of some writings published here. He also reported to me the essentials of your speech, in which you seemed more severe to me than your humanity would have led me to expect, especially as you knew from my letters (or rather: my letter; cf. post scriptum) how much hope I had placed in your affection for me. Even though the correctness of my cause forbids me to justify myself with an overly fussy discussion, I do not want my silence to pass for a sign of bad conscience either: so I thought I needed to explain what this is about in just a few words.

Two years ago, John Knox asked me privately what I thought of women governing. I simply answered that, insofar as it diverged from the first and original order of nature, it had to be placed with the other punishable items reserved for the defection of men, in the same way as slavery; and furthermore, that from time to time some women have received such gifts that the unique blessing that radiated from them clearly demonstrated they had been created by divine grace. With examples such as these, God either wanted to condemn the cowardice of men or he used the women to enhance his glory. I cited Olla and Deborah. I added that it was not in vain that God had Isaiah state that queens would be the foster mothers of the church, a prerogative that would not extend to private citizens, that is obvious. Finally, this was my conclusion: since mores, general consensus, and long custom have credited the idea that, by right of inheritance, kingdoms and duchies may fall to women, it did not seem to me that this should be questioned. Not only because that would be a most ill-received initiative, but because in my opinion it would be impious to overturn the states, the running of which has been regulated by divine Providence. I had no wind of the book itself and did not even know for a whole year that it had been published. Finally having been informed by some friends, I let it be known clearly enough the extent to which it displeased me to see contradictions of this kind be published. But, as the remedy would have come too late, I judged it better to bury an ill that could no longer be corrected. Ask your son-in-law what my response was when he alerted me through Bèze. Mary was still alive: therefore my allegation could not have been open to suspicion. I do not know the contents of the book, but John Knox himself would have to agree that I said nothing other than what I have told you here. As for the rest, despite the advice and the complaints of pious friends, as I had been alerted too late I did not dare debate any more for fear of inciting great turmoil. One might be offended perhaps by my forbearance, but I think I have every reason to fear that, had this thing come to judgment, through the inconsiderate action of a single man, an entire population of exiles might have been ostracized not only by this city but practically by the whole world. I am being unfairly and excessively scorned. It has astonished me all the more to see my own book rejected, as if at the first available pretext I am being blamed for the mistakes of another. If my gift displeased her, the queen could have refused it with just one word: that would have been more sincere and would have been a thousand times more pleasant for me than to be charged, in addition to the rebuff, with crimes of which I am innocent. For all that, I shall not cease to admire Her Most Serene Highness and to love and cherish you, my illustrious friend, for your peerless mind and for your other virtues, even though I have found you to be less than a good friend in this matter than I might have hoped and, heaven forbid, less inclined to bear me your good will in the future. Farewell then, most noble and respected friend. May God be with you, guide you, protect you, and bless you with his gifts. Geneva.

P.S.—Being not at all certain that my previous letter has been remitted to you, I thought it wise to have a copy made for you.

Calvin's analogy between the traditional Catholic definition of the Virgin Mary and queens as "foster mothers of the Church"—surprising, to say the least, coming from a Protestant—reveals the profoundly political or tactical character of the debates. Moreover, the idea expressed in the letter, according to which female succession to the throne would be legitimate because it rested on "divine providence," was repeated by almost all the defenders of gynecocracy. To be sure, even during the reign of Elizabeth I critics of female power, essentially for reasons of obedience to Catholicism, took up the pen to attack the queen. Still, after 1560 the storm of indignation died down. Henceforth, the defenders of female power essentially dominated; Elizabeth's political skills and her flair for staging her public appearances brought her such support that even in the middle of the 17th century, the political philosopher Thomas Hobbes commented on the "natural reign of mothers over children" and believed that female sovereignty was totally acceptable.

But what arguments did the defenders of gynecocracy invoke to counter the adversary's inventory? In contrast to the more extremist texts of the *querelle des femmes*, there was no attempt, or at least not a direct one, to refute the central thesis of woman's weakness and her subordination in the name of natural and divine laws. Most often, therefore, the writers believed that a man would always be better than a woman to assume a sovereign's functions. On the other hand, they generally upheld the legitimacy of the measures taken in England for the succession to the throne, and thus the legitimacy of the reigning English queen. Writers reminded their readers that God could allow for exceptions to the rules of the natural order, rules he himself had established. They also confirmed that the dignity of the office could compensate for the weaknesses of a woman—especially if good counselors were placed by her side. The *Mirror for Magistrates* (first edition, 1559), a collection of poetry written by several authors on the theme of reverses of fortune (making use of characters also to be found in the plays of Shakespeare and Marlowe) attested to the existence of female sovereigns such as Queen Cordelia. Some defenders of gynecocracy went well beyond the limits of theological and philosophical tradition, such as John Aylmer in *An Harborowe for Faithfull and Trewe Subjectes agaynst the Late Blowne Blaste, concerning the Government of Wemen* (1559). These writers argued that the Holy Scriptures did not constitute a basis for creating models of government, since in their accounts they most frequently incorporated only specific historical situations and facts long past!

What emerges from all these reflections is that despite the numerous women who successfully governed, struggled, and waged war in mythology and in history—examples cited most often to support a particular writer's own thesis—it was never deemed desirable to use the distinguished example of the queen who, in her office, owed no obedience even to her spouse to set a precedent on the road to a general transformation of the hierarchy between men and women. Even the most ardent supporters of gynecocracy never demanded that women in general be allowed access to public office or that the existing conjugal laws be corrected to reflect such a change.

The Position of Public Law: Jean Bodin

More terrified than convinced by the English model, the French legal adviser Jean Bodin (1529–96) formulated his thoughts on women's ability to govern and on female subordination in his *Six livres de la République* (1576; *The Six Bookes of a Commonweale*). In this voluminous and widely disseminated text, the erudite jurist appears as much as a humanist as he does an expert in the political questions of his time. His reflections center on the greatness and stability of royal power, at a time when the French monarchy found itself under growing pressure from the Calvinists and when the Saint Bartholomew's Day Massacre (24 August 1572) had seriously compromised royal authority, which was abandoning its role as arbiter.

Although linked to specific political events of his times, Bodin's *Six Bookes of a Commonweale* should be seen as the first modern constitutional theory. In systematic order, the author presents the foundations of the state and the community (book I), followed by the forms of the state (book II), the institutions (book III), the changing of laws and their control, as well as the indispensable adaptation of the state to circumstances and to missions of the moment (books IV and V), and finally the means of exercising power and the question of its guarantee and its transmission (book VI).

According to Bodin, the power of the state is legitimated by divine and natural law; its first objective should be to serve the true happiness of citizens, which resides in the knowledge of God and nature, and in the true adoration of God that results from that knowledge. The state has a hierarchic structure of which the home, "the household," is both the basic element and the model; as Luther also noted, various relationships of domination already exist in the home: domination of the master over the slaves, of the father over the children, and of the husband over his wife. The father of the family represents the members of his household when dealing with the state. On the other hand, his claims to rights and property limit and regulate the claim to power by the sovereign authority of the state (book I, chap. 2 and following), the best form of which is the monarchy—the form that most resembles the domination the father exercises over the family and is thus the most useful in terms of the requirements of the sovereign state. For its part, the sovereign state regulates the "civil order" in and among "households." Historically, as long as there were no communities, every father of a family had wielded unlimited power over those in his household, according to Bodin. Hunger for power, greed, and a thirst for vengeance had provoked the battle between clans until the chief of the conquerors became the master over all, until his allies became his subjects, and the vanquished his slaves.

While, in Bodin's view, inequality among princes, citizens, and the state is the result of an aggressive battle for power, the justification for the subordinate role or even the subordination of women and children is of an entirely different nature. In addition to the "law of nature," Bodin also invokes divine law, and with it theological tradition. The introduction of theology and the divine into the argument is particularly obvious when he justifies paternal domination:

> So the Prince (faith Seneca) hath power over his subjects, the Magistrat over privat men, the Father over his children, the Maister over his schollers, the Captaine over his souldiers, and the Lord over his slaves. But of all these the right and power to commaund, is not by nature given to any beside the Father, who is the true Image of the great and Almightie God the Father of all things. (book I, chap. 4)

The father's domination over his children is therefore not limited by any right to resistance on the part of the latter, nor by any form of outside intervention—and, in this sense, paternal domination is more "absolute" than the power of the prince over his subjects: it is rather the equivalent of the power of the master over his slaves. For Bodin, the relationship of power between husband and wife is barely less substantiated and impressive in its rigidity. Without a doubt, marriage is the basis of the home; the wife in her position as "mother of the family" plays a constituent role for the position of the father of the family, as Bodin emphasizes in chapter 2 of book I. The wife is also subordinated to the power of the husband and father of the family and owes him obedience, although the husband does not have the authority to enslave his wife: "so beseemeth it not the husband under the shadow of this power, to make a slave of his wife" (book I, chap. 3). Rather, the wife is defined as she "whom both God and mans law doth call his housefellow." Bodin is also eager to stress that "what change or varietie of lawes soever in such diversitie of Commonweals, there was never law or custome that exempted the wife from the obeysance, and not onely from the obeysance, but also from the reverence that shee oweth unto her husband" (book I, chap. 3).

In Bodin's view, the hierarchy of domestic power relations is of fundamental importance for political organization. In particular, a home or a state cannot function unless everyone obeys the will of a single master: for if there were several leaders, he posits, contradictory claims to leadership would appear, and the family would be exposed to constant disorder (book I, chap. 3).

Consequently, Bodin not only condemns any tendency toward "women's power," as he thought he was able to observe among the Spartans and at the end of the Roman Empire, but he likens "such women as take pleasure in commaunding their effeminat husbands" to people who "had rather to guide the blind, than to follow the wise and cleere sighted." In concluding these reflections on conjugal power in which "the husband is maister of his wives actions, and [is entitled] to take the profit of all the lands and goods that to her befall," he raises the ante by arguing that even agreements consecrated by an oath are invalid if they contravene the notion of women's subjection:

> I doubt not, but that women in their matrimoniall contracts have sometimes used to covenant not to be in any thing subject unto their husbands: but for as much as such covenants and agreements are contrarie to the lawes both of God and man, as also unto publick honestie, they are not to bee observed and kept, in such sort, as that no man can thereunto be bound by oath. (book I, chap. 3)

It should hardly come as a surprise, then, that Bodin shows himself to be in no way a proponent of female government in either the public realm or the state. He treats this question explicitly in chapter 5 of book VI, with the eloquent title "That a well ordered Commonweale dependeth not either of lot, either of choyce, and much lesse of women; but by discent to be derived from a most honourable stocke: and that it ought to be given but to one alone, without partition." Among other things, he emphasizes here that a "Gynecocratie" transgresses the natural order, which allots special talents, such as "wisedome, strength, courage, and power to commaund" to the male sex and not to the female. Divine law, too, opposes rule by a woman, for woman should be subordinate to man, and this situation obtains "not onely in the government of kingdomes and empires, but also in every particular mans house and familie." Inscribing himself within the same mindset as that of the English opponents to gynecocracy, Bodin reminds readers that God threatened his enemies with the terrifying curse of giving them women rulers.

If gynecocracy in his eyes transgresses positive law, and indeed international law, it threatens both the natural and divine order, and it also promises to have domestic and social effects as its logic infiltrates society as a whole.

> For it is a rule in policie, that whatsoever thing is found good, and sufferable in publike, the same is to be drawne into consequence and example in particular . . . For as the familie is out of order, where the woman commaundeth over the husband, considering that the head of the familie hath lost his dignitie to become a slave: even so a Commonweale (to speake properly) looseth the name, where a woman holdeth the soveraigntie, how wise soever shee be . . . (book VI, chap. 5)

In "the most true woman soveraigntie," in which a woman heir to the throne remains unmarried, her female weakness will expose her to the dangers of foreign appetites, and even to those of her subjects, and will become a cause for war and disorder:

> For that the people being of a great and courageous spirit, will deeme a womans government but ignominious, and not long to be endured . . . [W]hereas nothing is more daungerous unto an estate, than to have them which beare the soveraigntie contemned and derided of their subjects, of the maintenance of whose majestie, dependeth the preservation both of the lawes, and of the estate, which should bee troden under foot for the womans sake, against whome there shall never want mockings, reproaches, slaunderous libels, and so in fine rebellions and civill war . . . (book VI, chap. 5)

Although France's situation was wholly different from that of England, Bodin here reiterates the arguments of the most virulent English adversaries of gynecocracy. Nevertheless, he is unable to refrain from enumerating a large number of princesses and female regents who had governed and were still governing, thereby opening the way to a viewpoint more favorable to women.

To be sure, French jurists had long acknowledged the illegitimacy of the Salic-law based complete exclusion of women belonging to the royal household from the succession to the throne. But reasons of state, notably the fear of seeing the throne taken over by a "foreign" dynasty after the marriage of a potential heiress to the throne, caused even the most scrupulous jurists to recoil from the reestablishment of women in the order of succession (*Arrêt de la cour du Parlement de Paris contre l'établissement d'un prince ou princesse étrangère*, 28 June 1593 [Ruling of the Court of the Parlement of Paris against the Establishment of a Foreign Prince or Princes]). Bodin, in his capacity as French jurist and counselor to the king, adhered to the traditional interpretation of the Salic law all the more strongly because his ideas of the role and the position of the wife were hard to reconcile with the possibility of a female regency, and above all because of his prejudice against woman's predominance in marriage.

In addition to their presence in *The Six Bookes of a Commonweale*, Bodin's prejudices against women are especially evident in his text titled *De la démonomanie des sorciers* (1580; *On the Demon-mania of Witches*). In this voluminous treatise, which consists of four books and presents a detailed refutation of the ideas of the Low-German physician Johann Weyer on the persecution of witches, Bodin does not limit himself to inventorying the monstrous personalities of sorcerers and witches or to making his own pronouncements on the measures that authorities should be taking against them, but also delivers his vision of woman's nature. Basing his argument on the idea—already expressed in the Old Testament—that there are 50 witches for every male sorcerer, Bodin attacks the arguments that Weyer had invoked to exculpate the innumerable women accused of witchcraft: their weakness, their vulnerability to seduction, and their tendency toward melancholia. Countering these claims, Bodin argues that members of the female sex possess obvious physical strength—something that could be clearly noticed in their resistance when facing torture during a trial—and, moreover, that it is not melancholic blindness, but rather greed for pleasure and a thirst for power and vengeance that impels them to throw themselves into the arms of the devil and thereby to oppose God, his worldly order, and the authorities. In Bodin's view, women are in many ways closer to "wild animals" than men, who were endowed with reason; women are therefore not only unpredictable but also dangerous and the sources of sin. This judgment was particularly true for those who had joined the devil's sect and who, thanks to this diabolical help, could and wanted to cause harm to their neighbors—and, according to Bodin, there were 50 times more women than men in this category.

In conclusion, Bodin claims that women continuously come to reinforce the legion of the devil's partisans, and also contends that they are instrumental to Satan's entrapment of men and children. Therefore, to maintain the divine order and harmony in the home and in the family, and protect these entities from all chaos, it is necessary—and in this regard, the *Demon-mania* was very similar to Plato's *Republic*—to place women under strict male control, leaving no room for their desires and their diabolical instincts.

In fact, after the violent death of Henri III in 1589, Bodin's most extreme fears appeared to be coming true. In the struggle for the succession to the throne of Henri III, who had died without descendents, it was not only a question of blocking the influence of the Spanish, but also of preventing a woman, the Spanish infanta Isabella, from succeeding to the throne. Moreover, she was as openly declared a partisan of the Catholic cause as the unhappily famous Catherine de Médicis, accused of every evil.

While the Spanish infanta's claim to the throne was ultimately rejected, civil war could not be avoided. The function of the state—which, according to Bodin, constituted the true source of legitimacy and of the establishment and the preservation of peace—no longer existed. Although the coincidence of a woman's pretension to the throne and civil war was purely circumstantial, the two notions remained indissociable in the eyes of the next generations.

In a treaty by the counselor Cardin le Bret, one finds the same mistrust of women rulers (equated with periods of upheaval and instability), the same adherence to the benefits of the Salic law, and even the idea of subjecting female regents to a verification of their power in court, as if to limit their authority:

> France has rarely fallen into misfortunes of this kind; all the more so because under the laws of the kingdom, queens may not take part in the government of the State and have no authority whatsoever in the public arena . . . And even today (when queens have demonstrated their virtue and their merits) they may be given the regency and guardianship over their children until the oldest has reached his fourteenth year . . . But it is necessary that they have letters patent for this purpose, verified in court: for the guardianship over their children does not belong to them *jure proprio* for merely being either the wife or mother of the king. (*De la souveraineté du Roy*, 1632 [On the Sovereignty of the King])

This preventive judicial measure did not keep Marie de Médicis, mother of the minor Louis XIII, from fulfilling the role of regent of the kingdom of France for years. A few years later, Anne of Austria, who also became regent as the mother of a minor heir to the throne, the future Louis XIV, followed her in this role. It is true that in France after the long reign of Louis XIV, there were no further female regents, and that the constitution of 1791 reintroduced the Salic law, extending it even to the regency. In other European countries, however, women could sometimes accede to the throne. In vast territories such as Sweden or the empire of the Hapsburgs, for example, Queen Christina of Sweden (1644–54) and the Empress Maria-Theresa (1740–80), respectively, came to power. In their capacity as coregents or regents, and sometimes on the mere basis of their family relationships as wives of princes, widows, and mothers of the male heirs to the throne, women never played a greater role in politics than in the period between 1500 and 1800.

Bibliography

Sources

Agrippa von Nettesheim (Heinrich Cornelius), *Female Pre-eminence: or, The Dignity and Excellency of That Sex, above the Male*, translated by H.C., London: n.p., 1670

Boccaccio, Giovanni, "De claris mulieribus," 1361–1362, as *Famous Women*, edited and translated by Virginia Brown, Cambridge, Massachusetts: Harvard University Press, 2001

Bodin, Jean, "De la démonomanie des sorciers," Paris, J. du Puys, 1580, as *On the Demon-mania of Witches*, translated by Randy A. Scott, Toronto: Centre for Reformation and Renaissance Studies, 1995

Bodin, Jean, "Les six livres de la République," Paris J. du Puys, 1576, as *The Six Bookes of a Commonweale*, translated by Richard Knolles, facsimile reprint of the English translation of 1606, edited with an introduction by Kenneth Douglas McRae, Cambridge, Massachusetts: Harvard University Press, 1962

Calvin, Jean, *Institutes of the Christian Religion*, translated by Ford Lewis Battles, edited by John T. McNeill, Philadelphia, Pennsylvania: Westminster Press, 1960

Calvin, Jean, *Joannis Calvini opera quae supersunt omnia*, 59 vols., edited by Johann Wilhelm Baum, Edward Cunitz, and Edward Reuss, Brunswigae: C.A. Schwetschke et filium, 1863–1900; reprint, 59 vols., New York: Johnson Reprint, Corpus reformatorum 1964

de Pisan, Christine et al., *Le débat sur le Roman de la Rose*, translated and annotated by Eric Hicks, Paris: Champion, 1977

de Pisan, Christine "le livre de la Cité des dames," 1405, as *The Book of the City of Ladies*, translated by Earl Jeffrey Richards, New York: Persea Books, 1982

de Pisan, Christine *The Treasure of the City of Ladies; or, The Book of the Three Virtues*, translated by Sarah Lawson, London and New York: Penguin, 1985

Erasmus, Desiderius, *Familiarum colloquiorum formulae*, N.p.: Soteris, 1522; as *All the Familiar Colloques of Desiderius Erasmus . . . concerning Men, Manners and Things*, translated by N. Bailey, London: J.J. and P. Knapton, 1733

Institoris, Heinrich, and Jakob Sprenger, *The Malleus Maleficarum of Heinrich Kramer and James Sprenger*, Escondido, California: Book Tree, 2000

Luther, Martin, *Table Talk*, translated by Theodore G. Tappert, St. Louis, Missouri: Concordia, and Philadelphia, Pennsylvania: Fortress Press, 1967 (vol. 54 of Luther's *Works* below)

Luther, Martin, *Vom ehelichen Leben und andere Schriften über die Ehe*, edited by Dagmar C.G. Lorenz, Stuttgart: Reclam, 1978

Luther, Martin, *Werke: Kritische Gesamtausgabe*, 12 vols., Weimar: H. Böhlaus Nachfolger, 1906–61

Luther, Martin, *Works*, edited by Jaroslav Pelikan and Helmut T. Lehmann, 55 vols., St. Louis, Missouri: Concordia, and Philadelphia, Pennsylvania: Fortress Press, 1955–76

Reference Works

Brink, Jean R., Allison P. Coudert, and Maryanne Horowitz, editors, *The Politics of Gender in Early Modern Europe*, Kirksville, Missouri: Sixteenth Century Journal Publishers, 1989

Conti Odorisio, Ginevra, *Famiglia e stato nella "Républque" di Jean Bodin*, Turin: G. Giappichelli, 1993

Douglass, Jane Dempsey, *Women, Freedom and Calvin*, Philadelphia, Pennsylvania: Westminster Press, 1985

Ferguson, Margaret W., Maureen Quilligan, and Nancy J. Vickers, editors, *Rewriting the Renaissance: The Discourses of Sexual Difference in Early Modern Europe*, Chicago: University of Chicago Press, 1986

Fietze, Katharina, *Spiegel der Vernunft: Theorien zum Menschsein der Frau in der Anthropologie des 15. Jahrhunderts*, Paderborn: Schöningh, 1991

Hanley, Sarah, "Engendering the State: Family Formation and State Building in Early Modern France," in *French Historical Studies* 16, no. 1 (1989)

Jordan, Constance, *Renaissance Feminism: Literary Texts and Political Models*, Ithaca, New York: Cornell University Press, 1990

Jordan, Constance, "Woman's Rule in Sixteenth Century British Political Thought," *Renaissance Quarterly* 40 (1987)

Kelly, Joan, "Did Women Have a Renaissance?" in *Women, History and Theory: The Essays of Joan Kelly*, Chicago and London: University of Chicago Press, 1984

King, Margaret L., *Women of the Renaissance*, Chicago: University of Chicago Press, 1991

Koch, Elisabeth, *Maior dignitas es in sexu virili: Das Weibliche Geschlecht im Normensystem des 16. Jahrhunderts*, Frankfurt am Main: Klostermann, 1991

Maclean, Ian, *The Renaissance Notion of Woman: A Study in the Fortunes of Scholasticism and Medical Science in European Intellectual Life*, Cambridge and New York: Cambridge University Press, 1980

Portemer, Jean, "Le statut de la femme en France depuis la reformation des Coutumes jusqu'à la rédaction du Code civil," in *La Femme*, Brussels: Recueils de la Société Jean Bodin, 1962

Scalingi, Paul Louise, "The Scepter or the Distaff: The Question of Female Sovereignty 1516–1607," *The Historian* 41 (1978)

Thompson, John Lee, *John Calvin and the Daughters of Sarah*, Geneva: Librairie Droz, 1992

Vaillancourt, Pierre-Louis, "Bodin et le pouvoir politique des femmes," in *Jean Bodin: Actes du Colloque interdisciplinaire d'Angers*, 2 vols., Angers, France: Presses de l'Université d'Angers, 1985

Westphal, Siegrid, *Frau und lutherische Konfessionalisierung*, Frankfurt am Main: P. Lang, 1991

Wiesner, Merry, "Luther and Women: The Death of Two Marys," in *Discipline of Faith: Studies in Religion, Politics and Patriarchy*, edited by Jim Obelkevich, Lyndal Roper, and Raphael Samuel, London and New York: Routledge and Kegan Paul, 1987

Wunder, Heide, and Christina Vanja, editors, *Wandel der Geschlechterbeziehungen zu Beginn der Neuzeit*, Frankfurt am Main: Suhrkamp, 1991

Zimmerli-Witschi, Alice, "Frauen in der Reformationszeit," Ph.D. diss., Zurich, 1981

WOMEN'S POLITICAL AND MILITARY ACTION DURING THE FRONDE

To consider the issue of women's political and military action during the Fronde entails raising both questions of fact and problems of interpretation: it means not only revealing what this action involved, as can be seen through the events of the Fronde, but also attempting to elucidate the motives for such action and examining the various forms of political legitimization it assumed in pamphlets and manifestos, political treatises and theoretical writings, memoirs and correspondences.

The Fronde lasted five years, from spring 1648 (violent opposition of the Parlement of Paris and other courts of justice throughout the kingdom to the politics of Mazarin) until 21 October 1652 (the date of the king's return to Paris from Saint-Germain, where the royal court had taken refuge). It went on slightly longer in Guyenne (until the declaration of peace in Bordeaux on 31 July 1653). Owing to its long duration, the importance of what was at stake, and the range of its consequences in every area, the Fronde was the most serious of the internal crises that raged through France between the religious wars and the Revolution. Of course, in upheavals of such magnitude, in which civil war continues and intensifies the effects of a foreign war, women inevitably find themselves implicated, most often as victims but sometimes also as active participants in the great drama being played out.

The Fronde can be defined briefly as a movement of "officers"—what today would be called civil servants—who resisted Mazarin's absolutism and his fiscal policies brought on by the long conflict with Spain. This movement, known as the Fronde of the Parlement or First Fronde (1648–49), was soon followed by an open rebellion of the nobles against the regent queen and her minister, known as the Fronde of the Princes, or Second Fronde (1650–52). The aristocracy's strongest reproaches to Mazarin, as to his predecessor, were for having in a sense deregulated the monarchy, for having introduced, in the name of reasons of state, a despotism hitherto unknown and incompatible with the traditional freedoms of the kingdom. For convincing evidence of this, one needs only open the memoirs written by Jean François Paul de Gondi, cardinal de Retz at the end of his life (1675–77):

France has had kings for more than 1200 years; but they have not always been absolute kings to the extent that they are now. Their authority has never been regulated by written laws, as the authority of the kings of England and Aragon has been. It [French royal authority] has been tempered only by customs that have been accepted and, in a manner of speaking, deposited, first in the hands of the Estates General and later in those of the parlements.

In the context of the institutional tradition of the realm, absolutism was a new doctrine founded upon the collapse of old stabilities, notably the balance between the aristocracy's local powers and the central authority of the king; it was a governmental practice that was both irreconcilable with the French love of freedom and ruinous for the state. For Retz, who in this respect was representative of his generation, "the reversal of established laws, the annihilation of the middle ground these laws interposed between people and king, the establishment of a purely and thoroughly despotic authority," were the fundamental causes of the most serious of the "convulsions" France experienced in the 17th century.

The works known as *mazarinades*—an extremely rich corpus of more than 5,000 inflammatory pamphlets lampooning Jules Cardinal Mazarin and published during the Fronde—are a vast testimony to the resistance against the rise of absolutism. In one of these, Sandricourt, one of the most prolix of the pamphleteers, took pains to demonstrate that

Louis XI was the first to pursue this most lovable Aristocracy, ... the two last ministers of state, Richelieu and Mazarin, annihilated it, and the latter thinks only of tyranny and the absolute power of controlling everything, which means enslavement for us.

Thus, if there had been abuse of the traditional monarchy, the blame for this fell primarily on the ministers, as both memoirists and pamphleteers emphasized. In the words of Cardinal de Retz,

The first four years of the regency were as if swept away by this swift movement that Cardinal Richelieu gave to

23

the royal authority. Cardinal Mazarin, his disciple, who furthermore was born and raised in a country where the pope's authority knows no bounds, believed that this swift movement was the natural one, and this misapprehension caused the civil war. ... Within the most legitimate of monarchies, Cardinal Richelieu forged perhaps the most scandalous and most dangerous tyranny that ever subjugated a state.

Similarly, François, duc de La Rochefoucauld evoked "the ghastly image of the cardinal's domination" and "the established form of government Cardinal Richelieu had begun to destroy." Montrésor, one of the cardinal's main opponents, openly accused him of having used royal authority "in the way he considered most advantageous to his interests and most appropriate to his desires." And La Fare, who maintained the old aristocratic spirit toward the end of the century, wrote of the ministry: "That is when everyone began to adhere to the spirit of servitude."

If any significant protest against the rise of absolutism was impossible during the lifetime of Louis XIII's dreaded minister, this was no longer the case after the death of the king. The turbulence in parlementary circles and the aristocratic rebellion that soon followed were inseparable from the fact that the new sovereign was still a minor. It is well known that regimes of underage sovereigns are always periods of weakened monarchical authority, since those who hold the reins of power exercise it only in the name of a child unable to express his will by himself. Moreover, women of the upper nobility have always played an important political role in the turmoil that prevails during a monarch's minority. This trend, which had already been set during the regencies of Catherine de' Medici (1560–63) and Maria de' Medici (1610–14), would be repeated and intensified during the long and tumultuous regency of Anne of Austria (1643–51). We need only note one specific characteristic that may be explained by the succession of civil wars: the importance of the episodes of properly military action by women—the famous "Amazons of the Fronde" (to borrow the title of the book Marcel Pollitzer devoted to them), and their key role in the intrigues at court during a period when we should recall, "office" and administrative mechanisms had not yet been developed to the same extent as they would be during the personal reign of Louis XIV, when the court was limited to the immediate retinue of the king and remained the place where all decisions were made and all influences were exercised.

"Many Women Among the Men"

Can a revolution succeed without women? In any event, it was certainly not for lack of women's participation that the Fronde finally failed. All available testimonies on this subject show that women—and not just in Paris—by no means remained remote from the general passion for politics. In this regard, Tallemant des Réaux's anecdote about Madame de Montausier, the eldest daughter of Madame de Rambouillet, is as charming as it is significant. The story, set in 1651, involves Madame de Montausier's own daughter, Marie-Julie: "One day she took a little chair and placed it near the bed of Madame de Rambouillet. 'So, grandmother,' she said, 'now that I am five years old, let's talk about affairs of state.' 'It is true,' Tallemant des Réaux adds, 'that in those days people talked of nothing but the Fronde.'"

It should not be surprising, then, that women were passionate about politics at the time. The grandest ladies at court set the tone and the example. Nothing shows the importance of their role during the Fronde more clearly than the attitude of the secretary of state, Michel Le Tellier. He observed their attractions and their antipathies with scrupulous and penetrating attention, adducing motivations for their activities and watching for the least little sign they might show of change or development. The reports he sent almost daily in 1650 from Paris to Mazarin, who had left for Guyenne with the court to quell the rebellion in Bordeaux, are filled with commentaries on the inextricable tangle of their alliances and factions. "Madame de Montbazon does not like Monsieur the Coadjutor [Retz] for two reasons," he remarked in a note of 10 September,

> first, because she thinks that he is preventing her from having full power over the mind of Monsieur de Beaufort, and second, because he, along with Madame de Chevreuse, has taken sides with Madame de Guémené against her. The coadjutor hates Madame de Montbazon for the obvious reason that without her he would have greater control than he now has over the mind of Monsieur de Beaufort.

Any number of other, similar examples could be cited. The reports and dispatches sent to Mazarin throughout the Fronde by his agents in Paris—his librarian Gabriel Naudé, the lawyer Blue Silhon the abbé Foucquet, Bonneau, Ondedei, Claude Auvry, Bishop of Coutances, Father Paulin, and Father Léon, among others—were full of intimations of this sort, which affirmed, better than any other document, the importance that discerning observers attributed to the involvement of high-profile women in the everyday intrigues of the Fronde. Furthermore, it is significant that Gaston d'Orléans himself, in early summer 1651, when Anne of Austria seemed ready to give in to the advice that the duchesses d'Aiguillon and de Chevreuse had given her to have Condé arrested again, complained "loudly and in the presence of Their Majesties that the counsel of women prevailed over that of princes, who now no longer had the authority to offer their counsel for the good of the state, the preservation of which concerned them more than anyone else." It is understandable that in hindsight, in the memoirs he wrote at the end of the century, La Fare should cite, the continual meddling of women in the political intrigues as a characteristic feature of the regency of Anne of Austria. "It was," he states, "a period of license, of court intrigues, and gallantry throughout the time of this regency, for the queen herself was gallant and the women were heavily involved in the affairs of the court."

If one had needed merely to be both scheming and a duchess to meddle in politics, the phenomenon would not even have been deemed worthy of notice: for when was there ever a time when the noble ladies at court remained aloof from public affairs? What set the Fronde apart was that the passion for politics pervaded every sector of society, from 1648 on. In his memoirs, Guy Joly reports that in the beginning of the summer, while the Chambre de Saint Louis (an assembly of the Parlement with all other sovereign courts) was debating indispensable reforms, women from the common people

> gathered every Saturday at the doors of Notre-Dame Cathedral, when the queen went there to hear mass; since

these women were not able to get close enough to Her Majesty to speak with her, being prevented from doing so by the guards, they began to cry out repeatedly "To Naples, To Naples!" to indicate that, if they did not receive justice, the same thing would happen in Paris that had happened in Naples not long before . . . [at the time of the insurrection of the city under the leadership of the fisherman Masaniello (July 1647–April 1648)].

Of course, fervor for the Fronde did not stop there. Most of the accounts we have of the famous days of the barricades (26 and 27 August 1648) report massive participation of women from the lower classes. In his *Agréable récit de ce qui s'est passé aux dernières barricades de Paris* (Pleasant Account of What Happened at the Last Barricades of Paris), one of the finest burlesque lampoons of the First Fronde, Verderonne enables us to see and hear them, loud and clear, entrenched behind mountains of fruits and vegetables from where they hurled abundant abuse at the ministers:

> Behind, a multitude of fishwives,
> More hideous than any shrew,
> With hands on their loins,
> Were screaming: "By the head of onions,
> These traitors have really let us have it!
> Long live the King! Long live Broussel!
> Long live the Court of Parlement!
> And fuck the government!"
> They added other things as well
> That can only be said in prose.

One never-published *mazarinade*, entitled *Les harengères de Paris sur le retour de M. de Broussel* (The Fishwives of Paris on the Return of Monsieur de Broussel), presents the liberation of this most popular member of Parlement as a decisive victory by the women over the regent queen and her execrable minister:

> We've vanquished them,
> This queen of spades and her oddball! . . .
> We've made barricades and screamed out loud,
> Everyone will get knocked senseless, or give him
> [Broussel] back.

We can thus trust the maréchal d'Estrées's assertion that in every riot of the first Fronde "the women made as much noise as the men." Moreover, Dubuisson-Aubenay stated in his *Journal de guerres civiles* (Journal of the Civil Wars) that during the hostile demonstration when the Parlement's deputies were sent to the court on 28 February 1649, "there were many women among the men, armed with daggers and pistols."

It was during the blockade of Paris, imposed by Mazarin from January to March of 1649, that women's involvement in, and passionate curiosity about politics reached their apogee: "The only things people talked about were the affairs of state, no matter what their age or sex," the duchesse de Nemours observed in her memoirs. "The more ignorant one was, the more brazenly one made decisions." And, indeed, a number of *mazarinades* of the period, such as *La gazette des Halles* (The Gazette of Les Halles), *La gazette de la place Maubert* (The Gazette of the Place Maubert), *La Mi-Carême des harengères* (The Mid-Lent of the Fishwives), the *Plaintes d'une fruitière et d'une hareng-*

ère envoyées à la reine (Complaints of a [Woman] Fruit-Seller and a Fishwife, Sent to the Queen), the *Plaisant entretien de deux femmes de Paris* (Pleasant Conversation between Two Women of Paris), and 20 other pamphlets in the same style depicted the political discussions of lower-class women in the capital. In his famous *Lettre à Monsieur le Cardinal* (Letter to the Cardinal), a model of the parodies of the First Fronde, Laurent de Laffemas voiced his belief that the success of the Rueil conference between Parlement and the minister depended on "Perrette and Lady Alis" ratifying the concessions the deputies of Parlement made and putting up with Mazarin's return to Paris. One of these fishwives, the famous "Lady Anne," even made herself known by the role she played in 1651–52 in Condé's press team. She was quite brazen and accordingly enjoyed enormous prestige in her guild. A few years earlier in 1645, she had led a delegation of fishwives from Saint-Eustache (a parish of Les Halles) that had come to Anne of Austria to protest the nomination of a new parish priest. She was also cited as their standard-bearer in a song of 1652 on Mazarin's return from exile. She became famous for her zeal for the Fronde from the time of the blockade on, and she distinguished herself by her cries at the time of the riot of 13 March 1649 in protest of the agreement settled in Rueil between Parlement and the minister. Throughout the summer of 1651 she never left the great hall of the Palace, hurling insults and invective for days on end at Mazarin and all those she suspected of supporting him, sometimes provoking disorder and the beginnings of a riot, and even going so far as to sing dirty songs lambasting the queen in public. She became a force to be reckoned with in the streets of Paris. During the last phase of the Fronde, she was irreplaceable in the propaganda effort for the coalition of the princes in the popular districts of the capital city. Her loud voice, her insolence, her candid speech, her rough manners, her colloquial language, and her enthusiasm for the Fronde assured her an audience that no other crier of Monsieur le Prince could rival.

This type of involvement was by no means a specifically Parisian phenomenon. Women's political involvement in the Fronde was just as strong in the large provincial towns shaken by the insurrection. For example, in Bordeaux in the spring 1650, women participated in setting up the defense of the city in an atmosphere of popular celebration that recalled a joyful village fair. As Lénet recounts it,

> A man from each house was sent to work on the fortifications; even the ladies went there in crowds with small baskets to bring soil: the princess [of Condé] wanted to work there as well, to encourage others. The ducs de Bouillon and de La Rochefoucauld, who were laying out and leading the construction, treated the ladies to fruit and preserves and the men workers to wine.

The year before in Aix, while the comte d'Alais, governor of Provence, assailed the partisans of the provincial parlement in the home of President d'Oppède, "a girl of about 15 or 16 with a sword in each hand, stood all day and all night at the door of said Sieur Oppède and refused to leave no matter what anyone said to her, saying that she wanted to die for her country, which she saw as oppressed." The author of the *Relation véritable de ce qui s'est fait et passé dans la ville d'Aix-en-Provence* (True Account of What Happened in the City of Aix-en-Provence), who reported this gesture of feminine bravery, added that on that day in Aix "more than 800 women with sword in hand" had been seen. In Saintonge, too, women supported the party of the princes so actively that the king wrote to Montausier, the governor of the province, to order him to exile from Saintes the young ladies of Magezoy, Ladome, and Lossendières. Further, he was to convey to the young ladies of Saint-Seurin and Saint-André the king's displeasure with their attitude during the taking of the town by Condé's troops on 29 October 1651.

"Capable of Governing or Overthrowing" Great Kingdoms

Although women of any rank in the social hierarchy could become impassioned about the present state of politics of the Fronde and even became personally involved in supporting one of the parties struggling for power, a certain number of noble ladies distinguished themselves particularly well. When Don Luis de Haro, at the time of the Treaty of the Pyrenees, congratulated Mazarin on the relaxation he would be able to enjoy after so many storms, the cardinal responded to him by saying that a prime minister would never know any rest in France where even the women were redoubtable: "You Spaniards," he said to him, "can speak of these things in comfort. Your women concern themselves only with love-making, but the same thing does not hold true in France, and we have three of them who would be capable of governing or overthrowing three great kingdoms: the duchesse de Longueville, the Palatine princess, and the duchesse de Chevreuse."

Mazarin knew whereof he spoke: he had seen these women in action; he had been forced to outmaneuver their intrigues incessantly; and he had temporarily succumbed to those intrigues when the conjunction of the two Frondes, brought about by the Palatine princess in January 1651, forced him into exile. Here was an expert obliged to doff his hat to adversaries of his own stature, whose formidable efficiency he had been in a position to gauge on many occasions.

It was not without reason that Mazarin cited Madame de Longueville first. He constantly found her opposing him. There is no hyperbole in the title of Jeanine Delpech's 1957 biography, *L'Âme de la Fronde, Madame de Longueville* (Madame de Longueville, Soul of the Fronde).

More than any other, Madame de Longueville's example sheds light on the importance of the issue of lineage in taking political positions. Anne-Geneviève de Bourbon, sister of the princes of Condé and Conti, and herself a princess of royal blood, belonged to the family that was most closely related to the royal family itself: she was a Bourbon. It should be recalled that during the greatest part of the reign of Louis XIII the Condé princes were standing on the steps to the throne, so to speak. Until the birth of Louis XIV in 1638, it was Gaston d'Orléans, the brother of Louis XIII, who was heir apparent to the crown, and he had no sons. Thus the throne would have passed to the youngest branch of the Bourbons, that of the princes of Condé, in the case of a default by the oldest branch. This explains why the affairs of the kingdom had always been considered family affairs in the Hôtel de Condé. We should also bear in mind, however, that the house of Condé had been persecuted incessantly by kings and ministers from the time of the reign of Henri

IV. We should recall the senile assiduities of Vert-Galant toward the young Charlotte-Marguerite de Montmorency, our heroine's mother, which reduced her father, Henri de Bourbon, prince de Condé, to seeking refuge in Flanders with his young wife. We should recall the long detention of the prince during the time that Concini was in favor, until October 1619. Since Charlotte-Marguerite had obtained permission to share her husband's fate, it was in the dungeon of Vincennes that their daughter, the future Madame de Longueville, was born on 29 August 1619. We should also recall the execution in 1627, under Richelieu, of the princess's cousin, François de Montmorency-Bouteville (whose two orphaned daughters were raised with Anne-Geneviève in the Hôtel de Condé). Then there was the execution of the princess's own brother, the duc de Montmorency, with whom this illustrious lineage died out when he mounted the scaffold in 1632. Undoubtedly, the duke had rebelled against the king; but so had Gaston d'Orléans, who was left in peace, and the duc de La Force, who was marshal of France, and the duc de Rohan, who was able to take refuge in Bern. Why did Montmorency have to pay for everyone else? Why was there that exceptional tribunal, presided over by the guard of the Sceaux Châteauneuf that Richelieu had put into place for the express purpose of condemning him to death, when Montmorency, as a duke and a peer, should have been judged by Parlement alone? The house of Condé had ample right to feel persecuted, and it was the fear of Louis XIII's terrible minister that had pushed Henri de Bourbon to seek an alliance by marrying his eldest son, the duc d'Enghien, to the cardinal's niece, Claire-Clémence de Maillé-Brézé. This marriage went against the wishes of the young prince, who was in love with Marthe du Vigean. Anne-Geneviève knew that her brother, for whom she had particularly great respect and fondness, had long resisted a union imposed upon him by his father's weakness and the minister's tyranny. She herself had been obliged to yield to the same requirements and, in the blossom of her youth and the flowering of her beauty, to marry the old duc de Longueville. At the time of their marriage, on 2 June 1642, she was 22 years old, and he was 47. The poet Sarasin sang, "she is like a rose in the newborn season," while the duke already appeared an old man. It is easy to see that Anne-Geneviève had ample reason to detest a minister who had dominated her father, persecuted her mother, and imposed marriages upon both her brother and herself. It was the very system of the ministry that she abhorred, as did almost all of the aristocracy of her time. Certainly they were willing to obey the king, but they stubbornly refused to bend to the will of the cardinal-minister, and they denied him all authority over the princes of the blood. Moreover, the reasons they might have had for opposing Richelieu were equally valid against Mazarin, who succeeded the former during the regency (with the aggravating circumstance that Mazarin was a commoner by birth and not even French).

All this explains why in 1648, after the brilliant victory won by her brother in Lens (20 August), Madame de Longueville urged him to take advantage of the parlementary movements and the loathing for the minister in order to bring him down by an alliance with the Fronde. As far as Mazarin was concerned, it was primarily a question of annihilating Richelieu's heir and continuator: at the beginning of the Fronde, Madame de Longueville's hostility was directed less at the man than at everything the minister stood for, the institution he embodied. She was more than willing to adopt as her own cause the war the officers had declared against absolutist practices and the cardinal's omnipotence: her family had nothing but complaints after a generation of suffering the despotism of ministers. Thus, she dreamed of prevailing over the regent queen and restoring the former power of the great aristocracy. In principle, that objective was not displeasing to her brother, but he distrusted the *robins* (those who qualified as nobles by holding legal appointments), and his loyalty as prince of the blood won the day. He therefore remained faithful to the regent queen and to Mazarin during the first civil war of the Fronde and would lead the royal army assigned to set up the blockade of Paris. Having failed to mobilize her eldest brother, Madame de Longueville turned to her second brother, the young prince de Conti, who was only 19 years old and over whom she held great sway. This was the famous "Plot of Noisy" (December 1648), which she orchestrated together with Paul de Gondi, the boisterous coadjutor of Paris and future cardinal de Retz. In addition, she brought the support of her husband, governor of Normandy, to the Fronde as well as that of her lover, La Rochefoucauld.

During the blockade of the capital, the war councils of the Fronde took place in the Hôtel de Ville, where Madame de Longueville had taken up residence. She was like a queen of the Parisians, enormously popular, and no important decision was ever made without her advice or endorsement. Her first biographer, Villefore, later wrote:

> it was something quite flattering for her to see herself as someone whom Parlement was careful not to displease, to see so many lords loyal to her schemes, an entire population—so great in number in the capital—compliant with her commands, the queen herself alarmed by her ventures, a hero as great as her brother forced to be wary of her, and the prime minister of the state uncertain of his destiny because of her.

When the Peace of Saint-Germain (1 April 1649) put an end to the blockade, Madame de Longueville and Condé reconciled, and through him she came to terms with the court. However, this arrangement was purely formal, for her hostility toward Mazarin had not been laid to rest, as she continued to see him as an insufferable obstacle to the glory of her family and to the growing demands of her brother. The cardinal made careful note of this in his *Carnets* (Notebooks):

> Madame de Longueville has complete power over her brother. . . . She would like to see him prevail and have every favor at his disposal. . . . If she likes gallantry it is not at all with evil designs, but rather to insure that her brother has servants and friends. She instills ambitious thoughts in him.

When Mazarin—despite the fact that he owed his own safety the previous year to the support of Condé—had her two brothers and her husband imprisoned on 18 January 1650 in a true coup d'état, Madame de Longueville and her entire family had every right to feel that they were in a position of legitimate defense against tyranny. She succeeded in escaping (for she, too, was to be arrested as prisoner of the state) and fled to Normandy in the hope of rousing the province to defend its governor. But there she experienced the pain of human ingratitude: the majority of the duc de Longueville's vassals, fearful of the approach

of the comte d'Harcourt's royal army, closed their doors to her. She failed in Rouen, took refuge in the Château de Dieppe, and had to flee from the advancing royal army and hide. Finally, she boarded an English ship in Le Havre and reached Rotterdam, from where she wrote a letter to the king, justifying her conduct and denouncing the despotism by which she had been victimized. She then made her way to Stenay, a Condé stronghold in Argonne, arriving there on 28 February, after six weeks of restless wandering and incredible adventures worthy of the novels of Gomberville or La Calprenède. Here she found a certain number of loyalists, Turenne among them, for the bonds of loyalty were of great importance in the actions and positions taken throughout this entire period, particularly during the Fronde of the Princes. Madame de Longueville spent an entire year in Stenay, until her brothers and her husband had been set free. There she expended prodigious amounts of energy in the service of the prisoners, enticing some parties, mobilizing others, and rallying the reluctant. She galvanized others into action, playing on her own charms, for, as Madame de Motteville wrote "it was impossible to see her without loving her and without wishing to please her; . . . the power of her charisma extended itself even to our sex." She made a treaty with the Spanish, justifying her actions in a forcefully worded manifesto; she maintained an enormous correspondence with her friends both French and foreign; and she recruited troops—the only woman to have done so—and found money to pay them, even pawning her jewels for this purpose. With Sarasin, Conti's secretary, she wrote a remarkable *Apologie pour Messieurs les Princes* (Apologia for the Princes), arranging for its printing and distribution. In short, she fought on every front with an energy that sparked the admiration of her partisans and the uneasiness of the ministry.

To a large extent, these manifold actions achieved their goals: although she experienced military failure with Turenne's defeat at Rethel (15 December 1650), Madame de Longueville succeeded—and was not this the main point in a civil war?—in holding the public spellbound. With the help of Lénet in Chantilly, then in Bordeaux, she turned the tide of public opinion, which initially had been unfavorable to the princes (in Paris, bonfires had been lit to celebrate the arrest of the one who, a few months earlier, had led the blockade of the city). Finally, she contributed to the success of the negotiations with the "old Fronde" (Retz, Beaufort, Châteauneuf, Madame de Chevreuse, and the members of Parlement who were part of the Fronde), which would lead to the union of the two Frondes in late January of 1651 and to Mazarin's exile in February.

In April, after the liberation of her brothers and her husband, the duchess returned to Paris, where she was welcomed like a queen. This return had a decisive influence on the continuation of the Fronde, for it was Madame de Longueville who, out of visceral hatred for Madame de Chevreuse, thwarted plans for her brother Conti's marriage to Mademoiselle de Chevreuse, which was intended to seal forever the union of the cardinal's enemies. It was also she who pushed Condé to make ever-greater demands on the court, which made him more and more suspect in the eyes of the members of the Fronde. It may be said that, throughout spring and summer 1651, she was the main architect of the discord between those who had been recent allies. After Condé's break with the court and his retreat to Saint-Maur (6 July 1651), the duchess was among those who urged him most fervently into civil war. She "shifted the balance," said Goulas, "and was like a red-hot brand that set fire to the entire kingdom." This was the period in which she became the mistress of the duc de Nemours, whom she pulled into the civil war and with whom she managed to reach Bordeaux, where she rejoined Condé. Since the latter was more often leading his troops than he was present in the capital of Guyenne, it was actually Madame de Longueville who, under the ostensible authority of Conti and with the enlightened assistance of Lénet, maintained her camp's control of a city gripped by divisions and cabals. Condé's departure in March 1652 left her with a heavy burden; she had to reconcile and prevail over the rival factions that were stirring up Conti's entourage, and she struggled with ever-growing difficulties. As the opposition between the "Ormeé," an extremist movement, and the parlementary bourgeoisie turned more venomous, Conti and his sister gave in to public pressure and in May exiled from Bordeaux a number of magistrates suspected of loyalty to Mazarin. Madame de Longueville was forced to intervene incessantly between the Ormée and the provincial parlement, while little by little the royal army tightened its net around the city. As the situation grew untenable, she signed the Peace of Bordeaux on 24 July 1653, together with Conti, and retired to Montreuil-Bellay, her estate near Saumur. Having entered the Fronde during its earliest convulsions, she embodied it until its last days.

If one seeks to go beyond the sequence of events and daily life to understand the motivation of such constancy in opposing Mazarin—if one is not content to see Madame de Longueville as a mere accessory to the ambitions of her brother—one must examine the manifestos and apologies she herself composed or inspired during the Fronde to justify her actions and defend her ideas. These are very illuminating texts, most revealing of the political mentality of the high aristocracy of France in the middle of the 17th century.

First there is the manifesto she issued throughout all of Europe in May 1650 to justify herself for having concluded, together with Turenne, a treaty with the Spanish. If she was looking for their support, it was not only for reasons of legitimate defense against the tyrant. It was because

> the peace of France, the freedom of the Princes, the stability of the authority of the laws and of the last Declarations [of 22 October 1648, which signed into law the primary parlementary gains at the expense of absolutism], the solace of the people, the preservation of the realm and the peace of Christianity, to which Mazarin is opposed . . . cannot be obtained hereafter except through armed struggle.

All other forms of resistance to the tyranny having become impossible, reasons of state and the salvation of the country legitimized armed rebellion. "I have every reason to believe," she confirmed proudly,

> that since I found myself obliged to use legitimate force against injustice, and having done so in such a way that the responsibilities I assume are less for the deliverance of our own family than for the service to my prince and the usefulness to my country, there is no one of any conscience and good judgment who can fail to approve of this plan, concur with it, support it, and in some way consider me

happy in my misfortune for being the cause of the kingdom's reestablishment.

Several months later, these themes of aristocratic resistance against Mazarin were powerfully articulated in the *Apologie pour Messieurs les Princes*, written by Sarasin under Madame de Longueville's direction. One of the main ideas of this voluminous pamphlet (87 pages in quarto) was that Mazarin, like Richelieu before him, was practicing a despotic authority that was alien to the traditions of the land and contrary to its laws; for the minister, "who has everything but the title of Mayor of the Palace," was managing everything without restraint—he "unreservedly has the pen, the finances, the armies of His Majesty at his disposal," and was attempting "to raise his power well above the law." The ministry, a recent innovation, had no legitimacy whatsoever and was not part of the political tradition of the kingdom. Since he had not been invested with any official power, the minister was a private servant of the king, and consequently the nobles owed him no obedience. In Madame de Longueville's view, Mazarin was no more than an adventurer, an individual blinded by his good luck, a man whose ambition had made him lose his head, a "favorite" who, contrary to the princes of the blood, was in no way prepared to exercise such power, so that in his hands royal power inevitably became tyrannical. Moreover, the entire *Apologie* presents Mazarin as a man who cannot be trusted. Madame de Longueville, who in 1646 and 1647 had closely followed the negotiations in Münster, in which her husband had participated and which produced the treaties of Westphalia, boldly denounces the "perfidies of this foreigner," his continual deceitfulness, a duplicity that had prevented the peace concluded with the empire from being extended to Spain and from transforming this partial peace into a "general peace." Thus, Mazarin alone was held responsible for the continuation of the hostilities. "The war being waged at the frontiers," Jacques Debû-Bridel comments in the book he devoted to the duchess, "the war illuminated by Condé's victories is no longer a war of the nation. It no longer serves the public good. It is imposed by Mazarin's ambition alone. The Spanish are no longer the enemy of France or the king. They are Mazarin's enemy alone" (see Debû-Bridel). Thus, the treaty that Madame de Longueville and Turenne had just signed with Spain for the liberation of the princes and the "general peace," had been cleverly justified: there was no treason here, no connivance with the enemy of France, but a common struggle against the common enemy of both crowns.

What emerges above all else from the *Apologie* is a princely concept of the monarchical state, and it is, indeed, a crucial text for understanding the Fronde of the aristocracy. The kingdom is like an inherited patrimony: when its legitimate proprietor is a child, the princes of the family are his natural tutors; they have a right and a duty of guardianship where he is concerned. Thus, throughout any period of royal minority, they find themselves to be invested with national responsibilities: "Conscience and nature oblige the princes of the blood to watch carefully that the state not be injured in any way." The illustrious *Frondeuse* adds,

> I do not see how in this situation [that is, during a king's minority and in the midst of a foreign war] anyone dared to arrest princes who are concerned with the preservation of France, admitted to the administration of the state by

their birth, and whose detention could very well disturb the kingdom.

At the very least it was certain that during the period of a minority the regents had to consult the Estates General in all matters of such seriousness. "The power of our kings," the duchess continues,

> is entirely autonomous, they recognize only God above them, and to him alone do they owe an accounting for their actions. Nevertheless, these same kings, who consolidated the foundations of our empire and established such absolute rights in their monarchy, have deemed it necessary for its preservation that, during the minority of their successors and the tenderness of their age, the realm be led by the council of princes of the blood. In matters of greatest importance those who have been installed as regents would have to consult the states of the kingdom in order to resolve and assume such matters. In this case, can Cardinal Mazarin use the pretext of this omnipotence, given that the king is a minor and that the resolution of such a dangerous matter has been hidden from every order in the kingdom? Does this not mean, then, that the power of the monarchy lies in its ministry and that a man who, by his birth, should be excluded from participation in our affairs has the power to overturn the basic laws of our country?

If, among women, Madame de Longueville appeared as an emblematic figure of the Fronde because of her multifarious and tireless activity, the Palatine princess dominated it through cleverness and intelligence. Moresini, the ambassador of Venice, in one of his dispatches commented on her *capacissima di negocio* (extraordinary abilities as a negotiator). Cardinal de Retz was impressed with the breadth of her talents: "I do not believe that Queen Elizabeth of England had a greater ability for leading a state. I have seen her in a faction, I have seen her in the cabinet, and everywhere I have found her to be most sincere." His assessment was that of a connoisseur.

Anne de Gonzague de Clèves, the Palatine princess since her clandestine marriage, contracted in 1645 without the queen's knowledge, had received help and protection from the Longuevilles during the disgrace that had followed this union, and it was through Condé that she succeeded in being recalled to court. Loyalty thus bound her to the prince and his family: she helped Madame de Longueville escape to Normandy after the princes had been arrested, and she pledged her support toward their liberation. She devoted herself to this cause with extraordinary efficiency. It was she who, in December 1650 and January 1651, negotiated the treaty of alliance between the old Fronde and the coalition of the princes, and the only phase in the Fronde that saw the delicate union of the adversaries of Mazarin was the result of her action. One would have to read all the memoirs of the time to gauge the gifts of diplomacy and the genius for intrigue required for such success.

Once the princes had been released from prison, the Palatine princess considered herself cleared of her debt to them. Like Turenne, and like Bussy-Rabutin, she felt obliged to serve them only during their misfortune through laws of honor and loyalty, not to espouse all of their ambitions. She pointed out to them that it was not in their interest to push the queen to the limits, as their most ardent partisans and the most fanatical members of the Fronde wanted to do. During the last two years of the Fronde she actively supported Anne of Austria and Mazarin—without, however, abandoning either Retz or Condé, whom she always attempted to bring or hold back from the verge of rebellion. After the failure of the marriage plans of Conti and Mademoiselle de Chevreuse and the subsequent break between the two Frondes, she served as an intermediary between the queen and the old Fronde (Retz, in particular), who were drawing closer together as a way of countering the growing power of Condé. She tantalized the coadjutor with the prospect of his nomination to the cardinalship, in exchange for his support of the court against the prince, and she negotiated a treaty between the court and the old Fronde. It was during this period, from June to August 1651, that the princess rendered the most valuable services to Anne of Austria and Mazarin. It was she who convinced them, despite their reservations, to grant the coadjutor his nomination on condition that he allow the court the freedom to leave Paris to pursue Condé. Retz's secretary, Guy Joly, wrote, "it is certain that it was she who struck the final blow in the *affaire du chapeau* [the nomination of the coadjutor to the cardinalship] and that all the honor fell to her." She then again joined Anne of Austria in Poitiers in the winter of 1651–52 and remained loyal to her until the end of the Fronde. Even more than a woman of action such as Madame de Longueville, the Palatine princess thus appears to have been an exceptionally gifted negotiator. Bossuet, in his famous funeral oration, later said:

> The genius of the Palatine princess was equally great in matters of entertainment as in matters of business. The court has never seen anyone more engaging and, without mentioning her acumen and the richness of her wit, everyone succumbed to the secret charm of her conversation.

Isabelle-Angélique de Montmorency, duchesse de Châtillon, offers another brilliant illustration of the determining influence of lineage with respect to political choices. She was a Montmorency and a close cousin of the dowager princess of Condé. In 1645, she married Gaspard de Coligny, one of the famous young courtiers in the entourage of her cousin (himself still just the duc d'Enghien at the time). Coligny became the duc de Châtillon the following year. In other words, once the Fronde began, the duchess's side had been chosen for her in advance. After the death of her husband, who was killed during the blockade in the attack of Charenton (8 February 1649), the 20-year-old widow allowed herself to be consoled by the duc de Nemours before becoming Condé's mistress in 1651. The news of the princes' arrest reached her at her estate in Châtillon-sur-Loing. She joined the dowager princess in Chantilly and, after the dowager fled, she welcomed her in Châtillon, where the princess died on 2 December 1650, a few weeks before her children were released from prison.

In 1652, the duchess began to play an important role in the Fronde, owing to the influence she had gained over her cousin, Condé. Strengthened by the complete trust of the prince, she took it upon herself to negotiate on his behalf with Mazarin. Thus she left for Saint-Germain with a brilliant retinue; all she lacked, joked Nogent, was "an olive branch in her hand." But the shrewd cardinal appeased her with nothing more substantial than kindnesses. She took an active part in the battle of the

Faubourg Saint-Antoine on 2 July; it was she who passed a note to Condé during the battle, urging him to seek the help of Mademoiselle de Montpensier (Anne-Marie Louise d'Orléans, duchesse de Montpensier, daughter of Gaston d'Orléans and thus a niece of Louis XIII, known in her time and to posterity as "La Grande Mademoiselle"). It was the duchess who persuaded Mademoiselle to order the firing of the Bastille cannon fired against the royal army, thereby saving the army of the princes, which was under threat of being crushed. Throughout the summer, the duchess continued to negotiate on behalf of the party of the princes with the abbé Basile Foucquet (brother of the future superintendent), Mazarin's secret agent. After the king's return to Paris, too compromised to benefit from amnesty, the duchess was sent to live at Merlou, a property she had inherited from the dowager princess, and then banished to Châtillon.

Although for Madame de Chevreuse, as for Madame de Longueville, the Fronde coincided with a time of unbridled youth in which the heart's enthusiasms were strengthened by family ties and connection to a lineage in a romantic atmosphere of heroic exaltation, the impulse behind the political action of Madame de Chevreuse was very different. First of all, she was a woman of another generation. A daughter of the first marriage of Hercule de Rohan, duc de Montbazon (and thus the stepdaughter of Madame de Montbazon, who was 12 years younger than she), on her father's side she was a descendent of the illustrious princely house of Bretagne. On the side of her mother, Madeleine de Lenoncourt, she was descended from a very old and significant family in Lorraine. Born in 1600, she had in 1618 been named superintendent of the house of Anne of Austria, the young queen, and had become her favorite. In 1622, she married Claude de Lorraine, duc de Chevreuse, one of the sons of Henri de Guise.

Madame de Chevreuse was a born schemer: she had the both a vocation and a genius for intrigue. Involved in the conspiracy of Henri de Talleyrand, comte de Chalais (1599–1626) against Richelieu in 1626, she was exiled to Lorraine after his execution. She then became the mistress of the guard of Sceaux Châteauneuf, who was arrested on 25 February 1633 and imprisoned for 10 years in Angoulême; the duchess herself was then banished to Touraine (until 1637). There she continued her machinations. Richelieu was perfectly aware of her scheming, but he considered it too risky to banish her from the realm: "Her mind is so dangerous that, if she lives abroad, it could carry matters to new levels of unrest that we cannot foresee." Indeed, it was she who, having full control over the mind of Charles IV, duc de Lorraine, persuaded him to offer asylum to the duc d'Orléans. It was also she who pushed England to war, and she was the soul of the opposition to Richelieu. After she managed to flee from Touraine she went to Spain, later moving on to England and then to Flanders, where she participated in the conspiracy of the comte de Soissons to such a degree that Louis XIII, who said she was the devil incarnate, condemned her to permanent exile in his declaration of 20 April 1643.

However, Louis XIII only had a few weeks left to live. One of Anne of Austria's first gestures upon becoming regent queen was to recall her former favorite to court. Although Madame de Chevreuse expected her return to be triumphant, it turned out to be a disappointment. Her politics were those of the devout party: she did not forgive Richelieu for his coalition with Sweden and the Protestant princes of Germany against the Catholic house of Hapsburg. She advocated overturning the coalition, as she wanted the reconciliation of the two great Catholic monarchies. Upon her return from Brussels, she found the Spanish Anne of Austria, sister of the Catholic king, completely changed and totally submissive to the prime minister she had inherited from her husband. Mazarin, of course, had every intention of continuing his predecessor's policies against Spain. Seeing that she would not succeed in rallying the regent queen to the views of the devout party, Madame de Chevreuse entered the cabal of the "Important Ones" (August–September 1643). After the failure of this first conspiracy against Mazarin, she was banished to Touraine for two years, escaped, and went back to Brussels. During the Paris blockade, she naturally sought to win Spain's support for the Fronde. Back in Paris, she, along with Retz, Beaufort, and Châteauneuf, orchestrated the reconciliation between the old Fronde and Mazarin at the end of 1649. Then, when she saw that Mazarin was slipping through her fingers in the autumn of the following year, she actively applied herself to bringing the old Fronde closer to the party of the princes, who were by then in prison. She proposed to the Palatine princess to act as the negotiator of the union between the two Frondes that was to force Mazarin into exile. After the princes had been released from prison, and after the affront they inflicted upon her by not keeping their word to her daughter, she became the indefatigable instigator of a new reconciliation between the old Fronde and the court against Condé. Then, in all sincerity, she allied herself with Mazarin upon his return from exile early in 1652. "Too great a lady to deign to know any restraint," the 19th-century historiographer Victor Cousin would later say of her, Madame de Chevreuse truly was "the most formidable adversary faced by Richelieu and then Mazarin" (see Cousin 1856). More than any other woman, she exemplifies that somewhat crazy generation of great schemers of the Fronde: eager to dominate, entirely without scruples in their conquest of power, which they found intoxicating, ready to do anything to satisfy their interests and their ambitions, but fervent, "generous," impassioned, and tireless. These iron-willed women possessed a power of seduction that withstood the test of time, since Madame de Longueville still bewitched the serious Victor Cousin two centuries later (see Cousin 1859). In short, these were personalities strong enough to pull us in their wake into the whirlwind of events they so passionately lived and sometimes provoked.

Can the Kingdom "Fall to the Distaff"?

What space did the institutions of the monarchy leave for women to exercise political power during a regency? This question involves the limits of authority of a regent queen, and the issue lies at the very heart of the Fronde. In France, regencies by women had been accepted throughout the history: Blanche de Castille was regent queen twice, first during the minority of Saint Louis, then again when he left on a crusade; the regencies of Catherine de' Medici and later Maria de' Medici were on the minds of everyone during the Fronde. How, then, could the question of women's inability to act as regent have been raised?

In fact, this issue came up regularly every time the regency held by the mother of a minor king met with adversity. Already, during the regency of Catherine de' Medici, the eminent Protestant legal adviser François Hotman considered the absolute prohibition of women on the throne a fundamental law of the realm; he believed them to be totally incapable of assuming royal power, even in the diluted form of a regency. In his eyes this was a necessary consequence of the principle of the Salic law. There was thus a convergence of all the conditions needed for such a debate to arise again during the Fronde. "My dear mama," the little Louis XIV asks his mother in a *mazarinade* of the blockade entitled *L'entretien familier du roi et de la reine régente* (Conversation between the King and the Regent Queen), "why did you take the regency on, when my father forbade it at his death?"— an embarrassing and insolent question. "If my dear mama was not able to govern this kingdom during my youth," Louis XIV says again to his brother in the *Entretien familier du roi avec Monsieur le duc d'Anjou* (Conversation between the King and the duc d'Anjou), "she could have taken the advice of my uncle the duc d'Orléans, of my cousin the prince de Condé, or of several other princes and lords." "Intolerabilius nihil est quam femina regnans" (Nothing is more intolerable than a reigning woman), a regent of the College of Beauvais proclaimed in a *mazarinade* written in Latin verse. During the same period, Oudard Coquault, a bourgeois from Reims, wrote in his memoirs:

> We are being governed by a woman, who, because of her sex, will never be capable of leading a great state such as this one. The Gauls before us were quite wise to establish as a fundamental law that the kingdom should never fall to the distaff [be governed by women]. But they should also have ordered that the minority of kings could not be lived under the guardianship of their mother.

Then, after invoking the catastrophic regencies of Catherine and Maria de' Medici, fraught with civil wars, he concludes, "Our regent queen Anne of Austria does not handle it any better. I do not wish to accuse her of malice in her government, but of not being able to handle business matters." This was a common reaction, which the princes' imprisonment only strengthened. "Women are not capable of governing a state," the anonymous author of *La Politique sicilienne* (Sicilian Politics) categorically stated in May 1650. For the writer of the *Récit et véritables sentiments sur les affaires du temps* (Account and True Feelings about the Matters of the Period), the cause of all the difficulties was that Paris had forgotten

> The fundamental law of the French empire
> By allowing a woman to govern the state.
> In a word, a woman who cannot be queen
> Cannot command France as regent queen.
> The abuse that so often has brought trouble to the state
> Ought to make us rigorously protect our laws.

In March 1652, Dubosc-Montandré, Condé's official pamphleteer, devoted an entire lampoon to this question, tellingly entitled *Discours de l'autorité que les oncles des rois de France ont toujours eue pendant la minorité et bas âge de leurs neveux* (Discourse on the Authority That the Uncles of the Kings of France Have Always Had during the Minority and Youth of their Nephews). He wrote: "If we want to take the trouble of going through every regency placed in the hands of women, we will find they have been full of misfortunes and dreadful conflicts." For Mon-

tandré it was a logical and necessary extension of the Salic law that the regency be returned by right to the uncles of minor kings rather than to their mothers: "During the youth of our kings, their uncles or the most closely related princes of the blood are the true and natural tutors and regents. . . . The same Salic law that gives them their right to succession also gives them the right to tutelage and the regency." In *La franche Marguerite* (Marguerite Unbound), he again insists on showing that women, who under Salic law had been declared incapable of governing because of their incompetence in business administration, are therefore just as incapable of assuming the regency. This was the official viewpoint of the party of the princes and the most widespread opinion in the *mazarinades*; for example, in Sandricourt's *Le censeur du temps et du monde* (The Censor of the Times and the World). Only Henri d'Audiguier du Mazet, the queen's general counsel, took it upon himself to refute this in *Le censeur censuré* (The Censor Censored), establishing that women are just as capable of governing as men and arguing that, if there were frequent difficulties during their regencies, this was not because of their incompetence, but because of the minority of the king:

> It should by no means be said . . . that it is the government of women that is weak and causes the disorder, for during the illness of Charles VI, his uncles the princes caused appalling chaos, and the regency of the abbé Suger [the abbé of Saint-Denis, regent from 1147 to 1149 during the Second Crusade] was plagued by the revolt of the princes who would not obey him. Therefore, it is not the person or the quality of the regent at all that causes trouble, but rather the minority, the absence, or the illness of the king.

Furthermore, there is no reason whatsoever, d'Audiguier du Mazet continues, for women to be worse managers of public affairs than men, and if general opinion is mostly hostile toward the regency of queen-mothers, one ought not to look for the reason in an alleged political ineptitude of women, but rather in the French temperament, which chafes at authority in general, and particularly the authority of women:

> There is . . . no convincing reason why a woman's reign should be less prosperous than a man's, other than that men, and Frenchmen in particular, put up less patiently with the leadership of women, and that the nobles would rather take control, as we can see in the history of the regency of Queen Blanche and, since that is the case, one should no longer blame women nor their government, but rather our impatience and the ambition of the nobility.

France, adds d'Audiguier, is the only kingdom in which women are excluded from royal succession, and it cannot be denied that in those countries where women are able to reign they have sometimes proven to be great sovereigns (a possible allusion to the celebrated Queen Christina of Sweden, who was greatly admired throughout Europe at the time). Finally, d'Audiguier considers that there are fewer disadvantages in entrusting the regency to the mother of a minor king than to the princes of his family, because the latter are always tempted to usurp royal power, which invariably causes trouble and civil war.

A less theoretical and more concrete debate took shape during the Fronde over the possibility or the opportunity of taking the regency away from Anne of Austria and handing it over to Gaston d'Orléans, the king's uncle. Legally, this presented no problem whatsoever: all that was needed was a ruling of Parlement, and the latter had every latitude for reversing its preceding ruling of 18 May 1643, when it had set aside Louis XIII's last arrangements and removed all restrictions on Anne of Austria's power by excusing her from the council that had been imposed on her under the terms of her husband's declaration arranging her regency. Thus, *mazarinades* from the time of the blockade seized the opportunity to remind the queen that the same Parlement that had confirmed her regency earlier could now just as easily take it away from her. This sentiment is expressed, for example, in *La France à la Reine* (France to the Queen):

> It placed the scepter in your hand,
> Tomorrow it can take it from you:
> The rank you hold depends on
> Its sovereign power alone . . .

A song of 1649 even threatened Anne of Austria not only with being deposed but with confinement in a convent if she failed to get rid of Mazarin. In truth, however, a possible transfer of the regency in 1649 was hardly in question, for no one on the side of the Fronde was eligible to take it on. In fact, only Gaston d'Orléans could lay claim to it, and as long as he remained loyal to his sister-in-law—that is, until early 1651—there could hardly be a question of a transfer of the regency.

The situation changed completely when the two Frondes joined forces and Mazarin went into exile. At that time Anne of Austria had many reasons to fear that the regency would be taken away from her, and she resisted with all her might the request of the nobility, assembled in Paris, and the party of the princes that the Estates General be convened. "She had been warned," wrote Le Tellier to Mazarin, "that the purpose of the meeting of the Estates was to continue the king's minority for four more years and to establish a needed council for her." She was clever enough to play on the traditional hostility of Parlement to the Estates General, which wanted to relegate Parlement to the background, and to gain enough time for the ephemeral union of the two Frondes—organized by the Palatine princess—to go up in smoke. Subsequently, it became much more difficult to take the regency away from her, especially since the majority of the king in early September was approaching. According to Montglat, many people blamed Gaston d'Orléans for lacking the necessary resolve to get Parlement to hand the regency over to him as soon as Mazarin had fled and the princes had been set free. He then could have had Anne of Austria confined to a convent, and he himself assumed all the royal powers until the king was old enough to rule. In any event, that was the opinion of La Rochefoucauld in his memoirs:

> Several people believed that the duc d'Orléans and he [Condé] had committed a very grave error in allowing the queen to enjoy her authority any longer: it was easy to take it from her; the regency could have been passed on to the duc d'Orléans through a ruling of Parlement, and thereby not only would the leadership of the state be in his hands, but the king in person—the only thing lacking for the party of the Princes to become as legitimate in appearance as it was in reality. All the parties would have agreed to this, as no one either wished or was in a position

to oppose it, so greatly had the decline and the flight of the cardinal left his friends in dismay.

The question of Anne of Austria being deposed arose once again in 1652, but in appreciably different terms, since at that point Louis XIV had been of age for several months. The question was thus who would hold the power that belonged only nominally to a sovereign who was 13 years old. This was when the campaign of the partisans of the princes against Anne of Austria reached its most violent level. They went so far as to talk openly, Gaudin wrote to Mazarin, "about putting the queen on trial using strange [unusually audacious] words." Lampoons appeared more frequently than ever before. The very violent *Esprit du feu roi Louis XIII à son fils Louis XIV* (Spirit of the Late King Louis XIII to his Son Louis XIV) envisions for Anne of Austria only a safe retreat to Val-de-Grâce. In *Le coup de partie* (The Master Stroke), Dubosc-Montandré concludes that the queen should renounce the power and withdraw to her apanage, since she had been repudiated by the princes, the parlements, and the nation altogether; and in *La vérité prononçantses oracles sans flatterie* (Truth Pronouncing Its Oracles Without Flattery) he states purely and simply that she should be deposed: "Her hands should be tied; any and all power should be taken away from her; she should be placed in such a position that we no longer fear her." But by the time this lampoon appeared, in early August 1652, it was too late to conceive of a transfer of power into the hands of Gaston d'Orléans. Anne of Austria and her son were no longer quasi prisoners within the palace walls, as they had been in February and March 1651. They were free to move about, and they headed a powerful army that combed the countryside and held the princes' forces in check everywhere. The queen's long and stubborn resistance to all pressures had ended in triumph. The regency could easily have escaped her, particularly in February and March 1651. The only thing that saved her then was the characteristic indecisiveness of Gaston d'Orléans. In 1652, despite a furious press campaign by the party of the princes, the risk was no longer as great, because Louis XIV had come of age and Parlement, dreading the violence of Condé, showed itself to be more than reluctant to go beyond the general lieutenancy of the state that it conferred on Monsieur in its ruling of 20 July. Anne of Austria's relentless struggle for the continuation of her prerogatives as the king mother and the safeguarding of her power as regent queen was crowned with success in the end, and this outcome was of great importance in the history of the monarchical institution: had she been deposed by Parlement or the Estates General, a precedent would have been set to remove women from any official political power in the realm once and for all.

The War Expeditions

Finally, can one speak of women's military action during the Fronde? To be sure, this kind of action only rarely fell to them: a woman's place is not in the frontlines, and war in the 17th century was still almost exclusively the business of men. But extraordinary times call for extraordinary personalities. As we have seen, the era did not want for proud, fervent, and courageous heroines who were capable of vigorously taking command, if not actually donning armor. The impact such women's actions made on people of the time is clearly visible in contemporary representations—using the theme of Judith and Holophernes, for example—some of which have come down to us. A number of these "Amazons of the Fronde" were immortalized by engravers and painters in warlike poses, spurring a spirited horse, or helmeted and dressed in armor, like Mademoiselle in an engraving by Nicolas Poilly.

Madame de Longueville, in particular, seems to have distinguished herself in a specifically military role. During the Paris blockade, the generals—Beaufort, Noirmoutier, La Rochefoucauld, and La Boulaie—led the campaign, but Madame de Longueville, along with Conti, presided over the war council, which was held in her chambers in the Hôtel de Ville. In Stenay, it was she who recruited the troops, found the means with which to pay them, and organized the defense of the area. She undoubtedly had help from La Moussaie, its governor, and especially from the great warrior Turenne, but not a single military decision was made without the approval of the princess. When all this activity bore fruit in the liberation of her brothers and her husband, one of her admirers, Sommerance, who was civil and criminal lieutenant of Stenay, built a very strange *Temple de la déesse Bourbonie* (Temple of the Goddess Bourbonie) to glorify her and to celebrate her heroic virtue forever. "It is impossible for me," he declared there,

> to hide the fact from Your Highness that there is nothing in your admirable conduct that does not far exceed your sex, since in every war expedition you act like an Alexander or a Caesar, as much in those things that concern the army as in those that concern fortifications and the reestablishment of border areas.

In the *Apothéose de Madame la duchesse de Longueville* (Apotheosis of the Duchesse de Longueville), published a few weeks later by the same author, Condé's sister became "another Pallas Athena," a new Medea serving a second Jason, a "heroine who incorporates the strengths of Mars and the wisdom of Minerva."

As romantic as her cousin, Mademoiselle was burning to imitate her example and to leave memorable testimonies of her "generosity" to posterity. Her father's continual hesitation between the court and the Fronde did not allow her this opportunity until Gaston d'Orléans rallied the coalition of the princes in January 1652. Thereafter, Mademoiselle sought to distinguish herself through actions worthy of her birth, and she soon found the opportunity when she obtained her father's permission to go to Orléans, one of his apanages, to prevent the city from welcoming the court and force it to declare itself on the side of the princes. In her euphoria at playing a role commensurate with her stature, and a warrior's role at that, she left Paris on 25 March with her "brigadiers," the comtesse de Fiesque and the comtesse de Frontenac. Two days later, she entered the city by surprise—a city that had originally refused to open its gates to her and claimed to be observing a kind of neutrality between the two parties. The bold and unhoped-for feat compelled the court to stay on the left bank of the Loire and go to Gien instead of crossing the river and moving on to Paris. Immediately the *Triomphe des mérites de Mademoiselle* (The Triumph of the Merits of Mademoiselle) was celebrated. People compared her to Joan of Arc, calling her "the new Maid of Orléans"; her "generous sentiments" were lauded, the *Manifeste de Mademoiselle présenté aux coeurs généreux* (Mademoiselle's Manifesto Presented to Generous Hearts) was published, her exploits were sung in prose and in verse, and an engraving was made that depicts her

in a helmet, sword in hand, striking Mazarin down. Three months later, her active—indeed decisive—participation in the battle of the Faubourg Saint-Antoine, when she saved the army of the princes by opening the gates of Paris and ordering the Bastille cannon to be fired at the royal troops, brought her glory to a peak. The author of a *mazarinade* called *Le médecin politique* (The Political Physician) was unstinting in his admiration for

> . . . this adorable Amazon,
> This generous Bourbon blood
> Whose candid heart is so good to us.
> Oh gods! what marvels she has wrought
> Through her skill and her vigils,
> On that day when one favorable stroke of hers
> Saved Paris and its savior!

Mademoiselle was intoxicated by this abundance of praise, which swirled around her like incense, concealing from her view the ever-more precarious situation of her own party. She was idolized, and she played the heroine. According to her own assertion, this was the very word her father used when he left to go into exile at Blois at the end of the Fronde, while she herself retreated to Saint-Fargeau: "You have been so happy to play the heroine and to hear that that is what you are for our party, which you saved twice, that you may find comfort in that, whatever happens to you."

One might assume that such brilliant actions could have been achieved only by women of the highest rank, to which both Mademoiselle and Madame de Longueville belonged. How, then, was it possible for women whose social position seemed to remove them forever from any heroic feat to be inspired by the same moral code of glory? The answer is equally valid for women as for men: it is not necessary to hold the highest rank and play a central role for people to find themselves presented with opportunities to shine and surpass themselves, particularly during periods as agitated as the Fronde.

Witness Madame de Saint-Balmont, celebrated for her fearlessness, to whom Tallemant des Réaux devoted the better part of his little story on valiant women, and whom Claude Deruet depicted as a warrior, on horseback, brandishing her sword, in a painting now at the Musée Carnavalet in Paris. "Normally," Tallemant said,

> she wears a hat with blue feathers; blue is her color. She wears her hair the way men do, as well as a doublet, a cravat, men's double cuffs, knee breeches, very low men's shoes . . . a skirt over her breeches; she always has her sword by her side: when she rides horseback, she takes off her skirt and wears boots. . . . No one could be more valiant than she: more than 400 men have been killed or taken by her. When Erlac passed through Champagne (where his army wreaked great havoc in May 1649), she single-handedly attacked three German cavalrymen who were unhitching horses from her plow and held [the miscreants] until her servants arrived. She scaled the walls of a castle, pistol in hand, and, although her own people had deserted her, she entered without hesitation, hurled herself into a room, and single-handedly disarmed the 17 men she found inside.

Witness also Madame de La Guette, "the Saint-Balmont of Brie," as the soldiers of the duc de Lorraine called her in 1652.

She had a well-deserved reputation for courage and possessed an enterprising spirit: in her memoirs she herself recounted how she fended off "pilferers" and "marauders" from both sides during the Paris blockade and, in 1652, those of the duc de Lorraine. During the blockade, she wrote, "the soldiers knocked down all the doors and pillaged a great many places; there were even some women, not able to get away fast enough, who were violated." She had provided refuge to more than 200 women and girls at her estate in Sucy-en-Brie when 20 cavalrymen showed up at her door. "Someone other than myself would have been frightened," she declared proudly, "because I knew well enough that in those days they had no consideration for anyone. Nevertheless, I went to the door cheerfully and had it opened." Thanks to her sangfroid, everyone was safe and sound. In 1652, she calmly replied to an officer of the royal army who was pressuring her to leave her house immediately with all those who had taken refuge there because of the imminent arrival of the Lorraine camp: "Sir, you bring me a strange bit of news; but I have no intention of leaving until all the people here are brought to safety; and if anyone must perish it will have to be me; that is my resolve." She did not leave Sucy until the following day. A few days later, she performed another act of heroism: despite all the risks involved, she showed no compunction about deceiving the duc de Lorraine as to the position of the various parts of the royal army in order to deter him from attacking Turenne, allowing the latter time to prepare to defend himself in Villeneuve-Saint-Georges.

Another heroine of the Mazarin period, the comtesse de Jonzac, distinguished herself in Saintonge in January 1652. Since she had been unable to secure from Condé the exemption of her village from any garrisons, she armed her villagers and encouraged them to ply the soldiers with food and drink, the better overpower them afterwards. This tactic was so successful that the villagers managed to put 300 of the soldiers out of commission. The countess herself took charge of the officers and got them to drink so much that she was able to lock them up in a tower, the key to which she then sent to the queen, who in turn immediately sent a captain to take the officers prisoner. The news of this bold action soon reached Paris; not only did several governmental *mazarinades* extol the courage and presence of mind of the lady of Jonzac, but the newsmongers—Jean Vallier, Dubuisson-Aubenay, Loret—were full of praise for this wartime feat.

These were women who were not princesses of the blood, but simple wives of gentlemen who, in the absence of their husbands, were responsible for defending the family manor, the surrounding property, and the village, and who acquitted themselves of this difficult mission with a steadfast spirit worthy of going down in history. Besides these examples, sometimes preserved for us only by pure chance (we never would have known anything about the courage of Madame de La Guette without the details provided in her memoirs), we shall never know how many heroic acts achieved by women during these wars of the Fronde have remained buried forever.

"Are Women Not Every Bit As Worthy As Men?"

One may wonder whether women's political engagement and the role that some of them played during the Fronde actually contributed to a better opinion of them and whether it caused an evolution in the commonly held notion about their place in society at the time. In the slow progression of feminist ideas in the 17th century, it is revealing to examine the images of women that were offered in the texts dating from or inspired by the Fronde, and in particular in the immense corpus of the *mazarinades*

It is appropriate, first of all, to remember that the years preceding the Fronde had seen a multitude of apologies for the fair sex. After his treatise of *L'honnête femme* (The Honest Woman), published in 1635, the Cordelier Du Bosc published *La femme généreuse* (The Generous Woman) in 1643, followed in 1646 by *La femme héroïque* (The Heroic Woman). That same year, François du Soucy published his *Triomphe des dames* (Triumph of the Ladies), while awaiting the *Panégyrique des dames* (Panegyric of the Ladies), dedicated to Mademoiselle by Gabriel Gilbert in 1650, right in the middle of the Fronde. This was followed in 1654 by *L'honnête maîtresse* (The Honest Mistress) by Louis Couvay and *Le mérite des dames* (The Merit of Ladies) by Saint-Gabriel a year later. But we should have no illusions about this profusion of publications: just as much as it shows the increasing presence of feminist ideas, it reveals the deeply entrenched misogynist discrimination that needed to be combated.

The *mazarinades* do indeed bear ample witness to such misogynist prejudices. Reacting against Anne of Austria's complete control, a fair number of them deplored the more general phenomenon of the ascendancy of women, or even their presumption to encroach upon the rights of men. In *L'entretien familier du roi et de la reine regente* (Conversation between the King and the Regent Queen), the young Louis XIV asks his mother with false candor, "My dear mama, why do you tolerate women at the altar with the priest when, ever since the days of Saint Louis, they have not been allowed to enter the chancel?" To which Anne of Austria responds with quiet assurance, "My son, that was in the good old days of Saint Louis, but today everything is fashionable. Are women not every bit as worthy as men, and more so? Watch me and see whether I am not doing as I wish!"

In the mind of the lampoonist, this was apparently a scandalous thought: the traditional misogyny of the Gallic mind was much more frequently encountered in the *mazarinades* than were the new ideas. "A rational monkey" was the provocative definition of woman suggested in the *Catéchisme des courtisans* (Courtiers' Catechism), and Sandricourt went on to call them "an imperfect sex, without strength, without knowledge, without experience." As for Dubosc-Montandré, in *La vérité prononçant ses oracles sans flatterie*, he simply concludes his long indictment of Anne of Austria with these words: "By way of apology for the queen, I will say only that she is a woman," for, he continues in the second part of his lampoon, "one can never say that a woman is wise, but rather that she is less crazy than the others: the Holy Spirit, at least, knows no wise women."

With slight variations, this sums up the general feeling among the pamphleteers of the Fronde. And basically, this rather brutal misogyny is hardly surprising when one considers that the *mazarinades* essentially reflected the opinion of the common people and the bourgeoisie, who were far more traditional and conservative with respect to mores than the intellectual and social elite. Should we then infer that the women's emancipation movement and women's cultural achievements, so brilliantly represented during the second half of the century by the Hôtel de Rambouillet, left no trace at all in the pamphlets? In fact, these lampoons came from too many different personalities and backgrounds to be able to offer just one representation of women. Instead of adhering to the traditional prejudice—such as Montaigne proposed—regarding women's lack of ability for serious study and intellectual curiosity, some of the publications of the Fronde praised women's knowledge and their culture. For example, the author of the *Panégyrique de Monseigneur le maréchal de L'Hôpital* (Panegyric of Monseigneur the Maréchal de l'Hôpital) cites the example of the marshal's wife and her assiduousness in her studies. One should, he said to her, "Use, as you do, all curiosity that brings erudition/At every moment of the day/So that one progresses in gaining exquisite knowledge." In the *Mascurat*, composed for the defense of his master after the Paris blockade, Naudé takes a sharp stand against the misogynist prejudices of Juvenal and Accursio in defense of women of culture:

> The misgivings of Juvenal and Accursio were fine when learned women were visible as rarely as were monsters and comets, but today, when we find them everywhere . . . any blame put upon scholarly women should be attributed to men's fear that they themselves will be surpassed one day.

From a different point of view, a judicial and political one, Thomas Hobbes, another contemporary thinker, undertakes a forceful apologia on behalf of women in a chapter of his *Philosophicall Rudiments concerning Government and Society* (1649). He starts off by noting that control over children belongs initially to the mother and adds that he does not find "such a disproportion between the natural forces of male and female" that the male sex "should dominate the other without encountering any resistance." After citing the example of the Amazons, surely thinking of the regency of Anne of Austria, since he had taken refuge in France from 1644 on, he concludes: "And in our day have we not seen the most important matters in Europe managed by women, even in those states, I say, in which they were not accustomed to being sovereigns?"

No matter how interesting they may be in various ways, these attitudes that approve of women's advances in every area of social and cultural life, in her specific role within the family as educator of her children and, in the case of a regent queen, in her political power, remained altogether exceptional and expressed only the personal convictions of a few individuals. With regard to the political problems of the regency, we have just seen how violently the great majority resisted a woman's exercise of power. On those occasions when, throughout the immense corpus of the *mazarinades*, a few women took up the pen—for example, Suzanne de Nervèze, probably the sister of Antoine de Nervèze, a prolific novelist early in the century, or Charlotte Hénault, a relative of the printer Jean Hénault—it was not to offer an opinion on the problems of the time, much less to intercede as women in the political debate. Instead, it was to ingratiate themselves with those in power on the occasion of a promotion, a nomination, or a happy event, in eulogies and panegyrics full of the most flagrant flattery. Thus, although the beginnings of a change could be discerned within the intellectual and social elite, and

despite the influence of brilliant circles like that of Madame de Rambouillet, the *mazarinades* attested primarily to the social and cultural inertia that, from all sides, still impeded women's advancement. Moreover, was not the failure of the Fronde also a personal failure for the greatest female figures that embodied it, such as Madame de Longueville, Madame de Chevreuse, and Mademoiselle? In terms of politics, the Fronde finally resulted in a lasting setback in women's power. After the civil wars, it would take the sudden development of *préciosité* and its feminist demands to bring about, although on another level, a kind of women's revenge and a decisive change in ways of thinking.

Bibliography

Manuscript Sources

Archives des Affaires Étrangères, Paris. Mémoires et Documents (France), vols. 860–892 [Mazarin's papers from the period of the Fronde]

Archives du Musée Condé, Chantilly, France. Condé Papers: Series O, vols. I, IV, VII, and X [original correspondence from the period of the Fronde]; Series P, vols. II-XIII [letters and other documents addressed to the princes of Condé and Conti and their agents during the Fronde]

Archives Municipales, Bordeaux, France. Fonds Drouyn, vols. 13–16 and 26

Archives Nationales, Paris. Series KK, numbers 1217–1221 [papers and correspondence addressed to Mazarin on events in Guyenne, 1649–1653]

Bibliothèque Nationale, Paris. Collection Baluze: 174 [Mazarin's notebooks]; 343–350 [correspondence addressed to Gaston d'Orléans during the Fronde]; Manuscrits Français: 4177–4187 [letters and miscellaneous documents written by Le Tellier during the Fronde; 6702–6716 [Lénet's papers from the period of the Fronde]; 6881–6892 [Letellier's State papers 1648–53]

Reference Works

Amiguet, Philippe, *Une princesse à l'école du Cid: La Grande Mademoiselle et son siècle, d'áprès ses mémoires*, Paris: Albin Michel, 1957

Andreu, Anne, *La duchesse de Montpensier, ou la Grande Amazone*, Lausanne, Switzerland: Éditions Rencontre, 1965

Batiffol, Louis, *La duchesse de Chevreuse*, Paris: Hachette, 1913; as *The Duchess de Chevreuse: A Life of Intrigue and Adventure in the Days of Louis XIII*, London: Heinemann, 1913; New York: Dodd Mead, 1914

Carrier, Hubert, *La presse de la Fronde (1648–1653): Les Mazarinades*, 2 vols., Geneva: Librairie Droz, 1989–91

Cousin, Victor, *Madame de Chevreuse*, Paris: Didier, 1856; as *Secret History of the French Court under Richelieu and Mazarin, or, Life and Times of Madame de Chevreuse*, translated by Mary L. Booth, New York: J. Miller, 1871

Cousin, Victor, *Madame de Longueville pendant la Fronde, 1651–1653*, Paris: Didier, 1859; 7th edition, Paris: Perrin, 1891

Debû-Bridel, Jacques, *Anne-Geneviève de Bourbon, duchesse de Longueville*, Paris: Gallimard, 1938

Delpech, Jeanine, *L'âme de la Fronde, Madame de Longueville*, Paris: Fayard, 1957

Dulong, Claude, *Anne d'Autriche: Mère de Louis XIV*, Paris: Hachette, 1980

Erlanger, Philippe, *Madame de Longueville*, Paris: Perrin, 1977

Fagniez, Gustave, *La femme et la société française dans la première moitié du XVIIe siècle*, Paris: Librairie Universitaire J. Gamber, 1929

Fromageot, Paul, *Une cousine du Grand Condé: Isabelle de Montmorency, duchesse de Châtillon et de Mecklembourg*, Mâcon, France: Protat, 1913

Haase-Dubosc, Danielle, and Éliane Viennot, editors, *Femmes et pouvoir sous l'Ancien Régime*, Paris: Rivages, 1991

Herbillon, Émile Emmanuel, *Anne d'Autriche, reine, mère, régente*, Paris: J. Tallandier, 1939

Kleinman, Ruth, *Anne of Austria: Queen of France*, Columbus: Ohio State University Press, 1985

Knecht, R. J., *The Fronde*, London: The Historical Association, 1975; revised edition, 1986

Kossmann, Ernst H., *La Fronde*, Leiden, The Netherlands: Universitaire Pers Leiden, 1954

La Force, Auguste de Caumont, duc de, *La Grande Mademoiselle*, Paris: Flammarion, 1927; reprint, 1952

Maclean, Ian, *Woman Triumphant: Feminism in French Literature (1610–1652)*, Oxford: Clarendon Press, 1977

Magne, Émile, *Femmes galantes du XVIIe siècle: Madame de Châtillon (Isabelle-Angélique de Montmorency): Portrait et documents inédits*, Paris: Mercure de France, 1910

Melchior-Bonnet, Bernardine, *La Grande Mademoiselle: Héroïne et amoureuse*, Paris: Perrin, 1985

Méthivier, Hubert, *La Fronde*, Paris: Presses Universitaires de France, 1984

Moote, A. Lloyd, *The Revolt of the Judges: The Parlement of Paris and the Fronde (1643–1652)*, Princeton, New Jersey: Princeton University Press, 1971

Nativel, Colette, editor, *Femmes savantes, savoirs de femmes: Du crépuscule de la Renaissance à l'aube des Lumières*, Geneva: Librairie Droz, 1999

Payer, Alice de, *Le féminisme au temps de la Fronde*, Paris: Société des Éditions Fast, 1922

Pernot, Michel, *La Fronde*, Paris: Éditions de Fallois, 1994

Pollitzer, Marcel, *Les Amazones de la Fronde et le quadrille des intrigants*, Avignon, France: Aubanel, 1959

Raffin, Léonce, *Anne de Gonzague, princesse Palatine, 1616–1684*, Paris: Desclée-De Brouwer, 1935

Ranum, Orest, *The Fronde: A French Revolution, 1648–1652*, New York: Norton, 1993

Reynier, Gustave, *La femme au XVIIe siècle, ses ennemis et ses défenseurs*, Paris: J. Tallandier, 1929

Tillinac, Denis, *L'ange du désordre: Marie de Rohan, duchesse de Chevreuse*, Paris: Laffont, 1985

Wilson-Chevalier, Kathleen, and Éliane Viennot, editors, *Royaume de fémynie: Pouvoirs, contraintes, espaces de liberté des femmes, de la Renaissance à la Fronde*, Paris: Champion, and Geneva: Slatkine, 1999

FROM NATURAL SUBJECTION TO CONVENTIONAL INDIFFERENCE:

Women in the Political Thought of Sir Robert Filmer, Thomas Hobbes, and John Locke

GORDON SCHOCHET

THE SUBJECTION OF WOMEN and their exclusion from civic membership played extremely important, if not always apparent, roles in the patriarchal social and political theory of Sir Robert Filmer, the mid-17th-century apologist for Stuart absolutism. Yet he said surprisingly little directly about their status. While he was not altogether silent on the subject of women, most of his remarks seem to have been made almost in passing. Therefore, we must dig down to Filmer's presumptions about women and to the social and theoretical structures in which they were embedded to appreciate the importance of female inferiority in his political outlook. In this manner, we can begin to comprehend both the alterations in society and the shifts in political and social thought that would have to occur before women could emerge from their subordination in the traditional, western European household into a realm in which they had genuine civil entitlements and identities.

The first of these tasks, the social structural one, is accomplished by examining Filmer's society in terms of both what we know about its structure and the assumptions its members seem to have made about the ways their lives were to be organized. The theoretical analysis, by far the longer part of this essay, gives preeminence to Filmer and argues that his conceptualization defines the context within which the treatments of women by Thomas Hobbes and John Locke are most readily understood. One of the primary goals of that part of my discussion is to reveal the failures of these two political philosophers to address the strictures imposed on women by Filmer's presentation. Hobbes, I suggest, generally supported Filmer's conclusions; Locke, on the other hand, provided ample social space for women within the household but appears to have been indifferent to the larger issue of their civic identity. In all three cases, I indicate the ways in which their attitudes toward women were implicated in their more general theoretical doctrines and approaches.

Fundamental Social Structures

The translation of social structural assumptions into ideology and political theory is inherently difficult and deceptive. The assumptions on which societies rest are seldom recognized or fully understood by the people whose existences they govern and whose experiences they order, for such assumptions usually exist at the level of unconscious and unarticulated belief. When they are elevated to a plane of overt awareness, it is usually the case that the normative foundations of the society are under stress, if not actually in trouble. Merely talking about fundamental assumptions—even positively—is to risk opening them to question, and there is rarely any reason to make that move unless there is sufficient tension in the society to justify raising the issue of normative foundations. To have done this, as Filmer did, at a time of the expanding dissemination of ideas through print media is to magnify the speed and intensity with which a public debate over those foundations will take place; once something is in print and available for discussion, its components become more sharply defined, debated, and challenged.

Debates over foundations have unavoidable tendencies to become subversive, for there are important senses in which such discussions, once begun, cannot be stopped until they are somehow resolved. Unconsciously held beliefs are generally much stronger and irresistible than those that are based on reasoned acceptance; when unconsciously held beliefs are shared, they are among the most important normative factors that hold societies and other enduring social groups together and, at the same time, make them resistant to change. Unquestioned values are especially—but not exclusively—important with respect to the mass public, and they are among the reasons that traditional religious, nationalistic, and so-called ethnic values have more power to move people than do articulated, reasoned conceptions of justice. The intolerant tenacity—often mixed with and motivated by unwitting fear—with which people frequently defend deeply held prejudices and long-standing practices against perceived challenges can be explained in these same terms. To raise the normative foundations of society to the level of public examination and debate is to place them—and possibly the entire society—in jeopardy. Such a debate, once begun, is difficult to contain, and its consequences are almost impossible to predict.

Filmer is fascinating and important in several respects. His conscious and intentional articulation of patriarchal doctrine is a clue to the existence of some disturbance in the way Stuart society understood itself—that is, in its ideology—and probably an indication that the structural bases of that society were being pressured as well. Filmer apparently felt that it was necessary to defend a set of beliefs and principles that European culture had taken for granted almost without exception for nearly 2,000 years. Now, suddenly it seems, that ideology was in trouble.

Further, because he brought patriarchalism fully into the open as a political theory, Filmer is extremely helpful as a source of information about how early-modern English society implicitly conceived of itself. As Peter Laslett shrewdly notes in his edition of Filmer's works, "Filmer, for all his brash naivety and his obviously amateur outlook, was that extremely rare phenomenon—the codifier of conscious and unconscious prejudice."

While he was not particularly profound or complex as a theorist—not "deep" in the way we conventionally use the term to characterize thinkers—Filmer was virtually alone in his understanding of the fact that the foundations of English society and social structure were being challenged. Moreover, he seems to have grasped this situation, however intuitively, before anyone else did. It is precisely that awareness that foundations are being challenged and the process of defending them that raises such assumptions about society to the level of consciousness and therefore opens them to debate. In a sense, then, Filmer unintentionally gave rise to the discussion that, over the next 300 years or so, would subvert the traditional patriarchal household.

We cannot generalize directly from Filmer's views the social structural beliefs of Stuart England nor deduce Filmer's underlying assumptions from what we presume those social beliefs to have been; the correspondence between ideas and social structure is not exact. The most we can say is that there was a relationship between the ideas and the structure such that they supported one another. What we cannot say with certainty is which one came first and "gave rise" to the other or where crucial changes must have occurred. When we reach this ineradicably ideological component of Filmer's political thought, our abilities to determine precisely what he believed are severely limited, and we must resort to inference. Thus, unless there is a reason to the contrary—such as an overt rejection of, or quarrel with received opinion (which we find in Filmer only in works that have long been excluded from the Filmer canon, *An Advertisement to the Jurymen of England* [1652] and *Quaestio Quodlibiteca* [1653])— and so long as the analysis yields a reasonable degree of coherence, we must be permitted to presume that he accepted the standards and practices of his society.

In the world of the 17th century, people were generally presumed to have been born into statuses that were dictated and preserved by nature and God. The world was generally conceived as a harmonious, tightly organized structure in which every creature was assigned a place by nature. In a sense, this is rather an exaggeration, for the view of the world as natural and rigid hierarchy had been under serious challenge for some time. But the ideal view was one in which nature, God, socioeconomic status, and political hierarchy were all comprehended as parts of the same seamless whole. It was not a question of how or whether people could possibly "escape" the deprivations of their lowly status, or avoid the benefits and responsibilities of privilege, but of embracing the places that God and nature had provided. Again, extrapolated to the level of norms and expressed in something approaching a modern vocabulary, to the extent that there was a sense of "secular justice," it was an offshoot of the classic notion of giving each person her or his due. Thus, the crucial question was not why people occupied particular status but what their status was and what, accordingly, was due them.

Widows and daughters were allowed to inherit—in fact, the law preferred the direct line of a daughter to a collateral line of a brother—but married women had little standing as civil persons for most purposes and were considered "to bee one person" with their husbands, who represented them to the outside world (*The Lawes Resolutions of Women's Rights: or, The Laws Provisions for Women*, 1632). Although women were not permitted to sit in Parliament, queens regnant were an obvious exception, and England had twice been ruled by a queen in the 16th century. Filmer never commented on this apparent anomaly and referred to Elizabeth's and Mary's gender only once, in *The Freeholder's Grand Inquest* (1648), noting that they, "by reason of their sex, being not fit for public assemblies," stopped the practice of formally meeting with Parliament. Filmer mentioned Elizabeth with some frequency but referred to Mary, presumably because she was Roman Catholic, hardly at all.

Thus, Filmer was not nearly so extreme as the Presbyterian reformer John Knox, who had railed against what he called "the Monstrous Regiment of Women" in *The First Blast of the Trumpet against the Monstrous Regiment of Women* (1558), his attack on the Roman Catholic Queen Mary of England and Scotland. "To promote a women to bear rule, superiority, dominion or empire above any realm, nation, or city is repugnant to nature," Knox declared, "contumely to God, a thing most contrarious to His revealed will and approved ordinance, and finally it is the subversion of good order, of all equity and justices." These words could easily have been written by Filmer, for they are fully compatible with his derivation of all political power from God's grant of absolute, patriarchal authority to Adam, but Filmer avoided the entire matter, apparently content simply to presume that women were like children and servants in their lack of civil status. The only roles for women that Filmer's argument appears to allow are wife and mother, and it is the latter that makes fatherhood possible. Thus, it is not unreasonable—especially from today's perspective—to conclude with Carole Pateman that despite his explicit silence on the matter, "The genesis of political power [for Filmer] lies in Adam's sex-right or conjugal-right, not in his fatherhood. Adam's political title is granted before he becomes a father" (see Pateman).

When we look to the world around Filmer, which he showed no signs of rejecting, we see a patriarchal structure and a presumption of the inherent, natural inferiority of women. But we have to qualify this judgment somewhat, for the derogation or suppression of women was not an overt, intentional part of Filmer's design. Rather, female subordination was part of the unconscious prejudices on which his and his society's view of the world was built. However necessary such subordination may have been to that view and however accessible all the components of a fully antifeminist political theory may have been, there is no evidence to suggest that Filmer put these pieces together, or that many of his contemporaries were overtly and self-consciously antagonistic to the granting of full civil status to women. Inherent female inferiority was generally understood to be part of nature, and the principal reason for calling attention to a legitimate status which everyone can be presumed to know about and accept is to justify enforcing that status—or imposing the appropriate penalties on people who violate its requirements.

None of this is meant to deny the existence of what could be called "institutional sexism," to minimize its deleterious consequences for women, or to claim that women were treated with a kind of benign indifference in early-modern England. Quite the contrary, my point is that all this operated somewhere beneath the level of consciousness, where it was important in maintaining social order and could be called upon when that social order was threatened. And that is precisely what Filmer did, but without showing much concern for the restrictions that traditional European patriarchalism placed upon women.

For Filmer and his contemporaries, no less than for us today, it had to be very difficult to reject prevailing doctrines embedded in the self-conception of a society. Overcoming the constraints of one's own social structure requires enormous self-consciousness and strength of will, as well as the perspicacity to see that prevailing standards are in some way inappropriate—either because they no longer properly reflect the society's changing standards or needs, or because they do not correspond to the conceptual organization of the world. Part of the rhetorical structure of such claims is usually to insist that the "old" arguments were incorrect to begin with and were themselves based on misunderstandings of those governing principles. Rarely is the equivalent of "That may have worked in the past, but it is not the way we do things around here now" asserted on behalf of a new set of claims. Conceptual innovations are seldom presented for what they are, reformulating pointers to the future; rather, they are firmly tied to the present, and sometimes to the past as well.

In the final analysis, what was at issue in the mid-17th-century political debates to which Filmer contributed was the possession and control of the state. That problem was itself rooted in questions that the English had been able to avoid at least since Henry's VIII's Reformation had succeeded in making the religious establishment an arm of the polity. Thanks to the convenient but ultimately inadequate myth that England was ruled by the "king-in-Parliament," a tacit if uneasy constitutional accommodation had permitted the question of "fundamental law" to be sidestepped until king and Parliament finally found themselves theoretically at loggerheads and physically at war in 1642. Like all deep, conceptual conflicts that are not abandoned, this one had to be settled by force rather than principle.

Among the important subdisputes were questions of whether politics and the state are natural or the results of human artifice and, closely related, whether political origins are to be found in familial or patriarchal organization or in a so-called state of nature, and, if the latter, what makes people sufficiently free to establish civil society. In the short run, the patriarchal response was much the easiest of the alternatives, and Filmer attacked the notions of "natural freedom" and individual "rights" that the state-of-nature and contract theories presupposed as "a New, Plausible and Dangerous Opinion," which "was first hatched in

the Schools for good Divinity" (*Patriarcha: A Defence of the Natural Authority of Kings against the Unnatural Liberty of the People*, written c.1630–40; first published, 1680). In terms of the civil identity of women, his remark suggests that only a radical transformation in the way the social and political worlds were conceptualized could alter the status of women; nothing short of an overthrow of the naturalistic political theory that had undergirded European self-consciousness at least since the time of Plato and Aristotle would do the job.

Hobbes: From Nature to Convention

Both Thomas Hobbes, whose principal works were published during Filmer's lifetime in response to the same general problems of civil war and the disintegration of English politics that had inspired Sir Robert, and John Locke, whose attack on Filmer in the *Two Treatises of Government* (1690) is the primary reason that the latter was saved from near oblivion, rejected the naturalism of their day. But neither Hobbes nor Locke took the conceptually subsequent step of advocating the full civil emancipation of women.

Hobbes, it turns out, did not reject patriarchalism, but he did put it on a conventional footing. Nature played a brief and limited role in the construction of Hobbes's political system: it made all people equal—equally free, equally possessed of natural rights, equally entitled to all things, and physically equal (at least potentially, if one allowed for the use of weapons). This realm of natural equality, the state of nature, was short-lived; once people began to interact and to pursue their natural rights to all things, they realized how precarious their lives were and sought refuge in the artifact of civil society. But society, the setting in which human beings are actually found, is built on hierarchy and inequality of possessions and entitlements. This much of the Hobbesian political theory is generally known and understood; what is not fully appreciated is the artful way Hobbes dealt with the conceptual problem he had created for himself: how to justify the extraction of conventional or social inequality from natural equality. It is in the solution to this problem that Hobbes made his most forthright statements about women.

Hobbes was not truly interested in the question of the status of women, so he actually said very little directly on the subject. However, he was aware that the equality that nature had bestowed upon women was utterly eradicated by civil society. His explanation of this transformation is elegant and ingenious in its simplicity. Beginning with the premises that power and status are conventional, not natural, and that consent alone can make one person superior to another, he argued that in the state of nature mothers, not fathers, initially had power over children, since mothers were with their babies at birth and had the right as well as the ability to kill them, which they could do in full accord with the law of nature: according to Hobbes's argument in chapter 20 of *Leviathan* (1651), in the state of nature, one is permitted to kill all enemies, potential as well as actual, and a child could grow up to become a threat to the mother.

Theoretically, this supposition would make mothers the original sovereigns—the founders of commonwealths, a role that Hobbes sometimes ascribed to fathers in the state of nature— but sovereignty, as *legitimate* power, is a two-way relationship, and the mere ability and right of the mother to destroy the child could not extinguish the child's claim to natural rights; only the consent of the child itself could do that, which is precisely what Hobbes argued. He did so through what in chapter 15 of *Leviathan* he identified as the fourth law of nature, the law of gratitude, which stipulates:

> As justice dependeth on antecedent covenant, so does GRATITUDE depend on antecedent grace, that is to say, antecedent free-gift; and is the fourth law of nature, which may be conceived in this form, that a man which receiveth benefit from another of mere grace, endeavour that he which giveth it, have no reasonable cause to repent him of his good will. For no man giveth but with intention of good to himself, because gift is voluntary, and of all voluntary acts the object is to every man his own good; of which, if men see they shall be frustrated, there will be no beginning of benevolence, or trust; nor, consequently, of mutual help, nor of reconciliation of one man to another; and therefore they are to remain still in the condition of war, which is contrary to the first and fundamental law of nature, which commandeth men to seek peace. The breach of this law is called *ingratitude*, and hath the same relation to grace, that injustice hath to obligation by covenant.

Even presuming that gratitude is a sufficient basis for obligation and, hence, for authority, the gratitude of the infant child to its mother for not killing it is difficult to conceive, for a newborn does not have the capacities either to recognize or to act upon the natural law. Hobbes responded to this dilemma by projecting that gratitude into the future when the child had become sufficiently rational to appreciate its indebtedness to its mother.

But all this makes for matriarchy, not the patriarchal society of early-modern England. Women must still be suppressed for Hobbes's account to have been applicable to the political conditions of his day. As explained in chapter 20 of *Leviathan*, this next and crucial move was accomplished through a three-step process. First, conquest was a legitimate means of acquiring authority. Second, women were "conquered" or overpowered in the period immediately following the births of their children, when the mothers were weak and infirm, and their "conquerors" were usually the fathers of the children. The conquering male became sovereign to the child, who was already indebted to its mother, by virtue of his conquest of the mother. Finally, the inferior status of women was incorporated into civil society because commonwealths were established by men and because laws were made by men, not women.

Hobbes had taken a step away from hard and unyielding nature to malleable and potentially optional convention, and in the process he further opened up the possibility of discussion and debate of certain issues that were beyond question for Filmer. All that was left of nature when Hobbes was finished with it was the theory of rights, which was anathema to Filmer and those of his royalist persuasion. Admittedly, Hobbes's account of the place and function of rights in his absolutist civil society left no room for the assertions of individual liberty and limited government that we associate with the modern theory of rights, and there was no place in his doctrine of sovereignty for the civil status of women—unless, of course, the sovereign decreed it.

With the exception of ending the subjugation of women, these radical departures from the prevailing politics of 17th-century England were central to the platform of the Levelers, whose doctrine—to the extent that it was coherent—had rested in part upon the same appeals to rights and conventions as that of Hobbes. To a great extent, Hobbes's political writings aimed to show that such leveling and "democratical" claims were dangerous as well as false, but he had the genius to appreciate that the naturalistic, biblical metaphysics of a Filmer were equally inappropriate to his age. Hobbes's political and rhetorical task, then, was to provide new, conventional foundations for the same kind of absolutist polity that Filmer defended. And Hobbes certainly knew that conventions are an unsteady foundation for any political society.

Locke: Limited Entitlements for Women within the Household

Locke's doctrine was rather more ambiguous than Hobbes's. Locke, too, built upon rights and political conventions, but he retained rather more of nature than Hobbes had permitted. In the end, women were still denied a civil identity in Locke's view, but—because of his detailed criticism of Filmer—Locke ultimately had more to say than Hobbes about their general status, even recognizing somewhat limited entitlements for women within the household.

The starting point of Locke's argument was the insistence that power over children is not due to fatherhood but a consequence of the law of nature. He argued in *Two Treatises of Government* that all parents since Adam and Eve had been placed "*under an obligation to preserve, nourish, and educate the Children,* they had begotten, not as their own Workmanship, but as the Workmanship of their own Maker, the Almighty, to whom they were to be accountable for them" (book II, paragraph 56). It followed that "*The Power,* then *that Parents have* over their Children, arises from that Duty which is incumbent upon them, to take care of their Off-spring during the imperfect state Childhood." Parental power, he continued, "is but a help to the weakness and imperfection of their Nonage, a Discipline necessary to their education" (book II, paragraphs 58 and 60). Accordingly, the child was bound to obey whomever maintained and cared for her or him, whether that person was the natural parent or not.

Familial authority belonged to both parents, Locke asserted, and he chided Filmer for ignoring the fact that the Fifth Commandment named both parents, not just the father. Thus, even if parental power did come from generation, "This would give the *Father* but a joynt Dominion with the Mother over them [the children]. For no body can deny but that the woman hath an equal share, if not the greater, as nourishing the Child a long time in her own Body out of her own Substance" (*Two Treatises,* book I, paragraph 55). It followed, according to Locke, that paternal power ought "more properly [to be] called Parental Power. For whatever obligation Nature and the right of Generation lays on Children, it must certainly bind them equal to both concurrent Causes of it" (*Two Treatises,* book II, paragraph 52). But Locke violated his own injunction almost immediately, reverting to the phrase "paternal power" (book II, paragraph 69) and subsequently suggesting that the terms could be interchanged.

In general, Locke treated the husband as the superior mate but left a realm of freedom to the wife:

> But the Husband and Wife, though they have but one common Concern, yet having different understandings, will unavoidably sometimes have different wills too; it therefore being necessary that the last Determination, i.e., the Rule, should be placed somewhere; it naturally falls to the Man's share, as the abler and the stronger. But this reaching out to the things of their common Interest and Property, leaves the Wife in the full and free possession of what by Contract is her peculiar Right, and gives the Husband no more power over her Life than she has over his (*Two Treatises*, book II, paragraph 82).

Furthermore, this conjugal power did not provide the basis for civil government. If God's command to Eve that "thy Desire shall be to thy Husband, and he shall rule over thee" (Genesis 3:16),

> must needs be understood as a Law to bind her and all other Women to subjection, it can be no other Subjection than what every Wife owes her Husband, and then if this be the Original Grant of Government and the Foundation of Monarchical Power, there will be as many Monarchs as there are Husbands. If therefore these words give any Power to Adam, it can be only a Conjugal Power, not Political, the Power that every Husband hath to order the things of private Concernment in his Family, as Proprietor of the Goods and Land there, and to have his Will take place before that of his wife in all things of their common Concernment; but not a Political Power of Life and Death over her, much less over any body else (*Two Treatises*, book I, paragraph 48).

Quite simply, the complex society of the household, with its conjugal, parental, and master-servant relations "wherein the Master or Mistress of it had Some sort of Rule proper to a Family, . . . came short of *Political Society*" (*Two Treatises*, book II, paragraph 77). But the basic structure of the family remained essentially patriarchal, and the members of civil society were men who were heads of households or otherwise enjoyed economic and social independence. In this, Locke—like Hobbes— did not depart from the Filmerian understanding of the world. The important departure, also shared with Hobbes, was the movement out of nature and into convention. Locke's state, however, was the antithesis of all that Hobbes had defended; it was the constitutional, limited polity instituted to protect and maximize the rights and liberties of its members and derived from their consent that Hobbes had attacked in the *Leviathan*.

Theories of Politics: Divine-Rights Naturalism versus Individual Rights

The derivation of politics from a conception of rights and liberty, while certainly not original to Hobbes and Locke, was the theoretical target of Filmer's patriarchalism and a denial of his political naturalism. Filmer used the term "rights" throughout his writings, but he generally intended a kind of entitlement that came from and was attached to superior status (*Patriarcha*, para-

graphs 4 and 5). Rarely did he mean the natural or personal rights that belonged to each individual; he was aware of this meaning, and his criticism of Grotius was designed to condemn that usage for its incompatibility with political authority.

The appeal to individual rights suggests voluntarism and conventionality, a world in which each rights-bearing person has the capacity to make and be responsible for his—and ultimately *her*—own place. These notions are altogether absent from Filmer, whose theory could be described as a kind of divine-right naturalism; he looked to nature and the structures created by God for standards. But he appreciated the *logic* of the rights argument and saw that it would have to extend much further than its advocates intended.

Grotius had departed from the natural and original equality and common ownership of the state of nature and had endorsed the existence of private property and status in civil society. In a pointed criticism of that part of Grotius that is applicable to all natural law theories, Filmer said:

> dominion . . . was brought in by the will of man, whom by this doctrine Grotius makes to be able to change that law which God himself cannot change, as he saith. He gives a double ability to man; first to make that no law of nature which God made to be the law of nature: and next to make that a law of nature which God made not; for now that dominion is brought in, he maintains, it is against the law of nature to take that which is in another man's dominion (*Observations Concerning the Originall of Government*, 1652)

Filmer's arguments against the fictitious contract of government that ended the state of nature were even more telling and recognized that the exclusion of women would violate the law of nature. The majority cannot bind any but itself, he said; all who dissented from the pact would have to retain their original liberty. Anything short of this would violate the putative natural right of liberty. Second, it is inconceivable, he wrote, that a multitude of people freely living without the constraints of society should come together to make such an agreement; particularly unlikely to participate would be "infants and others under the age of discretion; *not to speak of women, especially virgins, who by birth have as much natural freedom as any other, and therefore ought not to lose their liberty without their own consent*" (*The Anarchy of a Limited or Mixed Monarchy*, 1648). Locke certainly knew of this argument but did not refer to it. However, his friend James Tyrrell inserted the following "Advertisement" to the first of the 13 dialogues that comprised his *Bibliotheca Politica* (1691–94):

> I Desire always to be understood, that when I make use of the word People, I do not mean the vulgar or mixt multitude, but in the state of Nature the whole Body of Free-men and women, especially the Fathers and Masters of Families; and in a Civil State, all degrees of men, as well the Nobility and Clergy, as the Common People.

If Tyrrell was aware of the problem, Hobbes and Locke should have seen it as well. At some level, they should have accounted for the relative absence of women from their conceptions of civil society and explained why women apparently did not have rights. Hobbes forthrightly acknowledged that women's rights had been extinguished by men. Locke seems to have ignored the question altogether, which his conventional theory of political society should have prevented. As we shall see below, there is a way of accounting for Locke's silence here, and that has to do with his understanding of the differences between "society" and politics.

In the end, of course, women were no more accorded civil status by Hobbes or Locke than they were by Filmer. In Filmer's case there are at least the excuses that his naturalistic conception of politics does not leave space for women and the fact that, in the final analysis, no one but the sovereign is a civil person. Even the patriarchal heads of households from whose God-given powers political power is derived do not enjoy civil status under the absolute monarchy Filmer envisioned.

In Filmer's view, the world is coherent, systematic, and orderly; it is structurally and naturally uncomplicated. To see this clearly is to appreciate the larger social and theoretical structures that supported the devaluation of women. According to Filmer, everything proceeds from God's will. Therefore, one must find where that will is most clearly expressed and subsequently manifested. Filmer argued from the Bible; human beings are obligated to obey God's will as it is expressed in the Scriptures, which "have given us the true grounds and principles of government" (*Anarchy*). The problem with an argument from Providence, as we shall see when Filmer's attempt to provide historical continuity is discussed below, is that it ultimately leads to the "whatever is is right" doctrine so brilliantly satirized in the next century by Voltaire's *Candide* (1759). In the end, it is impossible both to maintain a reliance upon Providence and to argue for standards or principles on which humans should base their conduct, for the latter implies a degree of freedom and volition that would seem to be incompatible with providentialism.

For Filmer, the model for political authority was Adam, whose sovereignty had been established by God in Paradise and was passed on intact to his lineal heirs until the division of the world among Noah's sons and the further division after the failed attempt to build the Tower of Babel:

> Most of the civilest nations of the world labour to fetch their original from some one of the sons or nephews of Noah, which were scattered abroad after the confusion of Babel. In this dispersion we must certainly find the establishment of regal power throughout the kingdoms of the world.
>
> It is a common opinion that at the confusion of tongues there were seventy-two distinct nations erected. All which were not confused multitudes without heads or governors, and at liberty to, chose what governors or government they pleased, but they were distinct families, which had Fathers for rulers over them, whereby it appears that even in the confusion God was careful to preserve the fatherly authority by distributing the languages according to the diversity of families (*Patriarcha*).

The larger, polemical point of all this was to undermine the increasingly popular political doctrine of Bellarmine, Francisco Suarez, and Grotius that looked to natural human liberty and equality as the basis on which society was voluntarily established. "This tenet was first hatched in the Schools for good Divinity," Filmer wrote, and has been adopted "by succeeding Papists," the "Divines of the Reformed Churches," and "the common people everywhere," none of whom remembers "that the desire

of liberty was the cause of the fall of Adam." This notion, which lay at the heart of the challenges to Charles I, contradicted "the doctrine and history of the Holy Scriptures, the constant practice of all ancient monarchies, and the very principles of the law of nature. It is hard to say whether it be more erroneous in Divinity or dangerous in policy" (*Patriarcha*).

To his providentialism Filmer added a Bodinian conception of sovereignty. One of his tracts, *The Necessity of the Absolute Power of all Kings* (1648), was a string of excerpts from the 1606 English translation of Jean Bodin's *Les six livres de la République* (1576; *The Six Bookes of a Commonweale*). It was an unquestioned truth of politics for Filmer that in every political society there must be an absolute, inalienable, and indivisible power to make and enforce laws. He was able to join divine-right absolutism and the doctrine of sovereignty by means of the simple assertion that since the "Kingly power is by the law of God, so it hath no inferior law to limit it" (*Patriarcha*). It was axiomatic that "There can be no laws without a supreme power to command or make them," from which it followed that "in a monarchy the King must of necessity be above the laws. There can be no sovereign majesty in him that is under them" (*Patriarcha*). Thus, he posits in *Anarchy*, the true question of politics

> is not, whether there shall be an arbitrary power; but the only point is, who shall have that arbitrary power, whether one man or many? There never was, nor ever can be, any people governed without a power of making laws, and every power of making laws must be arbitrary: for to make a law according to law, is *contradictio in adjecto*.

Filmer makes the same point in his *Observations upon Aristotles Politiques* (1652):

1. That there is no form of government, but monarchy only.
2. That there is no monarchy, but paternal.
3. That there is no paternal monarchy, but absolute, or arbitrary.
4. That there is no such thing as an aristocracy or democracy.
5. That there is no such form of government as a tyranny.
6. That the people are not born free by nature.

Yet another important ingredient in the structure of Filmer's political theory is the way that the household was used to prefigure politics. We are accustomed to regarding doctrines such as Filmer's analogically or metaphorically, such that the family suggests or implies things about the state, which can be seen as somehow like the household. Analogy is one of the standard modes of argument, and metaphors are among our principal means of assimilating and making sense of that which we might not otherwise understand or perhaps even perceive. The new or unfamiliar is presented as resembling or being a somewhat deviant instance of something that is already known to us, and we are "persuaded" to comprehend and eventually to accept it. This manner of arguing leaves room for discussion and debate about the ways in which the things in question do or do not resemble one another. In these terms, one might want to claim that while the modern state resembles the family in some respects (say, the existence of determinate responsibilities and expectations), it is sufficiently different in others—the absence of kinship ties, perhaps—to invalidate the comparison.

Initially, Filmer's argument would not be touched by such a response, for his theory was based upon identity, not similarity. Accordingly, the family was a polity, and the polity was a household, and the patriarchal, biblical family was not a prototype but was the wellspring of politics. Theoretically, there are two ways of responding to an argument from strict identity. One either accepts it, as Hobbes did, and then goes on to claim that both institutions are conventional, or one has the option of denying the identity altogether—a much more difficult strategy. Locke took the latter course and insisted that civil society was conventional and that the family was theoretically irrelevant to it, thereby avoiding even the question of the extent to which family and polity were related.

Only these two moves could have provided the opening that was necessary for the emergence of women as politically visible. Both loosened the stranglehold that patriarchal naturalism had on the politics of early-modern Europe and replaced divine-right absolutism with a political conventionalism derived from personal and natural rights. The fact that Locke himself did not carry his argument to the necessary next step and fully incorporate women into his political doctrine is altogether separate from the implications of that argument. Locke accepted a significant part of the patriarchal structuring of Stuart society, and he endorsed its exclusion of women from the political process, but at the same time he prepared the way for the eventual admission of women to the category of citizen. His omissions called attention to unresolved issues and placed them on the political agenda of the English people.

Filmer's Providentialism: A Denial of History

The weakest part of Filmer's argument was his contention that each successive sovereign had the same entitlements as every one of his predecessors; in the process, he was forced to ignore the impact of history on social and political institutions and practices. The logic of Sir Robert's insistence upon unlimited monarchical power meant that, apart from the commands of God and laws of nature, nothing other than the sovereign's own will could bind him. And even then, should the ruler give his word, there was no earthly power that could legitimately hold him to it. Thus, according to Filmer, the king could not be bound by the laws of his predecessors—unless he consented to them, but even that was questionable—and the coronation oath imposed no practical conditions on a ruler.

Certainly, wisdom, prudence, self-interest, even a concern for the welfare of his subjects all dictated moderation, and Filmer was well aware of the classical conception of a tyrant as one who ruled in pursuit of his own interests rather than those of his subjects. Nevertheless, in terms of the entitlements and powers of monarchy, only God could discipline a king, and humans should suffer whatever their rulers imposed while awaiting providential deliverance. Thus, each successive king was to determine for himself which laws of his predecessors he would retain and which prior limitations on the prerogative he would accept. Filmer had logic on his side, for it is difficult to see how a king

who is bound by the acts of his ancestors could be as fully a king as his predecessors had been. To have argued otherwise would have made Filmer as inconsistent as he had said Grotius was, for he would have allowed human actions to alter the commands of God.

For all its ruthless consistency—indeed, probably because of it—this hardheaded positivism was incapable of acknowledging the simple but profoundly important fact that societies are continuous over time and that each successive generation makes its own contributions to the process of maintaining social practices and institutions. In England, this was an exceptional difficulty, for it effectively eliminated the common law, the society's central political institution. In this respect, Filmer was truly the political theorist of reaction, not conservatism, more so perhaps than anyone else, even the ill-remembered critics of the French Revolution, Louis de Bonald and Joseph de Maistre.

Political practice is simply not logical and coherent in the ways that Filmer's patriarchal absolutism—or any architectonic theory, for that matter—requires. Rather, it is a continuing series of adjustments and accommodations, a mixture of persistence and change, and the invocation and partial or misapplication of principles, none of which can be fully captured by a theory. This is even more problematic for a providential theory that also has a political agenda. Filmer probably knew all this, for at the end of his life, with his beloved King Charles executed, the monarchy overthrown, and a republic (of sorts) established in its place, he halfheartedly defended taking the engagement to support Cromwell's government on the grounds that

> in usurpation, the title of the usurper is before, and better than any other than of him that had a former right: for he hath a possession by the permissive will of God, which permission, how long it may endure, no man ordinarily knows. Every man is to preserve his own life for the service of God, and of his King or Father, and is so far to obey a usurper as may tend not only to the preservation of his King and Father, but sometimes even to the preservation of the usurper himself, when probably he may thereby be reserved to the correction or mercy of his true superior (*Directions for Obedience to Governours in Dangerous and Doubtful Times*, 1653).

In *Anarchy*, a tract published in 1648, when Charles's fortunes had yet to be determined, Filmer remarked,

> many times by the act either of a usurper himself, or those that set him up, the true heir of a crown is dispossessed, God using the ministry of the wickedest men for the removing and setting up of Kings: in such cases, the subjects' obedience to the fatherly power must go along and wait upon God's providence, who only hath right to give and take away kingdoms, and thereby to adopt subjects into the obedience of another fatherly power.

It was a peculiar argument, but it was probably the best that could be made of the providentialist injunction to obey the powers that be because they are ordained by God (Romans, 13: 1). To this, Filmer added the more overtly prudential doctrine that "protection and subjection are reciprocal, so that when the first fails, the latter ceaseth" (*Directions for Obedience*). That was precisely the formula that Hobbes had employed in the *Leviathan*, which intended "to set before mens eyes the mutuall relation between protection and obedience." Thus, it seems to follow that the subject's duties to Charles I had ended when the king lost the Second Civil War—even before the Regicide—and were immediately transferred to the Parliamentary forces that had defeated and replaced him because they had shown themselves to be the effective civil government.

Filmer was certainly correct in seeing that the application and adjudication of the law requires discretion, an understanding that is generally accepted in modern common law jurisprudence. But he went from this unexceptionable insight, via the doctrine of absolute sovereignty, to a conclusion that is patently unacceptable in any political society that values law. The common law, by its nature, is indeterminate, if not altogether contingent. How it manages to function is always something of a conceptual puzzle, but Filmer's arguments rendered it even more mysterious. The common law is something other than the will of the sovereign, and its persistence is not merely a matter of its acceptance by successive generations of rulers.

As a matter of logic, of course, all law—statute law and the common law equally—must be backed up by some kind of legitimate force simply to make it law. Filmer fully appreciated this fact, as is evident from his pronouncements that "There can be no laws without supreme power to command or make them," and "What is hitherto affirmed of the dependency and subjection of the Common Law to the sovereign Prince, the same may be said as well of all Statute Law. For the King is the sole immediate author, corrector, and moderator also" (*Patriarcha*). His legal theories sound very much like those of the 19th-century utilitarian positivist John Austin, one of the last significant Anglophone contributors to the discourse of sovereignty. Austin, Hobbes, and Filmer alike were forced to deny history and could not adequately account for the continuity of changes in English legal and political practice. Again, Filmer's providentialist presumption partially rescued his patriarchal theory, but the cost of this coherence was historical and conceptual plausibility.

Admitting that it was "true [that] all Kings be not the natural parents of their subjects," Filmer nevertheless insisted that "they all are, or are to be reputed, as the next heirs of those progenitors who were at first the natural parents of the whole people, and in their right succeed to the exercise of supreme jurisdiction" (*Patriarcha*). Accordingly, "It skills not which way Kings come by their power, whether by election, donation, succession or by any other means, for it is still the manner of the government by supreme power that makes them properly Kings, not the means of obtaining their crowns" (*Patriarcha*). Finally, to clinch the point, "all Kings that now are, or ever were, are, or were either Fathers of their people, or the heirs of such Fathers, or usurpers of the right of such Fathers" (*Anarchy*). It was a neat, compact theory, but, as all of Filmer's critics pointed out, it had the effect of undermining patriarchalism and lineal succession altogether.

Civil Personhood for Women

A large part of what is involved in all this is Filmer's rather anxious attack on convention and what we see as "modernity." Filmer probably did not really understand modernity, simply defending the stable but declining traditional, natural order against challenges of precarious institutions and practices that

were subject to human will. It is in the nature of architectonic theories to reject uncertainty, and here, as elsewhere, Filmer provides an illuminating example of the kinds of ideological and structural changes that would be necessary before women could emerge into civil personhood.

Filmer stood for a conception of society in which the identities women were afforded were effectively derived from the males on whom they were dependent. Their status as wives and daughters rendered them radically different from men; they could never attain the familial headship that had been a prerequisite to membership in civil society at least since the time of Aristotle. From the standpoint of today's politics, it is ironic to realize that women in early-modern society needed a kind of individualism that would give them identities not inherently distinct from those of men. The transition to this modern outlook was already underway when Filmer was writing, but it was to be a protracted process of change, and Filmer stood somewhere near its beginnings.

One of the targets of Filmer's criticisms was the specter of discord, conflict, breakdown of government, and finally anarchy that haunts Philip Hunton's *Treatise of onarchy* (1643), which immediately became the center of an extensive debate. Claiming that the government of England was a mixture of monarchy, democracy, and aristocracy, Hunton believed—as did Locke some 40 years later—that the political process could not solve all the problems it confronted. When the moderation, accommodation, forbearance, and implicit trust that were essential to the political process broke down, Hunton reasoned, politics itself had reached an impasse that could only lead to revolutionary conflict. On that, Filmer and Hunton agreed, but Filmer placed the blame on the mixture itself, which he saw as an altogether improper and eventually disastrous form of rule.

Implicitly, Hunton accepted the modern conceit that authority is socially and culturally constructed and therefore controllable. One consequence of this view, which Hunton certainly did not embrace, is the distinctively modern assertion that the roles assigned to women are no less conventional and artificial than politics itself. More so perhaps than anyone else in the early-modern period, Hobbes represents that view. He is one of the most thoroughgoing social constructivists in history of western thought, particularly in the *Philosophical Rudiments Concerning Government and Society* (1651). We have already seen how he applied this perspective to the status of women. In the end, however, Hobbesian conventionalism did not emancipate women. In the first place, no one but the sovereign was freed from subjection; rather more to point, however, Hobbes left women in a condition of subjection to their male superiors, so their inferiority—however conventional it may have been—was one layer deeper than that of men.

Locke, as we have seen, stood somewhere between Filmer and Hobbes on this issue. He embraced that part of the conventionalist argument that applied to politics, but he was silent about the status of the family. What he did accomplish was the separation of politics from society, thereby rendering futile any attempt to infer the nature of the state from the household. The fact that the powers of a father and a civil ruler were sometimes resident in the same person was purely contingent, Locke insisted, in an effort to undermine Filmer's contention that because people are the natural subjects of their parents, they can never acquire enough freedom to be the authors of their own political obligations. The granting of Locke's point sets the stage for rendering all political relations indeterminate. His long-run legacy is the liberty that is required for humans to control their own destinies, and it is precisely that liberty that Filmer resisted.

Conclusion

It has been the genius of modern feminism to insist upon a place and identity for women independent of their memberships in households or families. For political as well as conceptual reasons, it has been a difficult struggle—the end of which is not yet in sight—but it is now possible to talk of women outside the structures of the family. This change is related to the growing dissatisfaction with "essentialist" formulations in general that was itself part of the 20th century's distrust of metaphysical speculation. And all this, in turn, is related to the malaise that is sometimes said to accompany the contemporary world's readjustment of long-standing identities and relationships. While it is far too early to determine precise causal connections, it is certainly clear that feminism has had something important to do with generating and perpetuating this entire series of complaints. What makes all this difficult is that the stakes are very high; members of modern society are being asked—and not only by their feminist critics—to reconsider some of their most fundamental self-understandings and to alter the relationships and social structures that have sustained the distributions of power and social advantage at least since the Reformation. Metaphysics, the essentialist conceptions of the self to which it gives rise, and the role-assignments that result function like "totalizing" institutions—society-wide, conceptual prisons that contain and restrain the inmates as well as the guards, with both classes appearing to have some interest in maintaining the system. For the "guards," the benefits are status, privilege, and power; for the "inmates," the psychological security of identity and stability are the principal advantages that derive from preserving the status quo.

All of which is to say that is it difficult, sometimes painful, and usually costly to bring about alterations in the characteristic ways societies describe themselves and their members. Resistance to such proffered changes is generally grounded in attempts to retain status and power, but even those who might benefit from the changes are often reluctant to adopt or endorse innovations they find too unsettling. The entire process rarely occurs at this level of consciousness, but desires to retain status and anxieties about potential dislocations help explain the often unwitting motives people have for preserving social order without in any way denying their possible sincerity.

In many respects, modern feminism has been unusually successful, for one of the most conspicuous consequences of the contemporary debate is that the meaning of women (and of men too, for that matter) is no longer stable. While this meaning is not quite up for grabs, as it were, it does appear to be on its way to being "lost" in the sense intended by James Boyd White, who, following Thucydides, remarks, "An alteration in language of the kind I mean is not merely a lexical event, and it is not reversible by insistence upon a set of proper definitions. It is a change in the world and the self, in manners and conduct and sentiment" (see White). It is now possible—not merely plausible—to talk about women apart from their traditional roles as wives, mothers, and daughters. What is more, our understanding of the family itself has been altered, partially in response to feminist criticisms and partially because the institution itself has changed. Although these reconceptualizations continue to be resisted by many people, they have fairly secure places in the social vocabulary of the Western world. These alterations continue to reverberate throughout society rather like an earthquake and its after-shocks, for the traditionally conceived household with its hierarchical arrangements is the part of the bedrock on which the entirety of modern social structure rests.

There is something fascinating about the entire business, for in the adult lifetimes of many of us, a set of linguistic convention and their surrounding and supporting and dependent institutions and practices that have held sway for more than 500 years have all been successfully modified as a result of the conscious efforts of feminist political reformers. It is an astounding accomplishment when apprehended from that perspective. This success would have been altogether lost on Sir Robert Filmer, for it represents the ultimate victory of his latter-day adversary, John Locke.

Bibliography

Sources

Filmer, Robert, Sir, *An Advertisement to the Jurymen of England, Touching Witches, Together with a Difference Between a Hebrew and an English Witch: or a Discourse Whether It May Be lawful to Take Use for Money*, London: n.p., 1653

Filmer, Robert, Sir, *The Anarchy of a Limited or Mixed Monarchy* (1648), in *Patriarcha and Other Political Works*, edited by Peter Laslett, Oxford: Blackwell, 1949

Filmer, Robert, Sir, *Directions for Obedience to Governours in Dangerous and Doubtful Times*, London: n.p., 1652

Filmer, Robert, Sir, *The Free-holder's Grand Inquest, Touching Our Soveraigne Lord the King and His Parliament* (1648), in *Patriarcha and Other Political Works* edited by Peter Laslett, Oxford: Blackwell, 1949

Filmer, Robert, Sir, *The Necessity of the Absolute Power of All Kings* (1648), in *Patriarcha and Other Political Works* edited by Peter Laslett, Oxford: Blackwell, 1949

Filmer, Robert, Sir, *Observations Concerning the Originall of Government* (1652), in *Patriarcha and Other Political Works*, edited by Peter Laslett, Oxford: Blackwell, 1949

Filmer, Robert, Sir, *Observations upon Aristotles Politiques Touching Forms of Government* (1652), in *Patriarcha and Other Political Works*, edited by Peter Laslett, Oxford: Blackwell, 1949

Filmer, Robert, Sir, *Patriarcha: A Defence of the Natural Authority of Kings Against the Unnatural Liberty of the People* (1680), in *Patriarcha and Other Political Works*, edited by Peter Laslett, Oxford: Blackwell, 1949

Filmer, Robert, Sir, *Quoestio Quodlibiteca: Or, A Discourse Whether It May Be lawful to Take use for Money*, London: Humphrey Mosley, 1653; as *A Discourse on Usury*, New York: Garland, 1978

Hobbes, Thomas, *Dialogue between a Philosopher and a Student, of the Common law of England* (1681), Chicago: University of Chicago Press, 1971

Hobbes, Thomas, *Elementorum Elementorum Philosophiae, sectio tertia, de Cive* (1642); as *Philosophical Rudiments Concerning Government and Society* (1651), Oxford: Oxford University Press, 1983

Hobbes, Thomas, *Leviathan: or, The Matter, Forme, and Power of a Common-wealth Ecclesiastical and Civil* (1651); reprint, Indianapolis: Hackett Publishing Company, 1994

Hunton, Philip, *Treatise of Monarchie*, London: John Bellamy and Ralph Smith, 1643

Hunton, Philip, *A Vindication of the Treatise of Monarchy*, London: John Bellamy, 1644

Knox, John, *The First Blast of the Trumpet against the Monstrous Regiment of Women* (1558), in Roger Masson, editor, *On Rebellion*, Cambridge: Cambridge University Press, 1994

Knox, John, *The Laws Resolutions of Womens Rights: or, The Laws Provision for Women*, 1632

Locke, John, *Two Treatises of Government in the Former, the False Principles and Foundation of Sir Robert Filmer* (1690), edited by Peter Laslett, Cambridge: Cambridge University Press, 1960

Tyrrell, James, *Bibliotheca Politica; or, An Enquiry into the Ancient Constitution of the English Government . . .. in Thirteen Dialogues*, London: n.p., 1694

Tyrrell, James, *Patriarcha non Monarcha*, London: Richard Janeway, 1681

Reference Works

Amussen, Susan D., *An Ordered Society: Gender and Class in Early Modern England*, Oxford: Blackwell, 1988

Barak, Aharon, *Judicial Discretion*, translated by Yadin Kaufman, New Haven: Yale University Press, 1989

Burgess, Glenn, *The Politics of the Ancient Constitution: An Introduction to English Political Thought 1603–1642*, University Park: Pennsylvania State University Press, 1993

Daly, James, *Sir Robert Filmer and English Political Thought*, Toronto and Buffalo: University of Toronto Press, 1979

Dworkin, Ronald, *A Matter of Principle*, Cambridge, Massachusetts: Harvard University Press, 1985

Eisenstein, Elizabeth L., *The Printing Press as an Agent of Change: Communications and Cultural Transformations in Early Modern Europe*, Cambridge: Cambridge University Press, 1979

Ezell, Margaret J.M., *The Patriarch's Wife: Literary Evidence and the History of the Family*, Chapel Hill: University of North Carolina Press, 1987

Fletcher, Anthony, "The Protestant Idea of Marriage in Early Modern England," in Anthony Fletcher and Peter Roberts, editors, *Religion, Culture, and Society in Early Modern Britain: Essays in Honor of Patrick Collinson*, Cambridge: Cambridge University Press, 1994

Gough, John W., "James Tyrell, Whig Historian and Friend of John Locke," *Historical Journal* XIX, 1976

Hart, H.L.A., *The Concept of Law*, Oxford: Oxford University Press, 1964, 1993

Judson, Margaret A., *The Crisis of the Constitution: An Essay in Constitutional and Political Thought in England, 1603–1645*, New Brunswick, New Jersey: Rutgers University Press, 1949, 1988

Orlin, Cowen Lena, *Private Matters and Public Culture in Post-Reformation England*, Ithaca, New York: Cornell University Press, 1994

Pateman, Carol, *The Sexual Contract*, Stanford, California: Stanford University Press, 1988

Pocock, John Greville A., and Gordon Schochet, "Interregnum and Restauration," in *The Varieties of British Political Thought, 1500–1800*, edited by J.G.A. Pocock with Gordon Schochet and Lois. G. Schwoerer, Cambridge: Cambridge University Press, 1994

Schochet, Gordon, "Constitutionalism, Liberalism, and the Study of Politics," *Nomos XX: Constitutionalism (1979)*

Schochet, Gordon, "The English Revolution in the History of Political Thought," in *Country and Court: Essays in Honor of Perez Zagorin*, edited by Bonnie Kunze and Dwight Brautigan, Rochester, New York: University of Rochester Press, 1992

Schochet, Gordon, "Intending (Political) Obligation: Hobbes on the Voluntary Basis of Society," in *Thomas Hobbes and Political Theory*, edited by Mary Dietz, Lawrence: University of Kansas Press, 1990

Schochet, Gordon, "John Locke and Religion Toleration," in *The Revolution of 1688–89: Changing Perspectives*, edited by Lois G. Schwoerer, Cambridge: Cambridge University Press, 1992

Schochet, Gordon, "Patriarchalism, Naturalism, and the Rise of the Conventional State," in *Categorie del Reale e storiografia: Aspetti di continuità e transformazione nell'Europa Moderna*, edited by F. Fagiani and G. Valera, Calabria, Italy: Franco Angeli, 1986

Schochet, Gordon, *Patriarchalism in Political Thought*, second edition, New Brunswick, New Jersey: Transaction Books 1975, 1988

Schochet, Gordon, "Sir Robert Filmer: Some New Bibliographic Discoveries," *The Library* XXVI (1971)

Schochet, Gordon, "Thomas Hobbes on the Family and the State of Nature," *Political Science Quarterly* LLXXXII (1967)

Schwoerer, Lois G., "Liberty Secured? Britain Before and After 1688," in *The Making of Modern Freedom*, edited by J.R. Jones, Stanford: Stanford University Press, 1992

Sommerville, Johann. P., *Politics and Ideology in England, 1603–1640*, London: Longman, 1986

White, James Boyd, *When Words Lose Their Meanings: Constitutions and Reconstitutions of Language, Character, and Community*, Chicago, University of Chicago Press, 1984

THE AGE OF
REVOLUTIONS

WOMEN'S ROLE IN THE ENGLISH REVOLUTIONS

ANN HUGHES

LOOKING BACK TO THE Restoration late in his life, the royalist leader and historian, Edward, earl of Clarendon, attributed the immorality of King Charles II to the attacks on all hierarchy and authority in the 1640s and 1650s:

> All relations were confounded by the several sects in religion which discountenanced all forms of reverence and respect, as relics and marks of superstition. Children asked not blessing of their parents; nor did they concern themselves in the education of their children. . . . The young women conversed without any circumspection or modesty, and frequently met at taverns and common eating houses; and they who were stricter and more severe in their comportment, became the wives of the seditious preachers or of officers of the army. . . . Parents had no manner of authority over their children, nor children any obedience or submission to their parents, but everyone did that which was good in his own eyes. This unnatural antipathy had its first rise from the beginning of the rebellion, when the fathers and sons engaged themselves in the contrary parties, the one choosing to serve the king and the other the Parliament . . . there were never such examples of impiety between such relations in any age of the world, Christian or heathen, as that wicked time, from the beginning of the rebellion to the king's return. (*The Life of Edward Earl of Clarendon*)

Clarendon's comments introduce two important themes for a discussion of the part played by women in the English revolutions of the 17th century: a parallel between political division and breakdown of order in the family, and a stress on the role of religious divisions in promoting a broader assault on social practices and conventions. In January 1649 Charles I—the "politic father of his people"—was executed after a public trial for betraying his people's trust; the House of Lords was abolished and the surviving House of Commons established a "Commonwealth" or republic, built on the declaration that the people, under God, were the source of all just power, and that this power was exercised through Parliament. The radicalism of this political transformation, at least in the short term, might suggest radical debate about familial authority also. Although the civil wars were in part the product of splits in the ruling elites over a variety of political and religious issues, significant elements from outside the normal political elite were also heavily involved—on both sides, but perhaps most importantly in support of Parliament. In the early 1640s Parliament's propaganda quite deliberately presented itself as the "representative of the people" and rallied those people (loosely defined) to the defense of true religion, law, and liberties. This appeal to "the people" was crucial in the later 1640s, but it remains to be seen how far it involved a politicization of women as well as men such as those serving in Parliament's army.

Women were clearly affected by the fragmentation of the established Protestant Church in the early 1640s. No generally acceptable reform of religion was achieved and in London, especially, but in most other parts of England as well, "gathered congregations" emerged, whose members believed the true church was to be found in separate communities of the godly, not in a national church with a parish structure and an ordained clergy. The end of episcopacy also meant the removal of the ecclesiastical courts that had supervised morality and religious orthodoxy before 1640 and the collapse of the system of licensing works for publication. Although Parliament after the early 1640s made periodic attempts to impose press licensing, throughout the 1640s and 1650s there was little effective censorship. This circumstance, in an atmosphere of political and religious crisis, contributed to an explosion of "print culture"—newsbooks, polemical pamphlets, broadsides, woodcuts—in which fundamental political and religious issues were debated by women as well as men.

We must also stress the practical impact on women of the civil wars: the military struggle of 1642–46, renewed in 1648 and 1651, was as extensive in its effects as the contemporary wars in continental Europe. It has been estimated that nearly 200,000 people may have died in England as a result of civil war, a greater proportion of the population than perished in either of the world wars of the 20th century. Perhaps as many as one in four English men served in the armed forces in the 1640s, some in garrisons near their homes, but others in marching armies. All this had important implications for women's roles in the household, especially as family economies were seriously strained by taxation, more than 10 times as heavy as in peacetime, and by the plundering and free-quarter of underpaid troops. The scale of the conflict, as well as its radical impact, justifies the term "revolution," although some modern historians prefer to write of the "Great Rebellion" or the "Fall of the British Monarchy."

Despite the restoration of the monarchy and the national Episcopal Church in 1660, the events of the interregnum had a lasting impact. Religious fragmentation, suspicion of monarchical powers and intentions, and lively printed polemics all contributed to continued instability after the Restoration. Finally, in the bloodless and much more limited Glorious Revolution of 1688–89, the Catholic monarch James II was deposed and replaced by his son-in-law and daughter, William of Orange and Mary, in practice if not entirely in theory through a contract with the political classes represented in Parliament. Thereafter England was a parliamentary or constitutional monarchy. Women continued to participate in printed debate, in political controversy, and in dissenting religious congregations after 1660. Most of the present essay, however, concerns women's involvement in England in the 1640s and 1650s; little work has been done as yet on women in Ireland or Scotland. The Restoration and the revolution of 1688–89 will be covered more briefly.

The English revolution has been regarded as a defining moment in dominant narratives of British or English political history and indeed in influential accounts of the development of the Western world in general. It is crucial to the story of modernization and has been deemed "the first world revolution," a major turning point with ambiguous but largely positive effects, ushering in such progressive developments as individualism, religious liberty, democracy, and capitalism. Such accounts are based on discussions of male political and property rights and on largely male economic enterprise. How well does this narrative hold up if one focuses on female activities? It is not necessarily the case that women's political influence is best appreciated through examining their participation in a crisis of formal male politics. In early modern England there were widespread assumptions, drawing ultimately on Aristotelian and medieval commonplaces, that women should be excluded from political life. Women were thought to lack the self-control and rationality of men and thus to be unfit for public affairs. Women's obedience to men was a religious as well as a natural duty. One zealous Protestant guide to family life, William Gouge's *Domesticall Duties* (1626), stressed that "subjection" was "the general head of all wives' duties." The ideal woman was modest, silent, and confined to household affairs. Within this framework, women could rarely be active in formal politics.

However, this understanding of the gendered nature of politics was qualified by rather contradictory notions—and by many practical ways in which public and private life could not be so easily untangled. Equally influential understandings of the political process in the early modern period were founded on notions of the body and the family. The king figured as the head of the body politic, the father of his people, or the husband of the realm. Early modern thinking was frequently analogical, understanding and explaining the world through a series of parallels. One of the most effective of these analogies was that between the family and the wider political community, as we have seen with Clarendon. The authority of kings and that of fathers in families were mutually legitimating; when the politic father was executed, it might be expected that the parallel authority of fathers, and of men over women, might be shaken too. Consequently, the civil war and its aftermath could easily raise questions about the gendered nature of politics, as well as offering extended opportunities for women to be politically active.

In practical terms, households were not the private realms of classical or humanist theory. Political power and influence depended on familial and friendship networks and on access to, or the offering of, patronage—gifts, office, and assistance of all kinds. Politics in this broad sense was not confined to office-holders or formal institutions but was carried on in aristocratic and royal households where women's influence and connections could be most important. At a humbler level, women's vital place in the household formed the basis for activity in the wider village or urban community—from attempts to discipline sexual deviants to collective action to defend family economies. In some ways, then, women's participation in the English revolutions was an extension rather than a transformation of their informal political role in the household or the community. Women were frequently prominent in direct action to prevent the export of corn in times of bad harvest or to oppose the enclosure of common land. In the 1630s they took a full part in the more widespread social protests in the fens of East Anglia and the forests of the West Country, where the king himself was backing attempts to transform small-scale local economies into capitalist agricultural economies by draining the fens and clearing the forests. Ordinary women participated in the attacks on symbols of Charles I's religious policies, pulling down the altar rails erected in the 1630s and destroying the pictures and stained glass that zealous Protestants had come to see as idolatrous or popish. When women of the radical Leveler movement claimed the right to a political voice in 1649, they appealed to the example of notable women from the Bible or from the distant British past—"we knowing for our encouragement and example, God hath wrought many deliverances for severall Nations from age to age by the weake hand of women"—but they also included the women of Edinburgh, Scotland, whose militant protests in 1637 had obstructed the king's attempt to impose a new prayer book on the Scots and had thus begun the overthrow of episcopacy in the British Isles.

Once the fighting began, the sheer scale of the conflict inevitably meant an expansion of women's responsibilities. This did not involve any radical transformation or a challenge to patriarchal authority, for it was widely accepted that women needed to be capable of taking over in the absence of men. Thus women raised money for the cause. Parliament's armies included "maiden troops" specifically financed by groups of women. Women built fortifications and defended cities during sieges by opposing forces, in parliamentarian Gloucester, Bristol, and Hull, or royalist Hereford and Worcester. In Bristol, a leading role was taken by Dorothy Hazzard, a "founder of a separatist congregation, a Deborah . . . with strength of holy Resolution in her soul from God, even a Mother in Israel." She helped to strengthen the city walls and, after the city's fall to the king's forces, testified in Parliament to the supposed cowardice of the commander who agreed to the surrender. The wives of Coventry army captains often acted as treasurers to their husband's companies, reproducing a role they played in merchants' households in normal times.

Similar developments took place at a higher social level. Aristocratic women rallied support for king or Parliament, acted as intermediaries, spies, or protectors of their family's interests. Anne Cunningham, dowager marchioness of Hamilton, was a zealous supporter of the Presbyterian Covenanting cause in Scotland despite the ambiguous stance of her courtier sons. She helped to organize the defense against Charles's threatened invasion of Scotland in 1639, raising and equipping a cavalry troop. She claimed she was prepared to shoot her own son if he led the king's army to Scotland. The stance of Lucy Hay, countess of Carlisle, was more equivocal, but her activities were typical of several aristocratic women. She was a friend of the queen, Henrietta-Maria, but had close connections with Protestant noblemen on the Parliament's side. From 1641 she leaked details of court discussions to parliamentarian kinsmen and friends, including her brother, the earl of Northumberland, her brother-in-law, the earl of Leicester, and the earl of Holland. In 1646–47 she tried to use her contacts to promote peace between king and Parliament, and by 1648 she was willing to conspire, unsuccessfully, with the Scots, London Presbyterians, and her old friend Holland to rally support for Charles in the second civil war. The royalist failure led to her imprisonment and Holland's death.

Other women engaged in spying and intrigue, usually on the royalist side. One of the best documented is Anne Murray, daughter of a provost of Eton College and a governess to the king's children, who wrote her memoirs in her quieter middle age. In 1647 Anne fell in love with Colonel Joseph Bampfield, a royalist secret agent, and thereafter assisted him in a variety of escapades; most notably she helped to engineer the escape of Charles I's younger son, James Duke of York, from imprisonment in London. James managed to evade his guards through a game of "hide and seek" and left the city dressed in women's clothes procured by Anne. The upheavals of civil war made it possible for Anne to travel independently in both England and Scotland during the 1640s and 1650s. In Scotland, like many other women, she became involved in treating wounded soldiers after the Battle of Dunbar in 1650. The disruption of war also made possible her deception by Bampfield, with whom she almost contracted a bigamous marriage: it took some four years for her friends to convince her that his wife was still alive.

Of course, the dominant female figure on either side was the queen, Henrietta-Maria. As a Frenchwoman and a Catholic, her influence over the king was deeply suspected; she was seen as the center of a "popish" or Catholic plot to undermine English religion and government. Henrietta-Maria was indeed active in rallying Catholic support to the king when he sought an army to put down rebellion in Scotland; she raised funds and troops on the Continent in 1642–43, and was generally believed to be one of the most extreme of Charles's advisers. The capture of the king's correspondence after the battle of Naseby in 1645 included much evidence of the queen's intrigues and helped to discredit the royal cause. One harsh judgment comes from Lucy Hutchinson, a republican whose husband was a colonel in Parliament's army:

the King [Charles I] had another instigator of his own violent: purpose, more powerful than all the rest, and that was the Queen, who, grown out of her childhood, began to turn her mind from those vain extravagances she liv'd in at first to that which did less become her, and was more fatal to the kingdom, which never is in any place happy where the hands that are made only for distaffs affect the management of sceptres. If any one object the fresh example of Queen Elizabeth, let them remember that the felicity of her reign was the effect of her submission of her masculine and wise counsellor; but wherever male princes are so effeminate to suffer women of foreign birth and different religion to intermeddle with the affairs of state, it is always found to produce sad desolations; and it has been observed that a French queen never brought any happiness to England. (*The Life of Colonel John Hutchinson*)

In the absence of their husbands, several aristocratic women conducted the defenses of their besieged homes. Brilliana Harley, a woman from a prominent parliamentarian family in Herefordshire, withstood two sieges of her home in 1643, while her M.P. husband was away in London, with brave words of defiance: "I must endeavour to keep what is mine as well as I can in which I have the law of nature, of reason and of the land on my side." The royalist Lady Mary Bankes, with only her daughters and maidservants to help, defended Corfe Castle in the summer of 1643 and then again for several months in 1645–46, when the war was almost lost. Charlotte de Tremoille, countess of Derby, a granddaughter of William the Silent and from a Huguenot background, was equally determined when Parliament's forces tried to take her Lancashire home, Lathom House, in 1643 and 1644. She declared that "though a woman and a stranger, divorced from her friends, and robbed of her state, she was ready to receive their utmost violence, trusting in God both for her protection and deliverance."

Women's responsibilities for the welfare of their families led them to become active in the public arenas of Parliament, its committees, and the law courts. Royalist property was confiscated by the victorious parliamentarians, and many royalist leaders went into exile. In these circumstances it was often women who engaged in lobbying and petitioning to preserve what they could of the family fortunes. The author Margaret Cavendish, duchess of Newcastle, whose husband was one of the most prominent exiles, returned to England to try to rescue some Cavendish property. She had a rather jaundiced view of the whole process:

I did not stand as a beggar at the Parliament door, for I never was at the Parliament house . . . neither did I haunt the committees, for I never was at any, as a petitioner, but one in my life . . . the customs of England being changed as well as the laws, where women became pleaders, attorneys, petitioners, and the like, running about with their several causes, complaining of their several grievances, exclaiming against their several enemies, bragging of their several favours they receive from the powerful, thus trafficking with idle words, bring in false reports and vain discontents.

Most comments were more positive: Thomas Knyvett of Norfolk argued that "women solicitors" were more effective than "masculine malignants," while for the Kent royalist Sir Roger Twysden, his wife was simply "the saver of my estate." The moderate royalist Sir Ralph Verney, in exile in France, was advised by a friend, "women were never so useful as now . . . instruct your wife, and leave her to act it with committees, their sex entitles them to many privileges and we find the comfort of them more now than ever." His wife should use "the juice of an onion sometimes to soften hard hearts."

Many humbler women also defended and supported their families. Unruly soldiers were frequently taken to court by the women in whose houses they billeted, and thousands of widows successfully petitioned central government and county magistrates for relief following the deaths of their husbands in Parliament's armies. The political debates of the time seem to have made such women bolder, for they did not beg for local charity, but presented eloquent arguments for proper pensions as their right.

So far we have considered how women's traditional responsibilities in the household and their care for their families were directed into new channels by civil war. Perhaps more interesting—and the focus for much feminist scholarship—are the ways in which female agency was prompted into new directions by religious and political upheavals. Numbers of women made overt claims to influence the course of events, particularly through collective petitioning of Parliament. In January and February 1642—a period of great crisis, following large street demonstrations which ultimately forced Charles from London—women petitioned on their own to urge the House of Lords to support the radical measures of the House of Commons against Catholics in general and the Catholic rebels in Ireland in particular. In August 1643, a group of women petitioned the Parliament asking for peace. A sympathetic observer described them thus: "women, who deplore the miseries of these times," came "to cry for peace, which was to the men a pleasing thing." According to Clarendon they were the wives of substantial London citizens; but to hostile commentators they were "two or three hundred oyster wives, and other dirty and tattered sluts"—"the very scum of the suburbs"—who "took upon them the impudencey to come to the honorable House of Commons." The women peace petitioners were ultimately dispersed by the city militia, and their treatment shows how reactions to women's public activities often depended on their political stance as much as on the fact that they were women.

The importance of their political orientation is clearly seen in presentations of the most notable interventions by women—their collective organization and petitioning as part of the democratic Leveler movement. Drawn mainly from the respectable middle classes of London, and given focus by men like John Lilburne and Richard Overton, who had a background in both religious radicalism and popular journalism, the Levelers from 1646 attacked Parliament for its betrayals of the people's cause, its interference with legal rights, attacks on religious sects, and the assault on freedom of the press. They acquired some influence in the army in 1647, and provided crucial backing for the revolution of winter 1648–49. Their angry and rapid disillusion with the Commonwealth seriously threatened political stability in 1649, but by the end of that year the Levelers had been defeated, with the elimination of their support in the army and the imprisonment of their leaders.

We know that women were very active in the Leveler movement as messengers, fundraisers, and petitioners. "Leveler wives" such as Mary Overton or Elizabeth Lilburne were imprisoned for distributing illegal pamphlets or for support of their husbands. Individual Leveler women petitioned for the release of themselves and their husbands from prison. It seems that the Levelers, like the royalist gentry, were well aware of the strategic value of female intervention. Writing of 1646–47, Richard Overton claimed that "for the better credence of our miserable condition" petitions for the release of his brother and wife from prison were "presented by a competent number of women" to the House of Commons. Most startling, however, were the collective petitions from Leveler women against the imprisonment of Leveler leaders and the punishment of army mutineers in the spring of 1649, and in support of John Lilburne during his second trial for high treason in summer 1653.

There is also some evidence of specifically female organization. All women who approved of the 1649 petition were urged to subscribe it, to deliver their copies to women representatives in every ward in London, and to meet at Westminster Hall to present the petition; according to the London newsbooks several hundreds turned up. Leveler female petitions made overt claims for women, based on religious and political grounds, to have some share in the formal political process. In 1649 they protested,

> That since we are assured of our creation in the image of God, and of an interest in Christ, equal unto men, as also of a proportionable share in the Freedoms of this Commonwealth, we cannot but wonder and grieve that we should appear so despicable in your eyes, as to be thought unworthy to petition or represent our grievances to this honourable house. Have we not an equal interest with the men of this Nation, in those liberties and securities, contained in the Petition of Right [a Parliamentary declaration of English liberties, passed in 1628], and other the good Laws of the Land?

The women received a contemptuous response: "Mr. Speaker (by the direction of the House) hath commanded me to tell you, that the matter you petition about, is of an higher concernment then you understand, that the House gave an answer to your Husbands, and therefore that you are desired to go home, and look after your owne businesses and meddle with your housewifery." The London newsbooks attacked the Leveler women as whores, "oyster-wives," the "civill-sisterhood of Oranges and Lemmons." In 1651 Leveler women petitioned against the iniquities of the laws on debt, and in 1653 they appealed to the example of Esther, who had intervened with a heathen king on behalf of the Jews, among many other notable women, to justify their right to petition:

> That we cannot but be much saddened to see our undoubted Right of Petitioning with-held from us, having attended several days at your House-door with an humble Petition . . . and it is ours and the Nations undoubted right to petition, although an Act of Parliament were made against it.

Although they were subject to much derision and opposition from Parliament and hostile newsbooks, the women's actions do not seem to have been controversial, or even particularly independent, within the Leveler movement itself. The movement's rituals and processions were differentiated by sex and age as at the funeral of Robert Lockyer, a Leveler shot after the army mutinies of 1649: "Officers, souldiers, Citizens, Maids etc every one having a black Ribbon and a small one fast'ned to it of a sea green colour." "Citizens and women," "youths and maids," marched separately embodying a complex, hierarchically organized, yet harmonious movement. The Levelers were a movement led by male householders, but householders who were supported by active, if subordinate wives, and servants. It is noteworthy that this conception of the household underpinned Leveler demands for a more representative Parliament and a broad parliamentary suffrage for men, but it also meant that the question of formal political rights for women was never even raised. Levelers believed that men and women were spiritually equal, that women had some share in the legal rights and liberties of the realm, and that women could intervene publicly to defend those liberties (especially in the absence of their husbands). This was not taken to mean that women had any formal public role in the making of law or the choosing of the representatives of the people.

It seems that women petitioners were not organizing for specifically female aims, but rather acting as women to support certain general initiatives—whether for peace in 1643 or for Leveler demands in 1649. It is perhaps misleading to look for a tradition of female petitioning or female activism as such. Rather, a series of women justified their involvement in a specific cause. Female interventions in the formal political arena were made possible by the upheavals of civil war, but the precise connections between the attack on patriarchy in the state, culminating in regicide, and a greater assertiveness by women against general patriarchal restrictions are hard to trace. Political satire testified to some alarm at the disruption of gender hierarchies. In August 1656, in a pamphlet, *Now or Never; or the Citizens' Wives Remonstrance*, these stirring words occurred:

> It is not unknown to all the world, how we have been and still are deprived of our liberties, living in the bonds of servitude, and in the Apprenticeship of slavery (not for terms of years, but during life). . . . We do and shall disclaim that tyrannical government, which men have over us, and to the utmost of our powers abolish, abrogate and destroy it, by being not subject and subordinate to it.

All women who have a "desire for freedom" are asked to assist, so "we may all enjoy such privileges as are fit for freeborn women." Attributing to women the radical rhetoric of the parliamentarian cause was a means of highlighting the absurdity of female political rights, and perhaps also a means of discrediting republican ideas.

Most parliamentary propagandists challenged the pre–civil war analogy between family and state, for two reasons. First, they saw no problems with fatherly authority in families, but they did not want patriarchalism to justify absolute monarchy in the state. Second, they did not want the overthrow of the politic father of the people—the king—to have any implications for family order. Henry Parker wrote in 1642 that "the wife is inferior in nature, and was created for the assistance of man, and servants are hired for the Lord's attendance, but it is otherwise in the state betwixt man and man, for that civil difference . . . is for civil ends." In 1650 the republican John Hall commented

succinctly, "as for the antiquity from Adam . . . what is this to civil government?"

There was some speculation over familial arrangements in the 1640s and 1650s: male members of the libertine Ranters were rumored to be promiscuous, as a sign that they were freed from normal understandings of sin. The poet John Milton wrote a notorious pamphlet in favor of divorce between incompatible partners. According to an alarmed conservative commentator, one London women, Mrs. Attaway, read Milton's work, and "decided to look more into it, for she had an unsanctified husband, that did not walk in the way of Sion, nor speak the language of Canaan." Following this research, Mrs. Attaway ran away with one William Jenney, another religious radical, who had an ungodly wife. But sexual liberty was not characteristic of these years; more typical were attempts at sexual control or reform, most notably in a parliamentary act of 1650 that established the death penalty for adultery with a married women (a sentence rarely enforced). In 1653 marriage was made a civil rather than a religious rite; this measure was not apparently very popular as many rushed to get married in church before it came into force. There was no widespread reform of family life or inheritance practices such as took place after the French revolution. The practical impact of men's absence and death during the war was more important than any ideological debate, and contributed to the population stagnation in England from mid-century.

Although, as we have seen, the upheavals of civil war offered new opportunities for women's initiative, in other ways political change seems to have restricted female influence. Ideologically and practically, the politics of the republic and of Oliver Cromwell's Protectorate were more overtly masculine than the household-based politics of hereditary "patriarchal" monarchy. In early modern England there was never a clear, uncontested distinction between the public and the private, and it is simplistic to trace a linear development of increasing separation between two "spheres" as part of the emergence of the modern world. Nonetheless, the 1640s and 1650s marked a moment, perhaps later reversed, when there emerged a much stronger sense of politics as a distinct, formal, and institutionalized aspect of life, as well as a sharp contrast between public service and private interest. This contrast was clearly gendered: the revival of classical and Machiavellian ideas in English republicanism involved a sharp distinction between the household and the public world, and public service was a crucial attribute of manliness. The republican citizen was an independent man—his own master—active in the service of the state. In contrast, royalism was portrayed as effeminate, because it meant dependency on the will of another. We have seen this idea in the comments of Lucy Hutchinson on the influence of Henrietta-Maria, and it is found also in the rhetoric of Milton's polemics in defense of the English republic against the attacks of foreign intellectuals. Milton claimed that the Dutch defender of royalism, Salmasius, was dominated by his wife; hence it was "no wonder that you wish to thrust royal domination upon others, since you are yourself so slavishly accustomed to endure feminine rule at home." Algernon Sidney, a leading republican politician of the 1650s and a republican martyr in Charles II's reign, wrote of "virtue and manhood" perishing under corrupt monarchies, while republics fostered "manly virtue." For Sidney, one of the major absurdities of the patriarchal arguments of Robert Filmer was that they allowed female or infant rulers through the vagaries of inheritance in families. The zealous Protestantism of many republicans worked in the same direction: Protestants stressed the spiritual equality of men and women, but men's religious duties were fulfilled in public affairs, women's in the household, where the ideal woman was often compared to a snail. The stress on the masculinity of the republican politician was no doubt a response to the anxieties produced by the execution of the monarch, as well as by men's alarm at the forward behavior of women in radical religious sects, petitioning in the streets of London or lobbying Parliament's committees.

In practical terms too, the regimes of the 1650s were largely male domains. Monarchist regimes focused on the royal household, the court. As we have seen, Charles's queen Henrietta-Maria, and other ladies as well, had a recognized political influence, for good or ill. Personal contacts and kinship were important to the parliamentarian cause: several of Cromwell's sons, sons-in-law, and brothers-in-law were important military and political figures, and the marriages of his daughters were an important index of political change. Oliver Cromwell's letters to his wife during his absence in Scotland in 1650–51 show that he trusted her with political matters, while she offered him political advice and kept in touch with influential allies on his behalf. But personal ties were less important within parliamentarianism than shared ideological commitment and institutional position. Political influence and advancement depended on success in male arenas—in Parliament and its committees, in the Council of State, and above all in Parliament's army. Male social mobility and political success left women behind. Elizabeth Bourchier, the daughter of an Essex merchant (albeit one knighted by James I) had married Oliver Cromwell when he was the son of an impoverished gentry family. As Elizabeth Cromwell, wife of the Lord Protector, who in 1657 refused the crown, she was treated with respect by foreign ambassadors, but had no apparent political influence. London newsbooks of the 1650s paid almost no attention to the protector's family; indeed there was more information on Queen Christina of Sweden or scandals in the French court. Much of the public ceremonial of the regimes such as funerals or receptions focused on the army, the Parliament, or the city of London. The public image of the protector's government was overwhelmingly male.

Formal "high" politics was not amenable to female influence; and indeed it seems that politics, narrowly defined, was less important than religion in empowering women. Milton's reader Mrs. Attaway was a notorious woman preacher in radical congregations in London—anathema to orthodox Protestants brought up on the New Testament injunction that women should be silent in church. For many women, it was the religious fragmentation of the 1640s and 1650s, rather than political conflict, that offered the better opportunities for independent expression and action. Religion, of course, was of crucial importance to politics and social life in early modern England, so the division is somewhat artificial. Nonetheless, it is within radical religious groupings that many assertive women can be found. This is not to say that most women were radical in their religious views. There is plenty of evidence that some women preferred the more traditional Episcopal or Anglican Church, with its focus on the parish community and its elements of ceremony and ritual. In gentry families it was possible for private ceremonies of baptism or churching (the rite of purification after childbirth) to be con-

ducted by deprived Anglican clerics according to the old rites. The wives of ministers expelled for royalism or adherence to Anglican beliefs were active in petitioning for maintenance and sometimes tried forcibly to keep their husbands' successors from taking possession of their parsonage houses. Local people in general were often suspicious of the zealous Protestant preachers "intruded" by the parliamentarian authorities, and women were among those who took direct action to keep them out. In Henley in Arden, Warwickshire, it was claimed it was the "custom" of local women "to disturb such as were authorized to preach there."

More significant, however, was the involvement of women in the radical sects, groups who rejected not only the Episcopal Church, but also the reformed national Presbyterian framework Parliament tried to put in its place. These radical groups varied greatly in their beliefs and practices but all rejected the idea of a "state church." The true church on earth should not be comprised of all people, whether godly or sinners, but was a separated, voluntary, "gathered" community of "saints." Saints were those who had felt (and could demonstrate) the direct impact of God's saving faith on their souls and hearts. Many sects had specific men set apart as their ministers, but all argued that it was gifts given by God, not official ordination or education, that made a person a minister. In these circumstances distinctions of sex seemed less relevant, and women were often prominent among the founders of these sects and outnumbered men among their members. Hostile conservatives attributed this to women's greater irrationality and gullibility; sympathetic observers and some modern historians have suggested that women were somehow more spiritual than men, or more in touch with fundamental issues of life and death, through their experiences of childbirth and motherhood. Perhaps it was simply that women could find in the radical religious groups an independent influence denied them in their families or communities. The sects all stressed the equality of souls, that Christ made no distinction between men and women, that God should be obeyed before man. Some groups, notably the Quakers, believed in a spiritual or mystical union between God and humanity and in the possibility that immediate revelation could be the basis of a public prophetic role, for women and men alike. Although the practical implications varied from congregation to congregation—and certainly no one argued that spiritual equality had civil dimensions—women's participation in the sects was evidence of female assertiveness, frequently resisted or resented by men.

One determined woman, for whom religious radicalism was part of a very broad involvement in the upheavals of the 1640s and 1650s, was Katherine Chidley. She had been prominent in a group of Shrewsbury separatists in the 1620s and after she moved to London became a noted polemicist against orthodox or Presbyterian opinion. In *The Justification of the Independent Churches of Christ* (1641) she urged

> that you would consider the text in I Corinthians, 7 which plainly declares that the wife may be a believer, and the husband an unbeliever, but if you have considered this text I pray you tell me, what authority this unbelieving husband hath over the conscience of his believing wife. . . . It is true, he hath authority over her in bodily and civil respects, but not to be a Lord over her conscience.

With her son Samuel, she founded a gathered church in Bury St. Edmonds in 1646, and with him she became a leader of the Leveler movement. Indeed, she is credited by some with the authorship of the women's petitions already quoted. Dorothy Hazzard, also mentioned earlier, was a major influence on the founding of a separate congregation in Bristol in the late 1630s and early 1640s.

The involvement of women in the sects led to a variety of tensions, negotiations, and conflicts over the precise extent of women's roles. The "particular" (or Calvinist) Baptists (who rejected infant baptism in favor of the baptism of believing adults), among the most respectable of the sects, depended on the Scriptures to define the proper limits in what was clearly a controversial area. In an association of Midlands Baptist congregations, the question of whether women could speak in the church was raised. It was agreed that women could testify to their faith and could act as witnesses or messengers, but they "may not so speak as that their speaking shall show a not acknowledging of the inferiority of their sex . . . a woman may not publicly teach in the church."

The independence of mind that had led women to join gathered congregations did not disappear once they became members, and in many groups women's continued religious speculation brought them into trouble with male ministers and elders. An independent congregation in Canterbury was founded by 14 men and 9 women in 1645, but women soon came to outnumber men, so that by 1658 there were 79 women and 43 men. The officers of the congregation were male, however, and dissident women were harshly dealt with. Two women developed anti-trinitarian ideas: they "followed seducers . . . drawn away into corrupt opinions . . . to deny Jesus Christ's remaining still in our humane nature . . . also that he was not distinct from the father." The women were not ashamed of their heresies; their "carriage" was described as "very pertinacious and obstinate." When the officials of the congregation admonished them, they argued back rather than submitting meekly, "uttering unfitting speeches" and offering biblical sanctions for their views.

Sometimes the women were less radical than the minister in their opinions, but equally brave in defending them. Susanna Parr, a member of a gathered congregation in Exeter, was encouraged to participate in religious discussions, but she felt uneasy about this, and after the death of her child she came to be unhappy about her separation from the national church: "when I considered the breach that the Lord had made in my family, I beheld how terrible it was to make a breach in his family." She then began to attend the Presbyterian Church instead, which prompted a public campaign against her, including a printed pamphlet of denunciation. Paradoxically, Susanna herself resorted to print, to attack the minister's pressure:

when I pleaded for my absence . . . from the meetings, that of the Apostle, "Let your women keep silence in the church, for it is not permitted unto them to speak" (I Corinthians 14.34); he replied he would do nothing without the consent of the whole. And when I was present, he would constrain me to speak my opinion of things proposed.

In other, more radical, congregations women's participation also caused conflict. John Rogers, the pastor of a Dublin congregation, was later associated with the millenarian "fifth-mon-

archy" movement. Its adherents believed the "last days" were at hand, when Jesus Christ would return to earth to rule with his Saints for a thousand years (and in some cases they were prepared to hasten the coming of the millennium). At his church in Dublin, Rogers encouraged women's participation: "most men do arrogate a sovereignty to themselves which I see no warrant for." As in other congregations, women delivered public affirmations of their faith, but Rogers also wished them to vote in church affairs. This led to "bitter contentions" from "such as would rob sisters of their just rights and privileges" and in the end Rogers decided not to put his views into practice: "that may be lawful to you [women] that is not (as yet) expedient." Some qualifications and ambiguities in Rogers's position are of general interest. For one, he stressed that he was concerned only with church affairs, not with politics: "there is a civil subjection" to men, but men had no power to deprive women of their Christian liberty. He also emphasized that these were extraordinary times, the last days when "God had care of the weakest contemptible vessels, viz women, that he would exalt them and pour out his spirit much upon them." Finally, it was the weakness of women—their more pliable nature—that made them more spiritual: "women are more readily wrought upon, and sooner persuaded and formed into the truth than men, who are for the most part like sturdy steel and iron, hard to work upon" (*Ohel or Beth—Shemesh. A Tabernacle for the Sun*, 1653).

Many of the gathered congregations were the political mainstays of the regimes of the 1650s (although some churches, like that of Rogers, were opposed to Cromwell's assumption of personal power), and thus many women were crucial to the local backing of England's new rulers. A more personal, and more direct, public influence for women could be acquired through prophecy. Here it was not women's own words, but women as conduits for God's warnings and messages, that were listened to. The prophetess Lady Eleanor Davies, an isolated, aristocratic woman, was confined as a lunatic in the 1630s but reemerged in the 1640s and 1650s with a series of obscure prophetic pamphlets.

Lady Eleanor's political impact is hard to judge, but the potential influence of prophetesses is shown in Elizabeth Poole's dramatic intervention in the debates of the Council of Officers of the parliamentary army in late December and early January 1648–49. This was during the supreme crisis of the revolution, when the officers were concerned with the proposed regicide and political transformation. Yet a woman was given "worthy consideration," not because of her own opinions, but because she might be transmitting God's message. Poole recounted her visions to the officers, warning against the regicide, with an interesting familial metaphor: "You never heard that a wife might put away her husband as he is the head of her body"; a wife could defend herself, as Parliament had defended itself against royal aggression, but neither she nor they could deliver a fatal blow. Poole's message was unpalatable, and ultimately rejected, but it is remarkable that a woman obtained a hearing on such an occasion.

The millenarian fifth-monarchy movement included women prophets, who were active in their campaign against the shortcomings of the republic in 1652–53 and in their bitter opposition to Cromwell's assumption of personal power at the end of 1653. Mary Cary argued, "The time is coming when not only men but women shall prophesy; not only aged men but young men, not only superiors but inferiors; not only those who have university learning but those who have it not, even servants and handmaids." Anna Trapnel was the most notorious of the fifth-monarchist women, first coming to public attention in London in 1654, when she uttered verses, prayers, and prophecies against the government during a twelve-day trance. Trapnel published four pamphlets in the same year, and she attracted great crowds on a tour of the West Country that culminated in her arrest in Cornwall. She was accused of being a witch—a common accusation against women whose public speech was seen as inappropriate—but found much support. As she wrote:

> many strangers were very loving and careful to help me out of the crowd; and the rude multitude said, "Sure this woman is no witch, for she speaks many good words, which the witches could not" . . . in all that was said by me, I was nothing, the Lord put all in my mouth, and told me what I should say, and that from the written word, he put it in my memory and mouth; so that I will have nothing ascribed to me, but all honour and praise given to him whose right it is, even to Jehovah, who is the king that lives for ever.

Cary's comments and Trapnel's experiences illustrate how prophecy was an activity fraught with danger and ambiguity. It was only the extraordinary nature of the times—the last days when normal social hierarchies were reversed—that justified female prophecy. Furthermore, it was the inferior rationality of women—their passivity and greater tendency to self-abnegation—that made women suitable conduits for God's words. Female prophets underlined conventional stereotypes of female weakness, even as they adopted an extraordinary public role. Audiences could reject their message by presenting women prophets as witches, in thrall to the devil rather than instruments of God. Yet it is undeniable that prophecy was a means by which women acquired public influence and engaged in public speech (which was often also written down and published for an even wider audience). This is remarkable in a society that stressed modesty and silence as crucial attributes of virtuous women.

The most successful of the radical sects established during the interregnum was that of the Quakers, or Society of Friends, who gained substantial support in both rural and urban areas, as well as establishing an organization that enabled them to survive the years of harassment after 1660. The Quakers gathered a disparate range of spiritual religious sects through a dynamic missionary campaign of preaching and the circulation of printed texts, seeking followers from the early 1650s. Rejecting the elitist Calvinism of many other radical groups, Quakers preached the possibility of general redemption for those who would recognize Christ's light within them and thereby achieve a mystical sense of union with Christ. Although they later became a pacifist and politically quietist group, the early Quakers mounted aggressive challenges to authority, with particularly defiant campaigns against "hireling priests" (the parish clergy), whose services they mocked and disrupted. Quakers refused to take oaths when brought before the courts, they refused to doff their hats to their social superiors, and they zealously opposed the levying of tithes, the compulsory "tax" paid to support the clergy. Quakers, men and women alike, were imprisoned and had their property confiscated for refusing tithes; they wrote and petitioned against

what was regarded as an exploitation of the poor and an infringement of religious liberty. One anti-tithe petition, from 1659, was signed by many thousands of women, for the Quakers' characteristic blend of fluid, emotional religion and sober organization seems to have been attractive to many audacious and energetic women. Quaker women engaged in verbal assaults on orthodox ministers, in ecstatic prayer and prophecy, in public preaching, and in writing for publication. Quaker women's works made up about half of women's publications in the 1650s and amounted to one-fifth of all female publications in the 17th century. The best-known Quaker woman was Margaret Fell, the wife and widow of a Lancashire gentleman who later married George Fox, the major figure in the first generation of Quakers. Her home at Swarthmore Hall in north Lancashire became the headquarters of the new movement and the crucial center of its international missionary activities, sustained through correspondence, the systematic use of printed pamphlets and declarations, and conscientious fundraising. Margaret Fell was one among many. One recent study of Quaker women has identified 243 girls and women active as missionaries, prophets, and authors. Many more were doubtless vocal at Quaker meetings. Quaker women claimed a public prophetic voice and engaged in extraordinary activities, traveling to continental Europe, the Americas, and the Ottoman Empire in attempts to win converts. A Yorkshire woman, Grace Barwick, traveled to London to deliver her message to the leaders of Parliament's army in 1659: "There is a great darkness over you. . . . There is a weight of blood, cruelty and injustice lying under this great mountain, and it is time to be cast down" (*To All Present Rulers, Whether Parliament, or Whomsoever of England*, 1659; quoted in Phyllis Mack, *Visionary Women*). Dorothy White and Esther Biddle were other Quaker women who addressed the powerful in peremptory terms, attempting to recall them to God's service. Biddle, imprisoned some 14 times for preaching from the 1650s to the 1690s, tried without success to win an audience with Louis XIV in 1694 to persuade him to make peace in Europe. Quaker women bravely endured much suffering and humiliation for their beliefs: when friends visited the Quakers Sarah Cheevers and Katherine Evans, who had spent three years in a Malta prison, writing verse, having visions, and appealing to their inquisitors, they found them quiet and composed, busy with their knitting. It is clear that Quaker women's dramatic interventions in public places aroused much male fear and hostility, linked often to a sense of sexual threat from aggressive women. Two Quaker women who visited the small Midland town of Evesham, at a time of fierce dispute between Quakers and other townspeople, were punished in a deliberately sexual way, placed in the stocks with their legs apart and above their heads. The magistrate ordered a block of wood "thrust between their legs, and said they should not have them between their legs which they would have."

It is interesting that leading Quaker women were often from comfortable social positions, whereas many of the men had more marginal social backgrounds. The women were frequently older, wives and mothers, and it was the strong, nurturing image of the "Mother in Israel" that underpinned much female Quaker activity, an image that sanctioned women's proffering warnings and advice to both men and other women. There was also a place, especially after 1660, for the younger, virginal, passive, mystical, female stance. After the Restoration, the Quakers became a more bureaucratic, more disciplined, and more passive movement, a process that no doubt helped them to survive the period of intermittent persecution between 1660 and 1689. This had a mixed impact on the role of women: a committee of male worthies supervised all Quaker publications, so that women after 1660 found it easier to get their introspective, mystical personal works published than the stern political denunciations more characteristic of the 1650s. Yet women retained a prominent, if more controlled, place in the movement: in 1671, as part of the move to greater institutionalization, specific women's meetings were established. Their functions were to visit and relieve poor Quakers, to aid those suffering persecution for their beliefs, and to supervise sexual morality and Quaker marriages. In some ways, this amounted to a marginalization of women's role, a confinement to traditionally feminine areas, for it was the male meetings that controlled public business and controversy. Nonetheless, within the Quakers women had the rare opportunity to take on formal, institutional authority, as opposed to the more common informal influence; and in their control of morality and marriage, they had oversight of men's as well as women's behavior. Some meetings were open to both men and women, and Quakers after 1660 still defended women's public preaching as in Margaret Fell's pamphlet, *Women Speaking Justified.* In both Britain and America, Quaker women were to be very important in later feminist and reform movements.

As the example of the Quakers amply shows, many women participated in the expanded print culture of the time, although women's works were never more than a tiny minority of all published works (the proportion was never more than 1.6 percent in the 17th century). Women always had to explain and apologize for their intrusion into the male world of print. Nonetheless, the 1640s and 1650s saw a significant and permanent expansion in the numbers of works published by women and in the range of themes women dealt with. Between 1616 and 1620, only eight new works by women were published; in 1646–50, there were 69. After 1660 women continued to publish plays, poetry, prose romances, and household advice books, as well as a wide range of religious and political works, whereas before 1640 the greatest concentration of works had focused on individual piety or on motherhood. Women participated in the production and circulation of printed material as well: in the Restoration period women made up about 1 percent of apprentices in the Stationers' Company, and about 4 percent of working printers and booksellers. Some were influential figures, such as the Whig publisher Anne Baldwin, who took over the family concern after her husband's death in 1698.

The distinction between published and manuscript work should not be drawn too sharply. The republican Lucy Hutchinson wrote a life of her husband, already cited, to justify the republican cause of the 1650s. It could not be published in the circumstances of the Restoration, but she may well have intended it to have an impact outside her family. Manuscript material was thus not necessarily "private" to an individual, but could be intended for circulation among a range of kin and friends, where it could influence opinion or bolster morale. "Secret" writing of this kind was characteristic of royalist circles in the 1650s: the poet Katherine Phillips made a low-key political intervention with her manuscript poem, "Upon the Double Mur-

ther of King Charles I; In Answer to a Libellous Copy of Rimes by Vavasour Powell." (Powell was a Welsh radical who visited her family home).

Women's participation in public printed culture, in the literary world generally, and in the Quakers and other religious sects, is one of the continuities before and after 1660. The return of monarchical government, and in particular the developing anxieties about the Protestant succession, highlighted the political role of some royal and aristocratic women, and others participated in the continuing political and religious controversies. Hereditary monarchy became problematic again in the 1670s, when it was clear that the heir to the throne, Charles II's brother James, Duke of York, was a committed Catholic. During the "exclusion crisis" (1678–81), when attempts were made by zealously Protestant Whig politicians to exclude James from the succession, there was increasing interest in his Protestant daughter Mary and in female rule in general, with the publication of several accounts of the reign of Elizabeth I. Aristocratic women played a role in "party" organization. The author Aphra Behn wrote propaganda for the Tory party, the supporters of the monarchy, and the established church. When James succeeded Charles in 1685, the radical Whigs mounted a futile rebellion led by Charles's illegitimate son the duke of Monmouth; two women were among those executed for their complicity. Alice Lisle, the widow of a regicide and prominent lawyer of 1650s, John Lisle, had sheltered two rebel soldiers. Despite being 70 years old, she was executed after a trial at Winchester presided over by the notorious Judge Jeffreys. Elizabeth Gaunt, a Baptist who kept a tallow chandler's shop in London, was burned at the stake in October 1685, for giving shelter to a fugitive from Monmouth's army. She was the last woman to be executed in England for a political offense.

These were isolated, individual actions, not really comparable to the general and collective initiatives of the 1640s and 1650s. The ambivalent political role of aristocratic women in a monarchical system was revealed in the controversy over the pregnancy of James II's Catholic second wife in 1688. Skepticism about the validity of the pregnancy was fueled by the queen's stepdaughter, the Protestant Princess Anne, in letters to her sister Mary, who was married to Prince William of Orange. When a son was born, his legitimacy was challenged by the Whigs, who claimed he had been smuggled into the Queen's room in a "warming-pan." As recent studies suggest, the warming-pan scandal showed that women could exert political power within a hereditary monarchy, for it was women's expertise about pregnancy and childbirth that was called on to decide a matter of crucial public importance. Aphra Behn expressed her hopes for a male heir in print, while aristocratic women like the countesses of Lichfield and Peterborough were called to give evidence in support of the queen. But the controversy also made women objects of suspicion and resentment, for it fed on male insecurity about paternity and showed how women might foist supposititious births on unsuspecting men. Here, opposition to Catholicism was linked to a misogyny that contrasted upright Protestant men with dependent Catholics in thrall to the Pope and the Virgin Mary.

The so-called Glorious Revolution, a limited, largely bloodless affair, was thus more important for the anxieties it revealed over the links or distinctions to be made between familial authority and the structure of the state, than it was for any openings it offered for women's political activism. Men were not removed from home by civil war in 1688–89, and the ruling elites moved quickly to limit political and religious speculation by replacing James II as quickly as possible. Women were present in the crowds that welcomed William of Orange at Torbay in November 1688, and isolated women intervened through the press to influence events. The Whig poet Elizabeth Singer Rowe wrote against James's supporters, while the Tory writer Aphra Behn made a last-ditch attempt to win favor from the new regime with a poem welcoming Mary to England. The Quaker poet Anne Docwra wrote in support of James because he had supported toleration for religious dissenters, while the Anglican prophetess Elinor James supported divine right monarchy and petitioned William to decline the throne. Their impact seems slight, although James was briefly arrested for her attack on William. Aristocratic women had some influence, as ralliers of support, letter writers, and intermediaries. Anne, countess of Sunderland, sent secret information about meetings of James's privy council to William in Holland, while Rachel Lady Russell, the widow of a Whig leader executed by Charles II, was very active on behalf of her family and party.

But it was only the two royal sisters, Mary and Anne, who had a real political impact. The revolution was in many ways a family drama, in which the daughters' defiance of their father was crucial. The desertion of Anne to William's army contributed significantly to James's demoralization, while Mary's preference for the role of obedient wife to that of dutiful daughter was immensely important to the political outcome of 1688–89. Several Tories were anxious that Mary should rule alone, as this minimized the disruption to their notions of legality and heredity. William would only accept joint sovereignty and the grant of executive power to himself alone; many male politicians also opposed a plan to subordinate William to his wife. Ultimately Mary herself would not agree; as one close associate wrote, she felt "as she was the Prince's wife, she would never do anything but in conjunction with him."

The Glorious Revolution produced some years of female rule, with Mary ruling jointly with William until her death in 1694 and Anne succeeding him in 1702. The prominence of female rule and the events of 1688–89 stimulated much debate about gender and political authority, especially after the collapse of the licensing laws in 1694. Anne's reign, in particular, seems to have empowered a variety of female authors to speculate about gender and power. It is perhaps not useful to describe them as early feminists, for this underplays the different opinions and strategies of such authors as Mary Chudleigh, Sarah Fyge Egerton, and Mary Astell, but there were ways in which female monarchy facilitated a sense of female intellectual community that combined assertion and obedience. In 1696 Mary Astell dedicated *A Serious Proposal to the Ladies*, a critique of women's educational disadvantages, to Anne; and in the 1706 edition of *Some Reflections upon Marriage* she drew an explicit contrast between female power in the state and subservience in marriage: "if by the natural superiority of their sex, they mean that every man is by Nature superior to every woman . . . the greatest Queen ought not to command but to obey her footman." "If all men are born free," asked Astell in the same work, "how is it that all women are born slaves?" But her use of the rhetoric of political rights was ironic, for Astell herself had no sympathy with the Whig or

dissenting cause. She was a Tory, an Anglican supporter of the established Anglican Church and of divine right monarchy, opposed to the revolution of 1688–89. For her, republican or "liberal" ideas had little attraction, and, like Behn, she saw no contradiction between Tory politics in the state and a critical stance on women's treatment within the family. This underlines the complex and ambiguous impact of the English revolutions of the 17th century on women and reveals how the traditional progressive narrative of English history becomes very problematic if women are our focus.

Bibliography

Sources

Gouge, William, *Of Domesticall Duties: Eight Treatises*, London: John Haviland for William Bladen, 1622; reprint, Amsterdam: Theatrum Orbis Terrarum, and Norwood, New Jersey: W.J. Johnson, 1976

Hutchinson, Lucy, *Memoirs of the Life of Colonel Hutchinson, Governor of Nottingham Castle and Town*, London: Longman Hurst Rees and Orme, 1806; new edition, edited by John Sutherland, London and New York: Oxford University Press, 1973

Hyde, Edward, earl of Clarendon, *The Life of Edward Earl of Clarendon*, 2 vols., Oxford: Clarendon Press, 1760; new edition, Oxford: Oxford University Press, 1857

Rogers, John, *Ohel or Beth-Shemesh; A Tabernacle for the Sun*, London: Eversden, 1653

Reference Works

Crawford, Patricia M., "The Challenges to Patriarchalism: How Did the Revolution Affect Women?" in *Revolution and Restoration: England in the 1650s*, London: Collins and Brown, 1992

Crawford, Patricia M., *Women and Religion in England 1500–1720*, London and New York: Routledge, 1993

Crawford, Patricia M., "Women's Published Writings, 1600–1700," in *Women in English Society 1500–1800*, edited by Mary Prior, London and New York: Methuen, 1985

Fraser, Antonia, *The Weaker Vessel: Women's Lot in Seventeenth Century England*, London: Weidenfeld and Nicolson, and New York: Knopf, 1984

Graham, Elspeth, editor, *Her Own Life: An Anthology of Autobiographical Writings by Seventeenth-Century Women*, London and New York: Routledge, 1989

Higgins, Patricia, "The Reactions of Women, with Special Reference to Women Petitioners," in *Politics, Religion and the English Civil War*, edited by Brian Manning, London: Edward Arnold, 1973; New York: St Martin's Press, 1974

Hobby, Elaine, *Virtue of Necessity: English Women's Writing 1649–1688*, London: Virago Press, 1988; Ann Arbor: University of Michigan Press, 1989

Hudson, Geoffrey L., "Negotiating for Blood Money: War Widows and Courts in Seventeenth-Century England," in *Women, Crime and the Courts in Early Modern England*, edited by Jennifer Kermode and Garthine Walker, London: UCL Press, and Chapel Hill: University of North Carolina Press, 1995

Hughes, Ann, "Gender and Politics in Leveller Literature," in *Political Culture and Cultural Politics in Early Modern England*, edited by Susan Amussen and Mark Kishlansky, Manchester and New York: Manchester University Press, 1995

Hughes, Ann, *Women, Men, and Politics in the English Civil War*, Inaugural Lecture published by the Department of History, University of Keele, 1999

Laurence, Anne, *Women in England, 1500–1760: A Social History*, London: Weidenfeld and Nicolson, and New York: St Martin's Press, 1994

Mack, Phyllis, *Visionary Women: Ecstatic Prophecy in Seventeenth-Century England*, Berkeley: University of California Press, 1992

Mendelson, Sara, and Patricia M. Crawford, *Women in Early Modern England*, Oxford and New York: Clarendon Press, 1998

Schwoerer, Lois G., "Women and the Glorious Revolution," *Albion* 18 (1986)

Smith, Hilda, editor, *Women Writers and the Early Modern British Political Tradition*, Cambridge and New York: Cambridge University Press, 1998

Sommerville, Margaret, *Sex and Subjection: Attitudes to Women in Early Modern Society*, London and New York: Edward Arnold, 1995

Weil, Rachel J., *Political Passions, Gender, the Family, and Political Argument in England 1680–1714*, Manchester and New York: Manchester University Press, 1999

Weil, Rachel J., "The Politics of Legitimacy: Women and the Warming-pan Scandal," in *The Revolution of 1688–1689: Changing Perspectives*, edited by Lois G. Schwoerer, Cambridge and New York: Cambridge University Press, 1992

THE AMERICAN REVOLUTION THROUGH WOMEN'S EYES

LINDA K. KERBER

"IS THIS LIBERTY?" ASKED Rachel Lovell Wells at the end of the American Revolution. The year was 1786—three years after a peace treaty with Britain had been signed, one year before the Federal Constitution would be ratified. Wells was probably 65 years old, a woman of the lower middle class. She was poor, but she was intellectually sophisticated. She could read and write (although her spelling was poor). Her sister, Patience Lovell Wright, was an accomplished artist who had served in a modest way as a spy in England, gathering information from the nobility whose portraits she sculpted in wax. Wells had bought war bonds from the state of New Jersey during the Revolution. Subsequently, she had moved to Philadelphia but returned to her New Jersey home after the war. In an effort to curb speculation, the New Jersey legislature decided that only state residents had a claim on interest payments. Wells's claim on her money was turned down because she had not been in the state at the war's end in 1783. Wells appealed directly to the Continental Congress. She believed firmly that she was entitled to a response from the patriot government: "I have Don as much to Carrey on the warr as maney that Sett Now at the healm of government." Wells urged the Congress to remember what her purchase of war bonds had accomplished: "If She did not fight She threw in all her mite which bought the Solgers food & Clothing & Let them have Blankets and Since then She has bin obligd to Lay upon Straw & glad of that." The Continental Congress did not respond to her petition, and it remains in the National Archives, perhaps the most moving witness to the Revolution left to us by a woman.

The mobilization of women is a significant index of the vigor of any revolutionary movement. Societies at war are societies engaged in a renegotiation of gender relations. Only in recent decades have U.S. historians begun seriously to evaluate the mobilization of women and to consider the ways in which relations between men and women changed in the era of the American Revolution.

The American Revolution accomplished a radical transformation in the relationship of ruler and ruled. Patriots reconceptual-ized both the sovereign and the subject. The Continental Congress, which began in 1774 as a cooperative assembly of colonial representatives, was transformed into the new nation's permanent governing body. The Articles of Confederation, passed by Congress in 1777 but not fully ratified by all the states until 1781, when the war was nearly over, preserved the "sovereignty, freedom and independence" of each state but gave the Continental Congress the power to declare war and peace, to raise an army and to finance its expenses, and to conduct diplomacy. For their part, the legislative assemblies of each state drafted new state constitutions (which generally included extensive bills of rights), passed new laws, devised new oaths of office, and replaced old taxes with new ones.

But while making all of these major changes in the public law, patriot legislatures and conventions retained two systems of inherited laws: the lawmakers strengthened the law of slavery and they continued the old law of domestic relations. Thus, into the new democratic order they imported the hierarchical relationships between master and slave, and the considerably softer, but still hierarchical, traditional relations between husband and wife. The meaning of American citizenship was thereby gendered and racialized; from the beginning it was composed differently for men and women, white and black. These continuations of prerevolutionary social relationships mark the limits of revolutionary creativity.

Women as well as men had a new relationship to civil authority: Rachel Wells described herself as "a Sitizen." As she understood, the newly constructed citizenship was a phenomenon in which all free people participated. But Americans entered the revolutionary era convinced that men and women have different social responsibilities. For men, political institutions—the army, the militia, the state legislatures, the Continental Congress, organizations of artisans—facilitated collective experience. But only Quaker churches had separate women's meetings, and Quakers, whose opposition to violence as a route to social change had the practical effect of aligning them with the English, were not usable as a political model for patriots. The political language of the patriots, inherited from the republicanism of Renaissance city-states and from English political tradition, reserved citizenship for men who had independent control of property and the ability to bear arms in the defense of the republic. Female imagery was used to describe what Americans should scorn: Britain was a cruel mother; virile men avoided effeminacy.

Yet the American Revolution was preeminently a crisis of authority. A democratizing society and a patriarchal family were discordant; in fact, patriot ideology challenged patriarchal relationships. Patriots excoriated the father figure of George III—in print, and also by destroying statues of the king. Denial of patriarchy infused a popular literature that called on women to assert their right to choose their own husbands and to demand of these men friendship and cooperation within marriage. The private roles of wife and mother came to be articulated as having an important political dimension. The republic relied on women to choose only virtuous men for husbands and on mothers to socialize the next generation of virtuous citizens. A reconfiguration of private relationships between husbands and wives was ideologically linked to the transformation of the public relationship between king and subject into a new set of relationships among citizens.

One set of changes—dethroning the king, substituting citizens for subjects—was rapidly inscribed in American law and social practice. The other set of changes—relationships between husbands and wives, parents and children—was left to develop in the sphere of custom. Indeed, while men were encouraged to claim the fruits of independence in their private lives and economic undertakings, women were simultaneously warned against the dangers of the new order. Novels and sermons warned women that to step outside of the patriarchal world into a world of individual independence and individual choice was to risk seduction, betrayal, and disaster. Revolutionary ideology held out many promises to women, but it would take many generations and much political struggle before women, white and black, could claim them.

1763–1775

Between 1689 and 1815, a period of time historians sometimes call the "long 18th century," England and France were pitted against each other in six wars. In these transoceanic conflicts, Atlantic trade control was at stake and the colonies of both states played a major role in supplying war provisions. The stakes continued to grow at the same rate as the immigration of Europeans to America: 250,000 people in 1700, 1.15 million by 1750, and more than 2 million by 1760. These migrants originated from many countries; they came not only from England but also from a variety of German principalities and included transplanted Scottish Protestants from Ireland. Very few came from France. When the British Parliament sized up the potential of the American colonies, it doubled its efforts to regulate commerce, notably by putting a heavy tax on the most profitable trade with the sugar-producing French islands. The Seven Years' War (1756–63) witnessed an intense confrontation between Great Britain and France on North American soil: in the west, where the French did their utmost to oust the English from the fur trade in the Ohio Valley, and in the northeast, where colonial soldiers fought for control of the fortresses of Nova Scotia, which protected the access to New France.

After the English victory in 1763, France ceded to England all of Canada and also all territory in North America east of the Mississippi except the city of New Orleans. This victory had ironic consequences. Stabilizing the frontiers of this expanded empire meant an expensive administrative system. The British Crown deemed that the stabilization of this enlarged empire, the maintenance of peace with the native inhabitants of America, and the regulation of trade required a reinforced presence of the British in the empire, and it increased taxes in order to assume the costs of this presence. Taxes seemed reasonable to the legislators in London, who had barely emerged from the expensive war with France.

But international relations do not allow for gratitude. To the colonists of America, who felt very removed from European rivalries and thought they had already made heavy sacrifices on behalf of the empire, the new taxes seemed exorbitant. Practically every workingman in Boston had fought in the conflicts, and many had died; the war had left a sorrowful legacy by reducing their widows and orphans to destitution. A whole generation of colonial merchants and traders had learned to dodge royal authority; from this the lawmakers who had successfully opposed the king's governors drew increased trust in their abilities. Although English colonists were lightly taxed, they resisted new taxes, partly because they believed they had already sacrificed enough during the war, and partly because they feared that Britain was preparing to exploit the American colonies as it was already exploiting Ireland. Thus, tensions between England and the colonies, instead of being resolved, were ironically exacerbated by English victory.

The next decade was marked by the imposition on Americans of a series of taxes, among them a "stamp tax" on newspapers, printed matter of all kinds including judicial documents, and playing cards. It was the first direct tax Parliament imposed on the Americans. Many questioned Parliament's right to tax a population that had no representation whatsoever in that body. Politicians throughout the colonies thus stressed the principle of "no taxation without representation." Secret organizations, including the Sons of Liberty, were created to fight the stamp tax; in many cities these groups intimidated with violence those who sold the stamps or imported British merchandise. In Boston crowds intimidated royal officials and destroyed the house of Lieutenant Governor Thomas Hutchinson. Everywhere in the colonies the Sons of Liberty organized boycotts of English goods until the Stamp Act was revoked. British merchants, hurt by this refusal to buy their wares, joined with the colonists in demanding that Parliament abrogate the Stamp Act, a goal that was achieved in 1766.

But in 1767 Parliament once again attempted to increase the revenues from the American colonies, this time by taxing many imported products, textiles in particular. And once again the colonists organized a boycott of English goods. These campaigns drew the population of the entire Atlantic coast into a unified movement of resistance against England. In 1770 the decrease in imported goods had reached such proportions that the Townshend Acts, by which these taxes had been instituted, were abolished.

Women were actively involved in the marketplace as shopkeepers and also as consumers. If the consumer boycotts were to succeed, it was clear that women would have to be mobilized to support them with enthusiasm. As one male patriot leader observed, unless we "persuade our wives to give us their assistance . . . 'tis impossible to succeed." In a consumer boycott, private behaviors suddenly became charged with public significance, political decisions might be ascribed where none were intended, and even those who wished to remain neutral might find themselves accused of aligning themselves one way or another. If patriots wore homespun, could one wear an old silk dress imported long before the boycott? Even children could shame their elders by setting a patriotic example.

Women as well as men signed pledges promising not to purchase imported goods or to patronize stores that sold them. In Boston many women signed these pledges; in 1768 and 1770 there were several agreements signed by hundreds of women. In 1774, when the Boston Committee of Correspondence distributed a "Solemn League and Covenant" asking all adults to pledge not only to boycott British imports but also to shun anyone who did, women as well as men throughout Massachusetts signed.

Not all women who enacted their politics by means of their consumption habits were patriots. Tories could also display their politics by their behavior as consumers. One loyalist, Peter Oliver, scorned the patriot boycotters as hypocrites:

> The Ladies too were so zealous for the Good of their Country, that they agreed to drink no Tea, except the Stock of it which they had by them; or in Case of Sickness. Indeed they were cautious enough to lay in large Stocks before they promised; & they could be sick just as suited their Convenience or Inclination.

Other women drank their tea privately or continued to purchase and sell imported goods.

If boycotting were to be effective, it would have to be accompanied by domestic production. Here, too, the efforts of women were consequential. In many towns and cities, the efforts of women to support the boycott of imported cloth by providing homespun material as an alternative was ritualized into public demonstrations. Bringing their spinning wheels to a central site—often the home of the minister—the women could simultaneously display their rejection of "foreign productions" and their support for the minister.

These public spinning demonstrations ensured considerable publicity for the cause. During one show in 1769, held at the home of Ezra Stiles, a pastor in Newport, Rhode Island, 37 women brought their spinning wheels while others came to help them. Dinner was served to 60 spinning women; throughout the day some 600 people came to watch them. It is known that between 1768 and 1770, in New England alone 1,600 women participated in spinning demonstrations; many more probably took part unnoticed by the newspapers.

Spinning demonstrations, historian Laurel Ulrich has noted, displayed "a form of political resistance built upon sacrifice, self-discipline and personal piety rather than on street action . . . and flamboyant self-assertion" (see Ulrich). Some women entered public space as consumers and producers; others entered it by publishing exhortations to support the boycott. In an era in which, as Jürgen Habermas has proposed, the public sphere of nongovernmental opinion-making was developed as a location situated between the private household, on the one hand, and legislative debate, on the other, newspapers were a central site of public argument. By their published expressions of opinion, private individuals in effect assemble themselves into a "public body" that positions itself "against the public authority itself." In a society in which men controlled the press and were using it to explain to each other how good republicans could retain their manhood while eschewing the patriarchal role, women faced the challenge of making space for themselves in the public sphere and participating in the task of opinion making. Patriot newspapers welcomed occasional contributions of women to the resistance movement and published examples of women's patriotic verses. Here is one example, from Philadelphia:

> Let the Daughters of Liberty, nobly arise,
> And tho' we've no Voice, but a negative here,
> The use of the Taxables, let us forbear,
> (Then Merchants import till yr. Stores are all full
> May the Buyers be few and your traffick be dull.
> Stand firmly resolved and bid Grenville to see
> That rather than Freedom, we'll part with our Tea.

Newspapers published some women's nonimportation agreements—such as the famous one of 51 women of Edenton, North Carolina, which was reprinted throughout the colonies in 1774—and reported on women's spinning demonstrations. In these ways, women learned of each other's participation in the argument with England, and, to a limited extent, entered into public dialogue with men.

When the resistance to England erupted violently into public spaces, women were also implicated. They were present in the crowds that protested the Stamp Act in 1764; they were present in protests against soldiers quartered in homes in Boston and New York. Eyewitnesses tell of women's participation in shaming and humiliating Tories. Women marched in ritual processions to jails in solidarity with political prisoners—for example, to support Alexander MacDougall in New York in 1770. They joined funeral processions to honor victims of British violence; in 1770 Boston women were mourners at the funeral of the murdered apprentice Christopher Seider. They also mourned for the victims of the "Boston Massacre," who were interred publicly after a confrontation between the city's workers and English troops who shot into the crowd, killing five people (1770). By bearing witness, these women conferred respectability on resistance and intensified the male opposition to England.

1775–1783

The disorders of war disrupted and endangered women's lives as well as the lives of their husbands, brothers, and sons. Enslaved women were particularly vulnerable; when masters felt endangered, they often made slaves even less secure. Although the British were not always protectors of slaves, they did understand that patriots would be weaker if slave systems were disrupted. A higher proportion of slave women were runaways during the war than before it. Occasionally, slaves received sanctuary behind the British lines. At the end of the war, when the British evacuated Savannah, Charleston, and New York, thousands of black women and children, as well as men, sailed with them to freedom.

The war in America developed in stages. The first battles—Lexington and Concord, Bunker Hill—were fought in New

England. The British evacuated Boston in 1776, and the main theater of war moved to New York and New Jersey. The British occupied New York City from July 1776 to the end of the war in 1783. There was little fighting in the south until 1778, but thereafter guerilla war in the region was especially violent. Throughout the country, as the war raged on, women were at risk. We do not have good documentation about the frequency of rape, but we do know of systematic and brutal attacks in Hunterdon County, New Jersey, in 1776, which may be associated with the anger felt by the British soldiers when George Washington escaped after the fall of New York City and it was clear that the war would be a long one. Other attacks on women were committed throughout the war.

Women in substantial numbers were made refugees by the Revolution. When the British occupied Boston, thousands of working-class women fled the city. Patriots rarely gave the families of loyalist men the opportunity to make their own independent political choices. In New York, New Jersey, and elsewhere, wives of loyalist men who fought with the British were expelled from their homes. "My feelings [are] . . . wounded for the sufferings of a Number of my Sex in this State," wrote Mary Morris of Philadelphia, "who are compeld to leave it, by that Cruell Edict . . . there is many whose conduct has not Merited it. . . . Mrs. Furgerson is determind not to go, she says they may take her life but shall never banish her from Her Country." Morris recognized that married women might wish to make a choice of what counted as their own country that was different from the choice made by their husbands, but often that choice was not respected.

Throughout the war, territory changed hands. The British army occupied Boston in 1775–76, New York City between 1776–83, and Philadelphia in 1777–78. They captured Savannah in 1778 and Charleston in 1780. In these cities they demanded that officers and sometimes soldiers be housed in private homes, forcing women to serve, in effect, as unwilling keepers of boardinghouses. The soldiers who moved in felt no obligation to be orderly; they could easily intimidate their hosts. Women whose homes served as lodging for strange men were physically vulnerable. For their part, American armies also demanded supplies and housing from fellow citizens when troops moved near their homes. Wherever armies moved, civilians were vulnerable to demands for contributions of food and shelter for soldiers; often these armies moved straight to pillage, looting, and physical abuse.

A very few women dressed as men and served as soldiers. We know virtually nothing about any individual except Deborah Sampson of Massachusetts. In 1782 she adopted men's clothing and the name of Robert Shurtleff. Already notable in her community for her height and strength, she enlisted for service with the Fourth Massachusetts Regiment, serving with that regiment in New York and possibly in Pennsylvania. She was wounded at a battle near Tarrytown, New York. After her return to Massachusetts she married and bore three children, but the fame of her exploits persisted. After a fictionalized biography was published, she went on a long speaking tour, perhaps the first American woman to undertake such an enterprise. She applied for the pensions to which her wartime service entitled her. These were awarded slowly and grudgingly, and she died impoverished in 1827.

Because women were not normally part of the armed forces, they could more easily play the role of spy. George Washington was very suspicious of wives of loyalists, who he thought smuggled information about patriot troop movements across British lines. In 1780, 32 women as well as 400 men were brought to the attention of the Albany County Board of the New York State Commissioners for Detecting and Defeating Conspiracies, accused of being spies or Tory sympathizers. Among the accused were women who had given sanctuary in their homes to loyalists and to British soldiers. Patriot women also smuggled information. Elizabeth Burgin was suspected of helping American prisoners of war escape from British jails; the British offered a reward of 200 pounds for her capture.

The American Revolution was one of the last of the early modern wars. As they had since the 16th century, thousands of women and children traveled with the armies, serving as nurses, laundresses, and cooks. Like the legendary Molly Pitcher, they made themselves useful where they could. They hauled water for teams of men who fired cannon; they brought food to men on the battlefield; they washed clothes. In British practice, with which the colonists had become familiar during the Seven Years' War, each company had its own allocation of women, usually, but not always, soldiers' wives and mothers. When the British sailed, women sailed with them. The ratio of men to women among the British troops ranged from 10:1 to 5:1. Patriots were skeptical about giving women official status in the army. But Washington recognized that his army needed women for the same reasons that the British did, and he established a ratio of 1 woman for every 15 men in a regiment. By the end of the war, between 10,000 and 20,000 women had served as "women of the army."

Some women, no doubt, came for a taste of adventure. Generals' wives, such as Martha Washington, took their right to follow as a matter of course, and spent the winter of Valley Forge with their husbands. But an overwhelming majority of the women who followed the armies, whether patriot or loyalist, were poor. Wives and children who had no means of support when their husbands or lovers were drawn into service followed after and cared for their own men, earning their subsistence by nursing, cooking, and washing for the troops, in an era when hospitals were marginal and the offices of quartermaster and commissary were inadequately run. Women who served these troops were performing tasks of the utmost necessity in an era when cleanliness was virtually the only guard against disease. One of these women, Sarah Osborn, applied for a pension long after the war was over. She had joined the army at West Point in 1780 and accompanied it on a long expedition south, marching proudly on horseback into Philadelphia and then continuing to Yorktown, where she witnessed the British surrender. On the battlefield at Yorktown she brought food to the soldiers under fire. When George Washington warned her of the danger, she told him she did not fear the bullets because they "would not cheat the gallows"; that is, she understood that her challenge to royal authority was not different from his. If the soldiers risked being hanged for treason, so did she.

Most women, of course, were civilians. They remained in their homes and tried to survive as best they could. As we have seen, many women had been politicized during the prewar boycotts of British goods. During the war women continued to be involved in the politics of production and consumption. State governments demanded that women turn in lead weights to be melted down for bullets, contribute rags for bandages, and supply clothing and blankets for troops, and the same governments penalized them if they resisted. Many women undertook to police local merchants who hoarded scarce commodities. Historians have identified at least 30 occasions in the first four years of the Revolution when crowds violently intimidated merchants who were selling food at excessively high prices. Most of these crowds were at least partially composed of women, and perhaps one-third were composed primarily of women. In July 1778, Abigail Adams reported that "a Number of Females, some say a hundred, some say more, assembled with a cart and trucks, marched down to the Ware House" of an "eminent, wealthy, stingy" Boston merchant who was rumored to be hoarding coffee. When he refused to give the women the keys to his warehouse, "one of them seazed him by his Neck and tossed him into the cart . . . he delivered the keys . . . they . . . opened the Warehouse, Hoisted out the Coffee themselves, put it into trucks and drove off. . . . A large concourse of Men stood amazed silent Spectators." In spring 1777, a crowd of women in Poughkeepsie, New York, made a notable series of destructive attacks on a loyalist merchant; others occurred throughout the country from time to time.

Some elite patriot women supported the Revolution by their words and fundraising. In 1780 Esther De Berdt Reed, wife of the president of Pennsylvania, and Sarah Franklin Bache, Benjamin Franklin's daughter, initiated the most vigorous project. They distributed a call for contributions, explaining their desire to offer "more than barren wishes" for the success of the Revolution. "If the weakness of our Constitution, if opinion and manners did not forbid us to march to glory by the same paths as the Men, we should at least equal, and sometimes surpass them in our love for the public good." These women were energetic; instead of passively waiting for contributions, they went from door to door to solicit them. Collecting contributions this way invited confrontation. One loyalist wrote to her sister, "Of all absurdities, the ladies going about for money exceeded everything; they were so extremely importunate that people were obliged to give them something to get rid of them." The campaign raised $300,000 in inflated paper war currency. Rather than let George Washington merge it with the general fund, the women insisted on using it to buy materials for making shirts. Each soldier who received a shirt would know that he had received an extraordinary contribution from the women of Philadelphia. Similar enterprises in some other states were modeled on the Philadelphia example. In New Jersey, women collected $15,000, which they remitted to George Washington to purchase stockings for the soldiers of that state. A more modest contribution, initiated by the governor's wife, came from the women of Maryland.

The connections between religious identity and political identity were complex. In most of the British colonies, the Church of England was the established church with the king at its head. To a certain extent, a political revolution hostile to the king had to be a religious revolution turned against the Church. Efforts toward separating church and state and laying the foundations for freedom of religion accompanied resistance to English domination. In state after state, the Church of England lost its official position: in 1776 in Pennsylvania, Delaware, and New Jersey; in 1786 in New York State, North Carolina, and Georgia; in 1790 in South Carolina. Virginia stopped collecting taxes intended for the Church in 1777. In 1785 the legislative assembly of Virginia adopted the Bill for Establishing Religious Freedom written by Thomas Jefferson. It stipulated that no person could be forced to attend or pay to support any form of worship, nor could individuals be subjected to discrimination based on religious convictions. In all the colonies, the Anglican clergy not surprisingly lined up on the side of the loyalists, but many members of the clergy, notably in the south, were patriotic. At the end of the war the Church of England lost what remained of its special status. Renamed the Episcopal Church, it was now merely one of the numerous branches of Protestantism.

In revolutionary America the Protestant churches had a role that was very different from the role of the Catholic Church in revolutionary France. In the case of France, the rejection of the Catholic Church led the revolutionaries to invent their own alternative public spaces and their own public rituals. In America, on the other hand, most of the Protestant churches, including the Congregationalists and Presbyterians, were in favor of the revolutionary movement. Many patriotic ecclesiastics happily held ritual demonstrations, sermons, and public ceremonies to show their support for the Revolution.

The American Revolution stimulated religious revivals, which had particular appeal to women. The percentage of women among the new members of Congregational churches in Massachusetts increased sharply in the early stages of the war, rising from a low of 54 percent in 1768 to a high of 72 percent in 1777 (see Shiels). Women were receptive to other forms of religious revival and recruitment. They made up large numbers of new Methodists, who honored John Wesley's mother, Susannah, as a founder of the sect and who welcomed women as exhorters and preachers. The Methodist denomination grew substantially during the war years and the subsequent generation, with a special appeal not only to women but also to black men and women. In some Methodist churches, blacks and whites shared the same space, and some black women became preachers. Mother Ann Lee, founder of the Shakers, arrived in America on the eve of the Revolution with a message that included equal rights for women and an equal role for them in the Shaker community. Lee's audiences were heavily female, as were those of Jemima Wilkinson, the "Publick Universal Friend." When new sects were pacifist or skeptical of war, however, they were likely to be regarded with suspicion. As the historian Ruth Bloch has written, "their repudiation of violence, their elevation of women to authority, their hierarchical distribution of power, their preoccupation with personal domestic life, were all directly opposed to the prevailing political ethos" (see Bloch). For these reasons, Shakers and Universal Friends were regarded with suspicion and linked to loyalists; Ann Lee was briefly jailed. Universalists, who formed in the United States during the war years, were also often regarded with suspicion even though their founder, John Murray, supported the Revolution.

Quakers were pacifists and did not believe in the use of violence to obtain their religious or political objectives. But in the revolutionary context, their rejection of violent changes placed the Quakers, as it did all pacifists, on the side of the British, even despite themselves. Some young Quakers broke with their church and joined in the fighting, but the majority kept their distance from the war effort. Quaker women were the only group of American women who were organized to run their own institutions, conducting "women's meetings" that ran parallel to "men's meetings," monitoring the moral behavior of their members and negotiating with men on a roughly equal footing in decisions to construct new meeting houses, and speaking from the floor in general meetings of worship. In the 1830s Quaker women were to play a leading role in the condemnation of slavery and the demand for greater rights for women, drawing their arguments from the logic of the Declaration of Independence. It is interesting to speculate on the influence they might have wielded in the revolutionary era had their pacifism not made them suspect and had it not taken them a generation to recover respectability.

Slave women of the revolutionary period have left us practically no texts other than the poems of Phillis Wheatley. Bought by a pious Boston family in 1761 when she was a child, she was taught to read and write, a rare experience for a slave. Her writer's talent was encouraged by her masters, who arranged for her poems to be published in England in 1773. Wheatley was one of the first women of any race in colonial New England to state in writing what she thought of the political problems. Freed shortly before the Revolution, she published a strong letter against slavery in the New England newspapers in 1774; she stressed "universal love of liberty." When the war broke out, she dedicated a poem to General George Washington. In it she depicted the whole world as attentive to the outcome of the American struggles:

Fix'd are the eyes of nations on the scales,
For in their hopes Columbia's arm prevails . . .
Proceed, great chief, with virtue on thy side,
Thy ev'ry action let the goddess guide.

Phyllis Wheatley married and had three children. She died in 1784, a free woman but destitute.

Slaves had a better chance of finding freedom by passing behind English lines than by entrusting themselves to the patriots. Although slavery was abolished in Massachusetts during the Revolution and in New Hampshire shortly after the Revolution, it persisted elsewhere. Pennsylvania, Connecticut, Rhode Island, and New York State established gradual emancipation, freeing adult slaves as of a given date, or when they reached age 21, while children born in slavery had to remain there until a predetermined age. Thus, it frequently happened that mothers and fathers were freed while their children were still enslaved. The system of slavery was actually strengthened by the Federal Constitution of 1787, which included a Fugitive Slave Clause and which permitted slave states to count three-fifths of the slaves as part of their population for the purposes of representation. The slave states continued the practice that children of enslaved women and free men (often their masters) followed "the condition of their mother" into slavery. Thus, Sally Hemings, by whom Thomas Jefferson almost certainly had several children, was his slave, although she was also the daughter of Jefferson's own wife's father.

The American Revolution was simultaneously a civil war and a war of national liberation. Both types of state violence are notable for their capacity to place women at risk and also for their power to recruit women in support of one side or the other. American women were not insulated from the disruption and violence of war. Even limited travel became hazardous, often impossible when armies were in the vicinity. Trade was dis-

rupted; prices rose precipitously; and maintaining the household economy became considerably more expensive and more difficult, even when there was no fighting nearby. Armies provided virtually no care for the sick or wounded, and injured and ill men were lucky if their mothers, wives, or sisters could come to the battlefield, find them, and take them home to recuperate. White women were not part of the political bodies that made decisions about when and how the war was to be pursued; they never were able to offer their own collective judgment on whether they thought the war worth the cost. (Enslaved women who found shelter and freedom with the British made their own statement about the meaning of the war and which side could be trusted.) Religiously devout women were deeply skeptical of violence and the drunkenness and cursing that accompanied it. Against that resistance, patriot leaders sought to persuade women to support the war effort and to sustain the recruitment of patriot men. Thus, women became part of the moral resources of the total society; they were mobilized by the state to mobilize their men. Sending men to war was in part women's expression of surrogate enlistment. They were shaming their men into serving the interests of the Revolution.

1783–1800

"[I]n the new Code of Laws which I suppose it will be necessary for you to make I desire you would Remember the Ladies, and be more generous and favourable to them than your ancestors," wrote Abigail Adams to John Adams three months before the Declaration of Independence. "Do not put such unlimited power into the hands of the Husbands. Remember all Men would be tyrants if they could."

The American patriots made the Revolution in order to found a republic, a government without a king. In a republic the people hold the sovereignty, and the executive agents are responsible to the people, usually by means of suffrage. The revolutionary generation gave proof of its greatest originality when it devised the *mechanics* of popular consent. As Robert R. Palmer has said, its principal contributions to political science were the concept of "people [as a] constituent power" (see Palmer), and the range of strategies meant to put this principle into practice (holding constitution-writing conventions and special ratification elections). The civil society that emerged from the war was a society in which citizenship belonged to every white adult and a few black adults; however, only white men's voices counted.

White men who held modest amounts of property thought of themselves as the makers of the Revolution, and it was to them—as voters, as soldiers, as citizens—that legislators felt themselves responsible when the war ended. In stabilizing the Revolution and eliminating many inherited class distinctions among whites, the legislators of the era created a social system that minimized differences among white men in comparison to what they had been before the war. White women had indeed served in and supported the American Revolution—as individuals, not in groups—but in 1787 women were not in a strong position to make collective demands as a group. When they wrote "new codes of law" during and immediately after the Revolution, male legislators paid little attention to women's distinctive situation. Indeed, the founders kept in place a legal system that emphasized legal differences between free women and men, especially between married women and men. If women had been "remembered," or if they had been able to participate in the making of the new codes of laws, would the laws have been different?

White women were divided between slaveholding and non-slaveholding families; it is not possible to predict whether, as a class, they would have changed or attacked the system of slavery. But white women who had lived through the revolutionary years *did* share some experiences with each other and did emerge with some common needs. Women had the right of petition, and they exercised it frequently. Lacking any other mode of approach, they flooded legislatures with petitions asking for redress for grievances and wrongs suffered during the Revolution. However, they had no control and little influence over what happened to their petitions once submitted. Rachel Wells's petition was one among many, and it met the usual fate; legislatures rarely responded to women's requests. If women had had the vote, surely they would have used it to demand pensions for war widows and orphans. But Congress provided modest pensions for wounded soldiers, not for their dependents; only the widows of Continental Army officers received very small pensions. Not until 50 years after the end of the war were widows of enlisted men, such as Sarah Osborn, included in pension legislation; by that time most of the widows were dead. Even women who had worked for the army were often reduced to begging and humiliation after the war. One woman wrote to Congress that she had suffered "the severity of Cold and heat in the Service of her Country—besides a greater [hardship], which was the loss of her husband, who was killed." She thought herself "entitled" to support from the nation, but she did not receive it. In the absence of legislative action, some middle-class women organized "ladies' benevolent societies" to raise money for widows and orphans. In these organizations they learned many skills of appealing to the public, of managing money, and of cross-class alliances. Some of these groups would be models for larger and more vigorous women's reform societies two generations later.

Although the Revolution was the occasion for a radical reappraisal of the laws by which they lived, Americans had no intention of relinquishing the entire British legal tradition. Many early state law codes specifically reenacted large portions of the common law and of equity practice.

British laws concerning domestic relations, adopted virtually without change in America, rested on the concept of "coverture," the idea that a married woman's identity was submerged in, or covered, by that of her husband. A married couple became a legal fiction; the pair was a single person with a single will. The will of the pair was always taken to be the same as the real will of the husband. The husband received control over all the property a wife brought to or earned during the marriage. He might use and dispose of it without her consent (saving only one-third of the moveable property, and the *use* of one-third of the real estate, for her in dower after his death). A married woman could not make a will; if she died before her husband, all her property would descend to him and their heirs.

For a generation after the Revolution, voting rights were commonly linked to ownership of property. So long as American domestic-relations law transferred to the husband control over all the property a wife brought to or earned during the marriage, married women were judged incapable of having an independent opinion or of making an electoral choice; it was thought that

their husbands could too easily dictate their political opinions. With the exception of Vermont, which gave the right to vote to all adult males who would swear allegiance to the new state, all the states feared those who, in John Adams's words, were "too poor to have a will of their own." Lawmakers feared that individuals without property could easily be pressured by those on whom their means of existence depended: employers could direct the votes of their employees without even having to resort to explicit threats; husbands could likewise dictate their wives' opinions.

Even though coverture was not consistent with republican theory, virtually no one proposed revising domestic-relations laws in order to give married women control of any portion of their property (whether they had brought it to the marriage, had been given it as a gift during the marriage, or earned it by their own labor). The married woman, "covered" by her husband's political identity, became politically invisible. Indeed, her primary obligations were to her husband; her major obligation to the state was to refrain from committing treason. After independence, American legislatures kept the old system of domestic relations in place. The system would not be explicitly attacked until the women's movement of the 1840s and 1850s. It broke down only slowly over the course of many years, and many elements of it were still alive in the late 20th century.

In every period, however, there was a large group of unmarried, widowed, and divorced women. If independence of mind depended on the property one owned, the argument that voting rights and the owning of even modest property should be linked was a persuasive argument. Indeed, the road to universal white male suffrage was facilitated by intermediate stages in which the requirement to own property was replaced by a requirement to pay taxes or, in some places, to serve in the militia. But even though unmarried women could often meet the taxpaying requirement, they were ignored in virtually all jurisdictions.

It was possible to imagine a different system. James Sullivan, a lawyer and politician in Massachusetts, observed: "Every member of Society has a Right to give his Consent to the Laws of the Community or he owes no Obedience to them." But only in New Jersey, where Quakers had made sure that the state constitutions would grant the vote to every free "person" whose property was worth 50 pounds, were unmarried women allowed to vote. When elections were hotly contested, party activists encouraged women to vote, and hundreds did. In 1807, however, the New Jersey legislature limited the right to vote to white male taxpayers only, thus excluding women, blacks, and the poor. The women of New Jersey would wait for the 20th century to regain suffrage.

Some legal changes, however, were put in place in the years during and immediately after the American Revolution. In Britain, divorce required a special act in Parliament and could be attained only by those with money and influence. Only in New England, where Puritan tradition regarded marriage as a civil contract, was full divorce (including the right to marry again) possible before the Revolution. In the other colonies, efforts to reform divorce law were denied as contrary to the law of England. After the Revolution, many states liberalized divorce law, although none as liberally as the French divorce law of 1792, which made divorce available on the simple condition of mutual consent. Since divorce was sought by women considerably more frequently than it was sought by men, these changes in American law were of particular significance for women. Some modest changes were made in inheritance practices after the war. Virtually all states ended primogeniture—the English tradition of giving a double portion to the eldest son. This reform placed sons and daughters on an equal footing.

In the decades after the Revolution, many aspects of economic life—with the exception of slavery—were fundamentally reconceptualized and reordered. The growth of commerce and the opportunities of empire after the Revolution seriously disrupted a 17th-century corporate worldview, which had assumed that population, money supply, agricultural practices, and forms of business association changed slowly, if at all. A new emphasis on the pursuit of self-interest, heightened expectations of profit, and new market opportunities—some created by the wars of the French Revolution—transformed the American economy. The earliest factories for the mass production of textiles—beginning with Samuel Slater's mill in Pawtucket, Rhode Island, in 1790—employed a workforce of women and children and signaled a major shift in employer-employee relations. In his 1790 *Report on Manufactures*, Secretary of the Treasury Alexander Hamilton took for granted the ready availability of impoverished and employable women and children for the first industrial workforce. Corporatist concepts were challenged by a more individualistic liberalism, which offered a vision of social and economic relations as both free and self-regulating.

In the years of the American Revolution, old boundaries on women's lives were stretched, making room for the questioning of hierarchies both within the family and in the public world. Buttressed by Enlightenment commentary on natural rights and by new definitions of citizenship that stressed voluntary allegiance rather the bearing of arms, many women had reason to feel that they were, as Rachel Wells was aware, citizens with their own relationship to the republic. In pamphlets and newspapers, some women and men, notably Mercy Otis Warren, Judith Sargent Murray, and Benjamin Rush, began to argue that women could sustain the republic in important ways associated with their gender position. They could monitor the behavior of their lovers and husbands in order to reward virtuous men and punish men who were irresponsible. As mothers, they could educate their sons and daughters not only in the basic skills of reading but also in morality, wisdom, and virtue, thus ensuring the civic virtue of the next generation. If they were to serve the republic in this way, however, women needed to be well educated. The new vision of the politicized mother supported arguments for heightened attention to women's education.

Simultaneously, the economy was increasingly relying on print. There were many reasons for the vigorous attention to the education of girls that characterized the early republic. Many new schools were formed, providing opportunities to adult women to be self-supporting; these women in turn taught girls to read and write. In some regions in New England, there was no gap between literacy rates for men and women; it is possible that the white women of New England were the most literate women in the world at the end of the 18th century.

The psychological implications of this educational development are obvious: the individual who masters the basic skills of reading and writing and the rudiments of arithmetic is less dependent on others to be informed. The growing literacy of women made them a little less intellectually dependent on the guardians of authority—ministers, parents, and husbands.

Women could read newspapers on their own and buy books and magazines published in distant places. Educated women were able to earn their living as teachers of young children and of other girls who, having become teachers themselves, would in turn contribute the dissemination of educational activities among the next generation. These same educated women prepared an audience for the authors of fiction, notably of novels, a literary genre new to the 18th century. Novelists—Susannah Rowson, the author of *Charlotte Temple*, or Hannah Webster Foster, author of *The Coquette*—warned women against the dangers of seduction.

White women's private choices as lovers, wives, and mothers were thus understood to have taken on an element of public obligation. The role of the "republican mother" asserted the responsibility of women to participate in building a new public order. But because women's choices were framed in the service of the men and children of their families, republican motherhood was also a conservative, stabilizing concept, deflecting the radical potential of the revolutionary experience. The woman who served the republic by raising virtuous children did not vote or serve in official positions in courts and legislatures.

There were few extended analyses of women's place in the new republic. Virtually no mention is made of women in *The Federalist Papers*, the classic defense of the new United States constitution written by James Madison, Alexander Hamilton, and John Jay. Mary Wollstonecraft's *Vindication of the Rights of Women* (1792) was reprinted in America shortly after its appearance in England. Americans particularly welcomed her endorsement of more education for women and her encouragement of women to prepare for economic self-sufficiency. In private correspondence, Abigail Adams also called for stronger education for women and the fostering in girls of their own sense of independence and integrity, but she wrote her observations in private letters that circulated only to her friends and family.

The most complex texts on women's place in the republic are those of Judith Sargent Murray, the wife and then the widow of the founder of the Unitarian Church of America. Born in 1751 into an eminent family in Gloucester, Massachusetts, north of Boston, Judith Sargent had been given a proper education by her family, according to the contemporary criteria for women. Nevertheless, all her life she was to regret not having been able to benefit from a Harvard education, as her brothers had done. At age 18 she married John Stevens, a navy captain, whose commercial speculations brought dramatic ups and downs to his state of wealth from one year to the next; he would die bankrupt. During the Revolution, Judith, her husband, and her father belonged to the Universalist Church. After Stevens's death in 1786, Judith married John Murray, the American founder of this church.

Judith Sargent Murray's "Gleaner" essays, published in newspapers between 1792 and 1794 and as a three-volume set of books in 1798, are nearly 700 pages long and touch on issues of education, manners, fashion, religion, and politics. There was much on which Murray and Wollstonecraft would have agreed, but there was also a great deal of Murray's work about which Wollstonecraft would have been bitterly skeptical. Compared to the Englishwoman's, Murray's message appears restrained. Her politics were conservative; she supported the Federalist party rather than the Democratic Republicans, whose positions on many issues were more progressive. She was skeptical of the

French Revolution, and even less confident of it once Robespierre made his appearance. Nevertheless, the two women would have agreed on many points. Like Wollstonecraft, Murray emphasized the need to educate women for independence and psychological autonomy. She urged them to show themselves as direct and practical. Like Wollstonecraft, Murray had had personal experience with adversity that had taught her that women should not base their entire futures on the marriage market. She knew from experience that a sensible woman had to be prepared for the most violent reversals of fortune.

Murray criticized Jean-Jacques Rousseau. "Rousseau said that even though a woman may *appear* to handle a pen, it is certain that some man of letters stands behind the curtain to guide its movements." She prided herself on being one of those women whom nobody helped with her writing and who earned her living with her work. She believed women were capable of sustained intellectual accomplishments and wanted to convince them that a solid education would make authentic independence possible. She tirelessly refuted the accusations thrown in the face of the "educated woman"—the lack of seductiveness, the relinquishment of her duties.

In the years of the early republic, Americans sustained the hierarchical patterns of family and work relations that contradicted some of the broad generalizations revolutionaries made about equality and citizenship. But Judith Sargent Murray's contemporaries were also probably the first generation in the cultural history of the West to recognize, indeed to encourage, women's ambitions and to support them to the extent that their objectives were developed within a framework in which the company of husbands and the education of children would also find their place. "I expect to see our young women forming a new era in female history," Murray wrote. These contradictions in American ideology would be addressed—slowly, with difficulty, against resistance—throughout the next two centuries of American life.

Bibliography

Sources

Butterfield, Lyman H., editor, *Adams Family Correspondence*, 6 vols., Cambridge, Massachusetts: Belknap Press of Harvard University Press, 1963–93

Dann, John C., editor, *The Revolution Remembered: Eyewitness Accounts of the American Revolution*, Chicago: University of Chicago Press, 1980

Murray, Judith Sargent, *The Gleaner*, Boston: Thomas and Andrews, 1798; reprint, Schenectady, New York: Union College Press, 1992

Warren, Mercy Otis, *History of the Rise, Progress and Termination of the American Revolution*, 3 vols., Boston: Manning and Loring for E. Larkin, 1805; reprint, 2 vols., Indianapolis, Indiana: Liberty Fund, 1994

Warren, Mercy Otis, *The Plays and Poems of Mercy Otis Warren*, Delmar, New York: Scholars' Facsimiles and Reprints, 1980

Reference Works

Applewhite, Harriet Branson, and Darlene Gay Levy, editors, *Women and Politics in the Age of the Democratic Revolution*, Ann Arbor: University of Michigan Press, 1990

Bloch, Ruth, *Visionary Republic: Millennial Themes in American Thought 1756–1800*, Cambridge and New York: Cambridge University Press, 1985

Juster, Susan, "Demagogues or Mystagogues? Gender and the Language of Prophecy in the Age of the Democratic Revolutions," *American Historical Review* 104 (1999)

Juster, Susan, *Disorderly Women: Sexual Politics and Evangelicalism in Revolutionary New England*, Ithaca, New York: Cornell University Press, 1994

Kerber, Linda K., *No Constitutional Right to Be Ladies: Women and the Obligations of Citizenship*, New York: Hill and Wang, 1998

Kerber, Linda K., *Toward an Intellectual History of Women: Essays by Linda K. Kerber*, Chapel Hill, North Carolina: University of North Carolina Press, 1977

Kerber, Linda K., *Women of the Republic: Intellect and Ideology in Revolutionary America*, Chapel Hill: University of North Carolina Press, 1980

Klepp, Susan E., "Revolutionary Bodies: Women and the Fertility Transition in the Mid-Atlantic Region 1760–1820," *Journal of American History* 85 (1998)

Lewis, Jan, "Of Every Age Sex and Condition: The Representation of Women in the Constitution," *Journal of the Early Republic* XV (1995)

Lewis, Jan Ellen, and Peter Onuf, editors, *Sally Hemings and Thomas Jefferson: History, Memory, and Civic Culture*, Charlottesville: University Press of Virginia, 1999

Norton, Mary Beth, *Liberty's Daughters: The Revolutionary Experience of American Women, 1750–1800*, Boston: Little Brown, 1980

Palmer, R.R., *The Age of the Democratic Revolution: A Political History of Europe and America 1760–1800: The Challenge*, Princeton, New Jersey: Princeton University Press, 1959

Salmon, Marylynn, *Women and the Law of Property in Early America*, Chapel Hill: University of North Carolina Press, 1986

Shiels, Richard D., "The Feminization of American Congregationalism 1730–1835," *American Quarterly* XXXIII (1981)

Skemp, Sheila L., *Judith Sargent Murray: A Brief Biography with Documents*, Boston: Bedford Books, 1998

Ulrich, Laurel, " 'Daughters of Liberty': Religious Women In Revolutionary New England," in *Women in the Age of the American Revolution*, edited by Ronald Hoffman and Peter J. Albert, Charlottesville: University Press of Virginia, 1989

WOMEN'S POLITICAL ACTION DURING THE FRENCH REVOLUTION

JACQUES GUILHAUMOU AND MARTINE LAPIED

ALTHOUGH WOMEN WERE LEGALLY excluded from political rights at the time of the French Revolution, some actively participated in the revolutionary process, while others, motivated primarily by religious convictions, tried to oppose it. Such active involvement on both sides admittedly concerned only a minority of women, but it does show that in times of crisis, women could play a role in the public sphere despite the traditional division of duties aimed at confining them to the private sphere.

In 1789 the French Revolution reached a new stage of political radicalism, becoming a veritable factory for new ideas from which women were not excluded. Women were present every time there were organized claims, protests, or insurrections where demands were being made, and they thus took part in the popular movement and in the shaping of a public sphere of exchange and reciprocity. Activist women engaged in the new political practices, participating in the social life of the clubs, joining the patriotic mobilization during the war, and, later, supporting the enactment of the Terror as a form of government.

The period from 1790 to 1793 witnessed new configurations of power relations. First, a democratic public sphere was established wherein women patriots might, in the name of an expanded conception of citizenship, participate in the culture of the clubs. Then, in 1792, such women joined the patriotic mobilization and contributed to the advances of the popular movement, making the first steps toward partial conquest of citizenship for women. These were admittedly ephemeral, but they were of great political importance during the spring and summer of 1793. Activist women wished to see themselves as full citizens, despite various exclusionary measures against them: they had no right to vote, no right to enlist (as of 30 April 1793), and on 30 October 1793 the women's clubs were banned. Dominique Godineau's pioneering historical studies have stressed the involvement of Parisian women in some of the fundamental events of the Revolution (see Godineau). But women's action was not limited to the capital. Recent research has brought to light a level of female participation greater than previously assumed collective undertakings in the provinces.

1789: A Turning Point

At the end of the winter of 1788–89 and in the early spring of 1789, tens of thousands of *cahiers de doléances* (lists of grievances) were written across the kingdom of France. Specific women's grievances made up only a small part of these, with groups of women merchants and religious communities being the most concerned with preserving their privileges and liberties.

On that occasion, and for the first time in huge numbers, French men stood up to make their voices heard and assembled to elect their delegates. As for women, on a strictly legal basis, only the female owners of a fiefdom (Article XX of the royal ruling of January 1789) and nuns' communities could be represented (that is, they could delegate their votes to the "bailiwick" assembly).

Nevertheless, within the vast current of public opinion circulating through petitions, lampoons, and pamphlets, women's voices could be heard. Aware that they had been excluded from future National Assemblies, women at first limited their demands: "We ask to be enlightened, to have employment," declared the *Pétition des femmes du Tiers-État au Roi* (Petition of the Women of the Third Estate to the King) of 1 January 1789. But their discourse, always proffered anonymously, became more radical when the Estates-General met. Asserting that the female mind had a "natural bent for political affairs," some women rose up against the political interdiction that had fallen upon them. The paradox of a nation that "has been finally enlightened on the question of natural rights" but that "somehow excludes the female sex" situates women's grievances in the perspective of "requested equality" (*Remontrances, plaintes et doléances des Dames françaises* [Remonstrances, Complaints, and Grievances of the French Women]). The activists' formal presentation of such a request as early as 1789 bespeaks women's assertion of the female sex as a legitimate political gender. In effect, nothing could be more real, more concrete, than women's participation in the protest movements that marked the beginning of the French Revolution. Through their practices, women helped enact the sovereignty of the people. The popular movements of 1788 and 1789, like those of the ancien régime, had an important female component. But women acted alongside men; they did not carry out actions of their own.

Women were present in Grenoble on the Journée des Tuiles (Day of the Tiles) on 7 June 1788, when the people took up arms to prevent the parliamentarians from being sent into exile as had been ordered by the king, holding in check the two royal regiments that were occupying the city. Women participated in the actions of that heroic day, signaling from the very start the importance of their role in revolutionary process. From the beginning of the insurgency, women described as fishmongers and secondhand traders but also as persons of "daring and determined character" astounded witnesses with their numbers and energy. They took possession of bell towers and sounded the tocsin, and they unhitched carriages to disable the vehicles in the middle of streets and intersections. Above all, they surrounded the magistrates of Parlement, who had gathered in the townhouse of the first president, and kept them there throughout the night by the light of bonfires. When the royal officers asked for a truce, it was a woman, armed with a cudgel, who seized a colonel of the royal navy. He had just pleaded that the officers were only obeying orders and would be delighted to see these orders revoked. She brought him to the commander and forced him to ask for just such a revocation.

In April 1789 women took part in the riot against the manufacturer Réveillon. This incident demonstrates one of the most consistent features of women's political involvement: their active role in inciting violence, urging men with their words to intensify punitive actions. After the events, a woman fishmonger was condemned to the gallows for having urged people to set fires and pillage, crying, "long live the Third Estate!" This outcome attests to the political dimension of the situation.

A strong and, it would seem, primarily female mobilization has also been documented during the food riots of the spring of 1789. Women were often at the origin of the gatherings that sparked the troubles, for generally it was grain shortages or high grain prices in the marketplace that provoked the fear and anger of the masses. Lower-class women, unable to procure food for their families, would stop to discuss the situation on the street or in the town square, and their indignation could quickly become a call to protest. The men would join them, and together they would demonstrate in front of the town hall, demanding assistance. The demands were accompanied by threats, which were immediately carried out if the authorities failed to satisfy the protesters. Thus, demonstrations could turn into riots aimed first and foremost at getting into the storage buildings containing the grain reserves.

In Provence, according to Monique Cubells, women and children were frequently present at large riots (see Cubells). Significant numbers of women took an active part in riots in Aix-en-Provence, Eyguières, Aups, Brignoles, Hyères, Manosque, Ollioules, Toulon, and Marseilles. In the Comtat it was common to see women among the insurgents. They instigated the riots that broke out in the marketplaces of Carpentras and Vaison to protest the lack of grain. In Avignon women participated in the attack on the house of the second consul, who had a reputation for hoarding stocks. Subsequent to this attack, one woman was sentenced to being branded and beaten with switches, but on the whole women were not as harshly punished as men.

A sergeant at La Ferté-Bernard, in the Sarthe, was unequivocal about the fundamental role played by women in the outbreak of violence there on 1 April 1789:

Without the women, I believe we could have made the men listen to reason. For that purpose, I had the women moved some distance away, but, seeing that during my harangue the carriage was already within view, the women started screaming and passed through despite us and our threats, getting the men to help them.

The mobilization caused by food shortages was accompanied by deep social hatred. In Nogent the wife of the schoolmaster, "who had not even taught his wife to sign her name," was heard to shout that if ever she got hold of the bailiff, "she would make his guts come out his gullet." In such cases, women occupied the same position they had in the popular uprisings of the ancien régime, in which they had always been present, albeit always alongside men. Demonstrating in small groups in those earlier revolts, women had undeniably played a very specific role in the violence, as they incited riots and goaded the men to finish off whomever they were attacking. The men considered it natural for women to participate in riots over food supplies, for they were acting as wives and mothers responsible for feeding their families. In the spring of 1789, however, the traditional women-led food riots acquired a markedly political orientation.

All the urban popular movements of the summer of 1789 included a female component, but women were far from dominant. In Paris women participated in every mass movement, but they were in the minority and their actions were indistinguishable from those of men. They did not lead, but nor were they barred from participating. Only one woman was listed among those who stormed the Bastille—Marie Charpentier, who was maimed in the uprising. No women were listed among the fatalities on that day, but women undoubtedly participated, as is shown by a number of testimonies, such as one woman's petition for a pension for her husband, mutilated during the attack, which states:

The woman citizen, his wife . . . she too "fought with all her might"—she too was ready to die. She too ran to several wine merchants to fill her apron with bottles, broken or not, which she ordered to be used as grapeshot for the cannon that was used to explode the rings of the Bastille drawbridge. (*Pétition de Marguerite Piningre au législateur* [Petition of Marguerite Piningre to the Legislator])

The role of women in propagating the Great Fear of 1789 has often been cited. However, they seemed to have played no more than a passive role, spreading rumors and then giving in to panic and the fear of being raped and slaughtered with their children. Some fled with their children to the forests or along the roadways. Accounts of men's preparations for defense speak only of women's lamentations.

Alarmed by the fact that "the provinces have been given over to the greatest of terrors," the deputies to the National Assembly endeavored to put the revolution on more solid footing, devoting themselves first and foremost to writing the Déclaration des Droits de l'Homme et du Citoyen (Declaration of the Rights of Man and Citizen). They made no allusion whatsoever to the status of women. Jean-Paul Marat summarized the virtually unanimous opinion of the deputies on this matter in his Plan of 17 August 1789 (published 23 August):

> Every citizen, as a member of the sovereign power, must have the right to suffrage, and birth alone must give him that right. But women and children must not take any part in public affairs, because they are represented by the heads of the family.

Women here seem very much reduced to a state of passive citizenship.

But although the abbé Emmanuel-Joseph Sieyès in his "Préliminaire de la Constitution" (1789; Preliminary to the Constitution), subtitled "Reconnaissance et exposition raisonnée des Droits de l'homme et du citoyen" (Acknowledgment and Reasoned Exposition of the Rights of Man and Citizen), placed women in the category of passive citizens (that is, among those "who must not influence public business in any way"), he also added the clause, "at least in the present state." Sieyès was recognized for his great constitutional ability: his draft of the Déclaration des Droits de l'Homme et du Citoyen was of great importance to the National Constituent Assembly. Was this legislator suggesting, by means of the qualifying clause, that women's citizenship was still a pending issue?

In the autumn of 1789, women made a much-remarked-upon eruption onto the political scene, giving rise to the image of the revolutionary heroine, with all its positive and negative connotations. Induced by both the economic situation, which was subjecting the lower classes of Paris to outright penury, and the attitude of the king, who continued to refuse to sign the texts that had been adopted on 4 August, the October events were a perfect illustration of women's revolutionary mobilization, featuring all those characteristics that would be further defined in the following years: women taking the initiative in the movement, soon followed by men organized in armed groups; the need for bread sparking the mobilization, but political demands being made as well.

In the climate of hostility maintained by the patriot press, particularly Jean-Paul Marat's *L'ami du peuple*, the announcement that the king's officers had trampled on the tricolor cockade during a banquet in the presence of the queen brought popular discontent to a peak. The first demonstrations in response to the announcement (5 October), originating in La Halle and the Faubourg Saint-Antoine, involved only women. These groups went first to the Hôtel de Ville, where demonstrators addressed the patriot authorities. Plebeian activists then joined the women, and together they left for Versailles, led by the "Volunteers of the Bastille." Later that night, 6,000 to 7,000 people arrived at Versailles, the march having grown along the way. The demonstrators forced merchants along their route to sell their wares at prices the protesters themselves had set. But the people's motivation was also political, and women stopped carriages to check the passengers' cockades, tearing up black ones and admonishing people to wear the patriotic model. Despite attempts to negotiate (a delegation of women demanding planned economy measures, specifically with respect to taxation of wheat and meat, was received by the Assembly), the demonstration turned into a riot, and the king was forced to leave for Paris.

Thereafter, women were present throughout the "revolutionary days," both in the provinces and in Paris, but their role was not so great as during the October events, which 19th-century historian Jules Michelet commemorates in his *Histoire de la Révolution française*; "The men took the Bastille, the women took the king. On October the 1st, everything was spoiled by the ladies of Versailles. On October the 6th, everything was repaired by the women of Paris"(book II, chap. 9; see Michelet). The anonymous author of a text dated 5 octobre 1789 and entitled *Les héroïnes de Paris* wrote: "it was the women who gave us back our liberty." This political reality, characteristic of the first "revolutionary days" clearly exposes the contradiction inherent in women's situation at the time: "You have justly handed down equality of rights? . . . Yet you unjustly deprive of [those rights] the sweeter and more interesting half among you!" (*Requête des dames à l'Assemblée nationale* [Ladies' Request to the National Assembly]). Without going so far as to ask for the abolition of the "privileges of the male sex"and thereby for a "deliberative voice" in the new assemblies, women addressed the National Assembly to ask for recognition as citizens: "Mothers of families can and should be citizens" (*Adresse des femmes bretonnes* [29 March 1790; Address of the Breton Women]); "And we, too, are citizens" (*Vues législatives pour les femmes adressées à l'Assemblée nationale* [Legislative Views for Women, Addressed to the National Assembly]).

It was the marquis de Condorcet, however, who actually made the members of the Assembly face their own contradictions, by means of a short but incisive text, "Sur l'admission des femmes au droit de cité" ("On the Admission of Women to the Rights of Citizenship"), published in the *Journal de la Société de 1789*. He explained at the outset that excluding women was "an act of tyranny," in that it violated the principle of equal rights. Written in the name of "equal rights for both sexes," Condorcet's critique of the existing legal inequality between men and women was a rejection of any reasoning based on the notion of women's natural inferiority, while expressing concern to define a specifically female type of rationality. "In truth, these [arguments] only oppose the admission of women to civic rights on grounds of utility, which cannot outweigh a true right. . . . There would be danger, we are told, of the influence exercised by women over men." In concrete terms, what Condorcet proposed did not go beyond granting the right to vote to female property owners and heads of households, in accordance with the criteria outlined by the Constituents with regard to active citizenship. Still, there was the expectation that educating women would ultimately permit them to gain the right to vote.

In any event, as early as 1789 there were demands that the word *citoyenne* (female citizen) be infused with positive meaning, as compared to *femme* (woman). It was in the field of militant action and the republican sphere of exchange and reciprocity that women would achieve citizenship, at least for a time.

The Fight for Democracy (1790–1791)

The historian Raymonde Monnier has shown how, in 1790 and 1791, a democratic public sphere developed, driven by Parisian public opinion (see Monnier). That unprecedented sphere of reciprocity brought a newly expanded concept of citizenship to the revolutionary political scene, in which patriot women occupied a significant place despite being excluded from the central discourse of the public assemblies. Thus, some French women saw themselves—and proceeded to behave—as citizens. Although they did not obtain political rights, they began to engage in new political practices. The number of such activist women was especially high in Paris, but they were present in the provinces, too. One of them, Louise de Keralio, clearly stated in *Le mercure national* the role of fraternal societies in the formation of that new space of communication:

> Every man being an integral part of the sovereign power . . . every society should, by right, be a deliberative society, deliberating about the nature and effects of law. . . . The fraternal society has sensed that the goal will not have been met if, after reaching an opinion within itself, it does not communicate this opinion to its fellow citizens.

Keralio—wife of the republican François Robert, a member of the radical Club des Cordeliers—was of noble birth. Highly educated, especially in the field of political science, she wrote numerous "patriotic views" in 1789 in the *Journal d'état et du citoyen*, of which she was the editor. In 1790 the newspaper changed its name to *Le mercure national*, and François Robert and Antoine Tournon joined Keralio as editors. Thus, from the very start, the figure of the female patriot within the new republican movement was embodied in individual personalities. Madame Roland, of whom Mona Ozouf has recently drawn a vivid portrait, played a particularly important role (see Ozouf). Born into the Parisian bourgeoisie, Manon Phlipon married Roland de la Platière in 1780 and by 1789 had become a fervent republican, as much through her reading as through her rejection of the system of privileges defining the ancien régime. Collaborating with her husband in his administrative and intellectual work, she became the source of his inspiration when he was named minister of the interior in 1792. The entire patriot circle came to her salon, which became the heart of the Girondist political activities. Roland's opinion was that women "should inspire the good [in men] and nurture and inflame every feeling useful to the *patrie* [fatherland], but should not appear to be contributing to the work of politics." A statement from her memoirs confirms that she voluntarily remained in the background: "I knew what role was appropriate for my sex, and I always kept to it. The conferences would be held in my presence without my taking any part in them; seated at a table outside of the circle, I sewed or wrote letters while they deliberated." She justified her attitude in terms of the risk that women who led a public life ostensibly ran of being associated with a "corruptive element," according to "the idea that existed about such matters under the ancien régime." Her aim was to avoid the trap of antifeminist rhetoric, which equated women who had a public life with bad mothers. We see from the outset how difficult it was for a female patriot to carve out a personal public role for herself in the midst of the restrictions and humiliations imposed upon her by male authority. A woman who spoke "the male language of virtue" was taking enormous risks.

Olympe de Gouges is a perfect example of this dilemma. Born in Montauban, the widow of an *officier de bouche* (officer assigned the task of supplying food for the administrators), she settled in Paris and then embarked upon a literary career. A patriot writer in 1789, bent on making "the voice of a just and sensitive woman" heard, she was aware of having "only very abbreviated notions of politic," owing to her lack of education, and "a style that was more naive than eloquent." But she added:

"My genius is ordinary, my talent mediocre, but I have long foreseen the present state of affairs." Highly sensitive to all kinds of injustice regarding the lot of women, an "all too unhappy and long dominated sex," that she deemed "so unfortunate in its torments," she set out to elaborate a number of "patriotic reveries." She unhesitatingly followed her "natural genius," and went so far as to affirm that women, herself among them, were endowed with a "visionary spirit":

> It must be agreed that the ladies at present are now endowed with an innate knowledge. . . . The fair sex makes women superior to men in ambition, sagacity, and politics. They have gathered up those advantages all at once, without study or profound knowledge.

Olympe de Gouges thus saw herself as belonging to no party but the one that "pleads the cause of women." She denounced the sexism of the men of the Revolution who wanted "to command the female sex like a despot." Her publication of a *Déclaration des Droit de la Femme et de la Citoyenne* (1791; Declaration of the Rights of Woman and the Female Citizen) represents a high point in the assertion of women's political personality within the Revolution. However, her involvement on the side of the Girondins in 1792, similar to Madame Roland's activities, made Gouges appear suspect to the Robespierrist Jacobins. Denounced as a moderate and suspected of seeking in her last writings to undermine the centrality of the law, she was guillotined on 3 November 1793, a few days before Roland.

Women were among those in the republican movement who denounced the royal executive's repeated betrayals, and some participated in the action aimed at bringing down Louis XVI after his attempt to flee. This mobilization took place in a turbulent social climate, since the emergency aid centers had been closed. Women had signed the collective petition to be presented on 17 July 1791, and they were present in great numbers on the Champ-de-Mars. After Mayor Bailly had proclaimed martial law, the national guard opened fire on both men and women. This bloody repression was violently condemned afterwards by the revolutionary press, in particular *L'ami du peuple*, which vigorously condemned the ghastly massacre of peaceful, unarmed citizens, women, and children.

Above all, women attended assemblies and club meetings. They also defended the revolution in the streets, marketplaces, and cabarets, and at club entrances. Indeed, women of the lower classes were very present in the streets, either for the purposes of their work or as family providers and nurturers. Marketplaces also became meeting places and sometimes the scene of arguments between urban and rural women.

In terms of ideological allegiances or activists' degree of involvement, the female component of the revolutionary movement was neither isolated nor monolithic. Real participation by women in political life through the associative movement was not a widespread phenomenon, but it was not insignificant either. Activist women had two options: gaining admission as members to mixed clubs or creating separate women's clubs.

Truly mixed-gender clubs were rare. In most cases, women could attend the meetings of popular societies but did not have a voice in the deliberations. The registers of the societies show that women's presence could mean problems: they were too noisy; they "distracted" male members. It was sometimes proposed that they be allowed to stay only if they sat separately. In

Vaison, where women were said to generate agitation, they were summoned to move into the side chapels of the church where the Jacobins met, under penalty of a six-cent fine or expulsion. In Arles, women were admitted as club members from the beginning. They initially represented 20 percent of the membership, but when the society's membership grew from 60 to 700 members, the number of women did not increase, so that eventually they made up no more than 1 to 2 percent of the total. From October 1792 to October 1793 an all-women's club was open, draining activist women from other places.

The possibilities for action available to women in the clubs varied. In some societies, they had to content themselves with merely attending sessions; elsewhere, and less often it would seem, they were considered full members. The Société de Largentière in the Ardèche granted its female members the right to vote, but the men monopolized elective offices, with the exception of a widow named assistant treasurer, whose job it was to collect funds to support the volunteers.

In Paris, La Société Fraternelle des Patriotes des Deux Sexes (Fraternal Society of Patriots of Both Sexes), defenders of the Constitution, was founded by a schoolteacher named Dansart in February 1790. Following this example, other fraternal associations were formed in the capital. In Dansart's group, women had membership cards and voted like men. Two of the six secretaries were required to be women, while the other offices could be held by either men or women, except for the presidency, which was reserved for men. Nuns participated in the important initiatives of the society, which was close to the Club des Cordeliers. After the king's attempted flight, the two associations led a joint campaign for the abolition of the monarchy.

Women's societies were founded fairly quickly in most large cities. Most frequently, those associations remained within the tradition of women's charities, focused on teaching, hospital work, and poverty-relief efforts. They played a primary role in the defense of the constitutional clergy. Still, some of these clubs were also involved in political struggles and supported quite radical views.

Archival records confirm the existence of 56 women's clubs between 1789 and 1793. In general, they maintained close relations with the men's clubs in the same city, of which the women's husbands, fathers, and brothers were members. Some of the men's clubs encouraged the creation of women's societies, and they collaborated in organizing celebrations and sometimes in setting up petitions. More often than not, members of women's clubs were from the bourgeoisie, but there were also some women artisans and shopkeepers, and the "less fortunate" female citizens, though a minority, were not completely absent. The clubs were first and foremost an urban phenomenon, although they were also widespread in the southwestern regions.

On 30 May in Dijon a group called the Dames Patriotes (Patriot Ladies) founded a club called Les Amies de la Constitution (Women Friends of the Constitution). The association had 400 members, the majority of whom were from the bourgeoisie. The goals of the Patriot Ladies, who had the flag of their club blessed by the Church, were to develop patriotism and civic virtues and to raise their children in the love of freedom and the fatherland. The president of the men's club underscored the importance of women's role within the family and in education. The women participated in the preparation of patriotic celebrations, were given a place of honor in the processions, took the patriotic oath, and sang hymns. The Women Friends of the Constitution supported the constitutional clergy, which was often under attack—mainly by women. The club, acting jointly with the men's club, was extremely vigilant when it came to helping people faced with problems of subsistence. They organized a number of philanthropic activities, including subscriptions to support soldiers, sewing soldiers' clothing, and providing replacements for hospital nuns who were caring for the sick. The role of the Patriot Ladies was above all a social one; when they were called upon to take a political stand, they followed Les Amis de la Constitution ([Male] Friends of the Constitution). Nevertheless, in September 1791, the women's club took the initiative of writing to the 83 men's clubs in the main towns of the department, urging women patriots to form societies to support the national effort, at least during the war period.

In Besançon, in the Doubs, a society called Les Amies de la Liberté et de l'Egalité (Women Friends of Liberty and Equality) was created in 1792, under the energetic leadership of one Citoyenne Maugras. The society's members developed a patriotic educational program for their children and established a workshop that employed indigent women to sew clothing and blankets for soldiers. The Women Friends of Liberty and Equality also supported the constitutional clergy, successfully worked to influence the municipality to encourage price controls, petitioned the Convention, and, early in 1793, asked that the new Constitution extend the right to vote to women. In the beginning, the Jacobin club in Besançon offered them enthusiastic support, but relations between the two clubs soon deteriorated, and the founder of the women's club was subjected to a number of personal attacks alleging she sought to use the club to serve her own personal ambitions.

In the city of Castellane in the Basses-Alpes, a women's society was founded on 3 June 1792 with the help of male patriots. In fact, after deliberating whether to invite the Patriot Ladies to attend their sessions, the men's club resolved instead to encourage the women to form their own Friends of the Constitution club. After doing so, the women affiliated themselves with, and were soon controlled by, the men's society: they requested two male commissioners to follow their work and instruct them. Still, they were not afraid to voice their views about female emancipation: "Until this day," declared the club's president,

> you have looked upon us as your idols, but even while you seemed to be accepting laws only from us, we were your slaves and you looked upon us as no more than your playthings, who served to entertain you and distract you from your deliberations and your affairs.

Later in her speech, however, the president made it clear that that though the women's patriotic feelings were just as strong as the men's, the members had resigned themselves to the differentiation in political roles: "Condemned by the laws of our sex to occupy ourselves inside with only those affairs related to our households, we can nonetheless be useful and maintain the Constitution, not only by inspiring courage but by preaching peace and unity."

In Arles a women's club was founded in October 1792 by two women: Citoyenne Philippeau (the housemaid of Guibert, a constitutional priest of Sainte-Croix), and Citoyenne Boisneaux, a woman separated from her husband and who was housekeeper to the elder Antonelle. The club's first meeting brought together a few of Guibert's parishioners, convened by Philippeau in the Église des Grands-Augustins; later the club received about 60 members from various social classes, 22 of whom had already taken part in working-class riots. Nevertheless, the society's activities remained very traditional: donations to the army and upkeep of hospitals. Numerous sessions were devoted to manual work. The members of the society were very close to the constitutional clergy and participated actively in revolutionary celebrations.

Early in the Revolution, attempts to organize women into clubs in Paris were not very successful. One such attempt was made by Etta Palm d'Aelders, a Dutch woman living in Paris, who had become known for her speeches on the political rights of women. In March 1791 she founded the Société Patriotique et de Bienfaisance des Amies de la Vérité (Patriotic Goodwill Society of the Women Friends of Truth) as a female counterpart to the men's Fédération des Amis de la Vérité (Federation of the Friends of Truth), but her group was not very active.

From the outset of revolutionary events, there were women who had reservations about them, and their reticence sometimes changed into open resistance, frequently motivated by their attachment to the Catholic Church. Just as there were women who participated in revolutionary riots, there were also women who participated in counterrevolutionary violence.

In Montauban, where, because of the strongly rooted Protestant presence and Catholic fears of Huguenot domination, the political struggles took on the appearance of a religious war, women played an important, or even driving role in a number of conflicts. The violence that erupted in May 1790 stemmed from women's attempt to bar municipal officers from entering convent and monastery gates to proceed with an inventory. In October 1791, women in Avignon played an active role in the murder of the revolutionary Lescuyer, the collective anger of a gathering having supposedly been sparked by a miracle (a statue of the Virgin Mary had ostensibly cried). Thirteen women were imprisoned after the episode; they subsequently fell victim to the revolutionaries' revenge in the massacres of La Glacière, in which women made up 22 percent of the victims. Three of the female prisoners came from the bourgeoisie, but the majority were women from the popular classes employed in the textile industry or practicing small-scale crafts or other occupations.

In Arles women represented a significant proportion of the *chiffonniste* party (so named to designate individuals from the lower classes, dressed in *chiffons* [rags]), which was violently opposed to the patriots, especially during the summer of 1791. They seem to have constituted about 25 percent of those who openly demonstrated their adherence to counterrevolutionary ideas, but only 8 or 9 percent of them actively participated in the struggles. Many of these women were associated with boutiques or the handcrafting of luxury items, while others were domestic servants. While the revolutionary party was in power, public condemnation was sometimes heaped upon such women. The devout among them were humiliated by being paraded on the backs of donkeys, subjected to insults and, in some cases, acts of violence.

In the Morbihan the resistance of peasant women soon took a religious turn, and they played a major role in the region's unrest. In February 1791 demonstrators protested against the inventory of titles held by the Ursuline convent of Muzillac.

According to a report by one of the members of the directory for the district of La Roche-Bernard, women led the movement:

> The moment we started going through the lists, we saw a great number of people coming up the staircase to the convent reception hall, a multitude of women and a few men, some armed with stones. . . . Having entered the hall, the crowd told us that we had already destroyed the monks of Prières, who no longer gave them alms, that we now wanted to do the same with the nuns of Muzillac, and that we had better bloody well get out of there.

There was a great deal of activism by women from the spring of 1791 to the spring of 1792, a time when religious concerns were a decisive factor in this area dominated by the Chouans, a group of counterrevolutionary insurgents. Women organized to defend the clergy and stood in opposition to the constitutional priests. When they resorted to violence, it was with the conviction that the salvation of a whole religious community was at stake.

Women's resistance to the French Revolution was less expected in matters closely linked to political matters, political knowledge being reputedly accessible to men only. In 1792 an eight-volume work entitled *Théorie des lois politiques de la France* (Theory of the Political Laws of France) was published; its author was Pauline de Lézardière (1753–l 835), a member of a noble family in Poitou. The work was a defense of monarchy as a moderating institution formed around a prince responsible for ensuring harmony between the different parts of the French nation. The author's concept of political power situated her work in the tradition of Montesquieu's *De l'Esprit des lois* (1748; *The Spirit of the Laws*). A member of the Parlement of Bordeaux, Montesquieu attributed the excellence of monarchic government to its moderation, the nature of its intermediary powers, and the speed with which its executive power could act. In a text unpublished in her lifetime (in fact, published only in 1927), Lézardière concurred: "The independence of the parlement with regard to the arbitrary power of kings is, of all prerogatives, the most precious to citizens. The security and stability of the Nation's judges are those of the Nation itself." In her opinion, the monarchy needed to return to the liberal foundations of the royal pact as it had presumably existed just after the kingdom was formed. Reissued in 1844 by Ministers Guizot and Villemain, Lézardière's writings are little known today, overshadowed by the image of her tragic destiny and her admirable perseverance in her work and convictions.

1792: Women and Patriotic Mobilization

As we have seen, women partisans of the revolution were hardly inactive. True, women activists' desire to assert themselves as full-fledged members of the sovereign body was not legally translated into the right to vote and participate in deliberation. In fact, the women citizens who protested against this legal exclusion remained very much a minority. But in the context of the call proclaiming that the fatherland was in peril, the "patriot ladies" (as they referred to themselves) asserted themselves through their will to take up arms and other concrete expressions of the "just demands" being made in the insurrectionist protests.

On 6 March 1792 Pauline Léon presented to the Legislative Assembly a petition signed by 300 Parisian women seeking to organize themselves into a female national guard. Added to the claim "it is weapons we need" was the statement "we are citizens—the extension of another declaration saying: "We are the sovereign." The petition was, of course, rejected by the deputies, but according to Harriet B. Applewhite and Darline G. Levy, it attests to the emergence of the concept of female citizenship in the spring of 1792 (see Applewhite and Levy 1990). That concept stems from an acknowledgment of a direct political relation between women's right to defend themselves and their civic obligation to protect and defend their homeland by taking up arms. The presence of women in armed processions, especially on 20 June, was a mark not only of their integration into the mobilizing theme of the "armed people," but also explains the irresistible strength of the republican movement against the royal executive power.

Within the female component of this radical movement, one personality soon stood out on the Parisian political scene: Théroigne de Méricourt, recently studied by Élisabeth Roudinesco (see Roudinesco). The daughter of farm laborers, Anne Terwagne, as she was legally called, regularly attended National Assembly debates from 1789 on. She dressed as an Amazon, the symbol of the woman warrior, as she wished to "escape the humiliation of being a woman." In a speech delivered on 25 March at the Société Fraternelle des Minimes (Fraternal Society of Minors), she called for the formation of an Amazon legion: "Citoyennes, why should we not enter into competition with men? . . . Let us take up arms. . . . Let us establish a list of French Amazons."

Since the right to bear arms symbolized membership in the sovereign body, some women had sought to organize sections of armed national guards, though this right was ultimately denied them. Nevertheless, the will to enlist as armed participants in the revolutionary fight continued to manifest itself. On 31 July 1792 the women of the Hôtel de Ville section asked that "true women citizens" be given arms to defend the capital.

The provinces were just as present as the capital on the front of women's patriotic mobilization. When regiments passed through Alençon, in the Sarthe, from March to August 1792, the main speeches were delivered by women, one of whom did not hesitate to suggest that French women of the 18th century should model themselves after the women of the old Germanic tribes "who cheered the soldiers on or even took part in battles." On 20 March 1792 a delegation of women patriots in Le Mans demanded and obtained the floor. In the words of an observer of the episode: "Proud of their origins, they asked to go to war, evoking the memories of the women and wives of the Gauls, our ancestors." Their motion to the town authorities, which won the support of the commoners, requested "as many pikes as there are patriot households," so that women could be armed. At the same time in Éguilles, near Aix-en-Provence, a man named Monbrion, known as the "patriot missionary" from Marseilles, proposed as a model to the devout women of that small village "the spectacle of the Amazons," gathered together in "a company of women." He attested to their patriotism, quoting the "brave female citizens" as (supposedly) saying: "Since our husbands will be busy working the soil, we need to be armed with their rifles so as to watch over the safety of the public good. And let traitors to the *patrie* find us standing and prepared!"

After 1792, numerous provincial societies became radicalized and took a more active part in local political life—for example, by mobilizing against federalism and sending petitions to the Convention. While there were very few demands for political equality and the right to vote, women continued to demand the right to bear arms. And women did fight for the country. We have evidence that there were at least 44 women soldiers, some of whom accompanied a relative, while others went into combat disguised as men. Their bravery was recognized by their comrades in arms. Félicité Duquet, for example, fought in the First Battalion of the Nièvre until July 1794 and was nicknamed "Va-de-bon-coeur" (Go-with-gusto) by her comrades. After leaving the army, she explained that she had disguised her sex and willingly marched to defend her country for the sacred love of the *patrie* that burned within her.

The revolutionaries acknowledged such cases of individual bravery, but they felt these women were transgressing their nature, as Collot d'Herbois expressed it in his praise for one of the women soldiers: "I don't even rank her among women, but declare this girl to be a male because, like the most intrepid warrior, she has confronted death on every perilous occasion." A decree of 30 April 1793 dismissed all women from the army, whether they were performing combat actions or not, with the exception of laundresses and sutlers. Nonetheless, cases of women soldiers can be found down to the time of Napoleon Bonaparte's military command.

When the Tuileries palace was attacked on 10 August 1792, the aggressors were primarily men, as had been the case when the Bastille was taken. But some women did take part, spurred on by the call to help the imperiled *patrie*, and three of them received a civic crown for their heroic actions. Women's participation was rather more noteworthy in the punitive actions of the summer of 1792, most particularly in the unrest linked to food shortages. There were women in the bands known as "the cutthroats of Arles," who organized punitive expeditions to neighboring towns such as Tarascon, Saint-Rémy, Eyrargues, Beaucaire, and Eyguières. They were organized into armed groups and rode donkeys. Attacking with firearms and swords, women participated in all the actions led by the Arlesian revolutionary party, the Monnaidiers, in a city where the counterrevolution was strong and the conflicts many and violent. In the Carcassonne region, where tensions were high because of the large quantities of wheat being exported after a good harvest, a crowd estimated at more than 1,000 men and women undertook violent action in August 1792, led by a working-class woman, Jeanne Establet (or Jeanne Nègre), a widow and day laborer. Having attempted to seize and unload grain and have it sold in Carcassonne at moderate prices, the rioters took over the town, attacking small shops and the department's administrative offices. Guillaume Verdier, the *procureur général syndic* (an executive officer in local government), was murdered. Most of the demands made during this riot reflect the traditional conception of grain commerce: control over circulation and taxation rates on prices. Added to this was the demand that payment in *assignats*, the special banknotes issued during the revolution, be accepted. When the action failed, three of the working-class leaders, including Establet, were condemned to death. According to testimonies at her trial, she had drawn attention to herself by crying that the administrators should be put to death and by striking Verdier. She went down into legend, becoming known as Jeanne la Noire (Black Jeanne), prototype of the swarthy wild woman.

In September 1792 in Lyon, provisions seized during attacks on food shops were sold at prices fixed by an improvised female court. According to the *Journal de Lyon* of 20 September, the women insurgents formed a "deliberating society" and armed themselves with pikes to control any excesses. They made a declaration that "[their] action was founded on the sovereignty of the people and the right to provide [themselves] with the basic means of subsistence without having to use the violent means often necessitated by the public calamities of the day." Such incidents marked by a strong female participation, of which many other examples could be given, must be placed in the context of the establishment of the French Republic.

1793

Insofar as the French Republic proceeded from the social contract between the people and the deputies to the Convention that had grown out of the insurrection of 10 August 1792, the force of the official proclamation of the Republic on 22 September 1792 was first and foremost symbolic. All that was decided at first was that the seals of the administration would henceforth bear the name and figure of the French Republic, "a woman leaning with one hand on fasces, while the other holds a lance crowned with the liberty cap [the Phyrigian cap]." Thereafter, the female figure of the Republic, associated with the equally emblematic figures of the Nation and Liberty, took on substance, becoming widely deployed after 1793, as Michel Vovelle has shown (see Vovelle 1986). Is this an indication that women's influence was growing as the revolution proceeded? According to the historian Lynn Hunt, the female allegory made it possible to avoid any confusion within revolutionary symbolism between the Republic and the traditional royal image of the father, and even prevented veneration of a single male individual, which would contravene the principle of political equality among brothers (see Hunt). It would seem that the very refusal to grant women a political role made it possible to give them such an important symbolic one.

It is also important to emphasize that, to the detriment of the women patriots, the woman judged by public opinion to have been the most politically active was none other than the queen, Marie-Antoinette, an emblem of the link between women and the political sphere. Indeed, the queen embodied the bad mother who concealed her hostility toward the revolution and by that very fact corrupted the body politic. As a consequence, the idea of feminized politics appeared monstrous and criminal and could only arouse the stern disapproval of men concerned with keeping women confined to the private sphere of the family. At the moment of the king's execution, the *Révolutions de Paris*, a patriotic newspaper marked by antifeminism, reported, not impartially:

Women, of whom it cannot be reasonably expected that they reach the level of political thinking, were generally rather sad. . . . There were some reproaches, even insults. All that is quite excusable coming from a shallow, weak sex.

The intrusion of the issue of female citizenship on the political scene in 1793 constituted the most important political moment for women in the entire French Revolution. It sparked a hostile reaction from men, who, as we have said, generally excluded women from political affairs. Colette Capitan has very personal views on this topic and has expressed them in a recent study (see Capitan). She argues that the fact that women were by law excluded from the armed forces, from the status of citizen, and then from political action in 1793, constitutes an "objectification of women" and implies their relegation to the "status of things." From that radical perspective, women would thereby be excluded from the process of shaping the national identity.

What arguments did men advance to justify refusing to grant women access to political rights in everyday politics? And what strength should be attributed to the opposing arguments proposed by some deputies, in particular Deputies Guyomar, Lequinio, and Romme? The arguments were presented in the course of a debate between deputies of the Convention, and it went on from the time of the quarrel over the new Déclaration des Droits de l'Homme et du Citoyen until the formation of the revolutionary government. Two opposing statements marked this exchange among men. On the one hand, Deputy Guyomar declared, "I do not imagine how a sexual difference could make a difference where equality of rights is concerned" (April 1793). On the other hand, Deputy Amar stated: "It is not possible for women to exercise political rights" (October 1793).

The great majority of deputies contested the presence of women in the political sphere on the basis of the "natural" qualities of females. Such recourse to "nature" made it possible to single out physical, moral, and intellectual differences between men and women—comparisons that were invariably unfavorable to the latter, who were judged unsuited to intellectual pursuits and, what is more, dangerous because of their whimsical character. In contrast, in the few speeches favorable to women, the differences between men and women were deemed secondary to the fact of their membership, as human individuals and regardless of sex, in the human community. In the name of a full, wide-ranging conception of the rights of mankind, Lequinio objected to the fact that the "lovable sex" was "the slave of the unjust sex." Guyomar stood up against "prejudice based on sex," which he considered "as prejudicial to justice as it is to sovereignty," allowing men as it did to affect superiority over women. As a matter of fact, those deputies' request to grant women political rights—gradually, of course —did not get much of a hearing. The cowardly relief of Lanjuinais—"I cannot help thinking that, all in all, no advantage would come of it for either men or women"—paved the way to the repressive stand taken by Amar, spokesman for the Convention Committees.

Nevertheless, it is the historian's role to describe in minute detail the importance of women citizens' indisputably political experience during the year 1793. She or he must temporarily set aside the effects of the marginalization imposed on them at the end of a revolutionary process that was particularly rich in terms of political experimentation by women, as Godineau has demonstrated to be the case in Paris (see Godineau).

In the provinces, as in the capital, women were being granted an increasing role in the popular societies. It is also a fact that in the provinces, their role became increasingly important through their participation, region by region, either on the side of federalist democratic experiments or in various movements to resist federalism.

In the summer of 1793, a woman citizen wrote a brilliant speech on Marat, which was read at the club of Le Mans by one of the society's male members. Her eloquence persuaded the club to accept her as a member on 21 July:

And wishing at last to banish the remainder of inequality and injustice that causes men to see themselves as so superior to women that they seek to reduce them to absolute nullity, the society has decided that it will welcome all women whose energy, understanding, and civic responsibility could be useful to the *patrie*.

In September 1793, the Société de Valognes in the Manche became a mixed-gender organization when 25 female Montagnardes were registered. A week later, an elected female president was made the adjunct to the society's male president. Until the month of Pluviose in Year II of the revolutionary calendar, women citizens participated in the work of the society, of which they made up 13 percent of the membership. Their zeal in serving the *patrie* was above all manifested in the specific tasks they performed. On 20 Brumaire, it was decided to organize women to prepare absorbent linen and bandages in a room above the meeting place where the men were discussing politics. Still, even though their presence in the society was mainly linked to charitable activities, women were not excluded from the meeting room, nor were they totally confined to manual work.

After the women's club in Arles was closed, many women joined the Club des Jacobins. Within a few months, 650 club members out of 1,100 were women–59 percent of the membership. After taking the oath, these women were considered fullfledged members and were officially granted the right to bear the same arms that the female Monnaidiers had seized during the punitive expeditions. In November 1793 women occupied a prominent place in the ceremony that took place when a statue was raised in honor of Marat in the Place des Portefaix. Moreover, women were an essential component of the intimidation groups that marched through Arles carrying a guillotine.

We do not have much direct knowledge of women's involvement in the federalist movements. Still, there are various indications of their presence both in federalist sections and in the resistance movement against federalism. In Marseilles, where the "section movement" took power in spring 1793, republican women requested and received permission to occupy the galleries at the assemblies of their respective sections. They were therefore present in these assemblies, speaking and applauding, without actually participating in the deliberations. Some stood up to speak and delivered energetic speeches advocating armed mobilization against the Convention. In Section 5, for example, a woman citizen spoke in particularly forceful terms on 7 August 1793: "Citizens! Do you prefer to die by assassination rather than to die fighting? No, I cannot believe that. If you must die, let it be as heroes, arms in hand: to live as slaves is to die each day." The president answered: "This is not the first time that the *Citoyennes* of Marseilles have demonstrated the truly republican Courage that inspires them." One of these young women of middle-class origins, 16-year-old Thérèse Clapier of Section 4, contributed to the shaping of a network of opinion that supported "the principles of the sections."

In Lyon, by contrast, a crowd of 200 women accompanied by club members banned the "permanent" members of the Saint-Georges section from their assembly on 2 July. That movement was in line with the popular resistance to federalism's regressive notions with regard to poor consumers. Arrests and disarmament followed before calm returned. Similarly, the women's club of Besançon penned an opinion against federalism in August 1793.

Suzanne Petersen has shown the magnitude of Parisian women's role in the protests in a city where the worsening of the food crisis fueled the radicalization of the popular movement (see Petersen). From the start, women's demands for subsistence provisions were a part of the sansculottes' program. Yet, from the spring to the fall of 1793, a growing awareness of specifically female alienation sparked action in the revolutionary movement in favor of political equality for women. Asserting that "the declaration of rights is common to both sexes" and that "men's rights are also our rights," the female citizens of Paris demonstrated their will to exercise popular sovereignty and enact their citizen status by appropriating the rights that men had denied them, despite their legal exclusion from the electoral body. At first, the women involved in the protest movement of early 1793 belonged primarily to the laboring classes; they were laborers, shopkeepers, and servants. Their firm stand on the taxation question was accompanied by a will to act against monopolizers of provisions and enemies of the Republic. At the time, the Parisian women's movement had close affinities with Les Enragés (Rabid Ones), a radical extremist group, and supported the ideas of the group's leader Jacques Roux.

On 24 February 1793, a group of women presented the Convention with a petition demanding bread and soap—and also the death penalty for those who seized supplies and speculated on them—but they were received coldly, and study of the petition was adjourned. The petitioners left the Assembly in a rage, proclaiming, "When our children ask for milk, we do not 'adjourn' until the day after tomorrow." The women decided to assemble in front of the Convention. The following day disturbances began, spreading outward from the central sections, where there were many grocers. As they had done the previous year, the rioters besieged the grocery shops and fixed the prices of soap, white and brown sugar, and candles before proceeding to sell them. Women were in the majority in those actions, but most often it was the men who took the initiative in breaking down doors and forcing the commissaires, overcome by events, to perform searches. We find here the usual division of roles in riots around primarily economic concerns: women instigating the riot with their words, then participating alongside the men they had won over, who generally took the initiative in the actions. The next day trouble was sparked in Les Halles but was quickly repressed. The Jacobins denounced these incidents as weakening the young Republic. Later, however, the Montagnards had measures adopted that were consistent with the people's demands. By opposing those measures, the Girondins distanced themselves even further from the popular movement. Women activists vigorously supported the Montagne's struggle against the Gironde.

The innovative aspects of the women's political practice became even clearer on 10 May 1793, with the official creation of the Club des Citoyennes Républicaines Révolutionnaires (Revolutionary Republican Women Citizens' Club). The purpose of the society, which admitted women only, was to "deliberate on a way to foil the plans of the enemies of the Republic." It operated like any other Parisian society. There were about 170 members, two-thirds of whom knew how to sign their names. The leaders belonged to the petite bourgeoisie but the club also recruited among the laboring classes. The members of this club proclaimed the desire to constitute themselves the guardians of the "interior," thereby reproducing on a national scale the traditional division by which men were associated with the external world and women with the internal, domestic sphere. The club played a major role in the fall of the Girondins and in the decision to institute the Reign of Terror. The Girondin deputies, who feared its influence, police observers, other clubs, and the revolutionary authorities all considered the club to be one of the primary forces of the revolutionary movement during the spring and summer of 1793. The republican women citizens sought to defend the revolution with arms. Accordingly, as early as 1 May, Pauline Léon led a delegation to the Club des Jacobins to request that weapons be distributed to women between the ages of 18 and 50 and that the female combatants be organized into regiments to fight against the Vendée insurgents.

The Revolutionary Republican Women Citizens' Club, which at the time maintained close ties with the Club des Cordeliers, worked to spread the anti-Girondin unrest. Its women activists propagandized other women and engaged in sustained agitation, calling for insurrection and intervening at every level and in all the sites of political life—the Convention, the sections, and the streets. In May a number of these women patriots gathered daily in front of the Convention, preaching insurrection against the Girondins, proclaiming, "we must repeat the day of 10 August and slit the throats of the rich." They followed the debates from the assembly galleries, applauding the Montagnard deputies and booing their opponents. The constant presence of women in the galleries was a means for them to integrate themselves into the political sphere. By observing the elected officials at work, these women underscored their own participation in the sovereign body. Later, the women took part in the insurrection of 31 May and 1 and 2 June, which they helped to instigate. Once again, it was in a time of insurrection that women were fully recognized as members of the sovereign body. In June activist women supported Roux's radical demands. Then, during the summer of 1793, they played a major role in making the Terror the order of the day, on the initiative of the revolutionary movement, especially the Club des Cordeliers.

On 25 June, the day after the Enragés' petition was presented to the Convention, turmoil broke out, first incited by laundresses who unloaded soap off the boats and shared out the merchandise after its taxation. Women occupied an important place in the ceremonies held in honor of Marat after his assassination on 13 July 1793. A complete pageant was organized around the body of the martyr for freedom, expressing a desire for defense and vengeance that ended in the formulation of the revolutionary slogan for instituting the Reign of Terror. The Citoyennes Républicaines Révolutionnaires swore to the Convention that they would "populate the land of Liberty with as many Marats as [they could possibly] possess." The club then turned its energies to organizing the cult of the martyr, but that task also removed them somewhat from the field of political debate.

Strongly influenced by Claire Lacombe and Pauline Léon, the majority of the Citoyennes Révolutionnaires supported the Enragés' program, but there was no real political homogeneity.

Since theirs was the only women's club in the capital, several points of view were to be found within it and members were sometimes opposed to each other. The women activists participated in the mass demonstrations to exert pressure on the Convention to institute the Terror, organize an executive power, and establish a planned economy. The revolutionary movement, of which the Citoyennes Révolutionnaires were a major component at that time, achieved partial satisfaction, but the women's clubs then fell victim to the Convention policy aimed at ensuring the primacy of the "national movement," embodied by the Assembly, over the "revolutionary movement," whose support came from the popular clubs and societies, the federalists, and the street movements, especially on 4 and 5 September. As the revolutionary government was being organized, the permanent committee of the sections was abolished, and Roux and Varlet, the leaders of Enragés, were arrested. Leclerc had to suspend publication of his newspaper; the Société des Citoyennes (Women Citizens' Society) was dissolved on 20 October 1793; and on 30 October women's clubs were prohibited by decree of the Convention as incompatible with a woman's natural vocation, which was to devote herself to home and children. Historians have explained this prohibition in different ways. Joan B. Landes attributes it to the mechanisms of exclusion inherent in the gradual constitution of a bourgeois public sphere (see Landes). Olwen H. Hufton, meanwhile, attributes it mainly to the legislators' desire to curb the protest movement (see Hufton).

However, by their presence in the revolutionary process, women citizens politicized the private sphere itself, forcing men to redefine the respective weight of public and private. Women showed they were just as able as men to reach and apply rational political judgments, contrary to received (men's) wisdom about the irrationality of female discourse. The repercussions of the failure to secure female citizenship were considerable, of course: the prohibition against citizenship for women was formalized as law. But the women citizens were able to affirm their presence in political practices until the Year II, asserting themselves as much in places traditionally reserved for men, especially the electoral arena, as on the borders between private and public spheres, which had been displaced by the new civil institutions.

It is thus appropriate to examine the issue of women's intermittent participation in the electoral process. Even though they were theoretically excluded from that process, women intervened often and loudly. Gathered in large numbers at the entrances to the premises where elections were held or in assembly galleries, they sought by their comments to influence the vote.

During the referendum on the Constitution of 1793, some women citizens made a point of expressing their approval. Numerous written declarations reached the Convention attesting to the support of women "deprived of the precious right to vote." Some women met among themselves to vote on the issue, thereby indicating their wish to be part of the sovereign body despite their legal exclusion from the national electoral arena. In the provinces women apparently participated in the vote in at least 30 electoral assemblies, either with the men or after them.

Without legally participating in the great national elections, women were still able to vote on certain occasions. The law of 10 June 1793 on the division of communal property stipulated that each community should make decisions on property division by means of a vote of an assembly of the inhabitants, composed "of individuals of both sexes" age 21 or older who had resided in the community for at least one year.

In Paris women voted in the general assemblies of the sections during certain crisis periods, but that was exceptional and contravened regulations. Parisian women also voiced their opinions in the popular societies of the sections, which formed the armature of the Parisian people's movement from the fall of 1793 to the spring of 1794. In reality, if not officially, activist women in Paris thus participated in the oversight of local political life and in the establishment of a new, revolutionary type of sociability. The same was true in the suburbs of Paris, which had been organized into an exceptional network of popular groups. The society of Belleville admitted women starting in May 1792; their presence was strongest during the winter of the Year II.

Despite women's interventions in the electoral process, the vote remained an exclusively male right. Should we then credit Mona Ozouf's contention that women in general did not demand the right to vote because the new republican marriage guaranteed them, within the framework of solidarity between spouses, a kind of indirect participation in the vote? After noting that "the great political upheavals" (a reference, of course, to the French Revolution) either "came from women" or "were deflected and considerably modified by them," the German philosopher Johann Gottlieb Fichte developed that position into a theory in his *Grundlage des Naturrechts nach Prinzipien der Wissenschaftslehre* (1796; *Foundations of Natural Right*):

> Thus women actually do exercise their right to vote concerning public affairs, only, they do not do so directly on their own, since they cannot will to do so without forfeiting their female dignity. Rather, they do so through the appropriate influence (grounded in the nature of the marital union) that they have on their husbands.(First Appendix to the Doctrine of Family Right.)

In this way, according to Ozouf, France's particularity was that of a "desired dependency" within a public sphere in which "the society of women schooled men's intelligence and mores," a notion that laid the way for the Republic's invention of equal rights to education.

As already noted, women were just as active in the resistance to the revolution as they were in its defense, particularly in the Vendée. At the time of the insurrection, the revolutionaries stressed the role of women in instigating events, explaining their resistance in terms of their ties to the nonjuring priests. In a letter of 21 Frimaire, Year II (11 December 1793) to the Committee of General Security, Jean-Baptiste Carrier indicated: "it is the women who have fomented and supported the war in the Vendée, together with the priests." In the 19th century historian Jules Michelet propounded the same thesis, while stressing the Vendéean women's submissiveness to their priests and the influence they later exerted on their husbands to instigate rebellion. Women accompanied the Catholic royalist forces, mingling with the soldiers along with children, old men, and priests. Some actually took part in the battles, and the republicans noted their ferocity in combat. The marquise de La Rochejaquelein also attested to the existence of women soldiers, and we know of some women fighters, among them one Renée Bordereau, nicknamed "Brave l'Angevin" (Brave Woman of Anjou), who claimed in her memoirs that she had killed 21 Blues (republicans) in a single conflict. Charette had female spies, and real Amazons sometimes

commanded his troops. It does seem, however, that only a small number of women engaged in active combat.

Women were part of the committees, made up of known local figures who had participated in the insurrection, responsible for regions "conquered" by the insurgent Whites, but only in the early stages of the insurrection when such organizations formed spontaneously. Once such committees had been made official and systematized, women disappeared from them. At numerous resistance sites, women were the first to engage in protest. This was the case in the Rouergue, where women, accompanied by their children and by adolescents, headed the revolt to defend the priests. On the other side, Protestant women launched violent harangues against the clergy. In Saint-Jean, Protestant women screamed in the streets that "priests were scoundrels who deserved to be hanged," and that they wanted "to wash their hands in the blood of Catholics" and profane their places of worship: "We will come and shit in the pulpit of your church; we will make a [Protestant] temple of it, and it will be your turn to go and pray to God beneath a tree."

In the Comtat, the constitutional priest Mathieu Mistarlet, a particularly vehement revolutionary, was chased out of the town of Malemort by a cabal of women. A midwife "known for her fanaticism," her daughter (a servant of the above-mentioned prior), a hospital nun, a woman known as "the Virgin," and two widows were denounced for preaching fanaticism and publicly opposing the new priest, while the former, nonjuring priest remained in Malemort. In this struggle, a sign was hung on the gate of the town, likening the constitutional priest and president of the people's society to Judas and the patriots to Cain. Women's resistance against the revolution spread, especially on religious grounds, when the revolutionary government was established in Year II.

Year II

The issue of women remained on the agenda throughout the Year II. With the establishment of the revolutionary government based on "legislative centralism," women found new opportunities for political action, as much on the side of the revolutionaries as at the forefront of the Montagnard resistance and the counter-revolution.

The establishment of civic institutions under the rule of the law—schools, philanthropy, the French language, public celebrations, and so on—fostered the development of new forms of civil individuality, particularly for women. In their case, paradoxically, the new civil individuality coexisted side by side with the clear antifeminism of the political legislation. The civil emancipation of women was already discernible in the Constitution of 1791, which defined marriage as "a civil contract." But it was above all two legislative acts in September 1792 that emancipated women as civilians: the 20 September law defining the civil state of citizens, which instituted symmetry between spouses, and the 25 September decree determining the causes, procedures for, and effects of divorce. Through these statutes, woman became "a civil subject capable of governance"; according to Élisabeth G. Sledziewski, Year II was characterized by the eminently political deployment of women's civil potential within the new revolutionary institutions (see Sledziewski). This civic elevation of women, associated with their status as individuals entitled to enter into contracts, was to be annihilated by the Civil Code of 1804.

It is important to stress the role of the family in the promotion of women as civil subjects in full control of their capacities. The family was, of course, regenerated in that both the father-son relationship and the maternal role came to rest on mutual recognition of rights and duties instead of undivided paternal power. The celebrations of Year II constituted the perfect laboratory for deploying sexual difference in the context of a family made up of citizens, in which women's presence made possible the symbolic representation of the community as a whole.

It should therefore come as no surprise that women's actions continued, not without internal contradictions, within the network of the patriotic societies. By this time, the only avenue for women activists was within the mixed-gender clubs, since women's clubs had been banned. In the mixed clubs women were received with mixed feelings, or even downright reluctantly, although they were sometimes authorized to speak and to propose texts and actions for adoption by the club. The town of Evron, in the Sarthe, has been studied by Christine Peyrard, who notes that women citizens who desired to become members of the society were admitted starting on 25 Germinal, Year II, "as were children over the age of 12," but they had to remain within an area reserved for women and youth (see Peyrard). Women represented 16 percent of the membership of the club, and, despite the weight of traditional attitudes, on 30 Germinal, women members obtained the right to introduce one motion per month. Collectively, however, they were still considered affiliated members rather than individual members with equal rights.

It was the role of mother that the revolutionaries most wanted to promote: women were to give birth to republican citizens—that is, bring them into the world and raise them in accordance with the revolutionary ideal. On that basis, as the mothers of reinvigorated future generations, women had an important place in the many revolutionary celebrations and participated in the construction of a new type of world. But this mission confined women to the private sphere; it was within their homes that women were deemed most useful to the revolution.

However, the tasks of surveillance and denunciation performed by women in the revolutionary committees show that they participated locally in the political life of their communities and that they were involved in the repressive aspect of the Terror and struggles between opposing groups. In villages where long-standing family rivalries and political antagonism coincided, certain women were relentless informers. Words exchanged by the village fountain or in the shops readily led to denunciations before the surveillance committee. In Paris the popular women's movement was characterized by the "cult of the holy guillotine." At Paris executions women made up the majority of the spectators who came to see enemies of the people punished.

Whatever the nature of women's involvement—since their presence has been documented in all the different parties confronting each other—their presence was smaller than that of men in the same regions. Women seem to have chosen their camp on the basis of family milieu, and, more generally, social background. Female suspects were frequently arrested along with male members of their families.

Still, the behavior of republican women in Year II cannot be reduced to terrorist attitudes. Women contributed in a decisive

manner to assisting the indigent, building networks of mutual aid, and making donations to the *patrie*. According to Bertrand Barère, it was through the accumulation of such civic actions that "women will finally take their place and arrive at their true destiny in the revolutions." Women did play the leading role in actions of patriotic benevolence. In that realm, moreover, no one stood in their way. After showing that "women's presence was central in the chain of civic solidarity," the scholar Catherine Duprat, echoing Barère, has understandably wondered, "are not women's roles par excellence to love, to give, to serve, and to nurture?" This emancipation in the form of civic participation, she argues, "may be seen as a kind of culmination or accomplishment" (see Duprat 1993).

The homage paid to women's civic self-abnegation attests to their importance. The national agent for Mont-de-Marsan wrote to the Convention: "After devoting their attention to their housework, republican women are spending all their time shredding linen for bandages and are thus making progress in truly Spartan character." As for the citizens of the people's society of Vic-en-Bigorre, they emphasized the complementarity between actions taken by legislators and those by male and female citizens in the defense of the *patrie*: "While you are making good laws, our women will nurse the wounded and we will fight." Women's exemplary action in the context of war sometimes gave rise to genuine veneration, as in the case of the "patriot saints" Perrine Dugué and Marie Martin, murdered by the Chouans for passing information to the republicans.

While no typically female political attitude seems to have developed, attachment to the Catholic faith did play a particularly important role in fueling women's resistance to the revolution. We have seen how, in the Vendée, women could become committed to the resistance, sometimes sacrificing their lives for their political convictions. Although the number of male inmates was greater, the revolutionary prisons did hold a large contingent of women, whose numbers grew continually after September 1793, for at that time women were often arrested on the mere basis of being the mother, wife, or daughter of an émigré. This was the situation for most condemned noblewomen. Their will to prevent the confiscation and sale of family property sometimes led them to illegal acts, the most frequent of these being the transfer of funds to foreign countries. Sometimes noblewomen aggravated their case by expressing overt hostility to the revolution or by preserving letters judged counterrevolutionary. Women's correspondence with émigrés or powers hostile to France was another frequent cause for arrest. Some were very active in the counterrevolution, providing their correspondents with political information; sheltering returned emigrants, nonjuring priests, and outlaws; and attempting to seduce or bribe deputies and administrators.

In Paris women who fell victims to the Terror do not seem to have been exclusively aristocrats; they could just as easily be commoners. Out of 9,294 suspects arrested in Paris between August 1792 and Thermidor, Year II, 1,315 were women. We know the occupation or social position of 427 of them: 240 belonged to the privileged classes and the upper bourgeoisie, 23 to the bourgeoisie, 159 to the petite bourgeoisie and the lower classes. Women of the lower classes were victims in the struggle against factionalism, especially after the radical Hébertists were eliminated. One-hundred twenty-six nuns also died, out of a total of 56,000 fatalities. The most renowned of the condemned nuns were the Carmelites of Compiègne and the nuns of Bollène, mostly Ursulines and Sacramentines. Most often, nuns were condemned for refusing to take the revolutionary oath, but there were sometimes other aggravating circumstances.

The 17 Carmelites from Compiègne sentenced in June and July 1794 had continued to live as a community after their convent was closed, enjoying the tolerance of the local authorities, who were called to order by the Committee of General Security in the context of the political maneuvering in Paris during the spring of 1794. Portraits of the king and correspondence in which they confessed their opposition to the revolution ensured the Carmelites' condemnation in a hastily organized trial, in accordance with the law of 22 Prairial.

Out of the 42 nuns sentenced in Orange, 32 were condemned to death. The nuns were brought before the People's Commission, because the Bollène surveillance committee deemed them to have set a pernicious example by overtly remaining together to live by their faith after the official closure of their convents. At their trial, some of the nuns openly affirmed their royalist convictions, and the judges were convinced they were sentencing these women for a political crime. In addition to accusing the nuns of denying the legitimacy of national representation, the judges charged them with attempting to dissolve a society in the process of shaping itself, and with opposing the freedom that was being established. Despite the judges' efforts to induce a change of heart, the nuns persisted in their refusal to become a part of the society that was emerging from the revolution. Among the republicans, "fanaticism and superstition" were considered crimes in themselves because they went hand in hand with, and indeed motivated, a refusal to recognize republican law, the expression of the sovereign people.

Among laywomen, an attachment to traditional religion was sometimes taken as an antirevolutionary attitude. Women mobilized to defend "their" priests and to prevent church bells from being taken down. They also manifested their opposition by refusing to observe the *décadi* (the last day of the new ten-day week), continuing to put on their best clothes on Sundays, and ostentatiously wearing crucifixes, considered "signs of superstition." On 9 Brumaire, Year III, for example, a woman called Magdelaine presented herself at Fort Nicolas in Marseilles to buy bread, wearing "the cross, sign of fanaticism." She was arrested for throwing stones at the guard, who told her it was forbidden to buy bread for volunteers. She is then said to have replied to the commanding officer that "if they were going to punish her, the Good Lord would avenge her."

Women sometimes went further, becoming deeply implicated on the side of the counterrevolution. In Sainte-Cécile, in the Comtat, Rose Delaye, a householder's wife, became an accomplice of the city's former rulers. She was accused of infiltrating the patriots to spy on them and report their words to the aristocrats, slandering the revolutionaries, and speaking bloodthirsty words against them during the time of federalism. Two other women were accused of disseminating pamphlets against the patriots, holding aristocrat assemblies at their homes, taking the side of the Marseilles camp during the federalist crisis, and participating in a distribution of images of the Sacred Heart. For their accusers, the Sacred Heart signified that the women were part of the Jalès conspiracy, since it was the counterrevolutionary emblem.

Many accusations attested to the importance of women's speech in village political practices. They were denounced for circulating false news, criticizing measures taken by the side in power, and threatening their adversaries.

In rural areas, women were more visible on the side of the conservatives than among the patriots, and their fundamental purpose in becoming involved was to defend religion. Church closures and the abolition of public worship had limited religion to the private sphere, which as we know was largely female. In defense of the faith, however, women managed to link private spirituality and public action, and, through their resistance to dechristianization, they sometimes attained the status of guides within their communities. This was the case of the order of the Béates in the Haute-Loire, who taught lace making and catechism to girls; they organized the clandestine survival of Catholic worship during the dechristianization period and were not afraid to ridicule the revolutionary cults. For the revolutionaries, such women represented a potential political threat because of the example they set and the influence they had over their immediate circles.

Women in the rural areas of southern Île-de-France also resisted dechristianization initiatives. At the time of the abdications of the clergy, they refused to let priests leave, opposed vandalism, and participated in secret worship services, where they made up the better part of the audience. In the region of Toulouse, those suspected of "fanaticism" belonged to various social strata—artisans, the poor, and well-off farmers. Women were the victims of fighting or repression throughout the war in the Vendée—for example, during the two-month episode known as the "virée de Galerne," when, from October into December, frightened mobs including women, children, and old men fled before the advancing republican troops; or when Turreau sent his army to ravage the region. According to the Convention decree of 1 August 1793, women and children were simply to be deported inland. In fact, they were roughly treated by the republican troops and paid a heavy tribute to the will to annihilate the "inexplicable, rebellious Vendée." Execution, the automatic punishment for male suspects, was often meted out to women and children as well.

Year III: The Last Movements

The end of the revolutionary government gave many women hope for a rebirth of the Catholic religion. Municipal accounts of events after Thermidor repeatedly describe women inciting people to practice public worship and voicing support for the nonjuring priests, who had begun to reappear. After the fall of Robespierre the Convention decided to release all suspects. Large numbers of women from the popular classes recovered their freedom and families, and in so doing also returned to the streets and sections where they had been accustomed to make themselves heard. Hatred for those who had denounced them became secondary when they found themselves once again confronted with the problem of subsistence. The new liberal approach in the revolutionary process made poor people angrier every day, and in particular the women of Paris. Women activists, who kept up their opposition in the galleries of the Convention, incited the female masses to mobilize against the bread shortages, and the mobilized women in turn pushed men into joining their battle. But the demands at this moment were also charged with political content: the people demanded that the Constitution of 1793 be applied and that all patriots imprisoned since 9 Thermidor be freed.

In the spring of 1795, Paris was struck by famine. The contrast between the lives of the lower classes and the more comfortable lifestyle of the bourgeoisie was visible to all. As their underfed children died, and as they waited interminably and often in vain for food, impoverished women began to speak in increasingly violent tones, calling for insurrection and accusing their men of cowardice. As during all periods of food shortage, women's demands came to the fore, and those claims had a political dimension.

Unrest rocked the poor districts of Paris at the end of March, with women and laborers being the main actors in the agitation. Meanwhile, in political developments, opponents to the Thermidorian reaction were beginning to unite and organize. Demonstrations took place in front of the Convention; the women citizens of the Gravilliers section marched on the Assembly carrying the engraved tablet inscribed with the Rights of Man, to show that it was the members of the Convention, not the insurgents, whose actions were illegal. But the representatives of the popular movement could not persuade the Convention to take their demands into account. With bread rations continuing to decrease, women once again made attempts to intercept provision carts and to fix prices.

The first day of Prairial (20 May 1795) marked the "apogee of the women's mass movement," according to Godineau. The riots began with crowds of women arriving in a steady stream at the Convention, calling for an insurrection. "I am only a woman," cried one protester, "but we must set fire to the Convention—scoundrels, all of them! At least the Jacobins gave us bread." The women were quickly joined by men of the Faubourg Saint-Antoine district—revolutionary activists and laborers. This mass movement, insurrectional from the start, lasted three days. The people demanded bread and the reenactment of the Constitution of 1793. The sansculottes wanted to reestablish permanent sections.

Despite support from a few of the last Montagnards in the Assembly, the movement failed for lack of real political direction. The demonstrators were fairly easily dispersed, and the police made some 1,200 arrests. The people of Paris were disarmed and the army was put in charge of a methodical "reconquest" of the working-class districts. The courts sentenced 36 people to death and many more to prison or deportation. The hope and dynamism of the popular movement had been broken, and after Prairial there was no further female mass movement, not even in response to the economic difficulties under the Directory.

Paris was the center of the insurrectional movements of Year III, but there was also much unrest in the provinces. As in the capital, the popular movements combined demands for food and political change. In Thermidor of the Year III, in the city of Coutances, in the Marche, women whose husbands, fathers, or friends had been arrested reacted against the war now being waged against the patriots. They allied themselves with the Volontaires Français (French Volunteers) against the royalist mayor and celebrated 10 August revolutionary style, with a republican banquet and dancing in the streets, to the tunes of *Ça ira* (Things Will Be All Right) and *La Marseillaise*. During this celebration,

the women attempted to persuade the volunteers to release the detained patriots. Though the celebration did not turn into a riot, the speeches prompted a judicial inquiry. Proceedings from the inquiry included the following declaration by a butcher's wife: "During Robespierre's time, we were better governed: we were eating bread at six or seven francs a bushel. . . . He had the rich guillotined, and the poor benefited from it."

Such mobilizations ultimately failed everywhere, however, and the patriots, men and women alike, suffered the effects of the backlash. In Arles a summary table of "terrorist patriots either in prison or in flight," dated 8 Vendémiaire, Year IV (30 September 1795), listed 65 women along with 359 imprisoned Jacobin men, the entire group referred to as "terrorist sansculottes Jacobins."

The Thermidorian initiative to apply the Constitution of Year III put an end to the revolution for the natural rights of man and citizen begun in 1789. That revolution had allowed women to "speak the language of natural rights and liberty," as Florence Gauthier justly observes (see Gauthier), and so doing, to affirm practically their access to citizenship, despite their legal exclusion from the right to vote. With the new Constitution, the people's sovereignty on which activist women had founded their claims became an empty phrase. By dispossessing human beings of their natural rights (life, liberty, existence, citizenship, and so on), the Thermidorians relegated women to an inferior status. On the one hand, the male proprietor of material goods, a "good father" and "good husband," could henceforth exercise power without sharing it (though women from the laboring classes did hold on to some degree of liberty); on the other, the words of women rioters were reduced to no more than "vociferation" and "howling."

Male political leaders would keep women in an inferior status for a long time to come. That was the price women paid for the two contradictory images that had come to be associated with their gender: the first, which haunted reactionary discourse, was that of the subversive revolutionary activist; the second, which continued to provoke republican mistrust, was that of the devout woman linked politically to the priests.

Had the French Revolution made women's existence in society even more uncertain by exposing them to the critical eye of men? What lesson did women themselves draw from it all? The attitude of Anne-Louise-Germaine Necker, baronne de Staël-Holstein (1767–1817) on the role of women during the French Revolution reflects the contradictory attitude of educated women about the events that had just unfolded before their eyes. In *De la littérature* (1800; *On literature*) she stresses that "women who cultivate letters," are also "the ones who gave the most frequent proof of devotion and energy." However, in *Considérations sur les événements principaux de la Révolution française* (*Considerations on the Principle Events of the French Revolution*), written in 1798 and published posthumously in 1818, she hardly has words strong enough to condemn the actions of the women of the popular classes during the events of the Revolution. Speaking of the bloody days of 5 and 6 October 1789, she invokes "the women and children armed with pikes and scythes [who] pressed in from all sides" and the men who "boasted that people called them head-choppers," characterizing them as a "hellish gang" of the "lowest classes of the people . . . even more benumbed by drunkenness than rage." Another anecdote she relates is equally revealing of her aristocratic contempt for women of the popular classes. She had decided to leave France in early September 1792, and her carriage was stopped in Paris by "a swarm of old women straight out of hell" who drew with them "common people with ferocious faces." Still, Madame de Staël's capacity for emotion, and even her enthusiasm, are undeniable with regard to "the independence and natural pride" of the educated women who became involved in the French Revolution and who thereby proved themselves capable of discussing ideas with men in a way that captivated their interest. Refusing to take into account the political action of revolutionary women citizens, and thereby demonstrating her blindness to those women's capacity to "manifest the truth" of the rights that she denied them (*De la littérature*), Madame de Staël dwells instead on the fate of Marie-Antoinette in an anonymous text of 1793, *Réflexions sur le procès de la Reine* (Reflections on the Trial of the Queen), seeing that event as one that should move "women of all countries" and "all classes in society."

In fact, Madame de Staël attributes women's "civilizing" role to their emotional capacity alone: "Without women, society can be neither pleasant nor enticing" (*De la littérature*). It was through sensitivity, such a fundamental value under the ancien régime, that she envisioned women enlightened in matters of public order having a potential influence on society, for they might effectively help to sweeten and smoothe civic customs and mores. Beyond the role imposed on the most learned women, that of mediation, Madame de Staël thought it "much better for women to devote themselves exclusively to domestic virtues" (*De la littérature*). In the name of domestic happiness, she denied them any access to political rights: "It is right to exclude women from political and civic affairs; nothing is more contrary to their natural vocation than rivalry with men. Public glory for a woman could only amount to loudly bidding happiness *adieu* (*De l'Allemagne* [1813; *On Germany*]). Nevertheless, her enthusiasm for the action, sensitivity, and mind of "distinguished women" placed her squarely in opposition to those "men who, since the Revolution, thought it politically and morally useful to reduce women to the most absurd mediocrity" (*De la littérature*).

Let us conclude with a more positive image of women's revolutionary political action, and consider the repercussions for women's emancipation that the French Revolution had in Europe during the Mayence Republic (1793) and during the Triennio Rivoluzionario (1796–99), in the sister republics created in Italy with the arrival of Napoleon Bonaparte's armies in Milan, Bologna, Genoa, and Venice, before the Treaty of Campoformio in 1797. Women patriots participated in the activities of the Mayence club, without intervening directly in the debates. Maria Ursula Thekla Zech was arrested after the Prussian conquest of Mayence, for "notoriously distinguish[ing] herself by her actions and speeches." Thérèse Forster and Caroline Böhmer, together with Georg Foster, also demonstrated their revolutionary enthusiasm.

But it was during the Neapolitan Revolution, through the figure of Eleonora Fonseca Pimentel, recently studied by M.A. Macciochi, that women's patriotism was granted the name of heroism (see Macciochi). A daughter of the Enlightenment, poet, and publicist, Pimentel was convinced that the virtue and education of the people could only be forged through struggle and that it was therefore necessary to use a language that would be understandable to them. Arousing the enthusiasm of her contemporaries, she directed *Il monitore napolitano del 1799* from 2

February to 8 June, proposing the formation of patriotic legions against the enemies of the people, an increase in the number of civic missions, and the adoption of measures for public safety in the name of "the imperiled *patrie*". Pimentel was hanged when the Neapolitan revolution failed. The Jacobin conception of revolutionary action (despite differences between the French and Italian versions), encouraged women to fight on the Italian peninsula as they had in France. This dimension of women's revolutionary political action, which remains largely unstudied, amply warrants further attention from historians and scholars.

Bibliography

Manuscript Sources

Archives Nationales, Paris. 4577 to F[7] 4745[53] [Commission of General Security, alphabetical index for 1793 (Year IV)]; F[1c] III Seine 27, 13–20: [police reports, Year II–Year VIII]; F[1c] III Seine 13 and 20 [police reports 1793 (Year II)]

Archives de la Préfecture de Police, Paris. AA48–AA264 [records of police commissariat]

Archives Départementales des Bouches-du-Rhône. Series L [files of the surveillance committees; section files; files on people's societies]

Archives Départementales du Vaucluse. 1L, 3L, 4L, 5L [administrative correspondence]; 6L [files on people's societies; files of the surveillance committees]; 7L [files of the criminal tribunal of Avignon]; 8L [files of the people's commission of Orange]

Archives Communales of Entrechaux, La Roque Alric, Maubec, Oppède, Saint-Romain-en-Viennois, Saint-Roman-Malegarde, Savoillan (Vaucluse, France)

Bibliothèque Municipale, Médiathèque Ceccano, Avignon, France. Collection Chambaud, Fonds Chobaut [collections of materials on the French Revolution]

Print Sources

Condorcet, Jean-Antoine-Nicolas de Caritat, marquis de, "Sur l'admission des femmes au droit de cité," 3 juillet 1790, no 5, Journal de la Société de 1789 "On the Admission of Women to the Rights of Citizenship," in *Selected Writings*, by Condorcet, edited by Keith Michael Baker, Indianapolis, Indiana: Bobbs-Merrill, 1976

Elyada, Ouzi, editor, *Lettres bougrement patriotiques de la mère Duchêne*, Paris: EDHIS, 1989

Fauré, Christine, compiler and editor, *Les Déclarations des droits de l'homme de 1789*, Paris: Payot, 1988

Fichte, J.G., *Grundlage des Naturrechts nach Prinzipien der Wissenschaftslehre*, 1796; as *Foundations of Natural Right*, edited by F. Neuhauser, translated by Michael Baur, Cambridge: Cambridge University Press, 2000

Les héroïnes de Paris, Paris: n.p., 1789

Lézardière, Marie Charlotte Pauline Robert de, *Écrits inédits de Mlle. de Lézardière*, annotated by Élie Carcassonne, Paris: Presses Universitaires de France, 1927

Sieyès, Emmanuel Joseph, "Préliminaire de la Constitution, reconnaissance et exposition raisonnée des droit de l'homme et du citoyen,"in *Écrits politiques*, compiled by Roberto Zapperi, Paris: Éditions des Archives Contemporaines, 1985

Reference Works

Applewhite, Harriet Branson, and Darline Gay Levy, *Women and Politics in the Age of the Democratic Revolution*, Ann Arbor: University of Michigan Press, 1990

Applewhite, Harriet Branson, and Darline Gay Levy, editors, *Women in Revolutionary Paris 1789–1795*, Urbana and London: University of Illinois Press, 1979

Azimi, Vida, "L'exhérédation politique de la femme par la Révolution," *Revue historique du droit français et étranger*, no. 2 (1991)

Badinter, Élisabeth, editor, *Paroles d'hommes 1790–1793*, Paris: P.O.L., 1989

Baker, Keith Michael, et al., editors, *The French Revolution and the Creation of Modern Political Culture*, 4 vols., Oxford and New York: Pergamon Press, 1987–94; see especially vol. 4, *The Terror*, 1994

Balayé, Simone, *Madame de Staël, écrire, lutter, vivre*, Geneva: Librairie Droz, 1994

Balayé, Simone, *Madame de Staël: Lumières et liberté*, Paris: Klincksieck, 1979

Bernet, Jacques, "Vitalité du clergé régulier picard en 1789 et réactions face à la sécularisation révolutionnaire: L'exemple des religieuses compiégnoises," in *Religieux et religieuses pendant la Révolution (1770–1820)*, edited by Yves Krumenacker, Lyon: PROFAC, 1995

Bertaud, Jean-Paul, *La Révolution armée: Les soldats-citoyens et la Révolution française*, Paris: Laffont, 1979; as *The Army of the French Revolution: From Citizen-Soldiers to Instrument of Power*, translated by R. R. Palmer, Princeton, New Jersey: Princeton University Press, 1988

Blanc, Olivier, *La dernière lettre: Prisons et condamnés de la Révolution, 1793–1794*, Paris: Laffont, 1984; as *Last Letters: Prisons and Prisoners of the French Revolution, 1793–1794*, translated by Alan Sheridan, New York: Farrar Strauss and Giroux, and London: Deutsch, 1987

Brive, Marie-France, editor, *Les femmes et la Révolution française*, 3 vols., Toulouse, France: Presses Universitaires du Mirail, 1989–1991

Brunel, Françoise, *Thermidor, la chute de Robespierre, 1794*, Brussels: Complexe, 1989

Burke, Peter, and Roy Porter, editors, *The Social History of Language*, Cambridge and New York: Cambridge University Press, 1988

Butta-Fuoco, Annarita, "Virtù civiche e virtù domestiche: Letture del ruolo femminile nel triennio rivoluzionario," in *L'Italia nella Rivoluzione, 1789–1799*, edited by Guiseppina Benassati and Lauro Rossi, Bologna, Italy: Grafis, 1990

Cantimori, Delio, and Renzo De Felice, editors, *Giacobini italiani*, 2 vols., Bari, Italy: Laterza, 1964

Capitan, Colette, *La nature à l'ordre du jour, 1789–1793*, Paris: Kimé, 1993

Capra, Carlo, *L'età rivoluzionaria e napoleonica in Italia, 1796–1815*, Turin, Italy: Loescher, 1978

Cazals, Rémy, *Autour de la montagne Noire au temps de la Révolution: 1774–1799*, Carcassonne, France: Clef, 1989

Colwill, Elizabeth, "Just another Citoyenne? Marie-Antoinette on Trial, 1790–1793," *History Workshop Journal* 28 (1989)

Cubells, Monique, *Les horizons de la liberté: Naissance de la Révolution en Provence: 1787–1789*, Aix-en-Provence, France: Édisud, 1987

Dauphin, Cécile, and Arlette Farge, editors, *De la violence et des femmes*, Paris: Albin Michel, 1997

Duhet, Paule Marie, editor, *Les femmes et la Révolution 1789–1794*, Paris: Julliard, 1971

Duport, Anne-Marie, editor, *Religion, Révolution, contre-révolution dans le Midi 1789–1799*, Nîmes, France: J. Chambon, 1990

Duprat, Catherine, "Don et citoyenneté en l'an II: Les vertus du peuple français," in *Révolution et République*, edited by Michel Vovelle, Paris: Kimé, 1994

Duprat, Catherine, *Le temps des philanthropes: La philanthropie parisienne, des Lumières à la monarchie de Juillet*, Paris: C.T.H.S., 1993

Dupuy, Roger, *De la Révolution à la Chouannerie, paysans en Bretagne, 1788–1794*, Paris: Flammarion, 1988

Edmonds, William D., *Jacobinism and the Revolt of Lyons, 1789–1793*, Oxford: Clarendon Press, and New York: Oxford University Press, 1990

Fauré, Christine, "Les Constituants de 1789 avaient-ils la volonté délibérée d'évincer les femmes de la vie politique?," *History of European Ideas* 15, no. 4–6 (1992)

Les femmes dans la Révolution française, 2 vols., Paris: EDHIS, 1982

Gambrelle, Fabienne and Michel Trebitsch, editors, *Révolte et société: Actes du 4e colloque d'Histoire au présent*, 2 vols., Paris: Publications de la Sorbonne, 1989

Gauthier, Florence, *Triomphe et mort du droit naturel en Révolution 1789–1795–1802*, Paris: Presses Universitaires de France, 1992

Godineau, Dominique, *Citoyennes tricoteuses: Les femmes du peuple à Paris pendant la Révolution française*, Aix-en-Provence, France: Alinéa, 1988; as *The Women of Paris and their French Revolution*, translated by Katherine Streip, Berkeley: University of California Press, 1998

Godineau, Dominique, "Pratiques politiques féminines et masculines et lignes de partage sexuel au sein du mouvement populaire parisien pendant la Révolution française (1793–an III)," *History of European Ideas* 10, no. 3 (1980)

Greisler, Beate, *Charlotte Corday: Die Mörderin des Jean-Paul Marat*, Bielefeld, Germany: Aisthesis-Verlag, 1992

Guibert-Sledziewski, Élisabeth, *Révolutions du sujet*, Paris: Méridiens-Klincksieck, 1989

Guilhaumou, Jacques, "Conduites politiques des Marseillaises pendant la Révolution française," *Provence historique* 186 (October-December 1996)

Guilhaumou, Jacques, *Marseille républicaine (1791–1793)*, Paris: Presses de la Fondation Nationale des Sciences Politiques, 1992

Guilhaumou, Jacques, "La mort de Marat à Paris," in *La mort de Marat*, edited by Jean-Claude Bonnet, Paris: Flammarion, 1986

Hufton, Olwen, *Women and the Limits of Citizenship in the French Revolution*, Toronto: University of Toronto Press, 1992

Hunt, Lynn A., *The Family Romance of the French Revolution*, Berkeley: University of California Press, and London: Routledge, 1992

Issartel, Jean-Louis, "Bourg-Saint-Andéol, cité carrefour et centre révolutionnaire dans la moyenne vallée du Rhône," Ph.D. diss., Université de Paris I, 1991

Landes, Joan, *Women in the Public Sphere in the Age of the French Revolution*, Ithaca, New York, and London: Cornell University Press, 1988

Langeron, Geneviève, *Le club des femmes de Dijon pendant la Révolution: La Révolution en Côte-d'Or*, Dijon, France: Rebourseau, 1929

Lapied, Martine, *Le Comtat et la Révolution française: Naissance des options collectives*, Aix-en-Provence, France: Publications de l'Université de Provence, 1996

Lapied, Martine, "Les massacres révolutionnaires sont-ils des événements? Réflexion sur les massacres de la Glacière à Avignon," in *L'événement*, proceedings of a conference sponsored by the Centre Méridional d'Histoire Sociale, Aix-en-Provence, France: Université de Provence, 1986

Lapied, Martine, "Les mouvements populaires à Avignon et dans le Comtat Venaissin au XVIIIᵉ siècle," *Provence historique* 145 (1986)

Lapied, Martine, "La place des femmes dans la sociabilité et la vie politique locale en Provence et dans le Comtat Venaissin pendant la Révolution," *Provence historique* 186 (October-December 1996)

Lapied, Martine, "Les victimes de la Commission populaire d'Orange," in *La Révolution française et la mort*, proceedings of a conference held in Toulouse, 9–10 March 1989, edited by Jean Mauride Bizière and Élisabeth Liris, Toulouse, France: Presses Universitaires du Mirail, 1991

Lefebvre, Georges, *La Grande Peur de 1789*, Paris: A. Colin, 1932; as *The Great Fear of 1789: Rural Panic in Revolutionary France*, translated by Joan White, London: NLB, and New York: Pantheon, 1973

Martin, Jean-Clément, *La Vendée et la France*, Paris: Seuil, 1987

Macciocchi, Maria-Antonietta, *Cara Eleonora*, Milan, Italy: Rizzoli, 1993

Marcelli, Umberto, "Donne giacobine a Bologna (1796–1799)," *Bollettino del Museo del Risorgimento*, anni XXIX-XXX, Bologna, Italy: Museo del Risorgimento, 1984–1985

Matharan, Jean-Louis, "Les arrestations de suspects en 1793 et l'an II, professions et répressions," *Annales historiques de la Révolution française*, no. 263 (1986)

Melzer, Sara E., and Leslie W. Rabine, editors, *Rebel Daughters: Women and the French Revolution*, New York: Oxford University Press, 1992

Michalik, Kerstin, *Der Marsch der Pariser Frauen nach Versailles am 5. und 6. Oktober 1789: Eine Studie zu weiblichen Partizipationsformen in der Frühphase der Französischen Revolution*, Pfaffenweiler, Germany: Centaurus-Verlagsgesellschaft, 1990

Michelet, Jules, *Histoire de la Révolution française*, 6 vols., Paris: A Lacroix and Company, 1868–69; as *History of the French Revolution*, translated by Charles Cocks, edited by Charles Wright, Chicago: University of Chicago Press, 1967

Monnier, Raymonde, *L'espace public démocratique: Essai sur l'opinion à Paris, de la Révolution au Directoire*, Paris: Kimé, 1994

Noack, Paul, *Olympe de Gouges, 1748–1793: Kurtisane und Kämpferin für die Rechte der Frau*, Munich: Deutscher Taschenbuch Verlag, 1992

Outram, Dorinda, *The Body and the French Revolution: Sex, Class, and Political Culture*, New Haven, Connecticut: Yale University Press, 1989

Ozouf, Mona, *Les mots des femmes: Essai sur la singularité française*, Paris: Fayard: 1995; as *Women's Words: Essay on French Singularity*, translated by Jane Marie Todd, Chicago: University of Chicago Press, 1997

Petersen, Susanne, *Frauen in der Französische Revolution: Dokumente, Kommentare, Bilder*, Berlin: Akademie-Verlag, 1987

Petitfrère, Claude, editor, *La Vendée et les Vendéens*, Paris: Gallimard/Julliard, 1981

Peyrard, Christine, *Les Jacobins de l'Ouest*, Paris: Publications de la Sorbonne, 1996

Proctor, Candice E., *Women, Equality and the French Revolution*, New York: Greenwood Press, 1990

Ragan, Bryant T., and Elizabeth A. Williams, editors, *Re-creating Authority in Revolutionary France*, New Brunswick, New Jersey: Rutgers University Press, 1992

Ressayre, Pascale, "Les Arlésiennes et la Révolution (1789-an IX)," master's thesis, Université de Provence, 1989

Roudinesco, Élisabeth, *Théroigne de Méricourt, une femme mélancolique sous la Révolution*, Paris: Seuil, 1989

Rudé, George, *The Crowd in the French Revolution*, Oxford: Clarendon Press, 1959; New York: Oxford University Press, 1967

Sgard, Jean, *Les trente récits de la Journée des Tuiles*, Grenoble, France: Presses Universitaires de Grenoble, 1988

Steiner, Gerhard, "L'engagement et le destin des 'Jacobines' de Mayence," *Annales historiques de la Révolution française*, no. 255–256 (1984)

Théry, Irène, and Christian Biet, editors, *La famille, la loi, l'État, de la Révolution au Code civil*, Paris: Imprimerie Nationale Centre Georges Pompidou, 1989

Veauvy, Christiane, and Laura Pisano, *Paroles oubliées: Les femmes et la construction de l'État-nation en France et en Italie, 1789–1860*, Paris: Armand Colin, 1997

Viennot, Éliane, editor, *La démocratie "à la française" ; ou, Les femmes indésirables*, Paris: Publications de l'Université de Paris VII, 1996

Vovelle, Michel, editor, *L'image de la Révolution française*, papers presented at the Congrès Mondial pour le Bicentenaire de la Révolution, Sorbonne, Paris, 6–12 juillet 1989, Paris, Oxford, and New York: Pergamon Press, 1990

Vovelle, Michel, *La Révolution française: Images et récits, 1789–1795*, 5 vols., Paris: Messidor, 1986

SEX OR RANK?

Women's Status in the Philosophy of the Enlightenment

CATHERINE LARRÈRE

THE AGE OF ENLIGHTENMENT, according to Immanuel Kant, meant the access to knowledge and the public exercise of freedom of thought that emancipated humanity from any guardianship and enabled it to come into its majority. Clearly, however, women did not wholly share in this liberation: they remained minors during the Enlightenment. The principle of legal individualism, as affirmed by modern natural law, was instated in the Déclaration des Droits de l'Homme et du Citoyen (Declaration of the Rights of Man and the Citizen) of 1789, but this did not lead to an affirmation of equality of the sexes—on the contrary. In Enlightenment thought, one is instead likely to find various justifications for depriving women of their civil rights, excluding them from the exercise of citizenship, and barring them from the most developed forms of knowledge. In his presentation of "Sophie, ou la femme" ("Sophie; or, The Woman") in book V of *Émile ou de l'éducation* (1762; *Émile: or, On Education*), Jean-Jacques Rousseau formally rejects sexual equality, states the beneficial effects of ignorance, and excludes women from politics and even from all autonomy. Women, he asserts, are not made *like* men but *for* men; it is their nature to be obedient.

To be sure, not all of Rousseau's contemporaries shared these views. Antoine-Léonard Thomas, in his *Essai sur le caractère, les moeurs et l'esprit des femmes dans les différents siècles* (1772; *Essay on the Character, Manners and Genius of Women in Different Ages*), reminds readers that "the important question of equality or sexual dominance" had been debated consistently for 150 years: indeed, the ideas of sexual equality and the importance of education and access to knowledge continued to be championed in the 18th century. In 1759, in his response to the letter Rousseau had written to him on theatrical performances, D'Alembert pleaded "the cause of women," denouncing "the slavery and the kind of degradation in which we have placed women," and he asked that parents give "their daughters the same education as they give their other children." In 1774, extracts from his works, published under the title *Pensées de M. d'Alembert* (D'Alembert's Thought), once again took up part of this defense. But this piece, which might have fueled the debate over women's

rights that Thomas had reopened, seems to have passed unnoticed. What made Thomas' book famous was Diderot's scathing criticism of it. Against all those who held that the difference between men and women lay in education, he asserted that female nature was dominated by a sexuality that made them inferior to men.

Only the French Revolution allowed for the full affirmation of the rights of women on an equal footing with men. In 1790 the marquis de Condorcet published an article, "Sur l'admission des femmes au droit de cité" ("On the Admission of Women to the Rights of Citizenship"), that was a rigorous demonstration of the equality of the sexes and the necessity for women to enjoy the same rights as men and above all of the right to vote. In *A Vindication of the Rights of Woman* (1792), Mary Wollstonecraft targeted Rousseau. However, opinions such as these were in the minority. When Condorcet presented his plan for the constitution to the National Convention, on 15 and 16 February 1793, he did not even mention women's vote, thereby abandoning the attempt to put into practice what he had advocated earlier. Wollstonecraft's criticism was all the more remarkable in that the female public had generally sided with Rousseau.

Condorcet himself acknowledged this. Even while he spoke to women on the equality of rights, he noted in his *Quatre lettres d'un bourgeois de New Haven sur l'unité de la législation* (1788; Four Letters from a Burgher of New Haven on the Unity of Legislation): "Since Rousseau has won their approval . . . I cannot hope that they would declare themselves in my favor." Such is the paradox of the Enlightenment: not only did the model of legal equality not prevail, it was superseded by another model, that of sexual difference and separation, which Rousseau exemplified with Sophie, and even more so with the heroine of *Julie, ou La nouvelle Héloïse. Lettres de deux amants habitants d'une petite ville au pied des Alpes, recueillies et publiées par Jean-Jacques Rousseau* (1761; *Eloïsa; or, A Series of Original Letters Collected and Published by Mr. J. J. Rousseau*)[1]. It is therefore not enough

---

[1] The French editors have elected to quote from William Kenrick's 1784 translation, in which the heroine is referred to as Eloïsa. Readers may also wish to consult Philip Stewart's recent translation, entitled *Julie; or, The New Heloise.*

to understand why (or how) Condorcet's model was not acknowledged, but it is also necessary to search for the reasons why (or how) Rousseau's model was deemed preferable.

Above all, we must come to understand *what* was deemed preferable. The exclusion of women from the public sphere raises the problem of the limits of individualism in the Enlightenment. In *Le sacre du citoyen* (1992; The Consecration of the Citizen), the historian Pierre Rosanvallon interprets this as a sign of the era's shortcomings: enclosed in "the traditional view of the relationship between the sexes," women belonged to the private, domestic, or natural sphere, while men alone made up the public arena (see Rosanvallon). In the 18th century, the issue of women's status was the determining point for the articulations between private and public spheres, natural relations and social relations. Montesquieu's merit was to have presented, in book VII of *L'esprit des lois* (1748; The Spirit of the Laws) two models of this nexus; reexamined and refined, these models remained in competition until the Revolution: the monarchic model and the republican model. Studying how the different currents of thought, from natural law to political economy, dealt with the condition of women allows us to see how the republican model came to supplant the monarchic model. At the same time, such an analysis allows us to see that sexual difference took on greater and greater importance. Was this a way of upholding a traditional view? Would it not have been more plausible that there should be, alongside the development of individualism in the 18th century, a new and increasing importance attached to sexual difference? The philosophical endeavor of the Enlightenment on the question of women—on the part of both Rousseau and Diderot—consisted precisely of seeking a definition of the female that avoided Condorcet's legal individualism. The place allotted to women, in the philosophy of the Enlightenment, would then attest not only to the incomplete achievement of individualism but also to the limitations of Enlightenment philosophy itself.

As we shall see, examining the condition of women in the philosophy of the Enlightenment makes possible advances in both thinking about women's identity and the understanding of the major articulations of political society. Although at the end of the Enlightenment women's condition did not offer them access to politics, the study of women's status is one of the keys to the understanding of politics.

Women's Rights or Women's Condition?

In efforts to explain why the Enlightenment granted women so little, a change in the very idea of nature—especially human nature—is often invoked. The egalitarian view of nature that corresponded to Cartesian intellectualism and mechanism was succeeded in the 18th century by a conception of nature that granted greater importance to feeling than to reason and that, above all, took sexual difference into account. Indeed, the latter was of great importance in the physiological and medical discourse of the second half of the 18th century, and this unquestionably had philosophical consequences, especially in Diderot's work, as we will see. Condorcet himself echoes this perspective in his article on the admission of women to the rights of citizenship,

when he challenges a detractor: "Let someone show me a natural difference between men and women that may legitimately serve as a foundation for the deprivation of a right." Here Condorcet demonstrates his line of argument: for him it is not a question of opposing one conception of nature to another, but of showing that naturalist objections are not acceptable in law. To reach this position, he merely applies the principles of legal individualism, those of natural law.

Modern natural law, established early in the 17th century by Hugo de Groot, known as Grotius, with *De Jure Belli et Pacis* (1625; The Rights of War and Peace: Including The Law of Nature and of Nations), which Samuel von Pufendorf systematized in 1680 with *De Jure Naturae et Gentium* (1672; Of the Law of Nature and Nations), was not naturalistic. To be sure, Pufendorf's conception of natural law refers to human nature, but it does not draw on a physical or physiological idea of it: "Let every man esteem and treat another as one who is naturally his equal or who is a man as well as he" (book III, chap. 2). In making equality into a natural law, Pufendorf uses two arguments, appealing to the oneness of human nature, on the one hand, and to the principle according to which ability does not make right, on the other.

Barbeyrac, who first translated Grotius and Pufendorf into French, disseminated the theses of natural law in Europe. He criticized the ancient philosophers, especially Plato and Aristotle, for having limited people's rights either to the Greeks alone (Plato) or to citizens alone (Aristotle). Only the modern period had posited, with Grotius and Pufendorf, that natural law extends to all humanity: this was how one differentiated humanity from animals without being forced to resort to positive knowledge taken from natural history. Every theoretician of natural law, until Rousseau and Kant, took care to show that the frontiers of humanity, whose rights were expounded, did not coincide with the differences between the species. Humanity, then, was a moral quality, to be carefully distinguished from any empirical anthropology. Locke demonstrated clearly in second of his *Two Treatises of Government* (1690) that, just because they do not use reason, children and madmen are therefore not any less persons of morality, that whether an individual belongs to a category of beings is not called into question through empirical determinations, accidental or permanent (chap. 6, "Of Paternal Power"). Therefore, from the moment one concedes that women are human beings, there is no reason whatsoever to exclude them from the rights of humanity: the argument, reiterated by both Condorcet and Wollstonecraft, is irrefutable.

On the other hand, the principle of natural equality did not postulate a de facto equality among men. Pufendorf does not deny the existence of natural inequalities between men—for example, that some are better equipped to command and others to obey—but the principle of ability does not make right: "a Natural aptitude, does neither give the one a right of imposing a condition of servitude, nor oblige the other to receive it" (book III, chap. 2). Furthermore, there is among men only that legitimate authority that is based on voluntary consent:

> For all Men enjoy a natural liberty in the same measure and degree, which before they suffer to be impaired or diminished; there must intervene either their own consent express, tacite [sic] or interpretative, or some fact of theirs, by which others may obtain a right of abridging them of

their liberty by force, in case they will not part with it, by a voluntary submission. (book III, chap. 1)

The argument, first used against the Aristotelian justification for slavery, was just as valid for rejecting the claim of establishing in nature women's submission to men. Louis de Jaucourt reiterates this line of reasoning in the article "Femme (Droit naturel)" (Woman [Natural Law]) in volume 6 of the *Encyclopédie*:

> It would be difficult to prove that the husband's authority comes from nature; for this principle is the contradiction of the natural equality of people; and it does not follow that, just because one is capable of commanding, one now has the right to do so.

Accepted authority is not necessarily weakened authority—on the contrary. Grotius uses marriage as the example of a relationship that, freely agreed upon between equal individuals, creates a situation of irreversible subordination: "Of this nature is that authority to which a woman submits when she gives herself to a husband" (book I, chap. 3). For Grotius and Pufendorf, the conjugal relationship is an unequal alliance that places the woman under the protection and safekeeping of her husband; she must promise him obedience and faithfulness unilaterally, in a communal life to which she commits the totality of her existence. In stating this, Grotius and Pufendorf do not deny the principles of natural law, those of equal liberty: the argument precluding the use of a de facto inequality as the basis for a legal inequality, at the same time allows this factual inequality to be acknowledged and consequences to be drawn from it. The fact that there are no natural slaves does not mean, for Grotius and Pufendorf, that there may not be conventions of slavery; the fact that man does not have a natural authority over woman does not prevent the sanctioning of the wife's submission to the husband under the conventions of marriage.

Thus, while he recognizes that nothing excludes spouses from being in an equal relationship, or even that a husband may be submissive to his wife, Pufendorf nevertheless considers it to be appropriate for the husband to be "head and director" of his wife. In so doing, he does not claim the existence of a female "nature" distinct from that of man, but his argument takes into account other considerations besides those of the rights of individuals: the purpose of marriage (the reproduction of the species), the proper order of society, and the patriarchal tradition, according to which it is the woman who comes into the family of the husband, not the other way around. It might be said, then, that what led Pufendorf to consider the wife not as equal but as subordinate to her husband was a holistic vision of social relationships in the sense that the anthropologist Louis Dumont defines this term: there are social totalities, and most particularly the family, that are anterior and superior to the individuals who are subordinated to them (see Dumont 1983).

Legal historian Alfred Dufour has shown how the concept of marriage changed in the 18th century in German natural law, especially in the work of its two main theoreticians, Christian von Wolff and Christian Thomasius (see Dufour). They went so far as to consider marriage an egalitarian relationship, replacing the old idea of marital power with the new concept of conjugal authority—an authority that is shared and in which the wife has as many rights and powers as her husband. Based on a reciprocal and contractual relationship, this conjugal alliance does not require a commanding power, as opposed to the situation in civil society. Marriage, then, is defined in terms of individuals; the spouses are subjects of law and freely contracted social relationships that have no other significance or existence than those their desires confer upon them: divorce, therefore, is lawful. Global entities are no longer taken into account, just individuals. In this instance, the progress of individualism on the question of marriage in natural law coincided with progress toward equality and liberty.

But when the problem is no longer framed in any terms other than that of individuals, one runs the risk of not being able to characterize them. This is what happened to Condorcet. In his plea for the admission of women to the rights of citizenship, he follows the same individualist approach: when recognizing a supra-individual characteristic, that of sexual difference, he declares it to have no legal effect: there are only individuals, certainly different, certainly unequal, but ability does not make right: one cannot allege natural inequalities in order to set women apart from a right that belongs to every member of the human race. But in the same logical move, individuals are rendered indistinguishable from one another. Condorcet himself recognized that the great scandal of excluding women from the rights of citizens of a state was not only that it had taken place, but that it had gone unnoticed—that it had not been necessary to justify it or even express it, at a time when the rights of man and the citizen, and indeed those of the human race, had just been proclaimed. This is an invitation to reexamine the manner in which natural law defines the individuals it considers.

When one reads, in book XIII of Hobbes's *Leviathan*, that "Nature hath made men so equall," one has every reason to suppose that "men" here are indeterminate human beings, men or women without any distinction being made between them. Such an interpretation, however, is completely erroneous. Gordon Schochet's study of Hobbes's conception of the state of nature has established that, in a state of war, it is the heads of the family who face one another in combat: all the other members of the family—women, children, domestic servants—do not participate in the struggle (see Schochet). This is not peculiar to Hobbes. Manfred Riedel has shown that this understanding is a common characteristic of the social contract theories of the 17th and 18th centuries: the individual who contracts and becomes a member of civilized society is the head of a family (see Riedel). The idea of civil society, until and including the French Revolution, maintained the ancient distinction of the political and the domestic, of the city or *polis*, and of the household or the family, the *oïkos*. The merit of Rousseau in the end is that he confirmed explicitly what was generally left implicit: when Émile is going to be married, his tutor solemnly declares: "When you become the head of a family, you are going to become a member of the state." But Rousseau said this in his treatise on education, not in his treatise on political institutions. When one reads, in *Du contrat social* (1762; *The Social Contract*),

> I assume men having reached the point where the obstacles that interfere with their preservation in the state of nature prevail by their resistance over the forces which each individual can muster to maintain himself in that state. Then that primitive state can no longer subsist, and humankind would perish if it did not change its way of being (book I, chap. 6),

one may reasonably think that this concerned every individual, not only the heads of families.

The pronouncements on "men" in social contract theories operate on two levels: on the one hand, when it is a matter of defining the universality of obligation, the term "men" certainly designates generic individuals, sexually indeterminate human beings. On the other hand, as soon as individuals are considered as active subjects, "all men" indicates only the head of a family. The first factor that allows for the confusion of two propositions on different levels is the inherently equivocal grammatical structure of the French language, which allows the masculine form to indicate both the entire species and male individuals of the species. Thus, the entire human race and the masculine gender can be referred to simultaneously, whereas the feminine, in order to have a discursive status, must be marked or given a special term: sexual difference must be stated. Added to this is the sociological perception of the family, a unit that exists as an individual embodied in the person who is the head of the family. Grammatical structure is conflated with social differentiation, so that in fact the category of the individual pertains only to men, and men as heads of the family, while women, defined through their belonging to the family, exist outside the field of political philosophy—without it ever having been necessary to describe this exclusion.

The overall logic of this process leads to the introduction of hierarchical relationships in the anthropological sense that Dumont uses that concept. The archetype of the hierarchical relationship, which Dumont defines as incorporation of the opposite, lies for him in the biblical account of the creation of man. From the moment that Eve is created, Adam is both the representative of the human species and the prototype of male individuals; Eve is a part of the whole, from which she distinguishes herself as woman. The exclusion of the female, in social contract theories, passes through the use of a hierarchical relationship that marks the limits of individualism under the social contract.

The fundamental proposition of all modern natural law, that of equal liberty, is an individualist proposition; it postulates that, since individuals draw their reality from themselves alone and not from some superior authority that might qualify them by granting them a status, what is true for an individual is necessarily true for all others: "either no individual of the human species has any real rights, or all of them have the same ones," as Condorcet so aptly expresses it in "On the Admission of Women to the Rights of Citizenship." At the same time, this individualism is expressed in a hierarchical grammatical structure, such as the term "man" indicating both the whole (the human race) and a part of that whole (male beings). It could be objected that this ambivalence reflects a defect in natural language that specific phrasing (or an adequate ruling of the he/she kind) could eliminate. But such an objection overlooks the main thing, which is that a pronouncement of this kind, which articulates two propositions that operate on different levels and still maintains them in one same unit, may actually be needed. The problem, then, does not lie in the equivocal nature of language, but in the fact that legal individualism is by definition incapable of describing individuals and that, when it needs to have recourse to definition, legal individualism cannot take specific descriptive criteria into account.

Thus the abbé Emmanuel Joseph Sieyès, encountering this difficulty during his drafting of the declaration of the rights of man and the citizen, made a distinction between passive and active citizens. On the one hand, in the "Préliminaire de la Constitution, reconnaissance et exposition raisonnée des droit de l'homme et du citoyen" (20–21 July 1789; Preliminary to the Constitution, A Recognition and Reasoned Exposition of the Rights of Man and the Citizen), he universally extends the category of the citizen: "All inhabitants of a country must enjoy the rights of passive citizens there," meaning that all individuals, in an undifferentiated manner, are subordinate to the law. On the other hand, he defines a subcategory of active citizens, "those alone who contribute to public matters." Between the two he excludes women, who "should not actively influence the public sphere." At least Sieyès names what he has just excluded; his putting aside "half of the human race" does not go entirely unacknowledged. But once the exclusion has been made, he is unable to give any valid reason for it. He explains that it was in "the present state" that this exclusion was made; elsewhere he attributes it to "prejudices." Similarly, Condorcet explains the exclusion of women through "standard practice" and "habit." When Condorcet's friend Pierre Guyomar, after defending the admission of women to the rights of citizens of a state, agreed to its restriction, he said that "the rigor of the law" must bend to "customs derived from mores."

Like all human beings, women have rights. But, according to the principle of equal liberty, they have rights not as women but as individuals, undistinguished from other individuals: strictly speaking, there are no women's rights, there are the rights of individuals. Such are the "rigors of the law," which prohibit characterizing particular individuals as women. That characterization amounts to "prejudices," to "standard practice," to "customs derived from mores." It is truly here that legal individualism meets its limits: the limits inherent in a social complexity that it cannot take into account, but within which women are characterized not only by an ensemble of empirical individual particularities but also by social norms that regulate their conduct, determine their social status, conventions, mores—everything pertaining to what Montesquieu, in *The Spirit of the Laws*, calls the "condition of women."

Republic or Monarchy?

Montesquieu contends that women's condition varies according to forms of government, which affect their liberty: "kept in extreme slavery" (*The Spirit of the Laws*, book VII, chap. 9) under despotism, women are free in republics and monarchies, but in different ways. This freedom does not consist of participation in power. With the exception—a very unique situation, as we shall see—of a woman's accession to a throne, women generally do not have a share in power. Everything pertaining to women in *The Spirit of the Laws* comes from the study of civil or religious laws, not political laws. If women's condition varies with the forms of government, it is because the political constitution— that is to say, the distribution of power and its mode of practice—informs social life as a whole, making every political society a complex unit in which political laws and civil laws vary in tandem.

Montesquieu separates political liberty from participation in power. He defines citizenship not in terms of the exercise of power but in terms of relationship to the law. The citizen is free because he has "the right to do everything the laws permit" (book XI, chap. 3); that is, the citizen is subject to the rule of law, not to an arbitrary will. Women are "citizens" in the same capacity as men, and their exclusion from power does not prohibit them from enjoying security. If women's liberty requires a specific study, it is because for women, far more than for men, what is permitted depends less on laws than on mores. Mores are what determine the difference between women's condition in republics and in monarchies: in the former, women are "free by the laws and captured by the mores" (book VII, chap. 9), while monarchy provides more freedom for women, because mores are freer there. Women's conduct is not only regulated by laws; it derives especially from a more diffuse social prescription, which escapes from deliberate action: "Mores and manners are usages that laws have not established or that they have not been able, or have not wanted, to establish." (book XIX, chap. 16). Essential to the understanding of women's condition, the study of these usages complements the study of governments: the process by which they are constituted allows us to grasp what such governments aspire to be; the study of mores should allow us to grasp what they are in reality.

Despotism is a regime of both political and civil slavery, and from this point of view the lot of women is the same as that of men. But women are "kept in extreme slavery" under that regime, owing to two additional characteristics that are specific to them. Under despotism, the husband's power adds a new form of slavery, which Montesquieu calls "domestic servitude" (book XVI, chap. 1) and which is linked to polygamy. Female slaves, moreover, are exposed to sexual abuses that make them into objects of the "voluptuousness" of their masters (book XV, chap. 12).

Montesquieu expresses universal condemnation of slavery and brings the longest part of his argument to bear against the justification of conventional slavery commonly given by theoreticians of natural law: the right of conquest, the relationship between conqueror and vanquished. He shows that the conqueror has no right whatsoever over a life that he never bestowed (book X, chap. 3, and book XV, chap. 2)—thereby placing himself on the very masculine terrain of warfare. It might be assumed that an argument that is valid for male captives would be even more valid for female captives. But, in addition to refuting this specific point, Montesquieu condemns slavery in the name of the principle of reciprocity, the "fundamental principle of all societies" (book XV, chap. 2), which is that of the priority of freedom over social utility. He examines the question from the point of view of the slave in order to reject slavery: "the law of slavery has never been useful to him" (book XV, chap. 2). Therefore, the condemnation of slavery is the very rigorous application of the individualist principle of equal liberty.

At the same time that he condemns slavery, Montesquieu seeks the reasons for its existence—reasons that prohibit its generalization inasmuch as they are linked to the specifics of a situation (such as climate). Moreover, the factor that explains the existence of slavery in certain places at the same time prevents it from becoming a generalized phenomenon and also makes the sexual use of slaves an unjustifiable abuse: "Reason wants the power of the master not to extend beyond things that are of service to him; slavery must be for utility and not for voluptuousness" (book XV, chap. 12). Thus, Montesquieu returns to the universality of natural law: "The laws of modesty are a part of natural right and should be felt by all the nations in the world" (book XV, chap. 12).

However, this is a particular universality that pertains only to the female sex. According to Montesquieu, this is because the sexes are not equal with respect to sexuality and its consequences. If modesty is "natural," it is because nature

> has established defense, she has established attack; and, having put desires into both sides, she has placed temerity in the one and shame in the other. She has given individuals long periods of time to preserve themselves and only brief moments for their perpetuation. (book XVI, chap. 12)

This way of rendering modesty natural has ambiguous consequences. It may lead to a finalistic and hierarchical line of argument, in the manner of Aristotle: if modesty is natural, it is natural to force women who stray from modesty to come back to it (book XVI, chap. 12). But the naturalization of modesty may also lead to individualist conclusions. Examining a law that required the public disclosure of sexual relationships outside of marriage, he criticizes it: "It is unreasonable to require a girl to make this declaration as to ask a man not to seek to defend his life" (book XXVI, chap. 3). In this way, Montesquieu grants sexual integrity the status of a right—a right specific to women—that is a particular instance of the generic right to preserve existence and to just self-defense.

Montesquieu also issues a sweeping condemnation of polygamy: "it is not useful to mankind or to either of the sexes, either to the one which abuses or to the one abused. Nor is it useful to children" (book XVI, chap. 6). However, he shows that imposing monogamy in a polygamous country, as the Catholic missionaries did, would risk placing former wives of the newly converted in a "deplorable" condition if one did not ensure that their civil status would be returned to them (book XXVI, chap. 10). Women's rights become more justified in such a situation. Thus it is important to understand how the institution functions: "One consequence of polygamy is that in the rich and voluptuous nations one has a very great number of wives. Their separation from the men and their enclosure follow naturally from their great number" (book XVI, chap. 8).

In despotic regimes, the seclusion of women is a consequence of both the abuse of male power (which wishes to hide the objects desirable to all men) and the abuse of political power, which reigns through fear only—in other words, through a sort of distancing. Such a reign, itself corrupt, must curb any freedom that might turn into corruption: "As the laws in these states are severe and executed on the spot, one fears that women's liberty could be a cause for doing business" (book VII, chap. 9)—that is, women's liberty could generate abuses of power among men. Therefore, cloistering women is the only barrier against generalized corruption—to such a degree that, in an ironic reversal of the situation, the regime of men's voluptuousness can be that of women's chastity: "In the various states of the East, the mores are purer as the enclosure of women is stricter" (book XVI, chap. 10).

In a republic, too, women live separated from men, but for a completely different reason, which Montesquieu mentions in the chapter devoted to English mores: "In a nation where each man in his own way would take part in the administration of the state, the women should scarcely live among men" (book XIX, chap. 27). In a republic, then, masculine and feminine correspond to a distribution of spaces and social roles: political and domestic realms, laws, and mores.

A republic links an egalitarian political structure (in which one is governed by one's equals) to a hierarchical social structure, a structure created by mores. What "maintains morality" is "the extreme subordination of the young to the elderly" and "paternal authority" (book V, chap. 7), and, to an even greater extent, the faithfulness of wives. The "purity" of conjugal morality is at the heart of the republican system. If virtue is the principle of republican government, it has two forms: women's domestic virtue—"simplicity" and "chastity" (book VII, chap. 9)—corresponds to men's political virtue, which is the love of equality.

The principle by which morality is maintained does not lie in seclusion, as under despotism, but, on the contrary, in publicity: "The Roman law that wanted the accusation of adultery to be made public maintained the purity of mores remarkably well; it intimidated the women and also intimidated those who kept watch over them" (book V, chap. 7). Thus, the republic is the regime that raises private morality, family life, to public dimensions. It makes morality an affair of the state: "Now, in republics private crimes are more public, that is, they run counter to the constitution of the state more than against individuals" (book III, chap. 5). Emanating from the conjugal and family home, morality is displayed for all to see and forms a public sphere, which requires control—the control exercised by censors. Censors are the custodians of morality, as the senate is the custodian of the law: "They must reestablish all that has become corrupted in the republic, notice slackness, judge oversights, and correct mistakes just as the laws punish crimes" (book V, chap. 7). The two forms of control do not operate in the same way: crime is punished after it has taken place, starting from a determination to which a text of law is applied. Control over morality is preventive and is practiced according to a moral code that brings collective opinion into play. Moral censorship is less discriminate and more severe than the code of law, for it does not aim at specific actions but at a state of mind:

> It is not only crimes that destroy virtue, but also negligence, mistakes, a certain slackness in the love of the homeland, dangerous examples, the seeds of corruption, that which does not run counter to the laws but eludes them, that which does not destroy them but weakens them. (book V, chap. 19)

Thus moral censorship is more severe than legal repression. Commenting upon a judgment by Areopagus, who had condemned a child to death "who had gouged out the eyes of his bird," Montesquieu cautions his reader: "Notice that the question is not that of condemning a crime but of judging mores in a republic founded on mores" (book V, chap. 19).

A republic, which from its constitution seems to be a regime of laws voted in by the assembled people, is in fact a regime of mores. The corruption of morality—that is to say, the subversion of the hierarchy—is potentially decisive in bringing about the ruin of the regime: "Women, children, and slaves will submit to no one. There will no longer be mores or love of order, and finally, there will no longer be virtue" (book VIII, chap. 2).

Without women's chastity there can be no political virtue. Between political equality and the social and moral hierarchy, in the end it is the latter that counts the most. This moral order is restrictive for women, who are always under guardianship, but men hardly profit by this, for the regime of their power is not in any way that of their pleasure.

Men seek elsewhere the satisfaction they do not find at home and will refuse marriage or its duties. In response, the Romans augmented laws that encouraged marriage and procreation. Thus, the extreme separation of the sexes favors homosexuality, which Montesquieu deplores, and it sustains misogyny. Montesquieu has a Roman say that "If it were possible not to have wives, we would be delivered from this evil" (book XXIII, chap. 21). This morose corruption was not peculiar to the republics of antiquity; in modern England, whose mores are republican, Montesquieu finds the same characteristics: separated from the men, women there are "modest, that is, timid" and virtuous, and the men, "lacking gallantry" throw themselves into "debauchery" (book XIX, chap. 27).

In this respect, monarchies are the exact opposite of a republic: it is possible for a woman to have access to power, and women there live together in mixed company with men. That a government run by a single person could be run by a woman was, first of all, a curiosity for Montesquieu: he collected scattered examples of this, in the manner of skeptical relativism. The intent was to show that what the French took for a law of nature was only an effect of custom: "If the Scythian women had continued their conquests, and if the Egyptians had done the same, the human race would be living under the servitude of women, and one would have to be a philosopher to say that another government would be more in keeping with nature," Montesquieu states in number 1622 of his *Pensées* (Thoughts [unpublished at Montesquieu's death in 1755, the *Pensées* did not appear in extenso until 1899–1901]). But government by a woman remains an exception from which no rule could be made. In truth, however, the rather positive evaluation Montesquieu brings to bear on the possibility that a woman's government would moderate despotism is not a favorable evaluation of the qualities of women, who are presumed to be gentler than men. Above all, he emphasizes the opposite effects that a related characteristic, weakness, has in a family (which a woman cannot command because of her weakness) and in the state, in which weakness may have moderating virtues: he aims to show that it is a question of two different powers that cannot be conflated. Rather than a reflection upon the abilities of women to exercise power, it is one element of his critique of the family model of political authority, which he formally rejects from the very beginning of *The Spirit of the Laws* (book I, chap. 3). Montesquieu returns to this distinction between the two types of authority when he examines the Salic law. He condemns it for having been "a purely economic law" and thus for having confused the ruling of the house (economy in its proper sense), which excludes the government of women, with that of the state, which allows for such a possibility: by insuring the male succession to the crown, "the provisions of the civil law forced the political law" (book XVIII, chap. 22).

In a monarchy, the morality of women develops along with court society, which gathers around the king an idle aristocracy that is distanced from power. Having left their homes, women mingle with men in a gallant society, based on the reciprocal attraction between the sexes, that cultivates conversation and the mind, thereby reproducing in jousts that are no longer anything but verbal the spirit of chivalry that previously brought men to distinguish themselves before a female public. "Enlightened judges of a part of the things that constitute personal merit" (book XXVIII, chap. 22), women foster in men the desire to please and to distinguish themselves, which is characteristic of honor—the principle of a monarchy. Like the development of court society itself, the liberty of women is synonymous with corruption. The critique of the pettiness of feminine flaws—"Women's quarrels, their indiscretions, their aversions, their inclination, their jealousies, their spiteful remarks, in short that art by which narrow souls affect generous ones, cannot be without consequence there" (book VII, chap. 9)—is a counterpoint to what Montesquieu says about masculine honor: "Ambition in idleness, meanness in arrogance, the desire to enrich oneself without work, aversion to truth, flattery, treachery, perfidy . . . the perpetual ridicule cast upon virtue, these form, I believe, the character of the greater number of courtiers" (book III, chap. 5). In gallant society, family virtues are turned into ridicule, appearances are cultivated to the detriment of being, and gallantry "is not love, but the delicate, flimsy, and perpetual illusion of love" (book XXVIII, chap. 22).

Women's liberty in a monarchy confirms Montesquieu's assessment of that form of government: virtue is not its principle at all (book III, chap. 5). This is because honor is not appreciated for its intentions but for its effects: "[E]ach person works for the common good, believing he works for his individual interests" (book III, chap. 7). The monarchy is that admirable mechanism in which the good is produced as a result without necessarily being seen as an end. Its effects are apparent on a political level, in the form of a guarantee of liberty, insofar as concerns the masculine value of honor. Insofar as women and their freedom are concerned, its effects are apparent in the moral sphere. Thus the masculine condition (honor) reveals something about political liberty, while the feminine condition reveals something about mores.

In a monarchy, mores have to do not with virtue but with manners: they deal with external behaviors and affect relationships with others. They are thus indicative of the "sociable" mood of those they govern. Manners polish and civilize more than they moralize. They enable exchanges to proliferate; they promote the dissemination of the social model of gallantry: "The society of women spoils mores and forms taste" (book XIX, chap. 8). The monarchic "civilization of mores" substitutes esthetics for ethics: it is the empire of good taste, of which women are the judges. As immoral or deceptive as it may be, monarchic gallantry is pleasing to women, who satisfy their desire for independence there and can exercise some power. But it is just as pleasing to men: "One is fortunate to live in these climates that allow communication between people, where the sex with the most charms seems to adorn society and where women, keeping themselves for the pleasures of one man, yet serve for the diversion of all" (book XVI, chap. 11).

More than a personal opinion, Montesquieu expresses here the judgment that an entire society makes on itself. With regard to mores and their appeal, monarchies unquestionably win out over republics: monarchic gallantry has more charm than republican coarseness. Won over by the monarchic model through his travels in France, Hume analyzes its civilizing effects, showing the link between the form of government, the role of women, and the development of the arts, and insists on the dissemination of aristocratic models from above. A republic is not conducive to a proliferation of the manifestations of social niceties: each citizen remains within the isolation of his independence. In "Of the Delicacy of Taste and Passion," Hume explains that the social hierarchy characteristic of the monarchy develops connections; it is

> sufficient to beget in every one an inclination to please his superiors, and to form himself upon those models, which are most acceptable to people of condition and education. Politeness of manners, therefore, arises most naturally in monarchies and courts; and where that flourishes, none of the liberal arts will be altogether neglected or despised. (*Essays Moral, Political, and Literary*)

Hume attempted to introduce the French model in England. In his first moral and political essays, he launches into gallant writing on topics that concern women: love and marriage, and shamelessness and modesty. He thus tries to attract the attention of women in the French manner of Descartes, who, by writing his philosophical works in French and not in Latin, sought to assure himself of a female readership and to move beyond the constraints of Scholasticism. In a similar fashion, Hume opines in "Of Essay Writing" that "the Ladies are, in a Manner, the Sovereigns of the learned World, as well as the Conversible, and no polite writer pretends to venture upon the Public, without the Approbation of some celebrated Judges of that Sex" (*Essays Moral, Political, and Literary*). He further increases his compliments in this essay by asserting that "I am of the Opinion, that Women, that is, Women of Sense and Education (for to such alone I address myself) are much better Judges of all polite writing than men of the same Degree of Understanding." His earliest essays thus present a little story of his own making in which the Scythian women liberate themselves from the oppression of men by giving up on pleasing them: they gouge out their eyes and, having become invisible to men, the women govern themselves just as they please.

Was this an allusion to the detrimental effects of segregation of the sexes? English women, in any event, did not receive his ideas well. Hume removed these frivolous essays from subsequent editions, which contained only the writings devoted to political subjects: the balance of power, jealousy, and commerce, as well as reflections upon the population. Although he reverted to a serious style, he did not abandon the condition of women as a subject. Indeed, questions of exchange, production, and population were crucial in the development of two rival social models that differed with respect to the place they allotted to women.

Commerce or Economy?

Bernard de Mandeville caused a scandal when he published the *Fable of the Bees; or, Private Vices, Publick Benefits* in 1714. In it one sees a beehive that is given over to corruption and the desire for wealth grow prosperous and powerful, while the nostalgia that leads it back to virtue induces only misery, laziness, and depopulation—a paradoxical thesis, by which "publick benefits" emerge from "private vices" and spending by the rich supports the poor. Mandeville's fable expresses the shift from an appreciation of the morality of intentions to an appreciation of effects. He turns luxury into the law of a humanity given over to satisfying passions and enjoying pleasure. But this universal lasciviousness has some positive consequences: those who knew how to look "may, in a hundred places, see good spring up and pullulate from Evil, as naturally as chickens do from Eggs." For the traditional vision of a society divided by distinctions of rank, Mandeville substitutes that of interconnected parts, a continual blending marked by the reciprocity of exchange: the world of commerce.

This was not a new thesis: it was already present in the works of the Sieur de Boisguilbert, where what we now call economic theories were formed on questions of the prosperity and power of political societies. Mandeville's originality lay in shifting these questions from politics to morality, placing himself in a literary tradition of critical observation of mores—social satire. Classical characters in this literary genre, women saw themselves in *The Fable of the Bees*, where they illustrated the central thesis. Mandeville recapitulates:

> I have shewn already that the worst of Women and most profligate of the Sex did contribute to the Consumption of Superfluities, as well as the Necessaries of Life, and consequently were beneficial to many peaceable Drudges, that work hard to maintain their Families.

But it is not enough to show that vice turns to the advantage of honesty. It is also necessary to throw doubt on the latter by showing that married women, even those "such as are counted Prudent and Moderate in their Desires" are a constant incitement to spending. No one is exempt from the merry-go-round of desire and appearance: husbands, for whom their wives are objects of vanity, "preventing their Wishes croud New Clothes and other Finery upon them faster than they can ask it."

Montesquieu thus borrows from Mandeville this schema of the rationality of effects, in which the general good is not the object of a deliberate design, but the involuntary result of actions devoid of any intentional morality. When he arrives at mores and women, after having applied it to the global political rationality of types of government, he returns to the very terrain in which this schema had been developed. Indeed, it is precisely from the perspective of advantages of commerce—that is, wealth—that Montesquieu finds license preferable to moral constraint, in a nation such as France, given to moral freedom: "One could constrain its women, make laws to correct their mores, and limit their luxury, but who knows whether one would not lose a certain taste that would be the source of the nation's wealth and a politeness that attracts foreigners to it?" (*The Spirit of the Laws*, book XIX, chap. 5). Originating in court life, the monarchic model thus becomes a commercial model—that of a generalized communication in which individual corruption goes hand in hand with beneficial global effects. If women are the privileged example of the generalization of commerce, it is perhaps because they express its spirit, which is frivolity, better than men: "Fashions are an important subject; as one allows one's spirit to become frivolous, one constantly increases the branches of commerce" (book XIX, chap. 8).

Frivolity, however, is not altogether identical to luxury. In the writings on commerce from the first half of the 18th century—of which the *Essai politique sur le commerce* (1734; *A Political Essay upon Commerce. Written in French by Monsieur M****) by Jean-François Melon is a good example—the classical example of luxury spending was the carriage: an ostentatious demonstration of power and rank, it was a masculine expenditure. Melon applies Mandeville's schema of private vice and public benefit to it: "What matter is it to a state if though a foolish vanity, a particular person ruineth himself, by vying with his neighbour, in Equipage?" he asks, since it makes industry run. He deems the dreary lament over the mores of the time not only myopic but pointless. When closely considered, from the point of view of the state—that of the general good—luxury does not exist. For Melon, "the term luxury is an idle name, which should never be employed, in considerations on Polity and Commerce: because it conveyeth uncertain, confused and false ideas, the misapplication whereof, might stop industry in its very source" (chap. 9, "Of Luxury"). This meant going back from the vanity of ideas to the seriousness of the state, to show the reality of things which the manufacture of a carriage puts into play: the consumption of raw materials, employment of workers, flourishing industry, merchandise sold the world over. . . . This was not a matter of just appearances, but also of being: the real lives of a great many men. "Since my childhood," recalls Ninon de Lenclos,

> I have thought about the unequal division of the qualities required from men and from women. I saw that they had charged us [women] with what is most frivolous, while the right to essential qualities had been reserved for men; from that moment on, I made myself into a man. (Quoted in Bret.)

The path of frivolity became possible in the 18th century. The affair of the *toiles peintes* (painted fabrics) in the 1750s, a critical moment in the debate on commercial freedom, illustrates the change. The painted fabrics were cotton calicos, originally dyed by hand and imported from India, and later printed and imitated in Europe. Their purchase and use were forbidden, but in the middle of the century, contraband fabrics nevertheless became so widely available that their use in furniture and clothing was endemic: common woman or duchess, everyone wore them or papered walls with them, even in the Louvre or at Versailles. Women's affairs, a matter of fashion, taste, or whimsy . . . the very definition of frivolity.

People grew worried about the situation. As recounted by François Véron de Forbonnais, they decried the scandal of a law not enforced, the threat to national industry, the "danger to the work of the people." They boasted of the simple woolen fabrics produced in France: "It might well be more useful for our land if it were to the liking of all its subjects to wear domestic fabrics." Women were scolded. Was half the nation—"the half more given to complaints and seduction" demanding the free use of "painted fabrics"? Let them be quiet! "Since they have left the difficult task of organizing matters of state to the other half, they have reserved only the glory of obedience for themselves." The mothers of those who were now making demands were the obedient women and "their finery did not cost the poor any tears at all" (*Examen des avantages et des desavantages de la prohibition des toiles peintes* [1755; Observations on the Consideration of the Advantages and Disadvantages of the Prohibition of Painted Fabrics]).

In 1751, Jacques Vincent de Gournay, a former merchant who had become intendant of commerce, along with the team he had gathered around him, promoted reflection on the benefits of free trade in France. He and his friends publicly defended free-trade policies with respect to the painted fabrics. They denounced as loathsome and ridiculous the practices of the repressive police, who would resort to placing an officer behind every consumer. Above all, they declared the futility of such practices. Against the contraband, "a continuous war was being waged on every border, which caused an unending armed population to perish, in the prisons, the galleys, and on the scaffold, and all of that only in order to force 20 million men to act against their inclination, rather than to make the best of this same inclination and take advantage of it" (Gournay, *Observations sur l'examen des avantages et des désavantages de la prohibition des toiles peintes*).

Not restraint, but accommodation—this was a radical shift in policy. Gournay was not looking for the serious hidden beneath frivolity. It was frivolity itself that interested him. Thus, when warranted, he added fantasy: "When will they be willing to believe in France that, since commerce is based as much on fantasy as on needs that vary constantly, no invariable laws should be made for the factories that serve these needs and fantasies?" (*Traités sur le commerce de Josiah Child avec les Remarques inédites de Vincent de Gournay* [see under Tsuda]). Need could always be arranged according to the hierarchy of the useful, the pleasurable, and the superfluous, while fantasy escaped from any grasp; it was variation itself, the ceaseless change in the quirks of taste that no regulation would ever manage to pin down.

Rules focus on being and its degrees of hierarchy; they seek to define perfection and fix its norms. Liberal criticism had no other rule than taste—that is to say, the absence of rules. It brought the first qualities in line with the second: the legislator can no more "prescribe perfection, form, and quality than price, color, design, or sort itself" (Clicquot-Blervache, *Considérations sur le commerce et en particulier sur les compagnies, sociétés et maîtrises* [Considerations upon Commerce and in Particular upon Companies, Societies, and Specialists]). This disintegration of human objectivity of being was followed by the subjectivity of association. There was neither good, nor bad, nor mediocre; there was only that which pleased the consumer: "if a fabric that seems ugly to us sells, then it is not bad" (Gournay, *Remarques*).

The shift from rules to freedom entails a loss of being but an increase in relationships. Philosophers conducted their critique of the perfection that the state wanted to impose in the manner of a metaphysical critique. Leibniz deals with "frivolous" or identical propositions, propositions that teach nothing about being but that one can "use" so as to "render them useful," for by suddenly presenting a totality of connections they offer the opportunity to think (*Nouveaux Essais sur l'entendement humain* [New Essays Concerning Human Understanding], book IV, chap. 8). Étienne Bonnot de Condillac, coming back to the frivolous, opposes innovative genius to the multiplicity of copies that spread out from it and meet with success: "Frivolous and ridiculous items that are born just for the moment multiply" (*Essai sur l'origine des connaissances humaines* [1746; *An Essay on the Origin of Human Knowledge*]). Ridiculous or ephemeral perhaps, but it was through this proliferation of insignificance, through this overabundance of things produced, that commerce developed. If Gournay and his friends unreservedly accepted the notion that one should model oneself on a taste for which no rules could be laid down, it was because this insignificance bolstered their critique.

There was no better obstacle to the seriousness of the state than frivolity itself, than futility. Could the state not understand women? Let it give up. Commerce thereby gained its independence. What some morose minds called "the empire of taste" was the incessant mobility, the constant variation of a network of connections—the world of women, taste, and sparkling wit. In the salons, unlike in the ministries, no serious business was discussed: every topic of conversation bore the irremediable stamp of futility. This was precisely why anything could be discussed, in total freedom, between equals, without any distinction other than individual talents. Frivolity and its insignificance marked the end of state-centered rationality—a form of organization whose absurdity and damaging incoherence were exposed by frivolity, leading the way to another form of organization, that of commerce and its reciprocal relationships.

Against the prohibition, Gournay and his friends posited "everyone's natural right to dress as one saw fit and at the best possible prices, a right that should not be taken away from citizens without some very good reasons" (Morellet, *Réflexions sur les avantages de la libre circulation des toiles peintes en France* [1758; Reflections on the Advantages of the Free Circulation of Painted Fabrics in France]). From Morellet's perspective, the authorities' searches for the contraband fabrics meant the "sacrifice" of a "precious portion of civil liberty," which he defines as "the free and tranquil possession of what is called one's home"—in other words, security. The campaign in favor of free commerce undertaken by Gournay and his team criticized prohibitions, regulations, privileged companies, corporations, and guildmasterships—everything that might be a restriction of individual freedom, that of choosing and practicing a profession. Condorcet—who assisted Turgot when the latter, having been appointed minister to Louis XVI, attempted to apply the ideas of his mentor, Gournay—remembered the campaign when he wrote his article "On the Admission of Women to the Rights of Citizenship." He was outraged that "yet up to 1776 [the year in which guildmasterships were suppressed], she (woman) could not be a milliner or dressmaker in Paris."

Reflections on commerce were thus the locus for a powerful affirmation of individual rights, including those of women. On this point, the Physiocrats continued Gournay's work, taking into consideration even those activities they called "economic," such as tasks of national interest that qualified those who carried them out as "citizens." They insisted specifically on the right to knowledge: *Les éphémérides du citoyen*, the Physiocrats' press organ, editorialized about the need for a "national education" for the peasantry: they are citizens, not slaves, and they have a right to instruction. The demand, articulated in 1765 in *Les éphémérides du citoyen*, included peasant women: "every daughter of the nation must receive a common and public education" (1765, vol. III and IV). In 1768 the marquis de Mirabeau devoted an article in *Les éphémérides du citoyen* to the "economic education of girls," because "the indispensable influence of women in society" made it necessary to bestow a "serious" education upon

young people who are destined to become mothers of a family, and who, together with their husbands, must be at the helm of the conduct of nations and the administration of goods and business; persons who may become widows and have all the responsibility for the economic government of the nation's patrimony and that of the community, and whose enlightenment and judgment must preside over the education and the establishment of their children. (1768, vol. III)

Thus, it was only by accident (widowhood) that women attained the position of independent economic agent. The move from commerce to agricultural production made by the Physiocrats gave rise to an interest in agricultural accounting and farm management more than commercial profit. Passing from commerce to the economy (the term was introduced and imposed by the Physiocrats), meant leaving the open space of commercial relations in order to come back to the "government of the household," back to the family. This was the space that defined women: "Daughter, woman, mother—such is the life course of the fair sex," Mirabeau concludes. While commerce continued the monarchic model and situated women in its networks of open exchange, Physiocracy imposed the return to what seemed to be a traditional view of society, based on the separation of the sexes and on the absorption of women into family duties.

But was it really a question of a traditional view? In ancien régime France, the separation between the idle elite and the popular classes at work was social, not sexual: men and women worked together. In *A Political Essay on Commerce* Melon has nothing to say against this; on the contrary, he encourages women working side by side with men. He posits that nature has placed men and women in a reciprocal desire to be together and to please and help one another. He cites the example of the construction of canals and roads, which would be facilitated by this type of reciprocal cooperation (chap. 8). Considering how arduous work on these large construction projects was, one can see that this apologia for mixing the sexes would not have made for any improvement in the condition of women. Nor in their rights. Melon considers women's labor in the same light as slave labor. He finds it beneficial in the colonies and wishes to introduce it in France. He considers work from the point of view of its overall utility, without taking the rights of workers into account. In *The Spirit of the Laws*, Montesquieu counters Melon's arguments with the principle of reciprocity: those who defend slavery in the name of utility would not want to be subjected to it themselves. "Do you want to know whether the desires of each are legitimate in these things? Examine the desires of all" (book XV, chap. 9).

In a mercantilist approach such as Melon's, human beings are resources or objects of wealth in the same way as gold or wheat. That is the basis of a country's power: the transformations of modern strategy require ever-greater numbers of troops. This resource is also the basis of a nation's prosperity: in preindustrial economies, where there is little accumulation of capital, human beings, as an available source of labor that can be cheaply put to work, were was the most important source of wealth, and an "inexhaustible abundance" of them, to use Antoine de Montchrestien's expression, was desirable. What was feared above all else was depopulation: regular disasters, both natural and social, food shortages (or worse, famines), epidemics, and wars endangered not only individual lives but the population at large. Reproduction of the species was a particularly imperative duty, and

populationist literature proliferated. These texts condemned all those who avoided the obligations of marriage, finding fault especially with monastic celibacy. They also sought to prevent the rural exodus, and encouraged immigration.

François Quesnay's articles "Fermiers" (Farmers) and "Grains" (Grain) in the *Encyclopédie* criticize mercantilism by defending the free trade of grain and by laying out the bases of physiocratic theory—the notion of "economic administration." In 1757 Quesnay prepared another article, "Hommes" (Men), which was not published because the *Encyclopédie* had been banned in the meantime. In the latter article, he does not dispute the idea that a strong population is an enviable benefit, the sign of a happy and well-governed people, but he criticizes the objectives of populationist politics. He condemns a warmongering politics that forcibly recruits soldiers, which is contrary to individual rights and turns men away from productive activities. It is agriculture and commerce, he argues, not war, that make the wealth of a nation. Above all, he reverses the prioritizing of men over wealth: it is not a matter of keeping men in until the countryside, he contends, but rather of investing wealth there; men will follow of their own accord, attracted by salaries or profits. This argument implies a definition of men as economic agents rather than a workforce. For Quesnay, work is not the primary human characteristic: he sees work as an expenditure of physical strength that animals or machines can accomplish better than men. He also criticizes generalized and indistinct employment, preferring a rational utilization of resources. It is in this context that he excludes women's work as an evil to be avoided: "The men do the work, or else women and children assist them, but [in that case] the work is very imperfectly done."

There was a change in the way women's work was regarded. In *Recherches et considérations sur la population de la France* (1778; Research and Considerations on the Population of France) Jean-Baptiste Moheau expresses his surprise at the manner in which work is divided according to sex, condemning "this division, which is as ridiculous as it is atrocious, of the functions in society." Men prevail over women, regardless of the qualities peculiar to each sex: "in the very work that, on the grounds of refinement of tact or the delicacy of taste, would seem to be the prerogative of the female sex, men are dominant to the point that women cannot even compete: writing, painting, engraving, watch making, and lens-crafting are all practiced by men." Women, on the other hand, are relegated to arduous physical labor: "One ought to be surprised and indignant to see a large and robust man wield a comb or a needle, unfurl fabrics, work on fittings, while a short distance away women can be found hitched up to plows with animals, or bare-armed, tending the vines, or carrying burdens that are not suitable for them, and meanwhile they cannot even earn the bread they eat" (book II, chap. 15). What Moheau finds most shocking is not only this counterintuitive use of abilities, but its effects on demography: women engaged in hard labor have few children, with many difficulties during pregnancy and childbirth. This constitutes the principal argument: when women are considered, it is not as workers, not even as consumers, but as reproducers, in the name of population requirements.

Demographic concerns thus explain the move away from the frivolities of fashion and the return to the seriousness of motherhood. The moralists had the last word in the quarrel over luxury, with arguments that its defenders were able to understand:

women's luxury might well bring salaries to the poor, but it was depopulating France. An abundance of writings began to appear that sought to "remedy the depopulation due to luxury, celibacy, and libertinism" and encouraged marriage, the sole mechanism that could give "a solid basis to demographic growth" in "civilized nations."

Populationist discourse tended to become specialized, targeting women in particular. An entire literature on marriage drew on new physiological and medical knowledge of sexuality, reproduction, and women's role in it. Texts gave advice on hygiene and on good demographic conduct. Writings of a naturalist orientation picked up where traditional theological and religious literature left off on the same issues. The Christian idea of marriage envisioned procreation as its final goal but also insisted on the obligation of friendship and mutual help between spouses. Procreation was a duty urged upon wives. In the *Dictionnaire des cas de conscience* (1733; Dictionary of Cases of Conscience), Fromageau discusses the case of a woman who was breast-feeding her baby and asked her confessor whether she could refuse to fulfill her conjugal duties "without sinning." He responds: "The wife should, if she is able, put her child with a wet-nurse in order to make herself available to her husband's infirmity by giving him what is his due, for fear that he fall into some sin that is contrary to conjugal purity." Public health literature supported a radically opposite point of view. In insistent propaganda for breast-feeding, the duties of motherhood prevailed over those of the wife. Thus, social relationships were of less importance than women fulfilling their natural functions.

When economy prevailed over trade, there was a dissociation between the functions of production and reproduction, economy and demography. Political economy entailed the promotion within the public sphere of chores that were basic to domestic activity: these were now activities that connected individuals and were socially appreciated and measured. The functions of reproduction originated in the private sphere, the intimacy of the family—a secret place in which individual behavior, far from being validated, was seen instead as an attempt at escaping from the collective duty of the propagation of the species. Thus, in *Recherches et considérations sur la population de la France*, Moheau expresses his outrage at attempts at birth control: "these disastrous secrets, unknown to all animals but mankind—these secrets have penetrated into the countryside; even in the villages they are deceiving nature." He calls for a "reestablishment of morality," that is to say, moral holism.

The economic perspective affirmed individualism and the capacity to build a human world in which the rationality of individual behavior was sufficient reason. In contrast, the demographic perspective entailed holistic reasoning, integrating individuals into overarching totalities. Population studies led to an understanding of how a natural function, the preservation of the species, was achieved with the help of social institutions that subjected individuals, women in particular, to norms that became more restrictive as their justifications became more complex. In his explanation of demographic phenomena in *The Spirit of the Laws*, Montesquieu brings together references to the individual and considerations that touch upon the species and the family, thus showing the interconnections between the natural and the social. The complexity of his explanation of the ban on incest, both universal and extremely variable, is a good example (book XXVI, chap. 14). According to Montesquieu, divorce

must not contradict the principle of free consent (he condemns the spousal repudiation practiced in Muslim countries because only the husband could take the initiative), but it can be justified only by a populationist objective: "the fundamental principle of divorce which suffers the dissolution of one marriage only in the expectation of another" (book XXVI, chap. 9).

The field of demography, pioneered in France by Moheau, was advanced in a highly moralizing discourse that called upon women to marry, incited them to procreate, and enjoined them to breast-feed their children, because by entrusting their children to a wet-nurse, they were "simultaneously betraying their duties as citizens, wives, and mothers" (Moheau book II, chap. 7). Prostitution was stigmatized, the general theme being that "debauchery does not populate the land in any way." In this regard Moheau's study merely continued what Montesquieu had already affirmed, namely that "Illicit unions contribute little to the propagation of the species" (*The Spirit of the Laws*, book XXIII, chap. 2). Similarly, Montesquieu had condemned debauchery in the name of nature: "Therefore, it is not true that incontinence follows the laws of nature; on the contrary, it violates them. It is modesty and discretion that follow these laws" (book XVI, chap. 12).

There was at least one person who took the opposite view: Diderot. In the *Supplément au voyage de Bougainville* (1772; *Supplement to the Voyage of Bougainville*), he presents the defense of Miss Polly Baker, brought before a court in Boston because, "pregnant for the fifth time," she owed her title of mother only to her "dissolute morals." She was incensed by the unfair law that imposed a fine on her: "Is it a crime to increase the number of His Majesty's subjects in a new country which lacks inhabitants?" This case, fabricated but presented as authentic in *L'histoire philosophique et politique des établissements et du commerce des Européens dans les deux Indes* (1770; *A Philosophical and Political History of the Settlements and Trade of the Europeans in the East and West Indies*) by the abbé Raynal (to which Diderot contributed), fits in with the general thematic lines of the *Supplement*, in which Diderot criticizes the moral and religious codes that constrict civilized societies and contrasts those codes with the mores of Tahiti, which are healthier because they follow only one code, that of nature.

In the *Supplement*, Diderot tells the story of Orou, a Tahitian, who has welcomed into his home one of expedition's members, a chaplain. After a "wholesome and frugal meal," Orou introduces "his wife and his three daughters, each of them naked" to the chaplain, suggesting that he spend the night with the one of his choice. "The chaplain replied that his religion, his holy orders, morality and decency all prohibited him from accepting Orou's offer." The chaplain ends up by letting himself be convinced. Orou explains to him that it would be very wrong to thank him. It is not so much a matter of his guest's pleasure as of the best interests of his country: "We didn't ask you for money; we didn't loot your ships; we cared nothing for your produce; but our wives an daughters drew blood from your veins. When you've gone you will have left children. Don't you think that this tribute seized from your person, from you very flesh, surpasses all others?"

At the beginning of the text, an old man salutes Bougainville's departure with a fierce and virtuous speech denouncing the enterprise of colonial domination: it is a pastiche of Rousseau's discourse on the need to keep virtue separate from corruption. Orou's discourse is more subversive: he radically reverses the connection between the savage and the civilized. Sexual relations with indigenous women are far from being one of the modes of the white man's domination; instead, the reverse is true, since it is the chaplain who has been appropriated by the natives and made to contribute. In this equivalence between sperm and money, the model of commerce and the generalization of networks of connection are maintained. The distinction between demography and economics does not have to be made: the circulation of women and men is homologous to the circulation of goods, and sexual behaviors can be construed as economic behaviors.

Nevertheless, this free exchange does not escape from normativity. Since the end is reproduction, sexuality is permissible only for young people of reproductive age. And while "[t]he birth of a child brings domestic and public joy" (the unfortunate Polly Baker notwithstanding), a sterile girl is held in disgrace. In his criticism of excessive moral codes in the *Supplement*, Diderot particularly condemns marriage, which makes a woman into the property of a man and requires the promise of a faithfulness that is impossible to maintain, and "which violates the nature and liberty of male and female alike in chaining them to one another for the whole of their lives." To be sure, the women of Tahiti were chained to no one, but they were compelled to procreate. Did that correspond to Montesquieu's principle of reciprocity? Would anyone choose to be a woman in Tahiti?

At the end of the *Supplement*, the two interlocutors who have presented the argument wonder what their wives would think of the topics they have just debated. "Probably the opposite of what they say," one of them suggests. In any case, the issue could not be avoided: when society began to question the nature and the identity of women, it was up to women to intervene.

Sexual Identity versus Family Life

In 1772 Antoine-Léonard Thomas, an Academician and a friend of the philosophes, published his *Essay on the Character, Manners, and Genius of Women in Different Ages*. This historical panorama owes a great deal to Montesquieu: the opposition between the virtuous austerity that ancient republics imposed upon women by isolating them, and the courtly model of monarchic gallantry is again in evidence. At the same time, Thomas presents the different themes that had been debated since the 16th century in the *querelle des femmes* (an ongoing debate about the condition of women). These themes include that of women "adored and oppressed," their access to knowledge, their nature, and their inferiority or superiority compared to men. Thomas himself does not take sides, juxtaposing opinions that are sometimes contradictory.

In a letter of 14 March 1772 to the abbé Galiani, sent along with Thomas's book, Madame d'Épinay reports seeing in it nothing but a pompous display of tired clichés about unimportant issues: "so many commonplaces! Are they more sensitive? More accountable in friendship than men? are they more this? are they more that?" Rejecting "all these details . . . small, ordinary, and not very philosophical," Madame d'Épinay firmly states her conviction that men and women are equal: "since men and women have the same nature and the same constitution, they are susceptible to the same failings, the same virtues, and the same vices" (*Correspondance*). She adds two corollaries to her thesis: the differences between men and women are attributable

not to nature but to education, and this "denatures" women by making them inferior and subordinating them to men. Madame d'Épinay lays particular emphasis on the "ignorance" to which women have been confined by turning their education toward the "pleasant talents." All this, according to Madame d'Épinay, is "obvious"; indeed, her arguments are the same as those of François Poulain de La Barre, who, in his treatise *De l'égalité des deux sexes* (1673; *The Woman As Good As the Man; or, The Equality of Both Sexes*), who saw in sexual inequality the very type of prejudice that attributes to nature what comes from common usage, namely the importance of instruction and access to knowledge.

However, denouncing inequality does not necessarily imply an affirmation of equality: one may also reverse the hierarchy of relations. Thus, D'Alembert condemns the oppressive relationship inherent in male tyranny, but he does so only to launch into comparisons between greater and lesser, male and female qualities that Madame d'Épinay mocks. Even with respect to intellectual qualities, he affirms not equality but difference, even when it is to the advantage of women: "Descartes," he asserts in his *Lettre de M. d'Alembert à M. J.-J. Rousseau sur l'article de Genève* (1759; Letter from M. d'Alembert to M. J.-J. Rousseau), "judged them to be more suitable for philosophy than us." The clear declaration by Madame d'Épinay in favor of equality thus stood out against a defense such as D'Alembert's, which seemed admirable more for its good intentions than for the rigor of its arguments.

In response to Madame d'Épinay, who sought Galiani's philosophical position since she was looking for "new ideas" on the question, the abbé sent her a "rough draft of a dialogue on women." In this, by setting up an inequality of nature, which has nothing to do with education, between men and women, he resolutely takes the opposite view of the theses she had expounded. He presents his ideas as "paradoxes," that is to say, as positions that fly in the face of the general opinion (whose spokesperson Madame d'Épinay became) by presenting the opposing view as a philosophical truth: women are, by nature, inferior to men, "sickly" beings. On this score, his views converge with the idea put forth by Diderot in his criticism of Thomas's book (published in Grimm's *Correspondence* and revised several times, Diderot's critique was eventually incorporated into an opuscule, *Sur les femmes* [1772; *On Women*]). Diderot posits a sexual identity that absorbs Woman entirely: "Woman carries within her an organ that is susceptible to terrible spasms; it toys with her and arouses all manner of phantoms in her imagination."

The Aristotelian tradition, seeing in the female body only a derivation of the male body, made woman into a "failed man," a "monster." Studies done in the 18th century on the physiology of sexuality and reproduction, especially on women's role in it, would insist on the difference between the sexes and allow a study of female sexuality that did not take the male as the norm. The physician Théophile de Bordeu related female sexuality to the totality of women's physiological functions. The conclusions he drew were of a femininity dominated by sexuality, to the point of pathological unbalance. Diderot borrows this idea, thus transforming the novelistic conceit used in *Les bijoux indiscrets* (1748; *The Indiscreet Jewels*)—women as talking vaginas—into a scientific truth.

The medicalization of the discourse on women ushered in the idea of female hysteria, which, in the 19th century, marked the way in which medical discourse invested women's bodies in the networks of psychiatric knowledge and power. Diderot instead adopted a question of naturalizing anthropological discourse: his *Supplement to the Voyage of Bougainville* focuses on the natural state of human beings ("male and female" rather than man and woman) in order to contrast it to the restrictive artificiality of moral and religious codes. The article entitled "Droit naturel" (Natural Law) in the *Encyclopédie* attempts to base the duties of social activity in what is natural to the human species—duties that the article "Droit de la nature et des gens" (Law of Nature and Humanity) instead endorses by means of a metaphysics that conforms to the theological dogmas of Christianity. One might well assume, then, that Diderot countered the thesis of equality with that of woman's sexual identity essentially for antireligious reasons.

The thesis of equality as expounded by Madame d'Épinay is not a legal thesis: she does not assert an equality of rights, but an identity of nature between men and women. Cartesian metaphysics is perfectly suited to uphold such a thesis. Separating soul and body, it posits that sexual difference, which influences only the body, has no effect on spiritual identity: "everyone knows that the difference between the sexes concerns the body alone and exists only in those parts that serve to propagate human nature" wrote Florent de Puisieux in 1750, in *La femme n'est pas inférieure à l'homme* (Woman Is Not Inferior to Man). This dualism, which proclaims the spiritual identity of man and woman, is in complete agreement with Christian dogma: the soul, which is purely spiritual, has no sex.

By way of its opposition to spiritualist metaphysics, Diderot's materialist thesis targeted Christian dogma. The soul has a sex; or, more precisely, that which is interpreted as the independent existence of the soul, freed from material weight, is nothing other than a manifestation of sex. In Diderot's view, from hysteria to devotion and mysticism, there is no interruption of continuity: "Nothing is more closely related than ecstasy, visions, prophesy, revelations, rapturous poetry, and hysteria" (*On Women*). Linking mysticism to sex explodes religious identity: it is in that place where souls communicate, oblivious of their bodies, that the difference between man and woman, the truth of sexuality, is to be found.

In order to convince religious thinkers of the innocence of sexuality and love, in his article "Jouissance" (Enjoyment) in the *Encyclopédie* Diderot uses a language familiar to religious discourse, that of identity:

Among the objects that nature everywhere offers to our desires, you who have a soul, tell me if there is anything more worthy of your pursuit, anything that can make us happier than the possession and enjoyment of a being who thinks and feels as you do, who has the same ideas, who experiences the same sensations, the same ecstasies.

The development of the article ruptures that equality; beginning with identity, it progressively specifies difference and otherness. Understood as a natural and purely physical connection, sexuality does not order the sexes, nor does it differentiate individuals: "Immodest Nature, if you think her so, impels each sex towards the other with equal force" (*Supplement*). But as soon as sexuality becomes more complicated by turning into love, the relationship then established no longer links an individual to a sex, but a woman to a man: "[W]hen woman began to discriminate, when she appeared to take care in choosing between several men upon whom passion cast her glances, there was one who stopped them, who could flatter himself that he was preferred." The love relationship is intersubjective, it mobilizes feeling and passion and extends to the spirit: "the soul was possessed with an almost divine enthusiasm."

Moving from the general and abstract finality of human reproduction to the individual reality of pleasure, Diderot's approach is antihierarchical. It so radically refuses the notion of sexual otherness being subsumed within a superior identity that Diderot actually speaks of women as "the being in nature most closely resembling men" (review of Robinet, *Sur le parallèle de la condition et des facultés de l'homme* [On the Parallel of the Condition and Faculties of Man]), as if men and women belonged to two different species. Thus, Diderot insists a great deal more on difference and otherness than he addresses equality. What he criticizes above all else in Thomas's work is the neutrality that affected the latter's discourse on sex: "He wanted his book to have no sex; and unfortunately he has succeeded all too well. It is a hermaphrodite that has neither the spirit of man nor the softness of woman." In Diderot's view, any discussion of sex necessarily involves a sexualized discourse, and he fully takes on the consequences of his position: it is from the vantage point of a lover that he speaks of women in *On Women*.

Diderot's discourse, necessarily masculine, called for a feminine counterpart of the same order. In the *Supplement* Diderot stages this feminine discourse, making Polly Baker speak. He provides an elegant rewrite of the story of the Indian woman of Orinoco who abandons her newborn daughter to die of exposure in order to spare her the suffering she would have had to endure as a woman. But, as we saw with the old Tahitian man, the solitary tirade was not the last pronouncement of truth for Diderot. His preferred philosophical mode is that of dialogue, of the multiplicity of positions in speech. *Le rêve de d'Alembert* (D'Alembert's Dream) shows the character of Bordeu, the physiologist, by his side, as well as Julie de Lespinasse, who continues the libertine tradition (illustrated by Bernard le Bovier de Fontenelle in the *Entretiens sur la pluralité des mondes* [1686; *A Conversation on the Plurality of Worlds*] of women's presence in scholarly debate. Not one of the speakers occupies a privileged position from which the truth may be spoken: certainly not the philosopher who is only heard to dream. Moreover, Bordeu, the physician, does not invoke scientific authority when philosophy is challenged: Julie de Lespinasse's presence prevents him from doing so. She intervenes not only through her ignorance, asking for explanations in layman's terms, but also as a woman whose sexual otherness challenges the very possibility of an objectively neutral discussion of sex.

Truth can emerge only when the various positions are put in relation to one another. This suggests a social model of access to knowledge that, rejecting any dominant or centralized position, places all positions on an equal level, without merging them into indeterminacy or exposing them to frivolity—that is to say, to the indifferent repetition of the same—for each position integrates its difference. This was the model of the *Encyclopédie*, that of "community of scholars" serving as a plural author: no one occupied a central position, especially not Diderot, since it was his role to "connect the links in the chain," to maintain communication between different contributors. It was in this way that Diderot proposed opening philosophical commerce up to women's commerce: the greater the number of discursive positions, the better the likelihood of arriving at the truth.

In his critique, Diderot mocks Thomas's serious style, countering that one should adopt the frivolous or gallant language one used in the presence of women also when writing about them: "You should dip your pen in the rainbow and sprinkle the dust of butterfly wings on the lines" (*On Women*). This was not merely a question of style or gallant frivolity, but an effort to integrate the position of women into the discourse about them, passing from unity to plurality. The remaining task was to persuade women to accept the invitation extended to them and get them to speak. Thus, when he was writing the article "Jouissance," he never stopped urging Sophie Volland to give him her opinion on different moral situations that involved the relationships between men and women. Considering the way in which Diderot received her answers, it does not seem that she satisfied his expectations.

The abbé Galiani used a light-hearted, conversational tone to offer his ideas on women. Responding to him in a letter of 20 June 1772, Madame d'Épinay congratulates him on "this charming dialogue"; they could not have done better in Paris. "It is too cheerful, just as light-hearted, just as frivolous as ever, but that touch of childlike gaiety is gone" (*Correspondance*). She thus recognizes the social success of a conception of women that is the opposite of her own, but she does not deign to respond to it: "Your dialogue pleased us greatly, it is cheerful, profound, and true," she acknowledges (23 May 1772). One is thus justified in doubting that in the 18th century gallant language was really the one in which women could speak about their own nature and position. On these questions, Madame d'Épinay published a series of pedagogical conversations between a mother and her daughter, *Les conversations d'Émilie* (1775; *The Conversations of Emily*). Indisputably a critique of Rousseau, these dialogues are pronounced from the very position he adopted to speak about women: the intimacy of the family and educational connections.

"To maintain vaguely that the two sexes are equal and that their duties are the same, is to lose oneself in vain declaiming": this opening of book V of *Émile* is addressed as much "women [who] do not cease to proclaim" that they are subjugated, as to "gallant partisans of the fair sex" who flatter them in their complaints. Rousseau was well acquainted with the longstanding *querelle des femmes*. Around 1748, when he was secretary to Madame Dupin, she had him compile more than 100 works for a book she intended to write on the question of women, the first draft of which (330 pages in length) she dictated to him. In 1735, while living with Madame de Warens, Rousseau himself wrote a fragment, "Sur les femmes" (On Women) in which he spoke of the "tyranny of men," and affirmed that they had "deprived" women of their freedom. The part of *Émile* that concerns Sophie might appear to be Rousseau's last word on this topic.

However, Rousseau's position is not only polemic and reactive. When he concludes, in *Émile*, that "there is no equivalence at all between the sexes as to the result of the sex act" and that only women should be held rigorously to conjugal fidelity because "[i]t is up to the sex that nature has charged with the bearing of children to be responsible for them to the other," he

is merely reiterating the arguments Montesquieu had already presented in *The Spirit of the Laws*. Montesquieu too opines that "the political and civil laws of almost all people, have with reason . . . required from women a degree of restraint and of continence that they do not require of men" (book XXVI, chap. 8). They based themselves on nature, which has "marked the infidelity of women by certain signs" (book XXVI, chap. 8). Here, Montesquieu is explicitly targeting the Christian Church, which, by looking at marriage "only according to purely spiritual ideas," imposes the same duties of fidelity on both spouses. Thus, the thesis of equality was once again perceived as a religious thesis, and it was criticized for not knowing the reality it claimed to inform. In the difference between the sexes, Rousseau sought an explicit principle on the basis of which he could construct the social order.

In the state of nature, as described in the *Discours sur l'origine de l'inégalité* (1755; *Discourse on the Origin of Inequality*), men and women lead the same solitary life. Motherhood is not an obstacle for women, who take care of their own needs; sexual relations are momentary and are not consolidated into lasting relationships. This situation derives, first of all, from the fact that sexual inequality, like all inequalities, is not active in the state of nature: only with the emergence of the family are male and female roles differentiated and prioritized. This is due above all to the fact that dependency, which is the essential condition of women, is not primarily defined by its link to nature: undoubtedly, woman is weaker than man, but this weakness is a relative, not absolute. Woman's dependency is a dependency in relation to others, a social dependency. Capable of destroying the family by her infidelity, woman is not only obliged to be faithful but to *appear* to be so: "What people think of her is no less important than what she actually is." Woman therefore finds herself continuously exposed to social judgment upon which she depends.

Émile has been educated to be independent. He obeys only nature, not his tutor. He bases his conduct on what is useful to him, and he learns a profession that will make him self-sufficient. His honor lies in himself alone. For Sophie it is quite the contrary: dependency is cultivated. Far from allowing her to rely on herself, those around her urge her to relate to others, to rely on her desire to please, in order to bring her to the point where she will conduct her life based on what others might think of her. The education of girls "disturbs" them, "subjugates" them, "constrains" them, and teaches them to keep themselves in a state of dependency from which they will never emerge: "they never cease to be subjected either to a man or to the judgments of men" (*Émile*). The education of girls is an education not just in service, but in enslavement.

By following these opposite paths, the education of boys and girls develops inequality into a polarity of male and female—the principle of organization and differentiation in social functions and structures. Men control the public sphere and politics; women are allotted the private domain of the family and, beyond that, everything that relates to "conduct," "preservation," and "manners"—in short, morality. Making sexual difference work entails the separation of men and women. Criticizing Plato's *Republic* in book V of *Émile*, Rousseau denounces "that civil promiscuity which throughout confounds the two sexes in the same employments and in the same labors." The description of life on Clarens's estate in *Eloïsa* emphasizes the separation of the sexes both in work and leisure time: "even husbands themselves are not excepted out of this rule," he explains (letter CXXXII [IV:XII])[2]. Womanly modesty maintains a distance between them and their husbands: Julie (referred to as Eloïsa in the 18th-century English translation) and M. De Wolmar live in the same house but do not spend their days together.

Of course, this sexually segregated society is a republican society: Claire, visiting Geneva, observes, "The manners of the English have reached as far as this country; and the men living more separate from the women than in ours"(letter CLV [VI: V]). From Paris, Saint-Preux sends the heroine a "letter on women" that is a presentation of the monarchic model of the "commerce of women" and court society. Eloïsa responds to this by calling for a separation of the sexes that is also a separation of social spheres. "What would become of us and the state? What would become of our celebrated authors, our illustrious academicians if the ladies should give up the direction of matters of literature and business and apply themselves only to the affairs of their family?" (letter XCII [II:XXVII]). Saint-Preux begins his critique by condemning the corruption of mores, but even more important, "They [women] are authorised to spend all their time in the company of men; and hence it is the behaviour of each sex seems to be copied from the other" (letter LXXXVI [II:XXI]): the promiscuity of the sexes erases their difference. That might be appropiate for monarchic government, which is characterized by uniform submission. However, political freedom has other requirements: "In a republic, men are wanted," Rousseau insists in his *Lettre à d'Alembert* (1758; *A Letter from M. Rousseau . . . to M. D'Alembert Concerning the Effects of Theatrical Entertainments on the Manners of Mankind*).

Here Rousseau returns to what had come out of Montesquieu's critique of Hobbes: by defining political relationships only in individualist terms, one ends up with despotism in which "man is a creature that obeys a creature that wants" (*The Spirit of the Laws*, book III, chap. 10). What Rousseau demonstrates, both in his depiction of the natural state and in his definition of the law as general will, is that if one pushes equality to its farthest extreme, one ends up with indeterminacy and jeopardizes the concept of the individual. This was why, to put an end to the inequalities that had developed with society, it was not enough to reestablish natural equality, for equality in the state of nature is identical to its opposite: the extreme despotism resulting from the degeneration of governments. Individuals under extreme despotism are equal because they are nothing. The loss of individuality means the loss of liberty. How, then, is it possible to reconcile equality and liberty, to reject inequality without instituting despotism? Modern individualism dissociates every traditional social entity into which individuals have been inserted and which qualifies them. However, this individualism cannot escape from the problem of qualification. Hence the interest in sexual difference, for "inequality is not a human institution—or at least, it is the work not of prejudice but of reason" (*Émile*, book V). Women are needed so that men may be citizens,

not individuals without distinguishing characteristics and subjected to a despotic power.

Of all political theoreticians of the modern age, Hobbes was perhaps the one who made the most radical attempt to generate a model of political relations from individual data alone. As we have seen, he did not succeed in this attempt, in that he brought hierarchical relations into play. Rousseau made the articulations between individualism and holism explicit by positing sexual difference at their pivot point, which allowed him to describe the individual subjected to the law as citizen and to link the political arena of equality to a social order with redefined components. The critique of the family model of political authority in the article "Économie politique" (Political Economy) in the *Encyclopédie*—which specifically targets Filmer—has as its correlate a reexamination of the political model of family relationships. A "good husband" is not "lord and master," Claire states in *Eloïsa*, The family, having become above all woman's sphere and the locus of maternal relations, was thus primed to serve as the pole for the moral reform Rousseau advocates at the beginning of *Émile*: he wants women to return to the home and breastfeed their children, and believes that society as a whole would find itself reformed in consequence. He thus attributes to women their own specific kind of efficacy in the realm of morality, customs, and the shaping of public opinion. Rousseau's *Letter . . . to D'Alembert* develops this link between mores and public opinion that endows women, who are simultaneously participants in and subjected to public judgment, with a censorship role in the old style. The complementarity of laws and mores then becomes apparent: it was by passing into mores that laws actually went into effect.

Rousseau's republican discourse mobilized women and the ordinary people into the same fight against the aristocracy. Where Montesquieu and Hume had spoken of the progressive dissemination of aristocratic mores to all of society, Rousseau exposes the differentiating practices that aristocratic women adopt in order to maintain social distinctions. Banking on the fact that "the minds of the people were deeply impressed with a sense of bashfulness and modesty," they have rejected all decency and all modesty in order to distinguish themselves from the people: "Thus they cease to be women, to avoid being confounded with the vulgar; they prefer their rank to their sex, and imitate women of pleasure that they themselves may be above imitation" (*Eloïsa*, letter LXXXVI [II:XXI]). Rousseau thus advocates reversing the hierarchy that valorizes rank over sex and tries to rally women around the joys of femininity: having children, loving a husband and keeping him close, and the companionship of other women. In contrast to the fierce competition among high society women who tolerate no rivals, Rousseau presents the complicit and tender friendship between Claire and Eloïsa.

At the same time that he disqualifies the monarchic model, Rousseau presents, in a social order based on the separation of the sexes, a completely renewed republican model in his depiction of the family: that of happy intimacy that pleases men and should appeal to women.

If girls are "quite drawn to marriage," Montesquieu writes in *The Spirit of the Laws*, it is because there is no other way to escape from the condition of being a girl, that of complete dependency; indeed, young women can hope to attain "pleasure and liberty only by marriage" (book XXIII, chap. 9). By affirm-

---

[2] In William Kenrick's 1784 translation, the letters are numbered continuously, whereas a fresh sequence of numbers begins in each of the six volumes of the original French. To facilitate cross-referencing of quoted passages, numbers of the letter from Kenrick's translation appear first in parentheses, followed by the corresponding French volume and letter number in brackets.

ing "our sex cannot purchase liberty but through slavery" (*Eloïsa*, letter CXXI [IV:II]), Rousseau's Claire rather soberly echoes him. It would seem that a woman's only opportunity to escape dependency on men—whether on her father or her husband—comes when she chooses the man she will obey. Only then, rejecting any holistic insertion, does Rousseau posit an individual right: he clearly states that it is people that ought to be wed, not conditions. All of *Eloïsa* is a plea against forced marriages.

This right to choose a husband freely, which Sophie's parents recognize without hesitation, is in fact denied to Eloïsa by her father because of his social prejudices. This is the substance of the novel, in the course of which the reader learns why the heroine does not marry the man she loves and instead marries the man her father has chosen. But this interval of time also allows Eloïsa to transform a dependency that is imposed upon her into a desired one. *Eloïsa* is a true educational novel, a bildungsroman, in which the heroine invents her liberty through the obstacles she encounters. She is a free subject who, as Jean Ehrard has shown, claims the rights of the heart and the rights of the body until her death: "A revolutionary morality that stands out against the ideological conservatism of Rousseau and contradicts—without canceling it, of course—the moralizing and spiritualist discourse that runs through the entire novel" (see Ehrard).

At the same time that she is being educated, Rousseau's heroine invents a "very intimate society" that unites, or tries to unite, those things that not one of the social models of the condition of women (despotic, monarchic, or republican) really manages to bring together: reproduction and pleasure, love and friendship. "A virtuous man cannot have a better friend than his wife" (*Eloïsa*, letter CLVI [VI:VI]), she declares. Dependency is thus transformed into equality—to such a degree that a complete reversal is achieved: "Incomparable Eloïsa who exercises in the simplicity of private life the despotic power of wisdom and beneficence" (letter CXLIII [V:VII]), Saint-Preux cries out, echoing Claire's earlier comment: "Eloïsa, you were born to rule. Your empire is more despotic than any in the world" (letter CXXI [IV:II]).

The heroine's "despotism," her "empire," are metaphors, and it is only because the family, for Rousseau, is not a political model that he can use them as terms of praise. But these metaphors reveal that relations between men and women continued to be analyzed in terms of power, as relationships based on strength. Attack, defense, victory, and weakness: sexual relations are a combat in which men have the advantage of strength. But women, playing on desire, can turn the situation around to their advantage. This is what Rousseau calls "the empire of women"—using a term frequently used in the *querelle des femmes*—in order to turn their condemnation of male oppression and their aspiration to equality back against them. Montesquieu echoes this idea in number 1726 of his *Pensées*: "It should be noted that with the exception of cases born from certain circumstances, women have never claimed equality: for they already have so many other natural advantages that equality of power is still an empire for them."

Equality of power implies an equilibrium that is necessarily unstable, and might cannot generate right, nor can despotism lead to freedom. In *The Social Contract* Rousseau shows that political liberty can only exist under a government of laws. That Eloïsa's condition may be one of "empire," "reign," or "despotism" not only attributes a rather ambiguous power to her, but, more important, shows that the conjugal union is regulated by holistic integration (she reigns in her family but does not leave it), rather than by a legal relationship between equal individuals. The polarization of society around the opposition of female and male, by separating the political from the domestic, places the domestic sphere beyond the application of the law.

Thus, women cannot simultaneously be situated within the discourse of empire and the discourse of rights. By choosing women's empire, would Rousseau have succeeded in seducing them? This is what Condorcet is suggesting when he takes it upon himself to defend women's access to the rights of citizens in his *Lettres d'un bourgeois de New Haven*:

> I am speaking of their right to equality not of their empire; one might suspect me of a secret desire to diminish it; and since Rousseau has won their approval, by saying that they were made only to take care of us and capable of tormenting us, I cannot expect them to declare themselves in my favor.

In *A Vindication of the Rights of Woman* Mary Wollstonecraft hurls the same accusation at Rousseau and pointedly refers him back to his own declaration in *The Social Contract*: "One believes himself the others' master, and yet is more a slave than they" (book I, chap. 1). From this perspective, seduction is a trap: whether despots or slaves, women will never be free human beings, but simple objects of men's desire. Thus Sophie is nothing but a "chimera," a "voluptuous reverie" on the part of Rousseau, the philosopher of "lasciviousness"; he has therefore never really escaped the discourse of gallantry.

Conclusion

Women's rights or women's empire? The strength of the opposition and the virulence of the criticism attested to the novelty of the situation. The American Revolution, and then the French Revolution, brought politics, hitherto strictly the "secret of the prince," into the public arena: it became the place of affirmation and realization of liberty. Why were women not there? Why did they wait for freedom to come from the slow transformation of their condition when they could have proclaimed their freedom right away? Why did they seek independence in the intimacy of the home when they could publicly affirm it? The tortuous or hidden paths to freedom seemed obsolete.

These were the paths that had been followed until the eve of the Revolution. Hume in his *Political Essays* and Montesquieu in *The Spirit of the Laws* had indicated the path of moral civilization: court society and the commerce of women did not suppress inequality but compensated for it with "politeness, respect, and generosity," to such a degree that, in Montesquieu's words, "a kind of equality between the two sexes has naturally been introduced" (book XVI, chap. 2). While affirming that men's domination over women was universal, Diderot believed that from the savage state to the civilized state this inequality tended to be attenuated: "Woman, unhappy in cities, is even more unhappy in the depths of the forest" (*On Women*).

Another path was that of the education of girls. In her reproach to Rousseau for perpetuating the slavery of women by cultivating the desire to please in girls, Wollstonecraft returns to one of the classical themes of reflections on education. Madame de Lambert, in *L'avis d'une mère à sa fille* (1728; A Mother's Advice to her Daughter) protests against the education of women: "They are meant to please, they are never taught any lessons in virtue." But would educating women in virtue suffice to lead them to independence? The way in which these themes were approached toward the end of the ancien régime, marked by a renewed interest in questions of education and especially the education of girls, leads one to doubt this. Rather, the defense of virtue seems indicative of the triumph of Rousseauist thought. A question inspired by *Émile* was posed by the Academy of Besançon in 1777: how could the education of women contribute to make men better? Jacques-Henri Bernardin de Saint-Pierre's response was purely Rousseauist: women were educated toward virtue for the moral improvement of men (male beings), without wondering for one moment whether women might not be educated for themselves. In 1783, when the Academy of Châlons-sur-Marne proposed researching the best means for perfecting women's education, Pierre Choderlos de Laclos, in the response he outlined and in the essay he later wrote on the subject, "Des femmes et de leur éducation" (1783; On Women and Their Education), attempted to turn Rousseau's themes on natural equality and its disappearance in the social state to the advantage of his defense of women's equality and their right to a liberal education, letting it be understood that it was not enough to oppose virtue to pleasure; virtue needed to be linked to knowledge as well.

In 1782, a new edition of *The Conversations of Emily* brought Madame d'Épinay the first Montyon prize for the literary work that might bring the greatest good to society. She had been in competition for this prize with Madame de Genlis, the author of another work on the education of girls. In the latter the triumph of Rousseauist thought is evident, for the framework of the family is never transcended: girls are raised to be wives and mothers. *The Conversations of Emily* thus proposes a rather austere preparation for the duties of women; this preparation keeps Emily occupied all day long with useful tasks and teaches her how to be respected by men—that is to say, how to safeguard her reputation. Still, by stimulating Emily to keep herself busy and especially by making her read and learn, Madame d'Épinay wants to enable her heroine to do without others, to escape from that dependency that Rousseau saw as the inevitable condition of women. In the ninth conversation her characters realize that knowledge and science are, indeed, "possessions that nobody can take away from you; that will free you from the dependency on others." In this way, Madame d'Épinay demonstrates that even in the very heart of the family—the place of women's holistic integration—it is possible to open up a space of freedom, which Virginia Woolf would later call "a room of one's own."

For their part, Condorcet and Wollstonecraft offered women the public space of freedom that the Revolution had made possible. That gesture supposes a complete redefinition of the relationship between men and women. Where Rousseau derives the organizing principle of relations between men and women from the difference between the sexes, Wollstonecraft rejects any sexual approach to the question of women, which she calls the "sensual error." In her view, the whole difficulty stems from the fact that men consider women to be feminine beings ("females") rather than human creatures.

In order to replace "rational fellowship instead of slavish obedience" (chap. 9) between the sexes, writes Wollstonecraft, "I do earnestly wish to see the distinction of sex confounded in society unless where love animates the behaviour" (chap. 4). This position is symmetrical to Rousseau's, which allows women access to the public arena only by relegating all sexual behavior to the private sphere, removed from all social relations. Wollstonecraft considers only rational human beings, writing in her introduction: "My own sex, I hope, will excuse me, if I treat them like rational creatures." Rational and not "sensitive": running through every stage of the meaning from "sense" to "sensitive," "sensation," and "sensuality," Wollstonecraft rejects all of these terms outright, criticizing the "fallacious light of sentiment; too often used as a softer phrase for sensuality" (chap. 3). In so doing, she rejects not just Rousseau, but the entire empiricist philosophy of the Enlightenment, which held that sensation was the source of all knowledge, and which was sometimes called "sensualism." Wollstonecraft does not return to intellectualism, but places herself on an openly religious plane: by referring to the duality of soul and body, and to the possibility of controlling one's passions, she links rationality to morality in a discourse heavily marked by Puritanism. She affirms the equality of the sexes from the standpoint of her religious belief in the spiritual oneness of humanity.

This is not Condorcet's position. Loyal to Condillac, in "On the Admission of Women to the Rights of Citizenship" he defines individuals as "sentient beings, capable of acquiring moral ideas and of reasoning concerning these ideas." He shows that women are rational beings like men not by referring to their common spiritual nature, but by establishing the rationality of their behavior, which is that of their interests in a given situation. Condorcet bases his axiological individualism (that of rights) on a methodological individualism, and he refuses to let himself be locked into Rousseau's opposition between sex and rank, acknowledging only differences between individuals, and thus the multiplicity of specific individuals, as relevant. Under these conditions, why should one submit to custom, why give pride of place to a difference between the sexes that had just been shown to be irrelevant?

A distinction must first be made between the rights of man and the rights of citizens, or, returning to the abbé Sieyès's distinction, between passive citizens and active citizens. In the first category, the principle of equal liberty works without limits: "Either no individual of the human species has any true rights or all of them have the same rights." But citizenship is not merely a right, it is also a function, a political act that affects public life. One must be qualified to practice it: throughout the republican tradition, from antiquity to modern times, there has been considerable reflection on the requisite qualities for a citizen: independence, the ability to take an interest in public affairs, and the leisure to do so.

This definition would have sufficed to disqualify women, busy in the home, if the republican model in style of antiquity—that of direct democracy and the assembled people—had prevailed in 1789. Such was not the case. As early as September 1789, Sieyès clearly stated that "France is not, and cannot be, a democracy," and he elaborated upon the distinction between direct democracy in the style of antiquity and modern representative government. In particular, he underscored the consequences of this for citizenship: representation, which entrusts legislative and executive abilities to only a small number of people, allows for the separation of the status of citizen and political capacity that had been combined in the democracies of antiquity. The right of citizenship was no more than the right to vote, and the abilities required for that were minimal: they were the capacities of every rational individual. Condorcet was able to show that the argument justifying the granting of the right to vote to any male individual, without any consideration of his capacities, implied that the same right should be recognized for women. If those men who had neither the leisure time nor the abilities needed to practice a political career could vote, why should women be excluded on the grounds that their domestic duties kept them from it or that they did not have the knowledge needed for legislative work? Abilities were to be demanded of those running for office—and elections certainly were a process of qualification—but not of those who voted; all "sentient beings, capable of acquiring moral ideas and of reasoning concerning these ideas"—women as well as men, without distinction—could fulfill this role.

Such reasoning justified the exclusion of children from the right to vote. But why women? Answering without really answering, invoking "prejudices" or the present state of affairs, Sieyès returns to the model of antiquity, even as he constructs a theoretical difference between the government of the ancients and that of the moderns. This difference, he argues, resides in the fact that modernity has had different effects on men and women. Admitting the rationality of the desire for wealth, modernity has developed production throughout Europe. Modern political systems are based on labor, Sieyès argues, and economic agents are certainly active citizens: they contribute to the social production of wealth. But the same movement that has brought the economy forth from the domestic sphere and allowed it to rise to political dimensions has kept the functions of reproduction inside the home and outside the public sphere. Hence the dissociation of the economy and demography that has led to the exclusion of women from the public sphere. Citizenship may be defined in terms of property or labor, the value of which is publicly determined by the market. Domestic tasks, peculiar to the reproduction of the family, are a private activity, an obscure area that eludes the sphere of exchange in the public realm. Once granted access to the public arena as economic agents, women would be qualified as citizens: for Condorcet as well as for Wollstonecraft, widows, as heads of households responsible for managing the family patrimony, did, in reality, have the independence of citizens.

Domestic servants, women, and children were disqualified from voting for the same reason: kept inside the home, subject to the authority of its head, they were reputed not to have a will of their own. The citizen's independence was first of all an independence of judgment. At this juncture, the discussion of equal rights comes back to the older theme of education, which simultaneously stated the reasons for the actual inferiority of women and the possibility of ending it. From the moment that women were educated like rational beings and not like gracious objects, they would become autonomous, according to Wollstonecraft: that which would cause them to escape from male oppression would at the same time qualify them as citizens. Condorcet expected the development of public education, which would take girls out of the cloister of the family, to reduce the

differences between the sexes and promote women's ability to enjoy their rights.

This led to the development, alongside the discourse on liberty, often based on the assertion that human beings are by nature—whether a metaphysical or theological nature—identical, of a parallel discourse on liberation, the development of the faculties, and the transformation of the conditions of existence. In *Über die bürgerliche Verbesserung der Weiber* (1792; *On Improving the Status of Women*), Theodor Gottlieb von Hippel, a friend and disciple of Kant, joins Condorcet in condemning the inability of the French Revolution to live up to its own legal principles when it excluded women from equal rights. At the same time, he develops a discourse on the improvement in women's condition, their emancipation, that would be a resolute course toward progress and not merely an observation of the involuntary benefits of the civilization of mores. Such a discourse rejects any naturalization of sexual inequality, and is therefore in opposition to Rousseau's thought. Nevertheless, this critique was built on grounds that the latter had opened up: that of human perfectibility and self-education, that of culture.

What prevailed in 1789, with the exclusion of women from citizenship, was not only the Rousseauist discourse on masculine virtue that would lead the 19th-century historian Jules Michelet to remark in *Nos fils* (1870; *Our Sons*) that "*Émile* is a very male book." That type of discourse would explain why the Jacobins adopted Rousseau's model, but not why Sieyès had a change of heart. To account for the latter, one must understand how the exclusion of women served as the foundation for the republican model of sexual polarization of the public and private spheres, and, the dissociation thus achieved, in modern times, between the two great ways of providing for the necessities of life (the preservation of individual existence and that of the species) and between the public sphere of the economy and the intimacy of the family. Slaves in antiquity, once they became free economic agents, could become citizens. This was not the case for women. The renewal of the family model at the end of the ancien régime, the importance of which during the French Revolution has been demonstrated by Lynn Hunt, was the main obstacle to the generalization of revolutionary individualism (see Hunt).

But if the discourse of equality remained a minority voice, this was also due to its own limitations. A universalist discourse that affirmed the individual and denied the feminine, it preserved the ambiguity of a hierarchical neutrality expressed in the masculine. It left open the possibility that a rupture of hierarchical inclusion might permit the emergence of woman capable of taking on, in the first person, her difference and her identity—in a discourse that was both sexualized and situated, and that is visible in the works of Diderot. The latter, indicating the place of that discourse, excluded himself from it and, at the same time, left it in abeyance. Furthermore, the concept of individualism within the discourse on equality excluded any collective understanding of women's condition. Rousseau's discourse, precisely because it was hierarchical and holistic, and because took into account the collective dimension of individual existence, was easily inverted into a discourse of liberation. Indeed, its highlighting of the relationship between sex and rank paved the way for the debates on the relationship between the emancipation of social classes and the liberation of women that were to mark the next era.

It might seem paradoxical that the century of human emancipation was one that pushed women aside and locked them into their condition. But the ultimate paradox is perhaps that, in the very place where their access to equality seems to have been most blocked, the basis for the discourse on women's identity and women's liberation was put into place.

Bibliography

Sources

Alembert, Jean Le Rond d', *Lettre de M. d'Alembert à M. J.J. Rousseau sur l'article Genève, tiré du VII° volume de l'Encyclopédie*, Amsterdam: Chatelain, 1759

Alembert, Jean Le Rond d', *Pensées de Monsieur d'Alembert*, Paris: Dufour et Costard, 1774

Bret, Antoine, *Mémoires sur la vie de Mademoiselle de Lenclos*, Amsterdam: Rollin et Bauche, 1751

Clicquot de Blervache, Simon, *Considérations sur le commerce, et en particulier sur les compagnies, sociétés et maîtrises*, Amsterdam: n.p., 1758

Condorcet, Jean-Antoine-Nicolas de Caritat, marquis de, "Sur l'admission des femmes au droit de cité," 3 juillet 1790, no 5, Journal de la Société de 1789, as "On the Admission of Women to the Rights of Citizenship," in *Selected Writings*, by Condorcet, edited by Keith Michael Baker, Indianapolis, Indiana: Bobbs-Merrill, 1976

Condorcet, Jean-Antoine-Nicolas de Caritat, marquis de, *Quatre lettres d'un bourgeois de New Haven sur l'unité de la législation*, in *Recherches historiques et politiques sur les États-Unis de l'Amérique septentrionale . . . par un citoyen de Virginie* [Filippo Mazzei], *avec quatre lettres d'un bourgeois de New-Haven* [J.-A.-N. de Condorcet] *sur l'unité de la législation*, 4 vols., Colle, France, and Paris: Froullé, 1788

Condorcet, Jean-Antoine-Nicolas de Caritat, marquis de, *Sur les élections, et autre textes*, Paris: Fayard, 1986

Diderot, Denis, *Denis Diderot's The Encyclopedia: Selections*, edited and translated by Stephen J. Gendzier, New York: Harper and Row, 1967

Diderot, Denis, *Oeuvres complètes*, 15 vol., edited by Roger Lewinter, Paris: Club Français du Livre, 1969–73

Diderot, Denis, *Supplement to the Voyage of Bougainville*, in *Political Writings*, by Diderot, translated and edited by John Hope Mason and Robert Wokler, Cambridge: Cambridge University Press, 1992

Diderot, Denis, *Sur les femmes*, in *Diderot, Oeuvres*, edited by André Billy, Paris: Bibliothèque de la Pléiade/Gallimard, 1951

Encyclopédie, ou dictionnaire raisonné des sciences, des arts et des métiers, 17 vols., Paris: Libraires Associés, 1751–65

Éphémérides du citoyen, ou, Chronique de l'esprit national, 1765–66; later *Éphémérides du citoyen, ou, Bibliotheque raisonnée des sciences morales et politiques*, 1767–72

Épinay, Louise de la Live, marquise d', *Les conversations d'Émilie*, Leipzig: Crusius, 1774; as *The Conversations of Emily*, London: Marshall, 1787

Forbonnais, François Véron Duverger de, *Examen des avantages et des désavantages de la prohibition des toiles peintes*, Marseille, France: Carapatria, 1755

Gournay, Jacques-Claude-Marie Vincent de, *Observations sur l'examen des avantages et des désavantages de la prohibition des toiles peintes*, Marseille, France: n.p., 1755

Grotius, Hugo, *The Rights of War and Peace: Including The Law of Nature and of Nations*, translated by A.C. Campbell, Washington, D.C., and London: Dunne, 1901; reprint, Westport, Connecticut: Hyperion Press, 1993

Hippel, Theodor Gottlieb von, "Über die bürgerliche Verbesserung der Weiber," Berlin: Voss, 1792 as *On Improving the Status of Women*, translated and edited by Timothy F. Sellner, Detroit, Michigan: Wayne State University Press, 1979

Hobbes, Thomas, *Leviathan*, edited by Richard Tuck, Cambridge and New York: Cambridge University Press, 1991

Hume, David, *Essays Moral, Political, and Literary*, in *Essays and Treatises on Several Subjects*, new edition, 2 vols., London: Cadell, 1777

Laclos, Choderlos de, "Des femmes et de leur éducation," in *Oeuvres complètes*, edited by Laurent Versini, Paris: Gallimard, 1979

Lambert, Anne Thérèse de Marguenat de Courcelles, marquise de, *Avis d'une mère à son fils et à sa fille*, Paris: Ganeau, 1728; as *A Mother's Advice to Her Son and Daughter*, Boston: Lord, 1814

Lambert, Anne Thérèse de Marguenat de Courcelles, marquise de, *Avis d'une mère à sa fille: Suivis des réflexions sur les femmes*, Paris: Louis, 1804

Locke, John, *Two Treatises of Government*, 1690; reprint, edited by Peter Laslett, Cambridge, England: Cambridge University Press, 1988

Maggetti, Daniel and Georges Dulac, editors, *Correspondances*, Paris: Éditions Desjonquères, 1992– (letters between Ferdinando Galiani and Louise d'Épinay)

Mandeville, Bernard, *The Fable of the Bees; or, Private Vices, Publick Benefits*, 2 vols., edited by F.B. Kaye, Oxford: Clarendon Press, 1924; reprint, Indianapolis, Indiana: Liberty Classics, 1988

Melon, Jean François, "Essai politique sur le commerce," 1734; as *A Political Essay upon Commerce*, translated by David Bindon, Dublin: Crampton, 1738

Michelet, Jules, *Nos fils*, Paris: A. Lacroix, Verboeckhoven et Cie., 1870

Mirabeau, Victor de Riquetti, marquis de, and François Quesnay, *L'ami des hommes, ou, Traité de la population*, 6 vols., Avignon, France: n.p., 1756–60; reprint, Aalen, Germany: Scientia, 1970

Moheau, Jean-Baptiste, *Recherches et considérations sur la population de la France*, 2 vols., Paris: Moutard, 1778; reprint, Paris: Institut National d'Études Démographiques, and Presses Universitaires de France, 1994

Montesquieu, Charles de Secondat, baron de, *Oeuvres complètes*, edited by André Masson, 3 vols., Paris: Éditions Nagel, 1950–55

Montesquieu, Charles de Secondat, baron de, *The Spirit of the Laws*, translated and edited by Anne M. Cohler, Basia Carolyn Miller, and Harold Samuel Stone, Cambridge and New York: Cambridge University Press, 1989

Pufendorf, Samuel, Freiherr von, *Of the Law of Nature and Nations: Eight Books*, translated by Basil Kennett and William Percivale, Oxford: Litchfield, 1703

Quesnay, François, *François Quesnay et la physiocratie*, 2 vol., Paris: Institut National d'Études Démographiques, 1958

Raynal, Abbé, "Histoire philosophique et politique des etablissements et du commerce des Européens dans les deux Indes," La Haye, 1774; as *A Philosophical and Political History of the Settlements and Trade of the Europeans in the East and West Indies*, 4 vols., translated by J. Justamond, Dublin: Exshaw and Halhead, 1779

Rousseau, Jean-Jacques, *Discourse on the Origin of Inequality*, translated by Franklin Philip, edited by Patrick Coleman, Oxford and New York: Oxford University Press, 1994

Rousseau, Jean-Jacques, *Eloïsa; or, A Series of Original Letters Collected and Published by Mr. J. J. Rousseau*, translated by William Kenrick, London: Baldwin, 1784

Rousseau, Jean-Jacques, *Émile; or, On Education*, translated by Allan Bloom, New York: Basic Books, 1979

Rousseau, Jean-Jacques, *A Letter from M. Rousseau . . . to M. D'Alembert Concerning the Effects of Theatrical Entertainments on the Manners of Mankind A Letter from M. Rousseau, of Geneva, to

M. D'Alembert, of Paris, concerning the Effects of Theatrical Entertainments on the Manners of Mankind, London: Nourse, 1759

Rousseau, Jean-Jacques, Oeuvres complètes, Paris: Gallimard, 1959–1995

Rousseau, Jean-Jacques, The Social Contract, and Other Later Political Writings, edited and translated by Victor Gourevitch, Cambridge: Cambridge University Press, 1997

Saint-Pierre, Jacques-Henri Bernardin de, "Discours sur l'éducation des femmes," in Oeuvres complètes, vol. 12, Paris: Méquignon-Marvis, 1818

Sieyès, Emmanuel Joseph, "Préliminaire de la Constitution [1789]," in Écrits politiques, compiled by Roberto Zapperi, Paris: Éditions des Archives Contemporaines, 1985

Thomas, Antoine-Léonard, "Essai sur le caractère, les moeurs et lèsprit des femmes dans les différents siècles," Paris, 1772; as Essay on the Character, Manners, and Genius of Women in Different Ages, London: Robinson, 1773

Tsuda, Takumi, editor, Traités sur le commerce de Josiah Child: Avec les remarques inédites de Vincent de Gournay, Tokyo: Kinokuniya, 1983

Wollstonecraft, Mary, A Vindication of the Rights of Woman: An Authoritative Text, Backgrounds, Criticism, edited by Carol H. Poston, New York: Norton, 1975

Reference Works

Badinter, Élisabeth, "L'éducation des filles selon Rousseau et Condorcet," in Rousseau, l'Émile et la Révolution, edited by Robert Thiéry, Paris: Universitas, and Montmorency, France: Ville de Montmorency, 1992

Benrekassa, Georges, Le langage des Lumières: Concepts et savoir de la langue, Paris: Presses Universitaires de France, 1995

Carrithers, David W., Michael A. Mosher, and Paul A. Rahe, editors, Montesquieu's Science of Politics: Essays on the Spirit of Laws, Lanham, Maryland: Rowman and Littlefield, 2001

Dufour, Alfred, Le mariage dans l'école allemande du droit naturel moderne au XVIIIe siècle: Les sources philosophiques de la scolastique aux Lumières, Paris: Librairie Générale de Droit et de Jurisprudence, 1971

Dumont, Louis, Essais sur l'individualisme: Une perspective anthropologique sur l'idéologie moderne, Paris: Seuil, 1983; as Essays on Individualism: Modern Ideology in Anthropological Perspective, Chicago: University of Chicago Press, 1986

Dumont, Louis, Homo hierarchicus: Essai sur le sysème des castes, Paris: Gallimard, 1966; as Homo Hierarchicus: An Essay on the Caste System, translated by Mark Sainsbury, Chicago: University of Chicago Press, 1970

Ehrard, Jean, "Le corps de Julie," in Thèmes et figures du siècle des Lumières: Mélanges offerts à Roland Mortier, edited by Raymond Trousson, Geneva: Droz, 1980

Fauré, Christine, "La pensée probabiliste de Condorcet et le suffrage féminin," in Condorcet: Mathématicien, économiste, philosophe, homme politique, edited by Pierre Crépel and Christian Gilain, Paris: Minerve, 1989

Fischer, Jean-Louis, "La callipédie, ou l'art d'avoir de beaux enfants," Dix-huitième siècle 23 (1991)

Flandrin, Jean-Louis, Familles: Parenté, maison, sexualité dans l'ancienne société, Paris: Hachette, 1976; as Families in Former Times: Kinship, Household, and Sexuality, translated by Richard Southern, Cambridge and New York: Cambridge University Press, 1979

Fontenay, Elisabeth de, "Pour Émile et par Émile: Sophie ou l'invention du ménage," Les temps modernes 358 (1976)

Geffriaud Rosso, Jeannette, Montesquieu et la féminité, Pisa, Italy: Goliardica, 1977

Habib, Claude, "Les lois de l'idylle: Amour, sexe et nature," Esprit 235 (August–September 1997)

Hochart, Patrick, "Le plus libre et le plus doux de tous le actes: Lecture du Livre V de l'Émile," Esprit 235 (August–September 1997)

Hoffmann, Paul, La femme dans la pensée des Lumières, Paris: Ophrys, 1977

Hunt, Lynn Avery, The Family Romance of the French Revolution, Berkeley: University of California Press, and London: Routledge, 1992

Larrère, Catherine, L'invention de l'économie au XVIIIe siècle: Du droit naturel à la physiocratie, Paris: Presses Universitaires de France, 1992

Mosher, Michael, "Spirited Commonality and Difference: I. The Judgmental Gaze of European Women: Gender, Sexuality, and the Critique of Republican Rule," Political Theory 22, no. 1 (February 1994)

Ozouf, Mona, Les mots des femmes: Essai sur la singularité française, Paris: Fayard, 1995; as Women's Words: Essay on French Singularity, translated by Jane Marie Todd, Chicago: University of Chicago Press, 1997

Pappas, John, "Condorcet, 'le seul' et 'le premier féministe' du XVIIIe siècle?" Dix-huitième siècle 23 (1991)

Piau-Gillot, Colette, "Le discours de Jean-Jacques Rousseau sur les femmes et sa réception critique," Dix-huitième siècle 13 (1981)

Raynaud, Philippe, "Les femmes et la civilité: Aristocratie et passions révolutionnaires," Le débat 57 (1989)

Riedel, Manfred, "Hegels Begriff der bürgerlichen Gesellschaft und das Problem seines geschichtlichen Ursprungs," in Materialien zu Hegels Rechtsphilosophie, edited by Manfred Riedel, vol. 2, Frankfurt: Suhrkamp, 1975

Rosanvallon, Pierre, Le sacre du citoyen: Histoire du suffrage universel en France, Paris: Gallimard, 1992

Schochet, Gordon Joel, Patriarchalism in Political Thought: The Authoritarian Family and Political Speculation and Attitudes, Especially in Seventeenth-Century England, Oxford: Blackwell, and New York: Basic Books, 1975

Steinbrügge, Lieselotte, Das moralische Geschlecht: Theorien und literarische Entwürfe über die Natur der Frau in der französischen Aufklärung, Weinheim, Germany: Beltz, 1987; as The Moral Sex: Woman's Nature in the French Enlightenment, translated by Pamela E. Selwyn, Oxford and New York: Oxford University Press, 1995

Steinbrügge, Lieselotte, "Qui peut définir les femmes? L'idée de la nature féminine au siècle des Lumières," Dix-huitième siècle 26 (1994)

FROM THE RIGHTS OF MAN TO WOMEN'S RIGHTS:

A Difficult Intellectual Conversion

CHRISTINE FAURÉ

H UMAN RIGHTS, THE SET of principles that Western societies readily display as their own and a state's guarantee of being recognized as a democracy, did not come to encompass recognized equality between the sexes until the 20th century. The 18th century, in different, disconnected centers, saw the appearance and expansion of the rights of man, but it took more than 150 years for two fields that should logically have overlapped, gender equality and human rights, to come into convergence. In principle, the universal recognition of the rights of man as an attribute or power with which the human person is endowed extended to all individuals regardless of historical, cultural, or religious differences. Why, then, should women have been such a constant exception? Approaching the issue from the margins of philosophy and intellectual history, certain men and women have sought in vain to answer this question over the centuries. Their attempts have taken hybrid forms, combining aspects of conceptual explanation with an effort to draw attention to the particular situation of women. Such thinkers and activists have exposed the tensions between contemporaneous representations of sovereignty in the political domain and in the family, on the one hand, and the logic inherent in the doctrine of the rights of man, mandating their applicability to all human beings, on the other. Such attempts are less important for any new information they might yield about the feminine condition than for their manifestation of these thinkers' desire to intervene in an area constitutive of modernity. The fact that the rights of man have come to be regarded as the quintessence of civilization, and therefore as virtually sacred, has helped to mask certain features of their origins and how they have been discussed and debated. The criticisms and interpellations we shall now consider shed light on fundamental questions raised in the historical development of the idea of human rights: human rights to what extent, within what limits?

Invention of the Rights of Man

The rights of man may be said to have been invented in three regions of the world: North America, England, and France. The American colonies made a pioneering contribution with the Virginia Declaration of Rights, adopted on 12 June 1776 (thus anticipating the Declaration of Independence of 4 July 1776 by a few weeks), which proclaimed for the first time, as the foundation and basis of government, "that all men are by nature equally free and independent and have certain inherent rights, of which, when they enter into a state of society, they cannot, by any compact, deprive or divest their posterity."

Following this declaration of rights came declarations by seven other states, adapting the terms of the former to local requirements. When the United States ratified its federal Constitution in 1787, some argued that it lacked a comparable statement on fundamental rights—a "bill of rights," to borrow the original British term. In 1791 James Madison (1751–1836) succeeded in getting such a bill passed, in the form of the first ten amendments to the United States Constitution. This pragmatic gesture ensured recognition at the federal level of the fundamental rights proclaimed by the states and endowed the American constitutional system with a capacity for growth and adaptation. It took until 1920 and the 19th Amendment, however, for gender-based restrictions on the right to vote to become unconstitutional.

As the term "bill of rights," alternating with the Latin-derived work "declaration," showed, the Americans were, paradoxically, appropriating ideological concepts about freedom that had been elaborated the previous century during times of turmoil in the colonizing power against which they had revolted—the English monarchy. In England the Petition of Right of 1628, the Habeas Corpus Act of 1679 against arbitrary arrests, and the Bill of Rights of 1689 declared the rights and liberties of subjects and established succession to the crown. Yet the continuity between the English and American paradigms should not be overestimated. Whereas in England the fundamental laws of the kingdom had to be continually reconfirmed because, like ordinary laws, they were subject to approval by the constituent powers, the American adaptation of those values within the framework of a written constitution considerably transformed the logic of common law, giving individual rights an inviolable character.

In the 17th century, according to the concept of coverture, English common law made married women totally dependent on their husbands. The legal status of women at that time is represented in an anonymous work entitled, *The Lawes Resolutions of Women's Rights* (1632), which presents laws and customs together with case studies in matters of succession, guardianship, marriage, property, and widows' rights.

A century later, the English jurist William Blackstone (1723–80), in his famous *Commentaries on the Laws of England* (1765–69), situated women exclusively within the sphere of private relations, which he distinguished from that of public ones associated with lawmaking:

> The three great relations in private life are (1) that of master and servant . . . (2) that of husband and wife; which is found in nature, but modified by civil society: the one directing man to continue and multiply his species, the other prescribing the manner in which that natural impulse must be confined and regulated . . . (3) that of parent and child. (vol. I, chap. 14)

Even though Blackstone subscribed to a civil definition of marriage (vol. I, chap. 15) that recognized reciprocal rights and duties for husband and wife, women remained confined to private relations. It was out of the question to envision any access by women to the sphere of public life.

In the American colonies from the 17th century on, the application of common law had been simplified, perhaps becoming more equitable with respect to women. In a few significant cases concerning property, wives were treated as virtual partners, equal to their husbands, rather than being subject to the principle of coverture. Women in such cases were unlikely to be treated as independent individuals, however, although this did sometimes happen.

As in the genesis of the English Bill of Rights, the writing in revolutionary France of the Déclaration des Droits de l'Homme et du Citoyen (1789; Declaration of the Rights of Man and the Citizen) took place within the tradition of parlementary opposition to royal power, the French parlements going so far as to appropriate for themselves the form of the "royal declaration." By designating man and citizen to be a rights-endowed being and by grounding this act of endowment in divine justice (with divine wrath guaranteed against any who might oppose it) in order to ensure a new political, social, legal, and fiscal order, the representatives of the French people appropriated and broadened the duty of *remonstrance* [grievance]. By 1787–88 this duty had become a right, traditionally used as a means of informing and counseling the king; it had become a means of expressing a will opposed to the monarch's—of deeming fiscal demands exorbitant, for example, or doing away with the lettres de cachet by which the king summarily imprisoned or banished subjects without trial. In the ensuing exchange of protestations and responses, a decree was issue by the Parlement of Paris (3 May 1788) containing a text entitled "Déclaration des droits du roi et de la nation" (Declaration of the Rights of the King and the Nation), which constituted a sort of transition between the right to remonstrance and the Déclaration des Droits de l'Homme et du Citoyen of 1789. The extent to which the Déclaration of 1789 broke with the past in the sense of being the

"expression of the general will"—a new legal notion—has often been overestimated. In fact, the text can be viewed as the culmination of monarchic public law. Given that the queens of France had been prevented from governing under Salic law, we should hardly be surprised by the silence on women's status in the text of the Déclaration and in the ensuing debate. Traditionally, this silence has been interpreted as pointing to a generalist, universalist spirit. Speaking in the name of all men, and not only in that of Frenchmen, meant breaking away from the France of privileges, a France characterized by rigid distinctions—and fundamental inequality—between social conditions. Yet elements may be found in texts leading directly to the Déclaration des Droits de l'Homme et du Citoyen of 1789 that suggest a very different underlying philosophy.

Ambivalence and Prejudice toward Women in French Revolutionary Legislation

Of the approximately 40 known preparatory drafts for a declaration of the rights of man, that of the abbé Sieyès, "Préliminaire de la Constitution, reconnaissance et exposition raisonnée des droit de l'homme et du citoyen" (20–21 July 1789; Preliminary to the Constitution, A Recognition and Reasoned Exposition of the Rights of Man and the Citizen), was the most frequently read and discussed, benefiting from its author's considerable intellectual and philosophical authority. The text expresses the idea of a two-tiered citizenry:

> All inhabitants of a country should enjoy the rights of the passive citizen: all have the right to the protection of their person, their property, their liberty, etc. But not all have the right to take an active part in the formation of public powers, not all are active citizens; women, at least in the present state, children, foreigners, and those who contribute nothing to the maintenance of the public establishment should have no active influence in public affairs.

Jean-Paul Marat's little-known, marginal draft, sent late (17 August) to the National Assembly and generally not much appreciated by the constituents because of its author's personality, placed women explicitly under the control of the head of the family: "Every citizen, as a member of the sovereign power, must have the right to suffrage, and birth alone must give this right. But women and children must take no part whatsoever in affairs because they are represented by the head of the family." These statements are in close harmony with the confirmation of Salic law found in the Constitution of 23 September 1791: "Kingship is indivisible and delegated by heredity to the reigning family from male to male, in order of birthright, with the perpetual exclusion of women and their descendants" (chap. 2, section 1).

Moreover, contrary to tradition, French revolutionary legislation also excluded women from the regency. On this point, the constituents even surpassed the exclusivity of the monarchic rules, as the decree excluded women in the name of reason: "The same reason that excludes women from ruling holds for the regency," proclaimed Thouret, a member for the Third Estate of Rouen, on 23 March 1791, to the great displeasure of certain deputies of the nobility, such as Clermont-Lodève and Montlosier. There was much impassioned resistance to this active disregard of tradition. This debate generated the notion that whereas women's influence had marked the past from which it was necessary to be delivered, the country's future would involve women's exclusion.

Preparatory drafts of the Déclaration des Droits de l'Homme et du Citoyen—for example, the constitutional charter drafted by Charles F. Bouche, deputy of the Third Estate for the seneschalcy of Aix—already included confirmation and renewal of the Salic law. In fact, not least among the paradoxes of the period was the constituents' ability to adhere to past measures excluding women without raising an eyebrow. For instance, Clermont-Tonnerre's report of 27 July 1789 on the content of the *cahiers de doléances* (lists of grievances) included "inheritance of the crown from male to male" as an established principle. Similarly, the constituents and the population at large felt no need to call into question the Salic law or the rules governing the transmission of land with respect to women. In this connection, it is highly instructive to study the specifics of contemporary discourse. The 10 April 1789 report by Barère, deputy of the Third Estate for Tarbes, on the alienability of royal domains gave thanks to the kings for having instituted male transmission of royal apanages: "The first attribute of the wisdom of our kings was to have restored male apanages under Charles V." Similarly, the decree of 21 December 1790, which eliminated the apanages, replacing them with an annuity, and abolished the right of primogeniture, vigorously excluded daughters in two articles (Article 11 and Article 13).

However, these examples may be contrasted with situations in which the civil legislature worked to equalize relations between the sexes. To bring about the breaking up of aristocratic landed property and wealth, it abolished both primogeniture and "masculinity" rights (15–28 March 1790). Furthermore, with regard to intestate successions, the legislature rescinded the customs that "excluded daughters or their descendants from the right to succession along with males or the descendants of males" (8–15 April 1791), thus moving toward legal unification of the country, which until then had been divided into regions ruled by customary law and regions ruled by written law. Henceforth, the true custom was to be the Déclaration des Droits de l'Homme et du Citoyen.

The high point of egalitarian revolutionary thought was the divorce law of 20–25 September 1792. When it was determined that dissolution of the marriage contract was a matter of individual liberty, women seemed to have been endowed, like men, with clear civil rights. In fact, this apparent recognition of women's civil rights was the result of lack of social foresight on the part of the legislators: to everyone's surprise, it was above all women who filed for divorce, refuting the adage, frequently repeated in the assemblies, that a woman had never been known to refuse marriage.

The will to establish equality between the sexes stopped short, however, at the threshold of an arena that symbolized the new way of regulating life—taxation, which was now to be regular, permanent, and grounded in consent. In this matter, it was no longer a question of liquidating the political and social organization of yesteryear, but of implementing the principles of the Déclaration des Droit de l'Homme et du Citoyen. He who had rights also had duties, and among these was paying taxes.

The fiscal reform was based explicitly on Article 13 of the Déclaration des Droits de l'Homme et du Citoyen: "For the maintenance of the public force and for the expenses of administration, a common tax is indispensable; it must be assessed equally among all citizens in proportion to their means." The contribution based on property ownership, instituted 23 November–1 December 1790, was to be divided "in equal proportions over all property owned, at the rate of net income." The tax based on movable assets, as established by the decree of 13 January 1791, on the other hand, consisted of two parts, one a contribution common to all inhabitants and another based on wage income, other revenues, and movable assets. The personal part of the contribution (though the term "personal" was deleted from the definitive version of the written law, perhaps because it was an unpleasant reminder of personal privileges) was to be paid by those who fit into the key category of active citizenship. This category had been defined in view of the constitution of the primary and administrative assemblies. Being of the male sex was not mentioned as a necessary condition for paying taxes, and the indeterminacy of the final speeches made it possible to associate clearly expressed prejudices against women with the financial demands of the Public Treasury, which sought the greatest possible number of taxpayers. Défermon des Chapelières's presentation of the draft decree of 19 October 1790 contains the following explanation:

> It seemed to us that it would be rational to include women in the arrangements we are proposing to you, because one cannot leave this weak sex with too many resources, and that it would be desirable to prefer their service, and to leave to the cultivation of land the men whom nature has destined to it.

Depriving the state coffers of funds for moral reasons seemed excessive to some—thus the amendment proposed by Lanjuinais, deputy of the Third Estate for the seneschalcy of Rennes, the spirit of which was maintained in the final version of the law: "[the following] movable means may confer active citizenship; otherwise, men who are deprived of that status by virtue of your laws, and all women, are excluded from contribution. A man does not owe taxes, his fortune does." Counted among movable property were male and female servants; saddle horses and mules; and carriage, cabriolet, and palanquin horses. Thus Aristotle's classification into animate and inanimate instruments (*Politics* I, 4) had been incorporated, despite the Déclaration's assurance of the inalienability of persons.

With respect to movable assets, women were taxed less than men. It had been suggested that they not be taxed at all, in the name of a particular understanding of the sexual division of labor, defined as follows on 22 March 1790 by Roederer, deputy of the Third Estate for Metz:

> The reasoning of the committee is that robust men should be left to the labor of the fields, to social functions, to the glorious profession of arms, for they are called upon to enjoy the most complete liberty. Women, by contrast, are nurses whom nature has given to children and the sick. We thought that imposing a tax on male servants would lead handsome and vigorous men, enervated by idleness, to leave our houses, and that this would put the two sexes in the proper place in the work of society.

Generally, the constituents did not elaborate on their vision of women's place in the new society, perhaps out of caution, out of fear of unleashing the female agitation that was so greatly dreaded and so hard to control. There are therefore few notable comments on this theme on the part of the constituents. Roederer (1754–1835), however, who had a long political career stretching from the Estates General to the Brumaire coup d'état, was an exception, and he had the merit of speaking in explicit terms. For him, the social division between men and women effected by the tax on movable property represented and perpetuated an unreserved adherence to the Roman doctrine of the paterfamilias. As he wrote in 1797 in his *Journal d'économie publique* ;

> It appears to me to be universally recognized, and above all recognized in France, that only heads of families are citizens. It must, of course, be understood that under this term, as for the Romans under the term *paterfamilias*, fall not only the father of the family but also he who may fill that role. It is by virtue of this principle that women, minors, domestic servants, and even soldiers are excluded from the rights of citizenship. And what more solemn recognition of the principle could there be than this exclusion?

Despite women's incontestable political mobilization during the Revolution, revolutionary events do not seem to have shaken the perceived legitimacy of this exclusion, which stood throughout the 18th century. In his article "Citoyen" (Citizen) in the *Encyclopédie* Diderot rejected the idea of attributing this title to women. Similarly, the constituent Antoine René Hyacinthe Thibaudeau, deputy for the Third Estate for Poitiers, refused to grant that there could be any valid use of the term *citoyenne* for, as he wrote in his memoirs, "never did the Latin word *civis* have a feminine form." The reference to ancient Rome was symptomatic of a general refusal to include women's action in any definition of public affairs. By nature, woman was not a citizen and did not enjoy political rights.

In the domain of rights pertaining to the private person, sexual equality had been attained—or was at least admissible. On the other hand, women were denied any legally recognized participation in political life. This explains the ambivalence about taxation, which at the time was being newly conceived as a voluntary and personal contribution of inhabitants instead of a charged imposed by the state. Neither the debate surrounding the final text of the Déclaration des Droits de l'Homme et du Citoyen (26 August 1789) nor the one concerning the first Constitution (3 September 1791) made any allusion to the status of women.

Nor did the draft of the so-called Girondine Constitution, presented to the Convention on 15 and 16 February 1793, recognize political rights for women. Its author, the marquis de Condorcet, who in 1790 had written a text in favor of granting women citizenship rights ("Sur l'admission des femmes au droit de cité" ["On the Admission of Women to the Rights of Citizenship"]), was not able as a legislator to impose his convictions. On 17 February, during discussion of the text, Gilbert Romme, deputy for Riom, proposed on the basis of the various drafts that had been submitted to the commission that a new declaration of rights be written, to be divided into three parts: the rights of man in society, political or sovereign rights, and civil or social

rights. In each article he was careful to specify that the proclaimed titles and faculties were valid for "both sexes," denouncing in this way the neutrality of the philosophical indeterminacy behind which the constituents and the Girondins had taken refuge. On 29 April 1793, in a similar spirit, Pierre Guyomar lambasted the legislators for their show of bad faith in manipulating the universality of the statements:

> Is the Declaration of the Rights of Man common to women? Choose in good faith: is the difference between the sexes any better founded than the color of Negroes as a foundation for slavery? . . . They [women] would henceforth have to be called daughters and wives of *citoyens*, never *citoyennes*.

The political exclusion of women signified the survival in revolutionary France of monarchic conceptions and prejudice, particularly the weight of the Salic law. The plea on behalf of women concerned not only their gaining the right to vote but also their eligibility to stand for election: "Voting women incontestably have the right to be elected."

The Convention gave these opinions no consideration whatsoever, as they represented a minority view in the Assembly. Lanjuinais put an end to the debate by invoking nature and common sense: "Women's physique, their purpose, their activity distance them from political rights and duties." There followed a cascade of sanctions against every form of female participation in public life: exclusion from the army, a decree (30 April–3 May 1793) ordering that superfluous women, termed "useless," be dismissed from any function in the armies, and mandating the closing of women's clubs and societies. After the riots of Prairial came the decree of 4 Prairial, Year III, which excluded women from political assemblies, and, on the same date, a decree that enjoined them to withdraw into their homes and ordered the arrest of any women found in groups of more than five. The legislators meant to establish a strict separation between public and private spheres and to keep the activities of men and women separate on the basis of that opposition. Henceforth, the public arena was to be restricted to a single gender—males—without any possibility of confusion on this point.

Offerings and Oaths: Forms of Activist Female Citizenship

Despite specific demands expressed in a few of the *cahiers de doléance*, women were not permitted to participate in the Estates General. They nonetheless continued to intervene in the Assemblies by means of offerings and petitions.

Historians have largely neglected the phenomenon of patriotic offerings. The link between the act and the individuals performing it has been studied only in terms of the geographic location of the donors, and though the important place of women in these gestures has been pointed out many times, no interpretation of their behavior has been proposed.

In 1789 the financial crisis in which the kingdom was plunged and the need to fill the state coffers gave credibility to the idea of a patriotic contribution applicable to all. On 29 September Jacques Necker, the first minister of finance, formulated the proposal for this extraordinary taxation, from which neither rich nor poor, men nor women were to be exempt:

I shall consider it a general and necessary possibility to allow all people without distinction to acquit themselves of their tax in plate or gold or silver jewelry, assessed at a favorable price for the taxpayers. The wife of a simple peasant will give her ring or her gold cross, if need be.

This proposal was ratified by the decree of 6–9 October 1789. In fact, a number of self-proclaimed *citoyennes*—artists' wives or daughters—had inaugurated the patriotic practice of making offerings as early as 7 September, invoking the exemplary behavior of the Roman women who gave their jewels to the Senate. Despite this reference to the nobility, the Frenchwomen's act was grounded in the constituents' idea of taxation as a transaction to which the taxpayer consented, one without inquisition and based on the citizens' good will. Participation in this national effort was therefore a form of activist citizenship—citizenship inhering in the strength of the act itself, for lack of any other form of recognition. The meaning of these acts was clear to contemporaries, as Chantreau's *Dictionnaire national et anecdotique* (1790; National Anecdotal Dictionary) attests: "The different donations of plate were nonetheless seen as patriotic restitutions that indicated a strong intention to become a citizen." For women, whose political future was already precarious at that date, the offerings were an ideal opportunity to express the wish for citizenship.

A range of objects were offered—precious metals, intangible assets, such as annuities and pensions, and gifts of linen in the Year II after the decree of 19 Brumaire (9 November 1793), which invited the population to make contributions to the *patrie* in the form of shirts, stockings, and shoes. Did the disparities in intrinsic value of these gifts correspond to different degrees of social obligation among the donors? Should we interpret women's gifts of fine metals to be the mere expression of an imposed situation, while viewing the donations of linens, linked to the war effort, as more closely connected to the traditional range of female tasks, "loving, giving, serving, and caring"? Any such attempt at classification seems misguided in many ways. First, it underestimates the new idea of exchange for services rendered that informed 18th-century revolutionary taxation policy, and the enthusiasm this conceptual changed aroused, at least in the early days. Second, it overestimates women's adherence to, and support for, the aforementioned female social roles. Women were as quick to ask the Assembly for monetary allowances for their own wounds received at the front as they were to request funds for their children's education upon being widowed. Still, the political investment expressed through these series of donations was indirect. In neither case did women themselves do the speaking. As the historian Catherine Duprat has noted, "the speeches that accompanied the offerings were almost always formulated and made by men" (see Duprat).

In addition to the practice of donations, women attempted other forms of investment in the political sphere, notably through oath-taking, the traditional means of guaranteeing the social reliability of acts and the possibility of exchange. On 29 March 1790, the woman delivering her "address by the wife of a municipal officer of the city of Lannion, endorsed by several others," asked that women be permitted to participate in civic oath-taking ceremonies: "Mr. President, not one word is said about women in the Constitution, and I confess that they would not be capable of being involved in public affairs. However,

mothers of families can and should be citizens." To this delegation of Breton women, having recourse to the solemn oath taken before municipal officers seemed the appropriate way to change their status and become citizens. Other demonstrations of women's belief in the power of the oath—and, moreover, at a time when the faith-based act of oath-taking had been weakened socially through the dissolution of the religious aspect of such perpetual bonds—attest to a will to integration based on the contractual nature of civil relations. At the end of the 18th century, the oath still had feudal connotations, but with political episodes such as the Tennis Court Oath, it became an allegory of the Revolution. Under attack from the philosophes, the automatically binding character of the obligation incurred by oath, tied to mere utterance of the name of God, had broken down. The oath had become a secular and profoundly rational act, practiced by every social group and thus by women. The theoreticians of natural law had made possible a convergence between existing practices and the ideal quest for the best of all possible governments.

The Declaration of the Rights of Woman

Olympe de Gouges' *Déclaration des Droits de la Femme et de la Citoyenne* (Declaration of the Rights of Woman and the Female Citizen) is to be situated in the context of this renewal, in the first years of the French Revolution, of the acts constitutive of society. This undated brochure, which brought posthumous renown to its author, was written in early September 1791, two months after the royal couple had been arrested at Varennes but also after the Assembly vote on the Constitution (4 September) and perhaps before the Constitution was approved by the king (14 September).

"For the National Assembly to decree in its last sessions, or in those of the next legislature" begins the text. Addressed to the queen, the *Déclaration des Droits de la Femme et de la Citoyenne* immediately makes clear its author's loyalty to the throne. It uses the traditional tone of a warning, even though the writer is calling for plain speaking. Gouges had already written, in a June 1791 text entitled, "Sera-t-il roi, ne le sera-t-il pas?" (Will he be king or will he not?), "I am a royalist, yes Gentlemen, but a patriotic royalist, a constitutional royalist," thereby distancing herself from the position of Jean-Pierre Brissot, who at the same moment, was proclaiming his republicanism in *Le patriote français* in the following terms: "I believe that the French Constitution is republican in five-sixths of its components; that the abolition of royalty is a necessary result; that that office cannot subsist alongside the Déclaration des Droits."

To better appreciate the path taken by Olympe de Gouges, let us quote a few texts that in theme and date of publication are close to her *Déclaration*, even though we cannot say whether she had any personal knowledge of them. On 10 August 1791, in the ephemeral *Journal des droits de l'homme* published by a certain Labenette, we read the following editorial comment: "Indisputably, the Declaration of the Rights of Man is the most beautiful work to have come forth from the head of our legislators. But they should have made its companion piece: they should, I say, have decreed the rights of woman." This editorial, written in gallant style, contained both an admonition to the legislators and a sharp plea on behalf of equality:

> History. . . . Well, read it. It will give you the list of famous women who have made themselves immortal. You believe only in great men . . . justice is needed in all things. If it is proven that there are as many educated women as there are narrow-minded men, we cannot without injustice deny them [women] access to the tiller of public affairs.

The following day, however, the editor broke off the discourse in favor of women because, he said, some men had threatened not to read his paper anymore. Whatever credence this allegation may be given, it attests to the strength of public sentiments on the subject.

In her introduction to Olympe de Gouges's *Déclaration des Droits de la Femme et de la Citoyenne*, the historian Dominique Godineau draws attention to an anonymous tract entitled *Du sort actuel des femmes* (On the Present Lot of Women), attributed on uncertain evidence by the bibliographer Brunet to Madame de Cambis and published by the Cercle Social (see Godineau). The content enables us to date this text to either early July or mid-August 1791. The exasperation engendered by the crawling pace of constitutional debate was at its height, and the tract's main target was the legislators:

> It is not a question of alleviating wrongs, it is a question of restoring property. To show groaning women is to arouse pity; and it is not pity they are asking for but a right they are having to demand, a right inherent in their being. . . . Is it permissible to keep silent when, after having decreed the Rights of Man, we have heard those who have collaborated on that work ostentatiously declare that the rights of woman were not included; that women were nothing and could be nothing other than humanity's beasts of burden? "My wife is mine as my dog is" is an expression that was uttered in our tribunals only a few years ago: the gravity of the magistrates was not affected by it. . . . Yes, Gentlemen, without meaning to, no doubt, you have equated French women and girls with men who are foreigners. What!—women are not citizens? Can you rob them of this title before they have proven themselves unworthy of it?

Although her underlying inspiration was similar to that found in these two texts, Gouges broke new ground. Her use of the declarative model, which represented the most radical form of generalization of her time, marked what might otherwise have seemed to be simply a critical mindset with a clear will to inaugurate new truths. Was the *Déclaration des Droits de l'Homme et du Citoyen*, which had been conceived to combat all the exceptionalist statutes that a society based on privilege had fostered, going to be compatible with an approach that claimed to ensure civil and political existence for women and recognize and grant them the right and power to legislate, while separating them from men? This was the question Gouges had to resolve.

The reference to the queen, whom she addressed in a highly individualized manner, played a key role in this undertaking, for Gouges had to give political anchoring to a declaration whose *déclarateur* (declaring subject), to use the term of the period, was part of a purely fictional entity: an Assembly of women representatives of a nation made up of mothers, daughters, and sisters, but not wives. In texts written in connection with her *Déclaration*, Gouges made numerous incursions. In a short introduction entitled "Les droits de la femme" (The Rights of Woman), she questioned, as a member of the female sex, the competence of men in matters of justice; and in both the "postamble" to her *Déclaration* and a text entitled "La forme de contrat social de l'homme et de la femme" (The Form of the Social Contract for Men and Women) she frequently used the first-person pronoun *je*. The *Déclaration des Droits de la Femme et de la Citoyenne* thus appears to be the only text by Olympe de Gouges to function by means of an imagined, hypostasized collective—women united in a national assembly—and in which the author does not speak directly in her own name.

In Article XI of her *Déclaration*, however, concerning "the free communication of thoughts and opinions"—which she related to the matter of paternity claims—she does use the direct style: "I am the mother of a child who belongs to you," says the female citizen. Herself a real or at least imagined bastard, Gouges voiced the concerns of the illegitimate woman, pregnant out of wedlock, who was forced by the laws of the monarchy to declare her pregnancy to a judge and thus to shine a spotlight on the troubles and disarray of her social and love life. Such forced display of one's private life, often humiliating for the women concerned even if justified by the reparative ends sought, was a response to the royal power's demand for demographic oversight and control. From the declaration of pregnancy, a condition which she desired to remove from public control, to the *Déclaration des droits de la femme et de la citoyenne*, Gouges invested the declarative act itself with an emotional intensity grounded in existing reality. Her declaration exceeded mere imitation of the 1789 *Déclaration* and revealed to the world, in a virtually prophetic mode, the sufferings of which the feminine condition was made. It was thus by addressing concrete situations that Olympe de Gouges brought about the intellectual conversion from the rights of man to the rights of woman—a conversion that may seem ordinary and almost natural to the contemporary reader but which, at the time, required a daring reformulation, a distancing of thought from the preconceptions of the day, attempted by very few.

At the time of its publication, Gouges's text went relatively unnoticed. The theme of women's rights was subsequently taken up by women sansculottes, but no allusion was made to the text, nor to the political liberation that this language act could, in itself, represent for women. Not until the writings of the socialist Flora Tristan (1803–44) would "declaring rights" be once again understood as a significant act in the emancipation of women. And even there, that emancipation was not conceived as the result of actions led by women themselves, as speaking subjects; it was instead mediated by the words of the proletariat, who, in declaring the rights of women, would accomplish a second revolution. In chapter 3 of *L'Union ouvrière* (1844; *The Workers' Union*), Tristan writes:

> Workers! In 1791 your fathers proclaimed the immortal Déclaration des Droits de l'Homme, and it is to that solemn declaration that you owe your being free and equal men before the law. . . . But, proletarians, there remains for you men of 1843 a no less great work to finish. In your turn, emancipate the last slaves still remaining in

French society; proclaim the rights of woman, in the same terms your fathers proclaimed yours.

Flora Tristan did not cite Olympe de Gouges's *Déclaration des droits de la femme et de la citoyenne*, and she even went so far as to credit herself with the invention of women's rights: "Women, the Workers' Union has a right to your gratitude. It was the first to recognize on principle the rights of women. Today its cause and yours are becoming one and the same." Should we suspect her of bad faith in this affirmation? Was she familiar with Gouges's text?

The first edition of the Michaud's *Biographie universelle* (1811–28; Universal Biography), which Flora Tristan frequently consulted, did not list the *Déclaration des droits de la femme et de la citoyenne* in its entry on Olympe de Gouges. On the other hand, E. Lairtullier in *Les femmes célèbres de 1789 à 1795* (1840; Famous Women from 1789 to 1795), gave long excerpts from Gouges's text. This information is insufficient for us to interpret Tristan's silence about Olympe de Gouges, but her undertaking, like Gouges's, may be situated in the field of practical citizenship. Tristan's focus on the constitutive moment of the act—the goal of the Union Ouvrière was to constitute the working class—underscores the similarity between the two women's views: "Workers [*Ouvriers, ouvrières*], . . . there is nothing more to be said, nothing more to be written, for your wretched position is well known by all. Only one thing remains to be done: to act by virtue of the rights inscribed in the Charter." Still, Tristan's unionism and her conception of the complementarity of the sexes were hardly in agreement with the avowed separatism of the fiery southern Frenchwoman.

"A Vindication of the Rights of Woman"

A Vindication of the Rights of Woman by the English writer Mary Wollstonecraft, published in London in 1792, was such a success that a second edition came out the same year. As the large number of foreign editions show, the work was recognized as decisive in the debate over the condition of women.

Wollstonecraft's text raised issues that went way beyond the preoccupations of the time. "An imperishable work," wrote Flora Tristan in her *Promenades dans Londres* (1840; *Flora Tristan's London Journal*). The treatise inspired an admiring Tristan to suggest what seemed to her an obvious affinity between Wollstonecraft and the economist and philosopher Saint-Simon (1760–1825)—a surprising notion since in fact the *Vindication of the Rights of Woman* is relatively unconcerned with any need for a constituted collective social subject.

Wollstonecraft seems to have been completely oblivious of the foundational import of declaring the rights of man and the rights of woman. For her, it was not a question of "stating" woman's rights, but of addressing the appropriate legislator, in this case the minister in charge of public instruction, to get the Constitution revised. Wollstonecraft had responded with indignation to the French report on education of September 1791 by Charles-Maurice de Talleyrand-Périgord (1754–1838), in which he developed a specious argument regarding girls' education. "Instruction must exist for all," Talleyrand wrote, "there-fore, no one can be legally excluded from it. . . . As for the object of instruction, it must be universal, for only then is it truly a common good." He concluded his analysis, however, by recommending mere "domestic education" for women:

> Let us raise women not to aspire to advantages the Constitution denies them, but to know and appreciate those that it guarantees them. . . . Let all your instruction, then, concentrate women's education within the domestic sanctuary: no other suits modesty better or prepares more gentle habits for her.

In the name of "the gift of reason," Wollstonecraft demanded sexual equality in education and instruction. From the moment that women were recognized as being endowed with the faculty of reason, could one legitimately perpetuate their social subjugation, even if one claimed to be promoting their happiness? Wollstonecraft condemned the French revolutionaries' attitude toward women as a tyranny that must be brought to an end in the name of logic and justice. Numerous cultural factors had worked to degrade women's condition. The responsibility of writers, however—particularly that of Jean-Jacques Rousseau—appeared to Wollstonecraft decisive. The author of *Émile, ou, de l'éducation* (1762; *Emile; or, On Education*) had given rein to his personal predilections when he advocated that girls be confined within the family. For Wollstonecraft, the popularity of Rousseau's ideas on education constituted a true danger to society. The state of moral debility in which women were kept had a deep negative effect on social happiness: "Weak, artificial beings, raised above the common wants and affections of their race, in a premature unnatural manner, undermine the very foundation of virtue, and spread corruption through the whole mass of society!"

In Wollstonecraft's view, women's social dependence was incompatible with the ideal of rationality as well as with practical solutions, notably the one she advocated: coeducation at school from the earliest age. Her criticism must be situated within the context of French revolutionary ideas, for she accepted and made her own the equation between equality and happiness, understanding it to mean—as she repeatedly underlined in the *Vindication of the Rights of Woman*—reason, virtue, and truth. In this understanding she was similar to the "rational dissenters" who were opposed to the Anglican Church and whose democratic ideas were founded upon a conception of God-given rights. Anglican by birth and education, she did not join the dissenters, but did remain close to them. She had met the most eminent among them in Newington Green in 1784, including the Unitarian Dr. Richard Price, who was in correspondence with the scientists and philosophers of the time, as well as Joseph Priestley. Her own publisher, Joseph Johnson, also published Thomas Paine's *The Rights of Man* (1791–92) and was the London distributor for Priestley's work, as Marilyn Butler notes in her work on the controversy that developed in England in 1789 around the French Revolution (see Butler).

And it is, indeed, within this framework that *A Vindication of the Rights of Woman* should be read. The work cannot be isolated from this debate, in which Wollstonecraft became personally involved when she published her response to Edmund Burke's *Reflections on the Revolution in France* (1790), entitled *A Vindication of the Rights of Men* (1790). In fact, *A Vindication of the Rights of Woman* takes up the convictions and argumentation already present in this defense of the rights of man against Burke's history and tradition. Wollstonecraft intervenes as a philosopher and moralist (chap. 2), adopting the perspective of radical abstraction, the political ravages of which Burke had condemned. (In *Reflections*, section 1, he had written: "The circumstances are what render every civil and political scheme beneficial or noxious to mankind.")

"Rational woman," Wollstonecraft wrote in *A Vindication of the Rights of Men*, required to manage her family and feed her children in order "to fulfill her part of the social contract," must find the conditions for her self-improvement in the means put at her disposal by the social community. School played a crucial role in this program for individual transformation. Wollstonecraft's past experience as a professional educator enabled her to substantiate her belief in progress with concrete proposals, and this places her work in the line of education manuals of the time, more concerned with morality than civil rights. Still, the book is political, as an essay on forms of voluntary subjugation. Why did "this half of the human race" accept its lot? That was the central question the author raised in this text. She did not hesitate to discuss—and attack—the established forms of sexual behavior and representations concerning how to please that were the arbiters of social relations between men and women. In the *Vindication of the Rights of Man* she had already upbraided Burke for propagating the female ideal of blushing and suffering beauty in his *Philosophical Inquiry into the Origin of Our Ideas of the Sublime and Beautiful* (1761). But her critical stance on Burke's thought was not central to the *Vindication of the Rights of Woman*. Her purpose here was to examine the various tyrannies that rendered women powerless. Among these, in chapter 10 she audaciously included parental love:

> Parental affection is, perhaps, the blindest modification of perverse self-love; for we have not, like the French, two terms to distinguish the pursuit of a natural and reasonable desire, from the ignorant calculations of weakness. . . . Parental affection, indeed, in many minds, is but a pretext to tyrannize where it can be done with impunity.

In this sense, her essay drew its inspiration from the earliest French revolutionary thinking, which condemned all forms of despotism.

An American writer of English origin, Paine took active part in the polemic against Burke, notably with *The Rights of Man*. In "An Occasional Letter on the Female Sex" (*Pennsylvania Magazine* August 1775), Paine focused attention on the paradoxical situation of women:

> Man with regard to them, in all climates and in all ages, has been either an insensible husband or an oppressor; but they have sometimes experienced the cold and deliberate oppression of pride, and sometimes the violent and terrible tyranny of jealousy. When they are not beloved they are nothing; and when they are, they are tormented. They have almost equal cause to be afraid of indifference and love. Over three quarters of the globe nature has placed them between contempt and misery.

Men had never let an opportunity go by to exercise their power while paying homage to women's beauty. For Wollstonecraft, the guileful invention of the beautiful woman—passive, flirtatious, and immoral, sometimes unconsciously cruel—seemed the main obstacle to women's exercise of reason and natural rights and to her sharing in "the sober pleasures of equality."

Olympe de Gouges and Mary Wollstonecraft, each in her own way, extended the rights of man to women—a daring intellectual move, to a large extent inspired by the constitutional debates that had just taken place in France. The first events of the French Revolution had solidified rifts in public opinion, as is attested to by the immense successes of two opposed works, Burke's *Reflections* and Paine's two-volume *Rights of Man*. The echoes of the revolutionary discourse were certainly far stronger in England than elsewhere because the debate spoke to truly English political concerns. As Philippe Raynaud emphasizes in his preface to the French translation of Burke's text:

> Religious dissenters were inspired by the French example either to advance a quasi-democratic interpretation of the English Constitution or to demand political or social reforms. The discussion was all the more complex because within Burke's own party the revolution had numerous admirers, who saw it as the natural sequel to the Glorious Revolution of 1688.

To appreciate Wollstonecraft's approach and work, we must bear in mind the heated debate between detractors and supporters of the French Revolution. We cannot discern any direct influence in her work of French supporters of sexual equality; their voices—a minority—were difficult to gain access to, heard as they were at the core of the event, during specific actions or through leaflets and brochures. It does not seem that Wollstonecraft knew of Olympe de Gouges's *Déclaration*; nor did she make reference to Condorcet's stand in "On the Admission of Women to the Rights of Citizenship," though Condorcet was close to Paine, whose house Wollstonecraft frequented regularly when in Paris. The French sources to which she did refer date from before the Revolution: *Lettres sur les ouvrages et le caractère de J.J. Rousseau* (Letters on the Writings and the Character of J.J. Rousseau), by Germaine de Staël, published in 1788 and reprinted in 1789 (Wollstonecraft relates that she came upon the book by chance) and, more generally, books by Madame de Genlis (1746–1830), who had been governess for the children of the duke of Chartres and whose publications—namely, *Adèle et Théodore, ou Lettre sur l'éducation contenant tous les principes relatifs aux trois différents plans d'éducation des princes, des jeunes personnes et des hommes* (Adelaïde and Théodore; or, Letters on Education, Containing all the Principles Relative to Three Different Plans of Education), published in 1782 and translated the next year into English, German, and Spanish—were highly successful.

The letters of Madame de Staël in particular fueled Wollstonecraft's egalitarian eloquence. She was hardly moved by Necker's daughter's plea for indulgence for Rousseau (see in particular letter 1), made in the name of love, emotion, and the primacy that Madame de Staël, together with the rest of the "elegant class," granted to love relationships. For Wollstonecraft, the "sycophantic" baroness's description of the amorous state could lead only to "the relaxation of men" and the "perpetuat[ion of] the species." "It is not empire, but equality, that they should contend for," she wrote ironically, condemning the famous prerogatives of love, which she saw as rendering impossible all mutual respect. It may be said, however, that Wollstonecraft bent this text written in Madame de Staël's youth to serve her own line of argument. In fact, in the second preface to her letters (1814), the baroness adjusted her position. While renewing her praise of feeling, she also affirmed her awareness of the social subordination of women: "Many men, however, give the preference to women merely devoted to household cares, and, to be safer still in this respect, they would not be sorry if their wives were incapable of understanding anything else."

Among her own countrywomen, Wollstonecraft greatly admired Catharine Macaulay-Graham (1731–91), an accomplished woman of letters, author of the eight-volume *History of England, from the Accession of James I to That of the Brunswick Line* (1763–83) and a pedagogical work; Wollstonecraft paid strong tribute to Macaulay in *A Vindication of the Rights of Woman*. Like Wollstonecraft, Macaulay had reacted immediately to Burke's theses, publishing observations (November 1790) in which she demonstrated her sympathy for the French Constituent Assembly and energetically defended the Déclaration des Droits de l'Homme et du Citoyen. Also in 1790, she published *Letters on Education: with Observations on Religious and Metaphysical Subjects*, which criticized the weakness of women produced by the dominant mores of society. In contrast, Wollstonecraft lambasted Anna Letitia Barbauld (1743–1825) for attributing a sexual vocation to women, an idea that the author of *A Vindication of the Rights of Woman* categorically, viscerally rejected. Love was a deceitful art in which women lost their dignity; and even though Pastor Price, in his celebrated speech on "love in our country" (4 November 1789), given for the centenary of the revolution in Great Britain, placed the poet John Milton side by side with John Locke in the pantheon of dissenters, this did not make the pamphleteering poet's sensualism any more acceptable to Wollstonecraft. In chapter 2 of the *Vindication*, she vigorously criticized the poet's contradictions: he abandoned his rationalist ideal when it came to women, granting them nothing but the right to please. "When he tells us that women are formed for softness and sweet attractive grace, I cannot comprehend his meaning," she declared, deaf to the charms of docility. There are many quotations from *Paradise Lost* in her essay, but in chapter 4, she did not hesitate to rank Milton among her adversaries: "Alas! Rousseau, respectable visionary! thy paradise would soon be violated by the entrance of some unexpected guest. Like Milton's it would only contain angels, or men sunk below the dignity of rational creatures."

As mentioned, *A Vindication of the Rights of Woman* was rooted in the ground of religious dissent and, like her Unitarian friends Price and Priestley, Wollstonecraft's thinking was nurtured by a rational reading of Scriptures. She frequently quotes Luke and Matthew. Nonetheless, her critique has an intensely personal tone, as shown in her analysis of Milton's ambivalence with regard to women, which she developed despite the recognized authority of his work. With the exception of Rousseau, her references to other writers were often indirect, when she did not modify them for the needs of her demonstration. Her particular talent resided in the force of the expression with which she tackled her preferred themes. In *A Vindication of the Rights of Men*, she occasionally used a kind of religious eloquence to persuade and make the human character of her concerns more tangible: reverence for the rights of man—these "sacred rights"—she wrote, was an intense personal experience that made her fear God. This fear of God was the secret pivot for passing from the rights of man to the rights of woman; it pushed her to respect herself and consequently all female beings, whose social existences often seemed so degraded: "This fear of God makes me reverence myself." Her first concern was thus not to situate herself in any historical line of learned women but to center and anchor her pedagogical and political project in an optimistic moral and religious experience. While she feared God, she believed in the perfectibility of mankind and distanced herself from the pessimism of Calvinists and Jansenists.

Wollstonecraft did make use of the popularizing works available to her, notably the famous women's dictionaries that were a flourishing genre in France at the time (no fewer than six were published between 1750 and 1789). The traces of this use may be found in a note where she provides a list of women who had acquired courage and decisiveness through their male-style education (chap. 4): Sappho, Heloïse, Macaulay, the empress of Russia, and Madame Déon, better known to the contemporary reader as the chevalier d'Éon. In fact, *Le Dictionnaire portatif des femmes célèbres* (1788; Portable Dictionary of Famous Women), following Boudier de Villemert in the *Nouvel ami des femmes* (1779; New Friend of Women), placed the distinguished transvestite known as the chevalier d'Éon in the ranks of famous women, recapitulating the diplomatic intrigues surrounding his return to France (1777), upon which he was made to dress as a woman and publicize his new official sexual identity. This comment brings us to the heart of the problem posed by the historical transmission of knowledge about women.

Between Historical Knowledge and Celebration

Alongside such dictionaries of illustrious women—mediocre literature in terms of the quality of information it provided, and undoubtedly written with a female readership in mind—there was a noble and erudite form of transmission in the 18th century, that of scholarly dictionaries and directories, but Wollstonecraft obviously was not familiar with that literature. Indeed, in her list of exemplary women, she put names that were either very close to her in time, such as Macaulay, or very distant, such as women of ancient Rome. Her lack of knowledge of the 17th-century English women who had preceded her in the desire to restore women's dignity is all the more striking given that her approach is comparable to theirs.

An early example is Mary Astell (1666–1731), listed in a widely distributed work by the scholar George Ballard (1706–55) entitled *Memoirs of Several Ladies of Great Britain* (1752, reprinted 1775). Like Wollstonecraft, Astell believed that women's incapacity was acquired, not natural; her *Serious Proposal to the Ladies, for the Advancement of Their True and Greatest Interest, by a Lover of Her Sex* (1694) expressed the need for rational education for women. For Astell, domestic tyranny was even more intolerable than political despotism: "If all Men are born free, how is it that all Women are born slaves?" she asked in *Some Reflections upon Marriage* (1700), written on the occasion of a court case between the duke and duchess of Mazarin, a trial that was the talk of the town in France and in England, where the duchess had taken refuge. Both Astell and Wollstonecraft belonged to the Anglican Church. However—and despite the difference in historical context—their attitudes diverged when it came to dissent. We know of Wollstonecraft's sympathy for radical dissenters, supporters of the French Revolution. Some 85 years earlier, Astell, on the contrary, had been concerned about the increasing number of sects. While she advocated moderation toward dissenters, she associated them with the causes of civil war (in 1704 she wrote: "But are Sedition and Rebellion no Grievances? they are not less, perhaps more Grievous than Tyranny, even to the People"). In fact, Astell joined the theorists of natural law in their general mistrust of any feeling of insubordination.

While Wollstonecraft, who surely did not have a vast library available to her while she was writing her work, did not make use of the major historical and political dictionaries of her time, this was certainly not true of the French Academician Condorcet. His "On the Admission of Women to the Rights of Citizenship" is replete with references to renowned women of the 17th century. The abundance of proper names is evidence that he had read these abbreviated biographies:

> Would not the rights of citizens in France have been better defended, [at the Estates General assembly] in 1614, by the adoptive daughter of Montaigne than by the counselor Courtin, who was a believer in magic and occult powers? Was not the princesse des Ursins superior to Chamillard? Could not the marquise du Châtelet have written a despatch as well as M. Rouillé?

Enlightened women against male obscurantism! There could be no uncertainty about the existence of these talented women, whose extraordinary abilities had been repeatedly recognized and celebrated. Even women who had wished to remain anonymous figured in these dictionaries. Gabrielle Suchon (1631–1703), for example, a nun who had renounced her vows and authored two works, *Traité de la morale et de la politique* (1693; Treatise on Morality and Politics), signed Aristophile, and *Traité du célibat volontaire, ou La vie sans engagement* (1700; Treatise on Voluntary Celibacy; or, Life without Commitment), was unmasked in Moreri's *Dictionnaire historique* (1674; Historical Dictionary), a great success with the public, reprinted and improved many times. In his *Dictionnaire historique et critique* (1697; A General Dictionary, Historical and Critical) also much read in the first half of the 18th century, Pierre Bayle did not limit himself to drawing up lists of women writers or those famous for some other reason, but also noted points of debate between them, and the refutations that had been elaborated to various arguments, thereby reconstructing for us the interactive sphere in which these women produced their texts. In the entry on Lucrezia Marinella (sometimes spelled Marinelli), Bayle wrote:

> A Venetian Lady who had a good deal of wit and, among other books, published a work entitled *La nobilità e l'eccellenza delle donne con diffetti e mancamenti de gli huomini* [*The Nobility and Excellence of Women, and the Defects and Vices of Men*]. For her sex she claimed not only equality, as some authors have done—note B—but even superiority. Mademoiselle de Schurman did not at all approve of the design of this work.

In note B he continued his remarks:

> I shall only name two of [these authors]. One is Mademoiselle de Gournai, who wrote a small treatise called *De l'égalité des hommes et des femmes* [On the Equality of Men and Women]. Her claim was disapproved by Mademoiselle de Schurman. . . . The other author is the man who in Paris in 1673 published a work entitled, *De l'égalité des deux sexes, discours physique et moral où l'on voit l'importance de se defaire des prejugez* [On the Equality of the Two Sexes: Physical and Moral Discourse in Which May Be Seen the Importance of Being Rid of Prejudices]. He thought he was being written against and was indeed threatened with this; but seeing no refutation forthcoming, he himself wrote against his own book; for in the year 1675 he published the *Traité de l'excellence des hommes contre l'égalité des sexes* [Treatise on the Excellence of Men against Equality of the Sexes]. Upon careful examination of all he says [in this last work], it appears that he had no design to refute his first work and that he was instead seeking to confirm it indirectly. However that may be, these two works were reprinted in Paris in 1679. It was a long time before we discovered who the author was. It was reported in the Nouvelles de la Republique des lettres of October 1685 that his name was Frelin, but some time afterward it was declared that it would be better to call him Poulain. This is, in effect, his true name, though he assumed that of La Barre for the third edition in 1691. . . . Let it be said in passing that he was a Lorraine clergyman who embraced the Protestant Communion at Geneva.

This is an admirable presentation by Bayle, who, despite his own reticence regarding the idea of sexual equality—in the entry "Gournai" (on Marie de Gournay) he reproached la demoiselle (the spinster) for having become involved in politics: "a person of her sex ought carefully to avoid that kind of controversies"—gives us a sense of where the question stood, by putting in context and perspective the work of the protagonists of that moment in intellectual life. Bayle put Poulain de La Barre, a theologian and philosopher of Cartesian inspiration and a Protestant, whose main work on sexual equality was translated into English under the title *The Woman As Good As the Man*, in the same line as Gournay, despite the strong religious and political differences between them. Gournay was known for her vigorous defense of the Jesuits, who, after the death of Henri IV, had been accused of inspiring the regicide. In this way, an international arena of controversy was defined, characteristic of this erudite literature whose authors so enjoyed intellectual exchange and debate.

Anna Maria van Schurman (1607–78), a Dutch Protestant knowledgeable in ancient languages, was one of the central figures of this female intellectual life. Her renown crossed borders and gave rise to numerous written notices and much praise. Following her example, the Englishwoman Bathsua Makin (1610–85), governess to the daughter of Charles I, wrote a work with the curious title *An Essay to Revive the Antient* [sic] *Education of Gentlewomen, in Religion, Manners, Arts, and Tongues* (1673), in which she set about cataloging the multiple facets of women's talents, practiced in the most varied disciplines—philosophy, mathematics, poetry, linguistics—and refuted one by one the arguments most often advanced against education for women. Her work, too, drew Ballard's praise. In a similar spirit, in Jacques Georges Chauffepié's supplement to Bayle's *Dictionnaire* (1750–56), in the entry on John Norris, a Platonist and disciple of Pierre Malebranche, Astell was mentioned for her philosophical activities. Was this undeniable recognition connected to the fact that these learned women put limits on the doctrine they defended? Schurman accepted that women be excluded from public responsibilities. That position elicited this question from her opponent, the Calvinist André Rivet, in *Question célèbre, s'il est nécessaire ou non que les filles soient savantes* (1646; A Famous Question, Whether It Be Necessary or Not for Girls to Be Learned):

> [S]ince it is beyond doubt and everyone agrees that women should not be admitted to political responsibilities at all, nor to the dignities of the church, and even less to university chairs, with what purpose would they obtain scientific knowledge with a great deal of effort when it is useless to them and its only goal is associated with ends forbidden to them?

Makin went no further than to grant women responsibility for defending the home in the absence of their husbands. Astell was even more timid, despite her stated desire to intervene in the public debate. Censors, who in France were particularly attentive to writings that attacked religion and royal authority, did not condemn the audacity of these women, whose intellectual excellence suited the ideals of the time. Of course, their undeniable proximity to the religious conflicts of their time sometimes rendered the task of later historians a delicate one, but memory of these women's works and actions was spared.

The situation changed during the second half of the 18th century. The archetype of the woman of letters, incarnated and perpetuated by the great women *salonnières* of the Enlightenment, ceased to be attractive and was ultimately exhausted. Those men who subsequently embodied independence and the dangers of modernity—notably the Encyclopedists—had placed beyond the pale all such attempts at instituting equality between men and women. They had given credibility to the increasingly popular idea that "each sex had a specific destiny that derived from its physical constitution" *(Nouvel ami des femmes)*. This social valorization of sexual determinism, which hardly fit in with the later constitutional debate that produced the defense of women's rights, marked the failure of the arguments that learned women of the preceding century had advanced—but without insisting on the implications of those arguments for the role of women in public life: identical abilities call for identical rights.

Bibliography

Sources

Alletz, Pons-Augustin, *L'esprit des femmes célèbres du siècle de Louis XIV, et de celui de Louis XV, jusqu'à présent*, Paris: Pissot, 1768

Archives parlementaires, 1787 à 1860: Recueil complet des débats législatifs et politiques des Chambres françaises, first series (1787–1799), Paris: Paul Dupont, 1862

Astell, Mary, *A Fair Way with the Dissenters and Their Patrons: Not writ by Mr. L———y, or Any Other Furious Jacobite, Whether Clergyman or Layman; but by a Very Moderate Person and Dutiful Subject to the Queen*, London: R. Wilkin, 1704

Astell, Mary, *The First English Feminist: Reflections upon Marriage and Other Writings*, edited by Bridget Hill, New York: St. Martin's Press, and Aldershot, Hampshire: Gower/ Maurice Temple Smith, 1986

Astell, Mary, *A Serious Proposal to the Ladies, for the Advancement of Their True and Greatest Interest, by a Lover of Her Sex*, London: R. Wilkin, 1694; reprint, edited by Patricia Springborg, London and Brookfield, Vermont: Pickering and Chatto, 1997

Astell, Mary, *Some Reflections upon Marriage, Occasion'd by the Duke & Dutchess of Mazarine's Case; Which Is also Consider'd*, London: John Nutt, 1700; reprint, New York: Source Book Press, 1970

Ballard, George, *Memoirs of Several Ladies of Great Britain, Who Have Been Celebrated for Their Writings or Skill in the Learned Languages, Arts and Sciences*, Oxford: Jackson, 1752; reprint, edited by Ruth Perry, Detroit, Michigan: Wayne State University Press, 1985

Bayle, Pierre, "Dictionnaire historique et critique," Rotterdam, R. Leers, 1967, as *A General Dictionary, Historical and Critical*, 10 vols., London: J. Bettenham, 1734–41

Blackstone, William, *Commentaries on the Laws of England* 3rd edition, Oxford: Clarendon Press, 1768–69

Boudier de Villemert, Pierre-Joseph, *Nouvel ami des femmes, ou La philosophie du sexe, ouvrage nécessaire à toutes les jeunes personnes qui veulent plaire par des qualités solides, avec une notice alphabétique des femmes célèbres en France*, Amsterdam and Paris: Monory, 1779

Brissot, Jacques-Pierre de Warville [founder], *Le patriote français, journal libre impartial et national par une société de citoyens*, Paris (8 July 1789–2 June 1793)

Burke, Edmund, *The Works: Twelve Volumes in Six (1887)*, Hildesheim, Germany, and New York: Georg Olms Verlag, 1975

Bury, Richard, *Histoire abrégée des philosophes et des femmes célèbres*, Paris: Monory, 1773

[Cambis, Madame de?], *Du sort actuel des femmes*, Paris: Imprimerie du Cercle social, 1791

Chantreau, Pierre-Nicolas, *Dictionnaire national et anecdotique*, Paris: Politocopolis, 1790

Condorcet, Jean-Antoine-Nicolas de Caritat, marquis de, "On the Admission of Women to the Rights of Citizenship," in *Selected Writings*, by Condorcet, edited by Keith Michael Baker, Indianapolis, Indiana: Bobbs-Merrill, 1976

Conway, Moncure Daniel, *The Life of Thomas Paine; with a History of His Literary, Political and Religious Career in America, France and England*, 2 vols., New York and London: G.P. Putnam's Sons, 1892

Gautier d'Agoty, Jean-Baptiste, *Galerie française ou portraits des hommes et des femmes célèbres qui ont paru en France: On y a joint un abrégé de leur vie prise dans les meilleures sources*, Paris: Herissant, Le Fils, 1770

Genlis, Stéphanie Félicité, comtesse de, *Adélaïde and Theodore; or, Letters on Education, containing All the Principles Relative to Three Different Plans of Education*, London: C. Bathurst, 1783

Gouges, (M. Gouze dite Olympe de), "Les droits de la femme, āla reine, s.l.n.d., *The Rights of Woman*, translated by Val Stevenson, London: Pythia, 1989

Gournay, Marie de Jars de, *Adieu de l'âme du roy de France et de Navarre Henry le Grand, à la royne avec la défence des pères jésuites*, Lyon: J. Poyet, 1610

Gournay, Marie de Jars de, *Égalité des hommes et des femmes A la reine*, 1622; as *Égalité des hommes et des femmes, le grief des dames, le proumenoir de Monsieur de Montaigne*, Geneva: Droz, 1993

Lacroix, Jean François de, *Dictionnaire portatif des femmes célèbres*, Paris: Chez L. Cellot, 1769; revised edition, Paris: Belin et Volland, 1788

Lairtullier, E., *Les femmes célèbres de 1789 à 1795, et leur influence dans la Révolution, pour servir de suite et de complément à toutes les histoires de la Révolution française*, Paris: n.p., 1840

[Labenette?], *Le journal des droits de l'homme* (8 July–28 August 1791, 30 in-octavo issues)

Makin, Bathsua, *Essay to Revive the Antient Education of Gentlewomen in Religion, Manners, Arts, and Tongues*, London: J.D., 1673; reprinted in *Bathsua Makin: Woman of Learning*, edited by Francis Teague, Lewisburg, Pennsylvania: Bucknell University Press, and London: Associated University Presses, 1998

Moreri, Louis, *Le grand Dictionnaire historique, ou Le mélange curieux de l'histoire sacrée et profane*, Lyon: J. Jirin et B. Rivière, 1674; new edition, Paris: Libraires associés, 1759

Norris, John, and Mary Astell, *Letters concerning the Love of God, between the Author of the Proposal to the Ladies and Mr. John Norris*, London: Samuel Manship and Richard Wilkin, 1695

Paine, Thomas, *The Rights of Man: Being an Answer to Mr. Burke's Attack on the French Revolution*, London: J.S. Jordan, 1791

Paine, Thomas, *The Writings of Thomas Paine*, edited by Moncure D. Conway, New York: Putnam, 1894–96; reprint, New York: AMS Press, 1967, and London: Routledge/Thoemmes, 1996

Poore, Benjamin Perley, *The Federal and State Constitutions, Colonial Charters, and Other Organic Laws of the United States*, 2 vols., Washington, D.C.: Government Printing Office, 1877

Poulain de la Barre, François, "De l'égalité des deux sexes, discours physique et moral où l'on voit l'importance de se defaire des préjugez," Paris, J. du Puys, 1673, as *De l'éducation des dames pour la conduite de l'esprit dans les sciences et dans les mœurs: Entretiens*, Paris: Jean Du Puis, 1674; reprint, Toulouse, France: Université de Toulouse le Mirail, 1980

Poulain de la Barre, François, *The Woman As Good As the Man: or, The Equallity of Both Sexes*, translated by A.L., London: N. Brooks, 1677

Poulain de la Barre, François, *De l'excellence des hommes contre l'égalité des sexes*, Paris: Jean Du Puis, 1675

Roederer, C. Pierre-Louis [founder], *Journal d'économie publique, de morale et de politique*, 5 vols., Paris: Imprimerie du Journal de Paris, An V–1797

Staël, Germaine Necker, baronne de "Lettres sur le caractère et les écrits de J.J. Rousseau," Paris, 1788, as *Letters on the Writings and Character of J.J. Rousseau*, London: G.G.J. and J. Robinson, 1789

Suchon, Gabrielle, *Du célibat volontaire, ou, La vie sans engagement*, Paris: Guignard, 1700; reprint, Paris: Indigo, Côté-Femmes, 1994

Suchon, Gabrielle, *Traité de la morale et la politique divisé en trois parties scavoir la liberté, la science et l'autorité*, Lyon: J. Certe, 1693; reprint, Paris: des femmes, 1988

Talleyrand-Périgord, Charles Maurice, prince de Bénévent, *Rapport sur l'instruction publique: Fait, au nom du comité de constitution*, Paris: Imprimerie Nationale, 1791

Ternisien d'Haudricourt, F., *Femmes célèbres de toutes les nations avec leurs portraits*, Paris: n.p., 1788

Tristan, Flora, "Promenades dans Londres," Paris, 1840; as *Flora Tristan's London Journal 1840*, translated by Dennis Palmer and Giselle Pincetl, London: G. Prior Publishers, and Boston: Charles River Books, 1980

Tristan, Flora, "Union ouvrière," Paris, 1843; as *The Workers' Union*, translated by Beverly Livingston, Urbana: University of Illinois Press, 1983

Wollstonecraft, Mary, *A Vindication of the Rights of Men, in a Letter to the Right Honourable Edmund Burke, Occasioned by His Reflection on the Revolution in France*, London: Johnson, 1790

Wollstonecraft, Mary, *A Vindication of the Rights of Woman with Structures on Political and Moral Subjects*, London: J. Johnson, 1792. Edited by Carol H. Poston, New York, London: W. Norton, 1975

Wollstonecraft, Mary, *The Works of Mary Wollstonecraft*, edited by Janet Todd and Marilyn Butler, 7 vols., New York: New York University Press, 1989

Reference

Blanc, Olivier, *Olympe de Gouges*, Paris: Syros, 1981

Butler, Marilyn, editor, *Burke, Paine, Godwin, and the Revolution Controversy*, Cambridge and New York: Cambridge University Press, 1984

Le Cour Grandmaison, Olivier, *Les citoyennetés en Révolution, 1789–1794*, Paris: Presses Universitaires de France, 1992

Duprat, Catherine, "Don et citoyenneté en l'an II: Les vertus du peuple français," in *Révolution et république: L'exception française*, edited by Michel Vovelle, Paris: Kimé, 1994

Fauré, Christine, editor, *Les déclarations des droits de l'homme de 1789*, Paris: Payot, 1988; second, revised edition, 1992

Fauré, Christine, "Rights or Virtues: Women and the Republic," in vol. 2 of *Republicanism: A Shared European Heritage*, edited by Martin Van Gelderen and Quentin Skinner, Cambridge: Cambridge University Press, 2002

Godineau, Dominique, *Citoyennes tricoteuses: Les femmes du peuple à Paris pendant la Révolution*, Aix-en-Provence, France: Alinéa, 1988

Godineau, Dominique, Madeleine Rebérioux, and Antoine de Baecque, editors, *Ils ont pensé les droits de l'homme: Textes et débats, 1789–1793*, Paris: Ligue des Droits de l'Homme, and Études et Documentations Internationales, 1989

Hill, Bridget, *The Republican Virago: The Life and Times of Catherine Macaulay, Historian*, Oxford: Clarendon Press, and New York: Oxford University Press, 1992

Levy, Darline Gay, Harriet Branson Applewhite, and Mary Durham Johnson, editors, *Women in Revolutionary Paris, 1789–1795: Selected Documents Translated with Notes and Commentary*, Urbana: University of Illinois Press, 1979

Robertson, David, *A Dictionary of Human Rights*, London: Europa Publications, 1997

Sapiro, Virginia, *A Vindication of Political Virtue: The Political Theory of Mary Wollstonecraft*, Chicago: University of Chicago Press, 1992

Thompson, Roger, *Women in Stuart England and America: A Comparative Study*, London and Boston: Routledge and Kegan Paul, 1974

Tomalin, Claire, *The Life and Death of Mary Wollstonecraft*, New York: Harcourt Brace Jovanovich, and London: Weidenfeld and Nicolson, 1974

Vincent, Bernard, *Thomas Paine; ou, La religion de la liberté: Biographie*, Paris: Aubier, 1987

Women Militants in the Brabant and Liégeois Revolutions

JANET L. POLASKY

Two anonymous pamphlets appeared in 1790 in the newly independent republics of Belgium and Liège, the *Réclamations des citoyennes de Bruxelles, tant démocrates qu'aristocrates* (Demands of the Women Citizens of Brussels, Democrats As Well As Aristocrats) and the *Réclamations des citoyennes de Liège, tant démocrates qu'aristocrates* (Demands of the Women Citizens of Liège, Democrats As Well As Aristocrats). Apart from the titles, the two pamphlets were identical. "We have groaned under the abuse of masculine authority for more than 17 centuries," the authors of the two pamphlets protested. They exhorted their Belgian and Liégeois readers to look to France, where women had taken up the pen against men, the enemies of their happiness. "Revolutions of every type tell us that our reign is coming," proclaimed the authors.

Nature had determined that women should be wives and mothers, the authors explained; reason demanded that they enjoy rights commensurate with these roles. Above all, women should regain control over the property they brought to their marriage, a right that they had not enjoyed for centuries. In particular, the authors called attention to the adverse legislation of the jurist Dominique-François de Sohet, a native of the village of Chooz in the principality of Stavelot. In his *Instituts de droit* (1770–81; Legal Institutions), Sohet proposed to allow women ownership of their personal attire and a spindle only, according to the authors. They suggested that Sohet must never have truly loved a woman, because if he had, "he would have felt the need for that delicate influence that we have always had on men." The unique nature of women would serve to complement that of men in society as in the family, they concluded.

Foremost among a long list of demands, the authors of the *Réclamations* called for the establishment of a national assembly composed of 600 members, of whom 300 were to be women. In addition, two academies were to be established and presided over by women, one for the French language, including eloquence and poetry—considered the natural subject of women—and the second to oversee the education of women and to teach *politesse* (refinement) to men.

All husbands who were unfaithful to their wives were to be severely punished by the revolutionary authorities. Men who harmed women's reputations were to be banned from employment in the revolutionary society. Finally, the authors threatened, "If you reject such well-founded demands, you will bring upon yourselves—through the just and deserved punishment we reserve for you—a second revolution, which will have an ending even more radical than your carefully laid plans, because it will bring the world to an end."

Despite all the attention paid to these two pamphlets in recent years by historians, I will argue that they are not typical of either the Brabant or the Liégeois revolutions. For example, the authors call for an end to the distinction made between aristocrats and patriots, defend the aristocrats as true patriots, and then proclaim the need for a national assembly. These appeals would have been incompatible with the revolutionary rhetoric of the Belgian provinces or of Liège.

The two revolutions actually differed radically one from another. Although both the Belgians and the Liégeois rose in rebellion against empires to the east, the paths followed in the two revolutionary societies were quite different. The subsequent political developments in the neighboring provinces would not seem to lend themselves to an identical treatment in the two pamphlets. The Belgians had revolted against their ruler, the Austrian emperor Joseph II, to protest against his plans for reforming their religious, judicial, and administrative institutions. In the midst of widespread prosperity, guild leaders, clergy, and nobles all felt threatened by Joseph's reforms. A number of provincial estates (governments) consequently refused to accord the Austrians their taxes, charging that the Austrians had violated the terms of the centuries-old constitutions of the Belgian provinces.

The confrontation came to a head in June 1789, when the Austrians barred the doors of the meeting rooms of the Brabant Estates in Brussels. Henri van der Noot, a counsel to the Brabant Estates, issued a formal protest. He then set out to negotiate support for an armed rebellion from the English, the Dutch, and the Prussians. Meanwhile, a group of lawyers, wholesale merchants, and a few nobles formed a secret revolutionary society, Pro Aris et Focis. These so-called democrats rallied village populations and distributed guns, ammunition, and pamphlets throughout the provinces. In the summer of 1789 the volunteer troops recruited by Pro Aris et Focis gathered and trained at Van der Noot's headquarters across the Dutch border.

In October 1789 the Belgian revolutionaries issued a manifesto of independence modeled after the American Declaration of Independence. They launched their military campaign from Breda. Much to everyone's surprise, this "army of the moon" succeeded in driving the Austrian troops from the Belgian provinces. Henri Van der Noot proclaimed Belgian independence from Austrian rule in December 1789.

Van der Noot, seconded by Prelate Pierre Van Eupen, declared the provincial Belgian estates sovereign. Adding the powers formerly exercised by the Austrian emperor and his governors-general to their own, the estates set out to rule in the name of the Belgian people as the États Belgiques Unis (United Belgian States). The leaders of Pro Aris et Focis charged the estates with usurping the people's sovereignty. "An exclusive aristocracy has arrogated all power in a manner incompatible with the true liberty and happiness of the people," leaders of the Société Commerciale de Bruxelles (Brussels Commercial Society) complained. Angry groups of artisans in the cities, supported by peasants on Sunday pilgrimages to the capital, chased the democratic critics of privilege and tradition through the streets and pillaged their homes. By May 1790 most of the democrats had been forced to seek refuge across the French border. The Austrians returned in October 1790 to defeat the ragged army of a divided Belgian republic.

The Liégeois revolted to declare their independence from the Holy Roman Empire in the summer of 1789. In contrast to their neighbors, however, they also revolted against privilege. César de Hoensbroeck had succeeded the enlightened François-Charles de Velbruck as prince bishop of the principality of Liège in 1785. Three estates shared legislative power with the prince. In 1789 the German prince, without seeking permission from the estates, prohibited the export of grain in hopes of alleviating the severe shortages that plagued Liège. The Second Estate quickly condemned the prince for failing to consult the estates. They seethed when he unilaterally limited gambling in Spa.

Pamphlets written by the Société Patriotique (Patriotic Society), a group formed in 1787 by Jean Nicolas Bassenge, Jean de Chestret, and Jean Jacques Fabry, and popular demonstrations in the streets of Liège broadened the conflict over the balance of powers between the prince and the estates. By August 1789, when the prince finally agreed to make concessions to the Liégeois, it was too late for reforms. Groups of bourgeois and workers employed in the rapidly industrializing region had joined the cause of the estates. Together they marched to the Hôtel de Ville on 18 August 1789 and declared Fabry and Chestret the new mayors. After they brought the prince back to the city from his chateau at Seraing, he agreed to a revision of the Liégeois constitution. The "Heureuse révolution" (Happy Revolution) appeared to be at an end, won it seemed by the workers and the bourgeoisie in the name of the principles of the philosophes.

However, neither the prince, who had taken up temporary residency in Trèves, nor the aristocrats were prepared to abandon their privileges without a fight. The Chambre de Wetzler (Chamber of Wetzler) ordered the directors of the Cercle de Westphalie (Westphalian Circle) to support Hoensbroeck. Meanwhile, the newly enlarged Liégeois Third Estate had decided that the program of the Société Patriotique was too moderate. Metallurgists signed a Déclaration des Droits de l'Homme et du Citoyen (Declaration of the Rights of Man and Citizen) and peasants denounced traditional forms of taxation. Prussian troops then moved in, ostensibly to protect the Liégeois from the Austrians who threatened to invade. When the Prussian troops withdrew in April, the Liégeois declared the end of the rule of Hoensbroeck as prince bishop, organized an army, and abolished the guilds. With the Constitutional Assembly of France as a model, the municipal government of Liège called on the citizens of the city to swear allegiance to the continuing revolution. The Austrians, joined by the Cercle de Westphalie, invaded Liège in January 1791 and reestablished Hoensbroeck.

Both the revolutionary regimes were short-lived. But the similarity ended there. At one point, the leaders of the Liège Revolution had considered asking the neighboring États Belgiques Unis to join together in an alliance. The Liégeois needed external support. The journalist Pierre Lebrun was skeptical, explaining that the divergence of principles between the two revolutions had erected "an impenetrable wall of separation." The Liégeois had founded a republic on the principles of liberty and equality, while the Belgians, especially the Brabançons, had returned to their medieval constitution safeguarding the privileges of the nobility, the clergy, and the guilds. In contrast to the alliance of the bourgeoisie and workers that coalesced as the leadership of the Liégeois Revolution, Belgian artisans, who enjoyed substantial privileges, supported the first two estates in Brussels. It is therefore surprising that the *Réclamations des citoyennes tant démocrates qu'aristocrates* appealed to the Belgians and the Liégeois in precisely the same terms. Furthermore, the calls for recognition of the property rights of married women and for equal representation of the sexes in a national assembly did not have even the faintest echo in either newly independent nation. These two *Réclamations* stand in marked contrast to the rest of the voluminous pamphlet literature generated by the Brabant and Liège revolutions.

Far more typical for the Belgians is another pamphlet, the *Précis historique sur les anciennes Belges en faveur et pour l'émulation des modernes: avec les preuves du droit qu'ont les femmes d'entrer aux États, de commander les armées, de traiter des affaires publiques et d'être consultées sur toutes les résolutions à prendre* (Historical Summary of Belgian Women of Old for the Edification of the Women of Today: With Demonstrations of the Rights of Women to Enter the Estates, Command Armies, Discuss Public Affairs, and Be Consulted on All Decisions to Be Made). This pamphlet expounded the centuries-old tradition of feminine involvement in public life in the Belgian provinces. According to the author (who styled himself "the friend of women"): "That the Belgians, the most ancient free people, have never lost their liberty is due to the fact that women no less than men have labored at all times for its preservation." The author supported his assertion with a multitude of examples of ancient and medieval Belgian women who had taken an interest in public affairs by deliberating in assemblies, arming themselves, or reigning as queens. Even though "their physical weakness" had sometimes forced them to delegate their duties to men—especially during the age of chivalry when they became the objects of admiration rather than actors—Belgian women had always been in the forefront of patriotic causes, the author explained. He despaired, however, that their 18th-century descendants no longer felt "the sacred duty to labor equally on the task of Liberty, in which they never ceased to cooperate throughout the centuries by all the sacrifices their sex was capable of." The author dedicated his call to revolutionary action to the comtesse d'Yve.

Anne Thérèse Philippine d'Yve, a 50-year-old unmarried countess, played a significant part in the Brabant Revolution. Initially, her home served as an informal salon where revolutionary guild leaders, nobles, and bankers could meet to discuss politics. In 1788, after the Austrians had arrested a number of suspected revolutionary leaders, the mayor of Brussels, who often visited her home, urged her to be more circumspect in her political activities. She ignored his advice and continued to distribute revolutionary pamphlets and information on the estates, troop movements, and treaty negotiations to her extensive network of correspondents. She was one of the very few revolutionaries who cooperated with both the democrats and the supporters of the estates.

The comtesse d'Yve also wrote her own pamphlets, in which she brought together ideas from both political factions. She defended the medieval constitutions, especially the Joyeuse Entrée (Joyous Entry) of Brabant, which, she argued, had served the Belgians well in the past and should be preserved as the foundation of the new state. At the same time, she called on the people of Belgium to fight for their natural rights and to secure their sovereignty for themselves.

Respected by the democrats and the leaders of the estates, the comtesse d'Yve often seems to have played the role of intermediary. By the spring of 1790, although both sides continued to confide in her, the countess had become increasingly critical of the democratic opposition to the newly independent Belgian state. She feared that their plans to reform the estates and to eliminate privilege would undermine the efforts of the États Belgiques Unis to secure recognition from the other sovereigns of Europe. The Brabant revolutionaries had overthrown Joseph II because he had violated the terms of their centuries-old constitution, she reminded the democrats. Who were they to presume to change that constitution so hastily? But while her attacks against the "democratic cabal" became more virulent, so too did her complaints about the stupidity of Van der Noot. One of her regular correspondents suggested in despair at the wrangling Belgians that if only the countess were not a woman, she herself could have led the revolutionaries along a more sensible and moderate course. As a woman, she participated not by governing, but by observing, discussing, and writing.

The comtesse d'Yve alluded once in her correspondence to the political rights of women. She suggested facetiously that if the democrats were really serious about granting the vote to propertyless villagers, nothing should prevent them from concluding that "women, who make up at least half of the nation, must also be represented." The propertyless villagers, like women, were already represented in the estates, she reasoned; they had no need for separate representation.

Women from two leading noble families, the duchesse d'Ursel and the duchesse d'Arenberg, also participated in the Brabant Revolution on the side of the democrats. Their husbands had corresponded with French philosophes, held high-ranking positions in the Austrian army, invested in mining and banking operations, and participated in processions at the head of the guilds' honorary volunteer units in Brussels before their outspoken support for the democrats led them to fear arrest by Van der Noot in the spring of 1790. The duchesses of Ursel and Arenberg remained in the Belgian provinces after their husbands fled. The duchesse d'Ursel had donated her family artillery to Pro Aris et Focis and driven her own horses to the gates of Brussels to welcome the victorious revolutionaries in December 1789.

Although the Austrian military commander despaired of the tenacity of "this party of Amazons," there is no evidence that the Belgians themselves considered the participation of the noblewomen to be extraordinary. The names of other noblewomen appear on the petitions and in the correspondence of both revolutionary factions. As the *Précis historique sur les anciennes belges* suggests, this participation of noblewomen in the public life of the Belgian provinces continued a long-established practice.

Perhaps the most visible woman in the Brabant Revolution, however, was Jeanne de Bellem, the mistress of the revolutionary leader Henri Van der Noot. Her participation in the Brabant Revolution could be characterized as a lower-bourgeois parody of the ancien régime tradition of court patronage. Before her liaison with Van der Noot, de Bellem had been a domestic servant, and according to some accounts, a prostitute. When Van der Noot started writing the petitions for the Brabant Estates in 1787, Bellem also took up her pen. She wrote a number of political pamphlets, often in verse, which she distributed with her daughter Marianne through the streets of Brussels. These pamphlets called on the Belgian people to rise up and throw off the tyranny of Austrian rule. "Belgian people/Tyrannical court / Follow the example of America," she urged in one of her typical verses.

De Bellem also served as go-between, carrying messages to Van der Noot from guild leaders and nobles who dared not be seen in public with the famous revolutionary. After Van der Noot fled Brussels for London in the summer of 1788, Austrian soldiers arrested de Bellem. She continued to relay political news to a number of correspondents, including Van der Noot, from her Brussels prison through an increasingly complicated chain of couriers. Van der Noot wrote to her, too, though infrequently, usually complaining about the weak English beer and the overcooked vegetables. At one point she complained of his failure to write more regularly to her in prison, "I wrote you that I have been very ill. I didn't write you that I was dead." De Bellem was feisty. When the first two Estates seemed about to cave in to the emperor's threats in November 1788 and to vote him his taxes over the resistance of the Third Estate, she wrote an anguished letter complaining that the nobles and the clergy "are like the gentile gods—they have eyes, ears, and mouths, but they do not see or hear and speak up no more. They have feet and hands, but they use them for nothing but presenting themselves to the Austrian minister." Liberated at last after a long and well-publicized trial, de Bellem accompanied Van der Noot on his triumphal entry into Brussels in December 1789. Together they paraded through Brussels in an open carriage and attended a pageant at the Théâtre de la Monnaie celebrating the Belgian victory over the Austrians. Pamphlets resonated with references to Van der Noot as the Belgian George Washington; however, there were no references to Jeanne de Bellem, his mistress, as a virtuous Martha.

Instead, the press regularly singled out the amorous liaison between de Bellem and Van der Noot for ridicule. To criticize Van der Noot's increasingly authoritarian rule within the Belgian estates, they attacked the political influence de Bellem was alleged to have over the self-appointed Belgian leader. Cartoonists, for example, portrayed de Bellem rocking an oversized wicker cradle full of sleeping guild leaders. She is depicted sitting on the throne, completely in control while the other revolutionary leaders look on. Another popular cartoon positions her driving a vehicle pulled by the revolutionary leaders, steam pouring forth from a cooking pan perched on her head. She is also portrayed concealing the plotting leaders of the estates under her ample skirts.

Pamphleteers joined the fray. The author of two of the more vicious satires, *Vie amoureuse de Jeanne de Bell—m, dite la Pin . . . u, Maîtresse en Titre d'un des célèbres Personnages du Brabant* (Love Life of Jeanne de Bell—m, Known as La Pin . . . u, Established Mistress of One of the Famous Persons of Brabant) and *Histoire secrète de la Révolution* (Secret History of the Revolution) argued that not only had Van der Noot declared himself duke of the Belgian provinces after the popular revolutionary victory, but his mistress, de Bellem, had continued the aristocratic parody by naming herself duchess. Neither had legitimate claim to their positions. A.J.D. Robineau, one of the less scrupulous pamphleteers, further accused de Bellem of inspiring the coterie of followers surrounding Van der Noot, all allegedly her lovers, to horrifying acts of terror against the democrats. According to his *Histoire secrète de la Révolution*, the evening after the leaders of the Brussels guilds refused to swear allegiance to Van der Noot, thus revealing their preference for an alliance with the democrats, de Bellem muttered vengefully, "Well. They should all be exterminated tonight." The ribald tales recounted in the multitude of pamphlets resembled the attacks written throughout early modern Europe against political mistresses who allegedly took advantage of their informal access to power. In form and content, they repeated the charges made against the French court, for example.

It is difficult to know how de Bellem perceived her own political role. Her correspondents wrote fawningly to her that they wished they could be planted as tulips in her garden so that they could admire her all day. She answered these letters, apologizing for her handwriting, which she compared to the scrawls of a cat, and for the mediocrity of her ideas. She added that they should not expect much from her as she was, after all, only a woman. Van Eupen noted in a letter praising her virtues to Van der Noot that when he was ill she had cared for him "like a mother."

The Liégeoise whose revolutionary role is most noted by historians is Théroigne de Méricourt. Her connection with the revolution in Liège was tenuous, however. She was born Anne-Joseph Terwagne in Marcourt, a village in the Belgian Ardennes, in 1762. In August 1789 she was following the debates of the National Assembly in Versailles. By then a resident of France, she appears to have had no contact with either Fabry or Bassenge during the revolution. After her death, the Liégeois razed her house; no streets were named in her honor.

In contrast to Théroigne de Méricourt, neither the comtesse d'Yve nor Jeanne de Bellem departed from the roles traditionally played by women of privilege during the ancien régime. Then again, it should be noted, few Belgian men assumed revolution-

ary roles not already sanctioned by practice under the ancien régime either. The political participation of these notable women reflected the complex web of economic and social roles played by women in the Belgian provinces and in Liège, as well as the mosaic of their legal position.

Unmarried women enjoyed legal privileges similar to men in the domain of private law. Noblewomen could inherit fiefs, for example. Since the 13th century, urban women had exercised a full range of commercial privileges as *marchandes publiques* (women merchants). Married women could legally act for their husbands in commercial affairs. They also had the power to draw up a will without the consent of their husbands, maintained quasi equality in disposing of goods during marriage, and enjoyed near equality in exercising authority over children. However, the husband's rights to correct his wife were quite liberal, and she was obliged to follow him wherever he chose to go.

In contrast to this near equality in private law, in neither the Belgian provinces nor in Liège were women admitted to public functions. The alleged physical weakness of women was cited as justification for excluding them from the exercise of political rights.

Given the participation of women in Belgian guilds and their presence in the markets and churches, it is not surprising, albeit also not well documented, that collective groups of women joined the revolution. Women did not serve as guild leaders, so they were not involved in an official capacity in defending the privileges of the Third Estate. Hence, they are invisible in the surviving files of revolutionary correspondence. However, from chroniclers' accounts, sketches, petitions, and pamphlets, we know that women made up the crowds that resisted efforts to collect taxes in Flanders. In July 1789 women carried statues of the Virgin Mary in procession through the streets of Namur and surrounding villages in defiance of Austrian decrees. Austrian commanders also complained about the guerrilla tactics of village women who dropped stones from housetops onto the heads of the Austrian soldiers below. In the region of Alost, women joined the pro-Austrian insurrectionary movements in the summer of 1790.

Once they had won their independence, daily cavalcades of women presented the Belgian Congress with cannon, ammunition, and arms to defend the new republic. They appeared costumed as Justice, Force, Prudence, and Harmony to celebrate the birthday of their revolutionary leader, Henri Van der Noot. This ceremonial presence parallels that of their French neighbors.

The richest documentation of the participation of artisan women comes from the revolutionary pamphlets. Women are frequently portrayed in the dialogues debating political grievances and plotting rebellion. They are to be seen in democratic pamphlets as well as those of the estates. It is significant that the women are depicted realistically, rather than allegorically. A visual echo of these pamphlets, drawings show women gathered in crowds in the marketplace and under fire from Austrian troops.

One pamphlet tells the story of a young Belgian girl who resolves to join her fiancé in the revolutionary army. Her mother applauds her determination, exclaiming in a statement that is reminiscent of the homage paid to the comtesse d'Yve in the *Précis historique*, "I would love to see you cultivate the ancient courage that forms the distinctive character of Belgian women."

The mother then summons a priest to marry the young couple before they depart for battle. When the priest questions the wisdom of sending her only daughter to the front, the mother replies that perhaps because he is a foreigner he does not understand that Belgian women differ from other European women. "They are no less suited to glory than to pleasure," she explains. In the last scene, the daughter Isabelle, armed with her father's sword and gun, departs for battle.

This story, exceptional as it was in its portrayal of female military participation, brings us back to the *Précis historique sur les anciennes belges*, Belgian women from all social groups apparently did participate in the Brabant Revolution in what they perceived as part of a proud national tradition. That is not to suggest that individual women were among the leadership of any of the revolutionary factions, nor that they joined the revolutionary army in any great numbers. But it is to argue that women acted collectively throughout the course of the revolution in the Belgian provinces.

These Belgian revolutionary women do not fit the clearly delineated patterns that we have come to recognize from the French Revolution. Examples of "domestic citizenship" are to be found in Belgium alongside the rough and ready images of ancien régime crowds and privileged *salonnières*, At the conclusion of the *Précis sur les anciennes belges*, for example, the author celebrates the happy mothers of sons who saved the revolution in the poem, "Voeux des mères belges" (Vows of Belgian Mothers):

> Our hands, our feeble hands, would have little power
> Against our enemies, if we were to take up arms;
> But there are our sons! Our tears must run copiously!
> If necessary, all will die, to save the country.

In contrast to the divide drawn by French historians between the bread rioters of the 1780s and the good mothers espoused by revolutionary leaders in the 1790s, these two images turn up side by side in the short-lived Brabant Revolution. They fit together in one complex whole.

All of this is not to argue for a vision of a golden revolutionary age of full female participation in the Belgian provinces. Rather, it suggests versatility among 18th-century Belgian women participating in what was predominantly a man's world. The comtesse d'Yve, Madame de Bellem, and an anonymous Liégeois all demanded "the right to propose one's ideas like everyone else" and deferred to the political wisdom of their correspondents because they were "only" women.

In Belgian society, poised on the edge of industrialization, women participated alongside men in part at least because the ancien régime institutions that had traditionally allowed artisans and nobles a role in the economic and political life of the community had been left largely unchanged. The less prosperous, but more industrially developed region of Liège presents a different picture. We have yet to discover the role of women in this revolution, which *did* fully question corporate structures and privileges. Nevertheless, the heritage of revolutionary activism would be picked up in the 19th century by working women in textile factories and mines throughout the Belgian provinces, including Liège.

Bibliography

Sources

Archives de la Ville de Bruxelles, Brussels. Bibliothèque 813/2: Les femmes belges; Précis historique sur les anciennes Belges

Archives des États Belgiques Unis, Archives Générales du Royaume, Brussels. Lettres adressées à la comtesse d'Yve [Correspondence addressed to the comtesse d'Yve]

Bibliothèque Royale, Brussels. Goethals 210: Anne-Philippe Thérèse, comtesse d'Yve, "A la nation, 10 novembre 1788"; *Réclamations des citoyennes de Bruxelles tant démocrates qu'aristocrates, Révolution belge*, vol. 3, pamphlet 33, and vol. 97, pamphlet 8

Rijkuniversteit Gent, Ghent, Belgium. G 12319: Anne-Philippe Thérèse, comtesse d'Yve, "Au comité de Steenhage, 17 février 1790"

Van de Voorde, Hugo, et al., *Bastille, Boerenkrijg en Tricolore*, Louvain, Belgium: n.p., n.d.

Reference Works

Borgnet, Adolphe, *Histoire de la révolution Liégeoise de 1789 (1785 à 1795)*, 2 vols., Liège, Belgium: De Their and Lovinfosse, 1865; reprint, Brussels: Culture et Civilisation, 1973

Craeybeckx, Jan, and F.G. Scheelings, editors, *La Révolution française et la Flandre: Les Pays-Bas autrichiens entre l'ancien et le nouveau régime*, Brussels: SC Press, 1990

De Peuter, Roger, *Brussel in de achttiende Eeuw: Sociaal-economische structuren en ontwikkelingen in een regionale hoofdstad*, Brussels: VUB Press, 1999

Dhondt, Luc, "La cabale des misérables de 1790: La révolte des campagnes flamandes contre la révolution des notables en Belgique (1789–1791)," in *L'Europe et les révolutions (1770–1800)*, Brussels: Éditions de l'Université de Bruxelles, 1980

Douxchamps-Lefèvre, Cécile, "La femme de la noblesse des Pays-Bas autrichiens et de la principauté de Liège devant la Révolution française," *Réseaux, Revue interdisciplinaire de philosophie morale et politique*, nos. 61–63 (1991)

Dupont-Bouchat, Marie-Sylvie, "Attitudes et comportements des femmes pendant les révolutions en Belgique (1789–1799)," *Réseaux, Revue interdisciplinaire de philosophie morale et politique*, nos. 61–63 (1991)

Gilissen, John, *Le statut de la femme dans l'ancien droit belge*, Brussels: Éditions de la Librarie Encyclopédique, 1962

Harsin, Paul, *La révolution liégeoise de 1789*, Brussels: Renaissance du Livre, 1954

Hélin, Étienne, "Un manifeste féministe à Liège en 1790," *Bulletin de la société royale le vieux Liège* 9 (1976)

Herne, Claude, *1789 dans les provinces belgiques*, Brussels: Contradictions, 1988

Lemaire, Claudine, "La comtesse Anne-Philippine-Thérèse d'Yve, figure de proue de la révolution brabançonne et grande bibliophile, 1738–1814," *Archives et Bibliothèques de Belgique* LXI (1990)

Lorette, J., P. Lefevre, and P. de Gruyse, editors, *Colloque sur la révolution brabançonne, 13–14 octobre 1983*, Brussels: Musée Royal de l'Armée, 1984

Mortier, Roland, and Hervé Hasquin, *Deux aspects contestés de la politique révolutionnaire en Belgique: Langue et culte*, Brussels: Éditions de l'Université de Bruxelles, 1989

Pirenne, Henri, and Jérôme Vercruysse, *Les États Belgiques Unis: Histoire de la révolution belge de 1789–1790*, Paris: Duculot, 1992

Polasky, Janet L., *Revolution in Brussels, 1787–1793*, Brussels: Académie Royale de Belgique, 1985

Polasky, Janet L., "Women in Revolutionary Brussels: 'The Source of Our Greatest Strength,'" in *Women and Politics in the Age of the Democratic Revolution*, edited by Harriet Branson Applewhite and Darline Gay Levy, Ann Arbor: University of Michigan Press, 1990

Raxhon, Philippe, *La révolution liégeoise de 1789: Vue par les historiens belges de 1805 à nos jours*, Brussels: Éditions de l'Université de Bruxelles, 1989

Raxhon, Philippe, "Théroigne de Méricourt; ou, La lecture historiographique d'un mythe révolutionnaire: Le cas des historiens belges," *Réseaux, Revue interdisciplinaire de philosophie morale et politique, nos. 61–63 (1991)*

Roegiers, Jan, "P.S. Van Eupen (1744–1804): Van Ultramontaan tot Revolutionair, Standen en Landen," in *Het einde van het Ancien Régime in Belgie: Colloquium van zaterdag 3 december 1988 te Brussel*, edited by P. Lenders, Kortrijk-Heule, Belgium: UGA, 1991

Roudinesco, Élisabeth, *Théroigne de Méricourt: Une femme mélancolique sous la Révolution*, Paris: Seuil, 1989; as *Théroigne de Méricourt: A Melancholic Woman during the French Revolution*, translated by Martin Thom, London and New York: Verso, 1991

Tassier, Suzanne, *Les démocrates belges de 1789 Étude sur le Vonckisme et la révolution brabançonne*, Brussels: Lamertin, 1930

Vanhemelryck, Fernand, editor, *Revolutie in Brabant, 1787–1793*, Brussels: Centrum Brabantse Geschiedenis, 1990

Van Impe, Éliane, *Marie-Christine van Oostenrijk: Gouvernante-generaal van de zuidelijke Nederlanden, 1781–1789, 1790–1792*, Kortrijk-Heule, Belgium: UGA, 1979

Van Kalken, Frans, *Madame de Bellem: La pompadour des Pays-Bas*, Brussels: Lebègue, 1923

WOMEN AND THE DUTCH REVOLUTIONS OF THE LATE EIGHTEENTH CENTURY

RUDOLF M. DEKKER AND JUDITH A. VEGA

"MUCH IN LITTLE," ROBERT R. PALMER commented in the title of his well-known article about the revolution that took place in Holland in 1795. Since that article's publication in 1954, numerous studies have broadened and complicated our knowledge of the political upheavals in the Northern Netherlands in the last quarter of the 18th century. Thanks to Simon Schama, Cornelis de Wit, Wayne te Brake, Stephan Klein, Maarten Prak, and others, we now understand that these upheavals were more momentous than Palmer believed. But while several aspects of the Dutch revolutions of the 18th century have been studied in depth, little has been written about the role of women. For the most part, women's contribution is still felt to have been marginal. In this essay we endeavor to provide a more substantial evaluation. We will discuss the available knowledge on women's participation in the revolutionary processes of the 1780s and 1790s, as well as on the shifting Dutch spectrum of ideas about women's place in politics, society, and culture. By way of background, we will first briefly sketch the specific nature of the Dutch state and the position of women in the Republic of the United Netherlands in the 17th and 18th centuries.

In 1780 the Dutch Republic experienced the first in the series of revolutions that would sweep through Europe during what Palmer in his major opus discusses as the age of the democratic revolution (see Palmer 1959–64). After the revolt against Spain in the 16th century, the Northern Netherlands had become a federal alliance of seven provinces. The highest authority in this republic resided in the Estates-General, particularly in matters of foreign policy. The provinces and towns were to a large degree independent and were governed by local political elites. For more than two centuries the House of Orange occupied the stadtholderate, the highest government office, which entailed leadership of the army and navy as well as administrative functions. This configuration gave the Orange stadtholders a quasi-monarchical status. Time and again, tensions between the various towns and provinces, and between the princes of Orange and local factions of bourgeois and aristocratic regents, sparked political unrest. Frequently such conflicts were fought in pamphlets, and occasionally on the streets. Continual contestation of the stadtholderate produced two long periods in which that office was suspended.

The revolt against Spain produced few changes in Dutch political institutions. Feudal law was not abolished, and the existing political bodies—the Estates-General, provincial states, town councils, guilds, and local militias—retained their privileges. Dutch society, on the other hand, had a fairly modern outlook, especially in comparison with other countries. Differences in income and wealth in Amsterdam, for instance, were small compared to Venice. The Dutch nobility had kept few political rights and had no privileges with regard to taxation. Nowhere else were tax revenues were as high as in the Netherlands; nowhere else were the army and navy so well organized and well paid. Nowhere else was the control of the political elite over the people as smooth as in Holland, which was partly the result of a well-organized social welfare system that provided aid to the poor and elderly, institutions for orphans, and, last but not least, uncharacteristically modern disciplinary prisons. Housed in magnificent buildings, such institutions became an attraction to visitors from other countries. When judged by these standards, in contrast to the stereotype of its tardiness in implementing modern decision-making processes, the Dutch Republic was perhaps the most efficient state in Europe.

The position of women in the 17th-century Dutch Republic was surprising to foreign visitors at that time, for Dutch women were very visible. They ran shops, operated businesses, and were often entrusted with the management of their husbands' lives and financial affairs. The Englishman Fynes Moryson wrote of Dutch women's "unnatural domineering over their husbands," while the Italian Antonio Carnero thought that they had to support themselves because their men were so often drunk. An English traveler wrote in 1622: "In Holland the wives are so well versed in bargaining, ciphering, and writing, that in the absence of their husbands on long sea voyages they beat the trade at home and their word will pass in equal credit" (see Schama 1987).

These judgments were surely exaggerated. Dutch women in no sense held a position equivalent to that of men. Tax registers show that women from the elite classes were rentiers more often than men, and that poor women were dependent on welfare relief more often than men. This means that more women than men remained outside the labor process, at the highest as well as the lowest levels of society. Nevertheless, most women did work for a living, and the possible changes in their position have led to discussions among historians. Labor, especially schooled labor, was mainly organized in guilds, and these trade associations were monopolized by men. Women's economic position and independence appear to have diminished in the course of 17th and 18th centuries. For example, in the Van Eeghen commercial house in the 18th century, female family members no longer played important roles, as they had before. Another example involves breweries: around 1700 there were many small beer breweries in Rotterdam, including some run by women; at the end of the 18th century, however, only a few big breweries remained, and these were all run by men.

Women's political role also diminished. In the feudal system, noblewomen could exercise power. That was especially true for women who were the wives, widows, or heiresses of the counts and dukes who governed the various political entities of the Low Countries. In the Middle Ages the position of Dutch countesses and duchesses had been based on the premise that governing was a family business. That personal element, however, became less important over time. In the process of state formation, a more rationalized and formalized functioning of political power took shape. This contributed to a withdrawal of women from the political scene. Historian Natalie Zemon Davis has suggested that women were worse off in a republic than in a monarchy (see Davis). One may indeed deem this true for the Netherlands.

As for women's juridical situation, no national legislation existed. Jurisprudence in the republic was based on local law, custom, the Bible, or still other sources. Feudal law remained in force in the Netherlands up to the end of the 18th century, and it was not unfavorable to women. They could inherit and manage feudal estates, which is to say that women could assume ultimate authority in rural communities and appoint sheriffs and clergymen. A woman could thus appoint men to functions that she herself was not allowed to hold. In the cities only a few lower civil offices were open to women, such as that of regent of charity institutions for poor women. But further possibilities were few, apart from the informal influence women could exert through their spouses. Such informal influence declined, however, as politics became increasingly rationalized (see Bosch; Wijs). Women of the lower classes could informally put pressure on the government by organizing protests. In the Netherlands women not only led food and tax riots but also political riots, such as those of 1672 and 1747–48. The leading role of women in demonstrations and riots must be seen in the light of their prominent role in local communities. Elderly women especially, who were often leaders of protests, also held pivotal positions in neighborhood networks, cities, and villages.

The diversity of the law in the Dutch Republic also applied to marriage laws, which were regulated by the provinces independently. The republic did not have a state church, but neither was there an actual separation of church and state. Civil marriage was the rule, although the Reformed Church exerted some influence. For example, marriages between Jews and Christians were forbidden, while marriages between Catholics and Protestants were strongly discouraged. In 1795 the Batavian revolutionaries would institute the separation of church and state. Civil marriage became the legal norm, and church weddings were reduced to private ceremonies. Immediately after 1795 new provincial marriage legislation was enforced. National codification of marriage laws did not come about until the 19th century.

While in most travel accounts it was alleged that women in the Dutch Republic enjoyed great freedom, this was hardly the case in the area of law. Married women came under the authority of their husbands. Before marriage, however, it was possible for a woman to set conditions enabling her to control her own property. In general, parental consent was required for marriage. Unmarried women who had reached legal majority (the age of 25) were no longer under parental guardianship. After they married, however, women were subjected to marital authority, which meant that they were unable to enter into contracts. Merchant women were the exception: they were free to draw up contracts within the limits of their business. In addition, in the case of conjugal difficulties, the wife could ask a judge for a matrimonial division of property. The actual legal status of a husband's "right of guardianship" in marriage was ambiguous; leading legal scholars in the Netherlands were generally opposed to it. In principle, there were only two grounds on which a marriage could be dissolved: adultery and desertion. In the 18th century, there were intense debates on divorce between jurists and moralists, but mere mutual consent was never considered a sufficient ground for ending a marriage. In practice, few divorces were decreed. The social position of married women compared favorably to their legal position: in the average household, they contributed an essential part to the family income and were not limited to domestic tasks (see Haks; Helmers; Huussen).

The role of Dutch women in cultural life was comparable to their place in politics and economy. At first glance it might seem they played only a marginal role in the arts, although there were one or two professional female painters and some well-known women poets. In the broader realm of culture, however, 17th-century Dutch women were active participants, notably in social meetings where poetry was read or music performed. The 18th century saw an increase in the formality of cultural life and the creation of various societies that, in the spirit of the Enlightenment, set cultural and scientific education as their goal. Most of these organizations were closed to women. In a study of several dozen of these societies, Cornelis Singeling identifies 1,487 members, only 38 of whom were women, most often admitted merely as honorary members (see Singeling). In The Hague one society admitted as many as 18 female honorary members, but mainly to fill its treasury with their contributions. A few famous female authors of the period received multiple invitations to become honorary members of learned societies. Petronella Moens (1762–1843) and Adriana van Overstraaten (1756–1828) each belonged to eight different societies. From about 1780 some modern societies, mainly devoted to the study of literature, opened up membership to women. In other societies women were not allowed as members, but they were sometimes allowed to attend lectures and concerts. In Felix Meritis, one of the most important societies in Amsterdam, the possibility of female membership was discussed in 1789. No action was taken, however, because the male membership believed women had duties other than studying the arts and sciences—an argument advanced by the well-known advocate of Enlightenment ideas Jean Henri Van Swinden (1746–1823) (see Hanou 1988). There were no famous salons in Holland, but in more informal circles women could still play a leading role as organizers, as is clear from the diary of Magdalena van Schinne, a woman from the haute bourgeoisie who lived in The Hague in the late 18th century.

The Dutch 18th century did produce several successful female novelists, among them Maria Geertruida Cambon-van der Werken (1734–96). Betje Wolff (1738–1804) and Aagje Deken (1741–1804) together wrote some of the best-known Dutch novels, and it can be said that they were the first professional female writers in Holland. Wolff and Deken's best-known novel, *De historie van Mejuffrouw Sara Burgerhart* (1782; The Story of Miss Sara Burgerhart) appeared in a French translation in 1787. The most internationally renowned woman writer of the period was Isabelle de Charrière (1740–1805), born in the province of Utrecht as Belle van Zuylen. Her first novel was *Le Noble* (1762; The Nobleman), published first in serial form in a periodical and later in book form. This satire of her own class caused a scandal, and her parents had the book pulled out of circulation. Living in Switzerland after her marriage, she was in touch with many personalities all over Europe.

When it comes to finding discussions of political and cultural issues specifically related to women, popular literature is a fertile source. The rights and duties of women became a theme repeatedly discussed in a growing number of periodicals that appeared regularly and contained articles and reviews on various cultural and scientific subjects, and that aimed at a wide public, known both in England and the Netherlands under the title of "spectators." The oldest spectator in the Netherlands, *De Mensch Ontmaskert*, published a letter to the editor sent by a ladies' club. The letter demanded that, henceforth, greater attention be paid to the female sex. This call elicited a strong response because writers were looking for a public of women readers. Justus van Effen (1648–1735), known as the founder of the most important of the Dutch spectators, *De Hollandsche Spectator*, had an ambivalent attitude toward women. On the one hand, he incessantly made fun of aging coquettes; on the other, he insisted on the need for better education for women. The group of writers who contributed to spectators also included some women. The important issue of education for girls was taken up by Betje Wolff, who wrote pedagogical and later political reflections in addition to her novels. In 1765 she published *Bespiegelingen over den Staat der Rechtheid* (Reflections on the State of Justice), a plea for better education and instruction of girls. She considered this a first demand, with future emancipation in view. However, at least at the beginning, she did not envision a role for women in the public arena; before all else, their tasks were to be those of the home.

Two Revolutions: 1787 and 1795

The last two decades of the 18th century were a stormy period in the history of the Netherlands, as in most European countries.

During this time, two revolutions took place in the Netherlands: the first, from 1781 to 1787, was the Revolution of the Patriots, which failed because the partisans of change were defeated by a foreign army, forcing thousands of revolutionaries into exile. The second, the Batavian Revolution of 1795, succeeded, and a democratic republic was instituted. Both revolutions had consequences for attitudes toward women and their potential to take political action.

The 1787 Revolution of the Patriots was the result of an opposition between interest groups, an opposition that already had led to repeated conflicts since the establishment of the Republic of the United Provinces of the Netherlands. On one side stood many of the regents of Holland who dominated the Estates-General, the supreme organ of power in the republic; on the other side were the Princes of Orange, who held the office of stadtholder. The stadtholderate had been suspended twice, in 1651 and in 1702. In each case, with the help of a popular movement, the House of Orange had been able to regain its position, first in 1672 and then in 1747. From 1780 on, discontent with the stadtholder, William V of Orange, increased, especially among many of the regents of Holland. From that year until 1784, the Dutch Republic entered into the war against England. After having chosen the side of the rebellious American colonies, which led to a political and economic crisis, the pro-American regents accused the stadtholder of being secretly on the side of the English.

Both camps had support in every social class. For a long time, historians believed that the political opposition could be reduced to social lines of division: it was assumed that the nobility supported the House of Orange and the regents and the bourgeoisie were patriots, whereas the common people supposedly had chosen the side of the House of Orange for sentimental reasons and from aversion to corruption. However, the historian Cornelis de Wit has convincingly shown that the demarcations were more complex and that, within the upper bourgeoisie, the regents were divided into "aristocrats" who wished to maintain the former relationships of power, and "democrats," who aspired to political renewal (see Wit, 1965; Wit, 1974; Wit, 1978). Moreover, even these distinctions do not do justice to the politically complicated map of the republic around 1780: the historians Wayne te Brake and Maarten Prak have drawn attention to the political awareness and existing divisions among the lower classes.

The stadtholder's adversaries called themselves "patriots." They did not form one coherent party. One wing was made up of regents, administrators of powerful cities who wanted to go back to a state in which they tranquilly held a monopoly on power. The other wing consisted of that part of the bourgeoisie which aspired to democratic power. For them, the successful American Revolution was a source of inspiration. There were also members of the nobility who agreed with these ideas, which further found some support among the lower classes, notably in the artisans' guilds. The House of Orange recruited its supporters primarily from the nobility and the lower classes, but also from part of the bourgeoisie. During the conflict, some of the regents were also to choose this side.

Thus, the rifts and alliances were not clearly delineated, as revealed by the problems of 1781, which occurred after the publication of an incendiary pamphlet by a nobleman from Overijssel, Joan Derk van der Capellen tot den Poll (1741–84). In the following years, the power of the stadtholder was more and more restricted by decrees that were issued by the provincial states and the Estates-General. In 1786 the patriots came to power in the provinces of Holland and Utrecht. From 1785 on, the revolutionary patriots organized themselves into *vrijkorpsen*— military companies modeled on traditional militia. They practiced the handling of weapons and met regularly at inns or elsewhere for discussions or reading. These organizations were open to men only. Women could only be donors to help finance arms, drums, or flags. When the conflict turned into a military confrontation, it did not take the form of a civil war against the supporters of the House of Orange, who in turn had created military companies; instead it became a battle with Prussian troops sent by the king of Prussia to bring the stadtholder William V and his wife, Wilhelmina of Prussia, back to power. The patriots did not offer much resistance and had to do without the support of the French, upon which they had built their hopes. Without much bloodshed, Prince William V and Wilhelmina were able to make a triumphant entry into The Hague the following year, in 1787. Numerous patriots, fearing repression, left the country and moved to Belgium or France. There were women among them, some just accompanying their husbands, while others, such as Betje Wolff and Aagje Deken, emigrated because they had openly chosen the side of the patriots.

After 1787, a few relatively calm years went by before the Batavian Revolution began. Many patriots had fled to the southern, Austrian Netherlands (Brabant) and to France, two countries where the revolutionary process had also started. These emigrants participated at close range in the Brabant Revolution and even more extensively in the French Revolution. France declared war on the Netherlands in 1793. The French troops were joined by a Dutch contingent eager to liberate its homeland from the stadtholder and bring about a patriotic revolution. In the meantime, the former patriots in the republic reorganized and a "revolutionary committee" was founded in Amsterdam in 1794. In 1795 the Dutch Republic was literally trampled by the French troops. On every level, from village administrations to the Estates-General, revolutionaries seized power. Stadtholder William V fled to England. In the Netherlands the revolutionaries established a new constitution, and thus the Batavian Republic was born. Politically, the situation remained troubled, chiefly because of the strong opposition between the Federalists—who wanted to preserve the Estates-General as it had been under the former republic—and the Unitarianists, who aspired to a unified state modeled after the French example. The Batavian Republic lasted until 1806, when the Netherlands became a kingdom under Louis Bonaparte, brother of Napoleon I.

One should not see the incidents of 1795 as a repetition of those of 1787, for the events in France in 1789 and the following years had exercised a great influence on the Dutch. For the Dutch revolutionaries, France was both a positive and a negative example. When the Batavian Revolution was underway in 1795, the most radical phase of the French Revolution had already ended. Few excesses of violence were counted in the Netherlands in 1795, but, as was the case in 1787, the struggle raged on through pamphlets and periodicals, where it continued until 1798, when the Batavian Republic took a more peaceful direction.

In judging these historical events, one cannot completely equate the opposition between the patriots of 1787 and the Batavian revolutionaries of 1795, on the one hand, and the

supporters of the House of Orange, on the other, with the opposition between French revolutionaries and the supporters of the king. It should not be forgotten that in 1787 the Dutch patriots allied themselves with France, when that country was still was a monarchy under Louis XVI. Among the Dutch patriots there was a conservative trend that aspired to its own version of the old regime and merely aimed at the stadtholder's departure in favor of a few regents' families. By the same token, several supporters of the House of Orange adhered to the ideas of the Enlightenment.

Significant, in this respect, was the criticism an Orange supporter, the Grand Pensionary L.P. van de Spiegel (1736–1800), made against the idea of the sovereignty of the people upheld by the radical democrat Van der Capellen, for example. Van de Spiegel attacked the concept of natural equality, pointing out that it deprived democrats of any argument for excluding the poor, minors, or women from government. He supported his criticism with quotes from Montesquieu confirming women's natural and rational ability to govern, and arguments from the legal scholar Huber (probably Ulricus Huber, 1636–94), who had asserted that it was not an absurd idea to admit women to government, since they were also admitted to the throne. It is difficult to establish where Van de Spiegel's own preference lay, but he was explicit about the halfheartedness of the democratic ideas and pointed out the difficulty of establishing coherent theoretical grounds for the political exclusion of women in a democracy (see Vreede 1874–77).

To particularize the situation of women in this debate, it should be remembered that in the political conflict in the Netherlands the opposition between aristocrats and democrats was far more important than the one that existed between stadtholder and patriots. Being a supporter of the House of Orange or a patriot was not a determining factor in one's adherence to or rejection of modernity or democracy. For certain authors, sympathy for the stadtholder could coincide with support for the idea of change in the situation of women.

The traditional account of Dutch political history, in which the crucial opposition is that between the House of Orange and patriot regents, is probably responsible for the general deprecation of Etta Palm d'Aelders (1743–99) that has long prevailed. This Dutch woman lived in Paris during the first years of the French Revolution, and was politically active on several fronts. She was a paid informer for the stadtholder of the Netherlands, a champion of the French republicans, and one of the most inspired advocates of women's rights and of their participation in the republican struggle. In view of her simultaneous revolutionary stand in Paris and adherence to the House of Orange, historians have frequently questioned her sincerity. But her ideas and actions accord well with recent historiography on the complex political relationships among the Dutch, both in France and at home. Her blending of republicanism, Orangism, and concern for women's rights is, moreover, instructive in the context of the complex political history of women's rights.

Gender-Related Enlightenment Ideas on Right, Virtue, and Opulence

The political crisis unleashed in 1780 by the Dutch war against England inspired various writings that applied the spirit of revolutionary liberty to ideas on transforming the role of women in society. Around 1780 *De Advocaat der Vrouwelyke Kunne* (Advocate of the Female Sex) appeared, a 44-page critique of the conventions that deprived women of their full rights and liberties, thereby compromising their personal happiness. The anonymous author, whose gender was not revealed, thought that women had been tormented by a retrograde "aristocracy of out-dated habits" even longer than the nation had. The author denounced the exclusion of women from "useful and instructive diversions" and from science, and criticized the double standard concerning freedom of choice of a partner and sexuality, arguing that women should be full members of cultural societies. A plea for equal rights, this critique did not proceed from a defense of the natural equality of men and women, but from emphasizing putative differences between the sexes, notably the greater emotional susceptibility of women.

In 1781 the article "Over de manlyke dwinglandy" ("On Male Tyranny") by Armida Amazone followed. In an ironic style, this text criticized the domination of women that men arrogated. Naming the American Revolution as her source of inspiration, the author cited Voltaire and condemned existing "marital power" in terms borrowed from the modern theory of law. Women's consent to the marriage contract was unlawful since it presumed their subjection to men. Although physical strength was frequently invoked as its legitimation, a legal right could never issue from such a source. Both of these texts were written in the tradition of the *querelle des femmes* that had stirred many thinkers to take pen in hand in the Netherlands during the 17th century—later than elsewhere. This critique of conventions and prejudices did not directly connect to more far-reaching democratic ideals. Armida Amazone explicitly directed her words to "distinguished ladies." Somewhat later in the revolutionary period, the debate on the sexes and the Dutch state became more systematically linked to Enlightenment philosophy: the debates linking modernity, citizenship, and sexual difference featured the doctrine of natural right, republican ideas, and Scottish philosophy.

Those who argued for Batavian civil rights usually grounded their arguments in the concept of the state of nature. Both conservative and progressive political theoreticians subscribed to the idea of a natural equality between the sexes, in accordance with the reasoning of Thomas Hobbes. Conservatives such as Dirk Hoola van Nooten (1747–1808) subsequently concluded that civil legislation should implement a distinction between men and women and place women under the "marital power" of men. The same point of departure could also lead to arguments in favor of civil equality of the sexes. In 1798 Frederik Adolf van der Marck (1719–1800), professor at the Faculty of Law of the University of Groningen, interpreted natural rights this way and pleaded for equality of the sexes in marriage and women's right to academic promotion. He argued that, in accordance with natural law, marriage is an association of equals in which "it did not behoove one to enjoy privileges over the other." He spoke expressly of "parental" instead of "paternal" power. Male privilege could be deduced neither from theological demonstrations, nor from any physical or intellectual superiority of men. According to natural law, no right could ever result from higher intelligence or greater physical strength. In addition, Marck noted, "experience teaches us that often woman is more intelligent than man and that, furthermore, she has greater physical

strength than her husband." In one of the spectators of 1799, a reader who was sympathetic to Marck's theses reacted by sending the translation of an English article in which the author discussed which sciences and arts might be practiced by women outside of the university.

As early as 1795, the first year of the Batavian Revolution, a person writing under the initials P.B.v.W. wrote a pamphlet entitled *Ten betooge dat de Vrouwen behooren deel te hebben aan de Regering van het Land* (Arguments in Favor of Women's Participation in the Government of the Country). The author pleads for equal rights, with a particular focus on the marriage contract. He claims to base his argument on the French Déclaration des Droits de l'Homme et du Citoyen (Declaration of the Rights of Man and the Citizen) of 1789. The crux of his argument is that in marriage men and women are equals; this writer thus reaches a more radical interpretation of the theory of natural law than the German legal scholar Samuel von Pufendorf, whom he cites. Like Armida Amazone, P.B.v.W. believed that the argument legitimizing marriage by citing women's consent to it used "the tone one uses to disguise violence." No less radical was his position that marriage should be dissoluble at all times. In addition, he demanded that the right to vote be granted to women and their access to public offices. The pamphlet concludes with an appeal to his fellow citizens in the Netherlands to take the initiative in this area, so that the French might one day be able say: "Holland, we have broken the chains! But you, you are putting Liberty on the throne."

In 1796 the theologian Ysbrand van Hamelsveld (1743–1812) translated Mary Wollstonecraft's *A Vindication of the Rights of Women* (1792). This translation has been lost, but a review of it appeared in 1797 in the *Algemeene Vaderlandsche Letteroefeningen*. In 1798 two democratic utopias on marriage followed: the publicist Gerrit Paape (1752–1803) published *Revolutionnaire Droom* (Revolutionary Dream), in which he sketched the ideal new family as it should exist in 1998, with complete equality between men and women; and the journalist Lieuwe van Ollefen (1749–1816) published *Het Revolutionnaire Huishouden* (The Revolutionary Household), in which a father who has his six daughters trained in male professions, prides himself on being a revolutionary, not only in political affairs but also in his private life.

In France Etta Palm-Aelders also took a stand in favor of equal rights for women and suggested changes in French legislation on adultery and succession rights. She insisted upon political equality for women as well, demanding in the National Assembly that civil and military offices be open to them.

Alongside the discourse on natural rights, the classical republican discourse on virtue was a source of inspiration for the Dutch debate on sexual difference. (In addition to the republican discourse on virtue, there was also, of course, a Christian one. In the Netherlands, there were various supporters a so-called Christian Enlightenment, who sought a religious underpinning of the enlightened state and virtuous citizenry. This trend does not seem to have produced a particular plea in favor of female citizenry, as far as we know.) Participants in the debate on virtue were just as interested in heroic virtues as they were in frugal republican ones. The heroic virtues attracted particular attention at times when revolutionary zeal was burning high. Between 1780 and 1782, when patriotism flourished after the outbreak of the war against England, it was accompanied by the appearance of a conception of militant female citizenry. One can interpret the pseudonym "Armida Amazone" in two ways. It could refer to the armed aspects of revolutionary practice at the end of the 18th century. It might also refer to the militant heroine Armida in Torquato Tasso's *Gerusalemme Liberata* (1580; Jerusalem Delivered), a character who reappeared in several operas of the 17th and 18th centuries. Madeleine de Scudéry, one of the 17th-century *précieuses*, included Armida among her "illustrious women" as "Woman Warrior" and as "Lover."

The year 1781 saw the publication of the translation of a letter attributed to the American Esther de Berdt Reed, who had organized a fundraising effort for George Washington's soldiers. Admitting that tradition and public opinion prevented her from calling women to take up arms, hers was nevertheless a call for direct, active intervention in the war by women, and she gave high praise to history's women fighters. In 1781 and 1782 the press mentioned the initiative of a women's fleet called "Heldinnenyver" (Zeal of Heroines). While intended humorously, the proposal showed that within republican revolutionary language, the idea of giving women a role had emerged. In 1786, shortly before the outbreak of the Patriot Revolution, a person writing under the name Androgina Plebeja wrote these verse lines in a poem against William V:

> I say this sincerely—it is your fall I desire
> And, with a lion's courage, I will defend
> the freedom of the Netherlands!
> Indeed, this hand, so used to handling the needle,
> will, strengthened by the blazing steel,
> then lead the people into battle.

In 1795, the first year of the Batavian Revolution, J.C. Hespe, publisher of the patriotic weekly *De Politieke Kruyer*, called upon "the Batavian sex" to look to "the Spartan sex" as a model. He continued, "Should their abilities be as great as their irresistible fervor for Equality, Liberty, and Fraternity, they would not leave it at these modest gifts, and would spring to arms." The idea of a female army was never realized, and it was revived only sporadically. More current were ideas such as this one articulated by Maria Paape: "Even if your hero's weapons are not suitable for women's hands, it is still Liberty to which our hearts pay homage." Another writer, who wrote under the initials H.F.A. and was probably a woman, continued to express ideas in the same vein.

The enthusiasm for a militant female citizenship was quickly abandoned in favor of numerous discussions concerning other republican virtues for women, in which the political and social aspects of female citizenship were emphasized. An article titled "Over de Geloofwaardigheid der Amazoonen" (On the Probability of the Amazons), published in 1788 in one of the spectators, made a rather original contribution to the debate on women and republican government. It asked whether a republic directed by women was conceivable and historically plausible.

Some texts expressed conservative aims when they held up the ancients and their "exemplary women" as an example to 18th-century society. Thus, the reviewer of *Geschiedenis der Vrouwlyke Sexe, bij de oudste Grieken* (*History of the Female Sex, among the Ancient Greeks*) by Carl Gotthold Lenz (1763–1809), a translation from the German, wistfully suggested that the simple virtues of the women of ancient times contrasted favorably with the present-day ones. But classical republican language was also used by the supporters of change. The pamphleteer P.B.v.W. recommended that all "display and vanity" be relinquished in favor of "competences." Etta Palm-Aelders, the best-known Dutch republican thinker on female citizenship, supported her arguments (as did other authors) by invoking the innumerable cases of women notable for their heroism and civic virtue that filled the annals of republican history. As was typical during that period, she combined the vocabularies of right and virtue. She insisted that men and women alike must train themselves in private as well as public virtues. She particularly advocated the practicing of public virtue by women. Palm-Aelders was among the initiators of the revolutionary women's clubs in Paris. One of her most ambitious projects concerned a plan for women's organizations with their own tasks in the creation of the new French Republic.

The Reformed minister Jacobus Kantelaar (1759–1821) explicitly established a link between the Enlightenment and women in a speech entitled "Redevoering over den Invloed der Waare Verlichting op het Lot der Vrouwen en het Huwelijksgeluk" (1793; Discourse on the Influence of the True Light on the Destiny of Women and on Happiness in Marriage), a text of decisively republican nature. This text closely followed the 18th-century republican doctrine according to which market society would lead to uncontrollable consumption and social chaos. Opulence and luxury were named as the main causes of an "antipolitical" civilization that paid more attention to science and the arts than to social equality: therefore, civilization should not be characterized in positive terms, but as barbarian and decadent. Employing this line of argumentation, Kantelaar stated that contemporary society should be lifted from its present barbarian state toward enlightenment. He concluded that "the refinement of manners has become the first cause of inequality among people," which for him included the inequality of the sexes. He could not uphold the conventional dichotomy between civilization and barbarism, as civilized men treated their women in the same way as "savages" did:

> There are no colors black enough, dear listeners, to depict the situation of women in nations where luxury has produced these disastrous consequences. Men, not knowing nor desiring conjugal happiness, expect nothing from women except the satisfaction of their bestial instincts, for which end they, like the savages, think women are solely created.

For Kantelaar, this same luxury was also the origin of the exploitation of savages reduced to slavery in order to make opulence possible. Interestingly, and in contrast to Jean-Jacques Rousseau's argument against luxury (which was presented as an indictment against women), Kantelaar posited that luxury caused the oppression of women as well as savages.

> You shudder, effeminate servants of sensuality! when you hear depicted the behavior of savage peoples. . . . And it does not occur to you that your wife, too, is a slave of your sensuality, just as theirs are; . . . how many of the products from the most distant regions of the world, products you devour daily, are splattered with the blood of poor Negro slaves, whose diligence procures these for you?

Among Kantelaar's references are the works of Seneca, *L'essai sur le caractère, les moeurs et l'esprit des femmes dans les différents siècles* (1772; *Essay on the Character, the Mores, and the Spirit of Women in Different Centuries*) by Antoine-Léonard Thomas, the *History of America* (1777) by William Robertson, and *Geschichte des weiblichen Geschlechts* (1788–1800; *History of the Female Sex*) by Christoph Meiners.

In the course of the debate on female citizenship during the construction of the new nation, the meaning of "Batavian tradition" also became a stake in the battle. What sort of women, who could deserve the pride of a new nation, do we encounter in the history of the Netherlands? Who was the "genuine" Batavian woman? One female reader of a spectator, who signed only as "geb. M.L.B," objected to the image of the servile and toiling Dutch woman sketched in this publication:

> If you had written this for German krauts who crawl like slaves at the feet of their Masters, it might have passed: but to write it about the women of the Netherlands who have drunk from Batavian liberty from the earliest days and would never let themselves be condemned to a mere nothing . . . that is positively intolerable!

The editors exhibited a different view of what was traditionally meant by Batavian femininity:

> Allow us, Madame, to remind you that our former Netherlands' women were in fact the most competent, the most diligent housekeepers, and that women of the then-higher ranks never felt too superior to prepare meals, wash their children, sit at the spinning-wheel, and please their husbands in every way.

By the end of the 18th century, this latter view of the essential nature of the Dutch woman as housewife (regardless of her social rank) had prevailed over the rival economic and political views of femininity.

As we have seen, the classical republican idiom of virtues and sobriety motivated debates in which historical and anthropological illustrations informed opinions on sex, and in which the implications of civilization and opulence for the position of women were a central theme. The "Scottish" response to civic humanism is well known. Philosophers of the Scottish Enlightenment such as David Hume (1711–76) and Adam Smith (1723–90) appreciated the very ideas the republicans reviled: in the first place, civilization, culture, and "sociability"; and, second, economy and luxury, which, according to the Scots, contributed to improving the lot of women. The historical, anthropological, and economic debates made a significant impact in the Netherlands. When the relationship of women or femininity to prosperity and the arts came up for discussion, Dutch authors often referred to the Scots, especially to William Alexander (d. 1783) and John Richardson (1741–l 811). They also referred—as we have already seen—to William Robertson (1721–1793), work by Montesquieu that was thematically close, and the previously mentioned 1772 book by Antoine-Léonard Thomas. In 1780 and 1781, a spectator published excerpts (translated into Dutch) from William Alexander's *The History of Women, from the Earliest Antiquity to the Present Time* (1779). They included his "Four Essays on Women's Clothing and on the Different Ways of Women to Please Men"; "Historical Dissertation on the Occupations and Amusements of Women"; "Historical Dissertation on the Specific Ways of Courtship among Different Peoples"; "Essay on the Beneficial Influence of Women on

Men"; and "Essay on the Education of Women." In 1782 the same periodical published excerpts (translated into Dutch) on the political influence of women in eastern nations, from John Richardson's *A Dissertation on the Languages, Literature and Manners of Eastern Nations, Originally Prefixed to a Dictionary of Persian, Arabic, and English* (1777), describing the excerpts thus: "Curious examples of the great importance and the influence of women in the Orient with details concerning their clothing, characters, and mores." Between 1783 and 1786, Montesquieu's *De l'esprit des lois* (1748; *The Spirit of the Laws*) was translated into Dutch. In 1796 another unidentified history of the female sex was translated from the English in a spectator.

The interest in Scottish historiography, in which the position of women was regarded as a decisive criterion of civilization, fit the broader interest of the spectators in historical and comparative anthropology. Treatises, often in translation, about the role of women in other cultures were readily published. This type of discussion could be framed in either a serious or a more sensational tone: women and foreigners were frequently discussed together, and not always in the earnest style of Scottish historiography or Kantelaar's republicanism.

Next to the history of civilization, other Scottish themes such as commerce, economic prosperity, and the just measure of luxury enjoyed lively interest in the Netherlands. Did luxury contribute to national prosperity, or was it rather responsible for national decline? In reflections on economic citizenship, women were accorded an important role. The links established between economy and female citizenship varied depending upon each author's attitude toward luxury, ranging from warnings against spendthrift coquettes and socially useless female scholars to schemes for involving women in realizing a balanced and prosperous economy. The following passage from a brochure entitled *Waarin bestaat, het egte Patriötismus?* (1789; What Is True Patriotism?) may indicate the moderately positive appreciation in the Netherlands of the importance of prosperity and commerce for the republic:

> As far as the female Sex is concerned, it, too, can in many aspects manifest its sacred attachment to the country's prosperity and thus claim the name Patriot in a most equitable manner. This supreme designation belongs to . . . every Lady, every Woman or Daughter . . . who sets herself as a sacred rule the wearing of fabrics manufactured in the country, thereby supporting the industry, the arts and sciences, providing thousands of inhabitants with a better life and the public Treasury with important revenue.

Women's Role in the Patriot (1787) and Batavian (1795) Revolutions

Women's participation in the Patriot Revolution remained limited. They did not engage in combat, although they did partake through writing. In 1784 an anonymous woman put her thoughts into a little song:

> For although I cannot fight
> By taking sword or rifle
> In these times I still do fight
> With my ink, pen, and paper.

The number of writings by women, insofar as they can be identified—for many appeared anonymously or under pseudonyms or initials—was limited by comparison to those written by men. In addition, women were surprisingly discreet when it came to matters that specifically concerned women. The *Post van den Neder Rhijn*, the most important patriot periodical, contained only six letters by women in its 12 volumes. The publishers declared that they had not printed one woman's letter because she had expressed ideas that were too radical. The letters by women dealt with general politics and not with women's rights. In another patriotic publication, *De Republikein aan de Maas*, which appeared from 1785 to 1787, there was only one letter written by a woman out of 46 letters from readers. Its writer proposed boycotting stores that belonged to the supporters of the House of Orange, taking a means of action from American revolutionary practice and bringing it to bear on a field of action that specifically belonged to women.

The 1780s and 1790s saw the rise of a kind of pamphlet that consisted of "dialogues" between women, between men, or between women and men. Both antipatriots and patriots published small newspapers (sometimes just a single issue, sometimes for several years and in many installments) in which political discussions took the form of dialogues between neighbors, male or female, or other "popular" contacts. Frequently, these publications reacted to one another. Most of the time, problems of general politics were discussed; occasionally, women's interests or rights were on the agenda. Some of the pamphlets had women's and men's names. Examples include the women interlocutors *Diewertje en Grietje* with their "male" counterpart *Louw en Krelis*, or the women *Teuntje en Pleuntje* rejoined by the men *Jaap en Teunis*—all publications with a patriotic leaning. *Klaartje en Trijntje* and *Neel en Mary* were two antipatriotic women's dialogues. Other publications had titles that expressly referred to gender, such as *Politieke Praatmoer* (The Political Gossip; the word *praatmoer* specifically refers to a woman) and *Politieke Praatvaar* (The Political Garrulous Chap); *Politieke Snapster* (The Political Babbler; *snapster* is the feminine form of "babbler"), an antipatriotic paper that reacted to the patriotic *Snapper* ("babbler" in the masculine form); *De Bataafse Burgeres en Boer* (Batavian Female Citizen and Farmer). *Het Anti-politiek Haspelstertje* (The Antipolitical She-Simpleton) explicitly discussed the political equality of women. Finally, the *Nieuwe Bataafsche Vrouwe Courant* (New Batavian Women's Newspaper) was written in a somewhat more serious style than the others and gave general political information intended for women readers, in particular.

The transposition of political oppositions in family conflicts between parents and children, men and women, had a longer tradition in the Netherlands. It is nevertheless remarkable that during the revolutionary decade, women could play a symbolic role of spokesperson for both political camps. Put differently, these dialogues convey an intuition that gender, while not through attribution of some substantial identity, is a relevant category in the debate on the political reassessment of the Dutch state.

In 1787 the old regime was restored in the Netherlands; the revolutionary events in Belgium and France erupted shortly thereafter. In the Batavian Revolution, women's status was discussed with more fervor than during the Patriot Revolution.

Some of the relevant texts have already been mentioned above; the press furnishes still more material.

In 1795 Etta Palm-Aelders was banished from France, accused of espionage. She returned to the Netherlands where she started to write again. In the *Oprechte Nationale Courant* she wrote a plea for the establishment of women's clubs, based on the French example. Her anonymous text was signed "A Friend of Truth," in remembrance of her Parisian days where she had been president of the Amies de la Vérité (Women Friends of Truth). She was in favor of the exclusion of men from these clubs because males would keep women from taking the floor. In a second letter, she developed rules for the allocation of the highest offices in the city of Delft, where she had settled. She was then arrested and imprisoned, officially because she was considered to be a political danger, but her characteristics as a political woman were manifestly taken into account. The French women's clubs were not unknown in the Netherlands, as the translation into Dutch of a French publication on the topic illustrates: *De Jacobijnse vrouwenclub, iets meer dan een roman* (The Jacobin Women's Club, More than a Novel).

In 1795 women's clubs came into being in the Netherlands, but the only extant documents on them are those on the creation of the Haarlem club, of which the women distinguished themselves by planting a tree of liberty. One newspaper, the *Revolutionnaire vraag-al*, published a letter signed by a "women's collective" asking "Why Could Not Women Lead the Country Also?" In a later installment, information on the constitution of a "women's society" can be found. On 4 January 1796, another periodical, *Janus Verrezen*, printed a "Message of Muliebra," a semiserious, semicomic account of the founding of a society of women called Wij zijn er ook nog (Don't Forget about Us). It contained the inaugural speech given by the president. Arguing against the absurdity of depriving women of the right to vote, the female author exclaimed in conclusion, "What is the reason that women could represent supreme power in monarchies, while in democracies they are excluded from the same?" The tone in which this fictitious meeting is described is one of irony, but the message was serious, and the subject obviously interested the readers.

The *Nationaale Bataafsche Courant* published five texts by women in 1797, while the *Oprechte Nationale Courant* published sixteen. The authors were well known, including Maria Paape, wife of Gerrit Paape, cited earlier. In 1795 she published a brochure entitled *Republikeins Gebed van eene vaderlandsche Vrouw* (Republican Prayer of a Patriotic Woman). Petronella Moens edited a periodical between 1798 and 1799, *Vriendin van het Vaderland*, in which her discussion of general political questions was oriented toward women. As early as 1792 she had already commented, with her friend Bernard Bosch, an eminent patriot pastor, on the new French Constitution.

One of the most remarkable Dutch women intellectuals of the period was Catharina Heybeek, originally a seamstress. With her friend Lieuwe van Ollefen, she edited the *Nationaale Bataafsche Courant* from 1797 on. In this paper, she reported on a visit to the National Assembly in The Hague. A bit disappointed in the debates, she wrote that she would have preferred to attend those in Paris. She wrote political columns on a regular basis. One of these sharp and humorous texts was so provocative it almost caused her to be sent to prison, but she was never put to trial.

Special mention must go to the Dutch novelist and playwright Isabelle de Charrière, who lived in Switzerland during the revolutionary decades but was an active commentator on the political events in Holland and France. Mainly a critic of the nobility, in 1788 she wrote essays that weighed the justified interests of the patriot insurrection against the equally consequential interest of preserving a unified state under a stadtholderate. She sympathized with the French Revolution in its early stages.

The year 1798 saw a political reversal. A coup d'état put an end to the first, revolutionary phase of the Batavian Revolution. The press was muzzled; no further work by Catharina Heybeek was published; and Petronella Moens restricted herself to domestic issues. Etta Palm-Aelders died. Isabelle de Charrière had become disillusioned with revolutionary politics in the course of the French Revolution. The only politically active woman writer at the time was Aletta Hulshoff (1741–1846). In 1804 she was arrested for having written anti-Orangist pamphlets, and in 1806 she was sentenced to two years in prison. Almost as soon as she was set free, she published a pamphlet against Napoleon Bonaparte, for which she was arrested a second time. She escaped and fled to the United States disguised as a man. There she pursued her career as a writer and translated the French Constitution of 1793 into English. In 1817 she returned to the Netherlands, but, like so many women and men, she had withdrawn from politics.

Women's Support for the Orangists and Counterrevolutionaries

Although some women sided with the revolutionaries of 1787 and 1795, others, especially in the 1780s, were prominently present in the counterrevolution. In 1787 Princess Wilhelmina of Prussia had played a decisive role. She was a more powerful personality than her husband, the stadtholder William. On her own initiative, she organized the resistance against the patriots. When the court was forced to withdraw from The Hague and go to the province of Gelderland, she planned a counterrevolution. Without having forewarned the advisers of the prince, and ignoring her husband's protests, in June 1787 Princess Wilhelmina traveled to the province of Holland with the purpose of instigating an Orangist rebellion after her arrival in The Hague. At the provincial border, however, she was stopped and sent back, like an ordinary citizen. Her brother, the king of Prussia, took this incident as an insult and used it as an excuse to send troops that brought the House of Orange back to power. Hatred of the patriots was directed more at the princess than at Prince William V. She was continually reviled in words or pictures, and the comparison with Marie-Antoinette, queen of France, is almost unavoidable.

Women of the lower classes, too, fought actively on the side of the House of Orange and were often more conservative than men. It was perhaps for that reason that, in 1784, the patriots created the above-mentioned periodical *Politieke Praatvaar*, against which the Orangist periodical *Politieke Praatmoer* was issued. In a caricature also circulated that same year, the conflict was reduced to a household quarrel in which the man was brandishing the *Praatvaar* and the woman the *Praatmoer*. The obser-

vation was not unfounded. The Orangist party was entrenched among the masses and among women. In the poor districts of the cities, many were eager to demonstrate their attachment to the House of Orange. Riots, traditionally led by women, now erupted against the patriot militia or the patriotic societies. In the 1780s one woman, Kaat Mossel, gained national notoriety. Around 60 years old, she worked selling mussels in Rotterdam. She lived in a poor district and was known for her solidarity and her staunch attachment to the Orangist party. After a confrontation between the crowd she was leading and the local militia, Mossel was arrested and interrogated. She then became a figure famous throughout the Dutch Republic. Through the engravings that represent her hanged on the gallows or looking like one of the Furies, it is clear to what extent the patriots feared her. A play even ended with a scene in which Mossel was punished by angels who threw boiling water on her head, pulled her hair out, and made her swallow flaming torches. She was the incarnation of the lower-class Orangist woman prepared to riot, who could be found in every city. This situation contrasted sharply with that of 1795, when the Batavian Revolution was hardly accompanied by counterrevolutionary violence. No women participated in pro-Orangist riots again until 1813, as a prelude to the return of the prince of Orange from his exile in England.

Women of letters also defended the cause of the House of Orange. One famous literary woman, Maria Geertruida Cambon-van der Werken, was an active Orangist. She was a novelist and translated *Le mariage de Figaro* (1784; *The Marriage of Figaro*) by Pierre Caron de Beaumarchais from the French. Her enlightened ideas and her support of Orange did not exclude each other—a blend we have already seen in the case of Etta Palm-Aelders. After the Restoration of 1787, she published a probably fictive interview with Princess Wilhelmina of Prussia and also a *Gedenkschrift ter huldiging van de Oprechte Vaderlandsche Societeiten* (Commemoration in Homage to the Sincere Societies of the Fatherland). The list of subscriptions to these texts reveals rather weak independent participation of women on the Orangist side of the political debate: 9 women as opposed to 228 men.

The context for this "female conservatism" may have been the aversion of the patriots to informal politics, which they associated with the old regime. An account in *Janus Verrezen* of a meeting of a women's club tells of a widow complaining that in the past she could suggest all sorts of "plans beneficial to the fatherland" to her husband, the mayor. Thus, she had been able to take part in the city's politics, for, she said, "my husband was nothing but my instrument." Such informal politics were successfully practiced by Orangists. Princess Wilhelmina of Prussia, at the top of society, and Kaat Mossel, at the bottom, both symbolized this form of politics, and both were favorite targets of patriot anger. The very different ways in which women could exercise power, in the street and in the palace, seemed to complement each other well.

The patriots wished to ground administrative reforms in a more rational pattern of decision making, but in practice their ideas on citizenship were oriented toward a military version of it and tailored to men. The patriots developed new frameworks of mobilization in the form of reading societies, discussion clubs, and volunteer militias, which reserved no place for women. New modes of collective action, especially the signing of petitions, were also closed to females. In the patriotic press, there were strong complaints about the fact that the Orangists, who had adopted the idea of petition campaigns, did allow women to sign. In Holland, no female petitions comparable to those in France were drawn up. In contrast to these new forms of collective action, there were the traditional structures through which the Orangists mobilized their adherents, the social networks that had served this function for centuries. In these family and neighborhood networks, women occupied a dominant place. They had already played an important role in the preceding waves of pro-Orangist riots, in 1653, 1672, and 1747.

On the basis of the available sources, we venture the following conclusions. During the two decades in which the Dutch nation-state took shape in accordance with Enlightenment ideas on a democratic or constitutional political order, there evolved various debates concerning the social and political relationships between the sexes. Contributions to this debate originated in different political groups and were grounded in different theoretical perspectives. In the 1780s, pleas in favor of female citizenship appeared in patriotic circles; after the Batavian Revolution of 1795, this debate was resumed on a broader scale. The arguments of male and female writers were comparable to those of authors in the rest of Europe, and the influence of political events in North America and later in France is obvious. Among Orangists, this debate was less noticeable, although positions that we would call "feminist" today could be combined with either Orangist or patriotic political views. In the social movement that supported the House of Orange, women played a more manifest and autonomous role than they did in the patriot movement. In the popular press on both sides, women fulfilled a symbolic role as spokespersons, which contrasted with their actual, restricted role in Dutch society.

The implications of natural rights theory for assigning political rights to women remained a controversial topic among both patriots and aristocrats. The assumption of a natural equality of men and women could lend itself to egalitarian as well as anti-egalitarian conclusions with respect to women's civil rights. The virtue-centered approach to citizenship led either to tentative notions of militant citizenship for women or to a critique of the oppressive and semibarbarian consequences that opulent societies had for women. The discourse on women's civic virtue was soon contested by a social discourse on virtue that established women's conjugal duties and domestic tasks.

What was the political fate of the various ideas under discussion? The sexually egalitarian interpretations of the doctrine of natural rights had no consequences for Dutch legislation. Only for a very short time were the militant, soldierly aspects of republican citizenship envisaged as an option for women. The republican criticism of luxury survived the revolutionary decade only in a very diluted form: beginning as a political critique of irresponsible citizenship and international relationships of domination, it was transformed into a call for temperance, and into channeling the desire for luxury into structures that would be profitable to the Dutch treasury. The political discourse in which ideas on female citizenship had been articulated was in time supplanted by an economic discourse that foresaw new private roles for women, and to this end the "tradition" of Batavian femininity was invented under the sign of excellence in domestic work. The actual role played by female merchants and entrepreneurs in the Netherlands was to change radically with the birth of a new normative discourse that redefined women's relationship to commerce, allocating to them the partly public, partly private role of consumers. Women were accorded national tasks in the caring for relatives and practicing responsible consumerism.

By 1800 the debate on a democratic transformation of the position of women had stagnated, and their public and political role had come to an end. Modern citizenship became marked as a male right and masculine practice. After 1800 women authors abandoned their political involvement. On the streets and in the forming of public opinion, women ceased to assume a role as leaders of collective protest, because the traditional local networks they had previously controlled had lost their significance. The new organizations that emerged, such as political parties, were created and ruled by men. During the first half of the 19th century, women in the Netherlands would occupy an even more subordinate place in public life.

Bibliography

Sources

"Aanmerkingen over de opvoeding en de studien der vrouwlyke sexe," *Algemeene Vaderlandsche Letteroefeningen* 2 (1799)

De Advocaat der Vrouwelyke Kunne; en wel voornaamentlyk, der jonge dochteren en weduwvrouwen: Met Artikelen van bezwaar, tegen de grillen van Mme de Verouderde Gewoonten, Die de vrouwelijke Kunne daar door, lange in haar aangebooren Recht en Vrijheid heeft verkort, N.p., ca.1780

Alexander, William, *The History of Women from the Earliest Antiquity to the Present Time,* London: W. Strahan and T. Cadell, 1779; reprint, Bristol, England: Thoemmes Press, 1995

Amazone, Armida [pseud.], "On Male Tyranny," translated by Judith Vega, *Journal of Women's History* 8, no. 2 (1996)

Berdt Reed, Esther de, "De Gevoelens eener Amerikaansche Vrouwe," *Den Hollandschen weeklykschen Nieuws-Verteller* (21 April 1781; 28 April 1781)

Charrière, Isabelle de, *Isabelle de Charrière: Une aristocrate révolutionnaire: Écrits, 1788–1794,* edited by Isabelle Vissière, Paris: Des Femmes, 1988

Charrière, Isabelle de, *Oeuvres complètes,* edited by Jean-Daniel Candaux et al., Amsterdam: G.A. van Oorschot, 1979–84

Hespe, Johannes Christiaan, *Vrijheid, Gelijkheid, Broederschap!* (21 April 1795)

H.F.A., *Aanspraak der Dordrechtse Maagd, voor derzelver burgerij, aan haare jufferschaar,* N.p., n.d.

Kaat Mossel voor den throon van Belzebub, Utrecht, The Netherlands: N.p., n.d.

Kantelaar, Jacobus, "Redevoering over den Invloed der Waare Verlichting op het Lot der Vrouwen en het Huwelijksgeluk, 13 augustus 1793," *Redevoeringen en aanspraken gedaan in de onderscheiden vergaderingen der Maatschappij tot nut van 't algemeen* (1799)

L.B. geb. M., "Korte aanmerkingen over de vrouwelijke waarde en bestemming," *Bijdragen tot het menschlijk geluk* (1789)

Lenz, Carl Gotthold, *Geschichte der Weiber im heroischen Zeitalter,* Hanover: Im Verlage der Helwingschen Hofbuchhandlung, 1790; as *Geschiedenis der Vrouwelijke Sexe, bij de Grieken,* Amsterdam: N.p., 1792

Meiners, Christoph, *Geschichte des weiblichen Geschlechts,* Hanover, Germany: Helwingsche Horfbuchhandlung, 1788–1800

Montesquieu, Charles de Secondat, baron de, *The Spirit of Laws,* translated by Thomas Nugent, new revised edition, edited by J.V. Pritchard, 2 vols., Littleton, Colorado: F.B. Rothman, 1991

Ollefen, Lieuwe van, *Het revolutionaire huishouden; naspel*, Amsterdam: N.p., 1798

Om op een andren Boeg te wenden ons vertrouwen, is dit Plan geschikt voor Neêrlands vrouwen, Ter oprichting van een singuliere Kaap-reedery [etc.] om die Reedery Heldinnen-Yver te noemen, Rotterdam: n.p., 1782

"Over de geloofwaardigheid der Amazoonen," *Algemeen Magazyn, van wetenschap, konst en smaak* 3, no. 2 (1788)

Paape, Gerrit, *De Bataafsche Republiek, zoals zij behoord te zijn en zoals zij weezen kan; of revolutionnaire Droom in 1798 wegens toekomstige gebeurtenissen tot 1998: Vrolijk en Ernstig* N.p., 1798

Paape, Maria, "Ter gelegenheid van het schenken van een koperen trommel: Aan de Leden des Genootschaps," in *Voor de Delftsche Schuttery*, N.p., ca. 1784[?]

Palm d'Aelders, Etta, *Appel aux Françoises sur la regénération des mœurs, et nécessité de l'influence des femmes dans un gouvernement libre*, Paris: L'Imprimerie du Cercle social, 1791; reprinted in volume 2 of *Les femmes dans la Révolution française*, Paris: EDHIS, 1982

P.B.v.W., "Arguments in Favor of Women's Participation in the Government of the Country," translated by Judith Vega, *Journal of Women's History* 8, vol. 2 (1996)

Plan voor Neêrlands vrouwen, ter opregting van een kaap-reedery, onder de zinspreuk Heldinnen-yver onder directie van Cornelis Balguerie, Ewoud van Son en Daniel Havart, Rotterdam: Gerrit Manheer, 1781

Plebeja, Androgina [pseud.], *Aanspraak van eene vaderlandsche vrouwe aan Willem de Vde*, Deventer, The Netherlands: n.p., 1786

Richardson, John, *A Dictionary, Persian, Arabic, and English: With a Dissertation on the Languages, Literature, and Manners of Eastern Nations*, Oxford: Clarendon Press, 1777–80; 2nd edition as *A Dissertation on the Languages, Literature, and Manners of Eastern nations, Originally Prefixed to a Dictionary Persian, Arabic, and English*, Oxford: Clarendon Press, 1778

Robertson, William, *The History of America*, London: Strahan, 1777

Schinne, Magdalena van, *Journal de Magdalena van Schinne: 1786–1805*, edited by Rudolf Dekker and Anje Dik, Paris: Côté-Femmes, 1994

Thomas, Antoine-Léonard, *Essai sur le caractère, les moeurs, et l'esprit des femmes dans les différents siècles*, Paris: Moutard, 1772; reprint, Paris: Champion Slatkine, 1987; as *Essay on the Character, Manners, and Genius of Women in Different Ages*, London: Robinson, 1773

van der, Marck, Friedrich Adolph *Schets over de rechten van den mensch, het algemeen kerken-, staats—en volken-recht, ten dienste der burgery ontworpen: Alsmede Tafereel van deelen, afdeelingen en hoofdstukken, tot een algemeen Bataafsch wetboek*, Groningen, Germany: Jacob Bolt, 1798

van Nooten, Dirk, Hoola *Vaderlandsche Rechten voor den burger*, Amsterdam: Willem Holtrop, 1793

"Waarin bestaat het egte Patriötismus?," *Bijdragen tot het menschelijk geluk* (1789)

Wolff, Elizabeth Bekker, and Aagje Deken, *Briefwisseling van Betje Wolff en Aagje Deken*, edited by P.J. Buijnsters, Utrecht, The Netherlands: HES, 1987

Wolff, Elizabeth Bekker, and Aagje Deken, *Historie van Mejuffroaw Sara Burgerhart*, The Hague: I. van Cleef, 1782; reprint, The Hague: Nijhoff, 1980

Wollstonecraft, Mary, *A Vindication of the Rights of Woman with Structures on Political and Moral Subjects*, London: Johnson, 1792; new edition, edited by Carol H. Poston, New York and London: W. Norton, 1975

Reference Works

Bosch, Jan Willem, "Le statut de la femme dans les anciens Pays-Bas septentrionaux," *La femme: Recueils de la Société Jean Bodin* 12 (1962)

Buijnsters, Pieter Jacob, editor, *Briefwisseling van Betje Wolff en Aagje Deken*, 2 vols., Utrecht, The Netherlands, 1987

Buijnsters, Pieter Jacob, *Spectatoriale geschriften*, Utrecht, The Netherlands: HES, 1991

Buijnsters, Pieter Jacob, *Wolff en Deken: Een biografie*, Leiden, The Netherlands: Nijhoff, 1984

Clark, Alice, *Working Life of Women in the Seventeenth Century*, London: G. Routledge and Sons, and New York: E.P. Dutton, 1919; reprint, London and Boston: Routledge and K. Paul, 1982

Davis, Natalie Zemon, "Women in Politics," in Natalie Zemon Davis and Arlette Farge, editors, *Renaissance and Enlightenment Paradoxes*, volume 3 of *A History of Women in the West*, edited by Georges Duby and Michèle Perrot, 5 volumes, Cambridge, Massachusetts: Belknap Press of Harvard University, 1993

Dekker, Rudolf, *Holland in Beroering. Oproeren in de 17e en 18e eeuw*, Baarn, The Netherlands: Ambo, 1982

Dekker, Rudolf, "Revolutionaire en contra-revolutionaire vrouwen in Nederland, 1780–1800," *Tijdschrift voor Geschiedenis* 102 (1989)

Dekker, Rudolf, "Women in Medieval and Early Modern Netherlands," *Journal of Women's History* 10 (1998)

Dekker, Rudolf, "Women in Revolt. Collective Protest and Its Social Basis in Holland," *Theory and Society* 16 (1987)

Dijk, Suzanne van, *Traces de femmes: Présence féminine dans le journalisme français du XVIIIe siècle*, Amsterdam: APA- Holland University Press, 1988

Dubois, Pierre H., and Simone Dubois, *Zonder vaandel: Belle van Zuylen 1740–1805: Een biografie*, Amsterdam: Oorschot, 1993

Frijhoff, Willem, "L'évidence républicaine: Les Bataves au passé, au présent et au futur," *Annales historiques de la Révolution française* (April–June 1994)

Frijhoff, Willem, and Joost Rosendaal, "La Révolution régénérée: Nouvelles approches et nouvelles images de la Révolution néerlandaise," in *L'image de la Révolution française: Communications présentées lors du Congrès mondial pour le Bicentenaire de la Révolution*, edited by Michel Vovelle, Paris: Sorbonne, and Oxford: Pergammon Press, 1989

Haks, Donald, *Huwelijk en gezin in Holland in de 17e en 18e eeuw*, Utrecht, The Netherlands: HES, 1985

Hanou, A.J., editor, *Revolutie in woorden*, Amsterdam: E. Querido, 1989

Hanou, A.J., *Sluiers van Isis: Johannes Kinker als voorvechter van de Verlichting in de vrijmetselarij en andere Nederlandse genootschappen 1790–1845*, Deventer, The Netherlands: Sub Rosa, 1988

Helmers, Dini, "Tweedragt in hun huisselijk koningrijk: Scheidende paren en huwelijkse deugden (1753–1810)," *Jaarboek voor Vrouwengeschiedenis* 13 (1993)

Howell, Martha C., *Women, Production, and Patriarchy in Late Medieval Cities*, Chicago: University of Chicago Press, 1986

Huussen, Arend H., Jr., *De codificatie van het Nederlandse huwelijksrecht, 1795–1838*, Amsterdam: Holland Universiteits Pers, 1975

Kerber, Linda K., *Women of the Republic: Intellect and Ideology in Revolutionary America*, Chapel Hill: University of North Carolina Press, 1980

Palmer, Robert R., *The Age of the Democratic Revolution*, 2 vols., Princeton, New Jersey: Princeton University Press, 1959–64

Palmer, Robert R., "Much in Little: The Dutch Revolution of 1795," *Journal of Modern History* 26, no. 1 (March–December 1954)

Rendall, Jane, *The Origins of Modern Feminism: Women in Britain, France, and the United States, 1780–1860*, New York: Schocken Books, 1984; Basingstoke, England: MacMillan, 1985

Rijn, Gerrit van, "Kaat Mossel," *Rotterdams Jaarboekje* (1890)

Schama, Simon, *The Embarrassment of Riches: An Interpretation of Dutch Culture in the Golden Age*, New York: Knopf, 1987

Schama, Simon, *Patriots and Liberators: Revolution in the Netherlands, 1780–1813*, New York: Knopf, and London: Collins, 1977

Singeling, Cornelis B.F., *Gezellige schrijvers: Aspecten van letterkundige genootschappelijkheid in Nederland, 1750–1800*, Amsterdam and Atlanta, Georgia: Rodopi, 1991

Sturkenboom, Dorothee, *Spectators van hartstocht: Sekse en emotionele cultuur in de achttiende eeuw*, Hilversum, The Netherlands: Verloven, 1998

Te Brake, Wayne P., *Regents and Rebels: The Revolutionary World of an Eighteenth-Century Dutch City*, Cambridge, Massachusetts: Basil Blackwell, 1989

Te Brake, Wayne P., Rudolf M. Dekker, and Lotte C. van de Pol, "Women and Political Culture in the Dutch Revolutions," in *Women and Politics in the Age of the Democratic Revolution*, edited by Harriet B. Applewhite and Darline G. Levy, Ann Arbor: University of Michigan Press, 1990

Tomaselli, Sylvana, "The Enlightment Debate on Women,"*History Workshop* 20 (Autumn 1985)

Vega, Judith A., "Feminist Discourses in the Dutch Republic at the End of the Eighteenth Century," *Journal of Women's History* 8, no. 2 (1996)

Vega, Judith A., "Feminist Republicanism. Etta Paelm-Aelders on Justice, Virtue, and Men," *History of European Ideas* 10, no. 3; special issue, *Women and the French Revolution* (1989)

Vega, Judith A., "Feminist Republicanism and the Political Perception of Gender," in *Republicanism: A Shared European Heritage*, edited by Martin Van Gelderen and Quentin Skinner, vol. 2, Cambridge: Cambridge University Press, 2002

Vega, Judith A., "A Stage of Conceptual Meaning: Isabelle de Charrière and the Republic," in M. van Gelderen and W.R.E. Velema, editors, *Republic. A Conceptual History from the 16th to the 19th Century*, Amsterdam: Amsterdam University Press, 2001

Velema, Wyger R.E., "Contemporaine reacties op het patriots politiek vocabulaire," in *De Droom van de revolutie: Nieuwe benaderingen van het Patriottisme*, edited by Hans Bots and Wijnandus W. Mijnhardt, Amsterdam: De Bataafsche Leeuw, 1988

Velema, Wyger R.E., "Revolutie, contrarevolutie en het stadhouderschap 1780–1795," *Tijdschrift voor Geschiedenis* 102 (1989)

Volz, Gustav Berthold, editor, *Die Erinnerungen der Prinzessin Wilhelmine von Oranien an den Hof Friedrichs der Grossen (1751–1767)*, Berlin: n.p., 1903

Vreede, George Willem, *Mr. Laurens Pieter van de Spiegel en zijne Tijdgenooten (1737–1800)*, Middelburg, The Netherlands: J.C. and W. Altorffer, 1874–77

Vreede, George Willem, *Frederike Sophie Wilhelmina, gemalin van den stadhouder Willem V, en Laurens Pieter Van de Spiegel, raadpensionaris eerst van Zeeland, dan van Holland*, Utrecht, The Netherlands: C. van de Post, Jr., 1868

Wijs, J.J.A., *Bijdrage tot de kennis van het leenstelsel in de Republiek*, The Hague: Die Residentie, 1939

Wijsenbeek, Thera, "Van pristeersters en prostituées. Beroepen van vrouwen in Delft en Den Haag tijdens de achttiende eew," *Jaarboek voor Vrouwengeschiedenis* 8 (1987)

Wit, Cornelis Henricus Eligius de, *De Nederlandse revolutie van de achttiende eeuw, 1780–1787: Oligarchie en proletariaat*, Oirsbeek, The Netherlands: Drukkerij Lindebauf, 1974

Wit, Cornelis Henricus Eligius de, *De strijd tussen aristocratie en democratie in Nederland 1780–1848*, Heerlen, The Netherlands: Winants, 1965

Wit, Cornelis Henricus Eligius de, *Het ontstaan van het moderne Nederland 1780–1848 en zijn geschiedschrijving*, Oirsbeek, The Netherlands: 1978

THE TRADE OF BLACK WOMEN SLAVES OF THE EIGHTEENTH CENTURY

HARRIS MEMEL-FOTÊ

Slavery and the Slave Trade from Antiquity to the Modern Era

A CLOSE EXAMINATION OF the notion of slave trade reveals several layers of complexity in its relationship to the ideas of transfer, violence, and slavery. In its etymological sense, the French word for slave trade, *traite*, refers to "extraction," while the economic meaning of the term is "commerce." Both meanings, however, refer to the same idea: transfer. In turn, the idea of transfer refers to three modes, two of them simple: the market; and violence as a physical force (*vis* in Latin) applied to extract or pull something from one point to another. The third is a complex mode: market violence, entailing material and/or symbolic violence, commerce through a form of violence. This latter mode can precede, accompany, or follow the market operation, or all three. To various degrees, this last dialectic is basic to every form of ancient and modern trade of human beings and especially to the trade of women.

From antiquity to the end of the Middle Ages, the black slave trade was relative in nature. On the marketplace that linked Africa, Mediterranean Europe, and the Orient, both black and white women were bought and sold, but in inverse proportions: many white and few black women were sold in the north, while many black and few white women were sold in the south (except in the Muslim east). In the 14th century the Moroccan traveler Ibn Battuta received a young black male slave as a present from the *farba* (lord) Süleyman, emir of a city in Mali. He bought a black female slave for 25 *mithkal* (equivalent to more than 100 grams of gold) and traveled back from Mali with a caravan of about 600 black women slaves. At the home of the *farba*, he had been served by one Arab slave woman from Damascus, among dozens of black female slaves.

Three differences appear to distinguish the black slave trade of antiquity from that of medieval times. First, the Muslim period increased the number of black women on the market. Second, the slave trade became associated with sugarcane cultivation. In the 9th century that association led to the great and famous revolt in Basra, Iraq, of the Zandj slaves, who created an independent state that lasted for 14 years (869–83). Finally, racial prejudice took shape: whereas, with Aristotle, Greek philosophy justified the enslavement of both white and black barbarians as natural, Arabic philosophy, with Ibn Khaldun, justified the slavery of black people as natural because of "their inferior humanity, closer to dumb beasts." The modern slave trade, in contrast to the ancient practices, acquired an absolute character. Africa became its principal source and the Americas its principal destination. The Khaldunian ideology was spread by theologians such as Bartolomé de Las Casas and Jacques Bénigne Bossuet, and philosophers such as David Hume and Montesquieu, who provided systematic justification for this black slave trade. Indeed, Africans were found to be sturdier than Native Americans, and thus better suited for labor in the mines or tropical agriculture of the Americas. In addition, it was held that the slave trade offered Africans hope of escape from three forms of death (tyranny, cannibalism, and hell) through European Christianization, and thus the possibility of complete salvation: political salvation through liberty, cultural salvation through civilization, and eschatological salvation through resurrection.

Still another complex dimension of the concept of slave trade resides in the notion of slavery itself. For Aristotle, who inspired the first historians of slavery (see Wallon, 1847; Blake, 1859) and most of the economists of the 18th and 19th centuries, slavery was a political category, and the slave trade was only one of its sources—the others being family dependence, debt, and warfare. Whereas in the *polis* (city-state) the negative status of the slave was determined by the positive status of the free man and citizen, in the *oïkos* (family), where the master administered the household and managed all means of existence, the slave had a positive status as an instrument of production and life—an economic status, in the primary, etymological sense of that term. However, inasmuch as the sociological distinction between warfare (the object of war studies) and commerce (the object of economy), and the historical distinction between the antiquity of the one and the later character of the other are now accepted, the conflation of the two orders is no longer possible today as it was in the 18th century. Thus slavery is treated here as a concept of economic anthropology and economic history, as Karl Marx was to see it. This concept includes every form of slavery, leaving aside idealistic distinctions between "mild" and "harsh" forms.

Slavery constitutes a social relation of absolute instrumentalization, in which three processes are combined: commercial appropriation, domination, and exploitation. The slave trade was the first expression of this form of appropriation involving the dehumanization of individuals. The capture it presupposed implied violence that was sometimes a fact of war, and that was always material and symbolic, inflicted upon women as daughters, wives, and mothers. It implied their being wrenched from their native society and culture, and their transfer to another society and culture. The mode of transfer, a total negation of dignity, was the industrial or small-scale treatment of the person as thing, first as a commodity and then as a medium of exchange. The use of the term "chattel" meant that the thing was seen as a cultural product endowed with mobility, in this case self-mobility. The trade in slaves—the long-distance commerce and transfer of human "goods"—represented a demographic and economic gain for the merchants and their societies or states.

The experience of slavery continued the process of desocialization, deculturation, and depersonalization that began with the trade, touching the very root of life, the sex organs or reproductive force. At the same time, slavery initiated a process of formation and reproduction of a new society and a new culture in which slaves were the instruments and products, but not the beneficiaries. Through this specific instrumentalization, the masters and their societies or states were enriched and enjoyed the good life, just as, for Adam Smith, parent states used their colonies for the accumulation and enjoyment of wealth.

The term "despotic society" (from the Greek *despotès*, master of the house and/or of slaves) will be used here in the socioeconomic sense to denote any society that is dominated by masters of slaves. According to a classification system based on modes of production, some of these despotic societies were slave societies in which women, who were part of the predominant producers, constituted a portion of the laboring class within the state. Other despotic societies, by contrast, were lineal: in these, women featured among the other slaves as secondary producers alongside the freeborn, particularly the younger men.

The notion of racial identity expressed in the term "Negress" to denote female slaves was more or less significant depending on whether these women were traded within Africa or exported beyond the continent. When black people were exchanged among black people, who did not have the same relationship to their race as did the absolute stranger—white or Native American—the term held no racist connotations, despite its Latin origin preserved in the Portuguese word *negro* (black). When traders exported slaves outside of Africa, the pejorative connotation of the term "black"—derived from the Atlantic trade and associated with the hierarchy of white, Indian, and black—was marked by a double connotation based on genetics or race for some and on physical appearance or skin color for others. This racist connotation, which was to be exorcised by abolitionism, was reintroduced in Africa by colonialism and led to the formation,

in the 20th century, of a symmetrical political ideology linking culture and race: the ideology of Negritude. On the Oriental market, the same framework motivated the ethnic opposition found in medieval Arabic between *mamelouk* (white slave) and *abd* (black slave; the feminine form of the latter, *ama*, appears in some later dialects as *abdeh, abde*, and *abda*, all equivalents of "Negress").

These connotations thus allow us to posit a cultural typology distinguishing between despotic societies where slaves and masters belonged to the same race and which were free of racial—but not of ethnic—prejudice, and societies divided between two or three races where this prejudice flourished. In the first case, women belonged to a multiethnic slave class facing a monoethnic despotic class, and in the second case, they belonged to a slave class identified with what was considered an inferior race (or two races placed in a hierarchy) facing a despotic class of a supposedly superior race.

It matters little that philosophers have diversely interpreted the subjectivity of the person who is bought and sold as the core of being and worth, a principle of autonomy and mainstay of dignity, or a subject of rights through the mediation of culture and political power. The fact remains that from the moment of the transaction, the individual sold into slavery engaged in individual or collective rebellion against the desocialization, reification, deculturation, depersonalization, and desexualization initiated by the trade. This meant that the primary instrumentalization applied by masters in despotic societies was countered by a secondary instrumentalization of the masters by the slaves, who sought to attain ends of their own. This was the path of tactical adaptation. Rather than the resignation of victims who accepted the status quo, it implied the critical and tactical behavior of those who used cunning to reach their ends, as in the African folktales of the Spider and the Hare, which celebrate the victory of intelligence or cunning over strength. Another path was resistance in the anthropological sense, as expressed in a general refusal and various kinds of revolt. Resistance took two main forms. The individual form used modes of civil action (theft, flight) or violence (murder, suicide). The collective form, class struggle, shook the despotic society in two ways: marooning and insurrection. To be a maroon was to revolt by deserting the despotic society; for the deserting slaves, it meant joining forces and organizing a separate society that was parallel to the despotic society, was itself a despotic society if need be, and was of greater or lesser duration. Through this separation and replication, runaway slaves could produce a revolution of a national nature. Insurrection, as a mass rebellion and an attempt at creative destruction, could lead to political and social revolution. Beyond these modes of adaptation and resistance, slaves participated over the long term in the invention of new societies in which, together with their masters, they were conscious or unconscious mediators.

The 18th century was a pivotal period in the history of the black slave trade. In a world market dominated by the capitalist economy, the slave trade and slavery peaked and began to see a decline. Who were the African women who fell victim to the slave trade? They were women whom a reductive theory based on the concept of "female civilization" has characterized as autonomous and complementary to men. In fact, they played all the roles, as merchants and agents, or commodities and medium of exchange. In the despotic societies that acquired, dominated, and used them, these women also assumed every function, as subject or as instrument, or sometimes as both together: proprietor, property, or even, simultaneously, property *and* proprietor of slaves. Furthermore, female slaves participated in every form and every phase of critical adaptation to and resistance against the despotic societies. Finally, their mediation in the invention of new social formations was notable on several levels: interbreeding and ethnogenesis, the creation of new gastronomic cultures, the establishment of a new religious pluralism, and the crusade for liberties. However, it will be seen how this autonomy was exercised within an overall framework of social inferiority.

The recent literature on this dialectic of autonomy and inferiority is of interest on several counts: it now includes works on lineal slavery in Africa; it sheds light not only on the lives of slaves, but also on the modes and the effects of their deaths; and, finally, it provides confirmation of the main hypotheses presented here. Nonetheless, its limitations, which also apply here, should be recognized: the field of inquiry is almost worldwide; available syntheses remain partial because of their national or regional character, and they lack data from the Arab world and the Far East; and documentation on different continents, hemispheres, regions and provinces, and historical periods is unequal. Above all, this literature is marked by the silence of slave women themselves, who, except in the United States in the last decades of slavery, and unlike their male counterparts in Africa, left no slave narratives; and, to our knowledge, by the absence of works on children and the elderly in the slave trade and in slavery.

The World Market and the Radical Dehumanization of Black Women

The economic context of the slave trade had three characteristic features. First, a worldwide market driven by capitalism linked Europe, the Americas, Africa, and Asia. Second, the international division of labor was structured as follows: Europe had the capital—circulation of which was facilitated by a continually improved credit system—and a variety of expanding industries (agroindustry, textiles, navigation, weapons, and munitions); the Americas had an abundant supply of land for agriculture (tobacco, cotton, sugarcane, cocoa, coffee, indigo) and mineral resources (gold, silver, copper, diamonds); Africa had an abundant supply of labor (farmers, artisans, herders, fishermen); and Asia had spices and silk. Finally, over time free trade and monopoly trade began to compete in both the old, expanding cities and new cities, led by merchant classes that sometimes entered into conflict with the planter classes and sometimes joined forces with them against the slave classes.

The political context, in which power, religion, and commerce remained inextricably linked, was marked worldwide by two contradictory trends. On the one hand, the old states of Europe were engaged in a struggle for world hegemony (to the benefit of England, France, and Portugal), while in Africa, a struggle for regional hegemony resulted in the militarization and feudalization of states to the detriment of lineal societies and city-states. On the other hand, another struggle developed in the Northern Hemisphere against the monarchy and in favor of democracy and the rights of man, while in Africa religious and political revolutions promoted Islamic theocracies (Fouta-Djalon), animist empires (Asante, Rozvi), or age-class organizations and secret societies, which were generally male-centered.

The political antagonisms in the northern states shaped contradictory views of the world and the law. On the one hand, theological antihumanism or exclusive humanism validated the white European male, and the defense of slavery was founded on what was held to be the natural inferiority of the black race, a prejudice that was legalized by the French Code Noir (1685, 1724) and the Codigo Negro Carolino o Codigo Negro Español (1784), the Spanish legal code in effect in Cuba and Santo Domingo. On the other hand, universal humanism validated humans of all races, and the humanitarian antislavery cause drew its inspiration from philosophical rationalism and the precursor to what would become known as socially progressive Christianity.

The last third of the 18th century marked the beginning of a protracted crisis in the slave trade and slavery. First, three types of nations emerged: the anticolonialist, proslavery nation (typified by the United States), the colonialist, antislavery nation (typified by France), and the anticolonialist, antislavery nation (typified by Haiti). Then, following on the ideological criticism expressed by progressive Christians (Quakers such as John Woolman and Anthony Benezet, and Methodists such as John Wesley), by philosophers such as the abbé Raynal, and by politicians such as the abbé Grégoire and William Wilberforce, political associations were formed in the colonies, England, France, and later the United States: the Pennsylvania Society for the Abolition of Slavery (1775), the Society for the Extinction of the Slave Trade (1788), the Société des Amis des Noirs (1788; Society of the Friends of Blacks), The American Anti-Slavery Society (1833), and the Société Française pour l'Abolition de l'Esclavage (1834; French Society for the Abolition of Slavery). Finally, legislative acts and political events of a revolutionary character followed: the unsuccessful Cormantin rebellion in Jamaica (1760); the abolition of slavery in several English colonies (1777–78); the French Déclaration des Droits de l'Homme et du Citoyen (1789; Declaration of the Rights of Man and the Citizen); the abolition of slavery decreed on 4 February 1794 by the French National Convention and then revoked by Napoleon (1802); the victorious revolution of the slaves of Santo Domingo (1791–1804); the abolition of the slave trade by Denmark (1803) and England (1807); and the abolition of slavery in Latin America (Chili, 1823; Mexico, 1829) and in Europe (England, 1833; France, 1848).

Merchants and Merchandise: The Slave Trade and Commercial Alienation

The world market system connected two kinds of slave trade: trade conducted within each continent, and interregional trade, which crossed the Sahara, the Red Sea, the Atlantic, and the Indian Ocean. The Atlantic trade, an expression of a capitalist economy, dominated all the others as a center dominates its periphery.

The African women who were to be subjected to the slave trade presented three dimensions in the context of their own cultures: complementarity, autonomy, and subordination. In many African worldviews, complementary female and male principles constitute the structure of the universe (earth and sky, moon and sun) as well as of human beings; in some regions, it was consequently deemed necessary to eliminate "androgyny" in humans by genital excision and circumcision in order to make copulation and biological reproduction possible. At the same time, the specific features associated with the female gender (the uterus in the magico-religious sense, menstrual blood viewed as dangerous, and motherhood as sacred) served as a basis for the development of a sphere of autonomy. This included the separation of property, gender-specific production tasks, therapeutic and artistic knowledge, and exclusively female ritual associations. Nevertheless, a global status of inferiority rendered women subordinate to men, in that they were generally excluded from control over the means of production (land, tools, younger men, and women), from political power, from warfare, and from administering the great religious rituals that ensured the circulation of the life force in the world. In the African numerology of the couple, the number 4 was assigned to women and 3 to men in one region, and 7 to women and 9 to men in another region.

Two types of factors could motivate the sale of women into slavery: general reasons common to both sexes (sorcery, adultery, debt, murder, warfare, political power) and specifically "female" reasons linked to an economic or demographic loss (refusal to marry, repeated divorces, infanticide). It was essentially for political reasons, for example, that Tegbetsu, king of Dahomey from 1728 to 1775, sold five priestesses, while King Adandozan sold three priests and Agôtime, the slave mother of Prince Gankpe, the future king Guezo, of whom he was jealous (see Manning).

African women, however, were not only the victims of the slave trade. One of the subject-roles they played was that of merchants who sold and bought their own kind. On the West African coast, from Senegal to Sierra Leone, rich and influential Afro-Portuguese women, surrounded by large courts, were known by variants of the same title: *signares, señoras, nharas, senhoras*. Some were highly renowned: Catti de Rufisque (late 17th–early 18th century), Bibiana Vaz de Cacheu (late 17th–early 18th century), Betsy Heard de Beira (late 18th–early 19th century), and E. Frazer Skeleton de Victoria and Mary Faber de Sanga (19th century). While only a small number of women were merchants, many others served as auxiliaries to the trade in the ports or the interior of the continent, playing a second subject-role, that of agent. In Madagascar, French administrators recommended concubinage with daughters of aristocratic families who would have some authority, could serve as interpreters or governesses, knew the country, and could strike a good bargain. This step was often taken and proved to be a success.

Nevertheless, the slave trade was marked by an internal contradiction. The first object-role that African women played on the market—the first denial of humanity—was that of the person-thing as merchandise. On the one hand, the productive humanity of the standard units of measure known as *pièces 'Inde* was exalted. The *Encyclopédie méthodique* (1782–1832) defined *pièces d'Inde* as the type of individuals the Portuguese customarily sought to buy as slaves for their colonies in the East Indies: "a man or a woman, aged 15 to 25 or 30 at most, who is healthy, well built, does not limp, and has all his or her teeth." Three children between the ages of 10 to 15 years were worth 2 *pièces d'Inde*; two children between 5 and 10 years, 1 *pièce d'Inde*. Black male or female children between the ages of 7 and 15 were called *capore* (boy) and *caporine* (girl) and those under 7

years of age, *négrillon* (little boy) and *négrillonne* or *négritte* (little girl). These units complied with universal criteria of an economic nature, as has just been seen (young adult, height approximately 1.76 meters, physically whole with perfect teeth, good health and sturdiness, sometimes a particular ethnocultural origin and good morality). They also corresponded to specific esthetic criteria, such as cleanliness and the quality of the breasts: "It is prescribed that women should have breasts that are not like that of the kid goat, nor pendulous or flabby." On the other hand, that same humanity was annihilated in and by commercial reification on the market.

The slaves' status as objects can first of all be seen in the language applied to this humanity, a language used for animals and materials: livestock, heads of cattle, warehouse, load, cargo, and holding pen. Object status is further expressed in the means of payment and finally in the price. The means of payment, equivalent to the merchandise, was composite and consisted everywhere of goods for production, consumer goods, and currency. On the African coast, it was sometimes what was known as the lot, package, or pieces (firearms, munitions, iron bars, liquor, fabric, tobacco, hardware, beads), and sometimes cash, depending upon the country (iron bars, gold, cowry shells, manillas); in the interior, payment was made in the form of kola, salt, copper, rifles, cows, and horses. In the Americas and on the islands, the pound, the piaster, the peso, the real, and agricultural and mining products were all used. An ounce of gold, the medium of exchange on the Gold Coast, equaled 800 pounds minted at Tours, which were worth 16 écus or *aqués* or 16,000 cowry shells, depending upon the locality; a single shell used essentially as "change" was worth one-fifth of a liard.

On the African and Arab markets, the price of female slaves exceeded that of males. In 1690 in Nioro (present-day Mali), when a man could be purchased for one ounce of gold, a woman was worth two ounces; in the same region in 1805, 40,000 cowry shells would buy a man or a boy, but a woman would cost 80,000–100,000 (see Robertson and Klein). In Cairo, the average price of a woman exceeded that of a man by 68 percent to 74 percent between 1720 and 1749, and by 174 percent between 1760 and 1769. However, that average price was lower than the price for an Abyssinian woman, an African of lighter skin, and corresponded to a sixth or a quarter of the value on the Cairo market of a white slave woman between the 17th and 19th centuries. This price ratio can be explained by a combination of several factors (although researchers continue to debate the relative weight carried by each). These were a female slave's productive capacity, obvious for slave societies; her reproductive capacity, significant for domestic economies; the ease with which she could be integrated and help integrate others, which was facilitated by domestic service; and the regulating function of concubinage recognized by Muslim families.

On the Atlantic, American, and Mascarene Island markets, on the other hand, the opposite was true: the prices of females were lower than those of males under the same circumstances. In the 18th century, Van Alstein, a slave ship captain, noted the following prices for his transactions: in Cabinda (Angola), from 20 September to 19 December 1766: 1 man: 21–30 coins; 1 woman: 18–22 coins; 1 little boy: 15 coins; 1 little girl: 8–22 coins. In Ardres (Gulf of Benin), on 12 December 1777, 1 man: 9–11 ounces of gold; 1 woman: 7–10 ounces; 1 child: 5–7 ounces. In Cap-Français (Haiti), on 29 April 1744, 1 man: 1,800 pounds; 1 woman: 1,500 pounds; 1 little boy: 1,200 pounds;

1 little girl: 1,100 pounds. The same price differences can be noted between 1684 and 1746 in Brazil, where "freedom charters," or certificates of manumission, were more expensive for men than for women: the average prices for a man went from 100,000 to 180,000 reals, and for a woman, from 80,000 to 130,000 reals. In 1796, 1 *molecão* (young man) was worth 90,000 to 110,000 reals, while 1 *molecona* (young woman) was valued at 70,000 to 90,000 reals. The same differences were found in Canada, where, in addition, an Indian male was worth half of an African male and an Indian female half of an African female.

The reasons for these disparities were both external and internal to Africa. The transatlantic demand was primarily for a male workforce adapted to the criteria of productivity of agricultural and mining activities. In Africa, by contrast, there was a considerable need for reproductive forces, and this determined the retention of women. This is demonstrated by the fact that, during that same period, the coastal regions that exported the most slaves—the Gold Coast, the Bight of Benin, the Bight of Biafra, and Angola—all presented a remarkable density of population that is still discernable today.

The second object-role that African women played on the market—the second denial of humanity—was that of the person-thing as a medium of exchange in the broad sense. In Africa and the Muslim states, women, together with men and various material goods, formed part of the tributes and taxes that vassals owed their lords. They were also used as gifts that superiors offered to their inferiors and to distinguished foreigners. Like men, women in this context could serve to guarantee a debt, as in Canada and Brazil. Above all, and well into the 19th century, women functioned together with the males as currency, in competition with other forms such as cowry shells or the Maria Theresa dollars used by the Egyptian state to pay civil servants. Women as commodities always formed part of a dowry or matrimonial compensation, where their function was associated with domestic service and reproduction.

A minimum of two sales and two purchases marked the passage from the slave trade to slavery, but no sale or purchase could be considered final, for the slave always remained alienable in law. In 18th-century Canada, for example, Marcel Trudel has noted the cases of three female slaves who were bought and sold five times—over a period of 12 years (1785–97), 9 years (1787–96), and 2 years (1785–87) respectively—and who were consequently unable to marry and have children (see Trudel).

Forms of Exploitation in Despotic Societies

Women in the Slave Population

During the 18th century, which marked the apogee of the slave trade and slavery, the exportation of slaves from Africa reached its highest proportions, totaling 7,433,000 slaves as compared to 2,868,000 in the 17th century and 5,442,000 in the 19th century, according to the figures cited by Curtin and corrected by Lovejoy (see Curtin; Lovejoy). The bulk of this population lived in slave societies, and slaves made up a majority of the total population in Jamaica, Santo Domingo, South Carolina, Goree, Saint-Louis, and the Mascarene Islands. From 1760 to 1800, there were 10 black people for every white person in Jamaica and 4 to 5 blacks for each white in Barbados; in 1770 there were 3 blacks for every 2 whites in South Carolina. The slave population was in the minority in other despotic societies (Congo, Cape Colony, Brazil, New Spain, New England, New York, Egypt), or became a minority at one period or another, as was the case in South Carolina, where black slaves accounted for 44 percent of the population in 1790.

African women comprised two-thirds of the 1,300,000 slaves exported via the Sahara, the Red Sea, and the Indian Ocean in the 18th century, and two-thirds of the 9,920,000 slaves held in Africa between the 16th and 18th centuries, according to Lovejoy. Inikori has estimated that their numbers in the Muslim world from 1500 to 1890 reached 4,590,000. According to the same author, women constituted about one-third of the 6,133,000 slaves exported across the Atlantic in the 18th century, and reached a total of 6,160,000 for the period 1500–1890 (see Inikori; Lovejoy).

The proportion of female slaves in the despotic societies differed from country to country. In Cuba, the slave population was 90.38 percent male and 9.62 percent female between 1746 and 1790, whereas in Santo Domingo there was a ratio of 150 men to 100 women from 1713 to 1754. The proportion of women also varied according to period and economic activity (mines or plantations). Thus, in Cuba from 1791 to 1822, there were 85 percent men versus 15 percent women, whereas in Guadeloupe the sex ratio was balanced from 1700 to 1715, and around 113 men for 100 women between 1734 and 1773 (see Gautier). In some Jesuit haciendas in Peru the sex ratio was even weighted toward women: the slave population was 56.8 percent female in 1771 at the Villa hacienda, 53.8 percent in 1776 at the hacienda of Vilacatioura, and 53.3 percent in 1775 at La Huaca. In 1870 in Cairo, the slave population of 10,481 comprised 8,674 women and 1,807 men.

Enslaved women came from all over black Africa. Those who were taken to North Africa and the Middle East came mainly from the Sahel and the Horn (Mali, Abyssinia, Nubia). The women slaves sent to North and South America and the Caribbean came primarily from the west coast of Africa (Guinea, the Bights of Benin and Biafra, and Angola). According to O. Patterson, the slaves of Jamaica (Fon, Arada, Nago, Igbo, Ibibio, Akan, Ga, Adangbe, Mossi, Congo) came mostly from the Bight of Benin and present-day Ghana between 1700 and 1730, from Ghana and Nigeria from 1730 to 1790, with a growing number from Nigeria at the end of the century (see Patterson). According to Gabriel Debien, Santo Domingo drew its slave population (Congo, Nago, Arada, Hausa, Senegal, Mandingo, Susu) from the Congo (1760–1790), Ghana, the Bight of Benin, Nigeria, and Middle Guinea (see Debien). Brazil was supplied primarily by Angola (68 percent), followed by West Africa (32 percent) between 1701 and 1810, according to Curtin (see Curtin).

In some colonies, however, Creoles (children of slaves born into slavery) outnumbered *bossales* (slaves who had come directly from Africa)—and in unexpected ratios attesting to the extent to which the slaves had settled and their level of reproduction: in Barbados the ratio of Creoles to *bossales* was 7 to 1, in South Carolina 4 to 1 (1740), in Martinique 9 to 1 (1746), and in the Chesapeake region 10 to 1 (1760).

Women Slaveholders

Alongside men of all races, the owners of female slaves included other black women of varying social rank. Highest in rank among such women slaveholders, in terms of the sheer volume of their possessions, came the aristocrats, such as the black mother of the Caliph Al Mustansir of Morocco in the 11th century, who acquired thousands of slaves of both sexes in order to reinforce her son's black army, and Queen Nzinga, head of the state of Ndongo in the 17th century, who received the viceroy of Portugal while seated on the back of a slave and surrounded by an armed guard. Generally speaking, the queen mothers of African monarchies and women chieftains, such as those of the Sherbro, were slaveholders. Next in rank came the merchant women, the *signares* mentioned earlier, and wealthy women from the lineal societies on the Atlantic coast of Africa in the 19th century. Finally, there were freed women, or even enterprising slaves of means, who owned slaves—a phenomenon that occurred in Peru, Brazil, Africa, and in the lineal societies.

The concrete and complete appropriation of slaves always involved ritual procedures of rupture and annexation. Certain groups in Africa invented new bodies for female slaves, who were absolute outsiders, by shaving their heads and dressing them in a new *pagne* (a type of garment). They breathed a new soul into the enslaved women, using the powers of medicine to make them forget their past; they gave them new "mothers" by entrusting them to the older women of the lineage and a new birth by imposing a new name upon them. European appropriation began with a stamp on the breast and an assigned number; it sometimes included baptism and always a new name. Upon arrival, female slaves would be placed under the guardianship of older slave women who initiated them into the master's language and the trials of servitude. Thiam, a slave in the Antilles in the 19th century, was allowed to keep her original African name, but this was very rare indeed. As was the case for male slaves, female slaves' names were almost always either inventions of the master (Egyptian Woman, Quinquionne), or borrowed from the master's mythology, history, and religion (Venus, Flora, Maria, Mary, Marie, Miriam). Thus, wholly and irrevocably appropriated and relocated in another time and space, female slaves and their descendants belonged unconditionally to the masters, and as possessions and multipurpose instruments they entered into the sexual division of slave labor, the "natural" structure of exploitation. There is a saying among the Peuls: "He who is owned does not even own what he wears on his head."

Women as Property

Slave women were instruments that fulfilled four functions: organ, factor of production, extension of power, and offering. As organs of pleasure, African women were subjected to extreme forms of abuse. Two examples among the innumerable instances that could be cited amply illustrate this phenomenon. These examples took place in two antithetical spaces, the slave ship and the family; they involved complete strangers in the former and relatives in the latter. For the victims the result was illness, depreciation, or death. In December 1776, on the vessel *L'Aimable Françoise* from Nantes, a deranged second captain sexually assaulted the crew, who were his compatriots, and the black captives who were part of the cargo. In particular, he

> mistreated a very beautiful black woman, breaking two of her teeth and putting her in such a state of indolence that she could only be sold at a very low price in Santo Domingo, where she died two weeks later. His brutality was

such that he even raped a little *négritte* of 8 to 10 years old, closing her mouth to keep her from screaming, and he repeated this on three different nights and put her in an almost mortal state; . . . this little girl, who would otherwise have been sold for at least 1,800 pounds in Santo Domingo, suffered so much harm from this mistreatment and violence that she could only be sold as one of the low-priced blacks who fetched 800 pounds each.

The second example is perhaps even more tragic. It was related by J. Girod de Chantrans, at the end of his seventh letter, dated 1782, in *Voyage d'un Suisse dans différentes colonies d'Amérique* (1785; A Swiss Traveler's Journey through Different American Colonies). A white colonist, about 50 years of age, unmarried but the father of several mulatto children, became enamored of one of his daughters. After failing to overcome the girl's refusal with caresses, and finding that his threats were equally unsuccessful, he began to persecute her. "Her brothers, witness to the horrors of which she was the victim, and carried away by pity and indignation, strangled the father in his bed." They boldly chose not to flee and were arrested and condemned to death; all of them were executed, including the daughter.

As instruments of procreation, enslaved African women were far from realizing their potential fertility. Nevertheless, their organic function was given priority in three kinds of despotic societies. Lineal societies, especially the matrilineal ones, sought to perpetuate lineages by assimilating women from outside the bloodline. In certain colonies, such as Virginia and Maryland, slaves were purchased to reproduce a social class. Finally, Muslim societies attached to the principle of concubinage, where concubines were accumulated in harems guarded by eunuchs, granted privileged status to the *umm-al-walad* ("mother of the child" or "concubine-mother"), whom they protected against ostracism, exclusion, or sale, and who was set free at the death of the master. Even the 1685 Code Noir, in its ninth article, legitimized marriage between whites and blacks, the freeing of slave concubines, and the freedom of children born to concubine mothers. It was only in 1724 that the Code forbade mixed marriages in Louisiana, on the grounds of racial corruption; the statutes authorized black people to marry only among themselves, following the example of the North American colonies.

The objective of population growth led other countries, such as Jamaica and Santo Domingo, or the Jesuit haciendas in New Spain, to introduce sanitary improvements and to offer rewards in money and in kind to encourage women to procreate. But all was in vain. Despite an unsubstantiated hypothesis to the contrary, and despite some localized progress, the general conclusion as confirmed by African studies on the 19th and early 20th centuries is that transatlantic fertility rates were low—even lower among the *bossales* than among the Creoles: the reproduction rate in the West Indies was about 1, as compared to about 2 in the lineal societies of Africa in the early 20th century. These low birthrates can be explained by the economic and social conditions that were the law of slavery: disintegration of the family, trauma caused by deportation and anxiety over being resold, precarious status, polygyny and infrequent marriage, excessive labor and insufficient sustenance, a high incidence of single mothers, and high infant mortality rates. Taken in combination, these factors explain why, until the source of slave labor was cut off at the beginning of the 19th century, the masters preferred the easy, continuous, and cheap importation of slaves from Africa to the natural, long, and costly process of breeding. Nevertheless, the childless concubines did ensure the masters' pleasure and provided domestic service, while the modest product of procreation entered into the category of factors of production.

The female servile class in slave societies was composed of three strata: palace slaves attached to the courts of kings and chiefs, domestic slaves attached to the households of plantation or mine owners (often known as the "big house," *casa grande*, or *habitation*), and lastly plantation or mine workers and unskilled laborers in commerce. House slaves, whose numbers depended upon the master's wealth, were relatively better housed, better fed, and better dressed. They were women "of talent," the most beautiful, the most intelligent and devoted; selected for the prestige of the household and the efficiency of its services, they worked as cooks, dressmakers, linen maids, laundresses, chambermaids, nurses, grain-millers, wet-nurses ("mammies," Arab *dadas*), or artists and poets in the harems. However, the proportion of skilled workers was always lower among women than among men, representing 1 to 9 percent of women as opposed to 7 to 28 percent of men in the slave class in the French Antilles from 1770–89 (with the exception of Martinique). Female workers in the narrow sense were laborers on the industrial plantations of the Caribbean and the Americas (known as haciendas, *engenhos, estancias, fazendas*), and in the broad sense those who worked in the agricultural villages (called *runde* in Peul) established around African cities and the villages of the free born (*misiide*, in Peul). Women in the agricultural villages were subjected to various regimes of exploitation. In Fouta-Djalon country, masters provided slaves with the means of production: land, seed, tools, lodging, and women. In addition to cutting wood, drawing water, cooking, and tending children, women devoted two days to gender-specific tasks (rice planting, hoeing, harvesting, and transporting) and feeding their families and five days to providing the masters with their sustenance and a surplus for the marketplace. In Malinke territory, where textiles and kola were the commercial staples, women would gin and spin cotton and collect and carry kola nuts, while the men did the weaving and packing and ran the commerce. Those slaves who were concubines of the masters (*jaariya*) were in the service of the first wife, who was always freeborn, and returned to the *runde* when they were repudiated; their sons remained free through their father but their status was diminished by the absence of a maternal family.

Slave labor in the industrial context of the Americas and the islands, where accumulation and the expropriation of surplus attained their maximum level, was organized in militaristic, concentration-camp fashion under the supervision of white or black overseers armed with whips. The slaves were poorly dressed, housed in clay and straw cabins with one door and one window (typified by the Brazilian *senzala*), and they received one insufficient daily ration of food. Most of the women worked in teams on gender-specific tasks for long, 14- to 18-hour days. On sugar plantations female laborers fed the mills, boiled down the cane, packaged the residue, and did the distilling. On coffee plantations they did the picking, fertilizing, and gleaning. This expropriation of surplus was not only carried out in agroindustry and mining, but also in the renting out of slaves and the toll imposed on them, and in prostitution, as seen in Brazil, Mexico, Santo Domingo, and Africa. Thus, while their efficiency as organs of reproduction was very limited, slave women were totally efficient factors of production.

Female slaves also served as auxiliaries to political power. For royal slaves, the famous Amazons of Dahomey, who abandoned their traditional feminine gender roles for military purposes, were exemplary in performing this service. Female slaves also served as spies. Finally, female slaves ensured the social balance of the military apparatus everywhere, even in societies where there was a deficit of women. This balancing function applied to the black units that hunted down maroons in Spanish America and to the black executioners' guild in the prisons of French Canada, where the authorities bought a 24-year-old black slave woman, Angelina Denise, for Matthieu Leveillé, an executioner in Quebec from about 1734. The same function was served by the black armies in the Muslim states, such as the army of Sharif Moulay Ismaël of Morocco (1672–1729); the *ajele* administrative and military system of the kingdom of Oyo in present-day Nigeria; and the *achikunda* military system on the Portuguese *prazos* (concessions) in the gold-mining region of the Zambezi. The *ajèle* was an administrative structure founded on a slave workforce operating in the provinces and directly responsible to the *alafin* (king) of Oyo. The *achikunda* (singular *tsachikunda*) referred to the slave soldiers used by the Portuguese in the Zambezi Valley from the 16th and 17th centuries to ensure the security of their slave trade networks in the interior of the country. Women not only satisfied the sexual appetites of the civil servants or the lords of international commerce, they also bore the children who would reproduce their social class, as well as the control apparatus, by ensuring the sustenance of soldiers and administrators through the cultivation of food crops.

The last function fulfilled by women was that of sacrificial offerings in the religious domain. Their physical destruction was exploited to honor the beautiful posthumous life of masters and mistresses or to preserve the health of society and the world. In animist societies such as the Asante or the Dahomey, numerous slaves were sacrificed at queens' funerals, including eminent women, wives, concubines or those condemned to death. Similar sacrifices accompanied the funerals of wealthy women in the lineal societies as late as the 19th century. While the sacrifice of men involved bloodshed, the sacrificial code required that the immolation of women involve no shedding of blood, because they were subject to menstruation and did not participate in the murderous activities of warfare and hunting. The prescribed procedures for their killing included hanging, poisoning, and live burial. The Abê people of the Ivory Coast, for example, customarily drugged the woman to be sacrificed, then buried her alive up to her neck and scattered ripe palm seeds around her. The red color of the seeds and the appetizing smell of fresh oil would attract voracious, flesh-eating ants that attacked the victim's ears, nose, and eyes, torturing her until she died. This ritual to ensure the safety of the polity was also addressed to the protective gods of agriculture, water, fertility, and peace.

Challenging the Despotic Society: The Invention of Societies without Masters

Three processes formed the basis for the expression of protest against the despotic society and the invention of societies without masters: tactical adaptation, resistance, and mediation during sociohistoric transitions. Enslaved black women made specific contributions to each of these processes.

Tactical Adaptation

The first area in which tactical adaptation was practiced was that of morality. Those women who submitted—whether as casual mistresses or long-standing concubines, and whether by force or not—to the desire of their white masters, asserted two rights: the right to ownership of their bodies, and the right to security. They enjoyed relative security in the reappropriation of their bodies and their reproductive power, as well as improved living conditions for themselves and their progeny. When times of crisis came, however, they showed a violent reversal of attitude.

The second area was that of religion. Sociologist Roger Bastide has documented the extraordinary place African women occupied in every form of trance-based religion: Candomblé (Bahia), Voodoo (Santo Domingo), Santaría (Cuba), Shangô (Pernambuco), and Macumba (Rio de Janeiro) (see Bastide). In the colonies where the masters' religion was also the state religion, African religion had no hope of surviving without some form of adaptation. Therefore, it was adapted to the undoubtedly less inquisitorial ideological context of certain colonies: in Catholic Brazil, for example, slaves adopted the Christian calendar and found a match for each *orisha* (god, in Yoruba) among the male or female Catholic saints, identifying Yemanja with the Holy Virgin and Ogun with Saint George. Deliberate syncretism was thus a mainstay, a means of remaining faithful to the past as well as of maintaining autonomy.

The third area in which tactical adaptation occurred was the economy. Contemporary historians correctly insist on the fact that slaves succeeded in creating an "internal economy" within the system of class exploitation, based on the "free time" they were granted daily, weekly, and on holidays. Within this framework, black female slaves, who were gardeners, retail sellers, paid dependents of their masters or mistresses, or sometimes unwed mothers or heads of matrifocal families, created an autonomous place for themselves on the plantation or mine, or in the city. These modes of adaptation were nonetheless not sufficient on their own, and were preceded, followed, or accompanied by forms of open resistance.

Resistance

At the individual level, women's record of moral achievements included transgressions that were common to both sexes (theft [which Booker T. Washington alleged his mother committed], possession of stolen goods, flight, arson, blasphemy against the official religion, adultery, poisoning, illegal meetings, suicide, or elegance and luxury in dress) or gender-specific (refusal to be separated from a child, abortion, infanticide). Attacks on the material property of the masters attested to the slaves' destitution, to their refusal to be exploited, and to their awareness of the rights to life, security, and justice. Their attacks on the masters' human property—murder of their mistresses, their children, or the masters themselves—were absolute aspirations to unattainable liberty and happiness. Female magicians condemned the Church's complicity in oppression, as in Spanish America under the Inquisition. Mention should be made of the antislavery prophetism of Kimpa Vita (also known as Dona Beatrice), an aristocrat of the kingdom of the Congo, who was idealized in *Béatrice du Congo* (1970; Beatrice of the Congo) by the playwright Bernard Dadié and in *Dona Béatrice: La Jeanne d'Arc congolaise* (1976; Dona Beatrice: The Congolese Joan of Arc) by the historian Ibrahima Baba Kaké. In 1704 Kimpa Vita preached a national African religion that was inspired by Saint Anthony; she identified Mbanza Kongo with Bethlehem and used local symbols associated with the female cult of healing (water, soil, vegetation). This was a black people's religion, a new Catholic religion without fetishes or foreign rites, which promised a free and prosperous society where the autonomy of the female peasants she symbolized would reign.

At the collective level, in Africa as well as on the slave ships, women participated in the demonization of white people. The latter were held to be cannibals who transported captives in order to eat them, and who used the blood of slaves to make their red wine and the ground bones of dead slaves to make gunpowder for the trade. "They imagine," wrote Giovanni Antonio Cavazzi in *Istoriaca descrizione de tre regni Congo, Matamban et Angola* (1687; Historical Description of the Three Kingdoms of the Congo, Matamban and Angola) with regard to captive Angolan women, "infinite suffering and torment, and they believe that in America they will be used to make charcoal and oil." African women attended illegal meetings, participated in messianic cults, and organized religious sisterhoods as forms of protest and resocialization. They also participated in three ways in the epics of the fugitive slave societies that accompanied the birth of slavery. First, whether at the level of gangs, villages, cities, or city-states, they were brought in as rare objects captured in raids to compensate for a population deficit that was fatal to new nations. Second, women of all ages were actors—from courageous little girls aged 8 to 15 to adult refugees, often traveling with their children—who fled for the same general reasons and under the same difficult conditions as the men. Jean Fouchard has estimated that 15 to 20 percent of the maroon population of Santo Domingo in the 18th century was female, of all ethnicities and occupations, with large numbers of *bossales* before 1760 (see Fouchard). In Jamaica the scarcity of women led to the severe repression of adultery and the adoption of a controlled system of polyandry. Through agriculture and craft industry, small-scale commerce and breeding of livestock, women contributed to both the sustenance and the defense of the societies of fugitive slaves. Lastly, they were political, spiritual, or political and religious guides. Some were queens to the kings and polygynous captains who had been elected to head the new societies. In the Caribbean, *bossale* women, as sorceress-healers and practitioners of *Obeah*, provided means of personal protection and contributed to collective cohesion and the sense of combat; they were replaced after 1760 by the antiwitchcraft cult of Hyalism, and then by Evangelism. In the *palancas* (forts) or *quilombos* (slave refuges) there were African sorceresses and priestesses, as in the *quilombo* of Palmarès (Brazil), and political leaders rose from their ranks: one in an Afro-Indian *quilombo* of the Malalis, and another, Filippa Maria Aranha, at Alcobaça.

Women's participation in insurrections was just as visible. For example, 14 African women on the *Soleil*, a ship out of Nantes, committed collective suicide by drowning on 23 March 1774. Women took part in all the slave ship rebellions, but in 1773 their role on the *Thomas*, a vessel from Liverpool, was particularly significant: it was they who found the armory open during the crew's dinner hour and armed the male slaves and made carnage of the whites (but whose lack of restraint caused the rebellion to fail). Another example took place in Fouta-Djalon: after the failure of the rebellion in Buyra in 1785, the defeated heroes took refuge in a fortress in Susu territory, where their survival—until the ruling classes of the Susu and the Peuls formed a coalition against them—was ensured by the productive activity and the political commitment of the women from the *runde*. Lastly, during the revolution of Santo Domingo, women's first role was that of ideological resource: it was a Voodoo priestess who officiated on 14 August 1791, at the ceremony of Bois-Cayman, giving full legitimacy to the pact of the general rebellion and to the political and military leadership of the slave Boukman. Another generation of priestesses and the so-called Amazon Company followed, spearheading the ideological struggle. Despite women's position of sociopolitical inferiority—they were excluded from carrying weapons—they were endowed with agency, acting as occasional spies, prostitutes who provided the fighters with arms and munitions, or fighters who divided their time between support to the rebels (as did Nanny Prosser, wife of Gabriel Prosser of Virginia in 1800) and production (as did the farm worker Suzanne Simon-Baptiste, wife of Toussaint Louverture). These women galvanized their men with their courage and their boldness in the face of death. Yet at the end of the social revolution, they globally remained subordinate in status. Arlette Gautier has shown how, in the sexist discourse of the insurgent generals, including Toussaint Louverture, women were merely victims to be protected, stakes in the battles between men, or objects to be given up or taken; and in the militarized society that had been established, they were only underpaid farm workers who, despite their demands for social equality, were denied the right to the same wages as those who held the monopoly on arms (see Gautier).

Even the punishments meted out for acts of transgression confirmed the common identity of the slave class, as well as the differences that set women apart in terms of inhuman treatment. The Code Noir did not establish a sexual classification of punishments: it reserved the same reprisals for all crimes falling into the categories of theft, acts of violence, or excess, including starting fires, marooning, conspiracy, magic, and blasphemy. When 11 maroons in Sarameca, Surinam, were executed in 1730, the six women among them were torn apart alive and the two girls decapitated, while one of the men was suspended from an iron hook in his ribs and the two others were chained to stakes and burned alive. Still, there was no specific treatment for women who were impenitent recidivists such as Zabeth, a Creole from Santo Domingo. In Spanish America, the heroines of the aborted Holy Week plot of 1612 in Mexico—8 of the 36 black slaves were women—suffered the same punishment as the men: they were hanged, quartered, decapitated, and exhibited. From the 16th to the 18th centuries, black women who had a fancy for silk clothing and jewelry in gold, silver, or precious stones were sentenced to 100 lashes and the seizure of the goods in question (Mexico, 1612; Asunción, Paraguay, 1762). To cite yet another example, in Peru between 1702 and 1736, three black female magicians were burned at the stake like their male counterparts, as was a Congolese prophetess. Similarly, in the English colonies, women engaged in resistance were executed in the same way as their male counterparts (for arson in Maryland, 1766 and Albany, New York, 1793; for murder in Saint Andrew County, Georgia, November 1774; and for conspiracy in North Carolina, 1805). Or they were burned while the men were hanged (New-ton, Long Island, 1708), or hanged while the men were quartered (the fate of the slave Samba, who led a revolt in New Orleans in 1730, and of insurgents in another incident in Louisiana in 1784; see Aptheker). In Montreal in 1734, the arsonist M.J. Angélique, who had sought to take revenge on the mistress who intended to sell her, was condemned on appeal to four standard penalties: she was to be tortured, forced to publicly confess her guilt before the church on the tumbrel taking her to execution, then hanged and her body burned at the stake.

But there were other offenses for which women received gender-specific treatment. In Santo Domingo, if a miscarriage was deemed criminal the midwife was whipped and the mother was not only whipped but also had to wear an iron collar that was not removed until her next pregnancy. In Cuba and North Carolina, the required precaution for the whipping of a pregnant slave was to dig a hole to protect her belly. Worst of all, women were burned after their breasts and genitals had been scorched and pierced. In Santo Domingo, women slaves suffered the extreme humiliation of being raped in front of their husbands or having to watch their children being hacked to pieces with machetes. In Brazil, a concubine had her eyes gouged, her nose torn off, and her ears cut off so that the jealous white wife could serve them to her white husband at mealtime.

Transitions

The persistence of marooning and slave resistance, the series of abolitions in the English colonies, and the advent of the three types of nations referred to earlier in this essay all heralded the development of a new era in despotic societies, particularly in the New World. The role played by black women slaves in this context was significant in at least four areas.

The first of these was ethnogenesis. Miscegenation between whites, Indians, and blacks gave rise to a biologically differentiated mulatto population that grew steadily in number (from 500 in 1703 to 28,000 in 1789 in Santo Domingo). On the African coasts, the Caribbean islands, and in the Americas, this population formed a social class whose interests diverged from those of other classes. Such circumstances shaped the political role this emergent class played during the Haitian epic, in what Aimé Césaire called the "mulatto revolt," after the "rebellion of the *grands blancs* [white plantation owners]" and before "the Negro revolution." Since the only tacitly accepted—if not necessarily legal—kinds of crossbreeding were between a white male and a black female or a white male and an Indian female, it may be concluded that black and Indian women were statistically the primary bearers of this mulatto population in the 18th century. In other words, such women were the principal cultural producers of this quasi-ethnicity.

Second, African women were the creators of national gastronomic cultures. Gilberto Freyre pays them this homage in his description of the formation of Brazilian civilization, and it could well be said to hold for other countries in the Western Hemisphere (see Freyre). This action initially involved women of the servile class, especially domestic servants, mine or plantation laborers, and paid workers in the cities. Later its scope became national: women of every African ethnicity were the creators of new products, and all the classes and races of colonial Brazil were the beneficiaries. Eventually, this creative activity influenced not only the materials and techniques but also the social framework of culinary practices.

The materials used for these culinary innovations were not limited to the African products and utensils imported through the slave trade (bananas, palm oil, malaguetta peppers and other condiments, stones used for grating), but extended beyond them both ecologically and culturally. From the technical point of view, primarily in Bahia, Brazil, a wide variety of preparations were used to transform the vegetable and animal foods of the area. Corn was used to make bread, rolls, dough, cake, or was roasted; rice was used in bread, cooked in coconut milk, or in balls with palm oil or honey; manioc flour was made into cake, tapioca, or added to fish or meat gravy. Fish was used for frying, as an accompaniment to couscous, and in fishcakes; chicken was used for grilled dishes and *xinxin*, a type of spicy stew flavored with dried shrimp. The same diversity in preparation techniques was evident in the various stews and pastries. As Freyre relates, the genius of this collective creation and its near-religious esthetic preoccupations are revealed in the preparation of pastries "decorated with multicolored paper flowers, and in shapes of hearts and animal figures" evoking "former phallic or totemic worship." Two dishes remain typical: *caruru* and *vatapa*.

Finally, slave women's culinary activities broadened the social framework of food preparation and consumption. From the domestic kitchen of the "big house" they moved on to cooking on portable stoves in food stalls in public squares, or they became strolling vendors who walked the streets with trays on their heads, like moving caryatids, in the same way as their free counterparts did in the cities of West Africa. Mother Eva, who continued this tradition in the 19th century during the preabolition era, symbolized the generation of the women who had founded it.

Third, slave women contributed to the development of new forms of religious pluralism. On a first level, African pluralism could be seen in the transatlantic coexistence of the priestesses and daughters of the gods who were central figures of the ethnic religions (Yoruba, Bantu). There was also pluralism on the national level, for despite persecution by the police and the church, African religions coexisted with Roman Catholicism, the official religion in much of the Caribbean and Latin America at the time. This was a significant new development: with the exception of the orthodox Christianity of Ethiopia (where it was coupled with the Judaism of the Falasha), Christianity was a minority religion everywhere in Africa, ranging from Catholicism in the Congo and Angola and on the islands, to Protestantism in the Cape. But in Latin America, the African religions were in the minority and coexisted with various indigenous Indian religions and Roman Catholicism. This unprecedented situation heralded another new development, that of ecumenical pluralism. On the one hand, the state religion during the colonial period in Latin America excluded all other forms of Christianity or monotheism. On the other hand, the various African religions were not historical religions, but rather, as Bastide has shown, living religions that continued to create new forms until the 20th century (see Bastide). At the dawn of the new era, in which the end of the first modern wave of colonization coincided with the beginnings of ideological liberalization, African religions were thus already prepared to encounter all the other religions, and indeed proved their ability to withstand competition. This cultural aptitude can be attributed primarily to the influence of the female clergy during the formative period.

Fourth, African women also played a leading role in the crusade for freedom. One example that can be cited is the role played by *signares* such as Bibiana Vaz de Cacheu in the struggle against monopoly commerce in Africa. Across the Atlantic, the primary form of the crusade was the emancipation movement. According to data on the Spanish, French, and Portuguese colonies, the majority of the freed slaves were women and children: statistics for Salvador show that between 1684 and 1745, 66.9 percent were females and 33.1 percent males, with 29.5 percent children and at most 10 percent elderly or infirm (cited in Mattoso de Queiros). The benevolence of the masters was not the sole source of emancipation. Slaves took initiatives of their own that were manifested in different forms: in self-sacrificing mothers who bought freedom for their children while they themselves remained slaves; in local or ethnic solidarity; in the love of freed husbands who purchased freedom for their wives; in urban brotherhoods that provided aid; and of course in the efficient Underground Railroad, a secret interstate network of solidarity that helped slaves to pass from slavery to freedom.

This was the context of the epic achievements of that exemplary figure, Harriet Tubman (1821–1913), a fugitive slave from Maryland. A key figure in the Underground Railroad, Tubman conducted 19 dangerous expeditions, leading more than 300 slaves to freedom while a price had been placed on her head. As a scout, she helped black troops to save 726 slaves. She became known as the "Moses of her people," leading them to "the Promised Land of liberty." But this social form of emancipation was accompanied by an ideological and political crusade. There was Phyllis Wheatley (1753–84), the first black woman poet of modern written literature, whose pious and moral condemnation of the slave trade and plea for freedom were to be continued and taken to another level in the 19th century by Sojourner Truth (1797–1883), an illiterate former slave. Sojourner Truth was set free in the state of New York and became a symbol of the struggle. She fought to recover her son from slavery, and then dedicated the rest of her life to the battle against slavery, racism, and sexism. She fought for the universal abolition of slavery, the equality of blacks and whites in a political democracy, and the equality of women and men in the religious, economic, and social spheres.

Conclusion

In summary, the black slave trade in the 18th century, and the process of dehumanization it imposed, radicalized the inferior status that was the lot of African women in their original societies and which they shared with the great mass of women in the world, especially in European, Native American, and Middle Eastern societies. The context of this process was worldwide, determined by the capitalist economy and dominated by a simplistic racial ideology and hierarchy (white, Indian, black), and, in concert with this, by social and gender stratification.

This radical exacerbation of African women's inferior status has a history: it was propagated from the coast into the interior of Africa, initiated by the Portuguese in the 15th and 16th centuries, continued by the Dutch in the 17th century, and brought to a conclusion by the French and the English in the 17th and 18th centuries. As an overall process, this radicalization related as much to the source of power of the slave trade and its means as to the object of the slave trade and its result.

This radicalization was linked to the source of power behind the slave trade: the male sex. Even if a minority of women participated in the slave trade, the international system was primarily controlled and managed by men of all races. Captive women, therefore, were subjected to three kinds of male violence that accompanied this activity. There was the African violence of social excommunication and political proscription. There was the combined violence inflicted by blacks and whites in the market of the coastal trading posts and Saharan cities. There was the European and Arab violence of the buyers and sellers on the Red Sea, the Indian Ocean, and in the Americas. This radicalization was also linked to the extreme means men used to turn the trade into an efficient industry: infrastructures, naval equipment, armed forces, cavalry, and firearms.

In addition, this radicalization was related to the ultimate object of the trade: the sexual body, which commercial reification both denied and exalted. The idea of the person as unit of measurement was based on the sexual body and in turn inspired that body as a norm; the requisite medical examination that preceded each purchase accepted the sexual body as a given, and that body was the obsession of the gender-specific treatment administered to the captive women on the slave ships (the absence of chains, as with children; segregated living quarters; specific surveillance by female quartermasters who were the prison wardens of the ocean crossing; sexual abuse inflicted upon young women, and the rape of girls). Finally, this radicalization lay in the result of the slave trade: the absolute ecological, social, and cultural distance that separated Africa, the point of departure, from the point of arrival, whether this was America, the Middle East or Asia, and the individual's death to the society of origin and rebirth in the society of exploitation.

Slavery continued and completed this radicalization, taking it to intolerable levels. Even if some women were slaveholders, they represented only a tiny minority, and the process of radicalization remained dominated by men. In the first place, this process was implemented by the economic and administrative system of appropriation-and-annexation, through which the slaves were integrated as members into the family body in the lineal societies, or as laborers into the concentration-camp system of the plantation or mine within the slave societies. In contrast to house slaves and concubines—that slave aristocracy of women "of talent"—the majority of women slaves were unskilled laborers who were subjected to four forms of hierarchical control at the place of production: black guardians, black or white overseers, white managers, and white lords and owners (whether present or absent). Exploitation was guaranteed by a military apparatus (itself sometimes made up of slaves) and justified by the state religion (Christian or Muslim monotheism, animist polytheism), or it was guaranteed by organizations based on age-classes or by secret societies and justified by ancestor worship. Finally, the radicalization of the inferior status of women can be seen in the end result of their oppression: disabilities caused by the sugar mills and mine labor, premature aging (although there were more women than men among the slaves who lived to 100 years of age), and the decline in fertility rates over the centuries.

Just as the beginning of this radical dehumanization had a history, so too did its end, which unfolded differently depending on space and time. Slavery's end began in the Caribbean, in Haiti, where black slaves participated in the greatest ever victory of slaves over one of the greatest military powers of the time. It continued in South America, in Europe, in the West Indies, and in North America until the end of the 19th century. For enslaved women in Africa, the end was only to come in the 20th century through the mediation of colonial subjugation, when the industrial violence that brought the slave trade to an absolute level became in turn a factor of the eradication of slavery.

The reaction against these processes of dehumanization helped disprove racist claims that a curse had struck the black race and, within that race, the female gender. In turn, the innumerable acts of refusal and social reinvention, under the banner of rehumanization, bore witness to universal rights and the rights of women. The universal dimension was first evident in the original acts of refusal (which were also bids for freedom) and their continuity over time and space. That dimension subsequently appeared in the forms of refusal identified in the historiography of resistance (flight, marooning, tactical adaptation, murder, insurrection; and literature and art) and the punishments shared by both sexes: whipping, iron collars, hanging, quartering, burning at the stake, death without burial.

However, in terms of class and race alike, secondary differences remained that were based on gender and revealed both by the ordeal of dehumanization and by the saga of rehumanization. The first kind of difference, which was of a structural nature and corresponded to the specific reasons for an individual woman's social excommunication and sale, concerned transgressions such as abortion and infanticide, which only women could commit. The second kind of difference, of a historical order, corresponded to actions specific to certain countries or certain periods but not to others (women's economic autonomy, the role of priestess in the religious sphere, the role of female guides in maroon societies, women's role in some insurrections, the part women played in the ethnogenesis of mulattos, in the creation of national gastronomic cultures, and in the crusade for freedom).

Thus, it may be concluded that the apogee of the great slave trade, with regard to the anthropology of the Rights of Man which was its contemporary, provides both the material and the justification for an anthropology of prerights or antirights (forms of dehumanization), for a differential anthropology (specific modes of dehumanization and rehumanization with regard to cultures, to class-races, and to gender), as well as for a general anthropology.

Bibliography

Aptheker, Herbert, *American Negro Slave Revolts*, New York: Columbia University Press, and London: King and Staples, 1943; 6th edition, New York: International, 1993

Bastide, Roger, editor, *La femme de couleur en Amérique Latine*, Paris: Anthropos, 1974

Bastide, Roger, *Les religions africaines au Brésil: Vers une sociologie des interpénétrations de civilisations*, Paris: Presses Universitaires de France, 1960

Berlin, Ira, *Slaves without Masters: The Free Negro in the Antebellum South*, New York: Pantheon Press, 1974

Blake, William O., *The History of Slavery and the Slave Trade, Ancient and Modern*, Columbus, Ohio: H. Miller, 1859

Bouhdiba, Abdelwahab, *Sexuality in Islam*, translated by Alan Sheridan, London and Boston: Routledge and Kegan Paul, 1985

Busby, Margaret, editor, *Daughters of Africa: An International Anthology of Words and Writings by Women of African Descent from the Ancient Egyptian to the Present*, New York: Pantheon Books, and London: Jonathan Cape, 1992

Césaire, Aimé, *Return to My Native Land*, translated by Emil Snyders, Paris: Présence Africaine, 1968

Césaire, Aimé, *Toussaint Louverture: La Révolution française et le problème colonial*, Paris: Livre Club Diderot, 1960

Crété, Liliane, *La traite des nègres sous l'Ancien Régime: Le nègre, le sucre et la toile*, Paris: Perrin, 1989

Curtin, Philip D., *The Atlantic Slave Trade: A Census*, Madison: University of Wisconsin Press, 1969

Davis, David Brion, *The Problem of Slavery in Western Culture*, Ithaca, New York: Cornell University Press, 1966; Oxford: Oxford University Press, 1988

Debien, Gabriel, *Les esclaves aux Antilles françaises, XVIIe–XVIIIe siècles*, Basse-Terre, Guadeloupe: Société d'Histoire de la Guadeloupe, 1974

Deschamps, Hubert Jules, *Histoire de la traite des Noirs: De l'antiquité à nos jours*, Paris: Fayard, 1972

Duchet, Michèle, "Reactions to the Problem of the Slave Trade: An Historical and Ideological Study," in *The African Slave Trade from the Fifteenth to the Nineteenth Century: Reports and Papers of the Meeting of Experts*, Paris: UNESCO, 1979

Engerman, Stanley L., and Eugene D. Genovese, editors, *Race and Slavery in the Western Hemisphere: Quantitative Studies*, Princeton, New Jersey: Princeton University Press, 1975

Filliot, J.M., *La traite des esclaves vers les Mascareignes au XVIIIe siècle*, Paris: ORSTOM, 1974

Fisher, Allan G.B., and Humphrey J. Fisher, *Slavery and Muslim Society in Africa: The Institution in Saharan and Sudanic Africa and the Trans-Saharan Trade*, London: Hurst, and Garden City, New York: Doubleday, 1970

Fouchard, Jean, *The Haitian Maroons: Liberty or Death*, translated by A. Faulkner Watts, New York: Blyden Press, 1981

Fraginals, Manuel Moreno, *L'Afrique en Amérique Latine*, Paris: Unesco, 1984

Freyre, Gilberto, *The Masters and the Slaves, A Study in the Development of Brazilian Civilization*, translated by Samuel Putnam, New York: Knopf, 1946

Gaspar, David Barry, and Darlene Clark Hine, editors, *More than Chattel: Black Women and Slavery in the Americas*, Bloomington: Indiana University Press, 1996

Gautier, Arlette, "Les esclaves femmes aux Antilles françaises 1635–1848," *Historical Reflections/Réflexions Historiques* 10., no. 3 (1983)

Gautier, Arlette, *Les soeurs de solitude: La condition féminine dans l'esclavage aux Antilles du XVIIe au XIXe siècle*, Paris: Éditions Caribéennes, 1985

Genovèse, Eugène D., *Roll, Jordan, Roll: The World the Slaves Made*, New York: Pantheon Books, 1974; London: Deutsch, 1975

Girod, François, *La vie quotidienne de la société créole: Saint-Domingue au XVIIIe siècle*, Paris: Hachette, 1972

Gordon, Murray, *Slavery in the Arab World*, New York: New Amsterdam, 1989

Grégoire, Henri, *De la littérature des nègres ou Recherches sur leus facultés' intellectuelles, leurs qualités morales*, Paris, Maradan, 1808. *An Enquiry concerning the Intellectual and Moral Faculties and Literature of Negroes, Followed with an Account of the Life and Works of Fifteen Negroes and Mulattoes Distinguished in Science, Literature, and the Arts*, translated by David Bailie Warden, Brooklyn, New York: Kirk, 1810; reprint, London and Armonk, New York: Sharpe, 1997

Inikori, J.E., editor, *Forced Migration: The Impact of the Export Slave Trade on African Societies*, London: Hutchinson, and New York: Africana, 1982

Landes, Ruth, *The City of Women*, New York: Macmillan, 1947

Landes, Ruth, "Negro Slavery and Female Status," in *Les Afro-Américains* 27 (1953) Lerner, Gerda, compiler, *Black Women in America: A Documentary History*, New York: Pantheon Books, 1972

Lewis, Bernard, *Race and Color in Islam*, New York: Harper and Row, 1971

Lovejoy, Paul E., *Transformations in Slavery: A History of Slavery in Africa*, Cambridge and New York: Cambridge University Press, 1983

Manning, Patrick, *Slavery and African Life: Occidental, Oriental, and African Slave Trades*, Cambridge and New York: Cambridge University Press, 1990

Mattoso, Kátia M. de Queiros, *To Be a Slave in Brazil, 1550–1888*, translated by Arthur Goldhammer, New Brunswick, New Jersey: Rutgers University Press, 1986

McDonald, Roderick A., *The Economy and Material Culture of Slaves: Goods and Chattels on the Sugar Plantations of Jamaica and Louisiana*, Baton Rouge: Louisiana State University Press, 1993

Meillassoux, Claude, *The Anthropology of Slavery: The Womb of Iron and Gold*, translated by Alide Dasnois, Chicago: University of Chicago Press, and London: Athlone, 1991

Meillassoux, Claude, editor, *L'esclavage en Afrique précoloniale*, Paris: Maspero, 1975

Memel-Fotê, Harris, "L'esclavage dans les sociétés lignagères d'Afrique noire: Exemple de la Côte-d'Ivoire précoloniale, 1700–1920," Ph.D. diss., École des Hautes Études en Sciences Sociales, 1988

Memel-Fotê, Harris, "Les sciences humaines et la notion de civilisation de la femme: Essai sur l'inégalité sociale des sexes dans les sociétés africaines," in *La civilisation de la femme dans la tradition africaine: Rencontre organisée par la société africaine de culture*, Paris: Présence Africaine, 1975

Mettas, Jean, *Répertoire des expéditions négrières françaises au XVIIIe siècle*, 2 vols., edited by Serge Daget, Paris: Société Française d'Histoire d'Outre-Mer, 1978; see especially vol. 1, *Nantes*

Miers, Suzanne, and Igor Kopytoff, editors, *Slavery in Africa: Historical and Anthropological Perspectives*, Madison: University of Wisconsin Press, 1977

Mintz, Sidney Wilfred, editor, *Esclave, facteur de production: L'économie politique de l'esclavage*, Paris: Dunod, 1981

Mullin, Michael, *Africa in America: Slave Acculturation and Resistance in the American South and the British Caribbean, 1736–1831*, Urbana: University of Illinois Press, 1992

Ogot, Bethwell Allan, editor, *Africa from the Sixteenth to the Eighteenth Century*, Oxford: James Currey, 1992

Patterson, Orlando, *The Sociology of Slavery: An Analysis of the Origins, Development, and Structure of Negro Slave Society in Jamaica*, London: MacGibbon and Kee, 1967

Peytraud, Lucien Pierre, *L'esclavage aux Antilles françaises avant 1789; D'après des documents inédits des archives coloniales*, Paris: Hachette, 1897; reprint, 1977

Raynal, Guillaume-Thomas, *Histoire philosophique et politique des etablissemens et du commerce des Européens dans les dèux Indes, Amsterdam, 1772–1774*; as *A Philosophical and Political History of the Settlements and Trade of the Europeans in the East and West Indies*, translated by J.O. Justamond, Dublin, Exshaw, 1779

Rinchon, Dieudonné, *Pierre-Ignace-Liévin Van Alstein, capitaine négrier, Gand, 1733– Nantes, 1793*, Dakar, Senegal: L'Institut Francais d'Afrique Noire, 1964

Robertson, Claire C., and Martin A. Klein, editors, *Women and Slavery in Africa*, Madison: University of Wisconsin Press, 1983

Sala-Molins, Louis, *Le Code Noir; ou, Le Calvaire de Canaan*, Paris: Presses Universitaires de France, 1987

Searing, James F., *West African Slavery and Atlantic Commerce: The Sénégal River Valley, 1700–1860*, Cambridge and New York: Cambridge University Press, 1993

Senghor, Léopold Sédar, *Négritude et civilisation de l'universel*, Paris: Seuil, 1977

Senghor, Léopold Sédar, *Négritude et humanisme*, Paris: Seuil, 1964

Shepherd, Verene, Bridget Brereton, and Barbara Bailey, editors, *Engendering History: Caribbean Women in Historical Perspective*, London: Currey, and New York: St. Martin's Press, 1995

Sindjoun, Luc, "Droit et idéologie dans le Code Noir et la Déclaration des droits de l'homme et du citoyen: La chronique d'une liaison intime," in *Le Code Noir et l'Afrique*, edited by Ambroise Kom and Lucienne Ngoué, Ivry, France: Nouvelles du Sud, 1991

Smith, Adam, *An Inquiry into the Nature and Causes of the Wealth of Nations*, London: Strahan and Cadell, 1776; new edition, edited by Kathryn Sutherland, Oxford and New York: Oxford University Press, 1998

Stedman, John Gabriel, *Narrative, of a Five Years' Expedition, against the Revolted Negroes of Surinam, in Guiana, on the Wild Coast of South America, from the year 1772, to 1777*, 2 vols., London: Johnson, 1796; reprint, Amherst: University of Massachusetts Press, 1972

Tardieu, Jean-Pierre, *Le destin des Noirs aux Indes de Castille, XVIe–XVIIIe siècles*, Paris: L'Harmattan, 1984

Thomas, Louis-Vincent, and René Luneau, *La terre africaine et ses religions: Traditions et changements*, Paris: Larousse, 1974

Thomas, Louis-Vincent, and René Luneau, "La traite des noirs par l'Atlantique: Nouvelles approches," *Revue française d'histoire d'outre-mer* 62, nos. 226–227 (1975)

Trudel, Marcel, *L'esclavage au Canada français: Histoire et conditions de l'esclavage*, Laval, Quebec: Presses Universitaires Laval, 1960

Wallon, H., *De l'esclavage dans les colonies, pour servir d'introduction à l'histoire de l'esclavage dans l'antiquité*, Paris: Dezobry, 1847

Watson, James L., editor, *Asian and African Systems of Slavery*, Oxford: Blackwell, and Berkeley: University of California Press, 1980

White, Deborah G., "Female Slaves: Sex, Roles, and Status in the Antebellum Plantation South," *Journal of Family History* 8, no. 3 (1983)

Williams, Eric Eustace, *Capitalism and Slavery*, Chapel Hill: University of North Carolina Press, 1944

Willis, John Ralph, editor, *Slaves and Slavery in Muslim Africa*, 2 vols., London and Totowa, New Jersey: Cass, 1985

Wright, Marcia, *Strategies of Slaves and Women: Life Stories from East/Central Africa*, New York: Barber Press, and London: James Currey, 1993

Yellin, Jean Fagan, and John C. Van Horne, editors, *The Abolitionist Sisterhood: Women's Political Culture in Antebellum America*, Ithaca, New York: Cornell University Press, 1994

WOMEN'S PARTICIPATION IN THE GREEK REVOLUTION, 1800–1827

ELENI VARIKAS

The National Revolution

THE SHAPING OF GREEK national consciousness was part of the awakening of nationalist feeling among the peoples of the Ottoman Empire. Throughout the 18th century these various national identities developed in conjunction with the emergence of an "inter-Balkan consciousness." In the second half of the century, the growing prosperity of the Greek communities scattered through the Balkans and the large European cities, their contact with the modern West, and the rebirth of Greek cultural life helped forge a national identity that profited from the external and internal problems facing the Ottoman Empire. The Russo-Turkish Wars, the separatist movements of local pashas, and finally, the outbreak of the French Revolution accelerated the formation of a nationalist movement by showing the vulnerability of Ottoman power and creating the conditions for a Greek political and military movement against that power.

In the 1760s, the peoples of Greece became the main instruments in Russia's eastern policies, which were designed to replace the Ottoman Empire with a "Balkan Empire" under a Russian prince. Invoking the "historical rights" of Hellenism over the former Byzantine Empire, Catherine II, nicknamed the "Great Siren" by the Greeks, began in 1763 to disperse Russian agents throughout the Balkans in order to contact the local Greek notables and officials, hoping to spark an insurrection. During the two Russo-Turkish Wars (1768–74 and 1788–92), the islands in the Aegean Sea and the Peloponnesus rebelled, while Greek communities abroad raised a flotilla to fight the Turks. At the same time, separatist initiatives of Ali Pasha, the Pasha of Janina, aimed at creating an independent Albanian-Greek state, revealed the vulnerability of Ottoman power and had direct repercussions on the development of the Greek nationalism. Ali Pasha's goal of establishing a centralized power (which at the end of the century extended as far as Thessaly and continental western Greece) came up against the autonomy of two regions, Chimara and Suli, whose fierce resistance (1790–1803) was to serve as an example in the struggles for independence yet to come. Fur-

ther, by entrusting to Greeks administrative posts formerly reserved for Turks, Ali Pasha made his court into a veritable place of political and military education for several future leaders in the struggle for independence.

The call for the liberty of nations issuing from the French Revolution and the French presence on the Ionian Islands, which passed from Venetian sovereignty to French sovereignty with the Treaty of Campoformio (1797), found an enthusiastic response among the Greeks. On Corfu, Bonaparte's armies proclaimed the abolition of privileges, publicly burned the Libro d'Oro of the Ionian nobility, and planted a tree of liberty. Despite the episodic nature of this French occupation—interrupted between 1800 and 1807 by Russo-Turkish domination, then replaced with the English Protectorate of the Seven Islands in 1814—its impact would endure. After 1800 republican groups nicknamed the *carmagnoli* (after the French *carmagnole*, referring to both attire of the French revolutionaries and a widespread revolutionary song) made their appearance in several self-administered regions (Kea, Samos), while Napoleon's policies seemed to be leading toward Greek independence under French protection. The majority of the leaders of the independence movement were to serve in the battalion of the "Chasseurs de l'Orient" (Eastern Hunters), formed for this purpose during Napoleon's Egyptian campaign.

Participation in the Russo-Turkish War and above all the uprising of the Peloponnesus had mobilized notables and prelates who envisioned an independent state modeled after the former Byzantine Empire. Meanwhile, the infiltration of revolutionary or liberal ideas associated with the French Revolution gave the nationalist movement a far more radical and democratic orientation. The movement led by Rhigas Ferraios (1757–98) was significant in this regard. Inspired by the French Revolution and in contact with the Directory, Rhigas Ferraios was the first to have conceived of a national Balkan movement with very specific objectives. Advocating the armed uprising of all the peoples of the empire, including the Turks, against Ottoman absolutism, he envisioned the design of a multiethnic and multidenominational republic under Greek cultural hegemony, to extend from the Balkans to Asia. Concerned about reconciling the indivisibility of the republic with respect for the diversity of Balkan and Asian peoples, he made provisions for annual provincial assemblies with the right to question the measures of the central legislative power. His New Political Constitution (the Charter), developed in 1797, was inspired by the French constitutions of 1793 and 1795, which he radicalized, reducing the executive power and proposing the abolition of debts, and instituting the right to work and social assistance for every individual. From his base in the wealthy Greek community in Vienna, he published poems and patriotic pamphlets and formed a secret society to prepare for the insurrection. Arrested with 17 of his comrades by the Austro-Hungarian police and handed over to the Turkish authorities, Rhigas Ferraios was executed by strangulation in 1798. But his political agenda, and above all his revolutionary songs inciting the subjugated peoples to imitate the example of the ancient Greeks and rise up against tyranny, continued to inflame the youth and intelligentsia of Greece throughout the following decades.

Neo-Hellenic Enlightenment and the Revolutionary Public Sphere

Rhigas Ferraios was a typical product of the "public sphere" critical of arbitrary authority that, according to the theories of Jürgen Habermas, paved the way for the end of absolutism in Europe and laid the foundations for modern political principles. Rhigas came from the growing merchant bourgeoisie, which, since the 17th century, had begun to challenge the Jews and Armenians for dominance in the empire's internal and external trade. Scattered in the harbors and commercial centers of western Europe, the eastern Mediterranean, and central Europe, and sheltered by endemic anarchy and the arbitrary power of the Ottoman authorities, thriving Greek communities had created a receptive environment for the development of what is known as the Neo-Hellenic Enlightenment—a phenomenon that was profoundly important to the shaping of the national Greek consciousness in the 18th century. The intelligentsia involved in it had been educated throughout the century in schools where instructors held degrees from European universities; they provided an education based on the teaching of mathematics and the natural sciences and on the study of the Greek classics. This educated class enthusiastically embraced Enlightenment thinking—and in particular that ideology's emphasis on the liberating potential knowledge and education—as a privileged path for the emancipation of the nation. In the view of this enlightened intelligentsia, thinking for oneself and no longer bending to anything other than the dictates of reason was the best remedy against despotism. Thus, they associated emancipation from all arbitrary authority with the objective of national liberation and at the same time targeted the governing "Christian" Turks—that is, the power of the Greek notables and the upper clergy. Adamantios Koraïs (1743–1833), the other central figure of this movement, complained that the Greeks, once governed by men of the caliber of a Miltiades or a Themistocles, were now governed by "riffraff, camel drivers or barbaric curates." His anger was directed not at religion in general but rather at the theocratic

Byzantine heritage of the Orthodox Church, which, especially since the French Revolution, had violently condemned Enlightenment rationalism and interest in classical antiquity, preaching voluntary submissiveness instead. The struggle against the Ottoman yoke was a struggle against ignorance and superstition, and it entailed educating an illiterate population oblivious of Greece's glorious past. References to ancient Greece, the cradle of civilization, progress, and democracy, created both a means to legitimize independence in the eyes of international opinion and a way of regaining national dignity. Thus, national independence was seen as a restoration of that classical golden age that would enable modern Greeks to join the "enlightened West," which had taken over the torch of the ancient heritage.

Raising the level of public culture and making the nation conscious of its destiny became a political task of the highest importance, and this project fed an unprecedented cultural and publishing activity. Dictionaries of the Greek language—of capital importance for a nation in formation—were prepared, new annotated editions of Greek classics were disseminated through an increasingly dense network of schools and libraries, and translations of authors such as Locke, Montesquieu, Beccaria, and Rousseau sometimes circulated in several thousand copies. Anonymous incendiary brochures, too, were circulated illicitly and distributed in the Ottoman Empire, thanks to the efforts of secret societies that had been formed to prepare for the revolution.

The "Philiki Etaireia" (Friendly Brotherhood)

The first two decades of the 19th century saw the formation of prohellenic secret societies, modeled after secret societies in Europe and closely linked to the Masonic lodges of the period. Notable among these were Hellenophone Hotel in Paris, established in 1809, and the Philomuse Society, established in Athens and Vienna in 1813; the latter's main activities included creating schools, financing archeological digs, and insuring that Greek youth studied in European institutions. Working to effect a renaissance and development of Greek culture, these societies contributed widely to the emergence of national awareness and helped pave the way for the revolution. But the most important and most famous of the secret societies was the Philiki Etaireia (Friendly Brotherhood), whose exclusive and explicit objective was "the liberation of the homeland." Founded in 1814 in Odessa, in the heart of a powerful Greek community, the Brotherhood within a few years had extended its activity to all the Greek communities in Europe and throughout the whole of the Ottoman territory. Based on a tightly closed and hierarchic structure, the society was directed by a supreme authority, the composition of which was not known by its members, who swore "to nurse eternal hatred for the tyrants of the homeland" and to preserve the secrecy of the organization under penalty of death.

In contrast to Rhigas Ferraios, the Etairists did not have a coherent ideology. While it was clear to all initiates that its final goal would be reached by a violent overthrow of the Ottoman yoke, the directors of the Friendly Brotherhood never developed a coherent political plan as to the kind of society it meant to put into place once independence was won. This allowed social groups, political agendas, and tactics of every variety to coexist in its midst. But it was precisely this political vagueness that made for a very broad membership base and enabled the widest and most heterogeneous recruitment possible in a society that was growing increasingly complex and stratified. Within this society, the higher clergy and Ottoman diplomats were hostile to the slightest social transformation that might jeopardize their privileges. Notables and local military leaders, working within the system of self-administration of the subjugated peoples, ensured order in the name of the sultan, and, having become a kind of hereditary nobility, dreamed of a liberated Greece in which they would replace the Turks in the exercise of power. The large merchants preached a "wait and see" approach and demanded guarantees of foreign support before any action was undertaken. The bourgeois youth abroad, along with some of the islands' ship owners, were open to liberal tendencies and the ideas of the Enlightenment, science and progress, while the local intelligentsia, infused with a secular, democratic spirit inspired by the example of the French Revolution, advocated immediate action. Finally, there were the masses of illiterate peasants, exploited both by the Turks and by Greek landowners. The peasantry's national and social aspirations were expressed in a popular messianism fed by post-Byzantine prophecies about the "reconquest of Constantinople" and by the rich tradition of popular songs celebrating the exploits of *klephtes* (bandits) unrestrained by the authority of the conquerors, or praising the feats of the Greek leaders.

The Revolutionary Forces

In 1821 the most radical wing of the Friendly Brotherhood, taking advantage of the rebellions by the pashas in Asia and in Janina against the central Ottoman power (1820), managed to impose its resolve for immediate action and proclaimed the revolution. While the numbers of insurgents appeared disproportionately small compared to the power of the Ottoman Empire, the forces available to the insurgents were not negligible. In the early part of the 19th century, the Greek population had grown to more than three million. The accumulated wealth of bankers, foreign merchants, and Aegean ship owners funded the early needs of the war. In military terms, the forces numbered an estimated several tens of thousands. They included *armatoles*, armed Christian militias that ensured order on behalf of the sultan; *klephtes*, or gangs of outlaws fleeing from the oppression of Turkish or Greek masters and living off crime and plunder in the mountains at the expense of the Turks and sometimes of the Greek property owners, while they presented themselves as protectors of the peasants; and finally, the small private armies of the *archons* and local notables of the Peloponnesus and the Greek continent. Many of these forces had been trained during the Russo-Turkish Wars in the military corps created by the French and the English on the Ionian Islands or in Ali Pasha's army. Moreover, the light and swift commercial fleet of the islands of the Aegean Sea (Hydra, Spetses, Psarra), armed against pirates and hardened by braving the innumerable blockades of the turn of the century, had often served under the Russian, French, or English flags and could fearlessly confront the Turkish fleet, which lacked experienced crews after the desertion of

Greek sailors. The small "explosive boats," whose legendary exploits were to sow panic among the Turkish and Egyptian fleet, were one of the techniques acquired during the Russo-Turkish Wars and perfected by the sailors from Hydra and Spetses.

Revolutionary Events and Civil War (1821–1827)

The Etairists decided to unleash the revolution in two places: the countries of the Danube and the Peloponnesus. Early in 1821, the leader Alexander Ypsilanti entered Jassi and proclaimed the revolution in Moldavia and in Wallachia. An uprising of Wallachian farmers was supposed to support the revolution, together with the society, but their leader, Tudor Vladimirescu, very quickly separated himself from the Greek cause because of Russia's disapproval, and also because of the Greeks' insensitivity to the social aspirations of the peasantry. Arrested by Ypsilanti, he was put to death. Faced with the indifference of the indigenous population, the revolution in Wallachia was rapidly quelled by the Turks and served only as a diversion to the revolution in Greece.

In March 1821, D. Papaflessas and other Etairists proclaimed the revolution in the Peloponnesus, on the Greek continent, and on the Aegean Islands. Initially, the revolutionary movement extended as far as Olympus and Macedonia, but it was very quickly limited to the Peloponnesus, the Greek continent, and the islands closest to the mainland. Of the rest of the islands only Samos would resist until the end of the war. In all of the rebelling regions, the Etairists had to overcome the hesitancy of local notables, and in several cases (Hydra, Samos), popular rebellions were quelled before the notables finally took up leadership of the national revolution. Between 1821 and 1824 the revolution progressed rapidly. Patras, Argos, and other large cities rose up against the Turks. In the Peloponnesus, fortresses of strategic importance (Monemvassia, Nauplion, Tripoli) fell into the hands of the Greek insurgents. Despite the bloody repression that came down on the rebellious islands (massacres on Chios and Psarra), the revolutionary troops managed to push back the Turkish forces at sea and by land, thanks to the concerted action of the irregular corps of the *klephtes* and of the navy of the islands.

At the same time, an internal struggle began for the leadership of the revolution and for the political and social principles that were to be the foundation of the independent state. Brushing the popular elements aside, the notables started leading the war and formed a series of local governments—the Senate of the Peloponnesus, the Senate of Western Continental Greece, and the Areopagus of Eastern Continental Greece—while the islands created their own local governments. The first National Assembly of Epidaurus (1822) proclaimed and officially legitimated the revolution, using for the first time the term "national revolution," which it distinguished from "demagogic and seditious movements." The constitution adopted by the National Assembly created the first general government without eliminating the power of local governments. Following the model of the French Directory, executive power was entrusted to five members who were to name the ministers, while the legislative power was exercised both by the executive branch and by a chamber elected for one year by a body of notables.

As the Constitution of Epidaurus left all the power in the hands of the notables, it soon ran up against the military leaders, whose influence and popularity was only increasing. This opposition led to an open civil war (1823–25) that depleted the forces of the revolution and discredited it in the eyes of the international community. Early on, the island notables, allying themselves with the notables of the Peloponnesus, managed to push aside the military leaders represented by the popular hero Theodore Colocotronis. This alliance carried the National Assembly of Astros (1823), where the foundations of the Greek state were established, abolishing local governments and formulating the rights of the people more clearly. But the coalition did not last long and the civil war grew all the more intense. In the course of this second stage, the island notables sought the support of the liberal elements and intellectuals with whom the great majority of the people were allied, in order to neutralize the more traditional caste of the Peloponnesian notables.

This new leadership, however, proved incapable of organizing resistance to the Ottoman counteroffensive. In 1825, when the revolutionary forces were depleted by the civil war and the coffers of the island ship owners drained, Muhammad Ali, viceroy of Egypt, became actively involved in the war, deploying his regular army and a European-style fleet. After the repression of the revolution on Crete and Cassos, Muhammad Ali's son, Ibrahim Pasha, ransacked the Peloponnesus for two years (1825–27). In 1826, after a long and arduous siege, the city of Missolonghi, which had become famous two years earlier when the philhellenic poet Lord Byron died there, fell into the hands of the Turks. With the fall of Missolonghi, the tragic exodus of whose inhabitants deeply moved the international community, and the storming of the Acropolis of Athens, continental Greece was restored to Turkish power. Demoralized, the leaders of Hydra and Spetses considered giving up the fight, and the revolution seemed to be on the verge of collapse. While the Greek government vainly placed all its hopes on foreign aid, especially that of England, popular forces grouped around Theodore Colocotronis in the Peloponnesus, Karaiskakis in continental Greece, and Miaoulis and Sachtouris on the islands, took over the resistance. The obstinacy of this unequal battle and the significance of the philhellenic movement forced the three great powers—France, England, and Russia—to intervene in order to settle the Greek question, which, since the beginning of the revolution, had been a troublesome diplomatic issue. In July 1827, with the Treaty of London, they concluded the Triple Alliance, demanding an immediate armistice between Greek insurgents and the Sublime Porte (the Ottoman government) and granting Greek autonomy under the sovereignty of the sultan. Thinking that the war had been practically won, the sultan refused to negotiate. On 20 October 1827, during the naval Battle of Navarino, the Turko-Egyptian fleet was annihilated by the Triple Alliance.

Independence

The Battle of Navarino was followed by the Russo-Turkish War (1828). Once conquered, Turkey recognized the autonomy of Greece with the Treaty of Andrinopolis (1829). Thus, Russian diplomacy triumphed in the Balkans, linking the liberation of Greece to the Russian victory. Elected to the National Assembly of Trezeno (1827), Ioannis Kapodistrias, a Greek from Corfu who had become a minister of the czar, became the first governor of independent Greece (1828–31). To neutralize the influence of Russia, English diplomacy organized the Protocol of London (February 1830) declaring Greece an "independent state under a hereditary monarchy." After Kapodistrias's assassination at the hands of a powerful family from Mani, the three "protecting" powers took advantage of the ensuing anarchy and confusion to impose an absolute monarchy on Greece with a monarch of their choice. Otto I, prince of Bavaria, arrived in Nauplion in 1832, having first received the official recognition of the independence of the Greek state from the Ottoman Empire.

Women in the Struggle for Independence

It is not easy to evaluate the role of women in the revolutionary process or the extent and substance of their participation in the revolution. Even today, theirs remains a history that is largely unknown, in which the scarcity of factual sources contrasts with the profusion of ideological arguments and representations that haunted the international imagination during the Greek War of Independence before entering into national legend. Disseminated through popular poetry, and above all in the literature and the iconography of philhellenic romanticism, images of the Suliote women dispersing Turkish troops, the mothers of Missolonghi killing their children rather than handing them over to the enemy, or the Amazons crossing swords with the pashas have acquired the enigmatic quality of popular icons. These images pose as many questions about women's place in the revolution as they offer answers.

A few preliminary remarks must be made. First, since this concerns a population of which the overwhelming majority was illiterate, the sources depicting the role of women in the revolution come from the most privileged social milieus, those capable of leaving written traces; inevitably, these sources provide us with only a partial image. They foreground certain forms of action, those associated with the presence of women in the public sphere, at the expense of others, such as military action, and they are not representative of the activity of Greek women as a whole.

In fact, on the eve of the revolution it was not possible to speak of Greek women as a homogeneous whole. Beyond differences of social class, their status and relative freedom depended on a multitude of factors that defy any attempt at generalization. Geographic factors differentiated the islands from the continent. Factors of age and family status differentiated women's positions across a lifespan. Cultural factors differentiated communities organized around father-centered or mother-centered principles—the Westernized circles of the diaspora and the traditionalist circles of the Peloponnesus and continental Greece, respectively. Political factors differentiated the regions under Ottoman domination from those under Italian or English domination, as well as differentiating regions where Ottoman domination was exercised directly from those that had acquired economic and political privileges from the Ottomans and enjoyed self-administration under guardianship. Finally, there were economic factors differentiating the agricultural economies of the Peloponnesus from the commercial centers of the empire and the diaspora. These differences had an impact on the extent of sexual segregation and the cloistering of women, patterns that were more entrenched on the continent than on the islands; on the gendered division of labor and women's potential to exercise control over resources; and on the physical demands of women's work, more crushing in the rural communities and among poor women than among the comfortable families of the manufacturing and commercial centers of northern Greece and the Balkans, where women's exemption from work was the main sign of conspicuous consumption.

A Profoundly Patriarchal Culture

Second, however, it must be stressed that on the whole, despite such variations in cultural practices, beliefs, symbolic rituals, and legal practices in the Greek communities of the 18th century confirm the existence of widely shared values. The cloistering of women, fear of and desire to control female sexuality, sexual segregation, denigration of little girls, and universal valorization of male children were common features of a shared, profoundly patriarchal culture in a heterogeneous world. In a predominantly father-centered society, where the status of children was broadly linked to their economic worth, a daughter was only passing through, since her dowry and labor were destined to enrich the family of her husband. Unmarried women were considered abnormal, sterility was a personal defect, and adultery was frequently punished with exposure and public stoning. In certain regions, the wife had no right to speak to her father-in-law before she had delivered her first child. Her status improved when she became a mother, especially a mother of boys. Honor, the supreme value, required not only chastity but also absolute obedience of the wife to her husband and to the male members of the family. This obedience was codified in daily gestures and behavior. On the rare occasions when spouses would go out together, the wife would let her hubsand go ahead, often on horseback, while she followed him on foot at a respectful distance. At dinner she would serve the men in the family at the table and would eat what was left over with the women afterwards.

Both European travelers of the 18th and 19th centuries and Greek historiography attributed these customs, so clearly indicative of the oppression of women, to the Ottoman conquest. Greek culture was presumed to have been contaminated by the oriental obscurantism of the conquerors, or else transformed by the fear of the *rayeas*, the Christian subjects of the sultan, afraid of seeing "their" women abducted or raped by the Turks. While this fear unquestionably served as a justification or rationalization for reducing women's freedom, it is important to remember—and this is our third preliminary remark—that the Greeks of the 18th century were the descendents of a world just as "oriental" as that of the Ottomans: the Byzantine world, which had practiced and even codified—for example, in the decrees of Leo VI, the Wise (866–912)—prohibitions against exposing "women to male eyes" and "encouraging them to participate in the affairs of men." These prohibitions remained valid until the 18th century, as is evident from accounts of foreign travelers who were surprised at the absence of women in the street. In 1751 in Athens, then a small town built around the ruins of the Acropolis, from which vantage point one had a sweeping view over the interior courtyards in which women circulated, visitors had to ask advance permission to go up to the Parthenon, so that the women could hide themselves from their view.

New Spaces for Freedom

However, this situation began to change in the second half of the 18th century. The development of social classes open to a Western lifestyle and Western social practices, along with the emergence of criticism of arbitrary authority, created cultural spaces of restrained but totally new freedom for some women and implied a dynamic of transformation of social relations between the sexes. In the flourishing communities of Trieste, Livorno, Florence, Vienna, and Odessa, well-to-do families began to be concerned about the education of their daughters, whom they entrusted to tutors or school establishments founded by the communities. The practices of mixed sociability of the European cities replaced the segregation of the sexes, and women began to make an appearance at cultural events and to participate in the debates of the literary salons. This pattern also held true among Greeks in the countries of the Danube, where, starting in the 18th century, the small Phanarian elite (named after Phanar, the elegant district of Istanbul from where they came) replaced the *hospodars* (the Moldavian or Wallachian princes in the semiautonomous principalities), reproducing in miniature the splendor and pomp of the imperial court. Despite the greed, corruption, and political conservatism with which their power was associated—aspects that became the main target of the radical wing of the Neohellenic Enlightenment—the Phanariots developed a kind of enlightened despotism, transforming the courts of Jassy and Bucharest into centers of Greek culture through the development of patronage, the establishment of prestigious schools, and the introduction of lifestyles and practices of Western sociability in which women played an increasingly important role.

These new practices were supported by the development and the dissemination of ideas of equality. In his famous novel *Scholeion ton delikaton eraston* (1790; The School of Refined Lovers), Rhigas Ferraios addressed the "sensitive" youth of both sexes, inevitably incurring the wrath of the Orthodox Church. This eulogist for an armed uprising of the peoples against Ottoman absolutism was markedly favorable to the idea of women's emancipation. His political constitution (the Charter) provided for not only obligatory education but also the apprenticeship in arms for both sexes. Rhigas Ferraios, who was well aware of the reactions that the bearing of arms and the wearing of the cockade by women had incited during the French Revolution, extended to women the rights to wear the symbol of the republic: three crosses on a club of Hercules, "the sign of recognition of free, democratic, and equal brothers." This symbolic recognition of women's full membership in the nation was interpreted as an affirmation of women's citizenship, even though the constitution confirmed the universal right to vote in abstract terms without specifying sex.

This ideological context had an influence on the status of women within the Westernized ruling classes and the revolutionary intelligentsia, and it encouraged women to feel actively involved in the movement for national emancipation. The development of the public sphere prior to the revolution facilitated Greek women's earliest form of activism for the national cause: they participated in the cultural awakening of the Greek people in the decade preceding the outbreak of the revolution, and would continue after 1821 in their efforts to promote international awareness of, and sympathy for, the Greek cause.

Spreading Enlightenment in the Service of the Nation

In the two decades preceding the revolution, the intellectual life of the countries of the Danube and the Greek communities in Europe was thus marked by the direct participation of a few women. First of all, these women played an increasingly central role in the crusade for the dissemination of the Enlightenment and in the publishing activity this entailed. National emancipation was furthered through the education of an overwhelmingly illiterate people. Adamantios Koraïs set an example by devoting himself to publishing the Greek classics. In his commentaries and prefaces to these works, he underscored the discrepancy between the glory of the ancestors and the present, fallen state of the Greek peoples. These texts were distributed free of charge to Greek schools, thanks to the generosity of the Zossimas brothers, rich merchants from Yannina. Koraïs's call "against ignorance and superstition" found an enthusiastic response among the Phanariot women. Subscription lists to books published in that period reveal that these women made up a substantial part of the cultivated public that financed editions both of the Greek classics and works by authors of the Greek and European Enlightenment.

Some of these women, such as Ralou Soutsou, Aikaterini Rasti, Roxani Samourcasi, and Aikaterini Guika in the countries of the Danube, and Maria Peretrini in Italy, themselves translated works that were "useful to the nation" and had them published at their own expense. For the most part these translations targeted a female readership, and they were mostly handbooks on childrearing for Greek mothers, works on female pedagogy, or edifying biographies of women from the past. But this gendered division in publishing activity was not a hard and fast rule. Women frequently translated the classics, as was the case with Smaragda Scarlatou Callimahi, wife of the *hospodar* of Moldavia, who translated Cervantes's *Don Quixote*. According to C. Dimaras, historian of Greek literature, Phanariot women during this period fully shared their male counterparts' enthusiasms and were influential voices in the linguistic quarrels over the use of language as a means of communication and of unifying an illiterate and culturally diverse people. Efrossini Hadzeri, daughter of Alexander Hadzeris, *hospodar* of Wallachia, even contributed to the writing of *The Ark of the Greek Language* (1819; untranslated) the famous dictionary conceived and compiled by the most influential scholars of the time, among them her tutor Nikolaos Logadis.

To be sure, these women belonged to the Phanariot elite and were for the most part wives, daughters, or sisters of the princes of Moldavia or Wallachia. But the crusade for the regeneration of the nation through education also opened possibilities of activism to women of far more modest origins. The case of Evanthia Kairi (1799–1866), sister of the most famous and respected

philosopher of the time, Theophilos Kairis, was an eloquent example not only of the new possibilities but also of the enthusiasm with which some of these women joined the national cause. Although she came from a family of very traditionalist priests, Evanthia Kairi studied at the Academy of the Kydoniai, where her brother taught. Possessing a perfect command of ancient Greek, Italian, and French, she wrote to Adamantios Koraïs when she was 15 years old, asking him to recommend a moral work that she might translate from the French in order to help her people "to the best of her ability." Her correspondence with the Greek scholar and his admiration for her work were to earn her great renown even before the revolution. In his account of his journey to Greece in 1817, the philhellenic publisher Ambroise Firmin-Didot recounts being impressed to find a young girl of such great philosophical and literary culture in a small hamlet somewhere in the middle of Asia Minor, where women had the right to go out only once a year. From 1815 to 1821, under the initials E.N., Evanthia translated pedagogical works, among others Abbé Fénelon's *L'éducation des filles* (1687; *A Treatise on the Education of Daughters*) and Jean-Nicolas Bouilly's *Conseils à ma fille* (1812; Advice to my Daughter). Following Koraïs's example, she wrote prefaces for these translations, directed at a female public, in which she reconstructed a female genealogy of philosophers and poets of antiquity such as Theano, Hypatia, Corinna, and Sappho, whom she contrasted with the wretched state of the Greek women of her time. In the preface to her 1820 translation of Bouilly's text, she exhorts her contemporaries to make themselves worthy and follow the example of their ancestors, "who, through their love of the homeland and their wisdom had made the race of woman famous during the glorious period of Greece." Renouncing marriage, Kairi decided to devote herself to the education of women and to allaying the suspicions of the Greek population regarding any substantial change in the status of women.

Literary Salons and Criticism of Absolutism

The capital importance of knowledge and education—the consensual foundation of all strategies of national liberation—informs the oppositions that shaped national consciousness: barbarism and civilization, obscurantism and progress, absolutism and liberty, and this emphasis on knowledge brought political content to women's activity in the public sphere. Won over by the ideas of the Enlightenment and taking advantage of their prestigious position, some wives and daughters of the Phanariot princes made their salons a privileged site for political ferment and established cultural institutions, such as discussion clubs and reading rooms, that developed into veritable hotbeds of criticism of arbitrary authority. At a time when theater was considered to be the best "school for educating the people," these women formed the first amateur theater groups, performing plays by Voltaire and Beaumarchais as well as by revolutionary Italian authors. Sometimes the critical spirit of these plays led to intervention by the authorities. Such was the case for Rallou Karatza, who with the financial help of Aikaterini Guika organized one of the first theater groups mounted with the Greek students of the Mangureanu School of Bucharest. After staging several tragedies by Euripides and Sophocles, in 1810 they produced a play whose critical allusions to Ottoman absolutism worried the Greek *hospodar* of Wallachia, who prohibited its performances. Rallou Karatza was not discouraged. When her father became *hospodar* himself two years later, she began her activities anew and in 1817 created a cultural club and a theater in which she presented patriotic plays by the Italian poet Vittorio Alfieri. At the same time, she financed the studies of young members of the Friendly Brotherhood in Paris.

Women's participation in the public sphere was even more pronounced in the Greek communities of Italy, where, early in the 19th century, the intensely patriotic activism of Italian secret societies against the Austrian power found an enthusiastic echo among the Greeks. Especially in the thriving community of Livorno, a multitude of small clandestine groups of Greek patriots were formed to lay the groundwork for the independence of their own country. Working closely together with Italian patriots, they used the literary salons to develop their influence and to find political and financial support for their action. At the end of the 1810s and early in the 1820s, some of the most famous salons were run by women who had originally come from the Ionian Islands, such as Maria Peretrini, Eleni Montsenigou, Angeliki Palli Bartholommei, and Isavella Theotoki Albriggi. The paths of Theotoki (1760–1836) and Palli (1795–1875), who were to promote the Greek cause in Italy and on the international front, clearly illustrated the close relationship between realms of literature and politics that enabled some women visibly to engage in revolutionary activism. Married to an Italian nobleman, then divorced, Isavella Theotoki was one of the foremost figures in Italian intellectual life during the years 1810–20. A personal friend of the precursor of romanticism and Italian national poet Alfieri, known for his writing and particularly for his biographical portraits of the intellectuals of his era, Theotoki hosted in Venice the most prestigious salon of Italy, frequented by the greatest personalities of the political and literary world of the country. She pushed her sympathy for the Italian national cause to the point of siding clandestinely with the Carbonari.

A resident of Livorno, Angeliki Palli was the daughter of a wealthy Greek merchant who managed the fortune of the duke of Tuscany. At age 20, she was already one of the best-educated women of her period; she spoke Greek, French, and Italian fluently, and had already begun a brilliant literary career that was to earn her the nickname "the new Sappho." Her famous poetic improvisations drew to her salon intellectuals from all over Europe, including Lamartine, Byron, Alessandro Manzoni, and the French publisher Firmin-Didot, along with apologists for Italian independence such as Gianbattista Niccolini, Giuseppe Mazzini, and Ugo Foscolo; the latter admired her dramatic work and introduced it to his students. Won over by the ideas of the Enlightenment very early on, Palli became involved in the struggle on behalf of Greek and Italian independence. Despite the efforts of friends who, like Foscolo, attempted to distance her from political involvement and convince her to "limit her action to the realm of art," Palli actively participated in Italian political life, as police reports from Florence and Sardinia reveal. Married to Gianpaolo Bartholommei, the future founder of the Carbonaria Riformata, she campaigned alongside her husband and was one of the officials of Mazzini's youth organization Giovane Italia. Her political involvement in Italy has been abundantly documented. The present state of research does not reveal whether Palli was involved in one of the Greek secret societies or even in the Friendly Brotherhood. What is certain, however, is her close and systematic relationship with Greek revolutionary refugees, the most famous of whom was the great national poet Andrea Kalbo, whom she helped financially.

Integrated into the intellectual and political life of Italy and having vast financial means available to them, Theotoki and Palli provided important financial and political support to the Greek national cause before and during the revolution. They organized and ensured the reception and material support of Greek refugees from the Ottoman Empire and the Ionian Islands, and they supported communication between Greek and Italian patriots. Inspired by Greek antiquity and then by the revolution, Palli's Italian and French writings continued to awaken international sympathy for the Greek cause and would be a valuable aid in the organization of the philhellenic movement during and after the revolution.

The Women of the Friendly Brotherhood

Inspired by the Masonic lodges, with which it shared its closed and hierarchical structure, the Philiki Etaireia was originally closed to women. In the first years of the brotherhood's activity, the wife of one of its initiates, the rich merchant Mihail Naftis, discovered documents revealing the existence of the secret society. According to the rules, her husband was supposed to eliminate her to protect the security of the membership. Unable to do so, Naftis sought permission from the highest Etairist authority to initiate her into the organization. His wife, Kyriaki Naftou, who brought a substantial financial contribution to the Friendly Brotherhood, seems to have been the first woman to be sworn in (K. Xiradaki, *Oi gynaikhes ste Philiki Etaireía* [1964; Women of the Friendly Brotherhood]). But from 1818 on, the society began a very broad recruitment that included a certain number of women. Before his death, Skoufas, one of the three founders of the society, suggested systematically contacting all women who, by their proximity to institutions of power, might be useful to the cause. He specifically mentioned the name of Vassiliki, the famous Greek mistress of the Albanian military leader Ali Pasha. In the present state of the research it is impossible to assess the numbers of women who participated or to confirm with certainty what functions or types of activities they assumed in the organization. What is certain is that they did not rise above the lowest level of the hierarchy, called *blames* and reserved for simple and illiterate initiates who paid dues but had only minimal information available to them. The names of known female members suggest that access was reserved for a minority of women whose wealth and connections were potentially valuable.

Indeed, as the revolution grew closer, the aid of women initiates proved to be priceless. Literary salons were not only privileged sites for recruitment but also ideal covers for clandestine action. Efrossini Negri in Wallachia and, in Jassi, Elisabeth Ypsilanti, the mother of the head of the society, Alexander Ypsilanti, hosted the secret meetings of the society. It was in Ypsilanti's salon that the decision for a national uprising was made. Elisabeth's daughter, Maria Ypsilanti, who had donated her immense dowry to the Etairists, was also present at this historic meeting.

While the majority of women initiates primarily contributed financial support, a fair number of them served as liaisons between the society and political and financial circles. Some, such as Roxandra Karatza, daughter of the prince of Wallachia, organized collections. Belonging to families dispersed throughout the empire and in the communities of European cities, they served as couriers during their travels. During the years preceding the revolution, the Ottoman repression that came down on male members of their family multiplied women initiates' opportunities for political action. In 1818, when the *hospodar* of Wallachia and Etairist Ioannis Karatzas was forced to go into exile in Pisa to escape the sultan's repression, his daughter Rallou Karatza accompanied him and continued her cultural activities on behalf of the cause. Her sister remained in Moldavia and relayed information to Pisa on the progress of the Friendly Brotherhood, as well as on Russian diplomatic activity and on the movements of the Ottoman troops in the countries of the Danube. Because women were less suspect in the eyes of the authorities and less closely watched than men, they were able to accomplish some missions more effectively. Marigo Zarifopoula, the sister of Hadjivassili Sarafis, an influential member of the society of Constantinople, often served as a courier. She set up a network that helped persecuted members to go underground or escape and organized campaigns to finance the society's activities. Shortly before the revolution, she was arrested by the Turks along with her brother, who was executed. Imprisoned and later deported, she escaped and went to the Peloponnesus, where Dimitrios Ypsillantis, the leader of the eastern armies, on several occasions entrusted her with dangerous missions during the sieges of Nauplion and Tripoli. Other women, too, were persecuted because of their revolutionary activities. In 1821, when her husband and her father, upper cadres in the Friendly Brotherood, were executed, Efrossini Negri Mavrogenous was deported to Asia Minor where she, together with her two daughters, was remarkably active as an organizer in the Greek community of Proussa. It was she who established that city's famous Greek school in 1826.

Calls for International Solidarity

The outbreak of the revolution in 1821 pushed women's activity for the development of Greek culture into the background. During this period, educated women devoted themselves mainly to praising the patriotic exploits of the insurgents, maintaining awareness and solidarity on the international front, and advocating for national cohesion, which had been sorely tried by internal strife. In March 1822 the burning and bloody destruction of Chios deeply affected public opinion both in Greece and on the international front. Of the 100,000 inhabitants of this well-to-do island, 40,000 were massacred or sold by the thousands in the slave market. Mado (sometimes spelled Mantō) Mavrogenous, one of the rare women commanders of the revolutionary army, addressed an appeal to "the Parisian women," whom she urged to support the struggle of Greek Christians against the "barbarism of Islam."

If the development of European philhellenism was a constituent part of the strategies of liberation before the revolution, it acquired enormous importance as international diplomacy distanced itself from the insurgents and their image became tarnished following the atrocities committed in the conquest of Tripoli and during the civil war (1823–25). In 1825, when the siege of Missolonghi was at its most intense, and when hunger and illness were killing off the populations already decimated by the Turkish counteroffensive, the mobilization of international opinion became vitally important in the attempt to offset the official policies of the great European powers, which were providing technicians, doctors, experts, and officers to the Turkish army. On the island of Andros, where she had taken refuge after the uprising of 1821, Evanthia Kairi drafted a petition appealing to the philhellenic women printed in Hydra with the signatures of several dozen women, most of them wives and mothers of notables and military leaders. Powerfully depicting the horrors of the war, the martyrdom of women on the islands burned by the Turks, and "babies nursing at the breast of dead mothers," Kairi vehemently condemned the inhumanity, indeed the savagery, shown by many of those who bragged about having been born in "civilized Europe." The courage with which so many of her sisters preferred to throw themselves off precipices or into the flames, or to become the prey of animals "rather than surrender one more time to the Turks" should come as no surprise: it was the price to be paid for the liberty of the homeland.

> But who, not only among our compatriots but even among the Turks themselves, would have believed that more than a hundred million Christians could watch with such incredible indifference, as if in a Roman amphitheatre, all Turkish nations together rushing to attack a handful of Christians?

None of the trials, she said, had been as hard for the Greek women as having to be subjected to this indifference people were calling "neutrality," which was in fact a policy of complicity with the Turks. She contrasted this policy, which she argued was unworthy of Europe, to the "only just policy," consisting of aid to the victims "of unjust oppression and inhuman tyranny." She thanked the "women friends of Greece" for promoting such a policy and assured them of the gratitude of the Greek women who were fighting for their freedom and for that of their daughters, who would be born into liberty. The appeal, translated into English, was to have a lasting echo in European and American public opinion, as attested to by the innumerable letters of solidarity from French, English, German, and American women published in the Greek press, as well as by the financial contributions that flowed in between 1826 and 1828.

. . . and for Revolutionary Unity

The organization of international solidarity was taken in hand in a more systematic manner by Greek women living in the large European cities. In Italy Palli and Theotoki used their fame and the prestige of their salons to support the cause of the insurgents within literary and political circles. During the same period, women's literature devoted itself to the revolution. Inspired by the struggles of the Cretan and Suliote fighters, Palli's *Odes* were published in Livorno in 1823. A year later, she herself translated them into French, adding some poems inspired by the tragedy of Psarra. The *Odes* on the events of Psarra were published by Firmin-Didot, who ensured their distribution in philhellenic circles. Two years later Palli published, in Italian, her first novel, *Allessio ossia gli ultimi giorni di Psarra* (1827; Alexis; or, The Last Days of Psarra), which was received with great enthusiasm in Italy. In May 1824 Psarra, one of the three most important islands for the revolution, was destroyed after fierce resistance. It was a setback of great strategic importance for the revolution, and it awakened the compassion of the international community. In a single day, this island of 7,000 inhabitants, where 23,000 survivors of Chios, Kydonia, and Smyrna had taken refuge, was transformed into a scene of massacre: 17,000 refugees and 4,000 inhabitants were killed or reduced to slavery. The horror of this carnage was witnessed by a French ship, which tried in vain to intervene and prevent the bloodbath and later brought the news to Europe. Psarra became a symbol of the suffering of the civil population in an unequal war. These events explain the impact of Palli's book, considered by the periodical *Anthologia florentina* to be one of "the most powerful defenses of the rights of the subjugated Greeks, bearing comparison to the most beautiful and most convincing pages of the most famous historians of Europe." Far from simply condemning the horror of the massacre, Palli in her novel uses the events of Psarra to develop her political beliefs about the right to national self-determination. Analyzing the causes of the civil war, she stigmatizes the race for power of military leaders, but she also lambastes the illusions of political leaders awaiting foreign aid. "Woe to the people that cannot trust its own forces. Woe to the nation whose liberty is dependent on foreign aid and which has not resolved to acquire this with its own blood." These words, which Palli put in the mouth of her hero, were directed both to international opinion and to her compatriots at war.

Palli was not the only one to intervene politically through literature during the revolution. The fall of Missolonghi and the tragic exodus had inspired the national poet D. Solomos to write the *Hymn to Liberty* (the future national anthem of Greece). In 1826, Kairi wrote *Nikiratos*, a play performed in the same year by a group of amateurs on the island of Syros. Inspired by the siege of Missolonghi, it was the first play of the modern Greek repertory to be staged on free territory and was to be performed several times after independence was proclaimed. Dedicated to the sacred memory of "the women sacrificed for Greece," Kairi's play is both an indictment of the thirst for power and the privileges that undermine the unity of the homeland and a hymn to those who struggle to "liberate and render the largest number of brothers equal and independent."

"I Wish for a Day of Battle As You Long for a Dance"

The pen was not the only weapon wielded by women during the revolution. In the combat zones, women often fought alongside men, sometimes arms in hand. Some of them attained positions of command and international renown. The best known and most celebrated among these, Lascarina Bouboulina, was 50 years old at the beginning of the revolution and already had considerable experience as a sailor and as a businesswoman. Born in a prison in Istanbul where her father was incarcerated for his participation in the Russo-Turkish War, Bouboulina was the widow of two great ship owners of Spetses who had been killed by pirates, and from whom she inherited an immense fortune. She increased her wealth by buying stock in many of the ships in the commercial fleet of her island and by building her own ships, which, armed against pirates, later braved the blockades. Initiated into the Friendly Brotherhood in 1816 in Istanbul, she returned to her island and began to lay groundwork for the revolution. She had built and equipped the *Agamemnon*, a corvette with 18 cannons, which was the first warship of 1821 and which went down in national legend for its exploits during the sieges of Monemvassia and Nauplion. During the years preceding the revolution, she collected a small private arsenal by clandestinely purchasing weapons abroad and secretly stockpiling them in her house. On the eve of the revolution, she also raised her own army corps, which she referred to as "my brave ones" and placed under the command of her oldest son. For years, she looked after these men as well as her crew and their families at her own expense. According to legend, she raised the rebel flag 10 days before the official proclamation of the revolution. In any event, the revolution found her totally ready, and she threw herself into the war at the head of her ships with an audacity that amazed her contemporaries. One of these, A. Hadzi-Anargyrou, historian of the revolution, described her standing on her ship, a superb silver pistol in her belt, braving the bullets and haranguing her men, who were yielding to the attack of the 300 cannon of the fortress of Nauplion: "Are you women or are you real men? Forward! Fire!" Seeing that the Nauplion fortress would need a long siege, she let her ships go on with the blockade and disembarked in the Peloponnesus in order to take part in the land battles. Her fiery speeches convinced the inhabitants of Argos to pursue the siege. Upon the death of her son, Bouboulina put herself at the head of the army, which she ran with iron discipline and such courage that her name alone was enough to sow panic among the enemy. Her role in the sieges of Monemvassia and Nauplion earned her enormous popularity, as was shown by the triumphant welcome reserved for her by the people of Nauplion, and thereafter she was called "the commander" or the "great lady." While her ships delivered fresh supplies to the besieged, at her own expense, she participated in the siege and taking of Tripoli (October 1822). In the midst of the massacre (more than 8,000 Turks were killed) and the pillage that followed for several days, Bouboulina managed to save the women and children of the harem of Kurshid Pasha, who were later exchanged for Greek hostages. Having spent the whole of her immense fortune in three years, Bouboulina returned to Spetses during the civil war and died there in 1824, assassinated in a vendetta of honor by the parents of the girl her son had abducted. A few days after her death, a Russian delegation arrived on Spetses to present her with the title of admiral of the Russian fleet.

"I wish for a day of battle as you yearn for a dance." These were the words with which Mado Mavrogenous, the other famous female fighter of the revolution, introduced herself to the women of Paris in her appeal for solidarity after the massacre of Chios. Born into a large family of Mykonos that had contributed several interpreters and dignitaries to the Ottoman court and daughter of Nicolaos Mavrogenis, who had been executed by the Turks, Mavrogenous found herself managing a huge fortune the day after the revolution. Having received a very careful education and having frequented the Italian and Swiss salons since her early youth, Mavrogenous was a true daughter of the Enlightenment, passionate about liberty. To those who were surprised that a girl of her age was unmarried, she would retort that she could love only a free man. Thanks to her uncle, an enlightened priest and himself an Etairist leader, she was initiated into the Friendly Brotherhood when still very young and contributed considerably to the organization. When the national uprising was announced, she left Trieste, where she had settled, and returned to Mykonos. Almost immediately after she arrived, she organized the defense of the island against Saracen pirates with surprising efficiency and convinced the hesitant notables to join the revolution. She had two ships built and put herself at the head of a military corps of 800 men, raised and equipped with her own money. She participated in several land and naval battles in Euboea, in continental Greece, and in Thessaly. In his *Histoire de la régénération de la Grèce* (1824; History of the Regeneration of Greece), François Pouqueville celebrates the inestimable help the ships of "the beautiful Mado" rendered to the villages of Pilion, besieged by Selim, pasha of Andrinopolis. Her enthusiasm, military exploits, contempt for danger, and her famous appeal to the women of Paris, as well as her youth and romantic beauty (disseminated through a series of portraits) and her love affair with Prince Dimitrios Ypsilantis made her into a legendary figure, celebrated in philhellenic poetry as "the heroine of Mykonos." Mavrogenous was the only woman to reach the rank of army commander.

Women's access to command was almost always linked to their ability to finance their ships or their own army, and also to their status as widow or unmarried woman, which freed them from male guardianship. For example, after her husband's death Domna Vizvizi, also a member of the Friendly Brotherhood, threw herself into battle with her ship and a crew made up of her four sons under her command. Widowhood could sometimes confer freedom of movement upon women of more plebeian origins, as in the case of Stavriana, the formidable fighter of Mystra, who sowed terror among enemy troops. It was to revenge the execution of her husband by the Turks that Stavriana took up arms at the age of 40 and signed on as a "simple soldier." Famous for her "virile appearance" and "her rough soldier's tongue," Stavriana was to distinguish herself by her military abilities in the taking of Tripoli; she left the army with the rank of colonel.

But if the revolution allowed a small number of women to participate in the same capacity as men, conferring prestige and authority on a few female fighters, the shifts it brought were far from overthrowing the patriarchal structures upon which women's position had rested for centuries. On the contrary, testimonies from the revolutionary period suggest that the status of women did not undergo any major change. In Kalamata, women did not even leave the house to do the shopping and were never seen at celebrations. In Nauplion, the few women who might be seen in the street "were always accompanied by armed men and were entirely covered" (K. Simopoulos, *Pōs eidon oi xenoi tēn Ellada tou 1821* [1978; How Foreigners Perceived the Greece of 1821]). On Hydra, the principal port of insurgent

Greece, women lived on the margin of the community under conditions of confinement.

To be sure, in the war zones women participated massively in the revolution. They played a strategic role in organizing the provision of new supplies during sieges and they often fought arms in hand. When the revolution of 1821 broke out, there was already a long tradition of women participating in combat, led by the Suliotes against Ali Pasha around the turn of the 18th century. Popular songs celebrating the exploits of the Suliote women rekindled this tradition, all the more so because a significant number of Suliote women had come to defend Missolonghi. A great many of them fell on the battlefield or collectively threw themselves from a cliff rather than to fall into enemy hands. But even those who fought in armed combat always found themselves under the control of the male members of their clan. The depictions of women in popular songs, one of the rare sources showing anonymous women participating in the struggle for freedom, confirm the persistence of the old patriarchal structures and traditional values that controlled the place reserved for the majority of women during the War of Independence. Most of the female figures are presented as passively suffering the ravages of war, passive victims of male violence inflicted by the Turks and, less frequently, the Greeks. Women's heroism and courage almost always emanate from their status as mothers or wives of great fighters who fought to defend their honor. In fact, as soon as one finds allusions to women in the source material, honor is the main preoccupation. When, in 1822, the Albanian pashas told the Suliotes that in the case of defeat their families would be taken hostage, their leader Yotis Danglis responded: "You don't need to be concerned about our wives and our children, for our army will not let you [harm them], and even in the case of a possible defeat, we will not leave them alive in your hands."

The Long Gowns of Slavery

The protection of female honor was as at least as important to Greek national identity as the polarity between Eastern barbarism and Western civilization that had inspired the democratic dreams of the ideologues of independence. The majority of the revolution's popular leaders identified themselves as *Roumoï* (Romans), heirs to the Roman Empire in the east, rather than as *Graïkoï* (Greeks), heirs to classical antiquity. Their idea of independence did not always coincide with the civilizing mission that some of their compatriots associated with the liberation of the nation. They were above all very suspicious of the Westernized mores of some of the revolutionary leaders. They accepted the participation in battle of women whose involvement was contained within the framework of family, as was the case of the widow Vizvizi. But they looked with hostility upon the autonomy of a woman such as Mavrogenous and her participation in the war counsels. Not able to endure the influence she had on Ypsilanti, which undermined the prestige of their leader, Ypsilanti's men decided to remove her from Nauplion and, with the complicity of other military leaders, they arranged her abduction and threatened to kill her if she came back to the capital. Mavrogenous wrote an accusatory report she submitted to the National Assembly of Trezeno (1827), but it was not read and does not show up anywhere in the accounts of the sessions.

Traditionalist perceptions of women were not limited to the lower classes. Although the majority of the women who distinguished themselves in the revolutionary action came from the upper and educated classes of the population, they were in no case representative of those classes, which, in the matter of relations between the sexes, largely shared the prejudices and practices of control of the popular classes. And although the process of national awakening and the spread of egalitarian and universalist ideas encouraged women to share the political and cultural preoccupations of their time and to feel actively involved in the patriotic cause, their will to action often ran up against very unequal power relations. The sole autobiographical testimony available from the period, the autobiography of Elizabeth Moutzan Martinengou, was written by a woman who belonged to the aristocracy of the Ionian Islands, the class of origin of women such as Peretrini and Theotoki. This document—today considered a perfect specimen of what was to become the demotic, spoken modern Greek, is significant in that it shows the corrosive dynamic of the revolutionary process on female subjectivity and demonstrates how little room women had in which to maneuver.

Daughter of the Greek prefect of Zante, the eminent collaborator with the English, Martinengou educated herself despite her father's opposition. She learned Italian and French almost entirely by herself, secretly reading books from her father's library. She gained admittance to the universe of the Enlightenment, which nourished in her a violent revolt against "all things tyrannical" and against all those "who defend them." She wrote plays for the theater, moral dialogues, and essays, and lived in the hope of publishing them. Confined to her house from the age of eight, as were most women of her caste, she learned the news of the Greek uprising while hiding behind a door. Her autobiography tells of her reaction:

> I felt my blood boil, I wanted to take up arms, to run to help those men who were fighting only for that precious liberty. . . . But as I looked at the walls of the house where they kept me locked in, as I looked at the long gowns of female slavery, I remembered I was a woman and I sighed.

If neither confinement nor family pressures could neutralize her need for freedom, it was because she learned very early on through her readings that "God has given us Reason so that we may use it." Preventing women from exercising that divine gift came close to "a barbaric and tyrannical command," and it was the result of fear of the liberty and education that "grant mankind great boldness and do not allow it to bend itself like an animal to the opinion of others." This was why her father's opposition to her education plunged her "into mortal despair: I felt swallowed up inside those thick and dark clouds that cast a shadow over life and the reputation of ignorant and uncultured men."

With her tendency to link political and domestic tyranny and to hate foreign domination just as much as the "pitiless custom" of her own land, Martinengou was undoubtedly an atypical case. But the enthusiasm with which she wanted to serve the national cause, the magical qualities she attributed to education, and finally, her eagerness to "make herself useful" to the homeland and even her hope of thus gaining "honor and glory" were undoubtedly widely shared by contemporaries who more successfully intervened in the public sphere of the revolution. In the end, her path illustrated in an exemplary manner the difficulty that most of her peers had in escaping from "the long gowns of slavery" even if they wished to do so.

Mavrogenous was to experience this difficulty in the 1830s. Left without any resources and rejected by her family for having sacrificed her fortune to the revolution, she asked to be integrated into the new army of the free state with the rest of the officers of the War of Independence. Despite her rank as leader of the army, she was to receive a "widow's or invalid's" pension. As she reminded King Otto in her petition,

> I have never been married and can thus not be a widow and I have never been wounded and can thus not be an invalid. Through its previously mentioned ruling, [the Secretariat] excludes me from the rights of the rest of the army's officers, as if my services to the homeland were of another kind than those of the other officers and as if the nation, in its calls and decrees, had made a distinction between men and women who served the homeland in the military area. (S. Aliberti, *Ai herōides tēs ellēnikēs hepanastaseōs* [1933; The Heroines of the Greek Revolution])

The domestic and international context in which national identity was constructed after Greek independence resulted precisely in an increasingly sharp differentiation of the "nature" of the services the homeland expected from each of the sexes. The petition by "the heroine of Mykonos" sealed the end of an adventure that was to serve as reference point for the first struggles for equal rights 50 years later.

Bibliography

Aliberti, Sotiria, *Ai herōides tēs ellēnikēs hepanastaseōs* (The Heroines of the Greek Revolution), Athens: 1933

Aliberti, Sotiria, *Mado Mavrogēnous* (Mado Mavrogenous), Athens: 1931

Comitato per le onoranze ad Angelica Palli Bartholommei, 1875

Dakin, Douglas, *The Unification of Greece 1770–1923*, London: Benn, 1972

Les femmes grecques aux femmes françaises, récit de leurs malheurs, traduit du grec par un philhellène, translated by J.-F.-T. Ginouvier, Paris: C. Béchet, 1826; Bruxelles, Brohez, 1927.

Dimaras, C.T., *Istoria ton Ellēnikou Ethnous* (History of the Greek Nation), vols. XII and XIII, Athens: 1977

Dimaras, C.T., *Neoellēnikos Liaphōtismos* (The Neohellenic Enlightenment), Athens: 1968

Foresi, Mario, "Lamartine e l'Italia in alcune sue lettere inedite," *Nuova Anthologia* (1916)

Hobsbawm, Eric J., *Nations and Nationalism since 1780: Programme, Myth, Reality*, second edition, Cambridge, England, and New York: Cambridge University Press, 1992

Kairi, Evanthia, *Eisagōgē. Symboulai pros tēn Phygatera mou* (Introduction to *Conseils à ma fille* by J.N. Bouilly), Kythoniai: 1820

Kandiloros, T., *E Philikí Etareía* (The Friendly Brotherhood), Athens: 1926

Kitromilides, Paschalis, "The Enlightenment of Womanhood. Cultural Change and the Politics of Exclusion," *Journal of Modern Greek Studies*, no.1 (1983)

Moschopoulos, N., *Istoria tēs ellēnikēs epanastaseōs kata tous Tourkous istoriographous en antiparabolē pros tous ellēnes istorikous* (History of the Greek Revolution, According to Turkish Historiography versus Greek Historians), Athens: 1960

Passamonti, Eugenio, "La famigla corsa dei Bartholommei e la Polizia Sarda," *Archivio Storico di Corsica* (1931)

Philikí Etareía (Friendly Brotherhood), *Paranoma Ntokoumenta. Apomnēmoneumata Agōnistōn* (Clandestine Documents. Memories of Combatants), Athens: n.d.

Simopoulos, K., *Pōs eidon oi xenoi tēn Ellada tou 1821* (How Foreigners Perceived the Greece of 1821), Athens: 1978

Svoronos, Nikolaos, *Histoire de la Grèce moderne*, Paris: Presses Universitaires de France, 1964

Varikas, Eleni, *Ē exergersē tōn kuriōn. Genesē mias pheniminsikēs syneidēsēs stēn Ellada* (The Women's Revolt: The Birth of Feminist Consciousness in Greece), Athens: 1987

Varikas, Eleni, "Gender and National Identity in Fin-de-Siècle Greece," *Gender and History* 5, no. 2 (1993)

Varikas, Eleni, "Les longues robes de l'esclavage: Stratégies privées et publiques dans le journal d'une recluse," *Les Cahiers du CEDREF*, no. 1 (1989)

Varikas, Eleni, "Question nationale et égalité des sexes," *Peuples méditerranéens* 50 (1990)

Vranoussis, L., *Rigas Ferraios* (Rhigas Ferraios), Athens: 1953

Xiradaki, K., *Evanthia Kairē 1799–1866* (Evanthia Kairi 1799–1866), Athens: 1984

Xiradaki, K., *Oi gynaikhes ste Philikí Etaireía* (Women of the Friendly Brotherhood), Athens: 1964

1826

Women in Philhellenism

<MAÏTÉ BOUYSSY>

IN 1826, FOR THE FIRST TIME, all of Europe was stirred by a distant cause, that of the Greeks. Some felt that military and financial help should be offered to a small and courageous nation seeking its freedom, while others saw it as a struggle of Christians against the despotic and bloodthirsty Turks. From Antwerp to Toulouse, from Saint Petersburg to Le Havre, a mobilized Europe was fired with passion and enthusiasm, that spirit of *Schwärmerei* (emotional turmoil and enthusiasm) so dear to German romanticism; and with this "crusade of humanity"—the expression was that of the duc de Choiseul—came radically new forms of staging protests. The ladies of Paris—that is, the women of the liberal upper class, the duchesses and bankers' wives—transposed the practice of collecting for charity onto a political plane; it was a practice that had up to that point been limited to salons or churches, or at best parishes, but had always been performed within the social context of their own neighborhoods. In Paris, Lyon, and Cologne, women even began to organize themselves; they did this on their own initiative, in stages, drawing both praise and sarcasm, but mobilizing to raise funds for a political cause was an innovative practice that indisputably brought them a new visibility.

This remarkable page in the political history of women shows that they took to the streets or went onstage in order to collect money, as if some subterranean political rift made it possible to exchange the cries and pure blood of massacred Greeks for their singing and the purified money of solidarity. This era marked the beginning of very modern forms of compassion for what Luc Boltanski has termed "distant suffering" (see Boltanski), and women played a key role in the process.

Jounalists and *chansonniers* (popular songwriters), lithographers and manufacturers of illustrated plates all seized on the story of women's fundraising efforts in support of the Greeks, yet it has been left out of all the writings on women's history, whether these be activist or scientific, for the general public or the specialized reader. Witness the *Histoire mondiale des femmes* (1966; World History of Women), edited by Pierre Grimal, and *Les grands événements de l'histoire des femmes* (1993; Major Events in Women's History), by Jacques Marseille and Nadeije Laneyrie-Dagèn.

Spring 1826: The Siege of Missolonghi and Parisian Emotion

On 13 July 1825, the Société de la Morale Chrétienne (Society of Christian Morality), which had already established a Greek Committee, proposed to

> reconstitute this committee on a broader footing. . . . Your new committee, in accordance with its means, will be concerned with *the application of the precepts of Christianity to the social institutions of Greece* [while] the French Philanthropic Society may be considered as the military and political Greek committee. The Greek Committee of the Society of Christian Morality, for its part, will be an essentially peace-loving, moral, and evangelical committee.

Here we see the double matrix of political philhellenism. Its origins did not lie in the scholarly and erudite enthusiasm of the 18th-century antiquaries, but rather in the liberal and philanthropic circles that have recently been studied by Catherine Duprat (see Duprat). However, this early emergence of women was connected to the particular political climate of the times stemming from public exasperation over the introduction of widely debated measures that were not always accepted by the government chambers, and which all served to reinforce the conservative symbolism of the regime: the union of the throne and the altar, and the restitutions made in 1825, under Charles X, to returning emigrés who had fled France during the Revolution and lost their property. Meanwhile, the comte de Villèle (ultraroyalist finance minister and head of the cabinet, 1822–27), although unanimously attacked, seemed to move through the different governments by his mere ability to manipulate influence.

In this context, François-René Chateaubriand's 25-page *Note sur les Grecs* (November 1825; Note on the Greeks) served far more effectively to revive interest in the Greek War of Independence than had Delacroix's *Massacres of Scio*, which had been exhibited at the previous Salon. The weight of words remained greater than the shock of images, and further, Delacroix's style had alienated the leaders of opinion and the liberal establishment. The vicomte de Chateaubriand, who continued to defend legitimacy although he had lost his ministry and his illusions about the Bourbons, developed his argument thus:

> Will our century see savage hordes stifling the rebirth of civilization within the tomb of a people who civilized the earth? Will Christianity calmly allow the Turks to cut Christian throats? And will European legitimacy suffer without indignation that its holy name be given to a tyranny that would have made Tiberius blush?

Until then, the French had largely been preoccupied with events in Spain. In 1821 a few works on the Greek struggle had appeared, such as the *Appel aux Français* (Appeal to the French) and the *Adresse au peuple français* (Address to the French People), among others, but such works remained rare. The following years, however, saw an increase: 18 such works appeared in 1822; 7 in 1823; and 11 in 1824. In 1825 their numbers increased to 27, and in 1826–27 to 43. These publications reflected the rhythm and pulse of French sentiment. Other writings, such as small brochures, poems, and topical works on the Greek theme followed the same curve, starting in 1821: 10, 18, 4, 26, 13, and then 34 in 1826, of which 12 alone were about the long and difficult siege of Missolonghi, a center of Greek resistance in the west, near the Ionian Sea. This became a focus for the attention given to a struggle which seemed to be lost but which no one wanted to see fail. In 1827 preparations for the Russo-Franco-English expedition, which was to destroy the Egyptian fleet at Navarino, eased the situation and the wave of mobilization subsided.

The press reported on these events with great enthusiasm. *Le Constitutionnel*—characterized by Stendhal as a liberal newspaper of shopkeepers—took up the cause of the Greeks. This newspaper functioned to a certain degree as the unofficial organ of the movement, recording all the events of which it had been notified, to the point that this eminently public source rather strangely overlapped with the (definitionally confidential) records of the Ministry of the Interior. The ministry's agents, at the request of the authorities, intervened, investigated, and evaluated events as soon as the authorized liberal newspaper reported items that aroused the suspicions of Prefect Delavau and the Ministry of the Interior.

The very serious *Globe* also gave extensive coverage to Greece, which as a topic of coverage took third place after France and England between 30 October 1824 and 19 February 1825 in the "History, literature, and statistics" columns. The overall cultural production inspired by the Greek War of Independence was substantial: Loukia Droulia has inventoried 2,070 items for 1821–33, of which 1,805 were published prior to 1829 (see Droulia). Some lines from the verse collection *Les Orientales* (1829; The Orientals) by Victor Hugo—although he was a staunch legitimist in his early days—are reminders of this Greek period of French sensibility:

> To Greece, oh my friends! Vengeance! Liberty!
> This turban on my brow! This sword by my side!
> Come! Saddle this horse!
> When do we leave? Tonight! Tomorrow would be too
> far off. Weapons! Horses!
> A ship at Toulon!

And especially:

> What do you want? Flower, fine fruit or marvelous
> bird?
> Friend, says the Greek child, the child with blue eyes,
> I want gunpowder and bullets.

Women sported shawls "à la Robelina"—the expression being an odd corruption of the name of the Greek heroine, Bouboulina. Blue and white, the Greek colors, were all the rage; the fashionable set wore blue and white sashes instead of precious chains, and, in 1826, donned "Missolonghi gray." In Saint Petersburg, high-society carriages, not to be outdone, were drawn by horses adorned with the Greek colors.

When the French Grow Bored, They Collect Funds: or, the Origins of the Practice

Members of the liberal public expressed their views by donating funds. They did so for General Foy, who died on 1 December 1825. A sum of one million francs was collected during the winter for the children of "the most eloquent defender of French liberty" and to erect a monument in the Père-Lachaise Cemetery to honor this valiant soldier of Napoleon. A competition was held for the design; the models were exhibited in the Grand Bazaar of the rue Saint-Honoré; and all of this was done in a remarkably modern way. At the same time, the press, especially *Le Constitutionnel*, published the names of the donors, sometimes together with the amounts subscribed. A counterculture was becoming visible. Women joined with men, especially when they seemed to be acting as the head of the household; a woman from Aisne, for instance, was listed together with the donations, in decreasing order, made by her sons, daughters, laundress, and kitchen and outdoor valets. Families frequently gave, distinguishing between the contributions according to the status of each member. The pedagogy of philanthropy in its ostentatious forms here became the premise for political education. The humble and the great, through the deliberate visibility of collecting funds, reunited a national community that had been crushed or stifled. Modest social standing was taken into account: six workers could contribute 25 centimes each, yet children, too, were called upon to make a donation. The consensus reigning within their social environment spurred women to take a stand; they became involved, moreover, not only because the situation called for their intervention in philanthropic matters—an indirect and privileged sphere for the exercise of their autonomy—but also, perhaps, because their inferior civic and legal status conferred upon them (as upon children) a greater independence. Thus it was that the private act of donating funds, with the promise of public recognition, became a subversive practice. The money collected expressed silent refusals and protest. This subterranean flow of humble actions, which redefined the notion of the patriotic act in terms of common usefulness, provided a counter to the majesty of the political powers, which grew more authoritarian and reactionary in their symbolic choices every day. Within this alchemy of emotion, women took a stand from the start.

The brief account of the funeral of General Foy in *Le frondeur* reported that, despite the rain, men of every class and every age stood, hat in hand, all the way from Notre-Dame de Lorette to Père-Lachaise, while at the cemetery, "More than three thousand women could be seen, and their sadness made the spectacle even more moving."

"This Holy Cause"

On 7 January 1826, philhellenism once again became topical in the fashionable circles of Paris when Delphine Gay, the muse of the literary world and the living incarnation of Madame de Staël's Corinne, donated 400 francs to the Comité Grec—the income sent from Munich for the translation of her poem "La quête" [The Collection]. That philhellenic work, published as a pamphlet, became known above all for the line, "Let us teach them victory, for dying is all they know." *Le Constitutionnel* followed up by declaring: "It is time to multiply donations for the defense of this holy cause."

On 25 February the Société Philanthropique en Faveur des Grecs (Philanthropic Society to Aid the Greeks) effectively launched the long-awaited, vast fundraising campaign. Appealing to "friends of religion and humanity," the society wrote:

> What Christian, what Frenchman would refuse to participate in this holy work? We implore every generous heart, every enlightened spirit, we invoke the pious charity of women, we ask for offerings from poor and rich alike, for it is a question of relieving terrifying ills, approaching nothing we know in our enlightened Europe, and which will only cease with end of the barbaric invasion that Greece is once again repelling.

This was followed by the names of the 24 committee members, all of them illustrious, including Chateaubriand and the literary historian Abel-François Villemain, together with the great names of the aristocracy and philanthropic bankers. On 6 March a neighborhood fund was started in the rue Jean Robert at the request of several young people employed in the hardware and wholesaling sections. This street ran parallel to the rue des Gravilliers, where the memory of the sansculottide priest Jacques Roux and the Enragés of the French Revolution hovered; it extended from the rue Saint-Martin to the rue Transnonain— of sinister memory because of the famous massacre perpetrated by the Army in 1834, a memory that is today literally covered up by the rue Beaubourg. This neighborhood was at the heart of the world of craftsworkers, the sansculottes of earlier days, whose attitude had "made" the days in Paris: their abstention on 9 Thermidor had been fatal for Robespierre, but the sector had risen up again in the year III.

Thus began a well-orchestrated campaign, which continued unflaggingly. On 14 March 1826, reported *Le Constitutionnel*, a letter from a young Greek was read at the rostrum: one little sentence, "What did we do to France?" was a resounding success, for it caused the French to question their passivity and lack of action. The following day, in the Chamber of Peers, Chateaubriand delivered a plea, and *Le Constitutionnel* of 15 March reported that women had joined the campaign:

> But public opinion has been expressed in an even more striking way. Women, who in France have always been associated with works of devotion and generosity and whose dedication has taken the lead in all that has been done that is great, noble, and patriotic in France, have, on this occasion, wanted to show themselves worthy of what they always have been among us. We have been told that the most distinguished ladies of the capital are forming special societies to support the fervor manifested everywhere on behalf of the Greeks. The duchesses de Broglie and de Dalberg, the marquises de Marmier and de Praslin, and all of the capital's most brilliant ladies by virtue of their rank, beauty, opulence, good taste, and virtue, are vying with one another to accept the honor of collecting money on behalf of the unfortunate Greeks.
>
> We have no doubt that this example will soon be followed in every department and that the ladies of Bordeaux, Lyon, Rouen, Marseille—daughter of Greece—Nantes, Bourges, Nancy, Metz, Strasbourg, Dijon, Aix, Avignon, and of so many enlightened cities will hasten to be associated with such an honorable act.

The facts established a fairly different political geography, however, for the underground networks of political connections took many forms. The size and wealth of the respective cities were not the only factors involved, and the provinces, like Paris, proved their capacity for inventing new forms of protest.

Meanwhile, *Le Constitutionnel*—which transmitted the sums collected to the bankers André and Cottier—had received 2,183 francs in less than three weeks. It reported a large deposit from Montpellier, clearly the balance of previous initiatives; 200 francs from Prince Constantin de Salm; then donations from "9 inhabitants of Saint-Hippolite-du-Gard," a predominantly Protestant town; and the remittance from a lodge in Vesoul, a city that was to become known for its opposition movements.

On 26 March a text by Félix Bodin, a member of the Philhellenic Committee of the Society of Christian Morality, gave the campaign new impetus. The donations grew in number. Some were large (1,000 francs given anonymously by "a lady using the modest name of Adélaïde"; others came with the donor's identity: the duke of Devonshire made a donation, and the duc d'Orléans gave 5,000 francs). Provincial cities such as Bordeaux and Angers started their own funds, with the notable participation of mistresses of households. On 27 March *Le Constitutionnel* reported: "In every society where there are no Turks or cabinet members, that is to say in 19 out of 20 salons, the mistress of the house is taking a collection for the Greeks." The newspaper's report of 3 April was more specific: "Every salon that is neither Turkish nor Jesuit has its collection box, and all put their offerings in with pious enthusiasm." Further, as if to legitimate the universality of the movement, the newspaper noted that anonymity was the fact of "shy benefactors who are obliged to shroud themselves in mystery and hide their good actions in order not to lose the good graces of a sensitive public." The highlight of this process of popularization within high society was represented by the announcement of a concert:

> For the benefit of the defenders of Missolonghi, a concert featuring the best amateurs in which the ladies of society who are the most distinguished for their talent and their singing will be heard. This performance by women who will overcome their timidity to pay the tribute of admiration and devotion to courage, will indeed be most worthy

of our interest. For these patriotic proceedings there will be 600 tickets available at 30 francs, and you may rest assured that in less than 24 hours there will not be a single one left.

An exhibition of paintings for the benefit of the Greeks was also announced.

The contributions continued to stream in (8,913 francs in one month). Philhellenic literature, published all the more readily when written by a woman of the upper classes, flourished. For example, the comtesse de Redem, née Montpezat, composed a brochure that was sold for 1.50 francs in the linen-drapers' shops, for everything produced "on this noble topic deserves the most favorable reception. . . . The Greeks can only add to the reputation of this lady."

The Vauxhall Concert

The great event of the month of April 1826 was organizing "the Vauxhall concert. . . . All the tickets taken for 20 francs over the past fortnight, have been bought this week for up to 150 francs each to be deposited in the Greek fund," related *Le Constitutionnel*. On 30 April, the paper's report of the event filled more than two-and-a-half columns, and in June, Stendhal devoted almost three pages of his chronicle in the *London Magazine* to it. Both of these reports clarified the social and political significance of the event. Stendhal wrote:

This concert afforded the first instance for these twenty-six years, of the upper ranks of society assembling for any object in opposition to the Government . . . [and it] has acquired a degree of historical importance. The plan was at first timidly broached by the Duchess of Dalberg and some other ladies, who trembled lest the massacres of Chio should be renewed at Missolonghi. The government opposed the project by a hundred little indiscreet measures. No clerk in any of the public offices dared to purchase a ticket; and so great was the dread of giving offence in this way, that it was feared not a thousand tickets at 20 francs each, would be disposed of. But suddenly a number of our ultra [ultraroyalist] ladies of rank began to evince symptoms of compassion, and in a day or two it became quite the fashion to patronize the concert. An English gentleman paid 300 francs for a ticket, and the seller immediately presented the sum to the fund for the benefit of the Greeks. This bargain, which was struck on the Exchange, completely established the fashion, and the rage rapidly increased. The duc de Dudeauville, minister of the king's household, and one of the short-robed Jesuits, who had opposed the concert by every possible means, found himself reduced to the necessity of paying five hundred francs for two tickets. Rossini, who, it is said, received orders not to direct the concert, took great pains in superintending the rehearsals of the duchesses, marchionesses and countesses, who vied with each other for the honour of singing in the choruses. . . . The hall was crowded with fashionable company.

Le Constitutionnel was even more eloquent in imparting information to its 20,000 subscribers. Its account of 30 April specified

the pieces that were sung by each performer (Gioacchino Rossini's *L'Italiana in Algieri* [The Italian Girl in Algiers] was most fitting), and it featured a truly political introductory paragraph on the front page, which clarified the analysis of the liberals:

From the first division of Poland, which saw the birth in France of the profound interest which any people's misfortune ought to inspire in all other peoples, to the American war, which so dazzlingly developed this generous feeling, we have had many occasions to sympathize with the lot of other nations or to share their triumphs in the pursuit of liberty, and a reciprocity of relationship has been established between them and us with the strength of family ties. These ties secretly bind the various populations of Europe who are so fully aware of the need to soberly oppose despotism with the impregnable barrier of freedom.

The reporter ended his detailed account with this very "patriotic" cry:

I have seen this concert and remain deeply touched by it, and proud of my country. Never has a pleasure of such keen appeal given rise to a more brilliant gathering; never have so many women of such remarkable beauty, grace, talent, and virtue been seen together. . . . The audience left filled with the satisfaction that only pleasures that are pure and mixed with noble actions can bring.

This event revealed a society unanimously rallied together in the consensual demonstration of its legitimacy, in the face of the dynastic legitimacy of the Bourbons under the Holy Alliance—or what was left of it around Vienna and Metternich—but loyal also to France's traditional Turkish alliance.

From Concert to Concert

The "entire country" offered a spectacle of communion and cohesion in a spirit of altruistic thought worthy of exalting the fine soul of each and all. Women were its ornament and melodic voice, its social and moral apparatus, the indispensable accompaniment that sanctioned and perhaps sanctified the holy cause. The voice of the female elite responded to the cry of Missolonghi.

In the course of time, similar benefit concerts were organized in Strasbourg, Nancy, Mons, and Brussels (where 2,000 tickets at 3 florins each were distributed), as well as in Germany, from Düsseldorf to Dresden. Records can also be found, although without further details, of funds coming in from Valence (two concerts), Colmar, Mulhouse, Nantes, Tours, Toulouse, Lyon, Bordeaux, Strasbourg, Mâcon, Amiens, Clermont, Dinan, Sedan, Valenciennes, Boulogne-sur-Mer, Avignon, Chartres, Lille, Rennes, Limoges, Angoulême, Charleville, Gray, Saint Quentin, Bolbec, Montargis, and Guebwiller.

The proceeds of a concert were sometimes supplemented by taking up a collection. In Dijon, two ladies organized an impromptu collection by passing "Greek caps" and, to great applause, Monsieur Chauvelin and the chevalier Montherot "were invited to give their hand" to Madame Saunac, wife of one of the deputies of the Côte-d'Or, and to Madame Hernoux, wife of Chauvelin's former colleague. In Antwerp, the same distinction was made between concert proceeds (1,763 florins) and the collection taken by the ladies (168 florins). Amateur concerts were also held in Tourcoing, Perpignan, Berlin (the Spontini concert, raising 7,966 francs), and Louvain, and on 15 June there was a celebration at the Montagnes Françaises, a well-known pleasure gardens in Belleville.

Women were the "natural" intercessors for the holy cause; ennobled by its tragic dimensions, they used their concert performances to demonstrate what their society was experiencing as a political emergency. This was the key to the great operas of the time, and Vincenzo Bellini and Esprit Auber made it a common theme of their dramatic art. Women, who had been deprived of all legal personhood by the Revolution and even more so by the Napoleonic Code, found themselves at the heart of a new civic venture that propelled them onto the stage. In this way, they were able to circumvent the actions of kings and diplomats, whereas their social rank did not suffice to include them in the political sphere.

The Ladies' Committee

While women made donations in their own names, such as Marceline Desbordes-Valmore, who contributed the proceeds (200 francs) from an edition of her poems, they also developed an unexpected means of action in the form of a Ladies' Committee. In that context they appeared under a collective name . . . and anonymously, acting as a delegation, as *Le Constitutionnel* emphasized:

Tales abound of the multitude of generous acts by this sex which displayed such heroic devotion during our civil strife. . . . Women are showing the most touching ardor for the Greek cause; forty of them, all endowed with a most touching union of virtue and grace, have begun a collection in every district of the capital, and never have their opulent parties and worldly pleasures had sweeter appeal for them than has this peace-loving mission on behalf of Christians who are suffering in the name of religion and liberty. Here is the letter (dated 12 March) addressed to them by the Philanthropic Society in Aid of the Greeks:

Dear Madame,

In its profound grief over the latest news received from Greece, the Philanthropic Society in Aid of the Greeks has placed its hopes in the pious charity of the ladies of Paris. Never will they find a more woeful occasion for the exercise of that religious and charitable zeal which is their glory: all the miseries of humanity, all the scourges of illness, destitution, and hunger have been brought to bear on Christian Greece. . . .

Pious women, happy and cherished mothers, do not be insensitive to such misfortune, give a piece of your finery or of your own handiwork to relieve their suffering, ask for gold, speak in the name of the religion that silently approves of you. Speak out, you will not be refused. We are hopeful of, indeed we await, the rapid success of your holy work.

And you, Madame, please permit us to call most particularly upon you to intercede, and accept our sincere respect.

The plea was signed by 23 members of the Greek Committee as well by the liberals, Chateaubriand, and the dukes of Choiseul and Fitz-James, all of them representing the finest of society: four dukes, seven counts, a baron, a general, seven bankers, the publisher Ambroise-Firmin Didot, and Villemain.

Thus, 40 ladies in their fine dress, a veritable academy of philanthropy, boldly ventured out into the rebellious streets of the small-shopkeeping neighborhoods of Paris. *Le Constitutionnel* of 7 April 1825 reported on the welcome they received, noting that "they knew no one there"; this might have constituted a social obstacle but did not exclude the possibility of a liberal network secretly taking the situation in hand:

The forty ladies who have so graciously and with such dedication accepted the honorable mission of appealing to people's generosity on behalf of the heroes of Greece, continue to walk the length and breadth of the various quarters of Paris, where they are paid tribute by many and meet with touching signs of interest.

These past few days, two of these noble collectors have been going through the merchant quarter of Les Bourdonnais, where they know nobody, but where they have been welcomed by everyone with the most attentive cordiality . . . from the wealthy store to the humble little shop, all gave more than they were able . . . there was the young girl who begged her parents to give the money intended for her new outfit, there were the children who came running to offer the small treasures of their savings; shop assistants took from their modest pay, and the collection box in the café, where gratuities for the modest employees are placed, was emptied into that of goodwill and misfortune.

These two ladies, whose names we will not mention because that is what they asked of us and because they are endowed with the modesty that is the inseparable companion of true charity, have nothing but praise for the welcome they received from Monsieur Michel, a most commendable merchant of the Bourdonnais district. He offered to guide them around, leaving his business and everything behind, and ensured that they were received everywhere in the same way as he himself had done. The names of every merchant and almost every resident of the rue des Deux-Boules, [rue] Bertin-Poirée, [rue] des Lavandières, [rue] Plat d'Étain, and of this whole quarter should be mentioned in order to make known the generous men who have not stopped at sterile wishes for the victory of the most noble of causes.

The former fourth arrondissement, running from the rue Saint-Honoré to the Seine and from Châtelet to Saint-Germain l'Auxerrois (to the east of where [the department store] La Samaritaine now stands), was a rebellious area, and a target for police harassment. Historian Maurice Agulhon has noted that in 1828, the authorities refused authorization to a merchant club in the rue des Bourdonnais, for it had immediately been suspected of liberalism (see Ahulhon). This action took on various levels of significance. Here, too, the memory of the Revolution hovered: the women from La Halle, the nearby market, were the symbol of fiery and uncontrollable actions, of dark and suspect forces. Now, other women—not just the local women but upper-class ladies with a moral mandate—were walking through and thus liberating a public space which Prefect Delavau was intent on controlling at the least sign of political opposition. It was as if the women were playing in counterpoint to the "shady-looking types" described by the press, who were hired to break the windows of the apartments and stores that were lit up at the announcement of the repeal of the law of primogeniture on 8 April—a law that would have permitted the creation of entailed properties for the few families who paid over 8,000 francs in property tax. The small shopkeepers—the "common people of Paris"—felt only the law's humiliating nature and its symbolism of inequality, for their immediate interests were in no way affected.

Of course, the collections were ridiculed, with ultraroyalists and supporters of the government giving full play to their satirical verve. An anonymous play, *L'Argent* (Money), commented on the persons with elegant carriages whose husbands played the stock market and who trod the streets to collect pennies in small boxes. On 12 May, *Le Frondeur* responded that these ladies were "not only generous but courageous as well, for they lay themselves open to rebuke." Other actions were also reported, such as that of the wine distributors who welcomed the collectors on 20 April "with eagerness and reverence." There again, a respectable merchant received them first and then accompanied them, as "the spirit of patriotism and charity" cut across the intricacies of civil society. This scenario was repeated in the rue Chapon and at the Saint-Nicholas cemetery, as *Le Constitutionnel* reported: "Several residents wanted to accompany these ladies. The contributions were plentiful and, we are sure, will not be any less so in the other streets of the sixth arrondissement." At notaries' offices, a customary place for taking collections, 3,500 francs had already been raised on 22 April by Mesdames Lambert Jeune (a notary's wife, 31 rue du Bac) and Bessas-Lamégy (née Boulay de la Meurthe, 30 rue de Bourbon); the presence of a name from the Revolution, Boulay de la Meurthe, that had rallied to the empire had its effect, while 10-year-old Lavinie Lefebvre-Desnouette, who gave 100 francs, was cited as an example to be followed.

"This Wonderful Zeal'"

From mid-April on, the provinces began to imitate Paris, as reports from *Le Constitutionnel* attest. In Louviers, supporters of the Greek cause collected 1,885 francs: "The inhabitants, manufacturers, property owners, craftsmen, and simple workers put the same enthusiasm into contributing to this good work as did the ladies to their task of collecting the funds." In Limoges, a collection "to hold our own jubilee without going to the procession" was reported, although the role of the women was not mentioned, doubtless because a trace of anticlericalism prevailed. In Troyes, on the other hand, the women's independent action was distinguished from the fundraising efforts of the city's merchants: "Eager to be associated with this charitable work, the ladies decided amongst themselves to receive personally, in their homes, the donations of the residents." Women's indepen-

dent fundraising efforts were also acknowledged in Nantes (22 April), while the philhellenic ladies of Rouen sent in 258 francs.

However, it was in the insubordinate and inventive city of Lyon, perpetual fomenter of plots, that a Comité Grec des Dames (Ladies' Greek Committee) declared itself with the most open autonomy. Its members addressed their female co-citizens in an appeal printed in *Le Constitutionnel:*

> Madame,
> The holy cause of religion and humanity, the cause of the Greeks, has just fueled the ladies of Paris with a pious zeal; they have collected money in every district of the capital, and the donations they have received give sufficient proof that charity is a virtue of the French.
> It is up to us, ladies of Lyon, to imitate the fine example they have set for us: let us hold collections in every district of our city. When it is a matter of saving old men from the swords of Muslims, women from slavery, timid virgins from infamy, and of maintaining children in the religion of their fathers, what woman, what mother could refuse the honorable mission of collecting donations destined to furnish arms, munitions, and even food to the brave defenders of so many innocent victims?
> It is acting in this conviction and in the knowledge of the pious feelings that inspire you, that we implore you to kindly accept the honor of being one of the collectors for your district.

The paper followed up with the report that there were already collection boxes in the salons of Lyon and that, by 15 April, more than 2,000 francs had been raised. This text broke away from those originating in Paris in that it explicitly dealt with the question of supporting the fighters, and went beyond the objectives that the Society of Christian Morality had set itself. On 24 April, it was noted that "'the zeal of the ladies of Lyon grows stronger with the success of their noble enterprise."

In Chalon-sur-Saône, a town reflecting the urban ostentation of the Rhône-Rhine crescent, the paper reported, "Twelve ladies spent several days going around the entire town. They slipped away from their homes and from the caresses of their young children with the honorable goal of helping to save mothers and bring aid to Christians." This "wonderful zeal" produced 2,000 francs—with a call for arms for the heroic Hellenes—and on 17 May the sum total announced amounted to 15,000 francs, "a prodigious sum for a community of 10,000 souls."

The ladies of Le Havre joined in and collected 9,088 francs. It was hoped that the ladies of Caen would be able to organize an amateur concert, but clearly liberal society did not have much sway there. In Metz, door-to-door collections were made, but women's action was not specified as such. In Mulhouse, by contrast, women activists raised 2,836 francs, which closely corresponded to the tradition of philanthropy of the Protestant industrialists.

Reports in *Le Constitutionnel* reveal that in other cities individual initiatives took on specific forms: "In Boulogne-sur-Mer, Madame Lesage-Fontaine, daughter of a former deputy, joined forces with an English lady, daughter of a minister of the king of England." Each was accompanied by a gentleman from her country, and collected funds from families of both nations. In Carcassonne, a collection was launched by Madame Tesseire (née Dejean) and the baronne Lamothe-Langon. In Cholet,

"Twenty-two ladies, all of them wives or daughters of men most respected for their industry, their fortune or their rank, went collecting door to door, and raised more than 1,500 francs." Colmar was noted for the remittance from the duc de Choiseul.

A sense of the multiplicity of the initiatives can be gleaned the column headed "Collections on Behalf of the Greeks" of 30 May: a Madame Delaporte, in Fontainebleau, was reported as having collected "300 francs from her family and friends"; "three ladies" were cited as having brought in 1,696 francs; three anonymous ladies from Tares, 55 francs; an impromptu concert following a wedding had been given in Clément-de-l'Oise; other women cited without place names had garnered 1,125, 2,000, and 1,000 francs; a Madame Boscary from Villeplaine had sent in 1,050 francs—and all this amid the efforts of the military, Masonic lodges, groups of young people from valleys such as that of Munster (Upper Rhine), and corporative banquets.

Abroad, funds were raised everywhere, but in Morat (in the canton of Fribourg, Switzerland), it was the ladies who sent in 500 francs. In Stockholm, the contributions came from a society of charitable ladies of which Princess Sophie-Albertine was the president. Places close to the French border, such as Ath, Lindau, or Saarbracken, also sent their remittances to Paris. In Cologne, on 13 May 1826, a women's committee was formed with ten of the most famous names in the city: Thérèse Schaffhausen (from an investment banking family), Agnès Steinberger (from a burgomaster family), Lisette Merkens (who shared the surname of a president of the Chamber of Commerce), the baroness of Lippe, and other names of the nobility. These women embodied the pride of this powerful Catholic city on the Rhine, which experienced its unification with Prussia as a misalliance. They were dynamic and their efforts were successful, whereas shortly earlier, a support committee that had wanted to give a concert had failed. These socially prominent women did not hesitate to go door to door, and they quite shamelessly approached the tables in the inns (something a good police force should never have tolerated), outraging the sober-minded. German solicitation texts of the time echoed the appeals of the women of Paris and Lyon.

On 15 June, women gave about another 1,000 francs. In Bercy, the comtesse de Nicolaï, accompanied by a Monsieur Louis Richard, collected 2,216 francs. *Le Constitutionnel* of 18 April published the result of the first Parisian collections: 36,153 francs, which meant an average of 2,582 francs per woman fundraiser. There appeared the names of the marquises de Praslin (4,420 francs), de Dalmatie (5,000 francs), and de Paravey (744 francs); the duchesses Decazes (4,037 francs) and Dalberg (2,690 francs); the comtesse Regnault de Saint-Jean-d'Angély (1,000 francs); Mesdames Delessert-Gauthier (2,025 francs), J. Peris (1,039 francs), Ternaux, (3,500 francs), Bartholdi-Walter (2,222 francs), Jules de la Rochefoucauld (1,160 francs), and de Carvalho (100 francs). An additional list gave the following names and figures: Madame de Dalberg (2,370 francs), Madame de Broglie (1,243 francs), Madame Georges La Fayette (1,700 francs), Madame Horace Say (1,941 francs), Madame Vatry (5,061 francs), Madame Grimaldi-Monaco (877 francs), and 1,561 francs for Madame Perin de Sérigny, elsewhere listed for 660 francs under the heading "privately collected." It is not known what proportions are to be attributed to the generosity of the women activists themselves, to collections organized in the semipublic sphere of the salon, or to canvassing the streets.

Neither is anything known about the activist fervor of the individual women, or the sectors they went through—which is why it is important to collect the scattered journalistic information whenever it enters into the concrete details of daily practices. Overall, the Ladies' Greek Committee raised a total of 1.2 million francs, and the women's action represented only the launching of this widespread movement.

Only the "Women Alone" on Their Own . . .

There is no doubt that the "authorities" were worried. In Auxerre, official inquiries were made about two female contributors, one a fashion merchant who had lived in Madrid and the other a Madame Baudesson-Villetard, who had given the first 100 francs. Police reports reveal that it was learned that the latter, far from being some formidable leader, was

> the widow of a chevalier de Saint-Louis . . . a woman with a very lively imagination, easily inflamed, who, on this occasion, acted merely for reasons of humanity. This lady, who is moreover in poor health and very old, exercises no influence whatsoever.

In fact, this elderly widow bore the surname of Montagnard, a member of the Convention and the Directory. This zeal for detail showed that, in May and June 1826, the police and the Ministry of the Interior were caught off-guard by a phenomenon that was deliberately public when their repressive tradition was more apt to think in terms of conspiracy. An "observer" wrote in a confidential note, dated 21 July 1826 and addressed to the prefect of the Upper Rhine, "I have been informed that the philhellenic committees, so numerous today, are replacing the *vendita* [lodges] of the Carbonari and are actively working to foment numerous disturbances."

The practice of collecting funds, particularly by women of the upper class, served to mark out a new kind of public space; it was part of a process of opinion building—a constitutive feature of liberalism. In 1827, furthermore, Villèle lost the elections and his power. This political shift was not produced by rioting or street uproar, although when the election results were announced, barricades did reappear for the first time since the 17th century, and this in the rue Saint-Denis, very near to the streets mentioned earlier. Seemingly, political visibility could not be achieved without some symbolic control of public space, and while liberalism sought to open up the barriers for free circulation, defensive action engendered entrenchment and barricades. The model that predominated in France was not that of the Germany of romanticism, as the zealous "observer" imagined it to be in this region along the border.

A new step was taken on 7 May, with the concerted plan to divide up the urban space into carefully supervised sectors: "Soon the need was felt to regulate [these collections] in order to prevent generosity from being deceived by fraud in the disguise of zeal." Twelve women were established as official collectors, one per arrondissement, reported the *Journal de la Société de la morale chrétienne*:

> They will be supplied with an official certificate, carrying a special stamp and signed by several committee members.

Each of these ladies will be assisted by and oversee a certain number of collectors in her arrondissement, who will also receive a certificate [a kind of "arrondissement" committee . . .]. Representative government is such a sensible thing that it slips in everywhere: we note with pleasure that the ladies are going to try their hand at this, too.

The only known certificate testifying to the institutionalization of these practices seems to be that of Madame Vatry, which can be found at the National Library in Athens. There is also evidence that the women collectors had certificates that they left for people who were absent. A single remaining example, preserved in the Museum of Pylos and bearing the names of Madame Georges Lafayette and Madame de Lasteyrie, attests to this.

Thus, under the aegis of a helmeted Athena and the signatures of the president of the committee (J.-L. Ternaux), the vice presidents (Alexandre Lameth and the comte de Lasteyrie), and the secretary (Firmin-Didot), a strange network was spread across Paris, departing from the Chaussée d'Antin and, to a lesser extent, the Faubourg Saint-Honoré, in which the investment bankers stole a lead over the liberal nobility; this conclusion is based on the addresses provided in *Le frondeur* of 7 June.

Madame Vatry of the rue Chantereine (which ran from the Faubourg Montmartre to the rue du Mont-Blanc) covered the area from the Chaussée d'Antin to Chaillot; from the Place des Victoires, while Madame Ternaux supervised her district (the parish of Saint-Roch) in the manner befitting the wife of the president of the committee. From her Faubourg Poissonnière and Saint-Denis, Madame André Jeune, a member of the collecting bank, was in charge of the neighboring Mail and the wealthy parish of Saint-Eustache. The duchesse Dalberg, at the political and moral heart of the project, was at work in the rue Saint-Honoré and around Saint-Germain-l'Auxerrois. More distant connections were also established: the duchesse Decazes was assigned to cross the city from the Faubourg Saint-Germain to the Faubourg Saint-Martin, and the marquise de Marinier went from the Madeleine to Saint-Nicholas des Champs and Sainte-Elisabeth, which took her almost to République.

From the Boulevard Poissonnière, Madame Davillier went south toward Saint-Gervais and Saint-Louis-en-l'Île; Madame Pillet-Will went into the Marais, and Madame de Paravey continued on to the Faubourg Saint-Antoine, a quarter near the Bastille that had become notorious for its riots during the French Revolution. Madame Bartholdi-Walter, also from the Madeleine, took on the working-class district of Montagne Sainte-Geneviève, while Madame de Chabrillat remained within the Faubourg Saint-Germain, and, very close by, Madame de Lasteyrie busied herself with the active and densely populated center of the Left Bank, her personal territory (the former 11th arrondissement—that is, Saint-Germain, Saint-Séverin, and Saint-Sulpice, formerly Cordelier). In this way, Paris and its areas of potential insubordination were placed under supervision, as if to construct a genteel political visibility. This visibility was noted by everyone at the time, and the general reaction is of particular interest, for the woman who left her salon—or the equally semi-public, but closed, space offered by the church—was viewed with a troubled eye.

Their audacity was praised. Bertrand Barère [de Vieuzac], a former member of the Convention living in exile in Brussels, who constantly sought to "penetrate the inner imagination of societies," noted, on the pages written as the ideas came to him according to the latest news: "Only the women in France have dared declare themselves the missionaries of liberty and of the human species in order to solicit help and bread for the besieged of Missolonghi" (April 1826). Or, in another instance:

> In France, the most brilliant notables, the peers of France, the deputies of the opposition, a few civil servants, merchants, manufacturers, all generous men, the middle and lower classes of society, and, above all, women of every rank are hastening to come to the aid of the Greeks in their heroic misfortune. . . . In the midst of the cruel indifference of cabinets and the hypocritical neutrality of kings, women alone have inspired and supported the zeal of nations. They have braved powerful prejudices and threats from those in power and have endured all kinds of fatigue in order to go [a word is missing here: perhaps "collecting"? "soliciting"?] aid of every kind on behalf of the Greeks oppressed by the Turks and the Gallo-Egyptians.

And more concretely:

> About the Greeks. The women in Paris have proven, by collecting money for the Greeks, that nothing is impossible for these sensitive beings when they undertake something noble and generous. Ladies, accustomed to pursuing delicacy and the capital's fine habits, are not afraid to walk the streets every day, streets which the police have not sanded over for them. These ladies penetrate into dark alleys and climb up to the highest floors, braving the fatigue of a task that they find possible only because of the idealistic goal they have set themselves and the results they hope to obtain.
>
> From the examples given in their reports, it can be seen what neglected districts, what classes of humble people show the greatest generosity and enthusiasm for the Greek cause.
>
> It was the lower classes that are the most sensitive to misfortune and also the most constantly generous. Artists, too, have come out in favor of the oppressed Greeks.

All of this shows that rumors and information were widely disseminated beyond the written press, and that the whole society had discovered a form of activism that was not built on the model of visits to the poor. On the contrary, in this case the poor were being solicited, and this was the guarantee of their subjective insertion into the political sphere.

Barère's papers include another 1826 leaflet evoking the military intervention of allied Russia, England, and France, which was to take place in 1827. The leaflet ends with these words: "Courage, generous orators, citizens of goodwill, compassionate women, inspired poets! One word can decide everything as one word can bring everything to an end." The values cited were in line with an enthusiasm that was defined, with increasing intensity, by generosity, a more structured charity, a more intimate compassion, and holy inspiration. Women's role as intermediaries in a highly political matter caused them to be seen outside of the usual sexual division of society. They had become actors, and this earned them visibility. Period representations of them, in lithographs or illustrated plates, were quite accurate. They were shown in the majesty of the finery befitting their social standing, in beribboned, plumed hats and flounced dresses, or as in the fashion plates, but—the detail is significant—counting stacks of coins (*Le Frondeur*, 31 May 1826). On the other hand, the historical plates by Bove show them only in the act of handing over a purse to a man from the Greek Committee (depicted as Chateaubriand, although it should have been Ternaux, the committee's president). Women had entered the realm of symbolic representation, and this, in itself, revealed a process of acknowledgement. It was a process that went beyond sentimental expressiveness, even though the very Christian context of the emotion surfaced everywhere, as on the collectors' certificates, under the heading "Appel aux Français" (Appeal to the French). These bore the verse from Paul's Epistle to the Hebrews (13:3): "Remember them that are in bonds, as bound with them; and them which suffer adversity, as being yourselves also in the body."

Policing Society the Polis

In France, then, the matter was transformed into a privileged form of political opposition that cut across society and was entrusted for a brief moment to women. This French peculiarity calls, nonetheless, for certain secondary considerations. French women of the time could be compared neither to Joan of Arc nor to Saint Geneviève, standing alone in the face of the enemy. Heroism was in the representations of the Greek adventure, such as the invention of Robelina attacking a ship with sword drawn, the engravings by Bove that put the women of Missolonghi in the breach, or a young girl battling face to face with a pasha, as on the plates from Montereau or Toulouse. If they were playing Joan of Arc in Paris, it was in performances of Soumet's *Jeanne d'Arc*, and it was in Zante that Sophocles' *Antigone* was staged. On the other hand, in Paris more than elsewhere in Europe, women were in the forefront because of the tense situation that was expressed in the *Villeliade*, a pamphlet attacking Villèle. Their heroic deeds may be analyzed this way: they were playing the part of moderators, as we would say today, by providing a means of expression for the rampant discontent, in the midst of the rebellious districts. When Prefect Delavau closed the highly respectable club in the rue de Gramont, where 400 fine notables of Paris met, he found himself one month later faced with an elusive network soliciting funds out in the streets and women who were untouchable because of their rank. When the repeal of the law of primogeniture was announced, sanctioning a governmental retreat, and the rue Bertin-Poirée, the rue Plat-d'Étain, the rue des Lombards, and the rue des Lavandières-Sainte-Opportune were lit, all they could think of doing was to send "rioters" to break some windows. When he used *Le Drapeau blanc* and *L'éltoile*, mockery of shopkeepers, or when he treated the collaborators of *Le Constitutionnel* as "proletarian rabble," he had to endure, in these same streets and in a vein of heroism and Pauline compassion, the quintessence of high society in the person of these women. It was not about throwing "women" into "the street," but about high-society women *being* out in the street, replacing provocation with a fully visible form of legal opposition. This opposition took place in the dual silence of the actors—that of the collectors and that of the donors—but this silent gesture put the potential barricades at a distance. At the banquet given at a restaurant called the Cadran Bleu in Paris on 4 July for the 50th anniversary of American independence, in the presence of La

Fayette and his son-in-law Lasteyrie, it was with a certain finesse that a Mr. Bradfort, from New York, made a toast "To the lady collectors of the Greek Committee of Paris! Their husbands must be proud to have such wives, and if France is asked to show her finest jewels, she will show her daughters!" It was as if he had fully grasped the success of a novel tactic: the occupation of the public arena by women. This, of course, was before the barricades—which went up again the following year, and then took over in 1830—framed the issue of the will of the people in completely different terms.

Elsewhere in Europe, as we have seen, fundraising efforts and concerts were organized in 1826. This was especially true in The Netherlands, where taking up collections was a customary practice, but usually under the control of male notables. At the end of May, a highly successful concert at Anderlecht was organized in a week: despite torrential rains, 2,500 tickets at 3 florins each were sold. In Liège, an appeal to the ladies seemed to have aroused interest, but youths from the university and local industry immediately formed a committee in order to better defend the interests of Walloon industry: the issue was to send locally manufactured arms and woolen cloth rather than money, and the speed of the reaction of the notables can be followed through the reports in the local daily paper, *Mathias Laensbergh*. Antwerp and a few northern cities gave benefit concerts that were supplemented by the collections taken by the women (whose autonomy, however, was never identifiable). Moreover, in the north of the country, Friesland and Groningen had been severely stricken by an epidemic that had spread from the port, and this drained some of the public charity. At the same time, the efforts by the baron de Damas, one of the great names of French legitimism, seem to have played only a marginal role. On 21 June, he requested from the king and the interior minister "the authorization to go through the states in the name of the most heroic misfortune." The minister, L. Van Gobbelschroy, merely acknowledged receipt of the letter, on 3 July: international diplomacy and its unofficial endeavors, like the local strategies, had their own reasons.

In the German territories, the modes of intervention were also highly fragmented and based on private initiatives. The approaches were very different: the king of Bavaria was philhellenic, even before he saw the possibility of a throne for his son; a lover of antiquities, the king was incensed not to have acquired the *Venus de Milo*, and then composed enthusiastic verses on the Greek cause, which he financed sometimes in relative anonymity and sometimes quite openly. Then there was the rest of southern Germany, where, as Christoph Hauser has shown, for the extraparliamentary opposition these actions served as an introduction to later forms of bourgeois and liberal organization (see Hauser). By 1821–22, 271 German volunteers had embarked at Toulon to go to the aid of the Greeks (France only supplied 118 volunteers out of a world total of 423). If considered proportionately to the population, the figures show that support from Frankfurt-am-Main, Hamburg, Bremen, and Lübeck took the lead over the rural states of Mecklenburg, Hesse, Württemberg, Saxony, Baden, and, especially, Prussia or Bavaria. Collections were taken to support the German volunteers who would go to the aid of the Greeks. The organizers and collectors came from different sociocultural configurations, depending on the state. In Württemberg, the majority belonged to the state apparatus; in Bavaria, the cultural world predominated; in Baden, the structure was mixed. From early on, Stuttgart was a dynamic center. In Frankfurt, the merchants and booksellers initiated the movement. Only Cologne had a women's fundraising committee in 1826—that is, when the first wave of enthusiasm had waned, based on the very critical reports that came from the philhellenes present in Greece or on their return. Part of the German funds went through Paris, but more frequently the funds passed through Geneva, where the retired banker Jean-Gabriel Eynard used his fortune and his competence to serve the Greeks with tireless zeal.

By 1826 the London committee had foundered due to negligence and lack of interest. In September, Colonel Stanhope was asked for an explanation: he had failed to mobilize public opinion and to carry through the large-scale operations he had, to a greater or lesser degree, sponsored. A loan (at 5 percent and floated at 59, or very much under par) returned only 454,700 pounds in 1824 on the original 800,000 pounds. The 84 members of the committee were eminent figures of the worlds of culture, politics, and business, and cut across Tory-Whig divisions. As the committee's function was technical, women played a very limited role, despite their notable presence around the figure of Byron.

This brief comparative overview shows clearly that the active presence of women in the political sphere depended heavily on local political circumstances. Women functioned as intermediaries when the liberal aspirations of the time were blocked, although these, at the same time, did not recognize their civic individuality. Women then set themselves up as substitutes, governed by a project in which they played a minor part.

Bibliography

Manuscript Sources

Archives Départementales des Hautes-Pyrénées, Tarbes, France. Fonds Barère: F 109

Archives Générales du Royaume, Brussels. Fonds L. Van Gobbelschroy, no.7, April–September 1826

Archives Nationales, Paris. F⁷6722 [records of the Ministry of the Interior]

Reference Works

Agulhon, Maurice, *Le cercle dans la France bourgeoise, 1810–1848: Étude d'une mutation de sociabilité*, Paris: Colin, and École des Hautes Études en Sciences Sociales, 1977

Athanassoglou-Kallmyer, Nina M., *French Images from the Greek War of Independence, 1821–1830: Art and Politics under the Restoration*, New Haven, Connecticut: Yale University Press, 1989

Bénichou, Paul, *Le sacre de l'écrivain, 1750–1830: Essai sur l'avènement d'un pouvoir spirituel laïque dans la France moderne*, Paris: Corti, 1973; as *The Consecration of the Writer, 1750–1830*, translated by Mark K. Jensen, Lincoln: University of Nebraska Press, 1999

Bikelas, Démétrius, "Le philhellénisme en France," *Revue d'histoire diplomatique* (1891)

Boltanski, Luc, *La souffrance à distance: Morale humanitaire, médias et politique*, Paris: Métailié, and Diffusion Seuil, 1993; as *Distant Suffering: Morality, Media, and Politics*, translated by Graham Burchell, Cambridge and New York: Cambridge University Press, 1999

Bouvier-Bron, Michelle, *Jean-Gabriel Eynard (1775–1863) et le philhellénisme genevois*, Geneva: Association Gréco-Suisse Jean-Gabriel Eynard, 1963

Bouyssy, Maïté, "Trente ans après, Bertrand Barère sous la restauration ou la rhétorique du Ténare," Ph.D. diss., Université Paris I, 1993; see especially the chapter entitled "Le mémorial européen sur la Grèce au siècle"

Canat, René, *L'Hellénisme des romantiques*, 3 vols., Paris: Didier, 1951; see especially vol. 1, *La Grèce retrouvée*

Corbin, Alain, and Jean-Marie Mayeur, editors, *La barricade* (exhib. cat.), Paris: La Sorbonne, 1997

Dimakis, Jean, *La guerre de l'indépendaance grecque vue par la presse française de 1821 à 1824: Contribution à l'étude de l'opinion publique et du mouvement philhellénique en France*, Thessalonika, Greece: Institute for Balkan Studies, 1968

Dimopoulos, Aristide G., *L'opinion publique française et la révolution grecque, 1821–1827*, Nancy-Saint-Nicolas-de Port, France: Idoux, 1962

Droulia, Loukia, *Philhellénisme: Ouvrages inspirés par la guerre de l'indépendance Grecque, 1821–1833: Répertoire bibliographique*, Athens: Centre de Recherches Néo-Helléniques de la Fondation Nationale de la Recherche Scientifique, 1974

Dünki, Robert, *Aspekte des Philhellenismus in der Schweiz, 1821–1830*, Bern, Switzerland, and New York: Peter Lang, 1984

Duprat, Catherine, *Le temps des philanthropes: La philanthropie parisienne des Lumières à la monarchie de Juillet*, Paris: CTHS, 1993

Échinard, Pierre, *Grecs et philhellènes à Marseille: De la Révolution française à l'indépendance de la Grèce*, Marseille, France: Centre National de la Recherche Scientifique, 1973

La Grèce en révolte: Delacroix et les peintres français (1815–1848) (exhib. cat.), Paris: Réunion des Musées Nationaux, 1996

Hauser, Christoph, *Anfänge bürgerlicher Organisation: Philhellenismus und Frühliberalismus in Südwestdeutschland*, Göttingen, Germany: Vandenhoeck und Ruprecht, 1990

Institut Français d'Athènes, *Le philhellénisme dans la vie quotidienne en France, 1824–1830*, Paris: Institut Français d'Athènes, 1982

Isambert, Gaston, *L'indépendance grecque et l'Europe*, Paris: Plon-Nourrit, 1900

Penn, Virginia, "Philhellenism in England (1821–1827)," *The Slavonic Review* 14, no. 41 (January 1936)

Quack-Eustathiades, Régine, *Der deutsche Philhellenismus während des griechischen Freiheitskampfes, 1821–1827*, Munich: Oldenbourg, 1984

Spaenle, Ludwig, *Der Philhellenismus in Bayern, 1821–1832*, Munich: Hieronymus, 1990

Stendahl, *Chroniques pour l'Angleterre*, edited by Renée Denier and Keith G. McWatters, volume 8, Grenoble, France: ELLUG, and Villeurbanne: Programme Rhône-Alpes Recherches en sciences humaines, 1995

Stendahl, *Esquisses de la société parisienne de la politique et de la littérature*, edited by José-Luis Diaz and Henri Martineau, Paris: Sycomore, 1983

Tischler, Andreas, "Die philhellenische Bewegung der 1820'er Jahre in den preussischen Westprovinzen," Ph.D. diss., Universität zu Köln, 1981

Vidalenc, Jean, "Quelques aspects du philhellénisme français," *Annales de la faculté des lettres d'Aix* 28 (1954)

Wagner-Heidendal, Lutgard, *Het Filhellenisme in het koninkrijk der Nederlanden, 1821–1829: Een bijdrage tot de studie van de publieke opinie in het begin van de negentiende eeuw*, Brussels: Paleis der Academiën, 1972

UTOPIA AND COUNTERUTOPIA

Women in the Works of Charles Fourier

SIMONE DEBOUT-OLESZKIEWICZ

*S*OCIAL PROGRESS AND CHANGES *of historical period are brought about as a result of the progress of women towards liberty; and the decline of social orders is brought about as a result of the diminution of the liberty of women.*

This "general thesis" proposed by Charles Fourier was the fruit of the rule he adopted at the outset of his investigations. As he declared in the first pages of his first book, *Théorie des quatre mouvements et des déstinées générales* (1808; *The Theory of the Four Movements*), he had set himself a rule of "absolute doubt and absolute divergence," that is, "absolute doubt about all prejudices, and absolute divergence from all known theories"; it was a twofold goal whose effects held together and reinforced each other: lifting the veil of prejudice was to uncover a different scene, and reveal all that was repressed and travestied beneath the masks.

Building on the Ruins of Revolutionary Ideology: The "Exact Sciences" and Passionate Harmony

In *The Theory of the Four Movements*, Fourier asserts: "The catastrophe of 1793 dispelled all illusions . . . no good was to be anticipated from any of the enlightenment accumulated thus far." In their drive to ensure social good and secure their own power, fanatical "agitators" had unleashed the blind fury of the crowds. And the philosophy of the Age of Enlightenment, which had served to mask this drive for power, had been tainted with the blood of the massacres. If Fourier continued, during the Empire and the Restoration, to inveigh against the "Executioner from Arras" [Robespierre], this was because, for him, the Revolution remained the decisive event, with all that followed being merely the consequence of its failure, its violence and disorder. The issue, then, was not to deny the revolutionary turmoil or its causes and effects, but to find another way of fulfilling its unaccomplished legacy—the demand for justice and the access of the masses to the public sphere. What was needed was a

balance between the passions of the multitude and reason; an understanding of the laws of social movement; and, finally, the creation of a just social organization that would bring out the hidden qualities of every individual and allow each person to achieve his or her particular perfection.

In *The Theory of the Four Movements*, Fourier, the architect of Harmony, contrasts the "inexact sciences" of philosophy and politics with the "exact sciences" of mathematics and physics; he replaces ideological abstractions with an affective, psychological reality, and provides a "calculus" of its full development "in society." He challenges "the economism that was invading the entire domain of charlatanism" and argues instead for the preeminence of a fundamental human relationship, the relationship between the sexes. "Other events," he concedes, "influence political vicissitudes, but there is no cause which produces such rapid social progress or decline as does the change in women's lot." This reversal in the order of causes changes both their meaning and their impact: what the philosophers and politicians have failed to heed is, for Fourier, essential—or in his terms "pivotal"—that is, the seat of social movement and its transformations. Thus, in his analysis in *The Theory of the Four Movements* of the history of humankind—which he traces from prehistory to the end of time—he distinguishes several "phases" which he divides into "periods," each characterized by a particular state of industry; but this industry (taken in its broad sense of activities producing goods), far from determining everything, expresses and reinforces the forms of human relations and variations in degree of liberty or oppression in society.

In the first period, "men emerged happy from the hands of God because they were able to organize a society with series," that is, a society that allowed "passions to develop." Yet, these happy, "confused series" of the earliest times became disorganized when the "too-rapid multiplication of clans produced poverty." Knowing no industry, theirs became but "the shadow of happiness," for "agriculture was hard, still in its infancy, and unable to provide the overabundance of food necessary to the mechanism of series." Such an abundance of food was necessary, yet not sufficient on its own. Knowledge and technology had made such enormous progress since then that the organization of society into "progressive" or "passionate series" should long have been possible. Fourier envisions these series as being constructed on the model of a musical scale, in which the different notes corresponded to the various passions. Progressively raised to their highest powers, and in one immense symphony "of several million instruments," the series will be organized to integrate and combine every social function and the entire range of individual characters or qualities, from the simplest to the most complex. And, doubtless, Harmony will be all the more resplendent for having been postponed. However, far from contributing to the advent of Harmony, "social industry is afflicted with scourges, such as poverty, unemployment, thriving dishonesty, piracy on the seas, commercial monopolies, the abduction of slaves, and so many other misfortunes." All these phenomena indicate, for Fourier, that there exists "in this industry some reversal of the natural order, ... and that the persistence of so many scourges could be attributed to the absence of some form of organization," or to an evil spell that has caused "industrial progress itself to turn into the seed of unhappiness," and "poverty to be born in a civilization of abundance."

Fourier's penetrating vision swept through space and time, from near to far and past to future, pinpointing the existence, at all times, of "the tenacity of subversive afflictions, poverty, deceit, oppression and carnage." It was a virulent criticism, which was generally better appreciated than his construction and dream of Harmony. Although the latter has tended to be overshadowed, both are the expression of Fourier's unique viewpoint, and the vision of the imagined good certainly served to heighten his ability to distinguish the reality of evil. May we not, then, pose the question anew: is Fourier's positive message as compelling as his diatribe?

Any attempt to answer this question requires a patient examination of the author's entire work, following him through the developments of his thought in order to seek out the full significance of those curt early declarations. His writings demand an active reading if we are to decipher and explicate the unwritten implications of the written text. Fourier's bold vision of material and spiritual movement, his interlacing of the course of events with individual and collective development, require from his readers an effort of imagination, the pursuit of a quest that will, by definition, be incomplete and resolutely turned toward the future.

In *The Theory of the Four Movements*, Fourier conjectures:

If human societies have, as Montesquieu believed, fallen victim to a "wasting disease, an inner vice, a secret, hidden venom," then the remedy might be found by diverging from the paths followed by our inexact sciences which, for so many centuries, have passed it by.

It is thus in opposition to the scholars, and "by endeavoring to address the problems they had never broached," that Fourier discovers both the vice and its remedy: the subjugation of women and their liberty.

The Relevance of Fourier Today

"The pivotal characteristic, which is always taken from amorous custom, leads automatically to the creation of all the others," Fourier posits in *The Theory of the Four Movements*,

but the secondary characteristics cannot give rise to the pivotal one, and they can only bring about a change of period very slowly. Barbarians could adopt up to twelve of the sixteen Civilized characteristics and still remain Barbarians if they failed to adopt the pivotal characteristic, the civil liberty of an exclusive wife.

On the other hand, he argues, "if we adopted the confinement and sale of women, we would rapidly become Barbarians as a result of that one innovation."

This argument should be less surprising for us today than it was at the time Fourier made it, since it is the logic of those women in some Islamic societies who are currently resisting fundamentalists, who seek to take back the liberties women have claimed. Such activist women object to the fact that women are forced to wear the veil, a symbol of submission; it is a shroud, they say, that turns women into ghosts, and, in the street, excludes them from the public space as the harem walls once did. The protesters assert that this social regression, together with economic difficulties, will precipitate the decline of society.

This present-day echo shows the continuing relevance of Fourier's writings and their connection to current events. Moreover, he deemed experience to be "a pivotal compass." However, since Fourier's conjecture about "barbarians" remained hypothetical, he instead lay claim to the guarantee of divine psychology:

If God gave amorous customs so much influence over the social mechanism and the transformations it undergoes, this was because of his horror of oppression and violence. It was his will that the happiness or unhappiness of human societies should be proportionate to the degree of constraint or liberty they allowed. (*The Theory of the Four Movements*),

Clearly, here, the utopian Fourier is projecting his own "horror of oppression" and his conviction that the paths of love lead to liberty. To stop at that conclusion, however, would be to miss the essential: in Fourier's view, God is the metaphor for the forces of love, "the most beautiful of passions," combining sexual desire and sentiment, the spirit and the body; without this, "for God himself there is no joy." This recourse to transcendence served to heighten a human experience. "God, fire, nature, passion" was the eminent representation of that primeval power of relationships, which, in its full and just development, would regenerate everything and lead societies and nature itself to their heights; but, if repressed, its "false and subversive development" would relentlessly drive the planet and all its inhabitants to disaster.

Fourier's metaphysics is form of metapsychology. It finds a surprising echo in one of Sigmund Freud's last works, *Das Unbehagen in der Kultur* (1930; *Civilization and Its Discontents*), in which he ponders the future of humanity:

The fateful question for the human species seems to me to be whether and to what extent their cultural development will succeed in mastering the disturbance of their communal life by the human instinct of aggression and self-destruction ... Men have gained control over the forces of nature to such an extent that with their help they would have no difficulty in exterminating one another to the last man.

Fourier, the visionary, expresses his own profound sense of the unhappiness of humanity and the dangers of science in terms of the fantastic. "A legion of stars has already set out to destroy the rebellious globe," he warns in *The Theory of the Four Movements*. An extravagant image, but the author left indications that its meaning was to be sought beyond words. In the margin of an unpublished manuscript (now preserved in the French National Archives), he noted succinctly, "proof that they are incapable of invention, take images literally." This lucid reflection was no doubt provoked by his critics, but it nonetheless indicates Fourier's use of "images" to represent what could not yet be made rationally explicit. Above all, he wishes to give tangible form and a sense of immediacy to the dire verdict of the universe, and to the dangers of the boomerang effect of the "noxious aromas" that civilized society discharges into the atmosphere.

More than a century after Fourier, these dangers remained relevant. "Men . . . know this," Freud argues, "and hence comes a large part of their current unrest, their unhappiness and their mood of anxiety." He also suggests the remedy: "And now it is to be expected that the other of the two 'Heavenly Powers,' eternal Eros, will make an effort to assert himself in the struggle with his equally immortal adversary," adding, "But who can foresee with what success and with what result?"

For Fourier, of course, the forces of dissociation and death do not stem from an immortal power, but from the reversal of passionate movement, from egoism—that is, from the "countermarch of Unityism, the source and synthesis of all passions," from a perverse withdrawal and a transference of desire to the self alone, which interrupts and depraves the natural movement toward others and the world. Evil is thus not rooted in the human being; it is contingent, the effect of ill will or a misunderstanding, and it can be not only neutralized and overcome, but totally "absorbed" by a full and just development of passion. However, Fourier believes that the danger is becoming acute. The growing disproportion between knowledge of the material and ignorance of the passionate threatens to drive everything into the abyss "after a fatal period of time": a time of reprieve during which all will be saved if the civilized do not persist in their iniquity, lies, and injustice.

Freud conceives of the life force and the death force as two basic instincts comparable to the pair of opposites—attraction and repulsion—that reign in the inorganic world. For Fourier, who was fascinated by Newtonian physics and particularly by the unitary science of Johannes Kepler (1571–1630)—one of the few books he owned, and which he kept throughout his life, was a copy of Kepler's *Harmonices Mundi* (1619; *The Harmony of the World*)—the opposition between attraction and repulsion is an active hierarchy: "Passionate movement is the typical movement and the model for all the other movements, instinctive, organic, and material."

Mocking philosophers, who believed they held the secret of existence, and scholars, who believe they have grasped reality when they are merely projecting their own constructions, Fourier elaborates a dynamic gradation that legitimates his goal of a universal mathematical science while confirming the preeminence of a human reality of the passions and its harmful or beneficial influence. Thus, nature's ferocious wild beasts, venoms, volcanoes, and putrid swamps are seen as "the end points" of human beings' deviated movements; nature itself is a demonic realm,

such as "hell in its fury" might have imagined, which human beings have been called upon to transform. Once they have progressed from their incoherent societies to Harmony, they will "act in concert with God," and lions and zebras will become marvelous servants, climates will become temperate, and the sea will turn into a delicious drink. In this dream we can see the interlacing of an ingenuous metaphysics with an acute awareness of the far-reaching effects of social order and disorder.

There is thus no dualism, no rigid Manichaeism, in Fourier's doctrine, but rather a unity of system in which happiness and misfortune, on earth and in the heavens, are the results of the two possible paths of development of passionate attractions. And since these attractions operate between two or more poles, their effects are not produced by isolated individuals, but rather by the relationships that are established between them and that give rise to one another, so that good and evil are spread without anyone directly causing or having control over them. Thus, the tyrant may believe that he is imposing his law, Fourier argues, but he merely finds himself entrapped in his own snares.

It is therefore necessary to distance oneself, to remove oneself from the system in order to detect the rampant poison that proliferates in a chain reaction and corrupts everything. That poison, Fourier declares, is contempt for women, the negative view of their difference as a deficiency of mind and body. This scornful misconception has been used to justify the domination of the male sex and injustice to women; it has endured throughout Savage, Barbarian, and Civilized societies despite the evolution of morality and culture.

For Freud, the only hope in the face of such dangers was that the forces of love would vanquish the forces of death. However, noting the tendencies to restrain sexual life and thus freedom in love, he, unlike Fourier, upheld the foundations of these tendencies "as though they were necessities of nature." In Freud's analysis of female deficiency and its development, female difference consistently represents the inferior and dangerous part of the human, the part that needs to be controlled and overcome, in constant reference to the masculine model and to the reigning phallus, symbol of the powers of body and mind.

Origins of Male Domination

Fourier poses a pertinent question that challenges the superiority to which men lay claim. Is it themselves they fear, he asks, or the women they have subjugated? In other words, are they afraid of that cursed part they have attributed to women, or of what women could be if they were free? "Men already seem to have a presentiment of this," he observes, "they become indignant and alarmed when women belie the prejudice that accuses them of inferiority." Fourier attacks this prejudice at its source—that is, the will to dominate, which finds its justification precisely in the effects it induces: "Any attempt to judge women by the vicious character they display in Civilization is akin to judging men by the character of the Russian peasant, . . . or to judging beavers by the stupefaction they show in captivity," that is, in situations where they became "so inferior to their destiny and capacities that one is inclined to despise them if one judges them superficially by appearances." By unifying all the oppressed, Fourier seeks to show that subjugation debases even animals and ravages all relations humans have with one another and with nature.

If, for him, "amorous customs" are the pivot of social progress or decline, this is because by treating women as goods that can be acquired, owned, and disposed of, men have perverted the primordial exchange that should have ensured human circulation. The prohibition of incest was nothing but a variant of commercial practices between male partners whose authority depended on what they could barter or convert into cash. Women, who in many societies bore the name of the currency, were merely the principal opportunity for or means of exchange. The dominant sex, by treating women as goods, had placed all relations under the empire of the marketplace.

> If the sale of women is indeed an institution in Barbarian societies, what is the "young girl" in Civilization, if not a piece of merchandise exhibited for sale to whomever wants to negotiate her acquisition and exclusive ownership? Is not the consent she gives to the conjugal bond derisory, and enforced upon her by the tyranny of all the prejudices that have beset her since childhood?

Albeit in a veiled and hypocritical form, with "chains woven of flowers," women continued to be bound and "fashioned from birth to stifle their nature." And men, fortified by the debasement they had caused, wondered whether women were altogether human.

"In those crude times," Fourier reminds us in *The Theory of the Four Movements*, "the Council of Mâcon, a true council of vandals, deliberated the question of whether women had a soul, and decided in the affirmative by a majority of only three votes." However, the legend Fourier invokes here is erroneous. The bishop who declared that a woman could not be called Man was, in fact, admonished by his peers with the objection that God had given his creatures of both sexes the name—and the reality—of human being.

Whatever the truth in those events may have been, Fourier singled out his targets and adjusted his fire. "The Turks," he wrote, "teach women that they have no soul, and the French, that they have no genius." Was physical strength then the measure of genius? he asked. Stendhal—who appreciated Fourier, calling him a "sublime dreamer"—provided a fitting rejoinder in his *Mémoires d'un touriste* (1838; *Memoirs of a Tourist*): "Any genius born a woman is lost to humanity," he wrote, for the seeds of genius are stifled before they can develop. "A man without education is inferior to a brute," observes Fourier along the same lines. "Unlike the lion, a man deprived of the lessons of education cannot become the equal of his fellow creatures." Women, however, were taught "to mind the stew-pot" or some other trifling accomplishment; their minds were dulled and then they were accused of ignorance and frivolity. Citing a famous text by Denis Diderot, *Sur les femmes* (1772; *On Women*), Fourier asks,

> What can be more inconsistent than Diderot's claim that to write to women *"you must dip your pen in the rainbow and sprinkle what you have written with the dust of butterfly wings"*? Women might reply to the philosophers: your Civilization persecutes us if we obey nature; we are obliged to behave artificially, and to attend only to promptings that go against our desires. In order to make us swallow your doctrines you have to play on our illusions and use the language of deceit, as you do with soldiers when you lull them with promises of laurels and immortality to make them forget their wretched situation.

Refuting this disdain and deceit, Fourier observes ironically, "A surprising thing is that women have always shown themselves superior to men when they have been able to develop their natural ability on the throne." Further, if some women's reigns had not been outstanding, it was because, like Mary Stuart, they had been "hesitant and evasive in the face of amorous prejudices," which they should have trampled underfoot; but when indeed they had resolved to take this course, which men could be said to have made better monarchs?

For Fourier, then, the seat of the feminine nature and its development was amorous freedom. Catherine the Great of Russia used and abused this and "trampled the male sex underfoot." "By her appointment of favorites, she dragged man through the mud and proved that he could . . . debase himself further than woman, whose degradation is forced on her and therefore excusable." In Fourier's view, voluntary servitude is more despicable than imposed slavery, and he rebukes men: "Would not you, the oppressor sex, surpass the faults with which you reproach women if a servile education had trained you like them . . . to crawl before a master that chance has brought you?"

Catherine the Great, by acting like a man, transferred the injustice: she was sufficiently powerful to confound men's claims to superiority but did nothing for the emancipation of women. Her contempt for prejudice thus had only a negative social value. Being the ruler, she had no need to fear the affront that "denied learned women honors" and relegated them "ignominiously to the home." But, Fourier adds, "Indeed, have they not deserved this disdain by seeking to ape their master" instead of "producing liberators, not writers, political Spartacuses, geniuses who could plan ways of leading their sex out of degradation?"

If female sovereigns and women who "had been able to spread their wings" had failed in this way, it was because they had "espoused philosophical selfishness"—male and philosophical being one and the same for Fourier. To clarify this collusion, he denounces the inflated use of a word that assigned a substratum to the reversal of desire: "The self, a new word that says nothing new, is a useless paraphrase for egoism." Fourier's sentence could have served as an epigraph to François de La Rochefoucauld's maxims (many of which deal with self-love), but it was René Descartes who was the butt of Fourier's taunts: "He raised absurd doubts" about the tangible world and his own body, admitting of only one unquestionable existence, that of the conscious self; this conscious self, it was true, existed as surely when it felt as when it thought, but since all that was perceived through the senses gave rise to doubt and therefore was to no avail, the "I" would be doomed to solitude and illusion if it did not miraculously possess the innate ideas from which all knowledge was developed.

This was a "partial and inappropriate doubt" which overevaluated the self and depreciated the contribution of the senses. "It is the soul that sees, and not the eye," claimed Descartes in the Sixth Discourse of *La Dioptrique* (1637; *Dioptrics*). The implication here is that the blind are better able to see the truth of the tangible with the eyes of the soul than the sighted, who are misled by illusory images from which they need to free themselves. All knowledge, thus, is no more than recollection, and all dialogue a monologue, the occasion to remember and to awaken to oneself. Whether the true unfolds separately, or immutable categories necessitate the intuition of the senses they inform, the subject can expect nothing new from others or from things, nothing that might transform the a priori assumptions that constitute the thinking being.

In opposition to this, Fourier advocates a moving out from the center and the thrust of inner latencies that incessantly call into question the identity of the self; "bombastic" philosophy, which relates everything to the rational subject, is only able to perceive the other as a lesser being or an inaccessible mystery.

Philosophers, according to Fourier, wish to control and possess nature, but are unaware of that inexhaustible, active impulse that challenges the mind and stimulates scientific invention. They know nothing of "the intentional nature of men," the expansive power that carries individuals outside of themselves toward what they are not, and yet is the source of their being and becoming. Reduced to the preservation of self, individuals can thus only assert themselves in struggle, not with and in the world, but against it. They transform trusting activity and the spontaneous drive to reach out to others and things into a defensive, aggressive reaction.

"The oppression of the weaker sex," Fourier stresses, "destroys justice at its basis." But his acid criticism of the aloof withdrawal of the philosopher and the pretension of the male sex is directed, beyond these, at the source of social division and injustice: the refusal, direct or indirect, passionate or premeditated, of otherness and of sensuality, and the cleavage that separates man from the world and from his own "intentional nature." In his analysis of the trials and tribulations of humanity, Fourier notes three "accidents" that have contributed to entrenching the spirit of the oppressor in modern men: (1) "The introduction of venereal disease, the danger of which has transformed sensual pleasure into debauchery, and tends to restrict the freedom of liaison between the sexes"; (2) the influence of Catholicism, and its "dogmas hostile to sensual delight"; and (3) "the birth of Mohammedanism [sic], which increased the misery and degradation of women in Barbarism, and thereby made the less deplorable condition of women in Civilization appear in a misleadingly positive light."

In this "fabric of fatalities," the diseases of the body and the mind had combined to "close the way to any improvement in the lot of women" and to any easing of amorous constraints. These "accidents" merely reinforced the fundamental prejudice and its repercussions. "Thus," Fourier argues in *Le nouveau monde industriel et sociétaire* (1829–30; The New Industrial and Societal World),

> the philosophers who tyrannically seek to exclude one of the sexes from employment are like those villainous colonists in the Antilles who first, with their torture, stupefy their Negroes who are already stupefied by their barbarian education, and then claim that these Negroes are not on a level with the human species. The opinion of philosophers about women is as just as the opinion of colonists about Negroes.

The cause of women went hand in hand with that of black slaves, or wage-earners constrained by poverty to do forced labor in "mercantile penal colonies," for they were all subjected to the same double injustice: their minds and their existences were diminished, and then they were accused of the vices this produced.

It was this cycle of oppression and debasement to which the 1789 Déclaration des Droits de l'Homme et du Citoyen (Declaration of the Rights of Man and the Citizen) had sought to put an end, with the proclamation of equality for all human beings. The declared universality, however, had remained abstract. To universal rights, which were widely flouted, Fourier—the realistic utopian—preferred the gradual achievement of personal rights in reciprocal progression. A caustic critic, he conceded that the social order was "still making some progress; but how slow they are to envision and execute the good!" When, at last, they put their minds to it, "the attempts of modern men to emancipate Negroes have resulted only in a torrential shedding of blood, and in exacerbating the misery of those they have sought to serve." Why? "Because our sciences, which boast of their love for the people, are completely ignorant of the means to protect them." Without this, progress can only be made at the price of centuries of turbulent experimentation:

> The progress of our societies is rather like that of the sloth, whose every step is marked by a groan. Like the sloth, Civilization moves forward with unimaginable slowness . . . with each generation, it tries new systems that serve only . . . to stain with blood the peoples that seize upon them.

Hence Fourier identifies the need to search beyond ideologies and to confound "those modern Titans," scholars, philosophers, and politicians alike.

The above developments and analyses serve to clarify the preliminary affirmations in *The Theory of the Four Movements*: "The seeds of social good all have no pivot other than the progressive emancipation of the weaker sex," Fourier declares, later noting: "To sum up, the extension of the privileges of women is the basic principle of all social progress." The words "progressive" and "privilege" are deserving of our attention, for they were not chosen at random. Fourier was not afraid of rhetoric; he could be verbose and appear disorganized, but he also knew how to find the right phrasing and to capture the essential with one stroke of the pen.

Disadvantages of Marriage and Paths to Freedom

If women play the role in Fourier's societal doctrine that proletarians play for Marxists, it was not his idea that these humiliated beings would suddenly rise from being nothing to becoming everything. That would be switching oppressors and perpetuating the constraints or exacerbating the disorder and depravity that, in Civilization, produced injustice and half-freedoms. Fidelity and chastity were demanded of women, while fickle men were called "lovable rakes." "What singular inconsequence, for the conduct that in one sex is found lovable and in the other odious is necessarily a reciprocal conduct, since men, unless they have a closed harem, cannot have 20 women consecutively without the women having 20 men consecutively." It was the husbands who paid the price of this incoherence, and their misfortune stimulated Fourier's satirical verve. In *The Theory of the*

Four Movements he establishes a "hierarchy of cuckoldry" in which he grades 60 (or 120) species of cuckolds in 9 degrees, and 3 main classes, these being: the "common cuckold," a respectable, jealous man unaware of his disgrace; the "short-horned cuckold," the husband who was "sated with love in his own household and who, wanting to take his pleasures elsewhere, turned a blind eye to his wife's conduct"; and "the long-horned cuckold," an absurdly jealous and wrathful man whose attempts to rebel against the decrees of destiny made him an object of ridicule, like "Molière's George Dandin."

But what about the lover, Fourier asks, "the athlete," who suffers "without a murmur" the husband's threats to pursue "seducers." Was he not often the more humiliated and ridiculous of the two? He was debased not only by his diplomacy toward the husband and the flattery he extended even to the lapdog of the house, but also by the "trickery of the lady who assures him she no longer lives with her husband." Yet, "can he really be unaware that she is redoubling her attentions [to her husband] in order to hide her intrigue" and possibly attribute paternity of her "heterogeneous offspring" to him? In the one case in which the woman was guilty, she enjoyed "the full protection of the law . . . and public opinion." "Oh! how can Civilized men, so persecutory when it comes to their wives' pleasure," show such good-natured tolerance of "the fruit of obvious adultery"? He concludes caustically: "Here indeed we see the fulfillment of philosophy's design, for it is truly in marriage that men form a family of brothers where possessions are [held in] common." Switching from his humorous tone, he declares: "If lovers find powerful motives for reconciling this sharing with self-esteem, delicacy, and sentiment," their accommodating attitude (and that of the husbands) is the sign of a "friendly sharing in love, a seed of direct or sociable development; this is the embryo that should be developed" instead of the scandalous constraints and contradictions "that reign in amorous matters." Did not religion and the theaters "publicly preach a contradictory morality," leading young women alternatively to take lessons in austerity from the church and in gallantry and deceit from the circus? And, he concludes: "God knows which of the two lessons bears the more fruit!"

There was thus no such thing as what Fourier ironically calls the "neo-perfectibility of perfectible civilization." Indeed, he believed that civilization was growing increasingly unstable, for it was beset by forces that were repressed but not destroyed, and was subjected to the "recurrent action" of constrained passions, "as harmful as, in their full blooming, they would have been beneficial." Yet, for Fourier, a consideration of the "valuable qualities" that amorous freedom developed in "the classes who most enjoy it" enabled one to foresee what a less oppressive order would produce. "Ladies of the court (the gallant ones, I mean)" he observes, "have frank, easy manners, and an exuberance which inspires friendship." Moreover, "high-class courtesans, leaving aside a degree of stratagem their kind of trade requires . . . are obliging, charitable, and cordial. . . . Their character would be sublime if they had a good income, witness that of Ninon." Finally, the "petty-bourgeois women, shopgirls, workers, etc." who were economically independent were completely free; before marriage, they flitted from man to man, and as a result, were all the better at their work.

These exceptional women possessed qualities that, when taken together, would raise "the female character to perfection."

"Being used to pleasure," they lose "that slyness, those sensual ulterior motives so noticeable in bourgeois women steeped in morality, in those housewives whose displays of sentiment constantly reveal a sensuality which they insist on denying," but which obsesses them and obliterates "the affections of the soul."

Fourier found that certain "gallant ladies" possessed "far more reason than did men." He notes:

> On several occasions, they have given me new ideas which provided me with most unexpected solutions. I have often been obliged to women of what is called the spontaneous class for valuable solutions to problems that had tortured me. I have never received aid of this kind from men.

In order to follow Fourier on the path to Harmony, what was needed was a lighthearted spontaneity or the ingenuousness of children, "the only class on which the full development of attraction can be safely tested."

Indeed, everything would be different if, from the age of three or younger, each child's promising seeds and latent riches were developed rather than being oppressed by rules and restrictions. "Education is a second mother," contends Fourier, capable of stifling what it should be bringing to life. Women, in particular, spent their childhood as "moral slaves," after which they were prepared for "shrewdness and guile" before finally being given up to the mercy of some "old fogey." They were deceived and deluded during their youth, then later abandoned and forgotten. Their nature, according to Fourier, had been so profoundly distorted that it would take two to three generations for them to achieve complete emancipation. Furthermore, the harmonious education of both sexes would require the transformation of educators and social environment alike, and could "only take place in the progressive series or combined order"; only then would it be seen that nature is not sparing of her talents, but is "on the contrary, prodigal far beyond our needs or desires." But it was necessary to know how to discover and develop the "seeds," and this was precisely what "the Civilized know as little about as the Savages knew about mining before the arrival of the Europeans." Since natural talents were distributed randomly between the two sexes, any individual, man or woman, was "virtually capable of equaling one of the most eminent figures." In Harmony, there would be thousands of poets equal to Homer, mathematicians equal to Sir Isaac Newton, and actors equal to Molière, and the same would hold "for all the talents imaginable." In order develop each person's hidden riches, education would be unitary, integral, and individual. All exclusive and uniform methods would be banished, the goal being both to link all individuals together and to lead each one to his or her own perfection: "All will be free, or none will be free."

In the new order, children would learn to harmonize their gestures and their voices in a well-ordered arrangement of ballets and choirs, and to organize these around the soloists whose perfection they would sustain. During adolescence, the majority of girls would be in "little Bands" and would be responsible for cultivating the flowers in the garden as well as those of a fine mind and beautiful language, while the boys, in their "little Hordes," would learn to transform their taste for danger and dirt into noble courage and devotion; their task would be to destroy vermin and refuse. There would be some exceptions: refined and delicate boys would join the little Bands, while bold and adventurous girls would be in the little Hordes.

"Toddlers" would be in the kitchen, boys and girls alike, where they would learn to recognize plants and animals and make themselves useful by doing small tasks appropriate to their age. Formal studies would begin later, toward the age of nine or ten, when "seraphim" of both sexes (with no distinction between them) would learn literature and science; they would be encouraged to subject everything they were taught to close scrutiny, criticism, and discussion.

At the age of 18, young people would attain their "amorous majority"; "damsels" and "squires" would choose lovers, whereas "vestals" (male *vestals* and female *vestales*), would devote themselves for a time to their studies and the arts. However, these options could be reviewed at any time. There would thus be an equality of freedom, which Fourier's terminology served to symbolize and to guarantee. There would be no more obligation for unmarried women to remain chaste virgins until their marriage, while young boys gained immediate access to the status of men and to sexual life. The words "damsels and squires" and the male and female versions of "vestals" served both to distinguish and to unify the chances of amorous liberty for each of the sexes.

Imposed relationships would thus no longer exist. Children would be raised in the open air of the world, and parents' only responsibilities would be to "spoil" them and love them. Furthermore, parents who wished to do so could choose adoptive children, just as children would be able to freely choose their parents. There would be no more enforced dissimulation or imposed reciprocal duties. Open families and the disappearance of marriage would do away with lies and oppression.

Fourier is tireless on the subject of the drawbacks of marriage, listing the most serious to the most futile, ranging from the risk of unhappiness due to incompatibility of character to increased expenses, which the association in the new order would reduce while improving the quality of meals and service. "The example I shall take," he states, "is care of the wine cellar"; for lack of "knowledge of enology, which is difficult to acquire," three-quarters of rich households have "adulterated and badly kept wines" because they are deceived by "wine merchants . . . and by hired cellarmen whose only skill is cheating."

His main emphasis, however, is on the monotony of marital life, which men flee to be with their mistresses, or to go to clubs where they can escape the constraints of the home but where they remain in a self-contained world of men, deprived of the contrasts that would liven up their encounters. Nonetheless, notes Fourier, "an embryonic form of the progressive household can be perceived in our large cities, in clubs or casinos for men and women" that provide "inexpensive balls and concerts, and a store of games, newspapers and other distractions." However, these places did not provide for self-fulfillment; they failed to organize unequal, rival groups, or to "balance" the exchange of partners; they were unable to imagine and even less able to put into practice the "amorous code" of the progressive household, which was soon to annihilate the Civilized order "without any political upheaval and to the great astonishment of all."

In the meantime, however, it was Fourier's turn to be astonished: "Stupid Civilization has only been able to imagine the worst of bonds, the forced bond, that of the couple. Could it do less than imagine what most animals discover about the question? He altars bend so servilely to prejudices about love, which are not even to the advantage of men?"

Fourier returns repeatedly to the issues at stake during those times of innovation and political upheaval: "It would have taken so little for the vandalism of 1793 to suddenly produce a second revolution as marvelous as the first was horrible. The whole of humankind was within sight of deliverance" (*Égarement de la raison* (1847; Reason Led Astray in "La Phalange," Rovue de la Science Sociale). But the prejudice of marriage had not been crushed during the Revolution. The deep motivations for this failure, he claims, lay in the refusal of the revolutionaries to cross certain limits. "The agitators unleash and use the universal tendency of wage-earners to reform 'the Horde,' a volcano waiting to swallow up Civilization," argues Fourier, "but they are quick to silence the people and subjugate them all the more." In 1793 the revolutionaries had crushed patriarchal authority and decapitated the king in order to establish the power of the sons, brothers in philosophy. But it was a Pandora's box they had opened, for by maintaining the oppression of one half of humanity and of the supposedly sovereign people, they had paved the way for a new despotism, of which women, once again, were the first victims.

During the Empire and the Restoration, the Napoleonic Code and the bourgeois order reduced the liberties that the women activists had won during the upheaval, and those that 18th-century women aristocrats had gained by peaceful means. Attacks on the institution of marriage were punished more severely in the courts of law than were licentiousness or libertine scenes or images. Nonetheless, notes Fourier, "the Civilized order is indeed increasingly insecure. The first eruption of the volcano created by the philosophers in 1789 will be followed by others as soon as a weak ruler makes the conditions right for agitation" and for the conflicts compressed by tyranny to emerge.

> There is no point in trying to stop them . . . Revolutions can be started with the very measures we take to ensure calm, and if Civilization continues . . . how many children will be begging at the door of their father's house? . . . I would not dare present this hideous prospect if I was not able to offer the calculus that will guide politics through the maze of the passions

and free "the whole Earth, not just the corner of it occupied by Civilized man." In passing from the inertia of savagery to industry, humanity had exchanged a state of apathy for one of active pain, "a disquiet gnawed by desire even in the midst of opulence."

To those who ask, "Which path can be taken? Which guide can be trusted to find the way out?", Fourier's answer is lucid and ironic:

> Apostles of error! Moralists and Politicians! After so much evidence of your blindness, do you still claim that you can enlighten humankind? The nations will reply, "If your sciences dictated by wisdom have served only to perpetuate poverty and destruction, give us rather sciences dictated by folly, as long as they calm the furor and relieve the misery of the people."

Fourier claims as his goal precisely that for which he was to be criticized—a calculated folly, not reactive but wholly active, a madness not of war but of love, which will replace repression and rejection with a generous espousal of the thousand splendors of a shared world. Since this was to be a world in which an unlimited, multifaceted freedom would revolve around women's privileges, it was Fourier's task to define these privileges. Bold pioneer that he was, his answers will not disappoint the intrigued reader.

Fourier's theory attributes to women, as to all human beings, twelve primitive passions: five sensory passions corresponding to the five senses; four affective passions—love, "familism" (family feeling or parenthood), ambition, and friendship—which draw them toward groups and connections with others; and three distributive passions—the Composite, the Butterfly (or alternating), and the Cabalist (or intriguing) passions—which tend toward the formation of series and the combined order. Women are dominant in love, just as men are in ambition. To promote their privileges would merely be to grant them the amorous freedom they themselves will put into effect once emancipated. "Men have other opportunities for superiority. If they want to dominate everywhere, this would no longer be liberal honor but despotism," a selfish and destructive claim. "The passions have already forced the Civilized to become their allies," but men only admit [the passions] partially, and continue to restrict love. And since "a cart cannot ride on three wheels," everything is being driven into the abyss.

Fourier notes, however, that love and familism, which are "passions of a minor order," determine relationships or "chords" that are fewer in number and more difficult to establish than those created by ambition and friendship, "the major passions." Major and minor, here, are terms borrowed from music and are not intended to convey superiority or inferiority. On the contrary, the minor mode is more intimately moving and resonates more deeply. Love exalts and concentrates individual energy. It is an ardent impulse that projects the subject outside of the self, and thereby endows the loved one with an even greater reality. When love brings the double mystery of presence to self and the other to a point of incandescence, the world heretofore exhausted by apathy and indifference will be reborn; it will become a world impossible to doubt and rich in unexpected "charms." Love is the child of both wealth and poverty; it reveals unnoticed qualities, unknown aspects of the loved one; it unites the desire to dedicate the self, to come together willingly and to admire, to see, and to marvel.

This is a conception of love that differs radically from subjective interpretations. The most powerful of the passions cannot be reduced to a sensation of excitement, pleasure, or intimate pain over an illusory object that may just barely be capable of keeping the dream alive. Love is the "lantern that guides us through the darkness of the world," because it is the highest manifestation of the creative power of "the intentional nature of men." Passions are not inner states that beings are subjected to, but different modes of the power of receiving and giving.

By calling five of the passions "sensory," Fourier implies that sensory perception, which appears to be essentially passive, presupposes an activity or an initiative and therefore the power of transformation. There can be no sensation, no perception, and thus no knowledge, without the desire to see, hear, touch, feel, or taste; there can be no access to things or to others that does not imply some form of love, whatever its degree of intensity or actualization. And the moving union of lovers, of the seer and the visible, the feeler and the tangible, will create "composite charms" not contained in the isolated elements. Interweaving the imaginary and the real, they will transform social life and relations with nature into a never-ending enchantment.

Since women are superior in the domain of love, "the secret of women is the secret of God," a secret Fourier relates to experience: "Is it not in the ecstasy of love that man reaches the heavens and identifies with God?" Because love unites what is different, "the shepherdess and the prince," the soul and the body, it is imperative to remember its essential condition, sensitivity; without this, the actors can only err or fall into the void. For Fourier, as for Dante, love moves the sun and the stars. Our cosmic dreamer, however, is not averse to dropping blithely out of his celestial skies and coming right down to earth. Once women are emancipated, he declares, they will coach men in all the domains "where bodily strength does not prevail."

With pure spirit, or "pure love called sentiment being nothing but a vision or jugglery for those in whom the material is not satisfied," Fourier imagines unlimited sensual pleasures. He may have been overly fond of a baroque abundance of images, but it is precisely this excessive quality that saves his metaphors of free love from triviality. Libertarian dreamer though he was, he was nonetheless attentive to protecting women—and society—from the consequences of total sexual license. Good food, he contends, will limit fertility, and "means as yet unknown" will, in Harmony, allow women to have control over their reproductive power.

The new amorous world, from the damselat or the vestalat to the progressive household, will know no limits or curbs. "A woman may, simultaneously, have a husband by whom she has two children, another partner by whom she has only one child, a favorite who has lived with her and retained the title, plus many possessors who have no rights by law." And this gradation of titles gives these commitments a large measure of urbanity and fidelity. A woman may refuse to give her various men the title to which they aspire. Men can do the same. This method completely obviates the hypocrisy generated by marriage.

There will be no limits. "If the Civilized have only been capable of imagining petty foursomes or six-somes where there is naught to exalt the soul," in Harmony, insatiable desire will go from six-way to eight-way combinations and more, and then on to orgy; "people are outraged, but would do better to understand the meaning of the most widespread need," the need for communion and "unityism." And while there is nothing "more repugnant or more foul" than Civilized orgies, "in which sentiment has no place," when the "phanerogamic" times arrive, spiritual pleasures will alternate with sensual festivities. Fourier envisages an evolution in the nature of sexual desire to the pleasure of the soul; he imagines "museum orgies" where the most beautiful women would be on display for contemplation. "The sight of 20 naked women should be even more charming than the sight of 20 statues." The beauty of a live composition will create an esthetic emotion without any deception or frustration, for "sometimes it is the following day that the full enjoyment of the beauties seen at the exhibition is achieved."

The combined order will introduce the total amorous freedom that the marquis de Sade had dreamed about. The only differences—although they are crucial ones—being that in Harmony arrangements will be absolutely free, and women will call the tune. It is not by chance, Fourier declares, that young girls have a taste for dissipation and for a variety of successive or simultaneous pleasures. And rather than sprinkling "the dust of butterfly wings" on the writing addressed to them, it would be better to grant them the privilege of the Butterfly, or alternating, passion, the one that "in Harmony, holds the highest rank," for it is the agent of transition and the courier of liberty. It expresses the need for variety and change, and the manifestation of an inalienable self that another's desire can never entirely capture and no object can hold, and which is always driven to move on. This was the movement that carried Fourier and the Harmonians to ultraworlds and other starry ways.

Against the Utopians

If Fourier had set out to exorcise the ineluctable, his journeys, he said, "into regions far distant from us, do not make up a body of doctrine." He wanted, moreover, to assert his difference from the utopians who "bend everything to fit their fantasy," for he was exploring a new, unknown moral continent that was buried, but altogether real and secretly at work. It harbored dangers or delights, depending on whether or not humankind would be able to understand its goals and harmonize their full song. He thus bore no relation to those builders of far-off islands, such as Thomas More, who invented the word "utopia," a non-place or good place; or Tommaso Campanella, whose *Civitas Solis* (1602; *City of the Sun*), was borrowed from the philosopher Iamboulos, who, in turn, was inspired by Plato's *Republic*; these were all builders of worlds outside of time that had been swallowed up as surely as had the mythical Atlantis. Such worlds were constructed upon immutable paradigms; they imposed perfect conformity on each individual, man and woman, and called for a rigid education, birth control, and eugenic practices. This was the kind of social justice that, for Fourier, was the height of injustice because it banished individual initiative and the unlimited individual rights and privileges that were his design.

Fourier had no time for 18th-century naturist illusions, for Montesquieu's Troglodytes or Rousseau's noble savage, and he heaped sarcasm on the "shepherds from Lignon" and the bucolic reveries in Honoré d'Urfé's *L'Astrée* (1607–27; *Astrea: A Romance*) Nor did he subscribe to the notion of the "perfectibility of perfectible civilization," although this did introduce the idea of time and social evolution. If he did not deny the confused memory of an original period of happiness, he objected to any nostalgia for a lost golden age. He wanted to retain the progress that had been made, but also to reach beyond prejudice and convention to find a new world in the freshness of its first dawn.

He was nevertheless interested in travel accounts and particularly in descriptions of Tahitian customs. He saw these as a surviving example of the archaic series and their amorous freedom, but it was out of the question, for him, to advocate a return to that state. He mocked pastoral idylls that claimed to recreate the imaginary ingenuousness and innocence of peasants. Such pastorals portrayed societies from which luxury, refinements of the passions, and all the composite charms of Harmony would be banished. His Phalanstery was closer to Rabelais' Abbey of Thélème and its rule of "Do as you will," than to the normative utopias of Dom Deschamp or Étienne Cabet. But it was above all with his contemporaries that Fourier's relationships were interesting and his conflicts violent. While he does not seem to have been acquainted with the work of the architect Claude-Nicolas Ledoux (1736–1806), whose designs prefigured his plans of the Phalanstery, Fourier obviously did know the social reformers of his time.

The socialist Pierre Leroux (1789–1871), in the sixth of his "Lettres sur le fouriérisme" (Letters on Fourierism), published in 1846–47 in *Revue sociale ou solution pacifique du problème de prolétariat*, stigmatizes Fourier's "erotic insanity" and accuses him of stealing his ideas from Restif de la Bretonne and Claude-Henri de Saint-Simon. He who so jealously guarded the originality of his inventions—"it is to me, and me alone," he claimed, "that present and future generations will owe the initiative of their immense happiness"—was being accused of plagiarism. Leroux, blinded by his near-biblical fury, was unable to appreciate the exceptional singularity of Fourier or the positive side of his rejection of abstract ideologies and religious dogmas. "What hatred for Christianity," Leroux exclaims, "for philosophy, for the Revolution, and for all that contributed to sustaining that Revolution," whereas in fact, Fourier went to the very source of the revolt, and found in the Gospel the confirmation of Harmony, of the realization on earth of the kingdom that "selfish priests" promised for the hereafter.

Fourier had doubtless read Restif de la Bretonne, but Restif's verve and vehemence, as well as his utopian ideals, have nothing in common with those of Fourier. It is true that in *Le paysan et la paysanne pervertis* (1784; *The Corrupted Ones*), Restif was the first to situate social happiness in the here and now of the French countryside rather than in some faraway place and time, but he imagines an exclusively rural life that will be preserved from the vices and corruption of the city. In *La découverte australe par un homme volant, ou Le Dédale français* (1781; Australia Discovered by a Flying Man; Or, French Daedalus), he rewrites the history of the planet based on materialist ideas selected at random, and constructs what is more of a work of fiction than a veritable document of social reform.

Restif had a passion for walking the streets, and his tales mingle his experience of seedy city neighborhoods with the immodesty of the countryside. He anticipated the turmoil to come—"I trembled every time I saw the lowly classes of humanity stirred by emotion. If ever this beast believed it might dare, it would overthrow everything." But what he envisaged to prevent this ugly violence—the rural refuge—has nothing to do with Fourier's vision of replacing violence with passions. More importantly, Restif's sensuality and sentimentality remain rooted in the mire he claimed to be combating. In *L'anti-Justine; ou, Les délices de l'amour* (1798; The Anti-Justine; or, The Delights of Love), which he hoped would supplant Sade's *Justine, ou Les malheurs de la vertu* (1791; *Justine; or, the Misfortunes of Virtue*), Restif depicts himself in the role of voyeur and the accomplice to a gruesome monk. After watching the spectacle of the monk cutting a woman to pieces to take his pleasure and then eat her, Restif goes off with his daughter to commit incest, satisfied at having saved her by providing the monk with a substitute victim. Sade rightly held him in contempt, calling him a low-class, seedy, and naively sentimental author. Restif had nothing of the speculative boldness that characterized Fourier, the optimistic utopian, or Sade, the cruel nihilist.

The comparison of Fourier to Claude-Henri, comte de Saint-Simon (1760–1825) is more significant. In 1803, when Fourier was writing his first articles, Saint-Simon evoked the existence of a law that would be more general than Newton's, and in 1808, the year in which Fourier published *The Theory of the Four Movements*, he elaborated an analogy between the phenomena of the material and social worlds in *Sur la science de l'homme* (The

Science of Man) and *Sur la gravitation universelle* (On Gravity). Saint-Simon's participation in the American Revolution, where, with La Fayette, he had fought side-by-side with woodcutters and planters, gave him the foresight "from that very moment, that the American Revolution marked the beginning of a new era in politics." He saw the French Revolution, too, as a turning point, the passage from a static, feudal theocracy to an era of industrial dynamism. He concluded in *L'industrie, ou, Discussions politiques, morales et philosophiques* (1817; Industry; or, Political, Moral, and Philosophical Discussions) that once the break with the old system was complete, society would have to be reorganized on a new basis: "The Declaration of the Rights of Man, which is seen as the solution to the problem of social liberty, has merely stated its terms." The Declaration was a demand that had no limits and was poor in content, and Saint-Simon opposed it with the concept of a diversity of economic agents. For Saint-Simon, the issue was to privilege not the passionate qualities of the individual, but those produced by industrial activity, and to replace the power of the idle rich with that of the masters of production.

This position is close to that of the English socialist Robert Owen (1771–1858). Owen had experimented with active, progressive management methods in his own factory, and he incorporated these new methods in the communitarian associations he created. It was after his triumphant tour of the Continent that Owen's ideas began to receive coverage in the French press. Fourier became acquainted with them through the *Revue encyclopédique* (founded in 1819), where, among other articles, he read a piece by Marc-Antoine Jullien on the "industrial colony" (April 1823). Fourier was very interested by Owen's *Address Delivered to the Inhabitants of New Lanark* (1817) and by plans for the new communities of Motherwell in Scotland and New-Harmony in the United States (Indiana), and he was eager to meet this "expectant" philosopher who was preparing "a half-exit from Civilization." Noting Owen's "speculative modesty," he hoped to rally the English socialist to his theory of passions in society. In 1823 Fourier began a friendship with Anna Doyle Wheeler, a beautiful and intelligent upper-class Irishwoman who was close to Owen. Although her attempts to arrange the meeting Fourier was hoping for were unsuccessful, she did bring him into contact with a number of Owen's followers. She also distributed Fourier's works among her English friends, and in particular to the Ricardian socialist, William Thompson, who translated a few texts and was probably the anonymous translator of a selection of pieces by Fourier published in 1810 by the Owenite London Cooperative Society under the title *Political Economy Made Easy*. In 1825 Thompson published the pioneering work, *Appeal of One Half of the Human Race, Women, against the Pretensions of the Other Half, Men, to Retain Them in Political and Thence in Civil and Domestic Slavery*, which was largely inspired by Wheeler (Thompson described himself as no more than her "scribe and interpreter"). The *Appeal* was written explicitly to refute James Mill's article "On Government" (1824) in the supplement to the *Encyclopaedia Britannica*, in which Mill argues that the political interests of women are "contained" in those of their fathers and husbands. Thanks to Wheeler, and to his own readings and translations, Thompson was, at least partly, familiar with the theory of Universal Harmony. He referred to Fourier only in one footnote, however. In this, he mentioned that while Owen was experimenting with the principles of a cooperative

society in New Lanark, Fourier was studying the same subject in Lyon, and publishing his *Traité de l'association domestique-agricole* (c. 1822; Treatise of the Domestic-Agricultural Association; later reissed under the title *Théorie de l'unité universelle* [Theory of Universal Unity]) in Paris. Thompson notes the agreement between Fourier and Owen on "the great leading features of the Co-operation of large numbers for the production of wealth and social happiness, and the improved, and industrious and equal education of all the children," but he also immediately highlights the point that separates the two: while Fourier's cooperative system is characterized by an inequality of distribution, Owen's is founded on the equal distribution of wealth and of "all the means of happiness." Thompson nonetheless acknowledges that for both thinkers, institutional protection is not sufficient to guarantee equality of happiness unless society is radically transformed. Only cooperation will create the conditions for mutual respect, and for the rediscovery of the fundamental, universal desire for happiness freed of the accidental, historically determined relations of domination. This is an optimistic, utopian affirmation to which Fourier would doubtless have subscribed. But, he would later object, if equality of civic and political rights do not ensure an equal chance of happiness to all men and all women, how can equal distribution do this? Owen, and Thompson too, he might add, neglected those motivating forces of interest and emulation to which differences or contrasts give rise. Instead of an abstract declaration of the equality of all human beings and its corollary, equality of rights, Fourier dared to advocate and encourage individual "privileges," that is, the unique qualities of each and all, together with the particular rights that these require to ensure their full development. Thompson argued that women are physically weaker than men and have the heavy burden of bearing and feeding children, but he did not dream of compensating for this natural inequality by transforming sex differences and female specificities into "privileges." There was no thought of amorous dominance for women, of a "Butterfly" passion capable of transforming what alienates and crushes women into a carefree, joyous freedom; and certainly no "foursomes, six-somes or eight-somes," orgiastic parties and "museum orgies," not even noble, pivotal love—that is, pure, sentimental, platonic, or, as Fourier calls it, "celadonic" love.

Thompson declared that his text was not concerned with Fourier's "eccentricities of speculation," and this was indeed true. While Thompson did attack marriage for subjecting women to the authority of men and relegating them to the status of minors, he was not in the least interested in total metamorphosis, nor in glorifying women and the "minor passions" of love and familism. He did not seek to unite the inconstancy of sensual and affective flightiness with mathematical idealities in order to turn free passional movement into truth, happiness, and harmony. Thompson was a bold, wise, rational optimist who wanted to reform morality and the relationships between men and women, but he did not wish to change his approach to the understanding of human nature. Published in London, his *Appeal* was not translated into French, and Fourier never made any mention of it.

However, in 1824 Fourier wrote to Owen to praise his initiatives and to offer his collaboration, sending a copy of his *Traité de l'association domestique-agricole* with the letter. Owen, who did not read French, had someone else send a polite reply expressing his reservations. Undaunted by this, Fourier reiterated the offer of his services a few months later, but this time he received no reply. Piqued, and better informed, he said, about Owen's methods, he now saw only their faults. According to Fourier, while Owen rightly appreciated the flexibility of human nature, he only related it to the external environment and not to the passionate latencies and inner resources that were secretly smoldering and becoming corrupted, but which would develop freely and openly in Harmony for the greater good of individuals and society. Saint-Simon and Owen gave in to the alleged necessity of things and to economic fatalism. Further, the equality they advocated was contradicted by the continuance and legitimization of the relationship between masters of industry and those who executed the work. The necessarily restrictive authority of the new managers called for the obedience of the workers, an austere discipline, and quasi-monastic rules, all of which were contrary to free, attractive activities—hence the satirical tract *Pièges et charlatanisme des deux sectes: Saint-Simon et Owen* (The Snares and Charlatanism of Two Sects: Saint-Simon and Owen) published in 1831. With remarkable acuity, Fourier points out the flaw in the doctrine:

> If the Saint-Simonist reign were to be organized, it is not at all certain that it would result in an improvement in the lot of the laboring classes; the only sure effect would be to concentrate all property, capital, and factories in the hands of the new priests. Once they have all in hand, they will doubtless treat the people in the same way as all theocrats have.

His forecast proved to be accurate with regard to those Saint-Simonians who became industrial leaders and, in their wake, even more so for the actors of economic necessity.

Fourier found the Saint-Simonians more inspired when, in order to maintain enthusiasm, they sought to renew religion; but their "New Christianity" was only a mediocre parody, and, given the absence of sensual attraction, it was doomed to failure, as were the revolutionary cults of the Supreme Being and the Goddess Reason. What should have been created was a religion of sensual delight, argued Fourier in *The Theory of the Four Movements*, to liven up "arid" economic "precepts," and "give some soul" to philosophical "dogma." He saw the importance of Freemasonry and the influence of its "network of societies in all Civilized regions," and pointed out its "still unknown properties" that "this century has not even glimpsed." It already possessed an organization that "lent itself marvelously to the foundation of a new religion." Had there but been a politically skilled leader capable of introducing women and sensual pleasure into the organization, the Freemasons would have gained invincible power; but they had not been able to take advantage of the political opportunity open to them, and they had missed their historic moment. Neither they nor the philosophers had been able to repudiate their own dogmas and "attack Civilization at its weak point, amorous servitude."

Some of the Saint-Simonians, it is true, had had the idea of founding a cult of sensual pleasure. Prosper Enfantin (1796–1864), known as Father Enfantin, priest and pontiff of the Saint-Simonist religion, stated its goals: "Our preaching thus consists in the emancipation of women and the rehabilitation of the flesh" (*Enseignements faits par le Père Suprême, extraits de morale* [1830–32; Teachings of the Supreme Father: Moral Excerpts]).

But the search for "the Mother" who would be the equal of "the Father" failed. In principle her words were to be listened to, and her revelations revered, but it was only those of the father that were heard; he remained in control of speech, pleasure, and even carnal beauty. Father Enfantin was brought to trial by the authorities, and on 27 and 28 August 1832 he appeared before the Criminal Court of the Seine, where he declared that the priest—that was to say, himself—had to be handsome: "Yes, Gentlemen . . . it is, above all, the beautiful bodies that I wish to call to a better life." This self-satisfied apologia for beauty denied any true recognition of female "privileges."

This male domination was later to become more pronounced with Pierre-Joseph Proudhon (1809–65), who was both fascinated and irritated by Fourier. While he admired the "undisciplined, solitary genius who, in one leap and by pure intuition, rose to the supreme law of the universe" (*De la création de l'ordre dans l'humanité, ou, Principles d'organisation politique* [1843; On the Creation of Order in Humanity; or, Principles of Political Organization]), Proudhon accused Fourier of ignorance and immorality and of advocating "a philosophy of big mouths and public concubinage" (*Qu'est-ce que la propriété? ou, Recherches sur le principe du droit et du gouvernement* [1840–48; *What Is Property? An Enquiry into the Principle of Right and of Government*]). This judgment contrasted sharply with that of Dostoyevsky, who at the Petrasevcy trial testified: "Fourierism is a peace-loving system; it enchants the soul with its subtlety, seduces the heart with that love of humanity which has always inspired Fourier, and strikes the mind with the harmony of all its parts" (Red Archive, Moscow, 1931, vols. 45 and 46).

Proudhon had no taste for the "phanerogamic" love of the Phalansteries. Considered an anarchist, he was an egalitarian who did not believe that the talents created by society and education deserved particular reward. He showered praise on women but made them minors for life, writing in *De la création de l'ordre dans l'humanité*:

> Woman, until she becomes a wife, is an apprentice, or at most, a second-in-command; in the workshop as in the family, she remains a minor, and has no part in the state. Woman is neither the other half nor the equal of man, as is commonly said, but she is his likable, living complement who finishes the work of making a person of him: that is the principle of the family, and the law of monogamy.

Woman is thus defined by Proudhon in this work to be a "housewife or courtesan"; there is no fluttering liberty for her, no "Butterfly" passion and no hope of a metamorphosis as natural and marvelous as that of the "hideous caterpillar" turning into a "brilliant butterfly." Proudhon praises women as "the ideal of humanity," but lays claim to "facts and evidence" to prove their "physical, intellectual, and moral inferiority." This contradiction and division maintains a double bondage, for this austere libertarian's system rivets woman to the home and man to his work. The amorous freedom of Harmony, on the other hand, transforms the lives of both sexes; it turns the biblical curse "you shall labor by the sweat of your brow" into a blessing, and coercive labor into attractive activities as varied as are individual tastes and aptitudes.

However, one of Fourier's contemporaries, Flora Tristan, did unite the cause of women with that of exploited workers. The two did not meet until 1835, two years before the prematurely aged Fourier died. Tristan went to see Fourier and wrote to him after her visit, "Every day I become more thoroughly penetrated with a sense of the sublimity of your doctrine." However, while she claimed to be a follower of Fourier, and indeed owed much to him, and used his declaration that "the extension of the privileges of women is the basic principle of all social progress" as an epigraph to her book *L'émancipation de la femme, ou, Le testament de la paria* (1846; The Emancipation of Woman; or, Testament of a Pariah), she did not want to identify exclusively with his doctrine. She believed that she was asserting her independence by being eclectic. Nonetheless, spurred on by a fervent desire to be useful, she sought an association with the Fourierists, and gave her support to the economic turn that Fourier's unfaithful disciple Victor Considérant (and his friends from the École Polytechnique) gave to "passionate Harmony."

Moreover, Flora Tristan ascribed a mystical filiation to Fourier that was essentially Swedenborgian. It is true that Fourier had had encounters with illuminist circles in Lyon. In the circle of the preromantic writer Pierre-Simon Ballanche (1761–1847), which brought together Freemasons, socialist mystics, and theocratic reactionaries, and followers of Mesmerism and the occult sciences, Fourier was appreciated as "a modest man, reputed for his knowledge of geography." However, some of his reading notes, together with precise similarities of vocabulary, prove that through these encounters, Fourier was introduced to, and read, the work of Louis-Claude de Saint-Martin, the "unknown philosopher," author of *Des erreurs et de la vérité* (1775; Of Errors and Truth) and *L'homme de désir* (1790; Desiring Man), among other works. Saint-Martin was highly esteemed in the Masonic lodges, and through him, Fourier was influenced by a heretical mystical current and in particular by the illuminato Jakob Böhme, the shoemaker from Görlitz, whose works Saint-Martin had translated into French and whose alter ego Saint-Martin declared himself to be. But there is no doubt that Fourier, the visionary of a new of social order, revised these contributions to fit his own exceptional needs; the kingdom of heaven, for Fourier, was to be realized on earth, in the here and now.

In *La société festive* (1975; Festive Society), the scholar Henri Desroche points to a certain convergence between Fourier's plans for Harmony and the Oneida experiment in the New York States, which began in the 1840s (see Desroche). This was a remarkable convergence, since the founders and members of Oneida barely knew Fourier's name. Under the impetus of J.H. Noyes, a pastor who became the head of the community, they introduced plural marriages, which gave free reign to the desires of the spouses and fixed no limits. They dissociated sexual desire and pleasure from reproduction and organized a new marital and parental system. The children, who were raised and educated by all, were reputed to be happy, well adjusted, and well educated. The community lasted more than 30 years and boasted a thriving industrial economy, but it did not take long for the initial commitment to free choice to be called into question and for discord to set in. Things came apart when the younger generation revolted against the ascendancy of the founding fathers, whom they accused of turning the principle of free love to their own advantage, and, on the pretext of initiation, of reserving the sexual awakening of young girls and boys for themselves. The community espoused Eastern philosophy and was waiting for a new effusion of the Spirit—a thwarted hope.

Oneida, the most daring of the experiments attempted at that time, could not equal the dream of Harmony, a "type and model" that was essentially imaginary.

On the other hand, modern anti-utopias have brought the motivating forces of the passions into play against an exclusively rational authority and totalitarian systems. In *My* (1924; *We*), Evgenii Zamiatin contrasts the arbitrary nature of power with the forces of love aroused by a woman of unusual beauty, while in *1984* (1949) George Orwell shows how love itself is vanquished by the fear of, and fascination for, an absolute master. Yuri Olécha, in his fine novel, *L'envie* (1934; *The Urge*), ironically praises the indifference which alone survives and triumphs under dictatorship, and imagined a last parade of "the old, obsolete feelings," the swan song of love with its marvelous brightness like a lamp about to go out. Fourier's battle was precisely against this indifference, and against the prohibitions that discourage the spontaneous, passionate impulse.

The Amorous New World: The "Composite Charms" of "Manias," Sapphism, and Prosapphism

The mocking critics and adversaries of his time knew nothing of the manuscripts contained in the five notebooks Fourier filled during the fertile time spent in his family retreat in Bugey while he was preparing his "grand treatise" on *L'unité universelle*. These were the manuscripts of *Le nouveau monde amoureux, synthèse finale* (The Amorous New World: A Final Synthesis); they were concealed after his death by his frightened disciples and neglected by scholars (Hubert Bourgin, in his thesis entitled "Fourier, Contribution à l'étude du socialisme français" [1905; Fourier: A Contribution to the Study of French Socialism] considered them to contain only useless repetitions) until Émile Poulat finally made an inventory of them. The manuscripts were subsequently filed in the French National Archives, where I discovered them, deciphered them, and then published them in 1967 (volume 7 of the Anthropos edition of Fourier's complete works). In these texts, which remained secret for so long, Fourier draws the reader to the ultimate point of the amorous quest, from the pure sentiment of platonic, "celadonic" love to the rare and bizarre particularities of "manias, ambiguities, transitions, or exceptions."

"If one exchanges ideas on amorous manias with women who have had many lovers and men who have had many mistresses," he observes in *Le nouveau monde amoureux*, "their tales teach us that there is an infinite variety of manias, material or spiritual, active or passive, or a mixture [of these]." Thus, if the common passions, which may be "subdivided into a multitude of nuances that are more or less dominant in each individual, resulting in an infinite variety of characters," are added to the manias, which are also of infinite variety, an inexhaustible "mumbo jumbo" of characters is obtained. Fourier limited their enumeration, and I will cite here only those that concern sex differences and "female privileges."

Our strange author gives the example of a heel-scratcher, a gentle fetishist whose friendship was much appreciated by a lady of beauty fully satisfied elsewhere by her "more audacious lovers." He then analyzes the cruelty of a Russian princess who tortured her beautiful slave. Was it jealousy? he asks. No, it was Sapphism. She was an unconscious "Sapphian." Powerful enough to keep the slave at her mercy, she did not have the freedom to break away from internalized taboos that suppressed the passionate message of the flesh—a desire that was all the more ferocious because it was "deprived of an ideal development." "Forced deprivation, when recognized, is not carried to such heights of fury," Fourier writes, and then adds: "Others practice on a collective level the atrocities that Madame Strogonoff practiced individually . . . Odin made a religious system out of this and Sade a moral one." Crimes, wars, massacres, and carnage are thus reintegrated into human life; they are the effects of repression, of an explosion of the passionate impulse, and of a perverted self-affirmation. Fourier upholds his optimistic premise: hatred is aborted love, but so well masked that it would have taken a mediator to enlighten the princess as to her true feelings and to reconcile her with the young woman she was persecuting because she did not know how to love her. Fourier thus envisions "male and female confessors," "older people of knowledge, subtlety and genius," who will intervene in order to resolve conflicts and facilitate "difficult matches." They will draw out unavowed secrets and intervene actively to decode obscure desires. Only with the help of experience and surprising encounters will individuals be able to liberate those innermost realms which they themselves keep imprisoned, and which the language of the confessors will interpret, yet without completely satisfying them or understanding the full extent of their depth and radiance.

Fourier himself discovered "by chance," on an occasion in which he was "an actor," that he had "the taste or mania of Sapphianism, the love of Sapphians and the eagerness to aid them in every way possible." Before that, he had railed "against Sapphians, as is the custom in Civilization," because he had not known how to be their "ally." He was an active voyeur who participated in "Sapphian" desire and pleasures, but did he penetrate the dark continent of female sexuality? Or, favoring phallic activity for himself, and the self-sufficiency of women together, did he still fail to perceive women's erotic uniqueness? Yet did he not discover, by accident, his own unconscious bisexuality and the bisexuality that other men and women harbor without knowing it, without wanting—or being able—to recognize and accept it? This mania of Sapphianism, he explains, is the special attribute of "omnigynes," great temperaments who are endowed with several dominant passions; they are devoted to the other sex, whose members they are "eager to satisfy, both ambiguously and directly."

Bisexuality, for Fourier, does not do away with sex differences, but it does tend to work in favor of Sapphians:

> We can already see that women in their state of liberty, like the women in Paris, have a great penchant for Sapphism. . . . This sex is more inclined than the other to monosexuality. Now, in the new order, where all female distrust and enmity will cease to exist . . . it will not be surprising if all, or almost all of them, will take to a liberty that is already common in the places where they are most refined.

Fourier's "manias" involve both participation and contrasts. They prove that there can be no relationships without an affinity between partners or a certain degree of resemblance, and that there could be no attraction without a certain degree of mystery and inherence in the unknown, in the movement of things offered or in the other's desire.

The composite pleasure of "co-manians" (individuals with the same manias) will reveal to each of them a hitherto unconscious passion, and thus unite the love of self, of the other in oneself, and of the other as stranger. These manias are considered perversions, but for Fourier the only perversion is the infatuated self that separates men from women and from their own nature, from bisexuality and the bizarre peculiarities that are the most intimate attributes of a subject, his or her individual—perhaps unique—features. Manias, moreover, are the offshoot of a principle of delicacy and are all the more numerous the more elevated the individual's character. Far from causing isolation or exclusion, they tend to form subtler, more complex ties than previously existed, a more tightly woven fabric of desires and pleasures. Manias, exceptions, ambiguities, and transitions do not open breaches into the void, but, like "dowels in a roof frame," they serve to consolidate social bonds.

"Without ambiguity, nothing would be connected." Taking his challenge to its limits, Fourier declares, "Everyone is right in love, since it is the passion of madness." This is a joking declaration, but also a rejection of cold, rational wisdom that claims to solve individual and social problems when in fact the remedy lies in the heart of the danger: "Passion," Fourier contends, "can only be treated by passion itself. Its highest manifestations absorb the discords that the inferior grades engender."

In order to confirm this "absorbing substitution" and the capacity of the highest form of love for plural liberties, Fourier creates the character of the beautiful giant Fakma. Fakma is the mythical mother and lover whose demanding sentimental principles become the pivot around which all other desires gravitate. The pure platonic love, or "celadony," that she demands and obtains from the heroic seraph, the chosen one among all her suitors, serves to redeem the exclusive love she has recently experienced with a Khan of Barbary, and with her, to redeem all the now permissible forms of amorous pleasure, from the rare and bizarre manias to the male and female "bacchantes" who "console the wounded," or the saints of both sexes who dedicate themselves to the forsaken. This sainthood is very different from "the useless sainthood in Civilization, which does good to no one, not even to those who dedicate themselves to it." In Harmony,

> only those people who have effectively contributed to the happiness of humans in this life will be admitted as saints and heroes, and since good food and love are the most common pleasures, it will be those who have powerfully contributed to the perfection of these pleasures who will be elevated to sainthood. (*Le nouveau monde amoureux*)

Fourier's heroism is somewhat similar in nature to what Charles Baudelaire called "divine prostitution." For Fourier, "minor heroism or excellence in the arts goes very well with minor sainthood or amorous prowess; similarly, major heroism, or excellence in the sciences, goes with major sainthood or preeminence in the gastronomic cabal."

For that matter, once the world has been delivered from convention and prejudice, from deceitful fictions and illusions, when perpetual peace and universal unity exist on the globe, there will be no more need for that Civilized heroism which consists in plundering, raping, ravaging, burning, and massacring. It will be necessary to replace that heroism of destruction with a heroism of production and enrichment. Then, the title of hero will only belong to those who excel in the sciences and the arts.

This excellence will be united with the fervor of desire and "amorous saintliness"; and, as women are superior in love, leading men along, the liberated female difference will exalt the primeval human difference, as well as the encounters in which that difference reveals itself while unveiling the other. In the place of the trickery of a mythical Reason that would tend to realization in history and contribute to bringing worldly externalization and evolution back into the initial idea, thus rendering them pointless, Fourier, the passionate dreamer, proposes a stratagem of desire that will endlessly create relationships—"objective chance" for the Surrealists, "composite charms" for Fourier—that unite the material and the spiritual, the life of the flesh and the forces that run through it. These multiple unions will progressively bring into play the inexhaustible reserves of passionate movement, so that individual and collective evolution will be a never-ending process in which the unpredictable, the accidental, and the unforeseen become essential—the sources of a limitless renewal of life and knowledge.

Bibliography

Sources

Ballanche, Pierre-Simon, *Essai sur les institutions sociales dans leur rapport avec les idées nouvelles*, Paris: Didot, 1818

Cabet, Étienne, *Voyage et aventures de Lord Villiam Carisdall en Icarie*, 2 vols., Paris: Souverain, 1840; 2nd edition, as *Voyage en Icarie*, Paris: Mallet, 1842; reprint, Paris: Slatkine, 1979

Enfantin, Prosper-Barthélémy, *Oeuvres de Saint-Simon et d'Enfantin*, Paris: Leroux, 1878

Fourier, Charles, *Oeuvres complètes de Charles Fourier*, 6 vols., Paris: Librairie Sociétaire, 1841–48

Fourier, Charles, *Oeuvres complètes de Charles Fourier*, 12 vols., Paris: Anthropos, 1966–68

Fourier, Charles, *L'ordre subversif: Trois textes sur la civilisation*, Paris: Aubier Montaigne, 1972

Fourier, Charles, *Pièges et charlatanisme des deux sectes Saint-Simon et Owen, qui promettent l'association et le progrès*, Paris: Bossange, 1831

Fourier, Charles, *La théorie des quatre mouvements et des destinées générales*, Lyon: Pelzin, 1808; new edition, edited by Simone Debout-Oleszkiewicz, Dijon, France: Les Presses du Réel, 1998; as *The Theory of the Four Movements*, edited by Gareth Stedman Jones and Ian Patterson, 1996

Leroux, Pierre, "Lettres sur le fouriérisme," *Revue sociale ou solution pacifique du problème de prolétariat* 9–12 (June–September 1846), 1–2 (October–November 1846), 4 (January 1847), 7 (April 1847)

Leroux, Pierre, "Réponse à l'école fouriériste," *Revue sociale ou solution pacifique du problème de prolétariat* 3 (December 1845)

Owen, Robert, *Selected Works of Robert Owen*, 4 vols., edited by Gregory Claeys, London: Pickering, 1993

Proudhon, Pierre-Joseph, *qu'est-ce que la propriété ou recherches sur le princique du droit et du gouvernement*, Paris, 1840; as: *What Is Property? An Enquiry into the Principle of Right and of Government*, translated by Benjamin R. Tucker, New York: H. Fertig, 1966

Restif de la Bretonne, Nicolas-Edmé, *Le dysan et la paysanne fevertis . . . La Hoye, 1784, 4 vols, as: *The Corrupted Ones*, translated and edited by Alan Hull Walton, London: Spearman, 1967

Restif de la Bretonne, Nicolas-Edmé, *La découverte australe par un homme-volant*, 4 vols., Paris: Leipsick, 1781; reprint, Paris: France Adel, 1977

Saint-Simon, Henri, comte de, *Oeuvres de Claude-Henri de Saint-Simon*, 6 vols., Paris: Anthropos, 1966

Thompson, William, *Appeal of One Half the Human Race, Women, against the Pretensions of the Other Half, Men, to Retain Them in Political, and Thence in Civil and Domestic, Slavery: In Reply to a Paragraph of Mr. Mill's Celebrated "Article on Government,"* London: Longman Hurst, 1825; reprint, Bristol, Avon: Thoemmes, 1994

Tristan, Flora, *L'émancipation de la femme, ou, Le testament de la paria: Ouvrage posthume*, Paris: Bureau de la Direction de la Vérité, 1846

Reference Works

Beecher, Jonathan, *Charles Fourier: The Visionary and His World*, Berkeley: University of California Press, 1986

Breton, André, *Ode à Fourier*, Paris: Fontaine, 1947; as *Ode to Fourier*, London and New York: Cape Goliard Press, 1969

Campanella, Tommaso, *La città del sole* [1602]: *Dialogo poetico; The City of the Sun: A Poetical Dialogue* (bilingual Italian-English edition), Berkeley: University of California Press, 1981

Considérant, Victor, "Fourier," in *Dictionnaire de la conversation et de la lecture*, edited by William Duckett, vol. 18, Paris: Belin-Mandar, 1836

Debout, Simone, "L'analogie ou le poème mathématique de Charles Fourier," *Revue internationale de philosophie* 16 (1962)

Debout, Simone, *Charles Fourier*, Paris: Presses Universitaires de France, 1970

Debout, Simone, "Invisible actif," in *Le charme composé*, by Charles Fourier, new edition, Fontfroide, France: Fata Morgana, 1993

Debout, Simone, "Légitime défense, légitime entente: Sade et Fourier," in *Libre: Politique-anthropologie-philosophie*, vol. 1, Paris: Payot, 1977, and vol. 4, Paris: Payot, 1978 (two parts)

Debout, Simone, "Saint-Simon, Fourier, Proudhon," in *Histoire de la philosophie*, edited by Brice Parain, vol. 3, Paris: Gallimard, 1974

Debout, Simone, *L'utopie de Charles Fourier*, Paris: Payot, 1978; new edition, Dijon: Les Presses du Reel, 1998

Debout-Oleskiewicz, Simone, "Fouriérisme," in *Encyclopedia Universalis*, Paris: Corpus, 1989

Debout-Oleskiewicz, Simone, "*Griffe au nez*"; ou, Donner "have ou art": Écriture inconnue de Charles Fourier*, Paris: Anthropos, 1974

Debout-Oleskiewicz, Simone, "Jacob Böhme et Louis-Claude de Saint-Martin," *Passé présent* 1 (1982)

Deschamps, Dom Léger-Marie, *Le vrai système, ou, Le mot de l'énigme métaphysique et morale*, Paris: Droz, 1939

Desroche, Henri, *La société festive: Du fouriérisme écrit aux fouriérismes pratiques*, Paris: Seuil, 1975

Dessignolle, Émile, *Le féminisme d'après la doctrine socialiste de Ch. Fourier*, Lyon, France: Storck, 1903

Freud, Sigmund, *Civilization and Its Discontents*, in *The Standard Edition of the Complete Psychological Works of Sigmund Freud*, edited by James Strachey, vol. 21, London: The Hogarth Press, 1961

More, Thomas, "Nova Insula Utopia," Louvain, 1615, in *Utopia*, edited by George M. Logan, Robert M. Adams, and Clarence H. Miller, Cambridge and New York: Cambridge University Press, 1995

Olecha, Youri, *L'envie*, Paris: n.p., 1934

Orwell, George, *1984*, London: Secker and Warburg, and New York: New American Library, 1949

Poulat, Émile, *Les cahiers manuscrits de Fourier: Étude historique et inventaire raisonné*, Paris: Minuit, 1957

Queneau, Raymond, "Dialectique hégelienne et séries de Fourier," in *Bords: Mathématiciens, précurseurs, encyclopédistes*, Paris: Hermann, 1963

Russell, Bertrand, *Marriage and Morals*, London: Allen and Unwin, and New York: Liveright, 1929; reprint, London: Allen and Unwin, 1976

Saint-Martin, Louis Claude de, *L'homme de désir*, Lyon: Grabit, 1790; reprint, edited by Robert Amadou, Paris: Union Générale d'Éditions, 1973

Scherer, René, *Charles Fourier; ou, La contestation globale*, Paris: Seghers, 1970

Silberling, Édouard, *Dictionnaire de sociologie phalanstérienne*, 1911; reprint, Geneva and Paris: Slatkine, 1984

Surine, Georges, *Le Fouriérisme en Russie*, Paris: Dupont, 1936

Théry, Irène, *Le démariage: Justice et vie privée*, Paris: Jacob, 1993

Vidler, Anthony, *Claude-Nicholas Ledoux*, Basel, Switzerland, and Boston: Birkhäuser, 1988

Zamiatin, Evgenii Ivanovich, *We*, translated by Gregory Zilboorg, New York: Dutton, 1924; reprint, New York: Penguin, 1991

1848 in Paris

MAÏTÉ BOUYSSY AND CHRISTINE FAURÉ

THE POLITICAL HISTORY OF women in 1848 may be located at the intersection of several historical accounts and assessments, all continually being revised. It is difficult to say whether we should celebrate the richness of these various histories or deplore their inadequacies. Comparative history in this case has often been called for but is never really practiced, while political and social historical study, with its mass of documentation, constantly renews its approaches in accordance with the shifts in sensibility that accompany changes in our ideological perceptions and preferences, themselves more or less in synchrony with fundamental social developments. In the absence of comprehensive studies of the "missing woman" of 1848, attempting to assess her role is somewhat perilous. She is hard to follow, hard to grasp. Everywhere present and active, in the daily misery of poverty and the heat of the riots, these women believed for only one springtime that they had linked up with history: from February to June, between the fraternal hope with which the revolution began and the terrible massacres that put an end to it, as Louis Eugène Cavaignac's artillery returned the streets to republican order. Subsequent French political life (Louis-Napoleon's coup d'état) and even literary life cannot be understood without taking into account this terrible ending to the events of 1848, which crushed men and women alike. Yet that ending, in French historiography as in French minds, has always been repressed.

During that brief spring, mainly in Paris and in the context of a violent economic crisis that showed no signs of subsiding, women became increasingly active and involved. The imperative they responded to was twofold: to provide, organize, and find work; and to invent ways of participating in this new republic that proclaimed the "Holy Trinity" of liberty, equality, and fraternity.

Resurrection of the Republic

On 23 and 24 February 1848, at the end of a campaign to broaden suffrage based on tax qualification, Paris rose up. Barricades were erected, and fighting took place in the direction of Château-d'Eau, around the Tuileries, and around the Palais du Luxembourg, in the heart of Paris. Louis-Philippe, who had been brought to power by the barricades of 1830, did not want to be responsible for a blood bath, and the regime fell. This is a fine example of a "surprise revolution," showing how, according to the aphorism devised decades ago by the historian Ernest Labrousse, "revolutions are made in spite of revolutionaries" (see Labrousse). Subsequently, the demonstrators in the streets had time to put pressure on the provisional government, which was made up of liberals such as Armand Marrast, mayor of Paris and editor-in-chief of the newspaper *Le national*; more advanced republicans, such as Ferdinand Flocon of the periodical *La réforme*; and, still further to the Left, the socialist theoretician Louis Blanc and "the laborer Albert," a former mechanic and veteran activist in Paris workers' societies. This team was dignified by the highly charismatic figure of the poet Alphonse de Lamartine. Its first task was to remedy an appalling unemployment rate, which was both the cause of the extreme poverty that prevailed and the reason for the consensus that had allowed the overthrow of the preceding regime, now held responsible by all parties for producing that situation through its great deficiencies and negligence. François Pardigon, a June insurgent who went into exile in Belgium, wrote in his *Épisodes des journées de juin 1848* (1852; Episodes from the Days of June 1848) of "the unanimous current of the population, the immense contempt poured upon an execrated king and a whole collapsing official world."

The right to work was proclaimed on 25 February: "The provisional government pledges to guarantee the livelihood of the worker with work; it pledges to guarantee work to all citizens" (*Le moniteur*, 25–26 February 1848). More concretely, the government promised the opening of national workshops and help for the associations that would direct them. The engineer Émile Thomas, with a few students from the École Centrale, was to be in charge of this.

Three days later a government commission for workers was created, under the pressure of demonstrations by an elite group of railroad mechanics. The commission was headed by the young railway worker Marche, who was known for his determination and physical strength. This was not, in fact, the Ministry of Labor the socialists had been expecting, but the commission did sit in the Palais du Luxembourg, under the direction of Louis Blanc and "the laborer Albert." Three days later, in an attempt to solve a major problem, the Luxembourg Commission banned subcontracting, for intermediaries and manual labor contractors had been taking advantage of the unemployment rate to put downward pressure on wages, forcing both men and women workers to increase their working hours inordinately just to be able to survive. A corresponding measure limited the working day to 10 hours in Paris and 11 hours in the provinces—a step the English government had taken the previous year.

Women, who were paid less than men and employed more often than men as domestic workers, were now suffering wage reductions of as much as one-quarter of their earnings, and on 4 March, underpaid labor in prisons and communes, convents, hospices, and army barracks came in for official indictment. On issues less concerned with material survival, however, significant changes were made. Universal male suffrage was granted on 4 March: "suffrage will be direct and universal without any requirement of property ownership" (*Le moniteur*, 5 March 1848). Freedom of assembly and complete freedom of the press were announced the same day. The latter measure entailed the abolition of the stamp tax on periodicals; clearly it was impossible to continue that practice in a climate of complete freedom of expression and debate of ideas—the requisite conditions for honest elections. In less than 10 days, an unprecedented space of liberty had been instituted, prefiguring the "free Paris" of 1871.

"Women's Work, One of Our Most Difficult and Serious Problems"

Although the actors in this new political order were primarily men, and while it is not at all easy for the historian to follow women's actions, demands, and itineraries during the revolutionary spring, women did participate in the new possibilities and opportunities offered. *La politique des femmes*, a newspaper "published by women workers," as the subtitle indicated, and bearing the inscription "Liberty, equality, fraternity for all men and all women," noted retrospectively, in August 1848, when the movement had been crushed, that

> after the February revolution, the provisional government was assailed by women. Some wrote letters, others offered proposals, others came in a troop bearing the flag up front, and all of them came to ask the Republic for protection. Women need to be helped and supported by a strong power . . . and since, for a long time now, among the working classes, men are at pains to provide even for themselves, women quite naturally turned their sights toward the state as the holder of supreme power.

The paper was edited by Désirée Gay and Eugénie Niboyet (1797–1883), seasoned activists who in the 1830s had been associated with various Saint-Simonian groups; the article from which the above quotation is taken appeared in the paper's second—and last—issue.

Rémi Gossez, the historian who has done the closest studies of workers and how they were organized in Paris under the Second Republic, has inventoried 640 petitions that workers in all industries throughout France had addressed to the Commis-

sion du Gouvernement pour l'Organisation du Travail (Government Commission for Labor Organization) before 2 May. Of these petitions, 63 came from women. At the head of the list came the laundresses (26), half from Paris proper, the other half from the surrounding areas where the laundries and floating washhouses were located. Then followed petitions from women employed in a variety of sewing and clothing trades (18), to which should be added petitions from women who worked in the textile industry and in the workshops of the clothing industry (8), and as midwives, florists, and in the small trades of the markets (11).

Only three petitions came from the provinces. The dominant issue was salaries (the subject of half of the petitions); the other half demanded labor-related guarantees, or, more modestly, asked for work and labor organization.

But when the Luxembourg Commission, which provided for three delegates per profession, drew up its list of *corps d'état* (recognized occupational categories), it excluded the linen and needlework trades. Of all the delegates listed, there was only one woman, cited (along with two male colleagues) as a "copper polisher." The following day Philippe Buchez, the president of the Constituent Assembly, convened the mayors of the 12 arrondissements at the Hôtel de Ville for a meeting whose stated theme was "women's work, one of our most difficult and serious problems." Clearly, women's unemployment and poverty were perceived to require specialized treatment. It was true that female workers suffered even more than men from the competition from convents, communes, and hospices, as well as from garment-making enterprises and the subcontracting of manual labor.

On 15 March, a sizable delegation of female garment workers came to demand that the government put an end to clothing manufacture in prisons, convent workrooms, and communes. Louis Blanc characterized competition as murderous, and M. Vidal, the reporter to the commission who received the delegates from the sewing workshops, said: "They presented me with shirts made by soldiers, the production of which is paid at 35 centimes and requires one working day. How do you expect a woman, under the same conditions, to be able to live from the work of her hands?" Blanc added:

> Note that the work done in convents under conditions that are impossible outside hits that part of the working population that most needs protection—women. Poverty leads a man to crime; think, Gentlemen, where, despite her delicate feelings, it might lead a woman. Protection, then, for the woman worker, whose plight is the most touching of all!

On 24 and 25 March a measure was published that limited competition from hospices and prisons, where people were also working for ludicrously low wages.

By April, abject poverty had reached staggering proportions, and proposals for remedial action acquired a new urgency. These suggestions juxtaposed or combined forms of traditional intervention and new aspirations in a climate that was alternately consensual and contentious. Madame de Lamartine, a friend of Eugénie Niboyet, proposed a benefit concert to raise funds for unemployed women workers. She was told that it was time for fraternity, not handouts; collective effort and mutual aid were preferable to charity. Eugénie Foa, a well-known author of historical novels for young people and a woman close to the Société de la Morale Chrétienne (Society of Christian Morality), presented a plan for a national workshop. *La voix des femmes*, the first French daily paper published by women and the publication that orchestrated women's initiatives from March until June, responded with the reproach that, for the project's proposed committee, Foa had chosen a body of 20 upper-class ladies rather than selecting working-class women. She in turn responded with a letter to the paper and its group of well-known activist women editors, who were finally obliged to concede:

> whatever the case may be, we shall support her generous efforts; if it takes 20 ladies, we will give them to her in order to provide work for the young girls who have awakened her sympathy. In generous efforts there is no rivalry possible; there is only the fertile competition of devotion. (*La voix des femmes*, no. 14)

On 27 March 1848 *Le moniteur* reported that Lamartine had received a delegation of women whom it called "Vésuviennes" (Vesuvian Women). The women had come to request the provisional government to provide shelter from public suffering for young homeless girls without bread. They asked that these young women be fed for a time at the government's expense and that the debtors' prison near the Barrière de Clichy—where inmates had enjoyed unusual privileges such as recreation halls, a cafe, and individual rooms—be made available to them for conversion into a garment-making workshop.

The image of the volcano was ubiquitous during the revolution, and women found ways of appropriating it to make themselves more visible. In fact, historians have wondered about the identity of the Vésuviennes. Available sources reveal that a certain Borme, Jr., a highly inventive young man, posted wall placards early in March calling for the formation of a military regiment of Vésuviennes: women were invited to come to the rue Sainte-Apolline, near the Porte Saint-Denis (a triumphal arch in what is currently the 2nd arrondissement) where they could enlist provided that they "unmarried and between 15 and 30 years old." This call for recruits and the often-satiric drawings in Paris journals were part of the fantastic constructions of the time that associated women, wretched poverty, and parade and public show in spectacular ways; the harsh realities, meanwhile, stayed the same for the women concerned. On 15 April the "women workers of the 1st arrondissement, in a manner similar to the Vésuviennes of March 27, brought a petition signed by Citoyenne Dubois" (*La voix des femmes*, 15 April 1848). These women, too, were seeking publicity and had resorted to staging a procession: "Forty strong, divided in two columns [they] presented the Citizen Louis Blanc with their demands: 'One franc per shirt or per day.'"

Most of the petitions, following the French tradition of pursuing social regeneration through government aid, called for the state to preside over the opening of national workshops, a costly initiative whose goal was to provide work for all. But in 1848—and this is perhaps what was new—women, and the people in general, also envisioned a variety of cooperative, fraternal, and mutual undertakings.

Under the signature "Anna-Marie"—a simple first name in the style customary for Saint-Simonian activists of the 1830s, for whom this practice was a way of breaking away from the father's or husband's name—*La voix des femmes* suggested a detailed plan for a communal family home. The building had to be close to the center of Paris and run by women, all of whom would continue to practice their specialties. Another project, proposed on 3 April, a kind of *maison du peuple* (community center) ahead of its time, seems a more cooperative conception, bringing together the efforts of all people, "great and small, men and women, within the limits of their strength." These associative projects were inspired by a combination of Charles Fourier's philosophy and barracks and dormitory living and labor practices.

National Workshops for Women

After the national workshops were opened, a second battle took place concerning wages and organization. Protests were heard; the problems looked insoluble. The workshops took in women suffering from every form of difficulty. More than 19 workshops had to be opened, each with many workers. All told, 22,000 women were registered—a considerable number, though modest compared to the approximately 115,000 workers registered for the men's workshops around 1 June. The women in the workshops were constantly moving in pursuit of larger quarters. They needed chairs, and they accused Émile Thomas, director of the national workshops, of not having had them manufactured. Women from the rue de Fleurus went to borrow chairs from the Luxembourg, while others worked on the floor. The government played along and put in orders for shirts to be sewn for the Mobile Guard, but the "ladies" consulted at the Luxembourg were not working-class women. Désirée Gay, a well-known activist and now a delegate of the sewing workshops of the 2nd arrondissement (Faubourg Montmartre), who had been elected to represent them to the commission by the women who worked in them, expressed the grievances of the seamstresses: the tasks had been defined by "ladies of the Luxembourg Commission . . . whereas intelligent workingwomen would have eliminated the unnecessary stitches." She then proposed a remedy: that working seamstresses should sit on the Luxembourg Commission as delegates. As a result of this proposal she was promptly discharged. *La voix des femmes* expressed its outrage.

Steady downward pressure on wages made it impossible to reinvigorate the economy on the basis of a policy of greater social justice. From then on, the hope for fraternal union was broken. But that political dream had touched people above and beyond the circles of the established, activist avant-garde. *Le volcan*, an "ultra-revolutionary" newspaper, according to police records, but which actually voiced a range of positions on the political spectrum, stands as excellent testimony of this. It seems to have been written single-handedly by "the fearless Citoyenne" Bassignac, the only editor mentioned (we do not actually know whether Bassignac was a man or a woman). This populist newspaper criticized the Assembly elected on 23 April and its "student confabs"; it lambasted the executive commission, "which does not act," and in its second issue criticized the national women's workshops for the abuse, preferential treatment, and petty tyranny that prevailed in them: the system engendered a vast monopoly that took away all resources from the very women for whom it had been created, while favoring the "monopolizers of furnishings and favoritism." The article devoted to the national workshops for women shows how class conflict ran all through that institution, with the following sketch of the female "general delegates," bourgeois directors of these improvised factories:

> These ladies with their hats swathed in expensive veils, draped in huge shawls bought in the rue Vivienne and their feet shrouded in long silk dresses; these ladies, who nonchalantly read the newspaper, accompanying each sentence with a strawberry dipped in sugar and Bordeaux wine—in no way do they help the ordinary workingwomen, whose thoughts are only that with piecework and their lack of speed they will have a mere 30 centimes, barely enough to buy bread.

The republican authorities showed themselves considerably less negative about women workers' prospects. As early as 15 April, Charles Duclerc, undersecretary of state for Finance and central director of the women's workshops, put an end to the daily subsidy of 50 centimes that had been allocated for unemployed female workers. The arrondissement mayors, meanwhile, appeared satisfied with deliveries of shirts that had been paid for at below-market price. On 4 July the mayor of the 4th arrondissement defended the principle of women's workshops in the name of the struggle against poverty and for morality. Nothing had been stipulated about closing them at this time, although for economic reasons the men's workshops had already been abolished on 28 June, and the announcement of their imminent closing had sparked riots on 23–26 June.

The battle for wages and work was not over, however. Désirée Gay and Jeanne Deroin preferred to renounce 12,000 francs in government subsidies rather than give up on the 1-franc daily minimum wage that the Association Fraternelle des Ouvrières Lingères (Fraternal Association of Women Garmentworkers) demanded as a guarantee for its members. They were not able to start their association up again until October, and then with only 30 women. They were greatly helped in that endeavor by the tailors and saddlers (the tailors, in particular, understood the need to struggle against competition from the privately owned clothing workshops through labor organizing).

People of both sexes working in numerous crafts took action to obtain additional wages that might compensate for the shorter legal working hours. Among the women who did so, there were textile workers, seamstresses, clothiers, and, especially women flax-strippers and makers of corsets, waistcoats, and trusses. Often a wage of 25 centimes is mentioned. Only the fringe-makers' contingent obtained satisfaction. Women tapestry makers (highly skilled by definition) asked for 50 centimes over and above their 2 francs; cobblers, who usually worked as families, demanded an increase for men and women; and goldsmiths demanded equal salaries for both sexes. The women who cut rabbit skins and those who made Falaise stockings asked that machines be banned since they caused unemployment—a concern shared by seven "male" crafts equally affected by the modernization of tools and equipment.

As of March and April, the women employed in the washhouses floating on the Seine on the outskirts of Paris managed to liberate themselves from the oppressive supervision of the foremen, who directed hiring and subjected them to all sorts of humiliating pressures. Wherever employment subsisted or the old crafts asserted themselves in a tradition of close professional solidarity between men and women, the women's struggles enabled them to become real partners. Generalized poverty and wretchedness, which had become a political concern and, secondarily, a moral one, permitted large numbers of women to enter the social arena in their capacity as workers.

Dreams and Rights in the Republic

From the first issue of her paper, *La cause du peuple*, George Sand (1804–76) underscored the presence of women in every demonstration in revolutionary Paris. She chided the bourgeoisie: "In July [1830] and in February [1848], did you not see the women and children of Paris go to meet the machine guns with bare chests and dirty hands? No, of course not; you did not see that; you were hiding; you were afraid." At that time she still believed in the heroism of the people. But how could women attain social justice when they were in a position of civil inequality? Perhaps the Republic was already being experienced and perceived as a progressive march toward equality, including small steps forward and more decisive progressive developments; but in France a group's demands were often satisfied on the spot, in the emotional heat of the event. Thus women hoped, demanded, drew up petitions, held meetings, and developed arguments—not only well-known writers and women known to be activists, but also obscure figures, who wrote to make their wishes and demands known (and also, as we shall see, to express their confidence in the new Republic). The first letter we present may be said to attest to the aspirations of all the anonymous women without rank who attended the meetings of the few clubs open to them, such as that of the utopian socialist Étienne Cabet.

Eugénie Avenard, who worked in trimming and soft furnishings, made so bold as to write an address to the provisional government—a "dream," as the official in the secretariat whose job it was to read such mail peremptorily noted. In her address Avenard recommended that machines be sent to the museums as a cause of unemployment. There was no question of plundering their owners, often "honest contractors": the employment thus recreated would allow for a debit of ten centimes per day and per worker to pay the owners for their machines—a debt of honor. Her handwriting is careful and her clumsy style carries the imprint of the years 1789–93:

> It is painful to be able to calm [sic] a crisis as great as the one we have just experienced. Our hearts are sickened by the suffering they were made to feel by a despotic and disloyal suffrage. Our brothers seemed to be annihilated under this destructive regime, all classes of society were in desperate straits; no more agreement between the poor and no more confidence in commerce. Then the immortal bell rang the hour of deliverance, and tyranny was overthrown, and the Republic came to dry our tears. All that you do, all that you propose to the people, is just and loyal.

From 16 March, other women more highly educated than Eugénie Avenard raised the point that women belonged to the people and thus to the universal electorate. The anonymous signatories of a call for women's suffrage identified themselves as "artists, workers, women of letters, or teachers." They met at 349, rue Saint-Honoré (at the time a major Parisian thoroughfare, in the vicinity of the Palais-Royal and the Louvre), at the house of Antonine André de Saint-Gieles, who presided over the meetings. After every argument in favor of women's suffrage appears the question, "How could we not believe it?" repeated six times like the liturgical responses in church, punctuating a text full of muffled anxiety and timid audacity (*La voix des femmes*, 23 March 1848).

Beginning on 26 March these initiatives were reported by *La voix des femmes*, launched and run by Eugénie Niboyet. She was a Protestant and had worked as secretary of the Society of Christian Morality. She visited prisons and regularly pursued her moral and political work on many fronts. In 1836 she wrote a pamphlet entitled *De la nécessité d'abolir la peine de mort* (On the Necessity of Abolishing Capital Punishment) and in 1838 another on the corollary issue of prison reform: *De la réforme du système pénitentiaire en France* (On the Reform of the Prison System in France). She also produced a more substantial work, entitled *Des aveugles et de leur éducation* (On the Blind and Their Education). Yet another text, written in 1842, shows the deeply Christian foundation of her thinking: *Dieu manifesté par les oeuvres de la Création* (God Manifested through the Works of the Creation). She also translated English literature, namely the works of Maria Edgeworth and Charles Dickens. In introducing herself to her readers, Niboyet underscored her experience as a journalist by listing the newspapers she had helped to found: "In 1834 in Lyon, we founded *Le conseiller des femmes*; in Paris in 1835 *L'ami des familles*, *La paix des deux mondes*, and *L'avenir, journal des intérêts de tous*."

In March 1848 she was joined by women with a more clearly socialist outlook, some of whom were Icarians (followers of Cabet). All of these women reinvested into the paper their capital of activist and journalistic experience. In the very first issue, *La voix des femmes* informed its readers of a declaration written by Madame de Saint-Gieles and delivered to the Hôtel de Ville in the name of the Comité des Droits de la Femme (Committee for Women's Rights). On 26 March the paper announced a meeting that same day at 16, rue Saint-Merri (near the Hôtel de Ville, in what is now the 4th arrondissement), at the home of Madame Bourgeois, one of the four women who had earlier been received by François Arago, member of the provisional government. At the same time, Jeanne Deroin sent four demands on women's rights to the government.

Jeanne Deroin (1805–94) was a militant socialist. She had met the socialist thinkers Pierre Leroux and Auguste Blanqui; had read the works of Saint-Simon, Fourier, and Cabet, and had discussed those of Pierre-Joseph Proudhon. She taught the children of the lower classes together with her own. She, together with Eugénie Niboyet and Désirée Gay, whom we saw in action earlier in 1848, comprised the "three critical figures of power" studied by Michèle Riot-Sarcey (see Riot-Sarcey, 1994); the three are also discussed by Edith Thomas in her pioneering study, *Les femmes de 1848* (1948: The Women of 1848; see Thomas). *La voix des femmes* brought the three women together and became the voice for a variety of initiatives they either launched or supported. In *La voix des femmes* every network was able to find a tribunal, a place for debate and the mutual confrontation of ideas. The success was such that the informal meetings at Niboyet's home soon grew into public assemblies connected with the newspaper. The participants in these assemblies were sometimes called "the women's club," and at least two of their meeting places are known, one in the rue Taranne on the Left Bank and another in the Salle des Spectacles-Concerts at the Bazaar Bonne Nouvelle, near the Porte Saint-Denis (in the present-day 2nd arrondissement). Other activists worked in their own sectors and spoke out only sporadically in *La voix des femmes*. For example, Suzanne Voilquin, a former Saint-Simonian embroiderer who had become a midwife, wrote to demand state remuneration for practitioners of that profession. Texts were also contributed by two women pioneers in education, Élisa Lemonnier and Pauline Rolland, the second of whom was close to Pierre Leroux.

"The Social Individual is Man and Woman"

These were Saint-Simon's dying words, according to report of the banker Olinde Rodriguès. The phrase marked the era with its Saint-Simonian sensibilities, and was turned into a sort of password. *La voix des femmes*, in the second paragraph of its declaration of faith, took up the same theme, which is crucial to an understanding of how the issues of women's suffrage, divorce, and, more generally, women's civil rights were thought about. The emphasis was consistently on union and fraternity, less on emancipation, though the notion of equality was at the heart of the debate. The half-Christian, half-Saint-Simonian utopia was to be based on the "Holy Trinity" of liberty, equality, and fraternity—and therefore, according to the texts, voting rights for women, whether immediately or in the long run. However, by emphasizing union—"Man and woman together, under the wise law of union, form the social individual, and they tend toward the same goal by different means, just as their natures are different" (*La voix des femmes*, 20 March 1848)—priority was given in the private domain to the family and in the public domain to the nation. This consensual utopia took on overtly mystical tones—"The voice of women is the voice of God, for God connects and unites all that has come forth from him" (*La voix des femmes*, 9 April 1848)—even in full electoral battle: "In the salons, the little attic rooms, around the hearth, every voter should find a woman's voice to guide him or serve as an echo. Union, union, that is our rallying call" (*La voix des femmes*, 24 March 1848). Women received support in their struggle from a variety of sources, notably Rodriguès (whose support was indispensable), and Robert Owen (1771–1858), who came at the age of 77 to salute the February Revolution. Then there was the support of Cabet and the Icarians, not to mention the electoral manifesto of the Fourierists. Debate over the theme of union was not restricted to France. Each country where Saint-Simon's thinking had penetrated and where the advancing Industrial Revolution allowed women to claim a role or status followed its own logic in this host of issues.

London and Brussels: "Unite, My Sisters, and Consolidate Your Rights"

Political Europe often sought refuge in London and Brussels, where liberal attitudes toward exiles prevailed. A colorful, variegated society lived in these cities, infused with passion for the new ideas. In the reverse direction, as was the case each time a revolution broke out in France, a small number of generally well-educated men and women crossed the Channel to participate in the event. One such person, the poet Elizabeth Sheridan Carey, wrote to the French provisional government, on 18 March 1848 from Boulogne-sur-Mer, a port city in northern France:

> New laws are demanded by social changes. Formerly, Woman depended upon Man: feeble, uneducated, and enslaved, her political existence is merged with that of her Father, Brother, Husband, next of kin.
>
> Now, liberated by the Religion of Christ, revered as the Mother, Sister, Friend, Counselor of Man; her moral position dignified, her intellectual character strengthened, her sphere of action, as of influence, enlarged, Woman is no longer a nullity. Often self-dependent, she becomes artisan, leader, merchant, professor, house and land owner; contributes to revenues, pays . . . taxes; [she] is a Citizen without the rights of Citizenship; [she] has the will, but is refused the power to serve her Country.

This journey, as so many other intellectual and political contacts, attests to the unprecedented international scope of the "woman question" in 1848.

Early English socialism, dominated by the unique figure of Robert Owen, found a zealous spokeswoman in Anna Doyle Wheeler (1785–1848). She was Irish, from a family of enlightened, land-owning Protestants, and after an unhappy marriage she came to live in Caen, where she met Fourier in 1818. Upon her return to England, she set about trying to unify Saint-Simonian, Fourierist, and Owenian socialists. She received Désirée Veret (Désirée Gay upon her marriage) and Flora Tristan when they visited London. Most important, Wheeler inspired the economist William Thompson to write a pioneering text on behalf of women's suffrage, a work that the author then dedicated to her. It was a response to an article by James Mill's 1824 article "On Government," in which, under the pretext of the then-current political doctrine of virtual representation, the author had included women as mere defenders of their husbands' and fathers' interests. Thompson's *Appeal of One Half of the Human Race, Women, against the Pretensions of the Other Half, Men, to Retain Them in Political and Thence in Civil and Domestic Slavery* (1825) gave primacy to political equality as the keystone of all social transformations necessary for the happiness of women. Thompson systematically examines Mill's arguments to bring to light the irrationality of excluding women from the vote. His demonstration was designed to hit home with Mill, an advocate of utilitarianism and disciple of Jeremy Bentham; both Mill and Bentham were firm believers in rational calculation. By favoring political rights over any other form of right, Thompson's article had a lasting effect on women's activism in England.

The vigor and scope of the battle against slavery, fought mostly through petitions, provided a visible social basis for this political analysis of exclusion. Clare Midgley, in her book on the antislavery campaigns in England from 1780 to 1870, distinguishes two waves of petitions, showing the growing involvement of women during the period with which we are concerned (see Midgley). The petition of 29 April 1833 amassed a total of 190,000 signatures in 10 days, while the 1838 petition against apprenticeships garnered 700,000 signatures. But when women antislavery activists, notably the Quaker Anna Knight, who was living in France during the events of 1848, were refused as delegates to the first World Anti-Slavery Convention (held in London in Exeter Hall in June 1840 and bringing together British and American abolitionists), these activists turned away from the abolitionist cause toward the one most immediately their own—women's rights. The Scotswoman Marion Reid, in her work, *A Plea for Women* (1843), was the first to articulate the link between slavery and women's rights, questioning whether man could be free if woman was a slave. Anna Knight wrote from a similar perspective to the French pastor Coquerel, who was close to the provisional government, to ask him to commit himself to the women's cause: "I have been struggling for twenty years against the oppression of slavery; this question and that of women's rights are one" (1848). Her plea was unsuccessful. The connection between the two causes was perhaps less clearly made in France than in England; in France, slavery had been legally abolished on 4 March. However, *La voix des femmes* did make its columns available to the abolitionist Victor Schoelcher, then France's undersecretary of state for the Navy.

In Belgium, liberal reform was won in 1847 without a revolution. It is difficult to follow the reactions of women, except for such extraordinary figures as Jenny Marx (Karl Marx's niece), who is described in the legal archives as "reciting democratic poems and songs" when she attended meetings.

We know that the Belgian Justine Guillery was a friend of Saint-Simon and that the sisters Zoé and Élise de Gamond styled themselves as priestesses of his doctrine "with zeal and success" before rejecting in horror the followers of Saint-Simon's disciple Prospère Enfantin. The sisters deemed him guilty of a concept of women's emancipation in which public opinion saw only unbridled sensuality. For Zoé Gatti de Gamond, as for a number of French women, early Saint-Simonian convictions were eventually supplanted by admiration for Fourier, and she became a recognized commentator on his work. A resident of Paris from 1837, she founded with Jean Czinski a dissident group called the Union Harmonienne and participated in the newspaper *Nouveau monde* before becoming involved in the realization of the phalanstery of Cîteaux, a financial disaster. This setback did not prevent her, however, from continuing her struggle for utopia through her writings, *Paupérisme et association* (1847; Pauperism and Association), and, in 1848, *L'organisation du travail par l'éducation nationale* (Labor Organization through National Education), in which she expressed the wish that the Revolution of 1848 would become "the era of the universal reorganization of societies." She never ceased to emphasize education, professional training, and the issue of women's civil status—all very different concerns from the struggle for female suffrage in England. The only proposal for women's political equality developed at this time in Belgium was that of Lucien Jottrand, a republican lawyer who in 1847 had founded the Association Démocratique (Democratic Association) with Marx. His intent was to fight "the abnormal situation of women in our societies." When calm returned to Paris, the situation of Belgian women seemed more than ever to have been relegated to the sphere of private life and charity work.

The Elections: "Let Us Live Life in Society"

The elections to the Constituent Assembly, which had been planned for 9 April 1848, were postponed until 23 April to allow the electoral campaign to develop. An ephemeral Club de l'Émancipation des Femmes (Women's Emancipation Club) shows that women wanted to participate. Its secretary was Jenny d'Héricourt, whose real name, as Karen Offen has established, was Jeanne Marie Fabienne Poinsard (see Offen). Born in 1809 in Besançon, Jenny d'Héricourt was then beginning in France the activist career she would later pursue across the Atlantic in Chicago. On 27 March Jeanne Deroin and *La voix des femmes* launched a public debate on women's rights and duties. On 28 March the candidacy of Ernest Legouvé was proposed. A professor at the Collège de France and the son of Gabriel Legouvé, author of *Mérite des femmes* (1804; The Merit of Women), full of conventional and sycophantic phrases, Ernest Legouvé was considered an apostle of the cause. "To work, my sisters, let us plant our flag, let us send whom we wish to the National Assembly. We have gained its voice; let us give it our suffrage," proclaimed *La voix des femmes* (28 March 1848).

"Let us live life in society, which will give a new impetus to the most noble faculties of the soul," pleaded Deroin in the same issue of *La voix des femmes*. We know that she worked with great energy on her own campaign for the legislative elections in 1849. In her "Pétition des femmes aux peuple" (16 March 1848; Women's Petition to the People), she wrote: "It is not only on behalf of women, but in the interest of the whole of society and in the name of a principle that includes the radical extinction of all privileges, that we have asked for the abolition of sexual privilege." Cabet intervened in public, urging that "each candidate be asked for a formal commitment to render justice to women" (*La voix des femmes*, 27 March 1848).

On another issue, Gabrielle d'Altenheym initiated the demand for divorce on 1 April 1848. She signed her demand with the initials "G. S." (corresponding to her maiden name: she was the daughter of the well-known poet Alexandre Soumet). The initials led some people to believe the author was George Sand— an identification that had its own complicated consequences, as we shall see. In connection with divorce, a correspondent for *La voix des femmes*, raised the issue of revising the Civil Code. From that time on, women's suffrage and divorce were the two main focuses of women's activism.

On 5 April, at a meeting of the Club de la rue Taranne, associated with *La voix des femmes* (which reported on the meeting in its issue of 6 April), George Sand was nominated for the elections—without her knowledge or consent. The author of the novels *Lélia* (1833) and *Indiana* (1832) responded by publicly distancing herself from the activists. The struggle for women's political rights was not her battle, and her social position and personal convictions combined to cut this celebrated woman, a progressive republican, off from any socialist affiliation. Her frequently quoted response to the nomination was published on 8 April in *La réforme* and *La vraie République*:

> A newspaper edited by ladies has proclaimed my candidacy for the National Assembly. If this little joke were hurtful only to my self-esteem, by attributing to me a ridiculous pretentiousness, I would let it pass, as with all such jokes, of which any one of us in this world may be the object. But my silence might lead people to believe that I adhere to the principles of which this paper seeks to become the instrument.

In addition to asking that no one vote for her, Sand stated explicitly that she "did not have the honor of knowing a single one of these ladies who form clubs or write papers" and that the articles signed with her initials were not hers at all. In her last sentence we hear the haughtiness of the renowned author: "Without my own acknowledgment, I cannot allow myself to be taken for the standard-bearer of a coterie of women with which I have never had the slightest association, either pleasant or disagreeable."

She revisited the issue in *La vraie République* on 7 May, continuing to reject the idea of women's taking a place in the public arena: "These ladies are wrong to want to throw themselves into the movement." This statement stands in contrast to the attitude of the comtesse Marie d'Agoult who, writing under the name Daniel Stern, acknowledged in her *Lettres républicaines* (1848; Republican Letters), that the "self-proclaimed free women" had "ideas that were just, but ludicrously misrepresented." Sand argued pragmatically that women were inexperienced: "I don't see why, as things presently stand, women should be in such a rush to participate directly in political life." Regarding the future, she expressed what is in fact highly perceptive caution: "It seems to us that the socialist ladies confuse being equal to with being identical to, a mistake for which they should be forgiven, since men often fall into the same confusion of ideas" (*La vraie République*, 7 May 1848).

In mid-April 1848, Sand had prepared—but never sent—an infinitely richer and more subtle appeal to the members of the Comité Central (Central Committee), the coordinating committee of the political Left which decided on nominees, in which she said that it was necessary to "discuss with great sincerity and good faith" the question of women's emancipation and their intervention in public affairs (letter 3910, *Correspondence*). As far as Saint-Simon, Enfantin, or Fourier were concerned, she could not find words harsh enough, and she stubbornly continued to caricature the idea of "these ladies [who] mean to destroy marriage and proclaim promiscuity." She declares that she finds this idea "hateful and revolting," then, correcting herself, calls it simply "strange"; a little further on in the letter she curses the "hideous doctrine" and the "esoteric dogma of promiscuity hidden in the shawl folds" of the women of the clubs.

Returning Civil Rights to Women

Sand belonged to the same generation as the activist women of *La voix des femmes*. She passionately aspired to equality, but had her own ideas about how it should be attained, which she developed at length in her unsent letter to the members of the Central Committee. First of all, women's civil status would have to be changed:

> Social conditions are such that women would not be able to fulfill a political mandate honorably and loyally. Since

woman is under the guardianship of man and dependent on him through marriage, it is absolutely impossible for her to give any guarantee of political independence without, individually and in contempt of law and moral custom, shattering that very guardianship which our moral customs and laws have established.

On the subject of divorce, she was outright pugnacious; where the exercise of this kind of liberty was concerned, nobody could surpass her. And she believed the objective was attainable:

> I think it easy and immediately realizable, and this within our present moral custom. It simply consists in giving woman back the civil rights which marriage alone takes from her and which celibacy alone preserves for her—through an abhorrent mistake of our legislation, which, in fact, places woman in a relation of grasping dependency on man and makes marriage a condition of everlasting minority for her. If young women had the slightest notion of our civil legislation at the age at which they renounce their rights, most of them would decide never to marry at all.

Sand derided the conservatives, who dared to include the words "family" and "property" in their deceitful mottoes, "since the marriage pact they so admire and proclaim shatters the property rights of an entire sex. Either property is not a sacred thing as they affirm, or marriage is not an absolutely sacred thing, and vice versa. Two sacred things cannot destroy each other." She declared divorce "one of the first questions a socialist republic will have to address," and she saw no risk in it for morality, conjugal fidelity, domestic harmony, or parental authority, all of which should be handled through "the arbitration of feeling or reason." Driving home her indictment, the writer underscored the "ridiculous and humiliating" situation of an 80-year-old mother, still a minor. She concluded with a powerful denunciation of the atrocity of everyday [married] life, blasting spinelessness and all forms of violence alike as the corollaries of "savage, atrocious, anti–human rights." It should also be noted, however, that Sand was also scathing on the topic of adulterous women, who had a lover on one sofa and a husband on another: "And you would claim to represent something when you do not even [honestly] represent yourself!"

Sand cited her advanced age as giving her the right to remonstrate so intensely. "Yes, as a woman I have the right, and as a woman who has sharply felt the injustice of the laws and prejudices I have the right to be roused to indignation when I see the reparation that is our due being pushed back by unfortunate ventures and attempts [on the part of women]." Although she did not wish to partake in the pervading bad faith, Sand said she was "in solidarity with those who mocked all that was extravagant and obscene in several such attempts [by women]."

It should be noted that as early as 1833, in her protest against the constraints of marriage on women, the Saint-Simonian militant Claire Démar (née Émilie d'Eymard) had defended a position similar to Sand's, criticizing the Civil Code and its dreadful sentence, "Woman owes obedience to her husband." "Is it recognized as legal, among you," she argued, "when you draw up a lease or a contract, that one of the parties imposes clauses upon the other, and that the latter does not have the right to discuss the conditions in which those clauses apply?"

Le moniteur reported that on 27 May 1848 Citoyen Crémieux, minister of justice, had proposed a law reestablishing divorce (previously abolished by Napoleon Bonaparte) to the Assembly, where it met with nothing but laughter, boisterous tumult, and resistance of all sorts. The vote was postponed on 29 May and the bill was sent on to 18 parliamentary committees, as Francis Ronsin has established (see Ronsin). The women were grateful to Dr. Eugène Villemin, who had argued that a repulsive union, whatever the reason, was tantamount to "legal assassination" (reported in *La voix des femmes*, 18–20 June 1848). Still, the campaign for divorce could not really be waged. On 3 June crowds began disrupting the meetings of the women affiliated with *La voix des femmes* in the hall of the Spectacles-Concerts of the Bazaar Bonne Nouvelle. Eugénie Niboyet had no other solution than to have the premises evacuated by the national guard, a cruel humiliation that *La liberté* did not fail to report on mockingly.

George Sand and "La Cause du Peuple"

Sand's positions are well known, but her way of responding to political developments warrants a few remarks, for her generous and complex populism heralded many traits of later political radicalism. It is interesting, moreover, that she never stopped shuttling back and forth between Paris and Nohant, between the circle closest to power and the provinces.

Concerning the day of 16 April, a complex affair, "an interweaving of meetings with various goals and in some cases tortuous intrigues," as the historian Maurice Agulhon has described it (see Agulhon 1973), Sand, insightfully diagnosed, in a letter written to Maurice Dudevant-Sand that night, that the dream of consensus had been broken; that this was the end of what might be called the "ascendant phase" of the revolution (*Correspondence*). The 200,000 people crying "Death to the communists, death to Cabet!" appalled and dismayed her. It should be said that Alexis de Tocqueville, though of a completely different sensibility, likewise grasped the importance of the moment. Sand's aristocratic contempt erupted before these hate-filled demonstrations, which she viewed as shamefully provincial: "Today Paris behaved like La Châtre," she wrote on the night of 16 April. But as she wanted to maintain solidarity with the ideal *peuple* she thought she had encountered in March, when she wrote, "The people were sublime in their courage and gentleness" (letter to René Vallet de Villeneuve, 4 March 1848, *Correspondence*). It was the extremist leaders whom she accused most vehemently in her April 16 letter to Maurice Dudevant: "The unfortunate Cabet, the despicable Blanqui, the wicked Raspail, and a few others of the same family . . . so unworthy to be speaking of truth!" Her responses point to an understanding of the situation on her part that is in fact not far removed from the ideals of Saint-Simon, as Geneviève Fraisse has shown (see Fraisse).

Sand criticized the selfishness of the bourgeoisie, which had "taken its revenge," and predicted, "the principle [of unity] has been violated and it is the bourgeoisie that will be looking at the scaffold" (letter to Maurice Dudevant, 16–17 April 1848). Here she was inspired by a combination of her solidarity with the provisional government team, some of whom were friends, and the Jacobin heritage according to which, beyond the line of one's own group, there were only sects and factions. More deeply, Saint-Simonian thinking was operative, working in the same direction. We need only consider what she wrote on 9 April 1848 in her paper, *La cause du peuple*, where she set out to reflect on the principles that might establish "the new social order." One of her first proclamations was that "the isolated man does not count at all before God and could not have any effect upon men." In that sentence two political horizons of the time converge: organization and the rejection of castes, whether aristocratic or ideological. We could say, then, that Sand condemned theocracies, even as she conceded, in the same article, that "there are always instances of great and beautiful clarity in a sincere fanatic's soul." In the name of the people as a whole, therefore, she chose to privilege issues touching on moral custom and civil status, such as divorce—a fundamental matter for the exercise of liberty in society—over the more controversial political issue of universal women's suffrage, which for her was a matter to be resolved at some future time.

Women on the Barricades

Just as, for the most part, they were auxiliaries of men in the workplace, women played an auxiliary role on the barricades; despite the spectacular imagery of the time, female combatants remained very much in the shadow of the insurgents. But we can nonetheless get a glimpse of them virtually everywhere in Paris, as Rémi Gossez has emphasized, and police statistics of July 1848 show that of the 600 women apprehended and brought to the Saint-Lazare prison, 222 had been wounded.

Clearly, then, women were not exempt from the cruel privilege of being shot at. Yet here again it is difficult for the historian to follow their actions. The women's press did not speak of these events; the social, moral, and ideological position of its writers made street violence abhorrent to them.

The newspapers *La politique des femmes* and, later, *L'opinion des femmes* thus participated in the collective repression of the horror that all men and women of that time and place experienced. The authorities responsible for charging the arrested insurgents performed that role in specially established courts and determined special penalties; the punishment of choice was "transportation"—that is, deportation without following standard procedures. The authorities' bias was against workers as such, and they assigned themselves the task of confirming and fulfilling the dreadful cry, "This must be brought to an end!" voiced by the entire frightened bourgeoisie, caught in the grips of a destructive fantasy of social dissolution, on the eve of the June events. The presumption of guilt of insurgency attached first and foremost to workers, specifically to workers from the east of Paris, those who had labored in the national workshops or who appeared to be "unstable" on the basis of having changed employment or lodging. Public order was the authorities' paramount concern. To have been in the national guard or an "African" (a line soldier in the ghastly campaigns of the Algerian conquest), or even, for those aged 50 years and older, a "Marie-Louise" (a drafted soldier in the last of Napoleon's armies) exacerbated a worker's case and increased the commission's fear. In fact, it is clear from police archives that the response to the

uprising of June 1848 was a case of the police and judicial system simply deciding that the categories of people it was interested in prosecuting were "dangerous." It was the authorities who had invented the crime, pinning it on a mass of defendants who had done little more than have the misfortune of being arrested.

It must also be remembered that Paris was taken back by military means. Estimates of the number of barricades built range from 600 and 2,400—an enormous gap, which can be explained by confusion about how the term should be defined: was any mere obstacle to be counted as a barricade, or did a barricade imply residents entirely closing off their street and district? The insurrection had no leaders; the individuals arrested and charged were simply those people who had been present at the locations of the last battles, in the Faubourg du Temple and the Faubourg Saint-Antoine. Cavaignac wanted to take back the center of the city before taking on the outer faubourgs, so the mass of people arrested did not reflect the true geography of political and social threat: the really determined insurgents were in the center of the city, while the people of the outlying faubourgs would have preferred to negotiate—and to work.

The Mobile Guard was open to all men who had been even minimally honored for their performance in the February battles against the old regime, but also to any man looking for a uniform and a salary. The guardsmen were a force of untested military efficiency but strong in number and will, and they were able to sweep away the barricades of the Faubourg Saint-Antoine one after another like professional soldiers on the line. They met with virtually no resistance.

The barricade was, above all, a politically defensive space, a sign that the people behind it had seceded. It seems therefore fair to say that people were arrested more out of retaliation than out of any tactical necessity. In fact, those who lived to be arrested could only be prosecuted—or defended—on the basis of their past records, and that is where game of appraising one's neighbor's character and representations of Parisian life at the micro level come in, with the related issues of neighborhood solidarity and enmities. Herein lies the ambiguity of the Marxist explanations that, for ideological reasons, posit that the Mobile Guard did not come from the same working-class world as the insurgents. Studies by Charles Tilly and Lynn Lees, followed by those of Mark Traugott, show on the contrary that both groups were grounded in the working class. Some 20,000 dossiers on the defendants at the Service Historique des Armées de Terre (Historical Archives of the Land Armies) in Vincennes permit us a glimpse of approximately 300 women who were either legally compromised by their solidarity with men or arrested because of their own autonomous acts. In themselves, these women were of no interest to the authorities, who were concerned above all with maintaining order. Some women leaders of the insurgency—in each case designated as "leaders" only by neighbors' testimonies or rumor—were in fact acquitted. The factor that weighed most heavily in the court trials was the testimony of soldiers and guardsmen, but what had they really seen of any plotting or preparations for an insurrection? For the historian this question is hard to answer. Everything in the documents suggests that such revolutionary "intentions" were trumped up after the fact. As for the convicted women, the authorities had no idea what to do with them. "Transportation," the terrible word that meant deportation to Belle-Île (an island off the coast of Brittany) or Algeria for the men who had come before the special commissions, signified, for women, incarceration at Saint-Lazare, the women's prison for common criminals. The overcrowding was terrible, and the prison administration found itself uncomfortably pressed by women's demands for rights and compassionate treatment.

Tocqueville, clear-sighted as always, saw the women involved—even in June—as wishing first and foremost to be able to live decently and raise their children. The first concern of the repressive forces, on the other hand, was to discredit the insurgents as the "dregs of the masses," the lowest of the low, "registered" girls (that is, registered as prostitutes in the police books) and, for the men, ex-convicts. This explanation fails: sources citing the investigative work of the commissions have found virtually no such people. Hard pressed, we can catch a glimpse of a convict in Melun, a town near Paris, and a few girls arrested in their home at five o'clock in the morning for not opening the door for the Mobile Guard fast enough. Two of these women, one 35-year-old former seamstress the other a former merchant, suffered for their past history: one had been condemned 10 years earlier for assault and battery, the other for being an accessory to theft. As for the others in their group of defendants, nothing could be held against them. Another woman, who had just left the widow Bouquet's establishment in the rue de La Reynie, proffered in her drunkenness a stream of inappropriate words against the guardsmen. After this public exploit, her female employer fired her.

During the riot, many male insurgents sought shelter for their wives and children. One brigadier took his wife to the gate of Reuilly, not yet under guard; others, including brush-makers and cobblers, went to the outlying villages of Bercy, Charenton, or Saint-Denis. Just as they stuck together at work, couples faced the storm in solidarity. For example, a 36-year-old bookbinder and bookstore clerk showed exemplary solicitude. He was reputed to be dangerous because of his "exalted spirit" and his role as delegate of the bookbinders. Nevertheless, during the rioting, between two shifts of guard duty in his company, the 12th Legion, he went to pick up his wife at the offices of *L'univers*, in the rue du Vieux-Colombier (in the present-day 6th arrondissement, near the church of Saint-Germain des Prés), where she worked folding newspapers. Clearly, nobody had foreseen the riot or made any arrangements in advance.

Women protected their husbands in all kinds of situations. When the insurgents wanted to make all the tenants of a multiple-dwelling building "march" to defend the barricades, the wife of a second captain of the Place Maubert (in the present-day 5th arrondissement), both of them shoemakers, said he was absent. In another case, neighbors testified, "the wife is as fanatical as the husband." The wife in question was a laundress; her husband, who had already been arrested once for assault and conspiracy, had directed the construction of the barricades in the Faubourg Saint-Antoine (near the Bastille, in the present-day 12th arrondissement), where he worked as a printer of wallpaper. In the rue du Grenier-Saint-Lazare (in the present-day 3rd arrondissement), a woman sent an apprentice with a meal for her husband, who was stationed on the barricades at the corner of the rue Michel-Lecomte. This couple worked at home as jewelers.

Women can also be seen to have acted autonomously. This seems to have been the case for a 48-year-old widow. Well read and financially comfortable (with an income of 8,000 francs a year), she was influenced by phalansterian principles and misunderstood by her family. She lived communally with a family called de Maer, headed by the director of the company La Fraternelle, and she was a shareholder in the *Représentant du peuple*, a workers' daily. She frequented socialist republican clubs such as La Révolution and a club in the rue Popincourt (near the Bastille); she knew people at *La réforme* and fully shared the progressive ideas of her time. In February and again in June, this woman ventured from her home near the quai des Grands-Augustins and went into the battle herself to recover the wounded, whom she treated in the ambulances. Nothing could be legally held against her, except for some correspondence with a prisoner from the Fort de Romainville east of Paris, but, according to archival material assembled by Rémi Gossez, she denied charges of complicity: "I had no wish to become better acquainted with that individual, for he looked like he was dealing in second-sale goods. I wanted to oblige him, and for that I am being punished."

Far more vociferous was a 60-year-old woman living in a furnished room in the rue de Lafayette, who had only her matronliness and age to give her any authority, and who shouted out what all were feeling. Her judges were less severe than they might have been because she had a reputation among the neighbors for being "dumb and chatty . . . ready to mind everyone's business just to make herself important." The court reporters on the case even had to acknowledge that she had tried to reconcile people who were fighting. Accustomed to mediating in working-class circles, she had taken the license to call out against national guards from the wealthy districts who, in the middle of the battle, were arresting a worker who had come down from La Chapelle in the northern part of Paris: "Leave that good man alone, what did he ever do to you? He might be your brother!" She also gave a piece of her mind to the Mobile Guard: "Ah! the snotnoses! The cowards! The rabble! They're firing on their own brothers!" When cross-examined, she swore to her innocence over and over again, but it was difficult for her to convince the judges of her populist brand of humanism.

Legend turned the women of 1848 into overexcited, dangerous furies. Archival sources provide records of vindictive words uttered by a few older women; they tended to be women who practiced their trades in the street, which made them the visible purveyors of rumors and information. As early as 23 June, a 53-year-old button maker near what is now the Marché d'Alligre (near the Bastille) shouted: "Make them come out! Force the men to march to the barricades—my husband and son are already there!" This eruption was later used in court against her husband. Then we get a glimpse, likewise in the Faubourg Saint-Antoine, of the 46-year-old widow Dufour, known as Décade. A fruit and vegetable vendor who worked with her 18-year-old daughter, she is said to have publicly vilified "the gardeners," who were "hiding and let our husbands go to the barricades alone." In another, even more poverty-stricken district near the river Bièvre, known for its dye-works and tannery, between Val-de-Grâce and Gobelins (between the present-day 5th and 13th arrondissements), another produce seller, a 40-year-old widow, was denounced by a 48-year-old woman dairy–shop owner for inciting the tenants of a building to take to the streets. A 58-year-old dressmaker named Louise Henri, mother of a Mobile Guardsman and the wife of a national guardsman named Cormery, seems to have been more vindictive still. A few days before the uprising she was already venting her exasperation: "When will we be rid of those people, the rich, who swindle and dominate us?" On June 25 she is said to have run wild in front of the door of the seed merchant's place, where General Bréa was being held, shouting, "They must be shot! Kill them—they've had our brothers executed!" Her words were reprinted repeatedly in the press. The good services her son had rendered made it possible for her to be pardoned in November 1848. Such practices were of no interest to the military authorities.

In fact, the military authorities did not believe there were any women leaders. Some proof of this may be seen in the case of a 76-year-old woman day laborer in Belleville who, with all sorts of evidence against her, was acquitted of all charges. Still, the court report on her was severe:

> Even on Monday, after the battles on the barricade of Ménilmontant, when the insurgents' cause had been lost and its defenders could have no further hope, this Fury still wanted barricades; she was still crying for murder and carnage when the good citizens, sure to be delivered soon and seeking to speed the hour of their deliverance, had started destroying the obstacles that held them prisoner. She went running to the city hall to denounce the audacity of these friends of order, bringing back with her hordes of the enraged, at whom she screamed for blood while indicating to them those who should be their victims.

Even closer to the image of the *pétroleuses*—the women who were to set off incendiary bombs during the Commune of 1871—was a 58-year-old woman who reportedly sold chemical matches along with her vegetables. She was apparently not quite right in the head anymore, but was said to have helped on the barricades in the rue Saint-Honoré, distributing cartridges, instigating acts of looting, and setting fires. She claimed that people were hearing nothing but lies, only what they expected to hear. "If this keeps up, the rich will have to give me some," she said, displaying a keen awareness of social relations and providing a fine example of the Parisian street talk of the time.

On the other hand, people did manage, with their fantasmatic fears, to construct a few "monsters." En route to her little garden in Belleville at five o'clock in the morning, a 49-year-old glazer was accused by two 19-year-old Mobile Guardsmen of having cut off the heads of their dead comrades with her knife at the barricade of the Faubourg du Temple, which they had just taken. If not drunk with battle, the guardsmen were no doubt full of anxiety about death—whence the powerful images they evoked of severed, discarded, and scattered limbs—signifying a loss of both body and identity. The only Parisian-born woman to be called before the War Council, the glazer was condemned to 10 years' hard labor.

Generally, women were not on the barricades because they were at home—where they could nonetheless be wounded or die at age 14 on the threshold of their houses. One woman was shot on the corner of the rue du Faubourg du Temple as she returned home, after having helped a soldier of the 59th line, isolated in the middle of the insurgents, to escape. There was also, however, the case of a young girl arrested with her hands and face black with gunpowder. A laundress of fine linen who lived with her parents in the rue de la Roquette (near the Bastille), this girl had been "adopted" by the 15th Battalion of the Mobile Guard. She was apparently arrested on the barricades in the center and held at the Hôtel de Ville; she seems to have escaped but later was finally spotted, thanks to her guardsman's uniform, and picked up as she was fleeing on the road to Neuilly, a village to the west of Paris. Another incarnation of the irrepressible woman in revolt was a 19-year-old fruit and vegetable seller, said to be a "streetwalker," because she lived with "the worst sorts of the area." Already arrested in 1846 for "inciting to rebellion," she insulted a musician of the 48th line on 20 June. On 24 June she got people to pour vitriol and gasoline from demijohns onto the bundles of straw she herself had brought to the entryway of the barracks at Reuilly, to feed a fire that was already burning, all the while shouting in unison with other assailants, "the dregs of the district's population." These words were not reported. Was this bad luck? Society's vengeance? This young woman was arrested in July, after denunciation by bandleader at the barracks near where she lived. It seems that only "old women" with the authority of age and matronly status had the right to speak out.

An Act Worthy of the Annals of the Revolution

The recorded examples cited above, all involving women born in Paris (with the exception of the "doyenne" of Belleville) do not give a complete idea of the situation, but on the basis of this sample we may say that there was a considerable gap between the facts of the 1848 uprising and constructed representations of it. With this in mind let us turn to the renowned story, codified in its narrative form from the very first days on, of the women on the barricade.

The event took place on one of the first barricades taken, at the intersection of the rue de Cléry, the rue d'Aboukir, and the rue de la Lune, close to the Porte Saint-Denis, Paris' noblest gate, on 23 June at 11 o'clock in the morning. Men from the wealthy districts ended up firing their weapons and killing women in order to advance toward the 6th arrondissement, where the city changed its aspect and the common people dominated, very close to the Vésuviennes' former meeting place in rue Sainte-Apolline (in the Porte Saint-Denis quarter). All the ephemeral elements in this event converged to fuel the imaginings and representations of the time, now an indelible part of the collective memory.

Historians can glean little from the written accounts of the event, which, taken together, present many contradictions. We can only say with the historian Maurice Agulhon in *Marianne au combat: L'imagerie et la symbolique républicaines de 1789 à 1880* (1979; *Marianne into Battle: Republican Imagery and Symbolism in France, 1789–1880*) that the entire press went repeatedly back and forth over the details of the event, and that it concerned women flag-bearers—as distinct from the two other possible occupations for woman during the revolution: elite combat fighting (this concerned very few) or dressing up and parading as a "living allegory" (see Agulhon 1979).

In all the aforementioned narratives, two women die. The archives, on the other hand, tell a completely different story: one of the women, 20-year-old Adèle Guerre, survived and was later interrogated. The accounts—still regularly quoted—variously depict her as a "young and beautiful grisette, . . . tastefully dressed, bare-armed," or else "a tall and beautiful young person, bare-headed, the front of her hair covered with a lace scarf, arms bare, in a dress of striped barège . . . [a] shopgirl." Another describes her as having "thick hair, her arms bare, wearing a dress of a dazzling color." In *Choses vues* (1887; *Things Seen*), Victor Hugo portrays her as a prostitute, hardening her features with gestures the others do not mention.

Adèle Guerre, a woman insurgent who left clear traces in the archives, resided in the rue du Faubourg Poissonnière, very close to where she did what she did. The previous evening, she had been given for safekeeping the flag of the 141st Brigade of the national workshops in the 12th arrondissement. On 23 June she reportedly planted or brandished the flag on the barricade, before helping a wounded person. Another woman, bearing another flag, was killed at her side. Adèle Guerre then took her own flag to a baker's at 18, boulevard de Bonne-Nouvelle in the Porte Saint-Denis quarter and went back to take care of the wounded in the ambulances of the Spectacles-Concerts (former venue for the meetings of *La voix des femmes*); the surgeon-major took notice of her devotion. When she went back to the bakery later to pick up the flag, the baker's wife threatened to have her arrested. "I have nothing to fear!" she retorted, "Ledru-Rollin is with me!" [referring to Alexandre-Auguste Ledru-Rollin, an influential member of the Chamber of Deputies who associated with Lamartine and Blanc in seeking social reforms]. Adèle Guerre was denounced by an artist residing on the boulevard de Bonne-Nouvelle. She was being supported by a male friend, a cabinetmaker in the rue de Ménilmontant, just inside the city gate. She had three brothers in Belleville. The oldest, who worked preparing wood for gilding, was sentenced to five years in detention.

The plot thickens when accounts by six different authors, many of whom we have already briefly quoted above, are compared. Hugo was not the only celebrated writer among them. In an article entitled "Der 23.Juni" (June 21) in the 28 June 1848 issue of *Neue Rheinische Zeitung*, Engels wrote:

> The boulevard Saint-Denis was heavily entrenched. . . . The people fought with an indescribable disdain for death. On the barricade of the rue de Cléry, a strong detachment of the national guard made a flank attack. The majority of the barricade's defenders retreated. Only seven men and two women, two young and beautiful grisettes, remained at their posts. One of the seven men climbed up on the barricade, the flag in his hand. The other men began to fire. The national guard returned fire and the flag-bearer fell. Then one of the girls, tastefully dressed, bare-armed, seized the flag, crossed the barricade, and marched on the national guard. The firing continued and the bourgeois of the national guard slaughtered the young girl, since she was close to their bayonets. The other grisette then immediately leaped forward, seized the flag, then raised the head of her companion, and furious, seeing she was dead, began hurling stones at the national guard. She, too, fell beneath the bourgeois' bullets. . . . It was the lions and wolves of the Stock Exchange [fighting] in the 2nd Legion who carried out this noble deed against seven workers and two grisettes.

Though it may seem less ideological, the second account of the event is no less partisan. It is the work of Adolphe de Bragel-

onne, a journalist and writer who as early as the summer of 1848 set out to write an apologia for General Cavaignac, entitled *Quatre-vingt heures de guerre civile; Histoire illustrée des journées de juin 1848* (Eighty Hours of Civil War: Illustrated History of the Days of June 1848). The gist of this apologia was that the general's brutal methods—together with his view of the insurgents as absolute enemies—could only be accounted for by his incompetence in matters of street warfare. The author criticizes Cavaignac's inaction on 23 and 24 June and the lack of preventive measures. Then we read:

> And then we witnessed one of those acts with which our revolutionary annals abound. A tall and beautiful young person . . . arms bare, from the class of shop girls, grabs hold of the flag, climbs up over the barricade, and moves forward to the entrance of the rue de Cléry, waving her flag and provoking the national guard with her words and gestures. The fire from the barricade did not stop, and, to their honor, it must be said that the national guardsmen, discovering the girl directly in front of their rifles, decided to return fire only after they had been fired upon for the third time. The girl dropped down dead and the other woman leaped forward, grabbed the flag and, after lifting the head of her companion, rose up, furious, and began throwing stones at the assailants. A terrible blast of shooting then brought her down and made the rest evacuate the barricade.

The third account was written later and was openly hostile to Cavaignac. In 1869 Hippolyte Castille, long won over to the Empire, remembered the episode in *Les massacres de juin 1848* (The Massacres of June 1848). His account is terse, beginning simply, "Toward noon, under a sunny sky . . ." The author indicates that nine national guardsmen were killed at the first assault and that at the second "few insurgents escaped. The national guard killed two women."

Marie d'Agoult, under her pen name Daniel Stern, used her own flair for the dramatic to erect a commemorative tomb for the women in her *Histoire de la Révolution de 1848* (History of the 1848 Revolution) published between 1850 and 1853:

> The national guardsmen charged back with vigor. The leader of the insurgents, standing on an overturned carriage, flag in hand, gave the order to fire and was mortally wounded. The fight was thought to be over, but as the flag slipped away from the leader it was seized by a young girl who had not been previously noticed. She raised it above her head and began waving it wildly. With thick hair and bare arms, wearing a dress of a dazzling color, she seemed to challenge death. At this sight, the national guard hesitated to fire; they shouted at the girl to retreat, but she remained there, dauntless, provoking the assailants with gesture and word. A shot was fired; she staggered and crumpled. But suddenly another woman leaped to her side; with one hand she supported the blood-soaked body of her companion while with the other she hurled stones at the assailants. A new volley was fired and she in turn fell, down onto the corpse she held in her arms. At that terrible moment, when the shooting was at its worst, a surgeon of the national guard broke rank to come help the women. Seeing them lifeless he returned, once again

in the thick of the bullets' crossfire, toward the wounded of the national guard. The barricade was taken by assault; the insurgents fled toward the Faubourg Saint-Denis. The shooting lasted at least half an hour.

We have two more views of the event, the first from an anonymous source, the second, and last, from Victor Hugo.

The first text, part of the unsigned *Histoire des journées de juin 1848* (History of the June days), was published in 1848:

From the neighboring houses, all occupied by the insurgents, came a terrible firing of shots; the national guard responded. After two hours of battle, in which the rebels' women showed the most terrible determination, following one another to hold the flag aloft on the barricade, the barricade was taken, at the cost of the blood of many national guardsmen.

Finally, in *Things Seen*, Victor Hugo clearly marked the social gap between notables (such as himself) and *le peuple* by introducing the gestures of a "whore":

The June uprising, right from the start, presented strange lineaments. It displayed suddenly, to a horrified society, monstrous and unknown forms.

The first barricade was set up by Friday morning the 23rd, at the Porte Saint-Denis: it was attacked the same day. The national guard conducted itself resolutely. They were battalions of the 1rst and 2nd Legions. When the attackers, who arrived by the Boulevard, came within range, a formidable volley was loosed from the barricade and strewed the roadway with guardsmen. The national guard, more irritated than intimidated, charged the barricade at a run.

At that moment a woman appeared on the crest of the barricade, a young woman, beautiful, dishevelled, terrifying. This woman, who was a public whore, pulled her dress up to the waist and cried to the guardsmen, in that dreadful brothel language that one is always obliged to translate: "Cowards! Fire, if you dare, at the belly of a woman!"

Here things took an awful turn. The national guard did not hesitate. A fusillade toppled the miserable creature. She fell with a great cry. There was a horrified silence at the barricade and among the attackers.

Suddenly a second woman appeared. This one was younger and still more beautiful; she was practically a child, barely seventeen. What profound misery! She, too, was a public whore. She raised her dress, showed her belly, and cried, "Fire, you bandits!" They fired. She fell, pierced with bullets, on top of the other's body.

That was how this war began.

[NOTE: The above-cited passage was expurgated from 19th-century translations of Hugo's work into English. The translation above is taken from Neil Hertz, *The End of the Line: Essays on Psychoanalysis and the Sublime* 1985.]

These narratives of furor and bloodshed are not merely charged with the sort of ideological passions and phantasmagoric recollections that prompted Pierre Leroux to comment, rather helplessly: "Passions, passions, always passions!" In fact, these accounts may be said to function as screen memories in response to the real butchery enacted to quell the uprising. The woman flag-bearer rises up on the barricades as an image of transgression against an order now in disarray—and as an annunciation, the emblem of a different promise. For whether she is seen as dazzling or destitute, she derealizes the history of the masses she has come to symbolize. With this in mind we can understand how readily the imagination of the time welcomed the image of another set of female figures: the Virgin Mary appearing to Bernadette Soubirous at Lourdes in 1858. The two appear as a kind of opposite to the women on the barricade, and as such they may be said to have served to exorcise French collective repression of the uprising's bloody end. Two women, one celestial yet speaking the language of the meek, the other the humblest of the humble, appear in the chthonic, regenerative shade of a grotto near a sparkling brook in the Pyrénées. Surely Baudelaire's *spleen*, as studied by Dolf Oehler (see Oehler), is not the only cultural invention to have been deeply informed by the collective forgetting of the events of June 1848. Other cultural forms employing the image of woman have likewise been fueled by that forgetting.

This brief view of persons and events shows that in 1848 in Paris, women were actors within a particularly mobile and contradictory social, economic, and political context. In this extreme situation, recourse to the traditional protective power of the state for labor organization went hand in hand with a variety of associative initiatives, while a female elite, often of philanthropic background and rich in experience, lent all sorts of assistance. In effect, the moral philosophy of the time sought to invest the social field under the Christian and socialist auspices of fraternity and union. Simultaneously, the question of women's right to equality was raised. Although there were no decisive gains for the women of France in 1848, they nonetheless won an identity for themselves in the economic realm—that of the *ouvrière*, or woman worker (often seen as "dreadful" and "terrifying" by bourgeois eyes)—and, in the civic realm, a moral cohesiveness that in turn makes it possible to understand their later struggles. It may be said that in 1848 in France, women as a coalescing social group entered the era of the multitudes.

Bibliography

The authors extend special thanks to Rémi Gossez for giving them access to his personal documentation and unpublished work. The authors are also very grateful to Eliane Gubin, Catherine Jacques, and Valerie Piette for Belgium documentation and to Bonnie Anderson for England documentation.

Manuscript Sources

Archives Nationales, Paris. BB[18] Justice; BB[30] 301 (items 2950 and 3419) [addresses and correspondence of the provisional government]; C934 [Ministry of War, various correspondence: Prefecture of Police and penitentiary administration]; F[9] [Ministry of the Interior: Commission on Damages of February and June 1848 (sometimes combined with reports for December 1851)]

Archives de la Préfecture de Police, Paris. Aa 427–429 [various reports]

Service Historique des Armées de Terre, Vincennes, France. F1.9 and F1.18 [documents on the insurrection of June 1848]

Print Sources

Bragelonne, Adolphe de Balathier de, *Quatre-vingts heures de guerre civile: Histoire illustrée des journées de juin 1848*, Paris: Martineau, n.d.

Cabet, Étienne, *La femme, ses qualités, ses titres, ses droits, son malheureux sort dans la société actuelle: Son bonheur dans la communauté*, Paris: Bureau du Populaire, 1844

Castille, Hippolyte, *Les massacres de juin 1848*, Paris: Les Principaux Libraires, 1869

Corbon, Anthime, *Le secret du peuple de Paris*, Paris: Pagnerre, 1863

Démar, Claire, *Textes sur l'affranchissement des femmes, 1832–1833*, Paris: Payot, 1976

Engels, Friedrich, "Der 23.Juni," *Neue Rheinische Zeitung*, reprinted in *Karl Marx, Friedrich Engels*, vol. 5, Berlin: Verlag, 1982

Histoire des journées de juin, Paris: Martinon, 1848

Hugo, Victor, *Choses vues*, Paris: Hetzel, 1887; as *Things Seen*, New York: Harper and Brothers, 1887

Pardigon, François, *Épisodes des journées de juin 1848*, London: Jeffs, 1852

Sand, George, *Correspondance 8: juillet 1847–décembre 1848*, edited by Georges Lubin, Paris: Garnier, 1971

Sand, George, *Politique et polémiques, 1843–1850*, edited by Michelle Perrot, Paris: Imprimerie Nationale, 1997

Stern, Daniel, *Histoire de la Révolution de 1848*, 3 vols., Paris: Sandré, 1850–53; reprint, 1 vol., Paris: Balland, 1985

Stern, Daniel, *Lettres républicaines*, Paris: Amyot, 1848

Reference Works

Abensour, Léon, *Le féminisme sous le règne de Louis-Philippe et en 1848*, Paris: Plon Nourrit, 1913

Agulhon, Maurice, *1848; ou, L'apprentissage de la République, 1848–1852*, Paris: Seuil, 1973; as *The Republican Experiment, 1848–1852*, translated by Janet Lloyd, Cambridge, England, and New York: Cambridge University Press, 1983

Agulhon, Maurice, "Classe ouvrière et sociabilité avant 1848," in *Histoire vagabonde*, by Agulhon, vol. 2, Paris: Gallimard, 1988

Agulhon, Maurice, *Marianne au combat: L'imagerie et la symbolique républicaines de 1789 à 1880*, Paris: Flammarion, 1979; as *Marianne into Battle: Republican Imagery and Symbolism in France, 1789–1880*, Cambridge and New York: Cambridge University Press, 1981

Agulhon, Maurice, *Les quarante-huitards*, Paris: Gallimard/Julliard, 1975

Anderson, Bonnie S., "Influence internationale sur les mouvements de femmes en 1848," in *Cent cinquantenaire de la Révolution de 1848*, edited by Jean-Luc Mayaud, Paris: Créaphis, 1999

Charléty, Sébastien, *Histoire du Saint-Simonisme*, Paris: Hachette, 1896; reprint, Paris: Hartmann, 1931

Corbin, Alain, Jacqueline Lalouette, and Michèle Riot-Sarcey, editors, *Femmes dans la cité, 1815–1871*, Grâne, France: Créaphis, 1997

Demier, Francis, and Jean-Luc Mayaud, editors, "Revue d'histoire du XIXᵉ siècle," *Cinquante ans de recherches sur 1848* 14, no. 1 (1997)

Dolléans, Édouard, *George Sand: Féminisme et mouvement ouvrier*, Paris: Éditions Ouvrières, 1951

Elhadad, Lydia, "Femmes prénommées: Les prolétaires Saint-Simoniennes rédactrices de 'La femme libre,' 1832–1834," *Les révoltes logiques* 4 (Winter 1977) and 5 (Spring-Summer 1977)

Fejtö, François, "Paris des années 40: Capitale de la Révolution," in *Actes du Congrès historique du centenaire de la Révolution de 1848*, Paris: Presses Universitaires de France, 1948

" 'La femme libre,' 1832–1834," *Les révoltes logiques* 4 (Winter 1977), and 5 (Spring/Summer 1977)

Fraisse, Geneviève, "Les femmes libres de 1848: Moralisme et féminisme," *Révoltes logiques* 1 (Winter 1975)

Gaillard, Jeanne, *Paris: La ville, 1852–1870:L'urbanisme parisien à l'heure d'Haussman[n]: Des provinciaux aux Parisiens: La vocation ou les vocations parisiennes*, Lille, France: Université Lille III, and Paris: Champion, 1976

Gossez, Rémi, *Les ouvriers de Paris*, Paris: Société d'Histoire de la Révolution de 1848, 1967

Hertz, Neil, *The End of the Line: Essays on Psychoanalysis and the Sublime*, New York: Columbia University Press, 1985

Labrousse, Ernest, "1848–1830–1789: Comment naissent les révolutions," *Actes du Congrès historique du centenaire de la Révolution de 1848*, Paris: Presses Universitaires de France, 1948

Michaud, Stéphane, *Muse et madone: Visages de la femme de la Révolution française aux apparitions de Lourdes*, Paris: Seuil, 1985

Oehler, Dolf, *Ein Höllensturz der alten Welt: Zur Selbsterforschung d. Moderne nach d. Juni 1848*, Frankfurt: Suhrkamp, 1988

Offen, Karen, "Femmes et suffrage universel: Une comparaison France-Atlantique," in *Cent cinquantenaire de la Révolution de 1848*, edited by Jean-Luc Mayaud, Paris: Créaphis, 1999

Offen, Karen, "A Nineteenth-Century French Feminist Rediscovered: Jenny P. d'Héricourt, 1809–1875," *Signs: Journal of Women in Culture and Society*, vol. 13, no. 1 (Autumn 1987)

Perrot, Michelle, "La morale politique de George Sand," in *Flora Tristan, George Sand, Pauline Roland:Les femmes et l'invention d'une nouvelle morale, 1830–1848*, edited by Stéphane Michaud, Paris: Créaphis, 1994

Ranvier, Adrien, "Une féministe de 1848, Jeanne Deroin," in *La révolution de 1848*, edited by Imbert de Saint-Amand, Paris: Dentu, 1894; translated in *The Revolution of 1848*, translated by Elizabeth Gilbert Martin, New York: Scribner, and London: Hutchinson, 1895

Rébérioux, Madeleine, "George Sand, Flora Tristan et la question sociale," in *Flora Tristan, George Sand, Pauline Roland:Les femmes et l'invention d'une nouvelle morale, 1830–1848*, edited by Stéphane Michaud, Paris: Créaphis, 1994

La révolution de 1848 (exhib. cat.), Paris: Bibliothèque Nationale, 1948

Les révolutions de 1848: L'Europe des images (exhib. cat.), 2 vols., Paris: Assemblée Nationale, 1998

Riot-Sarcey, Michèle, "1848, notes sur les Révolutions en Europe: La place des femmes contestée," in *Revue d'histoire du XIXᵉ siècle, 1848: Nouveaux regards*, edited by Riot-Sarcey and Jean-Claude Caron, 1997

Riot-Sarcey, Michèle, "De 'l'universel suffrage' à l'association ou l'utopie de 1848," in *Cent cinquantenaire de la Révolution de 1848*, edited by Jean-Luc Mayaud, Paris: Créaphis, 1999

Riot-Sarcey, Michèle, *La démocratie à l'épreuve des femmes: Trois figures critiques du pouvoir, 1830–1848*, Paris: Albin Michel, 1994

Riot-Sarcey, Michèle, "Le rêve d'une autre République," in *Révolution et République: L'exception française*, edited by Michel Vovelle, Paris: Kimé, 1994

Robert, Vincent, *Les chemins de la manifestation, 1848–1914*, Lyon, France: Presses Universitaires de Lyon, 1996

Ronsin, Francis, *Les divorciaires: Affrontements politiques et conception du mariagedans la France du XIXᵉ siècle*, Paris: Aubier, 1992

Soldani, Simonetta, "Les femmes et la nation au cours de la Révolution italienne de 1848," in *Cent cinquantenaire de la Révolution de 1848*, edited by Jean-Luc Mayaud, Paris: Créaphis, 1999

Strumingher, Laura, "The Vésuviennes: Images of Women Warriors in 1848 and Their Significance for French History," in *Women in European Culture and Society: History of European Ideas*, edited by Karen Offen, Oxford and New York: Pergamon Press, 1987

Sullerot, Évelyne, "Journaux féminins et luttes ouvrières, 1848–1849," in *La presse ouvrière, 1819–1850: Angleterre, États-Unis, France, Belgique, Italie, Allemagne, Tchécoslovaquie, Hongrie*, edited by Jacques Léon Godechot, Bures-sur-Yvette, France: Société d'Histoire de la Révolution de 1848, 1966

Thibert, Marguerite, *Le féminisme dans le socialisme français de 1830 à 1850*, Paris: Giard, 1926

Thomas, Édith, *Les femmes de 1848*, Paris: Presses Universitaires de France, 1948

Tilly, Charles, and Lynn H. Lees, "The People of June 1848," in *Revolution and Reaction: 1848 and the Second French Republic*, edited by Roger Price, London: Croom Helm, and New York: Barnes and Noble Books, 1975

Tixerant, Jules, *Le féminisme à l'époque de 1848 dans l'ordre politique et dans l'ordre économique*, Paris: Giard et Brière, 1908

Traugott, Mark, *Armies of the Poor:Determinants of Working-Class Participation in the Parisian Insurrection of June 1848*, Princeton, New Jersey: Princeton University Press, 1985

Voilquin, Suzanne, *Souvenirs d'une fille du people; ou, La Saint-Simonienne en Égypte, 1834 à 1836*, Paris: Sauzet, 1866; reprint, Paris: Maspero, 1978

Newspapers

La cause du peuple, 9–23 April 1848, se 1–3.

Le moniteur universel, Journal official de la République française, 25–26 February, 4–5 March, 27 March and 27 May 1848.

Neue rheinische Zeitung, 28 June 1848.

L'opinion des femmes, 1–6 August 1848–August 1849.

La politique des femmes, 1, 18 June 1848 and 2 August 1848.

La voix des femmes, 20 March–20 June 1848.

La vraie République, 26 March–24 June 1848 and 8–21 August 1848.

WOMEN IN THE GERMAN STATES, 1848–1849

BONNIE S. ANDERSON

"I ENLIST WOMEN CITIZENS IN the realm of freedom," proclaimed the title page of the *Frauen-Zeitung*, published on 21 April 1849 in Meissen by the 30-year-old Louise Otto. Declaring that "Freedom is indivisible," Otto began by asserting:

> The history of all times and especially of today teaches us *that those who do not think about themselves will be forgotten!* That is what I wrote in May 1848, when I aimed my words at the men in Saxony who were concerned with the question of labor. Speaking for my sisters, I thus admonished them to think of poor women workers, so that they not be forgotten. And that is why I am editing a women's newspaper. In the midst of the great upheavals in which we all find ourselves, women will be forgotten if they do not think about themselves!

These brave words, with their assertion of solidarity both with women of all classes and with like-minded men, represent a high-water mark of German female activism during the revolutions of 1848–49. Behind Otto's ability to publish a women's political newspaper and make such declarations in 1849 lay years of education, writing, and meetings aimed at inserting women into a particular political development—the *Sonderweg* (special path) of German history—which among other things excluded all women from any political participation whatsoever. Before the achievements of German women during the revolutionary years can be appreciated, their difficult politicization, during the *Vormärz*, the period from 1830 to 1848, which is defined by the revolutions to come, must first be examined. The political and economic situation shaped the ways in which German men and women were able to seize the moment in 1848–49.

The German Background

In Germany the multiplicity of states retarded both political and economic development throughout the first half of the 19th century. Although the Congress of Vienna in 1815 had con-

firmed Napoleon's consolidation of the more than 300 states of the old Holy Roman Empire into 39 entities, the divisions between these markedly unequal units dominated political life between 1815 and 1848. Ranging from tiny city-states such as Hamburg and Frankfurt to the two giants, Prussia and Austria—which also encompassed non-German Hapsburg lands in Central Europe and Italy—the German states after 1815 experienced a conservative resurgence that restored ancien régime conditions to most territories. Associating both liberalism and national unification with the conquering French, German monarchs and aristocrats reaffirmed the most reactionary elements within their individual societies. Absolute monarchy prevailed, supported by state churches and local aristocracies. While serfdom ended, feudal obligations remained. Everywhere, the middle class was excluded from all political processes. Well into the 19th century, the German middle class remained in the political position of the French bourgeoisie before 1789.

Social and economic conditions varied widely throughout the region that stretched from the southern Tyrol to Schleswig-Holstein on the Danish border, from the French-influenced Rhineland in the west to the plains of Polish Prussia in the east. Predominately rural, with 80 percent of the population living on the land, German states ranged from a majority with still wholly agricultural economies to the Rhineland and Saxony, which witnessed extensive industrial development in these years. However, all economic growth stopped at the local borders that crisscrossed the German lands. A complex system of tolls, tariffs, and individual currencies slowed large-scale economic development. Economic and political conditions depended on the inclination of individual rulers. Prussia, Bavaria, and Baden abolished child labor; other states retained it. Saxony and the Rhineland encouraged the growth of factories; others prevented it. Press censorship remained the norm—several states excised all mention of railroads, a sign of progress and change, from publications—but the proximity of more-liberal territories enabled radical literature to circulate illegally across borders. Although reactionary political conditions prevailed, substantial progressive opposition existed in the middle class, focusing on the intertwined issues of economic development and national unification.

This period in German history, from 1815 to 1848, is called the Biedermayer era, after a caricature of a middle-class "Papa" whose name came to exemplify the plain domestic style associated with the expanding bourgeoisie. These years saw slow but sustained growth in both the middle class and the German economy. Feudal obligations and the power of the guilds withered away. Population increased steadily, rising from 25 million in 1815 to 34.5 million in 1845. Cities grew, and railroad construction progressed. By 1850 Berlin had more than 400,000 inhabitants, and the German railroad system was the most extensive on the continent. The customs union of 1834, the Zollverein, laid the foundation for increased economic progress and unification. But political development remained frozen. Any attempts to raise issues concerning political representation, civil liberties, or national unification resulted in massive repression. Directed by Metternich in Austria and Friedrich Wilhelm III in Prussia, reactionary practices were implemented forcefully by local rulers.

Until the revolutions of 1830, such repression was standard in a Europe still controlled by the principles of divine-right monarchy, the denial of such fundamental civil liberties as freedom of speech or freedom of the press, and state churches, reinforced by armed international intervention when necessary. After 1830, however, German repression became more exceptional in western Europe, helping to create the unique German path of political development. While historians date the beginning of a German opposition movement to 1830, they agree that the combined efforts of the Austrian prime minister and the Prussian king stifled liberal development throughout the region. In the early 1830s a number of smaller German states adopted constitutions that proclaimed equality before the law, the sovereignty or cosovereignty of the parliament, and basic civil rights. Those wanting change—both the unification of the German states and political reforms that increased democracy—attempted to come together. Forbidden to attend political meetings, more than 30,000 Germans converged in May 1832 in Hambach for a "celebration" of nationalism and constitutionalism. Students and women participated in large numbers, listening to the debates and speeches on the "united free states of Germany" in a "confederate Republican Europe."

Hambach, the last such gathering before the 1848 revolutions, foreshadowed the events of that year in its debates, the inability of its participants to agree on a concerted program of action, and the ferocity of the repression it provoked. The Austrian and Prussian governments severely limited the authority of existing parliaments and curtailed freedom of the press. In Hanover the monarch abolished the constitution; when seven Göttingen professors objected, they were summarily dismissed and forced to leave the kingdom. Continued repression throughout the *Vormärz* ensured that German political development was delayed. Both Germans and others agreed that the Germans lagged behind France and England in these years. Conservatives, who wanted to retain crown and state while fostering economic development, and reactionaries, who wished to return to a feudal past, approved of this German "traditionalism." Liberals, who wanted some civil rights and wanted the middle class to share power with the monarch and the aristocrats, and radicals, who wanted democracy, freedom of religion, and, often, some form of socialism, sought to overturn this German "backwardness."

The Status of German Women

The situation of women in Germany in this era was seen by both Germans and foreigners as representative of an earlier period in other Western nations. German women comprised the most traditional sector of German society. In the lower classes, arduous physical labor remained the norm. As increasing numbers of women began work in the new factories, they often exchanged poorly paid exhausting rural labor for poorly paid exhausting industrial labor. In either circumstance, they retained primary responsibility for raising their children, who were usually brought to the fields and the factories by their mothers. During this period, the birthrate and family size increased among poor women, as did illegitimacy rates. Mothers bore more children under adverse circumstances. Such conditions, which intensified with the increased production demanded by early industrialism, resulted in a measurable "excess female mortality" among poor German women of childbearing age. In her 1848 Seneca Falls address, the U.S. activist Elizabeth Cady Stanton disparaged "the German who complacently smokes his meerschaum while his wife, yoked with the ox, draws the plough through its furrow."

In higher social strata, women continued to perform the physical labor connected with running a household long after most of their English or French counterparts had ceased such housewifery. Well-off German women continued to spin and knit, to do kitchen work and cleaning, and pressures on them to devote the bulk of their energies to such activities remained intense. Commenting on the Biedermayer era, the novelist Fanny Lewald (1811–89) wrote in her autobiography, *Meine Lebensgeschichte* (1871; *The Education of Fanny Lewald*):

> If any housewife of that period had dared to lighten her burden, bought her bread from the baker, her dried fruit from a grocer, her processed meats from a butcher, she would have been considered a heretic, a criminal, who was shirking her domestic duties. It would have permanently damaged her reputation and done irretrievable harm to the happiness of her marriage and her family.

Louise Otto later wrote that the prestige of the housewife eroded during these years, as families switched from home production to consumption. Others considered that housewifery had gained women little. "With all this most respectful sentiment towards a woman," wrote the English reformer William Howitt, who lived in Heidelberg from 1840 to 1843, "they only think of her as a *hausfrau* not a rational being and intellectual companion; a German never talks on any subject superior to common chitchat, to a woman" (quoted in Lee).

Howitt's observation confirms the 19th-century development of German political life into a "sphere" from which women were automatically excluded. Forbidden almost all forms of political meetings themselves, German men who wanted change met in organizations ostensibly centered around activities designated as exclusively masculine, such as sharpshooting and gymnastics. Even within the progressive political realm, among liberals and radicals, women were expected to function as appreciative supporters, to supply an enthusiastic audience for male achievements. Spaces that could provide women with an entry to political debate and discourse disappeared in Germany in these years. The salons of the early 19th century, often organized and maintained by women, many of them Jewish in origin, gave way to exclusively male secret societies or *Brüderschaften* (brother-hoods). "What has become of the time when we were all to-gether?" the influential salonnière Rachel (Levin) Varnhagen complained in 1818. "It has gone under" (quoted in Spiel). By the 1820s and 1830s, male Germans active in reform and nationalist groups routinely refused women any political partici-pation. Achim von Arnim, for instance, an important intellectual and nationalist, founded a Christliche-Deutsche Tafel-Gesell-schaft (Christian-German Table Society) that excluded "women, Frenchmen, philistines, and Jews" from membership.

In the quest to weave nationhood out of the tangle of 39 separate states, Germans needed to develop a national identity. In this period, idealized domestic womanhood became integral to German nationalism as well as to the identity of the growing middle class. The traditional housewife and mother came to embody national culture, to define the female contribution to national development. In Germany this phenomenon was seen as especially German, part of the *Sonderweg*, but in fact it oc-curred throughout the Western world in this period. Every-where, but "especially in Germany," declared J. Hillebrand in the influential essay *Über Deutschlands National Bildung* (1818; On Germany's National Development), "the women's destiny in common has always been: wife, mother, household." The conviction that women of all classes should remain at home, concerned only with family and household, pervaded German political thought. "Without woman, present-day life would be unbearable for every sensitive male soul," wrote the liberal Georg Gottfried Gervinus, "because the woman of today, like the Greek citizen of ancient times, is removed from the common bustle of life ... does not suffer the degradation of lowly occupations, the turmoil and heartlessness of work" (1853; *Geschichte der deutschen Dichtkunst* [The History of German Poetry]).

In Germany, with its national identity defined in large part by its divergences from French universalism, Enlightenment pro-posals for women's increased rights—even those by such Ger-mans as Theodor von Hippel—were rejected because of their French associations. German women were praised for rejecting "French" values in favor of the supposedly "German" docility, innocence, and dutiful industriousness displayed by Margarethe in Goethe's *Faust* (1832). Idealized domestic womanhood be-came the female sex's contribution to German national identity. Defining the political sphere as exclusively masculine, reformers and reactionaries alike condemned women's political involve-ment as another export of the hated French.

Writers and thinkers increasingly stressed the "character of the sexes," delineating the distinctive traits that supposedly sepa-rated male and female. Insisting that men and women were each other's opposites, cultural authorities asserted that the two genders were destined for entirely different social roles. "The female is a more feeling creature ... the man ... is a more thinking creature," wrote the German encyclopedist J. Meyer in the influential *Staatslexicon* (1845–48; Government Lexicon), in a typical formulation of the belief. Men were rational, women were emotional; men active, women passive; men aggressive, women gentle. And so they were destined for two "separate spheres"—men for "the world" and women for "the home." "While the woman in the main lays the foundation for the ties that bind the family," continued Meyer's encyclopedia article,

"the man is the link with the external world; he is the bond between family and family, it is he who is the basis of the state."

The growing middle-class German liberal and national move-ments defined themselves on the basis of such oppositions, which excluded women from the public realm and especially from poli-tics. Since male conservatives and reactionaries excluded women as a matter of course, entry into political life for German women was difficult and daunting. In France and England in the 1830s, radical socialist groups such as the Saint-Simonians and Owen-ites welcomed women to their enterprises and supported women's rights. There was no German equivalent until the mid-1840s. In Germany the Saint-Simonian call for the *femme libre* (free woman)—popular with male radicals of the "Young Ger-many" movement—was tainted for German women by originat-ing in France, as well as for being associated with free sexual behavior. Throughout the 1848–49 revolutions, even the most politically active German women were at pains to distinguish themselves from "French" emancipation, which they identified with smoking cigarettes, wearing men's clothing, and being sex-ually licentious.

In such circumstances, entry into political life was problem-atic for German women. However, during the *Vormärz*, increas-ing numbers of middle- and upper-class women began to engage in politics. They did so in two chief ways: by writing subversive literature that challenged the dominant political discourse and by participating in the radical new religious and political societies that increasingly defied the traditionalism of German culture and politics.

Women's Activities in the "Vormärz"

"Send girls to university and boys to needlework- and cooking school," wrote the anonymous author (Fanny Lewald) of the 1841 novel *Clementine*, and "in three generations they [the boys] will know ... what it means to be the oppressed." Growing numbers of German women challenged the status quo in novels and essays, public letters and poems, breaking the silence of their mothers' generation. Bettina (Brentano) von Arnim became one of the first to write political and social criticism, which she com-menced after her husband Achim von Arnim's death in 1831. Supporting a wide variety of dissident causes, she moved easily in the highest German cultural and political circles in part be-cause of her literary connections: her first book printed her corre-spondence with Goethe and her father and brother, as well as her husband, were important intellectuals. In 1843 she published *Dies Buch gehört dem König* (This Book Belongs to the King), a daring challenge to the new Prussian king Friedrich Wilhelm IV, to end the miserable poverty within his realm by adopting liberal policies and humanitarian values. (French feminists re-printed part of it in their newspaper, *La voix des femmes*, in March 1848.) Meeting only intransigence, Arnim came to be-lieve that "to help the poor now means preaching revolt," (quoted in Drewitz) and she actively supported democratic and socialist causes throughout the *Vormärz* and during the revolu-tion. Louise Otto, the future leader of the German women's movement, entered political life in 1843, when she responded to the radical editor Robert Blum's call for writings on the propo-sition that "Women's participation in the life of the state is not just a right but a duty." From then on, she published prolifically in the left-wing press, becoming well known as "the red (female) democrat."

By the eve of the revolution, German women writers had entered German political debate by creating a widely read radical literature that challenged political, social, and religious orthodoxy. They were integral to the dissident political culture that developed in the 1840s. In their writings they both claimed wider roles and options for women and championed nationalist, liberal, and socialist-democratic reforms. In the years just before the revolution, Otto published her fifth novel, the political *Schloss und Fabrik* (1846; Castle and Factory), and a poetry collection, *Lieder eines deutschen Mädchens* (1847; Songs of a German Maiden), which advocated nationalism, socialism, and women's rights: "All Humankind will struggle upwards / To found a renewed empire of love / To give women like men their rights." Often accepting the conviction of their time that women differed from men, these German writers nonetheless passionately asserted their right to political life. "Why shouldn't I [take part in politics]?" asserted Kathinka Zitz-Halein, "I am indeed only a woman but I love my fatherland not less than the best man" (quoted in Zucker). Others went further, challenging and discarding all remnants of female inferiority and subordination. Louise Dittmar, who had published two books anonymously in 1845, used her own name on a philosophic essay of 1847, *Vier Zeitfragen* (Four Timely Questions), where she claimed "a sense of self-worth for *every person*, for each *sex* equally."

In addition to claiming political equality, some women authors began to widen political discourse by raising issues of women's financial dependence and subsequent loveless marriages or recourse to prostitution, their lack of education, and their inability to achieve adult status. The case of Louise Aston focused discussion. Aston (1814–71), unhappily married at 20, had divorced and moved with her daughter to Berlin. There she frequented the male literary circles that met in cafes and taverns, as George Sand did in Paris. Upon the appearance of her passionate poetry collection, *Wilde Rosen* (1846; Wild Roses), which championed free love, republican government, and Sand, Aston was exiled from the city on the grounds that her way of life and ideas posed a threat to civic peace and order. Aston publicized her case in *Meine Emancipation, Verweisung und Rechtfertigung* (1846; My Emancipation, Proscription, and Justification), published in Brussels, and in her 1847 novel *Aus dem Leben einer Frau* (From A Women's Life). Mathilde Franziska Anneke, also a divorcée who supported herself and her daughter by writing in socialist journals, championed Aston in her 1847 essay, *Das Weib im Conflict mit den socialen Verhältnisse* (Woman in Conflict with Social Circumstances), which ridiculed the double standard of morality. Anneke herself, newly married to a radical military officer, presided over a "communist salon" in Cologne.

All these female German writers and activists had contact with and gained support from the dissident religious circles that challenged women's subordinate role during the *Vormärz*. Forbidden all political activity, numerous German progressives formed *freie Gemeinde* (free congregations) independent of the state Roman Catholic and Protestant churches. Usually identified as German Catholics or free Evangelicals, congregations often crossed the denominational divisions that so structured German life: Protestants met with Catholics; some groups had Jewish members; others included agnostics and freethinkers. Functioning as quasi-political bodies in a political culture that linked religious affiliation and citizenship, these new groups were seen as nuclei of social regeneration. In their weekly meetings, radical male clergy and their male and female parishioners considered the congregations as a mark of a new era of human development. Stressing peaceful growth, social justice, and the equality of all, congregations debated political, economic, and social restructuring in their weekly meetings. Since women's participation was seen as crucial for the effective reform of marriage, family life, and education, they were welcomed to the free congregations and joined in great numbers, making up 40 percent of the 100,000 to 150,000 Germans active in the movement between 1841 and 1852. Most congregations gave women equal voting rights within the group, and some congregations had women on their executive committees.

Joining a free congregation was a political act, for men as well as women. "For me this step was extremely important," recalled Malwida von Meysenbug (1816–1903) in her *Memoiren einer Idealistin* (1875; Memoirs of a Female Idealist). "It separated me forever from my past; by it I publicly renounced the Protestant church and joined a truly democratically constituted society." Free-religion circles overlapped with democratic and socialist groups and provided many German women with their initial entry to political life. Increasing numbers of women taught in the kindergartens and elementary schools established by the free congregations (a radical act, since elsewhere clergymen controlled primary education), raised funds for their growing communities, and managed their groups' social welfare programs. Such activities led many to claim more for women. "The spirit of the age cannot remain quiet even here," went a German woman's verses addressed to an 1847 meeting of the congregations, "It comes to slay ancient prejudice, / And will also elevate women to human dignity!" (quoted in Paletschek). The Frauen-Verein (Women's Club) of Hamburg reported a similar development:

> For three years we vigorously sought to further the cause of religious reform. We cannot, however, struggle for freedom of conscience without becoming free ourselves. For it is the blessing of all true human striving that a human being wins his own spiritual power when he works for the general good. The more clearly and self-consciously we came to an appreciation of the significance of our own spiritual lives, the more we felt called upon with joy and commitment to work for the intellectual and material well-being of our sex. (Quoted in Prelinger.)

By the eve of 1848, sizable numbers of middle- and upper-class German women had become politicized through their participation in the religious reform movement, which encompassed democratic and socialist circles as well, and through reading and writing critical and subversive literature. Some peasant and working-class women also had gained experience in popular rioting, which increased after 1846 as the effects of the Potato Famine were intensified by a second year of failed crops. While tens of thousands emigrated to the New World, many of those who remained behind resorted to traditional mob violence to express their suffering. Silesian weavers burned and looted the houses of employers whom they considered responsible for their exploitation. Elsewhere the poor seized foodstuffs from merchants and markets. The most important of these riots was the so-called Potato Revolution in Berlin of April 1847, where working-class women and men stormed the public markets and battled troops for three days. The Potato Revolution heralded the uprisings of 1848 in its street violence in the Prussian capital, but this sort of food riot was traditional. Throughout European history, women out in the streets participating in collective actions signaled the breakdown of social order under intense deprivation and suffering. The revolutions of 1848–49 were not traditional riots; they opened new political possibilities and hopes: unification, democracy, and even socialism. While German women participated frequently in the ferment of those tumultuous years, they were forced to continue their struggles of the *Vormärz* to take part in politics from which they were excluded by definition.

The German Revolutions: The First Phase: February–October 1848

The news of the 24 February 1848 uprising in Paris sparked revolutions in many German states. From late February on, demonstrations in Baden, Mannheim, Heidelberg, and other liberal areas demanded civil liberties, constitutions, and the convening of a national parliament. A number of smaller states acceded rapidly, curtailing royal power, introducing liberal policies, and creating new ministries. But as with other events in 19th-century Germany, the course of the revolution of 1848 was determined by the two giant states, Prussia and Austria. Their political developments shaped the opportunities for Germans to achieve their paired but often contradictory goals of political reform and national unification.

In Austria political revolution became coupled with nationalist rebellions against the Hapsburg Empire. Street fighting erupted in Vienna on 13 March 1848. Directed against the aged Prince Metternich, the uprising achieved an important symbolic victory when he fled to England. The monarchical government promised to convene a constitutional assembly and allow freedom of the press. Meanwhile, throughout the spring, national revolts triumphed in Budapest, Prague, Venice, and Milan, threatening the very existence of the Austrian Empire. In the midst of these upheavals, the Frankfurt Diet—which represented the economic confederation of the Zollverein and thus constituted a rare Germany-wide institution—requested that states send delegates to a constitutional assembly. Friedrich Wilhelm IV of Prussia resisted by insisting that any attempts at German unification must be undertaken by himself and his fellow monarchs and by planning to bring in the Russian army to quash the new revolutions in Germany and France.

Peaceful demonstrations in Berlin protesting these policies met with extraordinary brutality from the Prussian army, causing a number of civilian deaths. On 18 March the capital exploded into street fighting aimed at forcing the king to relent. Three days later, after the royal family had been made to view the bodies of dead revolutionaries, Friedrich Wilhelm granted a constitutional assembly and a liberal suffrage that enfranchised most men. Civil liberties and equality for men before the law—doing away with the traditional privileges of caste and property—became legal almost overnight. While the hopes of socialists and democrats for a republic had not been fulfilled, conservative absolutism seemed to have been speedily transformed into liberal constitutional monarchism.

The relative ease with which conservative policies seemed to vanish convinced many that other vast changes were also possible. In this hopeful atmosphere, it seemed possible to achieve German unification, and throughout the spring, elections were held for a German Constitutional National Assembly, which met in Frankfurt on 18 May 1848. Eight hundred middle- and upper-class men, many of them lawyers, convened to debate both unification and political reforms.

Severe splits rapidly appeared in the Frankfurt Assembly. The only decision that passed by a large majority was that the national constitution—as yet unwritten—should take precedence over state constitutions. But as soon as debate turned to what form national government should take, agreement became impossible. The few radical delegates—those who wanted a republic—left to organize uprisings to support their position. The summer of 1848 saw the greatest extent of revolution in Germany, as people struggled to achieve dramatic political changes and had not yet suffered major defeats.

Throughout this first, hopeful phase of the revolution of 1848, women attempted to enter into political activity and debate. They participated in the revolutionary crowds that thronged the streets, built barricades, and defied the army and police, although in far smaller numbers than men. To some degree, their behavior reflected the form of the traditional food riot, where women's presence signaled the people's outrage. But in 1848, women helped to construct the key device of the 19th-century urban revolution: the barricade of stone, earth, wood, and furniture, which carved cities into independent districts difficult for army or police to subdue. Women fed and sustained the fighters, nursing the wounded and raising morale. Legends quickly arose about the "brides of the barricades"—angelic revolutionary women who came to encourage men in their struggles. Like the men, women of the people suffered bullet wounds and fell before the cavalry charges and sword thrusts of government troops.

In addition, middle- and upper-class women immediately demanded a political existence within the newly formed assemblies and parliaments. By doing so, they became revolutionaries within the revolution itself, since the new governments excluded women as completely as the reactionary ancien régimes had.

At the Frankfurt Assembly, women were allotted 200 tickets to the opening ceremony, which allowed them to observe the proceedings from the balcony. In the lengthy debates over what form political rights and the suffrage should take for men, the issue of political rights for women was never raised. While the delegates were willing to overturn rank and property qualifications for male voters, they never challenged the prevailing view that politics was male territory. Women's petitions were not taken seriously, and indeed, often took the form of reproaching men for failing to do their job and thus forcing women reluctantly to enter the political arena. The "women of Bonn" wrote the German Assembly in June 1848 to this effect:

> In spite of our daily work that confines us to the house, it still cannot escape us women that in these difficult times our men in many ways lack the vigor to make a resolution, that, specifically, the deliberating members of the parliament lack counsel and courage, and that the assembly as a whole lacks unity in its highest form. In these circumstances, we dare to offer our help, which German women

have offered before in exceptional times of need and danger. We request that the representatives in question come home and for a short while dedicate their attention to the nursery, the kitchen, the wash house, and the cellar, while we women quickly determine how to mobilize and unify the threatened fatherland. (Quoted in Hummel-Haasis.)

Such criticism was ignored and women remained absent from the deliberations of the Frankfurt Assembly. The only female presence at parliamentary debates was a painting of Germania, the female personification of the German nation.

In the new Austrian Parliament, which met from May to October 1848, women's rights came under discussion only once, when a census-based suffrage was proposed. The male liberal and radical delegates who spoke agreed that women should not be included in the right to vote. They argued that women were already politically represented by their husbands and fathers and that giving women the vote meant it also had to be given to children and the insane. In October 1848 the Wiener Demokratische Frauenverein (Viennese Democratic Women's Association) presented a petition with more than 1,000 female signatures to the parliament. But this petition, the largest such effort by German women in this period, called not for women's rights, but for the government to rouse the countryside against invading conservative armies. It had no effect.

Barred from traditional political forums, German women made their presence felt in a variety of arenas. They sewed and displayed the red flag of socialism and the red, black, and gold banners of the new German nation that played so important a symbolic role in this period—many remembered the giant national banner that flew from St. Stephen's church in Vienna throughout the summer of 1848. Women dressed in revolutionary colors and attended and organized funerals and memorials for fallen male heroes of the revolutions, providing a symbolic but significant political presence. Restored governments later outlawed such demonstrations. A number of women joined in the actual fighting, especially in the urban streets. "Many women, who came from all ranks of society, took part in the struggle of the Saxon people in Dresden from 3 to 9 May [1849]" reported Louise Otto's *Frauen-Zeitung*:

Many helped build the barricades, dragging stones and furniture; others supplied the fighters on the streets with food that they distributed themselves. Still others took care of the wounded, bandaging their wounds in the rain of bullets on the open street or dragging them into their houses. A maiden, whose fiancé, a gymnast, had fallen on the first day, defended a barricade for three days with the courage of a lion, shooting down many soldiers before she herself was felled by an enemy bullet.

Women "no longer wish to remain alone in the quiet circle of the home," declared a newly formed Berliner Frauenverein (Berlin Women's Association), "but also [want] to be able to help and support outside as well" (quoted in Wittig). Barred from the brand-new parliaments and assemblies, which continued to be exclusively male and exclusively focused on male concerns, women created a wide variety of quasi-political institutions of their own. Generally formed during the first phase of the revolution, these newspapers, schools, women's associations, and democratic groups proved to be among the longest-lived of the period, enduring throughout the difficult second phase of revolution, which saw a resurgence of conservatism and the decline of both reform and national movements.

Women's Institutions of the Revolution

Throughout this tumultuous period, German women entered political life in support of the revolution. Refusing to accept their exclusion from the national and political battles unfolding in Germany, they seized the revolutionary moment to participate in politics in extragovernmental ways. What has often been seen as a "spontaneous" outpouring of women's activity during the revolutionary years of 1848 and 1849 came from women already engaged in the free congregations and radical socialist circles, or from women already published as authors participating in political and social debates. During the revolution, theoretical claims for participation became real as women fought, organized, and wrote on behalf of national and left-wing causes and in support of their own greater autonomy and options.

Wives sometimes joined their husbands in the radical uprisings. In Baden, for instance, Amalie Struve accompanied her husband, the revolutionary Gustav Struve, on three military campaigns in 1848–49, until they were separately imprisoned. Surviving harsh jail conditions, the couple went into exile together. Mathilde Franziska Anneke produced the radical newspaper her husband had edited when he was imprisoned in 1848, while caring for her newborn son and teenage daughter. She later rode by Fritz Anneke's side during the Baden uprising. Women who fought were severely caricatured and denounced as "Amazons" who had abandoned appropriate female behavior. Anneke complained in *Mutterland: Memoiren einer Frau aus dem badisch pfältzan Feldzuge 1848–49* (1853; Motherland: A Woman's Memoirs from the Baden/Pfelzen Campaign 1848–49) that her simple addition of linen trousers to her "usual women's clothing" when riding had been distorted by German journalists into "a massive cavalry saber, a hunting pike, a musket, and men's clothing." She appealed to other women to understand that she had acted because of her passionate feelings about "the struggle against tyrants and oppressors of sacred human rights."

Most "freedom fighters" were male, but thousands of German women took the political step of forming associations to help them. These women's groups provided important support networks for fleeing revolutionaries and their families, supplying food and money, escape routes and safe houses, bandages and nursing care to the thousands forced to emigrate. In Mainz the Women's Democratic Association created Humania, a group to aid "needy patriots" and their families. More than 1,600 bourgeois women contributed sizeable amounts to the organization, which sustained itself under the leadership of Kathinka Zitz-Halein for over a year.

More than 50 new German women's organizations formed in these years, in addition to the numerous free congregations in which women continued to be active throughout the revolution. Many of these groups not only supported male revolutionaries but also sought to improve women's lives. In Vienna working-class women demonstrated against low wages. In Berlin three middle-class women's groups formed to help women workers.

Female servants organized in a number of German cities, and for the first time German women arranged university-preparation classes for girls.

A number of these groups defined themselves as *Demokratische Frauenvereine* (democratic women's associations). In these sympathetic circles, which usually met once a week, women educated and politicized themselves, enlisting other women "in the realm of freedom." One of the most successful was the Viennese Democratic Women's Association. More than 300 women met in August 1848 to form a group with three aims—"one political, one social, and one humane." Under the presidency of Caroline Perin, the women pledged:

(a) politically, through readings and instructive lectures to become knowledgeable about the well-being of the fatherland, to spread the principles of democracy to all women's circles, to instill the love of freedom from the start of education in the breast of every child and thereby to strengthen the German [nationalist] element; (b) socially, to strive for the equality of women's rights through the founding of public primary schools and establishments of higher education to instruct women and to improve the position of poor girls through loving elevation; (c) humanely, to proclaim the deep-felt gratitude of the women of Vienna for the blessings of freedom won through the provident maintenance of all the victims of the revolution (see Hummel-Haasis).

Perin's women's association lasted only two months, but at least eight other such organized between 1848 and 1850 in the German states. Most documents about their existence have been lost, and their history is only now being pieced together.

In addition to banding together with other women, some female activists took part in politics through attending largely male associations of workers and democratic-socialists and by publishing manifestoes or letters in left-wing newspapers on political or economic subjects. In May 1848, for instance, Louise Otto wrote an address to the Saxon minister of the Interior, who had just convened a committee to examine the organization of labor. Otto declared that she wrote on behalf of her poorer sisters, and she urged that the committee not overlook women's situation:

You should not forget that it is not enough to organize work for *men*, you must also organize it for *women*.

Everyone knows that in the working classes, women as well as men must labor for their daily bread . . . Since women are admitted only to a few kinds of work, competition has so depressed wages that when you look at the whole picture, the fate of working women is much more miserable than that of working men. You all know that this is so . . . the worst state of the female proletariat is prostitution. I blush to use this word before you, but I blush even more over the social circumstances of a state that is able to give to thousands of its poor daughters no other bread than the poison of a hideous occupation, based on the depravity of men! (Quoted in Möhrmann.)

The left-wing press, which had published Otto during the *Vormärz*, reprinted this address widely, and women who had been active writers before the revolution continued to publish frequently after its outbreak.

In addition to placing their work with sympathetic publishers and in democratic and socialist newspapers, activist German women also produced at least five women's newspapers during the revolution. The year 1848 saw the launch of Mathilde Franziska Anneke's *Frauen-Zeitung*, Louise Marezoll's *Frauen-Spiegel*, and Louise Aston's *Der Freischärler*. In 1849 Louise Dittmar published her *Soziale Reform* and Otto her *Frauen-Zeitung*. Aston's, Marezoll's, and all but one issue of Anneke's newspapers have been lost. Only an edited collection of Dittmar's *Soziale Reform* remains, but it contains some extremely radical material: Otto published a plea in its pages for the German women's vote, and Dittmar severely critiqued German marriage and male guardianship laws that left woman "completely *without rights*."

Only Otto's paper succeeded in lasting more than a year, and in fact it became one of the longest running left-wing publications in the German states in these years, lasting from 1849 to 1852. Otto managed this feat by muting her radicalism somewhat—she did not demand the vote for women in the pages of her *Frauen-Zeitung*—and also by moving to the more liberal state of Thuringia in 1851, when repression in Saxony prevented her from publishing there. Otto's *Frauen-Zeitung* is the chief source for women's revolutionary participation in these years, and its pages are thronged with active women of all classes. Otto published socialist pleas for working-class women, news about women's associations in Germany and abroad, and critiques of women's existing situations and options. Consistently urging German women not to "forget to think about themselves," she printed a wide array of women's writings, including a call for a national union of women's associations, and two articles on the French feminist "Johanna" (Jeanne) Deroin.

In addition to their newspapers and public letters, their political and patriotic associations and activities, German women contributed importantly to the politics of their day by founding, staffing, and managing some of the most radical political institutions within revolutionary Germany: the new educational establishments of the religious reform movement. These schools, which were seen as the chief hope for a humanitarian, democratic, and socialist future, ranged from kindergartens to the first women's college in Germany. They deliberately challenged the religious and political status quo, since they were the first educational establishments in Germany not controlled by state churches and male, clerical teachers. Many found it shocking that young, unmarried women dared to teach in the new kindergartens and elementary schools. These new schools sought to inculcate humanistic, democratic, and socialist principles, often including both sexual and social equality.

Part of the impetus behind opening the first women's college in Germany, the Hamburger Hochschule für das Weibliche Geschlecht (Hamburg College for the Female Sex), was to train women to be teachers. Founded by members of Johannes Ronge's free German-Catholic congregation, the college's charter specified that two-thirds of its elected executive committee be female. Close to 100 middle- and upper-class women of all ages and religious denominations attended classes there from 1851 to early 1853. Women who attended testified that the experience profoundly influenced them. "When I retired to my room the first evening [at the college], I felt that I had found the true way to a new life," wrote von Meysenbug. "Sometimes a grandmother, a mother, and a granddaughter sat together at a lecture" (*Memoiren einer Idealistin*).

Women's schools, newspapers, associations, and publications proved to be among the strongest and longest-lived of the brief German revolutions. Many survived the second phase of the revolution, but all eventually dissolved before the repression that stifled all left-wing development in the German states by the early 1850s.

The German Revolutions: The Second Phase, November 1848–December 1849

By the end of summer 1848, the most radical phase of the revolution was over, and from then on counterrevolution gained force. Socialist uprisings in Baden and red flags in Frankfurt frightened the bourgeois representatives at the German National Constitutional Assembly. The chief effect was to make the Frankfurt Assembly more determined not to overthrow existing monarchies, but to work with them in German unification. The political scene became complicated as the armies of reaction began to triumph, first in the Austrian Empire. News that the imperial army had succeeded in subduing Budapest, where Louis Kossuth had led the Hungarian revolutionaries in a nationalist struggle against Austria, prompted a left-wing takeover in Vienna at the beginning of October 1848. Existing only a few weeks, this democratic, socialist regime capitulated to the conquering armies of Prince Windischgrätz. Revolutionary Vienna fell on 31 October 1848; the other Hapsburg capitals went under by the spring of 1849. Windischgrätz's brother-in-law, Prince Felix von Schwarzenberg, arranged for the 18-year-old Franz Joseph to replace the imbecile Emperor Ferdinand, withdrew Austria from the Frankfurt Assembly, and ensured the triumph of monarchy and reaction within the Hapsburg Empire.

In the midst of these tumultuous events, the Frankfurt Assembly wrangled at length about whether the new state should be a "little Germany" centered on Prussia or a "greater Germany" that also included Austria. In June 1848 the delegates elected Archduke John of Austria as "imperial regent," but by the winter of 1848–49, the Prussian king Friedrich Wilhelm IV seemed a more likely leader of the new German nation. Conditions in Prussia, however, kept changing, as the tide of revolution and nationalism ebbed. In March 1848 the national black, gold, and red banner flew alone over the Hohenzollern Palace in Berlin. In April a small black-and-white Prussian flag appeared below it. By August a large black-and-white banner flew over a small tricolor national flag. Many German intellectuals and burghers realized that they preferred the security of monarchy to revolutionary upheaval. "To a nature like mine," wrote the theologian David Friedrich Strauss,

> it was much better under the old police state, when we had quiet on the streets and were not always meeting with excited people, new-fashioned slouch hats, and beards . . . To this effusion on the part of boys and girls, this pouring out of wisdom on the streets, I can only respond with cutting irony or disdainful contempt. (Quoted in Hummell-Haasis.)

Lacking any wide base in favor of economic or political change, Prussians and other Germans retreated to a conservative defense of the existing monarchies. In November 1848 royal troops forced the Prussian National Assembly to disband. In December the king granted a constitution, which proclaimed divine-right monarchy and basic civil rights, as well as a bicameral legislature. Six months later a three-tiered voting system based on male property ownership was instituted. From early 1850 on, the revived Prussian monarchy directed its attention to extirpating from its domains all traces of revolution, including kindergartens and women's associations.

Meanwhile, the Frankfurt National Assembly wrote a new constitution for the German nation that included an emperor at its head. In March 1849 they narrowly voted to offer this position to Friedrich Wilhelm IV of Prussia. Disdaining this "crown from the gutter," the Prussian monarch denounced the Frankfurt Assembly and its constitution. Unable to rally sufficient opposition to Prussia, the Assembly was dispersed in June 1849. New revolutionary uprisings flared in the more liberal states, such as Baden and Saxony, but by late summer the Prussian army had crushed them all and, like Austria, left its troops in place to secure victory.

Women's institutions were among the longest-lived of the brief German Revolution of 1848–49, but they too were soon crushed by harsh repression. "Forbidding meetings of the 'Women's Circle for Needy Families' is already no novelty," wrote a Dresden woman in a letter published in the 27 April 1850 issue of Otto's *Frauen-Zeitung*. "But now they go so far as to oversee individuals—not just groups—and hold them responsible for all they say and do that is not completely ultramontane, reactionary, and 'gold-black' "—referring to the colors of the new German flag, minus the red. Otto first sustained her women's newspaper by moving it to liberal Thuringia, but eventually the "Lex Otto," a new German press law that forbade women to be editors, prevailed. There is no stronger proof of the importance of German women's political activity during the revolutions than the laws passed by the victorious conservative governments that ushered in the *stille Zeit* (silent time) of the 1850s. In addition to forbidding women to be editors, the Prussian government closed all kindergartens in 1851. Prussia and Austria forbade women (and boys) to attend any meeting where politics was even mentioned. The first provisions of the Prussian law of 11 March 1850 declared:

> For associations that intend to discuss political subjects in meeting, other regulations with the following limits apply. . . . They may have no females, students, or apprentices as participants. . . . Females, students, and apprentices may not attend the meetings or sessions of such political associations.

Such repression, coupled with house searches and arrests, harsh jail sentences, and continuing censorship, stifled the development of democracy, socialism, and liberalism for decades in Germany. Active women were punished as harshly as men, and the choices they faced were the same: to remain in Germany and be silent or to go into exile in a freer nation. Von Meysenbug went to England, Anneke and Struve to the United States. After 1850, Dittmar, Aston, and many others never published again. Otto wrote only on art during the *stille Zeit*. A sense of defeat permeates this era. Recalling the hopes raised by the black, gold, and red banner of the German nation, Anneke wrote in her diary: "*Black* death is our only wage, / Our *Gold* only the gold of evening, / Our *Red* a bleeding heart" (quoted in Schulte). Repression made any political life for women impossible throughout the 1850s. In 1865 the indomitable Louise Otto revived a women's movement in Germany. Far more conservative than women's efforts in 1848–49, the new movement bore the scars caused by the total defeat of the German revolutions.

Bibliography

Sources

NOTE: Most of the primary sources cited in this article are obscure and unlikely to be readily available to readers of the English-language edition. Listed below are only those works that have been recently reprinted or translated. Further bibliographic information on primary sources is provided in Bonnie Anderson, *Joyous Greetings: The First International Women's Movement 1830–1860* (Oxford and New York: Oxford University Press, 2000).

Anneke, Mathilde Franziska, *Mutterland: Memoiren einer Frau aus dem badischen pfälzischen Feldzug 1848/49* (1853); reprint, Münster: Tende, 1982

Arnim, Bettina von, *Dies Buch gehört dem König*, 2 vols., Berlin: Schroeder, 1843; reprint, edited by Ilse Staff, Frankfurt: Insel Verlag, 1982

Hippel, Theodor Gottlieb von, *On Improving the Status of Women*, translated and edited by Timothy F. Sellner, Detroit, Michigan: Wayne State University Press, 1979

Lewald, Fanny, *The Education of Fanny Lewald*, translated, edited, and annotated by Hanna Ballin Lewis, Albany: State University of New York Press, 1992

Reference Works

Allen, Ann Taylor, *Feminism and Motherhood in Germany, 1800–1914*, New Brunswick, New Jersey: Rutgers University Press, 1991

Anderson, Bonnie, *Joyous Greetings: The First International Women's Movement, 1830–1860*, New York: Oxford University Press, 2000

Böttger, Fritz, editor, *Frauen im Aufbruch: Frauenbriefe aus dem Vormärz und der Revolution von 1848*, Berlin: Verlag der Nation, 1977

Drewitz, Ingeborg, "Bettina von Arnim: A Portrait," *New German Critique* 27 (1982)

Fout, John C., editor, *German Women in the Nineteenth Century: A Social History*, New York: Holmes and Meier, 1984

Gerhard, Ute, *Unerhört: Die Geschichte der deutschen Frauenbewegung*, Reinbek bei Hamburg, Germany: Rowohlt, 1990

Götzinger, Germaine, editor, *Für die Selbstverwirklichung der Frau: Louise Aston in Selbstzeugnissen und Dokumenten*, Frankfurt: Fischer Taschenbuch, 1983

Hauch, Gabriella, *Frau Biedermeier auf den Barrikaden: Frauenleben der Wiener Revolution, 1848*, Vienna: Gesellschaftskritik, 1990

Herzog, Dagmar, *Intimacy and Exclusion: Religious Politics in Pre-Revolutionary Baden*, Princeton, New Jersey: Princeton University Press, 1996

Hummel-Haasis, Gerlinde, editor, *Schwestern, zerreisst eure Kettern: Zeugnisse zur Geschichte der Frauen in der Revolution von 1848/49*, Munich: Deutscher Taschenbuch, 1982

Joeres, Ruth-Ellen Boetcher, *Die Anfänge der deutschen Frauenbewegung: Louise Otto-Peters*, Frankfurt: Fischer Taschenbuch, 1983

Lee, Amice, *Laurels and Rosemary: The Life of William and Mary Howitt*, London: Oxford University Press, 1955

Lipp, Carola, et al., editors, *Schimpfende Weiber und patriotische Jungfrauen: Frauen im Vormärz und in der Revolution 1848/49*, Moos, Germany: Elster, 1986

Ludwig, Johanna, and Rita Jorek, editors, *Louise Otto-Peters: Ihr literarisches und publizistisches Werk*, Leipzig: Leipziger Universitätsverlag, 1995

Möhrmann, Renate, *Die andere Frau: Emanzipationsansätze deutscher Schriftstellerinnen im Vorfeld der Achtundvierziger-Revolution*, Stuttgart: Metzler, 1977

Möhrmann, Renate, editor, *Frauenemanzipation im deutschen Vormärz: Texte und Dokumente*, Stuttgart: Reclam, 1978

Paletschek, Sylvia, *Frauen und Dissens: Frauen in Deutschkatholizismus und in den freien Gemeinden, 1841–1852*, Göttingen, Germany: Vandenhoeck und Ruprecht, 1990

Prelinger, Catherine M., *Charity, Challenge, and Change: Religious Dimensions of the Mid-Nineteenth-Century Women's Movement in Germany*, New York and London: Greenwood Press, 1987

Schulte, Wilhelm, "Mathilde Franziska Anneke," *Westfälische Levensbilder* 8 (1958)

Siemann, Wolfram, *Die deutsche Revolution von 1848/49*, Frankfurt: Suhrkamp, 1985

Spiel, Hilde, "Rachel Varnhagen: Tragic Muse of the Romantics," in *Affairs of the Mind: The Salon in Europe and America from the 18th to the 20th Century*, edited by Peter Quennell, Washington, D.C.: New Republic Books, 1980

Wagner, Maria, *Mathilde Franziska Anneke in Selbstzeugnissen und Dokumenten*, Frankfurt: Fischer Taschenbuch, 1980

Wittig, Gudrun, *"Nicht nur im stillen Kreis des Hauses": Frauenbewegung in Revolution und nachrevolutionärer Zeit, 1848–1876*, Hamburg: Ergebnisse, 1986

Zucker, Stanley, *Kathinka Zitz-Halein and Female Civic Activism in Mid-Nineteenth-Century Germany*, Carbondale: Southern Illinois University Press, 1991

Supplemental Bibliography: Women and the Revolutions of 1848 in Europe

Belgium

Archives de la Ville de Bruxelles, Brussels. *Police, Meeting 1848* 3 (25 February 1848)

Bartier, John, *Libéralisme et socialisme au XIXᵉ siècle*, edited by Guy Cambier, Brussels: Éditions de l'Université de Bruxelles, 1981

Bartier, John, *Naissance du socialisme en Belgique: Les Saint-Simoniens*, edited by Arlette Smolar-Meynart, Brussels: Présence et Action Culturelles, 1985

Berger, Lya, *Les femmes poètes de la Belgique: La vie littéraire et sociale des femmes belges*, Paris: Perrin, 1925

Demuyter, M., *L'image de la femme à travers la presse féminine en Belgique, 1836–1850*, thesis for the License, Université de Louvain, 1977

Dhondt, Jean, *Les femmes et la Première Internationale en Belgique*, Brussels: Éditions de l'Institut de Sociologie de l'ULB, 1968

Gatti de Gamond, Zoé, "De la condition sociale des femmes au XIXᵉ siècle, par Marie de G***," *Revue Encyclopédique* (December 1832)

Gatti de Gamond, Zoé, *Fourier et son système*, 2nd edition, Paris: Librairie Sociale, 1839; as *Fourier and His System*, London: J. H. Young, 1842

Gubin, Éliane, "Le féminisme en Belgique avant 1914, de l'instruction à l'émancipation," in *Lieux de femmes dans l'espace public, 1800–1930*, edited by Monique Pavillon and François Vallotton, Lausanne, Switzerland: Université de Lausanne, 1992

Van Nuffel, Robert, "Zoé Gatti de Gamond," in *Biographie nationale*, vol. 38, Brussels: 1973–74

Van Nuffel, Robert, "Zoé Gatti de Gamond: L'enseignement et la religion," in *L'église et l'État à l'époque contemporaine: Mélanges dédiés à la mémoire de Mgr. Aloïs Simon*, edited by Gaston Braive and Jacques Lory, Brussels: Facultés Universitaires Saint-Louis, 1975

England

Bolt, Christine, *The Women's Movements in the United States and Britain from the 1790s to the 1920s*, Amherst: University of Massachusetts Press, and London: Harvester Wheatsheaf, 1993

Chedzoy, Alan, *A Scandalous Woman: The Story of Caroline Norton*, London: Allison and Busby, 1992

Davidoff, Leonore, and Catherine Hall, *Family Fortunes: Men and Women of the English Middle Class, 1780–1850*, Chicago: University of Chicago Press, and London: Hutchinson, 1987

Frow, Ruth, and Edmund Frow, editors, *Political Women: 1800–1850*, London and Winchester, Massachusetts: Pluto Press, 1989

Helsinger, Élisabeth K., Robin Ann Sheets, and William R. Veeder, editors, *The Woman Question in Britain and America, 1837–1883*, 3 vols., New York: Garland, and Manchester: Manchester University Press, 1983

Malmgreen, Gail, *Neither Bread Nor Roses: Utopian Feminists and the English Working Class, 1800–1850*, Brighton, East Sussex: Noyce, 1978

Malmgreen, Gail, "Anne Knight and the Radical Subculture," *Quaker History* 71, no. 2 (Fall 1982)

Mermin, Dorothy, *Godiva's Ride: Women of Letters in England, 1830–1880*, Bloomington: Indiana University Press, 1993

Midgley, Clare, *Women against Slavery: The British Campaigns, 1780–1870*, London and New York: Routledge, 1992

Pankhurst, Richard K.P., "Anna Wheeler: A Pioneer Socialist and Feminist," *Political Quarterly* 25 (1954)

Pichanick, Valerie Kossew, *Harriet Martineau: The Woman and Her Work, 1802–76*, Ann Arbor: University of Michigan Press, 1980

Reid, Marion Kirkland, *A Plea for Woman*, Edinburgh: Tate, 1843; reprint, Edinburgh: Polygon Press, 1988

Rendall, Jane, *The Origins of Modern Feminism: Women in Britain, France, and the United States, 1780–1860*, New York: Schocken Books, 1984; London: Macmillan, 1985

Rendall, Jane, editor, *Equal or Different: Women's Politics, 1800–1914*, Oxford and New York: Blackwell, 1987

Schwarzkopf, Jutta, *Women in the Chartist Movement*, New York: St. Martin's Press, and London: Macmillan, 1991

Sklar, Kathryn Kish, "Women Who Speak for an Entire Nation: American and British Women at the World Anti-Slavery Convention, London, 1840," in *The Abolitionist Sisterhood: Women's Political Culture in Antebellum America*, edited by Jean

Fagan Yellin and John C. Van Horne, Ithaca, New York: Cornell University Press, 1994

Taylor, Barbara, *Eve and the New Jerusalem: Socialism and Feminism in the Nineteenth Century*, New York: Pantheon Books, and London: Virago, 1983

Thompson, Dorothy, *The Chartists: Popular Politics in the Industrial Revolution*, Aldershot, Hampshire: Wildwood House, and New York: Pantheon Books, 1984

Thompson, William, *Appeal of One Half the Human Race, Women, against the Pretensions of the Other Half, Men, to Retain Them in Political, and Hence in Civil and Domestic, Slavery: In Reply to a Paragraph of Mr. Mill's Celebrated "Article on Government,"* London: Longman Hurst, 1825; reprint, London: Virago Press, 1983

Tyrrell, Alexander, "Woman's Mission and Pressure Group Politics in Britain (1825–1860)," *Bulletin of the John Rylands University Library of Manchester* 63, no. 1 (Autumn 1980)

General Sources

Anderson, Bonnie S., *Joyous Greetings: The First International Women's Movement, 1830–1860*, Oxford and New York: Oxford University Press, 2000

McFadden, Margaret H., *Golden Cables of Sympathy: The Trans-Atlantic Sources of Nineteenth-Century Feminism*, Lexington: University of Kentucky Press, 1999

The Emancipation of Women in the Works of Marx and Engels

MAXIMILIEN RUBEL

 WITH THE EXCEPTION OF a very few instances in scattered writings from different periods, the problem of women's emancipation conceived as a specifically female program of struggle was barely broached or treated by Marx and Engels. In their minds, the proletarian movement—an "independent movement of the vast majority in the interests of that vast majority" (*Manifesto of the Communist Party*, 1848)—was the common concern of workers of both sexes, and the cause of the working class was that of men and women equally subject to the laws of capital and the constraints of paid wages. If working-class women warranted special treatment, it was because their professional status was close to that of children doing the same work. In both cases, the physical frailty of the employed individuals demanded a combination of protective measures and regulations, in the employer's own interest, that were to constitute the matter of the first factory legislation promulgated in England as industrialization advanced.

As the International Workingmen's Association (IWA) became active on the scene from 1864 to 1873, the prospect of an autonomous women's movement was to become a subject of critical, or even polemical reflection for Marx and Engels, compelling them to broaden the horizon of their social vision. In the end, Marx's readings in ethnography led him belatedly to deepen his historical culture in the realm of the development of the social status of women and the family across eras and continents. His final studies and thoughts constituted a legacy that Engels executed, directing the principles of Marx's philosophy of history toward a posterity in crisis and facing the problems of that theory's generic survival.

Early Intellectual Development

Before embarking on their common struggle, Engels and Marx each went through an early stage of intellectual development, eventually discovering affinities that would forge a lifelong bond of friendship and produce a two-headed, or even hybrid work,

with unforeseen results both on the theoretical level and in terms of sociopolitical realities. Engels preceded Marx in the observation and the study of industrial working conditions under the rule of private property, competition, and the market economy. Engels was also the first to develop his criticism of the mode of capitalist production in a written work "based on direct personal experience and authentic sources" and entitled, *Die Lage der arbeitenden Klasse in England* (1845; *The Condition of the Working-Class in England in 1844*). The author revealed to the reading public the physically and morally destructive effects of work in the manufacturing shops, factories, and mines on all three categories of workers—men, women, and children. He drew heavily on reports by factory inspectors, which were rich in descriptions and statistical material on each of the categories of personnel and provided exact information on general working conditions and the duration, intensity, and rigor of the physical effort, accidents, mutilations, and work-related illnesses that workers endured. Although his conclusion announced the inevitable "war of the poor against the rich" (which in England would be waged under the battle cry, "War to the palaces, peace to the cottages"), and although Engels alluded to a "communistic party" that could "conquer the brutal element of the revolution and prevent a 'Ninth Thermidor,'" it remained true that the realities he described were, in the final analysis, reducible to an assessment and a profoundly negative picture, since workers of both sexes were rarely portrayed as being engaged in resistance and revolt—except in the case of a strike. The first signs that heralded an opposition movement were acts of resistance to the introduction of machines, soon followed by acts of destruction at the factories. Engels allotted a chapter of his book to labor movements, whose beginnings he placed in the first third of the 19th century, after a law voted in by a Tory Parliament had authorized workers coalitions and Chartism had become the formal opposition to the bourgeoisie.

In the chronicle of these first workers' struggles, there was no place for episodes of resistance specific to women. Quite the contrary, one might say, since throughout *The Condition of the*

Working-Class in England in 1844, Engels expressed his worry about the negative consequences of women's presence in the factories: "The employment of the wife dissolves the family utterly and of necessity this dissolution, in our present society, which is based upon the family, brings the most demoralising consequences for parents as well as children." These working mothers did not know how to be true mothers for their children, who, raised under such circumstances, would later be incapable of establishing a harmonious family, since they would have known nothing but a life of isolation. In some cases, women's work did not entirely dissolve the family but did distort its function: "In many cases the family is not wholly dissolved by the employment of the wife, but turned upside down. The wife supports the family, the husband sits at home, tends the children, sweeps the room and cooks." This was man "emasculated" and woman deprived of her femininity, a disgraceful state that was the last fruit of the so highly praised civilization: "the final achievement of all the efforts and struggles of hundreds of generations to improve their own situation and that of their posterity." The domination of woman over man, produced by the industrial system, was as inhuman as the primitive domination of man over woman. As for unmarried women working in factories, they were no better off than married women: "It is self-evident that a girl who has worked in a mill from her ninth year is in no position to understand domestic work, whence it follows that female operatives prove wholly inexperienced and unfit as housekeepers" (*The Condition of the Working-Class in England in 1844*).

It is obvious that behind the detailed description of the work done by women in the various branches of industry, a moral postulate of universal importance appeared: the emancipation of women. Marx had explicitly put forth this postulate in the essay "On the Jewish Question" (in *Early Political Writings*), a text that predated Engels's book. In that text Marx spoke of "*human* emancipation." By joining forces, the two authors were to discover together the specificity of woman's role in the process of the regeneration of the human race.

Critical Criticism: Fleur de Marie

By associating Engels with his first book, Marx undoubtedly sought to consecrate publicly a very recent friendship, formed during the few days the visitor from London spent in Paris. Indeed, *Die heilige Familie, oder, Kritik der kiritschen Kritik gegen Bruno Bauer und Konsorten* (1845; *The Holy Family, or Critique of Critical Criticism: Against Bruno Bauer and Company*; in *Karl Marx and Frederick Engels Collected Works* [hereafter, *MECW*, vol. 4), a work in which Engels's contribution counted for a mere 15 pages, presented Marx's first attempt at expressing the culmination of his philosophical and economic studies, in the form of a polemic against the "speculative idealism" of a few Hegelian disciples. It also presented the result of his political essays that had led him to adhere to communism, understood as a "real humanism."

In this first assessment of his publishing activity, Marx took the opportunity to approach the issue of women's emancipation with passionate interest on two occasions. First, he idealized the character of Fleur-de-Marie, who appeared in *Les Mystères de Paris* (1842–43; *The Mysteries of Paris*) by Eugène Sue. He later borrowed feminist "fantasies" from Charles Fourier.

A being dehumanized by the demands and the constraints of Christian morality, Marie primitively represents natural purity in an inhuman and corrupt environment. A prostitute in the middle of the underworld, she preserves a nobility of soul, an ingenuousness, and a human beauty that make her "a poetical flower of the criminal world and win for her the name of Fleur de Marie" ("Revelation of the Mystery of Critical Religion, or Fleur de Marie," *The Holy Family*). In contradiction to her Christian repentance, she adopts an attitude toward her past that is both stoic and Epicurean: her undeserved misfortune stifles neither her hope nor her enjoyment of life. "She measures her situation in life by her *own individuality*, her essential *nature*, not by the *ideal of what is good*." Her lot is an illustration of the destructive effects of religious alienation, as Ludwig Feuerbach analyzed it in *Vorläufige Thesen zur Reform der Philosophie* (1842; Preliminary Theses for the Reform of Philosophy) and *Grundsäätze der Philosophie der Zukunft* (1843; *Principles of the Philosophy of the Future*). Psychically broken by religious superstition, and yet the symbol of woman as the incarnation of all that remains of nature in bourgeois society, Marie finally adopts a wholly contrite and remorseful posture, becoming a living example of the corruption that society continually secretes. Villainous crime, prostitution, and the obligatory repentance for it were in some ways the modes of social regulation that became Sue's credo as reformer-novelist, although he did not suspect the sociological import of his fiction. If Marx was serious about extracting the consummately tragic female character from a popular novel, it was to argue her case with the "Young Hegelian" author who had reduced "Marien-Blume" (Marie-la-Fleur) to an "incarnation of an idea," a pretext for Hegelian speculation. The illegitimate daughter of Rudolph, a "prince of Gerolstein"—another character in the novel—Fleur-de-Marie became an opportunity for the "critical critic" to launch himself into the "Revelation of the Mystery of the Emancipation of Women, or Louise Morel" (*The Holy Family*). That revelation was motivated by the fact that Rudolph, "a petty prince" and "a *great* patroniser of servants' conditions" is in no way inclined to "understand that the general position of women in modern society is inhuman."

Marx's indignation was commensurate with the esteem he felt for one of the most visionary of French authors, Charles Fourier. Taking critical criticism to the extent of comparing Prince Rudolph to those thinkers who defended women's emancipation, Marx had no doubt consulted several of Fourier's writings. He had immersed himself in these readings to extract material that he used like aphorisms, to nourish the romantic inclinations that had almost drawn him into a poetic career. In "Revelation of the Mystery of the Emancipation of Women" (*The Holy Family*) Marx cites at some length Fourier's writings:

> Is not the young daughter a ware held up for sale to the first bidder who wishes to obtain exclusive ownership of her? . . . De même qu'en grammaire deux négations valent une affirmation, l'on peut dire qu'en *négoce conjugal deux prostitutions valent une vertu*. [Just as in grammar two negations are the equivalent of an affirmation, we can say that in the *marriage trade two prostitutions are the equivalent of virtue*.]

The change in a historical epoch can always be determined by women's progress towards freedom, because here, in the relation of woman to man, of the weak to the strong, the victory of human nature over brutality is most evident. The degree of emancipation of woman is the natural measure of general emancipation.

The humiliation of the female sex is an essential feature of civilisation as well as of barbarism. The only difference is that the civilised system raises every vice that barbarism practises in a simple form to a compound, equivocal, ambiguous, hypocritical mode of existence . . . No one is punished more severely for keeping woman in slavery than man himself. (Fourier)

Meanwhile, Fourier's "feminism" was of another order altogether—something that should not have escaped Marx, but that, for a reason yet to be clarified, did not hold his attention in this polemic, where he posed the problem of women's emancipation only on the level of the direct perception of the female proletariat's submission to the harsh conditions of factory work. To conceive of a form of emancipation in which women would assume the initiative in the social battle without waiting for exhortation and slogans from their companions of the "strong sex" was to move the debate onto a totally different terrain—the very one on which Fourier had dared to place himself. As touching as Fleur-de-Marie, a character in a novel, may have been, Fourier was presumably not thinking of that kind of woman when he wrote:

I have provided a basis for saying that women, in a state of liberty, will outdo men in all mental and physical functions which are not dependent on bodily strength . . . It is women who suffer most under Civilisation, and it is women who should be attacking it. (*Theory of the Four Movements*)

Critical Criticism and the Works of Flora Tristan

In addition to Fleur-de-Marie, Sue included in *The Mysteries of Paris* a character called Louise Morel. A servant, she is abused by her master, becomes pregnant, and gives birth. After committing infanticide, she is arrested—the occasion for the "socialist" novelist to voice his own critical ideas on the penal law through the mouth of Rudolph. "The criminal who has in fact driven a girl to infanticide is not *punished*," the prince declares, but he never questions the connection with domestic service as such. "Faithful in all respects to his previous theory, he deplores only that there is no *law which punishes* a seducer and links repentance and atonement with terrible chastisement" ("Revelation of the Mystery of the Emancipation of Women" *The Holy Family*).

Marx contrasted the thinking of the novelist as Rudolph—"the most pitiful off-scourings of socialist literature"—with "Fourier's masterly characterization of *marriage* or with the works of the materialist [fraction] of French communism." However, in *The Holy Family* another character emerged, a woman writer whom Marx could have placed in direct opposition to Eugène Sue's female characters: Flora Tristan (1803–44).

Mentioned three different times, Flora Tristan deserved a choice place in an apologia for women's emancipation, even if her writings did not truly rank her among communist materialists. In *The Holy Family*, Marx and Engels attacked the young Hegelian "critical critic" Edgar Bauer, the anonymous author of several descriptions of French writings, including *L'Union ouvrière* (1843–44; *The Workers' Union*) by Flora Tristan, whom he dubbed the "Woman-Messiah." Engels—for it was he who was writing here—spoke ironically about "Edgar's" position on non-organized work done in isolation and his defense of the need for organized work. "Flora Tristan, in an assessment of whose work this great proposition appears, puts forward the same demand and is treated *en canaille* [as a rabble-rouser] for her insolence in anticipating Critical Criticism"(*The Holy Family*). The text cites another critical remark by the "critic" Bauer: " 'Flora Tristan is an example of the feminine dogmatism which must have a formula and constructs it out of the categories of what exists.' " Engels replied that the brothers Bauer were constructing formulas with the existing philosophy of Hegel:

Formulae, nothing but formulae. And despite all its invectives against dogmatism, it condemns itself to dogmatism and even to *feminine* dogmatism. It is and remains an old woman—faded, widowed *Hegelian* philosophy which paints and adorns its body, shrivelled into the most repulsive abstraction, and ogles all over Germany in search of a wooer. (*The Holy Family*)

As for Marx, his vague allusions to *The Worker's Union* and its author added nothing that was essentially different from the remarks by Engels. It was as if both men had remained insensitive to Tristan's popular success and her reputation as a reforming pioneer, which she had acquired by then as much through her writing as through her propaganda activity. It was as if the theses and the revolutionary demands expounded in *The Worker's Union*—an opuscule already in its third edition when *The Holy Family* was being composed—had not yet been assimilated by the future authors of *The Manifesto of the Communist Party*. Did Tristan not deserve to appear among the representatives of "critico-Utopian Socialism and Communism," alongside Saint-Simon, Charles Fourier, and Robert Owen? Her presence in that company was all the more essential given that the misogynist Pierre-Joseph Proudhon was criticized as a "conservative" or "bourgeois" socialist for having written and published *Philosophie de la Misère* (1846; *The Philosophy of Wretchedness Poverty*), after he had garnered praise for his essay, "What Is Property?" in *The Holy Family*.

Construction of a Theory

The intellectual association between Marx and Engels took concrete shape and was demonstrated in a work that remained unpublished during their lifetimes. Although methodically constructed, it exhibited only the basic elements of a theory or an original philosophy of history. While Engels took care to attribute the discovery of this theory to Marx alone, the latter was content to speak of it modestly as a "vital lead" in his research, without seeing any more in it than a conception of the world, a Weltanschauung free from metaphysical presuppositions. Calling it "materialist and critical," Marx indirectly divulged his philosophical sources, his first teachers of thought, Epicurus and Spinoza.

It should come as no surprise that, once their philosophical apprenticeship had ended, Marx and Engels did not reserve a special place for the problem of women's emancipation when they decided to link their convictions and their theoretical standards to a movement of general emancipation, in which men and women of the same social class—the industrial proletariat—were engaged in a struggle for liberation. Subjected to a common servitude imposed by an economic system of exploitation and alienation that was becoming increasingly oppressive with the progress of mechanization, men and women workers had a common interest in defending the so-called rights of man without gender distinction, as much on the material level as on that of human rights. Transforming the postulates of the charter of human rights into daily reality was an immediate goal. The French Revolution, despite its failures and its terrors, had borne witness to the importance of political emancipation. With the gestation and dissemination of the writings of Saint-Simon, Owen, and Fourier, there emerged a new social doctrine, for the French thinker, Pierre Leroux, devised the name "socialism." Leroux was perfectly aware of socialism's debt to earlier utopian thinkers. Marx, who admired Leroux, retained certain lessons from utopian thought; once he had removed its mystical impulses, he was able to refer to "human emancipation."

Human emancipation necessarily involves a critique of political economy in concrete terms, for example, a critique of the division of labor:

> The division of labour in which all these contradictions are implicit, and which in its turn is based on the natural division of labour in the family and the separation of society into individual families opposed to one another, simultaneously implies the *distribution*, and indeed the *unequal* distribution, both quantitative and qualitative, of labour and its products, hence property, the nucleus, the first form of which lies in the family, where wife and children are the slaves of the husband. ("Social Division of Labour and Its Consequences,"*MECW*, vol. 5)

Marx extended Fourier's critique of bourgeois marriage to the entire economic system based on private property. Embodied in a still-rudimentary form within the family, slavery is the first form of property, as modern economists, for whom property is synonymous with availability of a foreign work force, admit. Division of labor implies antagonism between private interests and common interests, a state of affairs in which the action particular to man becomes for him an alien power that oppresses him and thwarts his hopes and anticipations. One of the main factors of historical evolution, this phenomenon of division and alienation culminates in the formation of the state: a model of autonomy detached from real interests, and at the same time the expression of the illusory community in which social classes are pitted against each other.

In the introductory part of *Die deutsche Ideologie* (1845–46; *The German Ideology*, *MECW*, vol. 5), Marx established the broad outlines of this critique of the state, which, together with his critique of capital, was to constitute the central theme of the work he had promised to a German publisher. Through his articles and essays in the *Rheinische Zeitung* (1841–42), in the *Deutsch-französische Jahrbücher* and in *Vorwärts!* (1844), he had gained adherents in Germany among the liberal and republican avant-garde, who would come into public prominence at the time of the revolutionary and parliamentary events of 1848. The slogans of this movement were limited to a single objective: political emancipation. It was this demand that made up the substance of the first part of the essay, "On the Jewish Question," in which the critique of political emancipation derived from the distinction between the rights of man and the rights of the citizen, and in which certain articles of the 1791 and 1793 French Déclarations des Droits de l'Homme et du Citoyen (Declarations of the Rights of Man and of the Citizen) were invoked, as were the state constitutions of Pennsylvania and New Hampshire in the United States.

In Marx's brilliant critical analysis of the charters of the rights of man and the citizen, the question of women's rights was never even touched upon. However, the connection between Jews ("inferior" citizens) and women (the "inferior sex") was obvious: Marx granted that Jews had the right to practice their religion by virtue of the recognized link between civil society and the state. He now needed new reading material to encounter a school of thought in which women, beyond their political and human emancipation, would see themselves raised to cult status with messianic overtones.

Among his readings at this time, Saint-Simon and his school were the most decisive for Marx. His admiration for the former had been demonstrated several times, beginning with his polemic against a German author who, in expounding Saint-Simon's doctrine, had resorted to secondary literature without specifying his sources. This had given rise to errors and unfortunate misunderstandings. For example, in one passage Herr Grün alleged that in "one of his books," Saint-Simon had uttered "mysterious words" about women's emancipation. Marx responded as follows:

> Of course, if in some work or other Saint-Simon had spoken of admitting and nominating women to some unknown position, these would indeed be "mysterious words." But the mystery exists only in the mind of Herr Grün. "One of Saint-Simon's books" is none other than the *Lettres d'un habitant de Genève*. In this work, after stating that everyone is eligible to subscribe to the Newton Council or its departments, he continues: "Les femmes seront admises *à souscrire*, elles pourront *être nommées*" [Women will be admitted, they may even be nominated]—that is, to a position in this Council or its departments, of course. ("Critique of German Socialism According to Its Various Prophets,"*The German Ideology, in MECW*, vol. 5)

At issue, of course, was a position on the council or in one of its sections, as a magisterial body of scholars and artists whose vocation it was to exercise spiritual power—a council of wise men charged with questioning facts and, by interpreting the law of "universal gravity," applying this unique law of the universe. Recalling that Olinde Rodrigues, one of the leaders of the Saint-Simonian school, "printed this message in large type in his 1832 edition," Marx agreed with the remark of a contemporary historian, confirming that with this single phrase Saint-Simon effectively launched the idea of women's emancipation.

It has been proven that the "woman question" was the source of the schism in the school of Saint-Simon. It is not impossible that the mystical feminism of Saint-Simon's disciples was rooted in the following evidence: the history of humanity in the political sense of the term had been that of the "strong sex" until then, woman having systematically been relegated to the background. Before Saint-Simon, Fourier had already sketched out the prefatory remarks of an ethics of the regeneration of the human race through the female element.

Departures from Utopianism

"It is through the complete emancipation of women that the Saint-Simonian era shall be indicated," wrote Sébastien Charléty in his *Histoire du saint-simonisme, 1825–1–1864* (1896; History of Saint-Simonism). By grappling with such a representative of "true socialism," neither Marx nor Engels wanted to stop at the associative model posited by Fourier, where all social functions were based on the couple. Marx contented himself with demonstrating that Grün's book was a mixture of plagiarisms, which allowed him to show off his own erudition in his review of it. His knowledge of the work of Saint-Simon prevented him from taking seriously the religious morality of the pretentious followers, who went so far as to deduce from the master's distinction between idlers and workers the expectation of the Woman-Messiah, called upon to heal the wounds of the family just as the followers themselves had discovered the secret of healing the wounds of the city.

As for Engels, who was a communist before Marx, he was preparing to set forth the principles of communism, having come to an agreement with his new companion, who was readying himself for the same task. What influence would the social order of communism exert over the family? Relations between the sexes were to be reduced to a purely private affair without interference from society. The elimination of private property would also bring about the disappearance of the two foundations of traditional marriage: woman's dependence on her husband and children's dependence on their parents (since the upbringing of children was to be a collective practice).

> Here also is the answer to the outcry of moralising philistines against the communist community of women. Community of women is a relationship that belongs altogether to bourgeois society and is completely realised today in prostitution. But prostitution is rooted in private property and falls with it. Thus instead of introducing the community of women, communist organisation puts an end to it. ("The Principles of Communism," *MECW*, vol. 6)

This theme was to be taken up insistently again in *The Manifesto of the Communist Party*, in which one can discern the influence of Fourier, his critique of the bourgeois family now extended to the proletariat family. The fully developed family existed only for the bourgeoisie, but there was a corollary in the absence of family life among the proletariat and in public prostitution. "The bourgeois family naturally declines with the decline of its complement, and the two disappear with the disappearance of capital" (*The Manifesto of the Communist Party*). The bourgeois phraseology on family, education, and the intimacy of parent-child

relations was all the more repulsive as big industry destroyed all family ties among the proletarians and transformed children into articles of commerce and instruments of labor. Distinctions of sex and age lost all social significance for the working class; all that remained were instruments of labor, the cost of which varied with age and sex.

The Manifesto of the Communist Party avoided emphasizing differences in the respective situations of men and women employed in modern industrial enterprises, and, accordingly, it refrained from attributing to each of the sexes a clear role in the struggle for the improvement of working conditions and in the movement of general emancipation. This absence of gender-differentiation was codified in the call to action that ends the text: "Proletarians of all countries unite!"

Far from bearing witness to any such triumphant proletarian unity, the year 1848 offered the spectacle of defeat in episodes of pitiless barbarity. The return of Marx and Engels to Germany had removed them from the theater of revolutionary and counterrevolutionary events in France, and there was to be no echo in the *Neue Rheinische Zeitung* (1848–49) of the political agitation of women such as Pauline Roland, Eugénie Niboyet, Jeanne Deroin, and others, notably George Sand. Equally ignored was the participation of a female avant-garde in the political movement in Germany itself, where a woman's press and women's democratic associations were being created.

Similarly, coming back to the years 1848–50 in France, Marx clearly focused on male figures in writing his assessment of class struggles and party conflicts. As a correspondent in London for the largest American daily newspaper for about ten years, he paid attention to the condition of workingwomen only to the extent that their work, like that of children, warranted an official application of the protection laws. He did not miss the opportunity to mention the case of a woman who, during a meeting of unemployed persons, rose up against wives working in the factory, which meant that children were neglected and household duties were trampled underfoot: with an honest salary for an honest day's work, every worker must be able to keep wife and children alive, etc. The working wives were summoned to strike in order to obtain fair wages for their husbands: a resolution that was unanimously adopted.

Women's and Children's Labor

Up until the creation of the International Workingmen's Association in 1864, Marx and Engels treated the subject of women's emancipation only in an indirect manner—a negative manner so to speak—by observing and recording the harmful physical and moral consequences of women and children working in factories and by taking to task industrialists who were guilty of violating factory laws. Reports by factory inspectors showed beyond all doubt that the laws meant to rein in the greed of industrial lords were pure sham, since the penalty imposed for infraction of labor laws represented only a minuscule part of profits. The sector of the workforce made up of women and young people—often minors—suffered the majority of work-related accidents.

Women's and children's labor was among the issues slated for discussion at the First Congress of the International Workingmen's Association in Geneva in September 1866. Neither

Marx nor Engels attended the congress, but the former did write the "Instructions for the Delegates of the Provisory General Council," where the issue appeared in point 3 under the theme "limitation of the working day." The working day was fixed at eight hours

> only [for] adult persons, male or female, the latter, however, to be rigorously excluded from all *nightwork whatever*, and all sort of work hurtful to the delicacy of the sex, or exposing their bodies to poisonous and otherwise deleterious agencies. By adult persons we understand all persons having reached or passed the age of 18 years. (*Documents of the First International*, vol. 2)

Under point 4 of the "Instructions," which dealt with "Juvenile and Children's Labour (Both Sexes)" Marx, as a follower of Robert Owen, expressed himself in favor of the participation in "the great work of social production" by children of either sex, from the age of nine and up, although as modern industry made that progress a reality "under capital it was distorted into an abomination." It was a question of a "rational state of society" in which "every child whatever, from the age of nine years, ought to become a productive labourer." The "Instructions" further specify that the working day should not go beyond two hours, after children have had their instruction in the elementary schools.

> We deal here only with the most indispensable antidotes against the tendencies of a social system which degrades the working man into a mere instrument for the accumulation of capital, and transforms parents by their necessities into slaveholders, sellers of their own children. The *right* of children and juvenile persons must be vindicated. They are unable to act for themselves. It is, therefore, the duty of society to act on their behalf (instructions)

Education to be combined with productive labor took three forms: mental, physical, and technological. In Marx's view, this combination would "raise the working class far above the level of the higher and middle classes." The idea was picked up again and developed in *Das Kapital: Kritik der politischen Oekonomie* (1867; *Capital: A Critical Analysis of Capitalist Production*), but during the 7 September 1866 session of the Congress of the International Workingmen's Association in Geneva, Marx's program referring to work by women and children became the object of a lively debate, which included the following resolution made by Citizens Chemalé, Fribourg, Perrachon, and Camélinat:

> On physical, moral, and social grounds the labour of women and children in factories ought to be energetically condemned on principle as one of the most prolific causes of the degeneracy of the human species and as one of the most powerful means of demoralisation put in motion by the capitalist caste. (Marx and Engels *Werke*, vol. 20–1)

The authors of the resolution added that women were "not made to work hard; their place is at the family fireside; they are the natural educators of the children; they alone can prepare their children for a civic and free life."

Capital is simultaneously a critical theory of capitalist economy and a martyrology of workers of both sexes. Like Engels in 1845, Marx turned to official documentation provided by factory inspectors. The concept of human emancipation was only suggested here, called for by a long series of indictments against personified "capital," the owner of money or the means of production and the buyer of the labor of men and women, young girls, and minors. "Previously, the workman sold his own labour-power, which he disposed of nominally as a free agent. Now he sells wife and child. He has become a slave dealer" (*Capital*). As for women's emancipation, where female labor power was concerned, the initiative fell to the male workers, who had succeeded in forcing the reduction of labor by women and children in the English factories, while the inspectors' accounts criticized the practices of parent-workers who trafficked in their own children.

With regard to factory legislation in England, Marx emphasized its interference in the lordly rights of capital, as may be noted in the case of work at home, where every regulation appeared as a direct encroachment upon parental authority. However, the violence of the facts had shown that, by undermining the economic foundations of the old family and family work, big industry turned the former family relationships upside down at the same time. "The rights of the children had to be proclaimed" ("Production of Relative Surplus Value," *Capital*, part IV). The mode of capitalist exploitation resulted in the degeneration of paternal authority. But however odious the dissolution of former family bonds in the capitalist system appeared to be, big industry nonetheless did create the economic basis of a superior form of family and the relationships between the sexes, thanks to the decisive role it assigned to women, young people, and children, beyond the sphere of the home, in the process of socially organized production.

> It was not, however, the misuse of parental authority that created the capitalistic exploitation, whether direct or indirect, of children's labour; but, on the contrary, it was the capitalistic mode of exploitation which, by sweeping away the economical basis of parental authority, made its exercise degenerate into a mischievous misuse of power. However terrible and disgusting the dissolution, under the capitalist system, of the old family ties may appear, nevertheless modern industry, by assigning as it does an important part in the process of production, outside the domestic sphere, to women, to young persons, and to children of both sexes, creates a new economical foundation for a higher form of the family and of the relations between the sexes. It is, of course, just as absurd to hold the Teutonic-christian form of the family to be absolute and final as it would be to apply that character to the ancient Roman, the ancient Greek, or Eastern forms which, moreover, taken together form a series in historic development. Moreover, it is obvious that the fact of the collective working group being composed of individuals of both sexes and all ages, must necessarily, under suitable conditions, become a source of humane development; although in its spontaneously developed, brutal capitalistic form, where the labourer exists for the process of production, and not the process of production for the labourer, that fact is a pestiferous source of corruption and slavery. ("Production of Relative Surplus-Value," *Capital*, part IV)

While stressing the priority role of men in the resistance to the dominant economic system, Marx did not go so far as to deduce from this a standard rule postulating the moral superiority of the male proletariat. Sometimes he even seemed to imply the opposite. For example, in order to illustrate the "general law of capitalist accumulation" with concrete examples, Marx reviewed the worst moments of pauperism in England, a country that offered the classic example by its rank in the world market. In a long chapter on the farming proletariat in the various British counties, the author of *Capital* began to indicate the harmful consequences of temporary or local lack of labor. Instead of causing salaries to be raised, this dearth of manual labor led to the forced hiring of women and children. One of the fruits of this "vicious cycle" was the gang system, the system of wandering gangs consisting of 10 to 40 or 50 people, mainly women, adolescents of both sexes, and children from 6 to 13 years of age.

> The farmers have discovered that women work steadily only under the direction of men, but that women and children, once set going, impetuously spend their life-force—as Fourier knew—while the adult male labourer is shrewd enough to economise his as much as he can. ("The Accumulation of Capital," *Capital*, part VII)

The International Workingmen's Association

The International Workingmen's Association was a predominantly male organization: most of its members and all of its leaders were men. During the constitution of the first General Council of the organization, the elected council members were men who represented a variety of nationalities, and the president and secretary general were named out of this group. In the inaugural address and the provisional statutes of the association—two documents remarkable for their high level of spirit and the universality of the expressed objectives—Marx made no specific place for workingwomen, whose oppression was considered to be simply a part of that of workers. No mention was made of the possibility of forging ties between the International and the emerging feminist groups in Germany and Great Britain.

Astonishingly, the presence of women in the IWA does not seem to have been accepted as natural at the outset: it took seven months after the founding of the International before the issue was submitted to the General Council and became the object of inscription in a few laconic lines: "A question being asked as to whether females were eligible as members, Citizen *Wheeler* proposed, *Bordage* seconded, that females be admitted as members. Carried unanimously" (Minutes, 25 April 1865, *Documents*, vol. 1). There was thus no debate, but if the business was so much a matter of course, why was the question posed and submitted to a vote?

The minutes of the session of the General Council of 3 October 1865 arouse our curiosity. The record states: "A letter was also read from Madame Jeanne Deroin. The letter had been addressed to the conference but had been delayed." A laconic remark that would seem to have warranted further clarification, in view of the personality of this self-made woman, a laundress by profession who became militant pedagogue, was active in the women's insurance movement, and who in 1852 emigrated to England, where she founded women's periodicals.

Two women's names appeared in the General Council on the occasion of a debate on the campaign initiated in England on behalf of imprisoned Fenians (Irish revolutionaries). The minutes of the session of 2 January 1866 record that

> *Fox* read from the *Cork Daily Herald* the appeal of Mrs. O'Donovan Rossa and Mrs. Clarke Luby to the women of Ireland for funds for the families of the state prisoners now or lately in Ireland and also evidence from the Dublin *Irishman* that collections were being made for this purpose in the manufacturing towns of the North of England. He remarked on the liberty granted by the British Government to Irish women, who were allowed to proclaim themselves Fenians without being prosecuted. He finished by moving that the appeal be sent to the *Workman's Advocate* by the Central Council with a request for its publication. (*Documents*, vol. 1)

Finally, more than two years after the creation of the IWA, a well-known female personality emerged: Harriet Law (1832–97), figurehead of the atheist movement in England, was first invited to attend the General Council's sessions and was later admitted as a full-fledged member. This is how the minutes of the General Council's session of 16 April 1867 recorded the first contact with the British activist:

> *Fox* read a letter from Mrs. Harriet Law on the subject of Women's Rights and expressed his opinion that perhaps Mrs. Law would go to the Congress at Lausanne if solicited. By mutual consent Fox undertook to write to Mrs. Law asking her if she would be willing to attend the Council meetings if invited." (*Documents*, vol. 1)

Law's admission into the General Council took place at the session of 25 June 1867, after the suggestion had been made at the 18 June session. Thereafter, the records confirm the presence of this sole woman at the sessions of the council throughout the next five years. It does not appear that she deemed it necessary to go beyond her role of observer except on two specific occasions. During the session of the council of 2 July 1867, Law announced her intention to establish a national association of workingwomen in London. Marx was absent from this session but was later informed of the announcement by Fox, the secretary general, who had advised Law to take up contact with "Miss Carroll, leader of the tailoresses of London and occupant of seat at the Tailors Executive" (Fox to Marx, 3 July 1867, *Documents*, vol. 2). At the session of 27 August 1867, during a discussion on the need for the IWA to strengthen its propaganda, Marx expressed his opposition to the transformation of the association into a "debating club," in view of the progress it had made in some countries, and he added that he was not opposed to the discussion of "large questions." Among the council members who were in favor of debates, Law's name is mentioned in the minutes. From February 1868 on a second woman, a Mrs. Morgan, was part of the General Council. No further details are given, but she may have been the wife of William Morgan, a bootmaker who had been a member of the council since October 1864 and was active in the Reform League. The minutes indicate Mrs. Morgan's frequent presence at the council sessions, but make no mention of her participation in the debates.

Both Harriet Law and Mrs. Morgan were present at the council session of 28 July 1868, in which Marx opened the debate on "the influence of machinery in the hands of the capitalists," a broadly developed theme in *Capital*, but neither woman is mentioned as having made any comment, while the speaker, talking of the harmful effects of the use of machines, emphasized the state of servitude of women and children in the factory, a match that traditionally reduced the female sex to an infantile state.

> The woman has thus become an active agent in our social production. Formerly female and children's labour was carried on within the family circle. I do not say that it is wrong that women and children should participate in our social production. I think every child above the age of nine ought to be employed at productive labour a portion of its time, but the way in which they are made to work under existing circumstances is abominable. (Minutes, 28 July 1868, *Documents*, vol. 2)

It was only at the session of 4 August 1868, when the debates on mechanization continued, that Harriet Law intervened with a few remarks that seemed to target Marx's thesis: "Mrs. *Law* said machinery had made women less dependent on men than they were before and would ultimately emancipate them from domestic slavery. She must enter her protest against the view taken of women's labour."

The debate was pursued on 11 August 1868. As the minutes for that session reveal, Marx stressed the reduction of working hours, a measure that was needed to offer the working class more time for self-betterment.

> Legislative restrictions were the first step towards the mental and physical elevation and the ultimate emancipation of the working classes. Nobody denied, nowadays, that the State must interfere on behalf of the women and children; and a restriction of their hours led, in most instances, to a reduction of the working time of the men. (*Documents*, vol. 2)

Law made a few more interventions during sessions of the General Council in 1868 and 1869. The most remarkable of these was her gesture on behalf of the *ovalistes* (workers who twist silk thread into strands) who were on strike in Lyon.

> A letter was read from Lyons announcing the adhesion of the *Ovalistes* of that town, consisting of about 750 women and upwards of 300 men, to the International Association. An official declaration accompanied the letter, the contributions are to be paid at the Congress at Bâle. The *Ovalistes* being on strike, they appealed for aid. (Minutes, 13 July 1869, *Documents*, vol. 3)

Minutes for the same session record that the *ovalistes* were accepted as members of the IWA, and that "Respecting the question of pecuniary aid Mrs. Law expressed an opinion that it would be advisable to communicate with Mr. Stuart Mill to bring the matter before the Female Suffrage Association who would meet on Saturday." Law agreed to act as the IWA delegate at the next meeting of the Women's Association and to collect funds for the strikers of Lyon there. "Mrs. Law reported from the Female Suffrage Association that the question of the *Ovalistes* of Lyons could not be officially entertained, but that she would have received private donations had she been provided with a

subscription sheet. The Women's Club in Union Street was willing to collect subscriptions if a sheet was forwarded" (Minutes, 20 July1869, *Documents*, vol. 3). She added that the Women's Club of Union Street was prepared to collect donations by means of a list of signatures. (It was in the course of this session of the General Council that Marx opened the debate on the question of inheritance rights, giving rise to a serious exchange of opinions.) During the session of 27 July 1869, Law handed the sum of two pounds, four shillings, and six pence over to Eugène Dupont, the secretary for France, for the silkworkers of Lyons, observing that "ladies did not like identifying themselves with strikes."

The topic of the silkworkers came up again at the session of 10 August 1869: "Declarations of adhesion were received from the Upholsterers' Society of Lyons, 200 from the *Ovalistes* of St. Symphorien d'Ozon (Isère), and an announcement that the adhesion of the *Ovalistes* of Lyons had been received" (Minutes, *Documents*, vol. 3). As proposed by Marx, the General Council decided to grant "special credentials" to Philomène Rozan, a member of the International and the president of the Société des Ovalistes de Lyon (Society of Silkworkers of Lyons). At the same session the issue of education was broached; that topic had already been discussed at three separate congresses of the IWA, in Geneva (1866), Lausanne (1867), and Brussels (1868). Taken up again at the 17 August session, it prompted an intervention from Law, described in the minutes as follows:

> Mrs. *Law* understood by education everything that would improve a human being. The working classes had to maintain all kinds of educational establishments, but derived no benefits from them. The property of the Church must be secularised and devoted to schools. We wanted fewer parsons and more schoolmasters. The *Law Times* prophesied that the Established Church would not last another ten years, and it was therefore time to stir in the matter. The dissenters would be on our side and it would induce the clergy of the Established Church to bestir themselves to find the means. Pope said the proper study of man was mankind. Milner wanted us to study what kind of a man a labourer was. Cit. Milner preferred that children should be taught what their labour was worth and how to get it. If they had been taught, they would not work so many hours. She proposed that the Church funds should be devoted to education as a part of our demand. (*Documents*, vol. 3)

We now come to Law's profession of communist faith, when she participated in the debate about unions and the struggle for fair compensation for work. She held that the system of competition prevented the worker from seeing his buying power grow. The market rules the supply and demand of work. In order to obtain the full value of his product, some power is needed to regulate production:

> [W]e must have communism as Robert Owen wanted it. The purchasing power could not be increased without increasing the raw material to work with. In a state of communism the directing power would know what was required and the labour would be distributed accordingly. Under no other form could the right to labour and the value of labour be guaranteed, it could not be done under

the competitive system; she was in favour of communism. (Minutes, session of 31 August 1869, *Documents*, vol. 3)

From August 1870 until October 1871, Harriet Law's name is missing from the minutes of the General Council of the IWA. However, it appears among the signatures of the new *General Rules and Administrative Regulations of the International Workingmen's Association* published 24 October 1871 (*Documents*, vol. 4). Meanwhile, it is worth noting that an earlier (October 1868) article written by Marx in response to a campaign of slander against the International, enumerating British organizations represented in the General Council, contained the following passage, after the names of cooperative societies, the Reform League, and the National Reform-Association: "lastly, the *atheist* popular movement [represented] by its well-known orator Mrs. *Harriet Law* and Mr. *Copeland*" ("Connections Between the International Workingmen's Association and English Workingmen's Organisations,"*Documents*, vol. 3).

Law's absence must have surprised the members of the General Council. In fact, the minutes of 21 November 1871 (after the defeat of the Paris Commune) reveal that George Harris, financial secretary of the council, wanted to know "if Mrs. Law [was] still a member of the Council." Engels replied that she had been "asked if she considered herself a member, and she said certainly" (*Documents*, vol. 5).

Several sessions of the council had been allotted to the issue of the refugees from the Paris Commune in London. At the session of 2 January 1872, "Citizen *Marx* announced . . . that Mrs. Law had sent two pounds, the proceeds of a lecture given by her for the refugees." Law's name is among the members of the General Council who signed the "Declaration by the General Council of the International Workingmen's Association on Police Terrorism in Ireland" (April 1872). Her signature also appears, alongside those of the other members of the council, in "*The Fictitious Splits in the International*," the brochure written in 1872 by Marx and Engels against Bakunin and his followers in Switzerland.

Lessons of the Paris Commune

It took a historic event with incalculable and unforeseeable political consequences for Marx to come to appreciate a form of revolutionary behavior among the women of the working class: the Franco-Prussian War and the Paris Commune (1870–71). The Commune also enabled him to enrich his political theory—which up until then had been faced with the repeated defeats of the labor movement—with a new dimension, barely begun in earlier writing: the actions and gestures of bourgeois and workers' self-emancipation. As a member of the General Council of the International and charged with representing the labor movements in Germany and Russia, he showed little sympathy for the "bourgeois" suffragettes, but he showed a great deal of admiration for the women of the proletariat who fought alongside the male militants. For example, in his "Address on the Commune" he showered praise on the "real women of Paris":

Wonderful, indeed was the change the Commune had wrought in Paris! No longer any trace of the meretricious Paris of the Second Empire. . . . "We," said a member of the Commune, "hear no longer of assassination, theft and personal assault; it seems indeed as if the police had dragged along with it to Versailles all its Conservative friends." The *cocottes* had refound the scent of their protectors—the absconding men of family, religion, and, above all, of property. In their stead, the real women of Paris showed again at the surface—heroic, noble, and devoted, like the women of antiquity. Working, thinking, fighting, bleeding Paris—almost forgetful, in its incubation of a new society, of the cannibals at its gates—radiant in the enthusiasm of its historic initiative! (*The Civil War in France*, MEGA, vol. 22–1)

The "Address on the Commune" unmistakably had the tone of a political pamphlet: Marx gave free rein to his passion as a militant communist, and, above all, the text presents what is essentially a condensed summary of the major theses of the social criticism he had developed in works such as *Die Klassenkämpfe in Frankreich, 1848 bis 1850* (1850; *The Class Struggles in France, 1848 to 1850*), "Der achtzehnte Brumaire des Louis Napoleon" (1852; "The Eighteenth Brumaire of Louis Bonaparte"), and *Herr Vogt* (1860; Mr. Vogt). In the last third of the 19th century, after several wars of continental and national dimensions and two aborted revolutions, an event occurred that, despite its tragic outcome, attested to a wealth of creative initiatives rarely encountered before in the annals of the movements of social emancipation. The momentous nature of the events of 1871 explains Marx's use of historical analogies to castigate the men of Versailles—defenders of civilization and the bourgeois order:

Even the atrocities of the bourgeois in June, 1848, vanish before the ineffable infamy of 1871. The self-sacrificing heroism with which the population of Paris—men, women, and children—fought for eight days after the entrance of the Versaillese, reflects as much on the grandeur of their cause, as the infernal deeds of the soldiery reflect the innate spirit of that civilisation of which they are the mercenary vindicators . . .

To find a parallel for the conduct of Thiers and his bloodhounds we must go back to the times of Sullaand the two Triumvirates of Rome. The same wholesale slaughter in cold blood; the same disregard, in massacre, of age and sex. ("The Commune,"*The Civil War in France*)

Once again Marx invoked the women of the Commune, whom he ranked among the "self-sacrificing champions of a new and better society," while a "nefarious civilisation, based upon the enslavement of labour, drowns the moans of its victims in a hue-and-cry of calumny," was changing the "serene workingmen's Paris of the Commune . . . into a pandemonium." Meanwhile, Marx speculates that the "bourgeois mind of all countries" would interpret the events of the Commune very differently:

The Paris people die enthusiastically for the Commune in numbers unequalled in any battle known to history. What does that prove? Why, that the Commune was not the people's own government but the usurpation of a handful of criminals! The women of Paris joyfully give their lives at the barricades and on the place of execution. What does this prove? Why, that the demon of the Commune has changed them into Megaeras and Hecates!

The two drafted versions of "The Commune" are rich in insights that Marx, being short on time, was not able to retain in the definitive text. For example, the first draft contains the following passage:

> [The] Commune has given order to the *mairies* to make no distinction between the *femmes* called illegitimate, the mothers and widows of National Guards, as to the indemnity of 75 centimes; the public prostitutes till now kept for the "men of order" at Paris but for their "safety" kept in penal servitude under the arbitrary rule of the police; the Commune has liberated the prostitutes from this degrading slavery, but swept away the soil upon which, and the men by whom, prostitution flourishes. The higher prostitutes—the *cocottes*—were, of course, under the rule of order, not the slaves, but the masters of the police and governors. (*The Civil War in France*, First Draft, *MEGA*, vol. 22–1)

In London, Marx changed the image of the Commune into the ideal prototype of the human city of the future, as he was able to construct it by combining extracts clipped from English and French newspapers and information sent by members of the Commune to the General Council of the IWA. Some of the leading principles of the book on the state, planned in his blueprint for the "Economy" (a work he never completed), were set forth in the "The Commune," both on the critical level and as viewed from the angle of expectation of the postcapitalist and post-state world commune.

The International and Women's Suffrage in the United States

On 11 September 1871, during a session of the subcommittee of the General Council in preparation for the the IWA conference that was to be held in London a week later, Marx proposed that the constitution of workingwomen's sections be recommended. At the congress itself, he read the following proposal: "The Conference recommends the formation of female branches among the working class. It is, however, understood that this resolution does not at all interfere with the existence or formation of branches composed of both sexes" (*Documents*, vol. 4). According to explanatory notes on the resolution, "Marx stressed the need for founding women's sections in countries whose industries engage many women."

As the IWA became increasingly influential, with the creation of several sections in North America, the emerging feminist movement in the United States did not lag far behind in challenging the founding charter of the organization, the statutes and regulations of which insisted on its exclusively proletarian character. In December 1870 representatives of these sections had come together in New York to found a Central Committee for the United States. In July 1871 two sections classified as Section 9 and Section 12 had joined this committee under the leadership of two "bourgeois" suffragettes, Victoria Woodhull, and her sister, Tennessee Claflin. Their followers sought to strengthen their influence in the International, with the intent of pitting them against other sections that were predominantly German, French, and Irish, and above all against Section 1 of

New York and its Central Committee, which had a direct relationship with Marx and Engels. Section 12 had its own organ, a publication with the significant title of *Woodhull & Claflin's Weekly*. The two sisters had established contact with Marx on the occasion of a rumor in the American press announcing his death. Thanking them for the "highly interesting papers" he had received, Marx sent them a lengthy correspondence from his daughter, Jenny, in which she recounted the police harassment she and her sisters had experienced during their vacation in Bagnères-de-Luchon. "This tragico-comical episode," he wrote, "seems to me characteristic of the Republic-Thiers" (letter to the editors of *Woodhull & Claflin's Weekly*, first published in No. 23/75, 21 October 1871. Jenny Marx's account ended with some sarcastic remarks:

> The French government are *capable de tout* [capable of anything]. They really believe in the truth of the wild pétroleum fables—the coinage of their own distempered brains. They do think the women of Paris are "neither brute nor human, neither man nor woman," but "pétroleuses"—a species of the Salamander, delighting in their native element—fire . . .
>
> One could afford to treat with silent contempt a government run mad, and to laugh at the farces in which the pottering pantaloons employed by that government play their muddling and meddling parts, did not these farces turn out to be tragedies for thousands of men, women and children. Think only of the "pétroleuses" before the court-martial of Versailles, and of the women who, for the last three months, are being slowly done to death on the pontoons. (quoted in *MECW*, vol. 22)

Marx's sympathy for the American periodical was short-lived. In December 1871 agitation by partisans of Section 12 resulted in a schism and led to the formation of two rival federal councils. The General Council in London, where Marx showed his extreme annoyance with this secessionist agitation, made a decision in favor of the Federal Committee of New York as representative authority for all American sections. The decision was published in *Woodhull & Claflin's Weekly*, accompanied by commentary that gave rise to misunderstanding. Accused of reducing the IWA to a tool for its own ends in contradiction to the objectives and tasks of the International, Section 12 was suspended until the following congress. The General Council emphasized one of the major demands of the general statutes of the IWA, namely the obligation imposed upon the sections to recruit exclusively from the working class, as the social conditions of the United States "peculiarly facilitate[d] the intrusion into the International of bogus reformers, middle-class quacks and trading politicians" ("Resolutions on the Split in the United States' Federation Passed by the General Council of the I.W.A. in Its Sittings of 5th and 12th March 1872," *Documents*, vol. 5). A recommendation was made that in the future no new section would be admitted that was not composed of at least three-quarters of salaried workers.

In their obstinacy in considering the United States only from the point of view of the interests of a working class in formation, Marx and Engels underestimated the role of the middle classes, which were then involved in the reorganization of the huge country that had just emerged from the more than ten-year-long Civil War. The women's suffrage movement was a part of these middle-class aspirations to achieve a full social and economic construction, in the spirit of the "historic" mission glorified by the authors of *The Manifesto of the Communist Party*. The aggressiveness with which Marx treated the suffragette sisters and their paper was communicated to Engels, who made the most of his friend's critical notes in composing "Die Internationale in Amerika" (The International in America), an article published in the 17 July 1872 issue of *Der Volksstaat* (in *MECW*, vol. 25). Here are some samples of Marx's indictments:

> *October 15th, 1871* was published in the journal of *Woodhull* (a banker's woman [sic], free-lover and general humbug) and *Claflin* (her sister in the same line) an Appeal of Section No. 12 (founded by *Woodhull*, and almost exclusively consisting of middle-class humbugs and worn-out Yankee swindlers in the Reform business; Section 9 is founded by Miss Claflin). [. . .] That the whole organisation for place-hunting and electoral purposes. [. . .] This appeal—and the formation thereupon of all sorts of middle-class humbug sections, free-lovers, spiritists, spiritist Shakers, etc.—gave rise to a split in which Section 1 (German) of the Old Council demanded the expulsion of Section 12, the non-admittance of sections in which at least two-thirds of the membership are not workers. (Marx, "American Split," *MECW*, vol. 23)

Marx seems not to have appreciated the fact that, among other things, Section 12 was demanding that each section have the right to set its own rules of conduct in full autonomy. He also did not accept the assertion that political equality and social freedom for all, without any racial or sexual distinction, were necessary preconditions for the more radical reforms called for by the International. Without comment, he quoted the following passages of protest from Woodhull and Claflin's *Journal*:

> "*The extension of equal citizenship to women*, the world over, *must* precede any *general change in the subsisting relations of capital and labour*. [. . .] Section 12 would also remonstrate against the vain assumption that the International Workingmen's Association is an *organisation of the working classes* . . ." ("American Split," *MECW*, vol. 23; emphases added by Marx)

In Marx's view, Section 12's entire campaign for the right to determine policy autonomously—contrary to the tactics decided upon by those in charge of Section 1—was motivated by just one goal: using the International as a propaganda instrument for the Victoria Woodhull's candidacy for the presidency of the United States. Marx's notes were intended for Engel's use in writing the article mentioned above. This time, the warning against the "two American ladies" went beyond the limits of an internal, local quarrel, since Engels chose the organ of the Social-Democratic Workers' Party as his forum to condemn the campaign of the two sisters, "millionairesses, advocates of women's emancipation and especially 'free love.'" Was it not the ambition of their followers to pass the International off as a bourgeois association? As for Woodhull's presidential campaign, Engels was careful to note: "The whole of America responded with resounding laughter" (*MECW*, vol. 25).

The few extracts from articles kept by Marx and Engels are far from doing justice to Woodhull's crusade for judicial, political, and social emancipation for women. Nor did they report on her general ideas, set forth in *The Origins, Tendencies, and Principles of Government* (1871), about the origins of civilization, the evolution of the social universe and its "sociological periods," the "mighty modifying influence of the civilizing power of modern Europe," the four determining powers of Europe—Russia, Prussia, France, and England—their rivalries, and the acceleration of the process of civilization in Asia. In this nearly 250-page volume of her collected articles, Woodhull showed herself to be closer to deist belief than to spiritualistic superstition. Pondering the causes of the Civil War from which her country had just emerged, she asserted that "the war was the necessary result of the growth of the principles of freedom within the general mind," principles that were opposed to private interests. However, although resulting from natural conditions, individuals incapable of mastering the situation had precipitated the catastrophe. As for her candidacy for the presidency in 1872, her decision was devoted to the affirmation of "a woman's right to occupy the highest office in the gift of the people" in accordance with the principles established by the United States Constitution, which guaranteed the right of suffrage for all citizens without distinction of race or color.

Social Progress and the "Feminine Ferment"

In a letter to Ludwig Kugelman dated 12 December 1868, Marx wrote:

> Everyone who knows anything of history also knows that great social revolutions are impossible without the feminine ferment. Social progress may be measured precisely by the social position of the fair sex (plain ones included). (*MECW*, vol. 43)

Almost a decade later, in a letter of 31 July 1877 to Sophie Liebknecht, Engels wrote:

> It's all very well for us here [in England] to talk and criticise, when in Germany any thoughtless or ill-considered work may entail imprisonment and the temporary disruption of family life. Fortunately our German women do not allow themselves to be deterred by this and prove by their deeds that the sickly sentimentality of which one hears so much is just a class affliction peculiar to bourgeois women. (*MECW*, vol. 45)

Many more examples of sympathy for women could be culled from the correspondence of Marx and Engels, but even taken as a whole these examples do not give an adequate sense of the result of the ultimate collaboration of the two friends. That work was both scientific and political, and, remarkably enough, it took shape after Marx's death, when, almost as a legacy from his collaborator, Engels published *Der Ursprung der Familie, des Privateigenthums und des Staats* (1884; *The Origin of the Family, Private Property, and the State*).

An eternal student, Marx had immersed himself for two years prior to his death in ethnological reading and was stimulated by the ideas of the American scholar Henry Lewis Morgan, the author of a work whose title alone could not help but catch the attention of any mind open to the problems of the historical destiny of the human species: *Ancient Society; or, Researches in the Lines of Human Progress from Savagery through Barbarism to Civilization* (1877). When he discovered one of Marx's notebooks referring to Morgan's work, Engels wrote to Karl Kautsky:

There is a *definitive* book—as definitive as Darwin's was in the case of biology—on the primitive state of society; once again, of course, Marx was the one to discover it. It is Morgan's *Ancient Society*, 1877. Marx mentioned it, but my head was full of other things at the time and he never referred to it again which was, no doubt, agreeable to him, wishing as he did to introduce the book to the Germans himself; I can see this from his very exhaustive extracts. Within the limits set by his subject, Morgan rediscovers for himself Marx's materialist view of history, and concludes with what are, for modern society, downright communist postulates. (letter of 16 February 1884, *MECW*, vol. 47)

The fruit of a post-mortem collaboration, Engels's *Origin of the Family, Private Property and the State* (notably in its 1891 edition) stands out for its enrichment of the materialist philosophy of history with a scientific foundation—a dimension that had been lacking prior to Marx's ethnological readings, but whose roots—with regard to women—were discernable in the works of thinkers such as Fourier, Saint-Simon, Johan Jakob Bachofen, and Morgan.

In the conclusion of his book, Engels quotes the following passage from Morgan's book, as if to appropriate the supreme lesson for himself and Marx.

A mere property career is not the final destiny of mankind, if progress is to be the law of the future as it has been of the past. The time which has passed away since civilisation began is but as a fragment of the past duration of man's existence; and but a fragment of the ages to come. The dissolution of society bids fair to become the termination of a career of which property is the end and aim, because such a career contains the elements of self-destruction. Democracy in government, brotherhood in society, equality in rights . . ., and universal education, foreshadow the next higher plane of society to which experience, intelligence and knowledge are steadily tending. *It will be a revival, in a higher form, of the liberty, equality and fraternity of the ancient gentes.* (*MECW*, vol. 26; emphases added by Engels)

This vision is essentially the same as that of Bachofen, who had written a work whose very title resembles the agenda of the communist ethic. Its categorical imperative can be summed up in these words: human emancipation of women: *Das Mutterrecht* (1861; *Matriarchy: Research on the Gynecocracy of the Ancient World According to Its Religious and Judicial Nature*).

In his ethnological readings—the last ones of his life as a researcher—Marx returned to some of Fourier's intuitions that he had already incorporated in his first book, *The Holy Family*, written some 30 years earlier. There Marx had adopted the pronouncement of the visionary genius who had prophesied that women, the first victims of bourgeois civilization and nevertheless superior to man, would be called upon to take men's place in the avant-garde of the struggle for human emancipation.

Engels, heir to Marx's ethnological papers, took it upon himself to develop a kind of supplement to the materialist theory.

He particularly relied on the work compiled by Marx, during his impassioned reading of Morgan's *Ancient Society*. Morgan had observed and studied the kinship systems and family types among North American Indians and had there found the key to the enigmas of the most ancient Greek, Roman, and Germanic history. According to Morgan, the family, far from being static, is continually evolving from an inferior form to a superior form, while kinship systems progress only after long intervals and according to radical family changes. "And," adds Marx, "the same applies to political, juridical, religious and philosophical systems generally" (*The Origin of the Family, Private Property, and the State, MECW*, vol. 26). Bachofen's work has been qualified as being "scientific prophecy," an assessment that could well be applied also to Morgan, his correspondent. As for Marx and Engels, they appropriated the fundamental thesis of the two explorers of primitive communities in order to nourish their own convictions, made up of prescience as much as science. Bachofen and Morgan discovered the existence of primitive communism in predominantly matriarchal societies. In a sense this constituted a heuristic demonstration of a form of women's emancipation rich with promise for a "revival in a higher form."

Bibliography

Sources

Bachofen, Johann Jakob, *Das Mutterrecht: Ein Untersuchungüber die Gynaikokratie der alten Welt nach ihrer religiösen und rechtlichen Natur*, Stuttgart: Krais und Hoffmann, 1861; reprint, Frankfurt: Suhrkamp, 1975

Bebel, August, *Die Frau in der Vergangenheit, Gegenwart und Zukunft*, Hottingen-Zurich: Schweizerische Volksbuchhandlung, 1883; 24th edition, as *Die Frau und der Sozialismus (die Frau in der Vergangenheit, gegenwart und zukunft)*, Stuttgart: Dietz, 1895

Engels, Friedrich, *The Condition of the Working Class in England in 1844*, translated by Florence Kelley Wischnewetzky, London: Sonnenschein, 1892

Engels, Friedrich, "Die Internationale in Amerika," *Der Volksstaat* (17 July 1872)

Feuerbach, Ludwig, *Principles of the Philosophy of the Future*, translated by Manfred H. Vogel, Indianapolis, Indiana: Bobbs-Merrill, 1966

Feuerbach, Ludwig, "Vorläufige Thesen zur Reform der Philosophie," in *Anekdota zur neuesten deutschen Philosophie und Publicistik*, edited by Arnold Ruge, Zurich: Verlag des literarischen Comptoirs, 1843; reprint, Glashütten im Taunus, Germany: Verlag Detlev Auvermann, 1971

Fourier, Charles, *Théorie des quatre mouvements*, 1808, as *Theory of the Four Movements*, translated by Ian Patterson, edited by Patterson and Gareth Stedman Jones, Cambridge and New York: Cambridge University Press, 1996

The General Council of the First International 1866–1868. Documents of the First International, Moscow, Progress [1976]

Marx, Karl, *Capital: A Critical Analysis of Capitalist Production: London, 1887*, Berlin: Dietz, 1990

Marx, Karl, *Early Political Writings*, edited and translated by Joseph O'Malley and Richard A. Davis, Cambridge and New York: Cambridge University Press, 1994

Marx, Karl, *Historiographie du socialisme vrai (contre Karl Grün)(1847)*, *Oeuvres*, vol. III, Paris: Pléiade, 1982

Marx, Karl, *Later Political Writings*, edited and translated by Terrell Carver, Cambridge and New York: Cambridge University Press, 1996

Marx, Karl, and Friedrich Engels, *Karl Marx, Frederick Engels: Collected Works*, London: Lawrence and Wishart, and New York: International, 1975–

Marx, Karl, and Friedrich Engels, *Karl Marx, Friedrich Engels: Gesamtausgabe (MEGA)*, Berlin: Diétz, 1975–

Marx, Karl, and Friedrich Engels, *Karl Marx, Friedrich Engels: Werke*, 39 vols. in 41, Berlin: Dietz, 1961–74

Marx, Karl, and Friedrich Engels, "Prosperity—The Labor Question,"*New York Daily Tribune* (30 November 1853)

Sue, Eugène, *Les mystères de Paris* (1843–44); as *The Mysteries of Paris*, New York: Fertig, 1987 (originally in French)

Tristan, Flora, *L'Union ouvrieère,* Paris, 1868, as: *The Worker's Union*, translated by Beverly Livingston, Urbana: University of Illinois Press, 1983

Woodhull, Victoria C., *The Origin, Tendencies, and Principles of Government*, New York: Woodhull Claflin, 1871

Zetkin, Klara, *Zur Frage des Frauenwahlrechts*, Berlin: Vorwärts, 1907

Reference Works

Auzias, Claire, and Annik Houel, *La grève des ovalistes: Lyon, juin–juillet 1869*, Paris: Payot, 1982

Benjamin, Walter, "Johann Jakob Bachofen,"*Les lettres nouvelles* 2 (1954)

Borneman, Ernest, *Das Patriarchat: Ursprung und Zukunft unseres Gesellschaftssystems*, Frankfort: Fischer, 1975

Charléty, Sébastien, *Histoire du saint-simonisme (1825–1–1864)* Paris: Hachette, 1896; reprint, Geneva and Paris: Gonthier, 1964

Fauré, Christine, *La démocratie sans les femmes: Essai sur le libéralisme en France*, Paris: Presses Universitaires de France, 1985; as *Democracy without Women: Feminism and the Rise of Liberal Individualism in France*, translated by Claudia Gorbman and John Berks, Bloomington: Indiana University Press, 1991

Lafargue, Paul, "Die Mutterrecht-Studie über die Entstehung der Familie,"*Die neue Zeit* 6 (1885–86)

Leroux, Pierre, "Lettre au docteur Deville, 1858," *Études de marxologie* 15 (1972)

Peuch, Jules-L., *La vie et l'oeuvre de Flora Tristan, 1803–1844*, Paris: Rivière, 1925

Rabaut, Jean, *Histoire des féminismes français*, Paris: Stock, 1978

Rubel, Maximilien, "Flora Tristan et Karl Marx,"*La nef* (January 1946)

Rubel, Maximilien, "Marx à la rencontre de Spinoza," *Études de marxologie* 19–20 (1978)

Rubel, Maximilien, *Marx: Life and Works*, translated by Mary Bottomore, London: Macmillan, 1980

Rubel, Maximilien, *Rubel on Karl Marx: Five Essays*, edited by Joseph O'Malley and Keith Algozin, Cambridge and New York: Cambridge University Press, 1981

Rubel, Maximilien, and Margaret Manale, *Marx without Myth: A Chronological Study of His Life and Work*, Oxford: Basil Blackwell and Mott, 1975; New York: Harper and Row, 1976

1871: THE PARIS COMMUNE

JACQUES ROUGERIE

WHEN THE THIRD REPUBLIC was proclaimed on 4 September 1870, and perhaps even more strikingly on 18 March 1871, the first day of the Paris Commune—the last of the three insurrections that rocked Paris in the 19th century—a "time of possibility" seemed to open up anew. The woman novelist and citizen André Léo could at last give herself over to a sense of immense hope, which she voiced in an article submitted to the Vallès newspaper, *Le cri du peuple*, on 12 April 1871: "All together, women with men. . . . It has been through women that, up to now, democracy has been defeated, and only women will bring the triumph of democracy."

Conflicting Opinions

Did the Commune truly constitute a significant stage in women's unending quest for their rights, as has been asserted? Two distinguished figures of the 1871 revolution, André Léo and the textile dyer Benoît Malon, despite the close ties between them, offer diametrically opposed testimonies on the subject. The novelist met the dyer in June 1868, at the time of the second trial of the International Workingmen's Association in Paris. André Léo (pseudonym of Leodile Champseix) contributed to Malon's political education and became involved in a half-maternal, half-love relationship with him. The couple married in June 1873, while in exile in Switzerland.

For Malon, a member of the Commune,

One of the most important facts the Paris Revolution has brought to light is women's entry into political life. Under the pressure of circumstances, through the circulation of socialist ideas, through the propaganda of the clubs, women have sensed that their support is indispensable to the triumph of the social revolution that has reached its fighting stage; that women and the proletariat together, the last among the oppressed of the old order, can hope for their enfranchisement only by strongly uniting against all forms of the past. (*La troisième défaite du prolétariat* [1871; The Third Defeat of the Proletariat])

By 8 May 1871, when Léo's article "La révolution sans la femme" (Revolution without Women) appeared in the newspaper *La sociale*, her tone was one of disenchantment. Her article reads almost as a preemptive response to Malon's words:

Once again women have nothing to gain in the immediate future from this revolution, for now the goal is men's emancipation and not women's. . . . From a certain point of view, going back to '89, a History of the Inconsistencies of the Revolutionary Party could be written. The woman question would make up its longest chapter, which would show how that party succeeded in making half of its troops, who had asked nothing more than to march with it, go over to the enemy side.

It is too often forgotten that while the Paris Revolution of 1871 was unquestionably tragic, it was an extremely brief event, lasting only 72 days. With regard to the role of women in the insurrection, the archives contain only minute traces. To better understand the part women actually played, one must first resituate the issue within a broader historical perspective.

The Women's Movement at the End of the Empire

"Women's rights . . . since the socialist movement of 1848 . . . have fallen into oblivion," Maria Deraismes noted in 1868. After the period of silence of the first decade of the Second Empire, which had put an end to every form of opposition and thereby to the progress of the women's movement, the demand for women's rights timidly resurfaced early in the 1860s, when imperial despotism began to abate. The salon of Charles Fauvety and his wife Maxime was an important meeting place for activist women, bringing the old generation of 1848 together with a new generation. Regular visitors included Jenny d'Héricourt, Juliette Lamber, Madame Auguste Comte, Angélique Arnaud (at the time Charles Fauvety's collaborator at the *Revue philosophique et religieuse*), Eugénie Niboyet, and Élisa Lemonnier with her husband Charles, the founder of the Ligue Internationale de la Paix et de la Liberté (International League for Peace and

Freedom). Also among the participants was Clémence Royer, the companion of the republican Pascal Duprat, known for her 1862 translation of Charles Darwin's *On the Origin of Species*.

A third generation of women activists had already appeared during the last years of the Second Empire. Its most noted figures were Julie Daubié, André Léo, Adèle Esquiros, Paule Minck (whose father was a follower of Henri de Saint-Simon), Élisa Gagneur (the wife of Vladimir Gagneur of the cooperative periodical *L'association* and a follower of Charles Fourier), Maria Deraismes, and a few others. In 1865 Deraismes published *Thérésa et son époque* (Theresa and Her Era) and *Aux femmes riches* (To Rich Women), and in 1869 and 1870 she participated in the series of "literary" lectures organized by the Grand Orient under the aegis of Adolphe Guéroult and Léon Richer of *L'opinion nationale*. There she addressed such issues as individual ethics, politics (women and law, women in society), private life (women in the family), education, and progress.

All of these women were women of letters, earning their living—seemingly quite well—from their writing. Their movement was one of "well-read" or even bourgeois women, as opposed to the women's movement of 1870 and 1871, which was deeply rooted in the popular classes. Indeed, none of these great women activists took part in actual combat. But the popular or proletarian movement was not without connections or affinities—direct or indirect—with the earlier women's movements. The complexities of this historical context are described below, as a necessary background to understanding women's involvement in the events of 1871.

André Léo and the "Revendication des Droits de la Femme"

Among the great activist women, few played as remarkable a part in the revolutionary movement of 1871 as André Léo did. She will be given a more prominent focus here than she has previously received.

In 1868 Léo was 44 years old (she coquettishly gave her age as 39, sometimes 36; like Louise Michel, she claimed to be younger than she was, since Malon was only 25). From 1866 on, Léo lived in the Batignolles district. Her novels, *Un mariage scandaleux* (1862; A Scandalous Marriage) and *Un divorce* (1866; A Divorce), had made her famous. A republican, she signed the manifesto published by *La réforme* in 1868, and she was a collaborator in Guéroult's journal, *L'opinion nationale*. Saint-Simon's influence was still discernable at that time, and Guéroult was one of the last of the Saint-Simonian "sect" to have remained in the leftist camp. Turning toward socialism, Léo published *Communisme et propriété* (Communism and Property) in 1868. As an activist for the women's cause, she published *La femme et les moeurs, liberté ou monarchie* (Woman and Mores: Liberty or Monarchy) in 1869. Other noteworthy facts include her unsuccessful attempt to launch a newspaper, *L'agriculteur*, and her authorship of the *Manifeste de la Commune aux paysans* (Manifesto of the Commune to the Peasantry), in which she compared the social and civic inferiority of women to the conditions of the peasantry under the domination of the Empire.

André Léo recognized the difficulty of her struggle: "The majority of democrats are the last to realize that all rights exist in solidarity and have one cradle, one common principle. And thus it is among them that women find their grimmest adversaries." In 1871 she stated harshly:

> Many republicans—I'm not talking about the real ones— have dethroned the Emperor and the good Lord . . . only to put themselves in their place. And of course, to that end they need subjects—or at least female subjects. Woman no longer has to obey the priests, but she must not govern herself, either. She must remain neutral and passive under the direction of man. All she will have done is change confessors.

The first women's organization that had any importance toward the end of the Empire was the Ligue en Faveur des Droits des Femmes (League for Women's Rights), which Léo created in 1868. In its issues of 20 July and the following days, *L'opinion nationale* published a manifesto signed by 18 women citizens, announcing the formation of a "league for a new declaration of rights, not only those of man but those of humanity, and for their social actualization." "Rights of humanity" was the expression Léo preferred to "rights of man." This handful of women citizens demanded "liberty in the religious, civil, political, and moral order," and equality before the law in marriage and at work—"in marriage as a guarantee of morality, love, and happiness," and "at work according to the abilities of each"—invoking "the brotherhood that must serve the law of the relationship between men and women, outside of marriage." The use of the term "brotherhood" is significant here: the socialist cause and the women's cause were to be defended together at last; woman was oppressed both as a worker and as a woman.

Definitively established early in August 1868, the League for Women's Rights held its first meeting on 4 January 1869. It may seem surprising that its goals were immediately strictly limited: "The majority of those here present are against claiming women's registration on the electoral lists." However, we should recall that any concrete opposition was impossible even under the liberalized Empire. Consequently, caution was essential. The league's first decision was to found an elementary school for girls, with the proviso that "men can participate as well as women" (*L'opinion nationale*, 30 January 1869).

Having slowly evolved, the league published a second manifesto on 18 April 1869 in the newspaper *Le droit des femmes*. It was signed by 38 women citizens, who, this time much more clearly demanded the civil rights "refused to half of the nation," access to secondary education, the right to work, and equal wages. "It is the duty and in the interest of all those who deem instruction to be preferable to ignorance, liberty to oppression, and justice to chance," they proclaimed. Malon found the manifesto all too modest in ambition, as revealed in a letter he wrote in March:

> You wish to follow a line of conduct that is carefully progressive, and you find yourselves caught between two obstacles. For those who adapt themselves to the present regime and practice politics as a pastime, it is too much; for those who are suffering, it is not enough. . . . Besides, in a country such as France, where the virus of authoritarianism has infected all levels of society, those grand ideas of enfranchisement can be effectively professed only during days of agitation, or at the very least after great

shocks—except of course by those who are struggling like us and have already broken with the past.

Such days of agitation were precisely what was to come.

On 10 July 1869, André Léo announced the founding of the Société pour la Revendication des Droits Civils de la Femme (Society for the Demand of Civil Rights for Women), more commonly known as the Revendication des Droits de la Femme (Demand for Women's Rights), the statutes of which were presented on 30 September. The organization turned its energies to the creation of a free, secular, democratic primary school for girls. Fund-raising began immediately, and 10,000 francs were collected and deposited in the Saint-Simonian Arlès-Dufour Bank. The history of the school will be taken up in detail later in our discussion.

A small but cohesive network of activists formed around André Léo and Benoît Malon. By reason of the names if nothing else, the connections are obvious between the Demand for Women's Rights and the Société Coopérative des Ouvriers et Ouvrières (Cooperative Society of Men and Women Workers) of Puteaux, Suresnes, and surrounding regions, known as the Revendication de Puteaux (Puteaux Demand). Of the 18 women who had signed the first manifesto of the League for Women's Rights, eight lived in Puteaux and were members of the cooperative, including Aglaé Jarry, the wife of a dyer, and Amélie Rahon, the wife of the society's secretary. Three women companions of militant cooperative members had also signed: Madame Rebierre; Aglaé Bedouch, also from Puteaux, and the wife of a shoemaker who was a member of the cooperative; and Madame Kneip, the wife of Louis Kneip, a piano maker and one of the founders of the Société du Crédit au Travail (Working Credit Union). Yet another signatory was a Citoyenne Poirier—who may have been Sophie Poirier, one of Louise Michel's collaborators in the 18th arrondissement.

Also included in the small circle were a number of Léo's friends or acquaintances: Marthe-Noémie Reclus, Maria Verdure, Élisa Gagneur, Louise Michel, Marie David, a schoolteacher, Julie Toussaint, and Caroline Demars, a machine-stitcher—all of whom signed the statutes of the Demand for Women's Rights. Some men were also associated with the group, among them an elderly professor, Gustave Francolin, known as "Dr. Francolinus," a friend of Louise Michel from her days at the seminary of women republican teachers on the rue Hautefeuille; Augustin Verdure, a future member of the Commune; Hippolyte Leval, a bronze fitter in Belleville (along with his wife, Élie Reclus, a shoe stitcher). It was a very small world indeed: records list the name Caroline Petit-Demars as the director of a poorhouse in the 10th arrondissement during the Commune.

Léon Richer and "Le droit des femmes"

At the same time, in 1869, Léon Richer, "the women's man," and Maria Deraismes established the Société pour l'Amélioration du Sort de la Femme et la Revendication de Ses Droits (Society for the Improvement of Woman's Lot and the Demand for Women's Rights). This society published the paper *Le droit des femmes*, of which 68 issues were printed between 10 April 1869

and 11 August 1870. Among its collaborators were all the leading female figures of the time: Deraismes, Marie-Louise Gagneur, Amélie Bosquet, Angélique Arnaud, and others who were less well known, such as Euphémie Garçin and Stella Blandy. Contributions were also made on a less regular basis by Marie Goegg, Julie Daubié, and Jenny d'Héricourt, who at that time was living in the United States and corresponding from there with André Léo. The latter's involvement was limited to providing the reports on the first popular meetings devoted to women's labor, in July and August 1868.

Then, on 16 April 1870, Richer formed an Association pour le Droit des Femmes (Association for Women's Rights), which set as its goal to "openly proclaim sexual equality before the law and moral standards" (*Le droit des femmes*, 24 April 1870). The association demanded equal rights for women in the family and at work; the right to file paternity suits; access to secondary and higher education; the establishment of professional education—in short, the same ever-present themes. The association, open to both sexes, probably had about 100 members.

As the revolution awaited by all true republicans approached, an in-depth and extensively argued analysis of women's status was published in *Le droit des femmes*: "We cannot be content with being 'underheard' " (Arnaud, 10 December 1869). "What women want is their fair share of rights and liberty" (Deraismes, 10 April 1869). "Right," they maintained, lay within the natural order, inscribed in the Declaration of the Rights of Man, and did not derive from duties (to family or household matters). "Duty is the obligation which stems from the exercise of a right" (Arnaud, 4 August 1869). Women's oppression was an artifact of culture; sexual inequality was a "social fiction, a human invention." The newspaper then proceeded to an in-depth study of the Civil Code and the legal inferiority it imposed upon women. Nonetheless, the editors conceded that certain functions were specific to women. There were female tasks. Woman played a valued private role: she was the finance minister of the household. Above all, woman was first and foremost a mother and educator. Motherhood was "work"—probably the most important and most respectable work. Women should be mothers—married mothers. Marriage—a "good" marriage, based on a well-balanced couple—was a necessary institution. For Léo: "Democracy must exist; it is still and only a dream, in the old monarchic body where it rests and through the brain of which it thinks. . . . It is waiting for the matrix that must shape it, the free mother who will give birth to it." However, she added ironically:

> Thus our democrats—who nevertheless maintain a monarchy within the home, and who have until now been neither more polite nor less despotic toward women than the Church has been—are making concessions: it is now a serious matter of making women capable of raising little democrats for the salvation of society.

The attitudes touching upon the political rights of women as they were expressed in the newspaper were varied and sometimes diverged. Deraismes came up with a powerful description of women's circumstances: "The democrats have created the universal for their own use, an unprecedented universal, a pocket-sized universal that leaves half of humanity aside" ("La femme dans la démocratie" [Woman in Democracy], *Le droit des femmes*, 18 February 1870). Yet she hardly believed in the virtues of politics, let alone "revolutionary" politics: "Whether government is changed, whether *senati-consulti* are promulgated, whether ministers are made responsible, society will nonetheless remain very sick; it promulgates laws with justice and iniquity simultaneously" (*Le droit des femmes*, 11 September 1869).

Olympe Audouard demanded complete equality, including the rights to vote and to stand for election; on the other hand, she wished to keep women away from the corruption that politics inevitably entailed. In any event, voting rights were second in priority, after education. She made comparisons between women and the downtrodden peasantry, as Léo had done earlier. At any rate, politics was an area in which to act with extreme caution: how would women vote? Jules Michelet had raised this problem as early as 1850: "Granting women the right to vote immediately would mean dropping 80,000 ballots for priests into the ballot box." Richer emphasized that "[women's] education has not prepared them for the special qualities that political action requires." Nevertheless, he was the newspaper's most vigorous supporter of women's political rights. Overall, there had been a tangible retreat from the clearly articulated women's programs of 1848—doubtless one of the crushing effects of imperial despotism.

Women and the Proletariat

These women were soon faced with a dilemma: should they demand their enfranchisement *as women* or simply as part of a general revolutionary enfranchisement? "Because of laws and prejudice, is woman not the last link in the chain of slavery, the oppressed of the oppressed?" asked Maxime Breuil in the first of her *Deux discours sur le travail des femmes* (1868; Two Discourses on Women's Work). "She is the sick limb of a sick body; their tight and fatal solidarity means that they will be saved or will perish together." Her likening of women's oppression to class oppression is significant for our discussion. The editors of *Le droit des femmes* admired the expanding activity of the women workers' movement. As Richer wrote in his article "L'exemple": "What is this 'woman question' after all, if not one aspect of the social question—perhaps the most important aspect? It does not merely touch a specific class of individuals, it concerns society as a whole" (*Le droit des femmes*, 18 December 1869). He returned to the topic in the following issue: "The law that subjugates them—daughter, wife, mother—weighs as heavily on rich women as on poor women. The [Civil] Code holds specific injustices for all women" (*Le droit des femmes*, 25 December 1869).

Obviously, most of these pronouncements and issues were being articulated by educated, independent women. One cannot help but wonder what "proletarian" women could possibly have understood of those analyses and debates. Surely working-class women were little concerned with Article 213 of the Civil Code, which demanded obedience to the husband, or with Article 214 on mandatory cohabitation, or Article 340 prohibiting paternity suits; nor did they have to worry much about articles concerning the division of property, the right of married women to relinquish and acquire property, or the problem of dowry and women's free management of wills. And most assuredly, some of the analyses of the people's condition by "women of letters" revealed a general incomprehension the realities of working-class life. The bourgeois women's movement was very attached to the notion of the family. The family, it was alleged, "is not at all a social invention, it is in the natural order. Even animals know what family is, at least in its most simple form." Family is "the root and founding principle of all human group . . . the primal society, that is, the embryonic society from which all others flow," including the nation (Deraismes). Consequently, prostitution—often seen as the fate awaiting female workers, and easily, albeit erroneously, equated with *concubinage populaire* (cohabitation outside of marriage, a frequent practice among the popular classes)—was absolutely inadmissible. Louise Michel herself, for all her familiarity with, and even fondness for, the working-class milieu, was an awkward or mediocre observer. In her *Mémoires* she writes:

> Why do so many women not work? There are two reasons. Some cannot find work; others prefer to die of hunger . . . rather than do work that barely brings in what they put into it. There are those who care about life. So . . . the unfortunate ones let themselves be recruited into the dismal army that roams around from Saint-Lazare to the Morgue.

What most people wanted was to see the unwed mothers married off—and into good marriages.

Fundamental Education for Girls

All the activist women agreed on the necessity of education: "Women's ignorance is the decline of the mother, it is the moral death of the child" (Richer, 15 May 1869); "Whereas the basis of man's education is science, the basis of woman's education is faith" (Richer, "La part des femmes" [Women's Share], *Le droit des femmes*, 3 July 1869). Julie Daubié presented the problem as a major one in her book *L'émancipation de la femme* (The Emancipation of Woman), published in 1871:

> When the instruction we receive becomes as sound and as strong as it is now weak and incoherent, when our curiosity is turned toward general ideas, only then will men have full knowledge of the facts and be able to make pronouncements on our faculties.

The overhauling of education for girls and women was thus the most fundamental task. *Le droit des femmes* devoted a series of articles to the teaching of girls, with the objective of training them as free human beings. The education of a new generation was a problem dear to the republicans, and the education of girls was just as important as the education of boys, if not more so, because girls would become mothers. Female education was set as a priority during the Commune, a revolution that was at the outset republican.

The initiatives for female education were not without precedent, and it is important to invoke the pioneering and major work of Élisa Lemonnier, the founder of the Société pour l'Enseignement Professionnel des Femmes (Society for the Professional Teaching of Women), who died on 5 June 1865. Madame Jules Simon, Madame Trélat, and Madame Vinçard were among the members of the society. Together with Madame Allard, who succeeded her, and with a teacher, Mademoiselle Marcheff-Girard, Lemonnier opened the first professional school for young girls at 23, rue de Turenne. In 1870 five of these schools existed. They offered courses in commerce, sewing, the manufacture of luxury items, and music. Although "free" in the sense that they were in principle open to all, the schools were unfortunately not tuition free, and consequently the instruction they offered was not readily accessible to girls of the lower classes. Other, more modest schools were created by republican women. Madame Cohadon, the wife of a mason in the cooperative, headed a boarding school that had a burnishing workshop, which was described in almost idyllic terms in an article in *La mutualité*: students there were housed, fed, and dressed, and they had the right to medical care. Their working days lasted 11 hours, but, as they were pieceworkers, most of the students finished earlier and could take advantage of their free time. Education was provided in the form of night courses. Half of each student's wages was deposited at the Working Credit Union, the popular bank of the cooperative labor societies.

Like other activist women, André Léo placed a very high importance on education: "An enslaved woman can only raise slave children." Hence her project for a democratic school for girls. It was as remarkable as the one formulated by Pauline Roland and Gustave Lefrançais in 1850: "work made attractive," concrete teaching "by means of objects," flexible discipline, and development of the child's initiative, reason, and strength. In addition to the basic academic subjects, courses were offered in gymnastics, the natural sciences, drawing, history, music, and home economics (including elements of accounting and law). The project was based on one moral doctrine, "the study of individual right that imposes duties with regard to others." A letter from Léo to Verdure, director of the republican-socialist paper *La marseillaise*, toward the end of 1869, specified the school's objectives, which were political as well:

> You know that it seems to us that the acquisition of equality, which we pursue and which aims at a reform of morality, cannot be better obtained than through the reform of the education of young girls. It is a question of basing education on liberty, science, justice, and equality, . . . of training the free female citizens of a free land.

The school was already the model of the democratic school of the future: open to girls and boys, and to every member of the future republic.

> School should develop the child, instead of restraining him or her. . . . It should instruct the child to think, but it prevents him or her from doing so, as much through inaccurate and absurd teachings as through authoritarian methods. . . . We want to establish the republic inside each human being, the only terrain from which it can never be torn away.

Still other women's organizations were started, of which little is known. Paule Minck, a teacher of languages and a linen worker, created the Société Fraternelle de l'Ouvrière (Fraternal Society of Workingwomen). Eugénie Niboyet is said to have established a Société de Protection Mutuelle pour les Femmes (Society for Mutual Protection for Women) in 1870. At the time, she was devoting her attention in particular to "the very large and interesting class of lady teachers" and proposed the construction of a "City of Ladies" in a strongly Fourierist vein. Marie Goegg created an Association Internationale des Femmes (International Women's Association) in Switzerland, linked with the International League for Peace and Freedom, of which Armand Goegg was vice president. At the Brussels Conference of the International Workingmen's Association in 1867, Marie Goegg's women's association requested, but was refused, affiliation with the latter. Presumably, Richer wanted to expand the women's association into France, but the plan does not seem to have had any results.

Women and Republicans

Bonds were close among the different women's movements and the republicans, the freethinkers, and the Freemasons. Angélique Arnaud defended women's rights in the Masonic periodical *Le monde maçonnique*, for which she also wrote a laudatory review of Léo's novel *Un divorce*. The Masonic lodges supported the work of Élisa Lemonnier. The lodge of the Élus d'Hiram (Elected of Hiram) was active in promoting the education of young girls. The families' Temple organized mixed clubs and accepted women initiates (although it is true that the upper leadership disavowed that practice). The presence of "sisters" was accepted in the Solidarité (Solidarity) lodge of the Orient d'Issy: "Woman was made to conceive and put the great philanthropic thoughts of Freemasonry into practice, to be associated with our noble work and to embellish our temples."

Moroever, the secular emancipation movement seems to have made progress even in the popular ranks. On 4 May 1870 civil funeral rites were organized for 23-year-old Émélie Dumesnil, a Puteaux worker who had organized a strike of laundresses when she was 18. In July 1870 some 2,000 people attended the solemn funeral of Augustine Ranvier, mother of the future feminist Adrien (who would thus carry on a family tradition) and young Henri Joseph, a budding Communard who was arrested in 1871 at the age of 13. The paper *La cloche* gave the following portrayal of this exemplary female citizen:

> [she was] one of those rare and courageous daughters of the people who know how to fight prejudices and abuses of all kinds and who encourage their husbands in the never-ending demand for their rights, against absolutism and the tyranny of despots. She was one of the very first to demand women's rights, and she wholeheartedly joined in every protest against abuse and injustice. She was able to shake off the numbing yoke of religious idiocy and earned the title of *citoyenne* and freethinker. She died as she had lived, in accordance with her principles. A good wife, a good mother, she is now mourned by all who knew her.

Women in the Labor Movement

At this point, we begin to approach the properly "proletarian" dimension of the "woman question." The radical theorist Pierre-Joseph Proudhon's fierce hostility toward women is well known. At the First Congress of the International, held in Geneva in 1866, the issue of female labor had been raised. People tend to emphasize the hostility to female labor, and to women's rights in general, displayed by the French delegation (with the notable exception of Eugène Varlin, a bookbinder, and Antoine Bourdon, an engraver). The report of the French delegates to the Geneva Congress reflects such hostility:

> Nature has clearly indicated the functions to which woman has been destined; her constitution, her faculties, her all-pervasive sensitivity, together with the family-oriented selfishness that is hers alone, constitute the most powerful means of preservation that could have been granted to human beings. . . . If devotion to the *res publica* [public affairs], if the preoccupation with collective interests are good points in men, they are an aberration in women. Science reached these conclusions long ago, pointing out the inevitable consequences for the child: mental decline, rickets, and finally impotence. (*Mémoire des délégués français au Congrès de Genève*; reprinted in Freymond.)

This type of argumentation—abundantly backed up by pseudo-scientific evidence—was commonplace at the time. Some of the most enlightened of activist workers shared these prevailing masculinist prejudices. However, after 1866, in the leading group of the Paris International, positions had very tangibly evolved under the influence of Eugène Varlin and Benoît Malon, whom André Léo had won over to the cause. He wrote her on 6 September 1868, while in prison at Sainte-Pélagie: "We are not allowing the women's emancipation league to slumber, and every day new members are joining. We have brought almost the entire International Association around to the idea; only Proudhon's pundits remain aloof." Malon admired *La femme et les mœurs*: "I have read *La femme et les moeurs*," he wrote in 1869. "You have seen right through all the sophisms they use to support inequality with a series of very clear and very conclusive reasons. I believe this book will help make giant strides forward."

What was the situation lower down the class ladder? There were a few women in the workers' societies, but they were still rare. They were accepted in the Société de Crédit Mutuel des Ouvriers de Céramique (Ceramic Workers' Mutual Benefit Union). The Société de Crédit Mutuel et de Solidarité des Ouvriers Relieurs et des Ouvrières Relieuses ([Men and Women] Bookbinders' Mutual Benefit and Solidarity Union) organized by Varlin is invariably cited as an example of mixed-gender labor unions, but it was not the only one. Moroever, it was not Varlin who actually opened this very small union (barely 100 members at the end of the Empire) to women: they had been admitted since its creation in 1857. The bookbinding profession was primarily made up of women: 2,500 women as opposed to 1,300 men. Still, it should be noted that the union's rules stipulated that "female members have the same rights as men, except for participation in administrative posts." According to its 1868 statutes, the tapestry makers' union admitted women, but, as they did "not attend general meetings, they should direct their requests or demands to the Syndicate [the union's committee of syndics], which, after hearing the explanations of the claimants, will submit them to the general assembly for evaluation." While membership dues were 2 francs for men, they were 1 franc for women—perhaps in compensation for their lesser level of participation. The Puteaux Demand seemingly admitted women on a more egalitarian basis. Aglaé Jarry managed one of the cooperative's stores. Among the organizers of La Marmite, a cooperative restaurant established by Varlin in 1868, two women held good positions: Nathalie Lemel, its secretary, and Mademo-

iselle Rozier, a bookbinder about whom little is known. Marie Vinçard was a member as well. Unemployed young *brocheuses* (stitchers in the bookbinding process) worked as waitresses at the restaurant. Lemel, a 45-year-old mother of three who was separated from her husband, had owned a bookstore in Quimper before becoming a bookbinder in Paris. She was a member of the bookbinders' union from 1865 and later became the director-secretary at La Marmite. As Charles Keller remembers her: "Citoyenne Lemel would philosophize and solve large problems with extraordinary simplicity and ease. We all loved her; she was already our duenna." Marguerite Tinayre was for a brief time secretary of the Société Coopérative des Équitables de Paris (Cooperative Union of the Equitables of Paris).

Varlin's case warrants examining in some detail. Unquestionably a seductive man, "he had a veritable squadron of young Amazons around him, who literally hung on his every word; for the most part they were stitchers." He was a confirmed supporter of women's rights and declared himself to be an "enemy of marriage." His "feminism" seems to have led him to go so far as to create (or at least help to inspire) what might well be called a "free milieu," according to the testimony given in 1907 to Lucien Descaves by Ralf de Nériet, a young apprentice in Puteaux at the end of the Empire, who had closely associated with the members of the International.

> In this milieu there reigned the true spirit of a phalanstery, not rationalized, but instinctively practiced. . . . As an example, I shall cite a house in the rue Taranne, near the passage du Dragon; . . . a group that had a rather odd relationship lived there. Each group was made up of six male members and one female president, married or unmarried—it mattered little, and you will see why. The space contained one bedroom with six small iron single beds —during the day this room also served as kitchen and dining room—and another room with a large double bed, in which every night a different member came to sleep beside the woman president. In addition to this special nightly service, she had to see to the laundry and the clothing of the members and prepare their meals. A common cash box, containing everyone's contributions, was entrusted to her. . . . No other woman was allowed to enter the apartment, and admission and expulsion were regulated by very strict but respected clauses. . . . The members, who were bookbinders and typographers, were very comfortable with the system. I should also add that beyond their one obligatory night, they were not bound by fidelity to the woman president, although some hygienic precautions were imposed upon them. It was in this milieu that Varlin evolved, who furthermore was in some way its founder and apostle.

The document carries a whiff of scandal that has shocked some. However, it is important. For within the small communal group, had not the primary role (sexual decision making) been bestowed upon the woman "president"? Such an arrangement was in direct line with the "communism" of the 1840s, which had also advocated what its opponents wrongly called "community" or the "sharing of women"; beyond the simple free sexual unions often practiced in the popular classes (and so often misnamed *concubinage*), such practices represented sexual freedom. Other traces of this communist tradition, although blurred by censorship, are to be found in records of debates in the public meetings of 1869 and 1870.

Work for Women: A Popular Issue

We are entering truly "popular" territory as we turn to consider the debates in these public meetings, which the government began tolerating in June 1868. There was discussion of any number of themes relating to the "woman question," a real concern at the time. Some of the most famous women activists voiced their opinions in these meetings, rubbing shoulders with unknown women, and here the "well-read" activists were indeed closer to women of the working class, such as Madame Désirée and Madame Piré. Were they listened to? Gustave Lefrançais had a categorically severe reaction:

> All this rhetoric from Mmes André Léo, Maxime Breuil, Maria Deraismes and others, who until then were the only ones to have stepped on the stage with their written texts on the question, is of only mediocre interest. The audience of workers remains cold, which is easy to understand. (*Souvenirs d'un révolutionnaire* [Memories of a Revolutionary], 1902).

The audience's cool reception is indeed easy to understand. On the men's side, the debates were sometimes stormy. There is no need to dwell on their hostility: their arguments were both familiar and commonplace. As the cabinetmaker Tartaret expressed them: "If women were to acquire political rights, they would lose more than they would gain. . . . I wish we were still 20 years old—they wouldn't be asking for equality then." Yet he did concede: "women's wages are insufficient; . . . there is much to be done. We often forget that we owe women assistance and protection and that they owe us obedience and faithfulness." This last sentence aroused "sustained grumblings from the crowd." Félix Chemalé, who no longer belonged to the International, summed up the retrograde arguments, saying: "Let women be women before they are men."

It was decided that work for women would be the first topic to be addressed, and the debates took place mainly in the Casino of the Vaux-Hall, rue de la Douane, from July to November 1868. The liberal economist J. Edouard Horn had suggested the theme. Some 1,000 to 1,500 people, about one-fifth of them women, attended the discussions. On 13 July 1868, Olympe Audouard, and especially Paule Minck spoke, as did Madame Piré, who opined that "the best society will be the one in which everyone works. Therein lies the foundation of equality itself." The discussion was confused and thoroughly awkward from the outset. Horn defended women working in the name of the principles of liberal economy, inevitably making the working-class participants bristle. Fribourg, a right-wing militant of the International, wanted "women to stay inside, not to desert their home, and not to be exposed to the moral and physical dangers of the workshops. . . . Women working leads to communism because it destroys the family." For Henri-Louis Tolain, "prostitution is increasing in the industrial nations where women have gone into the workshops. There, women's health deteriorates, and the workshops produce hysteria." Louis-Alfred Briosne, a "communist," defended only the narrow concept of work within the home. "Citoyen Pierron thinks that women should not work in factories, that her place is at home. He does, however, recognize that in the present state, owing to the wretchedness of the working class, women are obliged to work." And, we should emphasize, "he therefore invites women to follow the example of men and to form trade unions."

The speakers were unanimous on one point: their opposition to women working in plants or factories (rare in Paris in any event), which indeed posed a human and moral problem (we should recall Villermé's descriptions of women's working conditions, which Louis Reybaud recently updated and verified [see Reybaud]). Minck disagreed, arguing that what was needed was work that suited women's nature. The right to "any kind of work," which several female contributors to *Le droit des femmes* demanded, was too abstract a notion. On 31 August 1868, the discussants formulated a nine-point motion, reaching a compromise that was actually less "reactionary" than it might seem. "Equality of rights, consequently of duties. . . . In a democratic and social-minded society, work is a duty." However, women would not be able to take on any kind of work; they would practice only those professions that were in keeping with their aptitudes, notably in the liberal careers (although not in government posts). Participants in the debates concluded that "any useful occupation is work. The woman who devotes her time to being a wife and mother works in the most noble and fruitful sense. Any occupation that would be a detriment to this work would be socially harmful." Domestic work was "the most noble and the most fruitful." Someone—not necessarily with facetious intent—suggested that a part of the husband's salary be contractually handed over to the wife as compensation for "satisfying his needs."

At the Pré-aux-Clercs, another eight meetings were held from 14 July to 1 September 1868 on the problem of children born out of wedlock. Ten weeks were devoted to the topic of marriage and divorce, from 15 September to 17 November 1868, in the Salle de la Redoute. At the Folies-Belleville and the Pré-aux-Clercs, meetings dealt with marriage and free union, celibacy and family, and, at the Folies-Belleville only, with divorce. In the latter instance, the discussion was clearly derailed by the extremist presentation of the "communists," women included, who spoke out provocatively in favor of free union. Lefrançais declared he was "against divorce, because he was against marriage"—speaking theoretically, it would seem, since he was "a revolutionary on the outside and a family man on the inside," according to a police observer who was probably not altogether wrong. Briosne pronounced himself against "the family, which is crumbling; I would like to see it collapse." The educated women activists, we should recall, were also attached to the notions of family and true, good marriages. Everything was discussed. Mademoiselle Breuil (possibly Maxime Breuil) proclaimed "women equal in different capacities," asked for equality before the law, in marriage, and at work; she wanted "a complete regeneration of women." Others denounced subjugation to men, and wife-battery; "woman should shake off the yoke of man." Madame Désirée demanded that "women should have as many rights as men," and, since she was a communist, she also demanded the division of land and property for all, more concretely suggesting a general rent strike for April 1870. Minck was a great success, albeit not without her share of demagoguery. She invoked 1793, thereby drawing immediate applause from the male public; she asked for the abolition of inheritance and asserted that "when women have political rights, there will no longer be any rifles." She viewed women's struggle as being secondary to the social struggle. All the discussants, men and women alike, agreed on the need to develop women's secular and, especially, professional education.

Revolution in Paris

Paris proclaimed the Republic on 4 September 1870, but in the war against Prussia, defeat followed upon defeat. The capital city was besieged on 19 September. The siege lasted until the armistice of 28 January 1871—the prelude to a dishonorable peace that was intolerable to the Parisians, who had resisted to the end without weakening.

On 18 March, popular and republican Paris rose up against the National Assembly, elected on 8 February 1871, and against the government headed by Adolphe Thiers, which had just decided to sign the peace and was suspected of preparing a royalist restoration. Everything began in Montmartre. There, a typical crowd that included many women, among them Louise Michel, fought fiercely and retook the cannons of the national guard that government troops had tried to seize. It was this incident that unleashed the general uprising of the city. The government fled to Versailles and, on 26 March, Paris elected a Commune, a revolutionary municipality that immediately transformed itself into a genuine government; it was small but utopian, and above all ephemeral. The "Free City" planned to create new and more socially just republican institutions for a France that would be a federation. The newly created Commission du Travail et de l'Échange (Commission of Labor and Exchange) set up by Frankel, a Hungarian member of the International, went to work on that project. Another commission was established to work on educational reform. But it proved to be a time for fighting and dying rather than for building. From the beginning of April, Paris was surrounded by the regular army. The Commune came to an end in the final, so-called Bloody Week of 21–28 May, when 20,000 people were killed. Some 40,000 people, about 1,000 of them women, were arrested for alleged participation in the insurrection.

"The Women of Paris are Quite Turbulent"

The working-class women of Paris were not politically passive. The writer Émile Zola saw the women of the Commune in action. Working as a journalist for *La cloche* and *Le sémaphore de Marseille*, he shuttled between Paris and Versailles and left a remarkable series of articles on the events of 1871. He credited Parisian workingwomen with "having political potential." His almost sympathetic testimony—quite rare for the time—is worth quoting at some length:

> The women of Paris are quite turbulent. In the evening, in almost every working-class household, the wife states her political opinion right out loud and often imposes it upon her husband. They read the newspaper together, and

generally they are very hard on people in power, whoever they may be. This rebellious spirit really makes Paris into a city of opposition, a revolutionary city par excellence. . . . In no other city have I heard the weaker sex so imperiously settle government questions.

> I have often had occasion to talk politics with one of those ladies, driven by high literary curiosity. I hasten to state, furthermore, that many of them are perfectly honest women, a bit talkative, but good mothers and good wives. Only, they were born in the big city; they were raised amid political discussions in the street; they watch over their *pot-au-feu* [stew] while talking about the last session in the Chamber or the next change in the cabinet. It is in their blood, in the air they breathe, in those tall Parisian buildings that vibrate with the city's echoes. The women of whom I am speaking are familiar with the political personalities, M. Thiers, M. Guizot, M. Rouher, M. Émile Ollivier, and some of them still either detest or admire Lamartine. I am dwelling on this class of female citizens because in the provinces you are almost entirely unfamiliar with this species, and you might take them for women without virtue, who, under normal circumstances, would only be faulted with meddling in business that does not concern them. You should hear their reasoning. They are, as Michelet said, the exasperation of the just. . . . When a man takes a rifle, a woman feels her tongue itching, and, should she lose her head in a club, she too is quick to take up a rifle, or a saber or a simple knife. (Lettres de Paris [Letters from Paris], 14 May 1871, printed in *Le sémaphore de Marseille*, 15–270, 18–19 May 1871.)

This is indeed a fine republican counterpoint to all the many caricatures concocted in Versailles.

As many as 1,051 women were called before war councils, with 80 percent of them thereafter being dismissed for lack of evidence. These "females of the Commune," as Alexandre Dumas fils referred to them, could only be prostitutes or *pétroleuses* (women setting fire to buildings) in the eyes of military justice. "Almost all of the accused combined the most complete ignorance with a lack of moral sense. . . . All, or almost all of them, even the married women, are loose women." If we except the 246 "real" prostitutes the police had soon rounded up, this section of the female population nonetheless provided precise (although not new) information about the professions of the alleged Communardes: 37 percent of the female defendants worked in clothing and textiles, 8 percent in shoes and gloves, and 4 percent in fancy goods; 13 percent were laundresses or did ironing; 10 percent were day workers; 11 percent were domestic servants; and another 8 percent ran small businesses. These were just about the same proportions as one would find in a "normal" population of workingwomen.

We know relatively little about the popular households in Paris and about the place women held in them. The group associated with *Le droit des femmes* had created for itself an idealized image of the working-class woman and, more generally, of women's position in the working class. The "woman of the people" was seen as the good companion who shared everything in life. The popular household was nothing but brotherhood, solidarity, and dedication. "Once again, this should serve as an example to women who are asking for woman's enfranchisement," declared Richer. In this connection, a fairly accurate testimony is to be found in Denis Poulot's catalog of working-class drinkers, which is rich in concrete details and appeared in 1870 in *Le sublime* in 1870 (the heaviest among the heavy drinkers being called *sublimes*—forever dozing, bragging, hacking around, beating people up). Poulot's inventory of drunkards served as the primary inspiration for Zola's novel *L'assommoir* (1877; variously translated as *The Dram Shop*, *Drink*, *Drunkard*, and *The Gin Palace*), although the novelist darkened the picture even further.

Obviously, running the household was the first priority for working-class women. In fact, many households were "irregular" ones: cohabitation outside of wedlock was a widespread practice among the working classes. The worker "takes up" with someone, wrote Poulot, "he readily falls in with the laundress, the chambermaid or the nanny." "There are also the 'affairs' freely practiced between male and female workers; children arrive, and after much effort in assisting them, the Société de Saint-François-Régis manages to legalize the position of the innocents." Nearly one-third of the births in Paris were illegitimate, and it may reasonably be suggested that a good third, and probably more, of working-class households were "irregular." Of the women arrested in 1871, 60 percent were living with a man outside of wedlock, accounting for three-quarters of the single women, almost all the widows, and at least one-third of women legally separated from their husbands. To a great extent, this form of free union was a result of the impossibility of divorce. In addition, workers' relocation to the city was a source of social destabilization. Many migrant workers, married in the provinces, took up with another woman when they arrived in the capital. Such unions could be quite stable; it seems that on the whole, following the uncertainties of a long-lasting affair, people tended to set up house together, with or without marriage. However, in such circumstances women and their children lived with the constant risk of desertion. Sometimes a worker who had come from the province "suddenly decides to let everything go and gets married in his own region." For that reason, the ultra-Catholic Société de Saint-François-Régis actively devoted itself to legalizing popular unions, right from the end of the Restoration.

The Parisian worker drank, although less than Poulot claimed, and sometimes his wife did too: "The *sublimes*, or at least a great number of them, rubbed off on their wives; some of them really drink quite heavily." Domestic violence was far from exceptional, and women were easily given a black eye. Victorine Brochon recalled that her husband, although he had a "gentle character," would beat her when he was drunk. But the battering also happened in the other direction. Again according to Poulot, whenever a woman felt her husband was deceiving her "if she caught the lazybones red-handed, wham! a slap in the face. . . . She holds the purse-strings," even though the husband often "swipes" money from her.

Some housewives who were not docile in the least may have "turned the Civil Code around"—a typical 19th-century, more political way of saying these women "wore the pants." This was the case in the household—illegitimate, naturally—of the shoemaker Napoléon Gaillard, the great barricader of the Commune. Aged 55 at the time of the uprising, he lived with 30-year-old Augustine Clavelou. "His revolutionary ideas were remarkably well served, if not overstimulated, by his concubine, a hotheaded woman who had a certain hold over him" reported Poulot.

Often, women's jobs were simply a source of extra income for their families. As reported by Poulot, "Many workers set their wives up as sellers of dairy products, grocers, wine merchants, and laundresses. Most of them make a good living. The female companion's wages invigorate the business. . . . Some women are concierges." Proportionately, it seems that the number of women who worked did not increase under the Empire. A survey by the Chamber of Commerce counted 170,000 workingwomen in 1860 and 178,000 in "industry" (in its broadest sense) in 1872. About two-thirds worked in workshops, one-third at home. A more complete census documented the existence of some 350,000 female workers, of whom 80,000 were domestic workers (not counting the 20,000 or so concierges), while there were about 700,000 women of working age. No conclusions can be drawn from the apparently limited character of women's labor: the census could only keep imperfect track of work within the home.

Even more often than was the case with men's work, women workers faced the issue of work being subcontracted out by businesses. Department stores, which grew in number under the Empire, gave work to more and more dressmakers. Godillot, in the rue Rochechouart, had uniforms produced well into the Commune. In the clothing business, dressmakers were subject to severe competition from the work done in convents and prisons. Women's pay was always half that of men for analogous work.

"We Are Human, That Is All"

During the siege, working-class women were queuing up while their husbands did their duty in the national guard or, just as often, spent time in the bars. Victorine Brochon described her absolute misery that icy winter, conditions made even worse by badly organized rationing. The agony continued under the Commune. In an article that appeared on 8 May 1871 in *La sociale*, André Léo asked: "Who suffers most from the present crisis, from the high cost of food, from the work stoppage? Women, and especially women living alone, with whom the new regime is no more concerned than the old regime was." Women and men alike were employed in the tailors' associations, which, during the siege, produced clothes for the national guard under the aegis of their professional federation. In Montmartre, Sophie Poirier organized a sewing and production workshop that offered profit-sharing and could employ as many as 100 women.

Some prominent women had already become involved in revolutionary politics at the end of the Empire: André Léo and Louise Michel had attended the solemn funeral that republican Paris had arranged on 12 January 1870 for Victor Noir, who had been assassinated by Prince Pierre Bonaparte after a quarrel. Michel had returned from this funeral extremely disappointed that no one had sought to use it as an opportunity to help overthrow the Empire. Early in July, about 20 women signed the International's manifesto protesting against the war; for the most part, nothing is known about these women but their names.

With the proclamation of the Republic, women began to engage in activity that can properly be called political. As a matter of record, mention should be made of Félix Belly and the Amazons of 1870. Belly had made a plan for setting up 10 battalions, each consisting of eight companies of 150 women warriors. This attempt to create a new incarnation of the (largely mythical) "Vésuviennes" (Vesuvian women) of 1848 was unsuccessful. Belly's motivation, however, remains significant: to enable women "to earn their enfranchisement and their civil equality."

"It is not a question of our practicing politics; we are human, that is all," Léo declared in a lecture delivered on 13 November 1870. In fact, during the siege, women's activities essentially involved the formation of aid societies and groups of stretcher-bearers, following the example of what women in the United States had recently done during the Civil War. The Société de Secours aux Victimes de la Guerre (Society to Aid Victims of the War) was presided over by Madame Jules Simon; the group's members included the republican Madame Paul Meurice, Madame Goudchaux, and Léo. The society organized five community soup kitchens to distribute meals for children, and it established a workshop that could employ 600 women in the production of clothing for the needy. In that very cold month of December, the society expanded its activities to the distribution of ration coupons for heating, food, clothing, and medicines. During the same period, Olympe Audouard and Maria Deraismes organized an ambulance service at their own expense. This was not "bourgeois" charity but republican philanthropy.

On 8 September 1870, an appeal "Aux femmes de Paris" [To the Women of Paris] was signed by several women citizens, among them Madame Dereure, the wife of the future Commune member; Madame Lebéhot, the wife of a pharmacist who was himself a follower of the revolutionary theorist and future Commune president Louis-Auguste Blanqui; Louise Michel for the 18th arrondissement; and Octavie Tardif (whose name will come up again) for the 13th arrondissement. At that time the focus was still only on providing medical care for the wounded and helping the poor. Strong patriots, the women demonstrated on 22 September, demanding the right to go to the ramparts to help the wounded. Demonstrators included Adèle Esquiros, André Léo, Louise Michel, Blanche Lefèbvre (a milliner whose role during the Commune will be discussed later), Cécile Fanfernot (either the wife or the daughter of an old 1848 activist, and perhaps related to Julie Fanfernot, a heroine of July 1830), and Jeanne Alombert. Seemingly, the appeal and the demonstration were what sparked the formation of the Comité de Vigilance des Femmes de Montmartre (Vigilance Committee of the Women of Montmartre), modeled after the men's vigilance committees of the arrondissements, which were branches of the Comité Central des Vingt Arrondissements (Central Committee of the 20 Arrondissements). The women's committee was the only one of its kind. It was run by Michel, and by November its ranks included Esquiros, Léo, Alombert, and Poirier. There was considerable women's political activity in the 17th arrondissement, led by Léo, beginning in November, when Benoît Malon was elected as the arrondissement's deputy mayor specially charged with managing aid and assistance. A widow named Madame Fernandez directed the charitable activities of the Solidarité group in the Batignolles district. It was here that the most important section of the International was reconstituted around Malon and Varlin; Léo seems to have been a member. The program of the section, which was published in the 8 January 1871 issue of *La République des travailleurs*, included only a short sentence on women's rights, probably written by Léo: "It is now time for democracy fully to include women, whose foolish exclusion from it has made them into democracy's adversaries."

With Michel, women from the Batignolles and Montmartre participated in the last riot of the siege in front of the Hôtel de Ville on 22 January 1871. Women freethinkers organized a few other demonstrations that are seldom mentioned: on 21 September there was a demonstration at the foot of the statue of Strasbourg—which the Prussians had just taken—by "female citizens of free thought and women of the ramparts." Early in March 1871, some 50 women, "freethinkers all," attended the civil funeral of Léon Bousquet, one of the victims of the fighting of 22 January.

Jules Allix and the "Comité des Femmes de la Rue d'Arras"

A large-scale organization known as the Comité des Femmes de la rue d'Arras (Women's Committee of the Rue d'Arras) was inspired and created by the future Commune member Jules Allix. Apparently a bit touched in the head, he was a republican-socialist educator and an energetic supporter of the women's cause. In the first two weeks of October, his committee reportedly had 160 active district committees and 1,800 members. Confirmation is hard to come by: all we have is the list of the 20 delegates from the arrondissements. One of these was 29-year-old Anna Korvin-Krukovskaya, a young Russian aristocrat emigrant who was very close to André Léo and a part of the small network described above. Korvin-Krukovskaya was a populist in the Russian sense of that term: she had "gone over to the people" and had become a printer in Switzerland, where she had been a member of the Russian section of the International, before emigrating to France. She had just married Victor Jaclard, and, through him, she was also connected to the circle of the followers of Blanqui, who was influential in the north of Paris. The official headquarters of the committee was the home of the teacher Geneviève Vivien, at 14, rue du Cloître Notre-Dame; its offices were at 8, rue des Écoles at the Monge Ambulance service, which the committee had organized. Records indicate that every Thursday in November, the committee held general assemblies, open to the public, on the rue du Grenier-sur-L'Eau, in the girls' school near the town hall of the 4th arrondissement.

Allix's project was broad. It aimed at the achievement of "social solidarity" within the "social Commune" of Paris—envisioned as a "noncommunist, nonrevolutionary . . . socialist commune through liberty" primarily inspired by Fourier. Plans were made to create communal workshops and establish a committee on education. In 1869 Allix had defended the plan at the meetings of the Folies-Belleville: "Progress can only be fully realized through the social commune, which must be based on liberty, and must give man, woman, and child the full satisfaction of all their needs by ensuring the complete exercise of their rights."

Did the Commune, once established, truly concern itself with the lot of women? In truth, it did little for them. The importance of the decree of 10 April is commonly stressed: it granted a pension of 600 francs to the wife—legitimate or not—of any national guardsman killed in combat, and a pension of 365 francs to his children, recognized or not; their education would be paid for by the Commune. " 'Recognized or not, legitimate or not'—with those six words," the historian Arthur Arnould later contended,

> the Commune did more for women's enfranchisement, for their dignity, than any of the moralists and legislators of the past. . . . Thus, [the Commune] radically cut through a moral question and laid the groundwork for a profound change in the present constitution of the family. (See Arnould.)

Historian Édith Thomas views the decree as "one of the most revolutionary measures [of the] ephemeral reign" of the Commune (see Thomas 1963). This is probably an overstatement, but it is true that the measure—although one wonders whether it was ever applied—was highly appreciated by the Communardes. At least, a long-debated problem in the public meetings of the Empire had been formally addressed, if not resolved: the status of children reputed to be illegitimate. (In fact, far from all of them were really illegitimate, from the point of view of the popular classes.)

"L'Union des Femmes pour la Défense de Paris et les Soins aux Blessés"

Special mention should be made of the Union des Femmes pour la Défense de Paris et les Soins aux Blessés (Women's Union for the Defense of Paris and Aid to the Wounded). The association was established on 11 April 1871 by "a group of female citizens" that included a 20-year-old Russian emigrant named Elizabeth Dmitrieff together with Nathalie Lemel. The association's name was innocuous enough, and it can be argued that its mission involved nothing new: the groundwork for this type of activity had been amply laid by women's groups during the siege, and the union itself may well have been nothing more than "leftist" outgrowth of the rue d'Arras women's group. In truth, the union's political orientation remains difficult to gauge, since it really had no time to accomplish anything.

On 11 April the Women's Union for the Defense of Paris and Aid to the Wounded published a manifesto, and a few days later an address to the executive commission. On 8 May it designated a central committee of seven members and produced another manifesto that was a call to fight. The organization was to be short-lived—it lasted for six weeks at most—but its activity was intense; meetings were held every day, consecutively in each arrondissement. Early in May, the central committee set up operations in the town hall of the 10th arrondissement. Dmitrieff—about whom very little was truly known at the time—acted as secretary. The manifesto and address to the executive commission were presented as texts by "women workers and citizens"—the members of the Women's Union proclaimed themselves to be "patriotic citizens." They adopted the same slogan as the International: "No duties without rights, no rights without duties." Their goal: "We want work, and we want to keep the product of our labor. No more exploiters, no more masters. Work and well-being for all. Government of the people by the people." The strong significance the Commune had for these women was quite obvious: it represented

the fundamental principle proclaiming the annihilation of all privilege, of all inequality. By that very principle, the Commune is committed to taking into account the fair demands of the entire population without distinction based on sex—a distinction created and maintained by the need for the antagonism upon which rest the privileges of the ruling classes. . . . The triumph of the present struggle, which aims to suppress abuses, and, in the near future, to renew from top to bottom the social structure that will ensure the reign of work and justice, consequently is of interest to both male and female citizens.

These are strong words indeed. Very few among the innumerable proclamations by men are so radical. These women were determined "to work together for the triumph of the people's cause," "to fight and conquer or to die for the defense of our common rights," and, in the more prosaic present, to obtain an office in every arrondissement's town hall, with these offices to be used for "seriously organizing this revolutionary element into a force capable of giving effective and vigorous support to the Paris Commune," as well as "large premises for organizing public meetings." The goal was a generalized "social renovation." On the other hand, in all the foregoing there is still no articulation of a demand for women's rights in the real sense of the term, and notably the right to vote, as might have been expected.

The Emancipation of Women Workers

In fact, the major issue—the true issue, in the mind of these female citizens—was not women's rights or women's suffrage. Initially, as during the siege, they were concerned with setting up teams of stretcher-bearers and organizing visits to the sick and the wounded in combat. Very quickly they faced a serious but very different problem, that of organizing workingwomen. Dmitrieff had rightfully warned the Commune:

> In view of present events, with extreme poverty growing in terrifying proportions . . . it is to be feared that the women of Paris, who for the moment are revolutionary in spirit, may as a result of continual privations relapse into the more-or-less reactionary and passive position that the social order of the past marked out for them—a disastrous step backward that would endanger the revolutionary and international interests of the working class, thereby endangering the Commune.

The republic "of lawyers and defeatists" had already organized women's labor during the siege: 32,000 women, it was alleged, had been hired to sew uniforms on a piecework basis for the national guard. The government was criticized for the long lines women had to endure to get work or hand it in; moreover, since the armistice all activity had been interrupted. In any case, the Commune's revolutionary approach had to be better than that of the bourgeois government.

On 6 May Frankel, chair of the Commission of Labor and Exchange, whose disappointment as Dmitrieff's spurned suitor was so great he would later embellish her role, published a long report. "Women's labor being the most exploited, its immediate reorganization is therefore the most urgent." As of 10 May, the committee of the Women's Union began developing a meticulous plan for independent production cooperatives within the framework of the labor commission's planned general organization of labor. The commission formed a subcommission for study and organization that was meant to include delegates of both sexes from the trade associations. By 15 May the delegates included two women: Aline Jacquier and Lemel, both stitchers by trade and sent by the only trade association represented, that of the bookbinders. The Women's Union took part in the census provided for in the Commune's 16 April decree to requisition abandoned workshops. Once the abandoned spaces had been inventoried, one or several locations would be chosen for the distribution and receipt of goods. Arrondissement committees were formed, each theoretically consisting of 11 members; they were later to be replaced by women's labor unions. It was mainly the clothing industry that was organized, beginning with the production of uniforms for the national guard. In reality, a broader, more general reorganization was envisioned.

> In Paris the production of underlinens and fine lingerie is of enormous importance as a business; by ceasing production in convents and prisons, it will be possible to increase wages. The consumers in Paris will sustain the stores. Few of our men and women citizens will object to suppressing the middlemen and their exploiters. The export trade, too, will buy products from the federation, the provinces and foreign countries having been deprived of fancy goods from Paris for a long time now. . . . Although plumes and flowers are luxury articles, it is important to prepare a bright future for this industry. . . . Other women-led industries in particular need to be organized, and these cases will be studied over time as resources permit.

The goals here were obviously the same as those in the "socialization" process already envisioned for men's work: "reorganizing labor so that the producer is guaranteed the product of his own work . . . by freeing work from the yoke of exploitative capital"; entrusting to workers the management of their own affairs; a reduction in working hours; and "an end to all competition between male and female workers, their interests being absolutely identical." The organization was to include a central cutting room and a general sales store. Two delegates were to be designated for choosing the styles; a commission of bookkeeping cashiers would be responsible for establishing cost price and the earnings rate of the women workers, following a preestablished agreement with the administration and the tailors' union. It should be stressed that the plans did not involve a nationalization of labor. They stipulated that "prices should be based on a comparison among the best-known department stores in Paris, so that competition cannot harm the trade unions." Work was to be divided among the arrondissements, with warehouses for distribution and receiving "so that wages will not be diminished by significant loss of time." The plans also stipulated

> equal pay for equal hours of work. . . . Work is to be delivered to the homes of those who for serious reasons are not able to be part of a workshop. . . . Work is to be brought to the house every other day and in strict proportion to eight hours of work per day. . . . Work in the workshop is to be done during the day and by the piece.

There was to be a producers' association in each arrondissement. "Each local association is managed by a commission freely elected by the members. Each association preserves its autonomy concerning internal regulations in accordance with the general principles of the union." Members had to belong to the International. Then,

> through the intermediary of the central committee, the association will be in contact with similar associations elsewhere in France and abroad in order to facilitate transport and exchange of products; female agents and traveling saleswomen will be employed to manage these aspects.

At some indeterminate future time, the project would be broadened: "The producers' associations will be federated and will establish specific craft sections; they will meet each week in a general assembly of all the arrondissement sections." All of the Parisian, and later, provincial producer cooperatives would establish a "local and international federation of the craft sections in order to facilitate the exchange of products by centralizing the international interests of the producers."

It was a huge project. How much was actually accomplished in the short existence of the Women's Union? Work had begun to set up a commission responsible for the organization of "free work" for women at the Palais de l'Industrie (Palace of Industry). The commission was to purchase raw materials, set prices, divide the profits, and distribute the work among the 20 town halls. A central warehouse was opened on 21 May at 31, rue des Francs-Bourgeois, under the direction of the delegate Mathilde Picot, who was paid 2 francs a day "as an expert in the fabrics and supplies that arrived there." Beginning on 15 May, the union conducted a census of unemployed women in the 10th and 11th arrondissements. Some women's workshops received modest orders for sewing sandbags for the barricades. It was already late in the game. The 24th and last meeting of the patriotic female citizens of the Women's Union was held on 24 May at the boys' school in the rue de la Bienfaisance; undoubtedly because of the circumstances, it was specified that "male citizens were admitted."

All things considered, what real impact did this movement have on French society? The English historian Eugene Schulkind has traced a few more than 300 women who belonged to the Women's Union; only 30 of them can be identified and the files concerning them are all too often meager in content (see Schulkind 1950, 1985). Few female "militants" were systematically hunted down by the court of Versailles, which—a victim of its own stereotypes—was looking for *pétroleuses* and criminals. Logically enough, the majority of the Women's Union members were garmentworkers: dressmakers, linen drapers, seamstresses who used sewing machines (still rare in Paris), shoe stitchers, and so on. The laundress Alice Bontemps was a delegate of the 18th arrondissement, Aline Jacquier of the 17th arrondissement, and Blanche Lefebvre, the milliner, of the 10th arrondissement. At least six female arrondissement delegates came from the Women's Committee of the Rue d'Arras, including Marie Loup of the 11th arrondissement, Octavie Vataire, a linen draper, of the 7th arrondissement, and Mathilde Picot of the 8th arrondissement. A prisoner later testified that she had heard Madame Hardouin, a schoolteacher, speak to an assembly of the Women's Union: "She talked about work exchanges and the education of children. In addition, she said that one should not use priests to raise children, given that [priests] were good only for distorting the ideas and the character of those who came near them." Yet, the Women's Union did not gain the membership of all "republican-socialist" women for reasons that are unclear. André Léo, who contributed a few socialist-leaning articles to the newspaper *La sociale*, seems to have had only a brief and noncommittal presence within the organization. Anna Jaclard was not a member, although she was very active at Léo's side in the 17th arrondissement, and, as is well known, Louise Michel preferred to fight side by side with her male comrades.

Unsung Women Activists

There were also a host of minor neighborhood groups, known only by scattered traces here and there, in published appeals in the press, allusive notes in the documents of the war councils, and the like. Committees had been formed to collect funds on behalf of wounded national guardsmen, their widows and orphans. Toward mid-April, a Société de Solidarité des Dames du VIᵉ Arrondissement (Solidarity Society of the Ladies of the 6th Arrondissement), probably not very proletarian in its makeup, organized "aid to their wounded and unfortunate brothers." A Société de l'Union des Travailleuses (Society for the Union of Women Workers) was formed in the 10th arrondissement. Almost nothing is known about the local activity of a great many obscure militant women: most of them were the wives of male activists. During the siege, Citoyenne Marie Bertin organized a family council to collect and distribute aid given by the town hall, and in November she created a republican women citizens' club in the rue de la Maison-Dieu in the 14th arrondissement; in the minutes for 14 December 1870, a woman named Page reported that a "committee of women" was organized "to go out and collect funds from the rich." At the time, an association of women garment workers was operating in the same arrondissement, and under the Commune these little-known women grew even more active. Octavie Tardif was a *tailleuse* (female tailor) and member of the International (as was her husband), and in 1870 she served as secretary both to a commission of women citizens for secular teaching and to a group of freethinkers. In April 1871 she became secretary of the Comité des Républicaines (Committee of Republican Women) of the 13th arrondissement. A ledger clerk, she wrote a protest against the arrondissement's poor labor organization that was signed by nine other women, including the widow of General Duval; Julie Beauchery (wife of the secretary of the local section of the International); and Citoyennes Pouillet and Chantereine. They said they wanted "to work under the high leadership of your generous aspirations to the enfranchisement of Workers and to the regeneration of female citizens, because for us the issues of Progress and the Immobility of our sex are dependent on your cooperation." All of the women in the Piganiol family were fiercely political. The 72-year-old grandmother had been accused of saying that they should "throw the members of the National Assembly into the shit." The 42-year-old mother within the family, a capmaker and the "terror of the house" at 84, rue d'Enfer in the 5th arrondissement, would "every day sit down at the window to read *Le cri du peuple* out loud, emphasizing the most violent passages. . . . She said that the priests and nuns must be hanged and the convents burned to the ground; that people were fighting for equality; that there would be no more rich people, no more landlords; and that they had been working for this for 40 years." Her 19-year-old daughter helped her read *Le cri du peuple*.

Girls' Education: A Never-Ending Problem

As stated earlier, teaching under the Commune was above all secular. There was no schooling problem per se in Paris: almost all girls and boys between 7 and 13 years old attended school. There had been recent progress in girls' education in Paris, but less so in the provinces, where girls still received a mostly clerical education. For the revolutionaries of 1871, the real challenge was to institute secular education, since, to a great extent (almost two-thirds of all girls in 1870), the teaching of girls was still in the hands of *congréganistes* (religious authorities, priests or nuns, gathered in congregations). By contrast, the schools known as "free" schools, where the teaching staff was not required to swear obedience to the Empire, were usually secular. Vaillant, a delegate for education under the Commune, mobilized women republican schoolteachers to undertake reorganization and above all secularization. Marguerite Tinayre was inspector of the girls' schools of the 12th arrondissement. Hortense Urbain, the sister of a Commune member, was active in educational reform in the 7th arrondissement. Vaillant established a commission to organize and supervise education in girls' schools; its members included André Léo, Anna Jaclard, Madame Reclus, and Madame Sapia (*Le journal officiel* 22 May 1871).

Actual reforms were brought about on a limited basis at the local (arrondissement) level, as the municipal commissions saw fit. In the 7th arrondissement, where the former Women's Committee of the Rue d'Arras had survived, Allix was active. He opened a "new school" for girls at 14, rue de la Bienfaisance; on 8 May Geneviève Vivien, secretary of the Women's Committee, was appointed director of the school. In addition, provisions were made to convert the space allotted to the social Commune at 24, rue Monceau into a workshop for women and also a combination school and shelter for orphan girls and unemployed youth.

On 26 March a self-designated Société d'Éducation Nouvelle (Society for New Education) appeared and named its delegates during a meeting at the École Turgot: besides two men, Rama (a teacher dismissed by the Empire) and Manier, the delegates included Maria Verdure, Henriette Garoste, and Louise Lafitte. The latter two women are noteworthy in that their names appear again in women's organizations after the Commune. The society met every Sunday and every Thursday at the École Turgot. On 6 April it convened "male and female teachers of elementary schools, professors, as well as parents." It proposed to the Commune a general overhaul of programs, the use of new pedagogical methods, as proposed before by the Demand for Women's Rights (*Le journal officiel*, 26 April 1871). On 23 April, the Comité des Femmes de la Commune Sociale de Paris et Société d'Éducation Nouvelle (Committee of Women of the Social Commune of Paris and the Society for New Education) held a joint meeting for "a conference on public welfare and education."

Also active under the Commune was the Société des Amis de l'Enseignement (Society of Friends of Teaching) in the 11th arrondissement, run by Maria Verdure. The society's objective was to provide tuition-free professional instruction to prepare students for working life. Madame Manière was the teacher-director of a "workshop school" at 38, rue de Turenne, which she had opened early in April "for serious professional education." Initially, its staff was to be "formed through election among the workingwomen's groups, then with groups of educated women as instructors, with greater aptitude for intellectual work than manual activities." This effort was the direct descendent of the major achievements of Élisa Lemonnier, cited above. On 12 May the special drawing school on the rue Dupuyten, an extant institution that had once been directed by Rosa Bonheur, re-opened—this time on a tuition-free basis—as an "industrial arts" school for girls.

Women Taking the Floor, Women Taking up Arms

All of the foregoing amounts in some ways to great progress, and in other ways to very little. Again, at no time did the women of 1871 demand their political rights, which in any event men would most probably have refused to grant them. Not one woman was part of any committee that ran the arrondissements, while the Vigilance Committee of the Women of Montmartre was nothing but a small discussion group. However, women firmly took the floor in political clubs, which, at the end of April, had been set up in the churches (eliminating the word "saint" from the names of the respective churches). Through malevolent, though probably not wholly inaccurate descriptions from Versailles, we know what went on in the clubs; the descriptions have been confirmed by the minutes that have been preserved and are reconfirmed by the testimony of Zola, who attended the meetings. He seems to have been a bit amused at the difficulty putting the word "orator" in the feminine form—the neologism "oratrix" was recent at the time, perhaps coined by André Léo in her reports on the public meetings in *L'opinion nationale*. As Zola relates:

> Each club has its "oratrixes." A club in which women remained would resemble a comedy in which all the roles are played by men. Nothing could be more tedious. It is always necessary for a skirt or two to come and enliven the audience. I suspect that the organizers of clubs always arrange for the enchanting sex to appear at a given moment, just as a dramaturge does with ballets. I have seen two or three of these "oratrixes." For the most part they are young and pretty. They usually read their bits of speech, but with that self-assurance of women who know they are more looked at than listened to. Furthermore, they have merely changed catechisms: they believe in the republic with the same devout fervor, the same mystical blindness, they put into believing in the good Lord when they were little. (Lettres de Paris, [Letters from Paris], 14 May 1871, printed in Le sémaphore de Marseille 15–270, 18–19 May 1871).

As usual, women ran up against ill will from men: male Communards were no better than other men in this regard. Initially, in many clubs women were refused the right to vote: at (Saint)

Nicolas-des-Champs, they "could attend the sessions but they were prohibited from participating in the deliberations." Women had to carry an identity card—a measure that was cancelled after their forceful protests. Some clubs did not approve of women going out to fight; there were better things to be done in the hospitals, the men said. Nevertheless, most of the clubs were mixed, including those at (Saint) Jacques-du-Haut-Pas and at (Saint) Séverin. At (Saint) Sulpice, the assembly "was generally made up of a majority of women." At (Saint) Germain-l'Auxerrois, there was a "mixed club of freethinkers"; on 9 May a resolution in favor of divorce was made there—an issue which the Commune barely had time to touch upon. There were several clubs for women only: the club of La Délivrance in the Église de la Trinité (Church of the Trinity), the club of "lady patriots" at (Saint) Lambert de Vaugirard, and the club of Notre-Dame de la Croix in the Belleville district. The Club des Femmes de la Boule Noire (Women's Club of the Boule Noire), rue des Acacias, had been organized by the women citizens' vigilance committee of the 18th arrondissement. Sophie Poirier was president of that club, while its vice president was 20-year-old Béatrix Excoffon, known as "La Républicaine" (the Woman Republican) and listed as having no known profession. Even the bourgeois district of Passy had a women citizens' club.

The great activists, seemingly busy with other tasks, rarely spoke at the people's assemblies. André Léo was seen once at Saint-Michel des Batignolles. During the last days of the Commune, Nathalie Lemel came to the Trinity club to call women to the barricades. "Everyone to the front! Each and everyone to her duty !" But a few popular "oratrixes" were famous as being frequently seen or particularly loquacious: the widow Citoyenne Thyou, of the Club des Prolétaires (Proletarian Club) at (Saint) Ambroise, who did not tolerate the use of the phrase *Messieurs et Dames* (ladies and gentlemen), which she had heard used by the bourgeois on the Place de la Concorde; a woman named Lefèvre (not to be confused with Blanche Lefebvre, the milliner and organizer of the Women's Union), known as the "La Blanchisseuse" (The Laundress), a worker at the wash-house Sainte-Marie on the rue Legendre, at the Club de la Révolution. A woman named André, also a laundress, was secretary of the Club Ambroise, where "La Matelassière" (The Mattress-maker) "ruled by her word."

Anticlericalism and a resolve to dechristianize society were, if possible, even more virulent among activist women than among their male counterparts. At (Saint) Michel des Batignolles, the theme of the discussion was "Woman through church and revolution"; it was probably here that Madame Hardouin had developed the views cited above. La Matelassière reportedly suggested on 15 May "that all churchmen should be shot within 24 hours, from the beadle to the priest." It was further reported that "her favorite topic was the assassination of priests. . . . Priests should not be arrested, they should be declared outlaws so that every citizen can kill them like rabid dogs are killed." She held forth against marriage and for free unions, and had a 16-year-old daughter whom she "refused to marry off." At (Saint) Nicolas-des-Champs, an unknown woman proposed on 20 May that, to defend Paris, the sandbags be replaced with the corpses of 60,000 priests and 60,000 nuns, which she would take it upon herself to find in Paris. On 26 April at (Saint) Lambert de Vaugirard, the Club des Dames Patriotes (Patriot Ladies Club), an offshoot of the Women's Union, "a female citizen called the holy Virgin a harlot and maintained that every convent was a den of prostitution." At (Saint) Christophe de La Villette, a little old woman named Augustine valiantly held forth: "There is no more religion, no more prayer, no more God. So let us sing 'La Marseillaise' and 'Ça ira.' Those are the songs of the good guys."

Revolutionary Women Citizens?

The revolutionary women of 1871 intended to share everything with men. Women were battalion sutlers, stretcher-bearers, and finally fighters—fighters and therefore *citoyennes* (female citizens). The word *citoyenne* had great power in 1871 and "citizenship" should be taken in a broader sense, different from its conventional, narrowly political meaning. Citizenship meant participating in the work of "regeneration" and, if necessary, fighting for it in a "virile" way. The agenda of the Women's Union provided for this:

> It is our role, through virile energy, to lend moral support to those men who are step by step defending the soil of our dear homeland, at the price of their blood. . . . We want the European republic! With the universal republic, all people will be brothers, will hold hands. . . . You mothers, who each day moisten your children's bread with your sweat, a happy old age will be reserved for you amid your grandsons. And your sons will say: Our mothers won liberty for us.

Victorine Brochon, the wife of a shoemaker and a simple republican, was a stretcher-bearer for the Turcos of the Commune and, wholly devoted to her battalion, never wanted any contact whatsoever with women's organizations. On 14 May about 100 women came to ask the Commune for weapons. Citoyenne Reidenreth from the Club (Saint) Lambert had suggested putting together a battalion of Carabinières de la Mort (Women Carabineers of Death), but her suggestion never materialized. But there was indeed a women's battalion, the Légion des Fédérées (Legion of Federated Women) of the 12th arrondissement, organized by the arrondissement's Comité des Républicaines (Committee of Republican Women) and formed in the first two weeks of May. Adélaïde Valentin, known to us only as a "worker" and one of the founders of the Women's Union, was its colonel; Louise Neckbecker, a lace maker, was its captain; and Catherine Rogissart, a dressmaker, was its standard-bearer. All three of them belonged to the Club Éloi, where Valentin reportedly spoke with "rare energy": "I call on all women to rebuke their husbands and make them take up arms. If they refuse, shoot them." On 20 May Valentin invited "every female citizen to make herself useful to the cause that we are defending today; we are to guard the posts in Paris while the men go off to combat." Rogissart, "although uneducated, was a fluent speaker and exploited her talent to discuss politics"; she had two draft-dodgers arrested. In fact, the role of the women's battalion was to search for *francs-fileurs* (a pejorative term for Parisians who fled to the provinces or even abroad during the siege) and these fighting women were later severely sentenced for this. During the Bloody Week, a few women, among them Lemel, participated in the defense of the barricades at the Place Blanche and the Place Pigalle, with the intention of bringing aid to the wounded rather than fighting.

Women were also present, probably in larger numbers, at the Place du Panthéon, where the "federated women who were besieging the Law School" were fighting. The milliner Blanche Lefebvre was killed on a barricade in Montmartre.

Of course, the military role of these fighting women should not be overestimated, but it was highly symbolic. Women considered themselves to be citizens in patriotic fraternity with men. Was this really the revolutionary vision of citizenship? Priority was given first and foremost to the major, and urgent, problem of work, and later, by dint of circumstance, to combat. We should recall the observation by one of the unsung women of the Commune that the "regeneration of women citizens" and the "emancipation of workers" were closely interwoven; we might also recall the definition of the good female citizen that *La cloche* offered with regard to Alexandrine Ranvier. For the other newspaper *Le père Duchêne* also, "a good female citizen who is educated, who knows her business and does not let herself be led around by the nose by good-for-nothing holy joes —in a word, a true citizen—is a good mother." Here, one is not so far removed from the ideas of the Empire's activist "educated women." Had the issue of political rights been postponed indefinitely? André Léo seems to have been the only one to properly broach the subject, without any results.

Aftermath

Was the adventure of 1871 nothing but momentary glimmer of hope? The Commune, in Schulkind's view, was the first revolutionary government that gave real responsibilities to women. These responsibilities should perhaps be emphasized, but they were also inevitably without real consequences. The Commune was not the "revolution without women," but neither did it truly mark "women's entry into political life."

However, a growing momentum had been initiated, both by and throughout 1871. The Commune attempted to resolve several problems raised at the end of the Empire. As soon as the insurrection was over, the newspaper *Le droit des femmes* came out again under the new title *L'avenir des femmes*, with more or less the same collaborators. The one exception was André Léo, who, in exile, had just defended the Commune in a passionate speech at the Peace Congress of 1871 in Geneva. She was disowned by her former colleagues at *Le droit des femmes*: Amélie Bosquet demanded that Léo be denied the right to contribute to the newspaper. In June 1872, at a banquet for which the organizers had requested the patronage of Victor Hugo, there reappeared a Society for the Improvement of Women's Lot, whose members included Maria Deraismes, Hubertine Auclert, Jeanne and Léon Richer, Henriette Garoste, Louise Lafitte, and Julie Thomas. The last three had belonged to the Women's Committee of the Rue d'Arras and the Society for New Education. Auclert, only 21 years old at the time, would later become known as a militant activist for women's suffrage. Madame Hardouin and Citoyenne Manière, both elementary schoolteachers, attended the Labor Congress of 1876, which brought up for debate the two great problems that 1871 had already posed, women's work and education. Madame Manière again declared, "We want to replace charity with fraternity." The question continued to be formulated in the same terms, while men remained just as "masculinist," insisting that "woman's natural place is in the home." From 1870 through 1871, equality was very much "on the move," as has been observed, but it still followed unexplored, circuitous pathways that have here been marked out and dated as being essential. The time had come for a new generation: once the newly established Republic had been consolidated, women's struggle would evolve and take new forms.

Bibliography

Archives

Internationaal Instituut voor Sociale Geschiedenis, Amsterdam. Documents assembled by Lucien Descaves at the end of the 19th century, in particular those concerning relations between Benoît Malon and André Léo, about whom Descaves planned to write "twin biographies" (incomplete manuscript); a number of texts by Louise Michel.
Service Historique des Armées de Terre, Vincennes, France. Files on the insurgents of 1871 who were tried in Councils of War; of these, only about 100 pertain to women who played a real role in the insurrection.
University of Sussex Library, Brighton, England. Collection entitled "The Paris Commune, 1871."

Print Sources

Arnould, Arthur, *Histoire populaire et parlementaire de la Commune de Paris*; reprint, Lyon: J.-M. Laffont, 1981
Blanchecotte, A.M., *Tablettes d'une femme pendant la Commune*, Paris: Didier, 1872; reprint, Tusson, France: Du Lérot, 1996
Breuil, Maxime, *Mlle Maxime Breuil. Deux discours sur le travail des femmes prononcés aux réunions de la salle du Vauxhall et suivis de quelques réflexions sur le même sujet*, Paris: Le Chevalier, 1868
Brocher, Victorine, *Souvenirs d'une morte vivante*, Paris: Delesalle, 1909; reprint, Paris: Maspero, 1976
Daubié, Julie-Victoire, *L'émancipation de la femme*, Paris: E. Thorin, 1871
Daubié, Julie-Victoire, *La femme pauvre au XIXᵉ siècle*, Paris: Guillaumin, 1866; 2nd edition, Paris: Thorin, 1870; reprint, Paris: Côté Femmes, 1992
Deraismes, Maria, *Ce que veulent les femmes: Articles et conférences de 1869 à 1891*, Paris: Syros, 1980
Lefrançais, Gustave, *Étude sur le mouvement communaliste à Paris, en 1871*; facsimile reprint, Paris: Ressouvenances, 2001
Lefrançais, Gustave, *Souvenirs d'un révolutionnaire*; Bruxelles, Les Temps nouveaux, 1902, reprint, Paris: Tête de feuilles, 1972
Léo, André, *La femme et les moeurs: Monarchie ou liberté*, Paris: Droit des Femmes, 1869; reprint, Tusson, France: Du Lérot, 1990
Le Quillec, Robert, *La Commune de Paris: Bibliographie critique, 1871–1997*, Paris: Boutique de l'Histoire, 1997
Malon, Benoît, *La troisième défaite du prolétariat français*, Neuchâtel, Switzerland: Guillaume, 1871; reprint, Paris: Éditions d'Histoire Sociale, 1968
Michel, Louise, *La Commune: Histoire et souvenirs*, 2 vols., Paris: Maspero, 1970
Michel, Louise, *Je vous écris de ma nuit: Correspondance générale 1850–1904*, edited by Xavière Gauthier, Paris: Max Chaleil, 1999
Michel, Louise, *Mémoires*; reprint, Arles: Sulliver, 2000

Minck, Paule, *Communarde et féministe, 1839–1901*, Paris: Syros, 1981
The Paris Commune, 1871: Inventory of the Collection in the University of Sussex Library, Brighton: University of Sussex Library, 1975
Poulot, Denis, *Question sociale: Le sublime ou le travailleur, comme il est en 1870 et ce qu'il peut être*, Paris: Librairie internationale, 1870
Reybaud, Louis, *Études sur le régime des manufactures, condition des ouvriers en soie*, Paris: n.p., 1866–1879; reprint, Geneva: Slatkine, 1978
Simon, Jules, *L'ouvrière*, Paris: Hachette, 1861; reprint, Brionne, France: Monfort, 1977

Reference Works

Bossu, Jean, "Les républicaines du Second Empire," *1848 et les révolutions du XIXᵉ siècle* 38, no. 178 (Autumn 1947)
Dalotel, Alain, "La barricade des femmes, 1871," in *La barricade*, edited by Alain Corbin and Jean-Marie Mayeur, Paris: Sorbonne, 1997
Dalotel, Alain, "Des femmes dans les clubs rouges, 1870–1871," in *Femmes dans la cité, 1815–1871*, edited by Alain Corbin, Jacqueline Lalouette, and Michèle Riot-Sarcey, Grâne, France: Créaphis, 1997
Daubié, Julie, "Centre Pierre Léon d'histoire économique et sociale," *Bulletin* 2, no. 3 (1993)
Dictionnaire biographique du mouvement ouvrier français, Paris: Éditions de l'Atelier, 1997
Freymond, Jacques, *La Première Internationale, recueil de documents*, vol. 1, Geneva: Droz, 1962
Gaillard, Jeanne, "Communes de province, commune de Paris, 1870–1871", Paris, Flammarion, 1971.
Johnson, Martin Phillip, "Citizenship and Gender: The Légion des Fédérées, in the Paris Commune of 1871," *French History* 8, no. 3 (September 1994)
Klejman, Laurence, and Florence Rochefort, *L'égalité en marche: Le féminisme sous la Troisième République*, Paris: Presses de la Fondation Nationale des Sciences Politiques, 1989
Linton, Marisa, "Les femmes et la Commune de Paris de 1871," *Revue historique*, no. 603 (July–September 1997)
Perrot, Michelle, "L'éloge de la ménagère dans le discours des ouvriers français au XIXᵉ siècle," *Romantisme* (November–December 1976)
Rougerie, Jacques, *La Commune, 1871*, Paris: Presses Universitaires de France, 1988; 2nd edition, as *La Commune de 1871*, 1992
Rougerie, Jacques, *Paris insurgé: La Commune de 1871*, Paris: Gallimard, 1995
Schulkind, Eugene, "Le rôle des femmes dans la Commune de 1871," *Revue des révolutions contemporaines* 42, no. 185 (February 1950)
Schulkind, Eugene, "Socialist Women in the Paris Commune," *Past and Present* 106 (February 1985)
Shafer, D.A., "Plus que des ambulancières: Women in Articulation and Defense of Their Ideals during the Paris Commune," *French History* 7, no. 1 (March 1993)
Thomas, Édith, *Louise Michel; ou, La Velléda de l'anarchie*, Paris: Gallimard, 1971
Thomas, Édith, *Les pétroleuses*, Paris: Gallimard, 1963

WOMEN IN REVOLUTIONARY RUSSIA, 1861–1926

BARBARA ALPERN-ENGEL

IN THE SECOND HALF of the 19th and early in the 20th century, Russian women were among the most visible in Europe. Hundreds attended universities in Paris, Bern, and Zurich. Europe's first woman doctorate in mathematics and the first woman to occupy a university chair (in Stockholm, in 1880) was a Russian, Sofia Kovalevskaia. Kovalevskaia's older sister, Anna Zhaklar (née Korvin-Krukovskaia) was one of several Russian women who played an active role in the Paris Commune of 1871. Another Russian, Anna Kulishova, cofounded the Italian Socialist Party. At home in Russia, thousands of women tried to raise the socialist consciousness of peasants in far-flung villages and of workers in squalid factories. Some of the women took up arms, assassinating prominent officials as a protest against political tyranny and in order to rouse others to action. European and American newspapers carried accounts of their activities and printed their pictures. A minority of educated women, who in turned formed a tiny minority of Russian women, these activists were both more numerous and more prominent in movements for social and political change than women in the same kinds of movements elsewhere in Europe. Women's willingness to devote themselves to the cause of the Russian people enabled them to claim a share of the public space ordinarily monopolized by men. Far less visible or well known were the lower-class women who, in 1905 and again in 1917, participated alongside men in revolutionary upheavals that culminated in the Bolshevik Revolution of October 1917, the first socialist revolution in history. The Bolsheviks were the first revolutionaries who self-consciously attempted to liberate women, and one of them, Aleksandra Kollontai, wrote pioneering works that grafted analyses of women's subjectivity and a vision of their sexual freedom onto more conventional Marxist views of women's emancipation. The outcome of Bolshevik efforts with respect to women were complex, even contradictory. This article will trace the emergence and development of female activism in Russia beginning in the 1860s and concluding in the mid-1920s, after the death of Lenin but before Stalin came to power. I will also explore the relations between women activists of privileged birth and the lower-class women for whose sake they struggled to bring about social change.

Russia at the End of the 19th Century

To understand the unusual history of Russian women, it is useful to place them in their broader historical context. In the second half of the 19th century, Russia remained one of Europe's most backward nations economically, socially, and politically, in many respects more akin to the world of premodern Europe than to the industrialized societies of the West. Russia was an overwhelmingly rural and agrarian society. In the mid-19th century, barely 5 percent of the population were classified as urban; on the eve of World War I, less than 20 percent of the population lived in towns and cities. Over 80 percent of the people were peasants, emancipated from serfdom in 1861, but only partially, because peasants remained tied to the land by fiscal and legal obligations, and burdened by the requirement that they redeem the land that they obtained at their emancipation. The world of the Russian peasant was tightly knit and insular, and the needs of family and community governed the choices of individuals by custom as well as law. In the final decades of the 19th century, the growth of a national market and the expansion of nonagricultural employment, especially in industry, began to erode this insularity and to undermine family and community ties, but only a comparative minority of the population was affected. Most peasants continued to work and to live much as their ancestors had. Peasant insularity was sustained by the inability of most to read and write. At the turn of the century, about 21 percent of peasants (but only 14 percent of peasant women) possessed even the rudiments of literacy. Overall literacy had reached about 40 percent on the eve of World War I. Russia lagged behind Western Europe in other respects as well. Despite the fact that Russia's social composition had grown quite complex by the early 20th century, due in part to a government-sponsored program of rapid industrialization, Russia remained a hierarchical society of estates and not of classes until 1917, somewhat like France on the eve of 1789. People's public rights and obligations were determined by the social group to which they were legally ascribed, such as the clergy, the nobility, the peasantry, the merchantry, and the *meshchanstvo*, a category that translates roughly as "petty bourgeoisie." The estate system ignored the existence of Russia's middle and working classes and deepened the chasm between social groups by inhibiting social mobility. Russia's middle class remained tiny, fragmented, and powerless; men as well as women were disenfranchised, lacking not only the right to participate in political decision making, but also to play an autonomous role in public life. The autocratic czar monopolized political authority and public initiative, administering his vast empire with the assistance of his bureaucracy. Before 1905, the absence of civil rights such as freedom of speech, press, and assembly severely circumscribed the activities of Russians who sought to improve their social or economic situation through organizing. Unions and strikes were illegal. Professional and civic organizations had to gain the censor's approval for their publications and the police's permission for public meetings. Despite this inauspicious setting, by the early 20th century the rudiments of an *obshchestvennost'* (civil society) had emerged in Russia's major cities. From the first, it included women and women's groups and was concerned with the position and status of women—the so-called woman question.

Women's Struggles in the Intelligentsia in the 1860s

The particularities of Russian development stimulated women's activism and shaped it in complex ways. The profound social divisions that separated the "privileged" Russia of the nobility and educated elites from illiterate peasants in their villages or workers in the factories made it unusually difficult for advocates of women's rights to craft a program embracing all Russian women, although in the early 20th century feminists would attempt it nonetheless. At the same time, the exceedingly narrow range of public action, the visible suffering and misery of Russia's peasants and workers, and an ethos of service to the people shaped the mentality of Russia's elite women as well as men. This led many women who rebelled against their customary lot to focus on political and social issues and to embrace a radicalism only marginally concerned with women as a group.

Almost all the women who became politically active in Russia came from privileged backgrounds. Such women occupied a rather paradoxical legal and social position. On the one hand, they were powerless. In Russia, family law subjected women to men absolutely, defining parental power over children and husbands' power over wives as "limitless." Family law also enabled fathers and husbands to control the mobility of their wives and daughters. In order to travel any distance from their place of residence, Russians needed an internal passport; in order to obtain one, a Russian woman younger than 21 required her father's permission, and a married woman of any age required her husband's. Family law served a political purpose: it reproduced and reinforced the authoritarian social and political order, and fostered discipline and respect for authority. Because the family stability so essential to social and political order depended

especially on husbands' authority over wives, women's subordination to men served to maintain public order. But on the other hand, Russian women enjoyed greater access to public life than most of their European sisters. They could bear witness in court, could conduct a business independently, retained their rights to property even after marriage, and were liable for their own debts. Many played an important economic or social role. Depending upon their social status, women might fulfill a variety of responsibilities that were vital to maintaining their families' economic survival and social status. In the countryside, noblewomen administered estates that they themselves owned and sometimes oversaw the property of absent husbands. Women presided over urban salons in which men and women could discuss the issues of the day in relative freedom. Moreover, Russians did not glorify women's domestic role. Russia's comparative backwardness and weak middle class meant that the country never developed a pervasive ideology of domesticity that celebrated the virtues of home life and enjoined women to preside over it in their capacity as wives and mothers. Rather than expecting women to provide a haven in the heartless world of competitive capitalism, as middle-class and professional men so often did elsewhere, the Russian men who constituted the embryonic civil society were inclined to sympathize with, even identify with, powerless women. Some of the more radical accorded the woman question a distinctive political dimension. Recognizing the connection between domestic and public life, they believed that transforming Russia along more egalitarian and democratic lines would require transformation of not only the political and social structure but also the authoritarian family order.

These issues became more urgent in the aftermath of the emancipation of the serfs in 1861, a pivotal event that shook the economic and social foundations of Russia's traditional order by initiating the release of almost half of the peasant population of Russia from servitude to noble landowners. The loss of serf labor deprived many nobles of an easy living, forcing their children, daughters as well as sons, to seek their livelihood. Moreover, the ethos of the times encouraged women's economic dependence, even married women's, and their increased participation in public life. Progressive young men and women rejected the aristocratic culture and customs that had governed their elders: they tried to dress more simply and to simplify their way of life, rejecting the right of people to live idly on the fruits of others' labor. They believed that women and men alike were obliged to contribute to public life. In the language of the time, "A woman must advance her intellectual development just like a man, whether or not she is married, must be useful to society and must never forget the necessity of independently earning her daily bread."

In this turbulent era, as educated men and women attempted to extend the limits of permissible social and political action, intellectuals raised questions concerning the family order and women's role more explicitly than ever before. The woman question was debated in university hallways and on the pages of progressive journals, in student apartments and in the salons of the elite. One aspect of the woman question was the family, that "Realm of Darkness," to use the title of an article by the radical critic Nikolai Dobroliubov, first published in 1856. Both as a substitute for the autocratic order, which it was still dangerous to challenge and as a source of oppression in itself, the family became the object of numerous verbal and written critiques.

Elizaveta Vodovozova, whose memoirs provide a vivid account of the period as it was experienced by a young noblewoman from the provinces, remembers heated debates about social change that were suffused with the idea that before anything else, "the chains of the family had to be sundered." Men encouraged women to escape "family despotism" and become independent. Virtually everyone who claimed to be "progressive" agreed that women and men alike should engage in productive labor and contribute to the good of society. Nikolai Chernyshevskii's enormously influential novel *What Is To Be Done?* (1862) provided the most complete answer to the woman question, and a model for the "new" men and women to follow; it also inspired V. I. Lenin decades later. The novel's heroine, Vera Pavlova, escapes from an oppressive family situation and forced marriage with the help of her brother's tutor, whom she marries. In their egalitarian (and apparently unconsummated) marriage, she enjoys a room of her own, respect from her husband, and meaningful, socially useful work. She organizes a sewing workshop according to collective principles, sharing the profits with the women workers, who soon discover it is best to live collectively, too. Personal possessiveness has no place in the lives of these "new people," as Chernyshevskii called them. When Vera Pavlova falls in love with another man, her husband gracefully bows out of the picture, leaving her to marry the other, this time in the fullest sense. Toward the end of the novel, she trains as a physician and begins to practice medicine. She also becomes a mother, although it is never quite clear who cares for the children while she is at work. A satisfying and egalitarian family life; organization of labor and life according to collective principles; work for the social good—here was Chernyshevskii's formula for women's liberation, largely inspired by the writings of the French utopian socialists. Radical thinkers of subsequent generations would also emphasize the importance of a public role for women, and the connection between women's economic self-sufficiency and their personal happiness.

Chernyshevskii's novel inspired many young women to emulate Vera Pavlova's example and escape the confines of the domestic sphere and seek a public role. Daughters of nobles and government officials rebelled against "family despotism" in order to live as they chose. As a declaration of their independence from conventionally feminine demeanor, they cropped their hair, dispensed with crinolines, and simplified their dress. They sought to advance their education and to earn their own living. Young men encouraged and supported them, sometimes marrying the women solely in order to free them from the power of their parents. The fledgling women's movement, which emerged around the time of the emancipation, encouraged them too. The movement was led by three well-educated women from elite backgrounds, Anna Filosofova, Nadezhda Stasova, and Maria Trubnikova, whose personal connections and social skills helped them to overcome the government's limited tolerance of private initiative. They were especially successful in the sphere of higher education. Their efforts earned thousands of women the right to audit advanced lecture courses, the Alarchin courses (1869); to attend courses that prepared women for secondary school teaching (1872); and to earn a degree at medical courses exclusively for women (1872) and at a woman's university, the Bestuzhev courses (1878). The latter two were the first of their kind in Europe. These institutions were important because they enabled women to advance their education and to earn their own living;

but they also created social space where women could interact with each other without the constraints of family or the sometimes intimidating presence of men. Many of the women who became active politically during the following decades had spent time at one of these institutions.

Going to the People

Such women first appeared in substantial numbers in the 1870s. Although the majority of the women were young (under 20) when they became active, most had passed through the halls of the Alarchin courses, the women's medical courses, or the University of Zurich, whose relative freedom had become a magnet for young Russian women and men. Often, they had participated in the women's discussion circles that proliferated in the late 1860s and early 1870s. In these circles, from which men were barred, women discussed their position in the family and their place in society, in addition to other social questions such as the situation of the working class and the peasantry. Their discussions eventually led many to conclude that the oppression of Russia's lower classes far outweighed their own suffering as women of privileged backgrounds. As a result, hundreds of rebellious women, like the men of their generation, took up the cause of the Russian peasantry. Convinced that the Russian peasantry was inherently socialist by virtue of its communal land ownership and administration, these radicals (called populists, or *narodniki*, in Russian), aimed to foment a peasant-based revolution. They formed circles that were self-consciously egalitarian, and based themselves on the principles of honesty and mutual respect among comrades. Women were accepted as equals. Beginning in 1872–73, they went to "the people" (the peasantry) as the men did, in an effort to overcome the vast social chasm that separated them from the common people and to spread the message of socialism, some of them by disguising themselves as peasants or factory workers, others by taking positions in the countryside as teachers, midwives, and medical aides. Because discussing socialism, or even hinting at injustice in the existing order was sufficient cause for arrest, by the end of the decade thousands of populists were in prison, about 15 percent of them women. Political repression divided those still at liberty. While some held to the peaceful populist program, others turned to terrorism in 1878, in order to avenge themselves for their comrades' suffering and in the hope of forcing the government to make political concessions. In 1881, after five abortive attempts, the terrorists succeeded in assassinating the czar of Russia, Alexander II, under the leadership of a woman, Sofia Perovskaia.

Russian women brought distinctive qualities to their radical activity. In order to act upon their commitment to "the people," they neglected or denied the roles women were expected to adopt in private life, refusing to be dutiful daughters, submissive wives, or conscientious mothers. They also consciously rejected any self-interest and eschewed any feminist aspirations. Commonly, they justified their choices by claiming a higher calling: their duty to society, their debt to the common people. Although most of them were atheists, in explaining themselves they sometimes invoked principles rooted in the Russian Orthodox religious faith that remained a powerful element in their culture and was particularly important for women. Vera Zasulich can serve as one example. The daughter of an impoverished noble, she joined the movement in the late 1860s, and initiated its terrorist phase when she attempted to assassinate the governor general of St. Petersburg in 1878. She went on to become one of the founders of Russian Marxism in the 1880s, while in exile in Geneva. Later, reflecting on her own life, she attributed her first moral lesson to the Gospels, and wrote that it was her quest "for the crown of thorns" that attracted her to revolution. Vera Figner is another example. Also a noble by birth, she studied medicine in Zurich in the early 1870s and had come within a few semesters of earning her degree when she decided to abandon her studies and join the populist movement in Russia. When the movement split in 1879 she joined its terrorist wing, and after the assassination of the czar she led it until her own arrest early in 1883. Figner spent the next 20 years in prison, much of it in solitary confinement. Her decision to link her fate with the revolution was "the victory of a principle that had been imprinted long ago on my 13-year-old mind, when I read in the Bible, 'Leave thy father and thy mother and follow me,' " she would remember. This frame of mind led women radicals to subordinate personal interests and concerns to political struggle, sometimes rejecting marriage and family life, even sexual relations, for the sake of their commitment. Sofia Perovskaia, who began an affair with her comrade Andrei Zheliabov in the final year of terrorist struggle, had insisted to her brother the previous year that she would never become involved with a man so long as the fight continued. "That sort of personal happiness would be absolutely impossible for me, because however much I loved a man, every moment of attraction would be poisoned by the awareness that my beloved friends were perishing [in prison] . . . and that 'the people' still suffered under the yoke of despotism." Neither she nor Zheliabov allowed the relationship to interfere with their revolutionary work. Women who became involved with men and bore children usually left the children in the care of others and returned to the revolutionary movement. Women's selflessness and readiness to sacrifice themselves greatly endeared them to their male comrades, who regarded them as moral exemplars and inspirations. It also won them the sympathy of the educated public. "They are Saints!" declared the spectators at one political trial, the Trial of the Fifty (1877), which included women who had abandoned lives of privilege to take up factory labor. The women's altruism also set a standard of behavior that revolutionaries of subsequent generations would expect from women activists and that the women themselves would strive to emulate.

Ironically, their behavior and example had no visible effect on women peasants, the female half of the very "people" for whom women revolutionaries were prepared to sacrifice their lives. Such women had their own culture of resistance, very different from the culture that animated women of the educated elites. By contrast with elite women, peasant women drew upon the family as a source of resistance, and in most cases, they acted in their roles as wives and mothers, as well as members of their community. Women large with child or holding babies to their breast might confront the authorities with hunger in the village or articulate the community's collective rights. The nature of peasant women's resistance is illustrated by a quite typical incident which took place in early fall 1872, as peasants confronted an official who had come to survey their land and, potentially, to deprive them of some of it. The entire village stood facing the surveyor, but the peasant women with babies at their breast were in front. Shouting, "We don't agree, we'll force you to stop, you won't get away with this robbery," the women placed their infants on the ground in front of them and blocked the surveyor's path. Each time the surveyor tried to proceed in a different direction, the women threw their infants under a bush directly in his way, then screened the bush with their bodies. The police proved unable to disperse the women or to remove the children. Undeterred by the presence of the police, the women tore the surveyor's stake out of the ground and broke it, to the men's shouts of encouragement. The surveying party was forced to withdraw, overcome by the women's defiance, reinforced as it was by over 400 peasants who had congregated on the spot.

In many other instances, too, peasant women played prominent roles in acts of collective defiance. Police intending to confiscate village property were attacked by women brandishing hoes and pitchforks; efforts to survey disputed land were blocked by women with their bodies; peasant men cutting trees in noblemen's forests were joined by axe-wielding women. Such acts of resistance occurred in the 1870s and 1880s, and escalated in the 1890s as economic change brought increasing hardship to the village. Then, as earlier, defending the family rather than denying it provided peasant women with their rationale for assuming a defiant public role. The actions in which they participated were localized and spontaneous. There is no evidence that they ever responded positively to the political message of the populist women (or men) who went to the people in the 1870s, or that populist agitators ever noticed the women's potential for resistance. Populist women's memoirs portray peasant women as more suspicious of them than peasant men: Ekaterina Breshkovskaia was typical in her judgment that the women were "the more conservative element" in the village. The peasant women were often acutely aware of the enormous social and cultural divisions that separated them from the well-meaning young women and men who sought union with the peasantry as well as an improvement of the peasants' lot. The peasant women in the village where Breshkovskaia lived and worked continually frustrated her longing for acceptance by pointedly observing the ways that she differed from them.

Changes in the Peasant Outlook

Following the assassination of Alexander II and the ascension of his son Alexander III (1881–94), the revolutionary movement went into decline, decimated by the arrests that followed the assassination and by the climate of repression that ensued. Although some terrorist groups continued to operate, workers' circles began to form and a Marxist movement emerged among emigrants; radicals maintained a much lower profile and never attained the unity or visibility of the earlier period, and they attracted little support from educated society. Even as the czarist government sought to quell all signs of social or political discontent, however, it initiated massive economic changes that shook the traditional social order to its roots. Beginning in the early 1890s, Russia undertook a program of rapid industrialization and economic growth that greatly expanded the numbers of educated people and professionals; it also brought a million people into the industrial labor force for the first time. Most of them were peasants by origin, and a growing minority of them were women. As the industrial labor force increased in size, so did the proportion of women: their numbers grew from about one in every five workers in 1885 to about one in every three on the eve of World War I. Even greater numbers of peasant women left their villages to work as domestic servants, as day laborers, or to perform a variety of other poorly paid and back-breaking tasks in Russia's rapidly expanding cities. At the turn of the century, the census recorded 92,000 domestic servants in St. Petersburg in addition to 73,724 women employed in industry; in Moscow, there were 70,763 domestics and 57,818 women industrial workers.

The move brought dramatic change in some of these women's lives, although very few had sought change for its own sake. Most peasant women left home as a result of pressing economic need; in wage earning they did not seek the freedom to shape their own lives but the means to sustain themselves and, if possible, to contribute to their family economy. The vast majority lived apart from their families, experiencing demoralizing working and living conditions. Before factory legislation mandated a workday of 11.5 hours in 1897, women workers often labored 14 or more hours a day, six days a week. They either lived in factory dormitories, where dozens were crowded together in a single large room, or they rented a corner in an apartment just big enough for their bed. Factory women may have dreamed of a room of their own, but on their meager earnings it was an unattainable luxury. The working and living conditions of the domestic servant were even harsher. The domestic servant in urban Russia lacked even the modest refuge available to her servant sisters in the West. In crowded urban apartments, the servant usually spent the night behind a screen in the passageway, or in the kitchen, or even by the bed of her employer. Her wage was low, her position often insecure, her work never-ending. She would be on call 24 hours a day, rising at 6:00 A.M. to light the stove and clean up. She prepared all the meals and did the washing up, ran errands, and answered the door. The servant was more subject to the personal power of her employer than any other woman worker. A servant who got sick was likely to lose her job; a servant who broke things paid for the damage from her wages; a servant who failed to obey promptly risked losing the references she needed to gain another position.

Still, although her living and working conditions were often no easier than they had been in the village, the peasant woman who migrated to town or city experienced a new kind of independence. So long as she remained in the household of her father or husband, under ordinary circumstances a woman's relations with the larger society were mediated by men. When she left her village on her own, she was no longer directly subject to patriarchal control. To be sure, peasant women often remained psychologically and legally tied to their village. Most workingwomen sent a portion of their wages home, and they visited when they could. Marriageable women often planned to return, marry, and settle down when they had earned enough to pay for their dowry. Work left women little free time. This was especially true of the domestic servant, who was typically permitted two days off a month. Nevertheless, some laboring women took advantage of the opportunities offered by city life and an independent income, however small, to extend their horizon, deepen their understanding, and forge a new identity. Many dressed in urban fashions and enjoyed cheap urban amusements. Some attended evening classes and Sunday schools, and a few

developed cultural interests, participating in amateur worker theatrical performances, writing poetry, or spending their hard-earned kopeks on theatre tickets. This new self-assertiveness might take a more explicitly political direction. In Russia, strikes and labor organizations were illegal until 1905, but despite the legal prohibitions and the harsh punishments meted out to those who violated them, from the mid-1880s onward the labor movement grew and strikes became increasingly common. Women played a minor role in them and were also far less likely than men to take part in the underground workers' study circles that began to proliferate, many of which had a Marxist orientation. But a few working-class women organizers became active in the 1890s. One was Vera Karelina, born in 1870 and abandoned to a foundling home shortly after her birth. Following the death of her peasant foster-mother, Karelina became a hospital worker and then a worker at a cotton spinning mill. In a workers' study circle, Karelina read radical literature at the end of a 14 to 16 hour workday and on Sundays. Another activist was Anna Boldyreva, a peasant from Tver province. Born the same year as Karelina, Boldyreva began her working life at the age of nine. A weaver at the Paul cotton weaving plant in St. Petersburg, she attended a workers' Sunday School in the mid 1880s and was drawn into an underground workers' study circle. In the early 1890s, the two women collaborated in organizing a small circle of women workers, who read and discussed socialist literature. Boldyreva subsequently became a Bolshevik. As she describes it, their frame of mind at the time was shaped by the politics of their workers' milieu: "Were we socialists at the time? The revolutionary 'contagion' had infected each one of us, and if, perhaps, we had not yet assimilated for ourselves the theory and methods of class struggle, we were at least distinctly aware of who was the enemy of the working class."

The growing visibility of lower-class women in urban Russia elicited a response from intellectuals. As increasing numbers of women penetrated into public and previously male space, the woman question took on new and complex life. But the political atmosphere in which educated people debated was different from what it had been in the immediate postemancipation era. In the 1860s and 1870s, the struggle between the state and educated society had been more explicitly political, involving feminist, liberal, and radical movements aiming to wrest from autocracy some or all of its authority. In the politically repressive 1880s and 1890s, political movements of this sort did not disappear entirely, but their members experienced enormous difficulty expressing their ideas in print and they risked arrest if they acted on behalf of them. Most intellectuals were unwilling to take the risk; they found it easier to contest the state in less direct but nonetheless important ways. There were many more intellectuals equipped to do so. The requirements of an industrializing society had led to an expansion of both general and professional education. A new generation of educated persons, especially lawyers and physicians, asserted their right to operate outside state jurisdiction and have primary responsibility for the areas in which they claimed expertise.

Professional men sought greater rights for themselves, not for women, whose bodies became part of the terrain over which educated society struggled for power. Even as the basis for women's dependent status began to erode as a result of women's migration, jurists revised laws concerning sexual crime and prostitution so as to deny women's capacity for independent action and ensure that individual autonomy remained a male preserve. When they discussed abortion and infanticide, the only forms of birth control women had, male physicians and jurists expressed anxieties about uncontrolled women and sought to substitute their own authority for the power of the patriarchal state. For example, when they opposed state regulation of prostitution, male physicians rarely argued for complete abolition of the system of surveillance and registration; instead, they wanted it amended, and for medical authority to replace the authority of the police.

As a civil society took shape, women too claimed larger and more autonomous social roles. In some cases, women did so by extending their customary sphere. In Orthodox religious communities, for example, women moved from contemplation to acts of charity for the poor and to education of the young. Especially in rural areas, these women's communities remained relatively free of the bureaucracy, which continued to be suspicious of any private initiative or independent action. Around the turn of the century, women teachers in St. Petersburg fought for the right to enjoy their customary sphere, to be wives and mothers as well as professionals. Protesting regulations that forbade women teachers to marry, they banded together to claim that right and to control their personal lives. In their struggle with urban authorities, the teachers found allies in the reemergent feminist movement. Feminists defended lower-class women, too, contending, for example, that women had the right to make their own reproductive choices regardless of their social status; and they rallied to the cause of abolishing state regulation of prostitution.

The Revolution of 1905

In 1905 long-suppressed discontents finally exploded in revolution. Not only industrial workers but students, professionals, and even nobles and industrialists became caught up in the wave of resistance that swept Russia in the wake of Bloody Sunday (9 January 1905), when czarist troops fired on a peaceful demonstration of working-class men and women, killing over 100 people and wounding many more. In the months that followed, as opposition to autocracy mounted and spread, Russians gained an unprecedented sense of their power vis à vis the state, and, taking advantage of that power, demanded civil rights, political representation, and in the case of workers the right to a decent life and respectful treatment from others. Strikes broke out immediately following Bloody Sunday, and by the late summer they had become overtly political. Industrial workers, clerical workers, pharmacists, professionals, and even domestic servants joined unions and walked off their jobs to attend mass meetings and demonstrations calling for an end to autocracy and some kind of representative form of government. The revolution culminated in October, with a general strike that froze life in Russia's major cities, stopping presses and transport, halting the supply of electricity and gasoline, and bringing the autocracy briefly to its knees.

During the upheavals, women of a variety of social strata mobilized in very substantial numbers, joining the men of their class to demand an expansion of political rights and greater social justice. The intense politicization and pervasive use of a language of rights sometimes stimulated women to speak on their own

behalf and to claim a place in the expanding public sphere. Working-class women were among the first to raise their voices. They objected in print at the end of January 1905, when the government called for the convening of the Shidlovskii Commission to study the reasons for worker discontent and permitted women to vote for representatives to the commission but only male workers to be elected to it. In the first printed statement of their grievances that has come to light, the women outlined for their readers the particular oppression they experienced as laboring women and claimed that only women could represent themselves: "We women workers carry a heavier and heavier burden of work. Taking advantage of our helplessness and lack of rights, our male comrades oppress us and we are paid less." The women protested the dashing of their hopes that they would have the chance to speak in public, or, as they put it, to "loudly proclaim ... the oppression and humiliation that no male worker can possibly understand." However, it was not the Shidlovskii Commission, but the increasingly political strike movement that became the medium through which workers expressed their discontent and aspirations. Women participated actively in the strike movement, and at the factories where they worked strike demands often reflected their presence. Factory after factory raised demands for day care, maternity leave, and nursing breaks, and protection of women workers, reflecting the preponderance of women in certain industries as well as the influence of the Marxist Social Democratic Labor Party (SDLP) and liberals, both of which had long supported maternity-related benefits. Even as they claimed for women significant rights at the workplace, such demands also reinforced gender differences and a gendered division of labor: virtually all the demands that applied to women touched on their role as mothers, not on their actual working conditions, and only in a few known instances did workers claim that a woman should be paid the same as a man for doing identical work. Most commonly, the existing wage differentials and women's unequal status in the workplace were reinscribed in strike demands that called for raises maintaining women's earnings at a fraction of men's. In a few cases, male workers went even further, and sought to exclude women workers altogether from trades they claimed as their own, in an effort to assert a solidarity based on gender as well as class.

The record of women's political participation is equally ambiguous, at least in part because of their uneasiness in organizations that men dominated. Working-class men behaved as if public affairs were not the business of women, who belonged at home with their children and pots and pans. These attitudes had a chilling effect on women. When Vera Karelina encouraged them to speak their mind, women would respond, "Yes, I sometimes get the urge to speak, but immediately I remember that I'll have to speak in front of a lot of people, all staring at me, and that someone might start to mock me—look, she's putting in an appearance in our conversations!—and my heart goes cold at such thoughts." As a result, although in 1905 women played a far more visible role than in the earlier period, they were active in much smaller proportions than men, even where women constituted a substantial section of the workforce. In the summer of 1905, a soviet (workers' council) emerged in the textile town of Ivanovo-Voznesensk, elected directly by workers to coordinate strike activities and act as an organ of worker self-government. Women constituted over a third of the industrial workforce in Ivanovo-Voznesensk, according to the census of 1897; 25 of the

151 elected deputies to the soviet were women (17 percent), almost all of them workers elected directly from the factory floor. The proportion of women in the Ivanovo-Voznesensk soviet was significantly greater than elsewhere. A Soviet of Workers' Deputies emerged in St. Petersburg on 17 October. By mid-November, it consisted of 562 deputies, seven of them women, perhaps four of them of working-class origin. If the women deputies articulated needs and aspirations that differed from the men's, there is no record of it. Published documents and accounts of Soviet activity often bear the imprint of the official Soviet interpretation of 1905: they portray a united and class-conscious proletariat marching staunchly behind the banner of Bolshevism. Thus, we learn from male participants that "the women workers of Ivanovo-Voznesensk took active part in the revolutionary movement . . . They demonstrated complete solidarity and class consciousness" and that "the women deputies, representing the majority of textile workers, walked boldly alongside us to the [first] session of the Soviet, as if it were all a familiar business." Vera Karelina and Anna Boldyreva, two of the representatives to the St. Petersburg Soviet, proved tireless agitators on behalf of its policies. Boldyreva, already a Bolshevik, went so far as to castigate workers' wives for their husbands' insufficient commitment to struggle: "You accustom your wives to eat and sleep well," she accused an audience of metalworkers, "and it is therefore frightening for you to be without wages, but we are not afraid of that, we are ready to die to win eight hours of work." But Bolshevik organizers could also bring a message that supported the rights of working-class women, as did Klavdia Kiriakina, a seamstress in Ivanovo-Voznesensk and subsequently a deputy to the Soviet. In May 1905, Kiriakina lectured a crowd of striking workers about women's equality and the need to improve women's status. There is no record of their reaction. Whether or not they were aware of particular needs as women, it is clear that vast numbers of working-class women were swept up in the events of 1905 and came to embrace the working-class movement as their own. This became clear in the second half of October 1905. The general strike forced Czar Nicholas II to sign the October Manifesto on October 17, granting to his people civil liberties and a quasi parliament, the Imperial Duma, with unequal representation and circumscribed powers. These limited concessions satisfied moderate liberals, but not the working class, thereby dividing the opposition that had drawn its strength from unity. Thereafter, the workers, who insisted upon genuine democracy and universal, direct, and equal suffrage, fought alone, men and women together. On 6 November, working-class women of St. Petersburg, including both women workers and working-class wives, mounted a huge demonstration, demanding that the taverns that served liquor be closed, so that striking workers would not be tempted to drink. In December, during a last, desperate confrontation with the authorities, women and men took to the barricades. Single women, workers' wives, and domestic servants labored tirelessly, chopping wood, breaking up telegraph poles, and disassembling tram cars to construct barricades against government troops, who nevertheless crushed the working-class movement.

During the revolution of 1905, women of the educated classes took political action of a different sort. The feminist movement (or more precisely, feminist movements) reemerged on a much more substantial scale and embraced far larger numbers than before. The primary goal was women's suffrage, which became an issue as soon as men claimed a political voice. The largest and most visible feminist group, and the only one to be truly active in 1905, was the All-Russian Union for Women's Equality, a national women's political organization formed by 30 women liberals a month after Bloody Sunday. Their first public meeting on 10 April was also the first political meeting for women to occur in Russia, and it attracted about 1,000 people. By the time of their first Congress, held in Moscow, 7–10 May, chapters had formed. Feminist activists were mainly women of the emergent middle classes; however, independent professional women, such as journalists, physicians, and teachers (whom Soviet historians used to call the laboring intelligentsia), were far more numerous than they appear to have been in the feminist parties of Western Europe. Among the 30 women who founded the Union for Women's Equality were the journalists Zinaida Mirovich-Ivanova, Liubov Gurevich, Anna Kalmanovich, and Anna Evreinova, who was also the first Russian woman to obtain a doctorate in law; the historians Anna Miliukova and Ekaterina Shchepkina, both graduates of higher courses for women; the teacher Maria Chekhova, and the physician Olga Klirikova. The leader of the Mutual Philanthropic Society, a much more moderate feminist organization, was Anna Shabanova, a pediatrician. The Women's Progressive Party, which formed after the revolutionary movement had already peaked, was led by Maria Pokrovskaia, also a physician, who practiced among the urban poor.

The Union for Women's Equality was the most radical as well as the most visible of the three. From the moment it formed, it cast its lot with the broader liberation movement, embracing the idea that women's liberation was inseparable from the liberation of society as a whole. The platform the Union adopted in May 1905 echoed the platform of the liberation movement by calling for national autonomy, abolition of the death penalty, and the convocation of a constituent assembly elected by direct, equal, secret, and universal suffrage, in addition to its demands for specifically women's rights, such as equality of the sexes before the law, equal rights to the land for peasant women, laws to protect women workers, and coeducation at all levels. Their common ground of opposition to autocracy led members of the Union for Women's Equality to collaborate with liberal and leftist men far more extensively than feminists did elsewhere in Europe or in the United States. Many of the feminists were also active in liberal or professional organizations. The journalist Ariadna Tyrkova-Williams, for example, participated in the founding of the liberal Cadet (Constitutional Democratic) Party before she joined the Union for Women's Equality a year later. The Women's Union itself became a member of the Union of Unions, the umbrella group that embraced both professional and trade unions. Aware that success in winning women's rights depended upon changes in many other spheres of Russian society and politics, the women also sought support among moderates in organs of local government. They participated in radical demonstrations and openly supported workers' strikes, raising money to help the strike movement, unemployed workers, and political prisoners. In petitions and demonstrations they demanded amnesty for political prisoners and the abolition of the death penalty, as well as rights for women.

In addition, the Union tried to speak on behalf of all women, and not just the women of the middle class who were their main constituency. In St. Petersburg, they went into the factories to assist workingwomen in formulating their protest against exclusion from the Shidlovskii Commission, discussed earlier. Throughout 1905 and into 1906, the Union worked to transcend the enormous social chasm that separated privileged Russians from the laboring classes, by developing alliances with women factory workers and peasants. At its first conference in May, for example, the Union invited "women of the toiling classes" to draw up a platform articulating their own demands and pledged to support it, in an attempt to avoid the distrust that lower-class women inevitably felt for a platform devised for them by others. Feminist demands included laws for the welfare, protection, and insurance of women workers. They also tried to reach out to peasant women, who, like men, had become far more militant and aggressive in 1905–07, although as earlier, mainly on behalf of family and community. Feminists joined the Peasant Union and convinced it to adopt the plank of women's suffrage. Feminist efforts to expand their social base bore some fruit. Women domestic servants in Moscow and St. Petersburg joined feminist-organized unions and attended feminist-sponsored political clubs. Women workers added their signatures to feminist petitions favoring women's suffrage. A number of peasant women's groups were formed and some petitions signed by peasant men took up the demand for women's suffrage. In 1906 peasant women in Tver and Voronezh provinces sent petitions to the newly elected legislature, the Duma, laying independent claim to the political voice so recently granted their men and denying the prevailing stereotype of peasant women as backward and mute. Protesting the assertion of a peasant deputy that peasant women were not interested in the vote, 55 women signed a letter stating, "We learned from the newspapers that the deputy from Voronezh told the Duma that the peasant only recognizes woman's work in the family and assured them that peasant women themselves don't want any rights. There are no women deputies in the Duma who could represent all peasant women, so how does he know? He is wrong to say that the peasant woman doesn't want rights. Did he ask us? We, the peasant women of Voronezh province understand perfectly well that we need rights and land just as men do."

Despite these feminist efforts, the revolutionary year of 1905 brought women very little in the way of measurable political gains. To be sure, the granting of civil liberties, however limited, allowed more scope for their organizing, and the number of feminist newspapers increased, with Pokrovskaia's *Zhenskii Vestnik* maintaining a barrage of propaganda on behalf of women's rights. However, support for the liberation movement, so generously given, was rather less generously returned. The October Manifesto enfranchised only men, leaving women dependent on the loyalty of their former male allies. The Cadet Party, which dominated the first Duma, was divided over the issue of women's suffrage, while parties to the Left, because of their working-class orientation, although staunch advocates of women's rights, were with one notable exception, remaining suspicious of and reluctant to support "bourgeois feminism." Moreover, social divisions between women eventually proved insuperable. Working-class and peasant women felt more affinity with the men of their own class than they did with middle-class feminists, whom they tended to view as "bourgeois." Even when feminists succeeded in organizing women workers, they had trouble retaining their loyalty. As one feminist lamented in May 1906, it was relatively easy to establish circles among laboring women, but as soon as their political consciousness was raised, they wanted to work

with the men of their class. "They very quickly join the ranks of one of the parties and become party workers. In a number of cities, the Union [for Women's Equality] has acted as a kind of preparation for party work." Thus, the social divisions that weakened opposition to autocracy divided the women's movement as well. But more decisive than male ambivalence or social divisions was the fact that the revolution had ended and the czar was regaining control. The czar ordered the first Duma dissolved after three months, just as its members prepared to consider the fruit of feminist lobbying, a draft law on women's equality; the life of the second Duma was equally brief. On 3 June 1907 the government amended the electoral laws to give still greater weight to the propertied (and presumably less-volatile) sectors of society and finally got a Duma with which it could coexist. At the same time, it chipped away at civil liberties, making it increasingly difficult for oppositional groups to function and for unions to organize. The period following 1907 was a time of political demoralization: membership in radical political parties sharply declined, as it did in the women's movement. Despite the lack of concrete feminist achievements, women's experience of 1905, and, in particular, their participation in acts of protest and their use of the language of rights, left an ineradicable trace on the consciousness of thousands at all levels of society, from the most privileged to the most deprived. Nowhere is this clearer than in an extraordinary letter, signed by prostitutes in the provincial town of Vologda and published in the newsletter of the Union for Women's Equality in June–July 1907. Pointing out that everyone, including laboring men and women, "are gaining their rights," the signatories claimed rights of their own, including the subjection of their customers to venereal examinations, the right to leave a brothel when they chose, and the limitation of their customers to no more than five a night. Most of all, however, the women wanted the end of state regulation of prostitution, which greatly limited the ability of lower-class women to control their own lives. If regulation were abolished, in the words of the letter, "Then a girl could sell herself only when she pleased, and when she pleased, she could stop."

Between June 1907 and the outbreak of World War I, the women's movement splintered and lost membership and momentum. This period was distinguished primarily by the All-Russian Congress of Women, which took place 10–16 December 1908. Reflecting the repressive atmosphere, the organizers had had to submit the draft program to the Ministry of the Interior, which deleted certain sections of it; the police were present for the duration of the congress, aiming to intimidate those in attendance. The presence of the police did not keep participants from a lively exchange of opinions. The conference revealed differences within the feminist movement, but even more profound differences between middle-class feminists and the few workingwomen in attendance. Although the organizers had tried hard to attract a broadly based audience, the conference was overwhelmingly middle class in composition, with the exception of 30 women workers, who called themselves the Workers' Group and had been carefully prepared by the radical intelligentsia to disrupt the conference proceedings. Easily distinguishable from the other well-dressed and well-fed conference participants by their cheap clothing and undernourished appearance, the workingwomen spoke with a voice that was deeply inflected by class. Whatever their other differences, feminists agreed that women shared the need for equal rights in the family and society; their main opponents were men. By contrast, for the Workers' Group it was the crisis of capitalism that was primarily responsible for the problems of workingwomen. Although many of the women workers endorsed the feminist fight for women's suffrage, they believed that only a social revolution and socialism could provide a genuine solution to the problems of working-class women. The Workers' Group accused the feminists of trying to divert women from the struggle against capitalism and to divide the working class. The feminists retorted that they were fighting for the rights of all women, including women of the working class, and they criticized leftist parties for their ambivalence concerning women's suffrage. The two factions could not reach agreement. On the last day of the Congress, the Workers' Group read a declaration maintaining that it was impossible for hostile classes to collaborate and then demonstratively left the proceedings.

The apparent unanimity of the Workers' Group concealed significant divisions, not only among the women, but within the socialist movement itself, as well as tensions between the aspirations of some working-class women and the aims of the socialist parties that claimed to speak on their behalf. In 1903 the Marxist Social Democratic Labor Party had split into two factions, the Mensheviks and the Bolsheviks, and in the following years their differences intensified. The Bolsheviks were the more intransigent of the two: unlike the Mensheviks, who were receptive to the possibility of limited collaboration between classes and sought a broad democratic coalition of all forces that opposed the existing order, the Bolsheviks were separatists who rejected any kind of cooperation with nonsocialist elements. The Bolsheviks insisted that the woman question must be solved within the framework of socialist revolution, and their (male) leadership had accepted the idea of participation in the women's conference only very reluctantly. They sent one of their men to supervise the actions of the Workers' Group and attempted without much success to dictate the party position to them. At the conference, at least some of the working-class women had been affected by the speeches they heard or the contacts they made with participants from the "laboring intelligentsia." The Bolsheviks regarded this incipient feminist awareness with hostility and dismissed it as the "backwardness" of the women workers in the group. With regard to women's issues, the record of the Mensheviks was not much better. Although both parties adopted platforms that called for complete female equality and for reforms at the workplace, including maternity and childcare benefits, neither of them showed much concern for the woman question or the plight of laboring women as such; Mensheviks shared the Bolshevik stereotype of the woman worker as "backward." Men dominated both parties. Even educated and talented socialist women, like Nadezhda Krupskaia, Lenin's wife, tended to be relegated to secretarial or technical work and rarely participated in editorial boards or policy making. Moreover, activists and intellectuals in both parties, including women activists, did little or nothing to raise women's issues or to draw working-class women into party ranks. There certainly existed working-class female Bolsheviks, like the seamstress Klavdia Kiriakina, but such women were rare. The Bolshevik leadership in particular was fearful of dividing the working class and hesitant to "waste" scarce resources on efforts aimed at women.

Aleksandra Kollontai

Aleksandra Kollontai, who at the time was affiliated with the Menshevik Party and led the Workers' Group at the Women's Conference in 1908, was different. The most outspoken advocate of women's rights on the Left, she was also one of the most original feminist thinkers of her time. Like almost all women who occupied prominent positions in the socialist parties, her background was neither working class nor poor. She was born Aleksandra M. Domontovich in 1872 in St. Petersburg. Her father came from an old noble line and rose to be a general in the czar's army; her mother was the child of a wealthy timber merchant. She grew up in great comfort, amidst the typical amusements of a young noblewoman's life. Although she came of age in the 1890s, a time when Marxism was attracting increasing numbers of young women and men, her first rebellion was personal, not political: in 1893, when she was 21, she married against her parents' will a distant cousin, Vladimir Kollontai, an engineer. She fulfilled the role of housewife and, after the birth of their son, of mother, for five years, but she also read populist and Marxist literature. Increasingly, she grew restless with her narrow domestic horizons. In 1896, a visit to the Krenholm factory, where her husband worked, crystallized her political beliefs by bringing her into contact with the terrible conditions in which the working class lived and labored. Later that year, strikes of St. Petersburg textile workers confirmed her sympathies for workers. Kollontai became a Marxist; the distance between her and her husband widened. In 1898 she went off to the University of Zurich to study political economy and to deepen her knowledge of Marxism, leaving her husband for good.

She returned in 1903, a committed political activist, and devoted herself to organizing and public speaking. Her interest in women emerged somewhat later, although she had become sensitized to women's problems by her own personal struggle for freedom. Not until late in 1905 did she begin to work among laboring women, and only then because the feminists appeared so successful in reaching out to them; instead, she wanted to draw laboring women into the socialist movement. Like her fellow Marxists, Kollontai believed that the feminist movement was bourgeois; unlike them, however, she became convinced that socialist efforts to reach working-class women were insufficient. Much of her life as an activist and organizer would be spent trying to rectify the situation and to convince her party comrades of the need to devote resources to gaining the support of women workers. She herself took the lead. Between 1905 and 1908, Kollontai and a few associates worked hard at organizing a proletarian women's movement and winning laboring women over to social democracy. First, she organized lectures on the woman question from a Marxist perspective for servant and factory women; then, in the fall of 1907 she established a club for women workers that provided a reading room and a buffet. The club attracted several hundred laboring women. Both the Bolsheviks and the Mensheviks reacted indifferently, if not with hostility, to these efforts. On the day that Kollontai's club opened, Vera Zasulich, who had been one of the founders of the Menshevik Party, told Kollontai that she was wasting time and party resources. Somehow, Kollontai remained undaunted, her commitment to socialism undiminished. She wrote her first theoretical work on women, the *Social Bases of the Woman Ques-*

tion, in order to prepare women workers to resist feminist overtures at the women's congress of 1908. The book (not published until 1909) aimed to demonstrate that on issues such as marriage, motherhood, or the need for economic independence or political rights, for which feminists claimed a shared female experience and shared female aspirations, women were as divided by class as men, and it was the social democrats, not the feminists, who spoke most truly in defense of women workers. Ignoring the resistance she herself had experienced when she tried to gain her party's support for her efforts to organize women, in the *Social Bases of the Woman Question*, Kollontai urged women workers to fight alongside the men of their class.

Kollontai never abandoned this fundamental position, but in the following years she greatly expanded her ideas concerning women's situation under capitalism and her emancipation in the socialist future. Police persecution forced Kollontai to leave Russia at the end of 1908, and she remained abroad until 1917. During this time she developed an original socialist feminist perspective, in which she theorized with unprecedented sensitivity and understanding the position of the working-class woman both as a member of her class and as an individual. Her views and the response to them are worth exploring in some detail for what they reveal about the potentialities as well as the limitations of Russian socialist visions of women's liberation. Building upon the writings of earlier Marxist thinkers on the woman question, in particular August Bebel and Friedrich Engels, Kollontai went considerably further to explore women's psychology and to raise sexuality and sexual relations as proper topics for political discussion. As she sought to understand the ways that capitalist society shaped the most intimate feelings and the relations between the sexes, she drew upon her own experiences in several turbulent and ultimately unsatisfactory love affairs as well as on her reading. This effort to connect the psychological with the social can be seen in a pioneering essay entitled "The New Woman," published in 1913. Here Kollontai explored the evolution of literary prototypes of women as a reflection of women's changing lives. Until recently, she wrote, fictional heroines had been almost entirely preoccupied by love: it was their only source of happiness and they willingly abandoned their identity for the sake of it. But now a new type of heroine had appeared, a woman who found the meaning of her life in independence and in work, not in love. This heroine, unconstrained by "bourgeois morality" and its double standard, followed her sexual inclinations where they led her. The heroine also claimed new rights in the public world, "walking the streets with a businesslike, masculine tread." But she feared love. Love still had the power to waken "atavistic inclinations" in her, in particular, the inclination to surrender her hard-won identity to a man. And this she was not willing to do. In this transitional period, according to Kollontai, women had still not learned how to harmonize their inner freedom with the passion of love. Capitalism was responsible for the appearance of the "new woman," because for the first time it enabled single women to earn their own livelihood apart from the family. Such women derived from all social classes, but they were most commonly encountered among the working class, where hunger and need forced large numbers of women to adapt to changed economic circumstances and to develop a far more independent personality. In Kollontai's words, "By tearing women away from the home, by wresting them away from the cradle, [capitalism] transforms the submissive, passive family creatures, the obedient slaves of the husband, into a respect-demanding army of fighters for their own and general rights, for their own and general interests. The personality of the woman steels itself, grows." Kollontai linked her feminist analysis with class analysis, in the process denying the sexism that laboring women encountered daily in their relations with the men of their class. Independent workingwomen were welcomed and encouraged by their men, Kollontai claimed, because the men were developing a new, proletarian morality that valued women who rebelled against every kind of slavery and who were active and conscious themselves. By contrast, bourgeois women encountered only implacable hostility from the men of their milieu. Thus, Kollontai projected onto women workers her own hopes and struggles and fears. In this vision linking psychological to economic and social change, human beings could learn how to love as equals only under socialism.

Aleksandra Kollontai was unique among women on the Russian Left in her sensitivity to women's psychology and her concern for women's sexuality. Not since Chernyshevskii championed his heroine Vera Pavlova's emancipation had any Russian radical systematically addressed these topics. To be sure, sexual questions had begun to preoccupy educated society, especially after the revolution of 1905. Eased censorship enabled the press more freely to discuss sensitive issues, while the failure of the revolution to bring genuine political change served to politicize the "sexual question." But with a few notable exceptions, the post–1905 literature was preoccupied with male, not female, sexuality. One exception was the immensely popular boulevard novel, *The Keys to Happiness*, which might have provided Kollontai with a perfect prototype of the new woman had it not been completed in 1913, the year Kollontai published her essay. In six volumes and 1,400 pages, the writer Anastasia Verbitskaia explored the life of a sexually self-assertive modern heroine, Mania, who takes several lovers and struggles to retain her independence and artistic ambitions in the face of intense passion. Feminists increasingly addressed themselves to aspects of the sexual question. The most visible was the physician Maria Pokrovskaia, who fought unceasingly against regulated prostitution and who denounced punitive abortion laws as unwarranted restrictions on female autonomy. Invoking the concept of voluntary motherhood, she called for full decriminalization of abortion and claimed that only women were in a position to know their own needs. This was true even of the society woman who avoided childbearing because of a supposed devotion to pleasure, an example often cited by opponents of abortion. In Pokrovskaia's words, "Since the society lady risks her life in resorting to abortion, she obviously considers the birth of a child worse than death itself. Her arguments may seem pitiful to us, but to her they have enormous meaning." But even as she denounced the double standard, Pokrovskaia, like most of her feminist colleagues, urged that men adopt the female example of chastity, not that women emulate the sexually adventurous behavior of men. In her claims for women's right of sexual choice as well as in her efforts to theorize the link between personal emancipation and social change, Kollontai adopted a stance very different from the feminist one. Her behavior also challenged a radical political culture that for decades had emphasized women's capacity for self-sacrifice and self-abnegation when she insisted upon her right to follow her own sexual yearnings, even as she fought for social revolution. Although her references to "winged Eros," and the like may seem quaint or old-fashioned to the contemporary reader, she was far ahead of her time. Kollontai's efforts to incorporate intimate aspects of women's experience into the Marxist worldview won few converts among her colleagues; her romantic liaisons would be used against her later in intraparty political struggles.

Militant Women Bolsheviks before World War I

In the years before World War I, a handful of other leftist women awakened to the need to pay more attention to working-class women. Within a revitalized working-class movement, laboring women had become much more active and visible. Starting in 1912, there was a marked upsurge of work stoppages, in which women played a very dynamic role. Women strikers frequently demanded polite treatment from supervisory personnel, evidence of their growing resistance to humiliation, insults, and slights to their dignity; women also protested sexual harassment. Women workers were thus finding their own voice and raising it with unprecedented self-assertion. Increasing numbers of them wrote letters to socialist newspapers, complaining not only about working conditions, but also about the hostility they encountered from male coworkers, who tended to regard women as a lower order of being and to demonstrate their feelings in sexually demeaning ways. Women complained of men exposing their genitals, of being sexually assaulted by male coworkers in out of the way factory corners, or of being propositioned by male machinists upon whom they depended for repair of their machines. One woman employed in a carton factory described women's experience in the following terms: "The men [workers] treat the women workers and apprentices as if they were street prostitutes. All the time one hears from them [nothing] but insults and obscene propositions."

This new militancy prompted activist women to try to respond to workingwomen's particular needs and concerns and to draw women into their party fold. Three women, all members of the intelligentsia but from diverse backgrounds, played a leading role within the Bolshevik Party, with Konkordia Nikolaevna Samoilova taking the initiative. Born in 1876, the daughter of a village priest, Samoilova had attended the Bestuzhev courses, Russia's university for women, before resolving to devote herself full time to revolution. A Bolshevik from the first, she was an editor of the Bolshevik Party newspaper, *Pravda*. In the winter of 1912–13, she became convinced of the need for a special journal addressed to women workers. She was supported by Inessa Armand, who was actually French by birth. Born in 1874 in Paris, Armand was raised in Russia, when, after the death of her father, she accompanied her aunt, who found employment as a tutor for the wealthy Armand family. Treated as a member of the family, Inessa married one of the Armand sons when she became 18. She lived with him seven years and bore five children; like Kollontai, she eventually became dissatisfied with a traditional upper-class woman's life. After a Tolstoyan phase, she became a feminist and worked on the rehabilitation of prostitutes in Moscow. In 1904 she separated from her husband and went off to study socialism abroad. Although she returned a year later as a Bolshevik, she retained some feminist sympathies.

While in emigration in 1911, she attempted to organize a school for workingwomen; her male comrades, however, opposed the idea and forced her to abandon it. Armand eagerly embraced the proposal to start a journal for women. The third supporter was Nadezhda Krupskaia, the wife of the Bolshevik leader Vladimir Il'ich Lenin. Born 1869, the daughter of a leftist military officer, Krupskaia briefly attended the Bestuzhev courses, but, already politicized, she withdrew because she found the women's university too far removed from real life. She was far more satisfied to teach Marxism to St. Petersburg workers. Arrested in 1896, Krupskaia spent seven months in prison, then went to Siberia to marry the exiled Lenin, whom she had met four years earlier. Although she was very much in Lenin's shadow, she nevertheless had ideas and interests of her own. One of them was pedagogy; another, work among women. During their Siberian exile, she produced her first publication, *The Woman Worker*. This pamphlet, 24 pages long and aimed at ordinary workingwomen, drew on the work of August Bebel and Klara Zetkin to describe the oppression of lower-class women and to offer a vision of their liberation. In simple, accessible language it depicted the overworked and undernourished peasant woman and the factory woman, who enjoyed neither job security nor maternity benefits, whose low wages often forced her to choose between hunger and prostitution, but whose earnings nevertheless liberated her from a tyrannical husband or father. In the socialist future, the exploitation would end and only freedom would remain: factories would be clean and well lighted, children would be properly cared for. To attain this vision, the pamphlet urged laboring women to join the struggle for the victory of the proletariat. Despite its lack of originality, the pamphlet played an important role in the history of Russia's labor movement. Printed abroad and smuggled into Russia, it was the only Marxist statement on the woman question until the publication of Kollontai's *Social Bases of the Woman Question* in 1909. It proved very popular among agitators and among women. Evidently, the work she did on it influenced Krupskaia herself: she endorsed the idea of a journal addressed to women and tried without much success to win the support of influential male party members for it. None of them were enthusiastic. Lenin himself was deeply ambivalent and refused to devote party resources to it. But the party did not oppose the journal either, so when Armand succeeded in raising enough money from private sources, the project went forward. The journal *Rabotnitsa* appeared on International Woman's Day in 1914.

Despite the evident sympathy for workingwomen on the part of its female initiators, from the very first the journal *Rabotnitsa* revealed the dissonance between Bolshevik visions of women's role and the perspectives of the working-class women themselves. The record of *Rabotnitsa* on women's issues was mixed, to say the least. *Rabotnitsa* gave working-class women a forum to express themselves in print, anonymously if they chose, and it unleashed a flood of letters in which women wrote openly about their lives and the abuses they suffered, including abuse by male workers. But the editors never responded to this content. The editorial tone is revealed in an article penned by Krupskaia for the first issue. Reflecting the condescending attitude of most Marxist intellectuals, even those who advocated special work among women, Krupskaia wrote: "The woman question for men and women workers is a question of how to draw the backward masses of women workers into the organization, how to explain their interests to them better, how to make them better comrades in the general struggle sooner." Instead of acknowledging the difficulties working-class women endured, the editors ignored them or responded patronizingly and dismissively. The women workers complained about male hostility within and outside labor organizations; the editors insisted that the time of male-female competition at the workplace had ceased, and exhorted women to join unions. Women workers invited their sisters to "acknowledge that the time has passed when the woman was only a mother" and urged men to recognize that the woman worker had to earn her bread, too. By contrast, the editors emphasized women workers' maternal role. "We know that you have the heavy but great burden of raising and educating the new young generation, strong and staunch proletarian *sons*" (emphasis added). The journal faced other problems as well. Harassed by the police and always strapped for funds, it maintained a precarious existence, publishing only seven issues before the police shut it down.

1917

The outbreak of World War I in August 1914 did much more to set the stage for revolution, by mobilizing Russian women at unprecedented levels. New jobs opened up in factories that men abandoned for the front; by 1917, the proportion of women in Russian industry as a whole rose to 43.2 percent, although, as before, most women remained concentrated in trades that required no skill and paid low wages. Still, the numbers of women and children working in weapons factories grew dramatically, and in St. Petersburg, the heart of Russia's metalworking industry, women constituted 20 percent of workers in that elite trade by 1917. Peasant women shouldered all the responsibility for fieldwork in the absence of men, or they traveled for the first time to cities in search of employment. World War I thus helped prepare the way for the more profound transformations that the Bolsheviks would undertake after 1917. The conflict blurred gender boundaries and for the first time drew out to work hundreds of thousands, perhaps millions, of women.

The war years also markedly increased political discontent by creating severe dislocation. Prices rose sharply, and items of primary necessity such as bread and sugar grew scarce. By 1915, urban Russians experienced considerable hardship in their daily lives. When it became evident that the war effort would require enormous sacrifices from workers but bring few benefits in return, the strike movement resumed and quickly acquired an antiwar flavor. Thousands of workers went on strike daily; the strike movement cost roughly 4.5 million lost working days between fall 1915 and fall 1916, with skilled trades such as metalworking taking the lead. Trades where women predominated, such as textiles, tobacco, and food processing, were inundated with new and very youthful workers (many aged 12 to 14) and played a relatively minor part in the wartime protests. However, in metalworking and other war-related industries, women walked out on strike together with men. As the strike movement became politicized, some of these women workers, more educated and skilled than their sisters in other trades, also began to articulate demands of their own. Hundreds of them raised the question of equalizing men's and women's wages at two different meetings held in late February 1916, for example. Such meetings

suggest a growing self-assertiveness among a sector of women workers.

Lower-class women became more assertive in their traditional roles as well. In the cities, rising prices made it increasingly difficult for women to maintain everyday life and obtain food for their families. By the spring of 1915 women began to protest, sometimes by themselves, sometimes accompanied by men or youths. Russia's cities and towns were rocked by subsistence revolts. The participants were primarily women workers, soldiers' wives, and working-class housewives outraged by the escalating cost of essential goods. With an aggressiveness born of desperation, they attacked and destroyed the shops of merchants suspected of speculation. They broke into shops and appropriated goods for themselves at prices they believed to be just. Women resisted the efforts of police and cossack detachments to stop them, and in some cases the women responded by throwing stones and bricks. Women's anger at merchants and tradesmen for allegedly robbing the people reflected the growing alienation of Russia's laboring classes. This dissatisfaction took a political direction: they demanded that civil authorities force sellers to lower prices or take it upon themselves to provide food at affordable prices. The authorities failed to act. As a result, as the war continued and the food situation deteriorated even further, popular attitudes became fiercely antiwar and antigovernment. According to police reports, women complained bitterly among themselves in the marketplace: "They are slaughtering our husbands and our sons in the war, and at home, they want to starve us to death." Equally unnerving for the authorities, women's protests in the marketplace frequently spilled over onto the factory floor. In the wake of subsistence riots, thousands of male and female workers might walk off the job, demanding higher wages or lower prices. The situation reached a critical point on International Woman's Day, 23 February (8 March) 1917. In St. Petersburg, now renamed Petrograd, angry working-class women, both housewives and factory workers, ignored the pleas of labor leaders to stay home and staged a demonstration calling for bread and peace. The working-class response was decisive. Over the next few days, hundreds of thousands of workers joined them, while soldiers refused orders to fire on the demonstrators. The women's protest quickly turned into a full-scale revolution, forcing Czar Nicholas II to abdicate the throne on 3 March.

The system of dual power that followed the fall of the czar reflected Russia's profound social and political divisions. Formal authority was vested in the provisional government, composed of educated men of the privileged strata, mainly liberals who had participated in the fourth Duma. The provisional government quickly granted Russians unprecedented civil liberties, but chose to continue the war effort and postpone elections to the Constituent Assembly, whose task it would be to select a new government for Russia. For eight months, the provisional government tried to steer a moderate course, but proved unable to resolve Russia's most pressing problems or to obtain the allegiance of most of the population. The other, informal source of authority was the Petrograd Soviet of Workers' and Soldiers' Deputies, which emerged on 27 February. An enormous body elected directly by workers and soldiers, the Soviet was led by an executive committee composed of men from the major socialist parties. The Petrograd Soviet claimed to represent the interests of Russia's laboring classes. Initially, it granted the provisional government its conditional support. Other soviets soon sprang up in towns and villages all over Russia, but the Petrograd Soviet remained the most powerful. As 1917 proceeded, and the provisional government failed to satisfy lower-class demands for an end to war, a living wage, resolution of the subsistence problem, and distribution of land to the peasantry, the lower-class mood turned hostile to it. By the summer of 1917, cries of "Down with the provisional government!" and "All power to the Soviets!" could increasingly be heard in popular protests and demonstrations. Alone among the socialist parties represented in the Soviet leadership, the Bolsheviks embraced the demand for the overthrow of the provisional government and called for a workers' revolution. By the late summer of 1917, the mood of the lower classes had swung in its favor; in early September, elections to local soviets for the first time brought Bolshevik majorities in Moscow, Petrograd, and other important cities.

During the eight months that the provisional government remained in power, the mood of feminists and middle-class women, and working-class and peasant women diverged markedly. Women of the upper classes had enthusiastically supported the war effort, which offered them new opportunities to participate in public life. They volunteered and found work in nursing, as well as collecting gifts of clothing and medical supplies for troops at the front. Such opportunities increased dramatically after the fall of the czar, which brought an unprecedented upsurge of public activity. Newspapers of all persuasions proliferated, while speeches, demonstrations, and meetings for a wide variety of purposes occurred on a daily basis, as people gained for the first time a measure of genuine responsibility for their lives. Women became regular contributors to public funds such as those aiding released political prisoners; a few made a point of identifying themselves as "citizeness." Feminists launched a successful campaign for a genuine share of political power. When the provisional government failed to include sexual equality in its original political program, feminists mobilized women to defend their political rights. They held conferences and meetings that sometimes proved so popular that people had to be turned away. On 20 March they mounted a huge procession numbering up to 40,000 people, who marched to the palace where the provisional government was located in order to lobby it on behalf of women's suffrage. A female militia mounted on horseback accompanied the parade and marchers carried streamers reading, "Woman's Place—Is in the Constituent Assembly." The provisional government soon acquiesced to feminist demands. It granted women the right to vote, the right to serve as attorneys, and the right to act as jurors, as well as equal rights within the civil service—especially important for teachers. In so doing, it won the cautious support of the feminists, including support for Russia's continued participation in the war effort.

No doubt, lower-class women had other things on their minds. When one of the feminists approached a crowd of women lined up at a bakery after the suffrage victory and declared, "I congratulate you, citizenesses, we Russian women are going to receive [our] rights," she was met with indifference and incomprehension. Given their views on the eve of the February revolution, it is unlikely that lower-class women shared their privileged sisters' enthusiasm for war, or that they continued to support the provisional government after it became evident that they would gain neither the bread nor the peace for which they had demonstrated in February. In Petrograd, the socialist-led labor movement gained increasing influence over women's strikes after the February revolution, and women workers demonstrated impressive tenacity and self-discipline. In May, more than 3,000 laundresses walked out in a strike led by their new union. To their demands for an eight-hour day and a minimum wage of 4 rubles a day, employers responded with threats to lock them out and evict them from their dwellings. Some of the picketers were attacked physically; others were arrested. The owners organized a rival union; strikebreaking became widespread. However, the laundresses persisted and after a month won a modest victory. Another strike of mainly female dye workers lasted from 13 May to September, 1917. Led by the new chemical workers' union, the strike was widely supported by labor organizations, but despite the women's determination to resist, it ended in failure. Once the struggle was over, however, the women's interest in union membership declined. Aleksandra Kollontai, who took active part in both strikes, proposed to a Trade Union conference in June that they establish special women's sections, but the proposal was rejected without discussion.

The absence of organizations expressing lower-class women's interests contributes to the difficulty of saying with certainty what they believed or whom they supported. There are no books or serious studies on lower-class or peasant women in 1917. References to them in books treating the working class or peasantry are fleeting and tangential. In addition, the history of 1917 is politicized in every respect. Scholars continue to debate the question of whether the revolution that overthrew the provisional government in October 1917, was in fact a genuine workers' revolution or merely a Bolshevik coup. How one perceives this issue influences how one sees all antecedent events. As a result, even the new, revisionist histories that focus on the lower-class mood end up looking at workers or peasants in terms of their support for a particular political position. Such an approach yields very little information about women, because women were so rarely in the forefront of political action. Moreover, contemporary sources such as newspapers tended to ignore women, except when their activities, such as charitable work, fell within women's traditional sphere; accounts of events rarely tell us whether women participated or spoke. As a result, in the records of the eight months between the February and October revolutions, a time of widespread popular activism and intense political struggle, it is surprisingly difficult to detect lower-class women's voices or to discern their aspirations. And when the women's voices do become audible, it is often because they attended meetings inspired or organized by the Bolsheviks. In the late 1950s, Soviet historians published many volumes of archival documents, selected to emphasize the Bolshevik's leading role in 1917 and the extent of popular support for their positions. We can learn from such a document that on 17 March, a meeting of women workers in Petrograd passed a resolution demanding full equality for women, laws to protect the labor of women and children, and the abolition of night work, as well as a democratic republic, the eight-hour day, and land for the peasantry. Or that later in the month, women workers in the city endorsed a similar resolution in which they also expressed their solidarity with the workers' movement and distinguished themselves from "women of the bourgeois movement." But it is hard to know how representative such views really were or whether they persisted after the summer of 1917, when male workers in defense industries, threatened with layoffs, began to insist that women who had taken up work during the war should lose their jobs first.

What can be said with certainty is this: lower-class women took enthusiastic advantage of new political opportunities, but the greater the responsibility or commitment required, the fewer the numbers of women involved. Women joined meetings and demonstrations in record numbers. In the city of Moscow, they turned out to vote in municipal elections in numbers so large that they surprised observers. But only a few of the factories where women predominated formulated the resolutions on pressing economic and political issues that became ubiquitous in 1917. Women were poorly represented in trade unions and factory shop committees. Despite the high proportion of women in the factory labor force, only 4 percent of the delegates to the First Conference of Factory Committees were women. The same was the case with the soviets, the most important institution of popular democracy. Few women were chosen to run in elections to local soviets, and even fewer were elected even in cases where women numbered over half of the labor force that voted. The highest proportion we know of was in the district of Kineshma, Kostroma, where the textile trade prevailed and the workforce was overwhelming female. There, the March elections yielded 57 deputies, of whom seven (12 percent) were female. In Moscow province and in Nizhnii Novgorod, female representation was no higher than 5 percent. And elsewhere, it was even lower. We do not know these women's names, nor whether they were workers or intellectuals, nor with what party, if any, they identified. Women's low political profile was surely the result of their lack of political experience and long-standing habits of deference, as well as the assumption among women as well as men that active political participation was a male prerogative. The result was that apart from the feminist movement, men far outnumbered women in all the political organizations that struggled for political power and control over everyday life during the events of 1917.

The record of the Bolshevik Party is rather a mixed one in this respect. The party was preoccupied with organizing its forces and seizing power, and had little time or resources to spare for appealing to or organizing workingwomen. It also continued to consider them politically backward, conservative, and unresponsive to party propaganda. The party remained suspicious of efforts to establish separate sections within the party to coordinate work among women. Nevertheless, during 1917 the Bolsheviks paid more attention to working-class women than they had in 1905. This was partly because of the women's increasing activism, and partly because of pressures for the necessity of work among women from a few women Bolsheviks, including Aleksandra Kollontai, who joined the Bolshevik Party in 1915. The party agreed to revive *Rabotnitsa*, which appeared for the first time on May 10 and continued to publish for the rest of 1917. The paper soon became the unacknowledged center for Bolshevik work among women, organizing meetings, setting up a school for agitators, or attempting to popularize Bolshevik positions. These efforts did not succeed in drawing women into the Bolshevik Party. Membership grew dramatically during 1917, but the proportion of women dropped to around 2 percent. But they did succeed in earning women's support for party positions. The Bolshevik slogan, "Peace, land, bread," spoke directly to women's concerns. At meetings and demonstrations that attracted hundreds of women workers and on the pages of *Rabotnitsa*, organizers pointed out the reasons for the continuing suffering of lower-class women—the war and high prices—and promised to end them when the Bolsheviks came to power.

On 23 and 24 October 1917, the Petrograd Bolsheviks overthrew the provisional government in the name of a government of Soviets, and after several weeks assumed power in Moscow and other cities of Central and Northern Russia. One of the first acts of the new Soviet government was a decree on peace. In December it called a halt to fighting and demobilized the army. The Germans continued to occupy the western borderlands of the former czarist empire. On 5 March 1918, after considerable argument within the party, the government signed the humiliating Treaty of Brest-Litovsk, which ceded these lands to the Germans, including Ukraine, the empire's breadbasket. However, the revolution brought neither peace nor bread. From the outset, the new government faced armed opposition from within and without. National resistance and armed challenges by the parties excluded from power were supported by money and troops from Russia's former wartime allies, Great Britain, France, and the United States. The civil war continued until late in 1920. Men went off to war voluntarily or were conscripted by the Reds (the Bolsheviks) or their opponents, the Whites. About 1 million men perished in the civil war, in addition to the 2.5 million lost on the battlefields of World War I. The economy disintegrated almost completely. The food situation, critical at the time of the Bolshevik takeover, became catastrophic for urban dwellers. Many women were left to fend for themselves in desperate circumstances. Their men dead or off fighting in the civil war, women worked for wages all day, then searched for food and scrounged for fuel at night. People starved to death or froze. Epidemic diseases killed millions, typhus alone taking the lives of 1.5 million people between 1918 and 1919. Substantial numbers of urban inhabitants escaped back to their villages. By the end of the civil war, Moscow had lost half of its population, Petrograd, two-thirds. Millions of homeless children wandered the streets, their parents dead or unable to care for them. The Bolsheviks won the civil war, but for many lower-class women, the price seemed far too high.

In these grim circumstances, the Bolsheviks first attempted to carry out a vision of social transformation that included the emancipation of women. Although prerevolutionary feminism disappeared as an independent political and intellectual current after the revolution, a Bolshevik variety of feminism became part of the political discourse. The Bolsheviks proposed to equalize relations between the sexes by entrusting household tasks to paid workers, thus freeing women to become full and equal participants in waged labor. The party leader, V.I. Lenin, was particularly emphatic about the need to relieve women of household chores so they could participate in socially useful production. "Petty housework crushes, strangles, stultifies, and degrades" a woman, he wrote, chaining her to the kitchen and to the nursery and wasting her labor on "barbarously unproductive, petty, nerve-wracking, stultifying, and crushing drudgery." No longer needing to exchange their domestic and sexual services for men's financial support, women would encounter men as equals. Eventually, the family itself would wither away. However, during the civil war, the only real changes the new government could initiate were legal and organizational. In 1918, the government produced a family code that was extraordinarily advanced for its time. The code equalized women's status with men's, removed marriage from the hands of the Orthodox

Church, allowed a marrying couple to choose either the husband's or the wife's surname, and granted illegitimate children the same legal rights as legitimate ones. Divorce, virtually impossible in the czarist period, became easily obtainable at the request of either spouse. In 1920 abortion became legal if performed by a physician. The revolution also brought new opportunities for lower-class women to join and speak on their own behalf. In November 1918, the first All-Russian Conference of Workingwomen took place, organized by Aleksandra Kollontai and Inessa Armand. It attracted 1,147 women, far more than the 300 that organizers expected. Women's emancipation was a crucial component of socialism, the organizers reiterated. Armand lectured about the need to set up state-sponsored nurseries, laundries, and kitchens in order to free women to participate in public life. In August 1919, the Central Committee of the Communist Party granted permission for the formation of a *Zhenotde* (Women's Bureau) to coordinate the party's work among women. Inessa Armand, more moderate than Kollontai, was designated its first director. The party conceived of the Zhenotdel as an agency to mobilize women to support its objectives and to inform women of their new rights. It was to be a transmission belt, from the top downwards. In fact, it became far more. After the civil war had ended, the Zhenotdel sought to mobilize women on their own behalf. Despite a perpetual shortage of funds, the Zhenotdel did its best to establish a basis for women's liberation by setting up childcare centers, communal dining halls, and other services. Factory women, selected as delegates to the Zhenotdel, temporarily left the workplace to gain the political experience that would enable them to become more active in their local soviets, trade unions, and party organizations. Delegates attended literacy classes and meetings where they heard reports on political issues and learned how to organize facilities for workingwomen, such as factory day care centers. After three to six months, the delegate would return to full-time factory work, report on her experiences to her female coworkers, and be replaced by a new delegate. In this way, the Zhenotdel broadened the horizons of millions of women and encouraged them to take active part in political life.

But these waves of change encountered an undertow of conservatism from the first. Many Bolshevik cadres resisted women's emancipation and barely concealed their contempt for the Zhenotdel. Men resented working under women's direction and opposed their wives' taking responsibilities that might deprive the men of domestic comforts. Trade unions often disliked cooperating with the Zhenotdel or providing facilities for its meetings. In general, party bureaucrats tended to make work among women a very low priority or to dismiss it altogether. Because of this, the work of the Zhenotdel became increasingly isolated from the rest of party activity, inadvertently creating the separatism that party members had feared all along. The Zhenotdel was further weakened by the loss of its two most capable leaders. Inessa Armand died in a cholera epidemic at the end of September 1920. She was replaced by Aleksandra Kollontai, but Kollontai served only briefly. In March 1921 she spoke out on behalf of the Workers' Opposition, a faction of the Bolshevik Party that criticized it for losing touch with the masses, and proposed empowering workers by putting their trade unions in charge of the economy and industry. After the Workers' Opposition platform was decisively voted down at a party congress, Kollontai withdrew from political life. She was appointed advisor to the

Soviet legation in Norway and became ambassador in 1924. Her ideas came increasingly under attack, supposedly because she taught that having sex was like drinking a glass of water to satisfy one's thirst. This "glass of water" theory, a parody of Kollontai's thought, nevertheless remained identified with her ideas for years and served to discredit them and destroy their capacity to inspire women with a vision of their own emancipation. Postrevolutionary culture also undermined efforts to restructure gender roles by treating the proletariat as generically male. In the decade following the revolution, poster artists subtly reinscribed gender differences in revolutionary iconography by showing a distinct preference for the male form when they depicted the new proletarian hero who personified the Bolshevik regime. When artists did portray women, the women figured as helpers of men, unless the poster was specifically designed for a female audience. The attitude toward women of the Proletkult verged on hostility. An umbrella organization for working-class cultural groups between 1917 and 1921, the Proletkult attempted to devise new forms of art and culture that would reflect the spirit of the triumphant proletariat. Its artists and writers reinforced the image of the working class and its institutions as male, while they relegated women to the family. For them, as for much of the Bolshevik leadership, women's "backwardness" and their power in the family constituted a threat to the revolution. Even the Zhenotdel speakers avoided challenges to women's traditional roles when they addressed audiences of lower-class women, despite their devotion to the ideal of a genuinely emancipated woman.

Lower-class women themselves often showed little enthusiasm for their own emancipation, at least as they experienced it during the first decade of the Soviet regime. The revolution in many ways worsened their lot. The deaths of millions of men deprived them of husbands and lovers and destroyed their fragile family economies. Public dining rooms, childcare centers, and other state-sponsored efforts to assume domestic functions were miserable affairs, crippled by the terrible material scarcity of the civil war years, as well as by their ad hoc nature. After the civil war was over, women encountered difficulty finding or keeping work. Demobilization brought the return of millions of male workers who expected and received their previous positions. In 1921 Lenin declared a new economic policy that restored market relations on a small scale, in an attempt to restart a ruined economy and win back a peasantry seriously alienated by civil war grain requisitions. The effect upon women was mainly negative. State spending was strictly curtailed, cutting back public day care centers and other institutions for children, and leaving their largely female staffs without work. Factories and plants, now required to account for their costs, preferred hiring men over women, because women might require costly maternity leave and daycare centers for their infants. Despite decrees that forbade it, factory managers dismissed pregnant and nursing women on leave; they used laws banning night work for women as an excuse to lay off women workers. Unemployment escalated, and one-third to one-half of the hundreds of thousands of workers who lost their jobs were women. Moreover, the official figures on female unemployment did not include women seeking jobs for the first time. With no other recourse, thousands of women turned to prostitution to support themselves and their families.

Family instability compounded women's economic problems. In the period after the revolution, millions of Russians availed themselves of the new opportunity for easy divorce. In the early 1920s, 14 percent of Soviet marriages ended in divorce, twice as many as in Germany and almost three times as many as in France, which had the next highest levels. Divorce was heavily concentrated in urban areas: in 1926 there was one divorce for every two marriages in Moscow. When a couple with children divorced, it was left to the courts to determine the amount of child support. What kind of settlement could a court award when a man was seeking to end his fourth or fifth marriage? Reports circulated of men marrying and divorcing as many as fifteen times, leaving ex-wives and their children to fend for themselves. Unregistered unions had also become commonplace; if the woman bore a child, she had no legal means to obtain support from its father. In peasant villages, where the patriarchal family remained the basis of production, efforts to liberate women encountered fierce resistance from men and foundered on the lack of economic alternatives. How could a peasant household provide child support to the divorced wife of one of its members, when household property was collective and consisted mainly of land and a cow or sheep? How was a woman on her own to earn her livelihood in the village? To the many women more victimized than liberated by social change, promises of sexual equality rang hollow.

In 1925–26, working-class and peasant women articulated their dissatisfaction with the "new morality" in nationwide debates over a new Family Code. The code proposed to permit divorce at the request of either of the partners, even if the other opposed it; at the same time, it offered women in unregistered unions the same legal protections as women in registered marriages. Most of the working-class and peasant women who expressed their opinions offered a trenchant critique of the cost to women of family instability and male irresponsibility. Recognizing that, at least at present, women with children were in no position to enjoy sexual freedom, they demanded stricter rather than more lenient divorce laws. In the words of one working-class woman, "Women, in the majority of cases, are more backward, less skilled and therefore less independent than men. . . . To marry, bear children and to be enslaved by the kitchen and then to be thrown aside by your husband—this is very painful for women. This is why I am against easy divorce." Women pointed out how the benefits working men enjoyed might actually harm their wives: often men who took advantage of the opportunities that the revolution offered began to regard their wives as backward. One woman factory worker put it this way: "When you are working in a factory, you note a very unpleasant picture. As long as a guy doesn't participate in political work, he works and respects his wife as he should. But just a little promotion and already something stands between them. He begins to stay away from his family and his wife, already she doesn't please him." Another woman agreed: "I can't forgive a man who lives with a woman twenty years, has five kids, and then decides his wife no longer pleases him. Why did she please him before, but now she doesn't? Shame on you, comrade men!" She castigated men who betrayed their wives and claimed they were in love with someone else. "This isn't love," she declared, "This is swinishness!" Many of the women argued for a more serious and responsible approach to marriage and a much more restrictive approach to divorce. Rather than ensuring women's sexual freedom, they wanted to reduce the freedom of men. Here, their views seemed directly to contradict those of Aleksandra Kollontai, Bolshevism's foremost feminist theorist. Having read an arti-

cle by Kollontai in her local newspaper, a Zhenotdel worker from a rural area took issue with her:

> It seems to me that her view is directed toward the destruction of the family. She proposes "free love" and "free union." Her opinion is that the spiritual life of a person, insofar as it is vast and complex, cannot be satisfied by union with one, but that a person needs several "partners" . . . In our opinion in the countryside, this is simply called debauchery.

Regarding alimony or dependence upon a man as demeaning for women, Kollontai developed a plan to ensure them other means of support. She proposed to create a general fund, levying a tax of two rubles that would be used to support single mothers and to set up nurseries and children's homes. The plan, which would have weighed most heavily on the conservative peasantry, attracted few adherents. A more straightforward solution was to put the responsibility for their sexual behavior squarely on individual men. As one woman put it succinctly: "If you like tobogganing, you have to drag your sled uphill"

These exchanges occurred a year or two after Lenin's death in January 1924; a few years later, Joseph Stalin triumphed over his rivals for political power. The women's views resemble the ideas of party conservatives, who viewed the sexual question as marginal and emphasized disciplined and responsible family sex. In the words of the physician Aron Zalkind, a leading proponent of the view that sexual energy was limited and should be harnessed to serve society, "I am very much afraid that with the cult of 'winged Eros' we will build aeroplanes very badly." It is likely that lower-class women's views strengthened the tendency to marginalize Kollontai and to limit wide-ranging theoretical explorations of sexuality and sexual morality. At the same time, the fact that lower-class women articulated conservative views in public forums designed to elicit their opinion on the most pressing questions of everyday life in itself represented a triumph of the revolution; such forums would cease after Stalin's victory. Disagreements over such key issues as sex and marriage between the leading Bolshevik advocate for women and the lower-class women she had done so much to empower reminds us of the experience of earlier generations of radical women, who similarly articulated a vision of liberation that had far more in common with their own experience and needs than with the experience and needs of their lower-class sisters. These disparate visions are an important aspect of the history of the Russian revolutionary movement; they remain one of the many tragedies of the Bolshevik Revolution.

Bibliography

Sources

Armand, Inessa Stéphane, *Stat'i, rechi, pis'ma* (Articles, Discourses, Letters), Moscow: Politizdat, 1975

Balabanoff, Angelica, *Die Zimmerwalder Bewegung, 1914–1919*, Leipzig: Hirschfeld, 1928; reprint, Frankfurt: Neue Kritik, 1969

Kollontai, Alexandra, *The Autobiography of a Sexually Emancipated Communist Woman*, translated by Salvator Attanasio, New York: Herder and Herder, 1971

Kollontai, Alexandra, *Autobiographie: Suivie du roman "Les amours des abeilles travailleuses,"* edited and translated by Christine Fauré and Nicolas Lazarevitch, Paris: Berg-Belibaste, 1976

Kollontai, Alexandra, *Iz moei zhizni i raboty* (On My Life and My Work), Moscow: Sov. Rossiia, 1974

Kollontai, Alexandra, *Marxisme et révolution sexuelle*, translated by Claude Ligny, edited by Judith Stora-Sandor, Paris: Maspero, 1973 (an anthology)

Kollontai, Alexandra, *Polozhenie zhenschiny v evoliutsii khoziaistva*; as *Conférences sur la libération des femmes*, edited by Jacqueline Heinen, Paris: La Brèche, 1978

Kollontai, Alexandra, *Rabochaia oppozitsiia*, Moscow: 8-ia Gos. Tip., 1921

Kollontai, Alexandra, *Selected Writings of Alexandra Kollontai*, translated and introduced by Alix Holt, Westport, Connecticut Hill, and London: Allison and Busby, 1977

Kommunisticheskaia partiia i organizatsiia rabotnits (The Communist Party and the Organization of Women Workers), Moscow: Kn-vo "Kommunist," 1919

Reference Works

Bergman, Jay, *Vera Zasulich: A Biography*, Stanford, California: Stanford University Press, 1983

Bobroff, Anne, "The Bolsheviks and Working Women, 1905–1920," *Soviet Studies* 26 (1974)

Body, Marcel, "Alexandra Kollontai," *Preuves* 2, no. 14 (April 1952)

Bonnell, Victoria, "The Representation of Women in Early Soviet Political Art," *Russian Review* 50, no. 3 (July 1991)

Broido, Vera, *Apostles into Terrorists: Women and the Revolutionary Movement in the Russia of Alexander II*, New York: Viking Press, 1977; London: Temple Smith, 1978

Buckley, Mary, *Women and Ideology in the Soviet Union*, Ann Arbor: University of Michigan Press, and Hemel Hempstead, Hertfordshire: Harvester Wheatsheaf, 1989

Camparini, Aurelia, *Questione femminile e Terza Internazionale*, Bari, Italy: De Donato, 1978

Clements, Barbara Evans, "The Birth of the New Soviet Woman," in *Bolshevik Culture: Experiment and Order in the Russian Revolution*, edited by Abbott Gleason, Peter Kenez, and Richard Stites, Bloomington: Indiana University Press, 1985

Clements, Barbara Evans, *Bolshevik Feminist: The Life of Aleksandra Kollontai*, Bloomington: Indiana University Press, 1979

Clements, Barbara Evans, "Working-Class and Peasant Women in the Russian Revolution, 1917–1923," *Signs* 8 (1982)

Clements, Barbara Evans, Barbara Alpern Engel, and Christine D. Worobec, editors, *Russia's Women: Accommodation, Resistance, Transformation*, Berkeley: University of California Press, 1991

Donald, Moira, "Bolshevik Activity amongst the Working Women of Petrograd in 1917," *International Journal of Social History* 27, no. 2 (1982)

Edmondson, Linda Harriet, *Feminism in Russia, 1900–17*, Stanford, California: Stanford University Press, 1984

Efremova, [no first name on record], "Starshaia sestra Soph'i Kovalevskoi (The Elder Sister of Sophie Kovalevskaia)," *Voprosy istorii* (Questions of History) 6 (1994)

Elwood, Ralph Carter, *Inessa Armand: Revolutionary and Feminist*, Cambridge and New York: Cambridge University Press, 1992

Engel, Barbara Alpern, *Between the Fields and the City: Women, Work, and Family in Russia, 1861–1914*, Cambridge and New York: Cambridge University Press, 1994

Engel, Barbara Alpern, *Mothers and Daughters: Women of the Intelligentsia in Nineteenth-Century Russia*, Cambridge and New York: Cambridge University Press, 1983

Engel, Barbara Alpern, "Women, Men, and the Languages of Peasant Resistance, 1870–1907," in *Cultures in Flux: Lower-Class Values, Practices, and Resistance in Late Imperial Russia*, edited by

Stephen Frank and Mark D. Steinberg, Princeton, New Jersey: Princeton University Press, 1994

Engel, Barbara Alpern, and Clifford Rosenthal, editors and translators, *Five Sisters: Women against the Tsar*, New York: Knopf, 1975; London: Weidenfeld and Nicolson, 1976

Engelstein, Laura, *The Keys to Happiness: Sex and the Search for Modernity in Fin-de-Siècle Russia*, Ithaca, New York: Cornell University Press, 1992

Farnsworth, Beatrice, *Alexandra Kollontai: Socialism, Feminism, and the Bolshevik Revolution*, Stanford, California: Stanford University Press, 1980

Fauré, Christine, *Terre, terreur, liberté*, Paris: Maspero, 1979

Fauré, Christine, editor, *Quatre femmes terroristes contre le tsar*, translated by Hélène Châtelain, Paris: Maspero, 1978

Fauré, Christine, "The Utopia of the 'New Woman' in the Work of Alexandra Kollontai and Its Impact on the French Feminist and Communist Press," in *Women in Culture and Politics: A Century of Change*, edited by Judith Friedlander et al., Bloomington: Indiana University Press, 1986

Fieseler, Beate, "Russische Sozialdemokratinnen, 1890–1917," *Internationale Wissenschaftliche Korrespondenz zur Geschichte der deutschen Arbeiterbewegung* 21, no. 3 (1985)

Fréville, Jean, *Une grande figure de la révolution russe: Inessa Armand*, Paris: Éditions Sociales, 1957

Fréville, Jean, "Portrait d'Inessa Armand, révolutionnaire," *La nouvelle critique* 87–88 (1957)

Goldman, Wendy Z., *Women, the State, and Revolution: Soviet Family Policy and Social Life, 1917–1936*, Cambridge and New York: Cambridge University Press, 1993

Grishina, Z.B., "Dvizhenie za politicheskoe ravnopravie zhenshchin v gody pervoi rossiiskoi revoliutsii (The Movement for Political Equality for Women in the Years of the First Russian Revolution)," *Vestnik Moskovskogo Universiteta* (University of Moscow Messenger), series 8, *Istoriia* (History) (1982)

Hayden, Carol, "The Zhenotdel and the Bolshevik Party," *Russian History* 3, no. 2 (1976)

Johanson, Christine, *Women's Struggle for Higher Education in Russia, 1855–1900*, Kingston, Ontario: McGill-Queen's University Press, 1987

Kaplan, Temma, "Women in Communal Strikes in the Crisis of 1917–1922," in *Becoming Visible: Women in European History*, 2nd edition, edited by Renate Bridenthal, Claudia Koonz, and Susan Mosher Stuard, Boston: Houghton-Mifflin, 1987

Knight, Amy, "Female Terrorists in the Russian Socialist Revolutionary Party," *Russian Review* 38 (1979)

Koblitz, Ann Hibner, *A Convergence of Lives: Sofia Kovalevskaïa: Scientist, Writer, Revolutionary*, Boston: Birkhäuser, 1983

Lapidus, Gail Warshofsky, *Women in Soviet Society: Equality, Development, and Social Change*, Berkeley: University of California Press, 1978

Leiberov, A.I., "Nachalo rabotnitsy (The Debut of the Woman Worker)," *Voprosy istorii* (Questions of History) 9 (1985)

Lenczyc, Henryk, "Alexandra Kollontai," *Cahiers du monde russe et soviétique* 14, nos. 1–2 (1973)

Lindenmayr, Adele, "Public Lives, Private Virtues: Women in Russian Charity, 1762–1914," *Signs* 18, no. 3 (Spring 1993)

Massell, Gregory J., *The Surrogate Proletariat: Moslem Women and Revolutionary Strategies in Soviet Central Asia, 1919–1929*, Princeton, New Jersey: Princeton University Press, 1974

McNeal, Robert Hatch, *Bride of the Revolution: Krupskaya and Lenin*, Ann Arbor: University of Michigan Press, and London: Gollancz, 1972

McNeal, Robert Hatch, "Women in the Russian Radical Movement," *Journal of Social History* 2 (1971–72)

McReynolds, Louise, "Female Journalists in Prerevolutionary Russia," *Journalism History* 14, no. 4 (1987)

Meehan-Waters, Brenda, "From Contemplative Practice to Charitable Activity: Russian Women's Religious Communities and the Development of Charitable Work, 1861–1917," in *Lady Bountiful Revisited: Women, Philanthropy, and Power*, edited by Kathleen D. McCarthy, New Brunswick, New Jersey Rutgers University Press, 1990

Pavliuchenko, Z.A., *Zhenshchiny v russkom osvoboditel'nom dvizhenii: Ot Marii Volonskoi do Very Figner* (Women in the Russian Liberation Movement: From Mariia Volonskaia to Vera Figner), Moscow: "Mysl'," 1988

Pelletier, Madeleine, *Mon voyage aventureux en Russie communiste*, Paris: Giard, 1922

Ruane, Christine, "The Vestal Virgins of St. Petersburg: School Teachers and the 1897 Marriage Ban," *Russian Review* 50, no. 2 (April 1991)

Schiavi, Alessandro, *Anna Kuliscioff*, Rome: Opere Nuove, 1955

Schmieding, Walther, *Aufstand der Tochter: Russische Revolutionärinnen im 19. Jahrhundert*, Munich: Kindler, 1979

Smith, Steve, "Class and Gender: Women's Strikes in St. Petersburg, 1895–1917, and in Shanghai, 1895–1927," *Social History* 19, no. 2 (May 1994)

Steinberg, Isaac Nachman, *Spiridonova: Revolutionary Terrorist*, translated and edited by Gwenda David and Eric Mosbacher, London: Methuen, 1935

Stites, Richard, *The Women's Liberation Movement in Russia: Feminism, Nihilism, and Bolshevism, 1860–1930*, Princeton, New Jersey: Princeton University Press, 1978

Tishkin, Grigorii A., "Bestyzhevki v bor'be za idealy leninskoi partii (The Partisans of Bestyzhev in the Fight for the Ideals of the Lenin Party)," *Vestnik Leningradskogo universiteta: Seria istorii, iazyka i literatury* (Leningrad University Messenger: Series History, Language, and Literature) (1984)

Tishkin, Grigorii A., *Zhenskii vopros v Rossii v 50–60-e gody XIX v.* (The Woman Question in the 1850s), Leningrad: Izd-vo Leningradskogo Universita, 1984

Venturi, Franco, "Anna Kuliscioff e la sua attivita rivoluzionaria in Russia," *Movimento operaio* 4, no. 1 (1952)

Venturi, Franco, *Il populismo russo*, 2 vols., Turin, Italy: Einaudi, 1952; as *Roots of Revolution: A History of the Populist and Socialist Movements in Nineteenth-Century Russia*, translated by Francis Haskell, New York: Knopf, 1960

Wagner, William, "The Trojan Mare: Women's Rights and Civil Rights in Late Imperial Russia," in *Civil Rights in Imperial Russia*, edited by Olga Crisp and Linda Harriet Edmondson, Oxford: Clarendon Press, and New York: Oxford University Press, 1989

Waters, Elizabeth, "The Female Form in Soviet Political Iconography, 1917–1932," in *Russia's Women: Accommodation, Resistance, Transformation*, edited by Barbara Evans Clements, Barbara Alpern Engel, and Christine D. Worobec, Berkeley: University of California Press, 1991

Waters, Elizabeth, "In the Shadow of the Comintern: The Communist Women's Movement, 1920–1943," in *Promissory Notes: Women in the Transition to Socialism*, edited by Sonia Kruks, Rayna Rapp, and Marilyn Blatt Young, New York: Monthly Review Press, 1989

Waters, Elizabeth, "Teaching Mothercraft in Post-Revolutionary Russia," *Australian Slavonic and East European Studies* 1, no. 2 (July 1987)

WOMEN IN THE GERMAN REVOLUTION

Rosa Luxemburg and the Workers' Councils

CLAUDIE WEILL

THE DAY OF 9 November 1918 marked a watershed in 20th-century German history. In Berlin on that day, two rival social-democrat groups proclaimed, almost simultaneously, the German Republic and the German Socialist Republic. The political expression of the workers' movement was, indeed, divided at the end of World War I. Those who had supported the conservative Burgfrieden (Holy Union) regrouped under the banner of the Mehrheitssozialdemokratische Partei (MSP; Social Democratic Majority Party), while those who had opposed the war and had been excluded from the Sozialdemokratische Partei Deutschlands (SPD; Social Democratic Party of Germany) on that account had created a new party in 1917. This latter opposition party was the Unabhängige Sozialdemokratische Partei Deutschlands (USPD; Independent Social Democratic Party of Germany), which brought together the Left—that is to say, the Spartakusbund (Spartacus Group) and the Revolutionäre Obleute (Revolutionary Shop Stewards), an opposition labor organization that had taken root during the war, primarily among metalworkers. Further divisions occurred on 31 December 1918, when the Spartacists withdrew from the USPD to form the Kommunistische Partei Deutschland (KPD; German Communist Party).

The revolutionary workers' movement, which voiced its concerns in and through the workers' councils that were emerging in October and November 1918, sought to consolidate its ranks by the creation on 10 November of a Rat der Volksbeaustragte (Council of the People's Commissars), jointly composed of three representatives of the Majority Socialists and the same number of Independent Socialists. This organization was flanked by a provisional executive council, the extended Vollzugsrat (Executive Council) of Berlin, eventually to be replaced by a central council elected by the first Ratekongress (Congress of Councils) representing the entire Reich at its December session in Berlin. For want of a clear division of powers, the prerogatives of the Executive Council were scaled back by the Council of the People's Commissars. The USPD refused to be part of the central council and then also resigned from the Council of the People's Commissars. Hopes for unification of the two groups thus gave way to armed confrontation, and the revolutionary movement was suppressed by the Majority Socialists, supported by the army.

However, the civil war by no means ended when the Spartacist uprising was crushed at the end of the Bloody Week of January 1919 in Berlin. Other key events in the conflict included the assassination of the Independent Socialist revolutionary organizer Kurt Eisner in Munich (21 February 1919), the abolition of the Raterepublik (Republics of the Councils) of Bremen and Munich, and the suppression of the great strikes of 1919, particularly those aiming to socialize the industries in the Ruhr basin, Berlin, and central Germany. These upheavals were only one aspect of the German Revolution, which would continue until 1923.

The other salient political feature of the revolution was the faltering experiment of the council system, which came to an end with the Second Congress of Councils, held in April 1919 with little commotion, and the fall of the Second Republic of the Councils of Munich at the end of May 1919. These few months in Germany were marked by the uncertainties of what in Russia between February and October 1917 had been called the "double power," that is to say, direct democracy (with the attendant risks of corporatism) and representative democracy (dependent on the party system).

Women are strangely absent from accounts of the German Revolution of 1918–19. Correspondingly, in the history of socialist women in Germany, the "November Revolution" is accorded only minimal attention. Are such absences justified? In a speech delivered on 29 November 1919 at a women's conference in Leipzig, the political activist Toni Sender declared:

> We must conclude that until now, women have hardly played any role in the councils. In the workers' councils as such, there were only a very small number of women representatives, having no relationship whatsoever with the number of active women, those who practiced a profession, present in the most diverse enterprises, especially at the time when the councils were established early in the revolution. But above all in the executive councils: finding a female delegate was strictly the exception there.

Women's lack of representation in the soldiers' councils is logical enough. However, surprisingly few women were elected to the workers' councils in November 1918: there were 19 women (of these, it is known that eight were unmarried and five were married women, two of them the wives of permanent union members) out of the 370 members of the Workers' Council of Greater Stuttgart (the city where Klara Zetkin, the pioneer of the women's socialist movement, resided). There were two women in the Workers' Council of Göppingen in Württemberg, and there were also two women in Braunschweig in the first council, but they were not reelected to the second council, since it was felt that women had been overrepresented in the first. The Spartacists Auguste Lewinsohn, Frida Düwell (in Hamburg), Valeska Meinig and Herta Gefke (in Stettin), Rosa Morgner-Hollein (in central Germany), and Roberta Gropper (in Ulm) were apparently part of the councils. Finally, among the Independent Socialists and members of other parties on the Left, Toni Sender was a member of the Workers' Council of Frankfurt-am-Main, while Anita Augspurg and Lida Gustava Heymann gave speeches in the debates of the Second Congress of the Councils of Bavaria (March 1919). There was thus a mere sprinkling of women in these revolutionary organizations.

Yet, in innumerable branches of industry, women had taken the place of men who had left for the front, and women should therefore have had a far greater degree of representation in the councils, as Sender emphasized in her speech. Furthermore, women had been very much present during the rise of the first workers' councils in Germany in the form of strike committees, as in Russia in 1905. For example, Cläre Derfert-Casper was included in the 11-member workers' council that was established during the great strike of January 1918 in Berlin, with the slogan "Peace, liberty, bread." In Hanover around the same time, there were more women than men among the strike leaders. One may wonder whether women participated in the workers' councils elections in November 1918, and, if so, whether they voted mostly for their male colleagues. The outbreak of the revolution, the circumstances of the emergence of the workers' councils, and the manner in which delegates were elected are all likely to furnish parts of the explanation for women's scant representation on the councils.

The first stirrings of the revolution occurred in November 1918 in the ports, when sailors in Wilhelmshaven were put on alert for an intervention against the English fleet and mutinied. The arrest of the mutineers unleashed an uprising in Kiel (with women and children who participated in the great demonstration among the victims of the repression), and the conflict then spread to a large part of the Reich in a similar manner: soldiers and sailors would arrive in a town, neutralize the station guard, occupy public buildings, and free political prisoners. News of the Kiel revolt spurred the Revolutionary Shop Stewards and Spartacists to take the initiative in other areas. The uprising in Munich, anticipated by Karl Eisner, an independent socialist and a pacifist, which declared Bavaria a Socialist Republic, was actually precipitated by the capitulation of Austria—just across the border from Munich—rather than the Kiel uprising.

Soldiers contributed widely to the spread of the revolution, thus giving the impression that it had originated with the military. Inevitably, the involvement of soldiers reduced the participation of women. The soldiers created their own councils and fostered the emergence of their civilian equivalent, the workers'

councils. The coordination of the councils at a local level varied from place to place. In some instances the soldiers' and workers' councils merged; elsewhere, jointly composed executive committees included soldiers as collaborating parties, which allowed the soldiers' councils to maintain their autonomy.

The electoral system in the workers' councils contributed to the weak representation of women. The important role played by the political parties, and, consequently, their central and local permanent members, was yet another determining factor. As has generally been the case throughout history, the hierarchical organization of political parties has not been conducive to the presence of women at the higher levels. This was especially true for the MSP, which, in order to avoid being overrun by the revolution and lose control of the masses (from which it derived its legitimacy but which it feared at the same time) imposed parity representation of the parties on the councils wherever the MSP was in the minority and challenged the principle of parity elsewhere. However, in each of the four possible types of elections, there was in principle some room to maneuver that could have benefited women's representation.

1. In some cases, the members of the workers' council were jointly designated by the socialist parties (MSP, USPD) or after negotiations with the labor unions. Membership on the committee was confirmed by acclamation during a large meeting called by the parties.

2. In the large cities, where the Left was more solidly established, elections were held on the shop floor. The composition of the electorate was a matter for debate: should it comprise all the workers of the company or only those who were organized—that is to say, the class-in-itself or the class-for-itself? Since a party-membership card or union card was perceived as an entry ticket into the "legitimate" proletariat, those who were not part of an organization—especially women and youth—were automatically excluded, unless the parties recruited and enrolled members on the spot outside the polling places. In turn, the general assembly of workers' councils (or the Great Workers' Council) coming out of these elections elected an executive committee (or action committee) that had between five and 20 members. After 9 November 18 this pattern replaced the structure of the workers' councils as they had emerged spontaneously.

3. In some cases, elections took place by district, according to one's address. This procedure was frequently used in places where the MSP held a majority. Thus, the electorate was defined according to social criteria similar to those that had been adopted for the elections to the constituent assembly in Russia, the vote being reserved for "those who live off their own labor." In Braunschweig, for example, only those with an annual income of less than 1,000 marks were eligible to vote.

4. In rural communities or small towns, in those cases when elections actually took place, a committee was designated after 9 November during a large meeting, upon the suggestion of the local leaders of the parties and/or the union.

The jointly elected workers' councils imagined themselves to be more representative of their organizations (the parties and unions) than of the electorate. During the war, women's participation in such organizations did not keep pace with their presence in the workforce nor with the largely spontaneous upsurge in radicalism among women, which was not measurable in terms of enrollment and did not result from slogans coming from the party organizations. Even before, but above all after 1914, the SPD's efforts to curtail women's organizational autonomy were a decisive factor in this area. In some locales, the distribution of women in particular branches of production also helps to explain their limited participation in the councils. In addition, elections held by the company excluded housewives and the unemployed. The USPD pleaded in vain for a broadening of the electoral base.

Women thus had to make do with serving in support groups for the councils in the three main areas to which their immediate action happened to be limited: food supplies, demobilization, and maintaining order. The women who contributed their energies to the movement were therefore mainly involved in organizational and administrative tasks, the securing of food staples, and the provision of lodging to those soldiers who had been demobilized or soon would be.

Women's weak representation on the councils undoubtedly reinforced their demobilization, spurred by two measures taken immediately after the Republic was proclaimed on 9 November 1918. Without consulting the interested parties, laws to protect women workers were reestablished after having been suspended during the war, when manual workers were needed in industry. Following the demobilization of German troops, the departure of war prisoners did not ease widespread male unemployment, and women were thus gradually forced from their jobs, in a pattern that was ratified a posteriori by the "demobilization regulations." Women were sometimes laid off against the recommendation of their bosses, who had come to appreciate their work during the war—and who had benefited from paying them lower salaries than men. Women who had entered the workforce during the war were the first to be affected by the dismissals, which successively targeted: (1) women whose husbands drew a salary; (2) single women and girls; (3) women and girls who were financially responsible for only one or two people; and, finally, (4) all women and girls. In her 29 November 1919 speech at the Leipzig women's conference, Toni Sender invoked these layoffs to demonstrate the disastrous consequences of women's absence from the councils: if women had been represented, they could have tried to make the councils understand the injustice of these measures, which the male delegates, to whom such priorities seemed "natural," were unlikely to question spontaneously.

Although their presence on the councils was so limited as to be insignificant, large numbers of women took part in both the wartime hunger rebellions and the strikes demanding bread and peace, the principal demands of the revolution. On 4 November 1918 in Stuttgart, a crowd of young men and workingwomen who were striking and demonstrating overwhelmed the adult men present there. Indeed, women throughout Germany were involved in the demonstrations of 9 November: in Hamburg, Hanover, Braunschweig, Munich, the Ruhr Basin, and Berlin. They participated in the street fights of January 1919 in Berlin and in the armed struggles. Here, too, women almost invariably served as support troops. An exception to this was Cläre Derfert-

Casper, who contributed by furnishing arms she had acquired from arsenal workers to the Berliners. Women brought food to the fighters, served as couriers or nurses, transported arms and munitions concealed in baskets, beneath their aprons, or in baby carriages, and helped to set up barricades. In short, they contributed to the defense of the ephemeral Räterepublik (Republics of Councils) and participated in the movements for the socialization of industry.

Indeed, beyond the immediate tasks they had assumed, the councils aspired to the realization of a more ambitious program of democratization, including democratization of the state, which, for many, had been achieved with the elections of the National Assembly, fixed by the Congress of Councils on 19 January 1919; democratization of the army, conceived as a suppression of the privileges of the military elite, including a new system for choosing leadership that raised the fears of the ranking elite; and, finally, democratization of the economy, which was less a question of nationalization than socialization, since the workers' councils asked to be given a say in all important decisions affecting companies and their policies. Legislation providing for factory councils, adopted in 1920, represented a partial realization of this latter ambition.

By their very visibility, women labor activists—Luise Zietz, Käte Duncker, Klara Zetkin and, above all, Rosa Luxemburg—were exceptional figures. During the war, those who led the German socialist women's movement for the most part aligned themselves with the USPD.

Through her French mother and, later, her companion Ossip Zetkin, Klara (née Eissner) Zetkin (1857–1933) was in a sense an "existential" internationalist before being one out of political conviction. A teacher by training, Klara spent her twenties in Leipzig and Zurich; during this period she met the Russian revolutionary Ossip Zetkin and came into contact with an older generation of militant German feminists. In 1889 she traveled to Paris to join Ossip Zetkin, who had been expelled from Germany. That year she participated in the founding congress of the Second International and there spoke on behalf of women's concerns. After Ossip Zetkin's death, she returned to Germany and was one of the first women leaders of the SPD. In 1892 she founded and became editor-in-chief of *Die Gleichheit*, which at the time of the Stuttgart Congress of the Second International in 1907 became the press organ for the international socialist women's movement and remained one of the most radical press organs of German social democracy in the climate of censorship that prevailed in the next decades. (She remained editor-in-chief of the newspaper until 1917, when, as a result of the split in the SPD, she lost her editorship to Marie Juchacz.) At the Second International Congress of Socialist Women in Copenhagen in 1910, Klara Zetkin helped to establish an official International Women's Day in March. She was an organizer of the international socialist women's conference against the war held in Bern in 1915 and attended by 70 women from eight nations.

Women such as Klara Zetkin and Rosa Luxemburg played a signficant revolutionary role in the events of 1918–19. For example, Zetkin was one of the speakers during the 9 November demonstration in the courtyard of Stuttgart Castle and helped organize the general strike at Württemberg in the spring of 1919. Despite such actions, however, women in general had difficulty gaining access, if they participated at all, to the First Congress of Councils, which opened in Berlin on 16 December 1918; the number of female delegates was minuscule. Lacking a mandate in due form, neither Rosa Luxemburg nor Karl Liebknecht managed to gain admittance at the congress, even in an advisory capacity. Within the parties, by contrast, women enjoyed some degree of representation: Luise Zietz was a member of the leadership committee of the USPD, while Käte Duncker and Rosa Luxemburg were part of the central committee of the Spartakusbund and then of the KPD, which had 11 and 12 members, respectively. Nevertheless, the KPD was to be a party that had few women overall. Although she had somewhat recovered from an illness and from a period of depression following the defection of her husband, Fritz Zundel, Zetkin did not attend the Berlin founding congress of the KPD in December 1918 and early January 1919. She did not figure in the leadership either, as she was opposed to the schism with the USPD, particularly its Left wing, and accordingly postponed her own membership to the KPD for some time.

Upon her return to Berlin after her release from prison when the revolution broke out in 1918, Luxemburg's aims for publication included a women's supplement to the Spartacist paper, *Die Rote Fahne*, which she wanted Zetkin to edit. Luxemburg pushed Zetkin insistently, first to write an article on women ("it is so important at the present moment, and nobody among us here understands much about it"; letter of 29 November 1918) and then to take responsibility for the women's page. "Let us move on to propaganda among the women! Like yourself, we are convinced of its importance and its urgency." Luxemburg wanted the women's page of the Spartacist paper to be presented more in the style of a leaflet, "short, popular, propagandist, on the tasks of women in the Revolution," than in a theoretical style.

In her 22 November 1918 article in *Die Rote Fahne*, Zetkin called on women to show their gratitude to a revolution that had given them the rights to vote and to stand for election (granted 12 November 1918) without their having had to fight for it. Her counsel, however, was apparently contradictory: according to Zetkin, achieving the right to vote was a victory, but that did not mean that this right should be exercised (despite this pronouncement, incidentally, women voted in far greater numbers than men in January 1919). In Zetkin's revolutionary analysis, sharing power with the bourgeoisie was tantamount to giving up power; therefore, the proletariat could exercise power only if it did not have to share it. Women could best acquit themselves of their debt, Zetkin suggested, through the pursuit of revolutionary action: "Proletarian women helped to lead the first fights of the revolution against the monarchy, the domination of Junkers [nobility] and militarism . . . women are strong enough to stop the wheels of the economic machine if they have sufficient will." "In complete agreement with your point of view," Luxemburg wrote to Zetkin in a short note dated 21 November, the day before Zetkin's article appeared in print.

While she expressed doubts about voting, Zetkin was on the list of the USPD for the elections of the Diet of Württemberg (and she was elected). "[We] demand [that you] be struck from the list [of candidates]" was Luxemburg's message in a telegram (4 January 1919). Luxemburg's demand reflected the directives of the KPD, which had just come out for a boycott of the elections. The party felt that the 19 January election date did not leave sufficient time for the development of the revolution and sufficient radicalization of the Independent Social Demo-

crats. Opposed to the boycott decision herself, Luxemburg tried in a letter of 11 January 1919 to temper her friend's indignation:

> You overestimate the weight of this resolution enormously. . . . Our "defeat" [rejection of the boycott] was merely the victory over a somewhat puerile extremism, in full fermentation, without any subtleties. . . . Don't forget that the Spartacists are to a large extent a new generation, not burdened by the mind-numbing traditions of the "old" party, the party "that has proven itself."

Moreover, the question of the convocation of the National Assembly seemed likely to be swept aside in the onrush of events during the Bloody Week of the Spartacist uprising of January 1919. When she confirmed the need to bypass the political stage in order to reach the economic stage of the revolution, Luxemburg was most specifically in synch with Zetkin.

The relationship between Klara Zetkin and Rosa Luxemburg is rich in significance in terms of both revolutionary politics and women's rights. Born into a Jewish family in Poland in 1871, Luxemburg had obtained German citizenship through an unconsummated marriage in order to be able to militate in the SPD, the party that led the Second International. At one point, Luxemburg claimed to Zetkin (not without a certain false modesty) that she "understood nothing" about propaganda among women. She had never specifically militated for women's rights within the socialist movement: her ambition for universality was an obstacle to specialization in category-specific demands. "I am at home wherever in the world there are clouds, birds, and human tears," she wrote on 16 February 1917 to Mathilde Wurm, who shared her anxiety about the Jews.

Nevertheless, in 1913 Luxembourg was at Zetkin's side during the debates on pacifistic "belly strikes" (women refusing to procreate so as not to give soldiers to the state). She was arrested in February 1915 when, taking advantage of a suspended sentence granted for health reasons, she was on her way to accompany Klara Zetkin to a meeting in preparation for the Bern women's conference. Upon her release from prison in February 1916, a thousand socialist women came to pay homage to Luxemburg, who, although not a militant feminist, was an important symbolic figure for women, and to honor her antiwar activism.

Luxemburg was arrested again in July 1916; she remained in prison in "protective custody" for the rest of the war. During her incarceration she was formally prohibited from engaging in "political" writing and thus had to do it in secret; she expressed herself through letters, most written to women (Klara Zetkin among them). Her correspondence suggests a certain sensitization to women's issues during that time. The letters reveal her image of herself as a woman and especially her image of women in general. She believed that women need not be "propagandist or typist or telephone operator or anything else useful," provided they were "beautiful." In a letter to Sophie Liebknecht invoking the character Irene Forsyte in John Galsworthy's *Forsyte Saga* (1906–21), she wrote: "Beauty is not simply a pretty face but also inner refinement and grace." Luxemburg discerned in her friends the signs of unfulfillment characteristic of women who have reached maturity, "an unspeakable suffering and an inexpressible fear, the fear that the barriers in life had already closed and that [these women] had not touched or tasted real life," "astonishment, worry, groping around, searching, and grievous disappointment" which she refused to call hysteria (letter to

Sophie Liebknecht, 24 November 1917). One may wonder whether these thoughts echo her own frustrations, expressed throughout her correspondence, about having sacrificed her personal life, her relationships with men, motherhood, and serenity in nature, as well as reflections on the excitement of active militancy. Such feelings are clear, for example, in a letter she wrote to Klara Zetkin on 1 July 1917:

> After the war, I will very simply no longer allow you to participate in any session whatsoever and for my part these little meetings will be done with once and for all. There where large things are happening, there where the wind blows in your face, I want to be in the eye of the storm, but I've had it with the daily routine, and you too, no doubt.

Despite her imprisonment during much of the war, Luxemburg was close to those who led category-specific and particularly combative movements during the war, including Karl Liebknecht (who attended a secret youth meeting in Jena in 1916, between his return from the front and his arrest and incarceration for revolutionary activity) and Zetkin, whose broad dissemination of the manifesto adopted at the Bern Conference led to her own arrest. Luxemburg must have become aware during this time of the revolutionary potential these movements represented, perhaps at the same time that she became conscious of her own symbolic value as a militant woman. This consciousness may explain her subsequent insistence to Zetkin that the demobilization of women during the revolution must be stopped.

From the summer of 1918 on, Zetkin expressed her political views in the women's supplement to the *Leipziger Volkszeitung*, where she found a home after having been cast out by *Die Gleichheit*. In the supplement, she developed the theme of the power of the council system and insisted that the proletarian revolution should take the "soviet" form. Luxemburg, too, took a strong stand in favor of the council system, and she gained an awareness of the importance of her role as an emblematic figure for the women's movement.

In 1905 German social democracy had missed out on the experiment of the soviets, or workers' councils, in Russia. An account of that experiment did not appear in Germany until 1907, when an article by Leon Trotsky was published in *Die Neue Zeit*, the theoretical paper of German social democracy that was disseminated well beyond Germany's borders. In fact, the idea of councils was foreign to the party that Luxemburg had founded in 1893 and continued to head, the Socjal-Demokracja Krolestwa Polskiego i Litwy (SDKPiL; Social Democracy of the Kingdom of Poland and Lithuania). This group refused to recognize the workers' councils as organs of the revolutionary movement, considering them to be an archaic form of organization, valid for less-developed Russia, but rendered superfluous by the party organizations in a more evolved Poland. In fact, in Poland the 1905 revolution marked the meeting between the revolutionary workers' movement and the socialist parties. It was also at this time that the party slogans began drawing a widespread following. This public party victory undoubtedly overshadowed the importance of the emerging soviets. In her German writings, notably *Massenstreik, Partei und Gewerkschaften* (1906; *The Mass Strike, the Political Party, and the Trade Union*), drawing on her own observations of the Russian experiment, Luxemburg spoke of workers' committees and the spontaneous creation of

union organizations in the course of the revolution, contrasting these developments to the fetishism of German union organization. However, she did not mention the soviets.

Analyses of Rosa Luxemburg's revolutionary theory and her ideas about democracy have not sufficiently stressed the central importance she granted the councils. After all, in an article in *Die Rote Fahne* of 15 December 1918, she declared: "The Revolution will live without the councils; without the Revolution, the councils are dead." However, in 1918 she also proclaimed (*Die Rote Fahne*, 18 November 1918), aligning herself with Lenin's position, "All power in the hands of the working masses, in the hands of the workers' and soldiers' councils." While it might seem to indicate a political change of heart, the apparent divergence between the statements can be explained by the similarity of forms of the revolutionary movement in Germany (the workers' councils) and Russia (the soviets).

Internationalist that she was, Luxemburg launched a call for the creation of councils in other countries, together with her Spartacist friends Liebknecht, Franz Mehring, and Zetkin—the very same ones with whom she had declared her opposition to the Holy Union in 1914. In addition, in Luxemburg's view these forms of articulation of the collective will, having emerged spontaneously, traced the continuity of the Russian Revolution between 1905 and 1917, the very fact of their their resurgence in 1917–18 in Russia and in Germany being a gauge of their importance. "The workers' and soldiers' councils were therefore organs of the Revolution, agents of the newly created order, those who carried out what the laboring masses in workers' blue or in soldier's uniform wanted," she wrote in *Die Rote Fahne* on 11 December 1918. Such was her analysis of the councils' appearance in Germany. In this way, she cut through the controversy about whether they were instruments of the revolution or organs of revolutionary power (that is, established institutions). For her, incontestably, they were both.

Thus, in Luxemburg's revolutionary vision, council delegates could be called to convene as needed, but they were subject to dismissal at any time, as could those they in turn sent as delegates to the central council (or the Congress of Councils, or workers' and soldiers' parliament), which should meet at least every three months. (Luxemburg criticized the Bolsheviks for having extended the period between two soviet conferences from three to six months, in which she saw additional proof of the suppression of democracy.) The central council, in her perspective, should elect an executive council as the supreme seat of legislative and executive power, authorized to name and replace the people's commissars in a "constant and living interaction between the popular masses and their organizations, the workers' and soldiers' councils" (*Die Rote Fahne*, 14 December 1918). In short, the council system was for Luxemburg the expression of the dictatorship of the proletariat, synonymous with socialist democracy. The electorate of the workers' council comprised "the entirety of the workers of both sexes in cities and countryside," organized at their workplaces. It was envisioned that the soldiers' councils would emerge from the troops, "officers and capitulators excluded" (*Die Rote Fahne*, 14 December 1918). Luxemburg hoped to extend the essentially urban phenomenon of the councils to the countryside, among agricultural workers and peasants, thereby bridging the gap between the cities and rural areas.

Luxemburg held that socialist democracy should be founded as much on the expropriation of large estates and the creation of agricultural cooperatives (to be joined by small farmers only if they wished to do so) as on the socialization of industry. The latter was to be implemented in each plant by an election of councils, which in agreement with the workers' councils, would manage the internal affairs of the companies, regulate working conditions, oversee production, and, finally, take over plant management. What Luxemburg and her Spartacus organization proposed here was thus structured on the principles of socialist society.

Until the First Congress of Councils (16 December 1918), Luxemburg was violently opposed to convening the National Assembly, which she saw as an institutional embodiment of class collaboration and, finally, of the defeat of the revolutionary proletariat. But when the Congress of Councils expressed itself in favor of holding elections and fixed a date, she came to view these elections as a "new instrument of the revolutionary struggle" (*Die Rote Fahne*, 30 December 1918) that would serve to "mobilize the masses *against* the National Assembly" in order to "conquer the fortress of the counterrevolution" (*Die Rote Fahne*, 23 December 1918) it represented. This was precisely her argument in favor of Communist participation in the elections, since the boycott called for by the KPD—which actually represented taking a stand in favor of the council system—might not be understood as such by the masses.

Luxemburg resituated the councils in a double context, the political one of the representative assemblies, "empty envelopes" (*Die Rote Fahne*, 20 November 1918) in which each period of history places its own contents, and the economic context of the unions. During the war, the unions also appeared as instruments of class collaboration. Without being dissolved, they would progressively have to be emptied of their ideological content, "expropriated" by the factory councils. The second, economic phase of the revolution, expressed through massive strikes, was to contribute to this result. The only workers' organization likely to endure in the council system, she argued, was the party, whose role as "compass" appeared to be essential.

Women did not figure in the council system as Luxemburg conceived it, except as voters in their workplace. She undoubtedly would have solicited Zetkin's help in developing this aspect, had Luxemburg not been arrested with Liebknecht and savagely murdered on 15 January 1919. Her body was thrown into a canal and not found until two months later. Zetkin pursued her politics in the communist women's movement in Germany and in the Communist International, where she sat on the executive committee. On more than one occasion, she was ousted from the central committee of the KPD for her "rightist positions."

The radical feminist militants Anita Augspurg (1857–1943) and Lida Gustava Heymann (1868–1943) grew especially close to the USPD. With Zetkin and Toni Sender, who had been a member of the SPD since 1906 and then of the USPD, these women attempted to address the gaps involving women's issues that remained in Luxemburg's proposal. In recent years German feminists have exhumed these women as "ancestors." The memoirs of Augspurg and Heymann (edited by Heymann and published in 1973) sparked interest and discussion toward the end of the 1970s. Sender's memoirs appeared in 1939 and were reprinted in 1981. The partisan affiliations of these women were then obscured, as emphasis was placed on their contributions to the women's liberation movement.

Augspurg and Heymann preceded Luxemburg by a generation. A teacher, Augspurg had studied law in Zurich, where, like Luxemburg, she obtained a doctorate. Heymann was the daughter of a Hamburg merchant and became involved in charitable and professional institutions for workingwomen. In 1902 they launched a campaign for women's suffrage in Germany. The two women were pacifists during the war and were accused of "antipatriotism"; they later became the leaders of the German section of the Women's International League for Peace and Freedom. In January 1919 in Munich, they created the political women's magazine *Die Frau im Staat*, which continued to appear until 1933. They participated in the Republic of Councils in Munich. When the Nazis took power they emigrated to Zurich.

Younger than Augspurg and Heymann, Toni Sender (1888–1964) was a merchant's daughter whose first employment was in commerce. She participated in the 1915 Bern Conference and was a delegate to the party congress (the USPD and then the unified SPD) from 1920 to 1933 and served as a deputy to the Reichstag during the same period. In 1928 she assumed the editorship (replacing a man) of the women's journal of the SPD, *Die Frauenwelt*, and thereafter tried—albeit without great success—to give the publication a more "socialist" identity. What these three women had in common was their direct participation in the experiment of the councils.

All three deplored the weak representation of women on the councils. Heymann suggested that women be nominated to the commissions of the action committee charged with studying important economic questions. Augspurg proposed the creation of women's councils, to serve as political training schools that would cease to exist once the training had been achieved. Sender argued that the schools could also be tools for awakening women's interest in the development of the revolutionary process. Augspurg considered the presence of women indispensable in the farmers' councils of Bavaria in order to counter the influence of the Catholic Center in the countryside, since the reservations expressed in the social-democratic milieu toward women's right to vote referred directly to women's presumed susceptibility to the reactionary discourse of the clergy and local notables—a completely traditional approach. In 1919 Sender gave a speech on the proposed legislation on factory councils, which she criticized sharply; she suggested that women's representation on those councils should be at least proportional. On the level of political theory, Sender inverted Luxemburg's description of the succession of the economic phases (the movement for socialization) and the political phases (the reactivation of workers' councils).

These three militants were especially concerned with the plight of housewives, who were excluded from representation by their lack of integration into the economic system. Reaffirming the productive function of housewives in a traditional socialist analysis, Sender and Augspurg suggested that women's councils be organized, beginning in the administrative divisions of government—at the district or county level, and so on—up through a central council of women, at which point they would join the men in the political action committee or an executive council. In a more detailed contribution, Sender discussed the composition of this female electoral body, refusing the partisan approach adopted by her party, the USPD, as she rejected the suggestion (which she attributed to Zetkin) that women vote in the factories with their brothers or husbands. According to

Sender, the only solution was to have the women voters' lists drawn up by the electoral committee of the workers' council.

Women's councils devoted to education—with intellectual women being encouraged to act as teachers—were intended to bring together women only, in order to allow them to express their aspirations among themselves and to reflect upon the goals and means of the proletarian struggle for liberation. Sender also recommended that these councils consider a rationalization of housework and the rearing of children. Mothers were called upon to consider the political dimension of child-rearing, beginning with the damage inflicted by all-girls' schools. In this way, Augspurg argued, politics would make its way into the home, so that women could participate in equal measure in political life and would understand the potential efficiency of public institutions. These considerations would result in plans for the collective education of children and changes in the management of households, which under socialism would become partnership associations.

These activists soon ran up against the objections of their male counterparts. Augspurg's and Heymann's motion asking that women's councils be created was rejected by the Congress of Councils of Bavaria, which limited itself to presenting the motion as a suggestion to be studied by the action committee, despite support for the idea from the Left and particularly from the anarchist Erich Mühsam. Sender, conscious of the traditional outlook of militant workers, reintroduced the valorization of work for women outside the home but made no mention of men and women sharing household tasks.

Sender nonetheless painted a picture of a general and specific council system in every possible area of application. That picture was a plea for a specific practice of the proletarian dictatorship that would also be a utopia in which women's civic equality would be coupled with their social equality. Such women's councils were never created. Of the great movement that had given birth to a hope for everyday political, economic, and social activities carried out by all those who had an interest in the decisions made, all that remained were the factory councils, a portent of what would be called *mitbestimmung* (joint management) in West Germany later in the 20th century. Meanwhile, women's role in the German Revolution of 1918 has long been veiled in oblivion.

Bibliography

Sources

Luxemburg, Rosa, *Gesammelte Werke*, vol. 4, East Berlin: Dietz, 1974

Luxemburg, Rosa, *Gesammelte Briefe*, vol. 5, East Berlin: Dietz, 1984

Luxemburg, Rosa, *J'étais, je suis, je serai. Correspondance 1914–1919*, edited by Georges Haupt et al., Paris: Maspero, 1977

Luxemburg, Rosa, *The Letters of Rosa Luxemburg*, edited by Stephen Eric Bonner, new edition, Atlantic Highlands, New Jersey: Humanities Press, 1993

Luxemburg, Rosa, *The Mass Strike, the Political Party, and the Trade Union*, translated by P. Levin, Detroit: The Marxian Education Society, 190[?]

Luxemburg, Rosa, *Oeuvres II (Écrits politiques 1917–1919)*, translated and presented by Claudie Weill, Paris: Maspero, 1969

Luxemburg, Rosa, *Prison Letters to Sophie Liebknecht*, New York: A.J. Muste Memorial Institute, 1974–1985

Luxemburg, Rosa, *Rosa Luxemburg: Reflections and Writings*, edited by Paul Le Blanc, Amherst, New York: Humanity Books, 1999

Luxemburg, Rosa, *Selections. Rosa Luxemburg Speaks*, edited by Mary Alice Waters, New York: Pathfinder Press, 1998

Sender, Toni, *Die Frauen und das Rätesystem: Rede auf der Leipziger Frauenkonferenz am 29. November 1919*, Berlin: Verlagsgenossenschaft Freiheit, n.d.

Stenographischer Bericht über die Verhandlungen des Kongresses der Arbeiter-, Bauern- und Soldatenräte vom 25. Februar bis 8. März 1919 in München, Munich: Kongress der Arbeiter-, Bauern- und Soldatenräte, 1919; reprint, Glashütten im Taunus, Germany: D. Auvermann, 1974

Reference Works

Badia, Gilbert, *Clara Zetkin, féministe sans frontières*, Paris: Éditions ouvrières, 1993 Badia, Gilbert, *Les Spartakistes, 1918: l'Allemagne en révolution*, Paris: Julliard, 1966

Boll, Friedhelm, *Massenbewegungen in Niedersachsen, 1906–1920*, Bonn: Verlag Neue Gesellschaft, 1981

Bosl, Karl, editor, *Bayern im Umbruch: Die Revolution von 1918, ihre Voraussetzungen, ihr Verlauf und ihre Folgen*, Munich: R. Oldenbourg, 1969

Broué, Pierre, *Révolution en Allemagne 1917–1923*, Paris: Éditions de Minuit, 1971 Dornemann, Luise, "Die proletarische Frauenbewegung während des ersten Weltkrieges und in der Novemberrevolution," *Einheit* 13, no. 11 (1958)

Evans, Richard J., *Sozialdemokratie und Frauenemanzipation im deutschen Kaiserreich* Berlin: Dietz, 1979

Gabriel, Nicole, *L'assemblée des femmes: L'organisation féminine du SPD au temps de Willy Brandt et de Helmut Schmidt*, Berne: Peter Lang, 1992

Gabriel, Nicole, "Des berceaux aux tranchées: Les enjeux du débat sur la 'grève des ventres' de l'été 1913 en Allemagne," *Le Mouvement social* 147 (April–June 1989)

Gabriel, Nicole, " 'Des femmes appelèrent mais on ne les entendit pas': Anita Augspurg et Lida Gustava Heymann," in *Entre émancipation et nationalisme: La presse féminine d'Europe, 1914–1945*, edited by Rita Thalmann, Paris: Deux Temps Tierce, 1990

Gabriel, Nicole, "L'Internationale et les femmes socialistes," *Matériaux pour l'histoire de notre temps* 16 (July–September 1989)

Hagemann, Karen, *Frauenalltag und Männerpolitik: Alltagsleben und gesellschaftliches Handeln von Arbeiterfrauen in der Weimarer Republik*, Bonn: Dietz, 1990

Kolb, Eberhard, *Die Arbeiterräte in der deutschen Innenpolitik 1918–1919*, Düsseldorf: Droste Verlag, 1962

Kolb, Eberhard, and K. Schönhoven, editors, *Regionale und lokale Räteorganisationen in Württemberg 1918/1919*, Düsseldorf: Droste Verlag, 1976

Kuckuck, Peter, editor, *Revolution und Räterepublik in Bremen*, Frankfurt am Main: Suhrkamp, 1966

Mai, Gunther, "Die Sozialstruktur der württembergischen Arbeiter- und Bauernräte 1918/1919," *Internationale Wissenschaftliche Korrespondenz zur Geschichte der deutschen Arbeiterbewegung* 15, no. 3 (September 1979)

Neusüss, Christel, *Die Kopfgeburten der Arbeiterbewegung, oder, Die Genossin Luxemburg bringt alles durcheinander*, Hamburg: Rasch und Röhring, 1985

Oertzen, Peter von, *Betriebsräte in der Novemberrevolution: Eine politikwissenschaftliche Untersuchung über Ideengehalt und Struktur der betrieblichen und wirtschaftlichen Arbeiterräte in der deutschen Revolution 1918/19*, Düsseldorf: Droste Verlag, 1963

Strobel, Georg W., *Die Partei Rosa Luxemburgs, Lenin und die SPD: Der polnische "europäische" Internationalismus in der russischen Sozialdemokratie*, Wiesbaden, Germany: F. Steiner, 1974

Weill, Claudie, "Les conseils en Allemagne 1918–1919," *Le Mouvement social* 152 (July–September 1990)

THE WOMEN'S SECTION OF THE COMINTERN, FROM LENIN TO STALIN

JEAN-JACQUES MARIE

IN 1921 THE COMMUNIST International, or Comintern (established in Moscow in March 1919) began developing a "policy on women as an element of general strategy of the takeover of power and the revolution." The development of this policy was strictly subordinate to the internal transformations of the Soviet Union, its social changes—which Igor Gaydar, prime minister under Boris Yeltsin, summed up by calling 1937 the year of the "triumph of the *nomenklatura*" (*Literaturnaia Gazeta*, 30 November 1994)—and the policy's consequences for the Comintern, which was dissolved by Stalin on 15 May 1943.

The Russian Revolution began in February 1917 with a spontaneous demonstration and strike by women workers, independent of an order from any political party and beyond party control. Six years later, Bolshevik leader Vasily Kayurov still remembered this event as shocking and somewhat painful:

> The evening before "women's day" I was sent to a meeting of women workers in Lesnaya. There I gave them a definition of the meaning of "women's day," of the women's movement in general, and when I came to talk about the present moment, I was particularly intent on asking the workers to avoid any partial demonstration and to act only upon instructions from the party committee. . . . How surprised and indignant I was, then, when the next day, 23 February, in the hallway of the Erikson factory, Comrade Nikifor Ilyich came to inform me that a strike had broken out in several textile factories and that a delegation of women workers was on its way with a resolution demanding support of the metalworkers.
>
> I was outraged by the behavior of the strikers: first of all, [these women] had blatantly ignored the decisions of the regional party committee, and further, I myself had called for the restraint and discipline of the workers just the night before, and suddenly there was a strike.
>
> There seemed to be neither any goal nor any reason for this, other than the bread lines in front of the bakeries, basically made up of women and children. (*Proletarskaia Revoliutsia*, no. 13 [January 1923].)

A surprising text: six years after the events, while he could have assigned himself the more glorious role of organizer of the first day of the revolution, Kayurov could not contain his indignation, expressed twice in ten lines: the women had disobeyed orders! One cannot help but think that, had the strike involved men metalworkers and not women, Kayurov's anger in the face of this disobedience would have been less intense, or at least expressed with greater restraint.

After they seized power in October 1917, the Bolsheviks were faced with a gigantic tangle of problems: the collapse of industrial production, the sabotage of many thousands of state employees, the increasing disintegration of the army, difficult peace talks with Germany and Austria that were contested within their own party, uprisings organized almost everywhere by their adversaries, the insurrection of former Czechoslovakian prisoners of war, and civil war. In spite of volatile circumstances, they implemented a series of emancipatory measures—the right to divorce, the right to abortion, legal codes on egalitarian marriage, equal voting rights for men and women subject to social, not sexual limitations—which were a great deal more beneficial to women intellectuals and women workers than to peasant women.

Women's Issues and the Comintern's Positions of Principle

The Bolsheviks, who from the outset viewed their actions as a constituent part of an international revolutionary struggle, set out to establish the Communist International as quickly as possible, and it was proclaimed in Moscow during a founding congress in March 1919 by some 15 parties, of which only the Bolshevik Party was then a party of the masses.

The year 1919 was the high point of "War Communism"— a rigorously centralized system aimed at strict survival, relying on the requisitioning of agricultural production and subordinating the entire economy, which was channeled into funding the civil war.

The First Congress of the Communist International adopted a manifesto written by Leon Trotsky that aimed at establishing the objective necessity of the proletarian revolution. The inability of capitalism to continue developing the productive forces pitted states against each other in competition for a share in the world market that had become too tight, and this had created the war that ended up in revolution in the weakest of the belligerent states. Thus, seizing power was the order of the day in other countries. This objective gave a central role to the emancipation of colonized peoples, whose masters were undermined by the war and to whom Trotsky's manifesto devoted considerable space. Indeed, the struggle of these peoples was presented as a means of the revolution, while women's emancipation was seen as its result. In this perspective of imminent revolution, the "woman question" was thus only lightly touched upon. That issue was invoked as a position of principle in a short text that Aleksandra Kollontai submitted to the Congress. She was a Menshevik (a minority faction of the Russian Social-Democratic Party, in contrast to the Bolshevik majority) from 1908 to 1915 and, as stated in her autobiography, in 1905 she laid the foundations for an organization of women workers. She was the first woman to be elected to the Executive Committee of the Petrograd Soviet, a member of the Pan-Russian Executive Committee, then the first female people's commissar in the first Soviet government, and finally a member of the Central Committee from August 1917 to March 1918. Her text read as follows:

> The Congress of the Communist International notes that all tasks it has set itself, as well as the definitive victory of the world proletariat and the definitive abolition of the capitalist regime, can be carried out only through the common struggle of men and women workers. The enormous increase of women's labor in every branch of the economy, the fact that at least half of all the wealth in the world is produced by women workers, and, further, the important and universally acknowledged role that women workers play in the building of the new Communist society, in the reform of family life, and in the realization of socialist, communal, and children's education, the purpose of which will be the preparation of worker-citizens' councils, infused with the spirit of solidarity for the republic—all of the above imposes the urgent duty upon all the member parties of the Communist International to extend all their forces and energies to win women workers over to the party and to use every means to educate them in the direction of the new society and the Communist ethic from the point of view of society and family. The dictatorship of the proletariat can only be realized and maintained with the energetic and active participation of women workers. (First Congress of the Communist International, 5th day)

A peculiar text: focusing on the role of women as the educators who will train young generations of the "new society," it contained not a single demand, not a single platform, no call to action, not a single agenda item, and not a single allusion even to the measures taken in Soviet Russia for the equal rights of men and women likely to feed Communist propaganda in other countries. The text offered nothing in the way of guidance to the leaders of young foreign Communist parties, and the majority of them did almost nothing with regard to the "woman question."

Inessa Armand's Letter

A few months later, Lenin entrusted Inessa Armand, a French-born collaborator in the section of women workers of the Central Committee of the Bolshevik Party, with the responsibility of generating this faltering activity. On 2 January 1920, Armand sent a letter, written in French, to all the Comintern parties. It began with a description of the legal situation of women in Russia and then with resolute optimism affirmed the possibility of truly changing women's living conditions in a short period of time.

> In Soviet Russia, women workers and peasants absolutely enjoy the same rights as men workers and peasants. [Women] are voters and can be elected in any Soviet state and to any office, including the office of people's commissar. They also have full equality of rights in their civil status, and in marriage men and women also have full equal rights. All marital power has been completely eradicated by the Soviet Constitution and by decrees on marriage. The same holds true for paternal and maternal power. . . .
> Moreover, in the proletarian dictatorship we now have the possibility of establishing new forms of social and private life that will lead to the complete social liberation of women, in the sense that we will liberate her from domestic work and from the worries of rearing children. Consequently, we now face the possibility of breaking the last chains that still bind women.

She then emphasized that this specific activity should lead women into the general struggle against capital:

> For a year now, we have been leading rather strong propaganda efforts among women . . . workers. The purpose of this propaganda is, of course, *in no way feminist* [Armand's emphasis]. Our only goal is to attract the mass of women workers to the proletarian struggle against imperialism.

The long description she then gave of the Bolshevik Party's work of agitation and organization among women workers and peasants was plainly meant to convince the Communist parties, which were still completely inactive in this area, and to push them in that direction by the force of example.

> Each committee of the Communist Party has a women's propaganda section (mainly women workers and peasants) that organizes quarterly lectures by delegates from factories and plants. In addition, there are weekly assemblies of workingwomen's delegates representing all the factories and plants in the area.

The measures enumerated by Armand constituted an impressive legislative whole, but they ran up against two obstacles. First, there was the czarist Russian past in which women were considered inferior beings (a traditional Russian proverb states: "A hen is not a bird; a woman is not a person"), along with all the prejudices inherited from that past. Second, there was the dreadful destruction wrought by World War I and the civil war, which spread devastation, cold, hunger, typhus, and cholera, all of them material conditions scarcely propitious for a real emancipation of women factory and agrarian workers. In their

Azbuka kommunisma (1920; *The ABC of Communism*), Nikolai Ivanovich Bukharin and Evgenni Preobazhenskii stressed these circumstances. Listing the measures taken by the Soviet power in order to establish equality of men and women in marriage, family relationships, and political rights, they at the same time acknowledged the still partially formal characteristic of this equality:

> The task of our party now consists in making this equality work in practice. It is above all a question of making the large masses of workers understand that women's slavery can only be harmful to them as well. At the present moment, workers still consider women to be inferior beings: in the villages they still laugh at women who want to participate in public affairs. . . . Our women workers are much more backward than the men. Moreover, they are very scornfully regarded. A dynamic task is waiting, first to teach men to see women workers as equals of men workers, and then to enlighten women and incite them to use the rights they have been granted without embarrassment or fear. . . . The main thing is not to grant rights on paper only, but to open up the possibility of exercising them. How can a woman worker exercise her rights when she has to take care of household chores? The Soviet Republic must alleviate the lot of laboring women and to liberate them from the domestic obligations that are ancient history.

The authors listed the institutions that should be created in order to advance from formal equality to real equality:

> community centers . . . with communal laundry rooms, people's restaurants, day care centers, nursery schools, summer camps for children, school cafeterias, etc. All this should unburden women and give them the opportunity to occupy themselves with everything of interest to men. It is difficult to create these institutions during this period of misery and famine.

"Difficult" was a euphemism. Even when created, these institutions could do little more than socialize misery and famine. As Bukharin and Preobrazhenskii, as well as the other Bolshevik Party leaders saw it, the solution lay in the forthcoming world revolution, which would bring the aid of the rich countries to ruined Russia and thus allow formal rights to have real content.

> All of Europe will inevitably move on to the dictatorship of the proletariat and from there on to Communism. Consequently, Russia cannot stay capitalist when Germany, France, and England have moved on to the dictatorship of the proletariat. It is obvious that Russia will inevitably be led to socialism. Its lack of culture, the deficiency of its industrial development, etc., all of that will have little importance when Russia associates with the most cultivated countries inside a world republic, or at least a European republic of soviets.

This passage, taken from an authoritative popular handbook, sheds light on the thought and objectives of the Bolshevik Party leaders in the year 1920. Russia was a ruined capitalist country led by the party of the working class (a situation Lenin characterized as "a bourgeois state without a bourgeoisie"), which in fact could move toward socialism only within the framework of a victorious European revolution. Hence the importance assigned at the time to the Comintern and its activity. While awaiting the victorious revolution, the Russians had to hold on. At the same time, the distance between needs and realization was great. Thus Armand's letter ended with a simple request for news, coupled with a suggestion: "It would be of great importance for us to internationally have an understanding on the action to be followed. It therefore seems to us that an international Communist women's conference would be of the greatest significance."

To organize such a conference, a committee headed by German Communist Klara Zetkin proposed that an International Women's Secretariat be created and that it have the status of a special department subordinate to the International Executive Committee, which agreed to the proposal. The secretariat was to be composed of three to six activist women, elected at the Communist women's conferences and approved by a congress or by the International Executive Committee. The latter also was to approve the decisions of the International Women's Secretariat.

During the first years of its existence, the International Women's Secretariat enjoyed a much greater autonomy in the Comintern than any of its other departments, undoubtedly because its members were elected and because of the prestige of its women leaders, Aleksandra Kollontai and Klara Zetkin (who was also very close to Lenin).

Resistance from the Communist Parties

Communist parties in other countries showed little enthusiasm. The answers Armand received allowed her and her colleagues only to organize a first meeting, which took place in Leningrad on 16 July 1920 and was a "private meeting of women and men delegates" from nine countries (France, England, Italy, Russia, Sweden, Georgia, India, Mexico, and Bulgaria) on the eve of the opening of the Second Congress of the Communist International. The small meeting stressed the need to "convene the International Conference of Communist Women before the end of the congress, even if the number of delegates was not as substantial as might have been wished." The conference, which brought together women delegates from 19 countries, was held from 30 July to 6 August in Moscow, where the congress of the Comintern had moved. This congress adopted the statutes that the Comintern had previously lacked. Article 16 of these 17 statutes proclaimed: "The Executive Committee of the International sanctions the nomination of a secretary of the international women's movement and organizes a section of women Communists of the International" (*Theses, Resolutions, and Manifestos of the First Four Congresses of the Third International*). But the congress went into no further detail. While it adopted resolutions on the union movement and the factory committees, on the national and colonial question, on the agrarian question, and on the question of parliamentarianism, it adopted not a single text on women. Why? The answer lies in the first lines of the "Resolution on the Role of the Communist Party in the Proletarian Revolution," which affirmed that "The proletariat of the world stands at the eve of a decisive struggle, that is to say of the conquest of power." Thus, the congress examined only those problems that, in its view, were directly linked to this decisive struggle. That was why it adopted the famous 21 conditions for parties' admission into the Comintern. As the text itself stated, these conditions aimed in particular to avoid "invasion [of the Comintern] by indecisive and hesitant groups" (*Theses, Resolutions, and Manifestos of the First Four Congresses of the Third International*) incapable of preparing the takeover of power because closely linked to bourgeois democracy and its parliamentary institutions. For the Comintern, women's issues did not come under this immediate perspective. The Women's Secretariat of the Executive Committee of the International, which the congress had decided to create, took several months to come out of limbo. The Central Committee of every Communist party had to create a *Zhenotdel* (women's section), as did the Central Committee of the Bolshevik Party, which relied on a whole network of women's committees at different levels of the party. The International Women's Secretariat had to coordinate the international network that had been proclaimed but was still in gestation.

Armand, who had organized the first conference of Communist women and who was by then exhausted from the work, the deprivations, and the tensions of the moment, left for the Caucasus to recuperate but instead fell victim to the cholera epidemic ravaging the region. She died on 24 September 1920. At the same time, Kollontai, who had been ill with typhus for a long time, recovered. She was immediately appointed to head the women's section of the Central Committee of the Bolshevik Party, and thus "succeeded" Armand. Kollontai's various writings on the problems of women and the family had caused quite a stir because of her advocacy of "free love" and her apologia for motherhood as a social duty. She was then immersed in the struggle of the Workers' Opposition, which asserted that "the pinnacle of soviet administration and of the Communist Party [had] become a well-defined social class." As Kollontai put it: "The Workers' Opposition demands management of the various branches of industry by the producers organized within their unions." She nevertheless started working without delay.

The International Women's Secretariat

The International Women's Secretariat was initially intended to be composed of three to six members; in the end, it included eight women, six of whom were Russian: Nadezdja Krupskaya, Aleksandra Kollontai, Zlata Lilina, Konkordia Samoilova, Lyudmila Stal, a woman on record only as Similova, Henriëtte Roland-Holst, from the Netherlands, Rosa Bloch, from Switzerland, and the secretary general, Klara Zetkin. The latter, a veteran German Social-Democrat activist who became a Communist in 1918, had long been concerned about the specific problems of women's oppression in the German Social-Democracy Party, but all she had encountered was polite attention. Early in 1920 she had advised Lenin, who accepted the idea, to convene an international women's congress. There, according to her, Lenin had wanted to bring together "ladylike English pacifists, tempestuous French feminists, and pious Christian women who had the benefit of the pope's blessing or swore only by Luther" (*Battles for Women*). Lenin doubtless envisioned that such a "congress," which never took place, would be a simple

gathering of sympathizers or "women friends" of the Soviet Republic rather than a congress of a political movement of women. Shortly before, on 10 January 1920, he had addressed a message to the Bureau of the Women's Congress of the government of Petrograd, in which he presented a rigorous outline of the tasks of the women's movement in 1920 Soviet Russia. Unable to foresee the imminent attack by Poland under Józef Klemens Pilsudski (head of state from 1919 to 1922), Lenin insisted that the civil war was over and that all workers should henceforth concentrate their energies "on a bloodless war to conquer hunger, cold, and destitution. In this bloodless war, women workers and peasants are called upon to play a particularly great role" (*Complete Works*, vol. 40, Russian Edition). In short, women were urged to wage a social and political battle for the very survival of the Soviet state, without any specific female appearance.

However, the international Communist women's movement envisioned far broader tasks for itself in this context. The International Women's Secretariat met for the first time on 20 November 1920 under the aegis of Kollontai, who presented the introductory report to the Second International Communist Women's Conference. Presided over by Zetkin, the secretariat met from 9 to 15 June 1921, on the eve of the Third International Congress, at which "women's work" was to occupy a great place. Two months earlier, the first issue of the international Communist women's magazine *Die Kommunistische Fraueninternationale*, headed by Zetkin, had appeared in Stuttgart. Kollontai first emphasized the general objectives of the International Women's Secretariat:

> To develop the influence of the International among the broadest masses of proletarian and semiproletarian women workers and to help the strengthening of ties between the women's sections of the Communist Parties of Western and Eastern countries.

After six months of the secretariat's existence, an assessment of progress was discouraging. Not every Communist party had a women's section—far from it—and above all "we have received no political reports from any organization," Kollontai noted in a report entitled "The Work of the International Women's Secretariat." She went on to note that "only seven organizations bothered to bring documents to the conference: Sweden, England, the United States, France, Switzerland, Bulgaria, and Germany."

Kollontai suggested three lines of intervention: International Women's Day on 8 March, the struggle against prostitution, and the decriminalization of abortion, which had been authorized in Soviet Russia since 1918. In a great programmatic speech, Zetkin insisted that all the measures taken by capitalist regimes to ensure their survival came down particularly hard on women:

> women feel the vital needs that flow from the capitalist system even more strongly and these are becoming more acute in this period of decline. That is why women must intervene as pioneers of the revolution, of course not alone, not isolated from the broad masses of the proletariat, but as an avant-garde detachment of the revolution.

The lengthy debate at this conference was subtended by an analysis, implicit or not, of one's perspectives on the revolution. Was it imminent, or more distant in time? Kollontai, like many other delegates, believed it was imminent. She therefore brushed aside the fight for social demands, reducing them to propaganda elements for the revolution. She asserted:

> We should not address [the demands of] women servants and domestic workers by demanding the eight-hour work day for them and the allocation of a separate room; we should tell them that without the revolution, without the dictatorship of the proletariat, without Soviet power, you will not have these two demands.

If they were not to organize these women in order to help them force such demands, but instead attempt to convince them that the revolution was the requisite precondition for the satisfaction of those demands, "women's work" essentially had to consist of propaganda activity. Kollontai concluded the report by stating her hope that the secretariat's meeting the following year would be a conference of women from the Soviet countries.

What was needed to achieve that aim? The author of the report hardly answered the question. Leon Trotsky, in his presentation in the name of the Bolshevik Party, had tried to temper people's enthusiasm. Since the First Congress, he said, "we have lost certain illusions . . . which we have replaced with a clearer understanding . . . the struggle will be terribly difficult . . . matters are developing more slowly than we expected." His words of caution went unheard, at least by Kollontai.

During the discussions, she had been subjected to two series of criticism that undoubtedly tied in with Leon Trotsky's analysis. Zetkin reproached Kollontai for being uninterested in the work of women of the intelligentsia. Two delegates, one Korean and one Armenian woman, accused her of completely ignoring the situation of Eastern women, who had been released from their harems and who could not be approached in the same way as European women. Nevertheless, the conference indicated a turning point: first of all, it restructured the secretariat into a true international secretariat of six women: Zetkin, Hertha Sturm, Lucie Colliard, Kollontai, Zlata Lilina, and Varvara Kasparova. The latter, of Tartar origin, was codirector with Kollontai of the women's section of the Central Committee of the Bolshevik Party; she was named to head the Eastern section of the secretariat and was in charge of the established organizing bureau. A few weeks later the conference ended with decisions approved at the Third International Congress, where Zetkin presented a report on the work that had just been accomplished.

The Third Congress of the Communist International

In fact, this congress, held from 22 June to 12 July 1921, adopted no fewer than three resolutions on women (out of a total of 16 resolutions adopted by the congress). These were the "Theses for Propaganda among Women," a "Resolution on the International Relationship between Communist Women and the Women's Secretariat of the Communist International," and a "Resolution on the Forms and Methods of Communist Work among Women." Women's role was thus among the main concerns of the Third Congress that affirmed: "It is absolutely indisputable that at the present moment, the revolutionary struggle for power of the proletariat manifests a certain flexibility, a certain slowdown worldwide" (*Theses, Resolutions, and Manifestos of the First*

Four Congresses of the Third International). This cognizance of a slowdown explains the perceived twofold need to achieve a united front (between Communists and social democrats) and expand efforts in the way of agitation, propaganda, and organizing around the demands of the greatest masses.

The theses defined both the general principles that should guide Communist activity among women and the practical details of this activity. The core of the theses was unquestionably point 6:

> Women's struggle against their double oppression—capitalism and family and domestic dependency—must, in the next phase of its development, take on an international character as it transforms itself into a struggle of the proletariat of both sexes for dictatorship and the Soviet regime.

Considering that "women should always remember that their slavery has all its origins in the bourgeois regime," the theses specified there were no issues specific to women "and that Communism would be achieved only through the union of all exploited persons in the struggle and not through the union of women's forces from the two opposing classes." At the same time, the thesis stressed the need to "combat prejudices relating to women on the part of the masses of the male proletariat and struggle systematically against the influence of tradition, bourgeois mores, and religion." The congress declared itself strongly against any form of women's organizing separately within the party, the unions, or other workers associations, but "recognize[d] the need for the Communist Party to use special working methods with women and deem[ed] it useful to form special organisms responsible for this work in each Communist party," in various women's sections and commissions (*Theses, Resolutions, and Manifestos of the First Four Congresses of the Third International*).

The work to be undertaken with women was identified in three different sectors: countries under the Soviet regime, capitalist countries, and countries that lagged behind economically (the East). For latter region, the congress emphasized "the need to struggle against the influence of nationalism and religion on the minds of the people, to work above all with the masses of women workers in home industries, and on rice, cotton, and other plantations," and it anticipated special instruction on methods of working with women of the East (*Theses, Resolutions, and Manifestos of the First Four Congresses of the Third International*). The text ended with very detailed organizing measures that would direct this work throughout the years to come. The Stalinization of the USSR and the Communist parties was soon to reduce the program to purely exterior packaging, which was to be obliterated altogether in 1935–36.

In order to organize their work, the Women's Secretariat had tried to put together an international network of women "correspondents," who held an initial meeting on 25–26 January 1922 in Berlin. The second conference of the international correspondents met again in Berlin on 24–25 October 1922 and specified the direction of its activity. One of the ten points on the agenda dealt with the "Principal Questions of Agitation and Action among Proletarian Women." Discussions stressed social problems, the heaviest burden of which was borne by women: "the high cost of living, unemployment, and ever increasing poverty stand at the center of any agitation by women." In addition, a demand was made for "insurance for mothers-to-be," without any further details.

The Fourth Congress of the International met from 3 November to 5 December 1922. Unbeknownst to the delegates, a period of change was at hand: this congress was to be the last one at which Lenin spoke. At the same time, Stalin, then the new secretary general of the Central Committee and the future "Father of the People," never set foot on the congress premises even though he was his own party's official delegate. This congress devoted only one short resolution to "women's action," which emphasized the correctness of the direction decided upon by the preceding congress and, at the same time, the extreme reservations of the leaders of many (unidentified) Communist parties about implementing the proposed measures.

> Certain sections have not fulfilled, or have only superficially fulfilled, their duty, which is systematically to support Communist work among women. Until now, [these sections] have neither applied the regulations of organizing Communist women in the party, nor created the party organisms that are indispensable to the work with women and to the establishment of a connection with them. The Fourth Congress requires these sections to achieve as quickly as possible that which they have neglected to do. ... The proletarian united front cannot be realized unless women are part of it. ... A solid collaboration between the Communist parties and women workers will, under certain circumstances, allow the latter to open the way to the united proletarian front in the movements of revolutionary masses. (*Theses, Resolutions, and Manifestos of the First Four Congresses of the Third International*)

Varying Degrees of Implementation

No further specifics were added to this rather general statement of objectives. However, one of the targeted parties was the Parti Communiste Français (PCF; French Communist Party), which had remained almost impervious to the dictates of the Third International Congress in this and other areas.

A month earlier, the debates at the Second Conference of International Correspondents had made this clear. A report by Marthe Bigot, charged with covering the PCF's actions regarding "women's work," showed that the party had been dragging its feet. Its leading committee was flanked by a central women's commission, composed of eight women and two men, and about 15 local commissions throughout all of France. The party published a newspaper for women workers, *L'ouvrière*, with a modest circulation of 2,000 copies. Of the 1,800 party members, only slightly more than 2 percent (or 1 in 45) were women. In short, the paternalistic attitude characteristic of European social democracy was perpetuated within the French Communist Party.

The actions of the Parti Communiste Belge (PCB; Belgian Communist Party) with respect to "women's work" mirrored those of its big brother in France. At the time, the Belgian party had only one women's section, in the Federation of Brussels, led by Berthe Kestemot, a member of the party's Executive Committee. On average, the section held monthly meetings attended by only seven or eight women, who, moreover, were not very committed. Berthe Kestemot complained: "As a whole, the party does not understand the role or the usefulness of a women's section and, consequently, offers us no help at all."

The Kommunistische Partei Deutschland (KPD; German Communist Party) presented an equally absurd situation. Fascinated by extraparliamentary direct action—exemplified by the party's attempted minority insurrection strike of March 1921, which ended in a bloodbath—its leadership was reserved, to say the least, about any kind of "mass" activity, including women's organizing. Furthermore, the party was hostile to Klara Zetkin, whom they saw as a "rightist." At the end of 1920, Zetkin had created a propaganda publication targeting women, *Die Kommunistin*. Scholar Gilbert Badia writes, "Given women's political backwardness, Klara Zetkin had long been convinced that, to address them, it was necessary to offer special organizations, methods, and a propaganda different from those used to address workers" (see Badia). Zetkin believed that the weight of bourgeois and patriarchal ideology was much greater in a country like Germany than in Russia. In addition, she wanted to develop a specific propaganda campaign to reach intellectual women. In December 1920, the leadership of the KPD took the editorship of *Die Kommunistin* away from Zetkin, and, at the same time, it limited the activities of the women's section of the Central Committee to a maximum degree.

This woeful picture, however, contrasted with the actions of the Scandinavian Communist parties (although these were weaker than their French and German counterparts) and the Kommunisticka Strana Cech (KSC; Czech Communist Party). The leadership committee of the Suomen Sosialistinen Syövaenpuolue (Finnish Socialist Revolutionary Workers' Party, the legal cover for the forbidden Finnish Communist Party) was flanked by a women's section of five members, presided over by Elin Fagerholm, who had voting powers in the leadership committee on any question involving work for women. In December 1921 the section organized a women's congress. Party membership included 4,000 women, or 22.5 percent of the total, and 38 women's sections. Further, the party published a paper for women workers, *Työläisnainen*, whose circulation varied between 2,000 and 2,500 copies. Finnish women had the right to vote, and the party had six female deputies.

The Central Committee of the Sveriges Kommunistiska Parti (SKP; Swedish Communist Party) had a women's subsection with five members, presided over by Gerda Linderot, herself a member of the Central Committee; this subsection met twice monthly. If the subsection's president had not been elected to the Central Committee, the statutes guaranteed that she would have had to be invited there to discuss any question concerning women. Contrary to the explicit instructions of the Comintern, the party had separate women's sections that accounted for a little more than half of the 2,111 women members of the party in 1921; women paid lower membership fees than men.

Undoubtedly, the implementation of measures to promote women's political involvement was organized even more meticulously in the Czech Communist Party. Alongside the party's Central Committee, there existed a Women's Central Committee made up of German, Czech, and Slovak women. It was responsible for propaganda efforts directed at women throughout the country and published three papers for women. These were *Kommunistka* in Czech (circulation 9,000), *Kommunistin* (in German for the Sudeten, circulation 1,200), and *Zena* (for the women of the Brün region, circulation 7,000). There were plans for a fourth, Slovak-language paper, *Proletarka*, but these plans did not have an independent budget. The secretary of the women's committee was a member of the party's Central Committee in an advisory capacity, and she had the right to vote on those issues that pertained to women. Women's district sections and committees also existed. As in Sweden, women paid lower membership dues than did the men.

Communist parties in other countries, long entangled in the problems of their own structure and internal conflicts about orientation and developing a more or less cohesive agenda for action, became involved in implementing measures on women only later. This was very much the case of the Partito dei Communisti Italiani (PCI; Italian Communist Party). The first issue of *Compagna*, a bimonthly newspaper for women, came out in January 1922, 10 months before Benito Mussolini's March on Rome. The Fascist leader's climb to power rapidly reduced the labor movement to a clandestine activity. During the Second National Congress of the PCI in March 1922, a first women's conference was held; Antonio Gramsci gave a speech, which has been lost, on the importance of the struggle for women's emancipation. In three months, *Compagna*, with a circulation of 7,200 copies, gained more than 1,000 subscribers, but the paper was relegated to the margins owing to tensions among party leaders about the future general orientation of the party. Significantly, in April 1924, after the defeat of the PCI in rigged legislative elections (the PCI received only 266,145 votes against 4,690,000 in favor of the Fascist Party), a long, single-spaced, eight-page report by Jules Humbert Droz was silent on the work of women, as it was on union and youth activity, despite the existence of a youth organization (see Humbert Droz). This marginalization, and the fact that the Italian Communist Party was outlawed entirely in 1926, allowed it, like the French Communist Party, to painlessly put into effect the change in direction that accompanied the Comintern's growing Bolshevism—that is, the regime of strict, almost military-style discipline imposed after Lenin's death by Zinoviev in 1924–1925 and completed by Stalin.

The New Line of the Comintern

On 15 May 1925 the Executive Committee of the Comintern decided to rename the International Women's Secretariat—to reduce its status and its autonomy and call it the Women's Section of the Executive Committee. But the decision stated with some cynicism, "In presentations to a general audience it is good, for tactical reasons, to preserve the name International Women's Secretariat."

Perhaps this decision can be explained in part by Klara Zetkin's reservations about the triumvirate then in charge of the USSR (Stalin-Zinoviev-Kamenev) and by the fact that Kasparova belonged to the leftist opposition. In fact, there were also deeper reasons for this first retrenchment. A few months later at the Fourteenth Congress of the Russian Communist Party, during which he was to break with Zinoviev and Kamenev, leaders of a new defeated opposition, Stalin proclaimed, "We should not play with equality. For that is playing with fire" (*Complete Works*, vol. 7 Russian Edition, 1925). He was indicting social and political equality here, including equality between men and women. The parasitic bureaucracy, setting itself above society, fed on concealed privileges in the midst of generalized destitution. In August 1928, former Central Committee member Khristian Rakovsky condemned the mores of this proliferating caste as follows: "Robbery, deceit, violence, bribes, unprecedented abuse of power, unlimited despotism, drunkenness, debauchery." Vladimir Sosnovsky more concisely invoked the "harem-automobile factor"—the secretary-mistress and the fancy car being inseparable privileges and symbols of power. The exacerbation of social stratification accompanied the double oppression of women in the role of secretary (obliging, in the tradition of bourgeois vaudeville) and "decorative" worker, useful for her shock value and soon to be celebrated as mother of the largest possible family.

The ideological shift was marked in an almost caricatural way in the German Communist Party, which in that same year, 1925, created a Frauen- und Mädchenbund (Women's and Girls' Union), the women's section of the fighting organization of the party, the Roter Front Kämpferbund (Red Front Fighters' Union), which was the great organizer of virile paramilitary parades. There could be no clearer indication that "women's work" now centered on militant forms that could only distance the mass of women workers themselves, who were not at all ready to be transformed into service members of orders or fighting units. Despite her reservations, Klara Zetkin accepted the presidency of this women's section of the Red Front. At the same time, the International Secretariat definitively suspended the publication of her German-language paper and theoretical organ for Communist women, *Die Kommunistische Fraueninternationale*. This period marked the beginning of the Comintern's rapid relegation of "women's work" to the scrap heap. A Communist women's conference had been held in Moscow in 1920, then in 1921, and then, after an interval of three years, in 1924. One last women's conference was held in 1926. In November 1927, the Women's Secretariat organized in Moscow a conference of women who had come to attend the festivities of the tenth anniversary of the revolution; tourism took the place of a mandate at this purely ornamental conference.

This type of camouflage was, indeed, needed to conceal the neglect into which women's concerns had fallen within the party. In that same year, 1927, the Communist Academy of Moscow opened a research section on the concerns of women workers and gave Klara Zetkin the responsibility of developing the guiding documents for this new section. According to Badia, quoting an unpublished thesis by Gudrun Partisch on Zetkin's political activity 1923 to 1933,

> Klara Zetkin then developed three questionnaires: one dealt with issues relevant to married women (divorce, alimony, child care), the other with the application of laws (to verify whether discrimination against women had indeed stopped), and the third designed to document situations in which women workers had been laid off and how the courts of competent jurisdiction had received and treated possible complaints.

Badia goes on to state: "Unfortunately, no available document asserts that these questionnaires were even distributed, much less utilized."

Four months later, the ninth plenary meeting of the Comintern's Executive Committee mentioned "women's work" only on the occasion of a resolution on the union question, which affirmed the need to "recruit women and youth for the union [to] have them participate actively in union work." In August 1930, the Women's Secretariat organized a conference in Moscow of those in charge of women's sections of the central committees of the European and American parties. This conference was to be the last meeting organized by the secretariat—essentially a funeral service.

In part, that final meeting shed light upon the reasons for the secretariat's programmatically determined demise. The Moscow conference took place in the midst of the proclamation of what Moscow and the Comintern called the "third period." After the first, revolutionary period a second period was envisioned, that of the stabilization of capitalism. The third period was to see the final assault on the bourgeois order and its lackeys, of which the most dangerous were the social democrats—considered social fascists and deemed to be more dangerous the further they were to the left. The conference of 1930 defined "women's work" within a rigidly sectarian framework. On Moscow's orders, the German delegation, the most strongly committed, set the tone, discernible in their denunciation of the "social fascists," in the suicidal flirtation with the Nazis imposed by Stalin, and then in the obliteration of any gender-specific notion of "women's work."

The conference was placed under the direction of Ruth Overlakh, who headed the women's section of the Central Committee of the German Communist Party. Overlakh immediately criticized what she considered an excessive appeal to "women's issues."

> Our women's sections and our activist women often concern themselves primarily, and sometimes even exclusively, with so-called women's issues, and this undivided absorption in so-called women's issues inevitably leads them to lag behind in comparison to the work rhythm of the mass of the party and to find themselves in isolation in work with women, and this isolation in turn leads to sliding down the slope of opportunism ... which has ended up in the fact that the leading organisms of work of women have essentially been conciliators and right-wingers until recent years.

Overlakh nevertheless denounced the obstinate refusal to organize specific women's meetings in the various Communist parties of the world and defined six special tasks to be proposed to women. Surprisingly enough, she declared the most clearly "female" of these tasks to be action against scabs and strikebreakers: "Massive presence in the picket lines as a compact wall; the women will control any worker who approaches: is he a scab or not?" Overlakh praised the actions of women at a picket line who had half undressed and chased a Nazi near their factory, thereafter throwing themselves en masse in front of cars full of scabs in order to prevent their entry. Her description treated women workers simply as shock commando units at strikes. The Russian Serafima Gopner, head of the agitprop sector of the Executive Committee, went even further: "The wives of workers must be made to understand that there is no revolution without sacrifice, so that they will accept the fact there won't be any bread in the house and their children will be hungry when their husband participates in a strike." In contrast to this heroism by proxy, the national delegates' reports sometimes reveal a sense of real anxiety.

Pierre Allard, (pseudonym of Guilio Cerreti) a member of the Central Committee of the French Communist Party from 1932 to 1945, complained: "Where France is concerned, it may be said that the work among women is more undeveloped than in many other countries." His compatriot, Jeanne Bulland, who headed the women's section of the Central Committee of the PCF, specified: "It must be said openly that our Communist Party has basically not yet committed itself to organizing women's labor." In other words, in ten years nothing had changed. The PCF thus presaged the forthcoming abandonment of this "work" by Moscow and therefore by the Comintern.

This conference was marked, in fact, by a reining in that heralded definitive strangulation. The Executive Committee of the Comintern had sent two inspectors to the conference: a Finnish committee member, Otto Kuusinen, who reduced "women's work" to "participation in the economic struggle, and in the struggle of the masses in general" and Boris Afanessevich Vassiliev, whom the Russian delegate Varvara Moirova thanked for his way of "bolshevizing" women's work. He was even more brutal:

> The women's section, incapable of finding women workers suited to participating in organizing strikes, organizing physical resistance to the police, or organizing any form of self-defense during strikes, must be immediately dissolved without any further discussion.

A type of "women's work" based on physical "resistance" to the police and on "self-defense"—in short, on physical confrontation—could only be reduced to its simplest expression. To diminish the concept still further, Vassiliev disdainfully brushed aside "housewives, nurses, women lawyers," deeming them to be good only for use when needed. This deliberately self-destructive approach eliminated any notion of "women's work." In 1932 the German Communist deputy Maria Reese wrote to Klara Zetkin: "Our women's section is a disaster," while at that very moment massive unemployment was reducing hundreds of thousands of women to despair. This did not prevent the 12th plenary meeting of the Comintern's Executive Committee in September 1932 from repeating the ritual injunction

> resolutely to end the undervaluation of the work of the masses of proletarian women, this being a task of particular importance at the moment; it is important to develop the mobilization of women workers on the basis of delegate assemblies, as this is a task of particular importance at the moment. (Twelfth Plenum of the Executive Committee of the Communist International)

The sloppy writing emphasizes the offhand manner in which activity relating to women was henceforth regarded in Moscow.

The chaos of industrialization under Stalin and the brutal haste with which the collectivization of land was managed degraded the legal and material situation of women workers in the USSR. (Exceptions were *apparatchik* women, who nevertheless would soon be faced with anxieties brought by Stalin's reign of terror, which came down on many of their husbands and would drag whole families down into their bloody fall.) The degradation of women's condition required that the "women's work" in the Communist parties be quickly stifled. This degradation was manifested in three ways:

1. A worsening of housing and living conditions concurrent with forced collectivization and chaotic industrialization, since the transfer of millions of peasants, male and female, into the factories and the cities was not accompanied by any effort of serious housing construction. Under these conditions, even a communal apartment was a luxury. Millions of workers, male and female, piled themselves into wretched collective housing, even into abandoned train cars. In *Final Judgment: My Life as a Soviet Defense Attorney* (1982), Dina Kaminskaya recalled the "horrible wooden shacks resembling pigsties, without any running water or drainage, divided into minuscule cells" where she would defend "women who had tried to bring home a few pieces of sugar or teaspoons of jam from the Bolshevik candy factory where they worked, in order to feed their starving brats." Under a decree of 7 August 1932 signed by Stalin personally, such acts of petty theft were punishable by death, or, in the case of attenuating circumstances, a minimum ten-year sentence in a camp. In *Predannaia revoliutsiia* (1936; *The Revolution Betrayed: What Is the Soviet Union and Where Is It Going?*), Leon Trotsky commented: "The true emancipation of women is impossible on the terrain of socialized misery." Low salaries and the emergence of a new privileged class fostered the development of prostitution, which was officially just as nonexistent as the Gulags where free forced labor of women and men was organized. The construction of camps far outpaced the creation of day care centers and nursery schools. Women factory and office workers were subjected to social oppression and family slavery that were presented as the very actualization of socialism. At the same time, the wives of highly placed bureaucrats, released from the worries of everyday life by a network of special stores and low-cost, female domestic help, could be idle as long as police repression did not come to trouble this temporary state of well-being.

2. The woman worker was transformed into a mere producer. The 1935 launching of Stakhanovism included a promotion of female tractor drivers, textile workers, and milkmaids with broad hips and solid muscles, whose "family" life was carefully eclipsed, since their role was to produce in ever greater quantities and to be the incarnation of absolute devotion to the plan (although it was continually being rigged) and deified work.

3. The Kremlin wanted to stabilize the family socially, yet at the same time it encouraged police practices, such as children's denunciation of their parents, that were intended to prevent the family from offering a last refuge for free and uncontrolled thinking. In 1934 Stalin promulgated a new Family Code that heavily penalized divorce: the first divorce cost 50 rubles, the second 150, and the third 300, while the average monthly salary of a worker was around 200 rubles.

The Kremlin's new policies would easily be embodied in the slogans of Vichy France glorifying work, family, and fatherland, with one small difference. While in Marshal Pétain's National Revolution women were meant to stay at home and have and raise children there, women under Stalin were to have children at home, contribute to production in the factory or the fields, and entrust their children to collective institutions (few of which actually existed). The new cult of the family, then of fertility, resuscitated the archaic figure of the *babushka* (grandmother) raising the children. "High" society reverted to the mores of the czarist court: members of the Politburo, and particularly Mikhail Ivanovich Kalinin, the president of the Republic, had a notorious penchant for ballerinas.

The Stalinization of the Communist parties produced the decline of this "women's work" conceived of as a class or Communist activity rather than a women's activity, even in a purely formal or decorative way. The correspondence of the International Women's Secretariat with the women's sections of the Central Committees of Communist parties is edifying in this regard: the last exchange of letters with China dates to December 1930; with Spain and Poland to December 1934; and with England and, more surprisingly, with France, to March 1935. The termination of these exchanges also corresponded to the patriotic change of direction of the French Communist Party (Stalin then declared to Pierre Laval, France's minister of foreign affairs, that he understood the French war effort) and to the preparation for the Seventh (and final) Congress of the Communist International. This congress centered on alliances with "radical" and similar parties in the world and the denunciation, then the condemnation, of abortion in the USSR in 1936.

In spite of these developments, on 1 August 1935 the Seventh Congress of the Communist International again voted in favor of a resolution criticizing "the undervaluation of the labor of women workers." It was a ritual formula, within a litany about the "undervaluation of labor in reform and fascist unions and in the mass workers' organizations created by bourgeois parties . . . [and the undervaluation] of the importance of the work of farmers and the masses of the urban lower bourgeoisie." These resolutions were ritualistic, designed purely as demonstrations of correct ideology, and the congress made no decision whatsoever regarding "women's work."

Dissolution of the International Women's Secretariat

Three months later, in November 1935, the Comintern's Executive Committee dissolved the International Women's Secretariat (which, it should be recalled, had been renamed the Women's Section of the Executive Committee). Formally still active, the women's sections of the Central Committees of Communist parties disappeared as well.

The road was now clear to launch a campaign in the USSR against abortion. On 17 April 1936, the union newspaper, *Troud*, published an article by Stalin, whose rhetoric heralded word for word that of future "right to life" organizations.

We need people. Abortion, which destroys life, is unacceptable in our country. A Soviet woman has the same rights as a man, but that does not exempt her from the great and noble duty which nature has given her: she is a mother; she gives life. And that is certainly not a private matter but a matter of high social importance.

Aaron Soltz, a member of the Supreme Court and former president of the party's Control Commission, declared, "Since socialist society does not know unemployment, women cannot have the right to spurn the 'joys of motherhood'; therefore, abortion must be forbidden."

On 27 June 1936 a law forbidding abortion to terminate a first pregnancy was proclaimed. Two months later, in August 1936, the first of the great show trials in Moscow unleashed the terror against Trotskyites and against the hundreds of thousands of men and women labeled as such. This purge ended with the death penalty for 16 former leaders of the Bolshevik Party and the revolution, among them Zinoviev and Kamenev.

In the same month of August 1936, the *Stato Operaio*, the monthly of the Italian Communist Party, published a long and urgent call of the Central Committee of the PCI "to former fighters and volunteers in the Abyssinian War . . . to intellectuals, youth, women, to all Italian people!" The object: "For the salvation of Italy, reconciliation of the Italian people." The call forcefully proclaimed,

The Fascist program of 1919 has not been realized! People of Italy! Fascists of the old guard! Young Fascists! We, the Communists, will make our own the Fascist program of 1919, which is a program of peace, of liberty, of the defense of the interests of workers, and we say to you: let us wage a united struggle for the realization of this program.

Such a position required the liquidation of opponents, who were conveniently labelled as Trotskyites and denounced as fascist agents. In the Italy of Mussolini and the Lateran Treaty [the concordat signed in 1929, normalizing relations between the Holy See and the Italian state], the proposed "united struggle" entailed the abandonment even of any purely verbal policy in defense of basic rights for women, particularly women workers and peasants. From that time on, women were virtually reduced to *images d'Épinal* [a type of crude popular illustration]. This status is exemplified by Vera Mukhina's gigantic and endlessly reproduced stainless-steel sculpture, *Worker and Collective Farm Woman*, which topped the Soviet pavilion at the 1937 International Exhibition in Paris. Woman no longer served as anything more than a motif to exalt the happiness and the enthusiasm of Soviet women, to join in the male hymns of praise to the ineluctable victories (although these were often belied by facts), to denounce the enemy of the moment, and to stigmatize the infamy of the Trotskyites. Thus, the March 1938 issue of the magazine *The Communist International* published an article by Nadezdja Krupskaya, Lenin's widow, entitled, "USSR Women, Happy and Equal in Rights to Men" as well as two articles by Dolores Ibarruri, known as La Pasionaria, leader of the Spanish Communist Party. One of Ibarruri's pieces was a "Call to German Mothers to Prevent Their Sons from Being Sent to Spain" [to fight the republicans] and the other was a pompous ode in honor of International Women's Day on 8 March, described as a "Day of Hope." In her article, Krupskaya celebrated Soviet women

by denouncing those condemned at the third purge trial in Moscow: "The trial of the traitors to the cause of the working class, to the cause of socialism, the trial of the 'rightist and Trotskyite bloc'. . . . History has never seen such cowardice, such despicable betrayal." Ibarruri prophesied: "In our Spain, radiant with suns and flowers, with its splendid landscapes, marvelous mountains, burning plains and shaded valleys, etc., fascism will break its teeth." Endless paragraphs in the same vein followed. Further, since women really should be mentioned on this day devoted to them, La Pasionaria proclaimed: "With industrious hands and courageous in the face of the enemy, women will educate tomorrow's Spain." How, exactly, this would be accomplished remained a total mystery. In any case, republican Spain would fall a few months after the printing of this flood of emotion. La Pasionaria would pursue her bureaucratic career, the satisfied symbol of Stalinism and of the Comintern's elimination of work on women's issues. Five years later, in Moscow, Ibarruri was among the signatories of Stalin's decision to dissolve the Comintern.

On 15 May 1943, the Comintern, which Stalin disdainfully referred to as a "boutique," was actually dissolved. And soon, under the aegis of Communist parties, ideologically unanchored national organizations such as the Union des Femmes Françaises (Union of French Women) would flourish. Hand in hand with the church, these organizations led vigorous campaigns against abortion. Gone were the days when Klara Zetkin and Communist women led campaigns against Article 218 of the German Penal Code, which threatened proabortion women with prison sentences, or against the Papal Encyclic *Casti Connubi*. Stalinist art celebrated female brigadiers in shawls, while the Gulag was creating camps or zones for women, an ironic last refuge for women's rights.

After the dissolution of the Comintern, the much-vaunted return to the values of the past was completed semantically: in 1946 the Council of People's Commissars was renamed the Council of Ministers, and then the Red Army of Workers and Farmers became simply "the Army." A veritable national hysteria accompanied the anti-Semitic campaign, which culminated in the liquidation of the Jewish Anti-Fascist Committee (1948–1952). This was followed by the alleged plot of the white coats [resulting in the arrests of (mostly Jewish) doctors who were charged with medical assassinations], which was openly denounced on 13 January 1953. Reactionary politics had come full circle. One image remains especially symbolic of this culmination: the little Kazakh girl photographed in 1937 in the arms of Stalin, a bouquet of flowers in hand, symbolizing the joys of living under the Stalinist constitution, "the most democratic one in the world." The photograph graced an obituary for Stalin printed on the first page of the 11–17 March 1953 issue of *La vie ouvrière*, the weekly of France's Comité Général du Travail (CGT; General Labor Committee), but the little girl of 1937 was by then in the Gulag after her father's execution and her mother's death in one of the camps.

Bibliography

Manuscript Sources

Archives of the Russian Center for the Preservation of
Contemporary History. Moscow Collection of documents on the

International Women's Secretariat of the Executive Committee of the Communist International; Collection 507, files 1, 2, and 3.

Print Sources

Balabanoff, Angelica, *My Life As a Rebel*, New York and London: Harper and Brothers, 1938; reprint, Bloomington, Indiana: Indiana University Press, 1973

Bukharin, Nikolai Ivanovich, and Evgenni Alekseevich Preobrazhenskii, *The ABC of Communism*, translated by P. Lavin, Glasgow: Socialist Labour Press, 1921

Communist International, *The Communist International 1919–1943; Documents*, selected and edited by Jane Degras, 3 vols., London: Oxford University Press, 1956–71

Communist International, *7th Congress, Moscow (1935): Report of the Seventh World Congress of the Communist International*, London: Modern Books, 1936

Communist International, *Theses, Resolutions, and Manifestos of the First Four Congresses of the Third International*, translated by Alix Holt and Barbara Holland, London: Ink Links, and Atlantic Highlands, New Jersey: Humanities Press, 1980

Kaminskaya, Dina, *Final Judgment: My Life as a Soviet Defense Attorney*, translated by Michael Glenny, New York: Simon and Schuster, 1982

Kollontai, Aleksandra, *The Autobiography of a Sexually Emancipated Woman*, translated by Salvator Attanasio, edited by Irving Fetscher, New York: Schocken Books, 1971

Kollontai, [Alexandra], *Bulletin communiste* 23 (2 June 1921)

Kollontai, [Alexandra], *L'Internationale communiste* 19 (December 1921), *Le travail du secrétariat international des femmes*, Feltrinelli Reprint, 1967

Kollontai, [Alexandra], *Marxisme et révolution sexuelle*, Paris: Maspero, 1987

Kollontai, Aleksandra, *Women Workers Struggle for Their Rights*, translated by Celia Britton, 3rd edition, Bristol, England: Falling Wall Press, 1973

Kollontai, Aleksandra, *The Workers Opposition*, Reading, England: Morse, 1960 Trotsky, Leon, *The Revolution Betrayed: What Is the Soviet Union and Where Is It Going?*, translated by Max Eastman, Garden City, New York: 1937; 5th edition, New York: Pathfinder Books, 1972 (*Complete Works*, vol. 40, Russian Edition). (*Complete Works*, vol. 7, Russian Edition, 1925).

Trotsky, Leon, *Problems of Life*, translated by Z. Vengerova, London: Methuen, and New York: George H. Doran, 1924

Trotsky, Leon, *The First Five Years of the Communist International*, translated and edited by John G. Wright, New York: Pioneers Publishers, 1945–53, and London: New Park, 1973–74

Zetkin, [Clara], *Batailles pour les femmes*, translated by Gilbert Badia et al., edited by Gilbert Badia, Paris: Éditions sociales, 1980

Zetkin, [Clara], *Clara Zetkin: Selected Writings*, edited by Philip S. Foner, New York: International Publishers, 1984

Zetkin, Klara, *Reminiscences of Lenin; Dealing with Lenin's Views on the Position of Women and Other Questions*, London: Modern Books, 1929

Reference Works

Badia, Gilbert, *Clara Zetkin, féministe sans frontières*, Paris: Éditions de l'Atelier, 1993

Camparini, Aurelia, *Questione femminile e Terza Internazionale*, Bari, Italy: De Donato, 1978

Daniels, Robert V., *A Documentary History of Communism*, Hanover, New Hampshire: University Press of New England, 1960; 3rd edition as *A Documentary History of Communism and the World: From Revolution to Collapse*, 1994

Edmondson, Linda, editor, *Women and Society in Russia and the Soviet Union*, Cambridge and New York: Cambridge University Press, 1992

Fauré, Christine, "The Utopia of the New Woman in the Work of Alexandra Kollontai and Its Impact on the French Feminist and Communist Press," in *Women in Culture and Politics: A Century of Change*, edited by Judith Friedlander et al., Bloomington, Indiana: Indiana University Press, 1986

Hennen, Jacqueline, editor, "Kollantai Alexandra, Conférences sur la libération des femmes," Paris, La Brèche, 1978

Humbert Droz, Jules, *De Lénine à Staline: Dix ans au service de l'Internationale communiste, 1921–1931)*, Neufchâtel, Switzerland: La Baconnière, 1971

Lanérès, Catherine, *Les Femmes travailleuses dans le mouvement ouvrier*, Paris: La Vérité, 1994

Marie, Jean-Jacques, *Staline*, Paris: Fayard, 2001

Stites, Richard, *The Women's Liberation Movement in Russia. Feminism: Nihilism and Bolshevism, 1860–1930*, Princeton, New Jersey: Princeton University Press, 1978; revised edition, 1991

Porter, Cathy, *Alexandra Kollontai: A Biography*, London: Virago, 1980

Porter, Cathy, *Alexandra Kollontai: The Lonely Struggle of the Woman Who Defied Lenin*, New York: Dial Press, 1980

Waters, Elizabeth, "In the Shadow of the Comintern: The Communist Women's Movement, 1920–43," in *Promissory Notes: Women in the Transition to Socialism*, edited by Sonia Kruks, Rayna Rapp, and Marilyn B. Young, New York: Monthly Review Press, 1989

STRUGGLES FOR DEMOCRACY

WOMEN'S RIGHTS AND SUFFRAGE IN THE UNITED STATES, 1848–1920

FRANÇOISE BASCH

SUFFRAGE MOVEMENT, WOMEN'S RIGHTS movement, feminism—not one of these terms by itself offers a precise definition of the uneven but sustained progress of American women toward social and political emancipation in the 19th century. None can fully represent the century-long evolution of that permanent tension between sexual equality and male hegemony.

"Feminism," the term most commonly used today, only appeared at the end of the 19th century, and it is thus an anachronism—albeit a convenient one—to use it to describe the first steps toward emancipation. Furthermore, in the period between the 1840s and the American Civil War, the pioneers of emancipation referred explicitly to their struggle as a "woman's rights" movement. This first phase in the long march toward liberation corresponded to a struggle for social and then political rights in an era when traditional values were being questioned. In the America of Andrew Jackson, the mood was one of social reform and utopian aspirations toward change in the areas of religion and family, and with regard to what Elizabeth Cady Stanton and other abolitionist writers of the time called the "peculiar institution" of slavery. For many women who joined the various reform societies, the search for an identity and a status in their own right set them imperceptibly on the road to independence, even before they formed their own movement in 1848.

After the Civil War, in a radically changed political landscape and following considerable improvements in the legal and social status of women, the once-unified "woman's rights" movement gave way to a number of groups and organizations. A multitude of women's groups, clubs, and associations were created, with a broad range of activities. At the same time, women's rights advocates progressively focused on the single issue of the right to vote—obtained in several states after 1869—until the federal battle for constitutional suffrage was finally won in 1920. The once subversive demand for citizenship that had boldly contested the rights of the almighty husband, that possessor of patriarchal values, had lost its edge and its revolutionary character by the early 20th century.

Women's Rights: Radical Protest before the Civil War

The Beginnings

It is essential, if we are to understand this long march, to review the movement's period of gestation as well as the ideological influences that contributed to inspiring protest in the first decades of the 19th century.

Two English women exercised an undeniable influence on the American theoretical debate concerning female identity and emancipation. The first was Mary Wollstonecraft (1759–97). A staunch supporter of the French Revolution, she defended the idea of the rights of man, taken in the broad sense of the rights of individuals of both sexes, and opposed privileges of class and gender in the name of justice and equality. In 1792 she published *A Vindication of the Rights of Woman*, a fundamental text that saw several editions in the United States and England. Elizabeth Cady Stanton (1815–1902) and Susan B. Anthony (1820–1906) judged it to be sufficiently modern for publication in 1869. Opposing the views of Jean-Jacques Rousseau and other theoreticians of the "nature" of women, Wollstonecraft argued that the alleged weaknesses in female temperament—frivolity, flirtatiousness, and ignorance—were largely attributable to a process of socialization enforced by male hegemony and aimed at raising women to be obedient and seductive. Wollstonecraft nonetheless severely criticized the complicity of women who, through passivity or cowardliness, lent themselves to this endeavor. Through her insistence on the importance of the effects of social environment, Wollstonecraft seriously undermined the notion of "nature" and established the basis for a cultural and egalitarian approach to the condition of women.

The second notable English influence on the nascent women's movement in the United States was Scottish-born Frances Wright (1795–1852), a promulgator of utopian socialism, which had inspired numerous American communities. Closely connected to Robert Owen, the British industrialist and utopian philosopher, Wright collaborated in the creation of New

Harmony, Indiana, in 1824, and then founded her own community in Tennessee. She had planned to buy slaves in order to emancipate them and teach them how to live as free people—liberated from both servitude and the marital bond—in an environment redeemed from racism. But the subjects of her experiment did not live in conformance with her lofty vision and libertarian aspirations, and Wright's utopian project failed miserably.

The ideals of human rights and sexual equality inspired by the French Revolution and Enlightenment rationalism stimulated the American women who pioneered the movement for emancipation. But the revolutionary philosophy introduced by the "founding mothers" emerged only every now and then. What played a key role in the genesis of the drive for emancipation was the typically American religious phenomenon of evangelical Protestantism. This movement, which had its roots in the 17th and 18th centuries, found expression in the revivalist Awakenings that took place in New England and Virginia between 1730 and 1760, and then in the West around 1800. These "conversion" campaigns were led by itinerant preachers who admonished sinners to repent and devote themselves to Christ. The Awakenings created a climate of mystical and moral fervor that stimulated philanthropic action and inspired the temperance and abolitionist movements, both of which mobilized women in large numbers. This climate was further enhanced by the millenarian ethos of the late 18th century, which inspired sects led by women such as Ann Lee, founder of the first Shaker communities.

Reacting against elitism and intellectualism, sects and religious groups continued to emerge in opposition to the established churches and their hierarchical and secular concerns. Thousands of believers, brimming with optimism and enthusiasm and carried away by a kind of religious populism, began to search for salvation beyond Calvinist predestination. The drive for democratization and the surge of emotion provided particular encouragement to African Americans and women to express themselves. The latter converted in large numbers, especially in New England, where after 1790, with so many men leaving for the West, females soon outnumbered males.

The evangelical movement produced myriad charitable associations that encouraged the participation of women—as wives and mothers, and in the name of "domesticity" and "true womanhood"—thus giving women legitimacy and providing them with a field of action and an identity. The approval of spiritual and group leaders enabled women to free themselves from the "curse of Eve" and to become instead the dispensers of beneficial influence. In the popular imagination, Mary took over from Eve, for she was the guardian of faith and morality, particularly of the young. The American woman fulfilled her mission by participating in moral reform societies, and through the struggle against sin, female prostitution, and male lust.

In the 1830s the New England Female Reform Society was founded to "save fallen women," to ostracize sinners, and to raise boys and girls in sexual purity. The struggle against prostitution, based as it was on a staunch belief in female purity and male sensuality, evinced a certain disapproval of men. Through their visits to hospitals, hospices, and brothels, and through the distribution of brochures and Bibles from the early hours of the morning (including Sundays), the members of the Female Reform Society engaged in a "pious harassment," even going so far as to publish the names of suspect men. Two themes dominated their message: the uncontrolled, destructive sensuality of American men and the moral superiority of American women. The latter were called upon to create a vast union of mothers dedicated to raising their sons in sexual purity. In 1839 the society counted 445 auxiliary groups. In its progressive moments, it recognized the need for women to work and occasionally protested against the tyranny of husbands, those "Russian autocrats." It even maintained contact with such committed activists as Lucretia Mott (1793–1880), a women's rights pioneer, and Emma Hart Willard (1787–1870), who founded the remarkable secondary school, the Troy Female Seminary.

It was social action of this kind, inspired by their sense of moral mission, that kindled women's self-affirmation and their demand for autonomy. On a practical level, it was through their meetings, travel, and propaganda efforts that women learned how to organize and act collectively. Thus, the very forces that sought to confine these "angels" to the hearth incited them to public action out in the world, providing a contradictory pull that lay the groundwork for feminist demands.

The temperance movement was another outgrowth of evangelical Protestantism's emphasis on moral reform. The first temperance societies appeared at the beginning of the 19th century, and by 1833 the anti-alcohol movement counted thousands of local chapters. Like the crusade against prostitution, the temperance struggle was considered to be part and parcel of a female vocation and to provide a fitting sphere of action for women dedicated to the protection of the home. Although the movement came up against the difficulty of assisting women in distress who had no legal rights to divorce or separation, it served to highlight a microcosm of sexual inequality. It contributed to the emergence of a female culture based on the dualistic opposition between the violent alcoholic male and the victimized female. This social and symbolic dimension persisted in feminine and feminist sensibilities throughout the 19th century.

Amelia Jenks Bloomer (1818–94), editor-in-chief of *The Lily* and pioneer of women's dress reform (notably the famous "bloomers"), was active in the temperance movement, as was Susan B. Anthony. Anthony organized the Woman's New York State Temperance Society in April 1852, after she had been denied the right to speak at a temperance meeting the previous year because of her sex. In a letter written from Seneca Falls and dated 20 June 1853, Elizabeth Cady Stanton counseled her humorously, "Susan, I do beg of you . . . to waste no powder on the Woman's State Temperance Society. We have other and bigger fish to fry." Anthony had been raised in what was for the era a particularly egalitarian Quaker family, and had little tolerance for sexist behavior. She was not the only one: for many activists, the misogyny that reigned in philanthropic societies, coupled with the dogma of women's moral superiority, fueled demands for an independent movement.

The culture of the era was marked by a radical, multifaceted social reform movement steeped in the tradition of Christian evangelism. In the name of the perfectibility of man and the coming of the golden age, there was an upsurge in resolve to change life—to abolish slavery, the family, and marriage. People created alternative societies inspired by millenarian or socialist utopias (Shakers, Oneida, New Harmony, Modern Times). They went to war against the oppression of women and explored new remedies for their ills. The disciples of spiritualism attempted to soften the reality of death by communicating with the departed through a medium, who was often a woman. A powerful ferment of individual and collective energies, the reform movement played a considerable role in shaping the cultural profile of the women's rights movement.

The crusade against slavery was nourished by evangelical perfectionism and reformist enthusiasm. Women's abolitionist fervor enabled them to make the connection between moral action and awareness of oppression, and to take one more step on the road toward their own emancipation.

The abolitionists considered slavery to be a sin against God and the Gospel, and a violation of the "natural rights" of the individual. For white women activists, the fight against slavery highlighted their own oppression: subjugated, dispossessed by marriage of all their rights, deprived of education, an identity, and the ballot, women felt close to the slave, despite the chasm that separated them. An eloquent slogan imported from England, "Am I not a slave and a sister?" best expressed this growing awareness. The image of an imploring female slave in chains, published in 1832 by William Lloyd Garrison in his abolitionist newspaper, *The Liberator*, became a popular symbol of oppression and female solidarity.

The specificity of the abolitionist movement and disagreements within its ranks provoked contentiousness about the presence of women within that movement. In 1831 Garrison began his uncompromising campaign for the immediate emancipation of slaves; he viewed slavery as a national sin. He addressed this message to women, speaking to their hearts and moral consciences in a vehement and sentimental vein. He was, however, the only male abolitionist to recognize women as full-fledged activists. Maria Weston Chapman (1806–86), known later as "Garrison's Lieutenant," was one of the first women to respond to the call, followed by Lydia Maria Child (1820–80) and Lucretia Mott. In 1832 Chapman created the Boston Female Anti-Slavery Society, as an auxiliary to the New England Anti-Slavery Society founded by Garrison.

However, opposition to women remained strong within the ranks of the abolitionists. In 1833, when the founding convention of the American Anti-Slavery Society was held in Philadelphia, the local women abolitionists (including Mott) were not immediately invited to join, nor were they invited to sign the Declaration, although it had been written by Mott, whose Quaker family was active in the Underground Railroad. This prompted the excluded women to form the Philadelphia Female Anti-Slavery Society, whose membership was biracial and predominantly Quaker.

The case of Sarah (1792–1873) and Angelina Grimké (1805–79) shows how nearly impossible it was for women to engage in action without coming into conflict with the dominant model for female behavior. The Grimké sisters, daughters of a South Carolina plantation owner, were dedicated abolitionists. In 1837 Angelina Grimké wrote an appeal to the Christian women of the South, urging them to stand up against slavery; in 1838 the sisters embarked on a six-month speaking tour, often addressing large audiences of both races and sexes. This drew a swift reaction: in July of 1837 the Council of Congregationalist Ministers of Massachusetts issued a pastoral letter emphasizing the incompatibility of public activity and womanly nature. Catherine Beecher (1800–78), a well-known conservative educator, chorused her agreement. Sarah Grimké responded with her *Letters on the*

Inequality of the Sexes and the Condition of Women (1837–38), in which she sought to demonstrate that the Scriptures conveyed a message of sexual equality that had been distorted by translators and men of the church.

Paradoxically, recognition of equality between men and women in abolitionist groups was rare; Garrison's supporters, and a few other influential personalities such as Henry Chapman, James Mott, Theodore Weld, and Stephen Foster, all married to abolitionist women, were exceptions to the rule. Many of the (more orthodox) Quakers opposed female action. Women, on the other hand, generally favored active female participation, and the controversy sometimes boiled over—for instance, when Lucy Stone (1818–93) criticized the humiliating inequality of men and women in the teaching professions. Even at the end of the 1830s, the opposition to women activists remained unrelenting. In 1840 the appointment of Abby Kelley (1810–87; later Abby Kelley Foster) to the first position of responsibility in the Anti-Slavery Society to be held by a woman caused an uproar that ended in a split in the society.

That same year, the World Anti-Slavery Convention in London barred women delegates from participation, relegating them to a railed-off space where they were forced to listen to the debates in silence. William Lloyd Garrison, Wendell Phillips, and Henry Stanton were the only ones to express their solidarity with the excluded women. On that day, Lucretia Mott, one of the rebuffed delegates, and Elizabeth Cady Stanton, who had accompanied her husband to the convention, made a commitment to ensure that such a denial of justice would not occur again. Thus, the recognition of slavery as both a reality and a symbol of oppression, together with women's drive to play an active role in its abolition, forged the links between abolitionism and feminism. The phrase so dear to the activists, "Thine in the bonds of womanhood," neatly captured the double dimension of oppression and solidarity.

Nonetheless, all forms of oppression could not be seen as identical to one another. It fell to Sojourner Truth (1795–1883), a former slave whose noble stature and charisma enhanced her extraordinary eloquence, to highlight the difference between lived experience and metaphor. At the Akron, Ohio, women's rights convention in 1851, Sojourner Truth recounted her experience as a slave exposed to male brutality, demonstrating the absurdity of the conventional discourse on women's nature:

> Look at me! Look at my arm! I have ploughed and planted, and gathered into barns and no man could head me! And ain't I a woman? I could work as much and eat as much as a man . . . and bear the lash as well! And ain't I a woman? I have borne 13 children and seen them most all sold off to slavery. (*Reminiscences of Frances D. Gage*, cited in Stanton et al., vol. 1.)

Rarely had racism and sentimental rhetoric about women been so powerfully exposed. The members of the convention were moved to tears by this unlettered woman's irrefutable demonstration of the connection between slavery, racism, class domination, and feminine stereotypes.

Education unquestionably played a key role throughout the century in women's drive for their "elevation" and emancipation. Mere "feminine accomplishments" no longer fit the bill for the "republican mother" called upon to educate future citizens and, in the long term, to exercise her civil rights. Establishments for the secondary education of girls were created, such as Emma Willard's Troy Female Seminary, in 1821, and the famous school that Catherine Beecher (1800–78) founded in Hartford, Connecticut, in 1828. While the moral and domestic mission assigned to women continued to be a major objective, the new educators developed a more ambitious intellectual and scientific program—a program closer to the male curriculum—for their students.

The literacy rate for girls doubled between 1780 and 1840. New schools for women included Mount Holyoke (founded in 1837) and Vassar College (1865). Among the notable coeducational colleges were Oberlin (founded in 1833, and the first U.S. institution to award college degrees to women), Antioch (founded in 1853), and Swarthmore (founded in 1864). Teaching was the only postcollegiate career open to the women graduates, who were usually white Anglo-Saxon Protestants from middle- or lower-middle-class Quaker or Unitarian families in the Northeast. By 1850 there were already 55,000 women teachers; they tended to marry later than the average woman and have fewer children.

Such figures notwithstanding, the most widespread occupation for 19th-century American women was domestic service: there were 330,000 female household servants in 1850, many of whom were African-American or Irish. In addition, many young women from the rural areas were employed as workers in textile factories; in Lowell, Massachusetts, they were quick to organize the Female Labor Reform Association to demand the ten-hour workday.

Throughout the 1830s, then, women's active involvement in the philanthropic and reform movements, driven by a sense of moral mission, was strong. Their crusade for virtue and justice expressed the thirst for progress and reform that marked the era, while the philanthropic societies constituted a cultural model in which bonds of friendship, tenderness, and solidarity between women played a key role. In the two decades that followed, religious dynamism dwindled (although without disappearing entirely), and women's rights became a full-fledged objective.

The Women's Rights Movement

The formative, dynamic phase of the women's rights movement began with a convention held at Seneca Falls, New York, on 19 and 20 July 1848. It was called by a small group of women led by Elizabeth Cady Stanton and Lucretia Mott. Stanton and her husband had settled in Seneca Falls the previous year, and Mott was in the area to visit her sister and attend a Quaker meeting. Neither had forgotten the humiliation they had experienced at the Anti-Slavery Convention in London in 1840.

Men had been requested to abstain from attending the convention on the first day, but those who came were not turned away. And since none of the organizers felt sufficiently confident to take the chair, the task was entrusted to Mott's husband. A "Declaration of Sentiments and Resolutions" was presented to the convention for approval. This founding text had been written amid hesitancy and groping, but the idea of partially paraphrasing the Declaration of Independence to include women—absent from the original text—received unanimous support:

"We hold these truths to be self-evident, that all men and all women are created equal. . . ." While modern in outlook, the Seneca Falls declaration also laid claim to historical roots, and thus permitted the women rebels to assert their right to share in the legacy of the founding fathers and the American Revolution.

It was Stanton who stood up before the 300 people crowded into the small Seneca Falls chapel to read this historic text, which covered the full extent of women's subordination in the United States and detailed discrimination in the workplace, at school, in the family, in citizenship, and in religion: it was an act of accusation and provided a carefully considered catalog of demands. With characteristic audacity, Stanton proposed a call for women's right to vote, the only one of twelve resolutions not to be unanimously adopted. In 1848—a year that saw revolutions in Europe and the publication of Marx and Engels's *Communist Manifesto*—the women of Seneca Falls launched a blistering attack destined to transform American society.

The originality of the pioneers of Seneca Falls lay in their frontal attack on women's subjugation to male power, particularly in marriage. No mention was made of class or social structure in their plea against oppression: all the fire was directed at men. In 1848 in France, by contrast, women's analysis of their oppression emphasized political factors rather than the responsibility of the dominant sex.

Seneca Falls was to be the start of a long succession of women's rights movement conventions at the state or national level, where strategy was devised and where the stars of the movement, often brilliant orators, would deliver impassioned addresses to the activists and raise the morale of their troops. During these years, Stanton wrote for the only mainstream paper to take the movement's demands seriously, Horace Greeley's *New York Tribune*. Under the pseudonym "Sun Flower," she also contributed to *The Lily*, a temperance paper edited by the energetic postmistress of Seneca Falls, Amelia Jenks Bloomer.

The "Declaration of Sentiments" laid particular emphasis on the oppression of women in marriage. At that time, as under the English law of coverture, women upon marriage were *feme covert*—deemed to be under the legal protection of their husbands—and were thus deprived of all legal and social identity. They had no rights whatsoever to the property they had acquired by dowry, inheritance, or their own work. They could not sign contracts, sue or be sued, or gain custody over their children in the case of separation. In her 1860 address to the New York State legislature, Stanton pointed out: "Blackstone [celebrated author of commentaries of English law] declares that the husband and wife are one and learned commentators have decided that that one is the husband" (quoted in Schneir). Not the least of the paradoxes of the period was to see the acclaimed female ideal—the wife-and-mother—subjected to a servitude close to slavery, while widows and unmarried women enjoyed a higher status in the eyes of the law: as *feme sole*, they were endowed with a legal identity and the right to own property. Similarly, frontier women, owing to the harshness of pioneer life, enjoyed a degree of independence that sometimes received legal recognition: in 1850, for example, the State of Oregon authorized both women and men to acquire 320 acres per person.

In 1837 a few bold activists began campaigning against the injustice of the status of married women. They stepped in at a time when, for unrelated reasons, legislators were busy with the reform of marriage laws. In those days of economic depression, it was thought to be advantageous to grant a married woman a (limited) right to property in order to allow for the transfer of assets to her name, thereby avoiding bankruptcies and protecting private property. These reforms provided a favorable context for pioneers of the cause of married women's rights, such as Ernestine Potowsky Rose (1810–92), Paulina Wright Davis (1813–76), Stanton, and Anthony.

Despite the experience they had acquired through their political activities—organizing meetings, canvasing door-to-door, petitioning state legislatures—the women encountered enormous difficulties. Their tales have a heroic ring, even though Stone, the Grimké sisters, Rose, Stanton, and Anthony all recount their campaigns, their travels, the problems with transportation and lodging with characteristic modesty. And indeed, women were not well accepted in the role of political agitators, frequently meeting with hostility, insults, and physical threats. Rose, who began campaigning in 1836, obtained only six signatures for her first petition. She writes of her difficult experiences when canvasing door-to-door, and the indifference or blindness of women to their own oppression. She encountered xenophobia, racism, and misogyny at many an "anti-Bible" meeting, where she faced insults not only as a woman but also as a foreigner and a Jew.

Despite the obstacles to reform, the status of married women began to improve, notably through a series of property laws passed by certain state legislatures between 1836 and 1860. In 1848 the State of New York granted wives the right to dispose freely of assets acquired through dowry or inheritance, thus sheltering them from their husbands' creditors. This was an important measure for women of the wealthy classes, but meaningless for others; it nonetheless marked a significant step toward economic independence for women. In 1860 another law granted married women the right to file lawsuits, sign contracts, and dispose of their own property and wages. Anthony had been campaigning for this reform since 1853, and, with her 60 "captains," had succeeded in collecting 6,000 signatures. She was convinced that economic, social, and political power were closely related and declared that there could be no freedom for women as long as they were denied legal ownership of their property.

By the end of the first phase of the women's rights movement, considerable gains had been made in the status of married women with regard to property rights, custody of children, and recognition of their legal identity. Until then, and regardless of their marital status, activists such as Stanton, Rose, and Stone had viewed marriage as a symbol of women's slavery. Moreover, among the activists at least, there was a distinct reluctance to enter into the state of dependence or "civil death" which marriage represented at the time. Stone made her fiancé, Henry Blackwell, wait for several years before she consented to marry him. Tortured by migraines and anxiety, and paralyzed by the fear that she would be forced into idleness or her activities restricted, she dreaded entering the irremediable bond even with a man who promised her complete freedom and solemnly renounced his privileges as a husband. However excellent Blackwell's intentions may have been, their life together indicated that Stone's fears were not entirely unfounded.

For the majority of women, marriage was their lot in life, and a permanently binding one at that. Stanton firmly believed in the necessity of being able to end a marriage. Daring as always, she threw herself into the battle for the liberalization of divorce laws in 1860, at a time when even her comrades in struggle were reluctant to champion the cause. Robert Dale Owen had managed to get a law passed in Indiana that added desertion and habitual drunkenness to adultery as grounds for divorce; in New York State, a similar bill was defeated by only four votes. Stanton thus thought the moment had come to introduce the question at the tenth national convention of the women's rights movement in New York in May 1860. However, the ensuing debates on divorce brought to light the profound ideological disagreements that existed within the movement before it was to split.

Stanton had long been tormented by the destruction wreaked among poor families by alcoholism and the brutality of drunken husbands, and as early as 1860 she saw middle-class marriages as often nothing more than "legalized prostitution." Later, in 1894, she argued, "It is folly to talk of the sacredness of marriage and maternity, while the wife is practically regarded as an inferior, a subject, a slave" (*Eighty Years and More [1815–1897]: Reminiscences of Elizabeth Cady Stanton*, 1898). For marriage to regain its meaning, she believed, it should no longer be controlled by religious or civil institutions, but be treated as a simple contract between the parties that could instead be dissolved quickly and easily in case of incompatibility. Rose, her ally at the convention, demystified the sentimental and religious view of marriage with caustic irony, though denying any sympathy for "free love" or relaxation of morality. Anthony shared this point of view, as did Lucretia Mott, who in a letter of 30 April 1861 wrote to Lydia Mott that "there must be a total reconstruction of the system of marriage" (quoted in Stanton, *Eighty Years and More*).

But the majority of the members, including Stone, the Reverend Antoinette Brown (1825–1921; later Antoinette Brown Blackwell), and long-time abolitionist allies such as Wendell Phillips, Horace Greeley, and William Lloyd Garrison, disputed the validity of any secular and contractual conception of marriage. Reverend Brown, whose theological training at Oberlin College strengthened her position, declared that the only legitimate grounds for divorce would be a wife's subjection and humiliation. Torn between her feminist views and her religious convictions, she saw marriage as a union between equals, yet held the wife responsible for the redemption of her husband and the happiness of the family. After a stormy debate that some of Stanton's adversaries did not even want to see recorded in the minutes, the opponents of the liberalization of divorce won by a wide margin. Feminists and abolitionists opposed to religious interference in private life remained a minority.

Public opinion was outraged by this attack on the foundations of civil and religious authority and the family. Stanton, who had not really expected to cause such uproar, was stunned by the outcry of the press against the liberalization of divorce: "I began to feel that I had inadvertently taken out the underpinning from the social system" (*Elizabeth Cady Stanton as Revealed in Her Letters, Diary and Reminiscences*, 1922). She had underestimated the subversive nature of her initiative would later acknowledge its premature character. But her bold vision was beginning to undermine her popularity.

Toward Citizenship—Avatars of the Right to Vote: The Civil War and After

In 1860 South Carolina seceded from the United States, and six other slave-owning southern states rapidly followed suit. In 1861 the Confederates attacked Fort Sumter, and President Lincoln declared war on the rebel states. By 1863 he had come to the decision to free the slaves. In 1865, at the end of a difficult and fratricidal war—more than a million deaths for a population of 31 million—he had the United States Congress pass the 13th Amendment abolishing slavery.

As in all wars, women were called upon to assume many tasks normally reserved for men. Both in the North and the South, they collaborated in the war effort by collecting funds, clothing, and food supplies. They went to work in weapons factories. They organized sewing circles and soldiers' aid societies. Some even disguised themselves as soldiers in order to be able to fight. Harriet Tubman (1820–1913), a former slave and an exceptional recruit because of her familiarity with enemy terrain, served as an intelligence agent and guide to the northern armies. Having herself fled Maryland in 1849, she helped other slaves make it to the North. John Brown nicknamed her "General" Tubman. Women also proved to be particularly useful in the field of hospital care. Dr. Elizabeth Blackwell (1821–1910), Dorothea Dix (1802–87), and Clara Barton (1821–1912; known as "the Angel of the Battlefields") trained nurses and organized hospitals and care of the wounded. For Mary Livermore (1820–1915) and many other women of the middle classes, their participation in the war effort brought a new awareness. Through their work as volunteers in the hospitals and other organizations, or replacing the men who had left for the front, by mobilizing and organizing, they gained skills and independence—in short, a new personality. Livermore's war experience convinced her of the absolute necessity of women's enfranchisement.

It was in the name of patriotism and charitable duty that American women responded to the appeal to join in the war effort. Women's rights advocates temporarily put their specific demands aside, but, after years of militant action, the patriotic, charitable activities of making bandages or collecting clothing for the men at the front, or even caring for the wounded, were hardly satisfying tasks. "[T]he mass of women never philosophize on the principles that underlie national existence," wrote Stanton, somewhat condescendingly, in her memoir *Eighty Years and More*. By "principles" she meant the abolition of slavery, enlisting freed slaves as soldiers who could contribute to a more rapid victory, and suffrage for women. Anthony had long been critical of Lincoln's procrastination about emancipation and the priority he gave to maintaining the integrity of the Union over the abolition of slavery.

On 14 May 1863, Stanton and Anthony called a meeting in New York to form a National Woman's Loyal League in support of the abolitionist cause. Many of the women who attended were staunch patriots who did not want to hear any talk of abolitionism and even less of women's rights. Nonetheless, at the end of a troubled session, the assembly voted to support Lincoln if he promised to introduce concrete measures granting political rights to freed slaves and to women. Stanton was elected president of the League, with Anthony as vice president. After several months of frenetic activity, they succeeded in gathering 400,000 signatures (far fewer than their goal of 3 million) on a petition to Congress for an amendment abolishing slavery. Thus, women's rights activists temporarily renounced their own objectives in order to serve the nation and a great cause, convinced that they were working not only for the emancipation of slaves but also for their own freedom. Their intention was to show that in times of national crisis, women could prove their loyalty to the nation, their political maturity, and their ability to exercise the vote.

Abolitionists Proclaim "The Negro's Hour"

The political turning point that was to have a profound effect on the women's rights movement, its strategy, and its goals took place in the years immediately following the war. The Civil War and the ensuing period of Reconstruction brought a changed political environment that forced the suffragists to disassociate themselves from the abolitionists and count on themselves alone. This ultimately changed the face of the women's rights movement and cemented its autonomy.

The abolition of slavery brought the question of the vote for freed slaves to the center of the political stage. The abolitionists moved closer to the Republican Party and "temporarily" shelved the cause of women's suffrage. Campaigning for both women's rights and the rights of African Americans, they argued, would weaken the thrust needed to surmount the tenacious and widespread opposition to the latter: "One war at a time, one question at a time. This is the Negro's hour," the abolitionist Wendell Phillips declared. To which Stanton retorted by asking pointedly, in a letter to Phillips dated 25 May 1865, "Do you believe the African race is composed entirely of males?"

The suffragists were given cause for alarm when, in late 1865, they got wind of preparations for the drafting of a 14th Amendment to the Constitution aimed at securing rights for African Americans—an amendment that, in 1868, would grant rights to male citizens exclusively. This was not the time to defend the rights of one category or the other, the women argued, but to defend "human" rights. They decided to pursue the fight for women's franchise within a unified organization for universal suffrage, the American Equal Rights Association (AERA), presided over by Lucretia Mott. One of the contributions of this initiative was to attract attention to the predicament of African-American women, former slaves caught between abolitionists and feminists, and victims of both their race and their sex.

The creation of the AERA failed to resolve the controversy that crystallized over the issue of the right to vote and gave rise to sharp conflicts between abolitionists and feminists. The supporters of the AERA, notably Stanton and Anthony, felt betrayed by their long-standing allies among the opponents of slavery, whereas abolitionists such as Wendell Phillips and Frederick Douglass accused the feminists of selfishness and indifference toward the suffering of the former slaves. Douglass declared:

"When women, because they are women, are hunted down through the cities of New York and New Orleans; when they are dragged from their houses and hung upon lamp-posts; when their children are torn from their arms, and their brains dashed out upon the pavement . . . then they will have an urgency to obtain the ballot equal to our own." (Quoted in *The Concise History of Woman Suffrage.*)

Although short-lived, the AERA marked a significant stage in the evolution of suffragist politics, ending with the break-up of the feminist-abolitionist alliance and the launching of an independent women's suffrage movement.

Tensions between abolitionists and feminists came to a climax during the Kansas campaign in 1867. In March 1867, the Kansas legislature put two propositions on the ballot, one allowing for "Negro" suffrage and the other allowing for women's suffrage. A contingent of AERA members had been invited to Kansas; Stone and Henry Blackwell went first, with Stanton and Anthony following a few months later. They discovered that the Republican Party, both in New York and Kansas, was taking a more and more open stand against women's suffrage. Given this situation, Stanton and Anthony began to seek an alliance with the Democratic Party. The Democrat George Francis Train, a somewhat disreputable financier and politician who was ready to subsidize them, soon joined their campaign, sparking indignation in the ranks of the AERA: although he subscribed to women's rights, Train was an overt racist. This unnatural alliance violated a solid tradition of struggle, and, more than anything, it was revelatory of the sense of betrayal and confusion many of the suffragists felt. Greatly distressed, and convinced by the powerful argument of "the Negro's hour," Stone and Blackwell distanced themselves from Stanton and Anthony. Both of the Kansas propositions were hopelessly defeated, and this consummated the rupture between feminists and abolitionists as well as between the two feminist factions.

In January 1868, with Train's financial backing, Stanton and Anthony created their own paper, *The Revolution*. It was here that they now expressed their views—including the dubious demand for "educated suffrage." In her address to the National Woman Suffrage Convention on 19 January 1869, Stanton complained that ignorant immigrants such as "Patrick and Sambo and Hans and Yung Tung who do not know the difference between a monarchy and a republic, who cannot know how to read the Declaration of Independence" were making laws for "learned" women such as Lucretia Mott and Ernestine Rose (1810–92) (quoted in *A Concise History of Woman Suffrage*). Stanton was prompted by her anger and her absolute determination to defend women's enfranchisement, but racist arguments such as these alienated many allies. It should be remembered, however, that she was the daughter of a Presbyterian judge and the member of an elite class. Her commitment to and solidarity with women during the heroic period made her privileges of wealth and education, as well as a certain condescension toward ordinary mortals, less visible. The exclusion of women from the right to vote, and the defection of Republicans and abolitionists from the cause, provoked an understandably violent reaction. Stanton did not mistake her desires for realities, and she knew that this defeat was the responsibility of friends and enemies alike, and a great opportunity missed; the future was to prove her right.

In 1870 the 15th Amendment confirmed the 14th by stipulating that no United States citizen could be denied the vote on the basis of "race, color, or previous condition of servitude." By omitting the word "sex" from this list, the amendment effectively excluded women from political rights. Since the unfortunate Kansas campaign, the conflicts among the leaders of the suffrage movement had been on the increase. On one side, Stanton, Anthony, Parker Pillsbury (1809–98), and others were hostile to the Republican politics of Reconstruction because of the party's opposition to women's suffrage. On the other side, Stone, Blackwell, and a few leaders of the AERA, although equally disappointed, still felt obliged to maintain their allegiance to the Republican Party. These fundamental conflicts, along with personal rivalries, sounded the death knell for the AERA and gave birth to two distinct suffragist organizations, the National Woman Suffrage Association (NWSA), based in New York, and the American Woman Suffrage Association (AWSA), established in Boston.

The AWSA, under the leadership of Stone, Blackwell, Julia Ward Howe (1819–1910), Stephen and Abby Kelley Foster, and Frederick Douglass, was formed by members of the New England Anti-Slavery Association and was supported by the Republican Party. While convinced suffragists like Stone vehemently defended women's right to vote, the association gave priority to securing African-American enfranchisement, which continued to face violent opposition. It was argued that the vote was a question of life and death for blacks, while women were in no danger and had all the time in the world before them. The strategy adopted by the AWSA favored state-by-state voting campaigns, which would allow them to avoid clashing with Republican Party campaigns for the 15th Amendment. Membership was open to both men and women; the Reverend Henry Ward Beecher was elected president, with Lucy Stone as vice president.

In New York, the NWSA, under the presidency of Stanton and Anthony, pursued different objectives and followed a different strategy than the AWSA. The resounding failures of the campaigns in Kansas and New York State convinced the organizers to seek federal voting rights through a constitutional amendment, although of course they did not discourage gains on the state level. Furthermore, their goals were not limited to the vote for women but aimed at an overall transformation of society. During the two years that Anthony published *The Revolution*, the motto of the paper was: "Men, their rights and nothing more; women, their rights and nothing less." The issues addressed included the vote as political instrument, patriarchal oppression, and—in pieces written by Stanton—the sexual exploitation of women and the topics of marriage and divorce. After Anthony formed the Working Women's Association of America, a union of typists, secretaries, and factory workers, *The Revolution* demanded the eight-hour workday and encouraged women workers to unionize. The AWSA did not much appreciate this broad range of themes, particularly those with revolutionary overtones, and openly criticized them in the columns of the *Woman's Journal*.

Suffrage, Sex, and Socialism

Beginning in 1870, the "radicals"—that is, the NWSA—focused their action on three fronts: the right to vote; alliances with women workers; and sexuality and the reform of marriage. Victoria Claflin Woodhull (1838–1927) was to serve as a catalyst on all three fronts. This exceptional figure could not have been more different from the average American suffragist. Victoria Claflin came from an adventurous midwestern background. Born in Ohio, she began traveling around the United States from an early age with her sister and her charlatan father, who planned to live off the girls' real or imagined talents as spiritual mediums. Given America's passion for clairvoyance and spiritualism, a gift such as this was a gold mine, despite a few misadventures when the Claflin family only barely escaped the arms of the law. Victoria then pursued her bohemian life in California, until Demosthenes, her guardian spirit, urged her to head for New York. There, in February 1870, with the help of her sister and the millionaire Cornelius Vanderbilt, she set out on a career as stockbroker that served as a prelude to her brief but sensational political career.

The Wall Street adventures of the "bewitching broker," alone in a male stronghold and ridiculed by the press, brought her to the attention of feminists; a brief but intense period of collaboration between Victoria Woodhull and the NWSA ensued. On 2 April 1870, Woodhull announced her candidacy for the presidency of the United States, based on a gargantuan platform that included women's emancipation, the elimination of the death penalty, the abolition of poverty, and sexual freedom. The revolutionary content of her program bore the stamp of the International Workingmen's Association, which had been established in the United States by German Marxists. Victoria and her sister Tennessee belonged to Section 12 of the First International, known as the "Woodhull-Claflin" section, comprising mainly New York intellectuals and artists. The section defended women's suffrage and sexual freedom, and it was expelled in 1872 by Marx, who observed "the same section has never ceased to make the IWA the vehicle of issues some of which are foreign to, while others are directly opposed to, the aims and purposes of the IWA" (Resolutions on the Split in the United States' Federation passed by the General Council of the I.W.A. in its sitting of 5th and 12th March 1872, *Documents of the First International*, vol. 5). Yet it was the *Woodhull and Claflin Weekly* that had published the first U.S. edition of the *Communist Manifesto*, on 30 December 1871. But Woodhull and her friends espoused a socialism rooted in universalist and utopian tradition, attentive to human relations, sexuality, and women's rights—all of which were little appreciated by the leaders of the workers' movement.

The vast program of the "Woodhull Manifesto" put women's emancipation high on the list. Despite her profile as an adventurer, Woodhull's courage and the originality of her dissent attracted Anthony's and especially Stanton's sympathy in the beginning. After their bitter defeat regarding the 14th and 15th Amendments, the suffragists had run out of strategies and were fighting with little conviction for a 16th Amendment. It was then, on 11 January 1871, that Woodhull made an explosive declaration before a committee of the House of Representatives. In an argument whose logic was crystal clear, she contended that since the 14th Amendment stipulated that citizens of the United States had the right to vote, and since women were citizens, women could therefore vote. And since that right was already written into the Constitution, what was the point of fighting for a new amendment? This argument, in its sublime simplicity, seemed to offer the suffragist struggle a way out of its impasse.

In January 1871 the annual convention of the NWSA gave Woodhull a wildly enthusiastic welcome and decided to modify its strategy to demand application of women's right, as citizens of the United States, to vote. They began to demand their registration on electoral lists, their participation in the ballot when the case arose, and they harassed the courts. The most famous of these cases, *United States vs. Susan B. Anthony*, took place in 1872. Accompanied by 14 women from her hometown of Rochester, New York, Anthony had registered and then voted in the presidential elections of 1872. Brought to trial as an "illegal elector," she claimed her good faith based on the arguments of Woodhull and Virginia Minor, another protester, that women's right to vote was written into the 14th and 15th Amendments of the United States Constitution. In 1873 she was sentenced to a fine of 100 dollars, which she never paid. To her great disappointment, the administration carefully avoided bringing the case before the Supreme Court.

But Woodhull was aiming to go much further. In a lecture on constitutional equality delivered on 16 February 1871, she called for a mass mobilization of women "to frame a new constitution and to erect a new government," declaring, "we mean treason; we mean secession, and on a thousand times grander scale than was that of the South" (reprinted in *The Victoria Woodhull Reader*). With the backing of Stanton, Isabella Beecher Hooker (1822–1907), and Paulina Wright Davis, she planned to unite the NWSA with her People's Party. When Anthony happened to hear of this, she slammed on the brakes and finally managed to foil the plan, though not without difficulty. Scarred by her experience with the abolitionists, she had lost all confidence in men's commitment to women's suffrage. After the initial infatuation with Woodhull, Anthony also suspected, and not without reason, that the "terrible Siren" wanted to infiltrate the women's rights movement and pledge it to various other causes—spiritualism, the workers' international, free love, and so on—for which Anthony had little taste. Subsequent developments would justify Anthony's mistrust with regard to Woodhull's integrity and her loyalty to the women's cause. This was the most serious conflict to arise between the two greatest figures of the movement, Stanton and Anthony, and it attested to their ideological divergence. Stanton, who was keen to expand the women's movement, was not averse to an alliance with other political forces. While everything in their personal backgrounds separated Stanton, the New England patrician, and Woodhull, the midwestern adventurer, they did share a rebellious temperament and a creative imagination, which perhaps explains why Stanton defended Woodhull against her detractors so systematically and in the most exalted terms. Anthony was less imaginative and less creative, but she perceived with greater acuity the difficulties and constraints facing a movement as subversive as the NWSA.

Woodhull's political and feminist agenda included a vigorous attack on marriage and the hypocrisy of the sexual norms of the time. "Yes, I am a Free Lover. I have an *inalienable, constitutional* and *natural* right to love whom I may, to love as *long* or as *short* a period as I can," she declared in a speech on the principles of social freedom delivered on 20 November 1871 before an audience of 3,000. She had no fear of what people might say and even savored scandal. But her libertarian discourse was less original than it appeared. Since the 1850s Woodhull's own circles, as well as the occasional suffragist, had been criticizing marriage, demanding the liberalization of divorce, and protesting the sexual slavery of women. In communities like Modern Times and Unitary Home (both run by Stephen Pearl Andrews, a philosopher close to Woodhull), alternative models were being invented to replace the traditional family, which Woodhull viewed as a "community of small burning hells." On the whole, however, few suffragists subscribed to these utopian ideals in the realm of politics and sexuality. Woodhull's nonconformist image and her provocative discourse were seen as a taint on the prestige of the movement. But it was Woodhull's futile crusade against the brother of Catherine Beecher and Harriet Beecher Stowe that ultimately brought her downfall. She denounced the hypocrisy of Henry Ward Beecher, a minister who drew crowds to his Sunday sermons, and who feigned liberalism in sexual matters but nonetheless pursued in secrecy his affairs with his female parishioners, including the wife of his friend Theodore Tilton. In the prevailing climate of Victorian mores, "free love" continued to be synonymous with promiscuity and with all the fears aroused by women's emancipation. Given its focus on gaining the vote in an environment marked by an increasing conservatism, the movement was bound to reject Woodhull and leave her to her solitary adventures. The era in which pioneers such as Stanton believed in the need for reforms to ensure profound changes in women's position in the family and the working world, and in sexuality, became more and more remote.

After 1875 and the split between reformists and "radicals," the last decades of the 19th century ushered in a less adventurous era. In 1876, at the commemoration of the centenary of American independence, Anthony set the tone by arguing that the main adversary was not only men but legislators as well. A few years earlier, in 1869, the McFarland-Richardson affair, in which a husband who had murdered his wife's lover was acquitted by the court and granted child custody, had provided the opportunity for Stanton and Anthony to raise the issues of divorce and male violence once again. They organized a mass meeting in New York in order to protest the verdict and show how the case for the murderer's defense and the court's decision effectively confirmed the husband's property rights over his wife, proving that patriarchy was indeed alive and well.

Early feminism in the United States had been forged in a distinctly American cultural and historical context, but the movement was to undergo outside influences as the waves of immigration increased at the end of the 19th century. The influence of European socialism was apparent—for example, in Woodhull's manifesto of 1870. During this period of change within the women's rights movement, marking the end of the era of the pioneer suffragists, German socialist immigrants also showed their interest in women's situation, but from a different point of view and within a different context. Wary of radicalism and U.S. politics in general, and imbued with a romantic ideal of women and the principle of class struggle, these immigrants rejected the demand for two essential rights, the right to work and the right to vote. The role of women socialists essentially consisted of hastening the coming of a new era by helping their husbands and brothers in the home and in "auxiliary" associations. They were encouraged to acquire a few political notions, and to run various charitable and educational activities in order to create a congenial climate for the comrades. The stereotypical

roles of sister, wife, and mother were the rule in this type of organization. But in the next decade, under the influence of new waves of immigrants, the spectacular expansion in the garment industry, and August Bebel's *Die Frau und der Sozialismus* (1883; Woman and Socialism), the situation changed. Socialist women began to rebel against their auxiliary status, and, particularly in the cities, demanded a full place for themselves in socialist actions and leadership.

In the West, the struggle for social and political rights for women took a different form. Between 1840 and 1870, some 24,000 Americans had migrated toward the western states. Men set out on the great journey to the Rocky Mountains and California in search of virgin territory, gold mines, and adventure, and intent on colonizing these distant lands. Generally, the women in their families followed reluctantly, for the exodus to the Far West meant a break with family circles, a general uprooting, and facing the great unknown. These women lived more difficult but also a more adventurous lives than their counterparts in settled regions. For women, the dangers of travel not only increased the burden of such routine domestic chores as cooking, laundering, and childcare, but often meant the death of children, or having to give birth in wagons while on the move. Women also had to replace men or assist them in traditionally male tasks: driving the teams, fording rivers, fighting prairie fires, guarding the camp, and battling with Native Americans. Once they reached their destination, women homesteaders were faced with continuous hard labor in almost total isolation. On the other hand, to a certain extent they escaped from the yoke of sexual roles and stereotypical notions of womanhood. It was in bad taste, for example, to question a woman on the frontier about her "past"; some western women held unusual jobs as sheriffs or horse trainers, or became saloon waitresses, actresses, or singers. Few people in the West took offense at seeing women smoke or drink, in absolute contrast to settled regions. White women, moreover, enjoyed a certain prestige because of their scarcity on the frontier—they were outnumbered by men in the western territories throughout the 19th century; women of color were not shown the same respect.

The different mentality that reigned on the frontier was reflected in the fields of education and the law. Numerous western colleges and universities offered programs and degrees to both sexes. In order to encourage migration and the settlement of families, several western states granted married women the same rights as men to property, wages, and land. In Oregon, the Homestead Act authorized settler couples to own 640 acres; unmarried men or women could own half that amount. In 1890 some 250,000 women were operating their own farms or ranches.

Some of the western states were also on the vanguard in granting women the right to vote. Wyoming, with its nomadic population of cowboys, miners, railway workers, and gamblers on their way to Oregon and California, enfranchised women in 1869. During the campaign for Wyoming's law, Esther Morris (1812–1902), a suffragist and disciple of Anthony, argued for women's ability to create order, law, and peace; her plea was found so convincing that women were authorized to sit on juries, where their presence was much appreciated. The state was accepted into the union in 1890, in spite of the opposition of many members of Congress to women's suffrage. Utah granted women the vote in 1890 and was admitted to the union in 1896. The women of Colorado obtained the right to vote in 1893.

Philanthropy, Family, and Society

The end of the 19th century inaugurated a new phase in the struggle for women's rights that was reminiscent of the prefeminist era of 1820–30. The theory of the moral superiority of the "weaker sex" began to gain ground over that of sexual equality, and women were once again invested with the mission of reestablishing morality and equilibrium in a country destabilized by social upheavals and corruption. American women formed innumerable associations, defended their "difference" from a Christian point of view, and focused more on social reform than on achieving political objectives. The right to vote, once seen as an instrument for the transformation of society, now represented just one goal among many, such as the prohibition of alcohol and prostitution, the abolition of child labor, and the reform of the penal system.

Women's presence in the temperance movement was particularly strong. This movement, which had once rallied many of those who were later to become women's rights advocates, had exerted considerable influence and caused the consumption of alcohol to diminish earlier in the 19th century. But the Civil War had erased these results, and women entered the battle once again, directing their fire at the proliferation of saloons. The new generation of temperance activists, who were mostly evangelicals from rural areas and small towns, particularly in the West, saw alcoholism and corruption as abuses of male power that were encouraged by the sociability of the bar. They rose up in large numbers and, in the 1870s, led spectacular "crusades" through hundreds of small cities in the Midwest. Kneeling in the street and in bars, singing and praying, Bibles open on the counters, they would urge saloon owners to repent and close their establishments. Carrie Nation (1846–1911), the most famous of these temperance crusaders, would often come charging into the saloons wielding an axe and destroying everything around her.

The Woman's Christian Temperance Union (WCTU), a vast national association founded in 1874 by Frances Willard (1839–98), grew out of this wave of protest and moral regeneration. Willard, a Methodist, had first dedicated herself to higher education for women; she then turned to the temperance cause, convinced, like so many others, that it could serve as a powerful instrument for women's emancipation. While the WCTU was dedicated to the spread of Christianity and the struggle against evil, it was also involved in social and political causes. The temperance struggle, for example, necessarily affected the activities of the Democratic Party and the interests of the alcohol industry. As they carried out their battle against "demon rum," women acquired skills in direct action, harassment of political parties, and organizing. Willard devised an elaborate organizational structure, dividing the society into 40 sections, each directed by a woman who had an assistant in every state, and each section comprised thousands of groups. The WCTU objectives, summed up in the slogan "for God and Hope and Native land," attracted thousands of members. It was a tour de force when, in 1882, Willard succeeded in convincing the membership of the need for women's suffrage in order to protect their sphere—the family—and having this demand written into the agenda of

the WCTU. However, the ambiguous arguments of the specificity of the female "sphere" that she advanced in order to defend women's political rights were to have serious consequences. On the one hand, Nation's notion of femininity paved the way for her successors to abandon the demand for the right to vote and to concentrate exclusively on prohibition. On the other, for some groups, including the "liquor lobby," suffrage continued to be unshakeably associated with prohibition, which consolidated opposition to women's suffrage.

Between 1880 and 1920, a multitude of women's associations, clubs, and other similar organizations were active in a broad social field, with a certain degree of success. There were several reasons for this upsurge in social activism. Vast numbers of women from the middle classes were in search of intelligent and useful pursuits, for while many had studied in institutions of higher learning, they still had limited access to the professions. The syndrome of depression and boredom that had afflicted countless gifted young Victorian girls had not disappeared at the end of the 19th century—it simply expressed itself later in life. Philanthropic activities provided some of these women with an escape from the inherent boredom and uselessness of their lives. But such women's sense of a moral mission could dim their awareness of certain injustices, and the demand for sexual equality was not typically on the agenda. Many women who were uninterested in politics and alarmed by suffrage found shelter from conflict and controversy in this relatively neutral arena.

The women's clubs varied in substance and goals, but their extraordinary proliferation bore witness to the diversified and protean influence of women. In some clubs faithful to the tradition of "female accomplishments," gardening and other literary and cultural occupations were cultivated. Other organizations addressed social issues such as child labor, at the municipal or state level. Some pressure groups, often based in Washington, D.C., were effective in precipitating reform. In 1892 the clubs consolidated on a national basis into the General Federation of Women's Clubs (GFWC) and joined forces with the Women's Committee for Law Enforcement and the Southern Women's Educational Alliance. Charlotte Perkins Gilman (1860–1935), a feminist writer and sociologist, saw this movement as a unifying force that would be favorable to women.

Virtually all the associations, large and small, were founded on a belief in women's moral superiority, and in women's particular mission of disseminating Christian values—an idea that had never completely disappeared from the women's rights movement. Both the WCTU, with its close to 1 million members, and the Young Women's Christian Association (YWCA), with some 50,000 members, actively promoted chastity outside of the wifely duty of procreation. In the same conservative vein, the GFWC campaigned for the preservation of the life of the child, womanhood, and civic and national integrity. It was in this puritanical climate that Anthony Comstock, a member of the Young Men's Christian Association (YMCA) and defender of public morality, launched his successful campaign for the censorship of "obscene writings": in 1872 Victoria Woodhull and Tennessee Claflin were to find themselves in jail for infringing the Comstock Laws in their newspaper.

Woodhull's sexual protest did not receive the support of suffragist organizations. At the beginning of the 20th century, the campaign for contraception led by Margaret Sanger (1879–1966), through her lectures and brochures such as *Family Limi-*

tation, was to meet with a similar fate. In 1913 Sanger's efforts were still running headlong into the Comstock Laws, which by then had resulted in a total of 700 arrests, 333 jail sentences, and the seizure of thousands of "immoral" articles. It would take the opening of a clinic in October 1916, and Sanger's trial and sentencing to a month in prison, for public opinion to be alerted. In any event, the great majority of women steered clear of any form of sexual liberation.

The Progressive Era—a time of industrialization, accelerated urbanization, and massive immigration—saw the birth of a new breed of philanthropic associations. For members of these organizations, philanthropy's role consisted precisely in tackling the deviations and excesses of industrial capitalism. The notion of a "woman's sphere" of motherhood and moral vocation endured, but it now brought women closer to the world of work and politics. For example, the Settlement Movement founded by Jane Addams (1860–1935) played a prominent role. Despite her upper-middle-class origins and university education, Addams had struggled to find her way. Like Florence Nightingale (1820–1910), the pioneer of hospital reform and the professionalization of nursing in England in the 1840s, and like the writer Charlotte Perkins Gilman later in the United States, Addams was prey to boredom and dissatisfaction, manifested in psychosomatic symptoms such as fatigue, aches, and nervous exhaustion. She was brought out of her depression in 1887 when she discovered the work of Toynbee Hall in London, a project run by academics and students who lived among the poor to bring them assistance. In 1889 she founded Hull House in a working-class district of Chicago, the first establishment of its kind in the United States. Shortly thereafter, Lilian Wald (1867–1935) created the Henry Street Settlement in New York. By 1911 there were some 400 settlement houses in the United States. Thousands of women participated in this movement between 1895 and 1915. These "social feminists," even those who initiated the movement, generally knew nothing about the Italian, German, and Polish immigrant populations among whom they worked, or about their lifestyles and their needs. Addams and Wald had everything to learn, but it did not take them long to realize that good works and philanthropy were not enough to resolve social problems.

Two women helped Addams understand this new world. Florence Kelley (1859–1932), who was more politicized than Addams and had close ties to the Socialist Labor Party, helped expand the programs of Hull House to include day care, English classes, and union meetings, thus helping to change Addams from a philanthropist into a reformer. Mary Kenny O'Sullivan (1864–1943), a worker in the bookbinding industry and a union member, also helped Addams better to understand the problems of workers and immigrants. By 1900 Addams had become a national heroine. She was praised as "Saint Jane," the model of feminine virtue, but her talents as an administrator, a reformer, and above all as a pacifist of international caliber during World War I, were often overlooked.

The National Consumers' League (NCL), founded in 1898, was another organization that took an interest in workers, and especially women workers. Florence Kelley, as head of the organization, argued that women, as consumers, were better qualified to verify the quality of products, and therefore the conditions under which they were manufactured. It was thus women's duty to protect their families by boycotting products judged to be harmful to the health of consumers or workers. This was a hitherto untapped aspect of the maternal function; it implied contacts with factories and workshops, as well as knowledge of labor conditions and legislation. By 1913 the NCL's mobilization of middle-class women against ruthless capitalism had succeeded in rallying 30,000 members. Like Frances Willard and others before her, Kelley once again took the home as the point of departure for far-reaching activism by women.

Immigration, Labor, and Revolt

Toward 1900, 5 million women, or one-fifth of the nation, worked for wages; almost half of them were employed as domestic servants, and in the South almost all of these were African Americans. In big cities such as New York, Chicago, Rochester, New York, and Saint Louis, Missouri, women represented 55 percent of workers in the garment industry. While the female labor force was concentrated in the textile, garment, and cotton industries, food production, and laundering, U.S. industry as a whole discriminated against women workers by paying wages—even for unskilled labor and piecework—that were vastly inferior to those of men, for a working day that frequently exceeded 12 hours. A female cigarmaker or garmentworker would receive from half to a third of a man's salary. The large numbers of immigrant women (mostly Irish, Italians, and Eastern European Jews) who had been arriving since the end of the 19th century were primarily employed in workshops and factories, where they were subjected to the same exploitation with regard to wages and working conditions.

This situation prompted many women workers to take action, and the immigrants supplied their contingent of union activists. Mary Harris Jones (c. 1830–1930), known as "Mother Jones," was one of the most notable Irish women allied with the left wing of the labor movement. She began her career as professional activist and union organizer with the Knights of Labor, then helped found the Industrial Workers of the World, an anarchist organization, and participated in a great many strikes.

Many of the Eastern European immigrants had participated in the labor movements in the pre-1905 era, before leaving for the United States. Some, such as Emma Goldman (1869–1940), were anarchists; others, such as Rose Schneiderman (1882–1972) and Pauline Newman (c. 1890–1986), were Bundists. Schneiderman, who was born in Russia and immigrated to the United States in 1891, became the family breadwinner at the age of 13. She started out as a factory worker, organized women hatmakers, and quickly moved up in the union hierarchy. Schneiderman was a prominent figure in the "shirtwaist strike" that shook the garment industry in New York in 1909–10. At the time, some 20,000 to 30,000 women—mostly Jewish immigrants (55 percent), Italian immigrants, and American-born workingwomen—were employed in the city's numerous shirtwaist workshops (about 500 in all). They rose up in protest against their exploitation and, in a long and arduous strike, denounced the disparity between men's and women's wages (including their own ridiculously low pay); the 70-hour workweek in the busy season; and the innumerable humiliations they suffered at the hands of their employers (ranging from fines deducted for trifles to sexual harassment).

For 13 weeks these young women of different languages and cultures—many of whom spoke no English—continued their strike. They strategized, organized picket lines, and held fast against their employers, strikebreakers, and the police. Few of the women were unionized (less than 6 percent of female garmentworkers), partly due to their particular lifestyles and cultures, but also because of the blatant sexism of the International Ladies' Garment Workers Union (ILGWU). For many very young women, organizing was not a primary objective—they considered paid employment as a temporary phase in their lives before going on to establish a family. Others were from a rural background and had grown up far removed from any union tradition. The unions themselves, fearful of female competition, did everything they could to keep women at home or in unskilled jobs and generally made it difficult for them to become members. Despite the frenzy of excitement at the union meeting that voted for the general strike of the shirtwaist workers on 22 November 1909, the union leaders were less than overjoyed to see the women launch into battle.

The strikers ultimately won their case, and all their demands for improved working conditions and wages were met. This first massive strike held by women remains exemplary, and the participants' victory, heroism, and tenacity continue to be an inspiration for the labor movement. But the strikers lost one major battle, for they failed to obtain the official recognition of the garment industry union, and this shielded the large workshops from the obligation to apply security regulations. The consequences were to be tragic: in 1911 a fire broke out in the Triangle Shirtwaist Company in New York and within minutes had spread to the top floors, trapping the workers in their workshops; 146 young women perished in the flames or leapt from the windows to their death.

The women strikers received support from a variety of organizations and individuals, such the women of the Socialist Party of America (SPA), the Women's Trade Union League (WTUL), the unions, the ILGWU, and the suffragists. Since the creation of the Socialist Party of America in 1901 and its National Women's Committee in 1908, women socialists had strengthened their position and, like Schneiderman and Theresa Serber Malkiel (1870–1920), had fought the party's opposition to women's suffrage. During the shirtwaist strike, women socialists did their best to recruit women members for the party and for the ILGWU. They helped the strikers by organizing meetings, printing tracts, and initiating actions with other organizations. The entire socialist press, Jewish and otherwise, covered the events: a journalist for the *New York Call* described some meetings as a mixture of "suffragists, labormen, socialists and even some of the wealthy classes" (see Malkiel). In supporting the strike, socialist women were not only expressing their class solidarity, but also their solidarity as women and, for many of them, as immigrants. This was the case for Malkiel, author of the *Diary of a Shirtwaist Striker* (1910), whose heroine becomes a socialist during the struggle, and at the same time becomes aware that she is oppressed not only by capitalism but also by the patriarchy, her employers, and her family. On the whole, however, although the strikers occasionally worked with the Socialist Party and the union, they did not rush to join either of these organizations.

Significant support for the shirtwaist strikers was also provided by the Women's Trade Union League (WTUL). Established in the poor urban districts, the WTUL was run by middle-class women who, like Addams and her associates at Hull House, were eager to help underprivileged women. While their initial motivation was of a philanthropic nature, the "allies," as they were called, came to realize that the best way of assisting women and immigrants was to help them organize in the workplace. The WTUL did this effectively on a wide scale throughout the strike by collecting funds, intervening between strikers and the police, and taking charge of the legal aspects of the conflict. They worked quite successfully with Russian Jewish socialists such as Schneiderman and Pauline Newman, in spite of inevitable misunderstandings arising from social and cultural differences, for the members of the WTUL generally knew nothing about Jewish culture or religion. Of all the organizations that supported the strike, the WTUL was the most attentive to the needs of the women strikers and to their multifaceted identities as workers, immigrants, and women.

The shirtwaist strike, along with other textile strikes in Lawrence, Massachusetts, and in Patterson, New Jersey, in 1912 and 1913, served to familiarize middle-class suffragists with the problems of the working class. From 1910, Schneiderman and WTUL president Margaret Dreier Robins (1868–1945), both familiar figures to the suffragists, began to speak at suffragist meetings. In a homily reminiscent of the powerful words of Sojourner Truth in 1851, Schneiderman forcefully demystified the clichés of femininity. Some legislators were claiming that the ballot might undermine feminine delicacy? What about the women who worked stripped down to the waist in the foundry furnaces? Schneiderman asked. Were charm and feminine delicacy also expected of them?

The gap between the labor and suffrage movements was also illustrated during the shirtwaist strike. The women of the WTUL, who discreetly supported women's suffrage, stood daily by the side of the strikers. In contrast, wealthy suffragists such as Mrs. O.H.P. Belmont and Ann Morgan, daughter of the famous banker, both members of the "400 families," only offered sporadic, financial support. The "mink brigade," as Schneiderman called them, occasionally indulged in spectacular initiatives like the motorcade on 21 December 1909, or a reception for young strikers in the most select club of New York. Their action contributed to making the vote seem like a luxury foreign to the world of workers.

Despite Susan B. Anthony's concerted efforts, the cause of women's suffrage never really "took" among women workers. The immigrants who flocked to the United States at the turn of the century, and who were exposed to the xenophobic reactions of suffragists outraged by their defeat in 1869, hardly saw the right to vote as the solution to their immediate problems. As Mother Jones neatly put it, women were quite capable of protesting without the vote. Anarchist Emma Goldman failed to see how suffragist action—especially that of high society "ladies"—could help the cause of workingwomen. She also had little faith in the impact of the right to vote in general: once suffrage was obtained, she objected, the reign of money would still continue. "Red Emma" was doubtless not the only one using this language in the workshops and factories.

Socialist suffragists ran up against the ideological qualms of the party. In Stuttgart, in 1907, the Second International had urged socialist parties to work for women's suffrage but without collaborating with the "bourgeois" movement: a contradictory demand that gave rise to endless controversies about strategy and alliances among the activists. The relationship between class struggle and women's emancipation continued to be problematic, but the suffrage cause advanced nevertheless, and, in 1909, it was socialist women who introduced the annual celebration of International Women's Day.

African-American Women's Struggles at the Turn of the Century

The victory of the abolitionist northerners in 1865 had freed the slaves but did little to eliminate racial prejudice. African-American women continued to suffer discrimination because of their race and were still treated as second-class citizens, even in the North. The many women's clubs mentioned above had few or no black members. In the southern states, African-American women began to organize under the leadership of Ida B. Wells (c. 1862–1931). Born in Mississippi, Wells had taught for some years before she became the editor-in-chief of the *Memphis Free Speech*. Her systematic campaigns denouncing rape, lynching, and other segregationist practices earned her death threats and eventually dismissal from the paper. She nevertheless pursued her crusade, even traveling to England for the cause. She wrote *The Red Record*, a report on the wave of lynchings between 1892 and 1894, which was presented by Frederick Douglass, and once again provoked public ire. In Boston *The Woman's Era* continued her work and contributed to organizing women of color on a national scale.

In 1895 the National Federation of Afro-American Women was founded in Boston to unite the various clubs, with Margaret Murray Washington (1865–1925), Booker T. Washington's third wife, as the federation's first president. A year later, the federation merged with the National League of Colored Women to form the National Association of Colored Women. In 1900 the efforts of the African-American women's organizations to break the color barrier ran up against a major obstacle from the powerful General Federation of Women's Clubs. Meeting in Milwaukee, Wisconsin, the GFWC convention refused to grant delegate status to Josephine St. Pierre Ruffin, although she was mandated by two associations, one of them African American. For the membership of the GFWC, which was white, middle-class, and often racist, and which included a sizeable contingent of southern women, the mission of reconciling North and South was a larger concern than fraternization between blacks and whites. The other women's organizations were no more open than the GFWC: the WCTU and the YWCA admitted African-American women only on an individual basis.

The Final Battle for Women's Suffrage

The American social landscape changed considerably between the end of the Civil War and the Progressive Era, as did the female population, its education, and its occupations. The women's rights pioneers who had once sought far-reaching reform had given way to myriad organizations and clubs (although Anthony and Stanton were not to die until 1906 and 1902, respectively). The right to vote had lost the mobilizing force that had still been strong among American women in 1869,

when the two suffragist associations had confronted each other. In contrast to the suffragist groups, women's associations and clubs counted millions of members. This conservative development was related to the evolution of American society as a whole. In the wake of the numerous strikes that had shaken the textile, mining, and railway industries in the 1880s, the middle classes had come to shy away from anything that resembled radicalism. The arrival of new waves of immigrants helped highlight the breach between social classes in the ranks of the suffragists, some of whom still felt wronged for having been unjustly deprived of the right to vote during the Reconstruction era. The heroic days of the pioneers in the suffrage movement were long gone, and the heroines, even the least affluent ones such as Stone and Anthony, were leading a better life. The cause of suffrage, meanwhile, was gradually gaining acceptance.

As the 20th century approached, the distinctions between the two suffragist organizations began to blur. In 1890, after three years of negotiations, mostly handled by Alice Stone Blackwell (1857–1950), Lucy Stone's daughter, the Boston-based American Woman Suffrage Association and the New York–based National Woman Suffrage Association merged to form the National American Woman Suffrage Association (NAWSA). Stanton assumed the presidency for the first two years (she resigned in 1902, the year of her death). But her position became marginalized in the new association, which disagreed with most of her opinions—the importance of the vote as a means to exert political pressure, "educated suffrage," the liberalization of divorce laws, and, finally, her analysis of the role of religion and the Scriptures in the oppression of women, as presented in *The Woman's Bible* (1898). Although Anthony, who succeeded Stanton as president, battled valiantly to support her, she was unable to prevent the passing of a resolution completely dissociating NAWSA from Stanton's ideas. While she did not necessarily share Stanton's views on religion, Anthony was fighting a solitary battle on her end against "a narrow and intolerant agenda" and for the right of every individual to entertain broader views.

More of a realist and a tactician than Stanton, Anthony was a more acceptable leader for the younger generations. Nevertheless, she was defeated on one of her fundamental positions when the demand for federal legislation guaranteeing women the right to vote was dropped in favor of a state-by-state campaign. In line with this strategy, and to Anthony's great regret, the NAWSA decided to hold only one out of every two conventions in Washington, a move that inevitably relaxed the pressure on Congress. This policy of decentralization and its endorsement of "state rights" suited the southern states and their racist politics, while the prospect of a federal bill revived the specter of the 14th and 15th Amendments. Anthony, who remained loyal to the earlier NWSA strategy of pressuring the federal government, sadly noted that the cause of women's suffrage was losing its political impact.

Between 1870 and 1910, 480 campaigns for women's franchise were organized in 32 states, primarily in the West. Only two victories were won: in Colorado in 1893, and in Idaho in 1896. The 1896 campaign in California, although stimulating and well organized, lost by a narrow margin of 13,400 votes.

Anna Howards Shaw (1847–1919) and Carrie Chapman Catt (1859–1947), who succeeded Anthony to the presidency of the NAWSA, represented the second generation of suffragists. Shaw, a university graduate with a profession, came from a family of pioneers in the Midwest. A pastor and later a physician, she was a member of the WCTU, a suffragist, and close to Frances Willard. Catt, a journalist, had a similar profile; a suffragist activist from Iowa, she had proven her qualities as a strategist and organizer in the Colorado and Idaho campaigns. Catt was elected as the third president of the NAWSA in 1900, and in 1904 was succeeded by Shaw, who remained in that position until 1915. Anthony, the last of the giants, died in 1906, some years before women obtained the right to vote in the United States.

Between 1906 and 1913, suffragist activity under Shaw's leadership tended to mark time, with the exception of a petition addressed to Congress in 1910 with 404,000 signatures. But two dynamic women were to turn things around: Catt, now at the head of the International Woman Suffrage Alliance, and Harriot Stanton Blatch (1856–1940), one of Stanton's daughters who had contributed to the monumental history of the movement, *The History of Woman Suffrage*, when she was still a student at Vassar. Blatch spent several years in London and, on her return to New York in 1902, found the suffragist movement to be anemic and in a state of paralysis, in contrast to England, where Emmeline Pankhurst's "militant" organization, the Women's Social and Political Union (WSPU), was in the making. Blatch formed her own group in New York, the Equality League of Self-Supporting Women, which attracted 19,000 members, including Charlotte Perkins Gilman, Florence Kelley, Leonora O'Reilly (1870–1927), and Rose Schneiderman. The English example inspired these women to use more aggressive methods: mass outdoor meetings, parades, motorcades, and demonstrations in front of state capitol buildings. In 1910 Catt, who had also been in England, created the dynamic, well-organized Woman Suffrage Party.

During these years, advocates of women's suffrage placed particular emphasis on the civilizing mission of women, an argument that had served them in the 1820s and 1830s to clear a way into the public arena. "Yes, woman's place is in the home," they would repeat. But there were two sides to the message, for the notion of "social housekeeping," endorsed by Jane Addams, Frances Kelley, Frances Willard, and others, called for women to leave the confinement of the home and to make their voices heard in the political sphere.

The notion of female superiority and purity sometimes gave way to embarrassing errors in judgment. For example, Carrie Catt herself was not averse to using racist and xenophobic arguments, and, in 1894, she warned of the dangers for America of a foreign and ignorant electorate from the big city slums. Ten years later, it was Shaw's turn to deplore the fact that "American women were governed by men of every origin under the sun." Did they find no fault, then, with being governed by white, American-born males?

However, around 1910, the suffragist movement finally emerged from the consensual and apolitical climate created by the multitudinous associations and regained its energy. While it no longer championed a radical affirmation of women's rights as it had before the Civil War, it did express the firm determination to obtain the right to vote.

On the socialist front, women such as Theresa Malkiel (1874–1949) who were dissatisfied with the suffragist action of the Socialist Party of America had created a network of socialist clubs in the New York region. After a grand celebration in honor of International Woman's Day of 1912, they focused their energies on the referendum to be held in the State of New York in 1915. But once again, the electors rejected the proposition for women's franchise. Taking advantage of this defeat, the Sociality Party withdrew its activists and its financial support from the suffragist campaign. From then on, the Socialists played an insignificant role in the campaign for the right to vote, even if—and this was some consolation—such eminent suffragists as Alice Stone Blackwell and Harriot Stanton Blatch joined the party in 1920 and 1922.

A new event on the political scene occurred in 1912, when the recently formed Progressive Party put women's right to vote on its platform. At the same time, Blatch, Catt, and a newcomer, Alice Paul (1885–1977), all adopted the strategy of seeking an amendment to the federal Constitution. Paul, a Quaker social worker, had spent three years with the English suffragists, and came back to the United States in 1910 with the firm intent of resuscitating the American movement. She began by organizing a demonstration of 5,000 people on the eve of President Woodrow Wilson's inauguration in Washington in 1912; this gathering met with a hostile crowd and created something of a stir. Then, in 1913, together with Crystal Eastman (1881–1928), a lawyer and journalist specializing in labor issues, Paul created the Congressional Union for Suffrage, and founded a weekly publication, *The Suffragist*, that focused solely on obtaining a constitutional amendment securing women's right to vote.

The Congressional Union for Suffrage, although an auxiliary group of the NAWSA, disagreed with the latter's positions. Paul was not, of course, trying to introduce the tactics of the English suffragists in a country that already had 4 million women voters. But her dynamism, her aggressive style, the pressure she aimed to exercise upon the political parties, and her strategy on the federal level, all ran counter to the style of the NAWSA, with its objective of state-by-state campaigns and its model of the virtuous and apolitical female.

Expelled from the NAWSA in 1915, Paul created the Women's Party, a more radical group whose sole objective was to obtain the vote for all American women through a constitutional amendment to be ratified by every state by 1920. With the wind in their sails, the Women's Party sent delegation after delegation to President Wilson, organized campaigns in the 48 states of the Union, and launched a huge motorcade from San Francisco to Washington. The idea of a constitutional amendment progressively gained ground, especially after the defeats inflicted in 1915 by New Jersey, New York, Massachusetts, and Pennsylvania, the four eastern states that remained staunchly opposed to suffrage.

Catt's reelection to the presidency of NAWSA in 1915 further intensified and politicized the movement. Within a few months, she had put the organization back on its feet, but she did not succeed in rallying Paul's Women's Party. Catt's strategy was to win President Wilson over to the cause of a constitutional amendment through personal contacts and powerful state-level mobilization. In contrast to Paul, she considered it futile to put pressure on the Democratic Party.

The Women's Party, on the other hand, escalated its campaign against President Wilson after the United States entered the war in 1917; they posted "silent sentinels" in front of the White House and denounced the hypocrisy of his declarations on the international front when women in the United States remained deprived of their democratic rights. Accused of being "militant" and "antipatriotic," the Women's Party, with its large contingent of Quakers, firmly opposed the war. After several months, the police proceeded to make arrests. For lack of a more serious offense, the suffragists were accused of obstructing a public roadway, and a few were sent to prison, including Paul, who spent 22 days in jail. Following the example of the British suffragists, they demanded to be treated as political prisoners and began a hunger strike that the authorities attempted to break by force-feeding. But, just as in England, this ill treatment earned the imprisoned Americans the sympathy of public opinion. In March 1918 all legal action against the suffragists was dropped.

Many prominent suffragists were opposed to the war. Lilian Wald, the founder of the Henry Street Settlement in New York, was president of the American Union against Militarism. Jane Addams, the Chicago philanthropist and former president of NAWSA, founded the Women's Peace Party with Crystal Eastman in 1915; that same year, Addams was elected president of the International Congress of Women in The Hague. (In 1919, the Women's Peace Party was renamed the Women's International League for Peace and Freedom.) In 1931 Addams received the Nobel Peace Prize. Like Wald, both Eastman and Addams were active in the American Union against Militarism. None of the three, however, was averse to attending dinners at the White House with President Wilson and his advisers. The NAWSA, on the other hand, never made common cause with the Women's Party; it supported the war but did not relax the struggle on behalf of suffrage.

At last the goal of women's franchise was in sight. In 1918 the House of Representatives voted for the constitutional amendment by 274 votes to 136, only one vote over the required two-thirds majority. It took the Senate more than a year to approve the amendment and for its ratification by the states. On 26 August 1920, Tennessee became the 36th state to ratify the amendment, making it part of the Constitution. The "nay" votes came from the southern states and the East Coast states of Massachusetts, Pennsylvania, and New Jersey, as well as Ohio.

Conclusion

1920: Women obtained the right to vote relatively early in the United States compared to other countries. Even England, where a partial measure had been introduced soon after World War I, did not grant women suffrage until 1928. Although the rights of American women had progressed considerably by the beginning of the 20th century, opposition to their participation in the affairs of the nation continued until the bitter end, particularly on the East Coast, and notably in the state of New York. The sacrosanct slogan, "Woman's place is in the home" often served as a cover-up for fears of female competition and was used by certain financial interests (the liquor industry, the breweries), and by other sectors of society (southern Democrats and Catholics) that continued to express their hostility to women's franchise.

Certain major trends emerged in this long march for women's suffrage that lasted from 1848 to 1920, from the Jacksonian era until after World War I. The struggle for women's emancipation took many forms, with a diversity of actions and ideological dimensions, but an overall trend toward a growing conservatism

and an identification with society's dominant values can be discerned in the movement. After the Civil War, women began to distance themselves from the radicalism of 1848, which had questioned female stereotypes and debated the relationship between private and public spheres. The 1848 Seneca Falls "Declaration of Sentiments," with its demand for equality and justice, had shown that women did not exist only in relation to a family, a husband, and children, but that they were citizens whose relationship with the state should not be subject to male mediation. The notions of distinct spheres and gender roles were discarded, and with them, feminine stereotypes. In the years that followed, however, an essentialist vision began to eclipse this egalitarian aspiration. The discourse became dominated by the belief in a superior female nature, which had already been expressed, it is true, in the speeches of leaders as charismatic as Stanton. Organizations such as the WCTU and the YWCA, and philanthropists of all sorts, once again defined the relationship between woman and society through her moral mission and through her role in the family, which was still touted as her dominion. Women's demands for political rights were no longer voiced in the name of equality between the sexes and among individuals in the political sphere, but on the basis of their own prescribed responsibilities in the private sphere. The immense success of the Women's Christian Temperance Union confirmed the dominance of this vision, which even the socialist women, despite a radically different political horizon, did little to contest.

This feminine dynamic with its essentialist tendencies drew on the same mythical representations that, at the beginning of the 19th century, had encouraged women to pour their energies into charitable work. The view of the two sexes as equal was definitively lost: "difference" reigned. But the second generation of reformers—Addams, Frances Willard, and others imbued with their sense of female mission—were able to tap the resources and mobilize vast contingents of women. Putting their organizing talents to work in the service of their convictions, they amply proved their effectiveness in the area of social and political reform.

Bibliography

Sources

Malkiel, Theresa Serber, *The Diary of a Shirtwaist Striker: A Story of the Shirtwaist Makers' Strike in New York*, New York: Co-Operative Press, 1910; reprint, Ithaca, New York: ILR Press, 1990

Schneir, Miriam, editor, *Feminism: The Essential Historical Writings*, New York: Random House, 1972; new edition, New York: Vintage Books, 1994

Stanton, Elizabeth Cady, *Eighty Years and More (1815–1897): Reminiscences of Elizabeth Cady Stanton*, New York: European Publishing Company, 1898

Stanton, Elizabeth Cady, *Elizabeth Cady Stanton as Revealed in Her Letters, Diary and Reminiscences*, edited by Theodore Stanton and Harriot Stanton Blatch, 2 vols., New York and London: Harper and Brothers, 1922

Stanton, Elizabeth Cady, *The Selected Papers of Elizabeth Cady Stanton and Susan B. Anthony*, 2 vols., edited by Ann D. Gordon, New Brunswick, New Jersey, and London: Rutgers University Press, 1977

Stanton, Elizabeth Cady, *Elizabeth Cady Stanton, Susan B. Anthony, Correspondence, Writings, Speeches*, edited by Ellen Carol DuBois, New York: Schocken Books, 1981

Stanton, Elizabeth Cady, Susan B. Anthony, and Matilda Joslyn Gage, editors, *History of Woman Suffrage*, 6 vols., New York: Fowler and Wells, 1881–[1922]

Woodhull, Victoria, *The Victoria Woodhull Reader*, edited by Madeleine B. Stern, Weston, Massachusetts: M and S Press, 1974

Reference Works

Basch, Françoise, *Rebelles américaines au XIXe siècle: Mariage, amour libre et politique*, Paris: Méridiens Klincksieck, 1990

Bolt, Christine, *The Women's Movements in the U.S. and Britain from the 1790s to the 1920s*, Amherst: University of Massachusetts Press, and London: Harvester Wheatsheaf, 1993

Bordin, Ruth, and Birgitta Anderson, *Frances Willard: A Biography*, Chapel Hill: University of North Carolina Press, 1986

Buhle, Mari Jo, *Women and American Socialism, 1870–1920*, Urbana: University of Illinois Press, 1981

Buhle, Mari Jo, and Paul Buhle, editors, *A Concise History of Woman Suffrage: Selections from the Classic Work of Stanton, Anthony, Gage, and Harper*, Urbana: University of Illinois Press, 1978

Cott, Nancy F., *The Bonds of Womanhood: "Woman's Sphere" in New England, 1780–1835*, New Haven, Connecticut: Yale University Press, 1977

DuBois, Ellen Carol, *Feminism and Suffrage: The Emergence of an Independent Women's Movement in America, 1848–1869*, Ithaca, New York: Cornell University Press, 1978

Flexner, Eleanor, *Century of Struggle: The Woman's Rights Movement in the United States*, Cambridge, Massachusetts: Harvard University Press, 1959; enlarged edition, by Flexner and Ellen F. Fitzpatrick, 1996

Kerber, Linda K., Alice Kessler-Harris, and Kathryn Kish Sklar, editors, *U.S. History as Women's History: New Feminist Essays*, Chapel Hill: University of North Carolina Press, 1995

Kessler-Harris, Alice, *Out to Work: A History of Wage-Earning Women in the United States*, Oxford and New York: Oxford University Press, 1982

Lerner, Gerda, *The Grimké Sisters from South Carolina: Pioneers for Women's Rights and Abolition*, New York: Schocken Books, 1971; reprint, New York: Oxford University Press, 1998

Smith-Rosenberg, Carroll, *Disorderly Conduct: Visions of Gender in Victorian America*, New York: Knopf, 1985; Oxford and New York: Oxford University Press, 1986

Tax, Meredith, *The Rising of the Women: Feminist Solidarity and Class Conflict, 1880–1917*, New York and London: Monthly Review Press, 1980; new edition, Urbana: University of Illinois Press, and Wantage, Oxfordshire: University Presses Marketing, 2001

Wiesen-Cook, Blanche, "Female Support Networks and Political Activism: Lilian Wald, Crystal Eastman, and Emma Goldman," in *A Heritage of Her Own: Toward a New Social History of American Women*, edited by Nancy F. Cott and Elizabeth Hafkin Pleck, New York: Simon and Schuster, 1979

Yellin, Jean Fagan, and John C. Van Horne, editors, *The Abolitionist Sisterhood: Women's Political Culture in Antebellum America*, Ithaca, New York: Cornell University Press, 1994

WOMEN'S SUFFRAGE AND DEMOCRACY IN CANADA

YOLANDE COHEN

THE EXCLUSION OF WOMEN from suffrage at the very moment when the vote was extended to all adult men called into question the notions of universalism and popular representation that underlay the democratic system as it was being shaped in the West early in the 20th century. The principle of one man, one vote, which alone ostensibly embodied the abstract individualism so dear to the revolutionaries, meant that certain categories of the population, such as youth, women, Native Americans, and, in some cases, foreigners, Jews, blacks, and others, were excluded from the electoral process. Yet at the same time, it was the idea of political integration of the greatest number that legitimized the existence of the modern state. Contemporary with the development of that new model of government, women's demand for suffrage provides a striking picture of the ascendant ideology of democratic modernity. That demand exposed the ambiguities of a political ideology that aimed at inclusiveness yet practiced exclusion, that sought to establish equality while basing it on differences, and that produced several types of citizenship: passive and active, social and political. This paradox has been underscored by feminist historiographers, in particular by Joan Scott, who locates in it the theoretical and practical limitations of applying abstract individualism (see Scott 1994). It is this paradox, too, that has shaped women's approach to emancipation in their demand for the right to vote (equality) as well as in their concern with recognizing themselves as a distinct social group (difference). This calling into question, which most often pits the individualism and universalism associated with equality against the pluralism implicit in the expression of differences, lies at the heart of the crisis of contemporary democracy. That crisis is characterized by the divergent political philosophies of absolute liberalism, as articulated principally by the American philosopher John Rawls, author of the famous work *Theory of Justice* (1971), and communitarianism, whose main exponent is the Canadian philosopher Charles Taylor.

In this connection, analysis of one case enables us to understand how the suffrage debate was constructed. The history of women's participation in political life has always been deter-
mined by specific national conditions that cannot be summed up in the mere demand for the right to vote. Indeed, this demand usually seems to be linked to other forms of intervention: men and women's affirmation of individual rights, or, in the framework of a collective emancipatory process, such struggles as the civil rights movement the United States.

If, throughout most of the Western world, women are now considered full-fledged citizens, the ways in which they acquired the vote are very different and strictly dependent upon specific historical circumstances. The chronology of the attainment of the right to vote in the main industrialized nations between 1916 and 1945 clearly indicates the existence of rhythms and priorities particular to each country, rather than a chronological lag or lead relative to other countries. Moreover, possession of the right to vote is far from being synonymous with the exercise of that right. In short, the study of women's enfranchisement is most interesting for what it reveals about the political participation of excluded or minority social categories, and thus about the state of democracy at a given moment in a given country. The history of women's suffrage in Canada sheds light on the present debate between liberals or libertarians and communitarians in the United States as well as on the more European debate on citizenship versus national identity, for all of these traditions converge here.

In Canada, a country of colonization and immigration, the coexistence of distinct identity groups—French Canadians, English Canadians, and Native Americans—and of the British and French liberal traditions confers a specific timeframe and connotations upon the process of the acquisition of the right to vote. Three main periods can be discerned in this episode in the democratization of Canadian society: the crystallization of demands for women's right to vote, the establishment of women's suffrage legislation, and actual enfranchisement. The nation's confederate political structure as well as the very strong marking of Canadian identity (the eviction of the American Indians from the polity led to the supremacy of the two founding peoples, French and English), have led to major variations in the importance given to the acquisition of political rights. Discrepancies in the attainment of the right to vote according to province, marital status, gender identity, and so forth, illustrate the extent of these variations. Thus, as is often pointed out, the women of Quebec could vote in federal elections like all other Canadian women from 1918 on, but they had to wait until 1940 to vote in their own province, because the federal government granted this right earlier than the province of Quebec.

In addition to such variations (which must be decoded and taken into account), we must also consider the distinctions in social and cultural conditions inherent in the maturation of the demand for suffrage. It could be said that the two models, English Canadian and French Canadian, express two forms of rationality that are usually quite distinct and even diametrically opposed. In some cases, reference is made to the British tradition of individual rights, while in others the tradition of advancing the collective predominates. What must be identified is the way in which these different traditions interconnect in the Canadian mentality. In that regard we can assess relevance of the classical model of T. H. Marshall's analysis of the welfare state in Great Britain, by studying the particulars of the movement for women's political inclusion in Canadian society: did the demand for recognition of women's civil rights in the 19th century actually open the way to their political recognition and enfranchisement? Why was the franchise not uniformly accomplished through all the provinces of Canada? How does one explain the close overlapping of social and political demands at the turn of the century and into the 1930s and 1940s? This complex internal process of broadening female citizenship was further complicated by the immigration of women who brought with them American, British, or French experiences and ideas that were to play an important role in the debates.

Affirmation of Civil Rights in the British Colonies of North America

Before the acquisition of universal male suffrage, the issue of political rights in the British and French colonies of North America often appeared as the extension of those of the European capitals—at least in theory, and until the colonies acquired a personality of their own. Thus, in New France, historians presented a narrative involving a strict gender-based division of labor: women worked on every level of social life according to their rank and abilities, while the war and the fur trade kept their husbands, fathers, and brothers occupied. With the conquest of New France by the British army during the Seven Years' War (1756–63), the English judicial system was applied in the 13 colonies of North America. That system immediately encountered a major obstacle, namely the political disqualification of Catholics, who were in the majority in New France. The dilemma, described by the historian Hilda Neatby and quoted by Susan Trofimenkoff, quickly became obvious: "an English colony without an assembly seemed unthinkable, an assembly including Catholics seemed unworthy of trust and an assembly that excluded the Catholics seemed unjustifiable" (see Trofimenkoff). This dilemma was resolved through a special agreement, opening the door of political representation to Catholics, granted by the Act of Quebec, in 1774.

But in order to silence the protest movements in the colonies after the American Revolution and the French Revolution, Great Britain once again attempted to transform Quebec into an English colony: the Constitutional Act of 1791 organized the province after the British constitutional model, adapted to colonial realities. This act accorded only limited powers to the colonies and granted participation only to notables whose vote was based on tax qualifications. Indeed, with the Constitutional Act of 1791, the empire endowed Lower Canada with a parliament and rules of eligibility for participation in the electoral process: one had to be at least 21 years of age, own land or real estate that had a minimum annual value of 40 shillings sterling; or, in the city, one had to own a home or a building with an annual value of five pounds sterling or more, or else rent and have paid the annuity of one year (ten pounds sterling) and have resided in the city for at least a year. No mention was made of the voter's sex, and women were thus allowed to vote without any constraints.

Depending on region and year (from 1791 to 1849), hundreds of women, especially in Quebec (between 2 and 18 percent) claimed this right. They were highly aware of the privilege granted them by the Constitution: "The right to vote is not a natural right, neither for men nor for women, it is given by the law. . . . Property and not people are the foundation for representation in English government" ("Pétitions à la Chambre d'Assemblée du Bas-Canada" [1828; Petitions to the Chamber of Lower Canada]). Women voted en bloc with their families and they frequently held debates in philanthropic organizations, in which they were very active—an indication of their marked interest in political questions. The reality was therefore very different from the situation in Great Britain, where women did not claim these prerogatives, as the social hierarchy was more rigidly marked there.

Nevertheless, in 1834 restrictions were placed on women's right to vote. A new electoral law disqualified married women from voting by requiring ownership of the properties upon which tax was established. This legislation, a result of pressures from notables at the English court, reflected the development of liberal ideas on the issue of the vote. Property ownership was to be the sole basis for taxation, and property could no longer be family-owned because of the legal constraints such ownership imposed on freedom of exchange. Thus, an individual had to be sole owner of a property in order to vote. All the British colonies in North America, with the exception of Upper Canada, applied this law.

Paradoxically, women who owned property lost their voting privileges at precisely the same time that the notion of individualism inherent in the new bourgeois values was first gaining ground. In an international context marked by an increasingly rigid separation between law and morality, this reform contributed to the masculinization of politics. The new laws were symptomatic of a phenomenon that became increasingly significant in the political sphere, namely the growing individualism of English Canadian men and, to a lesser extent, English Canadian women, while French Canadians distanced themselves from the British model in order to better embrace the French model.

The civil rights of the women of Lower Canada, regulated by the *Coutume de Paris*, were further constrained by the more individualistic British concept of the family. In reality, the discriminatory measures regarding women in the *Coutume de Paris* nevertheless conferred numerous advantages on married women, including the dower's right. Under this right, which was widely used in Lower Canada, widows were entitled to hold certain properties that had belonged to their husbands. It was abolished in the aftermath of the Act of the Union of 1840. The adoption of the new Civil Code in 1866 confirmed the desire for unification of the two legal traditions, French and British, to the detriment of the recognition of women as individuals.

It is therefore not surprising that the electoral law confirmed this reality by formally taking the vote away from women altogether in 1849. As they took part in the broad debates mandating the separation of spheres, between political and economic, private and public, women and men, the British colonies engaged in a process of modernizing their structures and unifying the different laws at the heart of the new Canadian Confederation, constituted in 1867. The debate provided the juridical framework for the exercise of citizenship in the young nation. As in Paris, where the distinction between active and passive citizenship dated to the French Revolution, Canada created a list of qualifications required for eligibility to vote. The list of handicaps that excluded the poor, vagrants, and even the proletariat from full citizenship in Europe during the same period was quite long. Thoroughly imbued the new bourgeois morality, the ability to vote was the prerogative of a small, select group, sufficiently free from material and family obligations to exercise political functions with dignity. In this process, the masculinization of power went hand in hand with its growing identification with the middle class.

Similar moral criteria justified the political exclusion and legal marginalization of women of limited means or "dubious morals," such as prostitutes, day workers, or domestic servants, while at the same time a whole series of legal measures were being developed for the improvement of the condition of mothers and children. Thus, a political geography was drawn, based as much on the presumed moral capacities of certain men to lead public affairs as it was on the presumed capacities of some women to create the ideal conditions for the exercise of citizenship. The rearing of children and protection of the family were to be key concepts in the broad movement for social reform to which educated Canadian women committed themselves. The reform movement can be understood only by considering it alongside the suffrage movement; more than a complement to the latter, the reform movement was the feminized version of the suffrage movement. It attested to the democrats' belief that an individual's capabilities must be proven—first of all, by property ownership and then civic virtue—in order to take part in the affairs of state and city. Not everyone was naturally fit for civic responsibility. As a counterpart to these notions, and bolstered by the new laws restricting the electorate, which were justified by the goal of establishing a new, modern, political order, there emerged the perceived need to reform society as a whole in preparation for the new world. This task was immediately taken on by the women of the new social elites, who hastened to define their own area of influence and to locate the outlines of civic virtue in the family, which seemed to be its foundation par excellence. In tandem with a massive rhetorical campaign that consolidated the family in a separate sphere, there developed a veritable industry, almost exclusively women-run, devoted to philanthropic activity and behavioral reform. Depending on the cultural and religious traditions particular to different countries,

the reform movement was visible everywhere in the West at the end of the 19th century and took on connotations that could be predominantly religious, national, or political. In the United States, for example, the reform movement was first manifested in the struggle to abolish slavery and end racial segregation, while in England and Germany reformist energies were focused on women's suffrage. In every case, the movement was strongly anchored in maternal or social feminism, which recent studies have identified as the precursor to the welfare state. The Canadian example is significant in that it reveals the active presence of women's philanthropic groups in the transformation of the state, at the time that the latter was striving for the unification of Lower and Upper Canada. The philanthropic movement was closely involved in the establishment of the welfare state, contributing content and sometimes political personnel. In accordance with a strict division of tasks within the social and political sectors, the women and men of the educated elite shouldered the task of making Canada into a more just and equitable society and defining the modalities of the new citizenship.

Thus, at the turn of the century two ways of making this agenda a reality can be distinguished. One of these strategies relied on a strong associationist tradition that was secular but inspired by Presbyterianism and particularly present in English Canada; it attempted to put the state in charge of "the social" while at the same time professionalizing it. The other strategy, which considered aid to the poor, mothers, and families to be a private responsibility, assigned the role of social assistance to churches and charitable organizations; it was manifested in the upsurge of essentially French Catholic religious orders at the time. In the first case, the new welfare state considered the social-maternal function as the foundation of citizenship, while in the second case this function was considered to be a private activity. These two conceptions of women's role as citizens established the chronological rhythms that marked women's franchise in Quebec and Canada.

Inclusion of Mothers and War Widows in the Civic Realm in English Canada

The slow and gradual process that led to women's franchise was closely linked to the broad movement of social feminism, and it reflected the overlapping of the social demands proposed by the movement and changes within the state. In English Canada, the lead in the temperance movement was taken by reformers, physicians, and men of law whose concerns with curbing alcoholism and promoting public hygiene mirrored the agenda of the temperance movement in the United States. The Women's Christian Temperance Union (WCTU) played a front-line role in the transformation of the anti-alcohol campaign into a political movement for women's suffrage. An exclusively female organization founded in Picton, Ontario, in 1874, the Canadian WCTU counted 9,000 affiliated groups in 1891 and campaigned persistently in favor of government intervention against alcohol consumption, which was held responsible for crime, displacement of families, political corruption, and a great many other evils. Convinced of the importance of anti-alcohol reforms, the members of the WCTU became involved in highly publicized campaigns across the country to enforce compliance from governments that had remained impervious to their speeches. Imbued with belief in their cause and disappointed with the reception they were given, the main leaders of the WCTU quickly turned toward political action to demand rights equal to those of men. They joined the activist women who, as early as 1852, had demonstrated their desire to reform property laws with respect to married women. Anne McDonald and Elizabeth Dunlop asked that the legislation passed in the State of New York in 1856 be applied in Upper Canada.

The temperance movement, taken up by a number of other associations such as the Salvation Army, which recruited especially among working-class women, brought immediate results. Following the example of American suffragists such as Susan B. Anthony, who had been called upon to lend her support, groups of women demanded the franchise and, against all expectations, obtained it in British Columbia, where no organized group in favor of suffrage existed. In 1873 that province became the first in the nation to grant women partial suffrage (the right to vote on the municipal level). In Ontario, the process was a great deal slower and more complicated. In 1882 the provincial government granted the right to vote in municipal elections to female property-owners, unmarried women, and widows. Then, two years later, it proclaimed the equality of men and women where access to higher education was concerned by opening universities and medical schools to women, and finally it granted the right to vote in municipalities to unmarried women and widows without property. Married women remained without franchise even as the law emancipated them for the first time from their husbands' guardianship and authorized them to be sole property-owners. This situation led married women to intensify their efforts within mutual aid and assistance organizations in Ontario and the Maritime Provinces.

A veritable protection industry emerged and was to focus on childhood and the family; the socialization of children lay at the heart of the reformist effort. From their efforts to regulate the immigration process (where there was a marked tendency to separate little girls from their families) to the creation of orphanages in the large urban centers, the reformists were convinced they were attacking social evil at the root. These groups advocated rapid intervention, especially in working-class or underprivileged families, in order to do social work and to develop hygiene and education—in short, to ensure that minimal standards of children's education be met. In fact, these standards were largely inspired by bourgeois morality, but also by new ideas about the role of mothers that developed as the mothering function was increasingly professionalized. Juvenile delinquency, which was commonly attributed to the fact that lower-class women worked, sparked a protest campaign and a discourse on motherhood that perfectly suited the government and the women activists behind the campaign. Work was what distinguished virtuous women from depraved women. The work of women was here directly identified as the cause of juvenile delinquency: without close supervision, children left to their own devices progressed toward crime and prostitution. The ideology of motherhood and the call to vigilance, directed toward working mothers in particular, appeared as the essential condition for the survival of Canadian society. This mentality led to a high number of restrictions on women's employment and their exclusion from certain professions, including professions they had once

practiced exclusively, such as midwifery. With the professionalization and medicalization of the maternal function, the Canadian government and its representatives took charge of child welfare. At the same time, the dissemination of images of the model mother resulted in the recognition and reinforcement of her power over child welfare, giving women leverage with the state. And this was precisely the objective of the reformist women who had centered their national activity on these issues.

From the end of the 1880s, the WCTU enjoyed national stature while other groups, such as the Young Women's Christian Association (YWCA) and the Girls' Friendly Association, an Anglican organization, achieved similar levels of popularity. Entirely dedicated to providing social services and education to mothers and workingwomen, these associations intervened directly by taking charge of problem cases; for example, they assumed responsibility for caring for illegitimate children or children of single mothers. They developed a structure of family assistance that would serve as direct support to the state's intervention in this area. By adhering to and developing the ideal of motherhood and femininity, middle-class women who were strongly committed to the social reform movement publicized the specificity and the importance of their role in the building of Canadian society and provided the structure of the welfare state. They contributed to the redefinition of citizenship—a phenomenon that was current in many Western nations at the time, particularly in Great Britain and the United States.

Under the influence of these women, social activism spilled over into politics, as is evident from the inclusion of an equal rights agenda and the transformation of certain philanthropic associations into pressure groups promoting women's right to vote. Out of local centers of the WCTU, the YWCA, and other groups more specifically focused on suffrage, such as the Dominion Women's Enfranchisement Association, there emerged the political force of the National Council of Women of Canada (NCWC). Created in 1893 to promote recognition of women's essential role in the family, the council was led by Lady Aberdeen, the wife of the future governor general of Canada. The NCWC was a federal, nondenominational, and nonpartisan organization. It eventually became a national force that enabled numerous provincial women's groups to advance their campaigns for political and social emancipation.

To a large extent, this interlocking of social and political demands explains the progressive aspect of the legislation that guaranteed new rights for women. Without seeking to explain everything through the social movement, the remarkable coincidence of social activists' demands and laws recognizing the legal personhood of women must be noted: between 1872 and 1907 laws authorizing married women to own property were passed everywhere but in Manitoba and Quebec; all women could be elected to school boards and could vote in municipal elections.

Nevertheless, these legislative measures taken as a whole fell short of the movement's expectations. In every Canadian province, suffragists mobilized to make governments aware of injustices against women. They enlisted the Pankhurst sisters to give lectures, and they obtained the support of the International Alliance for Women's Suffrage. Demonstrations, especially the Mock Parliament, were opportunities for raising public awareness about the quibbling arguments men routinely invoked to reject women's suffrage. But it was World War I, with its attendant sacrifices and transformations, that played a determining role in women's access to the vote. Women's involvement in the war effort—whether through the Red Cross, the Victorian Order of Nurses, or the Suffragists' War Auxiliaries—was considerable, and their contribution was much more visible than in times of peace. The entire network of aid organizations was mobilized to defend the homeland. New members came flocking to all the women's associations, which consequently saw a surge in activity. Especially visible in work connected with health and family care, women also distinguished themselves in the areas of fundraising and the maintenance of services basic to the functioning of the national economy. They also filled the factory and office job vacancies created as men went to the front, in professions in which the workforce was not traditionally female.

The right to vote and to stand for election at the provincial level was granted to women in Manitoba, Alberta, and Saskatchewan (1916) and to women in British Columbia and Ontario (1917) in the middle of the war. With the exception of Quebec, the women in other provinces obtained this right a few years later: in 1918 in Nova Scotia, in 1919 in New Brunswick, and in 1922 on Prince Edward Island. On the national level, the right to vote would evolve from the granting of the vote in 1917 to nurses who had served in the war. This was broadened by the Wartime Elections Act of 1917, whose provisions included all women who had been affected by the war through a wounded or lost husband, brother, father, or son. Finally, on 24 May 1918, the law granting suffrage to women was adopted: the criteria for women's eligibility to vote became the same as those for men—to be 21 years of age and a British subject.

This process of enfranchisement was inscribed within the broader debate on women's suffrage. Arguments in favor of women's suffrage were clearly articulated in the Canadian Parliament a number of times (1883, 1885, 1898, 1916, 1917, and 1918). Women were taxpayers, like men, and should legitimately be able to express their opinions on the use of their money. Moreover, their presence in Parliament would provide a healthy purification of political morality. Further, with the acquisition of full rights women would finally be liberated from degrading inferiority, thus making Canada the first country to rise to the rank of a civilized nation. Opponents of suffrage, in particular conservatives, cited the sacrosanct sexual division of roles in order to push aside egalitarian arguments. However, such arguments were no longer tenable given the new realities the war had engendered. For one thing, the war had blurred the borders between spheres, since a good number of women occupied men's positions. For another, the war had fostered increased government interventionism and centralization, which disproved the ultimate argument that the women's vote would bring about a weakening federal power. In fact, in 1918 several western provinces and Ontario had already granted the right to vote to women, which risked giving them overrepresentation in the Canadian Parliament.

Thus, women's attainment of the right to vote at the national level in Canada (a short time before women's suffrage was achieved in Great Britain and the United States) can be explained in several ways. Political considerations must also be taken into account: the federal government of the national union led by Borden envisaged the political credit this measure would bring: the women's vote would help him contend with the intense controversy around the draft that threatened his position. In British Columbia and Manitoba, the new liberal governments

that had put women's suffrage on their agenda kept their promise, while the conservative governments of the other provinces were urged to follow the federal example. Nevertheless, partisan politics is not an entirely satisfactory explanation, just as suffragist pressure alone does not explain why the vote was obtained during the war. The federal state's new level of intervention in the war put it in a preeminent situation compared to that of the provinces, a situation that would continue after the war. The necessity of giving women the role they deserved derived from the social prerogatives newly given over to the state.

Abundant literature on the role of the war in women's emancipation has contributed to either underestimating or overestimating the war's impact in this area. In the case of Canada, one must conclude that obtaining the right to vote was directly connected to the recognition of women's changed role in postwar society. It was the culmination of the combined efforts of the women's associations to gain recognition for the specificity of women's social and political action. Indeed, it was first and foremost in their capacity as valiant women and devoted mothers that women won the right to vote, as Gisela Bock has concluded was also the case for German women (see Bock 1992).

In the provinces where women's associations were interventionist they used their position to achieve rapid political integration. In fact, the degree of osmosis with the state, to which these associations contributed, modified the perspective of all parties: the state took back some of the welfare prerogatives of the women's associations, while the associations facilitated the state's entry into the private family sphere by providing the structures and labor necessary for government intervention. In this context, the role of the state changed, as did the concept of citizenship, which became more inclusive and now rewarded services rendered. Citizenship, as foreseen by Sir William Beveridge, rewarding political and social responsibility, thereafter secured its full meaning: "The citizen . . . not only participates in the political life of the community and holds political rights but also contributes to its social and economic well-being, drawing from it social and economic entitlements" (*Social Insurance and Allied Services: A Report by Sir William Beveridge, Parliamentary Papers, 1942–43;* quoted in Pederson 1990). A similar logic was at work in the province of Quebec, sustained by the Anglo-Protestant organizations. Here, however, an additional logic was superimposed: that of the militant nationalism that drove the action of the French Catholic groups.

Philanthropy, Nationalism, and Voting Rights in Quebec

At the turn of the century, almost all social and philanthropic action in Quebec was concentrated within the chapters of national Anglo-Protestant associations (the YWCA, the Victorian Order of Nurses, and similar organizations) and French Catholic religious congregations. The Montreal Local Council of Women (the Montreal chapter of the National Council of Women of Canada), which campaigned openly in favor of suffrage, included Francophone women until 1907. These women decided in 1907 to establish the Fédération Nationale Saint-Jean-Baptiste (National Federation of St. John the Baptist), bringing together 22 affiliated societies. This regrouping within the federation of endeavors in the areas of philanthropy, education, and economic and mutual aid for women brought a new impetus to activists' demands.

Reform of the Civil Code to grant full legal status to women was on the agenda of the federation, which also subscribed to the suffragist views of the Montreal Suffrage Association, created in 1912. Women's attainment of the vote at the national level in Canada caused a rise in levels of women's suffrage activism in the province of Quebec: the Comité Provincial pour le Suffrage Féminin (Provincial Committee for Women's Suffrage) and the Alliance Canadienne pour le Vote des Femmes du Québec (Canadian Alliance for the Vote for the Women of Quebec), the latter presided over by Idola Saint-Jean, were founded in 1921 and 1927, respectively. In 1928, the committee was renamed the Ligue des Droits de Femmes (League of Women's Rights) under the presidency of Thérèse Casgrain. But despite support from Anglo-Protestant activists, Franco-Catholic Canadians were reluctant to shoulder the demand for the women's vote completely. They were not convinced of the validity of this battle, and even the soul of the Provincial Committee for Women's Suffrage, Marie Lacoste-Gérin-Lajoie, disagreed with the turn the movement was taking and withdrew in 1922. The ambiguity of this position was not due to some historic fatality, as Diane Lamoureux has emphasized (see Lamoureux 1989). Aiming first at the reform of the Civil Code, which they found to be particularly unfair toward married women, and following the example of Anglophone Canadian women, these groups tried to obtain recognition of their status as women based on their rights as citizens and their social duties, especially as mothers. However, in contrast to Anglophone Canadian women, Francophone Canadian women's demands were not directly translated into political capital for two reasons: the particular role of the Catholic Church and the close national cohesion of French Canada.

Suffragists ran up against the hegemonic presence of the Church in the social sector. Anxious to maintain its dominance in the areas of health, education, and aid to the poorest, the Church registered an unprecedented growth in its enrollment and influence in the course of the 19th century; between 1830 and 1870, the number of nuns doubled. Maintaining its autonomy from the state was the principal concern that helped set the course of the Church's interventions during this period, and that autonomy was readily conceded in view of the meager resources available. The Church, in turn, relied on networks of aid associations and groups to develop its work in both urban centers and rural areas. The convergence of interests at work here deserves emphasis. Taking into account the very strongly hierarchical structure of the Church and its power, it placed itself as the obligatory mediator between women and state—in contrast to Protestantism, which encouraged women's access to the state—and thereby short-circuited any possibility of women having recourse to government authorities. The numerous women's associations established at the end of the last century found themselves facing a single interlocutor and had to compromise with the immense prerogatives this situation conferred upon the Catholic Church.

Ultimately, the Church's discourse of distrust of government and the political realm restricted them to an exclusively social space. In Quebec, the dichotomy maintained between social and political citizenship was justified by the national question. The exclusion from political affairs, characteristic of the life of the great majority of the population in Lower Canada, led to lasting rifts between civil society and political life. Sociologist Fernand Dumont explains this divorce between what he calls the political and cultural character of the nation prior to Confederation by the absence of the state as much as by the supremacy of a politics of patronage, which he considers to be the prerogative of the federal state (see Dumont). As for Lower Canada and what was later to become Quebec, the ideological framework of a millenarian and then emancipatory utopia nurtured what Dumont calls the survival state, conducive to the birth of nationalism. The connection of this society to politics was constructed on a strong dualism between the society Dumont characterizes as "immobile," or apolitical, and that of the small world privy to the mysteries of federal power, the educated elite. The opposition seemed implacable between, on the one hand, the world of family, representing permanence, which at one and the same time ensured social reproduction and continuity of daily life in all its monotony, and, on the other hand, the world of politics, whether it be political, ecclesiastical, business-related, or federal. The Church's official suspicions about politics were presumably anchored in the prevailing mentality; these suspicions were clearly formulated when it concerned the women's vote.

The clerical and nationalist discourses against women's suffrage are well known: women were said to bear the foremost (and essential) responsibility for the survival of the French Canadian people—a responsibility best carried out in the community and not by politics and the vote, destroyer of sacred family values and national cohesion. In the name of communitarian and religious values and boasting the support of women who "prefer to practice the art of pleasing and indirectly exert political influence" (*Le coin du feu*, 1901), a common front excluded from suffrage tried to find other means for women to shape the nation.

Behind these discourses, however, a more subtle reality can be discerned. The partial retreat of some French Catholic organizations from the suffrage movement must be distinguished from the antisuffragist and anti-egalitarian campaign orchestrated by the Church for its own ends. Furthermore, it was at the moment when the Church's hold over its organizations weakened that it redoubled its efforts to publicize its views and maintain control over areas that were increasingly falling within the purview of the state. The Church was losing momentum particularly in the sectors of health and welfare. The rapid professionalization of these sectors involved a concomitant marginalization of the Church and growing intervention of the state as a regulatory authority. Transformations in the rural areas also led to a reconfiguration of the initiatives of the Catholic Church as it attempted to adapt to the new demands. While the Cercles des Fermières (Society of Farm Women), founded in 1915, kept its distance from the Church in order to enjoy closer ties to the state, the positions taken by some of the society's branches against the women's suffrage were widely publicized and were cited as evidence of "the opposition of women themselves" to the ratification of this right.

In fact, while it was true that social activism included the very great majority of women's groups, such activism was nonetheless not considered to be contradictory to action in favor of equality—even in the face of Church opposition. Following the example set by Anglophone Canadian women, organizations such as the National Federation of St. John the Baptist, the Association des Femmes Propriétaires (Association of Women

Property-Owners), the Canadian Alliance for the Vote for the Women, the League of Women's Rights, and the Conseil Local des Femmes de Montréal (Local Women's Council of Montreal), mobilized in support of reform of the Civil Code within the framework of the Dorion Commission (1929). Following the recent recognition of women as legal persons by the Private Council of London—which gave them the right to a seat in the Senate in 1928—these organizations obtained changes giving legal competence to women who were separated or divorced. The issue that remained crucial was still very much that of the rights of married women and mothers.

There was relative unanimity on this issue within women's groups (with the exception of a few marked figures such as the journalists Idola Saint-Jean and Eva Circé Côté) and even within political parties such as the Cooperative Commonwealth Federation (CCF) that were sensitive to the issue. Equality of the sexes began as something that could only apply to women who were not mothers. Concern for the reproduction of family and the survival of the French Canadian nation was common to all parties and groups, including those on the left, and this concern justified the exclusion of mothers from franchise. The notion of the protection of mothers, which also formed the armature of the social policies of the welfare state, was in full force at this time. It was this twofold debate, summed up in social policies, that in the 1940s led to the passage of women's suffrage laws in Quebec and the setting forth of principles for the reform of the federal welfare state.

In Quebec, the arguments advanced in favor of women's suffrage illustrate the connections between political and social, private and public aspects of the issue. On 13 separate occasions between 1927 and 1939, several groups of deputies, almost all from the party in power, sponsored amendments to the electoral law in order to include women. Each time the amendment was defeated by a majority of 65 percent or more. This record reveals that the parties in power seriously envisioned voting rights for women and were hoping to win their loyalties by being the party that had succeeded in making this reform a reality. The arguments for the rejection of the women's suffrage amendments are known and have been summarized in four points by the last call of Cardinal Villeneuve, published on the front page of the Franco-Catholic daily *Le devoir* on 19 March 1940:

> We are not in favor of women's political suffrage: 1) Because it goes against the unity and hierarchy of the family; 2) Because its practice exposes women to the passions and risks of electioneering; 3) Because, in fact, it seems to us that the very great majority of provincial women do not want it; 4) Because the social, economic, hygienic, and other reforms that have been advanced in order to advocate women's suffrage can just as well be obtained though women's organizations outside of politics.

It ultimately took a change in government and the election of the Liberal Party for the vote to be granted. Considerations around the attainment of women's franchise attest to the enduring nature of partisan and social concerns. Pressured by Thérèse Casgrain and the 40 delegates she had recruited to participate in the party congress in 1938, the Liberal Party agreed to include women's suffrage on its platform with a view toward obtaining women's support for getting the social reforms passed. As soon as he was elected, Prime Minister Adélard Godbout himself

sponsored the bill, a second reading of which he presented to the Chamber on 11 April 1940, thereby circumventing its return to committee, which in previous years had resulted in its repeated postponement. Invoking "the rights of all human persons," Godbout showed that it was not the vote but rather work that caused women to leave their homes (*Journal de l'Assemblée législative de la Province de Québec*, 1940). The vote would "only increase women's involvement in the public realm" he stated, arguing that

> they are a factor [that will help promote] order ... they will bring to it an enlightened patriotism and a broader range of perspectives than we ourselves bring to it. ... I demand the right to vote for women in order to ensure the protection of the family, of which they are the first caretakers.

Canadian women were granted the right to vote in accordance with the expansion of the state's prerogatives in the social sphere. Their active intervention in this area was rewarded:

> To pay homage to our young women, who work with generous hearts in our welfare and charitable associations to help solve our social problems, [and] to remove any obstacle from the beneficial influence of women in society, I ask the Chamber to adopt the second reading of this bill.

Ovations followed the reading of the bill. Adopted by 67 votes against 6, the law still faced opposition during its examination in plenary committee (*Le Canada*, 18 April 1940), but was finally adopted by the Legislative Council (*Le Canada*, 25 April 1940).

In Canada, the history of the demand for a broader notion of citizenship, for men in the 19th century and for women early in the 20th century, is framed in a context in which problems of identity overshadowed the citizenship debate. The dichotomy between civil and political society seemed to constitute the very foundation of citizenship, for the definition of citizenship is closely connected to an affirmation of a sense of identity by an entire people. The strong interdependency between the national and cultural constitution of Quebec society strongly suggests that the formal exclusion of women from political life led them to invest in an intense social and cultural life, in which the transformation of the world of the family was the primary stake. That is why it seems imperative in this case to dispense with the separation between private and public spheres, at least for analytical purposes, and instead focus on the interconnections among changes in the family and in social and political life.

Conclusions

On a more general level, the duality that has afflicted the Canadian Confederation from the beginning derived as much from the original sources of the model—the British Constitution and the French counterrevolution—as from the practical forms of resistance to its application. From very early on, this duality undermined the development of a true participatory democracy. In this connection, some divergences from the models of reference should be noted. The complex relationships maintained by the colony of New France with regard to the colonial power and feelings of ambivalence about Canadian unity from the Union Act until today have led to peculiar political arrangements that cannot be completely explained in terms of legal or narrowly political analysis. The originality of this situation is all the more remarkable in that the neighboring examples of emancipation, whether the United States or the other Canadian provinces, are hardly significant for the way in which the issue of Quebec's separatist tendencies resulting from the sense of a specific, Francophone national culture in that province should be considered. Moreover, Quebec's relationship to the original cultural and political model of the French Catholic society cannot be invoked unreservedly either. Close because of its language and culture, France became remote, to be fled and abandoned as soon as the French Revolution broke out. In France it was possible to trace the avatars of the demand for citizenship back to the French Revolution without too much difficulty; the initial exclusion of women was attributed to issues emerging from the political situation, from the republican rationale of abstract individualism, from women's limited and belated access to higher education, from ideological arguments, and so forth.

In Quebec as on the Continent, the law set rules that determined the government's mode of operation, leading many historians to conclude that the people of Quebec and even the Canadians as a whole were apolitical. By establishing a separation between the work and domestic realms of the people and the partisan character of the clerical and bourgeois elite, we preclude real understanding of the process that led to the particular formation of the Canadian state and confederation. Because political affairs emanated from a distant power, the colonies very quickly organized to make society function. It was in the movement of associations, whether inspired and run by the churches, political parties, or the unions, that civil society emerged. This movement led to Canada's emergence as the most sophisticated welfare state in North America. Women—mainly white, Protestant, and bourgeois—played an enormous role, both as men's equals and under the protection of their sexual difference. Their predominant place in the reform movement dedicated to hygiene, moral improvement of public life, and similar causes led them straight to the attainment of the vote for services rendered to society. This explains why the campaign for the right to suffrage in Canada did not pass through the same violent stages as it did in Great Britain and elsewhere.

The case of the campaign for women's suffrage in Canada also attests to the complexity of the situations middle-class women used as a springboard from which to gain access to public life. It illustrates the fundamental role of femininity, or maternalism as a discourse constructed on the notion of sexual difference, in the attainment of suffrage and political rights in a historical period that coincides with the construction of the welfare state. It shows the struggle for suffrage as an uneven process, where class and race played a strong role: initially only women of a certain class and status obtained the right to vote in Quebec, and American Indians had to wait until 1962 to obtain it there.

The account of women's enfranchisement in Canada thus allows for a reconceptualization of one of the dominant paradigms in contemporary feminist historiography, namely the irreducible opposition between equality and difference. Following Joan Scott, we believe, on the contrary, that the demand for equal rights proceeded from the different position of men and women in society: "The political notion of equality includes, indeed depends on an acknowledgment of the existence of difference. Demands for equality have rested on implicit and usually unrecognized arguments for difference" (see Scott 1988). Far from being essentialist, the historical analysis illustrating differences allows precisely for the deconstruction of assigned identities, whether feminine or masculine. On a secondary level, this analysis also permits a rethinking of the opposition between public and private spheres, a model that is less than helpful in understanding the fluidity of social relationships based on gender.

I would like to thank Erich Laforest for his contribution in compiling the data on the right to vote in Quebec. This research is part of the Research Project on Women and Democracy in Canada, which was subsidized by the Conseil de Recherches en Sciences Humaines du Canada (Social Sciences and Humanities Research Council of Canada).

Bibliography

Sources

Journaux de l'Assemblée législative de la Province de Québec 75 (1940)
Lettres patentes et arrêté en Conseil ayant force de loi dans la province de Québec, Québec: 1940
"Pétitions à la Chambre d'Assemblée du Bas-Canada, 4 décembre 1828," in *Documents relatifs à l'histoire constitutionnelle du Canada, 1819–1928,* compiled and edited by Arthur G. Doughty and Norah Story, Ottawa: Patenaude, 1935

Reference Works

Allen, Richard, "The Social Gospel and the Reform Tradition in Canada, 1890–1928," in *Readings in Canadian History,* edited by R. Douglas Francis and Donald B. Smith, vol. 1, *Post-Confederation,* 2nd edition, Toronto: Holt Rinehart and Winston of Canada, 1986

Arnup, Katherine, Andrée Lévesque, and Ruth Roach Pierson, *Delivering Motherhood: Maternal Ideologies and Practices in the 19th and 20th Centuries,* London and New York: Routledge, 1990

Bacchi, Carol Lee, *Liberation Deferred? The Ideas of the English-Canadian Suffragists: 1877–1918,* Toronto and Buffalo, New York: University of Toronto Press, 1983

Backhouse, Constance, "Shifting Patterns in Nineteenth-Century Canadian Custody Law," in *Essays in the History of Canadian Law,* edited by David H. Flaherty, vol. 1, Toronto and Buffalo, New York: University of Toronto Press, 1981

Baron, F.L., "The American Origins of the Temperance Movement," *Canadian Review of American Studies* 11 (1980)

Beito, David T., "This Enormous Army: The Mutual Aid Tradition of American Fraternal Societies before the Twentieth Century," in *The Welfare State,* edited by Ellen Frankel Paul, Fred Dycus Miller, Jr., and Jeffrey Paul, Cambridge and New York: Cambridge University Press, 1997

Bock, Gisela, "Pauvreté féminine, droits des mères et États-providence," in *Histoire des femmes en Occident,* edited by Georges Duby and Michelle Perrot, vol. 5, *Le XXe siècle,* Paris: Plon, 1992

Bock, Gisela, and Pat Thane, editors, *Maternity and Gender Policies: Women and the Rise of the European Welfare States, 1880–1950's,* London and New York: Routledge, 1991

Butler, Judith P., and Joan Wallach Scott, editors, *Feminists Theorize the Political,* London and New York: Routledge, 1992

Castel, Robert, *Les métamorphoses de la question sociale: Une chronique du salariat,* Paris: Fayard, 1995

Christie, Nancy, and Michael Gauvreau, *A Full-Orbed Christianity: The Protestant Churches and Social Welfare in Canada, 1900–1940*, Montreal and Buffalo, New York: McGill-Queen's University Press, 1996

Cohen, Yolande, *Femmes de parole: L'histoire des Cercles de fermières du Québec, 1915–1990*, Montreal: Le Jour, 1990

Cohen, Yolande, and Marie-Blanche Tahon, "Today's Women," in *Quebec Society: Critical Issues*, edited by M. Michael Rosenberg, Deena White, and Marcel Fournier, Scarborough, Ontario: Prentice-Hall Canada, 1997

Davies, Stephen, "Two Conceptions of Welfare: Volunteerism and Incorporationism," in *The Welfare State*, edited by Ellen Frankel Paul, Fred Dycus Miller, Jr., and Jeffrey Paul, Cambridge and New York: Cambridge University Press, 1997

De La Cour, Lykke, Cecilia Morgan, and Marianna Valverde, "Gender Regulation and State Formation in Nineteenth-Century Canada," in *Colonial Leviathan: State Formation in Mid-Nineteenth-Century Canada*, edited by Allan Greer and Ian Walter Radforth, Toronto and Buffalo, New York: University of Toronto Press, 1992

Dubois, Ellen Carol, *Feminism and Suffrage: The Emergence of an Independent Women's Movement in America: 1848–1869*, Ithaca, New York: Cornell University Press, 1978

Dumont, Fernand, *Genèse de la société québécoise*, Montreal: Boréal, 1993

Fecteau, Jean-Marie, *Un nouvel ordre des choses: La pauvreté, le crime, l'État au Québec, de la fin du XVIIIe siècle à 1840*, Outremont, Quebec: VLB, and Ville Saint-Laurent, Quebec: Diffusion Dimédia, 1989

Fraisse, Geneviève, *La raison des femmes*, Paris: Plon, 1992

Garner, John, *The Franchise and Politics in British North America, 1755–1867*, Ottawa: University of Toronto Press, 1969

Godineau, Dominique, *Citoyennes tricoteuses: Les femmes du peuple à Paris pendant la Révolution française*, Aix-en-Provence, France: Alinéa, 1988; as *The Women of Paris and Their Revolution*, translated by Katherine Streip, Berkeley: University of California Press, 1998

Guest, Dennis, *The Emergence of Social Security in Canada*, Vancouver, Canada: University of British Columbia Press, 1980; 3rd edition, 1997

Jones, Andrew, and Leonard Rutnam, *In the Children's Aid: J.J. Kelso and Child Welfare in Ontario*, Toronto and Buffalo, New York: University of Toronto Press, 1981

Jost, Hans Ulrich, Monique Pavillon, and François Vallotton, editors, *La politique des droits: Citoyenneté et construction des genres aux XIXe et XXe siècles*, Paris: Kimé, 1994

Kealey, Linda, and Joan Sangster, editors, *Beyond the Vote: Canadian Women and Politics*, Toronto and Boston: University of Toronto Press, 1989

Koven, Seth, and Sonia Michel, editors, *Mothers of a New World: Maternalist Politics and the Origins of the Welfare States*, London and New York: Routledge, 1993

Kymlicka, Will, *Liberalism, Community, and Culture*, Oxford: Clarendon Press, and New York: Oxford University Press, 1989

Lamoureux, Diane, *Citoyennes? Femmes, droit de vote et démocratie*, Montreal: Remue-Ménage, 1989

Lamoureux, Diane, and Jacinthe Michaud, "Les parlementaires canadiens et le suffrage féminin: Un aperçu des débats," *Revue canadienne de science politique* 21, no. 2 (June 1988)

Lavergne, France, *Le suffrage féminin*, Sainte-Foy, Quebec: Directeur Général des Élections du Québec, 1990

Levesque, Andrée, "Les Québécoises et leur citoyenneté: La citoyenneté selon Eva Circé-Côté," in *La politique des droits: Citoyenneté et construction des genres aux XIXe et XXe siècles*, edited by Hans Ulrich Jost, Monique Pavillon, and François Vallotton, Paris: Kimé, 1994

Lewis, Jane, "Motherhood Issues during the Late Nineteenth and Early Twentieth Centuries: Some Recent Viewpoints," *Ontario History* 75 (1983)

Marks, Lynne, "'The Hallelujah Lasses': Working Class Women in the Salvation Army in English Canada, 1882–1892," in *Gender Conflicts: New Essays in Women's History*, edited by Franca Iacovetta and Mariana Valverde, Toronto and Buffalo, New York: University of Toronto Press, 1992

Marshall, Dominique, *Aux origines sociales de l'État-providence: Familles québécoises, obligation scolaire et allocations familiales, 1940–1955*, Montreal: Presses de l'Université de Montréal, 1998

Mitchinson, Wendy, "The WCTU: For God, Home, and Native Land: A Study in Nineteenth-Century Feminism," in *A Not Unreasonable Claim: Women and Reform in Canada, 1880s–1920s*, edited by Linda Kealey, Toronto: Women's Press, 1979

Mitchinson, Wendy, and Janice P. Dickin McGinnis, editors, *Essays in the History of Canadian Medicine*, Toronto: McClelland and Stewart, 1988

Mongeau, Serge, *Évolution de l'assistance au Québec: Une étude historique des diverses modalités d'assistance au Québec, des origines de la colonie à nos jours*, Montreal: Éditions du Jour, 1967

Mossuz-Lavau, Janine, and Mariette Sineau, *Enquête sur les femmes et la politique en France*, Paris: Presses Universitaires de France, 1983

Parr, Joy, editor, *Childhood and Family in Canadian History*, Toronto: McClelland and Stewart, 1982

Parr, Joy, *Labouring Children: British Immigrant Apprentices to Canada, 1869–1924*, London: Croom Helm, 1980

Pedersen, Susan, *Family, Dependence, and the Origins of the Welfare State: Britain and France: 1914–1945*, Cambridge and New York: Cambridge University Press, 1993

Pedersen, Susan, "Gender, Welfare, and Citizenship in Britain during the Great War," *American Historical Review* 95, no.4 (1990)

Picard, Nathalie, "Les femmes et le vote au Bas-Canada, 1791–1849," in *Les bâtisseuses de la cité*, edited by Évelyne Tardy et al., Montreal: Association Canadienne-Française pour l'Avancement des Sciences, 1993

Pierson, Ruth R., "Gender and the Unemployment Insurance Debates in Canada, 1934–1940," *Labour-Le travail* 25 (1990)

Prentice, Alison L., et al., *Canadian Women: A History*, Toronto and Orlando, Florida: Harcourt Brace Jovanovich, 1988

Rawls, John, *A Theory of Justice*, Cambridge, Massachusetts: Harvard University Press, 1971; Oxford: Clarendon Press, 1972; revised edition, 1999

Rosanvallon, Pierre, *Le sacre du citoyen: Histoire du suffrage universel en France*, Paris: Gallimard, 1992

Saint-Jean, Idola, "Discours radiodiffusé sous les auspices de l'alliance canadienne pour le vote des femmes du Québec," in *Québécoises du XXe siècle*, edited by Michèle Jean, Montreal: Éditions du Jour, 1974

Scott, Joan, "Deconstructing Equality versus Difference; or, The Uses of Post-Structuralist Theory for Feminism," *Feminist Studies* 14, no. 1 (1988)

Scott, Joan, "Les femmes qui n'ont que des paradoxes à offrir: Féministes françaises, 1789–1945," in *La politique des droits: Citoyenneté et construction des genres aux XIXe et XXe siècles*, edited by Hans Ulrich Jost, Monique Pavillon, and François Valloton, Paris: Kimé, 1994

Skocpol, Theda, *Protecting Soldiers and Mothers: The Political Origins of Social Policy in the United States*, Cambridge, Massachusetts: Harvard University Press, 1992

Sutherland, Neil, *Children in English Canadian Society: Framing the Twentieth-Century Consensus*, Toronto and Buffalo, New York: University of Toronto Press, 1976

Taylor, Charles, "Le pluralisme et le dualisme," in *Québec: État et société*, edited by Alain-Gustave Gagnon, Montreal: Québec/Amérique, 1994

Taylor, Charles, *Sources of the Self: The Making of the Modern Identity*, Cambridge: Cambridge University Press, and Cambridge, Massachusetts: Harvard University Press, 1989

Thébaud, Françoise, "Sexes et guerres," paper presented at the XVIIIe Congrès international des sciences historiques," Montreal, 1995

Toupin, Louise, "Mères, ou citoyennes? Une critique du discours historique nord-américain, 1960–1990, sur le mouvement féministe, 1850–1960," Ph.D. diss., Université du Québec à Montréal, 1994

Trofimenkoff, Susan Mann, "Feminism, Nationalism, and the Clerical Defence," in *Rethinking Canada: The Promise of Women's History*, edited by Veronica Jane Strong-Boag and Anita Clair Fellman, Toronto: Copp Clark Pitman, 1986

Valverde, Mariana, *The Age of Light, Soap, and Water: Moral Reform in English Canada, 1885–1925*, Toronto: McClelland and Stewart, 1991

FROM WOMEN'S RIGHTS TO FEMINISM IN EUROPE, 1860–1914

FLORENCE ROCHEFORT

AT THE TURN OF the 20th century, European feminism enjoyed a veritable golden age. Inseparable from the progress of liberalism and the democratization of the European states, the rise of feminism as an autonomous force in the social, political, and cultural spheres was in itself a historic event. Although strongly contested, the demand for sexual equality shook the foundations of patriarchal tradition and contributed to the 20th century's evolution toward modernity. As new political forces emerged and unions and political parties began organizing, feminism made possible women's affirmation as active subjects and as a collective voice. As objects of male discourse and representation, women had scarcely had the opportunity to speak in their own name, much less defend their own interests, despite their massive participation in major political and national events. In response to the political exclusion and legal inferiorization of women, feminism kindled a collective aspiration to equality between men and women, drawing supporters of both sexes. From their beginnings, between 1850 and 1880, movements in defense of women's rights included both women and men. This remained the case at the turn of the 20th century, even when such movements were specifically established and were perceived as "women's movements."

Beyond particular national characteristics—which, to be sure, are fundamental to an understanding of the differences in chronological trends and tactical or theoretical choices—it is possible to view feminism as a Europe-wide phenomenon. Ideas were debated and activist structures emerged both nationally and internationally, often involving contact with groups in the United States. The only countries in Europe in 1914 not represented in either the International Council of Women or the International Woman Suffrage Alliance were Spain, Montenegro, Albania, and the Grand Duchy of Luxemburg. In spite of virulent antifeminism, the impact of which must be acknowledged, campaigns for women's integration into civil and political society began to bear fruit. The time was ripe for the reform of civil codes and women's triumphant entry into the public sphere. The success of the "first women" to force the doors of universities and enter liberal careers, along with the establishment of political equality in Finland (1906) and Norway (1913), were obvious indications of the transformations taking place within relations between men and women. The figure of the "new woman," which feminism helped to promote, crystallized the hopes and fears of the century to come. Indicative of this pervasive questioning of the future of sexual difference, the French neologism *féminisme* entered the culture throughout Europe.

Success of a Word

Long a strictly medical term used to designate signs of the abnormal development of female secondary sexual characteristics in a man, the adjective *féministe* was first used to refer to the champions of the women's cause by Alexandre Dumas fils in 1872. Ten years later, Hubertine Auclert (1848–1914), a pioneer of the French women's suffrage movement, adopted the term to describe the struggle for the franchise. *Féministe* and *féminisme*, and their antonyms *antiféminisme* or *masculinisme*, entered the common French vocabulary in the 1890s; their derivatives in other languages spread quickly throughout Europe. In 1891 the Fédération Française des Sociétés Féministes (French Federation of Feminist Societies) was the first association to incorporate the adjective into its name, as it aspired to "bring together every society of women and feminists." ("Règlement de la Fédération Française des Sociétés Féministes," Article I, reported in *Le droit des femmes*, 20 December 1891). These new "-isms" sometimes even became fashionable, and journalists, chroniclers, and publicists contributed widely to their dissemination. In France, "feminist columns" proliferated in the press, while feminist theater and novels began to appear. With its inscription into the language, the mobilization for women's rights changed status. From an issue that was hardly ever spoken about except to be ridiculed in the press—Honoré Daumier's caricatures of the women of 1848 are a prime example—the women's rights movement became an object of study. Derision was still inevitable and counterarguments were often violent, but a taboo had been lifted. In a period when people were impassioned about "social issues," this new terminology responded to the need to bring the "woman question" into visibility, to categorize and analyze what was now perceived as a sociological phenomenon.

Several scientific studies in France integrated the term *féminisme* into their titles without hesitating to apply it to earlier periods of history. Feminism entered the university, as large numbers of law theses were devoted to it. Any attempt to improve women's condition by moving toward gender equality and allowing women to be affirmed as free and autonomous individuals was called feminist. In 1898 François Alphonse Aulard, a historian of the French Revolution and the editor of a monumental series of documents on the Jacobin Society (1889–97), devoted a course at the Sorbonne to "Feminism in 1790–1791." Before publishing this study in the 19 March 1898 issue of the *La revue bleue* under the title "Le féminisme sous la Révolution" (Feminism under the Revolution), he solicited the opinion of the historian Léopold Lacour, author of *Humanisme intégral: Le duel des sexes, la cité future* (1897; Integral Humanism: The Battle of the Sexes and the Future of Citizenship) and a well-known lecturer on the French Revolution. In 1900 Lacour would publish a biographical essay entitled *Les origines du féminisme contemporain. Trois femmes de la Révolution: Olympe de Gouges, Théroigne de Méricout, et Rose Lacombe* (1900; The Origins of Contemporary Feminism. Three Women of the Revolution: Olympe de Gouges, Théroigne de Méricourt, and Rose Lacombe). "Feminism," Aulard asked in a letter to Lacour, dated 27 February 1898, "means a doctrine for the equalization of women's rights to those of men, does it not? I should not like to use the word incorrectly," adding that his question was "quite naïve and foolish." Not everyone had the same scruples, and sometimes "feminist" was used quite simply as an alluring synonym for female. The vogue for the term peaked between 1897 and 1900; once the fashionable effect had waned, the term "feminist" tended to regain activist and subversive connotations relating to the struggle for sexual equality.

Men and women to whom the adjective "feminist" applied were sometimes hesitant to embrace it. The new groups and militant newspapers did not systematically adopt it, and existing organizations did not feel the need to change their names. In German-speaking countries, where it seemed more difficult to purge the word *Feminismus* of its medical meaning, and in eastern European languages, the equivalents for "feminism" often retained a pejorative connotation. It nevertheless took hold in Hungary, where the main women's organization, established in 1904, took the name Feministák Egyesülete (Association of Feminists). For some, the term "humanism" corresponded better to an ideal of sexual harmony. That term was used by Léopold Lacour in *Humanisme intégral* and by the English suffragette Helena Swanwick in her magazine *The Common Cause*. The French activist Jeanne Oddo Deflou used the term *sexualisme* to indicate the oppression of one sex by the other. The expression "women's rights" was still in use, and the label "feminist" was most readily adopted by the most radical elements of the women's movement. Despite the hesitancy and confusion surrounding it, at the turn of the century the word "feminism" nevertheless accurately conveyed qualitative and quantitative change in the women's rights movements. Further, it offered the advantages of polysemy, simultaneously designating the desire to transform relations between men and women by inscribing sexual equality into the law and the struggle for the emancipation of women from the constraints of a traditional model of subservience and self-sacrifice. Finally, it was used to denote women's quest for individual and collective identity.

The Philosophy of Women's Rights

The feminist upsurge at the turn of the 20th century found its roots in the philosophy of women's rights that emerged in the 1850s and 1860s. John Stuart Mill's *The Subjection of Women*, published in 1869, became an essential reference throughout Europe. Rapidly translated into French (1869), German (1869), Swedish (1869), Danish (1869), Russian (1869), Dutch (1870), Italian (1870), Polish (1886), Spanish (1891), and even into Japanese (1878), Mill's text was in several countries the direct cause of the establishment of women's rights groups. Its success should not, however, overshadow the importance of discussions that raised public awareness of the issue of education for girls throughout Europe. Certain great figures had a decisive influence, even though in some cases their reputations barely crossed national borders. The following works were major contributions that were considered basic texts: the lectures of the philosopher Maria Deraismes (1828–94), delivered between 1867 and 1869 and collected in book form under the title *Ève dans l'humanité* (1891; Eve in Humanity); the work *La Mujer del Porvenir* (1868; The Woman of the Future) by the lawyer Concepción Arenal (1820–93), a specialist in the prison conditions of Spain; in Italy, *La donna e la scienza* (1861; Women and Knowledge) by the deputy Salvatore Morelli (1824–80) and *La donna e i suoi rapporti sociali in occasione della revisione del codice civile italiano* (1864; Woman and Her Social Relations at the Time of the Revision of the Italian Civil Code) by Anna Maria Mozzoni (1837–1920), John Stuart Mill's translator; and in Germany, numerous articles by Louise Otto-Peters (1819–95). The respective approaches of these thinkers were rooted each author's distinctive national political culture. Deraismes's thought should be understood in the context of republican opposition to the Second Empire, more egalitarian than the English liberal ideas of Mill. Italian reflections on women's rights must be situated in relation to the history of the Risorgimento and anticlericalism. Very active in 1848, Otto-Peters was faced with a most restrictive, repressive climate when she resumed her activism in Germany in 1865, and her writings reflect this. Nevertheless, these fundamental texts present common traits that are characteristic of the philosophy on women's rights in the second half of the 19th century.

The influences between this generation of supporters of sexual equality and previous generations, from 1789 on, were complex and have often been rendered unintelligible, blurred by the historical reconstructions and militant mystifications they underwent at the hands of feminists at the turn of the century. The earliest reference texts of the 1860s barely allude to the works that inspired them. Doubtless the authors' intention was more to demonstrate sexual equality philosophically than to inscribe themselves within a tradition of women's rights supporters. Undoubtedly, too, the rules of rhetoric did not encourage the quotation of contemporaries. However, one might well question the tendency essentially to reduce the past to a tabula rasa, as when John Stuart Mill did not deem it useful to quote Mary Wollstonecraft or even his wife, Harriet Taylor, to whom in his autobiography he nevertheless attributed his best thinking. Similarly, Maria Deraismes made no reference to Juliette Lamber's *Les idées antiproudhoniennes* (1859; Against Proudhon), Jenny d'Héricourt's book, *La femme affranchie, réponse à MM. Michelet, Proudhon, E. de Girardin, A. Comte et autres novateurs modernes* (1860; *A Woman's Philosophy of Woman; or, Woman Affranchised, a Response to Michelet, Proudhon, Girardin, Legouvé, Comte and Other Modern Innovators*), or Julie Daubié's detailed investigation *La femme pauvre au XIXe siècle* (1866; Female Poverty in the 19th Century). Daubié was the first French woman to hold a baccalaureate degree. No doubt Deraismes had already partially reinvented the issues of sexual equality by the time she discovered the texts of her precursors.

Yet from the French Revolution on there was some continuity in Western thought about women's rights. Ideas survived the sporadic movements that brought them into the first half of the 19th century. As different as they were from one another, the marquis de Condorcet and Olympe de Gouges in France, Mary Wollstonecraft in Great Britain, Theodor Gottlieb von Hippel in Germany, and Josefa Amar de Borbon in Spain offered a solid political analysis of sexual difference as early as the end of the 18th century. Their reasoning, which invoked reason, progress, morality, happiness, civilization, and natural law as the basis for demanding that the principles of equality and freedom be extended to women, must be resituated in the political and polemical context of their period—that is, that of a response to the political exclusion of women by the French revolutionaries. This philosophical tradition continued to be an invaluable tool for subsequent generations whenever an author felt the need to insert herself into a historical continuum. Still, many writers only retained ideas that would serve their needs, without concern for the historical coherence of the earlier authors' ideas. What did the disagreements among the rediscovered founding texts matter to them, since what remained on the agenda was their condemnation of a tyrannical and despotic male power, their comparison of women's condition to that of slaves, and their resolve to see women admitted as subjects of the law in the same capacity as men?

The connections between women's rights activists of the 1850s and utopian socialists, who enriched the thinking about women's emancipation enormously, were even more ambiguous. The women's rights movements of the second half of the 19th century clearly evolved in the context of a rupture of that political connection. The important issue was no longer one of mystifying femininity or exalting free love, as had been the case for the followers of Saint-Simonian leader Prosper Enfantin. Rather, the main concern was now to ensure that women's rights were written into the law. Thought on women's emancipation became detached from ideas on social emancipation and was articulated in terms of a program of political reform. Supporters of sexual equality were now inspired by the liberal and democratic currents that re-established the predominance of the notion of the law at the heart of political philosophy. But in contrast to most liberal and democratic currents, feminist thinkers were integrating women into the new concept of citizenship. They even conceived of sexual equality as the cornerstone of a societal transformation to be effected through legislative and moral reform and through a fair balance between the rights and the duties of all

citizens. It seemed obvious that women's rights deserved specific support without waiting any longer for a revolutionary transformation of society—a perspective that did not preclude commitment to both feminist and socialist causes.

Personalities such as Jenny d'Héricourt in France, Anna Maria Mozzoni in Italy, and Louise Otto-Peters in Germany formed the transition between the generation of 1830–48 and that of 1860. Héricourt's *A Woman's Philosophy of Woman*, published first in Brussels and then in Paris in 1860, resonated in France, in Italy (notably through Mozzoni) and in the United States, where she had spent time, but also in Russia through one of the organizers of the first circle of Russian women. While Héricourt paid homage to Saint-Simonian doctrine and continued to compare women's destiny to that of the proletariat, she nevertheless called for the creation of a paper "that must not bear the flag of any social sect and must eliminate all political and religious questions per se" (*A Woman's Philosophy of Woman*). A similar pattern of development was discernible in the thought of Louise Otto-Peters, who was a pioneer in the struggle for women's emancipation in Meissen in 1848. In February 1865, when she took up activism again by collaborating with the *Allgemeine Frauenzeitung*, a general women's publication, and then established her own paper, the *Neue Bahnen*, her romantic socialism gave way to a more pragmatic outlook. She remained interested in the plight of women workers, but she included this concern within the larger demand for the right to work and economic independence for all women and, more generally still, the resolve to make women's rights an autonomous demand. She explained her change in perspective since the end of the 1860s by comparing the two periods: "The first objective was to raise women's consciousness, now it is the right to professional activity," she wrote in 1869.

In Italy, a sudden interest in women's rights on the part of a great political figure, Princess Cristina Trivulzio di Belgiojoso (1808–71), showed the importance of the issue at the end of the 1860s. In fact, in 1866 the princess addressed the problem of women's condition, at the request, she said, of "persons of authority." In spite of her hostility to a "radical reform of the condition of women," Belgiojoso was opposed to the idea of women's intellectual and moral inferiority, and she wrote an article in favor of girls' education, entitled "Della presente condizione delle donne e del loro avvenire" (On the Present Condition of Women and Their Future, in *Nuova antologia di scienze lettere ed arti*, 31 January 1866).

Feminism's break with utopian and revolutionary idealism was accompanied in Catholic countries by a sharper criticism of Christianity and the trend toward secularism that touched political thinking generally. Salvatore Morelli believed that the way to counter the Church's obscurantism was through science and the rational education of girls. Maria Deraismes, although still a deist and a spiritualist in 1869, brilliantly exposed the misogynist prejudices of the Church fathers. The philosophy of sexual equality, however, was also in complete disagreement with those whose support might have been hoped for: the scientists and positivists who postulated women's inferiority or, at least, women's natural incapacity for any function other than that of wife and mother. Indeed, biological sexual difference was posited as a law of "social physiology" that would presumably govern the building of the modern state. Concepción Arenal, Deraismes, and John Stuart Mill devoted the major part of their demonstration to refuting this scientific discourse. Such rebuttals were still necessary in the 1880s, and Charles Secrétan (1815–95), a Swiss philosopher, resolutely took the side of women's rights in opposition to the positivists.

The first generation in the 1860s and 1880s particularly sought to explain the mechanisms of women's oppression at the hands of men and to demonstrate the absurdity of the sexual division of activity that had led to the exclusion of women from knowledge and, more generally, from the public sphere. The works of these thinkers left the double legacy of brilliant reasoning against sexual inequality and a program for legislative reform. The priority objectives were women's education and admission into male territory—especially in the professional realm—and the reform of the civil codes, notably regarding the status of married women subjugated by their husbands. What was envisioned was a plan for women's integration into civil and political society rather than a takeover of power by women. In order to achieve this goal of integration, Mill's parliamentary action seemed exemplary. As elements in their lobbying tactics, supporters of women's rights formed pressure groups of men and women, drew up petitions to force the passage of egalitarian laws, and sought allies among those elected.

Lobbying for Women's Rights

The first signs of a new wave of mobilization were perceptible first of all in Great Britain. English eyes were turned toward American antislavery activists, who, since their meeting in Seneca Falls in 1848, had sought to promote women's rights as an independent issue. In her article "Enfranchisement of Women," published in the *Westminster and Foreign Quarterly Review* of April–July 1851, the Englishwoman Harriet Taylor analyzed their declarations at length and wrote, "There are indications that the example of America will be followed on this side of the Atlantic." Indeed, a first women's rights group met in 1856 around the *English Women's Journal* and was primarily interested in reform in marriage and education. In Leipzig in 1865, Louise Otto-Peters founded the Frauenbildungsverein (Association for the Education of Women), which had a rather limited program, and convened the first assembly of women in Leipzig. The political context did not allow this group to deal officially with issues other than those of education and training. Even the question of civil rights was out of bounds under a law of 1851 that prohibited German women from any participation in associations or even meetings of a political nature. When Otto-Peters wanted to publish her theoretical work, *Das Frauen Recht* (Women's Rights), she was forced to change the title to *Das Recht der Frauen auf Erwerb* (1866; Women's Right to Professional Activity). Moreover, the women who supported Otto-Peters, particularly Auguste Schmidt, were far more moderate than she.

In France, a liberalization of laws under the Second Empire in 1868 legalized gatherings of supporters of sexual equality. The prohibition against tackling political questions too openly benefited the debate on women. In popular lectures, adversaries and supporters of women's rights were split around the question of women's employment. Advocates of work for women, close to the labor and socialist movements, met with the woman activist André Léo and planned to establish a school. The republicans, for their part, organized lectures at the Grand Orient of France

and decided to assert their originality by inviting a woman to speak. Léon Richer, a former notary clerk who had become an anticlerical journalist, along with Adolphe Géroult, the Saint-Simonian editor of a newspaper, turned to Maria Deraismes in 1867. She had never given a lecture, but her thorough knowledge of philosophy and her republican opinions were well known. After some hesitation, and finally prompted by her disgust at an offensive article on bluestockings by Jules Barbey d'Aurevilly, Deraismes decided to accept the speaking engagement. She enjoyed considerable success with her analysis of the principles and mores of her time before turning to the issue of women. In 1869 Richer founded the paper *Le droit des femmes*, in which he published opinion pieces by noted personalities who supported women's rights. The following year, together with Deraismes, he established the Association pour le Droit des Femmes (Association for Women's Rights). Their aims, according to the association's statutes published in the 24 April 1870 issue of *Le droit des femmes*, were to defend women as "human beings who have the right to be free and autonomous" and to have sexual equality written into the law and reflected in mores. Their agenda included reforms of specific articles in the Civil Code that diminished women, the right to work and to equal pay for equal work, and the right to file paternity suits. In a speech delivered to at an association banquet and printed in the 24 July 1869 issue of *Le droit des femmes*, Deraismes emphasized the movement's resolve to remain autonomous and stressed that it did not "depend on a particular doctrine, whether religious, philosophical or political." A trend toward internationalism was already discernable in the Ligue Internationale des Femmes (International League of Women) founded in Geneva in 1869 by the Swiss activist Marie Goegg Pouchoulin. Nevertheless, the international movement did not really come into being until after autonomous women's rights movements had been established in almost every European country between 1860 and 1890. Where there were no actual activist groups, a newspaper might serve as a rallying point, as was the case with the *Ladies' Journal* established in Greece by Callirhoë Parren in 1887.

In the Scandinavian countries, the first philosophical reflections endorsing women's emancipation were expressed in literature. *Hertha* (1856), a novel by the famous Swedish woman of letters Frederika Bremer (1801–65), is often cited as marking the birth of Swedish feminism. Indeed, the theme of woman's love and fulfillment found a field of infinite experimentation in the novel. The Norwegian novelists Camilla Collet (1813–95) and Amalie Skram (1846–1905) and the Finnish writer Frederika Runeberg (1807–79) used this medium to criticize the difficulties experienced by women in marriage. To a great extent the appearance of the first groups was connected to John Stuart Mill's work; this was particularly true of the Dansk Kvindesamfund (Danish Women's Association) founded in 1871 by Frederik Bayer, who would receive the Nobel Peace Prize in 1908. The Danish example was soon followed by Sweden, where the first organization, founded in 1873, devoted itself to the struggle to enable married women freely to dispose of their property; similar initiatives were taken in Norway and Finland in 1884.

Thus, the first activist groups stressed married women's right to exercise control over assets and wages, the establishment of quality secondary education and access to universities, the right to practice any profession, and civil equality (the right to bear witness, the right to guardianship, and the right to custody of one's own children). Political equality was not immediately considered a priority. In Great Britain, too, it was not until ten years after the initial campaigns led by the *English Woman's Journal* that the first suffragist groups appeared. With some chronological discrepancies, the same pattern of developments occurred in other European countries, where the demand for women's suffrage was eventually isolated from broader women's rights agendas and became the focus of a specific campaign from the 1900s on. In the early years, autonomy was the overarching theme of the campaign for women's rights. Access to knowledge and financial independence were fundamental concerns. The campaigns for various "firsts" achieved greater recognition because these events made an impact in the press of the period, and also because historiographers for a long time privileged class analysis as an approach to the women's rights movement. The struggle for "firsts" was seen as part of the far broader demand for the "right to work." At issue was the defense not only of women students, but also workers and employees; activists ran up against the hostility of a large part of the labor and union movement, which took the position that women's place was in the home and condemned the competitive threat posed by women's low wages.

In the liberal climate of the turn of the 20th century, the first wave of mobilization for women' rights enjoyed exceptional longevity. Beginning in the 1890s, "skeleton" movements made up of small groups evolved and broader movements began to take shape. Women of the urban middle classes rallied around the women and men who were vanguard champions of sexual equality, and that trend enabled feminism to take root as a political and social force.

Emergence of Feminism as a Political and Social Force

Women were essentially left out of the restructuring of civil and political society at the turn of the 20th century. It was as mothers of citizens, and not as female citizens in their own right, that they had an acknowledged place in the nation. While the labor and socialist movements solicited the involvement of women workers, particularly in Germany, middle-class women only very exceptionally had a place in the new political landscape. There seemed to be a growing imbalance between, on the one hand, political discourse, which advocated a gendered separation of the spheres of activity, and, on the other hand, the new economic and cultural needs created by an evolving society. Industrialization, urbanization, and the transformation of family models made financial and legal independence a vital concern for an ever increasing number of women. Although it was often rudimentary and inadequate as a preparation for either university or working life, the education of girls encouraged the expression of female individualism among the new generations of urban middle-class women. Women increasingly sought recognition of their value, no longer under the guardianship of their fathers or husbands but as autonomous individuals who wanted to assume financial and educational responsibilities on an equal level with their spouses, and who wanted to be recognized as adults, not only in the privacy of their homes but also in professional

and even political life. Following the example of American women, European women began seeking to break down the barriers that excluded them from universities and professions in the service sector. The injustice of the civil codes that gave them the same legal status as minors, madmen, and delinquents, along with the anachronism of the prejudices and customs that excluded them from all positions of power and knowledge, seemed increasingly unacceptable to them.

Women's growing involvement in philanthropic work also helped them to gain more substantial awareness of sexual inequality through the concrete experience of suffering. From the outset, English and American forms of feminism were closely united with the abolitionist and temperance movements. Following the Contagious Diseases Act passed in England 1864, which required every woman suspected of prostitution to undergo a medical exam, the struggle against legal control of prostitution was taken up under the leadership of Josephine Butler. In Geneva in 1877 she brought an international dimension to her struggle by founding the British Continental and General Federation, which was to become the International Abolitionist Federation in 1902. This organization played a vital role in sensitizing women's philanthropic groups throughout Europe to women's rights issues. Philanthropists gradually accepted finding themselves on political terrain by rallying around an egalitarian reforms agenda. It was the Swiss-born Émilie de Morsier who led French women onto this path. The 1888 formation, at the initiative of American women, of the International Council of Women, which brought feminists and women's associations together to defend women's rights in the name of women's duties, encouraged other countries to adopt this model. On several occasions the Americans sent emissaries to Europe to help create national councils. With 17 national councils in 1914, they considered Europe won over. Spain was one of the only countries in which the avant-garde, which had spoken out brilliantly in defense of women since 1860, did not manage to produce enough emulators to form a movement and join the international organizations. Concepción Arenal died in 1892, but a few other personalities nevertheless ardently pursued the fight on behalf of women's rights, notably Emilia Pardo Bazan, a woman of letters and the translator of John Stuart Mill's book into Spanish.

The feminist movements at the turn of the 20th century reflected women's new aspirations and helped radicalize feminist consciousness-raising. Activist groups proposed concrete solutions through carefully prepared and written legislative reforms. Free legal counsel, petitions, and press campaigns supported women who met with the refusal of administrative authorities to let them enter a university, take exams, or earn diplomas licensing them to practice as lawyers, journalists, or physicians. The same support was offered to women who found no place to have their work recognized, to those who were excluded from unions by reason of their sex—for example, the Couriau affair of 1913 in France, in which a woman typographer was excluded by the demand of the Lyon Printers Union executive committee, and her husband was expelled for having allowed his wife to practice her trade—and, finally, to all those women rendered helpless by legislation that permitted them no action without the authorization of their husbands. The copious feminist press offered a unique form of freedom of expression to women, serving as places of sociability, expression, and culture that responded to the marginalization and ostracism of which they were the victims in Western societies. The daily *La fronde*, which was entirely written, laid out, and printed by women, and which appeared from 1897 to 1903, was one of the most fully actualized and prestigious examples of a militant press that succeeded in making a national chorus of women's voices heard and offered a veritable tool in the struggle for equality. The earliest victories reinforced the credibility of feminist movements. Mobilization through petitions, press campaigns, meetings, lectures, and sometimes more spectacular forms of action led to certain reforms: women's admission to universities and the liberal professions (each department or profession requiring a specific struggle to obtain the relevant decree or law); the right of married women to dispose freely of their own property, savings, and wages; the right to bear witness in civil and notary acts; and women's voting and eligibility on the municipal level or, at least, in courts dealing with trade disputes.

Numerous theoretical works by activists, more-or-less benevolent observers, and even by antifeminists such as the Théodore Joran, in France, offer an account of the vitality of the women's rights movements. They clearly define feminist doctrine as a doctrine of sexual equality and analyze the cruelties of women's legal condition. The demonstration of the natural equality of the sexes henceforth commanded less attention than the study of the terms of the demand for equality and the sociological and historical analysis of the struggle to achieve it. A special 1896 issue of the *Revue encyclopédique Larousse*, put together by the Polish-born activist Marya Scheliga-Loevy, introduced feminism and its principal female and male figures worldwide to the French public. This work was widely cited in Adolfo Posada's *Feminismo* (1899), a well-known work that presented foreign feminist movements to support a plea for the rights of Spanish women. Charles Turgeon, Émile Faguet, and Madame Avril de Sainte-Croix in France in 1907, the Swiss Louis Bridel, and the Belgian Louis Frank also carefully studied the causes and effects of the mobilization for women's rights. Feminism was immediately understood to be a transnational entity, at least in the Western world, with contributions having been made by people of different nationalities, from the time of Marie de Gournay in the 17th century to Condorcet and Olympe de Gouges and on to the great contemporary figures. However, three distinct entities could be discerned: Anglo-Saxon feminism (women's condition in the United States is still presented as exemplary), French feminism, and finally, Scandinavian feminism. Supporters of sexual equality emphasized the presence of feminist men and even men's groups, which attested to the movement's humanist aspirations and allowed for a response to the frequent accusation of fomenting war between the sexes. Furthermore, male feminists, especially parliamentarians, undeniably played an indispensable intermediary role in the bastions of power and dissemination of information. Although feminism tended to be recognized as an autonomous force by those who devoted scholarly works to it, this was not always the case in the political world. In that arena, feminism had to win acknowledgment as the voice of women as a social group with common interests.

At a time when racist theories and colonial ideology were prevalent, European feminists said very little on the possibility of female solidarity beyond Western borders. Only a few isolated voices were heard, such as that of Hubertine Auclert, who followed her companion to live in Algeria and there took up the pen to defend Arab women. Nevertheless, the positing of Western women as a collective subject, despite their religious, political, and social differences, went against all political and philosophical ideas of the period. Conceiving of the autonomy of "women-as-subject" was just as shocking as claiming to make women autonomous on an individual basis. In both cases, the emergence of the collective and individual identities of women seemed to threaten to break the organic bond that united the sexes and indissolubly linked woman to family and the future of the "race." Among women themselves, feminism met with considerable resistance.

Limits of Success: The Marginality of Feminism

Feminist movements at the turn of the 20th century successfully exerted pressure to obtain reforms; they were often taken seriously as guardians of historical, sociological, and legal knowledge about women and called upon by governments to study legal proposals or to devise study committees. This critical acclaim and the winning of the first reforms stood in contrast to the isolation of the avant-garde of the 1860s, but that contrast should not lead us to overestimate either the numerical strength of the feminist movements or the degree to which they were representative. The current state of historiography does not allow for an exact count of the activists, and in any case the potential for confusion among the various movements, spheres of influence, and feminist milieus would make that difficult. The major suffragist demonstrations and petitions brought together several thousand women, while the national councils seized the advantage of adding together all the members of the affiliated associations and counting them in tens of thousands, although not all of the members were true activists. To be sure, feminism had appeared on the cultural stage, but it nevertheless showed quite a few signs of marginality. Although middle-class women were often the most receptive to feminism, the most combative activists were not always the most representative of the dominant groups of their country. For example, among the militants there were discernibly large proportions of Protestant women in France, Jewish women in Germany, freethinkers in Catholic countries, and members of dissident sects in the Protestant countries. Many of the feminist personalities in France who directed a newspaper, a group, or a congress were of foreign birth, notably two English women, two Polish women, one Russian, one Swiss, and one German woman. Marguerite Durand (1864–1936), the founder of the daily newspaper *La fronde*, which embodied French feminism with panache for five years, referred in the 1 October 1903 issue to "the formidable bluff that was my work." Created at the moment that the Dreyfus Affair got underway in December 1897, *La fronde* owed its existence to the secret financing of Baron Gustave de Rothschild. Thus, in contrast to other activist papers, until 1903 the publication enjoyed a rather luxurious lifestyle and could remunerate every article with a solid fee. In fact, subscriptions were not sufficient to sustain *La fronde*, and its success should be put into perspective and resituated in the context of women's political instrumentalization. However, it remains undeniable that in 1897 feminism was granted, or even entrusted with, the role of spokesperson for women and their concerns. Still, the notion of a collective women's identity radically eclipsed the existence of those women who did not identify with that group. Female personalities who belonged to the literary or artistic elite and whose names have been retained by history, such as Virginia Woolf, often remained indifferent or at least distant with regard to the movement. Women whose individuality had been revealed through the artistic process were unprepared to lose their uniqueness within a collective subject. Moreover, the enemies of feminism were not limited to men. There were women who took pains to block the way of "emancipated women": for example, Mary Humphrey Ward, famous woman of letters, who led the Anti-Suffrage League in Great Britain, or Colette Yver in France, who in her many novels endlessly wrote of the incompatibility of motherhood and professional activity.

Feminist movements also had trouble winning the support of women workers. The creation in France and Germany of women's unions in professions where women were excluded from the male unions, the active support given to women's strikes, and the organization in Paris of a congress of workingwomen and a labor office facilitated certain connections, but on the whole, women workers were not very receptive to feminist discourse. With the exception of Germany, the rate of women's membership in socialist organizations and labor unions was still quite low, and when they did mobilize, women workers were more drawn to the discourse of class struggle than to the logic of sexual equality. Workingwomen themselves could barely understand the debate, within international feminism, between antiprotectionists and protectionists over social legislation and night work (the antiprotectionists were opposed to the fact that the laws concerned only women). Meanwhile, women's demands for civil and political equality did not elicit much response in the world of labor. Great Britain, however, was an exception. British activists succeeded in creating a suffragist network among women workers. From the 1890s on, the radical suffragists of the National Union for Women's Suffrage Societies (NUWSS) devoted themselves to propaganda campaigns targeting working-class women and succeeded in bringing several committees to life. In 1903 Esther Roper and Eva Gore-Booth founded a suffragist labor organization. In addition, the fruitful alliance between the English Labour Party and the suffragists offered a counterexample to the enmity between socialists and feminists that often prevailed in other countries. In fact, feminist claims to political autonomy drew irritation from the socialist movements that were being organized at the same time. As socialist women, referring to August Bebel's *Frau und der Sozialismus: Die Frau in der Vergangenheit, Gegenwart un Zukunft* (1879; *Woman in the Past, Present and Future*) were beginning to mobilize on behalf of women's rights under the leadership of Alexandra Kollontai and Klara Zetkin, war was declared on the feminist movements. The socialists disdainfully dismissed feminists as "bourgeois" and considered them enemies of class struggle, which ruled out the possibility of forging an alliance with them. Feminist movements thus had to contend with many adversaries; in addition, they were also continually threatened with collapse under the strain of internal dissension.

Feminist Dynamics

Heterogeneity was one of the shared characteristics of the various feminist movements in Europe around 1900. Alongside the first women's groups, others quickly sprang up in connection with newspapers and associations. Some groups preferred to focus their activist efforts on a single issue, while others decided to target a specific public—for example, teachers, women workers, or the upper bourgeoisie and the aristocracy. The leader's personality was always a decisive factor in the growth and consolidation of any given group. Among the major figures who succeeded the first generation at the end of the 1890s, a great many women achieved the distinction of being the "first" to earn an advanced degree in their respective fields. Maria Vérone was one of the first French women lawyers, while Teresa Labriola was the first female lawyer in Italy. Marie Popelin in Belgium and Anita Augsburg in Germany defended their law theses, while Alice Salomon earned a doctorate in philosophy at the University of Berlin. Among the first female physicians were Aletta Jacob in the Netherlands, and Blanche Edwards Pilliet and Madeleine Pelletier in France. For the most part, however, activists of this period were employed women who in many instances had begun their studies as adults, sometimes under difficult material conditions. Given this great variety of circumstances and priorities, conferences were indispensable for tightening ranks among feminists and shaping the movement itself. The International Congress of Women's Rights, organized in Paris in 1878 by Léon Richer and Maria Deraismes, was the first in a series of 23 international conferences—20 of which were held in Europe and more than half of which were organized by the representatives of the International Council of Women or by the International Alliance for Women's Suffrage (IAWS).

Feminism was also combined with other currents of thought—spiritualism, socialism, neo-Malthusianism, and Christianity. The relationship between feminism and Protestantism was profoundly different in Protestant and Catholic countries. Women's rights advocates in the United States and Great Britain emphasized sexual equality before the Creator, while in predominantly Catholic France, Protestant-inspired feminist movements emerged in a context of secularism and were largely inspired by freethinking. Emerging from dissident sects such as the Quakers or the Unitarians, Anglo-Saxon feminists were predisposed toward proposing a feminist rereading of the Bible. In France, the active Protestant component of the movement did not seek to Christianize feminism. However, in 1896 a group of Catholic French women launched a group and a magazine, *Le féminisme chrétien*, which tried to reconcile sexual equality with Catholicism. This branch of activism, which in any case was hard pressed to find followers, soon broke with the feminist movement when it swerved off in a very xenophobic and anti-Semitic direction at the time of the Dreyfus Affair. Thereafter this Catholic feminist group existed in isolation, taking no further part in collective action or conferences. This was logical enough: the French feminist movement found its cohesion in the republican pact that was then defining the limits of its political neutrality, and furthermore, French Catholic feminists refused to accept the movement's religious neutrality. In Belgium, Louise van den Plas founded a Catholic feminist group and publication, also called *Le féminisme chrétien*, in 1902; she preferred to remain at a distance from the secular feminist movement. However, she was deemed to be too independent and daring in the eyes of the Catholic party. Thus, on the eve of World War I, Catholic feminism in Europe was only taking its first halting steps.

This profusion of activist structures allowed for a great wealth of approaches and modes of analysis. However, this same heterogeneity weakened the various feminist movements, which sometimes embraced contradictory strategic positions and which were further weakened by personal and emotional quarrels among the main figures in power. The contrast between moderate and radical tendencies was particularly acute in Germany, where the Bund Deutscher Frauenvereine (BDF; Federation of German Women's Associations), established in 1894, was taking more conservative positions than its counterpart in France, the Conseil National de Femmes Françaises (National Council of French Women), notably on the issues of prostitution and the right to vote. However, the range of feminist sensibilities, from progressive to conservative, should not lead us to overlook the extraordinary audacity it took in 1900 to be committed as an activist in any movement for women's rights. Meanwhile, tactical conflicts were at times implacable. Such was the case in Great Britain between suffragettes and suffragists.

British Suffragettes

With the exception of Great Britain, the choice of strategic priorities between civil rights and political rights divided feminist ranks between 1880 and 1900. In 1904 the suffrage movement gained remarkable momentum, owing not so much to increased radicalism as to tactical and political choices that became imperative when universal male suffrage became a crucial question on the agenda in almost all of Europe. The success of the suffrage movement in Europe was also strongly linked to the founding of the International Alliance for Women's Suffrage in Berlin in 1904. The French and Italian groups succeeded in forming national sections under the pressure of the international congresses. Once the right to vote had been accepted as a priority objective, tactical divisions appeared. In France, champions of total suffrage opposed those who advocated municipal suffrage. Many countries with restricted suffrage were divided between two options, either to demand women's suffrage under the same conditions as men (based on property-ownership qualifications), or to demand universal suffrage. This opposition solidified around different forms of action. The most striking split between advocates of moderate tactics and the suffragettes occurred in Great Britain, and indeed, the feats of Emmeline Pankhurst and her daughter Christabel Pankhurst were the talk of the town throughout Europe.

Since the 1850s the English suffrage movement had adopted a cautious juridical strategy for putting pressure on Parliament. Petitions, propaganda through lectures, newspapers, and increased memberships were still the principal modes of action of the most important organization, the National Union for Women's Suffrage Societies, founded in 1897 and presided over by veteran activist Millicent Garrett Fawcett (1847–1929). In 1905 the Women's Social and Political Union (WSPU), founded two years earlier by Emmeline and Christabel Pankhurst, drew comment for the first time when two of its activist women refused to leave a liberal meeting and were consequently arrested by the police and imprisoned. The press spread the news of the event widely and soon began to use the term "suffragettes" to designate other women who disrupted meetings. Despite the adverse reactions, new members flocked to the WSPU. The English Parliament's stubborn refusal to engage in discussion pushed the suffragettes to radicalize their tactics and use violence as a means of protest. In 1909 suffragettes regularly broke the windows of official buildings and became locked in a veritable arm-wrestling match with the authorities. There were intermittent truces, but the demonstrations grew more and more violent. On what became known as Black Friday, 18 November 1910, a demonstration turned into a riot that left more than 100 people injured. The arrests continued in 1911 and 1912, and the imprisoned suffragettes demanded political prisoner status, which they were refused. They then undertook a hunger strike; most of them were force-fed. The violence escalated. In 1913 the suffragettes placed bombs in public places on several occasions. After Mary Richardson attacked Velazquez's *Venus* in the National Gallery in London, women were forbidden entry into museums. Henceforth operating in semisecrecy, the suffragettes became increasingly cut off from reality. More than ever before, they now believed they were invested with a spiritual and purifying mission, and they exalted their sense of self-sacrifice. This took a particularly dramatic turn with the suicide attack of Emily Wilding Davidson, who threw herself under the king's horse during the Derby of 4 June 1913 and died of the resulting injuries. Her funeral became the occasion for a procession of more than 2,000 suffragettes.

The suffragette phenomenon continued to be specifically English; violent action found few advocates abroad. In France in 1908, Hubertine Auclert knocked over an electoral urn, and Madeleine Pelletier broke the windows of a polling office, but their examples were not followed. On the other hand, reports of suffragettes undergoing the torture of force-feeding in prison provoked the solidarity of foreign suffragists and left a strong impression on public opinion. If people hastened to criticize the violence of the suffragettes, they remained speechless in the face of the violence of the British government. Never had the political nature of the balance of power between the sexes appeared with such violence in the public arena. In the early days, the suffragettes lost allies to the cause in Parliament, but their notoriety helped to popularize the idea of political equality and open debate on the issue. Throughout Europe, suffragists benefited from the considerable impact made by the English suffragettes, whose radical activities helped publicize their own activism and, by contrast, showed it in a most respectable light. In fact, the suffrage movement succeeded where the feminist movement had failed: rallying forces and attracting a mass membership far larger than the usual activist recruitment. Based on demands that were sometimes reduced to municipal or poll-tax-based suffrage, ideological splits became less pronounced and gave way to a certain degree of unanimity, largely encouraged by the International Alliance for Women's Suffrage. The success of the suffrage movement to some extent eclipsed that of feminism, which continued to embrace its multiple concerns. Its objective remained the transformation of relations between men and women, not only in public life but also within the family and marriage. Central to this inquiry was the quest for new female and male identities.

In Search of Feminine Subjectivity

Feminism aspired not just to equality, but also to allow women to attain dignity and liberty—that is, the full development of their personalities. The recognition of women as full-fledged individuals endowed with the same rights as men was accompanied by recognition of women as persons who were ultimately responsible for their own self-redefinition. This dimension was already present in the 1860s: Maria Deraismes declared, in a lecture delivered on 18 November 1869 and later reprinted in *Ève dans l'humanité*, "We want to be what we are, at last, and not what they have made us be," while John Stuart Mill denied the possibility of any knowledge of women "until women themselves have told all that they have to tell" (*The Subjection of Women*, 1869). Only at the turn of the 20th century, when the feminist movements had solidified, did forums where women could speak about themselves begin to proliferate. Equal rights were understood as being absolutely fundamental, but they were also seen as a means to gain freedom—a freedom that remained to be discovered and constructed. The first step toward self-discovery was the deconstruction of misogynist (or even "philogynist") discourses on women and the construction of new forms of knowledge. Collective action generated a feminist culture that became an indispensable part of the birth of new sexual identities. Active valorization of women's artistic and intellectual production was a way to counter the systematic denigration of women's talents. Feminist publications promoted creative works by women, whether they were involved in activist ranks or not. The feminist library contained novels or essays by men who were taking up the defense of sexual equality. The rehabilitation of women called for a historical approach; the discovery of a history of women and their struggles was accompanied by the construction of a feminist pantheon. The criteria for selection were not very restrictive for the distant past, when any famous woman was considered to have made her contribution through her uniqueness alone. Among contemporaries, the great activist figures of both sexes were selected on a priority basis, but alongside them stood a few personalities who were totally extraneous to the movement. The Norwegian playwright Henrik Ibsen, for example, unwillingly found himself to be one of the most quoted men. His celebrated play *Dukkenhjem* (*A Doll's House*), published in 1879, was greeted as a revelation of the new woman. If feminism sometimes saw itself dispossessed of the themes it had brought into public awareness, activists also knew how to seize any cultural or political manifestation that could serve the movement's egalitarian agenda. Recording the memory of the present time was a primary concern. Several activists devoted themselves to this task of documentation and built extensive archival collections. The French schoolteacher and union leader Hélène Brion (1882–1962), whose feminist plea at her 1918 trial for disseminating "defeatist" pacifist propaganda at the beginning of World War I created a furor, set herself an immense task: to compile a universal encyclopedia of women.

Although there was consensus about the need to seek positive images of women, the analysis of the feminine identity inspired considerable debate. Deraismes's egalitarian premise, when she stated, "Between women and men there is absolute identity and equality" continued to be an exception—and even the philosopher herself tempered her thinking in later years. At the turn of the century, discourses valorizing woman's specificity were more prevalent in thought about sexual equality. Establishing legal equality remained an important goal, but increasingly, maternal qualities were invoked as the basis for demands for women's rights. The English suffragist Millicent Garrett Fawcett stated

in the November 1891 issue of *The Fortnightly Review:* "We do not advocate the representation of women because there is no difference between men and women; but rather because of the difference between them. We want women's special experience as women." Equality predicated on difference was an argument that more accurately reflected the egalitarian aspirations and identity politics of European women of the Belle Époque and more readily took hold in their political culture. The emphasis on sexual difference should also be understood in the context of a vigorous antifeminist polemic that demonized the "third sex." Fawcett was thus responding to an article that accused the suffragists of wanting to masculinize women. But for the vast majority of feminists, the main concern was not to promote androgyny, but rather to significantly expand the realm of experience of feminine identity without losing the possibility of affirming one's difference—a difference that then needed to be redefined. Motherhood, in particular, became the object of profound reflection.

For those intent upon rehabilitating the figure of the mother, the Swiss-German Johann Jakob Bachofen's theory of a primitive matriarchy that supposedly existed in the earliest human societies was seductive. Published in 1861 and widely translated at the turn of the century, Bachofen's *Das Mutterrecht: Ein Untersuchung über die Gynaikokratie der Alten Welt nach ihrer religiösen und rechtlichen Natur* (*Matriarchy: Research on the Gynecocracy of the Ancient World According to Its Religious and Judicial Nature*) lent impetus to the project of a rewriting of history that would encompass gender-specific concerns and valorize women's role. The notion of matriarchy made it possible to insist on the idea of feminine power; it revealed men's appropriation of power and gave a name to the adversary: patriarchy. The valorization of maternity and the specific qualities it bestowed on women—often viewed as "natural" qualities—led to an innovative analysis of motherhood as a social function. The structure of the family became the object of harsh criticism. Mothers' lack of legal rights, even over their own children, was condemned, and the issue of the gendered division of labor was also raised. Analysis and assessment of domestic work and the desire to relieve women of household duties by sharing them with men or through a collective infrastructure were recurrent themes of discussion at conferences. Although solutions varied, participants at any congress shared a fundamental concern: to win acknowledgment of women's work and experience in the home as valuable skills and to make these contributions visible. This concern in no way invalidated the model of the modern woman that emerged from feminist discourse—the model of a woman, working either professionally or in the home, who is autonomous, responsible, and present in civil society.

The actualization of women's potential remained of paramount importance. For the handful of feminists who espoused neo-Malthusianism, control over motherhood was the key issue. Nelly Roussel (1878–1922) traveled throughout France and Europe to advocate "unfettered motherhood" and Madeleine Pelletier (1874–1939) proclaimed the right to abortion, while Hélène Stöcker in Germany raised the same issues in the Bund für Mutterschutz (Society for the Protection of Motherhood). Reproductive choice was an issue on which radical and moderate feminists were clearly divided. Although the moderate contingent criticized the double sexual standard, the moderates also refused to challenge received notions of female sexuality or question a certain traditional image of maternity. In 1906, citing the altruistic function of the mother and the maternal mission, the National Council of French Women made a resolution against abortion; its German counterpart did the same in 1908.

At the turn of the 20th century, the quest for a new feminine identity drew upon the emerging philosophical currents that postulated the primacy of intuition over reason, began exploring the unconscious, and challenged patriarchal standards. Nevertheless, a deep rift existed between this intellectual and artistic avant-garde, rebelling against the established order, and the feminist movements that remained committed to reform projects and a much more pragmatic and political vision of the changes that were possible. All too aware of the risks women ran in the face of male egotism and the difficulties of being an unwed mother, even the radical feminist contingent remained fairly critical of supporters of free love and theoreticians of eroticism. A handful of feminists pushed the analysis of women's sexual oppression to extremes by personally refusing any contact with men and proposing virginity and chastity as the model of emancipation. In contrast to such divisions, it was relatively easy for the different feminist contingents to agree on the issues of identity intended to promote a new image of "woman." The transformation of women's dress, with the rejection of the corset and the adoption of a divided skirt or, at least, a shorter skirt, facilitated the freedom of movement that was absolutely indispensable to physically active women. It was strongly recommended that girls practice a sport from a very young age was to help prepare them for their new roles. These demands intersected with feminism but did not originate exclusively from its ranks. It was not rare for associations devoted to dress reform or the promotion of women's physical education to join the movement and support the suffragist campaigns.

The image of the new woman as sketched by feminists stood in contrast to representations of women in publicity posters for bicycles or automobiles, where there was no suggestion whatsoever of autonomy or liberation. Accepted as interlocutors by public powers and perceived in the public opinion as revealing a crisis between the sexes, feminist movements temporarily compensated for the failure of the law and prevailing mores to meet women's needs and for the inability of Western societies to accept women in a new public space. Early–20th-century European feminism contributed to women's partial integration into civil and political society and set in motion an egalitarian and democratic process that was to bear fruit. Feminism had not yet met with real competition from the modernist discourses of political power that emerged in the interwar years, and it had not yet reaped all the benefits of its success. The egalitarian message was heard but often reduced to a merely formal equality that did not encompass the resolve to effect an in-depth transformation in relations between men and women. Heralding the changes and mobilizations that would mark the 20th century, the feminism of the turn of the century appeared as a particular political culture that fundamentally clashed with the dominant values of its era.

Bibliography

Manuscript Sources

Archives Nationales, Paris. Letter of François-Alphone Aulard to Léopold Lacour; Lacour files, Box 2.

Bibliothèque Historique de la Ville de Paris, Paris. Fonds Marie-Louise Bouglé
Bibliothèque Marguerite Durand, Paris
Fawcett Library, London
Institut Français d'Histoire Sociale, Paris. Fonds Hélène Brion

Newspapers and Reviews

Le droit des femmes, Revrie internationale du mouvement féminin (1889–91). Le fronde (1897–1903).

Print Sources

Aguado, Ana M., Textos para la historia de las mujeres en España, Madrid: Catedra, 1994
Anteghini, Alessandra, Parità, pace, libertà: Marie Goegg e André Léo nell'associazionismo femminile del Secondo Ottocento, Genoa, Italy: Name, 1998
Arenal de García Carrasco, Concepción, La mujer del Porvenir, Madrid: Perié, 1868; reprint, edited by Vicente de Santiago Mulas, Madrid: Castalia, 1993
Auclert, Hubertine, La citoyenne: Articles de 1881 à 1891, Paris: Syros, 1982
Aulard, François-Alphonse, "Le féminisme pendant la Révolution française," Revue bleue, Revue politique et littéraire, no. 12 (4th series, vol. 9; 19 March 1898)
Bard, Christine, editor, Un siècle d'antiféminisme, Paris: Fayard, 1999
Belgiojoso, Cristina, "Della presente condizione delle donne e del loro avvenire," Nuova antologia di scienze, lettere ed arti, Fasc. 1 (31 January 1866)
Bell, Susan G., and Karen M. Offen, editors, Women, the Family, and Freedom: The Debate in Documents, 2 vols., Stanford, California: Stanford University Press, 1983
Bonacchi, Gabriella, and Angela Groppi, editors, Il dilemma della cittadinanza: Diritti e doveri delle donne, Bari, Italy: Laterza, 1993
Brion, Hélène, La voie féministe, Paris: Syros, 1978
Cohen, Yolande, and Françoise Thébaud, editors, Féminismes et identités nationales: Les processus d'intégration des femmes en politique, Lyon, France: Programme Rhône-Alpes de Recherches en Sciences Humaines, 1998
Corbin, Alain, Jacqueline Lalouette, and Michèle Riot-Sarcey, editors, Femmes dans la cité, 1815–1871, Grâne, France: Créaphis, 1997
Daubié, Julie-Victoire, La femme pauvre au dix-neuvième siècle, Paris: Guillaumin, 1866; 2nd edition, Paris: Thorin, 1870; reprint, Paris: Côté-Femmes, 1992
Deflou, Jeanne, Le sexualisme: Critique de la prépondérance et de la mentalité du sexe fort, Paris: Tallandier, 1906
Deraismes, Maria, Ce que veulent les femmes: Articles et conférences de 1869 à 1891, with preface, notes, and commentary by Odile Krakovitch, Paris: Syros, 1980
Deraismes, Maria, Ève dans l'humanité, Paris: Sauvaitre, 1891; reprint, with preface by Laurence Klejman, Paris: Côté-Femmes, 1990
Fawcett, Millicent Garrett, "The Emancipation of Women," The Fortnightly Review, vol. 1 (November 1891)
Frederiksen, Elke, editor, Die Frauenfrage in Deutschland, 1865–1915, Stuttgart: Reclam, 1981
Hellerstein, Erna Olafson, Leslie Parker Hume, and Karen M. Offen, editors, Victorian Women: A Documentary Account of Women's Lives in Nineteenth-Century England, France, and the United States, Stanford, California: Stanford University Press, and Brighton, Sussex: Harvester Press, 1981
Héricourt, Jenny P. d', La femme affranchie; Réponse à M. Michelet, Proudhon, E. de Girardin, A. Comte, et autres novateurs modernes, Brussels: A. Lacroix, Van Meeren, 1860; as A Woman's Philosophy of Woman; or, Woman Affranchised, a Response to Michelet,

Proudhon, Girardin, Legouvé, Comte and Other Modern Innovators, Newport, Connecticut: Hyperion, 1981

Lamber, Juliette, *Idées anti-proudhoniennes sur l'amour, la femme et le mariage*, Paris: Dentu, 1861

Mill, John Stuart, *The Subjection of Women*, London: Longmans Green Reader and Dyer, and New York: Appleton, 1869; reprint, in *Collected Work of John Stuart Mill: Essays on Politics and Society*, edited by J.M. Robson, Toronto: University of Toronto Press, and London: Routledge and Kegan Paul, 1977, vol. 21

Mozzoni, Anna Maria, *La liberazione della donna*, edited by Franca Pieroni Bortolotti, Milan: Mazzotta, 1975

Pelletier, Madeleine, *L'éducation féministe des filles*, Paris: Giard et Brière, 1914; reprint, as *L'éducation féministe des filles, suivi de le droit à l'avortement: La femme en lutte pour ses droits, la tactique féminine: Le droit au travail pour la femme*, with preface, notes, and commentary by Laude Maignien, Paris: Syros, 1978

Perrot, Michelle, *Les femmes; ou, Les silences de l'histoire*, Paris: Flammarion, 1998

Posada, Adolfo, *Feminismo*, Madrid: Fé, 1899; edited by Oliva Blanco, Madrid: Cátedra, 1994

Roussel, Nelly, *L'éternelle sacrifiée*, Paris: Syros, 1979

Scheliga-Loevy, Marya, "Les hommes féministes," *Revue encyclopédique Larousse* no. 169 (28 November 1896)

Taylor, Harriet, "Enfranchisement of Women," *The Westminster and Foreign Quarterly Review*, vol. 55 (1951)

Reference Works

Abensour, Léon, *Histoire générale du féminisme: Des origines à nos jours*, Paris: Delagrave, 1921; reprint, Paris: Ressources, 1979

Aerts, Mieke, et al., *Stratégies des femmes: Amsterdam, Berlin, Boston, Londres, New York, Paris, Philadelphie, Rome*, Paris: Tierce, 1984

Anderson, Harriet, *Utopian Feminism: Women's Movements in fin de siècle Vienna*, New Haven, Connecticut: Yale University Press, 1992

Anteghini, Alessandra, *Socialismo e femminismo nelle Francia del XIX secolo: Jenny d'Héricourt*, Genoa, Italy: ECIG, 1988

Banks, Olive, *Faces of Feminism: A Study of Feminism as a Social Movement*, New York: St. Martin's Press, and Oxford: Robertson, 1981

Bidelman, Patrick Kay, *Pariahs Stand Up! The Founding of the Liberal Feminist Movement in France, 1858–1889*, London and Westport, Connecticut: Greenwood Press, 1982

Bigaran, Mariapia, "Progetti e dibattiti parlemantari sul suffragio femminile: De Perruzi a Giolitti," *Rivista di storia contempoanea*1 (1985)

Bloom, Ida, "A Centenary of Organized Feminism in Norway," in *Reassessments of "First Wave" Feminism*, edited by Elizabeth Sarah, Oxford and New York: Pergamon Press, 1982

Bloom, Ida, "The Struggle for Women's Suffrage in Norway, 1885–1913," *Scandivanian Journal of History* 5 (1980)

Bolt, Christine, *The Women's Movements in the United States and Britain from the 1790s to the 1920s*, Amherst: University of Massachusetts Press, and London: Harvester Wheatsheaf, 1993

Bonacchi, Gabriella, and Angela Groppi, editors, *Il dilemma della cittadinanza: Diritte e doveri delle donne*, Bari, Italy: Laterza, 193

Caine, Barbara, *Victorian Feminists*, Oxford and New York: Oxford University Press, 1992

Conti Odorisio, Ginevra, editor, *Salvadore Morelli (1824–1880): Emancipazionismo e democrazia nell'Ottocento Europeo*, Naples, Italy: Edizioni Scientifiche Italiane, 1992

Conti Odorisio, Ginevra, *Storia dell'idea femminista in Italia*, Turin, Italy: ERI, 1980

Corbin, Alain, Lacqueline Lalouette, and Michèle Riot-Sarcey, editors, *Femmes dans la cité, 1815–71*, Crâne, France: Créaphis, 1997

Daley, Caroline, and Melanie Nolan, editors, *Suffrage and Beyond: International Feminist Perspectives*, New York: New York University Press, 1994

Edmondson, Linda Harriet, *Feminism in Russia, 1900–17*, Stanford, California: Stanford University Press, and London: Heinemann Educational, 1984

Evans, Richard J., *The Feminist Movement in Germany, 1894–1933*, London and Beverly Hills, California: Sage, 1976

Evans, Richard J., *The Feminists: Women's Emancipation Movements in Europe, America, and Australasia, 1840–1920*, London: Croom Helm, and New York: Barnes and Noble Books, 1977

Feministische Studien, *Die Radikalen in der alten Frauenbewegung*, vol. 3, no. 1 (May 1984)

Folguera, Pilar, compiler, *El feminismo en España: Dos siglos de historia*, Madrid: Iglesias, 1988

Fraisse, Geneviève, *Muse de la raison: La démocratie exclusive et la différence des sexes*, Aix-en-Provence, France: Alinéa, 1989; as *Reason's Muse: Sexual Difference and the Birth of Democracy*, translated by Jane Marie Todd, Chicago: University of Chicago Press, 1994

Fraisse, Geneviève, *La raison des femmes*, Paris: Plon, 1992

Gerhard, Ute, *Gleichheit ohne Angleichung: Frauen im Recht*, Munich: Beck, 1990; as *Debating Women's Equality: Toward a Feminist Theory of Law from a European Perspective*, translated by Allison Brown and Belinda Cooper, New Brunswick, New Jersey: Rutgers University Press, 2001

Gerhard, Ute, *Unerhört: Die Geschichte der deutschen Frauenbewegung*, Reinbek bei Hamburg, Germany: Rowohlt, 1990

Greven-Aschoff, Barbara, *Die bürgerliche Frauenbewegung in Deutschland, 1894–1933*, Göttingen, Germany: Vandenhoeck und Ruprecht, 1981

Gubin, Éliane, "Cent ans de féminisme," *Sextant: Revue du groupe interdisciplinaire d'études sur les femmes* 1 (Winter 1993)

Gubin, Éliane, "Le féminisme en Belgique avant 1914: De l'instruction à l'émancipation," in *Lieux de femmes dans l'espace public, 1800–1930*, edited by Francois Vallotton and Monique Pavillon, Lausanne, Switzerland: Université de Lausanne, 1992

Guilbert, Madeleine, *Les femmes et l'organisation syndicale avant 1914*, Paris: Éditions du Centre National de la Recherche Scientifique, 1966

Hannam, June, *Isabella Ford*, Oxford and New York: Blackwell, 1989

Hause, Steven C., and Anne R. Kenney, *Women's Suffrage and Social Politics in the French Third Republic*, Princeton, New Jersey: Princeton University Press, 1984

Hook-Demarle, Marie-Claire, *Femmes nations Europe*, Paris: Publications de l'Université de Paris VII Denis-Diderot, 1995

Jallinoja, Riitta, "The Women's Liberation Movement in Finland: The Social and Political Mobilisation of Women in Finland, 1880–1910," *Scandinavian Journal of History* 5, no. 1 (1980)

Käppeli, Anne-Marie, "Feminist Scenes,"in *A History of Women in the West*, edited by Georges Duby and Michelle Perrot, vol. 4, *Emerging Feminism from Revolution to World War*, Cambridge, Massachusetts: Belknap Press of Harvard University Press, 1993

Käppeli, Anne-Marie, *Sublime croisade: Éthique et politique du féminisme protestant, 1875–1928*, Carouge-Geneva, Switzerland: Zoé, 1990

Klejman, Laurence, "Les congrès féministes internationaux," in *Les congrès: Lieux de l'échange intellectuel, 1850–1914*, Paris: Société d'Études Soréliennes, 1989

Klejman, Laurence, and Florence Rochefort, *L'égalité en marche: Le féminisme sous la Troisième République*, Paris: Presses de la Fondation Nationale des Sciences Politiques, and Des Femmes, 1989

Lacalzada de Mateo, Maria José, "Concepción Arenal: Un perfil olvidado de mujer y de humanista," *Arenal: Rivista de historia de las mujeres*1, no. 1 (January–June 1994)

Lacalzada de Mateo, Maria José, *La otra mitad del generó humano: La panorámica vista por Concepción Arenál (1820–1893)*, Malaga, Spain: Universidad de Malaga, 1994

Lacour, Léopold, *Humanisme intégral: Le duel des sexes, la cité future*, Paris: Stock, 1897

Lacour, Léopold, *Les origines du féminisme contemporain. Trois femmes de la Révolution: Olympe de Gouges, Théroigne de Méricourt, et Rose Lacombe*, Paris: Plon, 1900

Maignien, Claude, and Charles Sowerwine, *Madeleine Pelletier, une féministe dans l'arène politique*, Paris: Éditions Ouvrières, 1992

Manns, Ulla, *Women in Sweden: Historical Facts from 1845 to 1921*, Stockholm: Center for Women Researchers and Women's Studies in Stockholm, 1987

Manns, Ulla, *Kvinnofragan, 1880–1921: En artikelbibliografi*, Lund, Sweden: Arkiv, 1992

Moses, Claire, *French Feminism in the 19th Century*, Albany: State University of New York Press, 1984

Nash, Mary, "Experiencia y aprendizaje: La formacion historica de los feminismos en Espana," *Historia social* 20 (Autumn 1994)

Offen, Karen, "Defining Feminism: A Comparative Historical Approach," *Signs*, vol. 14 (Autumn 1988)

Offen, Karen, *European Feminisms 1700–1950: A Political History*, Stanford, California: Stanford University Press, 2000

Offen, Karen, "Liberty, Equality, and Justice for Women: The Theory and Practice of Feminism in Nineteenth-Century Europe," in *Becoming Visible: Women in European History*, edited by Renate Bridenthal, Claudia Koonz, and Susan Stuard, Boston: Houghton Mifflin, 1987

Offen, Karen, "Qui est Jenny P. d'Héricourt? Une identité retrouvée," *Bulletin de la Société d'histoire de la révolution de 1848 et des révolutions du XIXe siècle* (1987)

Offen, Karen, "Sur l'origine des mots 'féminisme et féministe,'" *Revue d'histoire moderne et contemporaine*34(1987)

Perrot, Michelle, *Les femmes ou les silence de l'histoire*, Paris: Flammarion, 1998

Pieroni Bortolotti, Franca, *Alle origini del movimento femmile in Italia, 1848–1892*, Turin, Italy: Einaudi, 1975

Rendall, Jane, editor, *Equal or Different: Women's Politics, 1880–1914*, Oxford and Cambridge, Massachusetts: Blackwell, 1987

Rendall, Jane, *The Origins of Modern Feminism: Women in Britain, France, and the United States, 1780–1860*, New York: Schocken Books, 1984

Rochefort, Florence, "L'accès des femmes à la citoyenneté politique dans les sociétés occidentales: Essai d'approche comparative," in *Féminismes et cultures nationales: Les processus d'intégration des femmes au politique*, edited by Yolande Cohen and Françoise Thébaud, Lyon, France: Éditions du Programme Pluriannuel, 1998

Rochefort, Florence, "L'antiféminisme à la Belle Époque, une rhétorique réactionnaire," in *Un siècle d'antiféminisme*, edited by Christine Bard, Paris: Fayard, 1999

Rochefort, Florence, "La citoyenneté interdite ou les enjeux du suffragisme," *Vingtième siècle* 42 (April–June 1994)

Rochefort, Florence, "Démocratie féministe contre démocratie exclusive; ou, Les enjeux de la mixité," in *Démocratie et représentation*, edited by Michèle Riot-Sarcey, Paris: Kimé, 1995 en Sciences Humaines Rhônes Alpes, 1997

Rochefort, Florence, "Féminisme et protestantisme au XIXᵉ siècle, premières rencontres, 1830–1900," *Bulletin de la Société de l'Histoire du Protestantisme Français*, vol. 146, no. 1 (January–March 2000)

Rochefort, Florence, "La prostituée et l'ouvrière: Approches protestantes et catholiques du féminisme sous la Troisième République," in *Femmes et religions*, edited by Françoise Lautman, Geneva: Labor et Fides, 1997

Rochefort, Florence, "La séduction résiste-t-elle au féminisme?" *Séduction et sociétes: Approches historiques*, edited by Arlette Farge and Cécile Dauphin, Paris: Seuil, 2001

Sarah, Elisabeth, editor, *Reassessments of "First Wave" Feminism*, Oxford and New York: Pergamon Press, 1982

Scott, Joan Wallach, *Only Paradoxes to Offer: French Feminists and the Rights of Man*, Cambridge, Massachusetts: Harvard University Press, 1996

Sextant: Revue du groupe interdisciplinaire d'études sur les femmes 1 (Winter 1993)

Sowerwine, Charles, *Les femmes et le socialisme: Un siècle d'histoire*, Paris: Presses de la Fondation Nationale des Sciences Politiques, 1978; as *Sisters or Citizens? Women and Socialism in France since 1876*, Cambridge and New York: Cambridge University Press, 1982

Stites, Richard, *The Women's Liberation Movement in Russia: Feminism, Nihilism, and Bolshevism, 1860–1930*, Princeton, New Jersey: Princeton University Press, 1977; new edition, 1991

Stratégie des femmes: Amsterdam, Berlin, Boston, Londres, New York, Paris, Philadelphie, Rome, Paris: Tierce, 1984

Thalmann, Rita, *Être femme sous la IIIe Reich*, Paris: Laffont, 1982

Tulloch, Gail, *Mill and Sexual Equality*, Hemel Hempstead, Hertfordshire: Harvester Wheatsheaf, and Boulder, Colorado: Lynne Rienner, 1989

Varikas, Eleni, "La révolte des dames: Genèse d'une conscience féministe dans la Grèce du XIXᵉ siècle, 1833–1907," Ph.D. diss., Université de Paris VII Denis-Diderot, 1986

Walle, Marianne, "Contribution à l'histoire des femmes allemandes entre 1848 et 1920 à travers les itinéraires de Louise Otto, Hélène Lange, Clara Zetkin et Lily Braun," Ph.D. diss., Université de Paris VII Denis-Diderot, 1989

Wikander, Ulla, "International Women's Congresses, 1878–1914: The Controversy over Equality and Special Labour Legislation," in *Rethinking Change: Current Swedish Feminist Research*, Stockholm: Humanistisk-Samhällsvetenskapliga Forskningsradet, 1992

Woodtli, Susanna, *Gleichberechtigung: Der Kampf um die politischen Rechte der Frau in der Schweiz*, Frauenfeld, Switzerland: Huber, 1975

Zylberberg-Hocquard, Marie-Hélène, *Féminisme et syndicalisme en France*, Paris: Anthropos, 1978

Political Rights of European Women: An Assessment of the Two World Wars

ODILE RUDELLE

Women's Suffrage: A Contentious Issue

In "old" Europe, on the eve of World War I, only the women of Norway and Finland had the right to vote in both local and national elections. We should qualify this by noting that even so, Norway imposed certain fiscal conditions on women's suffrage, while Finland, strangely, was more liberal on the national than on the local level, where women had the right to vote but not to run for office. These peculiarities were more exceptional in Europe than in North America, where women at that time were already voting in municipal elections in many states but not yet in federal elections. For Norway and Finland, furthermore, this voting privilege was linked to incidents in recent history, a history in which the movement for women's emancipation, working alongside men, had been very active in achieving national independence. Indeed, at the turn of the century, united around the Lutheran Church, which had a long-established practice of elections to clerical councils, the Finnish nation had succeeded in asserting its autonomy against czarist Russia, just as Norway had regained its independence from Sweden, its old enemy.

It is nonetheless important to stress the fact that these exemplary voting rights, consecrated by the electoral laws of 1906 and 1907, were granted in countries on the European periphery, where population growth remained modest and balanced. At the time, Finland had some 3 million inhabitants and Norway 2.3 million. In both countries, the population had a fairly harmonious gender distribution: there was a "surplus" of only 18,000 women in Finland, while that figure was rising to 55,000 in Norway. More pronounced, the relative shortage of men in Norway therefore came closer to the shortage of men in Great Britain, where that topic was a matter of great debate. There, a total population of 45 million showed an imbalance of 1.5 million in favor of women—the human consequence of the colonial

emigration patterns of an imperial nation. Orchestrated by the Pankhurst family, which sought to influence public opinion with the double tactic of large, peaceful demonstrations alternating with acts of propaganda such as broken windows, disruptions of electoral meetings, or hunger strikes, the battle of the "suffragettes" had been raging since the early part of the century, and the demographic controversy weighed heavily in this debate. While the partisans of women's political rights insisted on the need for careers and political outlets for the innumerable unmarried women who lived, worked, and paid taxes in the nation, male opponents to women's rights were afraid of being outnumbered politically. Quite naturally, in order to protect themselves from this dreaded influx of voters, they invented criteria of age that would permit them to demonstrate the "risks" of women's suffrage and preserve their majority in the electoral body until 1929.

All these quantitative specifics have been drawn from a remarkable and militant booklet, *Woman Suffrage in Practice*, published in 1913 in New York, London, and Paris under the aegis of the International Alliance for Women's Suffrage, which, as an offshoot of the International Women's Council founded in Washington, D.C., in 1888, held its Fourth Congress in Stockholm in 1911. The booklet sought to reassure men by making a worldwide assessment of the issue of women's political rights— the right to be elected in all sorts of circumstances: to labor relations boards or boards of education, to positions in municipal life or, in federal countries, at state level, and in the life of the nation, of course. This "global" approach to women's rights in fact mirrored the expansion of Anglo-Saxon legal principles that followed the global expansion of English colonialism. Thus, the pioneering states for local elections were Australia and New Zealand, as well as individual states or provinces in the United States and Canada—including Quebec. But in order to properly understand these results, they obviously need to be weighed against the demographic situation of these countries: not only are the total figures modest, but women are vastly in the minority, since emigration was a predominantly male phenomenon. Let us take two examples at opposite ends of the world: according to statistics given in *Woman Suffrage in Practice*, in 1911 in New Zealand, the total population, not counting the local Maori, was 531,510 men and 476,558 women, while in the state of Wyoming, where men and women had enjoyed the same political rights since 1869, the electoral body consisted of 58,184 men and 37,347 women.

Whatever the implications of these figures (which should nonetheless be kept in mind in considering the evolution of the old world), the concrete presentation of numbers for these countries brought the issue of women's political rights out from the realm of utopia and into the realm of objective realities. In that spirit, *Woman Suffrage in Practice* presented a legislative assessment of their work in all places where women's political rights, whether local or national, existed. To lend it weight, this assessment was provided by an "impartial" authority—that is, a man, since the originality of the International Alliance for Women's Suffrage lay in accepting the assistance of "enlightened" male minds. The result was most convincing: the report of women's presence was favorable, belying stereotypes of French *tricoteuses* (knitters—a term dating to revolutionary times, when certain women activists knitted as they listened to the debates at revolutionary assemblies) and *pétroleuses* (women who threw incendiary bombs) and English suffragettes. Women's electoral participation in Norway and Wyoming weighed in favor of political moderation, the temperance movement, and social reform. France, incarnating a wholly different legal and political tradition, was very much present in this book in the remarkable woman Maria Vérone, who copublished the brochure with her foreign colleagues, Chrystal MacMillan, Marie Stritt, and Carrie Chapman Catt, president of the International Alliance. The dates of Vérone's life (1874–1938) almost coincide with those of France's Third Republic, so deaf to the demands of women. But by using the educational possibilities the Third Republic opened up, Vérone, a teacher if ever there was one, succeeded in advancing from her mother's shop to teaching and from there to political journalism with *L'aurore* and to feminist journalism with *La fronde*. Thereafter she went on to law school; in 1907 she became the fifth French woman to be admitted to the bar. Associated with the republican Left with its radical and socialist tendencies, in 1904 she became the secretary general of the old Ligue Française pour le Droit des Femmes (French League for Women's Rights), which she managed to revitalize while keeping it focused on legalist protest. Always ready to give of herself, she ran for election, specifically for the off-year election of Paris in 1912, and together with other suffrage organizations she ran the 1914 national campaign for the "female plebiscite," which had the remarkable success of collecting 500,000 votes in one week.

The suffrage movement was thus in full ascent when it was interrupted by the outbreak of the war in August 1914. Political priorities shifted to meet the needs of the moment, as national survival became the paramount concern of everyone, including women's rights activists. On both sides of the front—in Germany, where the movement was more exclusively linked to socialism, and in France and England—suffragists were enlisted for propaganda by the different governments. Proud to show their sense of responsibility, they responded with the same patriotic fervor everywhere, and their campaigns were heartily welcomed. It was thus necessary to wait for the return of peace and peacetime perspectives before the campaigns for women's suffrage would resume. Postwar activity, however, showed considerable variety in terms of results. In the wake of World War I, Scandinavian and British women achieved an emancipation that was already well under way, and in central and eastern Europe women generally benefited from the collapse of the old German, Austrian, Russian, and Turkish empires. By contrast, in southern Europe, where political continuity prevailed, nothing or almost nothing changed.

Thus, while Spain had its republican revolution in 1931, the women of France, Italy, and Belgium had to wait until after World War II to finally obtain full political rights, in concert with worldwide struggles against all forms of discrimination, whether religious, social, or sexual. Initiated by the United Nations Charter of 1945 and developed more specifically by the Universal Declaration of the Rights of Man adopted in 1948 in Paris, the human rights movement continued to gain strength, and the great, specialized organizations of the UN issued successive declarations. Although nondiscrimination against women in terms of employment actually dated to the former Bureau International du Travail (BIT; International Labor Bureau), created in Geneva in 1919, one cannot help but note that the World Health Organization was curiously silent on the subject of women, even though its constitution dates to 1946. On the other hand, in regional organizations, especially in the Council of Europe, which was born early in the cold war in 1949, the reaffirmation of the great, legal principles of equality and liberty went hand in hand with the establishment of the European Court of Justice. Thus, this new type of treaty created legal recourse for private individuals under certain conditions where appeals through national legislation had been exhausted. Far from being a mere ideal, where professional nondiscrimination against women (as well as for freedom of education and the death penalty) was concerned, this possibility turned out to be so restrictive for the member nations that parliamentary ratification often came long after governments had signed.

Given these general historical conditions, it understandable that there may be two readings of 20th-century history concerning the political emancipation of European women. On the one hand, there is the European reading and, on the other, the American reading, which, grounded in exclusive feminism, must be situated within the tradition of 19th-century legal imperialism that was already conceived as a form of universalism. The traditional European reading, by contrast, is more sensitive to chronological evidence and lived memory of the war experience. The war engendered such social upheavals in women's everyday life that hindsight tends to focus on the liberties opened to them. It is precisely against this latter interpretation that an exclusively feminist interpretation, influenced by the emergence of gendered studies of history in the United States, in the form of the five volumes of the monumental *Histoire des femmes en occident* (1991–92; *A History of Women in the West*) edited by Georges Duby and Michèle Perrot. The last of the five volumes opens precisely with the weighty influence of the wars on the destiny of 20th-century women.

Leaving essentially untreated the short chronology of the two postwar periods—moments of opportunity when European women's voting rights were officially sanctioned—this feminine-gendered approach to history, modeled after the pioneering work of Joan Wallace Scott, was intended to construct and even reconstruct a "sexed" (although in reality an exclusively feminist) reading of World War I (see Scott 1988). Against traditional historiography, then, this new form of history explained that, far from having emancipated women, the war and its violence had led, instead, to an exacerbation of the differentiation between masculine and feminine roles. Thus, in the face of grief and the death of soldiers, it was the woman nurse, caring and mothering, who was again and still is honored and celebrated. On the day that peace arrived, the dreadful human bloodbath further justified women's return to the family home, where children had to be raised while men returning from the front expected quite legitimately to find their work and their "manly" jobs waiting for them. To quote Simone de Beauvoir's famous phrase from *La force des choses* (1963; *Force of Circumstance: Autobiography of Simone de Beauvoir*), so frequently cited with regard to feminist movements, women were "cheated" (*J'ai été flouée.*) Giving further proof of the perverse weight of the two wars, the fifth volume of *A History of Women in the West* quite rightly explains that not until the 1970s—when cold war restrictions waned and colonial imperialism ended—would feminist movements again find an audience. At that time, formally recognized as nongovernmental organizations (NGOs), these movements were again able to take action in different international proceedings that offered them real influence.

While it is true that the (inevitable) debate over relations between the sexes was more ambiguous during those years of fire and blood than is commonly acknowledged, research on the evolution or stability of sex-role differentiation in the human species did not develop at the same rhythm as the emergence, practice, and consolidation of democratic political life. More sociological and anthropological than historical, a gendered approach is also more activist than descriptive, since the avowed and even required objective is a shifting of focus, in order to end up with a view of the whole that is tangibly different from that of the period, as its witnesses perceived it, spoke of it, and wrote of it.

Let us add, too, that this gendered approach to history, "sexed" in such a way that it benefits only feminists, unfolded over a long period of time, the almost biological rhythm of which is, in the end, more generational than electoral. Such an approach cannot, therefore, be of any great help in elucidating the political questions that are just as important and that we would like to emphasize here. For example: how to explain the persistent national differences in the ways in which advances in women's rights were made. For, if only a few Scandinavian women could vote in national elections before World War I, and if the fact of women's suffrage had become almost a generality in Europe after World War II, it should nonetheless be recalled that a country as democratic as Switzerland was to resist the women's vote in some of its cantons until the 1990s (not to mention the principality of Andorra, an archeological relic, or the Vatican, a theocratic state).

Another question is how to account for the discrepancy that has historically existed between the northern and southern European countries. The traditional explanation of religion, with the special weight of Catholicism, is insufficient, since Catholic women have been voting in Ireland and Poland since 1918. Even more surprising, Turkish women have had the right to vote since 1924. This was not the case in Italy, where the conflict

with the papacy weighed heavily, or in the secular nation of France, which nevertheless boasts of having been the land of the rights of man since 1789. Thus, France remains an oddity: a pioneer of universal male suffrage on the national scale in 1848, but a latecomer at the level of local government (where universal male suffrage was not granted until 1982) and with regard to women's suffrage, which did not make its appearance until April 1944, one year before it was applied—and under what conditions! This belated success was due neither to a regular parliamentary process as in Great Britain or in Scandinavia, nor to a revolutionary movement as in central Europe. In France, women's rights to vote and to stand for election were therefore neither proclaimed, nor voted upon by a regular assembly. After deliberation by a temporary consultative assembly, these rights were simply instituted by a French national liberation committee that was based in the offshore and equally temporary capital city of Algiers. We shall come back to this situation, for behind these exotic circumstances lies the potentially fruitful possibility of history that might be sexed without being biased.

Finally, an investigation is in order into the manner in which the women of Europe have used their ballot once their political rights had been voted in, proclaimed or instituted. It is known that subsequent to the study *Les Françaises face à la politique* (1951; French Women and Politics) by Mattei Dogan and Jacques Narbonne, numerous studies by both men and women have taken satisfaction in showing that for a long time women tended to abstain or to vote more "conservatively" than men (who enjoyed the privilege of setting the norm). But what does "conservatism" mean in the context of the threats on constitutional liberties made by the two forms of totalitarianism that successively erupted across the European Continent after World Wars I and II? Were there any countries or moments in which women, as bearers of a culture or an original memory, had their own means of exercising influence? And if so, were there any political, constitutional, or electoral configurations receptive enough to their influence to enable them to be decision makers? Finding answers to such questions will allow us to rebalance in women's favor the traditional historical account of 20th-century political developments in Europe, without rendering it unrecognizable.

Eschewing what might be called the "Cyclops syndrome"—meaning the one-eyed look of a uniquely male or a uniquely female perspective—this factual, chronological and quasi-procedural vision, to the extent that it takes into account the dialogue maintained between the two sexes by means of electoral consultations, should help to weigh and evaluate the political record of women's suffrage in 20th-century Europe.

Paths of Women's Suffrage in Europe: A National Revolution?

Strangely enough, very little has been done by way of a comprehensive study that treats women's acquisition of the right to vote throughout Europe. Those studies that do exist rapidly turn from the raw fact of women's right to suffrage to focus on results in the form of representation, whether in terms of the suffrage of the so-called progressive parties or, more recently, women's use of their right to stand for election. This does, in fact, allow for a precise measurement of the impact of women's suffrage in terms of numbers of women elected in local, national, and now European assemblies. But it must be emphasized that this strictly arithmetical approach risks neglecting the essence of life. Indeed, statistics transforms or reduces to a sociological equation what is in reality a question of history, mysterious and enigmatic in regard to the variety of processes that finally gave women the right to suffrage. Fruitful for purposes of shedding light on deficiencies and nurturing future mobilizations, a strict numerical comparison of electoral results will fail to satisfy those who seek to understand historical processes, which are far from having revealed all their key elements.

Since Auguste Comte, sociologists have known that "social facts" always have their own history. This is particularly true for Europe, Asia's small promontory, made up of once-imperial nations. Having once conquered and unified the planet, these nations today seek to state and reconstruct their unity by uncovering the outlines of a common history. This history, beyond the inexpiable and suicidal wars of the 20th century, gives Europe a uniqueness that all Europeans want to preserve in the world of the third millennium, in which the weapons that once enabled the conquest of the universe have now become commonplace.

In this recognition of Europe's uniqueness, the social, economic, and political role of women carries a great deal of weight—to such a degree that the details of women's attainment of political citizenship may serve as an indicator of the great moments of national histories. This hold particularly true with regard to each country's relation to political liberty and the slow emancipation of the democratic conscience that has given Europe's unique history its universal value. Against empires and churches, inherited from antiquity and the Middle Ages, the spirit of curiosity and questioning has, indeed, operated across the European Continent ever since the great geographical discoveries of the Renaissance. Causing the serious political and religious crises of the Reformation and the Enlightenment, this climate of curiosity and questioning preceded the new era of independence and revolutions that have always sought, albeit with varying degrees of success, to transform faithful believers and passive subjects into active and responsible citizens.

Failing to take this historical heritage into account is likely to render any knowledge of specific national differences unintelligible. Only the whole of European history can restore the soul of the different national destinies: that of northern Europe, where the influence of self-government, a model that there emerged from the Lutheran churches but which in other areas operated as a brake on women (in Calvinist Switzerland, for example). This practice is quite distinct from the everyday life of Latin Europe, long governed by a centralized administration inherited from Rome, which was to find unexpected reinforcement from the new male egalitarianism of the French Civil Code, written and disseminated by that Mediterranean soldier, Napoleon Bonaparte.

Closer to us in time, it is again a broad historical view that enables us to understand the tragic lot of central Europe, which was freed from the domination of the central empires after World War I, only to find itself captive to Communism and the cold war after World War II. Emptying institutional rights of all objective reality, the Soviet regime isolated countries as westernized as Poland or Czechoslovakia from their life-sources and thereby cut off the society of women from the social evolu-

tion that was being played out naturally in the West. There, once the joy of the liberation was accepted and the work of "reconstruction" complete, women were able to turn to their advantage the new resources of consumer society, which had avidly sought their labor, in order to reorganize themselves in keeping with modern demands.

Abandoning the long-resolved question of voting rights and strengthened by the academic and professional successes of its members, the feminist movement of the 1970s opened its eyes onto the world and focused on the encountered obstacles, and thus on the shape (and sex) of democratic representation in European countries. This was when the women of Western Europe, inspired by the great struggles waged across the Atlantic on behalf of different racial or sexual minorities, entered into a protracted campaign to institute quotas on the electoral lists by law or through regulation within the parties. This system was intended to ensure automatic "parity" between men and women in political representation.

But this battle, fought during the late 20th century, should not eclipse the importance of importance of 19th-century history, which taught us the extent to which women's political liberty was tied to the liberty of nations. Ireland and Poland, both prototypically Catholic countries, but which attained political independence on the rubble of the Great War, proclaimed as a gift of joyous advent that "no person may be excluded from Irish citizenship on the basis of his or her sex," or that "origins, religious persuasion or sex" cannot be a limitation to the rights of Polish citizenship. Very similar clauses exist in the constitutions of Germany, Austria, Estonia, Lithuania, Hungary, and Czechoslovakia, as they were published and annotated in 1928 by Boris Mirkine-Guetzevitch (see Mirkine-Guetzevitch). The great crisis had not yet worked its ravages, and Mirkine-Guetzevitch, an eminent member of the Institute of Constitutional History, still hoped that the legal work he had helped to shape might withstand the test—that is, that it might shelter and buttress liberty, which, for him, was intrinsic to the "parliamentary" regime he thought would be appropriate for the nations, which he even described as "aristocratic."

Governed by socialists (as in Germany or Austria), by Catholics (as in Poland, Ireland, or Lithuania), or by secular republicans (as in Czechoslovakia, Turkey under Kemal Ataturk in 1924, or republican Spain in 1931), these countries unhesitatingly proclaimed and put into effect equal political rights for men and women.

Further south, there was less progress on this issue. Emerging from the dismantled Turkish Empire and recognizing civil equality of the sexes in their constitutions, the two new kingdoms of the "Serbs, Croats, and Slovenes" and Rumania deferred ruling on women's equality in political rights to future legislation that proved long in coming. In 1931, the proclamation of the Kingdom of Yugoslavia changed nothing with regard to the issue, the urgency of which suggested that something of a regression had occurred since 1914.

As proof, there is the long article on Rumania by the young Mattei Dogan, published in 1953 at the Institut de Sociologie de Bruxelles (Brussels Institute of Sociology), on "L'origine sociale du personnel parliamentaire d'un pays essentiellement agraire" (The Social Origin of Parliamentary Personnel in an Essentially Agrarian Society). The article omits the "woman question"—an omission that is all the more surprising in that three years later the same author was a pioneer in gendered analysis of the political behavior of the sexes in France and Italy after the liberation. With regard to Rumania during the interwar period, the issue of gendered behaviors was not even mentioned. And yet, numerous variables were presented to explain the homogeneity of political personnel that still resembled that of a regime based on tax qualifications: the shrewdness of agrarian reform that satisfied the great mass of the farmers, proportional electoral laws, the weight of the Magyar minority, which elected journalists, the role of socioprofessional structures covertly informed by capitalism, and educational levels.

This exclusively male social problematic is best explained by making comparisons with England before 1914 or France in 1936. Those examples present two forms of "liberalism" and "socialist democracy" in which women's right to vote had, precisely, remained deadlocked within the regular course of parliamentary politics, and in which the existence of national minorities (for example, the Irish question, or the division of legislative power between two chambers, as in France in 1875) proved to be insurmountable obstacles to the advent of political rights for women. This was an obstacle the "national revolutions" had bypassed through their proclamations of independence that had brought the old systems down. Thus, the paradox of the years following World War I was to see young states, with new frontiers and new constitutions, reaping the benefit—sometimes better than long-established countries—of the struggles waged simultaneously by the suffragist leagues and the Socialist parties prior to 1914.

This does not mean that their path had been easy, as was shown by the example of the German Empire, paralyzed by the superimposition of its distinctive identities and the division of its women's organizations. Since the failure of the political revolution of 1848 and Prussia's rise to power, the uniqueness of the German Empire had resided in the linking of social emancipation with political emancipation. Taking into account the traditional hostility of a labor movement influenced by the very hostile theses of Pierre-Joseph Proudhon in France, this linkage was a significant innovation. It was a movement that only slowly would follow the principles of Karl Marx, who was willing to stall in order to preserve unity in 1864, or the ideas of August Bebel, who had prudently published his book *Die Frau und der Sozialismus* (1883; Woman and Socialism) in Switzerland. Bebel's book saw many subsequent editions. Founded in Paris in 1889, and on the urging of the German Socialist Party that had been ahead of it by two years, the Second International adopted a program of political, economic, and civil equality for women. This program was the result of the remarkable and diligent action of Klara Zetkin, who had founded her paper *Die Gleichheit* in 1892 and who for ten years served as the international secretary of the Socialist Women's Movement, established in 1907. But the hard-line demand of the Socialists was becoming a handicap in the German context, where local electoral systems based on property ownership—which enfranchised some 2,000 women on the condition that they vote by proxy—coexisted with an imperial system based on male universal suffrage (without a parliamentary system). In the long run, it would even have the odd result of isolating the German Socialists in their own International, for the hard-line demand had neither allowed alliances nor a development of common actions with

the more traditional women who came either from the liberal backgrounds of the Allgemeiner Deutscher Frauenverein (ADF; Union of German Women's Associations), which in 1894 had become the Bund Deutscher Frauenvereine (BDF; Federation of German Women's Associations), or from the Catholic Church.

The previous year, in 1893, led by Helen Lange, who belonged to the old generation that had been paralyzed by the German law of 1851 prohibiting women from participating in public meetings or associations, Germany's liberal women had attended the Chicago Congress of the International Council of Women. There they had discovered methods of legal advocacy, which were difficult to transpose into a Reich that ignored women to the point of depriving them of any initiative at the debate on the Civil Code, which had lasted 20 years, from 1873 to 1896. The contingent of German liberals had also had contact with women from the Anglo-Saxon countries, who were not shocked by a partial and progressive extension of the right to vote for women. In Germany, however, because of the importance of the female working class, the Socialists had immediately analyzed the vote as a class privilege to be maintained or broadened.

Back in Germany, the delegates acted to create a sufficiently representative association. In 1902 the National Council of Women of Germany was created and became the inviting power of a congress that took place in 1904 in Berlin. The event was marked by the establishment of the International Alliance for Women's Suffrage, which was to publish its well-documented brochures on this fast-evolving issue. The congress was successful: Empress Augusta Victoria and Chancellor Bülow honored it with their presence, so that for a time the movement pinned its hopes on the fortunes of the liberal chancellor. It was a wasted effort. Despite the verbal rallying of the liberal parties, which in 1907 agreed to write the demand for universal suffrage into their agenda so as to put an end to the criticisms of the Socialists, the movement did not manage to attain organizational autonomy.

Austria did better. A large demonstration took place in the streets of Vienna in March 1911, called for by the Socialists and mobilizing liberal women. In Germany, sustained respect for the British suffragettes did not lead to any such major demonstrations. The political movement contented itself with sending petitions to the Reichstag, which in 1913 deigned for the first time to take one "under consideration." Doomed to futility at the national level (in local parliaments the situation was more open), the debate on women had changed its focus and fluctuated between social considerations: the professional or maternal status of woman and polemics of a moral nature on prostitution in a country where so-called "protectionist" laws did nothing but reinforce the hypocritical social standards that absolved men and condemned women. Thus, on the eve of the war the situation had devolved into a stalemate. And as Rita Thalmann has somewhat humorously noted, with a total of 14,000 women, the movement for women's suffrage in Germany had mobilized fewer women than the number who belonged to the Colonial League! (See Thalmann.) In 1914 the outbreak of the hostilities only moved the still latent conflict toward a more radical split, first between liberal women who had turned toward nationalism and socialist women who had become pacifists and then, after 1917, between advocates of legal reform and revolutionaries. But the military routing of the Reich would in a single blow eliminate the obstacles that had blocked the way for so long: henceforth women's political right disappeared as a prize and became an obvious fact.

Following Catholic Bavaria's example in 1918, each new republic in the German lands honored itself by proclaiming universal and equal suffrage for men and women, although without accepting the idea of independent "women's councils," requested by socialist women. The same happened in all the countries of central Europe, whatever their history of women's suffrage activism. Paralyzed in earlier days by their imperial status, whether as center or satellite, the nations liberated by the defeat of the empires, from which they immediately dissociated themselves, all found they were equally young with regard to universal suffrage. Whether revolutionary, as in the Soviet Union, or legalist, as in the Czech Republic, the future was no longer envisioned without the political participation of women, who were everywhere called upon to join the election of the future constituent assembly, which was to be "one"—representative of all.

On the whole, the system of choice was a ballot based on proportional representation, organized by large conscriptions favoring the organization of parties, in accordance with ideas generated 20 years earlier by socialists and Catholics, who saw this system as a means of improving the fairness of representation by putting an end to the individual domination of liberals. In fact, the proportional electoral list was one of the commonplaces of the propaganda for the right of women's suffrage, and in France Joseph Barthélémy had been one of the most outspoken on the subject, saying that women's right to vote could take place only after proportional electoral reform. Abandoning the ballot for a single candidate, which elicited a single battle seen as too harsh for the weaker sex, the new elections—with equal suffrage for men and women—were therefore to be held with a proportionally representative ballot list intended to soften personal animosities. What was said less openly, but was nonetheless very real, was that proportional representation enabled the political parties to continue to be in charge of putting the lists together. Thus they were in control of choosing the order of precedence on these lists where, by definition, only the first places have a chance of being in a position of being elected.

The underlying intentions were praiseworthy, but during the interwar period this system did not meet with any success. Incapable of unblocking the government's majorities, the new diets or parliaments of central Europe became the victims of military, totalitarian, and fascist blackmail. The first years of these new democracies of mixed suffrage therefore were not happy ones, since dictatorship awaited them. Worse yet, their unfortunate fate was to serve as an alibi to the French senators of the Third Republic, who used it as a pretext for continuing to stand firm on the monopoly of their male privilege to political rights, trotting out the old saws about "defending the Republic." The argument only appeared truthful. In fact, recent critical works, including Paul-Marie de La Gorce's *La prise du pouvoir par Hitler, 1928–1933* (1983; Hitler's Coup), have proven what those best informed already knew at the time: that within the possibility of their means, German women of the Weimar Republic, who were more tightly integrated into the Catholic Church than men, had resisted the Nazi vertigo longer. Although not enormous, the difference remains meaningful. It is all the better known because in 1928 and 1930 experiments were conducted in when men and women used separate ballot boxes. The experiments involved 6,390,000 voters out of a total of 31,167,000 (or 20.5

percent of the electoral body) in 1928, and 5,938,000 voters out of a total of 35,226,000 (or 16.9 percent of the electoral body) in 1930. The results showed that the gender gap in votes for the Nazi party decreased from 15.6 percent in 1928 (57.8 percent of men voters as compared to 42.2 percent of women voters) to 1.8 percent in 1930 (50.9 percent of men voters as compared to 49.1 percent of women voters). Similar differences in the voting behaviors of the two sexes marked postwar France, where such differences could tip the balance in determining the political majority and thus played an important role during the two constitutive of 1945–46 and 1958–81. Such findings represent nothing new, since these particular cases merely illustrate the amply documented general rule that women's vote is typically more moderate than men's, whether on the extreme Left or the extreme Right (both of which are equally loathsome to women).

In order to gain a balanced view of the attainment of women's suffrage in Europe, one must also consider the respective histories of the old parliamentary democracies. For countries such as Great Britain and the Netherlands, the emotional impact of World War I facilitated or enabled the development of new procedures. In contrast, nations such as France, Italy, or Belgium, caught up in "aura" of victory, would have to wait for the shock of World War II in order to implement universal male and female suffrage.

The British Model of Parliamentary Reform

As a model, parliamentary reform is the opposite of the revolutionary process. The latter proclaims itself "in the face of the world" without concern for practical details—in this instance, legal obligations with their attendant civil, professional, educational, and social potentialities. The sad fate of the fine declarations of principle made in central Europe just after World War I was reminiscent of the disappointments of the French politics that was invented the revolutionary model in the name of the sovereignty of the nation. Four years after having proclaimed in August 1789 that "men are born free and equal," France found itself escorting Olympe de Gouges to the guillotine. Not content merely to write a *Déclaration des droits de la femme et de la citoyenne* (1791; Declaration of the Rights of Woman and the Female Citizen), she had sought to present a defense of the rights of the king, Louis XVI, as well.

Half a century later, the Revolution of 1848, which proposed as its goal "to walk more freely on the path of progress and civilization," showed a somewhat naive idealism in linking its destiny only to universal male suffrage. Like their revolutionary predecessors, representatives of 1848 neither welcomed nor wished to hear the lessons of English or American experience or the petitions of French women's associations, led by women's rights pioneers such as Jeanne Deroin, Désirée Gay, and Eugénie Niboyet. As for the regime of the Third Republic, "established" and consolidated after a series of political crises and still interpreted in terms of a "threatened" Republic that needed to be "defended," it could not understand that the stability and legitimacy gained by the victory of 1918 would finally open the doors to parliamentary reform implemented in stages.

For such is the heart of the difference between revolutionary process and parliamentary reform. This is not to say that extra-parliamentary means and concrete acts of militancy were eliminated, since in fact, female violence was to have much more power and reality in Great Britain than in France. But by reasoning in terms of "enfranchisement," the parliamentary system is able to sustain dialogue, negotiate, develop a timetable, and even experiment. These are all procedures that remain alien to the revolutionary method, which, concerned only with access to the exercise of "inalienable rights," continues to be wholly unfamiliar with any idea of local rights exercised before national rights. Even more alien to a revolutionary mindset are all changes that, seeking to gain time, start with women over the age of 30 or limit these rights to the unmarried, the divorced or, as in Belgium, to widows of men who died on the battlefield. This seemed especially discourteous to those women "fortunate" enough to have a husband who distinguished himself in battle.

The value of Pierre Rosanvallon's study, *Le sacre du citoyen: Histoire du suffrage universel en France* (1992; The Rite of Citizenship: History of Universal Suffrage in France), is that it focused on the filter of national cultures, which transformed the significance of the gesture of universal suffrage that could express contrasting feelings of either choice or communion from one country to another (see Rosanvallon). In France, the Catholic tradition for a long time meant that the vote was a solemn gesture that was less an "electoral" procedure, in the sense of choosing the best candidates, than a celebration of "social inclusion," a way for society to express a unity that could only be complete, perfect, and national—as opposed to distinct social, local, professional, and of course, sexual identities.

Elsewhere, the electoral process was seen as less sacred, more current. In addition to drawing upon church practice, voting procedures developed throughout the 19th century in the offices that grew out of Poor Laws or various boards of education in the countries influenced by British Common Law. In this sense, voting procedures were even to be found in France, where, as a vestige of the ancien régime, women's right to vote existed in the courts dealing with trade disputes and in the labor relations board. But this continued to be an altogether marginal practice in a country administered and still dominated by farmers. In Sweden, things were more natural: unmarried or widowed women who paid taxes voted in local elections from 1862. In Great Britain, it was the important 1984 law on local suffrage that abolished all distinctions in status of married, widowed, or unmarried women and retained only the requirement that women voters be "qualified" based on very simple residential conditions. In Denmark and Iceland, the right to vote in local elections was extended in 1908 and 1909; to attain women's suffrage on a national level, the governments had to progress to a "democratic" constitutional revision, concluded in 1915, that placed the two legislative chambers on an equal footing.

On the whole, the bicameral legislative model was a substantial obstacle to extending the right to vote to women. The system had been devised to protect liberty and to provide recourse against ill-considered decisions made in haste or under the sway of public opinion. Such parliamentary regimes were constrained to act under an organization of public powers that split the power between a chief of state (who could be a queen—a possibility that benefited women in the Netherlands) and a legislative power, itself in turn divided into two chambers. This distribution had

been conceived to put the forces of tradition—members of the established churches or the landowning aristocracy, who sat in the upper chambers—on one side, and on the other, the new forces that fed modern economic life and populated the lower chambers, which would be filled, successively, by members of the independent professions characteristic of liberal parties and then the contemporary Socialist parties of the Industrial Revolution.

In Great Britain, as in Germany or France, but with different constitutional modalities in each case, women's rights advocates had to create a space for the issue of national female suffrage within the parameters of three powers. First there were the Socialist parties, which assented rather quickly, although the question of the hierarchy to be established between union rights and political rights was never completely resolved. Occupying the center were the liberal parties, which, although intellectually in favor of extending individual rights, nevertheless feared undermining their electoral situation by granting the vote to creatures who remained under the "conservative" influence of the churches. Finally, there were the conservative parties, whose position evolved out of a principled hostility to an act that would bring women out of the private circle of family life and might lead her to the miraculous discovery that the electoral mass of women could serve as a useful counterweight to the temptation of revolution.

These situations offered many potentialities for the feminist movements that, in England as in Germany, were divided between the desire for autonomy and the need for alliances, between the common front and division, depending on whether or not they gave priority to winning civil rights (equality in marriage or divorce; educational, university, and professional rights; union rights or maternity protection) or political rights. An aggravating circumstance was that women might find themselves in competition with men in situations where the latter were still deprived of their rights, as in Belgium or Germany. In such cases, women were generally asked to subordinate their struggles to those of men or, taking an even greater risk, to invest their energies in helping to struggle to fulfill male ambitions. They did so in the hope of future gratitude—which, in the extreme case of Portugal, was delayed from 1911 until the Revolution of the Carnations of 1974.

The advent of the right to vote for British women constituted a sort of textbook case for the healthy functioning of parliamentary institutions capable of change, because in Great Britain the question of women's political emancipation was situated at the crossroads of all the stakes of modern politics. These stakes included the Irish national question, the potential position of the female electorate on the political frontier separating liberals from workers, campaigns of associations divided between mass demonstration and actions "against an unjust law," the moral status of women subjected to the provocation of "male lechery," and, last but not least, patriotic feelings in the face of a war in which women amply did their duty. Women's war contribution was such that the question of equal treatment of combatants on the front and those in the rear inevitably arose.

The need to develop a plan on a national scale was apparent from every point of view: from the perspective of social mobilization, where women had been put to the test to prove their representativeness to a male world that was split between skepticism and broad jokes; from the point of view of the legislative process, which put into play the collaboration of the highest authorities in the kingdom, including the monarch (whose support was sought), the House of Lords (whose powers had been redefined), the prime minister (who controlled the political agenda), the speaker of the House of Commons (who decided the agenda and the nature of parliamentary debate), and the creation, at the request of the government, of a large multiparty commission made up of peers and members of Parliament. Once the legal validity of the issue had been acknowledged, Millicent Garrett Fawcett achieved a tremendous initial success in 1916. She was a supporter of the legalist battle, who at that time obtained the first response indicating openness to her arguments from Prime Minister Herbert Henry Asquith, who had long been hostile.

These shifts in mindset were as much the result of prewar struggles as of the new realities of war; circumstances meant that for one thing, the labor employed in the weapons factories was largely made up of women. Further, given the long absence of sailors and soldiers overseas, there was in any case a clear need to revise the electoral requirement of a six-month period of residency before one could be registered to vote, to avoid penalizing combatants. These postwar projects, contemplated during wartime, benefited from the general climate of national union that eliminated the long-standing breaches between, on the one hand, the "legalists" represented by the members of the old National Society for Women's Suffrage (NSWS), which dated back to the Victorian era, and, on the other hand, the "activists" of the new Women's Social and Political Union (WSPU), founded in 1903 by Emmeline Pankhurst and her daughters, Christabel and Sylvia. The latter organization's name conveyed the newly forged ties between women's rights activists and a militant socialism able to mobilize female labor.

A 50-Year Campaign

The women's suffrage movement in Great Britain is generally perceived as having progressed in three waves. The first of these, from 1865 to 1894, extends from John Stuart Mill's highly publicized stand on the issue when he was elected to Parliament in 1865 to the "Local Government Act" of 1894, which established an initial framework that was limited to local politics, the actions of women activists mobilized to canvass for voter registration, and the social functions filled by charitable organizations and educational associations. The second wave, from 1894 until the truce of 1910–1911, included a ten-year period of intense activism; there appeared a veritable electoral lobbying process that proved costly to Winston Churchill (himself a supporter) in 1906 and 1908. Strong in its unity, the movement had won the sympathies of the public, and hopes for women's suffrage were all the more real since they were linked to the constitutional reform of the House of Lords. But in 1911, after the prime minister's about-face, the disappointment was great enough to justify the reprise of the "criminal" campaigns that would last until the outbreak of the war in August 1914.

Until the very end, the women's suffrage movement suffered from competition with the Irish question, which, justifiably, was considered to pose a more serious threat to civil peace than did women spitting in people's faces, shattering windows by throwing rocks, or even setting fire to the properties of hostile deputies. The interconnection of these two questions illustrates

the aforementioned relationship between women's liberty and the liberty of nations, as well as the difficulty of a transverse question that just as unexpectedly came to upset the traditional play of "representative" systems.

This configuration explains, on the one hand, the "blackmail" practiced by male unionists, imperialists, militarists, or Protestants, which presaged by 50 years the blackmail to which republican France was subjected at the hands of supporters of "French Algeria." The latter's separation from metropolitan France required a constitutional reform for which Algerian women would be invited to vote for the first time in 1958. On the other hand, however, in the very heart of the unionist city of Belfast, there had always been many courageous Irish women ready to be mobilized without making any real distinction between their campaign for women's right to vote and the hope that the ballot would serve to give expression to their national freedom. And in the case of Ireland, as for many European women, it was the war that cut through these truly Gordian knots of everyday politics.

Prehistory

In the United States, the suffrage movement was born in the aftermath of the Civil War, which, by abolishing slavery, had made the activists of the rights of man aware that the factor of race was paramount, surpassing even that of gender, in the abjection of the black slave, whose emancipation obviously required the liberty of all American women as a precondition. This antislavery precedent gave intellectual, moral, and political direction to the struggle waged on behalf of minorities by means of parades in the streets and legal petitions; the latter seemed quite natural, since in New Jersey women had voted from 1790 until 1807. In Great Britain, the precedent was instead that of the social struggles against protectionism, notably the efforts of Richard Cobden's "Anti–Corn Law" League. Cobden, who favored women's suffrage, initiated the "constitutional" tactic of legalist opposition, using itinerant lectures, meetings, a variety of tracts, and petitions to the House of Commons. The strategy was so successful that in 1869, for example, 225 petitions with a total of 61,475 signatures in favor of women's suffrage were submitted.

The movement eventually ran out of steam, after the disappointments of the years 1884 and 1894, when broader national suffrage was legislated, but only for men; this provision was confirmed in the Local Government Act of 1894. More serious still, efforts at moral improvement and democratic progress had actually produced perverse effects. For example, the 1883 anti-corruption law prohibiting paid electoral propaganda was interpreted and used as an invitation to feminists, henceforth called upon to voluntarily invest their activist energies in service of candidates of their party. This helps explain women's tactics in subsequent times, when they ran electoral campaigns, but on their own behalf, by selecting candidates to support—or to put out of commission—depending upon their having or not having promised to submit an amendment favorable to their cause.

Activist Politics of the Suffragettes

The convergence of the women's suffrage movement and the independent labor movement took place at in the Manchester region the end of the 19th century, around the activist couple Richard and Emmeline Pankhurst, both members of the Baptist Church; their story is related in Andrew Rosen's scholarly study (see Rosen). It was in meetings of the Labour Party that Emmeline Pankhurst learned the power of civil disobedience, which until 1914 often landed her in prison for having held and spoken at forbidden meetings in places where her great eloquence was deemed undesirable. She was widowed in 1898, and in 1901, through her daughter, Christabel, she discovered the near-dormant world of the 60 local associations of the National Society for Women's Suffrage. It had been founded in 1867 and had been barely rejuvenated by its reestablishment in 1897 by Millicent Garrett Fawcett. Along with Eva Gore-Booth and Esther Roper, the three Pankhurst women quickly grasped the futility of the quibbling and discussions on the status of married or unmarried women. They also understood the wisdom of going beyond the narrow world of the bourgeoisie to address the Labour Party, where women workers paid the same dues as men to the unions, which sent deputies to the House of Commons. Once the Women's Social and Political Union (WSPU) had been founded in 1903, they decided to participate actively in electoral meetings, where they resorted to interruptions and requests to take the speakers' platform in an attempt to force candidates to take a stand on their behalf.

From the start, these militant women accepted the risk of breaking the law—as did other activist women, among whom the best known were Teresa Billington-Greig (1877–1964) and Annie Kenney (1879–1953). They saw transgression as the most effective form of propaganda for shaking the bastions of male power. The desired result was very quickly attained, with the scandal of women molested by the police, called into court, and sentenced to fines they refused to pay—which landed them in prison (see Rosen). These events made headlines, and the two women's release from prison became a triumphant occasion, with 2,000 women awaiting them. Even though the moderate women of the NSWS were a bit shocked by these ways, they were forced to admit that the tactics paid off, and that even their own legalist organization reaped the benefits in terms of increases in membership and dues collected.

In 1906, after the electoral victory of the Liberal Party, when many thought that victory was near in the women's suffrage campaign, the Pankhurst family moved to London. There they established offices and used their know-how to mobilize the women workers of London's East End, where, as in Manchester, they managed to get these women to take to the streets to demand higher wages and recognition of their political rights. In these great marches, where middle-class and working-class women stood side by side, the discipline was excellent: music and uniforms were used to appeal to the imagination and to create the impression of an army on the march. In 1906, 1907, and 1908 they deliberately chose the days of the monarch's opening speech to Parliament to stage mass gatherings calling for a petition in support of the rights of women who requested to meet with the authorities.

In the fall of 1906, Christabel Pankhurst entered into an ambitious correspondence with A. J. Balfour, the leader of Conservative Party in the House of Commons, to invite him to come to a meeting to be held in November in Birmingham, so that he could announce his favorable intentions. He responded on 23 October, in a "private" letter, completely based on the "con-stitutional" ground of "government by consent," in which he asked women to prove that their not having the right to vote was truly felt as an "exclusion" by the majority of them, deprived as they would be of a "privilege they desired." In December 1906 Asquith, chancellor of the Exchequer and later the hostile and almost immovable prime minister from 1908 to 1916, would say the same thing:

> I am prepared to withdraw my opposition [known since 1892], which is a very unimportant factor in the case, to what is called female enfranchisement . . . the moment that I am satisfied of two things, but not before, namely, first, that the majority of women desire to have a Parliamentary vote, and next, that the conferring of a vote upon them would be advantageous to their sex and the community at large. (Quoted in Rosen.)

Thus challenged to prove their desire for suffrage, the women mobilized, launched subscriptions, and decided to organize a large meeting in Hyde Park on 21 June 1908. Estimates of the number of those attending ranged from 250,000 to 500,000 people. Empowered by this triumph, Christabel Pankhurst requested an audience with the prime minister. He refused, saying that he had already given his answer on 27 May: electoral reform was in preparation; the government's platform did not address the issue of women's suffrage, but the prime minister was willing to say that he would not oppose an amendment on the subject if it were written in a "democratic spirit, capable of assuring him of the majority of the country's women and men." Extremely disappointed, the women repeated their demonstrations and petitions at the end of the month. Turned down once again, they tried to take the floor and were then brutally manhandled by the police. Exasperated by this contempt, Edith New and Mary Leigh filled a sack with stones and threw them at the windows of 10 Downing Street, thereby inaugurating a two-year period of political activism filled with demonstrations, trials, and prison sentences.

The official position of the country, governed by parliamentary rule in which legislative power was divided between the House of Commons and the House of Lords, would not change until 1911. That year, in order to permit passage of a "budget of the people" granting workers a retirement pension, constitutional reform finally put an end to the constitutional crisis that had gone on for four years and which, since the government was dissolved in 1910, had forced Asquith's cabinet to rely on the support of Irish voters whose sole concern was Home Rule. Women thus had to make their way through an exceedingly complex political and parliamentary equation in order to voice their demands for suffrage. According first to Churchill and later to Lloyd George (both of whom nonetheless personally favored women's voting rights), the gradual introduction of women's suffrage, which was the only option then being considered, was likely initially to benefit the Conservatives. Tipping the balance in that direction would only further diminish chances for retirement benefits and Home Rule alike. Priority was thus given to the social budget in order to enable constitutional reform. Finally passed in August 1911, the reform was voted in only under the Louis-Philippe-style threat to nominate a large number of new Lords for the sole purpose of outnumbering the majority that was hostile to democratic progress.

Did women's hopes also lie in this measure? Would they benefit from the liberal government's appeals, which, thanks to Lloyd George, took into account the demands of social policy in an industrial country that was largely reliant on female labor? In any event, moderate or not, women were willing to put their faith in the government, and the activists decreed a one-year truce, from November 1910 to November 1911. For the next 12 months they followed the parliamentary meandering of a plan for electoral reform, called the Law of Conciliation, which succeeded in arousing real interest in the country. Voted at first and second readings in the House of Commons in the spring of 1911, it seemed to go so smoothly that its opponents began to invoke procedural difficulties: was it not better to prepare this plan through a commission made up of representatives of both houses of Parliament? Would the agenda authorize sufficiently deep discussion before the end of the session? Was it not better to proceed by special law or by a women's amendment proposed on the occasion of a broader plan?

On 7 November 1911, Asquith put an end to all speculation on the issue by declaring that he had reverted to his initial plan for a reform that was to extend men's right to suffrage, to which an amendment on women's suffrage could be appended. Appalled by this betrayal, the WSPU called a demonstration for 21 November. That event turned violent when the demonstrators, armed with bags of stones that had been distributed to them, physically attacked the seats of the ministries as well as the governmental parties. Three hundred women were arrested, sentenced, and imprisoned for a month. The radicalization began again and did not even stop when Churchill had the "in and out" law voted in 1913, which was instantly nicknamed the "Cat and Mouse Act." The law was intended to gain immediate release for women whose lives were threatened by the hunger strikes that they had begun upon their imprisonment.

After 21 November 1911, the women's suffrage movement would no longer be the same. The celebration had become a tragedy that culminated in the spectacular death of Emily Davidson, on 14 June 1913, when she threw herself beneath the feet of the horse that was pulling the royal carriage through the streets of London. Unity was shattered until the war. Worse yet, there was a split between activists and moderate women: the latter accused the activists of having sabotaged parliamentary procedure, since in March 1912 the House of Commons had revealed its hostility to a right the legislators had voted for the previous year, but which was now being demanded through the use of violence. The crisis even touched the activists, under the authoritarian direction of the Pankhurst family. Founding members, including William and Emmeline Pethick-Lawrence, were ousted. Christabel Pankhurst fled to Paris where she wrote intransigent editorials. Meanwhile, her mother, her sister, and her friend Annie Kenney continued to mobilize in Great Britain, holding illicit meetings and getting themselves sent to prison, from which they were taken out on stretchers.

World War I

The war put an end to the political impasse over the issue of women's suffrage—a measure of democratic justice that had been demanded with such violence that, paradoxically, it was denied in the name of the very democratic peace it intended to

institute. As soon as war was declared, the prisons were opened and the activists set free. Christabel Pankhurst returned to England and, along with her ever-eloquent mother, placed herself in the service of national politics. The Holy Union affected both England and France; everyone went to work, and, in 1918, women made up 90 percent of the labor force in the munitions factories. Earlier, in 1916, the hope of imminent peace had begun to cause people to imagine a postwar period that would be completely different from prewar times, in that women's patriotism and civic discipline would finally qualify them for the right to vote under the conditions stated by Asquith in 1906.

The last act was the revenge of the moderates—Millicent Garrett Fawcett, in particular. On 4 May 1916, she wrote to Asquith, then still prime minister, telling him that rumors of a new plan to extend male suffrage were circulating. She again requested that the question not be decided without considering women's suffrage, since the latter had mobilized during the war, just as men had done. Asquith responded on 7 May, saying that the rumor had no basis in fact and that issue of female suffrage would be weighed "without any prejudice of the past." This was a major step. Thereafter everything happened so quickly that no one could fathom how the issue could have remained intractable for so long. On 16 July it was decided that a committee would be set up to study the problems of voter registration and voting operations. The affair was facilitated by the "great coalition" in the government in which supporters of women's suffrage became the majority in the cabinet. On 3 August, Asquith made his last equivocal speech, saying that he favored women's suffrage after the war but not at the present time. On 26 September, he nevertheless gave the decisive impetus by asking the speaker of the House of Commons to establish a "great commission" made up of deputies and Lords to develop a proposal capable of rallying the majority in both houses.

In December 1916 Lloyd George became prime minister, but on 28 March 1917 Asquith still had enough influence to support the plan in the House of Commons with these famous words: "Some years ago I ventured to use the expression, 'Let the women work out their own salvation.' Well, Sir, they have worked it out during this War" (quoted in Rosen). The measure passed by 341 votes to 62. On 10 January 1918, it passed in the House of Lords by 134 votes to 71. Even the aged Lord Curzon, formerly president of the Anti-Suffragist League, gave up the struggle. Women aged 30 years and older would have the right to vote. In 1919 there were 8,470,000 women registered to vote, as compared to 12,910,000 men. The transition lasted until 1929. Although they became voters, Mrs. Pankhurst and her daughters would never themselves be elected to office. Mrs. Pankhurst died in 1928; in 1930 the eminent politician Stanley Baldwin inaugurated a statue in her memory in the garden of the Victoria Tower, in the shade of the House of Parliament that had finally imposed its conditions.

Great Britain, "the Mother of Parliaments," had followed a course very similar to that found in the Scandinavian countries or in the Netherlands, where, in 1917, the women's vote was the result of an original bargain that would transform the political life of the country. After 25 years of opposition, the Catholics finally rallied around the principle of women's suffrage, but in exchange for support for their parochial schools. At the same time, the electoral law was changed and the majority district ballot abandoned in favor of proportional representation, which, applied to the whole country, gave the parties the monopoly of selecting political personnel. In the northern countries, the model of parliamentary government was showing its flexibility and its adaptability to local circumstances. Unfortunately, developments were different in southern Europe, where women had to wait for a second war before reforms would be institutionalized.

Institutionalization of Reforms: The French Model

For more than a decade scholars have taken an interest in what the Americans were the first to call the "French exception." Various explanations have been proposed for France's unique situation, including centralization, the cult of revolution, the long existence of the Communist Party, the role of secularism in a traditionally Catholic country, the long resistance to accepting the independence of justice in general and of constitutional justice in particular, and so forth.

All these examples converge on the focal point of women's suffrage, the demand for which, always present and always camouflaged, and finally passed over in silence, in the end was satisfied in such an extraordinary way that even those who had been the first to ask for it—feminists and socialists—can no longer account for it. The matter is all the more inscrutable in that, for the nearly 40 years from 1946 to 1984, there was a difference in political behavior between the two sexes, so that the France of the second part of the 20th century is perhaps the only country in which the introduction of women's suffrage has changed outcomes, since on four decisive occasions a women's majority made the political decision against a men's majority.

A few major books have attacked the paradox of delay in France, nation of the rights of man. Curiously, though, these studies have never adopted either the constitutional angle (in which, as in Great Britain, the balance of powers is played out in dialogue with the electoral body) or the parliamentary angle (in which the decision—in this case, a nondecision—is made). Laurence Klejman and Florence Rochefort study the feminist movements under the Third Republic (see Klejman and Rochefort 1989), and Charles Sowerwine deals with their relationship with socialism (see Sowerwine 1978). Raymond Huard and Pierre Rosanvallon set out to clarify the legal or philosophical conditions of gaining universal suffrage (see Huard 1991; Rosanvallon), and Christine Bard gives an overall synthesis of all the women's movements from 1914 to 1940 (see Bard 1995). The study by the U.S. scholars Steven C. Hause and Anne R. Kenney is thus the best source to consult for an understanding of a form of parliamentary politics that was all the more difficult to grasp in that it erupted both in a Chamber of Deputies that sought to represent the interests of more than 500 districts and in a Senate heavily influenced by the restrictions of an unwritten "republican tradition" that dictated the career trajectory of each new applicant (see Hause and Kenney).

Such complexities are exemplified by the acts of sabotage—which, in the Senate, took the extreme form of refusal to register on the agenda—led by men such as Georges Clemenceau, president of the council of 1919, and Émile Combes (1835–1921), who until 1922 waged his final battle in favor of a secular society,

which he believed to be the battle of a statesman. Last but not least, there was Jules Jeanneney who, in 1932, won the president's seat of the Senate, which he held until 10 July 1940, when, mute and helpless, he attended his constitutional abdication. Faithful to the Clemenceau tradition that had been his life's honor, Jeanneney had nonetheless managed to incarnate the "republican tradition" all by himself, to such an extent that, won over by de Gaulle in 1942, he entered the government of national unanimity in September 1944, presided over by the "man of 18 June."

As minister of state in the provisional government (seated in Algiers), Jeanneney was charged with organizing local and national elections, and, of course, the two referendums of September 1945. The latter marked the first time that French women had been able to express themselves in a national consultation inquiring into the past (should they go back to the laws of 1875?), into the present (could the government of 18 June continue?), and into the future (should the Constitution written by parliamentarians be submitted for popular ratification?). This was a sensational novelty in France's constitutional history, where the only precedents for direct consultation with the nation's citizens were the constitutional ratifications initiated at the time of the Revolution or under the Bonapartes.

Clemenceau, the "father of victory" in World War I; Jeanneney, the symbol of the republican tradition; de Gaulle, the leader of the Free French, recognized late in June 1940 by Churchill, himself prime minister of a country at war, and the man who in 1944, having become the head of a national committee, signed the order giving women the right to vote. This past, weighty with historical references, avoided neither the divisions in the Consultative Assembly of Algiers nor the silence of a resistance movement that, in order to keep its unity and in the best radical tradition, had withdrawn the issue from the program of the National Council of the Resistance. Clearly, the fate of the women's vote in France calls into question the validity of every symbol of the country's national history in the 20th century: the war of 1914–18, in which the victory of arms preceded the failure of constitutional reconstruction; the war of 1939–45, with its disasters of defeat and decline, soon followed by the galvanizing of the resistance movement and the miracle of the liberation; those events, in turn, gave way to the tragedies of the wars of decolonialization. Under these conditions, it is easy to understand the reservations shown by biographers, who scarcely mention the issue of women's rights, or by historians, who have shown little inclination to examine the facts from the perspective of women's suffrage.

Not until 1994, when Pierre Guiral's biography of Clemenceau—the most recent of many—was published, had a biographer devoted a single line to the topic of his hero's hostile actions against women (see Guiral). The same goes for the only biography of Émile Combes, illuminated throughout with his devotion to his wife and his daughters; that book barely invokes the long-lasting hostility of the president of the democratic left (see Merle). Nevertheless, after a vote by the Chamber of Deputies that sought to link women to the emotion of the victory, he devoted his last strength to delaying the inclusion of a bill on women's suffrage on the agenda until 1922. In so doing, Combes had let pass the moment that was favorable to a desire for a different postwar period. Writers on the general history of 20th-century France do not often pose the question of women's absence up until 1939, or, conversely, that of their arrival on the scene after 1945. Is it possible to think that the sudden emergence of millions of women voters did not bear any weight on the destiny of the country? Imperturbable, the official institutions of the 200-year-old Republic continue to teach that universal suffrage was proclaimed in 1792 and put into practice by the Republic of 1848.

As is so often the case, these silences have their own history—one that reflects the acute difficulties of dealing with a situation in which all the players were miscast. That is why the examination of French history from a women-centered perspective allows one to trace the trajectory of very old demands. In addition, such an approach enables one to grasp the problems, peculiar to the French Republic, of effecting movement on a constitutional territory able to come to terms with its national history—that of the ancien régime and the Revolution, as Tocqueville put it.

In 1789 the proclamation of the rights of man "born free and equal" had been so momentous that, in 1791, its result was the electoral exclusion of women of the nobility or of the great religious orders, which, in France as elsewhere in Europe, had voted in the convocation of the Estates-General. In 1848 republican France had resorted to making a national proclamation to grant men universal suffrage. Women felt all the more excluded since, as in Germany, the right to associate and meet in clubs was expressly taken away from them after the days of social rioting in the years 1848–49. In France as everywhere else in Europe, political demands were made again under the Second Empire and became commonplace around the 1900s. Then, starting in 1910, such demands had been sufficiently achieved to exist as a proposed law, supported by the Commission of Universal Suffrage of the Chamber of Deputies. But there, the "rising tide of peril" brought things to a halt.

In 1919, when constitutional Europe legalized political rights for women, it was no longer the principle but rather the mechanism that was lacking in republican France. In fact, from defeat of Jules Ferry in the presidential elections of December 1887—a failure that was immediately followed by a crisis in 1888–89, when the popular General Boulanger pressed for institutional revisions—the world of radical republicans condemned in principle the very process of constitutional change. This meant that the French Republic entrusted its fate entirely to a "parliamentary government" in which the Senate was promoted as the sanctuary of a "republican tradition," and which no longer knew how to open up or how to evolve.

In France the political exclusion of women thus reflected a more general situation in which the executive power was incapable of bringing to fruition a constitutional change or an electoral program that did not have the senate's approval. Thus, republican France, which was also the France of universal suffrage, let itself be intimidated and paralyzed by the maneuvers of the "conscript fathers," instead of threatening a change in the manner of nominating senators, as Lloyd George had done for the House of Lords, and as Roosevelt did later with regard to justices of the United States Supreme Court. Worse yet, the governments tacitly accepted conditions of complicit silence and pejorative innuendo, thereby forming the habit of granting women's exclusion no more importance than was given to that of Jews, deprived of their citizenship in 1940, or to that of the indigenous peoples in the French colonies, who were to be excluded

from the right to national voting by the two consecutive Constituent Assemblies of 1946.

These are the reasons why the history of women's suffrage in France provides such an ample field for study. In contrast to the countries of northern and central Europe, where women's vote brought with it a system of proportional representation in which their impact dissolved, French history experienced women's political arrival at a time when great constitutional decisions were finally proposed and submitted to the free choice of the people. Thus, in 1945, as was also true for Belgium and Italy, France had to emerge from the provisional climate of the liberation. But in France, the dramas of decolonialization provoked a delivery of change "by forceps" in 1958, when the Fourth Republic, proportionalist and powerless, was replaced by the Fifth Republic. In the Fifth Republic, restoration of decision-making power went hand in hand with a rise in power of constitutional justice, which, in the end, was to upset the balance of powers of the old parliamentary regime. The transformation took place across an unprecedented succession of national consultations, of which the cumulative effect, thanks to women's return to the political scene, was to facilitate a calming of the nation's memories of a tumultuous past. The enduring paradox of French democratic society is that within it, a political present from which women were excluded could be made to coexist with a morality of the past in which women had had a solid place.

As Mona Ozouf has characterized this situation: from the pediment of cathedrals to the salons that were antechambers to the Academy, from the theater to the pairs of teachers in the public schools, one of the French society's distinctive features is that it has always known how to create spaces of sociability (see Ozouf). In these spaces men and women, on equal footing, could exchange elements in a very old intellectual commerce, through ceremony, the art of conversation, laughter, or professional experience. This is why, now that the political and constitutional evolution has been completed, it is possible to look at the whole of this history with a fresh eye, a history that, dying as we watch, marks the end of the French exception.

Women's Rights Activists of the Past

The happy outcome of the story of women's suffrage in France should not lead us to overlook the courage of the pioneers. Maria Vérone has already been cited as a prominent figure in the parliamentary battle. Other major figures include Hubertine Auclert (1848–1914), who broke with the socialists to devote herself exclusively to working for women's right to vote, and Maria Deraismes (1828–91), who challenged the notion that civil rights were a necessary precondition for women's suffrage and created a breach in a society locked into the Civil Code of 1804, in which married women, considered legal minors, were immured inside the family circle. In 1900, the modern turning point was made with Marguerite Durand, the organizer of the International Congress of Women's Rights attended by Ferdinand Buisson, René Viviani, and Joseph Bathélémy. In the 1930s, Louise Weiss picked up the torch; she was amazed to discover "emancipated women" who were so well integrated into the political parties—and even into Léon Blum's Socialist government—that they ended up forgetting that they were deprived of the right to vote.

Maria Deraismes represented the first republican generation that, under the governments of Napoleon III and the "moral order," developed the mechanisms for rehabilitating through "enlightenment" a universal male suffrage that had been abused. Rich and well educated, close to Freemasonry and the ideas that Jules Ferry was to express in April 1870 in his speech on educational equality that applied to women as well, Deraismes gave priority to the medium of law and coeducational schooling. She was associated with *Le droit des femmes* and *L'avenir des femmes*, publications created in 1869 and 1870 with Léon Richer, which survived until 1891. In 1878 she was also the organizer of the First International French Congress for Women's Rights. In addition to the issue of education for girls (including special responsibilities envisioned for women in the education of young children), the congress called for the opening up of the professions, equal wages, access to labor relations boards, and the ability to testify in courts of law. This was also the congress at which Desraismes broke with Hubertine Auclert, over Auclert's refusal to accept that general situation of the Republic might impose delays or restrictions upon women's political rights.

Auclert (1848–1914) incarnated a radical approach to women's suffrage and often found herself in a position of isolation. Thus, she wandered politically from Léon Gambetta, symbol of republican democracy who proclaimed the Third Republic on 4 September 1870 to Boulanger, and from *La fronde*, a daily newspaper (1897–1903) headed by Marguerite Durand (1864–1936), with Severine (1855–1929) who sought to unite the various women's suffrage movements, as far even as the nationalist and anti-Semitic *La libre parole*, founded by Édouard Drumont (1844–1917) in 1892. Then, in 1891, her own publication *La citoyenne* was taken away from her. Endowed with a small private income, she had arrived in Paris in 1872 to "enroll in the feminist army," which Victor Hugo and Deraismes had called for at a banquet organized by the editors of *Le droit des femmes*. Auclert devoted herself to this cause until the priority she gave to women's suffrage moved her away from it. In 1876 she established the Société du Droit des Femmes (Society of Women's Rights), shortly thereafter renamed Suffrage des Femmes (Women's Suffrage). When the Congress of 1878 barred her from speaking, Auclert resigned and began to take direct action. In 1879, she wrote to the president of the Republic to point out that women paid taxes without having the right of consent to those taxes; after an unsuccessful attempt to register to vote, she wrote the prefect to tell him she would not pay. Only after her furniture had been seized did she give up; a year later she burst into the middle of a civil marriage in the town hall of the 10th arrondissement to call the couple's attention to the injustices toward women written into the Civil Code.

Thereafter she began an independent life, barely interrupted by a marriage that took her to Algeria; her husband's death in 1892 brought her back to France. She resumed her activities among the deputies, lobbying them to vote for laws favorable to women, finally securing their rights to be elected to boards of labor relations and to sit down at work, especially in department stores. She continued to introduce petitions and campaigns, one of the most successful of which came in 1901. To protest against the issue of a stamp picturing a woman presenting the Déclara-

tion des Droits de l'Homme (Declaration of the Rights of Man), she countered with the image of a man holding the tablets inscribed with the Rights of Women on his lap. As time passed, the French suffragists engaged in more forceful means of action: in 1908 Auclert, together with Caroline Kauffman, overturned ballot boxes and ended up in court; the same fate awaited Madeleine Pelletier when she broke the windows of a polling place. In 1910 about 20 women presented themselves at the legislative elections, the last action in which Auclert participated.

The lot of French activists would have resembled that of the English suffragettes had it included mass participation on jubilant days or "martyrs" on days of mourning. Why was there such indifference on the part of French women, who did not truly become involved? Explanations vary. There was the weight of personalities and individualities. But there were more profound reasons as well. The socialists contended that women workers should mobilize for the union struggle, and that they did not need to place any more emphasis on the electoral ballot than did their comrades. The republicans, as Deraismes's case illustrates, were paralyzed by the fear of the Church's influence on "unenlightened" women. And the Catholic world, which had long been hostile, would not begin to understand the obligations of rallying to the vote, which the pope had been demanding for ten years, until the turn of the century. Thus, French Catholicism became receptive and one of the strongest supporters of women's suffrage during the interwar period but proposed a "family vote." The Church envisioned that the women's vote would help restore political equilibrium, offsetting the state clericalism that had become omnipresent since its victory against anti-Dreyfus nationalism, and which also served as a brake on the vote of legal measures such as taxes on revenue or the status of civil service.

This quasi-governmental turning point can be traced in *La revue bleue* during the early part of the 20th century in two articles that clearly evoke the destabilizing of a moderate world that was ostensibly to support a new generation. Accounts of the 1900 feminist congress were sympathetic, but even though women's civil and professional demands were considered legitimate, silence still reigned over their political rights. Two years later, on the other hand, Émile Faguet of the Académie Française cited books by the "feminist" Abbé Nolo and by Étienne Lamy, a Catholic republican, to remind people that French women had voted under the ancien régime as they were presently voting in state of Wyoming in the United States; he argued that "conquering the ballot box should be the first objective of French women." From that time on, important figures in French society participated in the fight.

In 1909, after ten years in power, the politics of the "Left bloc" was threadbare. Everyone sought a "reclassification of parties" brought about by electoral reform, which, more respectful of minorities, would be organized around an electoral list and some form of proportional representation. Led by Aristide Briand, a one-time Socialist and, above all, the man chiefly responsible for the draft law separating Church and state, the 1910 elections were held on this theme. In this new climate in 1909, Jeanne Schmal and Jane Misme founded the Union Française pour le Suffrage des Femmes (French Union for Women's Suffrage), which, as a member of the International Alliance for Women's Suffrage, was willing to break with French tradition and limit its demands to the right to regional or municipal voting. In the same spirit, Cécile Brunschwicg in 1911 founded the Ligue des Électeurs pour le Suffrage des Femmes (League of Voters for Women's Suffrage) along with Ferdinand Buisson; the latter, as president of the commission of universal suffrage, had just written an encyclopedic report, *Le vote des femmes* (1911; The Women's Vote).

It was thus against the politics of the "bloc" of secular radicals that extended from Combes to Clemenceau, and in the convergence of independent socialists and constitutional republicans around the issue of proposed electoral reforms, that Dussaussoy's proposal for women's suffrage slowly wended its way forward from 1906 on. Seemingly, the proposal had reached port when Raymond Poincaré became president of the council in 1912. Elected president of the Republic a year later, Poincaré seemed to show his steadfast support when he successively named to the presidency of the council Aristide Briand, the first independent socialist to achieve such responsibilities, and René Viviani, a lawyer well known for his battles on behalf of the professional and political rights of women.

Governmental Silence, a Prince's Decisions, and the "Dynamics of Difference"

Until 1914 French politics were not fundamentally different from those of the other European countries. Governed by republicans, France had a more open regime than Germany did, and the liberals in power were comparable to their English counterparts. The feminist movement existed and enjoyed broad support, and French women had devoted themselves to the Holy Union with the same ardor as Great Britain. Finally, after four years of war, the thirst for civil peace and renewal was equally great on both sides of the Channel. What was different was Lloyd George and Clemenceau.

While Lloyd George had always supported women's suffrage, Clemenceau for just as long had been hostile to everything that might strengthen the Constitution of the Republic, be it the right to dissolve the executive power or a change in the majority electoral law in the setting of the administrative division. He had been violently opposed to Jules Ferry's candidacy for president of the Republic. As president of the council from 1906 to 1909, Clemenceau sought to ensure the failure of the proposals for electoral reform. As president of the council in 1919, he kept silent during the week of 8–20 May 1919, when women's suffrage was discussed in the Chamber of Deputies—the same week that the preliminaries to peace were signed in Versailles. Christine Bard notes that on 17 February 1919 Clemenceau had received the feminists to tell them that he was in favor of a municipal vote. After the war years, during which many women had held the office of mayor or company director, this was ludicrous—all the more so because this half-measure was incomprehensible in a country used to reasoning in terms of access to rights and not in terms of progressive emancipation.

In any case, this argument was turned around by opponents of women's suffrage, who held that the idea of limiting women's vote to the local level was precisely an indication of the "danger" such a measure posed to the institutions of the Republic. Indeed, why limit the "danger" to municipal councils, the closest to

the population? Interpretations of the modest and reasonable proposal by Pierre-Étienne Flandin and the Socialist Alexandre Varenne became all the more twisted because the government remained silent. And the silence of the president of the council itself became an argument that was construed differently to suit the agendas of different people—even René Viviani and Aristide Briand, who contended that there was no "danger" at all and that, therefore, the Chamber of Deputies should have the courage to vote for universal suffrage for both men and women. Ultimately, the measure passed by 344 votes against 97. "Treacherous votes," announced the headlines in the "unofficial" paper *Le temps* the next day. In fact, this success was a trap set by the deputies, who, elected as senators at the end of the year, became hostile thereafter. Integral women's suffrage frightened the "secular" Senate, leaving the field open for stratagems of postponement that would continue until 1944.

This was how French politics isolated itself from the liberal politics of the Continent. Nothing could be done that would not have the endorsement of the "democratic Left" of the senate, a parliamentary group whose attitude on the women's vote was the exact opposite of its name. These senators were nevertheless a patriotic group that had to be handled carefully in the face of the "rising tide of peril" that coincided with an increase in pacifism. The utmost discretion was also necessary, since, as Claire Andrieu tells us, it was to gain the support of Paul Bastid, a member of the Radical Party and of the Comité Général d'Experts (CGE; General Commission of Experts) that the national council of the resistance left the quasi-mythical question of women's suffrage out of its agenda. Having fallen victim to the government's silences and refusals to make a decision for 20 years, the women's vote was finally attained through a supreme decision by General de Gaulle, announced on 23 June 1942 in the underground French press: "Once the enemy has been chased out of our land, all our men and all our women will elect the National Assembly, which will be sovereign in deciding the nation's destiny." This would be repeated in the ruling on the provisional organization of civil powers of 21 April 1944.

In his *Mémoires de Guerre* (c. 1955–60; *The Complete War Memoirs of Charles de Gaulle, 1940–46*), de Gaulle is brief, limiting himself to mentioning that women's right to vote and to be elected has put an end to a struggle that had lasted half a century. This terseness is understandable, given the ongoing debates within the resistance, where the former "Clemencist" radicals, supporters of the bicameral system and the exclusion of women, stood in opposition to the movements deriving from elements in the resistance dominated by "good-natured" socialism that hoped for a single legislative assembly elected by proportional and sovereign representation. The latter position was the exact opposite of the constitutional ideas on the necessary "separation of powers" that de Gaulle developed at the time of the liberation and that would motivate his departure in 1946. He would have to wait until 1958 to put these ideas into practice.

Unquestionably, de Gaulle's ideas were of a national and governmental order and were nurtured by his own prewar experience. In fact, in 1932, from his position at the Secretariat of National Defense, de Gaulle, then a colonel, had directly witnessed and been disheartened by Senate debates charged by calls to "defend" a Republic that was threatened by feminism, as in earlier days by Boulangism or nationalism, and this while Hitler had already entered his race for the chancellorship on the other side of the Rhine. The second scorching memory was the defeat of his friend Paul-Boncour's attempt to use the law on the organization of the nation in times of war (which would end up by being voted in 1938) to open career opportunities to a corps of women volunteers. This was an error that Free France would not commit since, when it was transformed into "fighting France" in June 1942, and thus at the time of de Gaulle's "Message to the Resistance" on the second anniversary of his celebrated 18 June appeal to the nation, there would be a special decree on the organization of French women volunteers. No better link could have been made between the defense of liberty and induction into citizenship. But, as was his custom, de Gaulle made things known by action rather than by proclamation.

From then on, the negative stratagems of the radicals mattered as little as the actions of Fernand Grenier, the Communist deputy who had rallied to London in 1923, and who liked to say that it was to him that French women owed their power to vote. Just as the continued activism of Louise Weiss had shown that not all women of the prewar period had been lulled into complacency by the honor of the few women members of the Radical Party, the speeches of Grenier or Louis Vallon showed that the Socialist and Communist Left had finally overcome the obstacle of secularism. That was a step forward for French political society rather than for General de Gaulle, who, far from using women in the exclusively negative chore of class anticommunism, instead knew how to enlist them in the very constructive work of establishing a Republic that, constitutional at last, would institute the separation of powers and the guarantee of rights inscribed in the Declaration of the Rights of Man.

Since the decision of principle had been publicly announced in 1942, and since the Assembly of Algiers was only consultative, it should be noted that the leader of Free France, so respectful of the future of sovereign decision-making power in the liberated

of difference"—comparable to the English expression "gender gap." In fact, it turns out that a change in constitutional regime allowed for a great variety of national consultations—referendum, presidential election, or dissolutions of the National Assembly on the initiative of the president. Such openness of the political system made it possible to observe and analyze the political consequences of women's access to political rights. It was possible to observe the effects of the female vote in France more precisely than in Italy and Belgium. In contrast to the latter countries, women's entrance into the political realm in France followed upon a century of exclusively male universal suffrage. A male world, fractured and "made absolute" by a political culture and memories—of the Revolution, Bonaparte's coup d'état, anticlericalism, and antifascism—with regard to which the memories of women, situated outside of the political center yet within the national community, were freer. The "dynamics of their difference" would come to play on four decisive occasions; their cumulative result would be the transformation of the "absolute Republic," a legacy from the past, into a "constitutional Republic," a conquest of the future.

It was known early in the century that women participated less frequently than men in elections and that they more often voted in favor of the "conservatives." In our day, Janine Mossuz-Lavau has refined the statistics on the gender gap (see Mossuz-Lavau). In particular, she notes that the gap between male and female voting behaviors almost disappeared in France around the 1980s. Those were also years when, as a result of electoral changes becoming commonplace, the constitutional transformation of the country was completed, and when revolutionary political parties had only a residual presence. It was precisely this transformation that was facilitated by the female vote, which on four occasions determined—or at least further strengthened—the results of an election.

	Women		Men	
5 May 1946	YES	NO	YES	NO
(referendum)	36	62	50	50
19 Dec. 1965	Mitterrand	De Gaulle	Mitterrand	De Gaulle
(presidential election)	39	61	51	49
19 May 1974	Mitterrand	Valéry Giscard-d'Estaing	Mitterrand	Valéry Giscard-d'Estaing
(presidentia election)	47	53	54	46l

country, nevertheless gave himself the permission to sign into effect two measures that were revolutionary with regard to "republican tradition." These were women's suffrage and government-initiated constitutional referendum. As in Italy and Belgium, the right to universal suffrage for French women came at the same time as the right to a constitutional referendum. In Belgium the referendum was used to protect the monarchy; in Italy it was used first to consolidate the young republic, and later, in the 1970s, to preserve the divorce law. France used it several times to defend its constitutional liberties: in 1946, and then on different occasions between 1958 and 1981. But the proportional electoral laws that were introduced at the same time in France as in other states prevent taking the comparisons further. Practically speaking, only France experienced to a measurable degree what Geneviève Fraisse has called the "dynamics

In May 1946 a female majority refused a Constitution presented by an exclusively Marxist-Socialist coalition. This first "NO" in French political history forced the election of a new assembly and the writing of a Constitution in which the president of the Fourth Republic reclaimed the freedom to "designate" the president of the council. This prerogative allowed President René Coty, in the face of the Algerian crisis, to call upon General de Gaulle, who was far outside the world of parliamentary representation. In December 1965, under the government of the Fifth Republic, it was again a female majority that reelected General de Gaulle to lead the state, after a run-off ballot that exorcised the Bonapartist specter of the 19th century a second time. In May 1974, differing for the third time, a female majority elected Valéry Giscard-d'Estaing, one of whose first gestures was to extend to parliamentarians the right of seizing of the Constitutional Council. The full implications of that procedure were not assessed at the time, but its beneficial effects would be felt after 1981 with the election of François Mitterrand, the most talented adversary of the 1958 institutions as head of state. In 1981 women played the same role in favor of constitutional liberties, since, after Mitterrand's election by a male majority, a gain of more than ten points in women's votes between the presidential and the legislative elections allowed the Socialist Party to have a large majority in the National Assembly. From the start, this result freed the head of the state from a debt to the Communist Party, which French women had already challenged in 1946, 1965, and 1974.

Today, the institutional revolution begun during the liberation is complete and France is reconciled with its past, thanks to the new practice of republican constitutionalism, which alternates direct consultations and representative elections under the higher control of Justice. In the mid– 1990s, French women, reintegrated into a political body that had long excluded them, voted more moderately, as in other European countries. Just as in earlier days they used to vote in lesser numbers than men for the French Communist Party, women in recent years have voted less frequently than men for the National Front, a movement whose violence calls into question the triumph over "ordinary sexism," as Mossuz-Lavau points out. This is yet another expression of women's "conservatism" with regard to a time-tested system of liberties. Today, now that constitutional acclamation has been completed, French women are beginning to watch the electoral results in terms of women elected, thereby joining the preoccupation with "parity" which, in the northern countries, has almost been achieved.

Conclusions: "Representation" or Decision?

By the end of the 20th century, the history of European women's attainment of political rights belonged to a bygone past—so distant that people may disregard the historic circumstances that made it possible, particularly the burden of the two world wars. But by eviscerating societies, by forcing them to superhuman efforts of mobilization, and by producing unparalleled suffering that required subsequent "reparations" of all kinds, the wars changed people's outlook in a very short period of time and, through "revolutionary," "parliamentary," or "institutional" means, enabled the advent of women's rights to vote and to be elected, which had long seemed unthinkable to male brains, prisoners as they were of ideas about a female "nature," ideas that originated more in prejudice and learned culture than in intangible laws.

Today the time for assessment has come. A landscape has emerged in which the power of the vote varies with the social-political and geopolitical climate. The potential of the vote is nonexistent if, as in so-called "socialist" Europe, it is not accompanied by any of the freedoms of assembly, association, publication, and candidacies known in our liberal democracies. That potential becomes more real when parties begin to reflect on the orientations best suited to winning and keeping the loyalties of a female electorate renowned for its volatility. Or again when governments take the trouble to submit true, simple questions

to direct universal suffrage. And above all, women, who dread conflicts and love peace, need a regular political life in order to initiate, organize, and see the politics of their choice succeed.

The assessment of women's attainment of political rights in Western Europe is therefore ambivalent and varies, depending upon the question asked. Has women's suffrage been favorable to women? Has their presence changed the course of politics or not? For an initial sense, one need only refer to an excellent synthesis by Joni Lovenduski and Pippa Norris, entitled *Gender and Party Politics* (1993). As the title indicates, the different chapters show the results of comparative research done in Western countries. The study provides strict and accurate statistics on party policy, measured by the yardstick of recruitment, promotions, and elections. The ideological environment in different cases is taken into account and helps explain the results. Whereas Socialist parties practiced a quota policy or that of a minimum of obligatory representation for women, conservative parties tended to prefer a top-down policy of appointment, which, in terms of parliamentary seats or ministerial positions, may have proven just as effective. Further, what was true in John Major's Great Britain was also true in Helmut Kohl's Germany and, early on, in the France of Jacques Chirac.

For the past 50 years there has also been another, ongoing questioning within the political parties, previously dominated by men: what should be done to gain the female vote? Early on, it was the social victory of the welfare state of the years of liberation or the measures of moral freedom of the 1960s. Later the problematic shifted: the figure of the stay-at-home mother was abandoned in favor of the woman employed outside the home, the woman entrusted with responsibilities, the woman as candidate for a position of power, and the series of measures taken to ensure more balanced female "representation" in the electoral body. This process introduced a kind of proportional obligation into electoral laws, although its potential impact on political decision making was not even mentioned.

A few examples are given here simply to elicit reflection on the political consequences of electoral laws that are majority or proportional laws. What has weighed more heavily in matters of political decision: women elected to the European Parliament thanks to the quotas, or Margaret Thatcher, a pure product of the majority system? Experience has shown that politics does not change in "nature" with the arrival of women in positions of political decision making in Norway and Sweden, where ideas about female representation and measures equalizing the possibilities of proportional access to positions of responsibility have been pushed very far. At very most there is an oscillation between the preference given to each of the two traditional women's roles: family role or professional role? Roles assumed alone or shared equally? But in the meantime, these questions continue to be marginal when compared to the totality of the problems that come up in the life of a nation.

At the same time, all those who hope that Europe will finally succeed in becoming a "decision-making center" in financial, diplomatic, and military matters know full well that this progress will happen only by extending the field of decision making to the majority. It is the decision of the majority that gives strength of conviction and drive to both our representative and our constitutional democracies, just as it is the succession of changes in different political forces that is the best tool for teaching citizens the constitutional value of public institutions. The point is only strengthened by the fact that historically, women's access to political rights has quite often been linked to the attainment of national independence. Loyal to these old memories even today, it is women who, throughout Europe, in their unassuming way, show the greatest skepticism regarding the achievements of the "European construction."

With the exception of Great Britain—and the United States, which is outside the scope of this study—the recognition of women's political rights has generally gone hand in hand with the introduction of electoral proportional representation. The result has not always been good. It has even been frankly bad at times, as in the Weimar Republic, the new republics of Central Europe, the Fourth Republic of France, or the First Republic of Italy. On the other hand, the institutional evolution of republican France shows that an electoral majority made of up women has, under certain serious circumstances, been able to put into play a "dynamics of difference" that has caused the balance to lean on the side of "constitutional patriotism," so highly prized today. In contrast to the Germany of the Weimar Republic, where their difference was crushed, the women voters of France at the liberation and in the Fifth Republic have been able on four occasions to have their weight counted in a political decision that has been favorable to the national community as a whole in terms of civil peace and the progress of freedom. Such is the assessment of 50 years of mixed universal suffrage, in which the political life of the nation has indeed been marked by the electoral dialogue of the voters, male and female, as the latter finally came back into the political body of a nation in which their social place had never been underestimated.

Thus, a fair desire for "representation" should not make one forget that politics is decision making as much as representation, and that the most important decisions, even when negotiated with the representative authorities, are more appropriate and welcome when they come from a political majority system than from an exclusively proportional system.

Bibliography

Sources

Auclert, Hubertine, *La citoyenne: Articles de 1881 à 1891*, with preface and commentary by Edith Taieb, Paris: Syros, 1982

Auclert, Hubertine, *Le vote des femmes*, Paris: Giard et Briére, 1908; reprint, 1983

Barthélémy, Joseph, *Le vote des femmes*, Paris: Alcan, 1920

Bebel, August, *Woman in the Past, Present, and Future*, translated by H.B. Adams Walther, London: The Modern Press, 1885; reprint, London: Zwan, 1988

Buisson, Ferdinand Édouard, *Le vote des femmes*, Paris: Dunod et Pinat, 1911

Deraismes, Maria, *Ce que veulent les femmes: Articles et conférences de 1869 à 1891*, Paris: Syros, 1980

Divoire, Fernand, editor, *La femme émancipée*, Brussels, F. Van Bruggenhoudt; and Paris, Éditions Montaigne, 1927

Engels, Friedrich, *The Origin of the Family, Private Property, and the State*, translated by Ernest Untermann, Chicago: Kerr, 1902; reprint, 1974

Fawcett, Millicent Garrett, *What I Remember*, London: Unwin, 1924; New York: Putnam, 1925; reprint, Westport, Connecticut: Hyperion Press, 1976

Lamy, Étienne, *La femme de demain*, Paris: Perrin, 1901; reprint, 1932

Macmillan, Chrystal, Marie Stritt, and Maria Vérone, compilers, *Woman Suffrage in Practice, 1913*, London: National Union of Women's Suffrage Societies, and New York: National American Women's Suffrage Association, 1913

Pankhurst, Estelle Sylvia, *The Suffragette Movement: An Intimate Account of Persons and Ideals*, London and New York: Longmans Green, 1931

Pelletier, Madeleine, *La femme en lutte pour ses droits*, Paris: Giard et Brière, 1908; reprint, 1975

Pelletier, Madeleine, "La question du vote des femmes," *La revue socialiste* (September–October 1908)

Pethick-Lawrence, Emmeline, *My Part in a Changing World*, London: Gollancz, 1938; reprint, Westport, Connecticut: Hyperion Press, 1976

Roussel, Nelly, *Paroles de combat et d'espoir: Discours choisis, 1903–1914*, Épône, France: Éditions de l'Avenir Social, 1919

Weiss, Louise, *Mémoires d'une Européenne*, 6 vols., Paris: Payot, 1968–76; see especially vol. 3, *1934–1939*, 1970

Witt-Schlumberger, Marguerite de, *La situation internationale des femmes en mars 1918*, Paris: Union Française pour le Suffrage des Femmes, 1919

Zetkin, [Clara], *Reminiscences of Lenin; Dealing with Lenin's Views on the Position of Women and Other Questions*, London: Modern Books, 1929

Reference Works

Agulhon, Maurice, and Pierre Bonte, *Marianne: Les visages de la République*, Paris: Gallimard, 1992

Albistur, Maïté, and Daniel Armogathe, *Histoire du féminisme français du Moyen Age à nos jours*, Paris: des femmes, 1977

Andrieu, Claire, *Le programme commun de la Résistance: Des idées dans la guerre*, Paris: L'Érudit, 1984

Andrieu, Claire, "Femmes," in *1938–48, Les années de tourmente, de Munich à Prague*, edited by Jean-Pierre Azéma and François Bédarida, Paris: Flammarion, 1995

Aulard, François Alphonse, and Boris Sergieevich Mirkin-Getsevich, *Les déclarations des droits de l'homme: Textes constitutionnels concernant les droits de l'hommes et les garanties des libertés individuelles dans tous les pays*, Paris: Payot, 1929; reprint, Aalen, Germany: Scientia, 1977

Bard, Christine, "Femmes (droit du vote des)," in *Dictionnaire du vote*, edited by Pascal Perrineau and Rominique Reynié, Paris: Presses Universitaires de France, 2001

Bard, Christine, *Les filles de Marianne: Histoire des féminismes, 1914–1940*, Paris: Fayard, 1995

Bartley, Paula, *Votes for Women, 1860–1928*, London: Hodder and Stoughton Educational, 1998

Berstein, Serge, and Pierre Milza, *Histoire de la France au XXe siècle*, 5 vols., Brussels: Complexe, 1995

Bossuyt, Marc J., *L'interdiction de la discrimination dans le droit international des droits de l'homme*, Brussels: Bruylant, 1976

Butler, L.J., and Harriet Jones, editors, *Britain in the Twentieth Century: A Documentary Reader*, 2 vols., Oxford: Institute of Contemporary British History, and Portsmouth, New Hampshire: Heinemann Educational, 1994

Capel Martínez, Rosa María, *El sufragio feminino en la IIa República Española*, Madrid: Horas y Horas: Dirección General de la Mujer, Comunidad de Madrid, 1992

Charlot, Monica, editor, *Les femmes dans la société britannique*, Paris: Colin, 1977

Commaille, Jacques, *Les stratégies des femmes: Travail, famille et politique*, Paris: La Découverte, 1993

De Gaulle, Charles, *Mémoires de guerre*, 3 vols., Paris: Plon, 1954; as *War Memoirs*, 5 vols., New York: Viking Press, 1955–60; see especially vol. 2, *Unity, 1942–1944*, translated by R. Howard, 1959

Del Re, Alisa, *Les femmes et l'état-providence: Les politiques sociales en France dans les années trente*, Paris: L'Harmattan, 1994

Dogan, Mattei, "L'origine sociale du personnel parlementaire d'un pays essentiellement agraire: La Roumanie," *Revue de l'Institut de Sociologie*, nos. 2–3 (1953)

Dogan, Mattei, "Il voto delle donne in Italia e in altre democrazie," *Tempi moderni dell'econmia, della politica e della cultura* 2, nos. 11–12 (February 1959)

Dogan, Mattei, and Jacques Narbonne, *Les Françaises face à la politique: Comportement politique et condition sociale*, Paris: Colin, 1955

Duby, Georges, and Michèle Perrot, editors, *A History of Women in the West*, 5 vols., Cambridge, Massachusetts: Belknap Press of Harvard University, 1992–94 (originally in French); see especially vol. 5, *Toward a Cultural Identity in the Twentieth Century*, edited by Françoise Thébaud

Duverger, Maurice, *La participation des femmes à la vie politique*, Paris: Unesco, 1955

Evans, Richard J., *Comrades and Sisters: Feminism, Socialism, and Pacifism in Europe, 1870–1945*, Brighton, Sussex: Wheatsheaf Books, and New York: St. Martin's Press, 1987

Fauré, Christine, *La démocratie sans les femmes: Essai sur le libéralisme en France*, Paris: Presses Universitaires de France, 1985; as *Democracy without Women: Feminism and the Rise of Liberal Individualism in France*, translated by Claudia Gorbman and John Berks, Bloomington: Indiana University Press, 1991

Fraisse, Geneviève, *Muse de la raison: La démocratie exclusive et la différence des sexes*, Aix-en-Provence, France: Alinéa, 1989; as *Reason's Muse: Sexual Difference and the Birth of Democracy*, translated by Jane Marie Todd, Chicago: University of Chicago Press, 1994

French, Marilyn, *The War against Women*, New York: Summit Books, and London: Hamilton, 1992

Fulford, Roger, *Votes for Women: The Story of a Struggle*, London: Faber and Faber, 1957

Galligan, Yvonne, *Women and Politics in Contemporary Ireland: From the Margins to the Mainstream*, London and Washington, D.C.: Pinter, 1998

Ghesquière, Ilse, et al., *Parcours singuliers: Portraits de 10 élues en 1921*, Brussels: Ministère de l'Emploi et du Travail et de la Politique d'Égalité des Chances, 1994

La Gorce, Paul-Marie de, *La prise du pouvoir par Hitler, 1928–1933*, Paris: Plon, 1983

Gruber, Helmut, and Pamela Graves, editors, *Women and Socialism, Socialism and Women: Europe between the Two World Wars*, New York: Berghahn Books, 1998

Gubin, Eliane, and Leen van Molle, *Femmes et politique en Belgique*, Brussels: Racine, 1998

Guiral, Pierre, *Clemenceau en son temps*, Paris: Grasset, 1994

Halimi, Gisèle, editor, *Femmes: Moitié de la terre, moitié du pouvoir*, Paris: Gallimard, 1994

Hause, Steven C., and Anne R. Kenney, *Women's Suffrage and Social Politics in the French Third Republic*, Princeton, New Jersey: Princeton University Press, 1984

Huard, Raymond, *Le suffrage universel en France, 1848–1946*, Paris: Aubier, 1991

Jordan, Glenn, and Chris Weedon, *Cultural Politics: Class, Gender, Race, and the Postmodern World*, Oxford and Cambridge, Massachusetts: Blackwell, 1995

Klejman, Laurence, and Florence Rochefort, *L'égalité en marche: Le féminisme sous la Troisième République*, Paris: Presses de la Fondation Nationale des Sciences Politiques, and des femmes, 1989

Krug, Charles, "Le féminisme et le droit civil français," Ph.D. diss., Université de Nancy, 1899

La Rochefoucauld, Edmée de, "Le vote des femmes," in vol. 10 of *L'encyclopédie française*, edited by Lucien Lebvre et al., 20 vols., Paris: Société de gestion de l'Encyclopédie française, 1935–66

Le Cour Grandmaison, Olivier, *Les citoyennetés en revolution, 1789–1794*, Paris: Presses Universitaires de France, 1992

Lewis, Jane, *Women in England, 1870–1950: Sexual Divisions and Social Change*, Brighton, Sussex: Wheatsheaf Books, and Bloomington: Indiana University Press, 1984

Lovenduski, Joni, and Jill Hills, editors, *The Politics of the Second Electorate: Women and Public Participation: Britain, USA, Canada, Australia, France, Spain, West Germany, Italy, Sweden, Finland, Eastern Europe, USSR, Japan*, London and Boston: Routledge and Kegan Paul, 1981

Lovenduski, Joni, and Pippa Norris, editors, *Gender and Party Politics*, London and Thousand Oaks, California: Sage, 1993

McMillan, James F., *Dreyfus to de Gaulle: Politics and Society in France, 1898–1969*, London: Arnold, 1985

Merle, Gabriel, *Émile Combes*, Paris: Fayard, 1995

Mirkine-Guetzevich, Boris, and Charles Eisenmann, *Les constitutions de l'Europe nouvelle*, Paris: Delagrave, 1928; 10th edition, 1938

Moghadam, Valentine M., editor, *Democratic Reform and the Position of Women in Transitional Economies*, Oxford: Clarendon Press, and New York: Oxford University Press, 1993

Mossuz-Lavau, Janine, *Femmes et hommes d'Europe aujourd'hui: Les attitudes devant l'Europe et la politique*, Brussels: Communautés Européennes, 1991

Mossuz-Lavau, Janine, "Le vote des femmes en France, 1945–1993," *Revue française de science politique* 43, no. 4 (August 1993)

Ozouf, Mona, *Les mots des femmes: Essai sur la singularité française*, Paris: Fayard, 1995; as *Women's Words: Essay on French Singularity*, translated by Jane Marie Todd, Chicago: University of Chicago Press, 1997

Perrot, Michèle, editor, *Une histoire des femmes: Est-elle possible?* Paris: Rivages, 1984; as *Writing Women's History*, translated by Felicia Pheasant, Oxford and Cambridge, Massachusetts: Blackwell, 1992

Rafroidi, Patrick, Pierre Joannon, and Maurice Goldring, editors, *Dublin, 1904–1924: Réveil culturel, révolte sociale, révolution politique: Un patriotisme déchiré*, Paris: Autrement, 1991

Riot-Sarcey, Michèle, *La démocratie à l'épreuve des femmes: Trois figures critiques du pouvoir, 1830–1848*, Paris: Albin Michel, 1994

Rosanvallon, Pierre, *Le sacre du citoyen: Histoire du suffrage universel en France*, Paris: Gallimard, 1992

Rosen, Andrew, *Rise Up Women: The Militant Campaign of the Women's Social and Political Union, 1903–1914*, London and Boston: Routledge and Kegan Paul, 1974

Rover, Constance, *Women's Suffrage and Party Politics in Great Britain, 1866–1914*, London: Routledge and Kegan Paul, and Toronto: Toronto University Press, 1967

Rudelle, Odile, "Boulanger, Boulangisme," and "Gambetta, Léon," in *Dictionnaire du vote*, edited by Pascal Perrineau and Dominique Reynié, Paris: Presses Universitaires de France, 2001

Rudelle, Odile, *La République absolue: Aux origines de l'instabilité constitutionnelle de la France républicaine*, Paris: Sorbonne, 1982

Rudelle, Odile, "République absolue, République constitutionnelle, en lisant Pierre Birnbaum," *Revue française de science politique* 45, no. 2 (April 1995)

Rudelle, Odile, "La tradition républicaine," *Pouvoirs* 42 (1987)

Rudelle, Odile, "Le vote féminin et la fin de l'exception française," in *XXe Siècle* 42 (April 1994)

Scott, Joan Wallach, *Gender and the Politics of History*, New York: Columbia University Press, 1988

Scott, Joan Wallach, *Only Paradoxes to Offer: French Feminists and the Rights of Man*, Cambridge, Massachusetts: Harvard University Press, 1996

Sineau, Mariette, *Des femmes en politique*, Paris: Economica, 1988

Sowerwine, Charles, *Les femmes et le socialisme: Un siècle d'histoire*, Paris: Presses de la Fondation Nationale des Sciences Politiques, 1978; as *Sisters or Citizens: Women and Socialism in France since 1876*, Cambridge and New York: Cambridge University Press, 1982

Strachey, Ray, *The Cause: A Short History of the Women's Movement in Great Britain*, London: Bell, 1928; as *Struggle: The Stirring Story of Woman's Advance in England*, New York: Duffield, 1930; reprint, as *The Cause: A Short History of the Women's Movement in Great Britain*, London: Virago, 1978

Thalmann, Rita, *Être femme sous le IIIe Reich*, Paris: Laffont, 1982

Thébaud, Françoise, *La femme au temps de la guerre de '14*, Paris: Stock/Pernoud, 1986

Toulemon, André, *Le suffrage familial; ou, Suffrage universel intégral: Le vote des femmes*, Paris: Recueil Sirey, 1933

Uzès, Anne de Rochechouart-Mortemart, *Le suffrage féminin au point de vue historique*, Meulan, France: Firmin Roger, 1914

Vianello, Mino, and Renata Siemienska, *Gender Inequality: A Comparative Study of Discrimination and Participation*, London and Newbury Park, California: Sage, 1990

Voet, Maria Christine Bernadetta, *Feminism and Citizenship*, London and Thousand Oaks, California: Sage, 1998

WOMEN'S ROLE IN THE SPANISH CIVIL WAR

MARY NASH

THE 1931 ESTABLISHMENT OF the Second Republic, a democratic regime, represented a significant change in Spain's political trajectory. That process of democratization soon made the Spanish forget the experience of the dictatorship of Miguel Primo de Rivera (1923–30). The long political course based on corruption and weakening of the constitutional system, which had begun with the Bourbon Restoration in 1875, had consolidated a cultural mistrust of the parliamentary system of representation and had created a political climate that was not conducive to the development of democracy. In fact, until the 1930s, with the political reforms implemented under the Second Republic, the social legitimization of individual political rights had not played an extensive role in the liberal and democratic tradition in Spain.

When the process of democratization under the Second Republic began in 1931, there were still tight restrictions on the social and political recognition of women. The law regulated women's conduct and established their complete subordination, especially where married women were concerned, guaranteeing the patriarchal power of male authority. The Civil Code of 1889, in force until the Second Republic, prescribed a married woman's obligatory obedience to her spouse and made the husband the administrator of the material property of the couple and the wife's legal representative. The Code of Commerce of 1885 required that a married woman seek her husband's authorization before starting a business or working in commerce, and it placed whatever wages she earned in the hands of her spouse. The husband's power was reinforced by measures that would punish any transgression of his authority. According to the Penal Code, disobedience or insults were sufficient cause for a woman's imprisonment, while a man incurred no sanctions unless he mistreated his wife—the same double sexual standard that allowed a man to engage in extramarital relations but severely punished such actions in women, and that was codified in laws on adultery and crimes of passion.

Toward Equality: Women under the Second Republic

The republican regime opened up a political context that was much more favorable to women. The policy of reforms undertaken under the coalition government (1931–33) brought tangible improvements to women's social status. The entire body of discriminatory and coercive measures affecting married women was changed under the legislative reforms of the Second Republic, thanks to the introduction of new laws on marriage and divorce. However, legislation ensuring the legal equality of spouses was introduced only in Catalonia, with a law of 20 June 1934. The political reforms instituted by the democratic government of the Second Republic established the principle of equal rights for men and women. They introduced profound legislative changes that, to a great extent, departed from the traditionally discriminatory treatment of women.

The establishment of a democratic regime immediately posed the problem of women's citizenship, and, consequently, the concrete political problem of women's right to vote. More than a decade earlier, "suffragist"-inspired groups had formed in Spain, but the Spanish suffrage movement was weak and found little political resonance. A few women, such as the socialists Carmen de Burgos, María Lejárraga de Martínez Sierra, Margarita Nelken, and the republican Clara Campoamor had posed the question of women's political rights. Organizations such as the Asociación Nacional de Mujeres Españolas (National Association of Spanish Women) and the Cruzada de Mujeres Españolas (Crusade of Spanish Women) were running active campaigns to eliminate the discriminatory legal measures then in force. These organizations, as well as the Unión Republicana Femenina (Republican Women's Union), created in October 1931 by Campoamor, were inspired by a suffragist politics. They demanded women's right to vote and their political equality with men. They were characterized by their adherence to the theses of egalitarian feminism—that is, liberal-inspired feminism, based on the principle of equal political rights for men and women.

Nevertheless, this demand for women's political rights, founded on the principle of sexual equality, was rather exceptional in the panorama of Spanish feminism. Most women's organizations were not concerned with suffrage and were not dedicated to the demand for women's voting rights. In Spain the women's movements, to the extent that they could be called feminist, were of a sociocultural rather than of a political nature for two reasons. In a setting that was largely unfavorable to constitutional values and to the practice of rights as an instrument of progress, women as a collective social entity did not focus their efforts on political demands or the defense of the principle of equality and individual political rights. In this respect, they resembled other social movements such as anarchism. Until the 1930s, Spanish political culture was unfavorable to the blossoming of a politically inspired liberal feminism comparable to what had developed in Great Britain or the United States.

However, the existing female culture, dominated by discourse centered on the home, contributed heavily, perhaps more than the political culture, to shaping the contours of Spanish feminism. Although prior to the Second Republic Spanish society had rested on a repressive power that mandated the subordination of Spanish women through a discriminatory corpus of laws, the influence of domestic values on women in the shaping of ideas was even more important. That discourse presented a prototype of the ideal woman—the "Angel of Hearth and Home," the "Perfect Wife," the "Woman on the Inside"—as the actualization of women's highest ambitions. Women's social options were limited to a family-centered life plan. Female identities were constructed on the basis of marriage and motherhood, with no possibility of forming independent social, political, or professional goals. The process of economic, cultural, and political modernization during the first decades of the 20th century entailed a more modern conception of a new female archetype—the "New Woman" or the "Modern Woman"—but without changing the traditional domestic values. Motherhood still constituted the essential basis of women's identity.

The maternal archetype served as an informal mechanism of social control and prevented the elaboration of an egalitarian discourse. Furthermore, it influenced the forging of Spanish feminism, which took sexual difference and not sexual equality as its point of departure. The driving force of many demands of Spanish women was precisely the discourse of sexual difference, which served as a justification for the demands of social feminism. This combination of sexual difference and political culture explains Spanish feminists' abandonment of the political arena to focus its aspirations on the social and civil realms instead. This was why socially inspired feminism made access to education and waged work the symbol of its struggle.

To a large extent, Spanish women in the 1930s continued to internalize the traditional norms of womanhood—a perspective that led them to see politics as something foreign to their sex. On the eve of the Second Republic, the suffrage movement still represented only a small minority and had little ability to mobilize. Thus, when Spanish women were granted the right to vote in 1931, this occurred not under pressure from suffrage groups or because of a mobilization of feminists, as in Great Britain or the United States, but within the framework of the overall legislative reforms undertaken by the new regime. It was for reasons of political coherence appropriate to democratic principles that discriminatory laws were revised and women obtained the right to vote.

Women's Right to Vote

The parliamentary debate on women's suffrage underscored the enormous ambivalence that weighed upon women's attainment of the right to vote. Political pragmatism put a brake on the enthusiasm of theoretical declarations on the principle of equality, for the debate dealt with the political significance of granting women the vote. The political forces of the parliamentary Left as well as those of the Right saw Spanish women as likely electoral allies of conservative forces. This assumption was significant when it came to distinguishing theoretical principles favorable to the women's vote from political practices that resisted granting women's suffrage when it would be inopportune. This contradiction even resulted in serious splits in the ranks of Spanish Socialism. It should be stressed that politicized women themselves were not entirely immune to these kinds of considerations. Margarita Nelken, a Socialist and a deputy from Badajoz, used such arguments to justify postponing the concession of women's right to vote. Like the Socialist Indalecio Prieto, she took an intransigent position: Spanish women were not ready for the right to vote, given that they supported the conservative forces. Victoria Kent, another Radical-Socialist deputy, shared Margarita Nelken's convictions. During the parliamentary debate, Victoria Kent systematically refused to concede the right to vote to women, invoking political timeliness. In contrast, Clara Campoamor, a deputy from the Partido Radical (Radical Party), defied the political line of her own party and defended women's suffrage. This suffragist leader insisted that the rights of the individual demanded egalitarian legal treatment. She postulated that the principles of the democratic regime itself should guarantee the creation of a Constitution consistent with the principles of equality and the elimination of sexist discrimination. Campoamor's line of reasoning was obviously feminist, for she attributed the refusal of women's suffrage to the desire to maintain a political order that guaranteed male political dominance—a political patriarchy. In her presentation to Parliament, she proclaimed that if the principle of equal political rights were not admitted, not only would the republic be discredited as a democratic regime, but it would reveal its desire to protect a patriarchal social order:

> The first article of the Constitution might well state that Spain was a democratic republic and that all its powers emanated from the public; but for me, for women, for men who see the democratic principle as an obligation, this article would state only one thing: Spain is an aristocratic republic that favors men. All its rights emanate exclusively from men.

Moreover, Campoamor's perception of women as rational individuals also led her to refuse any systematic association of women with conservative political behavior.

After intense public debate, the right to vote was finally granted to women and the principle of equality between men and women was written into the new democratic Constitution of 1931. This measure entailed ideological readjustments with regard to the political role of women and society's acceptance of their intervention in public life. During new elections, the desire to capture the women's vote contributed to renewed political problems. Far from promoting a true integration of women into country's political life at all levels, the different tendencies of the political spectrum instead attempted to use the women's vote for their own ends. Women's political presence was never conceived in the same terms as men's political activity. Gender still affected the exercise of citizenship, given that women's politicization had been envisioned in light of a differential female politics—different from that of men. Frivolous notions proliferated. Marin Civera of the Partido Sindicalista (Syndicalist Party) wrote:

> Woman, in a political party, should be consolation and compensation; her abundant sentimentality is worth more than all the harsh principles of the struggle for survival. I prefer her sweet, charitable, and trusting, and her moral and physical beauty does not merit the political disfigurement of her feelings.

Moreover, the traditional idea that women should exercise moral guardianship over society persisted. A few women defended the need for a greater humanization of politics through women's influence in the area of policy making. On the whole, however, it was clear that the idea of political activity as a male monopoly still prevailed. Despite their attainment of formal political rights, few women successfully integrated themselves into the world of politics. Despite their adherence to the principle of equality, practically all the forces in politics were hostile to women's political and social projection outside the private sphere of the home. This made women's presence in the political world extremely difficult.

Nevertheless, Spanish women did experience a political awakening during the 1930s. This phenomenon manifested itself in not only in the candidacy of women for the position of municipal counselors in many communities, but also in the accumulation of publications that dealt with women's political role. Works such as *La mujer española ante la republica* (1931; Spanish Woman before the Republic), by María Lejárraga Martínez de Sierra, or *La mujer y la urna* (Woman and the Ballot Box), by Victoria Priego, reflected ongoing political concerns. Although they were few, there were also some female deputies in Parliament under the Second Republic: Margarita Nelken of the Partido Socialista Obrera Español (PSOE; Spanish Socialist Workers' Party), María Lejárraga Martínez de Sierra (PSOE), Veneranda García-Blanco Manzano (PSOE), Julia Álvarez Resano (PSOE), Matilde de la Torre (PSOE), Victoria Kent (Partido Radical), Francisca Bohigas Gavilanes (agrarian), and Dolores Ibarruri of the Partido Comunista de España (PCE; Spanish Communist Party). On the Left, a small core of women occupied exceptional positions in public life. Some personalities, such as Dolores Ibarruri ("La Pasionaria") with the Communists and Federica Montseny in the anarchist movement, stood out as great leaders of the Spanish labor movement. Other women assumed public responsibilities, such as Victoria Kent (general director of prisons), Matilde de la Torre (general director of Industry and Commerce) or Clara Campoamor (general director of Public Welfare). On the whole, however, this phenomenon concerned a small elite that was not exactly representative of the influence the female collective had on the political dynamics of the country.

Throughout the Spanish Second Republic women's associations became more active, especially in the labor movement. One such case was Women against War and Fascism, founded in 1933 by the Spanish Communist Party to coordinate the antifascist struggle. This antifascist women's organization played a leading role in the support to the miners of the Asturias after the failed attempt at a social revolution in October 1934. On the initiative of Dolores Ibarruri, the group organized assistance to the miners' families during the severe repression that followed and coordinated the placement of miners' children outside of the Asturias. Later on the organization played an important role in bringing out the vote for the Frente Popular (Popular Front) in the elections of February 1936.

Women's social condition improved considerably during the 1930s. In the area of labor, the principle of equal wages for men and women was established by the law on *jurados mixtos* (mixed juries) in November 1931, but that did not mean that all wage discrimination against women had been completely eliminated. In fact, the view that women's work was complementary or transitory was invoked to justify continuing wage discrimination. Despite the important reforms of women's legal status under the Second Republic, the law of Labor Contracts of November 1931 still upheld the husband's right to control his wife's wages. However, it did stipulate that a woman could manage her own wages with her husband's authorization or in the case of a legal or de facto separation. Such limitations notwithstanding, many measures favorable to women were taken. Thus, under the new labor regulations all clauses forbidding women to marry or providing for their dismissal from jobs if they did marry were declared null and void. Similarly, dismissal on the grounds of maternity was also prohibited. Without any doubt, the most important measure taken was the application of obligatory maternity insurance, a measure that corresponded to the general policy of social planning to which the republican regime was committed.

In the area of education, schooling, particularly for girls, was clearly making progress. The rate of illiteracy decreased—although it was still very high—dropping from 47.5 percent in 1930 to 39.4 percent in 1936 (see Cortada 1988). The 1930s also witnessed greater numbers of women having access to higher education and to the cultural world. Yet in spite of these political, cultural, and social changes, many traditional attitudes still restricted the cultural, professional, and personal perspectives of Spanish women, while politics continued to be an area reserved for men.

Antifascism and Revolution: Women's Role in the Civil War

In July 1936 Franco's military uprising and the ensuing Fascist aggression provoked a three-year-long civil war. This period (1936–39) accelerated the transformation of the political and social structures of Spain. These years of upheaval, revolution, and antifascist struggle were the context of an unprecedented female mobilization, as thousands of women were transformed into active agents of the antifascist and revolutionary struggle. The civil war played the role of catalyst, forcing a readjustment of the traditional social role of women, which until then had been kept at a distance from political events. The period provoked a change in the gendered division of realms of action, bringing women into new public arenas and new services.

Throughout the war, women played a fundamental role in civil resistance, daily survival on the home front, work, social welfare and health, and even, in some cases, at the front. For many women, this period represented lived experience in liberty and development. Yet, despite the conditions of rupture in this era of conflicts, war, and revolution, it was clear that the cultural and social mechanisms that put a brake on women's emancipation continued to function, maintaining some continuity in sexual models and roles.

In the republican zone, an immediate change occurred in the way women were treated. Calls for the mobilization of men and women to resist Fascism proliferated, issued by various political elements, the republican and workers' press, and the numerous publications of the women's organizations. Orators such as the Communist Dolores Ibarruri, the anarchist Federica Montseny, or the young Teresa Pàmies and Aurora Arnáiz of the Juventudes Socialistas Unificadas (JSU; Unified Socialist Youth) specifically addressed women, inciting them to join the ranks of the antifascist struggle. The leaders of the umbrella group of antifascist women's associations, the Asociación de Mujeres Antifascistas (AMA; Association of Antifascist Women), along with leaders from the anarchist organization Mujeres Libres (Free Women) and the Women's Secretariat of the Partido Obrero de Unificación Marxista (POUM; Dissident Marxist Party), participated in numerous meetings and campaigns for antifascist mobilization and revolutionary transformation of society. During the first months of the war, thousands of women who had previously been isolated from the sociopolitical dynamics of the country mobilized in conspicuous ways. They were active in the fortification of barricades, caring for the wounded, organizing social welfare and healthcare on the home front, providing auxiliary war services or cultural and professional training, organizing clothing or military equipment workshops, and, in the area of labor, working in the transport industries and munitions factories. They made a highly significant contribution to civil resistance on the home front, making possible the civil population's survival throughout those long years of war.

Women's Organizations

Women's organizations, too, saw broad development during the war and were the primary instruments for mobilizing women in the antifascist struggle. The different cores of the Association of Antifascist Women, formed from the Unió de Dones de Catalunya (Catalonian Women's Union), the Unión de Muchachas (Girls' Union), and the Aliança Nacional de Dones Joves (National Alliance of Young Women), played a decisive role, as did the anarchist organization Free Women. The Women's Secretariat of POUM had less impact. This plurality of responses in the antifascist resistance reflected the strong polarization that existed within the republican forces and the Left during the war. This was why the programs and strategies of the different women's organizations had visibly contradictory ideas, not only in the political context but also regarding the role of women, despite the fact that in practice there was substantial consensus on fundamental points such as work, education, and women's mobiliza-

tion in the antifascist struggle. Despite the political cohesion that was created in republican society by the fight against Fascism, there emerged no common project among women's groups, nor any unified vision.

The antifascist women's organizations succeeded in rallying about 60,000 members, in addition to the 255 local associations in republican Spain. The Association of Antifascist Women (AMA) defined itself as the only unitarian, cross-political women's organization representing all antifascist women, no matter what their tendencies. It brought together Communist, Socialist, republican, and Basque Catholic women. However, it should be emphasized that despite this claim of transcending politics, the AMA's leadership clearly came from the Spanish Communist Party. Dolores Ibarruri was its president, and the successive general secretaries of the organization's national committee—Lina Ordena, Encarnación Fuyola, and Emilia Elías—were all militant Communists. The AMA's policy was perfectly aligned with the Communist Party's policy of refusing any revolutionary initiative. Its exclusive focus was the antifascist struggle and the defense of the democratic republic. Thus, the revolutionary transformation of society never played a role among the AMA's aims as an organization. The purpose of the unitarian antifascist organizations was first and foremost the antifascist struggle.

In addition to the main goal of women's unity in the mobilization against Franco, these organizations also incorporated some women-specific demands: women's right to education and culture, the abolition of women's subjugation and ignorance, and integration into political and social life figured among their specific objectives for women's emancipation. However, these more feminist-inspired demands, clouded by the pressure and constraints of war, were suspended. The conclusions of the First Congress of the Catalonian Women's Union, held in Barcelona in November 1937, were representative of the vast range of activities to which antifascist women had devoted their energies. The congress agenda included the following: women's incorporation into the army's auxiliary services, social-welfare services in hospitals, the war industries, and passive defense structures; professional training to enable women to replace male labor currently at the front; the fight against shirkers and spies; protecting and provisioning mothers and children; the creation of day care centers, hospitals, and schools for children of workingwomen; the creation of the women's clubs, a school for social work, and women-run farms; the organization of literacy classes and elementary instruction for adults; and the reform of the Catalan employers' group in charge of women's protection.

The discourse of the unitarian antifascist movements on women was hardly innovative; it stuck to the traditional concept of motherhood as the basis of women's identity. Moreover, antifascist women understood that the reality of Fascism was not felt directly by women as autonomous individuals but that this reality was mediated by their traditional condition as mothers and wives. Thus, women's perceptions of Fascism were filtered through its consequences for their sons and husbands. The aims of the AMA itself, as they appeared on association's membership card, clearly expressed this mediation of the Fascist experience:

woman is characterized by her constructive spirit and motherly love; and war and Fascism imply destruction and hatred. War destroys the home she has so tenderly constructed; it murders her companion and her son. And Fascism robs her of something that is worth more than life: liberty and the hope for improvement that every mother desires for her children.

The evocation of women as mothers and the adoption of the symbol of motherhood to emblematize women's mobilization were not new. Motherhood was a powerful, unifying theme with which women as a group identified. The figure of the militant mother allowed for the mobilization of women and their identification with a common cause: the antifascist struggle. Beyond political or religious differences, the figure of the mother outraged by Fascism served in turn as an element of common identity, not only on the home front of the republican camp but also on the international level, where maternity-centered discourse was used to call for the solidarity of other women, mothers of the world—an image that often appeared on the republican posters most frequently distributed abroad.

The myth of militant motherhood forged a collective identity for Spanish women and was much more effective than the novel image of women serving in the militia in the mobilization against Fascism. The image of the militant mother, the heroine on the home front—a cultural representation with which all women, biological mothers or not, could identify—could not bring about a change in social roles or create opportunities for action, because it did not challenge the existing bases of hierarchical organization of the sexes.

Acceptance of the principle of sexual difference and of social differentiation between men and women caused antifascist women to assume roles different from those of men in the war. They formulated their mobilization policy from the notion of spheres of action: the rear for the women, the front for the men.

The anarchist organization Free Women and the Women's Secretariat of POUM, the dissident Marxist party, presented a more clearly defined political structure. In contrast to the AMA, both those groups defended the need to stimulate a dynamics of revolutionary transformation in the framework of the antifascist struggle, in line with anarchist politics and notions of Marxist dissidence. Therefore, social revolution was an important part of their programs and strategies of antifascist resistance. While Free Women succeeded in mobilizing more than 20,000 women in their ranks and created more than 153 local associations, POUM's ability to rally women was greatly inferior.

Free Women clearly identified with the anarchist movement, but that group also showed original thinking, developing feminist postulates alongside its anarchist ideology. The anarcho-feminism of Free Women was original in the context of the Left and the Spanish and European labor movement: the group defended the feminist cause as the principal axis of the social struggle and demanded organizational autonomy within the libertarian movement. A strategy of struggle on two fronts was proposed: anarchist-inspired social mobilization to bring about revolutionary transformation of society, and a parallel feminist struggle to obtain women's emancipation. Free Women acknowledged the existence of a patriarchal system—"male civilization"—in which women were subject to a very specific form of subordination. One of its leaders, Suceso Portales, expressed it this way in an article in the tenth issue of the group's publication *Mujeres libres*:

Two things have begun to collapse because they are unjust, class privilege based on the parasitical civilization which gave birth to the monster of war; and male privilege, which turned half of mankind into autonomous beings and the other half into slaves; a male civilization based on power which has produced moral chaos throughout the centuries.

For Free Women, the revolutionary process undertaken during the civil war implied a profound change in the relationship between men and women. That was why the association developed a strategy linking women's emancipation with a revolutionary transformation founded on an anarchist model of an alternative social system. In practice, the organization did not succeed in systematically developing its strategy of twofold struggle, and its action was always clearly marked by the demands of war, as was the case for the other women's organizations. Even though Free Women ran up against the animosity of Federica Montseny, the most remarkable woman of Spanish anarchism, some anarchist women acquired resolutely feminist attitudes, even against the will of the majority of their male cohorts in the libertarian movement.

A charismatic anarchist leader and a propagandist and writer capable of mobilizing the working masses with her speeches, Montseny remains worthy of historical note for her intensive political and cultural action in the anarchist movement and her great rise in the Catalan and Spanish labor movement. In the 1930s she became a foremost personality in her country's politics. A fighter for human liberation and the first Spanish woman to be named minister, she was all the more important because she was a woman of extraordinary influence on the public stage, traditionally the exclusive patrimony of men. A major political figure during the civil war, Federica Montseny was minister of health and welfare from November 1936 to May 1937 in the socialist government of Francisco Largo Caballero. A strong defender of the egalitarian ideal postulated by the libertarians, she firmly opposed reformist republicanism but also the more centrist union politics of her companions in the Trentistas group. (*Trentistas* [the Thirty] was the name for the members of the Confederación Nacional del Trabajo [CNT; National Labor Confederation] who were opposed to the dominance of the Federación Anarquista Ibérica [FAI; Spanish Anarchist Federation] and who, in August 1931, published the *Manifesto of the Thirty*.) Montseny's political ascendancy made her one of the most important figures of Spanish anarchism, a supporter of the hardline radical revolutionary anarchism associated with the FAI. But, paradoxically, by agreeing to be the first woman minister in Spain, she went against one of the most sacred anarchist postulates—the need for an apolitical stand and criticism of the state. Her autobiography clearly reveals the difficulties she had in overcoming her anguish and her doubts about taking on the historically audacious task of accepting a ministerial responsibility as a militant anarchist, against all her convictions. In a lecture given early in June 1937, shortly after having resigned from this responsibility, Montseny admitted that she still did not know the meaning of her choice, but she justified it as a political decision to rally all the antifascist forces in the government in order to vanquish Fascism, even if that might mean postponing the realization of her anarchist ideals.

Montseny never defined herself as feminist, but, paradoxically, she was perceived as the incarnation of the emancipated woman. Despite her condemnation of the discriminatory treatment of women in society, Montseny never recognized the existence of oppression that was specific to women. She saw it as a problem of a general human order: the liberation of the person, applicable to all human beings without any distinction in sex. In denying the specificity of female oppression, Montseny believed that both sexes were oppressed by the capitalist system. For her the fundamental issue was the revolutionary change of society according to the anarchist model, which had to bypass the reality of misunderstanding between the sexes, given that man was "the enigma of woman and woman the enigma of man" ("La mujer, problema del hombre," *La revista blanca*, 15 December 1926). She relentlessly defended the dignity and the pride of her sex, proclaiming her personal esteem for women and her full confidence in them. She understood that a woman's life plan should pass through "the right to live her life and to be what she wants to be and not what man would like her to be" ("La mujer, problema del hombre"). But Montseny denied the need for a specific women's organization within the libertarian movement, and she always had reservations about the kind of collective proposal for libertarian feminism advocated by Free Women.

Women Fighting in the Militia: Symbol and Reality

In the first burst of war fervor, one of the symbols of the revolution and of the most socially and politically important antifascist resistance was precisely that of the figure of the militiawoman. The socialist realism of the war posters, largely influenced by the Soviet iconography of World War I, showed seductive young women, with a slightly masculine silhouette in their blue overalls (known as *el mono*), armed with their rifles, marching off to the front with determined step and with an expression of great self-confidence. Contrasting with the traditional images of the "Angel of Hearth and Home," the representation of women radically changed with the projected image of an active and enterprising woman, the militiawoman devoting herself to the war against Fascism. During the first years of the war, the heroic figure of the militiawoman became the symbol of the mobilization of the Spanish people against the Fascist regime. In the war rhetoric, militiawomen killed or wounded at the front became part of the popular mythology of courage, resistance, and hope, exemplifying the Spanish people's capacity to face the brutal assault of the Fascist rebels. The belligerent image of the fighting woman in blue overalls figured prominently on war posters and in propaganda photographs. The projected message was aggressive. For example, the famous poster by the illustrator Arteche showed a militiawoman in blue overalls against a background of militiamen holding signs. With raised arm, rifle in hand, her index finger pointed at the viewer, the woman combatant emphatically stated: "The militia needs you."

These images registered precisely because they broke with the traditional image of woman by representing her in an active, aggressive, and revolutionary attitude. One may wonder whether this novel and revolutionary image really reflected the social reality of women and whether the militiawomen in overalls were representative. In reality, there were very few militiawomen, but they were identified with the popular militia. The adoption of male clothing minimizing sexual differences might be interpreted as a break with traditional female dress and a demand for a more egalitarian status.

In fact, after a few months of war, the majority of women rejected the image of the militiawoman in overalls. Generally, female combatants wore a more traditional style of clothing, not as strongly associated with the extravagant morality and lack of respectability that later accrued to the image of the militiawoman. In the case of Barcelona, iconographic documentation shows that women dressed in overalls were a very small minority. Most of them, even the most active women, did not adopt the dress of the militia. Traditional fashion magazines, such as *El hogar y la moda*, did not adopt the revolutionary style, and women's clothing did not change much in comparison to the preceding years. Antifascist women's magazines, such as *Noies muchachas*, had fashion columns but preserved traditional styles of clothing, although in versions that were more easily manufactured. In her memoirs, the young Communist leader Teresa Pàmies enthusiastically recalled the freedom that the split skirt brought to young women: "What was important, essential for us, were the divided skirts, to jump into trucks, ride a bicycle, climb posts, leave in a 'brigade of aid to farmers,' or uncover the ruins after an air raid."

Some women's organizations eventually criticized women wearing revolutionary overalls, and the garment quickly lost its prestige. As early as October 1936, those who wore *el mono* were regarded with mistrust and accused of frivolity and coquetry, or at least of following a style that did not have much to do with the struggle against Fascism or a revolutionary mission. The author of "La frivolidad en los frentes y la retarguadia: La guerra es una cosa más seria" (Frivolity on the Fronts and in the Rear Guard: War Is More Serious), an article that appeared in the 3 October 1936 issue of *Solidaridad obrera*, wrote:

> Women who sport overalls in the streets in the center of town have confused war with carnival.

> We'd like a bit more seriousness. We should get rid of those magazines that publish photographs of women armed with rifles, who have never taken a shot in their lives. . . . Frivolity in war is a very dangerous weapon.

Although Spanish society at the time was more receptive to a change in the image of women, the militiawoman never succeeded in becoming a new female model associated with the resistance against Fascism, except during the initial phase of the war with that first thrust of antifascist and revolutionary fervor. From December 1936 on, there was a tangible decrease in the posters and propaganda depicting militiawomen. This retreat can be linked to the rhythm of revolutionary changes and to political and military developments of the period. Militiawomen were no longer evoked as praiseworthy heroines; instead, little by little they became associated with shameful and indecent images that impeded the war from taking its proper course.

In the first phases of the civil war, the novel image of the militiawoman seemed to be a significant departure from earlier models of standards and social female roles. However, a critical analysis, taking into account the double level of the image and

WOMEN'S ROLE IN THE SPANISH CIVIL WAR   353

social reality, underscores the fact that the new model of woman soldier that was so prevalent during the first weeks of the war was not actually representative of reality. Thus, the militiawoman did not appear as a new authentic female prototype, but rather as the symbol of the war and the revolution—an image that, moreover, was not necessarily meant to serve as a realistic model for other women. The projected model was not that of a "new woman" emerging from the sociopolitical context, but a model created in response to the needs of the war. The model did not mirror reality, nor did it represent women's enlistment into the military resistance at the front. In fact, the image of the militiawoman could be interpreted alternatively as representation that did not so much address a female public as transmit a message to men, urging them to do their masculine duty and enlist. She embodied a woman who made an impact, who was provocative precisely because she was playing a role considered to be masculine; consequently, she forced men to assume the military role, often characterized as "virile." Although heroines killed or wounded at the front, such as Lina Ordena, Antonia Portero, or the figure of Rosario "La Dinamitera" (the Dynamiter), were invoked by Miguel Hernández in his poems, militiawomen were not seen as examples to be followed. Rather, they were the symbolic incarnation of the courage and resistance of the Spanish people against Fascist aggression.

There was rapid agreement among the various women's organizations that women's mobilization should be channeled into the home front, but in the first weeks of the war a small number of women enlisted in the militia. In the first push of antifascist fervor, they spontaneously opted for a fighting role in the armed struggle at the fronts in Aragon, Guadalajara, the Basque country, the mountains of Madrid, Andalucia, Mallorca, and the Maestranza. In this initial phase of popular mobilization, women and men alike saw the taking up of arms as an immediate response to Fascist aggression. The Catalan anarchist Conchita Pérez, who later fought in Belchite, did not let distinctions stop her from choosing armed struggle. The young Communist Lena Imbert chose to fight at the front because she thought that the home front was for the wounded or children, while the Basque anarchist Casilda Méndez, who had participated in the social struggles of the Second Republic, followed her male companions into the armed battles in the mountains of Peñas de Aya. In a letter to her family, the young militiawoman Elisa García, killed a short time later in an operation at the front in Aragon, clearly showed that she refused a nonmilitary role for women, for she believed that women should be fighting like men and that only cowards refused armed struggle. For most women, the choice of armed struggle was connected to the defense of their political and social rights, acquired during the Second Republic, as well as to their rejection of Fascism. For many, it was the continuation of their involvement in union and social movements.

During the first months of the war, militiawomen filled various functions at the front, mainly devoting themselves to auxiliary support and assistance tasks. However, many women also fought as soldiers and engaged in fighting activities. Some of them played important roles as political consultants, like the Communist Anita Carrillo, the political coordinator of the Mexico Battalion. Still, at the front there was a clear sexual division of labor, since for the most part women assumed responsibility for culinary tasks, laundry, care of the wounded, and administrative duties. In the 5th regiment, they were given almost all the auxiliary tasks to do. As a general rule, gender-role segregation was quite clear at the different fronts, and with few exceptions armed combat duty was reserved for men. Assigning women noncombatant tasks was justified not only because of their lack of military training, but also because of their ostensibly greater aptitude for support tasks. On the whole, most women accepted this situation and agreed to take charge of cooking, laundry, cleaning, hygiene, and nursing duties. The broad scope of functions of militiawomen at the front demonstrated their ability to adapt to a variety of jobs.

The former militiawoman Conchita Pérez explained, however, that in some sectors female fighters in the militia demanded to be treated as men's equals, both with regard to the division of daily tasks and in military combat. For the same reason, two militiawomen of the 5th regiment decided to leave and join the column of POUM, under the command of a woman, Mika Etchebéhère, because there they would not be forced to wash and cook and would be assigned the same tasks as the male members of the column. In the words of one such woman, Manuela: "I have heard it said that in our column militiawomen have the same rights as men, that they neither did laundry or dishes. I did not come to the front to die for the revolution with a dishtowel in my hand" (quoted in Etchebéhère).

Even though Manuela was applauded by the militia, Mika Etchebéhère had experienced difficulties in her own column precisely because the militiamen expected the militiawomen to wash and pick up their laundry, do the dishes, and do all the other domestic work in the camp. Indeed, the militiamen went so far as to refuse to do "women's work," because in the 5th regiment it was women who took care of those chores. Finally, Etchebéhère managed to convince her men of the need to accept an egalitarian division of the domestic tasks in the column. This situation seems somewhat exceptional, but it is believable because one woman, very sensitive to women's demands, occupied a position in the military command. For the most part, however, women's presence at the front was legitimized by the idea that they would take up the "womanly duties." In the final analysis, the traditional gendered division of roles was not greatly challenged, even in the circumstances of trench warfare that were so very new in Spain.

During the first weeks of the war, images of the militiawoman in the press and in wartime rhetoric were associated with the "Heroine of the Fatherland." Heroism, courage, and strength were a part of the legend of the woman soldier taking up arms against Fascism. The initial choice of armed battle was acclaimed as a symbol of generosity, courage, and popular resistance to Fascism. As the poet Miguel Hernández wrote, many militiawomen associated their female identity with the character and duties of the male:

Rosario, the Dynamiter,
You could be a man and you are
The elite of women,
The spume of the trenches.

Nonetheless, in a very short time attitudes changed and propaganda directed at women demanded their presence on the home front exclusively. They were categorically made to understand that women were not equal to men, and it was emphasized that their role in the conflict could not be the same. Not only was there this obvious delimitation of social roles, but, as George

Orwell wrote in his *Homage to Catalonia: A Testimony of the Spanish Revolution* (1938), the attitudes toward the figure of the militiawoman changed dramatically. In a few months time, praise turned into contempt and caricature. Moreover, on this issue there was for once consensus between political parties and unions, usually so split on other points, and among the women's organizations themselves, on the need to force militiawomen to retreat from the front. Around September 1936, a coercive policy was implemented in order to compel them to leave the front, and in October 1936 a series of military directives required women to retire from the militia.

The slogan "Men on the front, women in the rear guard" became the watchword of the women's antifascist mobilization. Furthermore, although they recognized the positive role of militiawomen at the front, a certain number of women combatants in the militia withdrew because they were convinced they would be more useful on the home front, where their human attributes would be better utilized. Women's ability to adapt to the demands of war and, in general, their perfect willingness to get down to the tasks at hand should be stressed. As Manola Rodriguez, a former militiawoman, testified, women "were good at everything and, above all, they committed themselves willingly wherever they were needed to take up all types of activities."

One disconcerting element in these developments, and one of the most difficult to evaluate, is the fact that not a single one of the women's organizations publicly challenged the decision to restrict active combat on the front lines to men. In fact, one can discern both a kind of complicity and an unwillingness to debate the subject openly. There are a few sporadic references to the profound disappointment of many of the militiawomen when they were forced to leave the front, but there is no evidence of any open and concerted defense on their behalf, even in the women's magazines of the period. Very few texts are critical of the disdain toward these women expressed by men in the power structure. Furthermore, no one defended the militiawomen's competence for duty or questioned the validity of the argument that claimed that the lack of military and professional training prevented them from doing useful work at the front. This acquiescence in the face of the official attitudes showed glimpses of the persistence of ingrained behavioral norms, which prevented a break with traditional social roles. The result was that the militiawoman represented an atypical figure and a model of female behavior that was not to be recommended. In addition, the general tendency of women's magazines was to adopt an apologetic tone. Phrases such as "true women do not dishonor the front" (*Mujeres libres*, 10 July 1937) were quite frequently used. Even the Women's Secretariat of POUM, which had been the most vigorous advocate of military training for women, eventually declared that the duties of men and women during war time should not be identical and that the appropriate place for women was on the home front.

Most arguments justified limiting women's participation in the war to the home front. Essentially, these arguments held that women were effective there, for they had the necessary training for assuming war duties in that area, while their lack of military experience and their unfamiliarity with handling weapons made them unsuitable candidates for armed struggle. In fact, the militiawomen themselves appreciated the validity of this viewpoint and explained that they were actually devoting themselves to auxiliary work because they were better prepared

to assume those tasks. They did not attribute this sexual division of labor to women's innate qualities but to their lack of access to military training and to the difficulties experienced in handling weapons because of their weight. Moreover, reluctance to offer women military training even when they were at the front made their lack of competence in this area all the more apparent.

The women's organizations refused armed combat because it was an unacceptable imitation of men and "unsuitable" conduct for women. They also claimed that psychological and biological differences meant that women should be stationed on the home front exclusively:

> Woman . . . has reflected and understood that street skirmishes are a far cry from regular, methodical, and desperate combat in the trenches. Having seen things in this light, and recognizing her own value as a woman, she prefers to trade the rifle for the industrial machine and warlike energy for the gentleness of her WOMAN's soul. (*Mujeres libres*, 10 July 1937)

In any case, the central debate did not lie there. Toward the fall of 1936, women's retreat from the front was linked directly to the issue of prostitution. The progressive discrediting of the militiawoman meant that her dismissal from the front became a popular demand. The immediate and obligatory return of women from the front was justified by the assumption that women caused sanitary problems by spreading venereal diseases. This allegation was widespread in both the republican press and the pro-Franco press, and it had a decisive impact on the decision to billet women on the home front. During the campaign for the obligatory withdrawal of women from the front, the association of militiawomen with prostitutes was both implicitly and explicitly at work. Obviously, equating militiawomen with prostitutes was untenable when applied to the women's militia as a whole. It was true that a few prostitutes left for the front early in the war, as did a few male criminals who had been set free from prison. However, the latter did not cause the disrepute of all male militia or all soldiers. It is impossible to judge the exact number of prostitutes at the front, but they seemed to have represented a very small minority that, in any case, was there for only a very short time.

Verbal testimony from militiawomen confirmed that they saw no prostitutes and had no contact whatsoever with them at the front. It is true that wartime conditions brought greater freedom in relations between men and women. Some women began new love affairs, but many women already had stable bonds with the men they had accompanied to the front. Many couples married after the war. Other militiawomen asserted that they had no time to think about personal or sexual relationships, for they were completely taken up by survival and the struggle against cold, hunger, and the enemy. A few indicated that, although they even shared their bed with militiamen, they were never sexually harassed, while others affirmed the possibility of having sexual relations as a natural, conscious and, consequently, permissible decision between consenting adult men and women.

The argument that women should be withdrawn from the front to reduce the risk of propagating venereal diseases was frequently advanced and was used to support the growing discredit of the militiawoman's image. Admittedly, one of the most serious health problems of the war was controlling these diseases, which in 1937 posed a very grave risk. The central government and the Catalan government set up a policy to contain the diseases. Still, even though documentation is rare, it seems that the spread of venereal disease should be attributed to the unusual flourishing of prostitution at home, sustained by soldiers on leave, rather than to its propagation at the front itself. On the whole, there were sexist attitudes involved in the analysis of this issue in political circles.

Finally, an important piece of the logic underlying the campaign to withdraw women from the front was the problem of discipline and the policy of militarization of the armed forces. The rationalization of the military, entailing the creation of a regular army, brought with it the elimination of the militia, which was the popular armed response to the antifascist war. In fact, women found themselves implicated in a broader political struggle of confrontation between two forms of the military institution: the nonhierarchical voluntary service, run by the militia itself, versus the highly hierarchical and structured regular armed forces. The creation of a regular army meant that the militiawoman became a figure that was unacceptable to the structures of a highly stratified traditional army. The disappearance of the militia caused women's choice to participate in armed combat to become untenable.

Women in the Civil Resistance on the Home Front

Thousands of women participated in the war effort through their work in the weapons factories, volunteer work in social services, educational activities, cultural projects, or measures to support fighters at the front. Women ensured daily survival on the home front. This work of civil resistance was made even more difficult by the hardships linked to the war: hunger, problems of supplies, problems of the refugee population, and the deficiencies in sanitary and hospital aid services. Their efforts allowed the civil population to survive under adverse circumstances, including the unemployment, restrictions, and famine caused by the war.

On the home front, the main motto of all the women's organizations was "Men at the front, women at work." Women represented a reserve of manual labor that made it possible to maintain levels of production at a time when men were mobilized at the front. In addition, some women saw this situation as an opportunity to break the silence traditionally manifested toward paid work by women. However, in this area they ran up against resistance that was difficult to overcome. Indeed, professional training for women had very little success, owing to lack of collaboration from unions and qualified workers. The idea of incorporating women into the skilled professions or salaried jobs previously held by men aroused opposition from labor. Despite initiatives such as the Institut d'Adaptació Professional de la Dona (IAPD; Institute for Women's Professional Adaptation) set up by the Catalan government, which established bases for equal wages for men and women and started professional training of several hundred women during the war, there was no notable improvement in women's professional prospects on the labor market. Women were still confined to jobs in traditional sectors, and in many cases they were still kept away from paid positions. Gender segregation in jobs and salary discrimination

continued to exist even in collectivized enterprises. Women still had just as few professional opportunities, and, in the final analysis, the image of the woman worker in the munitions factories or the female mechanic or engine driver was exceptional and quite unrepresentative of the realities of work for most women. However, in rural areas, with military mobilization of the men, women's labor in the fields counted more heavily.

In the context of the devastation caused by war and the displacement of thousands of refugees, women found jobs in social services and public health. They played a decisive role in hospitals, dining halls, and laundries. They organized day care centers for the children of working women, schools, and a tight network to provide solidarity and aid to the innumerable refugees. They also played an important role in the organization of antifascist solidarity on the national and international level. Women's action was essential during the war when they threw themselves into new social, economic, and military activities.

The area of education and culture became an important place for women's activity. Women's magazines proliferated, attesting to their high levels of activity in education and culture. *Companya* was published by the Catalonian Women's Union, *Emancipación* by the Women's Secretariat of POUM, *Muchachas* by the Girls' Union, the four editions of *Mujeres* and *Pasionaria* by the AMA, *Mujeres Libres* by the anarchist women, *Noies muchachas* by the National Alliance of Young Women, and *Trabajadores* by the women of the Spanish Communist Party. Evidence of the intensity of women's journalistic activity during the war, these publications served not only as a means of disseminating the political line of their respective organizations, but also as a platform for debate and information on women's issues on the national and international level. They were an important vehicle for mobilization and cultural training for women, and they represented a clear expression not only of the response of women's response in the face of Fascism, but also of their organizational abilities.

Through their publications and their cultural initiatives, women broke their historic silence as a social group. They made their voices heard and publicly expressed their positions on topics that included politics, the war, antifascism, feminism, and women's needs. They published and wrote magazines, daily papers, and brochures. Through these organs of public expression, woman manifested their engagement in the antifascist struggle.

There was a remarkable development in cultural centers for girls and working women and Institutes of Free Women. The various women's organizations arranged courses, cultural and artistic activities in schools, and training centers in the countryside and villages. Awareness of the major handicap posed by high rates of illiteracy among women—close to 40 percent in 1936—led these organizations to center their activities on eradicating women's illiteracy and creating a cultural infrastructure. Their flexibility in finding ways to offer educational material, which in many cases was provided in the workplace, in the factories and workshops, attests to the organizations' deep sensitivity to the educational needs of working women. Women's access to public speech, writing, and general education was one of the decisive paths for women's emancipation established by women during the civil war.

The war had intensified the practice of prostitution, and one of the major health problems was the spreading of venereal diseases contracted on the home front. The anarchist organization

Free Women posed the social problem of prostitution not only from the point of view of hygiene and health, but also from the perspective of women practitioners themselves. However, their initiative to create Liberatorios de la Prostitución (health-care centers for prostitutes) could not be implemented owing to a lack of appropriate means. Repeating the proposal of Free Women, Federica Montseny, when she was minister of Health and Public Welfare, raised the issue of creating centers for the moral, medical, sanitary, and professional rehabilitation for female prostitutes. In practice, however, public health policy continued in the traditional vein, addressing the problem of prostitution in terms of the health and hygiene of the customer.

The war was a time of transformation of women's social condition, not only through broad legislative changes such as legal equality of the sexes and, in the Catalan region, legislation for voluntary termination of pregnancy, but also as a result of the extent of activity in the antifascist resistance. For many women, the battle against Fascism and their role in the activities on the home front were a new platform of training and consciousness-raising. Despite the fact that political rivalries among the various women's organizations impeded the development of common projects, what was produced was an awakening of women to political and social issues and to problems directly related to their own condition. However, this process did not have time to mature. The tragic end of the civil war broke the collective trajectory of the women of Spain.

Bibliography

Sources

Balius, J., "Elisa Garcia ha muerto en el frente de Aragon," *Solidaridad obrera* (3 September 1936)

Campoamor, Clara, *El voto femenino y yo: Mi pecado mortal*, Madrid: Librería Beltrán, 1936

Civera, Marin, *Partido Sindicalista: Sensibilidad femenina*, N.p.: Seccion Femenina del Partido, n.d

Etchebéhère, Mika, *Mi guerra de España*, Barcelona: Plaza y Janés, 1976

Herndández, Miguel, *Obra poética completa*, Bilbao, Spain: Zero, 1976

Ibárruri, Dolores, *Pour la victoire: Articles et discours, 1936–1938*, Paris: Éditions Sociales Internationales, 1938

Kaminski, H.E., *Ceux de Barcelone*, Paris: Denoël, 1937

"La frivolidad en los frentes y la retarguadia: La guerra es una cosa más seria," *Solidaridad obrera* (3 October 1936)

"Las mujeres en los primeros dias de la lucha," *Mujeres libres* 10 (July 1937)

Montseny, Federica, *Mi experiencia en el Ministerio de sanidad y asistencia social*, Valencia, Spain: Ediciones de la Comisión de Propaganda y Prensa del Comité Nacional de la CNT, 1937

Montseny, Federica, *Mis primeros cuarenta años*, Barcelona: Plaza y Janés, 1987

Nash, Mary, editor, *"Mujeres libres": España 1936–1939* (selections), Barcelona: Tusquets, 1976

Pàmies, Teresa, *Quan erem capitans: Memòries d'aquella guerra*, Barcelona: DOPESA, 1974

Portales, Suceso, "Necesitamos una moral para los dos sexos," *Mujeres libres* 10 (July 1937)

Oral Sources

Perez Collado, Conchita, interview by the author, Barcelona, Spain, 16 June 1981

Rodriguez, Manola, testimony presented at colloquium, "Las mujeres en la Guerra Civil española," Salamanca, Spain, 6 October 1989

Reference Works

Alcalde, Carmen, *Federica Montseny: Palabra en rojo y negro*, Barcelona: Argos Vergara, 1983

Capel Martínez, Rosa María, *El sufragio femenino en la Segunda República Española*, Madrid: Horas y Horas, 1992

Cortada Andreu, Esther, *Escuela mixta y coeducación en Cataluña durante la Segunda República*, Madrid: Ministerio de Asuntos Sociales, Instituto de la Mujer, 1988

Fagoaga de Bartolomé, Concha, *La voz y el voto de las mujeres, 1877–1931*, Barcelona: Icaria, 1985

Fagoaga de Bartolomé, Concha, and Paloma Saavedra, *Clara Campoamor: La sufragista española*, Madrid: Subdirección General de la Mujer, 1981

Grimau, Carmen, *El cartel republicano en la Guerra Civil*, Madrid: Cátedra, 1979

Jiménez de Aberásturi, Luis María, editor, *Kasilda, miliciana: Historia de un sentimiento*, San Sebastián, Spain: Editorial Txertoa, 1985

Nash, Mary, *Defying Male Civilization: Women in the Spanish Civil War*, Denver, Colorado: Arden Press, 1995

Nash, Mary, "Experiencia y aprendizaje, la formación de los feminismos en España," *Historia social* 20 (1995)

Nash, Mary, "Federica Montseny: Dirigente anarquista, feminista y ministra," *Arenal: Revista de historia de las mujeres* 1 (July–December 1994)

Nash, Mary, "Género, cambio social y la problemática del aborto," *Historia social* 2 (Autumn 1988)

Nash, Mary, "Maternidad, maternología y reforma eugénica en España," in vol. 5 of *Historia de las mujeres en Occidente*, edited by Georges Duby and Michelle Perrot, Madrid: Taurus, 1993

Nash, Mary, "Milicianas and Homefront Heroines: Images of Women in War and Revolution, 1936–1939," *History of European Ideas* 11 (1989)

Nash, Mary, *Las mujeres en la Guerra Civil: Salamanca, 1989* (exhib. cat.), Madrid: Ministerio de Cultura, 1989

Nash, Mary, *Mujer y movimiento obrero en España*, Barcelona: Fontamara, 1981

Núñez Pérez, María Gloria, *Trabajadoras en la Segunda República: Un estudio sobre la actividad económica extradoméstica, 1931–1936*, Madrid: Ministerio de Trabajo y Seguridad Social, 1989

Orwell, George, *Homage to Catalonia: A Testimony of the Spanish Revolution* (1938)

Radl Philipp, Rita, and Ma. Carme García Negro, editors, *A muller e a súa imaxe*, Santiago de Compostela, Spain: Universidade de Santiago de Compostela, 1993

Termes, Josep, *Carteles de la República y de la Guerra Civil*, Barcelona: Centre d'Estudis d'Història Contemporània, 1978

THE FEMININE CONDITION UNDER NAZISM

Tradition, Modernity, and Racial Hierarchization

RITA R. THALMANN

A Problematic Gathering

But the folkish [völkisch] state has not the task of breeding a colony of peaceful aesthetes and physical degenerates. Not in the honest petty bourgeois or in or virtuous old maid does it see its ideal of humanity, but in the robust incorporation of manly forces and in women who in their turn are able to bring men into the world. ("The State," *Mein Kampf*, Chapter 2, Volume 2; unabridged English edition: New York: Reynal and Hitchcock, 1941)

Reading these lines taken from Adolph Hitler's *Mein Kampf*, published in 1927—although who had read them or taken them seriously?—one may wonder what women could expect from such a movement, particularly since the party had proclaimed itself an exclusively masculine order from its first general assembly, in 1921. Its leader used only the archaic, biological term *Weib* (woman), which had become more or less pejorative in contrast to the sociocultural designation *Frau*. Its platform mentioned women only in connection with to the improvement of public health through mother-and-child care (point 21). By the early 1920s the decision had been made to exclude women from all party leadership offices, effectively confining them to the *Opferdienst* (service of sacrifice) characterized by the tripartite motto *Hegen, pflegen, erhalten* (breeding, nurturing, protecting). It is true that at this time Hitler was still nothing but an obscure political agitator whose party would barely attain 3 percent of the vote, in a republic where, between 1924 and 1928, the upheavals resulting from Germany's defeat in 1918—fratricidal splits on the Left, two aborted coups from the extreme Right, nationalist gatherings sparked by the French occupation of the Ruhr, runaway inflation, the growing wealth of speculators, the impoverishment of the middle classes and people of modest means, and so on—seemed to have been curbed.

However, the respite was short-lived. The world crisis of 1929 struck Germany full force, the country still being undermined by the consequences of the defeat of World War I, the instability of governmental coalitions, and the bankruptcy of an economy in which prosperity had been artificially maintained through short-term American credit.

To counter the unemployment that had skyrocketed from 400,000 to 6 million jobless workers, the only solution seemed to lie in austerity measures that in fact affected the most destitute, notably through a drastic reduction in social assistance, by virtue of Article 48 of the Constitution, which permitted legislation by edict. That was the context in which Hitler's party achieved its first great breakthrough in the legislative elections of September 1930. Of the 6.5 million votes captured by the Nazi Party (almost 13 percent), 3 million came from the female electorate.

Does that mean that German women had thrown themselves into Hitler's arms and had thereby ensured his victory? Between the myth spread by Hitler himself and upheld to this day by commentators both from the Right and the Left, and its repudiation by the German feminists of the 1970s, such as the Berlin sociologist Anne-Marie Tröger, who at a conference spoke of it as a "stab in women's back from the Left" (alluding to the myth spread against the Weimar Republic by the extreme Right after Germany's defeat in 1918), the reality is obviously more complex. According to the electoral statistics of the Reich, until 1930 there was indeed greater loyalty to the conservative parties from women voters than from men. This is a rather paradoxical phenomenon, but not unusual in those countries where women could vote, which partially explains the reticence of the French Left in granting women civic equality. Moreover, a 1975 study by Herbert Tingsten has shown that the vote of German women, especially for the Catholic Zentrum and the conservative Right, delayed the collapse of the Weimar Republic by more than two years and ensured the reelection of the empire's Fieldmarshall Hindenburg to the presidency of the republic, of which he was one of the main gravediggers (see Tingsten)—as Marshall Philippe Pétain would be seven years later in France. It should not be forgotten that in the last, still relatively democratic legislative elections of July and November 1932, half of the 17 million votes captured by parties that continued to oppose the Nazi program came from women. Still, it must be acknowledged that the votes in favor of Hitler's party, nearly 14 million in July and decreasing to roughly 12 million in November, were almost equally divided between the sexes.

To attempt to understand—although not to justify—this phenomenon requires us to relinquish the perspective of hindsight and to momentarily put aside what we now know about the ideology and criminal practices of the Nazis. The most vital concern for the 1932 electorate was Hitler's commitment to moving Germany out of the crisis and chaos in which it was submerged. Disseminated by massive propaganda and lavishly financed by industrialists and manufacturers for whom Nazi demagogy was preferable to the "Bolshevik peril," the promise to educate a pure, well-ordered, and sovereign *Volksgemeinschaft* (community of the people), to reestablish full employment, to go beyond the sterile party system, and to bring to an end Germany's humiliation by the victorious powers and the Versailles "diktat," appeared to these millions of men and women as the ultimate way out of an unbearable situation. In such a climate of material and psychological distress, what good were the objurgations of a Left that had proven its inability to construct a "strong and social state," the model for which, it now seemed, had been that of an empire? On top of those general motives, young German women, many of whom had not yet made use of the right to vote that their elders had welcomed enthusiastically in 1919, were attracted to the idea of a radical change in which, they were promised, youth would be the protagonist. Those women who did vote, and who were neither committed democrats nor "radical" feminists nor Jews, thought that the promised return to order, prosperity, and dignity was well worth the sacrifice of an emancipation that, in the final analysis, had benefited only a minority. Of what use had been the 1919 election of 9.6 percent women deputies, a proportion that along the years had been reduced to 3.6 percent in 1932? Or the 155 women elected to the regional Diets and the 10 percent elected to municipal councils? Their dependence on political parties, which outside of the electoral periods were rather insensitive to women's aspirations; the conviction, expressed in 1919 by Marie Juchacz, a Social-Democrat and the first woman ever elected to speak on the platform of the German Parliament, that from then on, her female cocitizens would no longer need to defend their interests outside of the normal framework of the parties; all of this had resulted in reducing the important network of women's associations, the jewel of the European women's movement since the 19th century, to the role of a mere "driving belt." Consequently, despite the fact that equality between the sexes was inscribed in the Weimar Constitution, with passive and active voting recognized by law as early as 1918—that is, 26 years before French and Italian women—German women had gained nothing but a few minor legislative measures such as social assistance for youth, official recognition of women's work in the home, mother-and-child care, and so forth. These measures had proven notoriously insufficient for the general improvement of women's living conditions, particularly during the major crisis of 1930. Unemployment at that time affected three times as many men as women, since, for equal work, employers preferred to hire women, whose wages were up to one-third lower than men's wages. As a result, many women not only had to provide

for the needs of unemployed family members, but also faced hostile unions denouncing "female job stealers."

In this context, two events marked a significant turning point. The first was the 1932 adoption by both the government and Parliament, dominated by the Catholic Zentrum and the Right, of a law against double wages in one household. The law was perfectly aligned with the logic of *Quadragesimo anno*, a Vatican encyclical of 1931 that aimed to send women back to their "natural vocation." The second was the failure of the campaign for the decriminalization of abortion, led by the Left and a minority of liberals. Together, these gave the signal for what Nazi ideologue Alfred Rosenberg was already calling "emancipating women from emancipation" in *Der Mythus des 20. Jahrhunderts* (1930; *The Myth of the Twentieth Century*). Women's emancipation, according to Hitler, was a Jewish—and therefore evil—invention.

Until its first victory in the legislative elections of 1930, when it discovered the importance of women's votes as an indispensable component in the legal conquest of power, the Nazi movement had in fact hardly been interested in the lot of women. Their only interest lay in assigning them the task of "breeding, nurturing, and protecting" the defenders of "Aryan purity" and their descendants, who would be called upon to build the thousand-year Reich and to conquer its *Lebensraum* (a space in which to live). Party official Gregor Strasser, at the time Hitler's heir apparent or even rival, but later assassinated on Hitler's orders during the Night of Long Knives in 1934, undertook to present a more attractive image of Nazism to the millions of conservative women who had still to be won over. His first task was to compel the small, relatively independent groups of activist women to join the "true" women's movement, the Nationalsozialistische Frauenschaft (National Socialist Women's Association). It was headed by Elsbeth Zander, founder of the German Order of Women and the "Red Swastika," who was promoted to the office of Sachbearbeiterin für Frauenfragen (Arbiter of Women's Affairs) by party leadership as a reward for her submission to the "superior interests of the party." Another noteworthy change was the introduction of a discourse that deftly promoted both the thesis of the "natural vocation of woman," including "social motherhood," and that of the social regeneration of a nation through selective breeding. Social Darwinism had been widely accepted by German society, including, since early in the century, the Bund Deutscher Frauenvereine (BDF; Federation of German Women's Associations), with the exception of its progressive wing, which had been marginalized since World War I. To better mask the radicalism of his plan, Hitler promised to restore the honor and dignity of the "German woman." Together with "German mother," the designation was first introduced into Nazi terminology as a title of nobility, and then, under the Third Reich, as a true "guarantee of origin." Another weighty argument invoked to win women voters was the danger of the "collectivization of women" in the case of a Bolshevik victory. To respond to their specific concerns, and undoubtedly also in the wake of the protest by a group of "Nordic feminist women" against the tendency of Hitler's movement to "extol a romantic cult of motherhood" borrowed from a "Pasha's oriental concept," while "the people have an inalienable right to the leadership by the best Germans of both sexes," the Nationalsozialistische Deutsche Arbeiterpartei (NSDAP; National Socialist German Workers' Party) published a "Call to Women Voters" at the legislative elections of July 1932. Mothers were reassured about their children's future, widows and retired women about the guarantee of their pension, and those who practiced a profession received assurances of job security. Similar assurances were given regarding the continuation of German women's legal rights and access to higher education and to all careers except those in the armed forces and in politics. All these promises were wrapped up in formulas and phrasings vague enough to allow any interpretation once the Nazis were in power.

Women's Position as Determined by the Nazi Regime's Objectives

Named chancellor on 30 January 1933, Hitler needed no more than two months to obtain from President Hindenburg the moratorium of constitutional rights, then the vote of full powers renewable for four years, by a parliamentary majority that went from the extreme Right to the Catholic Zentrum and the support of the liberals, in return for a few verbal assurances. Despite this blank check obtained through trickery, intimidation, and repression, a full-scale takeover of the country's levers of power required a long-term strategy combining the eradication of any residual opposition with pragmatism that was as conscious of obstacles to be overcome as it was of objectives to be attained. We should recall in this regard that despite the weakness of its democratic traditions, Germany embodied the European avant-garde in matters of economic and administrative management and in social, cultural, scientific, and technological accomplishments. The long-term Nazi strategy comprised four main stages: from 1933 to 1935, the focus was the struggle against male unemployment. The second stage, in 1936, saw the beginning of the first Four-Year Plan for the militarization of the economy and society in order to prepare for the conquest of *Lebensraum*. Next came Germany's headlong rush into war, punctuated by the euphoria of blitzkrieg victories, through air power and armored car vehicles, until 1941. Finally, there was a stage of extreme radicalization, proportional to the deterioration of the military situation. Nazism was a virile order par excellence, more akin to sibling clans or warrior hordes than to the patriarchal model, and this feature set it apart from other forms of fascism. Contrary to the assertions of some feminists today (see, for example, Bock; Kuhn), and while it considered "woman" a complementary and inferior being, Nazism could not allow itself to plan for her the same radical elimination it had programmed for other human groups deemed "unworthy of living." As Hitler stated from the end of the 1920s, the racial state needed "healthy" procreation in order to impose its hegemony. This did not imply a policy to decrease the birthrate but rather quantitative and qualitative pronatalist policies meant to optimize through selection the genetic potential of the "Aryan race." This idea had been developed since the turn of the century by German eugenicists who, in contrast to such scientists in other countries, already adhered to a principle of "racial hygiene." In this regard, it is significant that, alongside incentives to marry and have children and to the development of mother-and-child care decreed between 1933 and 1935, the Reich's legislation introduced the repression of contraception and abortion, even though it allowed eugenic abortion and also introduced forced sterilization

of all carriers of congenital diseases. Similarly, all sexual relations between "Aryans" and Jews were forbidden by the law of Protection of German Blood and Honor (1935). This measure was later extended to any human group that was decreed to be "of inferior blood."

While it was a determining factor in women's position under the Third Reich, the "racially valid" natalist policy did not imply women's general return to the home. To be sure, reestablishment of full employment for men was given priority during the first three years of the regime. However, by virtue of the law of 7 April 1933 on the Restoration of a Professional Civil Service—an example of the coded language the Nazis were so fond of to mask their crimes—the true priority was essentially the dismissal of civil servants either because they were of "non-Aryan" descent (a category that included Christians of Jewish origin), or because of "earlier activity that did not guarantee they would always devote themselves unreservedly to the nation's service" (Art. 4). The measure applied to both men and women. But while men dismissed from their posts could still benefit from dispensations as veterans or sons of veterans, women's dismissal went well beyond the stipulations of the 1933 law by also invoking the text of 1932 ruling against double wages in a household. Dismissal from the legal, medical, and dental professions was slower than the massive evictions from elementary and secondary education (exempted from the latter were Catholic schools, which were protected by the Concordat concluded between the Reich and the Vatican in July 1933). The dismissal of Aryan women was later rescinded, however, when mandatory military service and the militarization of the economy were introduced. The same was not true for higher education, where the regime could invoke the widespread ostracism of women in other industrialized countries. Already in the Weimar Republic, despite many interventions by women's associations and the association of women university graduates, there were only 74 women out of some 7,000 tenured faculty and senior researchers. In the wake of the forced retirements and the first wave of emigration, only 30 women lecturers remained in the universities, and—with the exception of one specialist in Christian archaeology excepted—those lecturers were soon confined to higher technical institutions.

The wave of discrimination and dismissals did not stop there. A law of 25 April 1933 addressing "overcrowding in schools" prescribed restricted admissions, aimed mainly at children of opponents not rallied to the regime, Jews, and girls, whose total number was not to exceed 10 percent of the 15,000 students admitted annually (see Stephenson 1975). Once students had cleared this first hurdle, a second round of selection criteria was applied. The criteria were particularly rigorous in sciences, law, and social sciences, where total enrollments dropped 50 percent up until the war, while attrition rates in medicine and dentristy—possibly in anticipation of the war—were only about 25 percent. Growing numbers of female students were directed toward specializing in languages, journalism, and physical education and were promised a fine future according to the regime's objectives. Thus, despite some later correctives resulting from the wartime economy, the regime's purpose in ousting female executives from civil service did not fundamentally change. The main consequence was to maintain women workers in a subordinate status.

Countering the official discourse from 1933 to 1935, with its incentives for women to return to the household, new generations of women replaced the approximately 900,000 women who took that path. Taking into account the increase in male labor, the proportion of women working outside the home decreased from 37.1 percent to 36 percent of the total labor force, but their number remained stable at 11.5 million (see Stephenson 1975). Out of this total, according to a study of the women's service of the Arbeitsfront (Labor Front), a substitute for dissolved unions, fewer than 1 million women were employed in the civil service and social sector. However, female labor accounted for 50 percent of the agricultural workforce (including 800,000 seasonal women farm laborers), and 33 percent in industry, commerce, and artisanal production. Another 1.3 million women held domestic jobs. In final analysis (omitting those singled out for elimination, who could only emigrate or be persecuted), the Nazi promise of a guaranteed living came down to a simple choice: going back to housework, or being relegated to subordinate activities. The most destitute workers, meanwhile, were driven back to their former lot: doing a double day's work. Deprived of any autonomous institution following the dissolution, self-dissolution, or integration of women's associations, women of the Reich henceforth depended exclusively and in every aspect of life on the decisions of the state and the Nazi Party. All laws, decrees, and ordinances that had a bearing on family, sexual life, education, and working women were issued by Nazi ruling politicians and experts, under the sole command of Hitler since the vote of full power of March 1933. In a pedantic and often comical style, through interminable consultations, meetings, and correspondence, and in the last instance arbitrated by the chancellor himself, these men debated questions such as the effects of menstruation on the work of women, ways to curb the frivolity of young girls, the frustration of housewives, and even the rationalization of home economics. It never occurred to any of them to consult their female assistants, who were confined to the role of "relaying" the decisions made. To cite a significant example of this monopolization of powers: women in charge of nationalist women's organizations—still tolerated until 1935—rose up against the dismissal of Gertrud Bäumer from her position as ministerial counselor of the Interior. She was a National-Liberal figurehead of the Federation of German Women's Associations, dissolved in 1933, and she was seen, not without reason, as a pioneer of an authentically German form of feminism. On the same occasion, women also protested against the nomination of men, as opposed to experienced militant women, to vacant posts that had previously been held by women. The secretary of state at the chancellery of the Reich issued this response (Bundesarchiv in Koblenz R 43 II 427): "The chancellor of the Reich appreciates the availability of the nation's women in cooperating with the service of the state and will gladly call upon this cooperation when the possibilities arise." This phrasing was as vague as the promises made in 1932 and committed no one to anything precise.

Worse: the primary female Nazi leaders, Elsbeth Zander and Käthe Auerhahn in particular, were simply dismissed from their positions for having protested against the decision to entrust the directorship of the Bund Deutscher Mädel (BDM; Nazi League of German Girls) to Baldur von Schirach, the leader and future minister of the Hitlerjugend (HJ; Hitler Youth). Other dismissals followed. In their place came Gertrud Scholtz-Klink, the incarnation of the pure, unconditional militant. She had taken up the torch upon the death of her husband in 1930, in order to lead the Nazi women of the Bade region. She was then 28, and already the mother of four children. She was put in charge of all the Reich's women's organizations, with the title of Reichsfrauenführerin (national women's leader) In addition, she became the expert in the Frauenfront (Protection Committee of Working Women) and the Rasse und Seidlungs Hauptamt (RuSHA; Committee for Demographic and Racial Policy). Despite her high nominal status, her authority actually depended on the chancellery of the party and on the chief of Social Affairs, while her budget depended on the party treasurer. Three years after her nomination, Martin Bormann, chief of the chancellery of the party, still had to remind others in a departmental memorandum, dated 6 October 1937, that "In accordance with the order of the Führer, Frau Scholtz-Klink has the rank of Hauptamtleiter [principal office director]. Consequently, when invited, she must be treated like the other Hauptamtleiter."

Militarization of the Economy and Selective Utilization of Women's Potential

With the reestablishment of mandatory military service in the fall of 1935 and the inauguration in 1936 of the first Four-Year Plan, which was meant to prepare a *Wehrwirtschaft* (defense economy) under the direction of Marshall Goering, for some women the situation underwent a tangible transformation. Significantly, in 1934, two years ahead of the general press, *Junges Deutschland*, the press organ of the Hitler Youth organization, replaced the official discourse on the "natural vocation of woman" with a plea in favor of women's involvement in production. The objective was to free up male labor power that was indispensable to the defense of the Reich. In order not to clash with what Goebbels called "the world of women," caution demanded at that stage that the appeal be addressed only to unmarried women and married women who wished to go back to work, even part time. Hence the perceived urgency of ensuring that female youth, largely neglected up to that point, would be ruled with a firm hand, if only to bar their access to higher education. Three decisions exemplify that new direction. First, in September 1936 Hitler ordered a controlled restructuring of the Reichsarbeitsdienst der Weiblichen Jugend (Work Service of the Reich's Female Youth). The organization was headed by a corps of women professionals—a new perspective in the area of social advancement—under the direction of Konstantin Hierl. Already recommended by some women's organizations at the end of the Weimar Republic, it remained relatively modest: 25,000 members in 1938, twice as many in 1940. Second, membership in the girls' branch of the Hitler Youth, the Bund Deutscher Mädel, became mandatory for all young "Aryan" girls in good health between the ages of 10 and 16, beginning in December 1936. This was recruiting on a wholly different scale, since the BDM, which represented only 22 percent of the youth organizations, came close to 50 percent two years later. Thus, 88 percent of the 3,893,000 girls of that age group, along with an additional 450,000 members, between the ages of 17 and 20, of the association Glaube und Schönheit (Faith and Beauty), were to be directly trained for the tasks assigned them by the masters of the Third Reich (see Klaus 1980). Third, the establishment of a year's *Landjahr* (mandatory public service) in the countryside or as family helper, a measure that made possible the transfer of agricultural or household servants to other sectors of the economy. The regime presented the measure as a "modernization" of women's condition, and they were seen as such by a the majority of girls, who were attracted to the prospect of escaping the shackles of family life and school. What could be more enthralling than the discovery of the new world of camaraderie transcending social barriers, united by the same uniform, the apprenticeship of the collective life "in the service of the people," days spent in ideological training, work in the fields or in farm families, the salute to the colors, sports, songs, and games? And there were rewards: distinctions and promotions, group outings, participation in official demonstrations—some of them, the supreme honor, held in the presence of the Führer himself. Some historians have construed this as a relative emancipation of women (see Schoembaum; Stephenson 1975 and 1981; and Frevert). In fact, this "modernization" was merely a step toward the implementation of the Nazi plan for a rational utilization of the female potential in view of the conquest and domination of a Germanic *Lebensraum*. To that end, the training of new female generations, including managers in special centers and the creation, in 1942–43, of three National Politische Anstalten (NAPOLA; National Political Institutions), which had been originally reserved for the male political elite, were measures aimed at replacing the "old guard"—the approximately six million members of the various Nazi groups and associations. "Modernization" involved physical, ideological, and technical training, all intended to produce docile minds in healthy bodies—characteristics that would facilitate ruling and controling the female population of the Reich and the territories still to be Germanized.

In addition, in the eyes of the Nazi leaders this particular training of female youth offered two advantages: first, it shielded them from the influence of older women, and, consequently, accentuated the generation gap; second, it introduced new forms of social advancement without challenging the sacrosanct principle, mentioned in a decree of 24 August 1937, that "access to higher positions must be reserved for men." On this issue, Reichsfrauenführerin Gertrud Scholtz-Klink wrote a letter to Martin Bormann on 24 January 1938, protesting against an instance of discrimination against a woman astronomer and expressing a broader anxiety about "the increasing tendency to deny advancement in their work to gifted, capable women and not to reward their achievements simply because they are accomplished by a woman" (quoted in Stephenson 1981). She firmly advocated bringing a woman's viewpoint on the issue to the Führer's attention; however, it seems that such discussions never took place. Aside from a few rare individual exemptions, the principle remained untouched. This was confirmed once again four years later, right in the middle of the war, when a woman physician specializing in pharmacy and botany at the Institüt fur Auslandische und Koloniale Forstwirtschaft (Institute of Foreign and Colonial Forest Economy) was denied promotion on the grounds that "the position of scientific advisor is not appropriate for a woman. The shortage of male candidates does not enter into the decision." By virtue of her own experience as a wife and mother, the Reichsfrauenführerin was closer to women of

the middle classes with little education, and she eventually gave in. However, she at least sought to have "her" intellectuals hired within her own services. On several occasions she even intervened, although in vain, on behalf of Gertrud Bäumer, who nonetheless until 1944 remained the editor of *Die Frau*, a women's paper of the dissolved women's movement, which, like all publications, was under the authority of Goebbels.

As they were frequently reminded, the first duty of true German women continued to be that of bringing healthy children into the world. Now, despite incentives and coercive methods, tangible increases in births during the first three years of the regime did not correspond to either the quantitative needs or the qualitative demands of a policy of territorial expansion and of "racial regeneration." As it became more and more difficult to reconcile the financing of the birthrate and rearmament, the regime turned to new initiatives that promised to be profitable and less costly. Thus, an October 1935 brochure issued by the Reichsjugendführung (Reich's Youth Leadership) recommended that the female leaders prepare young girls for "biological marriage," explaining to them that "you cannot all have a husband, but you can all be mothers." The result was immediate: in the fall of 1936 some 1,000 members of the BDM reportedly returned home pregnant from the Nazi Party congress in Nuremberg. In a country that was still strongly imbued with Christian morality, premarital sex generally remained taboo, and "illegitimate" childbearing was condemned by the majority. A piece in the 11 August 1934 issue of *Der Deutsche*, the press organ of the Labor Front, characterized it as a psychopathic aberration, harmful to the equilibrium of mother and child. An anonymous open letter, written to Goebbels in 1936 and clandestinely distributed, condemned the physical and psychological ruin of girls from 14 to 16 years of age after "biological marriages" in Hitler Youth camps. Kept aware of this public disapproval, the regime reacted in the usual way, with a tactical withdrawal; in this case, giving merely granting unwed mothers and adoptive parents those advantages enjoyed by married couples. This was a measure already advocated before 1933 by the women's associations and was thus readily accepted, as was the introduction of the title "Frau" for all women, legalized by a decree of the Ministries of the Interior and Justice in anticipation of the growing number of unwed mothers estimated by the medical profession. Additionally, we should recall that shortly after the recommendation of "biological marriages," Himmler had created an association initially open to wives, fiancées, or pregnant girlfriends of the SS and the police under its authority, with the poetic name of Lebensborn (Lifesource). He envisioned expanding the institution to include all mothers, in due time. Without referring to the earlier experience of Mutterschutz (League for the Protection of Motherhood) by the feminist Helene Stoecker, too tainted with liberal individualism, the head of the Black Order seemed to have been inspired primarily by the "*Mittgart* [human garden] of racial regeneration" founded in 1906 by Dr. Wilibald Hentschel. Hentschel was a disciple of Ernst Häckel, the father of monism and honorary president of the Deutsche Geselschaft für Rassenhygiene (Society for Racial Purity). For Himmler, a one-time animal husbandry expert and poultry breeder, and for the experts of the Third Reich, the objective was the establishment of a system of sexual intervention, developed and controlled by state and party in order to endow the Reich with 120 million healthy "Aryans" by 1980. But in 1937–38, Germany did not seem to be ripe for controlled procreation. The regime's efforts focused first on a more rigorous selection of large families and on legislative reforms. Accused of being Communist inspired, existing centers for family planning, with their 70,000 members, had been banned under the ordinance of February 1933 on "Protection of the People and the State." In contrast, the state-supported Reichsbund der Kinderreichen (Reich's Union of Large Families), which at the time had only 5,000 members, became one of the prestigious achievements of the Third Reich in a span of only four years. At the International Congress on the Protection of Children convened in Paris in August 1937, the delegates were so impressed with the accomplishments of the Union that they elected its president, Wilhelm Stüwe, as head of the organization and gave him the responsibility of preparing the 1938 conference in Frankfurt-am-Main. Insofar as Stüwe was content to state the traditional theses of family policy by stressing concrete achievements, the criteria of racial purity that the "new Germany" was applying do not seem to have held the attention of the participants—to the great displeasure of the SS observers, who were supporters of a selection of "worthy genetic heritage." The response was not long in coming: in a report of 7 February 1938, the SS medical inspectorate advocated that "Aryan" descendants be taken in as boarders in state-run schools after being selected as infants at the Mutterschulen (Schools for Mothers of the Reich) that would function on the Lebensborn model. The state and party leadership would thereafter take on responsibility for all material and ideological functions. In addition to the report, Martin Bormann suggested that Union president Stüwe be replaced by a two-headed directorship composed of a party physician and a superior officer of the SS. The restructuring of what would then be known as the Reichsbund Deutsche Familie (Federation of the German Family)—significantly subtitled the Kampfbund für den Kinderreichtum der Erbtüchtigen (Combat Union for a Large Progeny of Genetically Worthy Procreators)—would not occur until 1939. Placed under the personal authority of Himmler, its selection criteria were based on the eugenicist Francis Galton's three categories: worthy heredity, suspect biological worth, and defective heredity. During the war, the last of these categories was annotated with the term *ausmerzen* (to be eradicated).

Previously, under the pretext of bringing into conformance the laws of annexed Austria and the former Reich, a new law on marriage and divorce had been introduced on 6 July 1938. Recalling the earlier texts on "racial safeguarding" as well as the nonvalidity of any marriage of an "Aryan" person outside of the national borders, the new law in effect legalized "biological marriage" by recognizing the right of girls to marry at 16. Boys, who were considered head of the family, could marry at 21, with dispensations decreed possible at the age of 18. In divorce suits, the law stipulated that adultery was not to be taken into account "if it had been accepted, made possible, or facilitated" by the plaintiff, male or female. The birth-oriented policy was still more obvious in the denial of divorce "if the plaintiff is sterile or would not be authorized to contract a new marriage for reasons of health." On the other hand, divorce would be granted if the plaintiff's spouse was sterile or refused to procreate. The most "revolutionary" aspect of the text was Article 55, which provided for the separation of spouses who had not lived together for three years. Demanded by progressives of the 1920s in the name of individual freedom, the clause fit in with Nazi objectives, as it favored the dissolution of sterile unions (or those that had become so), thereby enticing fertile partners to remarry. In practice, almost 70 percent of the beneficiaries of the article were men "starting over in life," as Himmler did with his secretary after 20 years of marriage. The situation of the former female spouses was all the more precarious, because the alimony to which they had a right was subject to review or even definitive cancellation, should the former husband plead new family responsibilities.

Thus, on the eve of the war, the "new Germany" had emerged from the economic crisis, "thanks to" the dismissal of female managers, political opponents, and "non-Aryans," and to the militarization of the economy. Full employment had been reestablished. But the promise of a decent life was henceforth applicable only to "genetically worthy Aryans" and the "politically reliable." In this context, whether they were aware of it or not, women had no choice but to be supporters or to adapt. They were rewarded with the *Mutterkreuz* medal honoring "the German Mother" (the equivalent of the military Iron Cross decoration), provided that they had at least four healthy children, or with the sociocultural accomplishments of the Nazi regime such as leisure activities association Kraft durch Freude (Strength through Joy). For women who wished to escape the restraints, subterfuge was one option. Christian women found some refuge in the churches, which had become precarious since the 1927 campaign against religions. However, there were no choices at all for "reprobate" women: members of the opposition, Jews, and Jehovah's Witnesses who remained in the Reich were exposed to ever more merciless repression. As far back as 1933 (and up until 1937), several hundred such women had been placed in *Schutzhaft* (temporary detention) under guard of the SS and members of the NS Frauenschaft (National Socialist Women's Organization) in the special centers of Moringen, near Hanover, and then in the Fortress of Lichtenburg, in Saxony. Dozens had died, either slaughtered by the SS, like Wilhelmine Struth in Duisburg or Klara Wagner, an activist in the Kommunistiche Arbeiterjugend (Communist Workers' Youth) in Berlin, or had died in secret under torture or "by suicide" in the Gestapo dungeons. An unknown number of others, including the Social-Democrat deputies Toni Pfulf and her colleague Minna Bollmann or the young actress Margarete Köpke, committed suicide in anticipation of a frightening fate. Emigrants survived only thanks to odd jobs and help from aid committees. This class of women included "radical feminists" such as Lida Gustava Heymann, Anita Augspurg, Helene Stoecker, and Gertrud Baer; well-known philosophers and writers, particularly Hannah Arendt, Anna Seghers, Nelly Sachs, and Else Lasker-Schüler; and the academic Anna Siemsen, who was the only woman to have signed the call to the German Popular Front in exile in 1936—and of course thousands of other individuals. Alone, or with a companion in misfortune, some saw no way out of their situation other than flight into death. In the three summer months of 1933 alone, the police headquarters in Paris reported the utter confusion of 700 refugees from the Reich who, many with children, had been herded into old blockhouses just on the outskirts of the city, and the suicide in cheap hotel rooms of six German intellectuals, three of whom were women.

Yet, among these exiles, many men and women wanted to give assistance to another republic in danger, namely Spain, besieged at the time by Franco's followers with the help of Fascist Italy and Nazi Germany, while Great Britain and France advocated nonintervention. The story of Gerta Pohorylle, known as Gerta Taro Certa, is almost inevitably invoked in this connection. She was a young progressive student, born in Leipzig in 1910 of Polish Jewish refugee parents. She emigrated to Paris in October 1933, after a period in preventive detention in her hometown. Surviving only with the help of friends who were refugees like herself and by means of occasional work, she sometimes took to her bed " to save calories." Through her contact with André Friedmann, a Hungarian refugee and a photographer already known under the name Robert Capa, she started studying photography and soon had a passion for the press. With her companion and associate, she completed stories on the Popular Front for the progressive publications *Ce soir*, *Regards*, and *Vu* before leaving to join the Spanish republican lines. She was badly wounded on 25 July 1937 during a bombing by the Nazi Condor legion, and the French, and the international press two days later, headlined, with photographs, the death at the age of 27 of the beautiful young professional. She became a heroine overnight. In Paris, her remains, brought back from Spain by Capa and the writer Paul Nizan, were the object of an imposing funeral organized by the French Communist Party. There was an honor guard at the Maison de la Culture, a sea of flowers, messages from across the world, a funeral procession to the sounds of Chopin's Funeral March, followed by personalities from political, cultural, and media circles and by a large crowd overcome with grief marching as far as the Père Lachaise Cemetery. In his homage, the poet Louis Aragon glorified her as a "daughter of Paris" without mentioning the circumstances under which she had lived there. The Spanish republicans spoke of "the comrade in arms," while the poet José Bergamin called her "the huntress of light." Maria Rabaté spoke as the representative of the World Committee of Women against War and Fascism. In those uneasy times, the antifascist movement needed a Joan of Arc. Hemingway presented Gerta Taro as a femme fatale. Under the German occupation, the prefect removed from the tombstone that had been created for her by Alberto Giacometti the inscription recalling the circumstances of her death. Thirty years later, the myth resurfaced when the German Democratic Republic decided to name a street in Leipzig after Gerta Taro and had a stele erected in the cemetery to the glory of "the young Communist, cofounder of the International Brigade, fallen in the fight against the Fascists in Spain." Not until 1994 did a German woman biographer, Irme Schaber, reconstruct the true itinerary of the progressive young Jewish woman: a refugee from Germany, killed like thousands of others, although under more romantic circumstances, for having wanted to defend, despite all opposition, the right to live and be free, to practice a profession that she loved, and to get to know the world, the warmth of solidarity, and shared friendship (see Schaber).

The Decisive Turning-Point of 1938

It was not until 1938, referred to by the Nazis themselves as the "decisive year" for the realization of the Great Reich and the solution to the "Jewish question," that the radicalization of the regime began to become bluntly apparent. First in a long line, the Saarlander Katharina Kneup, 39 years old, and Liselotte

(Lilo) Herrmann, a 29-year-old Communist student from Berlin, were condemned to death for "high treason" by the People's Tribunal and, having been denied pardon by Hitler, executed on 20 June 1938 in the grim prison of Plotzensee. A few years later, the Social-Democrat unionist Johanna Kirchner would also be executed there, handed over by Vichy, in contempt of the right to asylum, under Article 19 of the Geneva Convention. In 1938 there still were international campaigns on behalf of victims of Nazism. The one undertaken for Lilo Herrmann, mother of a 4-year-old boy, had no effect on her executioners. As for Jewish women who lived by themselves or with their families, many had not been able to make the decision to leave a country to which they remained deeply attached in spite of daily ostracism and almost general indifference. What made them finally understand that their only chance of salvation would henceforth lie in flight were the following: the violence of the pogrom after the Anschluss, the confiscation of all Jewish property, and the expulsion in the space of a single October night of 17,000 coreligionists of Polish origin under horrendous conditions. November saw the unleashing of Kristallnacht (named for the broken glass of shop windows on the night of the pogrom), in the course of which 170 synagogues were burned, 7,500 Jewish stores and residences looted and destroyed, some 25,000 men arrested and sent to concentration camps, and 91 people—of whom 36 were women—killed, not counting the suicides. This was emigration through terror, toward a land possibly still inclined to receive the outcasts stripped of nearly everything they owned. When permits and financial means were not sufficient, married women gave priority to children and men deemed to be in greater danger, if arrested, or more easily set free in case of immediate emigration. For the most part, single or older women, as well as women without any relations abroad, remained in Germany, as did those who did not want to abandon ill relatives or their position in a community. These considerations explain why 60 percent of those deported from Germany and Austria were women.

After the Évian Conference in July 1938, the 14 July issue of the *New York Herald Tribune* featured headlines that read "650,000 exiled Jews refused by everyone," while the Nazi press ironically stated "Jews for sale at low prices? Who wants any? Nobody." After the Munich Accords in September, Hitler was convinced that neither governments nor international opinion, despite protestations, would curb the power politics that had brought him so many successes until that point. Hence the green light given to the pogrom, and a series of measures aimed at isolating the remaining Jews completely: they were concentrated in "Jewish homes," burdened with an accumulation of professional prohibitions, and expelled from schools. All special organizations were dissolved and forcibly integrated into a single Reichsvereinigung der Juden in Deutschland (Association of Jews of the Reich), a kind of self-managed administration under the control of the Security Services, which foreshadowed the future Jüdenrate (Council of Jews) in occupied countries. In that context, though they did not even have the right to vote or hold community offices, women played a dominant role—to such an extent that they were declared *unabkömmlich* (essential) by the Nazi authorities and made to be part of the last convoys of deportation with the community leaders. The deportations were announced with the usual sadism on the day of Yom Kippur, the highest of Jewish holy days. Begun in October 1941, the deportation campaigns were completed a year later in Austria, and in June 1943 in Germany. The Reich could then be officially declared *Judenrein* (purified of Jews).

Another sign of radicalization was the expansion of the world of concentration camps, in particular with the December 1938 construction of the women's camp of Ravensbrück. At first, German and Austrian women were transferred there, including 440 gypsies from Burgenland with their children. Once the war began, some 120,000 women of 23 nationalities were detained there; approximately 70,000 of them perished from hunger, ill treatment, or medical experiments, or by lethal injection, hanging, or gassing, even though this camp was not considered to be an extermination site (see Blau; *Frauen K-Z Ravensbrück;* Weisenborn). Meanwhile, as the eventuality of war became more and more probable, the status of women who were not "reprobates" sparked ongoing conflict between ideologues and technocrats—a conflict that Goering summed up in April 1942 to Fritz Sauckel, Gauleiter of Thuringia, who was responsible for mobilizing the labor force of the Reich and the occupied territories, in terms of the dichotomy "brood mares or draft mares?" (quoted in Heiber). According to the early estimates of 1939, out of the more than 30 million women over 14 years of age counted in the census was taken in the Greater Reich (Austria and Sudetenland included) in May 1939, only 3.5 million were unemployed (invalids, the sick, women over 60, and mothers of children under 14 years old being excepted from the count). These women could therefore be mobilized, and two million were transferable from the tertiary sector to the vital sectors of the war economy. However, the implementation of those measures did not bring the expected results. The output of this unqualified labor force, subjected to unaccustomed effort under bad working conditions and for low wages, did not meet the expectations of the experts. Countless reports indicated "lack of fervor at work," discontent, or even rebellion among the newly hired women. This translated into absenteeism, tacit work slow-downs, and the withdrawal of almost half a million wives of mobilized men, who preferred to keep their military benefits rather than perform hard, badly paid work. From the beginning of the conflict, the Gestapo did indeed receive the order to repress mercilessly any attack on "the German people's will to fight." This directive could not be applied to mothers, daughters, fiancées, and wives of mobilized men, for it would have been dangerous to demoralize them. This consideration, moreover, incited the military High Command to recommend in a brochure issued on 30 April 1940 that the demands of women workers be met: reduced hours to allow for shopping and housework, special days off to attend to family business or during their husband's furloughs, premiums for transfer to a new place of work, suitable housing and dining halls, and company nurseries and kindergartens. Three days earlier, Dr. Goebbels had reminded the press of his directive of September 1939 not to invoke problems that might "introduce new disturbances into the world of women."

It had been relatively easy for the regime to mobilize and control female youth: in 1936, the one-year mandatory *Landjahr* was "complemented" by an extra *Kriegseinsatz* (war service) of six months to one year. However, the same was not true for older women, who had not forgotten the promises of a peaceful future and a decent life. "Mistakes in this area," observed the state secretary of the Interior in a note dated 9 May 1936, "could

have dangerous repercussions, on the morale of people on the home front and men at the front." The regime felt an obsessive fear, shared by Hitler, of a repetition of the revolt of 1917. While twice renewing his admonitions to the *Volksgenossinnen* (women comrades of the race) in March and May 1941, to commit themselves to the "service of honor of the nation," Hitler had actually decided as early as the fall of 1940 to turn to foreign labor. Estimated at 1.2 million in May 1940, the foreign labor force would reach 7.6 million in 1944, or 21 percent of the total labor force of the Reich. Of those foreign workers, 1.5 million were female workers forcibly imported from the occupied countries in the East, and a minority of volunteers came from the West (see Petzina). Many of those modern-day slaves died from maltreatment or during the bombardments.

As long as the conquest of territories, occupation, and plunder of the better part of Europe shielded the Reich's population from the hardships of a war in which exploitation of the enslaved countries (with the complicity of collaborating political leaders, those of Vichy not being the least zealous) helped maintain the German standard of living, the hope for an imminent peace after the blitzkrieg victories, which had cost little in terms of human life, reinforced general faith in Germany's power and trust in the Führer. Although more often articulated by the younger generation of women, this mentality also had some currency among older women, even if they were more critical of some aspects of the regime. Unbeknownst to most of these women, after fall 1938, and especially since the outbreak of the war, the regime was free to radicalize its plan of directed procreation, an essential corollary to the eradication of the "inferior elements" in psychiatric centers, the camps, and the occupied territories. According to a 28 October 1939 order from Himmler, who in addition to his police functions had been promoted to Reichskommissar für die Festigung des deutschen Volkstums (Commissar of the Reich for Promotion of the National Character), the battle for births, a priority as absolute as military victory,

> must sometimes go beyond the limits of petty-bourgeois laws and customs, so that German women and young girls of good blood may become the mothers of children of soldiers leaving for battle, not fickleness, but a profound moral conscience prevailing.

In an open letter published in the 25 December 1939 issue of *Völkischer Beobachter*, Rudolf Hess, at the time still the "Führer's heir," adjured unwed mothers to "keep the racially unimpeachable child of the man who had gone to the front," They were assured that the state would "watch over the preservation of this precious national good." As months went on, while the mentally ill were systematically put to death, while the Nazi conquerors starved and massacred the Slavic and Jewish peoples of the East, Dr. Conti, the Reich's minister of Health, and his mother, president of the Vorsitzende des Nationalsozialistichen Hebammenverbandes (National Socialist Union of Midwives), "proposed the creation of marriage institutes" to be controlled by the party. These were intended to compensate through artificial insemination for the deficit of human potential that was "genetically and racially worthy." This proposal was rejected at a meeting on 16 July 1941 in Hitler's presence, because Himmler forcefully objected to the use of the vaginal swabbing techniques under development by doctors in the United States, which "risked inducing impotence, sterility, indeed the degeneration of genetic material." What was accepted, on the other hand, was the idea of party-controlled Forpflanzungsanstalten (Centers of Procreation and Maternity), which Himmler continued to establish right up until military collapse. The network of his Lebensborn program, too, was to be expanded. There his collaborator Inge Viermetz was prominent in taking ruthless action, assisted by medical and administrative SS experts and a staff of women who assisted in this barbarous work, willingly taking part in the elimination of "unworthy elements," just as women did in the centers where the mentally ill were put to death and in the concentration camps.

Must we conclude, in the words of historian Erika Weinzierl, that "too few were just"? In fact, it is difficult to evaluate the actual aid provided, which was anonymous and discreet under Nazism, as is generally the case under any authoritarian regime. There were some spectacular instances of resistance, such as that of Protestant vicar Käthe Staritz, who was sent to a concentration camp for having called upon her colleagues of Breslau to support the Christians of Jewish origin, or those known cases of women who helped to hide the persecuted or even helped Jews to escape deportation. Generally, however, it seems to have been a rare occurrence for women or men in hospitals, social welfare, and administration offices to refuse to participate in tasks of plunder, census taking, and selection linked to the racial policy of the regime, although such refusal might at worst have entailed sanctions such as transfer or demotion. This indifference to the fate of the victims was selective, however. By August 1941, churches, religious associations, and part of public opinion were sufficiently touched by the killing of mentally ill Aryans to have managed to curb the executions, which had already cost the lives of more than 70,000. The same was not true for "Operation 14f13," a gassing technique practiced later on the inmates of the Reich's concentration camps, followed by the deportations of the Jews of Germany and Austria, begun in the fall of 1941 under the code name "evacuation" or "transfer" to the East. There is only a single noteworthy—and successful—example of resistance: a demonstration by "Aryan" women in the heart of Berlin on 28 February 1943 in protest against the arrest of their husbands, who had previously been protected by a "privileged mixed marriage." Surprised and shocked by the mass demonstration, the Gestapo, whose headquarters was just a few dozen feet away from the demonstration, decided to integrate the approximately 6,000 "privileged ones" into the "community of the people." The incident would seem to prove that opposition was possible, on condition that it be large enough to worry the authorities. Similarly, very few French people reacted during the first two years, 1940 and 1941, to the measures of exclusion and internment of political opponents, Jews, and gypsies. Although people were shaken by the arrival of their compatriots expelled from the departments of Alsace-Lorraine in the fall of 1940, when the region had been annexed by the Reich, nobody was concerned with the approximately 7,000 Jewish men and women who were sent away from neighboring Bade-Palatinate at the same time. These people joined the thousands of internees in the French camps that were opened as early as 1939 under the Daladier government. Prisoners in the French camps were not in danger of being deliberately murdered, but several thousand people died for lack of food, hygiene, and medical care,

while the survivors were handed over for deportation by the Vichy state. The burst of indignation did not come until 1942, with the spectacle of thousands of Jewish men, women, and children who had been brutally arrested on the orders of the occupying enemy with the cooperation of the French authorities and police.

In the Reich, even responsibility for rescuing Jewish children seems to have fallen only to communities where they lived. In France, the intervention of the churches and their diocesan charities, along with the actions of professional and volunteer social workers, resistance fighters, and immigrants made it possible for three-quarters of the Jewish population to escape deportation. This proportion was exceeded only by Denmark and Bulgaria. Among so many others, the sacrifice of the young Marianne Cohn (aka Colin), a German refugee, is impossible to forget. Arrested with a group of children whom she was assigned to bring to Switzerland illegally, she turned down an opportunity to escape with the help of the resistance, because it would have meant abandoning her charges. The children were saved thanks to the mayor's intervention, but Cohn was pulled out of prison, raped, and beaten to death with a spade by her executioners. Young German-speaking emigrant women also participated in the "German work" of infiltrating the occupying troops. This was a particularly dangerous mission, and many of these women paid with their lives.

Twilight of the Idols

Not until the deterioration of the military situation and its consequences for the Reich's population did "nonreprobate, Aryan" women begin to express their discontent more openly. Their main grievances were shortages of supplies; having to work harder and harder for ever-diminishing wages, while the wives of the "mandarins" enjoyed privileges that seemed exorbitant; and the prohibition against sexual relations with foreigners, while mobilized men were free to have "girlfriends" from the occupied countries. This issues called into question Hitler's entourage without shaking the faith in him personally or public attachment to him. Protest was limited by many factors: the absence of a well-structured opposition, fears of denunciation, the omnipresent political police, a lack of solidarity (which in some cases went as far as refusing to share the restrooms in firms that employed foreign and Jewish workers), and, stirred up by constant propaganda, anxieties about the consequences of a possible Bolshevik victory. The more the German military and civil losses increased and the more the elimination of peoples designated as "inferior" or "unworthy of living" intensified in prisons, camps, and Nazi extermination sites—currently estimated at 10,000 (not all of them being permanent sites), of which 5,877 were in Polish territory (see Schwarz)—the more obsessed the masters of the Third Reich became with the birthrate. On 8 May 1942 Himmler confided to the SS General Pohl that he had secretly ordered the development of a Lebensborn project for 400,000 unwed mothers of "good blood" in order to compensate for the loss of human life. "The building," he added, "should be decent, and illustrate the noble idea of mankind and the unwed mother" (see Thalmann, 1982).

The term *anständig* (decent), of which Himmler and his people were particularly fond, also reappeared in his correspondence with regard to the establishment of brothels "in order to provide our men with worthy conditions for their sexual relations." The objective differed from his plans for foreign workers and "deserving" camp prisoners. "If I do not open these brothels," he explained to the state secretary of Agriculture, Herbert Backe, who refused to grant to prostitutes the special food-rations reserved for forced laborers,

> the thousands of foreign workers will throw themselves on our German women and young girls. . . . This particular problem is unappetizing, but it corresponds to a natural need, and if I can arrange this as a stimulant for a better yield, I believe that we have the duty to take advantage of the incentive. (Letter dated 30 July 1942, MA 65/520.)

On one side there were the sterilizations and forced abortions in the Reich and the Eastern occupied territories, the wear and tear of forced labor, the denial of medical care, the extermination of the sick declared to be incurable and of Slavic peoples, and the "final solution" for Jews and gypsies. On the other, there was frenzied imperative for growth in "genetically and racially worthy" human potential. In "Nehmt planmassig Urlaub!," a call to military men to plan their leaves, intended to reduce childless marriages and published in *Marine-Frontzeitung* on 10 December 1942, chief naval physician Hans Sievers declared: "Any unborn child signifies a drop of renunciation in our political ascension." This special "Aryan" procreation program was financed by SS headquarters from earnings realized on the confiscated belongings of concentration camp inmates. When women—even someone as well known as Guida Diehl, a conservative Protestant close to the Nazi movement since 1926—dared to protest against "animal procreation," they were forbidden to speak or publish their views.

Yet, the loneliness of German women, deprived of what the official speeches always characterized as as an indispensable companion, often led to what the Security reports called "forgetting necessary racial distance." This type of forgetfulness meant prison sentences or "reeducation" in a concentration camp for having "let oneself be loved by inferiors." Seen as the only one responsible, the "racial polluter" risked death penalty. By contrast, the German military in the occupied countries were absolved in advance. "If the German man," Hitler declared to the officers of his headquarters, "must be ready to die unconditionally, he must also have the right to love unconditionally." These were the words of a military man at war, which the loyal Himmler appreciated only moderately. Worried by the 7,000 cases of venereal disease in the German units brought back from the Russian front to France at the end of 1942 alone, the SS Reichsführer recommended to SS General Carl Oberg that brothels be established under medical and police control, saying that he understood that "men arrived from the East sexually starving." The control was extended to *Kontrolldirnen*, or "prostitutes"— a shocking expression to be avoided, he added, in case his "dear Carl" had not yet understood that France was not, and could not possibly be treated in the same way as the "primitive" Eastern lands (Letter; MA 21/5967–68).

This difference in treatment was also evident when it came to recuperating "racially worthy" elements from the occupied countries. Thus, in spite of their own doctrine, the purveyors of "human material" were quite willing to send into the Reich those young Polish and Ukrainian women deemed by the experts to come from "racial groups I and II." The policy had a double purpose: providing large families with inexpensive domestic help, otherwise hard to find, and training the young women to become "mothers of a good race," whose children would thus be removed from their country of origin. Depending on the experts' assessment, Lebensborn mothers from occupied countries were either sent to the Reich with or without their children, or separated from them when the latter were placed in German families to be raised as good Germans. In the occupied countries of Western Europe, to some extent the bonds between mother and child were still generally respected in the Germanization process, and women and their children were treated them accordingly. No such attention existed in the eastern territories; potential mothers there were brought to the Reich, after the SS had culled the population of children and torn them away from their families. These children were then sent to selection centers, and thereafter sent on to the Reich's adoption families or abandoned in death centers. In cases where there had been no forced abortion beforehand, abandonment was also the fate of babies born to foreign forced laborers or women in the camps.

The Nazi's obsession with the birthrate did not prevent the masters of the Reich from decreeing, on 27 January 1943, the total mobilization of women from age 17 to 45. The age limit was extended to 50 on 25 July 1944. Aware of the discontent of women workers, Hitler arrived at this extreme solution, which coincided with the defeat at Stalingrad, only after he had promulgated new measures for mother-and-child welfare that had been in preparation for two years. These measures, along with the order to care for sick workers and mothers, caused an increase in what armaments inspectors termed "the flight of women," which reached 40 percent in some businesses. This deficit was all the more worrisome since the Wehrmacht had begun to transfer young girls from production to its auxiliary services in order to free up the men needed to form new combat units. If the women already conscripted approved of total female mobilization, they remained skeptical about its realization, despite assurances that socially privileged women would not receive special consideration This skepticism was justified: out of 3 million women targeted by the law of January 1943, 1.1 million were actually hired, often on a part-time basis; another 1.9 million, many of whom had medical certificates or well-placed relations, received dispensations (see Petzina). Under pressure from military leaders, the experts then envisioned extending the mandatory service of young girls. Dr. Theodor Morell, Hitler's personal physician, was formally opposed: "If we want to stop the decrease in number of women desirous and capable of having babies, we should not think in terms of lengthening the period of work service" (BA Koblenz R43II 520A). There remained the possible solution that the technocrats had proposed in vain in 1939: offering women attractive wages. However, during a last arbitration meeting on 25 April 1944 in Berchtesgaden, Hitler adamantly declared that this was out of the question. Equal pay for women, if only in some sectors, would contradict the fundamental principles of the community of the people, based on the role of man as head and main support of the family, with woman essentially dedicated to household tasks. With the return of peace, this principle was even supposed to prohibit men from entering certain professions deemed too feminine, such as women's hairdresser or caretaker of young children. In Hitler's eyes, all that mattered was the preservation of the ideological model, even if, as in this case, it meant ignoring or contradicting economic interests.

From conversations of Himmler with his Finnish masseur (recorded in Felix Kersten, *Totenkopt und Treue: Heinrich Himmler ohne Uniform* [1952]) and from a memo of Reichsleiter Bormann on 29 January 1944, it it clear that Hitler and his entourage were still debating the future and the regeneration of the "Germanic race" while the Wehrmacht was retreating on all fronts. In this spirit, marriage was condemned as the "satanic work" of the Catholic Church; matrimonial laws were charged with immoral hypocrisy because they forced married men to hide their need to have other women. According to Bormann's memo, a system of applications and selection was to allow men, after the war, to have two households and two wives. In addition to bigamy, the population was to be prepared to accept free love. Appropriate speeches would incite men to have relations with several women. "Every woman," the memo concluded, "must be able to have an unlimited number of children if in twenty years the Reich does not want to be lacking in divisions that are indispensable to the survival of our people."

The most complete and most perfected model of dehumanization in the history of the so-called civilized world, Nazism, which from the outset judged women to be "naturally" inferior and relegated them to an auxiliary role, nevertheless established a systematic hierarchy among them. Some were thus slated for political mobilization, others for genetic mobilization, and a third group for slavery or eradication. This system was without precedent under any previous dictatorship, and was elaborated and actualized as a function of, and accordance with, the objectives of territorial and "racial" hegemony. It should not be forgotten that until 1939 the main victims were German and Austrian women who were members of the political or religious opposition or Jews; such "antisocial elements" were dismissed from their jobs, forcibly sterilized, driven into exile, thrown into prison or camps, slaughtered, or driven to suicide. Nevertheless, the fact remains that a majority of the women of the Reich, like men, accepted with varying degrees of enthusiasm a regime that, in spite of its "excesses," had restored full employment and the security and prestige of Germany. Neither the violence of the pogroms after the Anschluss and during Kristallnacht, nor the beginning of the war, dreaded as it was by those women who had not forgotten the suffering of the previous war, changed this attitude. The blitzkrieg victories of the Wehrmacht and economic benefits of exploiting the occupied nations further strengthened confidence in the Führer and his policies—with corollary increases in isolation and the numbers of victims. We should recall that German and Austrian women constituted almost 15 percent of the resistance groups and that 230 women resisters from every social, political, and denominational background were condemned to death and executed. Many people remember Sophie Scholl, of the Christian student resistance group Weisse Rose (White Rose), who was executed along with several other group members in 1943 (see Scholl). Another prominent woman resister was the American Mildred Fish-Harnack of the group Rote Kapelle (Red Orchestra), in which 18 of the 52 group members executed were women (see Brysac). There was an even higher proportion of women activists in Herbert und Marianne Baum, a group of young Jews, where 13 out of the 34 members who were executed were women. Until the final phase of the all-out war, while the Nazi death machinery was crushing millions of human beings—men, women, and children rounded up with the complicity of collaborating governments throughout occupied Europe—a majority of the female citizens of the Reich, although hard hit by the effects of war in their own lives, did not revolt as they had done in 1917–18. The sense of duty, fear, and 12 years of indoctrination and propaganda had done their work. While they did not operate the levers of command, female doctors, nurses, midwives, office workers, laborers, housewives, auxiliaries to the army or the SS, executives of the party's women's organizations, stars and activists of the regime, such as the film maker Leni Riefenstahl, the former actress Emma Goering or the aviator Hanna Reitsch, all contributed to the realization of the Reich's criminal objectives, simply by remaining at their posts. The women of Germany were politically better integrated than women in other fascist countries, and they did not have any independent women's organizations. These factors, in combination with nationalism and a long tradition of obedience to authority, had prevailed over a young democracy whose roots in German history had proven all too tenuous.

Notes

Rote Kapelle (Red Orchestra)
Resistance and information network that sought to accelerate the collapse of Nazi domination and weaken Germany's military by transmitting information, notably to the Soviet secret service. The network consisted of an outer circle based in Brussels and Paris, whose main leader was Léopold Trepper, a Polish Jew, and an inner circle based in Berlin and Hamburg, headed by David Harnack (b. 1902) and Harro Schulze-Boysen (b. 1909), both of whom were executed in 1942. The inner circle was active from 1932, initially around Harnack and his American wife, Mildred, and later (1934–36) around Schulze-Boysen. The outer circle became active in 1940. The Gestapo called this network the Rote Kapelle, having discovered, at the time of the first arrests in 1942, that its members came from very different political and religious backgrounds and that some even occupied key posts in the Reich. The inner circle included a large proportion of young women, 19 of whom were eventually executed. Mildred Harnack and Erica von Brockdorff were initially sentenced to six to ten years in prison, but after a second trial ordered by Hitler they were condemned to death. Ultimately, 55 members of the network were executed.

Weisse Rose (White Rose)
Underground resistance group made up of Christian students, created in Munich in 1942 by Hans Scholl, a student of medicine, and Sophie Scholl, a student of philosophy. The group wrote anti-Nazi tracts and distributed them in Munich and several other large German cities. Members were arrested in February 1943 for dropping their leaflets from an upper floor of the entrance hall of the University of Munich. Three of them—Hans and Sophie Scholl and Christophe Probst—were brought before a people's tribunal and sentenced to death on charges of high treason; they were executed in February 1943. Other

members were executed later the same year: professor of philosophy Kurt Huber and Alexander Schmorell (July 1943), and Willi Graf (October 1943). Following the execution of Hans and Sophie Scholl, the White Rose of Hamburg was formed; the group's tracts were recovered and duplicated.

Bibliography

Archives

BA: Bundesarchiv, Koblenz, Germany. Federal archive.
BDC: Berlin Document Center. American archive of Nazi documents in Berlin.
MA: Microfilm Archive, Alexandria, Virginia.

Reference Works

L'Allemagne nazie et le génocide juif, conference proceedings edited by François Furet, Paris: Hautes Études, and Gallimard-Seuil, 1985; as Unanswered Questions: Nazi Germany and the Genocide of the Jews, New York: Schocken Books, 1989

Badia, Gilbert, et al., Les barbelés de l'exil: Études sur l'émigration allemande et autrichienne (1938–1940), Grenoble, France: Presses Universitaires de Grenoble, 1979

Bédarida, François, editor, La politique nazie d'extermination, Paris: Albin Michel, 1989

Benz, Wolfgang, and Barbara Distel, editors, Frauen-Verfolgung und Widerstand, Dachau, Germany: Dachauer Hefte, 1987

Blau, Bruno, "The Last Days of German Jewry in the Third Reich," Yivo Annual of Jewish Social Science, vol. III, edited by Koppel Pinson, New York: Yiddish Scientific Institute, 1953

Bock, Gisela, Zwangssterilisation im Nationalsozialismus: Studien zur Rassenpolitik und Frauenpolitik, Opladen, Germany: Westdeutscher, 1986

Brès, Evelyn, and Yvan Brès, Un maquis d'antifascistes allemands en France (1942–1944), Montpellier, France: Presses de Languedoc, 1987

Bridenthal, Renate, Atina Grossman, and Marion A. Kaplan, editors, When Biology Became Destiny: Women in Weimar and Nazi Germany, New York: Monthly Review Press, 1984

Brysac, Shareen Blair, Resisting Hitler: Mildred Harnack and the Red Orchestra, New York: Oxford University Press, 2001

Diehl, Guida, Christ sein heisst Kämpfer sein: Die Führung meines Lebens, Giessen, Germany: Brunnen, 1959

Duby, Georges, and Michelle Perrot, general editors, A History of Women in the West, 5 vols., Cambridge, Massachusetts: Belknap Press of Harvard University, 1992–1994; see especially vol. 5, Toward a Cultural Identity in the Twentieth Century, edited by Françoise Thébaud

Elling, Hanna, Frauen im deutschen Widerstand, 1933–45, Frankfurt: Röderberg, 1978 "Émigration allemande sous la IIIᵉ Reich," in Émigrés français en Allemagne; Émigrés allemands en France, 1685–1945 (exhib. cat.), edited by Jacques Grandjonc, Paris: Institut Goethe and Ministère des Relations Extérieures, 1983

Frauen-KZ Ravensbrück. Autorenkollektiv unter Leitung von G. Zörner, Herausgegeban vom Komitee der Antifaschistischen Widerstandskämpfer in der Deutschen Demokratischen Republik, Berlin: Deutscher Verlag der Wissenschaften, 1971

Frevert, Ute, Frauen-Geschichte: Zwischen bürgerlicher Verbesserung und neuer Weiblichkeit, Frankfurt: Suhrkamp, 1986; as Women in German History: From Bourgeois Emancipation to Sexual Liberation, translated by Stuart McKinnon-Evans, New York: Berg, 1993

Gilzmer, Mechtild, Fraueninternierungslager in Südfrankreich: Rieucros und Brens, 1939–1944, Berlin: Orlanda Frauenverlag, 1994

Griebel, Regina, Marlies Coburger, and Heinrich Scheel, editors, Erfasst? Das Gestapo-Album zur Roten Kapelle (exhib. cat.), Halle, Germany: Audioscop, 1992

Guillaumin, Colette, Sexe, race et pratique du pouvoir: L'idée de nature, Paris: Côté Femmes, 1992

Hautval, Adélaïde, Médecine et crimes contre l'humanité, Arles, France: Actes Sud, 1991

Heiber, Helmut, compiler, Reichsführer! Briefe an und von Himmler, Munich: Deutscher Taschenbuch, 1970

Herlem, Didier, "Féminisme et antiféminisme en Allemagne: Étude de l'évolution des rapports hommes-femmes en Allemagne du XIXᵉ siècle à nos jours," 5 vols., doctorat-ès-État thesis, Sorbonne, 1990

Hilberg, Raul, The Destruction of the European Jews, Chicago: Quadrangle Books, and London: Allen: 1961; new edition, 3 vols., New York and London: Holmes and Meier, 1985

Hillel, Marc, and Clarissa Henry, Au nom de la race, Paris: Fayard, 1975; as Of Pure Blood, translated by Eric Mossbacher, New York: McGraw Hill, 1976; as Children of the SS, translated by Eric Mossbacher, London: Hutchinson, 1976

Hoock-Demarle, Marie-Claire, editor, Femmes, nations, Europe, Paris: Publications de l'Université Paris VII-Denis Diderot, 1995

Kandel, Liliane, editor, Féminismes et nazisme, Paris: Publications de l'Université Paris VII-Denis Diderot, 1997

Kater, Michael H., The Nazi Party: A Social Profile of Members and Leaders, 1919–1945, Cambridge, Massachusetts: Harvard University Press, and Oxford: Blackwell, 1983

Klaus, Martin, Mädchen im Dritten Reich: Der Bund Deutscher Mädel (BDM), Cologne, Germany: Rugenstein, 1983

Klaus, Martin, Mädchen in der Hitlerjugend, Cologne, Germany: Pahl-Rugenstein, 1980

Klee, Ernst, "Euthanasie" im NS-Staat: Die "Vernichtung lebensunwerten Lebens," Frankfurt: Fischer, 1983

Koehn, Ilse, Mischling, Second Degree: My Childhood in Nazi Germany, New York: Greenwillow Books, 1977

Kogon, Eugen, Hermann Langbein, and Adalbert Rückerl, editors, Nationalsozialistische Massentötungen durch Giftgas: Eine Dokumentation, Frankfurt: Fischer, 1983; as Nazi Mass Murder: A Documentary History of the Use of Poison Gas, translated by Mary Scott and Caroline Lloyd-Morris, New Haven, Connecticut: Yale University Press, 1993

Koonz, Claudia, Mothers in the Fatherland: Women, the Family, and Nazi Politics, New York: St. Martin's Press, 1986; London: Jonathan Cape, 1987

Kuhn, Annette, "Welche Geschichte wählen wir?" in Metis 2, Pfaffenweiler, Germany: Centaurus, 1993

Kwiet, Konrad, and Helmut Eschwege, Selbstbehauptung und Widerstand: Deutsche Juden im Kampf um Existenz und Menschenwürde, 1933–1945, Hamburg: Christians, 1984

Lingens-Reiner, Ella, Prisoners of Fear, London: Gollancz, 1948

Petzina, Dietmar, "Die Mobiliserung deutscher Arbeitskräfte vor und während des Zweiten Weltkrieges," Vierteljahrshefte fur Zeitgeschichte, 18 Jarhgang 1970

Pilgrim, Volker Elis, "Du kannst mich ruhig 'Frau Hitler' nennen": Frauen als Schmuck und Tarnung der NS-Herrschaft, Reinbeck bei Hamburg, Germany: Rowohlt, 1994

Poliakov, Léon, Le mythe aryen: Essai sur les sources du racisme et des nationalismes, Paris: Calmann-Lévy, 1971; as The Aryan Myth: A History of Racist and Nationalist Ideas in Europe, translated by Edmund Howard, London: Chatto and Windus Heinemann, and New York: Basic Books, 1974

Rinser, Luise, Gefängnistagebuch, Munich: Zinnen, 1946; as A Woman's Prison Journal: Germany, 1944, translated by Michael Hulse, New York: Schocken Books, 1987; as Prison Journal, translated by Michael Hulse, London: Macmillan, 1987

Schaber, Irme, *Gerta Taro: Fotoreporterin im spanischen Bürgerkrieg: Eine Biographie*, Marburg, Germany: Jonas, 1994

Schoenbaum, David, *Hitler's Social Revolution: Class and Status in Nazi Germany, 1933–1939*, Garden City: New York, Doubleday, 1966; London: Weidenfeld and Nicolson, 1967

Scholl, Inge, *Die Weiße Rose*, Frankfurt: Frankfurter Hefte, 1952; as *Students against Tyranny: The Resistance of the White Rose, Munich, 1942–1943*, translated by Arthur R. Schultz, Middletown, Connecticut: Wesleyan University Press, 1970

Schwarz, Gudrun, *Die nationalsozialistischen Lager*, Frankfurt and New York: Campus, 1990

Stephenson, Jill, *The Nazi Organisation of Women*, Totowa, New Jersey: Barnes and Noble Books, and London: Croom Helm, 1981

Stephenson, Jill, *Women in Nazi Society*, New York: Barnes and Noble Books, and London: Croom Helm, 1975

Stollwitzer, Gertrude, editor, *La résistance autrichienne* (special number), *Austriaca: Cahiers Universitaires d'Information sur l'Autriche* 17 (1983)

Thalmann, Rita, editor, *Entre émancipation et nationalisme: La presse féminine d'Europe, 1914–1945*, Paris: Tierce, 1990

Thalmann, Rita, *Être femme sous le IIIe Reich*, Paris: Laffont, 1982

Thalmann, Rita, editor, *Femmes et fascismes*, Paris: Tierce, 1986

Thalmann, Rita, *Frausein im Dritten Reich*, Munich and Vienna: Carl Hanser Verlag, 1984, and Berlin: Ullstein, 1987

Thalmann, Rita, "Hiérarchisation et traitement des femmes selon les critères nationaux-socialistes de la pureté raciale," in *Sexe et race*, vol. 4, Université Paris VII-Denis Diderot, 1989

Tillion, Germaine, et al., *Ravensbrück*, Neuchâtel, France: Éditions de la Baconnière, 1946; as *Ravensbrück*, translated by Gerald Satterwhite, Garden City, New York: Anchor Press, 1975

Tingsten, Herbert, *Political Behavior: Studies in Election Statistics*, New York: Arno Press, 1975

Vormeier, Barbara, *Die Deportierung deutscher und österreichischer Juden aus Frankreich; La déportation des Juifs allemands et autrichiens de France; The Deportation of German and Austrian Jews from France, 1942–1944* (trilingual German–French–English edition), Paris: La Solidarité, 1980

Weinzierl, Erika, *Zu wening Gerechte, Österreicher und Judenverfolgung 1938–1945*, Graz and Cologne, Germany: Verlag Styria, 1969

Weisenborn, Günther, *Der lautlose Aufstand: Berich über d. Widerstandsbewegung d. dt. Volkes 1933–1945*, Hamburg: Rowohlt, 1953

Weyrather, Irmgard, *Muttertag und Mutterkreuz: Der Kult um die "deutsche Mutter" im Nationalsozialismus*, Frankfurt: Fischer, 1993

Wickert, Christl, editor, *Frauen gegen die Diktatur: Widerstand und Verfolgung im nationalsozialistischen Deutschland*, vol. 2, Berlin: Hentrich, 1995

Wittrock, Christine, *Weiblichkeitsmythen: Das Frauenbild im Faschismus und seine Vorläufer in der Frauenbewegung der 20er Jahre*, Frankfurt: Sendler, 1983

Wobbe, Theresa, editor, *Nach Osten: Verdeckte Spuren nationalsozialistischer Verbrechen*, Frankfurt: Neue Kritik, 1992

Zimmermann, Michael, *Verfolgt, vertrieben, vernichtet: Die nationalsozialistische Vernichtungspolitik gegen Sinti und Roma*, Essen, Germany: Klartext, 1989

WOMEN'S COLLABORATION AND RESISTANCE UNDER ITALIAN FASCISM

CECILIA DAU-NOVELLI

BENITO MUSSOLINI WAS NAMED president of the council by King Victor-Emmanuel III on 28 October 1922 following the March on Rome, which was essentially a coup d'état. After removing the most extremist Fascists, Mussolini tried to normalize the regime by appointing a government composed of Liberals, Democrats, and Catholics. However, after only two years, he wanted to give the regime a more authoritarian character by changing electoral laws, substituting the majority system for the proportional system. His "national lists" received 65 percent of the vote in the legislative elections of 6 April 1924.

Not all Italians had been made subservient to the regime. The Socialist deputy Giacomo Matteotti was assassinated in June 1924 because he had criticized the fraud that had marked the elections. The opposition parties, disagreeing among themselves, left Parliament, seceded, and essentially withdrew from the political process. Mussolini, assuming the entire responsibility for Matteotti's assassination, turned the regime in an authoritarian direction in January 1925. The *legge fascistissime* (most extreme Fascist laws) reinforced the powers of the head of the government. Strikes were forbidden and unions suppressed, with the exception of the Fascist union. The regime installed a one-party system, drew up an election list, and created the Fascist Great Council, whose powers were more extensive powers than those of Parliament, as well as a special tribunal made up of military men to try political crimes.

Still, Fascist totalitarianism was an "imperfect" totalitarianism, for unlike Nazism it tolerated the existence of two powers independent of the power of Il Duce: the Catholic Church and the monarchy. The Fascists signed a concordat with the Church on 11 February 1929, to regulate their internal relationship. The monarchy, meanwhile, constituted an insurmountable internal barrier, since the king remained the highest authority of the state.

This was why the country could not become as fully Fascist as Mussolini had wanted. The regime advocated the formation of a "new man" through specific organizations such as the Opera Nazionale Balilla for youth, the Opera Nazionale Dopolavoro (National Recreation Service) for paid workers, and the Opera Nazionale per la Protezione della Maternità e dell'Infanzia (ONMI; National Service for the Protection of Mothers and Children), which were intended to accompany Italians from birth to death. In addition, as a result of special measures, very strict control was exercised over the press, radio, and cinema. The regime reacted to the economic crisis of 1929 with massive state intervention in the economy and with a self-sufficiency policy that anticipated exclusive recourse to the domestic market. In foreign policy, Fascist nationalism manifested itself through the conquest of Ethiopia, which was initiated in October 1935 and led to the proclamation of the empire in May 1936. This period marked the pinnacle of popular support for the Fascist regime, partly because of the favorable economic and social aspects that seemed to be opening up.

In October 1935 Mussolini signed the Berlin-Rome axis agreement, which gave him the illusion of being the leader of a great power. Galeazzo Ciano, who was Mussolini's son-in-law and had been appointed minister of foreign affairs, played a major role in this. The alliance between the two countries was reinforced in the fall of 1937 by Italy's participation in the Spanish Civil War and by Ciano's signing of the "Pact of Steel" in May 1939.

In reality, the racial laws of 1938 that excluded Jews from civil service and forbade mixed marriages were unexpected in a country that had never known anti-Semitism as it existed in Germany, Poland, Russia, and France. There was no popular mobilization against the Jews, as the regime had hoped, and the issue gave rise to serious disagreements with the Catholic Church.

Italy's entry into the war in 1940 was not received with the same enthusiasm by the people as the conquest of Ethiopia had been. Military setbacks in Greece, North Africa, and Russia ended up by completely isolating the regime. The landing of the Allies in June 1943 on the Italian mainland was a decisive blow. Defeated at the meeting of the Fascist Great Council on 25 June 1943, Mussolini was arrested. The king, who had escaped to the south of Italy, commissioned General Pietro Badoglio to form a new government. The latter signed an armistice with the Allies on 8 September 1943. Mussolini, having been freed by the Germans, was placed at the head of the Repubblica Sociale Italiana (RSI; Italian Social Republic), which controlled the north of the country.

For almost two years, until the liberation in April 1945, Italy was split in two: the north was under German control and was where the resistance developed; the south, meanwhile, had already been liberated by the Allies. Mussolini's execution on 28 April 1945 and the insurrection in the north of the country put an end to one of the most tragic pages in the history of Italy.

The Secular Cult of the Mother

The myth of motherhood certainly was one of the basic elements of Fascist ideology. The "new woman," the center of the family, was to be one of the pillars of the rebirth of the Italian nation. Her education had to take place under the control of the Fasci Femminili (Fascist women's groups) that would follow her from childhood to maturity in order to make her into a good mother.

Women's new role in the building of the fascist state was defined in 1924 when the Fasci Femminili were reorganized. Thus, two years after the March on Rome of October 1922, Fascism defined itself as a regime that needed women.

The exaltation of the woman-mother as the foundation of the life of the nation was a new element that had no precedent other than the idealization of Mary by the Church. In Fascism, however, this celebration was strictly secular. In an article published in *Augustea* in 1933, Wanda Gorjux, in charge of the Fasci Femminili of Bari, declared:

> The mother becomes the expression of the strength of the race and a sign of joy for the nation. Mother's Day is the celebration of the very race which feels sure of her, which is perpetuated, which is eternal: the Mother flourishes with her Child in her arms, she is the eternity of life, the symbol of the Nativity. . . . Thus, the responsibility for national life depends directly on women and women are directly involved in the life of the state. ("La festa del popolo che si eterna" [An Enduring Popular Feast])

Margherita Sarfatti, who published a biography of Mussolini and headed the magazine *Gerarchia*, declared that Fascism intended to defend the myth of motherhood, to which it rendered "a conscious homage of veneration and pride." Besides, every man owed not only his birth but his early education to his mother. "A man," wrote Sarfatti in the same issue of *Augustea*,

> should want a mother for his children and not simply a woman for himself. Man should not forget that he owes three lives to his mother: that of the blood in her belly, that of the first food at her breast, that of his first education in her heart. ("Italia d'oggi" [Italy Today])

In order to crown the myth of motherhood, the regime created the "Day of the Mother and Child," which was celebrated every year on Christmas Eve. The articles devoted to this day in the official Fascist publication, *Il popolo d'Italia*, celebrated the ideal identification between the people and Fascism through motherhood, with Mussolini thanking the mothers of large families and castigating those who did not yet have any children. According to Il Duce, the Italian people should model their conduct on the ancient Romans, who were accustomed to serving and obeying the family, since a nation without children was a dead nation. "I refuse to believe," wrote Mussolini, "that the Italian people of the Fascist era, when forced to choose between life and death, would choose the latter" ("La seconda giornata della madre et del fanciullo" [The Second Day of the Mother and Child], *Il popolo d'Italia* 1934).

For Mussolini, procreation—the perpetuation of the race—was a fundamental element of the collective national identity. Clearly, women were central in this ideology. Thus, with good reason, the myth of motherhood became part of the Olympus of Fascist mythology—to such a degree that slowly but irrevocably, the initially virile Fascist ideology took on female characteristics as well. Alongside the myth of the daring fighter, who had escorted the conquest of power, the regime espoused the myth of the woman-mother, symbol of security, fertility, and well-being.

It was again Margherita Sarfatti who recalled the Roman roots of the secular mother's day celebration. Writing in *Politica sociale* 12 (1933), she cited the example of the ancient Romans who celebrated a holiday called *Matralia*, or "Feast of Mothers," in honor of the Mater Matuta, a divinity of probably Etruscan origin, who was venerated among the Roman Olympians. Roberto Forges Davanzati, a high-ranking Fascist, established a link with Christian worship in order to make it into a secular celebration: "Our heroine is the mother. The fruitful mother, whose worship Fascism has restored in honor of the healthy, strong, and hard-working Italian people" ("Nello splendore cristiano" [In Christian Splendor], *Politica sociale* 12 [1933]). Wanda Gorjux, in the previously cited article, also exalted the observance, thereby contributing to the celebration of the myth: "The mother alone is able to create youth which will perpetuate the idea; and it is to her Fascist Mother's Fascist faith that Italy will owe generations of 'Balilla' and 'Avanguardisti,' who are already moving toward the conquest of the millennium."

Women's Integration into the Nation

Women were envisioned as being the driving force behind social regeneration and the artisans of national grandeur. But to that end they had to be trained in order to become new women—"true fascists." With this goal in mind, the regime in 1924 created the Fasci Femminili, of which every woman had to be a member.

From childhood on, members of the girls' organizations Giovani Italiane and Piccole Italiane were taught to love the fatherland through the family as intermediary. In the rhetoric of the regime's program, written by Augusto Turati, then the secretary of the Partito Nazionale Fascista (PNF; National Fascist Party), the fatherland was in fact presented as a great mother. The different goals of the program were phrased as follows in the Fasci Femminili's *Decalogo* (1929; Ten Commandments):

> 1) To accomplish one's duty as a daughter, a sister, a schoolgirl, a friend, with goodness and joy, even if this task is sometimes difficult. 2) To serve the fatherland as

a greater mother, as the mother of all good Italians. 3) To love Il Duce, who has made the country stronger and greater. 4) To obey one's superiors joyfully. 5) To have the courage to oppose those who are the advocates of evil and those who make a mockery of honesty. 6) To train one's body to conquer physical effort and one's soul not to fear pain. 7) To flee from vanity, but to love beautiful things. 8) To love work because it is life and harmony.

To be sure, the frame of reference was Catholic, with virtues and good feelings, the ethics of duty and of love, training of the body, education of the soul. However, the program included a cultivation of the body that was foreign to Catholic tradition. The importance assigned to physical education was to constitute one of the points of friction with the Church, because it would be interpreted as a glorification of the body that was unsuitable for a proper young girl's education. On the other hand, obeying and preserving the ability to oppose evil, keeping to that which is essential and rejecting the superfluous in everyday life, and devoting oneself to one's work with rigor and competence were totally acceptable precepts, even for Catholics.

During the 1920s, the Fasci Femminili had a very precarious existence, still associated with the revolutionary thrust of the first Fascist women. Nevertheless, in 1923, the year after the march on Rome, they still obviously appeared to play merely a helping role. According to the PNF's 1921 statute outline women were to "coordinate the work of propaganda, of charity, and of aid" while unreservedly accepting "the program, the statutes, and the discipline" of the party. In addition, the women's groups could not take any initiatives of a political nature ("Schema di statuto per il funzionamento dei gruppi femminili" [Statute Outline for the Operations of Women's Groups]; in Missori).

The duties of teaching were explained even more clearly in another party program that specified that it was a question of "organizing night courses, series of educational lectures and always with the goal of intensifying propaganda, facilitating charity and aid, and raising the level of instruction, especially for laborers and farmers" (*Programma statuto del gruppo femminile di Roma* [Program Statutes of Roman Women's Groups], 1921; in Missori).

The eradication of the most radical fringes of feminism was included in the larger project of reorganizing the PNF as Mussolini wanted. In March 1926, he appointed Augusto Turati as party secretary in order to complete this task. After the turbulent period, during which Roberto Farinacci had been party secretary, Mussolini was expecting Augusto Turati to produce a definitive "framework" for the PNF and to eliminate all "individualistic" positions that had marked it so far.

In 1926, the Fasci Femminili were integrated into other sectors of party activity in order to have them better controlled. The Fascist women's movement, which had been born with the intention of practicing politics and with such typically feminist objectives as winning the right to vote for women, was at that point integrated into the whole of the party and assigned exclusively to tasks of aid and propaganda. As early as January 1926, the body of female inspectors was suppressed. In the same way, the women's journal *Rassegna femminile italiana* was suppressed without the knowledge of its director, Elisa Majer Rizzioli. The same year saw the removal of all women who had been unhappy

with the way the issue of women's suffrage had been decided. In fact, in 1923 a plan had been adopted for a law granting women the right to vote in administrative elections, but this right was never applied for the simple reason that the elections were suppressed.

The new tasks for women were solely to be tasks of assistance. All women over the age of 18 could register in the groups known as Fasci. Each Fascio was led by a board of directors elected by its members and by a secretary appointed by the board. On the national level, each Fascio was controlled by the "Direttorio Nazionale" National Board of Directors of the Fascist Party and, therefore, by its secretary. Each Fascio included organizations for girls: a Gruppo Giovanile and a Piccole Italiane. The Giovani Italiane were young women between the ages of 14 and 18, while the Piccole Italiane were girls between the ages of 10 and 14. These organizations were responsible for "supporting and helping the moral, social, and patriotic action of the Fasci Femminili." The Fasci were charged with distributing books and newspapers published by the party, giving assistance to working women, advising families on hygiene, and recommending the purchase of Italian products.

Still, although they had now become an organization that depended directly on the party, the Fasci Femminili did not manage to gain the importance the regime had wanted the organizations to have. In 1928, they had only 80,000 members, to which should be added some 66,000 Giovani Italiane. The following year there were 100,000 members, but this increase still did not transform the Fasci Femminili into an organization of the masses (Foglio d'ordini , n°51, 28 October 1928). Moreover, their activities were still the traditional activities of women's associations in the early part of the 20th century: working in summer camps, clinics, cafeterias, day care centers, after-school activities, soup kitchens, and so forth.

Finally, in 1930, the organizations Giovani Italiane and Piccole Italiane were separated from the Fasci Femminili and placed directly under the control of the Ministry of National Education, as were the corresponding organizations for boys and young men: the Figli della Lupa, Balilla, and Avanguardisti. Essentially, this move meant taking female education away from the control of women—even Fascist women. This change in direction should be seen in the framework of a general reinforcement of the PNF, which Mussolini wanted and which was also manifested in the appointment of a new party secretary, Giovanni Giurati. One of the tasks entrusted to the new secretary was precisely that of "strengthening the PNF in those sectors the previous secretary, Augusto Turati, had least worked with, that is to say, youth, students, and women" (quoted in De Felice 1974–81).

But Mussolini was not yet satisfied with the success obtained. In December 1931 a new secretary, Achille Starace, was appointed with the goal of winning the entire Italian population over to Fascism and, according to the historian Renzo De Felice, he was a loyal administrator of Mussolini's program (see De Felice 1974–81).

The high priest in the enterprise of turning the country Fascist, Starace imposed uniforms on the men, and the Roman salute and a Fascist lifestyle on those women who belonged to party organizations. One of the first decisions made by the new secretary was to change the party statutes. The rules of the Fasci Femminili, the Fasci Giovanili (Fascist Youth) and the Gruppi

Universitari Fascisti (Fascist University Groups) were enforced. The establishment of the Fasci Femminili thus became obligatory in every town that had a male Fascio. In 1932, on the occasion of the tenth anniversary of the Fascist takeover, the regime reopened registration for the Fasci Femminili, which at that time became a mass organization. While they counted only 121,000 members in December 1932, their numbers had increased to 774,000 in October 1939, when Starace left the party secretariat (PNF, *Foglio d'ordini* 87; De Felice 1974–81).

The regime also organized a formal initiation ceremony called the "Leva femminile fascista" for young women, modeled on the existing practice for young male initiates into the movement. When they turned 18, the Giovani Italiane became Giovani Fasciste and thereby members of the Fasci. This rite of passage was the occasion for a feast celebrated on 28 October, the beginning of the year according to the Fascist calendar, and marked by the symbolic gesture of two young girls from the two groups kissing each other to represent the passage from adolescence to adulthood.

The regime had ambiguous attitudes toward education for women. It was held that wives should receive instruction in order to grow closer to their husbands, but their studies should not be so advanced as to cause them to become "unbalanced." The Gruppi Universitari Femminili (University Women's Groups) were considered to be too dangerous an instrument, because of the possible opportunities that study and work represented. These groups had a very difficult existence: early in the 1930s women were excluded from the *Littorali* competitions in sports and culture because these might offer the chance for excessive emancipation.

Fascist Policy on Women

This important program of integration in the nation naturally had to be sustained by an appropriate social policy destined to contain and help women complete their tasks. Thus, between 1923 and 1934, the Fascist regime adopted a group of laws intended to have a direct influence on women's lives. The logic of these laws went in two very specific directions: those designed to protect women, ensuring them the greatest security and thus encouraging the birth of multiple children, and those aimed at eliminating behaviors that deviated from the regime-approved norms for wives and mothers.

In the area of protections for mothers, one of the first significant measures was the creation of a maternity fund to pay benefits to working women. Protections for working women were broadened for the first time in 1932, then again in 1934. In addition, such protections were extended to the mothers of soldiers who had been killed during the war and to wives of veterans, who had constituted the most important core of the first members of the Fasci.

With a view toward shaping appropriate behaviors, secondary education was reorganized in 1923. In addition to scientific secondary schools, the regime created classical schools, teacher-training schools, and women's schools to train future mothers and housewives. As specified in Regio Decreto (royal decree) 1054, art. 65, of 6 May 1923: "The secondary women's schools make it their goal to extend additional general culture to young girls who do not intend to go on to higher studies or who do not plan to prepare a professional diploma." Alongside the usual curriculum—Italian, Latin, history, geography, philosophy, and political economy—the programs gave considerable space to artistic education: drawing, art history, music, and dance. They also included courses in women's work and home economics, so that young girls would learn to cut and sew clothes, manage the family budget and household records, decorate the home, deal with domestic workers, and be familiar with the tenets of sound nutrition.

This teaching of women extended to women of the working class as well, and in fact, the basics of home economics were even taught in the professional schools. "The apprenticeship schools or professional women's schools," a royal decree 2523, art.3, of 31 October 1923 stated, "prepare young girls to practice professions appropriate for women, but they also provide concepts important for properly keeping and managing a home."

Thus, immediately after the takeover the Fascist regime had established the general lines of its policy: maternity protection for large sections of the population and the preparation of women for their future maternal function. The interest in the multiple cultural and practical aspects of domestic education was so enormous that one might think Fascism wanted to make the role of the mother into a modern profession. The law that created the National Service for the Protection of Mothers and Children (ONMI), an institution endowed with substantial financial means to come to the aid of mothers and children, was most significant in this regard. As mandated by law 2277, art. 4, of 10 December 1925 on mother and child welfare, the service was responsible for tending to the

> protection and welfare of pregnant women and needy or abandoned mothers, newborns, and young children up to the age of 5 of needy families, physically or mentally disabled children, and minors who are materially or morally abandoned, corrupted or delinquent, up to and including the age of 18.

Admittedly, these arrangements were heavily influenced by a general philosophy of the nation's demographic development, of social control over and stabilization of deviants, and of isolation and marginalization of problem children. Nevertheless, no law of the liberal state had given so much attention to minors in need of aid and assistance.

In 1926 the regime launched a campaign against celibacy by establishing a tax for unmarried people, who thus had to contribute to the support of large families. In addition to providing aid to mothers, between 1929 and 1934 the regime reformed protective measures for working women and children. Fascist law, presented to the senate by Mussolini himself, extended the ruling to every workplace and limited the working day to 11 hours for women and 10 hours for children.

To assist working mothers, maternity insurance became obligatory for all women between the ages of 15 and 50. Maternity leave was no longer restricted to the last month before delivery and was extended to a month and a half after delivery. The law also made provisions for guaranteeing employment and paying maternity benefits. Further, it required employers to provide a room in the workplace where mothers could nurse their newborns, and guaranteed women the right to leave their work temporarily to nurse their babies.

However, in tandem with these measures of protection and guarantees for mothers, the regime also took a series of measures aimed at limiting the space granted to women. In particular, it removed them from professions considered decisive for the shaping of the Fascist nation, such as public administration and secondary education (Royal decree 2480, 9 December 1926). In 1926 women were excluded from teaching history and philosophy in secondary schools, and in 1933 (Royal Decree 1554, 28 November) the hiring of women in state administrative positions was tightly restricted. In practice, women's role had been limited to a very specific function, and although she was protected, any other desire on her part was discouraged. Still, the number of women in education grew tangibly. Whereas during Giolitti's era women were allowed to teach only at the elementary-school level, during the Fascist period they gained access to teaching in secondary schools. In the first cycle of education, female teaching personnel increased between 1923 and 1939 to the point of exceding male teaching staff by the end of that period. In contrast, and although their numbers had increased slightly, in secondary schools women were still very much in the minority. Women were formally prohibited from serving as school principals by a law adopted in 1934. Meanwhile, their right to vote in administrative elections ceased to be an issue at all once these elections had been suppressed.

Modernization of Daily Life

The 1930s in Italy were characterized by the beginnings of modernization in consumption and in the family life of the middle classes, albeit amid many contradictions. The regime did, indeed, make an effort to curb the effects of the Great Depression, which were felt in Italy from 1930 on, by establishing an economic policy of investments in great public works: the expansion of agricultural areas and the construction of roads, railways, and housing for the people. The gap between Italy and the other industrialized countries did not diminish, but the regime managed to limit the damage and even to achieve progressive improvement in the economy from the mid– 1930s on. Although the model family was large, it still had at least a radio, lived in an apartment or on a farm in the country with modern furniture, went on vacation in the summer by train at reduced rates, and could send the children to summer camp. The image of woman, so long revered by the regime, was changed by force of circumstance. The new model of the active woman was celebrated in newspapers and magazines: young Fascist women on skis, workers in the rice fields participating in meetings, women's world sports, and young mothers surrounded by their children. Public representations of women had never been so profuse. During the years of the totalitarian conquest of the country, Fascism was "feminized"—that is, it accepted the female image, more serene and reassuring than the male image, in order to ensure its dissemination to the farthest corners of the land.

But this massive propaganda, rather than encouraging the rebirth of the family as the regime wanted it to do, led to a decrease in births. In addition, women began to expand their activities and devoted themselves in particular to study and work. In this regard, the figures on women's fertility left hardly any doubt: in fact, they showed a clear reduction in birthrates between the early 1930s and the following decade. Moreover, in the big cities fertility was even lower than in the north of Italy on the average, according to the *Annuario statistico* (Statistical Yearbook) of 1939. Thus, it was precisely in the region where membership in Fascist organizations was strongest and consensus the most widespread, that private behavior was furthest removed from what the regime would have wished. During this period, almost all girls began to go to elementary school, which was truly becoming a school for the masses, and they started to attend secondary school, from which they had been practically absent until World War I. At the end of the 1930s, some 1,000 women had earned university degrees, according to the Istat *Annuario statistico* of 1939. In the working world, women's jobs were more skilled, and the number of teachers, saleswomen, and specialized workers increased, while the number of women agricultural workers decreased considerably. Fascist legislation designed to curtail the rural exodus and limit women's access to teaching proved not to be particularly effective.

Despite the Fascist regime's very obviously stated wish for women to devote themselves to the family, they began to behave quite differently: not that women abandoned the family, but they took care of it more freely and, above all, they managed a smaller family. In fact, despite the regime's insistence on the "demographic battle," the size of the Italian family continued to decrease. To grapple with the drop in population, the regime created a Direzione Generale per la Demografia e per la Razze (General Bureau of Demography and the Race) in the Ministry of the Interior to coordinate legislation and propaganda. The results continued to be disappointing, however. At this point one might wonder to what extent Italian women were truly in agreement with what Fascism wanted to impose upon them. This can only be answered in approximate terms. Nevertheless, it is obvious that the most widespread models of behavior reflected women's desire for modernity and a wish to distance themselves from traditional female roles. An opinion poll on the aspirations of a group of young Roman women, based on a questionnaire from the Istituto di Orientamento Professionale (Institute of Professional Orientation) completed in 1939 by 1,000 young girls between the ages of 16 and 18, confirmed this hypothesis. Even though it represented a limited sample, the poll was quite significant in that it dealt with young women who had lived in the midst of Fascist propaganda in the city that was the symbol of the regime. Against all logical expectation of conformity to the national collective identity, the poll showed that what predominated was the desire "to command and not to obey," and that young women stating "that they wanted many children" were rare. What also appeared clearly was a desire for consumer goods and entertainment, a desire strongly counteracted by both Fascism and the Church. The true aspiration of young women was not to get married and have many children but to practice a profession and be economically independent. It can thus be said that, at that point in time, the Fascist regime had lost its control over Italian women and that the attempt to integrate them into the nation had worked in the realm of public conduct but not in that of private behavior.

Housewives and Gymnasts

One of the reasons for the partial failure to shape the mentality and behavior of women lay in the contradiction between an adamantly antifeminist ideology on the one hand, and, on the other, propaganda that tended to exalt women's role. The model of the modern and efficient housewife of which Il Duce dreamed, the worthy wife of a husband who was both father and soldier, and the mother of athletic and energetic daughters, was difficult to reconcile with the secondary role allotted to women.

Admittedly, the "demographic battle" was a metaphoric war, but it was nevertheless deemed just as important as the war with Libya. The mother and housewife was comparable to the infantryman in the sands of the desert, and the specter of the falling birthrate was comparable to the hordes of Libyan Bedouins. Such metaphors sustained an image of the strong and active woman in private, which was a contradiction with the model of passivity and obedience that was idealized by the Fascist regime.

Thus, the true Fascist woman was not only a mother bringing several children into the world, but also a model housewife who personally took care of home and family. The image of woman, without class distinction or type, was to become the main element upon which the making of Fascist families would rest.

In 1927 courses in home economics began to be offered in the setting of the Fasci Femminili, and such training was destined to become one of the most important themes of Fascist propaganda during the years that followed. The first experiment took place in the province of Latium. After a stop in Rome, a school-train made up of four cars—a classroom, two rooms for the instructors, a kitchen, and a facility set up for making butter and cheese—was supposed to go to the small villages in the region to disseminate the basic rudiments of home economics to girls.

In addition, Augusto Turati, the party secretary, increased efforts for the organization of the Fourth International Conference on Home Economics in Rome, which was held from 14–16 November 1927 and was also the occasion for an international exhibition. The first such conference, which had been held in Fribourg, had drawn the participation of official delegates from nine of the most industrialized countries. At the end of the Fribourg conference the decision had been made to create an international bureau for the teaching of home economics in the various countries. The third home economics conference, held in 1922, welcomed delegates from 35 countries. The Rome conference drew participants and attendees from almost every industrialized nation. Angiola Moretti, secretary of the Fasci Femminili, and Wanda Gorjux, of the Fasci Femminili of Bari, made presentations there.

Thus, Italian Fascism presented itself to Europe as a regime that wanted to modernize and renew family and domestic life. One of the first conclusions drawn by the conference dealt with the professionalization of the housewife. One motion, reported in *Il popolo d'Italia* on 15 November 1927, stated: "All educational authorities must see to it . . . that domestic work is raised to the dignity of a profession to be learned in a cycle of study of several years." It was also proposed at the conference that exchanges be made between different European countries. The latter were invited to compare their kinds of education and schools so that the progress made in any given country would be profitable to all. In another resolution the conference insisted on the role and development of scientific research in the improvement of technologies for domestic use. In short, Fascist women were to renounce all specific demands and think only of improving their professional training as housewives and integrating themselves into the process of modernization.

In 1929 the Fasci Femminili were reorganized once again: young women between the ages of 18 and 22 became Giovani Fasciste (Young Fascist Women) before becoming full-fledged Donne Fasciste (Fascist Women). In the course of those four years, they received special training that would lead to their fulfilling the role of wife and mother. In addition to home economics, sports had a definitive place in their program. The first Accademia Femminile (Women's Academy), responsible for training teachers of physical education, opened its doors in Orvieto in 1932. Home economics also appeared in the curriculum of this academy.

In May 1928 the first national gymnastics and athletic competition was held in Rome. Three thousand young women participated, divided over different disciplines. It was on that occasion that young women were seen carrying rifles in public for the first time, which caused polemics and discussions both within the regime and with the Church. That same year, many Italian women participated in the Olympic Games, which the regime interpreted as the sign that the country had caught up with the most advanced European nations.

For the four years that Turati was party secretary, enrollment in the Fasci Femminili was closed, in accordance with party directives. The only new registrants came from the "Leva fascista." Throughout this entire period, the secretary of the Fasci Femminili was Angiola Moretti, who scrupulously followed Turati's directives.

By 1930, according to statistics given by Ester Lombardo in the *Almanacco della donna italiana* (Almanac of Italian Women), there were 3,000 Fasci Femminili with a total of approximately 100,000 members, mostly from the middle classes, wholly satisfied with their role as modern women. The organization ran completely parallel to that of the party, with women in leadership roles at the municipal and provincial level, under the control of their male peers. The whole system showed a skillful balance between modernity and tradition, transgression and respectability. If young Fascist girls participated in sports on the one hand, they were learning home economics and carrying rifles on the other, and they also wore elegant uniforms: a white pleated skirt and a very chic black cape.

In order to ensure strict control over the entire organization, the regime decided to form an elite of Fascist women. Also, the Direttorio Nazionale (National Bureau) opened three schools in Rome that admitted members of the Fasci Femminili, chosen from among those most deserving and most devoted to Fascism throughout Italy. The courses, lasting ten months, were free of charge. Life in the boarding schools was of particular importance to the "spiritual training" of these young women.

The Scuola Superiore Fascista di Assistenze Sociale (Fascist School of Higher Learning for Social Welfare) was open to young women who had a degree of higher learning and to those who had taken the courses of an institution preparatory to the teacher's college and who wanted to become Fascist assistants in factories. The Confederazione Generale dell'Industrie (Confederation of Industry Employers) ensured their being hired in the factories. The Scula Superiore Fascista di Economia Domestica (Fascist School of Higher Learning for Home Economics) admitted young women with a diploma in elementary teaching and trained them to teach in secondary schools and all establishments where home economics were taught. Finally, the Scuola Fascista per la Preparazione delle Maestre Rurali (Fascist School for the Training of Elementary School Teachers in Rural Areas) admitted young women who planned to teach in the country. These teachers subsequently benefited from career advantages.

Every year, the newly graduated women of these three schools were received by Il Duce who lavished "final advice" upon them before they were to begin their professional assignments. At the end of their training, these young women thus represented the elite of fascist women. As A. Felici Ottaviani wrote in the 1937 *Almanacco della donna italiana*: "They are the unknown but precious apostles of the true fascist faith, because they love the people in whose service they work with absolute devotion."

The training of female "Fascist visitors" was simpler. These women, comparable to caseworkers, were the most direct means of propaganda and of penetration into families of the lower classes. They provided moral and spiritual assistance to these families, and they were responsible for helping them find solutions to their problems. As they were very familiar with the laws and the institutions of the regime concerning welfare aid, they practiced their activities as volunteers for the Ente Opere Assistenziali (Office of Welfare Work).

The courses in home economics for women preparing to leave for the colonies assumed special importance. The Istituto Coloniale Fascista (Fascist Colonial Institute) was in charge of providing training courses to facilitate women's integration in these countries. The courses offered dealt with hygiene, dress, home organization, and the use of water. All this propaganda activity culminated in a great day of collective mobilization: the "Day of Alliance" was celebrated on 8 December 1935. Over the course of the day married men and women were compelled to offer their alliance to the fatherland in order to participate in the resistance against sanctions. The call was directed particularly to women whose husbands or sons had died for the country. "The mothers and widows of heroes who died have formed a sacred phalanx around Il Duce," declared *Il popolo d'Italia* on 5 December 1935, "united by an oath that has thrilled the conscience."

On 8 May 1936, at the time when consensus was at its strongest because of the conquest of Ethiopia and the proclamation of the empire, Il Duce—during a great gathering in Rome—expressed his gratitude to Fascist women for their attitude and spirit of sacrifice, which they had proven during the colonial war and the economic blockade. He practically thanked them for having renounced any demand for emancipation and for having fervently committed themselves to the path of colonialization. In his speech of praise, printed in that day's edition of *Il popolo d'Italia*, Mussolini declared: "Surrounded by the siege organized by 52 nations, Fascist Italy entrusted you with a delicate and decisive task: making every family into a fortress in order to resist the sanctions" ("Elogio alle donne italiane" [In Praise of Italian Women], 1936).

In 1934 the regime had also begun to organize housewives in rural areas, where each of the Fasci Femminili had been given the responsibility of creating a section to this end. These sections saw a rapid development and quickly became the arm of the party in the countryside. The objective was to raise the standard of living in order to curtail the rural exodus. In October 1936, according to an article, "Massaie rurali" (Rural Housewives) by Ottaviani in the 1936 *Almanacco della donna italiana*, there were about half a million members of the party organizations Fasci Femminili, Giovani Fasciste, and Massaie Rurali. Nevertheless, it should be noted that being a registered member of the PNF, in whatever form, provided a series of advantages that made participation in these different activities quite attractive. In fact, in order to take part in Italian society, party membership was obligatory. But women thus mobilized chose to behave in a way that was not totally in agreement with what the Fascist regime wanted.

Catholic Women and Fascism

Another reason why the regime had little success had to do with the existence of a strong Catholic affiliation whose organizational structure precisely paralleled that of the Fascist regime. The Catholic organizations did not have a line in opposition to Fascism, but they sought to promote a different female model, and this factor was what systematically caused the regime's efforts to create a modern, warrior youth to fail.

At the end of the 1920s, the group Azione Cattolica Italiana (ACI; Italian Catholic Action) had been organized in a form decided upon by Pope Pius XI for the conquest of civil society. Thus, Fascism had to struggle against what was already a fairly effective structure. After different forms of restructuring, the regime, too, managed to create a satisfactory organization by the early 1930s, modeled on the Catholic structure. Fascism used the same separations by sex and age that the pope had wanted for Catholics. The general spirit of the two structures reflected the same principle of wanting to exercise control over everything in order to acquire a mass membership of the entire population.

It was precisely the Unione Donne (Women's Union) of ACI and its younger branch, Gioventù Femminile (Young Catholic Women), that most faithfully corresponded to the plan of Pope Pius XI. As early as the end of World War I, Pope Benedict XV had thought that the action of the former Unione fra le Donne Cattoliche d'Italia (Union for the Catholic Women of Italy) was insufficient because it was unsuitable for the new requirements of a mass society. That was why in 1919 he created the Unione Femminile Cattolica Italiana (Italian Catholic Women's Union), which consisted of two branches, the Unione Donne (Women's Union), presided over by Maddalena Patrizi, and Gioventù Femminile, directed by Armida Barelli.

The early mass orientation of the new organization had already become apparent with the consecration of soldiers at the Sacred-Heart, directed by Armida Barelli and Agostino Gemelli, the founder of the Catholic University of Milan. This campaign had marked the first manifestations of the new Catholic presence in Italian society.

The early relationship of the Catholic youth group Gioventù Femminile with nascent Fascism was extremely tempestuous. Armida Barelli was opposed to the double membership in the Fasci and Gioventù Femminile. In 1921, in an article published in the ACI bulletin she wrote: "The Gioventù Femminile cannot be together with those who, forgetting or denying the law of love preached by the Gospel, sow and propagate discord; that cannot be. . . . That is why the Gioventù Femminile must not enter the Fasci" (reprinted in Barelli 1948).

But when, after taking power, Mussolini demonstrated that he was capable of keeping his most violent partisans under control, there was a significant change in the attitudes of the Catholics and of Gioventù Femminile. There were moments of friction, which culminated in 1931 in the dissolution of ACI, but throughout the 1930s a kind of armed truce was established that allowed for broad consensus on the issue of women.

However, the debate on organizational planning did not progress without difficulty. Although the Concordat of 1929 had recognized the full legitimacy of the affiliation between the Catholic Church and Fascism, the regime retracted a part of the concessions it had made as soon as it realized the undeniable superiority of the Catholics' organizational abilities. In the Concordat it had been established that the Italian state would recognize "the organizations that depended on Azzione Cattolica Italiana." However, following the serious splits that appeared in 1931, the regime decided to reduce what appeared as a breach in its totalitarian claim. At the end of the agreement made on 2 September 1931, it was specified that ACI had a diocesan disposition and would depend directly on the bishops, who were to choose the organization's leaders.

The program of Gioventù Femminile had already been defined in 1922 at its Second National Congress. The organization planned to struggle against the process of secularization by reinstating the moral values of Christianity in the family. Within a few years the new organization created an extremely rigid structure intended to insure the religious training and social preparation of future Italian mothers. In the desire to leave a lasting imprint on Italian society, Gioventù Femminile made every effort to train a whole generation of women so that they would then transmit their ideas to the men and women of the generations to come. By 1928 the movement had nine publications: *Squilli d'apostolato* for the diocesan leaders, *Squilli parrocchiali* for the leaders of the local organizations, *Squilli di resurrezione* for members, *Squilli d'aurora* for benefactors, *Squilli argentini* for youth, *Squilli di consolazione* for the sick, *Squilli studenteschi* for students, and *Squilli dell'assistente* for social workers.

Between 1920 and 1923 sections for Catholic youth had been created as well, first for "candidates" (from 12 to 16 years old), and then for "benjamins" (from 6 to 12 years old). Gioventù Femminile also included an athletics component: in 1923 the gymnastics and sports association Forza e Grazia (Strength and Grace) was created to promote the harmonious and well-balanced development of young girls. This association was dissolved in 1928 because it was competing with the organization Opera Balilla.

The propagandists represented the elite of the Catholic women's associations. After training in specialized schools, they would go into different milieus to teach courses and give lectures. By 1923 there were already 115 training schools throughout Italy, of which some were run solely by Gioventù Femminile, others in collaboration with the branch for older Catholic women, Unione Donne. Courses dealt with questions relating to social and religious culture: the history of ACI, the catechism, and social issues, with talks on Marxism and Catholic doctrine. After this training period, the propagandists would stay in contact with each other and from time to time continue their training with further courses.

The members of the association also participated in competitions in religious culture, organized on an annual basis throughout the entire Fascist period, beginning in 1928. Gioventù Femminile essentially targeted middle-class women artisans, employees, elementary-school teachers, and young women who wanted to work while continuing to take care of their families. The model targeted by Gioventù Femminile was the woman who devoted herself fully to motherhood. One of the movement's papers praised these

> blooming young girls who devote their day to the humble and happy work of sewing and to domestic tasks in close and peaceful contact with their mothers, young girls who are the guardians of healthy traditions and of Christian wisdom, who take care of the vigor of their own bodies for the sake of their children, who smile at the pure expectations of the future. (*Squilli di Risurrezione* 6 [1 April 1925])

In 1929 Gioventù Femminile welcomed the signing of the Concordat with great enthusiasm. The 17 February 1923 issue of *Squilli di Risurrezione* devoted a full-page article to it, written by Armida Barelli, its president. "Let us kneel, my sisters, let us kneel," she wrote, "to give thanks to God for such a large and beautiful blessing, a blessing we have passionately awaited and that is so dear to our Catholic and Italian hearts" ("Te Deum laudamus! Il tratto di pace ed i Concordato tra la Sante Sede e l'Italia" [Praise God! The Peace Treaty and the Concordat between the Holy See and Italy]). But all this enthusiasm had a sharp fall: indeed, on 30 May 1931, the dissolution of ACI was a harsh blow to the members of Gioventù Femminile. Nevertheless, their faith in their ideal did not weaken and the association's members were able to carry on their work simply by not wearing the insignia of the association. Even after it had been dissolved, ACI was able to proceed with its activity at the local level.

The measure intended to break the youth sector was a proof of the regime's weakness rather than of its strength, as it did not manage to overtake the Catholic organizations with its own. Gioventù Femminile came out of the ordeal a stronger group. Even if it had lost some of its distinctive exterior signs, it held on to its full capacity of intervention in civil society.

By 1936 Gioventù Femminile had become a mass association. Indeed, at that time it counted 310 diocesan centers organized in 57 percent of the parishes. According to ACI statistics, membership in Gioventù Femminile rose to 863,000 in 1939, a figure slightly above that of the Fasci Femminili. In substance, the Fascist and Church organizations were equal in numbers and in strength. When, after the nomination of Starace as party secretary, each section of the PNF had to establish a group of Fasci Femminili, the two organizations fought over control of the territory and not without coming to blows—with the slight difference that, while the Fasci were backed and supported by the state, ACI could count only on its own forces and the organizing structure of the parishes. At the end of the Fascist period, an entire generation of women had grown up in the worship of peace and not war and had been spiritually shaped in the Catholic faith.

Antifascist Women and the War

Alongside this multitude of women who, perhaps unconsciously, had not been trained to believe, obey, and have babies but instead to make more conscious and well-considered personal choices, there was a small minority of women who were consciously active against Fascism. Such women were very few in number and were not very important in the course of the prosperous years of the consensus, but when the misgivings about the war began to create rifts in the certainties of Italian women, their influence increased.

These women had lived abroad and had gained political experience during the Spanish civil war. Not having been influenced by Fascist propaganda, they had seen its limitations and could call on other women to rid themselves of the troublesome burden of inferiority and submissiveness.

Between 1927 and 1943, the special tribunal sentenced 122 primarily Communist women, but their history was linked mostly to emigration. Moreover, their choice, dictated by heroism and exceptional quality, was limited to a small number by force of circumstance. Some wives of members or leaders of the Communist Party or the Socialist Party identified their lives with the party and chose emigration. Others, in particular after 1930, were busy in clandestine activities in their workplaces or in residential sections.

Almost all of the members of the leading women's group of the future in the Italian left-wing parties spent those years abroad. Adele Bei, Teresa Noce, and Camilla Ravera, early Communists, were emblematic from this point of view. In 1923 Bei emigrated to France with her husband, returning secretly to Italy in 1930. She was arrested in 1934 and sent to a residence under surveillance on the island of Ventotene. She then participated in the resistance. Noce, a member of the Communist Party from its foundation in 1921 on, participated in the Spanish civil war with her husband Luigi Longo. She was later arrested in France and deported to a concentration camp. Ravera had belonged to the Communist Party from its beginning as well. For several years she was the leader of the inner center of the Italian Communist Party. Back in Italy in 1930, she, too, was arrested and was placed under house arrest. Two other younger women, Nadia Gallico Spano and Maria Maddalena Rossi, who had registered in the party just before the war, participated in the clandestine struggle before being arrested.

The Socialists Rosa Fazio Longo, Giuliana Nenni, and Angelina Merlin experienced the same fate. Fazio Longo took part in the resistance and at that point began to organize the Movimento Femminile Socialista (Socialist Women's Movement), while Nenni, who had left Italy with her family, returned in 1943. Merlin had belonged to the Italian Socialist Party in 1919 and, as a teacher, had refused to sign the loyalty oath the regime required from all civil servants, which caused her to be fired from the teaching profession. At first she took part in the clandestine struggle, then in the armed struggle against Fascism. All these women were subsequently elected to the Constitutional Assembly and then to Parliament.

The action abroad was primarily characterized by the struggle for peace in collaboration with women from other countries. In 1934, together with 1,500 other women, Italian women participated in the First Women's World Congress against Fascism and the War. Among the Italian women there were seven Communists but also 15 other women who had fled Fascist Italy. Among the latter were some Catholics. It was at that moment, too, that the fight against the Fascist regime in Italy grew more intense, thanks to the creation in Paris in 1937 of the Unione Donne Italiane (UDI) as well. That organization's publication,

Voce della donna, headed by Teresa Noce, was secretly sent to Italy, hidden between the covers of French fashion magazines. In 1937 the paper changed its title and became *Noi donne*. It played a coordinating and organizing role in the clandestine women's movement that was in the process of being formed in Italy.

Thus, at the end of the 1930s, the antifascist struggle grew stronger, and women then played an important role because in all sorts of tasks they were less noticeable than men: printing and distributing tracts in factories and among private individuals, organizing the Soccorso Rosso (Red Aid), a group that came to the aid of antifascists, and holding meetings in apartments. These were preparations for the resistance that exploded later while carrying off whatever remained of Fascism.

When Italy entered the war in the summer of 1940, antifascist activism gained new energy and women reclaimed their place in the foreground, which they had lost during Fascism. In fact, they were almost immediately called upon to replace men in jobs from which they had been fired during the preceding years. Food shortages, extreme cold, and the bombing campaigns of the winter of 1942–1943 contributed to depleting the morale of the Italian people even more. When the Fascist regime fell, on 25 July 1943, Italian women came together again in the streets to celebrate the end of a nightmare.

The Resistance

After the signing of the armistice on 8 September 1943, Italy was sliced in two. The Allies had already landed in Sicily, and a Kingdom of the South was established in the south of Italy, while in the north Benito Mussolini, recently set free by the Germans, proclaimed the Italian Social Republic in Salò.

The myth of the Fascist woman fell apart with the birth of the republic in Salò. The Fascists abandoned everything, including their families. After 20 years of adoration of the mother, the women of the Italian Social Republic found themselves to be neither wives nor mothers but simple soldiers. Restricted to the Servizio Ausiliare Femminile (Women's Auxiliary Service) they asked to be given the same status as men and to participate in the armed struggle. In the name of Fascism, they had relinquished their home and their family, and for these reasons they demanded to be treated equally. Early in 1945, they acquired almost everything—the right to participate in raids and even the right to vote—knowing quite well that from then on the end was near. The right to vote was included in the constitutional plan of the Italian Social Republic, which in fact was never approved or even opened for discussion.

The "woman question" was not discussed among resistance workers. The men who joined the underground left their personal and family feelings behind and gave priority to politics. However, women's solidarity supported them both directly and indirectly. Women took part in the resistance not only by acquitting themselves of their traditional tasks but also by filling other roles. Apart from any political considerations, the women of northern Italy helped the resistance workers because they, too, were living the existence of the oppressed, crushed by a pitiless power, whether of the Germans or the partisans of the Italian Social Republic. The atrocities committed against women and children caused Anna and Battistina Aimar, two peasant women from Piedmont, to say that the Germans were "cowards, monsters, wild animals, but not men" (quoted in Revelli). Therefore, they helped the resistance workers in the name of the same natural sense of solidarity that had caused Italian soldiers to be aided abroad. Similarly, early in 1944 Caterina Brunetto, another woman from the Piedmont Alps, said that she was helping the resistance workers and refugees because her husband had himself received help: "When my husband was a soldier and was wounded in Greece, if nobody had helped him, he would be dead. They helped him and I help others" (quoted in Revelli).

These women asked for no declaration of political belief whatsoever: all fleeing Italians found someone willing to hide them. Francesca Giraudo, speaking of the round-ups, was to say later: "The people who had been arriving so far, we didn't know who they were. Mostly they were Italians. We dug a shelter in the courtyard and hid the entrance with stones" (quoted in Revelli).

Later, in the course of the winter of 1944, the resistance grew stronger as it was organized into brigades. At the same time, women's participation was managed in a more orderly fashion, even if spontaneous help continued to be available. The birth of the Gruppi di Difesa della Donna per l'Aiuto ai Combattenti della Libertà (GDD; Women's Defense Groups to Aid the Freedom Fighters) dated exactly from the beginning of 1944. In its tracts, the Comitato Liberazione Nationale (CLN; National Liberation Committee) called for the first time on women to become involved in politics and to organize the Voluntarie per la Libertà (Volunteers for Freedom). One of these tracts, entitled *Perchè la politica le devono fare anche le donne* (Why Women Should Also Engage in Politics), stated:

The war arrived, and with its procession of horror, massacres, destruction, it has shaken women and awakened them. Women are seeing that it is men who practice politics, but that politics concerns them as well, to the extent that they suffer its consequences, and perhaps even more than men. The great majority of the victims of bombings are women; during invasions, in the countries where fighting takes place, where fires are set and looting occurs, are women spared from all that? (Quoted in Beltrami Gadola and Bruzzone.)

Early in 1944 in northern Italy, women's defense groups formed that completed many functions, from simple aid through actions of political liaison to armed struggle. In "red" Emilia-Romagna, the women of the defense groups provided support on the organizational level, but they also took part in armed attacks on the fascists. According to testimony by Laura Polizzi, a Communist resistance worker, the participation of the population in the summer of 1944 was extremely important.

The results of our work went beyond any expectation. With the wool of dozens and dozens of mattresses, which they were spinning by hand, women produced shawls, gloves, socks, and berets for the resistance workers. Inside the gloves and shawls, they would slip words of encouragement. . . . They collected money, medications, cigarettes, and food supplies. (Quoted in Pieroni Bortolotti.)

There were also women liaison officers who would collect information, as Silvana Lodi remembered, and who also participated in the resistance: "We were in touch with the farmers in the country and we would transmit the information we received" (quoted in Pieroni Bortolotti). Then, too, women were fighting with arms in hand, such as Germana Bordoni and Novella Albertazzi, who led a brigade completely made up of women. Similarly, in Liguria in the summer of 1944, women organized themselves into a defense group in order to make armbands and tricolored insignia, to care for the wounded, and to help the families of resistance workers.

All in all, according to the official figures, the Volunteers for Freedom numbered 125,000, of whom 35,000 were women fighting in the partisan groups, 20,000 patriots, and 70,000 women organized into defense groups (see Brizzolari). But these figures are quite certainly below the real ones, because a certain number of women refused to be officially recognized as resistance workers and some even asked not to be mentioned as such at all. One may well assume that the number of women participating directly or indirectly in the resistance was barely lower than that of the men.

Organized as resistance workers, women accomplished all sorts of tasks: from the most traditional, as liaison officers or nurses, to the less obvious ones as fighters. In such a situation, the demand for the right to vote was seen as appropriate recognition of their participation in the resistance.

Thus, the resistance gave birth to a new subjectivity that led women out of the private microcosm in which they had lived. For Italian women, the liberation in April 1945 meant the definitive conquest of their status as citizens. The law granting women the right to vote, which was approved in Italy in 1945, was the official recognition of a right to political citizenship won in armed struggle.

In Fascist Italy, women had been called upon to play a public role connected to the state. They were political subjects only to the extent that they adhered to the model the Fascist regime desired. They all had to identify with the woman as wife and mother. In order to be a political subject they had to be made "Fascist." With the proclamation of Republic, women at last won the right to be citizens. There no longer was a unique identification model, and nobody asked women for a profession of political loyalty. Moreover, this recognition was also a simple recognition of right, since a woman was already an autonomous subject. She was such a subject during the spontaneous modernization period of the 1930s and in the struggle for survival during the civil war, and she was such a subject in the postwar reconstruction period.

Bibliography

Sources

Barelli, Armida, *La sorella maggiore racconta*, Milan, Italy: OR, 1981

Barelli, Armida, "Te Deum laudamus! Il trattato di pace ed il Concordato tra la Sante Sede e l'Italia," *Squilli di Risurrezione* 3 (17 February 1929)

Beltrami Gadola, G., and A.M. Bruzzone, "La Resistenza sulle spalle," in *Esistere come donna. Volantino del movimento femminile, September 1944*, in Carlo Brizzolari, *Un archivio della Resistenza in Liguria*, Genoa, Italy: Di Stefano, 1974

Benedettini Alferazzi, Paola, "Organizzazioni femminili fasciste nell'anno X," *Almanacco della donna italiana*, Florence, Italy: R. Bemporad, 1920–1936

Bizzarini, Giotto, "La donna attraverso i tempi e la donna italiana nel regime fascista," *La Stirpe* 2 (1934)

Brizzolari, Carlo, editor, *Un archivio della Resistenza in Liguria*, Genoa, Italy: Di Stefano, 1974

Catholic Church, *Treaty and Concordat Between the Holy See and Italy; Official Documents*, Washington, D.C.: National Catholic Welfare Conference, 1929

"Congresso internazionale di Economie domestica inaugurato con un discorso di Turati," *Il popolo d'Italia* (15 November 1927)

Felici Ottaviani, Ada, "Le tre scuole fasciste del partito," *Almanacco delle donne italiana* (1937)

Forges Devanzati, Roberto, "Nello splendore cristiano," *Politica sociale* 12 (1933)

"La giornata della fede," *Il popolo d'Italia* (11 December 1935)

Gorjux, Wanda, "La festa del popolo che si eterna," *Augustea* 23 (1933)

Istituto Coloniale Fascista, *Corso di preparazione coloniale per la donna*

Istituto Nazionale di Statistica, *Annuario statistico: 1939*, Rome: Istituto Nazionale di Statistica (ISTAT), 1939

Istituto Nazionale di Statistica, *Compendio statistico*, Rome: Istituto Nazionale di Statistica (ISTAT), 1931

Istituto Nazionale di Statistica, *Note riassuntive sui risultati delle indagini sulle famiglie numerose*, Naples, Italy: Istituto Nazionale di Statistica (ISTAT), 1936

Italy, Legge, 10 December 1925, no. 2277, *Protezione e assistenze della maternità e dell'infanzia*, Art. 4

Italy, Regio decreto [R.D.] 6 May 1923, no. 1054, *Ordinamento della istruzione media e dei convitti nazionali*, Art. 65

Italy, Regio decreto [R.D.] 31 October 1923, no. 2523, *Ricordinamento della istruzione industriale*, Art. 3

Lombardo, Ester, "Rassegna del movimento femminile italiano," *Almanacco della donna italiana* (1926)

Lombardo, Ester, "Sei anni di attività dei Fasci Femminili," *Almanacco della donna italiana* (1929)

"Maternità feconda," *Politica sociale* 12 (1933)

Ministero dell'Educazione Nazionale, *Dalla riforma gentile alla Carta della Scuola*, Florence, Italy: Ministero dell'Educazione Nazionale, 1941

Missori, M., editor, *Gerarchie e Statuti del PNF: Gran consiglio, direttorio nazionale, federazioni provinciali: Quadri e biografie*, Rome: Bonacci, 1986

Mussolini, Benito, "Elogio alle donne italiane," *Il popolo d'Italia* (8 May 1936)

Olgiati, Francesco, *I nuovi orizzonti della Gioventù Femminile*, Milan, Italy: Consiglio superiore della Gioventù Femminile Cattolica Italiana, 1929

Ottaviani, A. Felici, "Massaie rurali," *Almanacco della donna italiana* (1936)

Ottaviani, A. Felici, "Le tre Scuole fasciste del partito," *Alamacco della donna italiana* (1937)

"Pagina studentesca," *Squilli di Risurrezione* 6 (1 April 1925)

Partito Nazionale Fascista, *Decalogo, I Fasci Femminili*, Milan, Italy: Partito Nazionale Fascista (PNF), 1929

Partito Nazionale Fascista, *I Fogli d'ordini* (31 July 1926–28 October 1935)

Partito Nazionale Fascista, *Programma statuto del gruppo femminile di Roma*, Rome: Partito Nazionale Fascista (PNF), 1921

Partito Nazionale Fascista, "Statuto dei Fasci Femminili (1929)," in *Statuto del fascismo, a cura dell'Ufficio propaganda del PNF*, Rome: Partito Nazionale Fascista (PNF), 1929

Relazione e statistica della Gioventù Femminile Cattolica Italiana, Triennio 1922–1925, Milan, Italy: Azzione Cattolica Italiana, 1925

Revelli, Nuto, *L'anello forte: La donna: Storie di vita contadina*, Turin, Italy: Einaudi, 1985

Sarfatti, Margherita, "Italia d'oggi," *Augustea* 23 (1923)

Reference Works

Bravo, Anna, et al., editors, *Donne e uomini nelle guerre mondiali*, Rome: Laterza, 1991

Bravo, Anna, and Anna Maria Bruzzone, *In guerra senza armi: Storie di donne: 1940–1945*, Rome: Laterza, 1995; 2nd edition, Rome: Laterza, 2000

Dau Novelli, Cecilia, *Famiglia e modernizzazione in Italia tra le due guerre*, Rome: Edizioni Studium, 1994

Dau Novelli, Cecilia, *Sorelle d'Italia: Casalinghe, impiegate e militanti nel Novecento*, Rome: A.V.E., 1996

De Felice, Renzo, *Mussolini l'alleato 1940–1945*, Turin, Italy: Einaudi, 1990

De Felice, Renzo, *Mussolini il Duce 1929–1940*, Turin, Italy: Einaudi, 1974–81

De Felice, Renzo, *Mussolini il fascista 1921–1929*, Turin, Italy: Einaudi, 1966–68

De Felice, Renzo, *Mussolini il rivoluzionario, 1883–1920*, Turin, Italy: Einaudi, 1965

DeGrazia, Victoria, *The Culture of Consent: Mass Organization of Leisure in Fascist Italy*, Cambridge and New York: Cambridge University Press, 1981

DeGrazia, Victoria, *How Fascism Ruled Women: Italy, 1922–1945*, Berkeley: University of California Press, 1992

De Luna, Giovanni, *Donne in oggetto. L'antifascismo nella società italiana 1922–1939*, Turin, Italy: Bollati Boringhieri, 1995

Detragiache, Denise, "Il fascismo femminile da San Sepolcro all'affare Matteotti (1919–1925)," *Storia contemporanea* 2 (1983)

Dogliani, Patrizia, *L'Italia fascista 1922–1940*, Milan, Italy: Sansoni, 1999

Duby, Georges, and Michelle Perrot, general editors, *A History of Women in the West*, 5 vols., Cambridge, Massachusetts: Belknap Press of Harvard University, 1992–1994; see especially vol. 5, *Toward a Cultural Identity in the Twentieth Century*, edited by Françoise Thébaud

Fraddosio, Maria, "La donna e la guerra. Aspetti della militanza femminile nel fascismo: dalla mobilitazione civile alle origini della Saf nella Repubblica Sociale Italiana," *Storia contemporanea* 6 (1989)

Gabrielli, Patrizia, *Fenicotteri in volo. Donne comuniste nel ventennio fascista*, Rome: Carocci, 1999

Gentile, Emilio, *Il culto del littorio: La sacralizzazione della politica nell'Italia fascista*, Rome: Laterza, 1993

Passerini, Luisa, *Mussolini immaginario: Storia di una biografia 1915–1939*, Rome: Laterza, 1991

Pavone, Claudio, *Una guerra civile: Saggio storico sulla moralità nella Resistenza*, Turin, Italy: Bollati Boringhieri, 1991

Pieroni Bertollotti, Franca, "Le donne della Resistenza antifascista e la questione femminile" in Emilia Romagna: 1943–1945, Milano, Vangelista, 1978

WOMEN IN VICHY FRANCE

FRANÇOIS ROUQUET

War's Disorder

THE CATASTROPHE THAT WORLD WAR II represented for humankind, both on a global scale and by its two deadly innovations—industrialized genocide and the entrance of atomic weapons into political conflict—made itself felt with very little distinction between the sexes. In France, as in most of Europe, Nazi barbarism was experienced by everyone. An acknowledgment of gender roles and the inequalities between men and women in countless circumstances not mask this overall brutal reality. Nonetheless, in the light of what has been conveniently called "sexual difference," other aspects of the phenomena of crisis, violence, and repression have emerged, putting the role and image of women in perspective and contributing to an understanding of changes in their status and position since the Nazi occupation. Applied to the Vichy period, such a gender-conscious analysis provides a complement to a historiography that has already been broadly reexamined and enriched over the past three decades.

The violent disorder of war was all important in the first half of the 20th century, when twice in a span of little more than 20 years millions of people died. The war, according to Michelle Perrot, "by mustering virile energies . . . was profoundly conservative" and thus "put each sex back in its place" (see Perrot). In civil society, the memory of World War I, which had killed 1.3 million men and overturned the lives of an even larger number of women—mothers, sisters, wives or fiancées—remained an open wound. Some of these women forced themselves to believe that nothing was irreversible, despite the first mobilization flyers that, from 1 September 1939, touched their personal lives like the finger of death. Without a doubt many of them, like Célia Bertin, were racked by a sob when they heard the alarm sound in the afternoon of 3 September 1939. While the incomprehensible Phony War had already shaken the morale of the French (who were nonetheless prepared ready to fight), the fiasco of the German invasion in the spring of 1940 was total and left France dumbfounded. It is worth emphasizing the magnitude of this trauma, which caused the majority, often in shame and relief, to acquiesce in the request for armistice, at least in the early stages. But Marshall Pétain, "the conqueror of Verdun," called back to the business of the land in the febrile desperation following the Blitzkrieg from 10 May 1940, was not content simply to offer his services to his country. Renouncing the pursuit of struggle at the same time as Charles de Gaulle, at the time an obscure undersecretary of defense, was making his appeal for an implausible hope—an appeal that went largely unheard—Pétain summoned France to assume, with him, the great task of national reform. The Republic disappeared. A new order had begun.

Vichy, Fatherland, National Revolution, and the Role of the Sexes

Vichy has been called a "strange regime," "hybrid," "heterogeneous," "opaque," "a bizarre syncretism," a "special case," "an arbitrary and incoherent dictatorship." These are some of the terms noted by Jean-Marie Guillon in the historiography of the Vichy regime and the political philosophy of the Vichy revolution, which began in the summer of 1940. The references to heterogeneity and syncretism show how complex a regime Vichy was, and despite its authoritarian aspect, it would be simplistic to reduce it to a homogeneous totalitarian regime. Vichy was more complex than the product of a mere conservative reaction emerging from the Front Populaire (Popular Front). Further, over the course of the occupation, Vichy radically evolved into becoming a militia state governed through terror. Its nature reflected a conservatism tinged with ideas of integral nationalism (of the type promoted by Charles Maurras of the far-Right group Action Française, notably), mixed with a planned economy and a real concern with organizing society. It was a blend of archaism and modernity, "of old Romans and young cyclists," in the words of Henri Moysset, secretary of state in 1941 (see Azéma 1979), fitted out with a multiplicity of socio-ideological components ranging from the Left to the extreme Right, even if the latter was far more widely represented. The relationships between these diverse components evolved throughout the occupation, and generally speaking, the supporters drawn to the sometimes vaguely defined Vichy regime were not immune to contradictions. The French state was not totalitarian in the strict sense, but was rather a regime reeking of what Gérard Miller calls "cozy fascism" (see Miller), which reviled Communists, Jews, and Freemasons, as well as parliamentarianism and unbridled capitalism. It was the hostage of illusions supplied by the occupying enemy. It was a regime, markedly clerical in its earliest phase, that suggested a kind of post–Popular Front purgatory to France, opposing joy to pleasure: "pleasure demeans and joy elevates. Pleasure weakens, joy strengthens!" Pétain exhorted the French in his celebrated address of 29 December 1940 (reprinted in *Les cahiers Révolution nationale*, vol. 1). It was a regime that, in the name of renewal and tradition, assigned each sex a place in society: women should become mothers and concern themselves with their children at home; men were to provide for their families.

Discourse and politics, too, should be separated. Vichy discourse disseminated a morality in which motherhood was the only approved female identity. The regime was more concerned with the family than with mothers, and its policies were largely inspired by the measures advocated in the Family Code established under the Third Republic. But one of the regime's characteristic features was the continued discrepancy between its declared politics and the lot of women and the whole of French society. Although Vichy glorified women and the family that justified their existence, women and families alike were abused throughout the occupation, in contrast to what the propaganda proclaimed. Malnourished, sometimes starving, people had to tolerate the difficult conditions of the occupation and generalized, ever worsening poverty. This forced march toward destitution disguised as national recovery was accompanied by intense campaigns of indoctrination throughout the National Revolution (or "National Renewal," the term Pétain preferred). *Travail, Famille, Patrie* (Work, Family, Fatherland) was the motto of Vichy, at the price of ever growing deception. To begin with, work was hard to find, especially for women without any job skills. They became a controlled labor force abused by the regime, for all its speeches. The family unit suffered from the absence of innumerable fathers. The families of opponents of the regime and Jewish families were broken and decimated. Finally, the very "national" idea of an exclusive fatherland—not the least of the contradictions in an occupied and amputated country—was used to justify the persecution of undesirables, including Jews (some of whom were deprived of their citizenship), Freemasons, and Communists, aided and abetted by spiraling repression. The role of the French state, in singling out these "undesirables" and supporting the destiny that awaited them, destroyed two centuries of humanist tradition and continues to be painful in the national memory.

After the collapse, the exodus, the defeat, and the armistice, reform was focused on the regeneration of the fatherland and its people. Vichy propaganda opposed the values of morality, order, and duty to the democracy that had brought the Popular Front to power, and even incorporated some of the misogynist imagery used in the prewar rhetoric of the antirepublican right, with its metaphorization of the Third Republic as "La Gueuse" (The Harlot). In Vichy propaganda, women who had failed in their moral duties were considered one of the causes of the defeat: women who had "aped" men, wore pants, cut their hair, or smoked cigarettes; women whom the "spirit of pleasure" had led to the movies to see American films or who used make-up, and who were thus frivolous and unworthy; and women who had left their homes to go to work. Vichy's beginnings thus took shape under the sign of guilt. "Let us examine our conscience

harshly and let us note that many have sought the least effort, the least risk; the raw laws of life take their revenge, they impose themselves today," commented the 4 August 1940 issue of the popular women's weekly *Petit écho de la mode* (nos. 25–31). The propaganda system conceived by Vichy was, furthermore, unprecedented: a High Commission for propaganda was created, later to become the General Secretariat for Information and then a true Ministry of Information directed by Paul Marion. As Denis Peschanski has shown, its means were proportionate to the plan of complete control over society (see Peschanski 1988). Central among the themes of propaganda was the cult of Marshall Pétain: a veritable mystique around the figure of Pétain as the savior and father of the nation. Women were celebrated as mothers; girls were invariably healthy, dreamed of children, and chose a life in the open air of the countryside rather than an urban existence, the source of deviation from moral values. A return to the land, the great theme of early Vichy, became the almost obligatory solution in an economy of values founded on the cult of a mythical past in which the fatherland verged on the sacred.

From early on, youth was a central concern of the regime. In the summer of 1940, Chantiers de Jeunesse (Youth Work Camps) replaced national service for young men, who were required to live outdoors for eight months and work in the country, in a spirit inspired by scouting. Moreover, the majority of existing organizations were brought together into the scouting movement. The newly created Compagnons de France (trade confraternities) surpassed the political youth organizations (which had been suppressed) and secular work. This merging of groups worked well, even though the divisions between these diverse organizations had not disappeared. The Guides de France or Éclaireuses (Girl Guides) supervised girls in an education that privileged action and group interests, with a prevailing ethos of sanctified patriotism combined with unswerving morality, discipline, and the cult of national reform. From the Catholics—despite undeniable vigilance with respect to the Nazi peril (from the Jeunesse Étudiante Chrétienne [JEC; Christian Student Youth], and L'Action Catholique [Catholic Action])—came a traditional benevolence for the Vichy values of order, morality, tradition, restoration of religion, and so forth. School, too, was to be a place of supervision inspired by the same precepts underpinning the new order. But generally speaking, with the exception of a few specific measures (among them training in "family household management," which was made into a requirement in March 1942), Vichy did not challenge sexual equality within the educational framework. This was not a deliberate decision, and in any event there were tangible conceptual rifts from one minister of education to another (there were five of them, only two in office more than a few months: Jérôme Carcopino from February 1941 and then Abel Bonnard after April 1942). Although it was under surveillance, the educational system, beyond any political will, constituted a force of inertia that proved difficult to overcome. Moreover, some of the initiatives taken under the Vichy regime were actually beneficial to women. December 1940 saw the creation of Écully, a national school for female managers, training personnel responsible for the direction of the newly established centers and training programs for young working women, in the unoccupied southern zone. This school, like its male counterparts Uriage and Sillery, was not just a simple channel for communicating the propaganda of the General Secretariat to all youth, and it enjoyed considerable autonomy until the end of 1942.

The National Revolution constructed an image of women to match its project of putting her back in the home, in keeping with an old order that was more imagined than real. The weight of this tradition—already a contradictory justification of the "renewal" the regime wanted to impose upon women—stood in opposition to any social reality, since 36 percent of French women were working before the war. Fundamentally, the whole art of Vichy discourse was meant to justify the suffering and the frustrations of the war and the occupation, presenting these as a necessary penitence, a purgatory needed for the regeneration of France. In the end the results were few. Studies on propaganda show that, all in all, it was largely ineffectual, especially given its scale and means. The development of the National Revolution regime into a military state widened the gap, separating Vichy rhetoric and its practice even more. To give but one example, this practice translated into an ever tighter control of communications and correspondence: in December 1943, according to Michael Marrus and Robert Paxton, 2,448,554 letters were censored, as well as 1,771,330 telegrams and 20,811 telephone conversations (see Marrus and Paxton). Control grew in proportion to distrust of the regime. Censorship must have reinforced a feeling of isolation in the population, especially among women separated by circumstances from their spouses. One had to learn how to speak without speaking in order to avoid censorship, how to lie in order not to worry one's beloved, how to read between the lines he wrote, while wanting to believe that all was well with him. It was the same for all social relationships. The practice of lying became commonplace, and mute anxiety began eroding communal trust, even if silence and laconic half-truths were capable of hatching the first clandestine conspiracies.

The fatherland according to Vichy was telling lies. "For women the project of the National Revolution," Hélène Eck summarizes, "constructed a symbolic and ideal universe of motherhood, family, and home, while the state in its actual functioning regulated and managed wholly different collective and concrete situations: poverty, aid, and manual labor for Germany" (see Eck). Yet another possibility was pure and simple annexation, as was the case for Alsace and Moselle, which suffered the German Reich's politics of Germanization. This policy, described by the Germans as "reintegration," caused much grief. Nevertheless, faced with annexation, Vichy did not react in a meaningful manner. Women's organizations, uniforms, informing, political sessions, the reluctance of young men (The "Malgré Nous" in Alsace–Moselle) to take up arms as against their will in the German Army as their fathers were obliged to do in the First World War, and so forth, were so many acts of aggression against the now elusive integrity of the nation. It seemed that the homeland of France had never been glorified as much as when, carved up into six separate zones, it no longer existed.

On the Family Front

The family was a central for the Vichy regime; indeed, it had already been a particular focus under the government of the Third Republic. The Family Code was passed into law on 29 July 1939—the same year that the war was declared. It was a series of measures meant to curb the population decline that had accompanied the crisis of the 1930s—in 1938 there were 612,000 births against 647,000 deaths—and to strenghten the family generally. These measures, as Antoine Prost has explained, were the result of pronatalist and populationalist concerns and favored rapid family growth and large families—that is, families with at least three children and a stay-at-home mother (see Prost). Most measures taken after the defeat were not really initiatives taken by Vichy but rather an inheritance from the Third Republic, and some of their instigators would retain their positions even after 1944. "Once she had become a mother, a woman gained access to the Pantheon of Vichy's social models," comments Eck. She became the receptacle of life and the nation's continuity, the guarantor of the moral order. Medals were awarded to French mothers of large families: bronze for five children, silver for eight children, and gold for ten children or more. The notion "family virtue" embodied in the women who won medals obviously excluded illegitimate births, but measures were nevertheless taken to legitimize children born out of wedlock. In 1941, it was decided that 25 May would henceforth be the "day of national gratitude to French mothers," heavily reinforced by propaganda and school activities: posters, medals, speeches, demonstrations, and performances. For example, Laurent Gervereau notes that a play entitled "Le plus beau métier du monde" (The Most Beautiful Profession in the World) was performed in Bordeaux before an audience of 3,200 girls (see Gervereau and Peschanski). Mother's Day in France, first introduced in 1926, had never before been celebrated as it was under Vichy, when it was inscribed in the logic of the propaganda that hammered away at the absolute necessity of having children— "a national duty." Posters loudly proclaimed: "A household without a child is a couple adrift"; "An only child is a sad child"; or "Your expenses will be less burdensome with the wife at home," while childless and flirtatious women were vilified as useless. Under the Vichy government, as in any conservative regime, woman and family were conflated. This trend grew progressively stronger in Pétain's France, following a tendency of all fascist or fascist-leaning regimes to substitute the mother for the woman, thus favoring community over the individual.

To strengthen the family unit, different structures responsible for stimulating its development were created: Secrétariat d'État à la Famille et à la Jeunesse (12 July 1940; State Secretariat for Family and Youth), Comité Consultatif de la Famille (June 1941; Family Advisory Committee), Commissariat Général à la Famille (September 1941, directed by Philippe Renaudin; General Family Commission), Secrétariat d'État à la Famille et à la Santé (March 1943; State Secretariat of Family and Health), and the Conseil Supérieur de la Famille (June 1943; Higher Council for the Family), not to mention various secondary or regional offices. Moreover, some of these entities were maintained after the war. For example, at the liberation the General Family Commission, responsible for initiating laws to ensure family protection and for propaganda, was headed by Father Chaillet of the Témoignage Chrétien (Christian Witness). A variety of social measures were taken, such as development of family benefits or the single salary, which came to replace benefits for stay-at-home mothers, or the Gounot Law on family associations (November 1942). Some provisions were incorporated into the regulations of 1945. For example, there was the *carte de famille nombreuse* (large-family card), created with the Ministry of Agriculture, that had originally been issued to families with at least five minor children living under the same roof. There was the *carte nationale de priorité* (national priority card) issued to nursing women, and various measures designed to protect women in childbirth and to reduce the numbers of abandoned children. What the rules devised by Vichy had in common was their strengthening of the family institution more than the protection of individuals, and in that sense, the regulations went against the individualism of French legislation. A law such as the one of 22 September 1942, which specified the prerogatives of spouses, came less from the desire to confirm the husband's position as head of the family (nothing new) than from the wish to stress what Aline Coutrot characterizes as "the predominance of family interests over the point of view of one or the other of the spouses" (see Coutrot).

Alongside such measures for social protection, the Mouvement Populaire des Familles (MPF; People's Family Movement) was born in 1941. This organization replaced the Ligue Ouvrière Chrétienne (LOC; The Christian Workers League), whose objectives included providing activists with social training, maintaining a presence in the districts in order to help women, and helping them "become aware of their maternal vocation." The MPF supported the creation of associations of prisoners' wives, brought together in 1942 into a federation with some 30,000 members. The MPF increased services families and health care: the Service Populaire de Santé (People's Health Service), family centers and people's assistance centers, the Service d'Aide Familiale (Family Assistance Service), the Service Enfance et Jeunesse (Childhood and Youth Service) or the Centre Ouvrier d'Étude et d'Information (Workers' Study and Information Center), and so forth. Generally speaking, Vichy's family and corporatist ideology helped stimulate the development of social and family policies. Its first result, according to Michel Chauvière, was to promote representation of the family's interests among those who held public power. The second result, says Geneviève Dermenjian, was directly connected to current circumstances, since "it was during the war that the women of the MPF put themselves outside the home in large masses in order to respond to the needs of the time" (see Chauvière and Dermenjian, 1985). This progress can be linked to other measures favorable to women, such as those allowing them to play a role in the social committees of institutions or in municipal management. There was even a proposal in the National Council to grant them the right to vote. Social policies outlived the National Revolution, which was quite short, and even the Vichy government, which lasted four years. Perhaps women's participation in the social services influenced by the ideology of Vichy implied a vague sympathy for the values of the National Revolution. The symbolic universe of Vichy and organizations like the MPF overlapped on more than one point. Still, this closeness, which does not necessarily apply to all French women, was undoubtedly tempered by the harsh reality of everyday deprivations.

Other measures made social practices that undermined family life more difficult or punished them more severely. The divorce law of April 1941 prohibited divorce during the first three years of marriage. Desertion of the conjugal home became a criminal offense, for which wives were punished more severely than husbands. The law of 23 December 1942 provided for the protection of "the dignity of the home from which the husband was far removed as a result of the circumstances of war." Faithfulness to one's spouse became an almost "sacramental" virtue for wives, while for husbands it was a simple duty. Laws punishing abortion were made more severe, following the wish of Alliance Nationale contre la Dépopulation (National Alliance against Depopulation), which since 1939 had demanded the death penalty for professional abortionists of either sex. Numerous brochures written by the Alliance and targeting youth presented abortion as a crime. One such brochure, *Le Massacre des Innocents* (Massacre of the Innocents) by Fernand Boverat, described the fetus as a "prenatal child" and explained the tortures it underwent during abortion: "crushing . . . asphyxiation . . . the prenatal child is pierced by the probe . . . and burned alive in the abortionist's fire." While the law of 29 July 1939 provided for prison sentences of up to ten years for abortionists (six months to two years for those undergoing the operation), a new law enacted on 15 February 1942 made abortion analogous to assassination of the fatherland, punishable by death. Thus, as Francis Szpiner relates, Marie-Louise Giraud, age 40, a wife and mother and an abortionist, was put to death by guillotine in the morning of 30 July 1943, in the courtyard of the prison of La Roquette. Marshall Pétain had refused to grant clemency, in the name of defending the family and in contempt of the old tradition of French justice that spared women from capital punishment. Aside from this extreme case, prosecutions for abortion steadily increased: there were 1,225 convictions in 1940; 2,135 in 1941; 3,831 in 1942; 4,055 in 1943; and 3,701 before the liberation in 1944 (see Szpiner).

In the name of the family, the central theme of its propaganda and its politics, Vichy thus implemented a series of social measures that were directly inspired by the philosophy of the Family Code and that were extended into the Fourth Republic. Above all, the family was a central element in the Vichy paradigm. The family served as absolute proof, the foundational evidence used by an essentially patriarchal ideology that sought to construct its own legitimacy. The cult of the family was inscribed in the logic that naturalized national rootedness and conservatism. It established the legitimacy of a Pétain–father figure and his authority over "his" nation-family, demonstrating the perceived need for a return to methodical moral values and presenting social immobility as "natural," in contrast to an earlier and disturbing open-mindedness.

Hardships and Suffering

The context of war is a decisive element for understanding what life was like for French women under the Vichy government. The war was associated with the trauma of defeat, a more or less vague feeling of betrayal, experienced primarily, but not exclusively, among the elite classes, and which, accompanied in many cases by the absence of an imprisoned family member, fed into the anxiety of the early days of the war. Added to this, women faced a cluster of uncertainties to adjust to: work or, worse, unemployment; for those who were mothers, having to raise children by themselves; organizing to cope with poverty; and, generally, speaking, having to cope with the absence of men. Of more than 1.5 million prisoners who remained in Germany, almost half were married. Women in agricultural areas faced the problem of having to replace missing laborers. In administration and in some companies, some privileged women were able to receive their husbands' salary, but many others needed to find a means of subsistence. For the majority of women charged with the responsibilities of domestic life, the change was radical, and the difficulties of everyday life came fast and furiously. For example, the first rationing cards appeared in September 1940. Shoe sales were regulated from January 1941 on, and a system of points to determine allotments of textiles was instituted in July of the same year. Food rations diminished throughout the occupation. Jewels of ingenuity had to be used to keep the home alive. "Sleuths, virtuosos of deliverance, of domestic and daily miracles," writes Colette in her wartime memoir, *Paris de ma fenêtre* (1944; Paris from My Window). Poverty concerned women directly and often led them to deprive themselves. "I have not known any women who did not sacrifice some of 'her share' for others when there was nothing else to do," one witness reported. The deprivations made for a difficult life in which, according to Célia Bertin, "there was no longer any occasion to laugh wholeheartedly, the few jokes that were heard while standing in line were sinister and were received with more of a grimace than a smile" (*Les femmes sous l'Occupation*, 1993). A study specially commissioned by Marshall Pétain, undoubtedly to measure the breadth of the "ill wind" blowing in the autumn of 1941 in 2,500 homes of the working population in the Paris region, registered 48 percent of the people identifying themselves as "not happy," basically because of the material hardships of everyday life (see Gervereau and Peschanski). This daily humiliation of hunger and material frustrations, linked to the never-ending labor of women who had to feed their families, weighed heavily in their perception of the regime and its credibility. These women were the first to notice what Jean-Pierre Rioux describes as "an erasure of familiar reference points, in . . . a kind of social weightlessness of wartime" (see Rioux). Added to these torments was, for the wives of prisoners, the frequent feeling of living in forced isolation, no longer having any "social existence," and the ruin of the best years of their womanhood. Yet another hardship was sexual frustration, an issue rarely dealt with in postwar investigations though it unfailingly filled the "letters from readers" columns in women's magazines. No breach of conduct was allowed on the part of prisoners' wives. One wife, a postmistress in the Mayenne suspected of having an affair with a German soldier despite contradictory testimonies, was harassed in the spring of 1941 by the administration, which sent an investigator. The moral strictness of which the state had made itself guardian in the husband's absence was thus combined with concern for preserving the administration's image—and this was even before the law of 22 September 1942, which protected the rights of imprisoned husbands whose wives were unfaithful. Generally speaking, the increase in divorces after the war illustrated the depth of the trauma in civil society. Many women opted to postpone marriage until better days had arrived.

Very few did not suffer under the occupation. "They really had to be in a privileged position to profit from the advantages handed out by the government of the French state, or else they had to be as blind as they were rich not to know what was going on," comments Célia Bertin. From 1943, a growing fear of the occupying enemy, the plunder and hostage-taking, and the spectacle of raids was compounded by fear of militia violence and anxiety over Allied bombing campaigns, which intensified until 1944. The year of the liberation was also that of numerous dramas borne by the civil population: more than 300 people died in Amiens, another 300 in Nice, twice that number in

Lyon, and almost 2,000 in Marseilles—so many tragic situations for a wounded and weakened population. Worse still, perhaps, the war years struck at what the majority of women hold dearest among life's values, the sacred one of children. The infant mortality rate increased steadily from 68.3 per 1,000 births in 1939 to 113.7 per 1,000 birth in 1945 (see Sauvy). There is no doubt that for many women these dramas, caused by the war and the occupation—the occupying enemy generally being perceived as responsible for food shortages and their consequences—compensated for the frequent lack of a more "political" approach to the situation. It was first of all in the shops and in the street that Vichy lost the trust of the French. And French women, the primary managers of daily life, were the first to be disillusioned.

Women's Labor or State Opportunism

The law of 11 October 1940 was intended to send women back to their homes by forbidding the hiring of married women. It encouraged voluntary resignations from posts in administration, and in the civil service even allowed for retroactive dismissal of already tenured married women. Women over the age of 50 were forced to retire. Only mothers of at least three children or women whose husbands could not meet the needs of the family were left untouched by these measures. Moreover, some women had perceived the danger well before the month of October. In the 16 August 1940 issue of the *Journal de la femme*, an editor was already critical of the fate awaiting her peers:

> Only a few weeks ago the press did not have enough to say to praise women's work and the help it provided to national defense; voluntary service was encouraged, and official texts even threatened a return to mandatory service if voluntary service should prove insufficient. Now that unemployment has returned, they say, menacingly . . . they are preparing to lay off the majority of those women who are presently working and to prevent younger women from causing men any problems in the job market in the future.

Work for women became a burning issue in the early stages of the war, with the slow decline of male labor that accompanied the demobilization in the summer of 1940. The dismissal of certain categories of salaried workers was thus encouraged. State employees were threatened, and their dignity was hurt. Early in September 1940, when schools were opening, the teachers, whom propaganda had accused of being responsible for the moral decline of the land and thus for the defeat, had to sign statements that they were not Jewish or members of a secret society. This was required of all civil servants. Many must have found themselves in the same situation as a schoolteacher in Charentes, who, refusing at first to sign, had to swallow her pride when she was faced with the cruel dilemma between dignity and the need to provide for herself. Should she sign out of pragmatic realism, or should she refuse this indignity no matter what the cost? Circumstances certainly made the choices less clear cut, and the banal administrative forms undoubtedly passed like a bitter pill, but one that it was better to swallow unflinchingly while waiting for better days to come. Simone de Beauvoir signed the form and regretted it for the rest of her life (it must be said that there were those who made sure to remind her of it). France Hamelin reports what happened to Hélène Mabille, who refused to sign a declaration of allegiance to the Marshall; her case says a great deal about the severity of repression. Sentenced first to ten months in prison, by "implementation of the decree against dissolved leagues," she was sent to the Tourelles camp. When she was transferred the Aincourt camp, she sang the "Marseillaise" and the "Internationale" with her companions while crossing Paris, after which she was tried in special court on charges of "attack on morale and seditious singing." This time a sentence of ten years was handed down. (See Hamelin.) Teacher-training colleges were closed and some 20 left-wing teachers were dismissed daily during the first semester of 1940.

In October 1940 women represented 26 percent of the unemployed. In the postal services 19,000 agents were relieved of their posts, and the young assistants who had been hired when war was declared were fired in mid-July. But beginning in the spring of 1941, many women had to be rehired to offset the German refusal to authorize personnel movements between zones and to compensate for the lowering of individual productivity owing to difficult living conditions and lack of job skills on the part of replacement personnel. These new deficiencies canceled out the effects of the October law. Having attempted to confined women to their homes in the turmoil of the National Revolution, officials again began proposing auxiliary posts in administration or industry, and more and more often to women. The war continued, and the 1940 October law was completely suspended in September 1942. It is worth noting that unemployment had dwindled in the meantime: with about a million unemployed in October 1940, the number had been reduced to 300,000, more than half of whom were women, in July 1941; in July 1942 there were only 77,000 unemployed, 60 percent of whom were women (see Bordeaux). The Germans were also more and more interested in the labor force of young, mobile women likely to leave voluntarily for the Reich under the system called "La Relève" (relieving), which had been announced on 22 July 1942, through Pierre Laval's much heralded propaganda. The system provided for the exchange of three qualified French workers emigrating to Germany for the return of one prisoner to France. Despite the propaganda, the operation was a failure. Even though it allowed for the return of more than 90,000 prisoners, the program disappointed many women who had hoped to see the return of a son or a husband and, as Dominique Veillon writes, it "made the existing gap between the different layers of the population a little wider" (see Veillon 1992). The law enacted on 4 September 1942 was then presented as a law relating to "the use and orientation of labor," of interest to all men between the ages of 18 and 50 and all unmarried women between 21 and 35. With this law, the Vichy government planned to assign French women and men who fulfilled these conditions to all work it judged useful to national interests. But its application was suspended until the law of 16 February 1943 was published, much more radical in the face of the failure of the voluntary work policy, which instituted obligatory work service for three age categories (20, 21, and 22 years of age), and tangibly increased the number of departures to the Reich: in October 1941 14,500 French women worked there, while in 1944 the figure was 44,000 (see Pollard). The use of female labor to compensate for personnel shortages was very clear cut in a variety of sectors, notably in the large public enterprises.

Women's labor was indispensable to the functioning of the postal services or the national railway services, where 45,000 women, or more than half of the auxiliary personnel, were working late in 1943—an increase of 57 percent in one year (see Delvincourt and Durand). Vichy, wanting to send women back to their homes, in fact practiced short-term management of the constraints of the occupation and the war, the fluctuations of which were the only determining factors.

A Resistance of Solidarity and Commitment

French historiographers in recent years—notably through a series of university colloquia in Toulouse (1993), Rennes (1994), and in Besançon and Paris (1995)—have emphasized the variety of processes that led individuals toward a mentality of refusal, as well as the complexity and contradictions of many attitudes. The failure of the National Revolution and the policy of collaboration were signs of the population's rejection of the regime—a rejection that did not apply in the same manner to the person of Pétain. In this dynamic of refusal, women played a role that was often obscured after the war. Rarely in the foreground, they contributed to a passive form of resistance, at one and the same time colorless but indispensable, a form of refusal that Pierre Laborie has called "resistance based on community solidarity" (see Laborie 2001). That is, it was a solidarity of proximity, a form of daily and informal mutual aid that, often on individuals' initiative and in an almost "natural" manner, constituted the fabric of a collective reaction in the face of German and Vichy aggression. The survival of those who escaped the Final Solution by remaining on national soil is to be credited to this type of solidarity among the rest of the population. These attitudes could also be organized into various forms of civil resistance, branching out in mutual aid networks that included or called upon a large proportion of women. There were the religious associations such as the Consistoire Israélite (Hebrew Consistory) or the Oeuvre de Secours aux Enfants (OSE; Children's Aid Operation), a Jewish organization that saved thousands of children. There were also Catholic organizations such as Amitié Chrétienne (Christian Friendship), the previously mentioned Témoignage Chrétien (Christian Witness), under the leadership of Father Chaillet, and the Comité des Oeuvres Sociales de la Résistance (COSOR; Social Action Committee of the Resistance), organized under his initiative in order to come to the aid of families of resistance workers, all of them with the support of many women. The movement's press organ, *Les cahiers du Témoignage chrétien*, later in 1943 retitled *Le courrier français du Témoignage chrétien*, was distributed by activists of the Chronique Sociale (Social Chronicle), a Catholic social organization in Lyon headed by Sylvie Mingeolet. Many women of the Christian Friendship group took children into their homes, as did the sisters of Notre-Dame-de-Sion, who hid Jewish families and children in Grenoble. What might appear as a duty of solidarity from the religious point of view was much less frequently decreed by the Catholic hierarchy. A few rare prelates, such as Monsignor Saliège and Monsignor Gerlier—who had written the famous adage "France is Pétain and Pétain is France"—took a stand in support of the outcast Jews in the summer of 1942.

Solidarity emanating from Protestant circles was more consistent. Pétain had not shaken the convictions of Protestants. Persecution, which was part of Protestants' history and culture, had enabled them to see clearly and prepared them to react effectively. In some places, expressions of solidarity were far more common than in non-Protestant environments and also involved more women. Famous examples of this type of expression include the small village of Le Chambon-sur-Lignon in the Haute-Loire, which became a refuge for Jews and persons evading the obligatory work service, or the actions carried out by the Comité Intermouvement auprès des Évacués (CIMADE; Inter-Movement Committee for Evacuees). Women were abundantly present in these charitable organizations and often played a key role. But their involvement remained ambivalent, in that it did not always reflect mistrust of Vichy. Thus, forms of action that today would readily be called humanitarian, toward outcast Jews, which involved true risk taking, might be superimposed upon a wish not to question the established order of Vichy, based on fears of Communism, foreigners, and Jews (the entity depicted in propaganda, not the persecuted child). Also to be mentioned in the resistance to anti-Semitism is the firm opposition of the Conseil Protestant de la Jeunesse (CPJ; Protestant Youth Council), which consolidated the youth movements of reformed and evangelical churches, including the Union Chrétienne des Jeunes Gens et des Jeunes Filles (Christian Union of Young Men and Women), the Association Chrétienne d'Étudiants (Christian Student Association), the Girl Guides, and the Éclaireurs Unionistes (Unionist Boy Guides). What the majority of these mutual aid networks had in common was that they did not frame their actions as an open struggle against the regime. Even if they might later provide the resistance with support, they limited themselves to a role of defense and protection.

Women's Involvement in the Resistance

The number of women detained during the occupation grew sixfold during the same time period in which that of men doubled. There was thus a clear increase in illegal acts committed by women under the Vichy government, even if all of them were not necessarily acts of resistance (abortions, in this regard, could be assessed in different ways). Women's involvement in the resistance should, nevertheless, be approached carefully in that their contributions were less clear cut than those of men. Undoubtedly, women who were visibly involved in the underground groups or in the liberation fights were fewer than men, and they rarely had the same role in the resistance from the point of view of paramilitary involvement. But the risks women ran were almost entirely the same whatever actions they were engaged in, be it informing, liaison work, logistical support, safeguarding outcasts, or any other possible acts of solidarity. Simply lodging a Jew, a Communist, or some other "terrorist" could lead the person in question directly to a concentration camp. And women in the resistance who accompanied Allied pilots out of the country to facilitate their escape, for example, could not claim the protection offered by the laws of war if they were arrested (unlike the pilots themselves). "Unquestionably," writes Hélène Eck,

the Resistance used women and their presumed innocence, frailty, and ignorance, separating them from the stronger sex, as a cover, and it was precisely because the occupying enemy shared the same cultural and social representations of female behavior that this cover could be effective.

Olga Bancic, of the Manouchian group of the FTP-MOI (Francs-Tireurs et Partisans, Section Main-d'Oeuvre Immigrée; Snipers and Partisans, Section of Immigrant Labor), hid weapons in her shopping bag before assassination attempts. A young girl like Célia Bertin was contacted by Pierre de Lescure (1891–1963), cofounder, along with Vercors (pseudonym of Jean Bruller), of the clandestine Éditions de Minuit, who was in contact with the British, to accompany agents or Allied flyers during their crossings. "They needed a young girl who could speak English," she explains,

and a couple aroused less suspicion than a man alone—especially if he did not speak French or only barely. And in spite of the fear that had me in its grip, when I was alone in the metro or the street with my myopic look, not wearing any glasses, my fine hats and my high heels, I certainly did not look like a "terrorist," as the Gestapo and the French working for them were already calling us.

Members of the Communist Party were specifically targeted as "terrorists." Communist women, on the other hand, were better habituated to both secrecy and underground organizing generally, since the French Communist Party had been dissolved in September 1939, after its refusal to condemn the German-Soviet Pact. Its activists, persecuted during the Phony War, had been plunged into the dangers of repression well before the advent of Vichy. Their political convictions—which led all party members to accept paramilitary discipline—also helped to reinforce the efficiency of the largest clandestine organization of the country. By May 1940 some 5,500 Communist activists had been arrested. But in spite of this, it is not certain that the motivation of Communist women did not differ from that of the men. "The political aspect of the Resistance escaped most of us," recalls Bertin, in whose eyes political commitment was primarily a concern of men. "Young Communist women seemed to be in the same rush as I was to find peace again."

The desire for peace did not exclude the fervent wish to contribute to the construction of a more just society after the war. Lucie Aubrac's case exemplifies both desires: a young history teacher whom nothing had predisposed to commando action, she became a specialist in rescue operations for resistance workers, and several members in charge of the Mouvements Unis de Résistance (MUR; United Resistance Movements) owe her their lives. She organized the escape of her husband, Raymond Aubrac, in an incredible manner. Several months pregnant, she acted out of love before anything else, she explained ("everything always brings me back to him," she wrote in her journal), without being burdened by "political" considerations. The realities of life and the absolute imperative to survive were surely what counted most in women's involvement. That perhaps explains why women of radically different political sensibilities sometimes took action, even though nothing predisposed them to insubordination. This was the case of a few factory superintendents who, in Annie Fourcaut's words, "were employers' most reliable allies, blind in 1936, apostles of good form and unmarried by duty and vocation, they welcomed the Vichy regime and its motto, 'Work, Family, Fatherland,' as a divine surprise" (see Fourcaut). About 15 such women were shot or deported. Despite contradictions, developments, and divisions of all sorts, the professional environment continued to be a privileged place of trust and solidarity. Still, "fully engaged" active resistance of this type concerned only a tiny minority of the population. The mass heroism that figures in collective representations of the resistance after the war—which Gaullists and Communists had a common interest in encouraging—was hardly true to reality.

To be sure, there were great female figures, and their celebrity sometimes obscured the invisible role played by the larger number, anonymous and overshadowed. Marie-Claude Vaillant-Couturier is an example, or Danièle Casanova, who was in charge of the Union des Jeunes Filles de France (Girls' Union of France) before the war. At the end of 1940, Casanova organized several demonstrations for the return of prisoners and the improvement of living conditions; her activities were emulated in both the occupied and free zones. Another Communist, Lise Ricol, paid very dearly for her initiative, already mentioned, to incite the rebellion of August 1942. She was arrested a few days later, then deported to Ravensbrück after delivering a baby in the prison of La Petite-Roquette. In contrast, Elisabeth de La Bourdonnay, an upper-middle-class woman, joined the network of the Musée de l'Homme (Museum of Man)—where the paper *Résistance* was published from 15 December 1940—very early on. She pursued her clandestine activity after the network had been dismantled and Boris Vildé, together with six other resistance workers, had been shot on 23 February 1942. Still other women were a direct part of the resistance from the beginning: Bertie Albrecht, who, after her work publishing the clandestine paper *Les petites ailes*, became copublisher with Henri Frenay of *Combat*; Lucie Aubrac of *Libération*, another large movement; or Marie-Madeleine Fourcade, who directed the network Alliance. Madeleine Braun, a militant antifascist and a member of the Comité Amsterdam-Pleyel (Amsterdam-Pleyel Committee), was in charge of the southern zone of the National Front. Simone Michel-Lévy created a resistance network in the French postal services and was arrested and deported to Ravensbrück, where she was hanged. Another decidedly atypical case was that of Jeanne Bohec, a young chemist who eventually titled her memoirs *La plastiqueuse à bicyclette* (1975; Bomber on a Bicycle); she became a military specialist in sabotage and was parachuted into France in February 1944 to train Breton resistance workers. The list could be much longer. But these few examples, while they reveal undeniable dispositions, remain exceptional. And even if many of these women were to agree in saying that they were on an equal footing with men in the resistance —"the responsibilities were divided without any sexual discrimination, but rather in accordance with what seemed to be the best use of competencies and abilities," recalls Aubrac—it was nevertheless rare for women to hold a top-ranking position in a resistance organization. Equally rare were women who were active without their husbands' knowledge. Despite progressive thinking among the great majority of resisters, there continued to be a kind of dichotomy between the image of women and that of war. Virility seemed obligatory in combat, as a kind of perceived guarantee of effectiveness.

In London, the beginnings of Free France were difficult, as is well known. Out of some 700 French people on assignment at the time of the armistice, Élisabeth de Miribel notes that one could count on the fingers of one hand the high-placed people who rallied around de Gaulle. Still, a Corps Féminin de la France Libre (Women's Corps for Free France), later renamed the Volontaires Françaises de la France Libre (Women Volunteers for Free France) was formed by Simone Mathieu, a tennis champion. In November 1940, she put out a call to French women in Great Britain in order to create a "women's contingent for Free France." Rachel Windsor describes the situation as follows:

> there were students, a cook, the daughter of an embassy attaché, merchants, a schoolteacher, some middle-class women, a cabaret artist, wives of English military men, a saleswoman from Lancel, an avant-garde theater actress, a teacher of Spanish, a children's governess, the daughter of a Polish sculptor, a Norwegian woman from Paris, etc.

Modes of Action

One mode of refusal, simple but not without risk, was the participation in public protests of all kinds. Danielle Tartakowsky has inventoried 239 demonstrations by housewives during this period, 53 of which took place between November 1940 and October 1941, and another 96 between November 1941 and March 1942 (see Tartakowsky). Sometimes these demonstrations took an adamantly political turn, with speeches by activists protected by the Organisation Spéciale (OS; Special Organization), then by the Snipers and Partisans. During the demonstration of 1 August 1942, Lise Ricol addressed women who were standing in line in front of a store in the 14th arrondissement in Paris. Protesting against the propaganda, the food shortages, and the first departures for Germany, they sang the "Marseillaise." The event was picked up and widely quoted by Radio-London. Operations of this kind, generally organized by Communist women, found a resonance in proportion to the growing weariness of a starving urban population. More than 30 demonstrations of the same kind took place in the coal basin of the north, presaging the great miners' strike that occurred between 28 May and 7 June 1941. The miners' wives increased support actions, demonstrations of all kinds, and processions in front of city halls. Émilienne Mopty, considered a leader, was executed by the Germans. Elsewhere traces can be found of various popular women's committees, established on the initiative of Communist activists, developed before the Union des Femmes Françaises (Union of French Women) was created in 1943. The material nature of most of the demands induced the sympathy, even the mobilization, of an ever larger fringe of housewives. The spirit of resistance thus welled up from the realities of poverty.

This was the recurrent theme developed in the minuscule, women-oriented district papers that sprang up in Paris and the suburbs. The year 1943 saw the publication of *La ménagère de Paris, Femmes de Belleville, Femmes d'Ivry, Femmes de Soissons*, and so forth. Most often emerging under Communist influence, these publications criticized problems with the food supply, general poverty, the absence of prisoners, Vichy's policies intended to raise the birthrate, and other common themes. Some flyers were created in prisons by women resistance workers who had been caught. This was the case of the monthly *La patriote enchaînée*, which circulated through the prison of La Roquette starting in July 1943 or, in Marseille, a handwritten flyer titled *Le trait d'union des Baumettes*. Other publications with a larger distribution were developed, such as *Les Mariannes*, put out by the Snipers and Partisans, the Communist monthly *Femmes françaises*, or *Les femmes patriotes*, put out by the United Resistance Movements, although in absolute terms their circulation remained moderate. Counterpropaganda slogans were disseminated through small, often handwritten posters, as were calls for demonstrations in front of the food warehouses under German control. For women who, in one way or another, felt committed to the resistance, life changed and was daily interwoven with fear they had to learn to control or accept. Besides the growing dangers, as the French state grew more radical, people had to contend with mistrust of acquaintances and neighbors and with various brutally abrupt changes. "There was also the pain created by unexplained disappearances," recalls Bertin,

> people one knew, others one simply used to run into. Where had they gone? You would phone friends or relations, no answer; or else an anonymous voice would give an embarrassed explanation. You would question people's motives. Sniffing out someone else's involvement seemed a threat for those who had not taken any stand, as well as for those who approved of Pétain. They could already see themselves being accused of complicity.

Complicity against Vichy's anti-Semitism, for example, which transcends the issue of sexual difference. It must be acknowledged that despite the explicit spiraling of discrimination, the policy of excluding Jews was an extension of a continuous tradition of anti-Semitism within one part of French society. Accordingly, the policy was granted a legitimate facade for some time. In addition there was the fact that, as Renée Poznanski points out, "the approval of abstract legislation would not exclude personal sympathy for a victim with whom one had daily contact" (see Poznanski 1994). This legislation came to blur the points of reference a little and was not always understood for what it was. One example is that of a farmer's wife in the Eure-et-Loire region who, having taken two Jewish children of disappeared parents into her home in June 1943, wrote in all naïveté to the local police prefect to ask for supplementary food ration cards for her protégés.

The first statute on Jews, issued on 3 October 1940 and establishing a whole array of restrictions against the "Israelite population" (as they were then called), did not elicit much in the way of public reaction. The second statute, in June 1941, intensified the earlier measures. In any case, the French camps had already been filled well before that. The exact figure is difficult to establish when transfers, permanent variations, and imprecision linked to circumstances are accounted for, but it is known that at the end of 1940, there were fewer than 1,000 persons interned in the north, while there were between 50,000 and 60,000 internees in the southern zone. In February 1941, in the camp of Gurs in the Basses-Pyrénées, which held many foreigners, there were 4,300 women and 350 children under the age of 14 out of 12,000 inmates, a majority of whom had fled Hitler's Germany (see Peschanski 1992). Between October 1940 and June 1942, more than 1,000 deaths occurred there. Some

camps, such as the one at Rieucros, opened in January in 1939 to receive Spanish refugees, were inhabited mostly by women.

With the decree of 7 June 1942 mandating the wearing of the yellow Star of David, the seal of shame materialized in a bit of fabric. The tag created a shudder in public opinion. "This morning I saw the first Jewish star," wrote Edith Thomas,

> on the chest of two little girls who were coming out of school in the rue des Archives: sewn neatly onto their apron right where the heart is. What tears of anger, rage, and despair the mother who sewed this on must have wept. I felt a sudden blow, as if, in spite of everything, I couldn't understand, as if I couldn't believe that this possible infamy was becoming a reality. (*Pages de Journal 1939–1944*)

During the round-ups in the Vélodrome d'Hiver of 16 and 17 July 1942, organized by the French police under the direction of Darquier de Pellepoix, general commissioner of Jewish questions, 3,031 men, 5,802 women, and 4,051 children were arrested. The disproportionate presence of women was the result of the Jews' excessive trust in the French state: only some men had fled upon hearing rumors of the coming raids. The Jewish community was convinced that women and children had nothing to fear. The anti-Semitic death knell had sounded and was justified in extreme terms by some collaborators. "We must be separated from the Jews as a whole and not keep the little ones; humanity is in agreement here with wisdom," wrote Robert Brasillach in the 25 September 1942 issue of the weekly *Je suis partout no 589*. Terrible words. But in spite of everything, most of the French, beginning with the Jews themselves, did not imagine that a fate beyond all comprehension lay in store for them, announcements and rumors notwithstanding. Michael Pollak's exemplary studies on the attitudes of some women in the concentration camps help clarify both the importance of the preservation of their identity and their need to fulfill a particular function, as part of a survival strategy (see Pollak). Precisely because of the fundamental role of identity in the process of survival, everything in the concentration camp system was conceived to annihilate the individual, man or woman, including the individual's self-awareness. While in the early stages internees might still have some self-respect, after a few weeks of internment, they were watching the last moments of the dying in order to eat their bread. "When we arrived here, the majority could still think of something other than hunger," according to internee Robert Antelme. Our present gender-specific focus means that we must stop at the gates of the camps.

Women and Collaboration

The deportation of Jews from France sealed the abjectness of Vichy and its policy of collaboration at the same time that it gave shape to what very rapidly became the cynical plan of a vassal state. The gap between Vichy and French society—the latter having fostered the Enlightenment, the Republic, and the Popular Front—arrived at impossible political and moral extremes. The notion of political collaboration, however, is hardly adapted to the situation of most of the women who were judged or sanctioned as collaborators after liberation. Under Vichy, they were "by nature" absent from the political structures of the state, as they were from the parties of the collaboration—even more absent than they were from the resistance organizations. This is not to say that there weren't any women at all in these parties. Here and there some traces of women, usually young, are to be found in the Parti Populaire Français (PPF; French People's Party), led by Jacques Doriot, and others in the ranks of friends of the Légion Française des Combattants (French Fighters Legion). A few rare teachers were part of the Rassemblement National Populaire (RNP; People's National Assembly) led by Marcel Déat, with its more intellectual approach. There were women members employed in the militia offices, whose presence in those times of material hardship was frequently linked to the few advantages they might draw from their involvement. An overwhelming minority in the political parties, women were active there to varying degrees but almost never held any post of responsibility. There were 6,091 women out of a total figure of 29,401 arrested for "acts of collaboration" in March 1946; and 1,191 out of a total figure of 6,715 in January 1950. In 1958, there was only one woman left. Two penitentiaries were reserved for women, in Jargeau in the Loiret and in Schirmeck in the Lower Rhine. Apart from these rather rare cases—particularly if one does not associate activities in official organizations with a social vocation (such as the People's Family Movement) with collaborating, although the role of such organizations was sometimes ambivalent in being joined to a system the regime had conceived—women accused of collaboration came from two large groups. First, there were the famous or highly placed women whose names were associated with high-society life. In that capacity, they often served as support for Vichy or for Franco-German collaboration. Then there was the anonymous multitude whose attitude (if one excludes women who denounced others) often reflected a kind of vulgar misbehavior in the presence of the occupying forces, but who represented a large part of the purged population after the liberation.

There is little to say about the former group. The majority of these high-society women chose comfort and ease without always carefully weighing what impact their compromises with the notables of Vichy or the powerful of the Reich might have on public opinion. They still made the first pages of the press at the liberation, and several of them wrote their memoirs. Corinne Luchaire, a prominent actress, the daughter of Jean Luchaire, and a regular at the German-Parisian soirées, had a taste for the easy life before anything else; she was also very young. Others, such as the singer Germaine Lubin, or actresses such as Mary Marquet or Mireille Balin, compromised themselves, but without directly harming their compatriots. For those who were in business this was not always the case, as is shown by the example of Gabrielle (Coco) Chanel, who, taking advantage of the anti-Semitic laws, attempted to recover the rights to perfumes (including the famous Chanel No. 5) she had sold to the Wertheimer brothers before the war. Still other women, more discreet or opportunistic, and nameless, in some cases worthy of a role in airport novels, played around with the big traffickers dealing with the occupying enemy and his purchasing agencies. Mathilde Carré, known as "La Chatte" (The Cat), also resembled a character out of fiction. She betrayed her compatriots when she went to work for the Germans in 1940 and was later responsible for the dismantling of several resistance networks. She was arrested in England, accused of spying, and condemned to death

in January 1949. Her sentence was eventually commuted, and she was set free in 1954.

The second group, ordinary women, defined a form of collaboration that was generally apolitical, where the ambiguity of the relationship with the occupying enemy, in the form of seduction or adultery, often constituted the common denominator of the acts of which they were accused. "My heart belongs to France, but my ass is international," the film star Arletty is credited with saying (quoted in Claudine Brécourt-Villars, *Les mots d'Arletty*, 1988). That comment, besides its impudence, sums up the question of the limits of patriotism and, in essence, of the role reserved for women in the country's situation under the yoke of the conqueror. To a great extent, the women harassed after the liberation were implicated for having been mistresses. Moreover, this observation implies an important remark: the data on common collaboration are essentially known only through the filter of the purges, a context and process that ignored some individuals while others were counted in the ranks of the "collaborators" for trivial offenses. Although it is still impossible to know the precise gender distribution of those purged, we do have specific indications concerning the areas of communications and public education, the two administrations most heavily female. In those fields, many, often young women were harassed and sanctioned in large proportions. In the postal services, where personnel were equally divided between the two sexes, 26.5 percent of the files on the purged concerned women, and in public education this figure was 37.1 percent. Therefore, women were proportionally charged less frequently than men. However, they were more harshly treated by certain purge committees. Women represented as much as 40 percent of the sanctions taken by the postal administration and were, thus, much more severely punished than men. After the offense of "fraternizing with the enemy," the principal motivations for punishment were betrayal or threats of betrayal, and to a lesser extent, public expressions either unfavorable to the Allies or the resistance, or admiring of the Germans, generally related to a more "consistent" motivation (fraternizing with a German, denunciation, or even suspected denunciation). Offenses of opinion were many but were very seldom sufficient to consider the accused a collaborator. It is noticeable, however, that the term "collaborator" was most often applied to women on the lower rungs of the social ladder.

In Alsace and Moselle, where the purges were most intense, the concept of collaboration had a very particular meaning, one that cannot be dissociated from the intense policy of Germanization to which the population had been subjected for four years. There, things had changed very rapidly. The French language was outlawed, and French civil servants were either removed from their positions or relegated to very basic tasks, while all that was a reminder of France and French culture was forbidden. Above all, civil society as a whole was fettered by myriad organizations of every kind that depended, directly or indirectly, on the Nazi Party. Included in this were social welfare associations such as the Elsässicher Hilfsdienst (Alsace Aid), the Opferring (Circle of Contributors, which became the Circle of Offering and later still, when the war was at its height, the Circle of Sacrifice), and the Volksgemeinschaft (Community of the People), which became efficient recruiters of Nazi Party members. Women's organizations were numerous there; they supervised and oversaw the women while constituting one of the wheels of the enormous Nazi propaganda machine. What all these entities had in common was that they presented Nazism with a human face, and for their members they were the first step toward a personal involvement in National Socialism. Innumerable women who had belonged to the Nazi Party or had played an active role in the many women's organizations that were part of it were hit with sanctions ranging from national humiliation to the revocation of civil service. Those who had been implicated in more serious affairs were imprisoned. Many were sentenced because they had accepted responsibilities in these organizations, had worn the uniform and insignia of the party, had raised their arm in salute when arriving at work, had led propaganda actions, or had become *Blockleiterin* or *Zellenleiterin* (block or district supervisor), and so forth. Similar sentences were meted out to those who had succumbed to the many official incitements to inform and had betrayed their opponents.

The political involvement of women accused of collaboration in the annexed departments was real, but it was connected to the policy of Germanization. Further, part of the phenomenon of membership in the Nazi Party reflected a defense strategy and stemmed from a kind of commitment of convenience. It was the most Francophile cantons that most readily handed their contributions over to the police, merely so as not to be suspected of dissidence. For those who crossed the line into membership it was very difficult to retreat and to withdraw from the spiral of compromised principles.

Purged Women More than Collaborators

In contrast, other places suggest radically apolitical but even more troubling female "collaborators." Such is the case for the pocket of Lorient which, for strategic reasons, was not liberated until May 1945, and where 379 arrests were made, 87 percent of them women, as were almost all of those called to appear before the Civil Chamber. The women here (and this concerns only people of the lower classes who worked for the Germans as domestic servants) figured prominently in the system of collective representations studied by Luc Capdevila (see Capdevila). Such women were considered not French citizens accused of a crime, but "women of Krauts," "Krautized" women who had betrayed their country: they were practically all accused of having sexual relations with Germans. They were seen first and foremost as women and sustained a collective fantasy which, besides unbridled sexuality, saw in them every sign of pleasure, in contrast to the suffering endured under the occupation. Even if the case of Lorient is undoubtedly exceptional, this kind of female "collaborator" turned out to be abundant. Who cannot call to mind the image of the woman whose head was shorn at the time of the liberation? She often played a role of release and participated in a complex phenomenon that intermingled political collaboration, social designation, and a more-or-less improvised ritual of reclaimed liberty. At the same time, this practice isolated and returned the shorn women to their sexual specificity. Recent studies have shown that the phenomenon occurred across the land, most frequently in rural areas, sometimes well before or long after the liberation. This shaving or "shearing" of women, dealt with philosophically by Alain Brossat, took different forms and had a variety of violent modalities, but could go as far as

the execution of the victims, although this was rare (see Brossat). The shearing of women's heads constructed a kind of opposition figure, both simple and reassuring, that eroticized, as if better to exorcise, the collaborator-prostitute. She stood in symbolic contrast to a virtuous Marianne and thus seemed to shoulder the shameful femininity of the collaboration. This was a "horizontal" collaboration, in contrast to the virile "verticality" of the resistance, erected against the enemy in a gendered economy of symbolic space that has been evoked by Pierre Laborie. There were troubling reversals in this situation, which sometimes stressed certain contradictions: thus, there was the discourse, dominant in the resistance press, that fluctuated between the desire to preserve the image of the liberation and thus to minimize acts of violence against women, and the exultation of the victory over the enemy unfolding in the ritual shaving of women's heads. "The balancing act between the description of ugliness and the preservation of the image of the liberation," writes Fabrice Virgili, "leads to the paradox of seeing the execrated symbols of Nazism become 'magnificent swastikas' when they decorate the cheeks of the shorn women of Albi" (see Virgili 1992).

In some places, collective frenzy could attain dimensions that far surpassed the prevailing excesses linked to violent acts of the liberation. In Pamiers, in the Ariège, 50 people were condemned to death by a people's tribunal during the first few days of the liberation. Among them were ten women who were first shorn then executed. The incident once again reflects the idea of collaboration—and also that of purging, the one and the other obviously linked—in the complex prism of a gendered, interdisciplinary reading. The question raised by women and their role in these phenomena necessitates evaluation at the level of both a long-term political perspective and immediate impact. While both aspects remain open to interpretation, one observation must be made: women were essentially absent from the political arena, in the sense that it can be understood when evoking collaboration. Those women who were stigmatized as "collaborators" were far more often the objects of a process of social marking, sometimes violent, than they were active and responsible subjects. From this point of view, being shorn was a punishment that in and of itself was less humiliating than was the fact that it sent women back to their "natural," thus political, irresponsibility.

Vichy and After

"The problem of women has always been a problem of men." This statement by Simone de Beauvoir, which gave *The Second Sex*, the work from which it came, its well-known fame, was true during the occupation—and indeed, doubtless found one of its best illustrations in that context. The law of 11 October 1940 and its subsequent suspension, quickly accompanied by oft-repeated encouragement to get women back to work, and even—with the help of the spiral of collaboration—to send young women to Germany to run the war industry, are there to prove it. The fate that awaited opponents of the regime and Jews obviously emerged from the same inhuman logic. They are as many traces of the permanent gap between the Vichy regime's rhetoric and the treatment it reserved for the female population and for society as a whole. In any event, women's daily reality was quite far removed from the National Revolution's ideal of woman in the home. This was a pipe dream more than a real plan and, at best, would have convinced the most gullible that Joan of Arc, the muse of Vichy, was a *garçon manqué*, a "failed boy."

State sexism, however, was not the sole prerogative of the Vichy regime. The example of the purging and its disparities toward the weakest of women, those without any status—maids and domestic workers, auxiliary workers in public service sector, prostitutes, and the disenfranchised—seems significant of the role assigned to them. This was notably true in the administration, where the practice of purging appeared above all as one embodiment of the cold efficiency of state logic. From the professional point of view, liberation's return to order put women back in the tasks of implementation, tasks of mastery at best, they had fulfilled before the war—despite the proven ability of those women who had had the opportunity to take on unusual responsibilities for four years running. The return to the old order should not have greatly surprised the older women, who had experienced a similar situation in the years after World War I. Yet, in these new times when the resistance newspapers berated the defunct regime and magnified revolutionary acts of faith, they might have hoped to obtain full rights of citizenship in their professional careers, voted by the Consultative Assembly on 23 March 1944. "It is true," wrote Célia Bertin bitterly, "they have granted us the right to vote but nothing else has changed."

Finally, the newly restored Republic showed hardly any gratitude toward those women who had distinguished themselves in the resistance. Out of 1,060 Compagnons de la Libération (people honored for their role in the resistance) only six were women. This proportion clearly has very little connection with the reality of women's participation in the struggle against Vichy and the occupying enemy. Common modes of thinking had little taste for honors and decorations for women, which explains this iniquity but cannot hide the basic martial sexism that prevailed in the awarding of decorations and, beyond that, in the national memory. But what was most important surely lay elsewhere for most women, as it did for certain men. Those who had fought for the country's liberation, like everyone else, were doubtless less preoccupied with the claim of "great deeds of arms" reeking of death than with the urgent need to live again, at last—even at the risk of forgetting. To live out what remained of their lives and their hope.

Bibliography

Sources

Aubrac, Lucie, *Ils partiront dans l'ivresse: Lyon, mai 1943, Londres, février 1944*, Paris: Seuil, 1984

Berberova, Nina, *The Italics Are Mine*, translated by Philippe Radley, New York: Harcourt Brace and World, and London: Longmans, 1969

Bertin, Célia, *Femmes sous l'Occupation*, Paris: Stock, 1993

Bohec, Jeanne, *La plastiqueuse à bicyclette*, Paris: Mercure de France, 1975

Bood, Micheline, *Les années doubles: Journal d'une lycéenne sous l'occupation*, edited by Jacques Labib, Paris: Laffont, 1974

Carré, Lily, *On m'appelait "la Chatte,"* Paris: Albin Michel, 1975

Colette, *Paris de ma fenêtre*, Geneva: Milieu du Monde, 1944

Colombel, Jeannette, *Les amants de l'ombre*, Paris: Flammarion, 1990

Fourcade, Marie-Madeleine, *L'arche de Noé*, Paris: Fayard, 1968

Kriegel, Annie, *Ce que j'ai cru comprendre*, Paris: Laffont, 1991

Marquet, Mary, *Cellule 209*, Paris: Fayard, 1949

Maurel, Micheline, *Un camp très ordinaire*, Paris: Éditions de Minuit, 1957

Thomas, Édith, *Pages de journal: 1939–1944*, edited by Dorothy Kaufman, Paris: Hamy, 1995

Thomas, Édith, *Le témoin compromis*, edited by Dorothy Kaufman, Paris: Hamy, 1995

Tillion, Germaine, et al., *Ravensbrück*, translated by Gerald Satterwhite, Garden City, New York: Anchor Press, 1975

Vallotton, Gritou, and Annie Vallotton, *C'était au jour le jour: Carnets, 1939–1944*, Paris: Payot, and Rivages, 1995

Windsor, Rachel, "J'e tais une volontair," Paris, Cahiers de l'office français d'édition, no. 54 (s.d.)

Reference Works

Adler, Karen H., "Reading National Identity: Gender and 'Prostitution' during the Occupation," *Modern and Contemporary France* 7, no.1 (February 1999); special issue entitled *Gendering the Occupation of France*, edited by Hanna Diamond and Claire Gorrara

Ariès, Philippe, and Georges Duby, editors, *Histoire de la vie privée*, 5 vols., Paris: Seuil, 1985–87; as *A History of Private Life*, 5 vols., Cambridge, Massachusetts: Harvard University Press, 1987–91; see especially vol. 5, *Riddles of Identity in Modern Times* Azéma, Jean-Pierre, *De Munich à la Libération: 1938–1944*, Paris: Seuil, 1979; as *From Munich to the Liberation, 1938–1944*, translated by Janet Lloyd, Cambridge and New York: Cambridge University Press, and Paris: Éditions de la Maison des Sciences de l'Homme, 1984

Azéma, Jean-Pierre, and Bédarida, François, editors, *Le régime de Vichy et les Français*, Paris: Fayard, 1992

Bolle, Pierre, editor, *Le plateau Vivarais-Lignon: Accueil et résistance 1939–1944: Actes du colloque du Chambon-sur-Lignon, 12–14 octobre 1990*, Le Chambon-sur-Lignon, France: Société d'Histoire de la Montagne, 1992

Bordeaux, Michèle, "Femmes hors d'État français (1940–1944)," in *Femmes et fascismes*, edited by Rita Thalmann, Paris: Tierce, 1986

Brive, Marie-France, "L'image des femmes à la Libération," in *La Libération dans le Midi de la France*, edited by Rolande Trempé, Toulouse, France: Eché, 1986

Brossat, Alain, *Les tondues: Un carnaval moche*, Levallois-Perret, France: Manya, 1992

Burch, Noël, and Geneviève Sellier, *La drôle de guerre des sexes du cinéma français, 1930–1956*, Paris: Nathan, 1996

Burrin, Philippe, *La France à l'heure allemande: 1940–1944*, Paris: Seuil, 1995; as *France under the Germans: Collaboration and Compromise*, translated by Janet Lloyd, New York: New Press, 1996; as *Living with Defeat: France under the German Occupation, 1940–1944*, translated by Janet Lloyd, London: Arnold, 1996

Capdevila, Luc, *Les Bretons au lendemain de l'Occupation: Imaginaires et comportements d'une sortie de guerre, 1944–1945*, Rennes, France: Presses Universitaires de Rennes, 1999

Chauvière, Michel, and Geneviève Dermenjian, *L'action familiale ouvrière et la politique de Vichy*, Cahiers du Groupement pour la recherche sur les mouvements familiaux (GRMF), no. 3 (1985)

Coudert, Marie-Louise, and Hélène Paul, *Elles: La résistance*, Paris: Messidor/Temps Actuels, 1983

Coutrot, Aline, "La politique familiale," in Rémond, René and Bourdin, Jeanine (eds), *Le gouvernement de Vichy, 1940–1942: Institutions et politiques*, Paris: Colin, 1972

Delvincourt, H, "Problèmes relatifs à l'emploi dans les P.T.T."; Durand P., "La politique de l'emploi à la S.N.C.F.," in Revue d'Histoire de la Deuxième guerre mondiale, janvier 1965, no. 57.

Dermenjian, Geneviève, *Femmes, famille et action ouvrière. Pratiques et responsabilités féminines dans les Mouvements familiaux populaires*, Cahiers du Groupement pour la recherche sur les mouvements familiaux (GRMF), no. 6 (1991)

Diamond, Hanna, *Women and the Second World War in France, 1939–1948: Choices and Constraints*, London: Longman, and New York and Harlow, Essex: Pearson Education, 1999

Douzou, Laurent, "Notes de prison de Bertrande d'Astier de La Vigerie (15 mars–4 avril 1941)," *Les Cahiers de l'Institut d'Histoire du Temps Présent*, no. 25 (October 1993)

Dupâquier, Jacques et al., editors, *Histoire de la population française*, vol. 4, Paris: Presses Universitaires de France, 1988

Eck, Hélène, "French Women under Vichy," in *A History of Women in the West*, edited by Georges Duby and Michelle Perrot, vol. 5, *Toward a Cultural Identity in the Twentieth Century*, edited by Françoise Thébaud, Cambridge, Massachusetts: Belknap Press of Harvard University Press, 1994

Femmes dans la Résistance, proceedings of a conference organized at the Sorbonne by the Union des Femmes Françaises, 22–23 November 1975, Paris: Rocher, 1977

Fishman, Sarah, *We Will Wait: Wives of French Prisoners of War, 1940–1945*, New Haven, Connecticut: Yale University Press, 1991

Fourcaut, Annie, *Femmes à l'usine en France dans l'entre-deux guerres*, Paris, Maspéro, 1982.

Francos, Ania, *Il était des femmes dans la Résistance*, Paris: Stock, 1978

Gervereau, Laurent, and Denis Peschanski, editors, *La propagande sous Vichy, 1940–1944*, Nanterre, France: Bibliothèque de Documentation Internationale Contemporaine, and Paris: Diffusion, and Découverte, 1990

Gilzmer, Mechtild, *Camps de femmes, chroniques d'internées, Rieucros et Brens, 1939–1944*, Paris: Éditions Autrement, 2000

Grynberg, Anne, *Les camps de la honte: Les internés juifs des camps français, 1939–1944*, Paris: La Découverte, 1991

Guidez, Guylaine, *Femmes dans la guerre, 1939–1945*, Paris: Perrin, 1989

Guillon, Jean-Marie, "La philosophie politique de la Révolution nationale," in Le régime de Vichy et les Français, edited by Jean-Pierre Azéma and François Bédarida, Paris: Fayard, 1992

Hamelin, France, *Femmes dans la nuit: L'internement à la Petite Roquette et au camp des Tourelles, 1939–1944*, Paris: Renaudot, 1988

Higonnet, Margaret R., et al., editors, *Behind the Lines: Gender and the Two World Wars*, New Haven, Connecticut: Yale University Press, 1987

Koos, Cheryl A., "On les aura! The Gendered Politics of Abortion and the Alliance Nationale Contre la Dépopulation, 1938–1944," *Modern and Contemporary France* 7, no. 1 (February 1999)

Laborie, Pierre, "Entre histoire et mémoire, un épisode de l'épuration en Ariège: Le tribunal du peuple de Pamiers, 18–31 août 1944," in *Pays pyrénéens et pouvoirs centraux: XVIᵉ–XXᵉ siècles*, vol. 2., edited by Michel Brunet, Serge Brunet, and Claudine Pailhès, Ariège, France: Association des Amis des Archives de l'Ariège, 1995

Laborie, Pierre, *L'opinion française sous Vichy*, Paris: Seuil, 1990; new edition, as *L'opinion française sous Vichy: Les français et la crise d'identité nationale, 1936–1944*, Paris: Seuil, 2001

Marrus, Michael R., and Robert O. Paxton, *Vichy France and the Jews*, New York, Basic Books, 1981

Miribel, Elisabeth de, *La liberté souffre violence*, Paris, Plon, 1981

Miller, Gérard, *Les pousse-au-jouir du maréchal Pétain*, Paris, Seuil, 1975

Muel-Dreyfus, Francine, *Vichy et l'éternel féminine: Contribution à une sociologie politique de l'ordre des corps*, Paris: Seuil, 1996; as *Vichy and the Eternal Feminine: A Contribution to a Political Sociology of Gender*, translated by Kathleen A. Johnson, Durham, North Carolina: Duke University Press, 2001

Paxton, Robert O., *Vichy France: Old Guard and New Order, 1940–1944*, London: Barrie and Jenkins, and New York: Knopf, 1972

Perrot, Michelle, "Sur le front des sexes: un combat douteux," *Vingtième siècle, revue d'histoire*, no. 3 (July 1984)

Peschanski, Denis, "Exclusion, persécution, répression," in *Le régime de Vichy et les Français*, edited by Jean-Pierre Azéma and François Bédarida, Paris: Fayard, 1992

Peschanski, Denis, "Vichy au singulier, Vichy au pluriel. Une tentative avortée d'encadrement de la société (1941–1942)," *Annales ESC* 43, no. 3 (1988)

Pollak, Michael, *L'expérience concentrationnaire: Essai sur le maintien de l'identité sociale*, Paris: Métailié, 1990

Pollard, Miranda, "La politique du travail féminin," *Le régime de Vichy et les Français*, edited by Jean-Pierre Azéma and François Bédarida, Paris: Fayard, 1992

Pollard, Miranda, "Women and the National Revolution," in *Vichy France and the Resistance: Culture and Ideology*, edited by Harry Roderick Kedward and Roger Austin, London: Croom Helm, and Totowa, New Jersey: Barnes and Noble, 1985

Poznanski, Renée, *Être juif en France pendant la Seconde Guerre Mondiale*, Paris: Hachette, 1994; new edition, as *Les juifs en France pendant la Seconde Guerre Mondiale*, 1997; as *Jews in France during World War II*, translated by Nathan Bracher, Hanover, New Hampshire: University Press of New England, and Waltham, Massachusetts: Brandeis University Press, 2001

Poznanski, Renée, "Shield-Bearers of the Resistance? Women in the French-Jewish Underground," in *Women in the Holocaust*, edited by Dalia Ofer and Lenore J. Weitzman, New Haven, Connecticut: Yale University Press, 1998

Prost, Antoine, "L'évolution de la politique familiale en France de 1938 à 1981," *Le mouvement social*, no. 129 (October–December 1984)

Rémond, René, and Jeanine Bourdin, editors, *Le gouvernement de Vichy, 1940–1942: Institutions et politiques*, Paris: Colin, 1972

Rioux, Jean-Pierre, "Le clair-obscur du quotidien," in *Le régime de Vichy et les Français*, edited by Jean-Pierre Azéma and François Bédarida, Paris: Fayard, 1992

Rossiter, Margaret L., *Women in the Resistance*, New York: Praeger, 1986

Rouquet, François, *L'épuration dans l'administration française, agents de l'État et collaboration ordinaire*, Paris: Centre National de Recherche Scientifique, 1993

Rouquet, François, "Épuration, résistance et représentations: Quelques éléments pour une analyse sexuée," in *La Résistance et les Français: Enjeux stratégiques et environnement social*, edited by Jacqueline Sainclivier and Christian Bougeard, Rennes, France: Presses Universitaires de Rennes, 1995

Rouquet, François and Danièle Voldman, editors, "Identités féminines et violences politiques, 1936–1946," *Les cahiers de l'Institut d'Histoire du Temps Présent*, no. 31 (October 1995)

Sauvy, Alfred, "La population française pendant la Seconde guerre mondiale," in Dupâquier, Jacques et al. (eds), Histoire de la population française, vol. 4, Paris: Presses Universitaires de France, 1988

Schwartz, Paula, "Partisans and Gender Politics in Vichy France," *French Historical Studies* 16, no. 1 (Spring 1989)

Schwartz, Paula, "The Politics of Food and Gender in Occupied Paris," *Modern and Contemporary France* 7, no. 1 (February 1999)

Sohn, Anne-Marie, *Du premier baiser à l'alcôve: La sexualité des Français au quotidien (1850–1950)*, Paris: Aubier, 1996

Szpiner, Francis, *Une affaire de femmes: Paris, 1943: Exécution d'une avorteuse*, Paris: Balland, 1986

Tartakowsky, Danielle, *Les manifestations de rue en France, 1918–1968*, Paris: Publications de la Sorbonne, 1997

Thalmann, Rita, editor, *Entre émancipation et nationalisme: La presse féminine d'Europe, 1914–1945*, Paris: Tierce, 1990

Thébaud, Françoise, "Femmes dans la Deuxième Guerre Mondiale," in *L'année 43: Guerre totale*, Caen, France: Lys, 1994

Thébaud, Françoise, editor, "Résistances et libérations: France, 1940–1945," *Clio: Histoire, Femmes et Sociétés* 1 (October 1995)

Veillon, Dominique, "Elles étaient dans la Résistance," *Bulletin de l'agence femmes information*, no. 59 (30 May–5 June 1983)

Veillon, Dominique, *La mode sous l'Occupation: Débrouillardise et coquetterie dans la France en guerre, 1939–1945*, Paris: Payot, 1990

Veillon, Dominique, "Résister au féminin," *Pénélope*, no. 12 (Spring 1985)

Veillon, Dominique, "La vie quotidienne des femmes," in *Le régime de Vichy et les Français*, edited by Jean-Pierre Azéma and François Bédarida, Paris: Fayard, 1992

Veillon, Dominique, *Vivre et survivre en France (1939–1947)*, Paris: Payot, and Rivages, 1995

Virgili, Fabrice, *La France virile: Des femmes tondues à la Libération*, Paris: Payot, 2000

Virgili, Fabrice, "Tontes et tondues à travers la presse de la Libération," DEA thesis, Université de Paris I, 1992

Weitz, Margaret Collins, *Sisters in the Resistance: How Women Fought to Free France, 1940–1945*, New York and Chichester, West Sussex: Wiley, 1995

Yagil, Limore, "La politique familiale de Vichy et la conception de la 'femme nouvelle,'" *Guerres mondiales et conflits contemporains, Revue d'histoire* 47, no. 188 (December 1997)

WOMEN AND SALAZARISM

ANNE COVA AND ANTÓNIO COSTA PINTO

I F THE SOUTHERN EUROPEAN dictatorships of the interwar period had anything in common, it was their attitudes toward women. Although these regimes were initiated during a period characterized by democratization, the emergence of feminist movements, and significant increases in women on the labor market, they all emphasized that women's place was in the home, glorifying motherhood and the primordial role of the family. At the same time, these dictatorships faced the "problem" integrating women into politics. Some would elevate this objective to a nationalist goal and an important means of mobilizing their regimes. This article addresses Salazarism's attitudes toward women and their organizations, providing some basis for comparison with the other dictatorships (for example, that of Benito Mussolini in Italy), by which, to some extent, some institutions of the Portuguese Estado Novo (New State) were inspired.

The Family: Cornerstone of Society

The Portuguese Constitution of 1933 laid down equality for all citizens before the law and denied all privileges accruing from birth, nobility, sex, or social status. However, it also pointed out "women's differences resulting from their nature and their duty toward the good of the family" (Article 5). By comparison with the First Republic of 1910, the peculiarity of Salazarism is that it introduced this important nuance into the principle of equality between the sexes. The Constitution of 1911, and the laws governing the family, drawn up on 25 December 1910, contained no such provisions.

Salazarism thus invoked female "nature" to deny women complete equality with men. The idea of "nature" went back to the old discussion of culture versus nature, in which the public sphere dominates the private sphere. Salazarism was deeply rooted in the traditional idea that women were situated on the side of "nature" and men on the side of culture. Salazar's New State thus remained faithful to the messages reiterated by the Catholic Church in the encyclicals *Rerum novarum* (1891) and *Quadragesimo anno* (1931), according to which "nature" destined females to stay at home, bearing babies and devoting themselves to housework. Based on the assumption that men and women do not possess the same physical strength, *Rerum Novarum* stated, "There are tasks less suited to women, whose destiny, by nature, is to work at home." *Quadragesimo anno* carried a similar message: "The duty of mothers lies above all in the home and in housework." According to the laws of "nature," women were conceived to be mothers. Salazarism added that the female was the pillar of the household.

A publication of the Secretariat for National Propaganda, *Economia doméstica* (Domestic Economy), written in 1945, compared the art of running a home to that of running the state—a comparison that illustrates the tenuous character of the boundaries between public and private. In fact, under this logic women could potentially penetrate the public sphere by saying that they were very good at taking care of their families and were therefore fit to hold public office, since the state was nothing more than a conglomerate of families. The New State, however, preferred to maintain the established ideology concerning the "natural difference" between the sexes, which paid an implicit tribute to the differences between, and the complementary nature of, the roles of men and women. The notion of the complementarity of masculine and feminine functions was consistent with the principles of the encyclical *Casti connubii* (1930), which stated that women had a different temperament and posited that within the family, the "husband is the head and the wife is the heart." The New State was equally interested in seeing the complementary roles of spouses as a guarantee of the stability of the family, which always had priority over individual rights. If the mother was glorified, it was because of her important role within the family. Her mission was to take care of the home and be its guardian. Her beneficial influence was not limited to just her children; it concerned the whole house. She was meant to ensure her husband's peace of mind and harmony within the household. The slogan "Women's place is in the home" was particularly resonant during the economic crisis of the 1930s. In many European countries, women who worked outside the home became a particular concern because they were taking the place of male workers. The "solution" offered was that women should stay at home. In Portugal, however, the situation was different: the country had a very low unemployment rate, and the insistence that women should stay home had no direct link to the crisis of the 1930s.

This vision of the mother's predominant importance in the family was a distortion, since by law and in reality, the father had the power. The Constitution of 1933 declared that the husband was head of the family and that it was he who should wield the authority while his wife played her role as mother, devoting herself to the home. As father and head of the family, a man's task was to guide the upbringing and education of his children, to look after them, and to defend and represent them, even before they were born. For Salazarism, the most important thing of all was the family, which it was the state's duty to defend. The family was "the source of the preservation and development of the race" and "the foundation of all political order"; it ensured that society would function properly and be "regenerated."

Rerum novarum posited the primacy and priority of the family over civil society. However, only the legitimate family was sanctioned: "the constitution of the family is based on marriage and legitimate children." Marriage, which was the origin and foundation of the family, assumed a transcendent significance, and its purpose was procreation. The emphasis on the legitimate family is not peculiar to Salazarism and should be situated in the context of the high rate of illegitimate births in Portugal. At the beginning of the 20th century this rate stood at about 12 percent, and the phenomenon continued thereafter, as witnessed by the fact that, by the end of the 1950s, Portugal had the third highest rate of illegitimate births in Europe.

The declining overall birthrate was another phenomenon that characterized the Portuguese New State, although the birthrate in Portugal remained higher than in other European countries, even those of southern Europe. Nevertheless, Salazarism also participated in the recurring populationist debate, closely related to the idea of the "mystique of the nation," that was especially visible in countries such as Germany and Italy. Demographic obsession was not the monopoly of fascist regimes, however. France, for example, shared the same concern.

In Portugal's 1910 laws on the family, marriage was considered a contract between two persons of different sexes in order to establish a legitimate family. Salazarism undercut the gains for women's rights in marriage that had been made during the First Republic. For example, under the earlier regime, a woman could not be forced to return to her conjugal home. This clause was abolished by the Civil Code of 1939. In accordance with legislation drawn up on 3 November 1910, the civil contract of marriage could be dissolved. The law authorized divorce, and, in the areas of grounds for divorce and rights regarding children, gave the same privileges to men and women. A real subversion of tradition, this divorce law remained in force for 30 more years and was only abolished by Salazarism in 1940. After that date, people who had been married by the Catholic Church were not allowed to divorce. (Prior to the 1940s, divorce was an essentially urban phenomenon. In 1930, 51 percent of all divorced people were city dwellers; most of them [40.7 percent] lived in Lisbon and Oporto. Still, there were some differences: in Lisbon the majority of those suing for divorce were female, while in Oporto the opposite was the case.)

With a law on the defense of the family, enacted on 12 October 1935, the New State sought to ensure the "constitution and the defense of the family in its function as the source of preservation and development of the race." In order to protect and preserve the family, the New State set various priorities,

although not all of them were respected. For example, rhetoric valorizing the protection of motherhood was undermined by a 10 March 1937 law cutting maternity leave to one month (half the previous length) and granting employers discretion to refuse to pay a subsidy to a mother on leave if "the employee was not worthy of such a subsidy or did not need it."

Similarly, the New State's express desire to promote the adoption of a family wage—a demand which was dear to European social Catholics and which would contribute to the rehabilitation of the family—was not realized. Other goals of Salazarism also remained unachieved. The government saw fit, however, to promote propaganda efforts such as "Family Mothers' Day," and founded a national organization called Defense of the Family, whose president, António de Sousa Gomes, was from the Catholic movement. Official speeches constantly proclaimed he importance of moral conduct and the promotion of moral virtues: morality was posited as the basis of the family, and it fell to state to promote the moral unity of the nation.

Strongly inspired by social Catholicism, the New State followed the various papal encyclicals and reinforced ties with the Church through the Concordat of 1940. Salazarist ideology mandated various roles for women within the family: wife and mother, household manager, and upholder of the family's morals. This glorification of women's mission in the domestic sphere, however, was a far cry from the real life of women, who were beginning to work outside the home. In 1926, according to official statistics, female participation in the labor force was 17 percent. In 1950 this percentage had reached 22.7 percent. In 1926 Italy had a similar percentage, 23 percent, while France had already reached 36 percent (the same as Germany in 1933).

Throughout the New State, a very significant portion of the active population, including women, was employed in the primary sector. It was only after the 1960s that there was a real explosion of female labor in the tertiary sector. During the 1960s the percentage of female workers in this sector was already estimated at 33.9 percent, while 26.2 percent were employed in industry. At the end of the Salazar era the majority of women working outside the home were not married: 53.7 percent were single, 9 percent divorced or separated, and fewer than 1 percent widowed; only 36.3 percent were married. Considerable numbers of women were employed as unskilled laborers: more than half of employed single women performed unskilled or manual labor.

The majority of women lived in the countryside, as did over half of the working population: in 1930, 55 percent of the active population was working in agriculture; in 1940, 52 percent; and in 1950, 51 percent. After the 1950s Portugal experienced a significant drop in the proportion of all labor made up of agricultural workers owing to the heavy emigration of rural laborers. This affected the female workforce as well: in 1950 women represented 20.6 percent of the active population in agriculture; ten years later only 9.1 percent were women. This marked decrease resulted in part from the practice of taking into consideration only paid women workers when compiling statistics, which left out the many housewives who worked in the fields without pay. From the 1960s on there was a pronounced increase in female employment, mainly because of male emigration, which peaked during this period, and because of the colonial wars at the time. A marked feminization then followed in agriculture: in 1970, 24.2 percent of the agricultural workforce was female. These cyclical increases in female employment in Portugal did not necessarily coincide with those in other European countries. Notably, unlike other European countries, World War II did not prompt an increase in female labor in Portugal, because the country was neutral.

High rates of illiteracy prevailed throughout the regime of the New State. In 1930, 61.8 percent of the population aged seven and above was illiterate. Thirty years later this percentage had been reduced by half, but it continued to be fairly high: in 1960 the percentage was still 31.1 percent. Women were especially likely to be illiterate: in 1930, 69.9 percent of women were illiterate, whereas the rate for men was 52.8 percent. In 1960 these percentages were, respectively, 36.7 percent and 24.9 percent. The differential between men and women thus decreased, although it was still significant, and Portugal continued to have one of Europe's highest illiteracy rates in that period.

These consistently high rates of illiteracy must be seen in relation to low rates of urbanization compared to other European countries, reflecting Salazar's fierce hostility to urbanization and industrialization. Throughout his regime, Portuguese society had a low rate of urbanization and was strongly dualistic, with important differences between the rural majority and the urban-based social, economic, and political elites. Industrialization and economic development were limited, and this lag had a different effect in the south, which was poor and suffering from desertification, than in the north, which was richer and more densely populated as a result of emigration. Significant disparities existed between women who lived in the countryside and the urban elite, from which the militants for various women and feminist organizations were recruited.

Despite the rhetoric proclaiming that "women's place is in the home," women continued to enter the labor market during the New State. Although a law was passed in 1966 to address the inequality between men's and women's salaries, women's salaries were lower than men's in all sectors. During the 1960s, because of the emigration of the male labor force and the number of men fighting in the colonial wars, the feminization of certain branches of industry (such as the textile industry) grew rapidly. On the other hand, strong social stratification and a shrinking of the elite classes resulted in an element of reduced educational and professional discrimination against women of the upper middle class.

Compared to Salazarism, the First Republic represented a period of freedom and legislative innovation for women, especially with the new family legislation, namely the divorce law. In the political arena, however, the Republic excluded women from the formal political system, whereas Salazarism opened some doors, although still in a very limited way.

The New State and Women's Movements

Predating Salazarism, the first Portuguese feminist organizations were created at the beginning of the 20th century under the influence of the Freemasons and the republican and socialist movement. This was the case for the Grupo Português de Estudos Feministas (Portuguese Group for Feminist Studies) in 1907, and of the Liga Republicana das Mulheres Portuguesas (LRMP; League of Republican Portuguese Women) in 1909. With the proclamation of the Republic in 1910, relations between the republicans and the latter organization became complicated because of the republicans' denial of women's right to vote, whereas innovative legislation about the family gave women some new rights. Between 1910 and 1920 these organizations went their own way, although the republican and Masonic matrix still dominated. In 1914 Adelaide Cabete, a gynecologist and militant in the cause of women's rights, spurred on by the liberal Republic, founded the Conselho Nacional das Mulheres Portuguesas (CNMP; National Council of Portuguese Women). Cabete had already participated, with Ana Castro Osório and Fausta Pinto de Gama, in the creation of the LRMP in 1909. This movement had connections with the Republican Party and helped to bring down the constitutional monarchy. The league's first leaders, including Castro Osório and Cabete, were members of various women's Masonic lodges. Adelaide Cabete, for example, headed the Human Rights Lodge. These women belonged to the upper-middle classes and were active within the republican movement.

According to the statutes of the League of Republican Portuguese Women, its objectives were to "guide, educate, and instruct the Portuguese woman along democratic principles." The league had between 400 and 800 members during its ten-year existence, until it was dissolved in 1919. Although it had rural sections, the overwhelming majority of its followers lived in Lisbon. From the social and professional point of view, teachers were its most significant constituency of members. During the first years of the Republic, the LMRP supported the new republican power, particularly with respect to new legislation affecting the family, and the league took a stand in favor of the divorce law. However, disagreements arose within the LMRP regarding women's participation in politics. Some leaders wanted their list of demands to emphasize women's right to vote, whereas others were more inclined toward social and economic rights. These dissensions caused Castro Osório to leave the league. Without waiting for women to obtain suffrage, Carolina Beatriz Angelo, a female doctor, a militant advocate of woman's suffrage, and the founder of the Associação de Propaganda Feminista (Association of Feminist Propaganda), exercised the right to vote on 28 May 1911, claiming to be the "head of the family" since she was a mother and widow. The republicans, however, soon remedied this "loophole" with a law passed on 3 July 1913 that gave the right to vote only to male citizens who could read and write.

The National Council of Portuguese Women (CNMP) formed the Portuguese section of the International Council of Women (ICW), which was founded in Washington, D.C., in 1888. The Portuguese council established special ties with its French partner, the Conseil National des Femmes Françaises (CNFF; National Council of French Women), created in 1901, through Ghénia Avril de Sainte-Croix, secretary general of the CNFF and vice president of the ICW. The statutes of the CNMP, approved in April 1914, described this organization as "a women's institution not following any philosophical, political, or religious school or faction." It aimed to form a federation of women's (not only feminist) associations that "deal with women and children" and to "coordinate, direct and stimulate all efforts toward dignifying and emancipating women." Additional objectives were to "advocate everything concerning the improvement of women's material and moral condition, especially those of the female worker" and to secure equal pay for equal work. Like similar movements, the CNMP tried not to use the word "feminism," proclaimed itself to be apolitical, and tried to incorporate various philanthropic movements into its activities. This organization also represented the International Alliance for Female Suffrage.

The military dictatorship, established in 1926, did not ban the activity of women's movements and even—albeit only slightly—opened the political sphere to a small elite of women. The New State did nothing to change this. However, this modest opening took place in an atmosphere hostile toward the women's social and civil rights that had been granted during the First Republic.

With regard to political citizenship, Portuguese women were given some slim rights by laws passed under the dictatorship. On 5 May 1931, when the government wanted to organize municipal elections (which in fact were not held), women age 21 and over with a secondary school or university diploma received the right to vote. Here the new regime followed the lead of other dictatorships such as Primo de Rivera's in Spain and gave women who were the heads of their families a limited right to vote.

Only a very restricted group of Portuguese women were granted suffrage: widows, divorced women, married women with husbands abroad, and women with a secondary or university education. In 1934, when the first legislative elections of the New State were held, women whose names were on the electoral rolls exercised their right to vote. In 1946 a new law extended this right to married women who were either literate or, if illiterate, liable for taxes. Only in 1968, after Marcello Caetano replaced Salazar, were all women given the right to vote. A memorandum of the Corporatist Council stressed the advantages of this change, stating that "women were more conservative than men." Nevertheless, the right to vote still did not apply to municipal elections, in which only family heads had the right to vote. Moreover, these political rights were granted only after 1945, under a single-party regime that allowed only a controlled opposition to emerge, using rigged elections and with restricted suffrage.

The União Nacional (UN; National Union) was a party of notables that benefited from a well-entrenched organization in the provinces and close ties to the local administration, and which was dependent on the state. The number of women in the National Union remained very low during the regime of the New State: on average, they formed 3.7 percent of the total membership (from the foundation of the National Union until the end of the New State 44 years later). After Salazar's removal from power in 1968, his successor broadened women's suffrage and promoted their admission into the single party, which was now called the Acção Nacional Popular (National Popular Action). It was on 11 January 1935, in Salazarism's first National Assembly, that three female deputies set foot in the Portuguese Parliament building for the first time. Women deputies were never very numerous throughout the New State, but the arrival of the first three was welcomed by the press that was connected to what remained of the feminism of the 1920s. As he prepared to choose the first deputies of his regime, Salazar regarded women's presence in government as a novelty, declaring in his remarks to a Lisbon daily: "In both the upper and lower houses there will be some women—which does not mean that the state or the women have converted to feminism."

The first three deputies, although they were unmarried and conservative, practicing Catholics, did not come from the single party or from the small fascist movements. They certainly did not come from the moderate feminist movement of the liberal Republic. Maria Baptista dos Santos Guardiola, the 40-year-old principal of a girls' secondary school in Lisbon, played a central role in the creation of women's organizations during Salazarism. Domitila Hormizinda de Carvalho, age 64, was a doctor and teacher and had headed the first girls' secondary school in Lisbon. Maria Candida de Bragança Parreira was a teacher and lawyer. Their speeches in the National Assembly were mainly about education; in particular, they proposed the introduction of courses on general hygiene and childcare in secondary schools and the reform of the school system, guided "by the principles of Christian doctrine and morals, traditional to the country." Guardiola, who had a long career in the service of the New State, defended the introduction of a single history and philosophy text book. Of the three, it was she who had the most political influence.

Women's Organizations under Salazar's Regime

During Salazar's regime, official women's organizations were created within the framework of the nationalist and Catholic reform of the educational system. The New State had an ideological obsession with education, but this did not mean that it wanted to modernize education. It was only in the 1950s that there was an incipient attempt to achieve educational reform. The debate about the advantages of illiteracy in 1938 became famous; in 1933 Salazar himself had declared that it was "more urgent to form the vast elites than to teach the common people how to read." The priority was to reorganize what had been the liberal republicans' pride: the secular state schools, and especially primary education.

Ideological control of teachers, single school books, the arrangement and decoration of classrooms, all reflected the "ideal type" of Salazarism's ideology: "God, Homeland, Family, Work," which also inspired the French Vichy regime, particularly its Maurrassian component.

More than any combative, imperialistic mystique, it was the values of resignation, obedience, and, above all, a conflict-free "organic society," on the one hand, and politics reserved, as it was, for a paternalistic elite led by Salazar, on the other, that characterized the new primary education. Christianization was another official obsession, expressed everywhere from syllabi to the decoration of the classrooms and school rituals. It was in this framework of educational reform, particularly in an area of growing feminization of certain sectors of the workforce (in 1940, women comprised 76 percent of primary school teachers and 33 percent of secondary school teachers, illustrating that women's numbers decreased at higher levels in the hierarchy), that sex segregation was introduced in the secondary schools and the Ministry of Education founded its official women's and youth organization.

On 15 August 1936, under the Ministry of Education, the New State created Obra das Mães para a Educação Nacional

(OMEN; Mothers' Service for National Education); in 1937, the entity Mocidade Portuguesa Feminina (MPF; Portuguese Female Youth) was organized. Most of the leaders of OMEN were the same as those in the official organization for young women. Maria Guardiola, national commissioner of the latter, led the MPF for 30 years, until 1968.

OMEN was mainly modeled after the least politicized organization founded by Italian Fascism, Opera Nazionale per la Protezione della Maternità e dell'Infanzia (ONMI; National Service for the Protection of Mothers and Children), which had been founded in 1926 and placed under the Ministry of the Interior. The law that created the Italian organization stressed the protection of motherhood and childhood through the introduction of scientific hygiene and was part of the pronatalist policy of Mussolini's Fascist regime. To coordinate a number of agencies that aided Italian mothers, ONMI celebrated the Day of the Mother and the Child but possessed a much larger assistance network than its Portuguese counterpart and was not even initially run by women. Of all the organizations in Fascist Italy dedicated to the family, ONMI was the least political and was not a mass organization. Its Portuguese counterpart never grew to be very large and had few pretensions to political mobilization.

Dependent on the Ministry of Education, OMEN included a small group of women devoted to Salazar and his regime. Its patrons and leaders were mainly Catholic figures from Lisbon's social elite or aristocracy. The law that created OMEN described it as an association that would "stimulate the educational influence of the family and ensure cooperation between family and school." Its regulations defined the organization's goals: "to guide Portuguese mothers in the raising of their children," instilling in them the principles of hygiene and childcare, to stimulate "a family upbringing"; to promote "the beautification of rural life and the comforts of home as an educational environment"; to organize the girls' section of the Portuguese youth movement, and to promote "the nationalist education of youth."

A few years after the creation of the Portuguese Female Youth (MPF), OMEN, which had initially been linked to the area of education, turned to granting "awards" to large families and support for mothers; it was not very active in its new mission, however. Focusing mainly on rural areas, OMEN cultivated the image of the happy, Catholic, domestic countrywoman. Its goal was not far from the ideal image of corporatist society conveyed by the school system in the 1930s. Nevertheless, OMEN was never very close to rural society, nor did it grow far beyond its small core of leaders. Delegations were created in the big cities, but their activity was predominantly ideological, providing courses in communities and *casas do povo* (public community centers).

After the creation of the MPF, which was one of OMEN's goals, OMEN still officially remained an autonomous organization, but it never really grew. In addition to supervising MPF, it maintained functions such as the annual organization of Mothers' Week and others with the participation of the official youth movement. District delegations organized information sessions and gave awards to large families, defined as those having more than five children born to parents married by the Church. The awards were mainly given by the provincial clergy, who eliminated those candidates who did not live according to Catholic morals. OMEN survived until the 1970s. When Marcello Caetano came to power, the organization went from lethargy to

paralysis and was abolished soon after the regime was overthrown in 1974.

Without organic links to its male counterpart, MPF was supposed to include all Portugal's female youth, but in fact it only interacted with school-age girls, for whom membership was compulsory up to the age of 14 and voluntary after that. Its founding leaders came from OMEN and the Catholic influence was strong: education in "love for God, homeland, and family" was the first motto of MPF's statutes, and its aim was to train "Christian Portuguese women." As its top leader declared in 1941, moral education was most important, as it prepared girls for "the elevation of home life, love for the family, and the acceptance of the duties it imposes." Only after such priorities came attention to physical attention, but MPF regulations banned "all sports that are harmful to females' natural mission" or "offend womanly modesty."

No matter what typology one adopts for the analysis of fascist youth organizations, MPF will always be the most similar to those in which the presence of Catholicism and the traditionalist family mystique was strong, such as, for example, its counterparts in Franco's Spain. Nationalistic education, visibly more important in the male sector, was almost totally replaced in MPF efforts by the cult of the Portuguese medieval queens, such as D. Leonot, founder of charitable organizations, and by the worship of the Virgin Mary. Home economics—principles of hygiene and nursing and "the science of mothers, the most useful of all sciences for the family and the homeland"—was fundamental to the training offered by MPF. For those members who were interested in political activity under Salazar or in contacts with the male organization, the propaganda pamphlets did not leave any doubts that, although born of "the same great patriotic thought," the boys' youth movement "uses its political and social education to prepare active collaborators for our statesmen," while the girls' movement "prepares them for work at home, within the family, which their love, work and Christian spirit will turn into the solid basis of the New State."

Although its most important activity was limited to high schools, which, in 1940, were attended by 14,600 girls (as compared to 21,800 boys), the hypothesis that MPF was mainly intended to control girls from the urban middle classes, on the grounds that they were more susceptible to dissident influence, seems credible. However, with the important growth in the number of secondary school pupils, especially girls, from the 1950s, MPF was probably paradoxically much more progressive [as the Catholic youth often were] than the rest of a backward-looking society. At least until the 1960s, most girls attending secondary school went to private schools, where the Church played a central role. Some of the women who stood out on the Corporatist Council or at the universities in the final years of the New State had held positions in MPF but maintained a parallel Catholic militancy. Maria de Lourdes Pintasilgo, for example, the first woman to hold the office of prime minister in democratic Portugal, was one of these.

The Movimento Nacional Feminino (MNF; National Women's Movement) was the last women's organization created under Salazar. Launched in 1961, its objective was to support Portuguese soldiers fighting in the colonial war, which was then starting in Angola and would quickly spread to Mozambique and Guinea-Bissau. The movement was founded by Cecília Supico Pinto, the wife of one of Salazar's ministers. Its initial manifesto, signed by 25 women, described MNF as an association created to unite all Portuguese women interested in giving "moral and material support to those who are fighting for the integrity of our homeland's heritage."

This organization, sponsored by the Ministry of the Interior and Overseas and by businessmen with interests in the colonies, represented an attempt at politically mobilizing women for the regime's last battle on the African front. Some of its promoters worked with Catholic charities, and its initial network was based on that of the Order of St. Vincent. The movement organized sessions in mainland Portugal to show solidarity and raise funds, arranged visits to the African fronts (especially at Christmas), and organized the "war godmothers." In the 1960s the regime's media, especially television, gave substantial coverage to the organization's activities. Shortly after the fall of the dictatorship, Portugal's military involvement in its former colonies ended and MNF was abolished.

Female Catholic Organizations

Although the "Catholicization" of institutions was a founding element of Salazarism, the Church feared the possible totalitarian tendencies of some state organizations, especially those that were partially inspired by Fascism, and the possible "forced integration" of Church youth organizations into official state ones. This fear, however, never became a reality. On the contrary, from the beginning of the 1930s, the regime "gave" the Church a role in shaping the symbolic and ideological framework of large sectors of society, in particular those closest to traditional rural society, and provided the Church with social space for its own organizations. When Salazar institutionalized the New State and its Catholic Center Party was abolished so that it could be integrated into the single party, he gave the Church the task of "rechristianizing" the country after decades of republican and liberal secularization.

The organization Acção Católica Portuguesa (ACP; Portuguese Catholic Action) was created by the episcopate in 1933 and would long remain the Church's guarantee of collaboration with Salazarism and its institutions, mainly the corporatist ones, from a position of relative autonomy. Depending strictly on their hierarchy and with links to some government organizations, such Catholic institutions formed a powerful instrument of conservative socialization, with sporadic dissident elements mainly after 1945. The very strong presence of the clergy within the effective management of the movement's nucleus helped prevent tensions with the regime on the part of more "social" sectors, though some did arise.

As regards women's organizations, ACP inherited old experiences from the period of the liberal Republic, but its organizational structure, dating from 1934, grew remarkably until the end of the 1950s. The Liga de Acção Católica Feminina (LACF; Women's Catholic Action League), subdivided into socioprofessional sectors, organized married women older than 25 or holding university degrees. The Juventude Católica Feminina (JFC; Female Catholic Youth Organization) was also divided into specific organizations for university and high school students, and rural and industrial workers. Besides these, there were also other Catholic organizations such as the União Noelista (Noelist Union), which considerably developed its activities in teaching

catechism and providing social assistance in the 1940s and 1950s.

The number of women in Portuguese Catholic Action was very high throughout the long Salazarist period. In 1960, women accounted for 76 percent of the total 95,000 members in ACP organizations. The high number of women members was particularly evident within the youth sector of the organization, which always had more female than male members, with female youths representing 77.5 percent of the total.

The female Catholic movement was most strongly represented in the provinces in the north and center of Portugal, the most religious areas of the country. In the south, in regions such as the Alentejo with its latifundia, membership was minimal. The autonomous Catholic apparatus probably possessed recruitment and organizational networks that were more effective than the official ones, especially when it came to young people, because other girls' movements, such as the Catholic Girl Scouts, had always coexisted with the official organizations and were particularly strong in private schools.

No research has yet been carried out into the activities of female Catholic organizations. In the ideological and educational realm, the JFC press, at least until 1945, did not show any major differences from the official state organization, although former insisted more on Christian morality than the latter. In any event, it is worth noting that some female Catholic leaders were also the leaders of the official state organizations, OMEN and MPF, which shared not only the same doctrine, but some of the same leaders as well.

This complementary relationship between state and Church activities was mainly evident between the 1930s and 1950s, and was not merely a coincidence. The area of "family and assistance" was a prime example: OMEN, MPF, ACP, and other organizations inspired either by the state or the Church, such as the Social Service Institute, embodied an ideological commitment found less in other dictatorships, particularly in Fascist Italy or Nazi Germany. It was only from the 1950s, and always in minor deviations from the hierarchy, that tensions sometimes arose, mainly in the university sector.

The Survival of Reformist Feminism

Although its activity was severely limited—practically reduced to the publication of its bulletin—the National Council of Portuguese Women (CNMP) was not outlawed by the New State when the regime created its own official women's organization. The CNMP survived until after World War II and was abolished only on 28 June 1947. In addition to the CNMP, the regime allowed the creation of another organization, the Associação Feminina Portuguesa para a Paz (AFPP; Portuguese Women's Association for Peace), founded in 1936 and dissolved in 1952.

During the 1930s the CNMP operated inconspicuously, publishing its magazine, maintaining a small network of members (two hundred in 1933, corresponding to the number of subscribers to *Alma feminina*, the organization's magazine), and managed to participate in the last international women's congress before the outbreak of World War II. Adelaide Cabete left in 1930 and was replaced by young professionals, including writers and journalists such as Maria Lamas and Elina Guimarães.

The strategy of the CNMP during the first years of the military dictatorship and the New State consisted of petitions and protests addressed to the government and the National Assembly. Some of these protests were against the abolition of coeducation in primary schools or restriction of the right to vote; others targeted the notion of sexual differences based in "nature" inherent in the 1933 Constitution's definition of rights. With little room to maneuver, the CNMP did not antagonize the official women's organizations and described the entry of the first Salazarist women deputies into Parliament as "a notable step in the march of women's demands." The council also supported some proposals made by these deputies in the National Assembly, such as the proposal by Maria Luisa Van Zeller, leader of MPF, prohibiting child prostitution.

At the end of the 1930s, the activity of the CNMP had nearly been reduced to the irregular publication of its bulletin. But in 1944 the council significantly revived and broadened its organization. Maria Lamas was elected president in 1945, and a group of young anti-Salazarist university students joined the association. International contacts were taken up again and socioprofessional nuclei were created in order to expand the association's membership base into different social milieus. The 200 associates of the 1930s grew to 2,000 in 1944, with delegations opened in various districts of the provinces. After an international exhibition of books written by women organized by the National Society of Fine Arts in January 1947, the dictatorship abolished this organization. The Catholic and government press denounced the organization's dissident character in a wave of articles, even saying it was "a disguised instrument of communist propaganda." Maria Lamas and other members had meanwhile enrolled in the youth section of the Movimento de Unidade Democratica (MUD; Democratic Unity Movement), an antidictatorship electoral front.

The Portuguese Women's Association for Peace was born in a time of radicalization within the regime, exemplified by the Popular Front's victory in Spain. It seems strange that this association, which was created by a group of women who did not support Salazarism, was authorized, although it had a moderate program of activities. According to some sources, it never had more than 300 members. Its objective was women's dignity and their participation in the struggle for peace. The association organized courses in reading, writing, and needlework. During World War II it coordinated the shipment of food to refugees. Some members of the movement, such as Maria Lamas, were also in the CNMP, but the decisive influence of militant Communists was increasingly visible, mainly during the organization's final phase between 1945 and 1952. It was the association's close relations with the peace movement during the first years of the cold war that served as a pretext for the government to close down the organization. But the real reason for the dissolution of both organizations was the new political situation after the war, characterized by the defeat of fascism in Europe and by the emergence of stronger legal and illegal efforts to oppose the New State. In 1945, to a great extent deluded by the new international situation, part of the opposition believed that the fall of the regime was imminent. Salazar announced that there would be elections "as free as in free Britain." Some women from the National Council of Portuguese Women and the Portuguese Women's Association for Peace appeared in public to support candidates from the democratic opposition and would later suffer from repression because of it. Lamas participated in the democratic opposition and was arrested several times.

The structure of the underground opposition to Salazar changed markedly after the 1930s. The old anarcho-syndicalism, dominant in the period of the liberal First Republic, disappeared as a political and unionist power. The republican movement, after the defeat of the military conspiracies at the end of the 1920s, fell into a state of lethargy, and the small Partido Comunista Português (PCP; Portuguese Communist Party) progressively became the main force of underground resistance. In the 1940s the PCP was already the main organized force of resistance and had substantial student and intellectual sectors. Various young women, working together with the two women's organizations, supported the party. One notable young woman was Alda Nogueira, who was a member of the Central Committee.

Although small at first, the number of female political prisoners grew. These women were associated with the PCP and demonstrations, strikes, and protests, where the party already had considerable influence. Between 1932 and 1945 more than 400 women were imprisoned for political reasons. But their number only started to be significant after 1935, growing from 14 between 1932 and 1935 to 204 between 1935 and 1939.

Although the "woman question" had always been included in the political programs of the legal and underground opposition and became an even more prominent concern beginning in the 1960s, it tended to be merged with other opposition concerns and almost disappeared as an autonomous theme until just before the fall of the regime. In 1969 the Movimento Democrático de Mulheres (Democratic Women's Movement), associated with the PCP, appeared. In 1972, immediately following the publication of *Novas cartas portuguesas* (*The Three Marias: New Portuguese Letters*) a book written by three women writers who criticized marriage and the dominant morality, the organization was banned, which inspired a movement of international solidarity. Known as the period of the "Three Marias," this era marked the rebirth of Portuguese feminism during the 1970s, the development of which was an indication of the process of transition toward democracy, initiated by the military coup of 25 April 1974.

Fascism, Catholicism, and Women

The European Fascist regimes of the first half of the 20th century were characterized by the contradiction of mobilizing women and trying to keep them at home. The Italian case is particularly enlightening. After its initial heterodoxy, and after it had assumed power, Italian Fascism reverted to a conservative discourse, limiting women's political rights and even forbidding them to enter certain professions (mainly in secondary schools) that were already strongly feminized. This did not happen in Portugal. On the other hand, the "demographic battle" and the more totalitarian wave of the 1930s in Portugal imposed female mobilization and the effort to subordinate the "family" to the state.

Just before World War II, Italian Fascism had many women's organizations, in addition to ONMI, most of which were run by the party, the state, or a corporatist apparatus. In 1939 about

3.18 million Italian women (or 25 percent of all women over 21) were members of Fascist organizations, which included youth organizations that were made compulsory for all students at state schools. Observing the kinds of Italian organizations and the social influence of the most important ones, their differences from the Portuguese case are quite obvious.

The first women's organization directly linked to the Italian Fascist Party was the Fasci Femminili, which mainly addressed middle-class women. When the organization was initially founded, in 1920, it met with the distrust and even hostility of the regime's hierarchy. After periods of tension the group was reorganized at the end of the 1920s and became a mass voluntary organization. In 1939 the Fasci Femminili had 750,000 members. The organization Massaie Rurali, founded in 1933, targeted rural housewives and farm workers. At first these groups were led by the rural Fascist unions, but in 1934 their management passed into the hands of the Fasci Femminili. These groups were also of a voluntary nature and had 1.48 million women members in 1939. The Sezione Operaie e Lavoranti a Domicilio (SOLD; Section of Workingwomen and Domestic Workers) created in 1938, included women factory workers and the wives of male factory workers. In 1939 these groups had 500,000 members and continued to grow, mainly after women had entered the wartime economy. The Picole Italiane (for girls between the ages of eight and twelve) and the Giovani Italiane (for girls between the ages of thirteen and eighteen) were at first placed under the control of the Fasci Femminili. In 1929 these organizations passed to the Ministry of Education; in 1937 they were reabsorbed by the Fascist Party.

Salazarism shared with the other dictatorships a fundamental nucleus: the ideology of "women's place is in the home." However, this ideology was not particular to Fascism, for it was also a preoccupation of the more conservative nuclei of the political sphere and particularly of the Catholic Church, which provided Salazarism some of its fundamental premises. Further, since the Portuguese New State was not subjected to the same totalitarian tension as German National Socialism or Italian Fascism, Salazarism did not attempt a similar mobilization of women with regard to the "nation" and therefore did not organize women to the same degree as was seen in Germany or Italy. In Portugal the repression of moderate feminist organizations was not linked to the creation of official movements in the 1930s. Rather, such repression was part of the more general repressive aftermath of legal resistance following World War II, when the New State was already trying to rid itself of associations with the "age of Fascism."

Another important comparative dimension, central in the Portuguese case, is the weight of the Catholic organizations. In Italy women's Catholic organizations simultaneously formed a collaborating alternative and a pole of resistance to the totalitarian temptations of the Fascist state. The Church supported many of the measures for "the protection of the family" and the discourse that went with them. Militant Catholic women helped implement such measures in official organizations. However, from the 1920s tensions became more pronounced, as attacks on and limitations of the autonomous activity of the Catholic Action grew, imposing new, unstable compromises.

At the beginning of the 1920s, the women's organizations of Italian Catholic Action were by far superior in number to the Fascist ones. When Mussolini met the Fasci Femminili in 1927,

he advised them to "control the sacristy," but the Catholic and Fascist organizations shared a large common nucleus. It was only in the mid 1930s that the Fascist organizations began to grow bigger than the Catholic ones and tensions were expressed more openly. The campaigns for women's mobilization during the war in Abyssinia and the totalitarian wave of the 1930s, as Italy prepared for its participation in World War II, coincided with the reinforcement of the monopoly of organizations linked to the National Fascist Party and with a new wave of repression resulting in the abolition of various organizations in civil society. In this perspective some associations, already lethargic despite their collaboration with the regime (such as the National Council of Italian Women) were dissolved and the organizations of Italian Catholic Action were once again attacked. Some of these groups were obliged to close down, while others were forced to accept severe limitations on their organizations.

In the case of Salazar's New State, it seems clear that Portuguese Catholic Action not only maintained and developed its autonomous associations but was also part of the female Catholic elite that formed the fundamental nucleus of the official organizations. These organizations remained small and elitist, like OMEN or MPF, and were Catholicized expressing their commitment to the Church, reinforced by the Concordat of 1940.

Bibliography

André, Isabel Margarida, "The Employment of Women in Portugal," *Iberian Studies* 20, nos. 1–2 (1991)

Antunes, José Freire, editor, *A guerra de África (1961–1974)*, 2 vols., Lisbon: Círculo de Leitores, 1995

Baptista, Virgínia, "As mulheres no mercado de trabalho em Portugal: Representações e quotidianos (1890–1940)," Master's thesis, Istituto Superior de Ciências do Trabalho e da Empresa, 1998

Barbas, Manuela de Sousa, "Mocidade portuguesa feminina (1937–1945)," Master's thesis, Instituto Superior de Ciências do Trabalho e da Empresa,1998

Barreira, Cecília, *História das nossas avós: Retrato da burguesa em Lisboa, 1890–1930*, Lisbon: Colibri, 1992

Barreno, Maria Isabel, Maria Teresa Horta, and Maria Velho da Costa, *Novas cartas portuguesas*, Lisbon: Estúdios Cor, 1972; as *The Three Marias: New Portuguese Letters*, translated by Helen R. Lane, Garden City, New York: Doubleday, 1975

Beleza, Teresa, *Mullieres, direito, crime ou a perplexidade de Cassandra*, Lisbon: Faculdade de Direito, 1990

Belo, Maria, et al., "O Estado Novo e as mulheres," in *O Estado Novo: Das origens ao fim da autarcia, 1926–1959*, vol. 2, Lisbon: Fragmentos, 1987

Bock, Gisela, and Pat Thane, editors, *Maternity and Gender Policies: Women and the Rise of the European Welfare States, 1880–1950s*, London and New York: Routledge, 1991

Comissão do Livro Negro sobre o Regime Fascista, *Presos Políticos no Regime Fascista*, 6 vols., Lisbon: Comissão do Livro Negro sobre o Regime Fascista, 1981–82; see especially vols. 1 and 2

A concordata de 1940 : Portugal-Santa Sé, Lisbon: Didaskalia, 1993

Costa, Fernando Marques da, *A maçonaria feminina*, Lisbon: Vega, 1981

Cova, Anne, and António Costa Pinto, "O Salazarismo e as mulheres: Uma abordagem comparativa," *Penélope*, no. 17 (October 1997)

Cruz, Manuel Braga da, *O partido e o estado no Salazarismo*, Lisbon: Presença, 1988

De Giorgio, Michela, and Paula Di Cori, "Politica e sentimenti: Le organizzazione feminile cattoliche dall'età giolittiana al fascismo," *Rivista di storia contemporanea* 3 (July 1980)

De Grazia, Victoria, *How Fascism Ruled Women: Italy, 1922–1945*, Berkeley: University of California Press, 1992

Delgado, Pedro, *Divórcio e separação em Portugal: Análise social e demográfica: Século XX*, Lisbon: Estampa, 1996

Esteves, João Gomes, *A Liga republicana das mulheres portugueses: Uma organização política e feminista (1909–1919)*, Lisbon: Comissão para a Igualdade e para os Direitos das Mulheres, 1992

Esteves, João Gomes, *As origens do sufragismo Português: A primeira organização sufragista portuguesa, a Associação de Propaganda Feminista (1911–1918)*, Lisbon: Bizâncio, 1998

Ferreira, Ana Paula, "Home Bound: The Construct of Femininity in the New State," *Portuguese Studies* 12 (1996)

Ferreira, Virgínia, "Engendering Portugal: Social Change, State Politics, and Women's Social Mobilization," in *Modern Portugal*, edited by António Costa Pinto, Palo Alto, California: Society for the Promotion of Science and Scholarship, 1998

Fiadeiro, Maria Antónia, "Maria Lamas (1893–1983): Uma mulher jornalista: Tentativa e tentado biográfica," Master's thesis, Universidade Aberta, 1999

Fraddosio, Maria, "The Fallen Hero: The Myth of Mussolini and Fascist Women in the Italian Social Republic (1943–45)," *Journal of Contemporary History* 31 (1996)

Gorjão, Vanda, *A reinvidicação do voto no programa do Conselho nacional das mulheres Portuguesas (1914–1947)*, Lisbon: Comissão para a Igualdade e para os Direitos das Mulheres, 1994

Guinote, Paulo, *Quotidianos femininos (1900–1933)*, 2 vols., Lisbon: Comissão para a Igualdade e para os Direitos das Mulheres, 1997

Ipsen, Carl, *Dictating Demography: The Problem of Population in Fascist Italy*, Cambridge and New York: Cambridge University Press, 1996

Koon, Tracy H., *Believe, Obey, Fight: Political Socialization of Youth in Fascist Italy, 1922–1943*, Chapel Hill: University of North Carolina Press, 1985

Lamas, Rosmarie Wank-Nolasco, *Mulheres para além do seu tempo*, Lisbon: Bertrand, 1995

Luque, Concepción Campos, and Maria José González Castillejo, editors, *Mujeres y dictaduras en Europa y América: El largo camino*, Málaga, Spain: Universidad de Málaga, 1996

Mónica, Maria Filomena, *Educação e sociedade no Portugal de Salazar : A escola primária Salazarista, 1926–1939*, Lisbon: Presença, 1978

Moreira, Isabel Alves, "Mocidade Portuguesa feminina: Um ideal educativo," *Revista de história das ideias* 16 (1994)

Muel-Dreyfus, Francine, *Vichy et l'éternel féminin: Contribution à une sociologie politique de l'ordre des corps*, Paris: Éditions de Seuil, 1996; as *Vichy and the Eternal Feminine: A Contribution to a Political Sociology of Gender*, translated by Kathleen A. Johnson, Durham, North Carolina: Duke University Press, 2001

A mulher na sociedade Portuguesa: Visão histórica e perspectivas actuais, 2 vols., Coimbra, Portugal: Instituto de História Económica e Social, Faculdade de Letras da Universidade de Coimbra, 1986

Nóvoa, António, "A educação nacional," in *Portugal e o Estado Novo*, edited by Fernando Rosas, Lisbon: Presença, 1992

Organização das Mulheres Comunistas, *Subsídios para a história das lutas e movimentos de mulheres em Portugal sob o regime fascista, 1926–1974*, Lisbon: Avante, 1994

Pimentel, Irene, "Contributos para a história das mulheres no Estado Novo: As organizações femininas do Estado Novo: A obra das mães para a educação nacional e a mocidade portuguesa feminina, 1936–1966," Master's thesis, Universidade Nova de Lisboa, 1997

Pinto, António Costa, "L'État nouveau de Salazar," in *Le régime de Vichy et les Français*, edited by Jean-Pierre Azéma and François Bédarida, Paris: Fayard, 1992

Pinto, António Costa, *Salazar's Dictatorship and European Fascism: Problems of Interpretation*, Boulder, Colorado: Social Science Monographs, 1995

Rezolla, Maria Inácia, "Breve panorama da situação da Igreja Católica em Portugal (1930–1960)," in *Portugal e o Estado Novo*, edited by Fernando Rosas, Lisbon: Presença, 1992

Rodrigues, Julieta Almeida, "Continuidade e mudança nos papéis das mulheres urbanas portuguesas: Emergência de novas estruturas familiares," *Análise social* 19, nos. 3–5 (1983)

Silva, Maria Regina Tavares da, *A mulher: Bibliografia portuguesa anotada (monografias: 1518–1998)*, Lisbon: Cosmos, 1999

Silva, Maria Beatriz Nizza da, and Anne Cova, editors, *Estudos sobre as mulheres*, Lisbon: Universidade Aberta, Colecção de Estudos Pós-Graduados, 1998

Vicente, Ana, "Do autoritarismo e das mulheres na Segunda e Terceira Repúblicas," *Revista de história das ideias* 16 (1994)

Willson, Perry R., *The Clockwork Factory: Women and Work in Fascist Italy*, Oxford: Clarendon Press, and New York: Oxford University Press, 1993

LIBERTY AND EQUALITY FOR WOMEN IN THE SOCIALIST COUNTRIES OF EASTERN EUROPE, 1960–1980

SVETLANA AIVAZOVA

The "New Woman"

BEGINNING IN OCTOBER OF 1917, liberty and equality for women were among the principal objectives of the program of societal improvements envisioned for Socialist Russia. These same aims were unhesitatingly adopted by all the countries of Eastern Europe, which in the aftermath of World War II became the Socialist bloc. Today, the most radical detractors of the Soviet Socialist system view the phenomenon of "women's emancipation" in these countries as a "complete myth." Although this judgment is to a great extent justified, it does not reflect the whole truth. But there is even less truth in the countless scientific and literary descriptions of Socialism's real-life successes in bringing about equality between men and women—descriptions that were massively published until the early 1990s and whose only outstanding feature was their use of "Newspeak," the mark of their participation in the official ideology. The true situation of women in Eastern Europe was more complex and more contradictory than either past or present ideological schemas would lead us to believe. Women's circumstances differed from country to country and from society to society. Nevertheless, within the general picture one can discern certain essential, common traits, which were conditioned by the manner in which the goals and means of women's emancipation were initially formulated.

To reach an in-depth understanding of the problem of women's circumstances in the Eastern bloc countries, we must go back to its sources. Unquestionably, the Bolsheviks were the first regime in history to found a system—or indeed, a world—that sought to reconstruct basic human relationships: social relationships between the sexes as well as the representations and symbols attached to them. Several decrees adopted in December 1917 gave women full civic rights and liberties and made them equal to men before the law. The Bolsheviks believed that in and of itself, this legislation would suffice—or nearly—to ensure true equality for women in society. Ideologues of the women's

proletarian movement, such as Aleksandra Kollontai, Inessa Armand, Nadezhda Krupskaya, and Klaudia Samoïlova, counted on achieving a new revolution in Russia—that is, transforming the daily existence of Soviet women and definitively eliminating the sphere of "private life" and its main refuge, the family, as obstacles to women's liberty.

The credit for these new ideas on social relations between the sexes, as they were supposed to be formed in socialist society, goes primarily to Kollontai, a well-known Bolshevik theoretician. A true Marxist, Kollontai started out from the principle that the old patriarchal power, which oppressed women, was the product of women's alienation—itself the result of women's being cut off from productive labor within society. From that point of view, Kollontai believed that women's progressive entrance into industrial production during the capitalist era made undeniably positive sense: it would deal an irremediable blow to the family—the basis of patriarchy—while at the same time destroying the economy of production within the family and the unequal relations between husband and wife, between man and woman. Kollontai was convinced that the "woman question" came up in a society precisely at the moment when women entered the field of social production and that this issue was the result of, on the one hand, a contradiction between the true equality of women and men in collective labor, and, on the other, "the absence of equality in marriage, society, and the state," as she wrote in *Trud zhenshchiny v evoliutsii khoziaistva* (1923; Women's Work in the Evolution of the Economy). The legal recognition of women's civil rights was supposed to put an end to that contradiction and thus automatically resolve the woman question, putting a definitive end to the primitive division between men's "productive" work and women's "unproductive" task, that of reproducing the species.

As Kollontai envisioned it, the path to be taken after the first decrees of the Soviet power structure was to be very short. The life of citizens had to be organized on a new and collective basis by purging it once and for all of every habit and instinct of private life. The new life was to be a collective and communist life: people would eat in cafeterias, laundry would be done in state facilities, children's education would take place in kindergartens and schools, and care for the elderly would be provided in homes designed for this specific purpose. Kollontai's new ideas on marriage came from this line of thinking as well. Communist marriage would be freed from all the mundane burdens of daily life. The labor collective would replace the old institution of the bourgeois family, absorbing it little by little until it was completely dissolved into the collective. Along with the bourgeois family, the last vestiges of the social division of work between "male" and "female" would disappear, and so, consequently, would the asymmetry and the inequality in the social relationship between the sexes. Thus would be inaugurated an era of authentic love, liberated from "any aftertaste of calculation and material profit." What would then distinguish women from men on the social level? One function alone: women's maternal role. Still, even that role was to be transformed and evolve into a social function.

For Kollontai, the new marriage would be a wholly personal act, fairly insignificant in the social realm, while "maternity would become a social obligation in its own right, an important and essential obligation." In the course of her many presentations during the first Soviet years, Kollontai never tired of emphasizing this:

> Work provides the means to take the measure of woman's condition: within the economy of the private family, this work has chained her down; work directed toward the collective carries within it her emancipation. . . . Marriage is evolving, the family straitjacket is weakening, motherhood is becoming a social function.

Kollontai incorporated a fully elaborated version of her new conception of social relationships between the sexes in her novel *Liubov' pchel trudovykh* (*Love of Worker Bees*), written in 1922 and published the following year. The novel's subject seems very elementary: Man and Woman, their love and their new and free marriage, followed by a love triangle, and ending with the heroine alone and pregnant. She awaits the birth of her child without tears of despair, as would have been the rule in the past, but with hope and joy. Why? Because this woman's social situation is radically different: she is a factory worker, a member of the party, and she is a participant in the revolutionary battles and the building of socialist society. All her plans are geared toward a new daily life, toward a residential cooperative she has created, toward the factory where she works, and toward the day care center she is about to establish. Love is only one aspect of her existence, which comprises many other dimensions. This is why she gives up the man she loves to another woman for whom love is everything. The heroine draws support from her work collective and her party cell, which are her true family. The hero of the novel is also an active Bolshevik, but one who is subject to "deviations," submitting to sometimes anarchist, sometimes bourgeois influences, and whose instincts as a private-property owner are still very strong. The party condemns him for his lack of judgment in both politics and love. The hero is incapable of appreciating the qualities of the "new" woman, as embodied in the heroine. He leaves her for another woman who represents typical bourgeois life, for she is dependent and greedy.

Such is the plot. Its simplicity should not, however, conceal what was a grandiose plan of social transformation. The sexual division of labor here took on unprecedented forms: in this couple, the woman has the dominant role. She is not merely a "production unit," a worker who labors for the good of society; she is also a mother, fulfilling the function of reproduction, and thus a "unit" that is doubly useful to society. This "unit" no longer has any property instinct; she readily and joyfully accepts the party's idea that the labor collective is her family. She feels no need for another family—the one that a private life, removed from the party and the state, would offer her. In this couple, the man is the secondary character and, what is more, he is suspect, for his need for a private and personal life is much greater than the heroine's. He shows some hesitation as he considers the guidelines of the party-state; he reflects, he dreams, and he questions Socialism instead of believing in it immediately. What emerges above all else from the novel is the idea that this man is not indispensable: he can be relinquished along with the shadows of the past that he still carries within. For the work collective and the party cell are there to support the heroine. These are the true guarantors of the new life, ensuring a future both for the heroine and for the child she is awaiting. It is clear that for Kollontai, these radical changes meant above all a reconfiguration of relationships in the triangle "man-woman-state." Kollontai proposed that the revolutionary state make woman its privileged partner in creating new forms of communal life, a new communist society. In every speech and every article from the early 1920s, Kollontai repeats this idea insistently, noting in her *Trud zhenshchiny v evoliutsii khoziaistva*: "Soviet power is the first in the world to have taken mother and child under its protection." Thus, Kollontai proposed that the new power should eradicate the patriarchal system of family relationships and everything that system entailed. What was the reaction to these demands? They were included in the general educational agenda of Soviet Socialism, but the measures outlined toward achieving this goal were undoubtedly not those that Kollontai was expecting.

In the final analysis, all the Soviet states used the idea of recasting relations between the sexes in order to crush the individual, whether male or female, and to establish the total dominance of state power. As soon as relations between the sexes began to change, a third force—the party-state or even the clan-state—took the upper hand. In other words, patriarchal hegemony was taking on new forms: the paternalistic state, aspiring to totalitarianism, vested itself with "paternal power" by alienating man as husband and father, depriving him of the very basis of masculine identity. Such a state sought to subjugate the individual completely by annihilating the forms of his personal and private life: love and family. It is no accident that the great anti-utopias of the 20th century, from Yevgeny Ivanovich Zamiatin's novel *My* (completed 1920; *We*) to George Orwell's *1984* (1949), featured plots centered on love, a love that resisted the rules imposed upon individuals by the power structure. Nor is it an accident that Stalin, more than any other honorific, liked to be called "father of the people." He meticulously perfected this role, tailoring his image to it and even taking on the responsibilities of real paternal functions, guaranteeing food and shelter for women and children, as well as education for the latter. He decreed measures and privileges that had the force of law, meant to support the "new" woman in her socially useful work. He communicated with women through governmental committees for the "protection of maternity and childhood"; meanwhile, the notions of "father" and "paternity" were disappearing from official documents. Women had the right to address their concerns to Stalin through his local representatives—party committees, unions, administration—and to complain about their husbands, so that Stalin could call the men to order if they persisted in demanding divorce, cheating on their wives, beating them, or getting drunk.

The supreme power of the state meddled in every detail of private life, assuming decisive power in the area of births, abortions, marriages, and divorces. Men, heads of families, became the focal point of this close watchfulness. They were humiliated, destroyed by mass arrests, forced labor, poverty-level wages, almost chronic food shortages, fear, and life under conditions of bare survival. But women were subjected to the same style of existence, an endless obstacle course that forced them to struggle with difficulties of all kinds, described as "daily life" Soviet style. This lifestyle equalized the relationship between the sexes by force of circumstance, for both men and women were hostages, not to say slaves, of the same power system. This "erasure" of the boundaries between the sexes translated, for example, into what at first glance might have seemed to be a small detail: the forms of address the two sexes used for each other. The word "comrade" became the norm, making no distinction between men and women, just as they were no longer distinguishable in reality. In "Gumanism i sovremennost'" ("Humanism and the Present"), the poet Osip Mandel'shtam describes this period as "an era that did not take man into account at all, that used him like brick and mortar, like construction material, instead of building for him." Thus, a new Soviet reality was formed, and with it the myth of women's liberty and equality, a myth that was widely used by official propaganda, for, on the emotional level, it was a particularly sensitive point in the general myth of the "Socialist paradise."

Woman as Citizen

In accordance with this initial ideological orientation, women were invested with two roles: "worker" and "mother." These roles continued to be obligatory throughout the 70 years of Soviet Socialism and guaranteed her the status of citizen. However, during each period of the history of Soviet Socialism these roles were interpreted differently and set down in civil law, the Constitution, decrees, and edicts.

Invariably, the hidden motivation behind these legal changes was the need to make the roles of worker and mother compatible. In fact, the ideal combination of the two could and can exist on paper only: in reality, there is often a tension between a woman's professional activity and her maternal obligations, and vice versa. Individual families and their organization might minimize this contradiction or, on the contrary, aggravate it to the extreme. In its early stages, the Socialist state declared that the traditional family was an institution made ponderous by the unequal relationship between the sexes, and that socially useful work would guarantee liberty and equality for all citizens, regardless of their sex. By this very fact, the state set a new institution, the soviet (labor collective), in opposition to the family, and it declared its intention of guaranteeing women "social protec-

tion," to replace what in former days had been offered above all by the family and its head, the husband and father. The solidarity of comradeship within the labor collective was to replace the traditional family relationship and to enable women to reconcile more successfully their contradictory roles and obligations. It was in this spirit that the first Soviet legislators treated the new social connections. Only one month after the revolution, the women of Russia were liberated from all restrictions on rights to their children and possessions upon dissolution of their marriage. They received the right to choose freely their profession and their place of residence, to get an education, and to receive equal pay for equal work. The first Constitution, adopted in July 1918, ratified the equality of political and civil rights for men and women. In 1920 abortion was legalized. The 1918 Civil Code of the Russian Soviet Federated Socialist Republic (RSFSR), and later the 1925 law on marriage, the family, and guardianship, recognized only civil marriage as legal, while prior to that time only religious marriage had been legal in Russia. The act of registering a marriage became a purely statistical procedure. The process for divorce was just as simple. This was a truly revolutionary recasting of all the foundations of social life, vital for the establishment of the new power.

But during the second half of the 1920s, this trend began to shift, albeit very slowly and gradually. The country was entering the era of industrialization, of collectivization, of the "great construction sites" of Socialism—all things that needed inexpensive female labor. Indeed, women's labor became a symbol of that period. But the state proved unable to keep its promises, either in the matter of social infrastructure or in the matter of children's education. In part, there were purely economic reasons for this failure. Thus the public powers slowly but surely came to the conclusion that the manner of dealing with the problem of the family and, consequently, of the role and destiny of women in society, had to be reconsidered. Another compelling factor was the erosion of the family, which was generating a greater demographic awareness; as a result, a precipitous decline in the birthrate threatened normal reproduction of the population. Since its very inception, the world's only socialist state had been expecting war, and it therefore could not afford a severe drop in its population. In the mid-1930s, the problem of falling birthrates became critical, and this was immediately reflected in legislation.

In 1936 the famous Soviet Constitution solemnly proclaimed: "In the USSR a problem of enormous magnitude has been resolved: for the first time in history, authentic equality for women is assured." Article 122 stipulated:

> In the USSR women receive rights equal to those of men
> in every area of economic, political, and social life, as well
> as in that of the state. These rights are realized concretely
> in women's rights, equal to those of man, with respect to
> work, wages, leisure time, social insurance, and education,
> and in the form of state protection of mother and child,
> state aid to mothers of large families and single mothers,
> paid maternity leave, a vast network of maternity clinics,
> day care centers, and kindergartens.

Finally, Article 137 of the Constitution emphasized: "Women have the right to vote and the right to be elected in the same capacity as men."

Alongside the Constitution, however, a decree was adopted on 27 June 1936 by the Executive Central Committee of the

Soviets and the government of the USSR, reflecting another spirit altogether and pursuing a very different goal. It was entitled "Prohibition of abortion, improvement of aid to young mothers, establishment of state aid to mothers of large families, expansion of the network of maternity clinics, day care centers, and kindergartens, reinforcement of penal prosecution against those who do not pay their alimony, and some modifications to the abortion law." This decree essentially wiped out earlier practices and theories of "free love" and the "free family." Little by little the state brought the family under its wing, making it into a "social cell." This was a sign of the stabilization of the socialist system. Having seized control of society, the state needed the solid bases, links, and stable social relationships that have always and everywhere been ensured by the family. With the onset of World War II, this need became a necessity of primary urgency and, in order to satisfy it, on 8 July 1944 the Presidium of the Supreme Soviet of the USSR adopted an edict according to which "only registered marriages entail the rights and obligations of the spouses."

This edict was significant in several respects. First and foremost, it concretized a decisive shift that had already occurred in state policy concerning relations between the sexes within the family and in marriage. Henceforth women's inequality was brutally obvious as soon as she entered into an extramarital relationship or when she chose free love—which socialist ideology itself had nonetheless cultivated for almost a quarter of a century. This edict prohibited the establishment of paternity in such unions, even with the free consent of the father. The sole responsibility for such a relationship, the full weight of its consequences, thus fell completely on the woman and ultimately redounded onto her children. In addition, every free union or unregistered marriage was treated as an extramarital relationship. By refusing to recognize these unions, the state divested itself of all responsibility for providing social protection to these families. A certain number of measures were adopted following this edict, severely complicating the process of divorce and signifying a radical change in the way divorce was understood. Divorce became a sign of "social instability" in an individual, which brought unpleasant results, such as administrative penalties or penalties within the Communist Party, from which the guilty person could even be expelled (an event that would mean the end of any career). These steps accelerated the institutionalization of the Soviet family and changed woman's civic status. In exchange for her liberty and her equal rights, the state henceforth expected woman not only to fulfill her roles as worker and as mother, but also to be the main educator of her children, the preserver of the Soviet family, and faithful wife who would shoulder the entire weight of domestic concerns.

The state, which had failed in "revolutionizing everyday life," burdened woman with all of these "everyday" concerns and legalized the double load that women, deemed "free and equal in rights," had in fact always borne in any case. It is true that the state promised to use all possible means to develop the social infrastructure. However, this promise was not to be fulfilled right away but only progressively, after other, more urgent tasks were achieved, such as the industrialization of the country, the collectivization of agriculture, economic reconstruction after World War II, the reforms of the 1960s, and so forth. In the meantime, women were granted additional rights and assistance, especially paid maternity leave and family allocations, as compensation for their double burden.

If one analyzes the consequences of this "swerve" in Socialist legislation, it is important to note that, after the new orientation was adopted, the Soviet family once again became asymmetrical: the figure of the mother, whose function was complicated considerably, was becoming more and more important. She was responsible for the birth and the education of the children and the family's everyday existence, and she bore the whole weight of domestic work. In addition, she supported her family with her salary, for in most Soviet households the husband's salary was insufficient even to ensure a minimal level of subsistence, as the French legal sociologist Chantal Kourilsky has so clearly shown. The school reforms decided upon in 1943, right in the midst of the war, reinstated separate education for girls and boys and revealed more openly the radical changes that had occurred in state policy concerning relations between the sexes. Henceforth, the state deemed it necessary to raise and educate children from their school age on by inculcating them with the "natural" destiny of their sex. In this new paradigm, the boy was to be ready to fulfill the functions of "father" and "combatant," while the girl had to be trained as a "mother" and the "conscious educator" of her children. The "father of the people" personally directed this reform. Nevertheless, it in no way altered state propaganda, either with respect to women's rights and equality or to the family, which it continued to present as a cell within the great labor collective, open to all forms of state interference. The state did not consider it a good idea to suppress the obvious contradictions of this propaganda, whose main themes had almost become articles of faith, and, like all symbols of faith, could be contradictory and even incompatible.

This openly patriarchal orientation of state policies did not begin to be corrected until after Stalin's death, just as, little by little, the contradictions of the law were erased or concealed. This correction was based, to a great extent, on the legislative experience of the "brother" countries of Eastern Europe. Owing to a variety of circumstances, these countries did not experience the period of "revolutionary romanticism" that Soviet Russia had known in its first decade, with its recasting of relations between the sexes, its disdain for everyday realities, and its radical rejection of the old forms of social life. In the Eastern bloc countries, legislation was reshaped in accordance with the Soviet manner of regulating the woman question. As the official texts emphasized, "the solution to the woman question in the USSR and in other Socialist countries is based on the fact that women's participation in social production is the determining factor in women's equality in society and the family" (Assessment of the Tenth Anniversary of the United Nations Organization, 1985). Women's participation guaranteed them economic independence and

> serves as a basis for the instruction of social qualities in women: responsibility for her actions and for collective life, understanding of her civic duty, the feeling of belonging to the society, and energy in social activity. All this shapes the personality of women and reinforces their prestige in the family.

An orientation such as this forced lawmakers in all the Eastern bloc countries to resolve the same problem: they had to act in such a way that the principle of liberty and equality of the citizens of both sexes would be compatible with that of the protection and reinforcement of the socialist family as a basic cell of society. In order to respond to this demand, a whole range of solutions was proposed, and each legislator's choice was determined by the cultural particularities of his country and by the degree of resistance to socialist innovations posed by social standards and traditional institutions.

Of all the countries, the German Democratic Republic created the most consistent and thorough laws. Article 20 of the 1968 Constitution stated the equality of men and women in every area of social life and specified that the state would commit itself to helping to raise the standards of professional training for women. At the same time, Article 28, which was dedicated to the protection of marriage, family, and motherhood, made provisions for helping large families, even when the mother or father was a single parent. Moreover, medical and material assistance was guaranteed to all women during pregnancy and childbirth. The GDR's Constitution was the only Socialist constitution that relinquished sexual distinctions in family obligations. Its measures conformed to the Family Code of 1966, in which Article 9 stipulated: "Spouses have the same rights. They live together and manage their home. All questions of communal life and of the development of each person are regulated by the spouses on the basis of their mutual consent." And Article 10 stated, "both spouses take part in the education of the children and in the management of their home."

The constitutions of Hungary (adopted in 1949 and modified in 1972) and of Rumania (1965) guaranteed both the defense of women's civil rights and the protection of the family, motherhood, and childhood; lastly, they prohibited any sexual discrimination. This final point also appeared in the constitutions of Bulgaria (1971) and Poland (1952, 1976). These constitutions and that of Czechoslovakia (1960, 1968) gave the woman the obligation of safeguarding the family home, specifying that the state guaranteed her its full support and promised her improvements in the service sector. In three countries—Bulgaria, Poland, and Yugoslavia—the constitutions specified that children born out of wedlock were fully recognized by the law.

Despite the differences that separated these constitutional texts and independently of their degree of coherence, these fundamental laws reflect a single trend, in the opinion of legal specialists: in every case, legislators sought to formulate and establish measures pertaining to the family and relations between the sexes in ways that would not contradict the principle of women's liberty and equality. Legal language needed to be found to formalize the idea of an egalitarian family based on partnership. The stumbling block of this search was the notion of "woman-mother," which the lawmakers neither wished nor were able to abandon.

Soviet law took the same direction during the years of the post-Stalinist "thaw." Educational reforms, begun in 1954, restored mixed-gender schooling; in 1955, abortion was again legalized; in 1965, divorce procedures were simplified considerably; in 1967, alimony obligations were regulated. Finally, in 1968, a more general law was adopted, entitled Foundations of Marriage and Family Legislation in the USSR and in the Republics of the Union. For the first time in the history of Soviet legislation, this document focused not so much on women's duties and obligations as on their rights. It specifically stressed

notions such as "motherhood and a happy childhood," "encouragement of motherhood," and so forth. The text of the law explicitly stated, "the Soviet woman receives all social and material conditions necessary to combine a happy motherhood with an active and creative participation in productive, political, and social life." Article 3 particularly referred to "the equality of rights of women and men in family relationships." Yet, to some extent, this article contradicted the fourth paragraph of Article 1, which mentioned "measures of all kinds, meant to protect the interests of mother and child," and also Article 5, in which state assistance to families was referred to as aid to the "woman-mother."

This legislative quest was set forth in the Constitution of the USSR adopted in 1977, after lengthy debates in society. In the 1977 Constitution, the status of every Soviet citizen was defined independently of his/her sex, by the two main functions of "worker" and "family member." This was why one of the central themes of the discussion became the equal sharing of family obligations between spouses—that is to say, the egalitarian family based on partnership. Article 35 was devoted to women's liberty and equality and Article 53 to the family. Article 35 stipulated:

> In the USSR, women and men have equal rights. These rights are realized in women's free access to education and professional training, to work, in their right to remuneration for work and to promotion equal to that of men, in their right to political and cultural activity as well as to special measures of protection in women's work and health, under conditions that allow them to combine work and motherhood: legal protection, material and moral support for motherhood and childhood, including paid leave and other advantages conferred upon pregnant women and mothers, and a progressive reduction in work time for women with young children.

In the constitutional plan submitted for discussion, the first line of this Article was presented in a different form: "In the USSR, women have rights equal to those of men." In the course of the debates, this version was criticized because the rights of men were taken as a standard, to which those of women had to conform. The wording was changed on these grounds. The initial formulation had repeated the phrasing of the constitutions of Poland (Art. 78) and Rumania (Art. 23) and the definitive version reproduced the constitutions of the German Democratic Republic (Art. 20), Bulgaria (Art. 36), and Hungary (Art. 62).

The detractors of the initial plan observed that Article 35 of the 1977 Soviet Constitution, pertaining to the protection of motherhood and childhood and to the advantages granted to women with young children, contradicted Article 53, which stated, "in family relationships, whether it be in connection to persons or material goods, women and men have equal rights." What was more, critics suggested completing the text with a measure on "the equal obligations" of spouses, but the authors of the legislation preserved the initial and contradictory text. It corresponded to the contradictions in social life and to the true model of the Soviet family, which had ceased to be purely patriarchal but nevertheless had not become egalitarian. In order for it to become so, two obstacles, raised by the official ideology and the mentalities it had shaped, had to be overcome. First, the "classic" notion of "woman-mother" had to be abandoned:

woman had to be taken as a full-fledged citizen, whose public recognition did not depend on complementary functions. And second, man had to be recognized as a full-fledged member of the family, a father endowed with the same rights as the mother with respect to the upbringing of children. The Constitution of 1977, like the "Foundations of Marriage and Family Legislation" cited above, was not able to overcome these obstacles.

Aware that they needed to offer, at least in appearance, some coherence between the constitution and the other legislative acts dealing with women's liberty and equality, Soviet jurists explained that de jure equality between women and men had never been considered as an identity of their legal status in the Soviet state. Simple equalization of rights did not guarantee true equality of women, who, while fulfilling the same functions as men in society, still fulfilled another quite specific one, namely that of motherhood. It followed then that true equality between men and women was possible only if women, being endowed with the same rights as men, also benefited from supplementary rights and advantages. These were the general outlines of Soviet legislation, called upon to resolve the woman question and to guarantee women's rights in liberty and equality with men in socialist society. These laws served as a model for the laws of the Eastern European countries and, in turn, were inspired by them. In any case, this was "protective" legislation, built upon the principle of advantages and, as a result, fundamentally discriminatory (that is, in favor of women). But when, in 1979, the United Nations adopted the convention meant to put an end to all forms of discrimination against women (CEDAW), Soviet propagandists proudly affirmed: "In our country, all the measures foreseen by the convention have already been applied for a long time. . . . Soviet legislation is in total conformity with it and even goes much further than the established standards." What was the reality?

Women in the Workforce

During the 1960s and 1970s, the idea that a woman might opt not to work in production had completely disappeared from the culture. All official and propaganda publications, textbooks, and scientific studies were unanimous on the issue of women's work. For example, it was affirmed in *Zhenshchiny mira v bor'be za sotsial'nyi progress* (1972; Women of the World Struggling for Social Progress. See Koval'skii) that

> The essential, determining factor of the true equality of women with men in society is that she take part in the work of society. Work is the foundation of women's emancipation and their economic independence. Work helps to develop women's personality, it increases their role in society and the family, and it gives them moral satisfaction.

In reality, placing women in production did not respond so much to the demands of their emancipation as to the needs of the modernization of the Soviet economy and its passage into the industrial era. The same phenomenon occurred in the other Eastern European countries. Any form of modernization, even when it is produced in the framework of a natural evolution, is accompanied by social upheaval. It is a process involving conflict, and it is painful—especially when the natural evolution is

superseded by a planned revolution, as was the case in the USSR and, later on, in all the countries of the Socialist bloc.

From the early 1920s on, women's participation in paid labor grew continuously in the USSR. It is true that this phenomenon fluctuated along with economic conditions: during the New Economic Plan, in the course of the years following World War II, and again in the early and mid 1960s, when the Kosygin reforms were applied, women's work declined proportionately. On the other hand, during the 1930s, when the country was undergoing accelerated industrialization, and then during World War II, and finally during the 1970s, women's participation in the total number of workers grew considerably. A statistical overview in *Narodnoe khoziaistvo SSSR za 60 let* (1977; The Soviet Economy in the Course of the Last 60 Years) provides the following picture:

Year	1922	1926	1940	1945	1950	1955	1960	1970
Percent of Women	25	23	39	56	47	46	47	51

According to the statistics collected in *Zhenshchiny v SSSR* (1975; Women in the USSR), women represented as much as 51 percent of the labor force during the 1970s, and this level was sustained until the end of the 1980s. In the same period, 92 percent of all Soviet women of working age were either working or studying. The numbers did vary slightly in the different Soviet Republics: women's employment rate was highest in the RSFSR, Byelorussia, Latvia, and Estonia, and lowest in the Central Asian republics and Transcaucasia. For example, in Kyrgyzstan 48 percent of the workers were women, while in Turkmenistan the proportion was 40 percent. Women's work was concentrated especially in industry, which employed the most women in absolute numbers and where growth in female labor was greater than that in male labor. In 1974, the number of women working reached 49 percent in industry and 45 percent in state agriculture. Women constituted the majority of workers in health care, social insurance (84 percent), education (73 percent), culture (70 percent), communications (68 percent), commerce, and public food service (76 percent). In other words, women were working in all areas of the economy and played an enormous, sometimes decisive, role everywhere.

Increases in the numbers of women working in productive labor were similar in the other Socialist countries, as the following figures, taken from Koval'skii, reveal. In the German Democratic Republic in the early 1970s, 78 percent of adult women were working and they constituted 47.4 percent of the total labor force. In Hungary during the same period, the proportion reached two-thirds of adult women. In Rumania, women constituted 47 percent of the total working population and 30 percent of the factory and office workers. In Czechoslovakia, women made up 46 percent of the total workforce; in industry their numbers grew to 42 percent; in science it was 30 percent; in the area of education and culture it was 62 percent; and in health and social welfare, 78 percent. In Bulgaria, women in industry accounted for 43 percent; in commerce 50.2 percent; in health and social welfare, 70.9 percent; in science 48.2 percent; in education, culture, and art, 64.7 percent; and in agriculture 67 percent. In Poland, women made up 37 percent of the workforce;

this figure reached 70 percent among health-care workers and 66 percent among those working in education and culture.

The quantitative data concerning employed women are informative in terms of the process of social modernization, but insufficient for testing the influence of this increase in female labor on women's emancipation and equality. In this regard, the qualitative data, which reveal the nature and the content of women's work, are far more meaningful. Sociologists have noted that the kinds of women's occupations changed with the times: in the USSR, from the 1930s to the 1970s, the number of women employed in agriculture decreased almost by half, primarily because of the rural exodus. During the same period, the portion of women employed in industry, information, production, and administration grew by approximately 300 percent (see Gruzdeva and Chertikhina 1986). In other words, the quantitative increase in women's work was accompanied by a rise in their levels of education and skills.

At the same time, women's work continued to be rather unskilled, especially in the USSR, with many women workers doing extremely tedious manual labor that required no professional training whatsoever. According to official statistics, in the early 1980s this type of work was done by nearly 40 percent of the women workers, whereas these unskilled jobs accounted for only around 30 percent of the labor force as a whole. This meant that women constituted the majority of the workforce employed in heavy physical labor. Women made up almost half of the construction and agricultural workers employed in manual or unskilled labor; 97 percent of the workers in the textile and light industries, noteworthy for their dust and other noxious by-products; 98 percent of the workers in cleaning, nursing, day care, and so on; 90 percent of the assembly line workers; and 70 percent of the jobs in warehouses. Moreover, a very large number of women were working in industries that presented significant health hazards: almost 1 million women worked in conditions with higher than average levels of noise and vibrations; almost 700,000 women worked in conditions of insufficient lighting; almost 1 million worked in production, where the air was contaminated by dust and gases; more than 1 million worked in abnormal temperatures. In the early 1980s, the proportion of women-held jobs that did not meet safety standards and regulations rose to 50 percent in the chemical industry, 46 percent in the radio-technical industry, 46 percent in the shipyards, and 34 percent in forestry and the paper industry (see Shineleva).

During the same period in Bulgaria, one-third of workingwomen worked under conditions that did not meet sanitary and hygienic standards. Almost 50 percent of the jobs filled by women posed health risks. In Hungary, close to 5 percent of the women workers were subjected to high temperatures, 6 to 8 percent to harmful chemical vapors, and 10 percent to above-normal noise. In Czechoslovakia, according to official figures, 2 to 3 percent of the women workers were forced to violate the regulation prohibiting them from lifting weights above 15 kilos, 4 to 5 percent of the women workers worked night shifts on a permanent basis, and in many industrial enterprises the maximum length of night work, as set by law, was exceeded by 100 to 300 percent.

Sociologists who have studied these issues have determined that barely skilled women knowingly chose industries that were hazardous to their health because such jobs were better paid

and gave workers the right to shorter work days and to early retirement. Thus, it was with women workers' tacit consent that the bosses disregarded the existing laws on the protection of women's work, which, at the time, were quite advanced.

In Socialist countries, the principle of "equal pay for equal work" was legally codified. And in fact, in industry and the other economic areas, women were paid the same as men in similar jobs. However, problems emerged in other areas. First, there was a "feminization" of low-wage work; then, to the extent that women occupied positions in a particular field, it would lose its prestige and become poorly paid. Thus, a disparity in salaries between different branches—sometimes even in the same branch of the industry or services—was recreated. The discrepancy attested to a real inequality in the remuneration of "female" and "male" work, but it remained concealed. In the early 1980s, the specifically "female" sectors were commerce and public food services, health care and social welfare, education and culture, and other areas in which wages were a great deal lower than in others, such as industry, construction, or transport. If one takes 100 as the base figure of pay for work in industry, the average wage in the area of commerce and public catering would come to 71, in health and social welfare 64, in national education 69, and in the cultural professions 56. But in those industries in which the workforce was predominantly female—that is, light industries such as food production, textiles, and the pharmaceutical industry—the average wage was one-third lower than the average Soviet wage overall. This disparity could even be seen within a profession, where the average salary for women came to less than two-thirds that of men. Gaps of this sort were evident in almost all Socialist countries: in Czechoslovakia, the wages of women with high levels of seniority only reached two-thirds of that of men; in Hungary, the proportion was between 70 and 80 percent.

Sociologists were inclined to explain these gaps by the fact that women had come to professional training belatedly. However, such explanations struck a paradoxical note, especially when compared to other statistical data concerning the level of women's training.

Women's education has always been seen as a sign of the success of socialism. All women were subject to the law on general and mandatory secondary education. That was why, beginning in the 1960s, 59 percent of the specialists who had secondary- or higher level training were women, according to the *Vestnik statistiki* (Statistical Bulletin), no. 1 (1982). In 1981, 52 percent of the students in higher learning and 56 percent of the pupils in specialized secondary schools were young women. Among all professionals—engineers, agronomists, physicians, and teachers—there were more women than men. These figures attest to the enormous role women played in the life of the country and to their place in the Socialist labor economy. This role was so extensive that in the event of a general women's strike, especially in sectors where the majority of workers were women, the economy would have been threatened by chaos or even complete disintegration. For 66 percent of the Soviet Union's physicians, 74 percent of its teachers, 60 percent of its engineers, 87 percent of its economists and accountants, 45 percent of its agronomists and cattle-breeding technicians, and 40 percent of its scientific researchers were women.

How to explain women's attraction to university-level education? First of all, there is the factor of Russian traditions. The foundations for women's education were laid in the ancien régime and were one of the victories of the Russian women's movement in the 19th century. Thanks to the vitality of this movement, higher education for women was officially recognized by the Russian state and received considerable support from society in the 1870s. In 1876 courses at the Academy of Military Physicians were opened to women. In Saint Petersburg in 1878, courses of higher learning, known as Bestuzhev, named after the professor of history Konstantin Bestuzhev-Ryumin (1829–97), were opened to women. In 1913, 37 percent of the students in St. Petersburg were women.

Other factors were the society's needs and its extreme mobilization of human resources. Economic necessity produced a jump in women's educational levels in almost every Socialist country, for the most part during the 1960s. For example, in Czechoslovakia and Poland, by the 1970s the majority of workers with a secondary education were women, and equal numbers of women and men received a higher education (see Koval'skii). In Rumania during the 1970s, 59 percent of the students in specialized secondary schools, including technical schools, and 43 percent of all university students, were young women. Moreover, these young women showed a strong tendency to choose technical professions such as physics, chemistry, mathematics, and electronics.

Early in the 1980s, women made up 51 percent of the student population in Bulgaria, 51 percent in Hungary, 50 percent in the Germand Democratic Republic, 50 percent in Poland, and 45 percent in Czechoslovakia. In the same period, women's educational levels in the technical professions advanced as well. In the GDR, for example, when they had finished their general and required secondary education, four-fifths of the nation's young people, 45 percent of them women, acquired professional credentials through the system of technical education. In Czechoslovakia, 38 percent of the students in professional and technical education were girls; in Bulgaria this figure was 36 percent, and in Hungary 32 percent (see Cherednichenko). It follows that where general and specialized training was concerned, women in the Socialist countries had practically attained equality with men. Their high level of education and their professional training should have ensured their equality with men in the workplace and in pay. The official publications, notably *Zhenshchiny mira v bor'be za sotsial'nyi progress* (Women of the World Struggling for Social Progress) emphasized—not without reason—that "the solution of the problem of general instruction and its development on the basis of specialized and higher education offers women every possibility of becoming a qualified worker, a specialist, and rising to cadre-level positions in the economy."

And yet this was not the case. Why? What was the source of the inequalities in pay, the difficulties that prevented women from applying their professional training, the obstacles that stood in the way of their promotion, their underrepresentation in leadership positions, and their overrepresentation in subordinate jobs, identified either by poor pay or by difficult working conditions? In fact, all of these traits, which sociologists have defined as sexual segregation in the professional realm, were characteristic of women's work as a whole.

All these problems that appeared so clearly in the period between 1960 and 1980 stemmed from the fact that women's work was modeled on that of men, in such a way that women's professional activity was incompatible with their tasks as moth-ers, educators of children, and housewives, which society expected them to perform as well.

Mother and Educator of Children

As they completed their secondary or higher studies and or received their professional training, young women were at the same time assimilating the principle of equality between men and women that was the foundation of the socialist system of education—an integral part of the socialization that created the ideal socialist personality. Then, sometimes before they had finished their studies, women would typically marry and have children. In the Soviet Union three-quarters of births occurred among women younger than 30 (see Cherednichenko). Having a family and the arrival of children profoundly changed women's existence, much more profoundly so than it did that of their partners. As a general rule, this was the moment when women became aware of the inequality between the sexes—the discrimination against them to which they had not been subjected before, and which, according to received wisdom, came from the natural particularities of their sex. A young couple with university degrees at the beginning of their careers and family life would share domestic tasks equally. They would work in comparable jobs with the same assiduousness and demonstrate equal abilities. Nine months later, the wife would deliver a baby and stay at home with it, while the man would continue to work. The young woman's career was interrupted for some time, while she fulfilled the responsibilities of child and home. To compensate for these additional responsibilities that fell on his wife, and also to support his family materially, the man would work more hours. His career would take off. His knowledge base would increase, as would his professional experience, his efforts, and his salary. His time became more "valuable" than that of his wife. When the child grew older, the wife would go back to work, but the burden of domestic work still fell to her, for her time "brought in" less than that of her husband. This disparity between men and women would become deeper and permanent: the career was his, the domestic concerns, the children's upbringing, and the professional work in whatever time remained were hers. The traditions and the patriarchal mindset that were still current in society, which the woman had not noticed during her student years, were now weighing on her heavily and prevented her from protesting against the order of things. Women's resistance was manifested above all in declining birthrates. A wife could still hope to resume her career after the birth of her first child, but a second child would deal an irreparable blow to her professional ambitions unless she had outside help from another person. No family benefits, no advantage conferred upon mothers, could resolve these contradictions. Worse still, state aid aggravated the dilemma if it were granted to the mother alone and not to the family as a whole, which was the case in all Eastern bloc countries except the GDR.

According to statistics, in the Soviet Union the number of women who temporarily interrupted their professional activity after the birth of a child was low, but these numbers were fairly significant in Hungary, Poland, the GDR, and Czechoslovakia. In the early 1980s in Hungary, 4.6 percent of the women of working age, or 12 percent of all women employed in the economy, chose to take advantage of postnatal support: in other words, they stopped working for a period of up to three years. During the same period in Czechoslovakia, 10.2 percent of the women employed in the economy fell into the same category. It was in precisely those countries with declining populations that the state adopted an active demographic policy, the principal measures of which were paid maternity leaves and family support. In 1967 the Hungarian government decided to provide working mothers with state benefits until the child reached the age of three. The same measure was adopted in Czechoslovakia in 1971, except that there benefits ceased once the child reached the age of two. In Bulgaria, women had the right to a paid maternity leave from six to eight months, then to an unpaid leave of three years; the unpaid leave did, however, count toward their seniority. In Poland from 1972 on, women wage earners had the right to an unpaid leave of two years to raise their child and received state support, the total amount of which depended on the family's income per person and amounted to 50 to 100 percent of the minimum wage. In the USSR, women workers had the right to a partially paid leave until the child had reached the age of one.

Official discourse stressed that measures of this kind were of inestimable importance for mother and child, for such provisions allegedly attested to a public recognition of maternal work. In reality, other issues were involved. The partial compensation for family expenditures in the matter of the children's education and giving women the option to temporarily interrupt their professional activity during the first years of their child's life served, for one thing, to stimulate the birthrate—that is, to improve the demographic health of the countries concerned. For another, the measures helped strengthen the family. Of course, these two results were very important for both the society and the state. The measures listed also allowed for greater compatibility between women's professional activities and her family and maternal obligations. But this was true only to a certain extent, and only when the state benefits were consistent and, at very least, comparable to the minimum wage. In the other cases, women were forced to interrupt their leave and return to work. Sociological polls taken among women with children below the age of one and who, in the mid 1970s, were working in enterprises in Moscow and the Soviet Far East showed that not all women took advantage of the unpaid leave to which they were entitled—far from it. Among them, 17 percent took from four to six months leave, 14 percent from seven to nine months, 63 percent from nine to twelve months, and 6 percent stayed home with their children for 18 months. They cited material difficulties in the family and the impossibility of living on the husband's salary alone to explain their choices (see Lantseva and Markova).

As it massively integrated women into production, the state also had to develop the school and preschool network. Until 1960 the USSR was deficient in this respect: early in the 1960s, only 12.6 percent of the preschool-age children attended day care centers and kindergartens or nursery schools. By the early 1980s the situation had improved: more than 45 percent of the children were placed in such institutions while their mothers were working (see Gruzdeva and Chertikhina 1983). In this respect, the GDR had made greater efforts, with the result that in the mid-1960s, 23 percent of all children below the age of three attended day care centers, 61 percent of the children between three and six were registered in nursery schools, and in the elementary schools more than half of the children stayed

after classes to do their homework under supervision. At the end of the 1970s, almost all children of working mothers in the GDR were attending preschool institutions, which was the highest figure in the Eastern bloc countries.

Women with jobs also experienced difficulties when their children were sick and during summer vacations, as well as in the areas of housing, food, and housekeeping—all of which involved domestic labor. The Socialist state, having initially promised to free women from this burden, had not kept its promise in all cases. Even in a country like the GDR, where the most favorable conditions for employed women had been created, they were obliged to devote more than 40 hours a week to household tasks in a family of four. According to the Dortmund Institute of Physiology, the physical energy expended by housewives, even if they owned electric appliances, was the same as that of a worker doing arduous physical labor. Soviet women were particularly badly off, for in the USSR, what A.I. Kurganov has called "organized poverty" reigned in every area related to family needs. These difficulties specific to Soviet daily life were caused above all by the tasks of building socialism in this enormous, still largely agricultural country, which was rapidly becoming a superpower by systematically robbing its own population. The average Soviet family was continually threatened with the specter of destitution, aggravated by a chronic shortage of all merchandise. In order for families to survive, both wife and husband were forced to work, even when the children were very small. For the most part, it was the wife who did the housework. Thus, her normal day consisted of an eight-hour work day, not including time spent commuting to and from her job (an average of 1.5 hours in Moscow), while, in the early 1960s, the time spent doing her housework could amount to as much as six or seven hours (*Kommunist* [The Communist] 12, no. 9 [1963]).

These figures and facts concealed the phenomenon of the "double" workload, typical of workingwomen, whatever their country might be. The burden was lighter in areas where services were better developed, where household work had been mechanized, and where all members of the family equally shared the domestic work.

But when these ideal conditions had not be met, a woman's daily life was filled with every imaginable and unimaginable difficulty—her job, household chores, the lack of a comfortable residence, insufficient income, shortages of food staples, and so on—and all that was left to her was to limit the number of children in her family. After the first birth, each new pregnancy would become a problem for her, regardless of her desire to have more children. When circumstances were a bit more favorable, she might decide to have a second child, and in exceptional cases a third. These conditions explain the fact that large families, so typical of Eastern European societies, became rare during 1960s and 1970s. Preventing births was a great concern for women, all the more so since contraceptive methods were quite rudimentary, and information about these methods was even less available. For example, in Russia, even today, only 20 percent of the women who need contraception actually have access to it. According to a poll in 1990—the first of its kind—three-quarters of Russian women were not using any contraceptive methods regularly; among these women, 6 percent (12 percent in the rural areas) knew nothing about such methods. Even in the maternity clinics, almost two-thirds of the women surveyed had very little or no information on family planning. Oral contraception was not used in the Soviet Union; imported products were very limited in quantity and were expensive, and only 2 percent of the women using contraceptive methods used the Pill. Intra-uterine devices (primarily the copper T-type), used by 15 to 20 percent of those women who practiced birth control, were manufactured but not available in all locations. According to Monica Fong, 15 to 20 percent of those women practicing birth control used condoms, and 15 to 25 percent practiced coitus interruptus and the temperature method (see Fong). Most physicians and women were convinced that taking hormonal contraceptives was extremely harmful. They used only the most archaic formulas, and even the best-trained doctors in the capital city had only a very remote idea of modern hormonal methods. The number one method of birth control was and still is abortion, and Russia has long held the dubious honor of having the world's highest abortion rates. During the 1970s there were 250 abortions for every 100 live births; this figure fell to 170 in the mid-980s. It was considered normal for a woman to have undergone two or three abortions during her fertile years, and it was not uncommon for a woman to have had eight or ten abortions.

As we have seen, Soviet law has not always tolerated the practice of abortion. Legal changes have been less the result of following changes in mores and the population's behavioral standards, and even less so of heeding women's demands, as happened in the Western countries, than of responding to socio-economic and demographic imperatives. It is worth noting that before the October Revolution, abortion in Russia was prosecuted, and the distribution of contraceptive methods was almost negligible. Public opinion in Russia resolutely condemned any attempt at introducing a new sexual practice based on "owning one's body" and on desire. The timidest mention of birth control, motherhood by conscious choice, or family planning elicited storms of indignation.

Even the women's movements disapproved of attempts to reflect on this issue. As the texts of the first women's conferences early in the 20th century reveal, Russian feminists desperately but vainly tried to sketch out a path by which women, as individuals, might free themselves from the principles of clan-based culture. Feminism thus ran headlong into the obstacles put in its way by cultural tradition, archaic on its deepest levels, which sublimated motherhood, the procreative force, and the life force in women. The protomother, the earth mother, and the Mother of God were the cultural archetypes that defined women's place and functions in society. Russian feminists could not ignore the moral imperatives of this culture, the severity of which bordered on hypocrisy, and which stringently regulated sexual life according to the needs of the clan. Many of them were convinced that motherhood alone would raise women above the level of the everyday and that it was only as mothers—a spiritual and profoundly moral force—that women could transform the world, social life, and political practice. Hence the refusal, so characteristic of the eulogists of Russian feminism, to call on women to take charge of themselves and their bodies, to control their lives by controlling births. On the eve of the revolutionary upheavals of 1917, a passionate debate opposed supporters and adversaries of these ideas within the women's movement in Russia.

After the October Revolution there was nothing further to debate. Civil war, famine, bitter cold, society's general decline, and the dissolution of family ties turned every newborn into a burden, not only for the woman but also for the state. The civil war increased the phenomenon of child abandonment, which became a veritable scourge. This was the determining factor in the state's decision to authorize voluntary terminations of pregnancy. On 18 January 1920, a law was proclaimed allowing doctors to perform abortions under hospital conditions, free of charge. Urban women, and later rural women, made extensive use of this right. In the middle of the 1930s, the number of abortions took on threatening proportions. In Moscow, for example, there were three abortions for every live birth. The government could not fail to see the demographic consequences of this phenomenon. There were two ways possible to neutralize or mitigate the trend: encouraging births with material assistance, or banning abortion. The former would have required a heavy financial investment. The result of the latter might be an increase in clandestine abortions and, consequently, serious threats to women's health and even lives. The government opted for the second choice. Anticipating an inevitable war with its "capitalist environment," the Socialist state used its financial resources first and foremost to develop the country's military defenses, even at the expense of the health of women or the future of children.

A new law passed in 1936 banned abortion, providing for prison sentences of one to two years for those who broke the law. The result was a temporary and very slight increase in births, which soon came down again dramatically. During World War II and the period of economic reconstruction in the 1940s, illegal abortions became very widespread. The harm they did to women's health was obvious, as was the economic loss they caused to the country, whose workforce was almost 50 percent female. Even if illegal abortions went relatively "well," women had to spend a few days at home to recuperate instead of going to work. The government began to understand that it would be more cost-effective to authorize abortions in a hospital setting than to prosecute illegal abortions. Still, although the repressive method had proven to be futile, it would take years before this conclusion was translated into legal action. On 23 November 1955, a law lifted the prohibition against abortion and immediately authorized voluntary terminations of pregnancy in hospitals. But beyond prohibition pure and simple, there were other methods to lower abortion rates, including contraception in all its forms. Why did that remain at such a lamentable level?

Doubtless because contraception meant the freedom of women, who would no longer be forced to reproduce, and for whom motherhood would no longer be a necessity but a right, a desired and consciously chosen path that formed part of the right to plan their own lives. The Soviet state, totalitarian by nature, neither could nor wanted to encourage this liberty and these rights to take root, even to the detriment of immediate economic profit. The authorities even went so far as to use the standards and rules of the traditional culture in order to put moral pressure on women who decided to have an abortion. The whole process of abortion was humiliating for a woman. The doctors and other medical personnel of the establishments to whom she turned received her with blatant crudeness. In accordance with tradition, she was thus punished for the "sin" of her sexual life, which she wished to dissociate from the birth of a child. In this regard, it is almost impossible not to invoke Leo Tolstoy's famous story "The Kreutzer Sonata," whose hero categorizes carnal love as one of the basest aspects of human existence. Speaking through his hero, Tolstoy wanted to show that carnal love was a sin for which the full responsibility lay with women, notoriously immoral creatures, devoid of spirituality and faith, who turned men away from the path of truth. The same attitude toward women was characteristic of the state's politics in the era of Stalin and Brezhnev. In "The Sexual Revolution in Russia" (*Zhenshchina plius* [Women Plus], 1995), the sociologist and sexologist Igor S. Kohn defines this politics as "Soviet sexophobia" and emphasizes that, in Russia, following this sexophobia, "sexual culture and education were completely eradicated in the 1930s, as was erotic art. This intolerance was explained first of all by the control over the individual by means of the power that it [intolerance] allowed."

The ban on sexual freedom was accompanied by an undeclared ban on the distribution of contraceptives, even when abortions had been relegalized. This same prohibitive mentality made abortion into a moral and physical torture for women. When a woman decided to have an abortion, she would have to obtain any numbers of special certificates, each of which would require a long wait. She would be subjected to the rudeness of doctors, while the operation itself would often be done without anesthesia. After such an operation, any semblance of sexual desire would disappear. But some time would pass, and, when the woman discovered to her horror that she was pregnant once more, the whole thing would start all over again. Having an abortion meant that a woman risked everything, including her own life. Public opinion punished her, equating abortion with licentiousness. Quite often, the woman tortured herself as well. This is how the journalist, Tatiana Beliaeva, described her experience in the feminist journal *Maria* in 1982:

> The sin of infanticide torments me. But what can I do when desperate friends come to me asking for help? I try to dissuade them but *the fear of reality* overshadows everything, I remain helpless in coming to their aid and all I am left with is compassion. We already have the greatest difficulty in feeding and raising one child. The complete absence of contraceptive methods, the impossibility of following the prescriptions of hygiene in the conditions of communal housing, and pure and simple medical ignorance [push women to abortion].

One can say without exaggeration that for the women of Eastern Europe, abortion was no longer a medical operation but a difficult existential problem, upon which both her personal life and the life of society depended in a great many ways.

The debates over women's issues at the end of the 1970s in every developed Socialist country slowly but surely led to these conclusions. These debates were intermittent and would sometimes die down, only to flare up again with renewed force. They addressed questions such as the "destiny" of each sex and woman's place in society, or traditions and their influence on the modern family. Journalists called for "preserving the family" or "preserving men." The prevailing mindset was limited to clichés about bringing woman's personality back to motherhood or to the role of the modern workingwoman (always in connection with the needs of the family). Almost no one mentioned the problem underlying these discussions: the real contradictions that emerged when one sought to apply the principle of woman's liberty and equality in socialist society, and her everyday relations with the world when she introduced her own interests and requirements into that world. It could not be otherwise in a society where the interests of the "clan"—that is to say of the Socialist state—were placed above the individual, whether woman or man. In its own interest, the clan perpetuated the traditional division of labor: the home for women, everything outside the home for men. This division hurt the interests of women and men alike. The most perceptive observers who dared to mention the problem ran into a wall of general incomprehension. The Czech sociologist Ivo MoÂni stated: "The family is much less accessible to the man than the sphere of paid work is to the woman" (paper given at the International Colloquium on Women, UNESCO, Prague, 1991)—a very precise and very correct observation. What was much less obvious was that certain areas of the work of society remained almost inaccessible to women.

The "Cook" Who Runs the State

The exclusion of women was most conspicuous in the area of state administration. The complete absence of women in the places where real political decisions were made was camouflaged by grand declarations boasting about women's political equality, the active part they were taking in building socialist society, and their presence in the presidencies of conferences and official assemblies, as well as in the intermediary and upper echelons of legislative power. In the official speeches, reference was readily made to the precepts of Lenin: "If women do not independently take part not only in political life but also in the permanent, political daily work of all citizens, there can be no question of speaking of socialism, or even of a solid and true democracy." To show that such a democracy had become a reality in the USSR, the following figures were cited: by 1939, 33.1 percent of the locally elected Soviets were women, and in 1971 this proportion went up to 45.8 percent; in 1952, 26 percent of the deputies of the Supreme Soviet were women, and in 1970 this figure was 31 percent (see Koval'skii). It was also stressed that Soviet women were widely using their right to vote and to stand for election. For example, 99 percent of the women voted in elections; women participated in nominating candidates for elections, and then in the electoral campaigns, either to support candidates or to campaign on their own behalf. The authorities argued that women played an important role "in mass organizations such as unions, especially at the level of companies, as well as in the cooperatives and in youth organizations." They explained that "women make an important contribution to the political life of the country, in the companies' councils of women, in the women's committees of the unions and friendship associations with foreign countries" (*Zhenshchiny i deti v SSSR* [1969; Women and Children in the USSR]).

Official statistics in the other Socialist countries showed similar results. For example, in Bulgaria, 41 women were elected to Parliament in 1961, and 70 women in 1966, which was 17 percent of the total number of deputies; in the same year, 20 percent of the new municipal counselors were women. In 1970, women made up 20 percent of the Hungarian Parliament, 31.4 percent of the East German Parliament, and 13.5 percent of the Polish Parliament. These were impressive figures when compared to the same statistics for Western countries. The problem, however, was precisely that these data were not comparable. In the Socialist countries, legislative power was not elected and the electorate voted for the only candidates selected by the party beforehand. Moreover, Eastern European parliaments had no real power and were nothing more than purely decorative assemblies that met from time to time in order to approve decisions already made by the Communist parties. Under these circumstances, it was not all that costly to introduce women into such structures.

Real power lay in the Communist parties of the Eastern European countries. To be sure, there were women party members. For example, 26.5 percent of the members or the candidate members of the United Socialist Party of the GDR were women (Seventh Congress of the United Socialist Party of Germany, Moscow, 1968). In the Hungarian Socialist Workers Party the proportion was 22.9 percent (Ninth Congress of the Hungarian Socialist Workers Party, Moscow, 1967). In the Polish Unified Workers Party the figure was 20.5 percent (Fifth Congress of the Polish Unified Workers Party, Moscow, 1969). The Communist Party of the USSR, which originally defined itself as the "avant-garde detachment of the working class" (statutes of 1934), then as "the union of combat and Communist ideas" (statutes of 1952), and finally as "the avant-garde of the Soviet people," counted 3 million women in its ranks, according to the official data. To what extent did these 3 million women exert an influence on the party's decisions? In 1966–67, women made up 54.2 percent of the Soviet population and 20.9 percent of the Communist Party. In the Central Committee of the CPSU, however, women accounted for only 2.8 percent, while the Politburo and the Secretariat of the Central Committee were composed entirely of men. Thus, women were absent from the leadership bodies that truly governed the country. It was extremely rare for women to hold positions of leadership in municipal or regional committees of the party, which were the administrative bodies of the daily life of the country.

Generally speaking, the higher one moved in the administrative hierarchies, whatever they were, the fewer women there were to be found. For example, of the total number of researchers in the Academy of Sciences as of 1 January 1966, women made up 51 percent of the researchers, 23 percent of the directors of research, and 8.8 percent of the academicians. In the area of education, women composed 87 percent of the teachers of the first classes, 68 percent of the teachers of the last two classes, 74 percent of the principals of elementary schools, and 21 percent of the principals of secondary schools. In industry, as of 1 January 1961, women made up 59 percent of company technicians; 37 percent of the engineers; 24 percent of the construction managers; 12 percent of the foremen; and 6 percent of the company directors. The same picture emerges in the realm of agriculture. The 26 November 1967 issue of *Izvestia* contained an article entitled "The Work of the Female Farmer," which observed: "One recalls the dozens of work brigades of the collective farms, in which the subordinates as a general rule were women, while the head of the brigade was invariably a man." In 1965, in the Russian Federation women made up only 1 percent of the directors of the state farms, while 2 percent of the directors of the collective farms were women (*Partiinaia zhizn'* [Party Life] no. 3, 1965). It is obvious that Lenin's plan to "teach a cook how to govern the state," to "introduce women into politics" (see Lenin, vols. 34 and 42) had been disregarded. In the early 1960s, Khrushchev complained that there were almost no women to be found among the leaders of the country and con-

cluded demagogically: "In short, we have men for leading and women for working" (Speech to the Assembly of Agricultural Workers of Ukraine, *Izvestia*, 24 December 1961). Khrushchev was right: in spite of all the mass organizations, councils, and committees, women were kept far from any real participation in the process of decision making, both in the USSR and in the other Socialist countries. The true power structures that developed domestic and foreign policy in these countries were closed to women. And even when a woman such as the Bulgarian Tsola Dragoicheva, who was endowed with a most uncommon organizing talent and with a rich activist experience, managed to reach the heights of power, her presence there did not change much. It was still a "male" politics conducted by a paternalist state, in which woman was an object and not a subject. Leonid Brezhnev's speech to the 25th Congress of the Communist Party of the Soviet Union illustrated this state of affairs very clearly: "The Party deems it to be its duty to be continuously concerned with women, in order to improve her situation as an actor in the work process, as mother and educator of children, and as a housewife" (25th Congress of the CPSU, Moscow, 1976).

In fact, women in the Eastern bloc countries demanded no other power than that of mother and wife. The powerful feminist movement that took off in the West during the 1960s did not appear to have touched Eastern Europe. However, this was in appearance only.

Feminism in Eastern Europe

In Russia, feminism was born in the middle of the 19th century and, as everywhere else, the movement raised the issues of female solidarity and mutual aid in the defense of women's right to work, to education, to civil recognition, and to equality in political rights. In 1917 the women's movement was already a recognized political force, with its leaders and its network of organizations, its publications, and its press. As soon as the movement got off the ground, however, Soviet power prohibited all women's and feminist organizations and the publications originated in their ambit. It even forbade the very term "feminism" and took full responsibility for connecting women to political and social life.

The rebirth of feminism did not occur until the end of the 1970s, in the wake of the human rights movement, partly under the influence of Western neofeminism, but above all as a reaction to "Soviet emancipation." During this period, the human rights movement counted numerous women in its ranks. Not only were they the mainstays of the movement—typists, copy editors, and readers—they also suggested new ideas and demonstrated their initiative. Citing the names of Natal'ia Gorbanevskaia, Ludmila Alexeieva, Malva Landal, and Tatiana Khodorovich, among many others, should suffice to measure women's contribution to these efforts. In Leningrad, other women of particular note included Yulia Voznesenskaia, Tatiana Goricheva, Tatiana Mamonova, and Natalia Malakhovskaia, who were in fact the founders of the feminist movement within the human rights movement.

In 1979, there were several samizdat magazines in Leningrad—clandestine publications primarily devoted to questions of culture and unofficial religion. The best known of these were *The Clock* and *37*. They collaborated most ungraciously with women who wanted to write about "women's" subjects, on the grounds that such articles were too closely tied to current events and that they broke with the generally distant and reflective tone of the Leningrad samizdat. The female authors who were close to these publications insisted precisely on the need to treat "women's" subjects. Having been turned down by the editors, they decided to establish their own magazine, *Maria*. The goal stated in the first issue, in 1981, was to "unmask the myth according to which the lot of women in the USSR was free of problems"—to tell the truth about women's situation in order to improve it.

Why was this publication born in Leningrad? Perhaps because, in that city, the human rights movement was closely connected to the one that opposed official culture, which counted many more women than in other cities, so that people at the time often referred to the "feminization" of Leningrad culture. Another possible reason is that in Leningrad the everyday life of dissident families differed greatly from life in Moscow. Leningrad was an impoverished, uncomfortable city where women carried a double burden: that of the struggle for freedom and, at the same time, that of exhausting daily worries. Finally, as the dissidents said at the time, in Leningrad it was impossible to find real men except among the women.

In a very short time, a group of women prepared an almanac on women in Russia for publication by the end of 1979. In addition to Voznesenskaia, Goricheva, Malakhovskaia, and Mamonova—all cited above—noteworthy contributors included E. Doron, L. Vasilieva, G. Grigorieva, N. Lazareva, A. Lauva, D. Levitina, N. Lukina, T. Mikhailova, R. Romanova, A. Sariban, S. Sokolova, and G. Khamova (later there would be others). The KGB seized the almanac as soon as it appeared. However, these women received support from Western feminists and prepared to publish a new magazine, entitled *Maria*. This magazine became the nucleus of the first Soviet feminist club, which took the same name. The first issue of *Maria* appeared in 1981. It opened with an "Address to the Women of Russia" stating the following:

> We are on the brink of utter loss, on the spiritual, moral, and physical level. A monstrous wave of nihilism and numbness is sweeping away every cultural and spiritual value: families are becoming dislocated, the people are drowning in alcohol, crime has risen catastrophically, and the birthrate is plummeting. . . . Under these conditions, the Russian woman suffers not less, but more than others. As before, she continues to be the slave of a slave, and the rope she wears around her neck pulls at her twice as painfully as it pulls at men. . . . Humanity, directed at the acquisition of material goods, is being shipwrecked both in the West and in the East. But in Russia we have gone even further: we have tried, at the price of a bloody revolution, to let justice reign on earth, we have killed God, we have exterminated millions of people—and the very best among them, and presently we are reaping what we have sown: our life is mutilated, torn to shreds, and it holds no light or consolation. . . . If humanity does not turn its gaze away from expansion and wars, if it does not turn to the "feminist" values so disdained today, it will be sentenced to inevitable destruction and death.

Thick and chock full of information, the magazine provided documentary evidence of a feminist consciousness that was caught up in restless wandering, in search of spiritual solace in a despiritualized world. This quest developed in every possible direction, from theory and religion to practical everyday problems.

The women of Leningrad presented themselves as a "democratic community in action," a community that refused all forms of hierarchy and subordination. According to them, it was precisely hierarchy and subordination that that formed the structural basis of totalitarianism—which they considered evil incarnate on earth and saw as the very nature of the Communist system. In their view, the system was strong because it penetrated every pore of society; it permeated everyday human relationships. The metastases of the system were even corrupting the human rights movement:

> The groups that defend the rights of man and the literary and artistic associations of the "second culture" have been contaminated with the following evils: the thirst for power, with its attendant vices, and the thirst for a leader whom one can follow, whom one can blindly obey; the intolerance of any different thought (including from those who pride themselves on thinking "differently"); and severe demands imposed upon those of lower rank and complete lack of control of the leaders, with their total power, their dogmatism, and their demagogy. There is no way out of this nightmare!

The group also presented itself as a "feminist community" that was close to, but also different from, Western feminism. The connections with Western feminism were apparent in the promotion of "feminist" values such as nonviolence and creativity. The difference lay in the Leningrad feminists' attitude toward men:

> We do not consider our movement to be anti-male, and we feel no hatred whatsoever toward the other sex. But we reject, we declare war, on hermaphrodism as a means of shaping "the state-controlled human being." Our counter to Bolshevik hermaphrodism is the development of woman in the fullness and beauty of her sex. . . . We do not reject the traditional union of man and woman, but we believe that it can be real only between a free man and a free woman.

Maria was thus a feminist and educational magazine, devoted to the defense of human rights, calling for a "religious rebirth of Russia as a brotherhood founded on Christian love." In other words, the magazine was an expression both of feminism and of the spiritual values of the Orthodox Church, the combined image of which was that of the Virgin Mary, "the merciful, eternally feminine power, rising up high above the world."

This clear orientation toward religous orthodoxy—a strange one for feminism, which is by nature a movement of the Left, formed in a struggle against the patriarchal society consecrated by Christianity—was far from accidental. This spiritual bent was a reaction against vulgar, materialistic ideas and the practices of emancipation as they had been set in official Soviet politics and culture. During the first theoretical lecture organized by the magazine's editors, Tatiana Goricheva said:

Without any doubt, we must fight for the political and social rights of women, we must demand equality in rights and equality in fact with men, but for all that it must not be forgotten that this equality can become an equality of slaves equally deprived of rights, that no social revolution will be able to emancipate women if it is not also a spiritual revolution.

In this revolution, according to Leningrad feminists, women were destined to play a major role. They were called upon to bring "feminine" values to the world and consolidate them there—the ability to love and to sacrifice everything for that love, in the name of that love, to live by one's heart and not by one's reason. They saw this sacrificial self-affirmation as the road to freedom, for the individual and for all humankind.

This road involved a quest for spiritual truth and a denunciation of the official lie about "work and daily life" of Soviet women. By analyzing and describing the realities of women's work and everyday experience, the magazine—the only one in the country to do so—gathered and published a great deal of concrete information on divorces and abortions, the true state of nursery schools and hospitals, homeless women, prostitution, drugs, alcoholism, and incest: all topics that attested to the social violence inflicted upon women. The Leningrad feminists were the first to speak out loud and clear about this violence and about the complete absence of defenses for women within Soviet society. Their prognosis was rather pessimistic: "It is unlikely," stated the magazine, "that women's situation can improve. The economic crisis is worsening, the prices of food staples are increasing, there is ever more drunkenness and crime, and daily life grows more and more hellish." What, then, were the editors of *Maria* hoping for? "We expect changes in the spiritual life of women," they wrote, "for the feeling of inner freedom is growing within them, as is the desire to break forth from the tomb in which they are being buried alive."

The magazine also dealt with themes of general politics. Articles mentioned the place of women in the human rights movement and the profound crisis that gripped the USSR in the early 1980s. The writers of *Maria* were among the courageous, almost desperate, few to openly express their indignation at the war in Afghanistan and protest against it.

The feminist movement has taken the lead in the protest of mothers against the war, and one of its first objectives is to fight for peace, by explaining to mothers what the war in Afghanistan really is, urging them to tear up the summons from the army, and calling upon them to realize that for their sons, an honorable prison sentence is preferable to a shameful death as a soldier-aggressor.

Naturally, the feminists' stance aroused an immediate reaction from the authorities. The KGB kept a close eye on the activists, and its agents "looked after" the editors 24 hours a day. Shortly after the publication of *Maria*, its editors were told to leave the country and threatened with heavy jail sentences should they refuse. Voznesenskaia, Goricheva, Mamonova, and Malakhovskaia emigrated, while those who remained continued the work of gathering information and preparing subsequent issues of the magazine. Despite all their efforts, *Maria* ceased to exist at the end of 1982. According to Malakhovskaia, six issues of the magazine had been published, three of them abroad with the help of Western feminists, and these can be consulted today. It is not known what happened to the other three issues, as it is difficult to know the fate of the women who remained in Russia.

The magazine *Maria* apprised its readers of the existence of Polish feminists. Its third issue (1982) contained a long letter by Sabina Gweiman, one of the founders of the Neofeminist Association created in Warsaw in 1960. The author wrote: "All in all we were just a handful of young girls who, in October 1980, organized the first feminist meeting in the student club Sygma." The Polish feminists, like their Russian friends, were united by the idea that their compatriots had to be educated in the spirit of resistance to the hidden discrimination the authorities wanted to pass off as emancipation. In the course of their monthly meetings and discussions, the Polish feminists put together an action program and a manifesto of their movement. These documents stressed several essential problems, phrased as demands. First, they required paid maternity leave for three years after the birth of a child instead of the 16-week maternity leave or the paid maternity leave of three years demanded by the Solidarity movement. Second, a new policy with regard to pregnant students or those who were already mothers, who should be given the option of finishing their studies and taking their exams. Third, general improvement in gynecological, obstetrical, and pediatric services, as well as changes in the traditionally harsh and insulting attitudes of health care personnel toward women in childbirth and other female patients. Fourth, a change in women's wages, which averaged 60 percent of men's wages, in violation of the constitutional principle of equality in work. Fifth, an improvement in the quality of contraceptive methods, and sufficient supplies and correct information about birth control. Sixth, the end of all hidden discrimination against women in both university entrance and hiring practices.

The Polish feminists put these requirements forward as social demands and saw their task as forcing society to recognize them as such. In other words, they posed the problem of the social nature of the relations between the sexes and the awakening of a social conscience in men and women.

From the beginning of their activity, both Polish and Russian feminists experienced not only persecution by the power structure but also the hostility of public opinion, which saw these women as nothing more than ridiculous, irritating, and ignorant failures who had fallen short in their private lives. Nevertheless, it was precisely the feminists who set the example of resisting the state-controlled, bureaucratic "emancipation" that made women into asexual robots, machines programmed to fulfill productive and reproductive "social functions." Their discourse evoked concrete, living people and the daily life of their compatriots, who were very far removed from the myth of the most liberated, most emancipated woman in the whole world.

The appearance of the first feminist groups in the USSR and in Poland, also in Hungary, Czechoslovakia, and Yugoslavia, can be considered a covert progression toward female emancipation in the Eastern European countries. It was with difficulty that these women broke a path through the reinforced concrete of official mythology, with its images of the "working woman" and "reproducer of the species" that had been imposed on women. Their feminism grew out of these women's desire to understand how to exist in the new world of work, how to defend their human dignity, how to remain full-fledged human beings—subjects and not objects in history. Added to this were women's thoughts on ways in which to combine work and domestic responsibilities, children's education and career, to build new relations based on partnership with their spouses, and finally to influence the process of decision making in society, to change the world in which they were living. It was quite a solid basis for a new feminist consciousness, a social consciousness that was the only guarantee that true equality and freedom would come into being. This new feminist consciousness, born under the leaden blanket of Communist ideology, was nourished by the unofficial culture and the counterculture that survived even during the terrible years of Stalinist terror. The brief period of the "thaw," and then the years of the quest for "socialism with a human face," which posed the problem of the living individual as the measure of any social system, had in their own ways stimulated the appearance of this consciousness. In response to this search, the official ideology increasingly looked to Charles Fourier's famous formula, according to which extending rights to women was a general measure of all social progress. The feminist movement, in turn, proclaimed that equalization of rights was impossible if opportunities were not equal. Such were the end results of the Eastern European attempt to bring about equality between women and men by means of, and under, the aegis of state ideology.

Bibliography

V s"ezd Pol'skoi ob"edinennoi rabochei partii (The Fifth Congress of the Unified Polish Worker's Party), Moscow: Izd-vo Polit. Lit-ry, 1969

VII s"ezd Sotsialisticheskoi edinoi partiii Germanii (The Seventh Congress of the Unified Socialist Party of Germany), Moscow: Izd-vo Polit. Lit-ry, 1968

Cherednichenko, G.A., "Molodaia zhenshchina v sotsialisticheskom obshchestve" (The Young Woman in Socialist Society), in *Rol' zhenshchiny v sovremennom obshzhestve k itogam X-letiia OON: Sbornik statei* (The Role of Women in Modern Society on the 10th Anniversary of the United Nations Organization: Collected Articles), parts 1 and 2, Moscow:1985

Fong, Monica S., *The Role of the Women in Rebuilding the Russian Economy*, Washington, D.C.: World Bank, 1993

Gruzdeva, E.V., and E.S. Chertikhina, *Trud i byt sovetskikh zhenshchin* (Work and Daily Life of Soviet Women), Moscow: Izd-vo Polit. Lit-ry, 1983

Gruzdeva, E.V., and E.S. Chertikhina, "Professional'naia zaniatost' zhenshchin v SSSR i oplata ix truda (The Professional Occupation of Women in the USSR and the Payment for Their Work)," *Rabochii klass i sovremennyi mir* (The Working Class and the Contemporary World) 16, no. 3 (1986)

Kollontai, A., *Trud zhenshchiny v evoliutsii khoziaistva* (Women's Work in the Evolution of the Economy), Moscow: Gos. Izd-vo, 1923

Kollontai, A., *Liubov' pchel trudovykh*, Moscow: Gos. Izd-vo, 1923; as *Love of Worker Bees*, translated by Cathy Porter, London: Virago, 1977; Chicago: Academy Press, 1978

Konstitutsiia (Osnovnoi Zakon) Soiuza Sovetskikh Sotsialisticheskikh Respublik (Constitution [Basic Law] of the Union of Soviet Socialist Republics), Moscow: Politizdat, 1977

Kourilsky, Chantal, "La Constitution de l'URSS de 1977 et la famille," *Annuaire de législation française et étrangère* (new series) 26 (1977)

Koval'skii, N.A., editor, *Zhenshchiny mira v bor'be za sotsial'nyi progress* (Women of the World Struggling for Social Progress), Moscow: Mysl', 1972

Kurganov, I.A., *Zhenshchiny i kommunizm* (Women and Communism), New York: n.p., 1968

Lantseva, M.S., and V.I. Markova, editors, *Voprosy oplaty truda i urovnia zhizni naseleniia* (Questions of Wages and Living Standards of the Population), Moscow: Nauch.-Issl. in-t Truda Gos. Komiteta SSSR po Trudu i Sots. Voprosam, 1978

Lenin, V.I., *Polnoe sobranie sochinenii* (Complete Collected Works), 55 vols., Moscow: Gos. Izd-vo Polit. Lit-ry, 1958–65; see especially vols. 31, 34, 42

Mandel'shtam, O.E., "Gumanizm i sovremennost [1923]," in *Izbrannoe* (Selections), by Mandel'shtam, Tallinn, Estonia: Eesti Raamat, 1989; as "Humanism and the Present," in *Mandelstam: The Complete Critical Prose and Letters*, edited by Jane Gary Harris, translated by Jane Gary Harris and Constance Link, Ann Arbor, Michigan: Ardis, 1979

Maria 1981, n° 1; 1982, n° 3.

Materialy XXV s"ezda KPSS, Moscow: Politizdat, 1976

Mayzesova, D., "Situation présente de la femme en Tchécoslovaquie QcF, intervention au Colloque international sur les femmes, UNESCO, Prague, 3–6 December 1991

Narodnoe khoziaistvo SSSR v [1965] gody (The Economy of the USSR [in 1965]) (1966)

Narodnoe khoziaistvo SSSR za 60 let (The Soviet National Economy in the Course of the Last 60 Years), Moscow: Statistika, 1977

Nikol'skii, A., *IX s"ezd Vengerskoi sotsialisticheskoi rabochei partii* (The Ninth Congress of the Working-Class Socialist Party of Hungary), Moscow: Izd-vo Polit. Lit-ry, 1967

Rol' zhenshchiny v sovremennom obshzhestve k itogam X-letiia OON: Sbornik statei (The Role of Women in Modern Society on the Tenth Anniversary of the United Nations Organization: Collected Articles), parts 1 and 2, Moscow: 1985

Shineleva, L.T., *Zhenshchina i obshchestvo* (Women and Society), Moscow: Izd-vo Polit. Lit-ry, 1990

Statisticheskii spravochnik po Leningradu (Statistical Guide to Leningrad), Leningrad: 1930

V.I. Lenin o roli zhenshchiny v obshchestve i opyt resheniia zhenskogo voprosa v sotsialisticheskikh stranakh (Lenin on the Role of Women in Society and the Attempt at Solving the Woman Question in Socialist Countries), Moscow: n.p., 1972

Zakonodatel'stvo o pravakh zhenshchin v SSSR (Legislation on Women's Law in the USSR), Moscow: IUrid. Lit-ra, 1975

Zhenshchiny v SSSR (Women in the USSR) (1975)

Zhenshchiny v SSSR (Women in the USSR) (1989)

Zhenshchiny i deti v SSSR (Women and Children in the USSR) (1963)

Zhenshchiny i deti v SSSR (Women and Children in the USSR) (1969)

FEMINISM IN THE 1970S

DOMINIQUE FOUGEYROLLAS-SCHWEBEL

Emergence of the Feminist Movement

THE EMERGENCE OF THE feminist movement at the end of the 1960s generated a veritable shock wave. It marked the convergence of a series of transformations in the economic, social, and cultural spheres, as well as transformations in the balance of political power. The emerging feminist movement also coincided with several "breakthrough" political phenomena that affected society as a whole, from the radical critique of the extreme Left to the mobilization of women as a potentially united political force, embracing those women who were involved in promoting women's issues within national and international organizations, those who fought to make contraception available, and those who struggled in unions and political organizations. The feminist shock wave began in the United States and very quickly spread to Great Britain and Germany in the 1960s. The widespread and explosive student unrest of 1968 provided fertile ground for the dissemination of feminism, and the highly publicized appearance of the American women's movement in 1970 lent impetus to European movements. Anglophone feminists in Canada generally shared the perspective of feminists in the United States, while for the women of Quebec the feminist movement was a part of the claim to nationhood. Feminist movements in Portugal, Spain, and Greece grew out of the planning and realization of the International Year of Women celebrated in 1975.

In the 1960s, the polemics surrounding the development of "mass culture" enabled the sociologist Edgar Morin, in his work *L'Esprit du temps* (1962; The Spirit of the Times) to show the new requirements of modern life: a liberalization of mores, a new quest for happiness through sexual fulfillment, and the development within the mass media of a women's mass culture— a true and specific "subculture." In concrete terms, however, this new ideal resulted in exaggerated expectations with regard to private life, and it was essentially reduced to the status of a commodity within the vast marketplace of leisure consumption. This brought further criticism of capitalist society, charged not only with the exploitation of the working classes but with being technocratic and repressive. According to Herbert Marcuse, who collaborated in the work of the Frankfurt School before fleeing

Nazi Germany in 1933, the forces of freedom and social dissent were no longer limited to the organized labor movement but were expressed in every movement that challenged norms of any kind, whether economic or cultural. There thus arose the need to seek new forms of social solidarity capable of embodying the struggle against what Marcuse termed "one-dimensional alienation" (*One-Dimensional Man*, 1964). It was within this theoretical context that feminism took root. This meant that issues relating to private life—conjugal happiness, parent-child relationships, sexuality within the couple, and childhood sexuality— were topical and widely discussed, not only in women's magazines but in the major weekly news magazines as well.

In the 1960s the appearance of the birth-control pill—sold first in the United States and the Scandinavian countries, while the Catholic countries placed restrictions on its distribution— lent fresh vigor to family-planning movements. For the first time, women's control over contraception was discussed, and the major newsweeklies as well as women's magazines devoted long articles to the future of the family and women's attainment of sexual independence. When the new study of sexual behavior by William H. Masters and Virginia E. Johnson (*Human Sexual Response*, 1966) was published, it was widely distributed both in the United States and abroad. Sustained by increasingly precise knowledge and descriptions, debates on female sexuality revealed new demands with respect to orgasm. These debates engendered greater freedom to deal with sexual issues—a freedom that is one aspect of what is generally called the "sexual revolution."

The feminist movement thus arose in the climate of heightened awareness and concern that attended the condemnation of the malaise and many neuroses of consumer society. When young women voiced their protests, sexual issues were the very first concerns pushed to center stage, whether explicitly or less directly.

The earliest impetus to the rise of the women's movement came from student movements and groups of the extreme Left, or the New Left. These leftist groups had been reinvigorated by their actions undertaken in solidarity with national liberation movements in Africa, Latin America, Cuba, and Asia, and quite specifically by the large-scale uprisings that, throughout the 1960s, took place in reaction to the escalation of the Vietnam

War, mainly at the time of the deployment of American expeditionary forces and later during the bombings of North Vietnam in February 1965 by President Lyndon B. Johnson's government. In the same period, the split between pro-Soviet and pro-Chinese factions polarized the Communist world, leading to its reorganization. The fall of 1965 marked the outbreak of the Cultural Revolution—a revolution within a revolution that resulted from the clash between the concerted actions of the core of leaders directed by Mao and a groundswell of criticism of the regime expressed in the youth movements. The Red Guards of the youth movement embodied the revolutionary dynamic of the masses and became a widely disseminated symbol in the protest movements of Western students. Finally, China's foreign policy positions made it into the privileged defender of Third World countries—a posture that kept the realities of the autocratic Chinese regime largely hidden from view. Nevertheless, the Cultural Revolution also served as a source of symbols for feminist movements, for it granted women—"half of heaven" according to the Chinese expression then in vogue—an important role in the critique of society.

In the United States, as in Canada and Europe, feminism emerged in the context of a bourgeoning counterculture, including the hippie movement and the activities of various underground groups. This cultural evolution entailed a condemnation of the most normative and repressive aspects of the social values of Western societies: the monitoring and restrictions of juvenile sexuality and the repression of homosexuality. The denunciation of sexual repression became became specifically channeled into a public protest movement for the rights and freedom of homosexuals, first in New York in the spring of 1969, then in the rest of North America and in Europe. The paradox here was that the feminist movement would claim as its mandate the politicization of questions that had been pushed to the margins of traditional politics at the very same time that the radical protests against society that all liberation movements entail—the refusal of norms of any kind, the call for spontaneity as instinctual truth—also called for the rejection of all politics. Since all forms of institutionalization were considered tantamount to death, the protests did not aim at building a new society: a political system capable of resolving social issues simply did not exist. Caught up in this paradoxical logic, the feminist movement of the 1970s bore the mark of contradiction in its early stages. Thus, on the one hand, there were calls for reform or for the creation of new rights to ensure women's complete integration into society, and concomitantly, on the other hand, a rejection of all forms of institutionalization, which was seen as the source of the alienation of the individual.

The schisms in the organizations of the New Left in North America and extreme leftist groups in Europe occurred because of the reiterated refusal of these organizations to recognize women's issues as political issues. These movements, and particularly the organizations of the extreme Left in Europe, condemned the traditional parties of the Left as reformist and called for a renewal of Marxism, for a return to radicalism that the practice of social-democratic power had supposedly corrupted. But these extreme leftist factions were blinded by their perception of women's demands as bourgeois. While they criticized as illusory the concept of equality formally espoused by capitalist society, they nonetheless believed that the rights women had obtained would lead to real equality in practice. Thus, in the

early stages, the radical Left rejected the "woman question" as it had been paternalistically posed by the traditional Left.

In the case of the youngest female activists, confrontation with their party's comrades actually constituted their first experience with discrimination. These were female students who had not yet entered professional life and who had received an education that was relatively equal for girls and boys; they came from families aspiring to social promotion of their children through study. Once the gendered division of labor in militant endeavors had been pointed out, women's place within activist organizations became a topic of discussion throughout the world. Militant work resulted in a split between relatively menial tasks, which were often performed by women (secretarial tasks, responsibility for equipment and facilities, administration), and, on the other hand, political responsibilities (public speaking, decision making, the drafting of motions). Of course, women were not excluded from this second category of tasks, but few women were involved at this level—among them those who would later protest against discrimination.

The first feminist demonstrations drew a chorus of invectives from different quarters: leftist groups condemned feminism as being bourgeois in its concerns, while American activists decried the reduction of feminist issues to a merely individual or personal level. The attacks that characterized feminism as a concern of middle-class or lower-middle-class women exemplified the kind of sexism that Simone de Beauvoir's analyses in *Le deuxième sexe* (1949; *The Second Sex*) had helped bring to light: as soon as women express themselves politically, she argued, they are not criticized based on the logic of their analysis; instead, they are expected to account for their social status. Naturally, this kind of sexism was not the sole prerogative of the male members of activist organizations and political groups, as female comrades also played a powerful role in the name-calling among different groups or tendencies. What was specifically "macho" and could be found in various countries—notoriously so, for example, in the United States, Germany, and France—was the insulting accusation that women activists were "frustrated," "needed to get laid," and so forth. Such insinuations undoubtedly should be viewed as a caricature of relationships between men and women. The fact remains that they attested to the social legitimacy of the strong humiliating the weak: the "stronger" sex ridiculing the other.

Feminists had no trouble responding to these attacks. Irony, sarcasm, humor, and derision became the weapons of choice in a struggle in which the manner in which otherness was articulated would henceforth appear not only as a philosophical question but clearly as a societal issue as well. More or less insulting terms were then claimed and parodied by feminists as group names: WITCH (Women's International Terrorist Conspiracy from Hell, a group created in New York in 1968, which developed in various American cities such as Washington, Chicago, San Francisco, and Boston, as well as on the campuses of several universities); Bitch; the group Weiberrat (Meddler's Council) in Frankfurt; the Redstockings (a play on "bluestocking"), a New York group whose name was later taken up by Danish feminists; the Chimeras; the Gouines Rouges (Red Dykes) in France, and so on.

The time had come to avenge the usual discrediting of autonomous women's ventures; a veritable catharsis was being played out on the public stage. The first demonstrations in public buildings and in the streets were among other things demonstrations of exuberant joy. Media coverage helped to propagate and amplify the demonstrations. Feminists came into the spotlight through scandal and provocation: counterdemonstrations during the Miss America pageant, protests at the election of Miss World in Great Britain, demonstrations on the Tomb of the Unknown Soldier in Paris, invasions of the French Estates-General by the weekly *Elle*, takeovers of buses in Copenhagen. The forms of provocation differed from country to country. It was often noted that such demonstrations with their eccentricity and their excesses potentially alienated some women. This is no doubt true. But it should also be reiterated that the feminist demonstrations drew immediate sympathy from other women, and this became an asset. The resonance among women as a group was soon translated into broad participation in and support for the mass campaigns of the women's movement. If endless articles were able to assert that the new women's movements had been born spontaneously, it was in part because these movements indeed did not claim any affiliation with existing groups. Quite the contrary; the new movements proclaimed their break with earlier women's associations and criticized the reformist and paternalistic practices of those earlier associations. The emphatic valorization of spontaneity by the new women's movements should be interpreted not as an effect of their appearance "out of nowhere," but rather as a sign of their resolve to restore to women the responsibility for their own destiny rather than relying on what "experts" had to say. The new feminism appeared at a juncture when considerations and conjectures on the transformation of women's condition were omnipresent. What new status should women have? What would become of children if women started working? Would love be changed? Where did the fight for family planning stand? What was the future of relationships between men and women?

To understand the imperative need for a condemnation of the place traditionally allotted to women, the feminist protests of the late 1960s must be placed in the broader context of economic and social developments following World War II. Indeed, for all countries of North America and Europe, in contrast to the days after World War I, economic development in the wake of World War II relied on a growing demand for labor, first in the industrial sector and then in the service sector. In all of these countries this translated into an increase in wage-earning labor by women, which meant a growing participation of married women in the workforce, generally until the birth of a first child. The escalating demands for waged workers, a new phenomenon of the postwar period, was of course directly related to the modes of industrialization in local economies, but it was the dominant feature of the postwar period everywhere. As is well known, the growing demand for labor coincided with the development of the Ford-style assembly-line mode of production, predicated on the mass production of consumer goods. The industrial production of household appliances as well as the expansion of social services contributed to the transformation of household life styles.

In the immediate aftermath of the war, with the expansion of the job market and the perspective of qualified female labor, there was general optimism about the possibility of economic change; this is what Beauvoir, for example, expresses in *The Second Sex*. However, the 1950s began with much more alarmist assessments of the actual situation of women. Of course, women

were working more and more outside the home and were thus gaining certain forms of independence. The legal status of married women was amended in many countries to try to ensure the equality of both spouses in marriage. But the realities of women's employment were very somber. While jobs were developing that were identified as male and female work, the gap in salaries for equal work continued to be considerable in some countries, notably in the United States, where gender-based differences in income and salaries became even more pronounced. Access to work was intended to represent economic and social equality, but the 1960s brought a vast disappointment of these expectations. In reality, given the existence of different statistical curves, different job markets, and different forms of discrimination, the new feminisms would have to contend with demands from women whose condition had in fact not been transformed by work: "equality through work" seemed to be an empty phrase.

On the initiative of national or international organizations such as the Organization of Economic Cooperation and Development (OECD) and the United Nations (UN) and its commission on the condition of women, women in each country participated—as experts or by representing various women's associations—in the development of new policies to accompany the development of paid work for women under the best social circumstances. It was an opportunity to formulate new demands for the reforms that would lead to genuine equality between women and men. In *Women's Two Roles, Home and Work* (1962), the sociologists Alva Myrdal and Viola Klein, OECD experts attuned to the issues of women's psychological equilibrium as represented by classical Freudianism, advocated that, in order to bypass the social prohibitions against work for married women, women adapt their professional aspirations to the demands of motherhood by choosing so-called female careers or half-time careers. These women were to be the first to realize a new ambition, namely that of reconciling domestic tasks with professional tasks. Their role in the articulation and reinforcement of women's difference was in fact a contradictory one. Myrdal and Klein's arguments became the target of feminist protest as examples of the reduction of the feminine condition within functionalist rationalizations.

As in Betty Friedan's analysis in *The Feminine Mystique* (1963), feminist protest is often—inaccurately—understood as having begun in the United States, based solely on the discontents of suburban housewives. However, although the critique of the housewife's feminine mystique was essential, it must be recalled that women's return to the home did not entirely become a reality after World War II. Women were taken out of certain jobs only to be massively rehired in the service sector. Thus, in the United States as in other countries, the postwar period saw a growing trend toward paid work for women. Naturally, this trend was not uniformly manifested in all countries, but corresponded to the phases of industrialization in each one, according to its own place in international competition. The changes in women's double role, as housewives and as paid workers, took different forms in different countries.

Throughout the 1960s discrimination against women was analyzed in terms of employment and, in particular, discrimination in wages, among other issues. There were numerous attempts to enact national and international laws to put the principle of equal pay for equal work into practice. In the United States, this issue prompted the formation of the National Organization for Women (NOW). In Europe, Article 119 of the Treaty of Rome, stipulating equal pay for men and women, referred to the same concept. However, the main objective of this treaty, as Jacqueline Nonon, who has occupied various posts in the European Commission, reminds us, was not to improve the situation of women. Instead, it had a purely economic objective—that of trying to forestall any potential for bending the rules of competition within the Common Market. But the existence of international legislation, which was more favorable than the national regulations of the various countries, constituted a strategic point of support for women's demands. Thus, in February 1966, the women workers of the National Arms Factory of Belgium in Herstal in the French-speaking region went on strike. In *Histoire et sociologie du travail féminin* (1968; History and Sociology of Women's Work), the sociologist Évelyne Sullerot called this "the first European strike, the first workers' movement that had a 'European' text as its point of departure," referring to Article 119 of the Treaty of Rome. The entire European press gave broad coverage to this strike and to the broad international movement of women's solidarity that formed in its wake. The women workers of Herstal did not even demand complete parity of pay, merely the adjustment of wages of specialized women workers to match the lowest wages paid to male workers—those of manual laborers. This dispute became something of an exemplary case because of its duration (three months, during which there were seven successive votes in favor of the initiative); it revealed the real consequences of classifying work as "male" and "female": overvaluing the physical strength needed for "men's" jobs and ignoring, not to say discrediting, the skills associated with "women's" jobs. The increase in paid jobs for women essentially coincided with the trend toward greater numbers of married women working outside the home, but what the protest movements and studies by experts would reveal was that this massive integration of women into the workforce was in fact achieved by maintaining, or even reinforcing, gender-based discrimination against them.

In addition to the growth of the female workforce, factors such as the growing demand for skilled jobs, an increase in women's educational levels, and an increase in the number of female students must be cited as part of the context of the feminist renewal of the 1960s. If the resurgence of the women's movement emanated in part from the student movement, it also issued from a broader group of economic and legal changes that placed women at the heart of reflection on social change, and from the stakes involved in new demands: protests by unskilled laborers and strikes by women workers became increasingly common in European countries. These actions exerted a strong mobilizing influence, and were a tangible expression of the new forms of solidarity among women workers.

For European feminist movements—those of Germany, France, Italy, and Great Britain—relations with left-wing political parties were essential, and the dialectic of inclusion and exclusion was an ongoing phenomenon. Constant elements in this dialectic included recognition, tactical integration of women's groups by left-wing political parties, confrontation appropriate to each country depending upon the kind of relationship that existed between the Communist and Socialist parties, assessing the political capacities of social democracy, the development of the welfare state, and recognition of women as a workforce.

What was obvious for the women's liberation movement at the end of the 1960s was the radical will to break with everything it found in the present: there was no acknowledgment of the legitimacy of earlier feminist currents. On the contrary, feminists now considered it a priority to mark a break with earlier women's movements. If the suffragists had left their traces in history, feminists of the late 1960s perceived the need to present themselves as distinct from the suffragists (who were thereafter somewhat unfairly labeled as bourgeois feminists). The search for continuity or an explanation of the differences between contemporary feminism and the movement that developed during the second half of the 19th century is a present-day concern and an obvious result of advances in feminist research, especially in political history. Today's scholars are examining the continuity from one wave of feminism to the next and the phases of emergence and greater calm as they may relate to other jolts or social crises. On the other hand, according to Sheila Rowbotham in *Women in Movement* (1992), the appearance of the expression "liberation movement" had to indicate the desire to be freed from a feminism that was seen as too restricted in its aims, limited to a demand for rights and specifically the right to vote. In truth, many of those who participated in the creation of the first autonomous women's groups were rather ill informed about earlier feminist movements. However, some of these groups asserted themselves as feminist groups but used the term with the adjective "radical" (in the American tradition) or "revolutionary" to set themselves apart from the earlier feminists. The term "liberation" signified less a demarcation from earlier periods than the desire for analogy with the national liberation movements against colonialism and imperialism, or with the black liberation movement in the United States.

It will fall to historians to put the rise of feminism into a long-term perspective and to show that the movement that became neofeminism actually began right after World War II rather than in the 1960s, as is commonly and summarily asserted. However, one should be careful not to reconstruct the long term in such a way as to underplay the importance of late-1960s feminism and the social upheavals of the time. The struggles against colonialism, imperialism, and most especially against the impasse of the imperialist war in Vietnam, as well as the victorious struggles of national liberation movements, were an important source of ferment for women's massive intervention in the political arena. There can be no doubt that to establish a long-term perspective—whether in general or in the particular context of the history of feminism—it is not enough to reduce the emergence of feminism only to its break with the New Left: the value of establishing a long-term perspective is precisely to reconstruct the totality of social conditions of the period. However, to downplay the importance of feminism's break with the New Left at that particular juncture would be just as reductive.

Feminist Movements in the United States

Feminism in the United States was characterized by high levels of participation in collective activism and by the existence of countless groups capable of exerting political pressure. In *Born for Liberty. A History of Women in America* (1989), Sara Evans, a historian of American feminism, observes that women's associations, and then the feminist movement as an extension of the civil rights movement, were instrumental in reminding to America of its democratic heritage and reinvigorating public life throughout the decade of the 1960s: "By pioneering in the creation of new public space—voluntary associations located *between* the public world of politics and work and the private intimacy of family—women made possible a new vision of active citizenship." She cites as an example the 1962 "defeat" of the House Un-American Activities Committee (HUAC) in the face of the determination of the women of the Women Strike for Peace (WSP) movement and its founder Dagmar Wilson, who loudly and clearly "proclaimed their concern for peace in the name of mother love." In fact, the example is significant, for, as Evans affirms with a touch of emphasis, "the politicized feminity of Women Strike for Peace was not the source of the new feminism, but it helped create an environment in which the passivity and apolitical nature of the feminine mystique could be challenged."

Analyses of the founding of the feminist movement stress the appearance of two constituent branches of the new feminism. On the one hand, there was the organization NOW, representative of a feminism that focused on the struggle for the transformation and improvement of women's rights; this was essentially a revival of the women's rights movement that had been the main current of feminism at the end of the 19th century. On the other hand, there was the trend that could be called the women's liberation movement, composed of a number of different groups. These two trends were the expression of two quite different political philosophies, but distinctions between the two remained nebulous except in very large cities. Both currents carried the ferment of the new feminism but they remained unaware of their latent strength, owing to the lack of a political climate that would have allowed for a reassessment of the potential power of women's associations as pressure groups. This phase of U.S. feminism in the 1970s was a reactivation of what the feminist movement of the 19th century had been, but with contemporary concerns addressed by the different Kennedy-era commissions entrusted with revalorizing women's social role. This was when new battles for equality in the workplace began, notably with the publication of the government report *American Women* (1963), which exposed innumerable forms of discrimination, particularly in employment. These campaigns, which showed the restrictions brought into the workplace by earlier protective laws, dealt with equal pay and equal career opportunities for women and men. The President's Commission on the Status of Women, created by President John F. Kennedy in 1961, officially declared itself in favor of women's advancement. But in reality it was opposed to egalitarian policies and rejected the proposed Equal Rights Amendment (ERA), a battle that feminists—especially those of the National Women's Party (NWP)—had begun in 1923.

Among the various studies of American feminism, Ginette Castro, in *Radioscopie du féminisme américain* (1984; *American Feminism: A Contemporary History*), sees the idea of actions for women's equality as purely instrumentalist. Tantamount to taking a position unrelated to any concrete results, this abstract notion simply aimed to attract women's vote at a time when, in the cold war climate of rivalry with the Soviet Union, the United States lagged behind in advancing female resources. But very rapidly the gap between, on the one hand, the expectations created by official positions, and, on the other, the actual experience of women, many of them involved with activist groups, became a source of growing tensions. And thus in 1966, in the face of this official resistance and delaying tactics on the part of the Equal Employment Opportunity Commission (EEOC), which failed to provide any substantive investigation of sexual discrimination cases, the National Organization of Women was born. It then became possible to tackle these cases, for at the last moment the word "sex" was inserted into Title VII, the 1964 civil rights laws, which prohibited discrimination in employment on the basis of race, religion, or national origin. The idea that some jobs were necessarily appropriate for women while others were not was so widespread in the United States at the time that at the time of the vote on the amendment mentioning sex, the *New York Times* ironically referred to Title VII as the Bunny Law (in reference to the bunny costumes worn by hostesses at the Playboy Club) and wondered what would henceforth constitute "men's" work.

In the series of key dates in women's history, encyclopedias most often cite 1968 as the year of the first public demonstration. Acting on the initiative of the New York–based WITCH movement, a group of women protested against the Miss America beauty pageant in Atlantic City, New Jersey, and disrupted the show by awarding the crown to a sheep and piling girdles, curlers, and copies of *Ladies' Home Journal* into a garbage can. Disrupting an event widely covered by the media guaranteed instant publicity, and this particular protest inaugurated the "spectacular" approach that was advocated by many feminist groups and subsequently adopted in many other countries. In a spirit closer to that of the mass gatherings associated with the peace movement and the condemnation of the Vietnam War, other authors prefer to cite the January 1968 action by the Jeanette Rankin Brigade (named for the first woman elected to the U.S. Congress in 1919) during the great Peace March in Washington. Betty Friedan, meanwhile, considers the creation of NOW in 1966 the beginning of the second wave of feminism.

The success of the demonstration on 26 August 1970 surprised observers, and, undoubtedly, many participants as well. For feminists most determined to build an autonomous and organized women's movement, this largest of the women's rights demonstrations marked the beginning of the women's liberation movement as a mass movement. The commemoration of the 50th anniversary of American women's right to vote, planned as a "women's strike for equality," represented the joining of the two main branches of the American movement. The event was an unequivocal meeting between the new demands, as articulated by women whose activism was shaped in the radical movements, and the radicalization of women in traditional organizations focused on women's rights, and it marked the origin of the renewal of feminist demonstrations at the end of the 1960s. The organization of the 1970 demonstration has provoked many debates that reveal that, far from being a beginning for American feminists, the event was the culmination of a long effort of agitation and activism that had been particularly pronounced over the preceding three years.

Finally, other authors prefer to go back to the rift that occurred within the Left as a key date for feminism. In an article published in *Esprit* in 1992, Michel Feher argues that this rift represented, beyond the feminist question, the end of the civil rights movement and the beginning of multicultural demands (see Feher). Feher takes up the analysis proposed by Sara Evans in *Personal Politics: The Roots of Women's Liberation in the Civil Rights Movement and the New Left* (1979) of the double schism that occurred in Chicago in August of 1967, when, during the National Conference for New Politics, the Black Power group asked that half the votes be reserved for blacks. The women used this same argument on their own behalf and demanded 51 percent of the vote because they, too, were subjected to a specific form of oppression and represented 51 percent of the total of the American population. The proposal was not technically rejected, since it was not even on the agenda. Shulamith Firestone, who together with Jo Freeman tried to present a motion on this issue, was "paternally" removed from the platform. Using the Chicago conference as the point of departure for her analysis of the feminist movement, Evans emphasizes the emergence of feminist strategies modeled on the Black Power movement—an autonomous movement resolved not to allow anyone else to define the priorities and conditions of emancipation; a segregated movement resolved to escape from subjection to the dominant culture, male and white, and determined to provoke a radically new way of thinking. The emphasis placed on the organization of the women's movement starting from women's own oppression was, indeed, directly borrowed from the separatist ethos of the Black Power movement, which no longer demanded equal rights or racial integration, but fought in the name of "black power."

Despite the importance of ideological connections between feminism and the Black Power movement, in the beginning few black women participated in the women's movement. Thus, the women of the Black Panthers, who were waging their fight together with the men of their party, stressed the fact that their struggle was directed against the racist, capitalist system that oppressed all minorities. The experience of racism demanded that these women give priority to their sense of racial identity. For many analysts, this circumstance explains the limited participation of black women early in the feminist movement. Black women were quick to take a stand on women's rights, but undoubtedly, the media did not give them the same publicity as that devoted to women's movement protesters.

Evans, in her analysis of the historical origins of the movement in *Personal Politics*, insists very specifically on the gulf separating the political effectiveness of women from men in the political practice of the radical student movements. She locates the roots of the feminist movement in the protests of the 1960s and sees the civil rights activists and the militants of the New Left as the instigators of the women's movement: the liberating experience of the civil rights activists within black communities was called into question by their loss of power in the New Left. In Evans's view, the Students for a Democratic Society (SDS) was the locus of the most conspicuous tensions between aspirations to put the more democratic new relationships into immediate practice and the competition to preserve power relationships in the organization, as well as the definition of roles and responsibilities.

In the early stages, women formed groups within activist organizations, and they individually questioned their participation in the movement and women's place as sexual objects. Numerous accounts underscore the contrast between, on the one hand, the highly aggressive atmosphere that reigned within leftist organizations whenever women's issues were discussed, and, on the other, the atmosphere of trust within women's groups, which

led some of these groups to discover how little they knew about one another even though they had struggled together for a long time. According to an article on the women's liberation movement by Marcia Salo and Kathy McAffee that appeared in French translation under the title "Histoire d'une longue marche" (History of a Long March) in a special issue of *Partisans* (1970), the obstacle to true discussions on women's liberation inside the movement on the Left—besides the rivalry between leadership figures—was, in the final analysis, the issue of sex—a topic that was taboo and divisive for women: "But since sexual liberation is part of the ideology of the Left . . . women recoil from recognizing their own oppression for fear of a threat to their relationships with their men." Seen from this perspective, one might be tempted to read the oppression of activist women within the political Left as nothing more than a long litany of victims. "We have been led to look at our life without self-indulgence. The contradiction is blindingly obvious; in the name of building a new society, we all play the role of the oppressed in capitalist society," states the article. However, such an emphasis obscures these women's experience of affirming their political independence by breaking with the established Left. Following Jo Freeman's precedent in *The Politics of Women's Liberation: A Case Study of an Emerging Social Movement and Its Relation to the Policy Process* (1975), it has become customary to distinguish between the two branches of the American movement—the branch oriented more toward liberation as opposed to the branch oriented toward legal rights—by using the respective shorthand designations "new" and "old" movements. Care should be taken not to paint this opposition in absolute terms. As soon as one takes into account the breadth of the movement in all the cities of the United States and goes beyond the conflicts between the high-profile personalities most frequently seen in the media spotlight, the enormous variety of women participating in the movement becomes apparent. The difference in tendencies then becomes far less relevant. In "Gauchistes, théologiennes et majorettes: Itinéraires féministes à Dayton, Ohio, U.S.A." (1991; Leftists, Theologians, and Majorettes: Feminist Itineraries in Dayton, Ohio, U.S.A.), her study of an average city in the United States, Judith Ezekiel shows that only slight differences existed in the participation in the two branches of the movement, which fluctuated according to circumstances. What Ezekiel's study brings out more clearly are the differences between the social backgrounds of the activists, which varied according to the forms of their involvement and commitment. At this level, there were distinctions to be drawn between radical feminism, whose adherents tended to follow marginal and heterodox life trajectories, and liberal feminism, whose adherents were characterized by professional profiles more or less in keeping with their social background.

The feminist movement spread to other countries. In Canada, Great Britain, and Germany, developments were initially in synch with the evolution of feminist movements in the United States.

Canada

The development of feminism in Canada can be understood only in relation to the oppositions and connections inherent in the communities to which women belonged, beginning with the intimate link between feminism in Quebec and the broader development of the Quebecois separatist movement. According to feminist ideas as they have generally evolved, social affiliation was not supposed to create divisions among women. Seemingly, some women went so far as to deny the reality of such divisions, lest uncategorizable and thus insurmountable tensions and conflicts emerge: social divisions, they held, proceeded from male-dominated, capitalist society. In reality, however, a sense of community identification—among black and Chicana women in the United States, women of communities in Quebec that were culturally dominated, and, in other ways, women in Northern Ireland—created considerable resistance against the idea of common identification with all women. On the one hand, the feminist movement in the English-speaking part of Canada was actively involved in the very first demonstrations of the American feminists. Several publications thus associated the feminist groups from Toronto with the American groups. On the other hand, the Quebec movement when it first appeared continued to be deeply attached to its differences from the English-speaking community, which was seen as dominant; in some ways solidarity among women did not arrive until later. Thus, Quebec nationalism, because it was often represented as anticapitalist, served as the foundation for a nationalist feminism that stressed the ethnic and cultural aspects of domination in Quebec: some Quebec feminists refused to campaign with English-speaking women. The Front de Libération des Femmes (FLF; Women's Liberation Front) appeared in 1969, just after the Montreal Women's Liberation Movement, which had been in gestation since 1968 among the women students of McGill University. The determining influence in the formation of such groups was American feminism, which began to be known abroad by the late 1960s. As Diane Lamoureux emphasizes in *Fragments et collages. Essai sur le féminisme québécois des années 70* (1986; Fragments and Collages: Essay on Feminism in Quebec in the 1970s), the FLF was conceived within leftist organizations as an appendix to the socialist plan and did not evolve into a truly independent movement until later.

Nurtured by the nationalist movement, feminism in Quebec developed alongside that movement in a parallel and noncontradictory fashion. Consequently, the break between the women's movement and leftist organizations was far less hostile there than in other countries. It would be wrong to characterize the interest shown in feminism by the political Left in Quebec as paternalistic, for that interest reflected the Left's broader desire for social transformation. Quebec's cultural production—especially its cinema, which was focused on transformations in relations between men and women—attested to this concern. "No women's liberation without a free Quebec, no free Quebec without women's liberation," affirmed a well-known feminist slogan.

Institutionalized feminism was omnipresent in Quebec, where, to a greater extent than in any other region of the world, the burgeoning numbers of feminist groups were partly supported by state funding. "In the beginning, the federal state, and then later, when the Quebec Party came to power, the provincial government, too, played an active role in the transformation of these collectives into service-providers," Lamoureux emphasizes. But these somewhat privileged conditions of institutional recognition were a strength as well, and the institutionalization of feminist scholarship, for example, encountered no direct opposition. In consequence, links between institutions and the more

militant forms of feminism seemed much better protected than in France, for example, where institutionalization was more difficult: feminism in France was less readily recognized as legitimate by the university, and constantly had to distance itself from any suspicion of militantism.

The women of Quebec first condemned the feminism of English-speaking Canada as a more "bourgeois" feminism than their own, one less attuned to social transformation. This condemnation was used to justify their reservations about collective action. However, many authors, acknowledging that these oppositions did not give way to true hostilities but, on the contrary, developed common forms of mobilizing, particularly around the question of abortion, believe that the opposition that today is perceived as a difference was not in any way an obstacle to the development of feminism, but instead provided a ground for mutual recognition and the legitimization of two forms of feminism. For there were definitely two feminist movements in Canada, functioning side by side and faithfully replicating the country's linguistic-political split. Actively involved in the nationalist movement and Quebec identity, which was posited in an antagonistic relation to the rest of Canadian society, feminism broke with a universalist approach of women's oppression in order to make preserving cultural specificities a priority from the start. This embrace of multiculturalism prefigured later postmodernist thinking.

Great Britain

Connections between U.S. and British feminist movements developed immediately, exchanges of ideas being facilitated by the common language and, in particular, by extensive travel back and forth, including some long visits. In Great Britain itself, American feminist publications were rapidly distributed, while one of the first theoretical texts by an English scholar became a major reference work in emerging corpus of analyses by Marxist feminists in Great Britain as well as in the United States and in other European countries. This work was "Women: The Longest Revolution" by Juliet Mitchell, published in the *New Left Review* in 1966. This long article recalled the positions of socialist movements toward women since the 19th century and stressed the need for a political reevaluation of their practices—a project that was undoubtedly relevant on a constant basis yet constantly relegated to the back burner.

In Great Britain, the renewal of the feminist movement grew out of multiple sources that were revealed in 1968. In Hull, for example, demands by the wives of fisherman for safety on trawlers attracted the support of activist university women. Seamstresses employed by Ford in Dagenham and Halewood demanded recognition of their skills, ultimately resulting in a law for equal wages. Union leaders reacted and created the National Joint Action Campaign for Women's Equal Rights (NJACWER), which campaigned in the union confederation and organized an impressive demonstration in Trafalgar Square in May 1969. During the same period, demonstrations against the war in Vietnam and against South-African apartheid contributed to the emergence of a feminist movement within organizations on the Left and the extreme Left, as well as in the unions. Conflicts over nationalism and collective identity led women to think about their own identity. The Trotskyite movement was particularly active and led to the creation of one of the first women's groups in Nottingham. In all of these currents the prevailing question was that of solidarity with the working class, and researchers such as Anna Coote and Beatrix Campbell (*Sweet Freedom: The Struggle for Women's Liberation*, 1982) or David Bouchier (*The Feminist Challenge: The Movement for Women's Liberation in Britain and the United States*, 1984) emphasize the importance of the great strikes and active militancy of women workers in the elaboration of the debates of the Left, as well as women's need for an organization of their own. In that context, Marxism was often revisited, using as a springboard questions of ideology and alienation. Another frequent reference was the work of Wilhelm Reich (a psychiatrist and psychoanalyst, but also a political activist, who left Germany in 1933 and settled in the United States in 1939) and antipsychiatric thought. The interface between a culture dominated by neo-Marxist thought and the radical thought that filled texts from America shaped the emerging feminist groups in Britain. Here, as elsewhere, the high stakes involved in women's sexuality were a motivation to action, whether it was a question of women rediscovering their bodies or refusing a "liberation" that transformed those bodies into objects of consumption and liberated only the men. Sheila Robowtham gives a very personal account of this cultural foment (*Woman's Consciousness, Man's World*, 1974).

The first gathering that attempted to form an association of these groups and bring together their various points of view took place at Ruskin College in Oxford in February 1970. The initiative came from women academics who had participated in "history workshops" on the labor movement and who were outraged by male domination of the debates on the historiography of workers. This first National Conference of the Women's Liberation Movement brought together nearly 600 participants from all over Great Britain. The conference established a national organization committee (which did not ultimately survive maneuvers to seize power by organized groups on the extreme Left) and concluded with a compromise between the more traditional demands for equal pay, equal work, and training, and the new demands of the radical movement for free contraceptives, abortion on demand, and day care centers that would be open 24 hours a day. Recognition of the demands of homosexuals did not come until the conference of 1975. The first conference planned a large demonstration for 8 March 1971. In both London and Liverpool, several hundred women marched, joined by many men and children; the event marked the beginning of the growing number of activist groups in Great Britain. Subsequent national conferences sustained the organic links among the various groups and successfully prevented the degree of fragmentation that occurred in other countries. This cohesion ensured a wider potential for mobilization, although each group retained its autonomy and no one voice was authorized to speak on behalf of the movement as a whole. The British women's movement thus protected itself from the dissension that hindered the development of its different components elsewhere. National conferences were held each year, but in the first instance the British women's movement developed on a local level, through the creation of women's centers in most of the cities of Great Britain. These centers were usually a space open to all groups for the purpose of holding meetings or coordinating demonstrations. Some of these centers soon began to receive municipal funding and served as a prototype for future shelters for battered women.

Germany

In considering this first period of feminism, it is interesting also to take into account the beginnings of the women's movement in West Germany, which occurred concomitantly with its rise in the United States. Owing to the policies of the German government, the very active student protests in Germany closely paralleled the protest movements against the Vietnam War by students in the United States and included protests against the maintenance and development of U.S. military installations on German soil. This new generation of German youth, the first without any direct experience with Nazism, came to political action by asking the preceding generation to account for its past. Some authors have commented at length on the idea that the head-on protest by the young against the state was in reality a protest against parents guilty of having participated in Nazism. Even with the benefit of greater historical distance, the question of women and Nazism is a point that is obscure and in fact often occulted by feminists, who may perceive it as an immediate threat to the notion of women as single, undivided political entity.

Because of the close ties between West Germany and the United States, the German youth demonstrations against the imperialist politics of the United States immediately caused a confrontation with the government in Bonn. In her analysis of the German feminist movement, *Contemporary Western European Feminism* (1992), Gisela Kaplan gives the reader to understand that the underlying frontal opposition between "us," the protesters, and "them," the government, evolved into a politics reminiscent of civil war, as illustrated in the terrorist movement founded by Andreas Baader and Ulrike Meinhof, the Rote Armee Fraktion (RAF; Red Army Fraction). The development of terrorism on the extreme Left, then on the extreme Right, led the government to adopt antiterrorist laws that became a new ground for the condemnation of German legislation as being antidemocratic. This context needs to be taken into account to understand what some authors have noted as the lowest visibility of feminist demonstrations in Germany, when compared to other countries in the same period.

One of the priorities of the main German student movement, the Sozialistischer Studentenbund Deutschland (SDS; League of Socialist Students of Germany) was the condemnation of the authoritarian nature of all institutions. The SDS declared itself to be strongly opposed to all forms of government and posed the relationship between the movement and the state in terms of confrontation. Following Wilhelm Reich's analyses of the postwar period, the German student movement attempted to eradicate every connection with authority. It thus established links between the various manifestations of fascism, locating one of fascism's original causes in the core of family life. The SDS defined itself as an egalitarian and emancipatory movement and shared in the common ideology of the student movements that claimed the cultural revolution of the late 1960s as an international phenomenon. As participants in an antiauthoritarian movement, SDS members soon began to implement communal living structures and devise methods of nonauthoritarian education, offering the first *hauss für kinder* (antiauthoritarian kindergartens).

In this case, as was generally true in the United States, meetings in all-women groups within the SDS gave women the occasion to criticize their place in the leftist movement for the first time. Thereafter they established independent groups outside the SDS. Helke Sandler's presentation at the conference of SDS delegates in Frankfurt is seen as a key historic event in the process of the creation of a new women's movement in Germany. Criticizing the power relations between the sexes in the student movement and the continuation of male domination throughout the so-called sexual revolution, feminists also carried the legacy of the activist movements in their quest for new and more democratic relationships. Traces of these links can be discerned in the development of alternative solutions, which were especially widespread in Germany. Such solutions included nonauthoritarian educational programs for children, the creation of alternative structures, the implementation of structural autonomy in children's homes, and so forth. However, the real crystallization of the women's movement and its spread through all aspects of German political life occurred in 1971, around the question of abortion. At the initiative of Alice Schwartzer, a manifesto of self-accusation, patterned after the "Manifesto of 343" circulated in France in 1971, appeared in the magazine *Der Stern*. The struggle against Article 218 of the penal code, which criminalized abortion, mobilized all German women's organizations, both parliamentary and extraparliamentary.

English and American historical accounts have no doubt tended to date the beginning of the German feminist movement only from the time of Schwartzer's press campaign on abortion and to minimize the presence of this issue in debates in the parties of the Left, the extreme Left, in the German unions, and in the student movement of the late 1960s. The political situation of Germany, then divided into the Federal Republic of Germany (West Germany) and the German Democratic Republic (East Germany), lent a very particular tone to the first feminist debates, and every discussion entailed inevitable comparisons between East and West. For the German feminist movement, the situation of the women of East Germany was a reference point in the debates that could not be ignored. Some German feminists triumphantly cited the high employment rate of women in East Germany as an example of socialist transformations in society. Others, in contrast, argued that the permanent absence of women in areas of political and economic responsibility and their predominance in domestic work and child care demonstrated that women's oppression was independent of the class structure of society. Thus, the priority given to antiauthoritarian and alternative projects in the women's movement, as well as women's wish to set themselves apart from any ideology, even more strongly than in the student movement, corresponded partly to the peculiar, double position of the women's movement in Germany: critical with respect to social democracy, but just as critical of what was known as real socialism in East Germany. Of course, this perspective acquired fresh urgency with the political demonstrations and unfolding events of the "Prague Spring" of 1968. As compared to Great Britain, the action of autonomous Socialist feminists in Germany was not very developed, as Socialist women remained affiliated with the traditional party, the Sozialdemokratische Partei Deutschlands (SPD; German Social Democratic Party). In *L'assemblée des femmes. L'organisation féminine du SPD au temps de Willy Brandt et de Helmut Schmidt* (1992; The Women's Assembly: Women's Organization of the SDP in the Era of Willy Brandt and Helmut Schmidt), Nicole Gabriel stresses the fact that the unions, political parties, and leftist groups of more traditional as well as less dogmatic persuasion were regarded distrustfully and were at the very most partners of solidarity in isolated struggles. Here, perhaps more than elsewhere, independence was seen as the top political priority.

From 1970 on: France, Italy, the Netherlands, and the Scandinavian countries.

France

The women's liberation movement in France, or Mouvement de libération des femmes (MLF), was directly linked to the student movement of the 1960s, and then to the events of May 1968, but it was not openly manifested until 1970, when the U.S. women's movement underwent an explosive expansion. The first public expression of feminism in France was the presentation of a bouquet to the wife of the Unknown Soldier at the Arc de Triomphe on 26 August 1970, an action to manifest solidarity with the massive women's strike in New York. The direct affiliation of the women's movement with the student movement of May 1968 was first of all the burst of revolutionary fervor, the belief that change was possible and that it was possible right away. The MLF's first manifestos, published in *L'idiot international* and then in the special issue of *Partisans*, were a self-styled declaration of war against oppression and a radical condemnation of the system—in this instance, the system that oppressed women: patriarchy. In this early phase, the emerging women's movement in France experienced a series of clashes with the movements of the Left and with leftist extremists. Indeed, the first years of the decade of the 1970s saw the resurgence of activist practices and the proliferation of extreme Left, Maoist, or Trotskyite groups. Different fronts of struggle proliferated, leading to the creation of corresponding action committees: the Comité Vietnam (Committee on Vietnam), Secours Rouge (Red Aid), the Front Homosexuel d'Action Révolutionnaire (FHAR; Homosexual Front for Revolutionary Action) and the Comité d'Action des Prisonniers (Prisoners' Action Committee).

In *Libération des femmes. Les années-mouvement* (1993; Women's Liberation: the Movement Years), Françoise Picq characterizes the women's movement at this time as "one leftist group among others." This argument undoubtedly holds if one bears in mind that the criticism of the avant-garde and the demand for a new politics were in some ways an actualization of the hopes of the May 1968 movement. The condemnation of the activists' machismo in the beginning dominated many meetings of women, who then broke with organizations such as the Gauche Prolétarienne (GP; Proletarian Left), or Vive la Révolution (VLR; Long Live the Revolution). Initially, many of these activist women came to swell the ranks of the group Psychoanalyse et Politique (Psyc et Po; Psychoanalysis and Politics). But the women's movement in France, as in other Western countries, was also the result of the struggles for equality in the workplace, for reforms in family law, and for the right to contraception—goals that were attained throughout the 1960s after debates that were bitter in varying degrees depending upon the case. In fact, although women in the Scandinavian and Anglo-Saxon countries had had access to contraception for years, or even decades, French women had to wait for the Neuwirth Law of 1967 for a first liberalization of the law. We should recall that one aspect of the student demands at the end of the 1960s concerned policies in university residences regulating visits among men and women.

In France, as elsewhere, many women had been active participants in the social and legal changes that had taken place since 1945 and accelerated during the 1960s, whether through public organizations such as the Comité pour le Travail Féminin (Committee for Women's Labor), or through the action of the Mouvement Français pour le Planning Familial (MFPF; French Movement for Family Planning), political parties, and most especially the Mouvement Démocratique Féminin (MDF; Women's Democratic Movement), connected with the Fédération de la Gauche Démocratique et Socialiste (FGDS; Federation of the Democratic and Socialist Left), in which Colette Audry and Yvette Roudy played a role. Thus, by focusing on abortion as a pressing concern, feminists immediately encountered a potential for broad mobilization well beyond the student movement. When the "Manifesto of 343" was published and the *Nouvel Observateur* made public the "list of the 343 women who had the courage to sign the 'I have had an abortion' manifesto" on 5 April 1971, there ensued a bitter struggle for the legalization of abortion, which continued until the new law was decreed in 1974.

As a movement connected with the student movement, the women's movement in France from the outset recruited among the intellectual and artistic elite and more broadly from all of the intellectual professions, including journalists, lawyers, and teachers. The writers Christiane Rochefort and Monique Wittig and the actress Delphine Seyrig were among those actively involved in the movement's first public actions and demonstrations. The same urgent criticism of the constraints that impeded women appeared both in Rochefort's works (*Le repos du guerrier* [1958; Warrior's Rest]; *Stances à Sophie* [1963; Stanzas to Sophie]) and in those of Wittig (*L'Opoponax* [1964; The *Opoponax*]; *Les guérillères* [1969; *The Guérillères*]) and in their activism very early on in the movement. Rochefort's writing offered caustic humor in the portrayal of alienation, while Wittig produced experimental texts in which the formal qualities of the writing itself reflect the author's feminist utopian aspirations. As early as 1960, in a commentary on marriage for the book *La Française et l'amour* (1960; Frenchwomen and Love), Rochefort insisted on showing "the revolting indulgence" that jurors showed for men in their verdicts on crimes of passion:

> For, if one looks at [crimes of passion] carefully, the principle (considering a living person as exclusive property, with the right of life or death over slaves, except that here the person was not even purchased, in most cases) is infinitely more immoral than that of villainous crimes, which originate in a protest against the distribution of goods that are merely material.

These observations were still relevant in 1970 and surely still are today. Rochefort and Wittig participated in and encouraged the early productions of the movement: articles in *L'idiot international* and in *Partisans*, then publication of the work *Le livre de l'oppression des femmes* (1972; The Book of Women's Oppression), and so forth. Indeed, naming, revealing, and describing women's oppression were priority concerns at this moment in the evolution of the women's movement. Continuing in the vein of the poetic activism of May 1968, many women drew from the sources of surrealism and embarked on "the adventure

of words." To condemn oppression there was nothing like irony, humor, the diversion or the "undressing" of words, and these were the issues addressed in the column "Le sexisme ordinaire" (Ordinary Sexism) first published in December 1973 in *Les temps modernes*. This column also attested to the close relationships Beauvoir had established with feminist groups.

Feminism in France was nourished by concomitant debates in the area of psychoanalysis, strongly marked by the predominance of the theories of Jacques Lacan. But the reciprocity of intellectual borrowings and thus of indebtedness characterized the exchanges between such feminist psychoanalysts as Luce Irigaray and the psychoanalytic movement as a whole. This proximity to the best-known developments of French philosophy, notably the work of Michel Foucault, Gilles Deleuze, and Jacques Derrida, became the aspect of French feminism that was cited most frequently in its dissemination abroad, thereby occulting contributions from materialist feminists in France.

As in other countries, theoretical debate was important, although impugned by those women who saw every theoretical perspective as terrorist. More strongly in France than in other countries, antagonisms within radical feminism gave rise to irremediable conflicts and accusations that hurt common initiatives. Nevertheless, with the exception of Paris, collaboration between opposing groups was without a doubt more extensive than has often been thought. Although in France, as elsewhere, the strategy of the small group and its autonomy were avowed priorities, the movement continued to be centralized in Paris during the early years. The spread of feminism to the provinces often began with the establishment of mixed-gender groups supporting the Mouvement pour la Liberté de l'Avortement et de la Contraception (MLAC; Movement for the Right to Abortion and Contraception). To a lesser extent, the movement was spread by the efforts of the Psyc et Po group to disseminate its ideas, notably by opening a network of bookstores called "des femmes" and affiliated with the publishing house of the same name. The denunciation of crimes against women in May 1972, originally intended as a continuation of the manifesto on abortion, soon transcended that one aspect, generating a multiplicity of initiatives that gave the measure of the real propagation of the movement and its spread beyond Paris. The categorical opposition of some women to any form of institutionalization whatsoever limited any initiatives oriented in that direction. The more organizational initiatives, such as the MLAC and, to an even greater degree, Choisir (Choice), existed only as projects outside the movement. This situation would prevail later on as well, though to a lesser extent, in the case of the Ligue des Droits des Femmes (League of Women's Rights).

While some analysts have suggested that Sara M. Evans's perspective was somewhat naive in her analyses of the rejection by American activist women of intellectualism as a purely male form of expression, conflicts and verbal sparring were endemic within the Parisian movement and are often cited as the reasons for the failure of that movement. Undoubtedly, as Sandrine Garcia suggests in "Le féminisme, une révolution symbolique? Étude des luttes symboliques autour de la condition féminine," the thesis she wrote under the direction of the sociologist Pierre Bourdieu, such infighting was precisely an expression of the search for constitutive positions of power of the women's movement as an independent arena. In Bourdieu's analysis such confrontations are not specific to feminism but are characteristic of all power relations, symptomatic of the polarization between the dominant and the dominated in every social arena.

In countries other than France, the autonomy of women's groups did not need to be affirmed, and when the confrontations between fractions were violent, the constitutive role of any group was not implicated anyway. The Parisian movement was paradoxical in that it participated in this ideology of autonomy of initiatives, while tensions over the monopoly on authenticity went beyond the usual strategic positions and became concentrated in a fight at the level of theory. Specifically, materialist feminists were opposed to the Psyc et Po group, the latter being effectively dependent on the theoretical positions of Antoinette Fouque. At the end of these confrontations, Fouque's social prominence enabled her to secure for her publishing house (Éditions des femmes) the exclusive use of the acronym MLF; in consequence, this group in some ways came to monopolize the legitimacy of the struggle for women's liberation. Naturally, the other groups did not disappear, but their capacity for action was somewhat reduced, especially in the channels of print distribution, both in France and abroad. One of the effects of this head-on opposition was that it sterilized and ossified part of the theoretical debate for some time. The objective of *La revue d'en face* (published in Paris 1977–83 by the Éditions Tierce, a preeminent feminist publishing concern headed by Françoise Pasquier) was then not so much to provide a vision of the happy medium but to suggest analyses that were less dogmatic. Similarly, mention should be made of the prominence of *Les cahiers du Grif* (published in Brussels and Paris 1973–93, also under the aegis of the Éditions Tierce) in contributing to theoretical production in France and Belgium and of the important role played by Françoise Collin, the director of this publication, to encourage "thinking and acting" from a feminist perspective.

Italy

The women's liberation movement, as a group distinct from mixed-gender political organizations, emerged publicly in Italy in 1970. Even more than in other countries, the Italian women's movement drew from sources that went beyond student movements and the occupations of universities, beginning in 1967, to include the dissemination of articles by women intellectuals and journalists who wrote left-wing criticism of the Italian Communist Party. Equally important is the fact that Italian feminism also arose in a broader context, where women's issues were omnipresent within political discourse on the modernization of society: in the mid 1960s, women union activists s protested against their responsibilities being limited to traditional "women's jobs."

Compared to other women's movements, one of the often-cited characteristics of the Italian women's movement was the high degree of politicization of its activists. Two main factors are usually cited to account for this profile. The first was that feminism was a part of the lively political debate ongoing in Italy at the end of the 1960s and the early 1970s. Specifically, and in contrast to other European countries, the student protests in Italy were followed by new labor struggles in 1969 that went beyond union demands, advancing a more radical critique of organized labor itself and expressing the need for a new and different quality of life. This social and political context meant that Italian feminism met with a broad current of public opinion

that had been sensitized to the entire process of social transformation.

The second factor, a complement to the first, was that the new feminists of the 1970s, associated with the Italian New Left, opposed the liberation movements that were very much present in the traditional Left. "Autonomy and antireformism are their two watchwords," comments Bianca-Maria Frabotta in her article, "Une autre façon de faire de la politique?" (1978). But in Italy, unlike in France, differences in opinion did not necessarily lead to invective, and the different factions appeared together in large common demonstrations. For the new Italian feminists of the 1970s, the conflict was not with the reformist feminist movement, as in other countries and especially in North America, but with the women's organizations within the political parties. In Italy more than elsewhere, feminists practiced a double militancy: in the New Left and in the women's movement. These practices did not prevent the fragmentation of the New Left at the end of the 1970s. Through their criticism of the New Left or through their break with it, a great number of Italian feminist activists were therefore highly politically engaged. Frabotta also points out the contradictions inherent in this attitude, particularly a schizophrenic attitude toward the Unione Donne Italiane (UDI; Union of Italian Women), a mass women's organization that predated feminism.

> When we accused the women of the UDI of lacking autonomy and of being too subordinate to the parties, we were in fact alluding to our superior level of feminist consciousness. But in reality, the unconscious guarantee of our political line, different because antireformist and non-institutional, also came from our membership in the New Left. This meant that we reserved for ourselves a small corner in which our alliance with males could serve as a weapon against other women. This painful perception has certainly been the most contradictory and the most dramatic aspect of double activism.

The women's movement in Italy—its spectacular ability to mobilize women for mass demonstrations in the main Italian cities often hailed as exemplary—was characterized by its ability to join important theoretical practice together with a practical involvement that was just as striking, and by the joining together of intellectuals and the labor movement. The latter, for feminists, testified to closer ties and a capacity for effective collaboration between left-wing intellectuals and union organizations. Such collaboration flourished especially in 1973, thanks to an agreement on a new arrangement of working hours, commonly referred to as the "150 hours." The metallurgy workers were the first to obtain this agreement; it was later extended to all workers. These events gave women activists in universities a rare opportunity to help bring feminist issues to the attention of the unions as an important subject among the traditional topics of left-wing politics. In Italy even more than in France, the egalitarian principles of the Constitution and the legal texts associated with Italy's participation in the European Community were expressed in sufficiently ambivalent terms to preserve women's de facto unequal status and to establish the priority of family in their responsibilities. Feminists thus helped in intensifying demands for the transformation of family law, still highly unequal at the end of the 1960s. Among its achievements, the Italian feminist movement gained recognition by means of major demonstrations for the revocation of the laws that prohibited divorce and, just as significantly, for its role in demanding laws liberalizing abortion.

The Netherlands

The development of feminist movements at the end of the 1960s in the Netherlands was similar to the developments the movement would experience in the Scandinavian countries: Denmark, Sweden, and Norway. All of these countries are comparable in that the level of social benefits was (and remains) high there and the traditional women's organizations were relatively well represented. Of course, there are also significant divergences among these countries, in part linked to the very different forms of women's participation in the job market. In the Netherlands, feminist movements had to situate themselves in relation both to the student protest movement, which they continued, and to government measures for the equality and support of women, which were put into effect through a large number of women's organizations.

In terms of employment, the Netherlands was very different from the Scandinavian countries, with one of the lowest rates in Europe of women with children engaging in paid work. For a long time high salaries across the board, a lack of day care centers for young children, and a strong ideology in favor of mothers staying at home could be invoked to explain the low employment rates among women. But at the end of the 1960s, a movement emerged demanding equal rights for women, asking for a more egalitarian share in social as well as family responsibilities, and with these demands came the request for a shorter workweek. The mixed-gender group Man–Vrouw–Maatschappij (Man–Woman–Society), which provided the impetus for this movement, and which aimed to establish a pressure group to push for legal change, could be compared to NOW in the United States. Man–Vrouw–Maatschappij activists were the first to be concerned with institutional measures on behalf of women, and they participated in the different committees on the status of women. Dutch feminist associations, in alliance with the government, created various educational initiatives for the benefit of mothers.

The first demonstrations of Dutch feminists in 1969 and 1970 sought to differentiate themselves from the action of traditional women's associations, particularly through the activism of the Dolle Mina's. The Dolle Mina's were a group that had been created during the occupation of the University of Amsterdam in May 1969. They took the name in honor of one of the pioneers of feminism at the end of the 19th century, Wilhelmina (Mina) Elizabeth Drucker, known as Dolle Mina, or Mad Mina, an early critic of the law forbidding married women to work. Influenced by anarchism and the Situationist movement, the Dolle Mina's used public spectacle and street theater—means also used by students and the *provo* movement—to criticize the extant power structure. Grand gestures, demands for public toilets for women, and also campaigns for abortion on demand and against pornography, gained recognition for the movement and ensured the dissemination of its ideas. These activists advocated the forming of small consciousness-raising groups, and their actions basically dealt with plans for opening houses and cafes for women, self-managed clinics, and shelters for battered women.

Denmark, Norway, and Sweden

In Denmark, Norway, and later in Sweden, an independent women's movement grew out of the student protest movement and the influence of American activism. Those antecedents are obvious in the development of the Danish feminist movement and the name Redstockings, taken from the New York group. In her article "Is the New Women's Movement Dead? Decline or Change of the Danish Movement" (1986), Drude Dahlerup particularly emphasizes the importance of the international diffusion of ideas as a factor that shaped the emerging feminist movement in Denmark: it was after a big meeting in which three Danish journalists had spoken about the movements in the United States, Great Britain, and the Netherlands that the idea of a new women's liberation movement became concrete. As in other countries, the emerging women's movement in Denmark was inscribed within with the break with the student extreme Left, but here the movement was also inscribed within a break with traditional feminist movements established during the first wave of feminism, centered on the demand for women's suffrage. In the Scandinavian countries these traditional groups had remained active in varying degrees beyond the establishment of the welfare state in which they had directly participated.

In the same article, Dahlerup describes the Danish movement, by comparison with other Nordic movements, as being more anarchist, giving greater priority to alternative projects, and presenting itself as revolutionary feminist force dedicated to transforming class society. Thus, the women's liberation movement in Denmark opposed not only patriarchal society but also earlier feminists, who were accused of reformism because of their concern with legal reforms. From this perspective, the model of the career woman was just as heavily criticized as the confinement of women to the home. The primacy of solidarity with the working class was apparent from the time of the Danish movement's first slogans demanding equal pay. One of the movement's first demonstrations in May 1970 was a sit-in in the buses of Copenhagen, in which participants refused to pay more than 80 percent of the fare since women's wages were only 80 percent of men's wages.

As with autonomous women's groups in other countries, the Redstockings and their agenda were criticized by Socialist feminists, who urged women workers to mobilize en masse. However, according to Dahlerup, such autonomous groups hardly grew in size. Additionally, a sizeable movement developed in support of alternative projects of women's homes and communal living. In 1971, in order to reach as many women as possible, the Redstockings organized a feminist summer camp run exclusively by women (the only males admitted were boys under the age of 13). The success of that gathering, which attracted feminist participants from many European countries, was a symbol of women's autonomy. Dahlerup also credits the movement for holding the first feminist festival in August 1974. Almost 30,000 women, men, and children attended, and the festival still takes place annually, drawing large numbers of participants.

The development of the women's liberation movement in Norway seems analogous to events in Denmark in many respects.

In "The Impact of the Women's Liberation Movement on Public Policy in Denmark and Norway" (1983), comparing the two movements through an approach that is perhaps somewhat mechanical but nonetheless interesting, Dahlerup and Brita Gulli examine the relationship between the presence or absence of a women's branch within the political parties and the breadth of the women's liberation movement as an extraparliamentary movement. Their findings indicate that women's branches within political parties were more active in Norway than in Denmark, and that this led to the formation of a women's liberation movement in Norway that did not oppose the actions of traditional, party-affiliated women head on. These more pronounced divisions within the movement in Norway made the type of unified mobilization that occurred in Denmark more difficult.

In Sweden women's participation in the life of the political parties, and more specifically, their active presence in the Social-Democratic Party of Sweden, was to a large degree instrumental in the establishment of social policies for women. According to some analysts, the massive presence of women in that party in effect precluded broad development of the feminist movement in Sweden.

The beginnings of the women's movements in Ireland, Spain, Portugal, and Greece, and the impact of international organizations.

Ireland

Even more than in other countries, not only was the development of feminism in the 1970s in the Republic of Ireland linked to the international propagation of the movement, exchanges of ideas between feminists, and travel, but the movement only really generated a favorable public response in connection with the nation's desire for integration into the European economy. In that latter connection, one of the first developments, on the eve of membership in the European Community, was the government's establishment of a Commission on the Status of Women, which presented women's situation in the various areas of work and family. Thus was initiated a period of debates on sexual equality, frequently supported by the Brussels Commission, in which feminist movements participated. In Ireland as in other European countries, the women's liberation movement had connections to the radical Left, although the Left in Ireland was much less prominent than in other countries. The political radicalization at the end of the 1960s and the beginning of the 1970s was more closely associated with the movement for civil rights and the republican activists in Northern Ireland. In 1970, the first feminist activist group, commonly known as the Irish Women's Liberation Movement (IWLM), was created by a small group of intellectuals and journalists. Their familiarity and connections with the media assured them immediate success in their public presentations.

Tracing the history of the Irish movement in "The Women's Movement in the Republic of Ireland 1970–1990" (1993), Ailbhe Smyth shows that when viewed in retrospect 20 years later, the manifesto of these first feminist militants was far from having the same radical tone as similar manifestos in other countries: it contained no mention of sexuality, dependency, or the sexual domination of women. It thus provides a standard of measure

for assessing the course of events during those two decades in Ireland. Closely akin to the predominant social concerns of the Left at the time, one of the priorities of this manifesto was the condemnation of the deficient housing conditions rampant in Ireland, and the text reiterated the republican motto: one family, one house. The IWLM militants took a stand against the activities of many women's associations that had been revitalized by the government's activities involving the Commission on the Status of Women, criticizing them as being reformist. Nevertheless, many actions were carried out jointly, women could circulate from one of the movement's branches to another, and the presence of the more radical IWLM forced the members of the commission themselves to take more advanced positions than they had done in previous years. Thus, Smyth argues that one of the characteristic traits of the women's movement in Ireland is the fact that it is often irrelevant to the attempt to draw a clear line of demarcation between its most radical and its most reformist aspects. And indeed, although here, as elsewhere, radical feminists favored direct action and strategies that bypassed the usual parliamentary practices, the militants also demonstrated from the start their firm will to urge the government to speed up the legal transformations that were necessary for social change. Feminists could base their arguments on the discrepancies between the new proposals in European politics and Irish realities in need of change.

With regard to employment, membership in the European Community undoubtedly accelerated the promulgation of new laws on equal pay, professional equality, nondiscriminatory allocation of social security benefits, and unemployment insurance. But in Ireland, just as in other countries, these laws did not change the differences between women's jobs and men's jobs: women's position in the labor market was more precarious, with a focus on service employment that paid the least, and so on. As Élisabeth Gaudin, a specialist on Ireland, has shown, recourse to the European Court of Justice in matters concerning private life often has an impact on changes in the law, but owing to widespread reluctance to run counter to the particularities of each nation's culture, questions of morality nevertheless remain an area in which resorting to international law is not necessarily effective.

Spain and Portugal

The Spanish feminist movement was not simply a response to the dissemination of the American movement: the public appearance of an independent feminist movement in Spain coincided with the governmental activity of the International Year of Women declared by the UN in 1975. In fact, even earlier antecedents can be cited. The imprisonment in December 1974 of Eva Forest, Lidia Falcon, and several other people accused of complicity in the attack on Admiral Carrero Blanco unleashed a vast international solidarity movement among feminist groups. This became the occasion for renewing the criticism of women's position, for through these arrests the beginnings of the women's liberation movement, which was just starting to organize, were targeted as well. In Portugal, the prohibition of the publication of *Novas cartas portuguesas* (1972; *The Three Marias: New Portuguese Letters*), a work by three dissident nuns (Maria Barreno, Maria Horta, and Maria Velho Da Costa), also prompted large demonstrations of solidarity and condemnation of Fascist regimes. Concomitant with the establishment of a democratic regime, Portuguese feminist groups were active participants in the elaboration of the new constitutions. Thus, the feminist movement appears to have been very institutionalized in Portugal, even though the most libertarian forms of feminism emerged during the early moments of the Revolution of the Carnations. In Spain, by contrast, there were independent manifestations of feminism.

To a far greater degree than the dissemination of European feminist publications, the celebration of the International Year of Women encouraged the formation of the first feminist collectives and revitalized Spanish feminism at the very time that Franco's Fascist state was dying and the transition toward democracy had begun. Analyzing the participation of feminists in this process of democratization in "La transition vers la démocratie en Espagne" (1987; The Transition toward Democracy in Spain), Judith Astelarra reports that in 1974 women of the opposition affiliated with the Movimiento Democratico de Mujeres (MDM; Women's Democratic Movement), together with feminists, decided to organize their own demonstrations to coincide with the official U.N.-sponsored events. The MDM was founded in secrecy in the mid 1960s; many of its members were close to the Spanish Communist Party, including Lidia Falcon and Carmen Alcade. Authors disagree as to the exact date of its founding: 1963 in Madrid and Barcelona, according to Maria Angeles Duran and Maria Teresa Gallego; 1965 according to Astelarra. In December 1975, shortly after Franco's death, "women's liberation days" were held, giving all the women's organizations present the opportunity to develop a platform asking the government for ratification of the United Nations Convention on the Elimination of All Forms of Discrimination against Women (CEDAW). These debates, which initially took place in an atmosphere of semisecrecy, nevertheless drew large crowds and were the occasion for differences of opinion between, on the one hand, feminists who recommended granting priority to the organization of an independent women's movement, and, on the other hand, women members of traditional political parties who insisted on participation in the general process of democratization. In the end, the majority favored activism on both fronts. Meanwhile, the autonomous feminist movement was developing on the regional level as well as on the national level, which provided coordinating structures. The latter allowed for substantial mobilization during the early years in order to demand amnesty for women who had been found guilty of crimes associated with the feminine condition (abortion or adultery) as well as women recognized as political prisoners. However, the active mobilization that characterized the early years of the transition period was not sustained, and, according to Astelarra, the failure of Spanish feminist groups to continue to participate in the political process was presumably due both to their lack of representation within political parties (with the exception of two female deputies) and to the distancing with respect to institutional politics that had taken place within the feminist movement.

Greece

The manifestations of feminism in Greece are comparable to developments in Spain and Portugal insofar as they were linked to the general political period of transition toward democracy. However, in contrast to events in Spain, the autonomous feminist movement in Greece remained seriously marginalized precisely because of opposition from the women's organizations connected with political parties, according to Eleni Varikas in "Les femmes grecques face à la modernisation institutionnelle: Un féminisme difficile" (1985; Greek Women Facing Institutional Modernization: A Difficult Feminism). Today, as at the end of the 19th century, feminism is assailed in Greece as an ideology that imitates foreign models. Thus, Varikas stresses the double bind in which the radical feminist movement in Greece found itself, forced to defend itself against attacks from the parliamentary Left. Worried about accusations of being apolitical, writes Varikas,

> feminists had a tendency to use the traditional model of politics in order to legitimize their feminist intervention. This deprived them of the theoretical means necessary for the elaboration of *a politics of their own*, based on an analysis of social relations between the sexes, which would have allowed them to differentiate themselves clearly from a concept of women's liberation as a tool, seen as a superstructural complement to democratic and socialist struggles.

And yet, despite their very limited numbers, feminists were not absent from the political stage. In the meantime, Varikas emphasizes, although feminist activity was criticized for being "xenophilistic," feminist ideas were being redeveloped and stripped of their quality of systematic social critique in order to become an element of the discourse of modernization, in Greece as in Ireland or Portugal, serving national development in the new setting of the European Community.

The dissemination of feminism in these countries fit completely into the political borders of the Western world of the 1970s—that is to say, before the collapse of the Soviet system and the reunification of Germany in 1989. These borders marked the ideological landscape of the time. Among the various connections beginning to be forged between the feminisms of the West and the East, one of the most striking examples was the publication, beginning in 1980, of the *Almanac of Women* of Leningrad and Moscow, first in samizdat and then in translations in different European countries. Part of the emerging protest movement, these authors revealed the failures of the Soviet system and condemned the situation of women. Moved by international opinion and actively involved in the demonstrations in support of the dissidents, Western feminists pledged solidarity with the women of Eastern Europe. This solidarity was not without its paradoxes, in that it was established beyond the revalorization of religion that was among the anchors of the new Soviet dissidence, and which many Eastern bloc women advocated. The situation was yet another example of solidarity among women initially being given priority over ideological oppositions, even though the latter became a source of contentions later on.

The Formalism of Antiformalism

At the heart of feminist demands lay the eradication of any association with violence and the denunciation of male power as the archetype—although not the sole form—of relationships of domination. Consequently, the issue of powerful personalities within the movement was inevitably a constant source of tensions. The fact of such and such a woman's dominance in the various feminist groups in each country was not mentioned for a long time, and even today the issue is only discussed reticently—or even purely and simply expunged. However, theoretical disagreements, and also the approach to organizing the movement and its strategic oppositions, unquestionably derived from the positions taken and choices made by the first women to play a basic, initiatory, and historic role. In *Le nouveau féminisme américain* (1972; The New American Feminism) Rolande Ballorain systematically shows that this was true with regard to the American movement: the increase in and proliferation of women's groups gave direction to and defined the development of the feminist movement. All historical accounts focus on this aspect to describe the distinguishing features of the feminist movement, which had to demonstrate clearly its difference from all other forms of political organization—a requirement emphasized in ways that were almost incantatory. Many authors have interpreted this rejection of all forms of structure, beginning with representation and the possibility of delegation, as an impediment to the lasting presence of feminist groups in the political field. However, any such interpretation is mechanical in that it obliterates all the other, purely historical and political factors.

Another very illuminating aspect of the history of feminism is the propagation, among militant women all around the world, of psycho-physiological metaphors to describe their participation in feminist groups. These semantic choices sought to restore the intensity of lived events, an adherence not to exterior ideas but the common sharing of what one always believed inside oneself and now dared to express at last—thoughts of emotional and bonding relationships between women and groups seen as a living body, a matrix of action, an ebb and flow of energies and a means of harnessing those energies. In every group, ongoing experimentation to forge new types of relationships between people was led by women who were well versed in the theories and practices of group dynamics. Such experimentation meant that in practice, and no longer just in theory, the principles of democracy were placed in opposition to the creative potential of individual initiatives. These situations were inevitably sources of antagonism and conflict. The inability to cope with tensions between the collective and individuals was soon cited as a causal factor in the development of impasses or, more simply, in the necessarily circumscribed character of feminist activism in the 1970s. Many examples could be given. The New York group The Feminist, in which Ti-Grace Atkinson, among others, played a major role, exemplified the ceaseless desire to inscribe rules that would ensure democracy within the general context of a movement that was forever condemning every rule as an institutionalization of power. The objective of these rules was to give each woman an equal place, for, as stated in the group's brochure, *Organizational Principles and Structures*:

the aptitude for politics is a general human ability and we think that the possibilities in this area are about the same in everyone. We cannot prove this assumption, but its opposite (that inequalities are natural) cannot be proven either as long as we have not eliminated oppression, which creates artificial inequalities among us. (Quoted in Ballorain.)

Here one sees the paradoxes and paroxysms of a voluntaristic egalitarianism so extreme that, for example, group members were assigned turns to speak during meetings—a measure that did not prevent violent outbursts and in some ways even restricted speech. In the context of the indictment of "alienating" practices, the wish to "banish the phallus from our minds," as the slogan of Parisian feminists put it, it became difficult to distinguish between, on the one hand, attacks on the processes feminists saw as being imposed from the outside and subsequently interiorized, and, on the other hand, the denunciation of individuals and their choices. Françoise Picq's account of the "movement years" bears the many and multiform traces of the exhilaration and elation but also of the rages and wounds of that period (*Libération des femmes. Les années-mouvement*).

In reality, the political debates were nothing short of a quest for identity. The first debates were a gently explosive mixture of the precepts of the cultural revolution—"power to the people"—and the search for an authentic self, a quest informed by the theses of English antipsychiatry, as put forth in the works of David Cooper or R. D. Laing. The preferred introduction to any participation in the movement was the consciousness-raising group. Notwithstanding the opposition often maintained between consciousness-raising groups and the "political" and structured organization of a mass movement, the consciousness-raising groups, based (although not exclusively) on personal testimonies of sexual experiences, initially appeared to be the requisite path for understanding the common roots of women's oppression. But, coming from the movements of the New Left, the objective of the first activists was to build a new mass movement. "For the time being, our first task is to awaken a 'class consciousness' in ourselves and in others on a massive scale," Kathy "Sarachild" Amatniek explained in a text translated into French and published in a special issue of *Partisans* (1970), containing the methodical description of the rules by which a consciousness-raising group was to function. Very quickly, however, the groups that saw themselves as being more "political" became critical of the consciousness-raising groups. Trotskyite militants criticized the discussions held in consciousness-raising sessions, which they saw as too limited in scope, as being merely an activity of "petites bourgeoises." In contradistinction to other extreme leftist groups, the Trotskyite groups advocated a policy of infiltration into feminist groups; this eventually led to more or less vituperative accusations and denunciations of ideological recuperation. In the United States the majority point of view in the consciousness-raising groups was that through their practice weapons were being forged against the influence of psychology and psychoanalysis. In France, the practices of consciousness-raising groups were somewhat mitigated, being strongly marked by the split within the movement regarding the place of psychoanalysis. As in other countries, the propagation of feminism in France occurred by way of groups that would meet for a limited period of time around a specific project and then be dissolved. More permanent groups were created on the basis of neighborhoods or a communal workplace, such as groups within a company. But, in contrast, many feminists were receptive to the contributions of psychoanalysis, which was not rejected in France as it was in the United States, as a symptom of what might be called hyperconsumption, but instead constituted a sign of belonging to enlightened intellectual circles. In France, therefore, there was a greater focus on the unconscious in the expression of feelings. Widespread at first, this focus on the unconscious eventually became more circumscribed as a result of tensions within the movement as a whole regarding the increasingly sectarian influence of the Psyc et Po group. Beyond the direct effects of this polemic, it may be noted that in Italy, on the other hand, consciousness-raising groups practiced in a more widespread and highly esteemed way. These Italian groups sought both to promote collective feminist consciousness-raising and to bring to light the most hidden mechanisms of the unconscious. Italian women thus engaged in an "auto-unconscious" practice, examples of which are discussed in Louise Vandelac's *L'Italie au féminisme* (1978; Italy's Feminism).

Adhering to feminist ideas cannot be reduced to a purely instrumental role, an element in the strategy for the transformation of social roles given to men and women. Participation in the women's movement represented putting a new ideology into praxis, the search for a common direction and values. This new ideology was given the name of sisterhood: "Womanhood is Sisterhood." Established as a prerequisite, sisterhood proved to be more difficult to live than had been foreseen in the early days of the movement—as numerous pamphlets and articles attest. An article by Cathy Bernheim and Claire Brisac, entitled "Liberté, égalité, sororité, ou: Le troisième mot" (Liberty, Equality, Sorority: The Third Word) published in *La revue d'en face* 1981, shows that women's groups passed through a more or less precarious period of ambiguity, as was true for many other constituent aspects of the feminism of the 1970s. On the one hand, there was sisterhood devised as an instrument of solidarity in order to deconstruct the myths of femininity and, on the other, the paradoxical limitation of autonomy, which was nonetheless the foundation of liberation, which sisterhood—lived as a moment of fusion of shared oppression—involved. In the words of Bernheim and Brisac:

> If the word Fraternity unites men in a common energy, a common *happiness*, it should first of all be noted that Sorority is rather a common bringing together of our misfortunes. Let us observe also that, if Fraternity allows men to reinforce their own identity and to come close beneath a same banner, that of the Human Being, Sorority is for us a weapon with which to deconstruct Woman, that strait jacket in the name of which they oppress us and challenge our identity as women. Sorority helps us to combat the universal legitimacy of the hatred of women in this male world.

Questions of racial or national identity compartmentalized the women's movement. Each of the groups maintained its autonomy and yet recognized common forms of solidarity. But sisterhood, the common solidarity of women, was badly hurt everywhere by the suspicion that the concept did not acknowledge the specific problems of lesbians, and by the fear that new forms of domination would be created between homosexuals and heterosexuals, or between mothers and women without children. In addition, the taking of positions in response to the perhaps more predictable political reflections polarized activists who defined the struggle only as integrated into the class struggle and those who refused to define one struggle as a prerequisite

for another. The latter disagreements very quickly resulted in the formation of ideologically distinct groups. By contrast, the issue of gay women's place within the movement did not immediately result in the formation of completely autonomous lesbian groups, but instead remained the object of acrimonious quarrels and internal fragmentation.

Throughout the 1970s, alongside the expansion of the demands and movements of homosexual men, lesbians formed separatist groups in the women's movement or in homosexual organizations. Since the first demonstrations in the United States of the Gay Liberation movement in 1969, homosexuals, advocating the liberation of all sexuality, participated in the revolutionary movements critical of "bourgeois" morality. Before lesbian radicalism affirmed its positions, female homosexuals were the victims of a double invisibility: rendered invisible by the sexism of gay male activists, and kept silent by the fervor of antihomosexual prejudices among even sincerely feminist women. For some of them it was a question of distancing themselves from the lesbian stereotypes that clung to feminists. Meanwhile, the broad distribution of Anne Koedt's text, "The Myth of Vaginal Orgasm" (originally published in 1968, then in a more elaborate version in 1970, and translated for the special issue of *Partisans*), allowed all feminist groups to reevaluate sexual practices and expose the submission to the male order that heterosexual social constraints had covered up. The practices of the small groups based on personal testimony quickly led to concrete concern with the taboos surrounding women's knowledge of their own bodies. These practices became widespread thanks to the enormous success of the book *Our Bodies, Ourselves* (1971) published by the Boston Women's Health Book Collective. After several new editions in the United States and various translations across the world, more than 3 million copies of the book had been sold by 1995, with profits still being transferred to different women's health organizations. *Our Bodies, Ourselves* was conceived as a tool of practical information on sexuality, contraception, abortion, venereal diseases, sports, and so forth, and it gave directions for gynecological self-examination and the use of a speculum. In the same spirit, alternative and women-run health care centers were created and women began actively taking charge of their own health in North America—the United States and Canada—as well as in the Netherlands. It was in these centers that illegal abortions were performed prior to the reform of abortion laws. Occurring within the more general climate of sexual liberation, on a more immediate level these debates on sexuality and choice also entailed a reevaluation of lived experience. But the question of homosexuality was not merely a question of personal pleasure, as some women discovered through feminist encounters, it was also a political question that served as a stumbling block and a point of friction within some groups. In most countries lesbians banded together in autonomous groups that participated in international gatherings. As in other countries, some French groups restricted their membership to lesbians only (les Gouines Rouges [The Red Dykes], for example), but in the early days of the French feminist movement homosexual women participated widely in all initiatives, and it was not until 1977–78 that independent groups of lesbians began to develop. Moreover, in France lesbian separatism continued to be a minority position. The conflicts that arose within the *Nouvelles questions féministes* team were most revealing of the positions involved. Beyond interpersonal conflicts, the opposition was not between homosexual and heterosexual women but instead concerned the acknowledgment of lesbianism as a political choice—which would necessarily diminish the impact of heterosexual feminism. Those homosexual women who envisioned feminism as a political organization of all women rejected the politicization of lesbianism, and they assailed the break that would then separate feminism and women. Claudie Lesselier's analysis in "Les regroupements des lesbiennes dans le mouvement féministe parisien, 1970–1982" (1991; Lesbian Groups in the Paris Feminist Movement, 1970–1982) presents a very mixed assessment of the recognition of lesbians' contributions to feminism, even though they played a major role in the movement's large demonstrations and mobilizations. Their contribution, explains Lesselier, continued to be marginalized: "Groups of lesbians could 'coexist' with the rest of the movement, the image and tenor of which continued to be heterosexual."

The history of feminist groups is punctuated by quarrels with the press. This relationship was caught in the tangles of contradictory injunctions—a blend of attraction and rejection, in the words of some women. As we have indicated, a large proportion of feminist activists came from the middle strata of the new intellectual classes; many journalists took an active part in the movement's initiatives, as in the campaign to legalize abortion in the United States, France, and Germany. One of the first public demonstrations of the women's liberation movement in the Republic of Ireland was mounted by a group that included several journalists. At the same time, however, relations between the women's movement and the press bore the stamp of distrust: a majority of feminists indisputably condemned the press's ideological function in propagating the "feminine mystique." Thus, the press played a major role, both as a place of expression and a means of dissemination of feminist texts and as a simple organ of information helping to increase public awareness of feminism as a new cultural phenomenon.

As is emphasized in studies on feminism in the United States, or in Liliane Kandel's analyses of the situation in France in "Journaux en mouvements: la presse féministe aujourd'hui" and "Post-scriptum: une presse 'antiféministe' aujourd'hui: 'Des femmes en mouvements'" (1980; "Newspapers in Movement: The Feminist Press Today" and "Post-scriptum: An Antifeminist Press Today: Women in Movement"), the relationship between feminists and the media shed light on two issues that were of crucial importance to the women's movement: "that of writing and that of 'organization.'" On the one hand, there were denunciations of the cult of stardom surrounding certain individuals, even as, on the other hand, some of the women participating in the movement's early initiatives came from intellectual circles and were already close to the media, and many groups were using public performance and spectacle as a means of gaining media exposure and thus public recognition. How could the press be used without putting this or that individual personality into the limelight? Very quickly one of the challenges facing groups was the promotion of their own means of expression, essentially through writing but also through radio, television, and cinema. The publication of newspapers, magazines, and the establishment of independent publishing houses accompanied the early enterprises of the movement worldwide. An exhaustive list cannot be produced, for in each country many projects of variable duration emerged, including ephemeral publications of a few issues that were supported only by activist and volunteer

work and had a hard time surviving in the face of periodicals that met with true commercial success, such as *Ms.* magazine in the United States, *Emma* in Germany, *Effe* in Italy or *La vie en rose* in Quebec. In the mid 1970s some publications focused exclusively on the theoretical viewpoint, at a time when feminist research was developing and being institutionalized in the academic world. Parallel to this, new magazines appeared based on a new image of femininity: the liberated woman.

The Feminism of the 1970s as a Conceptual Shift

Feminism is above all a highly diversified ideological product, and its greatest impact has unquestionably been in its critique of conceptual categories—regardless of whether feminists' contributions have been recognized. The priority task continues to be to expose and condemn the mechanisms that favor and maintain the subjugation of women and to act upon these mechanisms in order to change them. Feminist criticism has thus dealt with all scientific disciplines and with the construction of sexual categories as categories of discourse and elements of the self-perpetuation of the patriarchal system. Feminism proposes a double critique of science: women as the object of knowledge on the one hand, and, on the other, the recognition of women's viewpoint as subject of science. This feminist critique of knowledge and the sciences was very quickly institutionalized through the establishment first of courses, and then entire curricula and degree programs in women's studies in the universities. This work continues today, as a critical feminist perspective is brought to bear in the various disciplines in which sexual difference intervenes. Alongside this theoretical production we should acknowledge all the cultural and artistic productions, in literature, the fine arts, and filmmaking, that have contributed to the conceptual shift brought about by feminism—all the more so since many women's groups eschew all hierarchical systems in their productions, each manner of expression being considered as a way of inscribing one's presence in the world.

Valerie Solanas's 1967 manifesto for SCUM (Society for Cutting Up Men) is a model of this type of hybrid between literary production and political stance. The manifesto was widely distributed among feminist groups, undoubtedly with fewer reservations in Europe than in the United States, where judgments and declarations of anathema against Solanas herself were instantaneous. It should be recalled that not long after the publication of her text, Solanas was arrested for shooting Andy Warhol, one of the best-known painters of Pop Art in the New York underground. Her book was translated into German in 1969, into Dutch in 1970, and into French in 1971, with an introduction by Christiane Rochefort. Extracts were frequently used as quotations at the head of feminist texts: "The oppressor does not hear the words of his oppressed as language but as noise. . . . When the oppressed realizes this he pulls out his pistol. Then it is understood that something is wrong." Solanas's text, which may be compared to those of Swift, Sade, Céline or Leroy Jones, attacked our societies based on the exploitation of women. "The solutions Valerie proposes in order to put an end to this state of affairs are, in fact, in the image of her revolt: violent and desperate," as Annie-Elm, Catherine Crachat, and Rose Prudence wrote in one of the columns of *Le sexisme ordinaire* (1979), written in response to the words emanating from the paranoid personality that the text seems to reveal.

In its most radical version, feminism presented itself as a critique of dualism and a total refusal to be confined in the straitjacket of the most conventionally accepted dichotomies: between theory and practice, infrastructure and superstructure, women and men, nature and culture, heroic women and oppressed women.

> [As] feminists, we must show the historical and social—therefore arbitrary and reversible—character of the hierarchy of the sexes, and that there are "women" only insofar as relations based on inequalities of strength make the oppression and exploitation of one social group into the condition of power of the other. (*Questions féministes*, 1977)

In complete opposition to this radical and materialist current of feminism, there was another feminist current that, far from attacking the notion of differences between the sexes, called for the acknowledgment of sexual difference as an ontological principle. Adherents to this current sought to transcend the inauthentic femininity defined by the phallocentric culture and to bring authentic womanhood to light. As Françoise Collin expresses it:

> The specificity of the feminine . . . is no longer simply concerned with experience, but also with the constitution of a way of thinking and a creation, in short, of a culture that will bring about a true break with traditional phallocentric culture. ("Différence des sexes," 1990)

This current, often called "difference feminism," thus extends through its gender naturalism and essentialism the conceptual tradition that has long been the most common one where sexual difference is concerned.

Two characteristics emerge very strongly from the first wave of feminist theorizing, and both are evident in the two works that signaled the beginning of the theorization of the relationships between the sexes as a political relationship: *Sexual Politics* (1969) by Kate Millett, and *The Dialectic of Sex: The Case for Feminist Revolution* (1970) by Shulamith Firestone. First, both of these works brought a critique of Marxism and Freudian thought to bear on the trends of critical thought of the period. Second, both writers sought to produce explanatory analyses of male domination, but they had a hard time abandoning the impulse to understand the why and how of that domination through a reconstitution of its genesis. This quest for an explanation of the origins of the subordination of women took several forms that tied in with the 19th-century theories of a mythical matriarchy in which power belonged to women. Whether male domination stemmed from men's victorious struggle against matriarchal power or from women being socially hindered by reproduction, these first analyses retained a biological definition of sexual difference. Still, these overly deterministic analyses later gave rise to new examinations that rejected the search for the mythic origins of sexism in order to study the multiple forms of gendered divisions in society. Instead of the permanence of the differences between the sexes, the focus would henceforth

be an analysis of their variability. In order to distance the analysis of the relationships between the sexes from biological characteristics, research replaced the isolated analysis of women and the time-honored expression "the feminine condition" with the notions of sexual categories and gender.

The first article of faith of radical feminist theory was the definition of women as a caste, as a class. The second basic characteristic of radical feminist analyses was the characterization of male domination as an exercise in material violence: the material exploitation of women's bodies. This domination became systematic and constituted the foundation of the patriarchy. Economic exploitation of sexuality and reproduction thus established the exploitation of women as the first form of economic exploitation. Understandably, then, neofeminism began to reevaluate Friedrich Engels's analysis in *The Origin of the Family, Private Property, and the State* (1884), a work that had been reprinted a number of times in North America and Europe. However, recognizing the economic exploitation attached to sexuality and reproduction is not sufficient grounds to infer that sexuality was the *original* form of economic exploitation. A nondeterminist perspective of feminism should recognize that no historical reconstruction of the origins of domination is possible, but that the domination of women is inscribed in a complex whole of social relationships.

Standing in opposition to this materialist current, which was heavily stamped with Marxism and post-Marxist critique, was the current of difference feminism that located the basis for male domination within the system of representation. Notably in France, this rested on the most radical currents of psychoanalytic criticism. The approach embraced in Luce Irigaray's works—notably *Speculum de l'autre femme* (1974; *Speculum of the Other Woman*)—sought to open new fields of symbolization that recognized the feminine not as the deductible of the masculine, but, on the contrary, an entity based in the biological or morphological understanding of the female body as it is experienced in relation to oneself and also in relation to other women. The key issue was that of reestablishing the connection with the mother. Irigaray's works, translated in the United States as well as in Italy, were widely disseminated within the academic field of women's studies in the United States. Irigaray's theories met with a more politicized reception in Italy, where women's groups took up the idea of women's inherent differences in order to establish specific civil rights for them. Women were redefining their position with respect to nature, the economy, and government.

In "Différence des sexes" (1990; Sexual Difference), her philosophical critique of sexual difference, stressing the two directions that Beauvoir's founding thought ("one is not born a woman") took in neofeminism, Collin shows that, beyond their opposition, equality feminists ("one is born neuter") and difference feminists ("one is born a woman") converged because both were seeking a definition of women: a false question to which only false answers can be offered. This point of view can be compared to the analysis of "feminine nationalism" proposed by Ti-Grace Atkinson, who also maintained that when feminists constitute as a unique physical class those persons who share the same consciousness, they do not automatically abandon all biological considerations in making their argument.

Sexual Dependency and Sexual Autonomy

One of the principal stakes of contemporary feminism, as we have seen, involves the body and a political critique of sexuality. Reiterating the criticism already proposed by Simone de Beauvoir, radical feminism attacked the most normative aspects of Freudian thinking—the supposed imprisonment of the female libido in the idea of the "failed male" as an element of "phallocentrism"—and developed a political theory of sexuality. This was part of Kate Millett's project in *Sexual Politics*. However, the path opened by radical feminism was not the only analysis of sexuality. It should be remembered that in France, the project of the Psyc et Po group was that of exploring the points of articulation between those two disciplines. One of the strong points maintained by Antoinette Fouque within that group was the assertion of innate homosexuality among women. As Élisabeth Roudinesco relates in her history of psychoanalysis in France, for Fouque

> [T]o think the continent of womanhood is to displace the issue to the terrain of a *homosexual* women's sex, defined as a second libido and inductively derived based on the relationship with the mother. . . . This doctrine continues to be structural: it is based on the Lacan's notion of the supplement and Derrida's notion of différance. (See Roudinesco.)

Meanwhile, Irigaray advanced a critique of Freudian and Lacanian theses as manifestations of logocentrism and suggested, as Roudinesco also reports, "a 'deconstructive' reading of the Dark Continent: through the emergence of her repression, woman becomes *a* woman and thus gives birth to her radical otherness." In conjunction with this redefinition of female sexuality there emerged a sexed conception of writing, in which the active search for this "being-woman" would pass through the practice of writing to bring forth "the plural inscription of language."

In contrast to the perspective of difference feminisms, the radical theoretical view minimized any reference to the differentiation of the sexes in favor of an analysis of patriarchal institutions as the foundations of sexual difference and male domination. Marriage, in which the exchange of women is institutionalized, imposes complementarity of the sexes through the gendered division of labor that it puts into place. This view was developed in particular among feminist anthropologists, including Gayle Rubin in the United States, Nicole-Claude Mathieu in France, and Paola Tabet in Italy. It was henceforth possible to challenge the institutionalization of heterosexuality as a social constraint, as suggested in the analyses of radical feminists such as Atkinson. This viewpoint assailed sexuality as a social imposition and thus overturned the theoretical perspective on the sexual revolution offered in the works of Marcuse and Reich. This radical perspective posited lesbianism as a tactic. Once heterosexuality has been established as a social norm, the radical view denounces heterosexuality as a form of submission to the oppressor and calls upon women to struggle against men. According to Monique Wittig, the critique of socially imposed heterosexuality necessitates a critique of the categories of thought, structuralism in particular. The struggle against what she calls "the straight mind" involves not only the transformation of economic relationships but also a political transformation of language.

> [F]or us, this means there cannot any longer be women and men, and that as classes and as categories of thought or language they have to disappear, politically, economically, ideologically. If we, as lesbians and gay men, continue to speak of ourselves as women and as men, we are instrumental in maintaining heterosexuality. ("The Straight Mind")

Economic Exploitation

At the heart of the analysis of the economic exploitation of women, several issues exist at the same time: that of women's specific relationship to production and to reproduction, and that of the points of articulation between the patriarchal system and capitalism. These issues are central concerns both in the formation of feminist strategy and in determining whether or not privileged bonds with the working class should be maintained, depending on whether one's perspective tends toward "class struggle" or toward Trotskyite militantism. In France, Christine Delphy's analysis in "L'ennemi principal" (The Principal Enemy), published in *Partisans* in 1970, was decisive in the definition of domestic production as the foundation of the patriarchal system and the definition of women as a class. Meanwhile, part of the women's movement in Great Britain, the United States, Canada, and Italy drew on the analyses of authors such as Mariarosa Dalla Costa and Selma James, coauthors of *The Power of Women and the Subversion of the Community* (1973). The campaigns advocating "wages for domestic work" in various countries—with the exception of France, where these positions never garnered much of a response—did not seek greater integration of women into the capitalist system, since they were already implicated in it. The subversive power of this demand lay in using the demand for wages to denounce the current feminine role and its manifestations in acts of "servility" and "sacrifice" on the part of women.

From Direct Action to Campaigns of Mass Mobilization

While the extraparliamentary character of the women's liberation movement, beyond the bounds of traditional political organizations, has been emphasized, the movement also succeeded in organizing large protest demonstrations demanding support for the exercise of existing rights and the creation of new rights. Demonstrations were a powerful means of political action to shape public opinion, to exert pressure on political parties, and to instigate new policies and establish new rights.

Initially the campaigns for the legalization of abortion constituted the most important and the most striking of such mass events. Later came the mobilizations to protest against violence inflicted upon women—rape, sexual harassment—and to demand legal changes, such as the recognition of conjugal rape.

In Europe, feminist action in accelerating successive reforms in family law for greater equality in the treatment of men and women contributed to bringing different national laws closer together and to bypassing the oppositions often made between predominantly Catholic and Protestant countries. The conquest of new rights for women in the private sphere went hand in hand with renewed demands in the public sphere for effective measures to achieve true equality in the workplace. The latter kind of demand could really be expressed only in association with unions and political organizations. Women's liberation movements organized few initiatives directly linked to questions of work, although, as we have seen, feminists demonstrated as soon as they were able their solidarity with women struggling in the workplace: women workers, office employees, employees in commerce and department stores. In addition, in the United States a large proportion of feminists participated in the campaigns to adopt the Equal Rights Amendment (ERA), which would affirm sexual equality in every area. After innumerable struggles, this constitutional reform has still not been achieved at the beginning of the 21st century.

In France, by contrast, a constitutional law on political parity between women and men was adopted on 28 June 1999 by the Congress of Parliament in solemn proceedings that brought together the National Assembly and the Senate. The new law modified Article 3 of the Constitution, dealing with national sovereignty, and Article 4, dealing with the role of the parties, by affirming equal access for women and men to all electoral mandates and functions. The law on parity, while it benefited from extraordinary media coverage, nevertheless had little effect on the sexist workings of the French republican tradition. Its intended effect of achieving gender balance was not achieved in the legislative elections of June 2000 (when only 11 more women were elected than in 1997, bringing to 71 the total number of women deputies, out of a total of 577).

The most significant fact during the 1970s was that feminist movements were able to join forces with and mobilize vast numbers of union women and women affiliated with left-wing political parties, but also women of right-wing parties who agreed with the demands for freedom of abortion or, in Italy, of divorce. This capacity to mobilize generated new ways of spreading feminism, which became diffused throughout society. Thus, the feminism of the 1970s found new intermediaries in the unions, for it would be wrong to limit the period's feminism to mere cultural manifestations. In the United States and Great Britain, new measures were put into place aimed at counteracting the discrimination against women perpetrated through the adoption of so-called "positive" laws. Similar measures were implemented in Europe. This spread of feminist demands in professional and union organizations as well as in political parties occurred in all of the countries of Europe and North America, with more or less pronounced forms of integration into the traditional institutions of political and union life. The connections between feminists and the labor movement marked the evolution of feminism in Italy in an important way. Great Britain exemplifies the case of a broad diffusion of feminism within one party, the Labour Party, because of the organic links that bound that party to the unions, where these demands were first adopted. On the other hand, the integration of feminist demands into the French union movement was stamped with the usual seal of the French political universe: conditional integration. Feminism appeared to be

conceivable only if its assimilation was complete—which would also mean the loss of all its ability to criticize the space allotted to women in the workplace as well as in the unions. Thus, in the early days there were many women's commissions in the various union bureaus, of both the Confédération Générale du Travail (CGT; General Labor Confederation) and the Confédération Française Démocratique du Travail (CFDT; French Democratic Labor Confederation), albeit mostly on the local level. But when the issue of sexism in the organization itself came up, it met with paternalistic smiles, dismissal out of hand, or disdainful rejection. And yet, when it came to women's strikes, for instance, union thinking did take into account the "fallout" from night work in factories in terms of its impact on the sharing of domestic and family tasks; the unions did include the struggle for abortion rights in their agenda of actions. Nonetheless, union activism had trouble integrating women's issues into its core considerations and confined women's issues to the sector of social questions: improvements to be demanded so that women could best reconcile their dual roles as workers and mothers. The conflict that broke out in 1982 at the magazine *Antoinette*, the women's publication of the CGT, was an example of the difficulties of the central organization in taking into account women's expectations, which had been renewed by the women's liberation movement. Here again, just as in the early 1970s in the extreme Left organizations, the issue of women's place within the organization brought the question of democracy and the critique of centralism to the heart of the organization.

Feminism, a New Social Movement?

A sociological analysis of feminism as a social movement emphasizes the gap between legally confirmed equality and observable difference in society—the basis for all feminist demands. The new feminism is fundamentally not a demand for equality but instead an acknowledgment of the social impossibility of establishing equality in a patriarchal system. Taking this radical demand of neofeminism into account, recent sociological analyses of social movements, such as Alain Touraine's *Critique de la modernité* (1992; *Critique of Modernity*), classify feminism as "new" in the sense of a movement of cultural rather than economic demands:

> Whereas the social movements of old, and especially the trade unions, degenerated in to being either political pressure groups or agencies for the corporate defense of sectors of the new wage-earning middle class rather than the defense of the underprivileged, the new social movements are already revealing a new generation of social and cultural problems and conflicts, even though they are unorganized and do not have any capacity for permanent action. The conflict is now not one over who controls the means of production, but one over the goals of cultural productions such as education, health care, and mass information.

The insistence on feminism's "newness" seems a rather inadequate notion to the extent that contemporary feminism is continuing the expectations of 19th-century feminism. Feminist demands, as Geneviève Fraisse demonstrates in *La raison des femmes* (1992; *Women's Reason*), are essentially based on the two-fold question of women's economic and political autonomy. At stake is the individuation of the democratic and economic subject (the individuation of the democratic citizen and the wage-laborer), and that process was already included in 19th-century demands. Today's feminism is thus not innovative in that regard. It has been innovative, however, in pushing more strongly for greater autonomy within female sexuality: motherhood is not women's sole horizon, and further, the wish not to be a mother may be expressed positively; childlessness is no longer equated with failure.

According to Bourdieu's analysis in "La domination masculine" (1990; Male Domination), the feminist movement is wholly characterized as a "symbolic revolution" to the extent that male domination is strong enough to dispense with self-justification:

> Only a collective action intended to organize a *symbolic struggle* capable of *challenging* practically every tacit assumption of the phallo-narcissistic vision of the world can bring about the break of the quasi-immediate agreement between incorporated structures and objectified structures, which is the condition of a true collective conversion of mental structures.

There is no cause to deny the importance granted to the symbolic, but women who are entirely caught in the tangles of symbolic power games are, in Bourdieu's view, in some way removed from other social practices, which nevertheless establish the reproduction of sexual relationships. Feminism is also a demand for social change, as the struggles to legalize abortion, an active ferment in women's mobilization, have shown.

The views developed by Touraine and Bourdieu converge with those of sociologists in other countries, particularly Claus Offe and Jürgen Habermas: all these writers privilege the ideological and cultural aspects of feminist demands. Are feminists' own analyses so opaque to readings by sociologists that the latter can explain women's political engagement only in ideological terms? According to Nicole Gabriel's formula in her analysis of women's movements in Germany, *La question féminine depuis les années 1970: Féminisme et "nouvelle féminité"* (The Feminine Question since the 1970s: Feminism and the "New Femininity"), the ideological dimension is only the rhetorical surface that accompanies every expression of social movements. The novelty of the discourse may capture the attention of these sociologists, but women's demands are not rhetorical. Gabriel argues that in situating women's revolt merely on the ideological plane, it is almost as if these analyses still do not manage to consider women as social agents responding to an emergency in their social situation. She views this as a denial of the situation of oppression visited upon women.

Other analyses focus not on the cultural dimension of women's movements, but rather on their ability to call for new rights, reproductive rights, rights to a citizenship differently formulated. Such analyses continue in the vein of T. H. Marshall's theories on the new demands for social rights or new citizenship in contemporary societies. Feminism is also the profusion of alternative plans offering the citizen new expectations outside any earlier appeal for law, for the feminism of the 1970s was above all a demand for liberty. From that perspective, there is no power strategy, not so much because feminists reflect a uniquely negative image of power—although one might easily point to the trap some women have fallen into in reproducing stereotypes such as the one that negatively defines power as male—but because feminism propagates libertarian perspectives against the state and every form of power. These alternative projects are especially characteristic of the development of the feminist movement in Germany.

The impact of feminism in the 1970s was perhaps not so much that of generating new forms of demands and requests for rights as that of reassessing political arenas. Since the women's liberation movement continued the counterculture movements of the 1960s, for which everything was political, one of feminism's priorities, which could summarize many of these expectations, was the affirmation that "the personal is political." Indeed, feminism was defined in the analysis and the questioning of the conventional relationship between the public and the private in women's lives. In *Free Spaces: The Sources of Democratic Change in America* (1986), Sara M. Evans and Harry C. Boyte contend that the most crucial aspect of the traditional ideology of feminism inhered in its struggle for an appropriate definition of women's role in the public arena. A first version of feminism in the American movements of the 19th century corresponded to the integration of women into the political arena as it had been defined by men, emphasizing women's individual rights as citizens. This was republican feminism, a legacy from the American Revolution. Other feminist currents departed from the traditional roles and responsibilities of women in the family and the values attached to these as a basis for a critique of the public arena and of an alternative vision of politics. Historically, neofeminism emerged out of the tensions between the rejection or the preservation of tradition, between the affirmation of equality and the affirmation of difference, between the female counterculture (community) and individual liberty, between public and private spheres. The task of feminism thus not only entails taking cognizance of the evolution of the two poles of such tensions, but also necessitates a critical understanding of the public/private dichotomy itself. In fact, feminists have a hard time achieving critical distance from that dichotomy, and one need only privilege one of the poles for the other to represent a "mortal" danger for women's liberation.

On Woman as Subject

A paradox in the feminist movement is that it is a collective movement for individual affirmation. Feminism is a common identity in oppression: it is rooted in an acknowledgment of women's community of identity, but very quickly it inevitably abuts against the need to recognize the absence of a common interest among women. Radical feminists attack a society that promotes belief in equality even when its own foundations are based in inequality. Community of interest among women, they argue, is an illusion constructed by their alienation as women. The category of "otherness" is a construct of male domination. What must therefore be at stake is the subversion of this alienation. A first stage consisted of the demand for equality as access to the universe of the human species. The second stage represented the denunciation and the deconstruction of this universe. The ideological reversal of this critique thus involves a rejection of masculine productivist thinking and the valorization of the feminine values of motherhood.

Feminism in the 1970s can be schematically presented in terms of a combination of different currents of thought, all of which sought to respond to the urgency of social changes. In the first place, one can identify a form of feminism that was presented as the culmination of liberal thought, based on the promotion of individual values. This type of feminism was expressed either in a struggle for true democracy, for complete equality of women and men, or in "pro-women" feminism, which proposed giving women priority treatment in order to reduce gender-based discrepancies. Second, a large part of feminism consisted of the critique of ideological productions, the objective being to provoke a "symbolic revolution" that would allow new values to be established. This trend was manifested as much in lesbian separatism as in the approach of revalorizing femininity/femaleness. Finally, many aspects of the feminist movement derived from the libertarian tradition.

Analyses of feminism usually distinguish three currents that differ from one another in their definition of women's oppression and in their political strategies: radical feminism, socialist feminism, and liberal feminism. In terms of the presentation we have just given, this typology fails to mention the libertarian dimension of feminism—both as it was initially expressed during the 1970s and also as it can be seen in the anarchist tradition generally and in specific struggles against institutions and the state. As is the case with other aspects of libertarian movements, it is difficult for historiography to trace the development of this tradition.

For some, the political weakness of feminism is that it has not yet managed to subvert and redefine on its own terms femininity or "being-woman"—a concept that remains caught up within the dialectic constructed by oppression. And yet, the definition of "being-woman" continues to be the unsurpassable horizon of both egalitarian feminism and difference feminism. In her conclusion to *The Second Sex*, Beauvoir, in the somewhat pessimistic vein common to many aspects of existentialist "humanism," depicts women's destiny as a frantic search for equality within inequality: a dead-end quest and thus one that produces intense frustration. But fortunately, Beauvoir did live to see a glorious transcendence of this situation: as an expression of the battle between the sexes, the feminism of the 1970s, in its "warrior" mode and its "dialogue" mode alike, was an exultant critique of the oppressors.

Bibliography

Albistur, Maïté, and Armogathe, Daniel, *Histoire du féminisme français du Moyen Âge à nos jours*, 2 vols., Paris: Éditions des femmes, 1977

Altbach, Edith Hoshino, compiler, *From Feminism to Liberation*, Cambridge, Massachusetts: Schenkman, 1971; 2nd edition, 1980

Astelarra, Judith, "La transition vers la démocratie en Espagne," in *Femmes et contre-pouvoirs*, edited by Yolande Cohen, Montreal, Quebec: Boréal, 1987

Atkinson, Ti-Grace, *Amazon Odyssey*, New York: Links Books, 1974

Atkinson, Ti-Grace, "Le nationalisme féminin," *Nouvelles questions féministes* 6–7 (Spring 1984)

Ballorain, Rolande, *Le nouveau féminisme américain: Essai: Étude historique et sociologique du Women's Liberation Movement*, Paris: DenoëlGonthier, 1972

Barreno, Maria Isabel, Maria Teresa Horta, and Maria Velho da Costa, *Novas cartas portuguesas*, Lisbon: Estúdios Cor, 1972; as

The Three Marias: New Portuguese Letters, translated by Helen R. Lane, Garden City, New York: Doubleday, 1975

Beauvoir, Simone de, *Le deuxième sexe*, 2 vols., Paris: Gallimard, 1949; as *The Second Sex*, translated by H.M. Parshley, New York: Knopf, 1953

Benoît, Nicole, Edgar Morin, and Bernard Paillard, *La femme majeure: Nouvelle féminité, nouveau féminisme*, Paris: Club de l'Obs, 1973

Bernheim, Cathy, *Perturbation, ma sœur: Naissance d'un mouvement de femmes, 1970–1972*, Paris: Seuil, 1983

Bernheim, Cathy, and Geneviève Brisac, "Liberté, égalité, sororité; ou, le troisième mot," *La revue d'en face* 11 (1981)

Bonnet, Marie-Jo, *Un choix sans équivoque: Recherches historiques sur les relations amoureuses entre les femmes, XVIᵉ–XXᵉ siècle*, Paris: Denoël, 1981; new edition, as *Les relations amoureuses entre les femmes, du XVIᵉ au XXᵉ siècle: Essai historique*, Paris: Jacob, 1995

Bouchier, David, *The Feminist Challenge: The Movement for Women's Liberation in Britain and the USA*, London: Macmillan, 1983; New York: Schocken Books, 1984

Bourdieu, Pierre, "La domination masculine," *Actes de la recherche en sciences sociales* 84 (September 1990).

Bourdieu, Pierre, *Masculine Domination*, Sanford, California: Stanford University Press, 2001

Castro, Ginette, *Radioscopie du féminisme américain*, Paris: Presses de la Fondation Nationale des Sciences Politiques, 1984; as *American Feminism: A Contemporary History*, translated by Elizabeth Loverde-Bagwell, New York: New York University Press, 1990

Centre Lyonnais d'Études Féministes (CLEF), *Chronique d'une passion: Le mouvement de libération des femmes à Lyon*, Paris: L'Harmattan, 1989

Collin, Françoise, "Différence des sexes," in *Encyclopédie philosophique*, edited by André Jacob, vol. 2, *Les notions philosophiques*, edited by Sylvain Auroux, Paris: Presses Universitaires de France, 1990

Collin, Françoise, "Féminitude et féminisme," in *Le féminisme pour quoi faire?* Brussels: Transédition, 1973

Coote, Anna, and Beatrix Campbell, *Sweet Freedom: The Struggle for Women's Liberation*, London: Pan, 1982

Costain, Anne N., *Inviting Women's Rebellion: A Political Process Interpretation of the Women's Movement*, Baltimore, Maryland: Johns Hopkins University Press, 1992

Crispino, Anna-Maria, "Le féminisme et la gauche: La route des collisions," *Peuples méditerranéens* 67 (April–June 1994)

Dahlerup, Drude, "Is the New Women's Movement Dead? Decline or Change of the Danish Movement," in *The New Women's Movement: Feminism and Political Power in Europe and the USA*, edited by Dahlerup, London and Beverly Hills, California: Sage, 1986

Dahlerup, Drude, and Brita Bulli, "The Impact of Women's Liberation Movement on Public Policy in Denmark and Norway," *Institute of Political Science Paper* (University of Aarhus, Denmark) (1983)

Dhavernas, Marie-Jo, and Liliane Kandel, "Le sexisme comme réalité et comme représentation," *Les temps modernes*, no. 444 (July 1983)

Duran, Maria Angeles, and Maria Teresa Gallego, "The Women's Movement and the New Spanish Democracy," in *The New Women's Movement: Feminism and Political Power in Europe and the USA*, edited by Drude Dahlerup, London and Beverly Hills, California: Sage, 1986

Evans, Sara M., *Born for Liberty: A History of Women in America*, New York: Free Press, and London: Collier Macmillan, 1989

Evans, Sara M., *Personal Politics: The Roots of Women's Liberation in* the Civil Rights Movement and the New Left, New York: Knopf, 1979

Evans, Sara M., and Harry C. Boyte, Free Spaces: The Sources of Democratic Change in America, New York: Harper and Row, 1986

Ezekiel, Judith, "A Contribution to the History of the American Women's Movement: The Case Study of Dayton, Ohio (1969–1980)," Ph.D. diss., Université Paris VIII, 1984

Ezekiel, Judith, "Gauchistes, théologiennes et majorettes: Itinéraires féministes à Dayton, Ohio, USA," in Crises de la société: Féminisme et changement, by Groupe d'Études Féministes de l'Université de Paris VII, Paris: Éditions Tierce, 1991

Falcon, Lidia, Cartas a una idiota española, Barcelona: Editorial Dirosa, 1974

Feher, Michel, "1967–1992: Sur quelques récompositions de la gauche américaine," Esprit (December 1992)

Les femmes s'entêtent, Paris: Gallimard, 1974 (reprint of a special number of Temps modernes [1974])

Ferree, Myra Marx, and Beth B. Hess, Controversy and Coalition: The New Feminist Movement, Boston: Twayne, 1985; 3rd edition, as Controversy and Coalition: The New Feminist Movement across Three Decades of Change, New York: Routledge, 2000

Firestone, Shulamith, The Dialectic of Sex, New York: Morrow, 1970; London: Jonathan Cape, 1971

Frabotta, Bianca-Maria, "Une autre façon de faire de la politique?" in L'Italie au féminisme: Recueil de textes, edited by Louise Vandelac, Paris: Tierce, 1978

Fraisse, Geneviève, La raison des femmes, Paris: Plon, 1992

Freeman Jo, The Politics of Women's Liberation: A Case Study of an Emerging Social Movement and Its Relation to the Policy Process, New York: McKay, 1975

Friedan, Betty, The Feminine Mystique, New York: Norton, 1963

Gabriel, Nicole, L'assemblée des femmes: L'organisation féminine du SPD au temps de Willy Brandt et de Helmut Schmidt, Bern and New York: Peter Lang, 1992

Gabriel, Nicole, "La question féminine depuis les années 70: Féminisme et 'nouvelle féminité,'" Revue d'Allemagne (1988)

Garcia, Sandrine, "Le féminisme, une révolution symbolique? Étude des luttes symboliques autour de la condition féminine," Ph.D. diss., École des Hautes Études en Sciences Sociales, 1993

Gaudin, Élisabeth, "Communauté européenne et droits des femmes en Irlande: Quel impact?" L'Irlande politique et sociale 4 (1991)

Hervieu-Léger, Danièle, Le féminisme en France, Paris: Le Sycomore, 1982

Irigaray, Luce, Speculum de l'autre femme, Paris: Éditions de Minuit, 1974; as Speculum of the Other Woman, translated by Gillian C. Gill, Ithaca, New York: Cornell University Press, 1985

Kandel, Liliane, "Journaux en mouvements: La presse féministe aujourd'hui," and "Post-scriptum: Une presse 'anti-féministe' aujourd'hui: Des femmes en mouvements," Questions féministes 7 (1980)

Kandel, Liliane, "Du politique au personnel: Le prix d'une illusion," in Crises de la société: Féminisme et changement, by Groupe d'Études Féministes de l'Université de Paris VII, Paris: Éditions Tierce, 1991

Kaplan, Gisela, Contemporary Western European Feminism, New York: New York University Press, 1992

Katzenstein, Mary Fainsod, and Carol McClurg Mueller, editors, The Women's Movements of the United States and Western Europe: Consciousness, Political Opportunity, and Public Policy, Philadelphia, Pennsylvania: Temple University Press, 1987

Koedt, Anne, "The Myth of the Vaginal Orgasm," in Notes from the First Year, New York: New York Radical Women, 1968

Kuhn, Annette, and AnnMarie Wolpe, editors, Feminism and

Materialism: Women and Modes of Production, London and Boston: Routledge and Kegan Paul, 1978

Lamoureux, Diane, Fragments et collages: Essai sur le féminisme québécois des années 70, Montreal: Éditions du Remue-Ménage, 1986

Lesselier, Claudie, "Les regroupements des lesbiennes dans le mouvement féministe parisien (1970–1982)," in Crises de la société: Féminisme et changement, by Groupe d'Études Féministes de l'Université de Paris VII, Paris: Éditions Tierce, 1991

Le livre de l'oppression des femmes, Paris: Belfond, 1972

Lovenduski, Joni, Women and European Politics: Contemporay Feminism and Public Policy, Brighton, Sussex: Wheatsheaf Books, and Amherst: University of Massachusetts Press, 1986

Malos, Ellen, editor, The Politics of Housework, London: Allison and Busby, 1980

Marcuse, Herbert, One-Dimensional Man: Studies in the Ideology of Advanced Industrial Society, Boston: Beacon Press, 1964

Masters, William H. and Virginia E. Johnson, Human Sexual Response, Boston: Little, Brown, 1966

Maternité esclave: Les chimères, Paris: Union Général d'Éditions, 1975

Millett, Kate, Sexual Politics, Boston: New England Free Press, 1969

Mitchell, Juliet, "Women: The Longest Revolution," New Left Review 40 (1966)

Mitchell, Juliet, and Ann Oakley, editors, What Is Feminism? Oxford: Blackwell, and New York: Pantheon Books, 1986

Morin, Edgar, L'esprit du temps, vol. 1, Paris: Grasset, 1962

Myrdal, Alva, and Viola Klein, Women's Two Roles, Home and Work, London: Routledge and Kegan Paul, 1962

Offe, Claus, "New Social Movements: Changing Boundaries of the Political," Social Research 52 (1985)

Partisans no. 54–55 (July-October 1970), special issue entitled Libération des femmes: Année zéro; see especially "Groupe de conscience," by Kathy "Sarachild" Amatniek, and "Histoire d'une longue marche," by Marcia Salo and Kathy McAffee

Picq, Françoise, Libération des femmes: Les années-mouvement, Paris: Seuil, 1993

Randall, Vicky, Women and Politics, New York: St. Martin's Press, and London: Macmillan Press, 1982; 2nd edition, as Women and Politics: An International Perspective, Chicago: University of Chicago Press, and London: Macmillan Education, 1987

Rémy, Monique, Histoire des mouvements de femmes: De l'utopie à l'intégration, Paris: L'Harmattan, 1990

Rochefort, Christiane, "Le mythe de la frigidité féminine," Partisans 54–55 (July–October 1970)

Roudinesco, Élisabeth, La bataille de cent ans: Histoire de la psychanalyse en France, vol. 1, Paris: Éditions Ramsay, and vol. 2, Paris: Seuil, 1986; see especially vol. 2, 1925–1985; vol. 2 as Jacques Lacan and Co.: A History of Psychoanalysis in France, 1925–1985, translated by Jeffrey Mehlman, London: Free Association, and Chicago : University of Chicago Press, 1990

Rowbotham, Sheila, Women in Movement: Feminism and Social Action, New York: Routledge, 1992

Rowbotham, Sheila, Woman's Consciousness, Man's World, London: Penguin, 1974

Le sexisme ordinaire, Paris: Éditions du Seuil, 1979

Smyth, Ailbhe, "The Women's Movement in the Republic of Ireland, 1970–1990," in Irish Women's Studies Reader, edited by Smyth, Dublin: Attic Press, 1993

Solanas, Valerie, SCUM Manifesto, New York: Olympia Press, 1967

Sullerot, Évelyne, Histoire et sociologie du travail féminin, Paris: Gonthier, 1968

Threlfall, Monica, editor, *Mapping the Women's Movement: Feminist Politics and Social Transformation in the North*, London and New York: Verso, 1996

Touraine, Alain, *Critique de la modernité*, Paris: Fayard, 1992; as *Critique of Modernity*, translated by David Macey, Oxford and Cambridge, Massachusetts: Blackwell, 1995

Touraine, Alain, editor, *Mouvements sociaux d'aujourd'hui: Acteurs et analystes*, Paris: Éditions Ouvrières, 1982

Tristan, Anne, and Annie de Pisan, *Histoires du M.L.F.*, Paris: Calmann-Lévy, 1977

United States President's Commission on the Status of Women, *American Women: Report*, Washington, D.C.: Government Publishing Office, 1963

Vandelac, Louise, editor, *L'Italie au féminisme*, Paris: Éditions Tierce, 1978

Varikas, Eleni, "Les femmes grecques face à la modernisation institutionnelle: Un féminisme difficile," *Les temps modernes* (December 1985) (special issue entitled *La Grèce en mouvement*)

Veauvy, Christiane, "Le mouvement féministe en Italie," *Peuples méditerranéens*, nos. 22–23 (January–June 1983)

Wittig, Monique, "La pensée Straight," *Questions féministes* 7 (1980); as "The Straight Mind," *Feminist Issues* 1, no. 1 (1980)

UNIVERSAL SUFFRAGE AND DIRECT DEMOCRACY

The Swiss Case, 1848–1990

BRIGITTE STUDER

IN THE AREA OF political rights, Switzerland undeniably stands out as a unique case. It was the first modern democracy to grant universal male suffrage in 1848, and while this right remained unquestioned, Switzerland was also the last country in Europe to grant the right to vote to its female citizens. Women's suffrage did not receive approval at the national level until 1971. Moreover, it was not until 1990 that every political body at the cantonal and municipal level finally recognized women's voting rights, and this only because the canton of Appenzell Innerhoden was forced to capitulate in the face of a decision handed down by the federal court. All told, close to one hundred votes had been needed for the measure to pass electorally. How should we interpret Switzerland's exceptionalism in this matter? For the persistence of its refusal to grant women's suffrage was certainly an anomaly, even though women's political representation in Switzerland quickly caught up with European averages after 1990.

Any analysis of the question must obviously take into account the specificity of the Swiss political system, particularly its founding principles of federalism and direct democracy. Swiss direct democracy incorporates two unusual features, both of them independent of the founding of the federal state in 1848. First, there was an old democratic tradition known as the *Landsgemeinde*, which periodically assembled all citizens eligible to vote. Political theorists of liberalism in 1848 had been highly critical of this form of democracy (which predated the founding of the federal state in certain rural regions), arguing that it did not provide the appropriate mechanisms to control the exercise of political power. Dian Schefold has shown that as a result of this criticism, liberal theorists opted instead for a mode of representational democracy, which was the model for the new Swiss confederation (see Schefold). Nonetheless, the form of federalism adopted allowed the *Landsgemeinde* to subsist in some cantons of central Switzerland. Second, there are the two mechanisms that specifically define Swiss direct—or, more accurately, semi-

direct—democracy, namely, the citizens' right of referendum and their right to introduce constitutional amendments by a citizen's initiative. These rights were introduced later, in 1874 and 1891, respectively. Thus, women's exclusion from the political process was determined prior to the implementation of the rights granting ordinary Swiss citizens the means to participate directly in government through their ability to introduce their own particular interests into the shaping of the general will.

These circumstances limit the relevance of the main argument in the debate about women's suffrage in Switzerland, that is, the notably participatory nature of Swiss citizenship and the extent of Swiss democratic rights. The latter issue must therefore be put into historical perspective. While it is true that the rights to referendum and to introduce citizens' initiatives have weighed heavily in the denial of women's suffrage during the 20th century, this was not true in the 19th century. In fact, while the committee of the Diet charged with drafting the constitution of 1848 was concerned at the time about the political inequality reserved for Jews (only to comply with it in the end), not one word was ever uttered about women's legal rights. By instituting a system of universal male suffrage, the liberals of 1848 were guided by a premise that seemed perfectly self-evident at the time. All Swiss men were considered perfectly "competent" to fulfill this function of citizenship. This was considered an established principle from the outset, even though its implementation on a practical level would take several decades. In contrast, the supposition of "competence"—that is, personal qualifications of a moral or intellectual nature—was not extended to Swiss women. Woman's lot in this case shows that in reality, Switzerland in 1848 had not really given up the notion of the right to vote based on "competence," even though it had eliminated property ownership as a criterion for eligibility to vote. Of the two categories of exclusion from access to political rights—property and competence—mentioned in 1932 by Karl Braunias in his massive comparative study of European parliamentary systems (see Braunias), the second had remained in force in Switzerland. The determining factor for exclusion was gender—although it was never explicitly stated as such.

The presumption of women's incompetence in political life in reality hides a number of contradictions with regard to their relationship to the state and to citizenship. These contradictions provided fertile ground for feminist argumentation. While women were ineligible to vote, they were nevertheless subject to taxes. This logical inconsistency—which was continually criticized until the introduction of women's suffrage—had already been raised by a group of women in 1849. They realized they were penalized by a special tax levied upon the elites of the Sonderbund—the association of Catholic cantons opposed to the creation of the federal state—and after the association's defeat, they filed a complaint with the Federal Council on 5 January 1849. They expressed their surprise at finding themselves on equal footing with men of state and military officers: "It is unheard-of that women should be made responsible for the outcome and the success of battles or political maxims, when their legal status is that of minors." As noted in a government report to both houses of Parliament in 1850, these women rose up in protest against such hypocrisy. "If they are just holding (our) luck against us and applying the doctrine of might makes right, let them come out and say so, instead of invoking the inflexible tenets of a higher justice." Because the measure penalizing the Sonderbund elites also included stripping the people subject to the special tax of their political rights, the women asked pointedly how the authorities could take away from them "political rights they have never abused, because they don't have any."

Gender was seen as a self-explanatory reason for assuming that women did not have the necessary capabilities to vote responsibly. With this in mind, one wonders whether Switzerland's exceptionalism might not, in fact, prove the rule. That is to say, does this case not point to the normativity of the structure that regulated gender relations according to an asymmetric distribution of power, defined by the bourgeois social order of the 19th century? From vantage points almost a century apart, two Swiss feminists drew precisely this conclusion. In the 12 May 1872 issue of *Zur Bundrevision*, Julie von May (1801–75), an aristocrat from Bern, complained Mabout the "destiny" reserved for the female sex by "Switzerland, the cradle, the very model for movements of liberty and equality throughout Europe." Yet this was the very model that kept "its girls" in "a more wretched and enslaved condition than [did] the monarchies that surround[ed] it." In 1958, Iris von Roten (1917–90), whose radicalism foreshadowed that of the Women's Liberation Movement of the 1970s, echoed von May's judgment:

> No other form of government besides democracy so pitilessly illustrates women's subjugation as when it refuses them political rights because of their gender. And democracies are more likely to do this in proportion to the degree to which they are "pure" democracies, democracies without intermediaries. In this sense, Switzerland represents the most striking example of women's subjugation.

This interpretation is obviously somewhat general, given the particular conditions that shape each nation-state and its political system. Nevertheless, the Swiss political system provides what is perhaps a particularly clear illustration of the principle of dif-

ference that structures social relations between the sexes in modern industrialized societies—despite declarations of universalism on the part of democracies. Whereas the instruments of democracy are intended, precisely, to make equality a reality, in fact they serve to maintain the status quo, demonstrating the extent to which the principle of sexual difference is culturally entrenched. Moreover, the emergence of a majority that favored the introduction of women's suffrage was made even more difficult by particularities in the Swiss political system. Through its specific mechanisms of direct democracy, Switzerland's political system has historically given primacy to the political expression of particular concerns, which, in turn, have been given an institutional space. The resulting multiplicity of interests made it very difficult to achieve the majority needed to pass women's suffrage. Furthermore, the political system has a built-in safeguard that discourages constitutional change: the principle of the double majority. A popular majority in itself is not enough to enact a constitutional change; constitutional changes must also be ratified by a majority of the cantons. A final factor must be taken into account: the logic of Switzerland's institutional structures, which are designed to promote continuity. No major political change has occurred since the federal state was constituted in 1848. Therefore, no party or government has felt the need to appeal to women to legitimate its power or to help resolve a social or political crisis through the extension of the electoral body.

The factors outlined above do not imply that the issue of women's suffrage has been unmarked by changing circumstances. The debate about the inclusion of women in the civic process has evolved through several phases and through shifting historical contexts. During the first phase, prior to the 1890s, the problem of women's suffrage remained on the back burner. Other aspects of women's status as "second-class citizens" seemed more pressing.

Women as Citizens but Not Voters

As the British sociologist T.H. Marshall has underscored, the notion of citizenship comprises several dimensions. Rights—political, civil, or social—are not the only issue. Modern states also have a vested interest in the functions performed by individuals and are cognizant of the economic contributions of their citizens. Accordingly, the indispensable role of women's labor in the household economy encouraged certain politicians to advocate the institutionalization of women's groups in cantonal debates prior to the 1848 Constitution. Women's groups would be responsible for the implementation of welfare policy. Immediately following the birth of the confederation, social reformers—mostly men—began a campaign to protect children, and later women, against the most damaging effects of industrial exploitation. This effort culminated in the 1877 passage of the factory law, which banned work at night and on Sundays for all women and children. Considered at least as important during this period was the issue of girls' education and their chances for professional training. Slowly but surely, between 1830 and 1850, every canton introduced compulsory education. In fact, education—which was in the cantons' jurisdiction—was one of the first tasks addressed by the new authorities. Education was considered a precondition for the responsible exercise of political rights. Although their education did not measure up to that of their brothers, Swiss girls did quite well compared to international standards at the time. When Julie von May joined the fray in pushing for constitutional reform in 1872 and again in 1874, she interpreted the high levels of education among females as an indication that Switzerland was ready for women's emancipation. Her conclusions were a little hasty, as it turned out, although the fact that educational reformers like Johan Jacob Binder were advocating women's rights only seemed to confirm von May's position. Yet, when the time came actually to demand women's suffrage, most voices fell silent. It seemed better to pursue this goal more gradually: to attend to education first and then to wait and see. This prudent and reasonable position—the pragmatic strategy of asking for only one thing at a time—proved to be typical of political action in Switzerland. In a system that allows for the expression of many diverse positions, no position has a chance of passing unless it creates consensus and, from the outset, holds out the potential for compromise. In the end, such a system privileges the political and social agents who already hold power.

Even Marie Goegg-Pouchoulin (1826–99), the founder of the International Association of Women (IAW) in 1868, had to bend to this political reality. When push came to shove, despite the international scope of her organization (Switzerland was the home of the Central Committee and several branches, but branches were also founded in France, Italy, and Germany) and her egalitarian feminism, she relinquished her demands for women's political rights during the debates on constitutional reform at the beginning of the 1870s. This advocate of women's individualism, who dreamed of the free and equal development of men and women alike, limited her demands to civil and economic rights. As Beatrix Mesmer has shown in her history of Swiss feminism in the 19th century, in the end, the practical solutions adopted by the International Association of Women barely extended beyond those spheres that had traditionally belonged to women (see Mesmer 1988). Nevertheless, Switzerland's first women's organization was different from those that followed it in one crucial respect: it never felt that women's equality needed to be justified. The IAW painted a bold social portrait in the broadest strokes, one in which the question of women's rights was of a piece with aspirations that "ensured freedom, instruction, morality, economic well-being and fraternal union." Above all, the association "demanded equal pay and education as well as equality in the family and before the law."

During the 1870s and 1880s, a whole series of feminist organizations emerged. However, most of them limited their scope to social and moral issues. For example, the Association of Swiss Women for Moral Improvement (Association des Femmes Suisses pour l'Oeuvre du Relèvement Moral), founded in 1877 by Josephine Butler (1828–1906), devoted its energies exclusively to abolitionism. Offering more immediate practical help, the International Association of Friends of Girls, the Swiss chapter of which was established in 1886, struggled to end prostitution. There was also the influential Society of Swiss Women for Social Welfare (Schweizerischer Gemeinnütziger Frauenverein/Société Féminine Suisse d'Utilité Publique), created in 1888, which combined the promotion of home economics with the development of so-called women's professions. As Catherine Fussinger's prosopographical outline has shown, these various pursuits did not preclude a certain amount of permeability between traditionally oriented organizations and more progressive women's groups (see Fussinger).

The only other egalitarian feminist discourse that protested against discrimination during this initial period came from Meta von Salis-Marschlins (1855–1929), an aristocrat from Graubünden, a doctor of history at the University of Zurich and a personal friend of Friedrich Nietzsche. Von Salis-Marschlins was the first to pose the question of women's rights in terms of citizen's rights and their duties toward the state. On New Year's Day of 1887 she published her treatise, "A Woman's Heretical Reflections," in the democratic daily, the *Züricher Post*. If women achieved the right to vote, she argued (going against the usual arguments used to legitimate claims for women's suffrage), it should not be on the basis of their special merit or superior moral qualities. Rather, women should vote simply because they paid taxes—like men. She dismissed the well-worn mantra that women needed to be educated before they could vote responsibly. "Expecting free human beings to teach those who are not free how to make good use of their freedom," she wrote "is tantamount to expecting human nature to change." She reiterated this point in a series of public lectures given in 1894. Although the issue of women's suffrage had become a widespread concern in Switzerland by this time, her radical egalitarian position remained marginal even as it continued to provoke her contemporaries.

Women's Issues Come into Prominence

During the 1890s, the Swiss suffrage movement entered a phase in which its emphasis shifted toward organization. During this period, which extended until the eve of World War I, the "woman question" emerged as an important societal issue. Once again, von Salis-Marschlins was first to bring the issue of suffrage to the fore, not as an issue specific to women, but as a universal concern. And indeed, global debate about the integration of women was resonating throughout society at that time. The issue of women's suffrage, although it occupied an increasing place in the public discourse, was only one of several women's issues being explored. For example, the project of protecting women workers was taken up by the Swiss Union of Workingwomen (Schweizerischer Arbeiterinnenverband/Union Suisse des Ouvrières), founded and presided over by Verena Conzett (1861–1947); the Society for the Legal Protection for Women (Frauenrechtsschutzverein/Société de Protection Juridique des Femmes) championed the cause of salaried women workers; and the Society for the Reform of Female Education (Verein Frauenbildungs-Reform/Société de Réforme de l'Éducation Féminine), created in Zurich in 1893, championed the cause of women's education. Other burning issues included the status of married women in the context of debates over the new Civil Code about to be unified at the national level, and women's changing roles in the context of a government whose responsibilities and budgets were both increasing. Meanwhile, the importance of political parties was on the rise, provoking debate about the place allotted to women within them.

This period also witnessed the emergence of several organizations whose objective was to go beyond the spheres of activity traditionally allotted to women. Several examples are worth mentioning: the Geneva Women's Union (Union des Femmes de Genève), founded on 17 September 1891; the Bern Women's Committee (Frauenkomitee Bern), whose initial constituent assembly met on 5 April 1892; and in 1896, the Zurich Union for the Women's Cause (Union für Frauenbestrebungen/ l'Union pour la Cause des Femmes). The Bern Women's Committee eventually became a major political consultant for government authorities seeking advice on how to deal with women's issues. This informal status as "expert consultants" came about as a direct result of the committee's survey on women's philanthropic activities in Switzerland, a project the government had decided to subsidize despite its initial rejection by Parliament. For the first time, this study revealed the extent of women's participation in the public sphere. Almost 6,000 charitable women's organizations were registered in Switzerland. Given the rapidity of industrial development in Switzerland, these groups played a considerable role in compensating for the deficiencies of a welfare state that was still in its infancy. Indeed, the government welcomed—and even encouraged—charitable initiatives sponsored by women's groups, because they helped keep public expenditures to a minimum. Moreover, women's groups provided a means for encouraging social integration at a time when the status of women—especially single women—was a prominent concern. Thus public authorities delegated a portion of the government's growing responsibilities to women. This allowed women to establish their own fields of expertise, which provided them with new public status; in turn, they gained increased access to the corridors of power. Thereafter, thanks to their know-how in matters of social welfare, women would be counted among the special interest groups regularly consulted by government authorities on certain questions. Furthermore, women's groups gradually gained access to political institutions after the turn of the 20th century. They were often invited to send a representative to take a seat on extraparliamentary committees of experts. A woman representative first sat on a committee charged with revising the laws regulating factory operations, which began its work in 1907. Such cases notwithstanding, women's participation in these political forums was dependent upon the good will of the heads of the relevant departments, and until the postwar period, women's organizations were routinely excluded from several important committees. Nevertheless, women's organizations gained a considerable political foothold during this period, generally attaining a place in the circle of organizations recognized officially by the state. Moreover, associations devoted to the defense of women's rights also had more informal ways of gaining access to power. Most of the women running these associations came from social backgrounds that afforded them influence through politically powerful brothers, fathers, or husbands.

At first, the increased importance of the women's issues was manifested through public opinion—to such an extent that in 1897, Carl Hilty (1833–1909), a professor of constitutional law at the University of Bern and a leading proponent of women's voting rights, felt compelled to write that in his opinion, too much ink had of late been devoted to women's issues. Of course, given the intensity of the debate, not all of this ink had been put to the service of supporting women's cause. In 1895, for example, Zofingia, a student association, initiated an internal debate about women's suffrage. In the end, apparently, the debate consisted of little more than homilies in the vein of "the state for men, the family for women." But on the whole, academic elites were far from being unanimously hostile to women's rights. For example, most of Switzerland's universities were open to women by the 1860s. Academic elites also contributed significantly to shaping turn-of-the-century debates. Hilty, for example, was the first person to propose a federalist strategy for breaking down opposition to women's right to vote by beginning at the cantonal and municipal level and addressing issues such as schools, churches, and public assistance, all of which fell under cantonal jurisdiction. Some of the great academic defenders of women's rights included Charles Secrétan (1815–95), a professor of philosophy at the Lausanne Academy and the author of a book entitled *Women's Rights* published in 1886; law professor Louis Bridel (1852–1913), deputy for Geneva and also the author of *Le mouvement féministe et le droit des femmes* (1893; The Feminist Movement and Women's Rights); and André de Maday (1877–1958), professor of social legislation and sociology at the University of Geneva, who advocated women's right to work, as the title of one of his 1905 publications made clear. These intellectuals also embodied a new social type: the feminist man. Alongside academics, Socialists and Protestant activist groups were also generally sympathetic to women's demands. Even Parliament showed some encouragement of women's equality in 1900, when its members voted to make women's access to courses a precondition for receiving federal grants for professional training programs in the commercial sector.

Women had also begun to show their own political mettle during this period. In 1896, the Congress for Women's Issues (Kongress für die Interessen der Frau/Congrès pour les Intérêts Féminins) suggested that women possessed both strong organizational acumen and the ability to express themselves. Another step was taken in 1900, when Helene von Mülinen (1850–1924) oversaw the creation of the Alliance of Swiss Women's Societies (Bund Schweizerischer Frauenverein /Alliance des Sociétés Féminines Suisses) which was the first national umbrella organization to champion women's legal and professional equality. Meanwhile, the Swiss Association for Women's Suffrage (Schweizerischer Verband für Frauenstimmrecht/Association Suisse pour le Suffrage Féminin)—founded in 1909 by Pauline Chaponnière (1850–1934) and Auguste de Morsier (1864–1923), an engineer who was also the association's first president—was organized with the specific goal of achieving women's political equality.

The Contradictory Origins of the Issue of Women's Suffrage

The distribution of issues between various organizations expressed not only a certain division of labor but also the adaptation of different political objectives and strategies. This said, some qualification is necessary on this score. The boundaries between the various women's groups hardly followed a strict line dividing egalitarian feminists and "difference" feminists (who endorsed the idea of essential gender differences). While de Morsier advocated total political equality for women, this position was far from being unanimously held by the Alliance of Women's Societies—or even, for that matter, by the Swiss Association for Women's Suffrage. From the beginning, two conceptions of the social relationship between the sexes overlapped and competed. On one side were the partisans of suffrage as a fundamental human right. They refused to countenance any material restrictions of this right as it applied to either active or passive forms of citizenship. Their egalitarian vision thus led them to reject any restriction of their political rights to questions of "feminine" interest. "The right to vote implies the right to be elected," stated de Morsier in a brochure published by the Association for Women's Suffrage in 1912. "We see absolutely no reason why these rights should be abrogated in any way or in any field. . . . If the right to vote is a right, then it should be given with all of its consequences." The other side of the question was taken by those who believed that men and women had fundamentally different natures. According to their understanding, men and women were different from one another in their intellectual interests, their psychological orientations, and their spheres of activity. Nonetheless, the two sexes were complementary, and society benefited directly from the specificity of women's contributions. Proponents of this viewpoint did not feel it was essential that women be given a political voice for every issue; the right to vote could be limited to matters pertaining to religion, education, and welfare, at least in the initial stages.

According to political scientist Sibylle Hardmeier, the suffragists' political practices reveal that the differences between these two strategies often dissolved (see Hardmeier). In fact, gender difference was an axiom for both groups: "Women synthesize and are intuitive, men analyze and reason," observed Secrétan. Nevertheless, some, including the philosophers from Lausanne, insisted on the equal value of male and female character traits. But this argument could always be turned back on itself and against equality. Since women are different, it was countered, why should they enter into masculine spheres of activity, especially politics? Of course, for those who advocated women's voting rights, the whole point was to enrich the public sphere with women's special qualities, but this was the very same reason invoked by the opposition in their campaign to keep women at home, shielded from the "baseness" of political questions. In order to counter this logic, Swiss suffragists adopted a compromise strategy, one that consisted of limiting their demands to a progressive introduction of women's voting rights. This strategic position was designed not only to navigate the particular contingencies of Swiss federalism, but also to take advantage of the most commonly held understanding of women's roles. It was crucial to secure a foothold in specific important domains—at the level of both the municipal political bodies and the cantons—that coincided with the capacities presumed to be proper to women. Questions of education, religion, and public assistance were considered close to the reality of women's lives, as were the general political questions affecting local government. Indeed, the latter was often described as a larger-scale family household. "If we are serious about women's political participation," declared a cantonal deputy from Bern in 1917, "granting the vote at the community level is a good place to start . . . because the community is a large family and women know how it works just as well as men." This argument, first voiced as early as the1890s, was reiterated throughout the struggle for women's suffrage. It paralleled the gradualist strategy advocated by Louis Bridel and Carl Hilty. Moreover, the consistency of the respective arguments put forward by both sides is one of the most striking features in the history of women's voting rights. The large Zurich daily, the *Neue Zürcher Zeitung*, re-

minded readers of this in 1919, when it complained that positions on these issues were all too familiar and that it seemed impossible to imagine that new elements might be introduced to the debate.

From this point of view, the first Swiss ballot on the question of women's voting rights is particularly instructive, since it already ran along the general lines of this split. On 4 November 1900, the citizens of the canton of Bern were asked to vote on a draft of legislation that would make women eligible for election to school boards. This law proposal was defeated by an almost two-thirds majority. Even in the cities, a majority voted to reject the measure, though their rejection was less cut and dried than in rural areas. The debate in the Great Council (the legislative body of the canton), along with the newspaper campaign that had preceded the vote, had already defined the arguments of both sides and drawn the dividing line between their positions. When the opponents of the proposal actually got beyond expressing their phobias about women's emancipation, they fell back upon the arguments about a woman's function as a wife and mother—which was a discourse that both sides shared. But one side argued that it was precisely as mothers that women naturally possessed the talents to be good educators, while the other side claimed her role as mother and wife demanded that she limit her activities to home and hearth as destiny had intended. According to the social constructions of the day—and their impact on the question of the vote—it was femininity that made women either compatible or incompatible with politics.

The two decades that preceded World War I witnessed not only the rise of organized feminism in Switzerland (with its strong international links), but also the emergence of the intellectual and political framework for the debate thereafter. Hardmeier has pointed out three basic characteristics of the debate on women's suffrage that persisted throughout the century. First, the discourse on women's citizenship was marked by arguments about women's full electoral rights as opposed to partial voting rights; this distinction was a great source of tension within the women's movement itself, while offering opponents of emancipation a power tactical instrument, helping them to block initiatives on this front. Second, there was a widely held assumption that any new political rights acquired by women should be predicated upon their first having proven themselves worthy of the responsibility. Finally, it was during this phase that the model for discursive legitimacy was established, which insisted that women's interests should coincide with meeting social needs.

At the end of the war, the proponents of women's suffrage were full of hope. Had they not proven their worthiness to serve their country? Had they not accomplished many of the tasks vital to national defense? Had they not proven themselves indispensable in the social sector, especially in terms of the practical and moral support they provided for soldiers? They discovered quickly that their hopes were to be dashed. While successfully meeting the needs of their nation may have been a precondition for obtaining the right to vote, it still did not provide any guarantees that this right would be granted. The swelling ranks of the Association for Women's Suffrage did nothing to change this. In fact, the question became increasingly politicized, to the point that it turned into a platform distinguishing one political party from another. While the Socialists approved of it, Catholics rejected it overwhelmingly. As for Radicals, conscious of their role as referees, they generally preferred to keep a low profile in order to avoid polarizing society on this issue. The demand for total political emancipation became a standard feature of Socialist interventions, and by 1912 it was made into part of their official program. In 1917 Socialist-sponsored citizens' initiatives demanded women's suffrage in several cantons. But the politicization of this demand—in terms of its discursive appropriation by a specific political party—only became really conspicuous at the time of the General Strike. Of the nine points on the call for action posted as the strike broke out on 12 November 1918, the demand for women's political equality was listed second. The association of this demand with the most explosive political and social conflict in 20th-century Switzerland, as well as with a leftist party, put feminist organizations in a difficult position. The Genevan egalitarian feminist, Émilie Gourd (1876–1946), the president of the Association for Women's Suffrage at the time of the strike, personally sent a telegram to the government. She distanced herself from the methods being used by the strikers. But she also "urgently recommended that the High Federal Council (the Swiss government) adopt point II of the Olten Action Committee's agenda, that is to say, active and passive political rights for women." Gourd's personal initiative provoked a leadership crisis within the women's suffrage association, whose membership was largely made up of women from the middle and upper classes. The strike was broken only three days later in the face of an ultimatum issued by federal authorities. The political option of extending the vote to women in order to help stabilize democracy—an option chosen by other European countries—was not exercised here. Undeniably, the first vote in the cantons on this matter served as a test case—especially since the usual arguments were now bolstered by the added threat of Bolshevism.

The Triumph of Gender Conservatism

The antifeminist shift that marked the interwar period was not immediately apparent. In December of 1918, following the strike's collapse, Emil Göttisheim and Hermann Greulich, who were members of the lower house of Parliament (the National Council), affiliated with the Radical and Socialist movements respectively, each put forward a motion in support of women's suffrage. These motions were supported by every feminist organization in Switzerland, with the exception of the Swiss Union of Catholic Women (Schweizerischer Katholischer Frauenbund/ Union Suisse des Femmes Catholiques) founded in 1912. Both parliamentary houses accepted the motions as a *postulat* (a parliamentary resolution instructing the government to examine the need for legislation) in 1919. But then everything remained on hold until 1951, when the government finally issued its report, which only concluded that women's suffrage had not yet matured into a pressing current issue. In fact, the year 1920 marked the beginning of a long series of failures for the women's movement, accompanied by a cultural trend back toward a very traditional model of femininity. That trend was particularly obvious throughout the 1930s and World War II, and it reemerged again during the 1950s with the advent of the cold war and the baby boom. It was not until the mid 1960s that this traditional representation of women began to break down.

More than half a dozen referenda were held on the issue of women's suffrage at the municipal and cantonal level during the 1920s. They all failed to pass. The last of these took place in the city-canton of Basle in 1927. There was then a total eclipse of this issue until the 1940s, when at last the subject finally resurfaced on the political horizon. There was one exception: a petition of unprecedented magnitude had been circulated in 1929 to remind political leaders and the general public that support for women's suffrage was widespread. Two hundred fifty thousand people signed the petition, including 170,000 women, which was roughly one-seventh of Switzerland's total female citizens of voting age. The 80,000 male signatures would have been enough on their own to sponsor a citizens' initiative on the issue, leading us inevitably to wonder why Swiss women's groups did not pursue such a course of action. They could have held the first national vote on the women's suffrage issue based on the petition. As it turned out, this did not happen until 1959. It is difficult to formulate a clear picture of what motivated their decision not to press the issue, since the Association for Women's Suffrage at that time only argued that the petition provided a means for the will of the general population, both male and female, to be heard. We can nonetheless advance a few hypotheses about why a citizens' initiative was not pursued, based on who signed the petition and how it was organized in the first place. The petition was initially planned as part of the Great National Exhibition on Women's Labor in Switzerland. But the initiative proposed by the Association for Women's Suffrage was rejected by the exhibition's organizing committee. This was not the only problem the project faced: among the hundreds of women's organizations contacted, only a handful indicated any willingness to collect signatures. A few trade unions and the Socialist and Communist parties added themselves to the meager list. Given this initial lack of enthusiasm, no one was more surprised than the organizers at the sheer number of signatures gathered on the petitions. Despite this, so many of the signatories were associated with the Left and with temperance movements— the French-speaking Swiss League against Alcoholism (Ligue Suisse contre l'Alcoolisme) as well as a women's organization of similar aims were among the petition's active participants—that they did little to legitimize the suffrage movement more broadly. Besides, these signatures made it difficult to predict anything, since the Socialist Party, and to a lesser extent, the Communist Party, showed patchy support on the issue from within their ranks. This was verified when a citizens' initiative was rejected in the city-canton of Basle, where both parties held strong constituencies. Finally, a geographic breakdown of the figures revealed a divide between country and city, Catholic and Protestant cantons, as well as between Swiss Germans and French-speaking Swiss.

An elaborate ritual was staged to mark the presentation of the petition to authorities at an official government reception. However, despite this gesture, which was quite unusual at the time, the petition languished at the bottom of a drawer for many years. Generally speaking, the question of women's suffrage went underground until the end of World War II. A few small incursions were made at the communal and cantonal levels, where women were made eligible to serve on school boards, in parishes, and on social welfare committees. But these functions corresponded perfectly to the traditional conception of women's roles. This was equally true of the "family vote" proposed in 1934–35 by Carl Doka, the "theoretician" of the Conservative-Catholic Party, in discussions surrounding a corporatist-inspired citizens' initiative for a complete revision of the Constitution. While his proposal to double the vote for the head of the household did not explicitly exclude women a priori, it is clear that widows with children would be the only women likely to benefit from his plan. The political climate during this period was extremely hostile to the expression of any interests that might be considered particular interests—and women's political rights were classed in this category. In the context of World War II, which demanded great social solidarity, and which followed so closely on the heels of an economic crisis that affected employment up until the outbreak of hostilities, women's suffrage was perceived at best as a kind of individualist luxury, and more often as a provocation in the face of national unity. At the time, moreover, many feminists essentially shared this perception. At a time when the legitimacy of their paid work was on the shakiest ground and when democracy itself was under threat both internally and internationally, women simply had other priorities.

After 1945, the battle over women's suffrage picked up where it had left off in 1919. This occurred not only on a social level, but also on the institutional level. For example, in 1944, a parliamentary intervention, spearheaded by Socialist Hans Oprecht, saved *in extremis* Greulich and Göttisheim's 1919 *postulats*—which were still pending—from being permanently dismissed. Although they were more cautious than they had been in 1919, women's groups remained moderately hopeful. But the first postwar ballot held in 1946, again in the city-canton of Basle, was once more a total defeat. Compared to the previous 1927 ballot, support for women's suffrage had increased only from 29.2 percent to 37.1 percent. Six other votes between 1946 and 1948 were also unsuccessful. The Association for Women's Suffrage thus returned to the tactic of campaigning for partial rights. In order to demonstrate its civic maturity, in 1949 the association requested that women be given the right to vote but without the right to hold office. In the meantime, the cold war had started, providing a new, anti-Communist, justification for denying women's rights; after all, weren't women in all Soviet bloc countries emancipated? We all know where that led! Even the Swiss government hinted at this in its February 1957 address, which laid the groundwork for the first national referendum on women's suffrage two years later. Predictably, the referendum was again defeated, being rejected by two-thirds of the citizens and all but three cantons. Generally speaking, it would seem that in 1959 the political strategy of taking small steps, securing partial political rights, and making modest demands (which always risked being limited still further), had not paid off.

According to historian Yvonne Voegeli, propaganda produced at the time by the political action committee on the suffrage question showed some signs of change (see Voegeli). With the exception of the Society of Swiss Women for Social Welfare, all of Switzerland's women's groups united in 1957—including Catholic groups, which signaled an important shift—to form a single political action committee, the Working Community for the Promotion of Women's Political Rights (Arbeitsgemeinschaft der schweizerischen Frauenverbände für die Politischen Rechte der Frau / Communauté du Travail en Faveur des Droits Politiques pour les Femmes). This coalition expressed a new consciousness in the suffrage movement and allowed a more egalitarian argument to be put forward. Their first line of reasoning was no longer that women should be allowed to vote because they were useful to state and society. While this argument did

not completely disappear, it was relegated to the background. The argument that now prevailed was women's affirmation that the legitimacy of their claim was based on basic rights—on human rights. If women met their responsibilities toward the public good, they also deserved to enjoy all the benefits of citizenship. This new attitude attests to a slow change in mentalities, but it was also precipitated by a political event.

The referendum on women's voting rights had been preceded by a campaign for the introduction of a mandatory civil defense plan that included women. The Association for Women's Suffrage and the Alliance of Swiss Women's Societies were joined—at least on this issue—by two Catholic organizations. They immediately protested the plan, arguing on that there should be "no new responsibilities without new rights." For a series of reasons, not all of which had to do with women's suffrage, the government's proposal was rejected in a referendum held on 3 March 1957. The growing confidence of advocates for women's political equality was reinforced by polls of the female population in the canton of Geneva (1952), the city-canton of Basle (1954), and the city of Zurich (1955). These polls showed that a clear majority of women wanted the vote and put paid the notion that women themselves did not really care about the issue. Furthermore, an assessment of the constitutionality of women's political exclusion by eminent legal expert Werner Kägi (commissioned by the Association for Women's Suffrage in 1955) concluded that such exclusion was indeed unconstitutional.

Kägi stipulated, however, that a new interpretation of the federal Constitution (by the Federal Court) was not enough—the issue demanded a popular vote. The Association for Women's Suffrage saw things differently. In three French-speaking cantonal chapters, members of the association submitted requests that they be registered on electoral lists, but their requests were denied in the Federal Court in June 1957. This was the third time this strategy had failed. In 1887, the Federal Court had rejected a complaint brought by Switzerland's first woman lawyer, Emilie Kempin-Spyri, that her rights were being denied according to Section 4 of the federal Constitution. The Constitution stipulates that "All Swiss citizens should be considered equal before the law," and Kempin-Spyri argued that the definition of Swiss citizen included both men and women. During the 1920s, lawyer Leonard Jenni (1881–1967), future founder of the Swiss branch of the League for Human Rights, launched two new campaigns against the courts. His challenges were prompted by the fact that in another, unrelated case the Federal Court had reversed its own historic line of interpretation (which was based on the intentions of the framers of the Constitution) and approved an interpretation more in step with contemporary society. But the Association for Women's Suffrage distanced itself from Jenni's initiatives. In the words of its president at the time, Émilie Gourd, the association's position was motivated by its respect for "the political institutions of our country."

In contrast, by the 1950s suffragists showed far less conformity in terms of institutional norms. They were themselves the authors of strategies designed to circumvent the obstacles presented by direct democracy. The outcry provoked by Iris von Roten's feminist writings in the late 1950s, illustrates, however, that this transformation was only a relative one. In 1959, she published a book called *Frauen im Laufgitter* (Women in the Playpen), a caustic but extremely substantive indictment of male domination. It created such a storm that even women's groups distanced themselves from the critique. When she later published her "breviary" on voting rights, women's groups hardly thanked her for the publicity. Von Roten was considered threatening because she adopted an approach that women's groups had avoided like the plague—she suggested that political rights were only the first step in the march toward women's eventual equality on all fronts, that "gender parity" should follow in every part of the government, including federal administration. As it turns out, it was this maximalist strategy that eventually prevailed.

Escalating Demands and Intergenerational Encounters: From Suffragists to the Women's Liberation Movement

The breakthrough for women's federal voting rights finally occurred on 7 February 1971. In a national referendum, 65.7 percent voted "yes," as opposed to 34.3 percent who voted "no." The ratio of supporters to opponents had been reversed in the years since 1959. What had happened? Why were women given in 1971 that which had been denied to them in 1959? Many factors contributed to this, but space allows for discussion of only the most important ones here. Without going into depth, let us first recall the tremendous structural transformations that redefined industrial societies in the 1960s. Switzerland was no exception. Economies were internationalized, the tertiary sector ballooned, governments developed and diversified their social infrastructures, and women went to work while birthrates fell, among other changes. Shifts in mentalities and mores must also be taken into consideration. An increase in the standard of living was a contributing factor in these shifts, but a major change also took place as a result of family planning and the institutionalization of birth control during the 1960s, including the introduction of the Pill, which was used by an estimated one-sixth of all Swiss women by 1971.

An analysis of debates, both in the media and in the political arena, shows a general awareness of the changes in women's roles, as well as an awareness that the separation between public and private spheres had also been eroded. In looking back at the debates in Parliament, what is striking is that even those who described these changes as regrettable—which included many Catholics—no longer perceived them as a threat to the social order or even to social relations between men and women. What was important to them was that women kept their "femininity." In reality, the notion of "difference" invoked by the representatives of the people concealed the hierarchical principle that they sought to preserve. Almost without exception, members of Parliament insisted that the right to vote would do nothing to change "female specificity," which was proved by foreign examples as well as those provided by the women's vote already established in the cantons of Vaud, Geneva, and Neuchâtel. Femininity and politics were thus no longer conceived as mutually exclusive. In the end, whether or not the members of Parliament really believed their own rhetoric to justify this political action is irrelevant: what matters is the fact that the rhetoric disarmed the opposition. When the proposal for a referendum on the issue was actually brought to the floor in Parliament, both houses voted for it unanimously.

The question remains: was the political conversion of Parliament and the people rooted more deeply in practical or intellectual considerations? On one level, the introduction of women's suffrage represented only a minor institutional reform. The electoral system was not modified in any way; the only change that occurred was in the number of citizens voting. However, the symbolic weight of women's suffrage was very important, especially in the context of Switzerland's democratic tradition. During the late 1960s, both internally and in terms of new international standards, Switzerland's democratic prestige had begun to slip. In 1968–69, at the time of the ratification of the European Convention on Human Rights, the Swiss experienced a brutal awakening when it became clear that their nation was no longer considered a model democracy. In fact, Switzerland discovered that it was not even eligible to sign the convention until it passed a series of constitutional reforms, including women's suffrage. This realization coincided with the emergence of the second-wave feminism that catalyzed the movement to finally pass the reform.

Despite the disdain the Women's Liberation Movement (Frauenbefreiungsbewegung [FBB] / Mouvement de Libération des Femmes [MLF]) expressed about the issue of women's political rights, it was hardly an accident that the first problem the new organization tackled was suffrage. On 10 November 1968, in the Schauspielhaus, Zurich's main theatre, a young woman grabbed the microphone during an anniversary celebration for the Association for Women's Suffrage. The entire press corps and many public representatives were in attendance. Her call to arms made the intended impact. For one, she and other radical feminists felt there was nothing worth celebrating. These feminists believed that even with the eventual granting of the right to vote, formal equality would not be enough. Not only that, they charged that traditional methods of political mobilization were not sufficient for achieving the kind of changes women were now demanding.

The Swiss Women's Liberation Movement quickly demonstrated what it meant by a new style of politics. The radical nature of their demands combined with the provocative and innovative kinds of political actions they staged—which were often funny and playful, but also scathing and ironic—could not have been more different from the somewhat muffled protests voiced by women's groups from the previous generation. Even their frames of reference were fundamentally opposed. The new feminists overwhelmingly tended to come from the New Left, which systematically attempted to distance itself from Swiss society and its institutions, while the suffragists, by contrast, had never ceased protesting their alliance to these things. Nonetheless, the two generations forged a fruitful political alliance on a series of questions surrounding women's rights. During the 1970s, militants from the Women's Liberation Movement gathered signatures and made common cause with more traditional feminists on a citizens' initiative to decriminalize abortion launched in 1971. They also joined forces in 1975 for a citizens' initiative to recognize the equal rights of men and women, although they had boycotted and even disrupted the conference sponsored by traditional women's organizations that had initiated the campaign. In fact, the collaboration often proved to be a difficult one. The first demonstration they jointly organized following the action at the Schauspielhaus provides an excellent example of the kinds of difficulties they faced.

Energized by the enormous media response provoked by the young woman's actions in Zurich, a portion of the older women's rights movement organized a "March on Bern" to protest the government's proposal to ratify, with reservations—in particular on women's vote—the European Human Rights Convention. The proposal was to be debated in Parliament during the spring session of 1969. Despite the refusal of many women's organizations to participate, not least the Association for Women's Suffrage, the demonstration mobilized a large number of women. The Women's Liberation Movement, which had been enthusiastic at first, finally ended up backing out as well. The younger women's movement found it inconceivable that the demonstration's organizers had planned for it to take place one day prior to the opening of the parliamentary session, rather than during the session. Nonetheless, the demonstration caused enough pressure that the Council of States (the upper house of Parliament, which gives equal representation to the cantons) decided to abandon the ratification proposal and that the government felt compelled to pass a law legalizing women's suffrage quickly. By December of 1969, this was done. In the summer and fall of 1970, both houses of Parliament debated the issue, and the national referendum on women's suffrage was finally passed in February of 1971. The majority of cantons quickly followed suit, with 17 cantons passing legislation for political equality as early as 1972. The cantons of Solothurn and Graubünden would pass such legislation in 1983, followed by the last two cantons of the Appenzell in 1989 and 1990. All told, then, it took more than 100 years for the world's "oldest modern democracy" to concede political rights to women, from the earliest demands of Meta von Salis in 1887—taking that as a pivotal date—and the final ratification of women's suffrage in every part of Switzerland. At the federal level, more than 120 years elapsed between the time when "universal" suffrage was granted to men and the final granting of the vote to women. The question remains, is there a causal connection between these two facts?

The Effects of Direct (or Semidirect) Democracy

Most authors who have studied the institutional dimensions of women's suffrage in Switzerland, especially Neumayer, Banaszak, and Hardmeier, tend to lay the blame for its belatedness at the feet of direct or semidirect democracy. This was also the conclusion of that most lucid and committed observer, Iris von Roten. In her contribution to the debate of 1959, she observed that direct democracy had given women's rights opponents a peerless legal weapon. This observation would seem to bear out in at least two ways. First, and this is incontrovertible, the fact that the question had to be submitted to the popular vote and possibly to a referendum, created a breakwater against institutional change for a very long time. Second, specific features of Swiss political culture, for example, the tendency toward creating consensus and a certain normative pressure for modesty and discretion, seem to have contributed to limiting the opportunities and the capability of suffragists to mobilize politically. These features have been closely analyzed from the perspective of history and political science by Banaszak, as well as by Hardmeier. We can also conclude that these factors helped to delegitimize

women's suffrage by branding it "radical." This label, in turn, encouraged supporters of suffrage to minimize their demands in the aim of achieving consensus.

This portrait becomes increasingly complex the more one looks at it. Switzerland's political system has other institutional particularities, among them a strong interpenetration between the administration and interest groups and relatively easy access to the decision-making process thanks to the decentralization of political power. Political science tells us that any opportunity to participate institutionally has an effect on both the forms and the content of political mobilization. One could say, then, that the political opportunity structure of the Swiss federal state, which opened its doors to moderate feminist groups, also contributed to limiting the general orientation of the women's suffrage movement by helping to delegitimize more radical demands.

All of these elements obviously privileged a tendency toward compromise, but they also afforded women access to the political arena at a relatively early date. Are these grounds for concluding that had the popular vote not existed, female suffrage would have been passed earlier? Such a conclusion is contested by Voegeli's historical research. She argues that the executive, the administration, and Parliament were as responsible for resistance to women's suffrage as the people. Before World War II, only eight law proposals had been submitted for voting at the cantonal and municipal level, while 12 such propositions ran aground at the government or parliamentary levels. We could object that the reverse was also true. The first vote on women's suffrage in 1900, which took place in Bern, occurred as a result of the cantonal government's initiative in response to women's petitions. It should be added, however, that at that time parts of the dominant classes tended to regard feminism with a fair measure of benevolence.

It seems to me that this question cannot be reduced to institutional responses alone; it must also take historic and cultural dimensions into consideration. The first problem is to determine why the vote did not happen before the end of the 1960s, and then to examine why it happened at that time. The major cause lies most likely in the Swiss conception of national identity. If this conception was left untouched by the problem of women's exclusion, it is precisely because the construction of Swiss national identity was based in large part upon the belief of the special nature of Swiss democracy. Swiss democracy was considered not only the oldest democracy in Europe, but also the world's most extensive democracy—one that hardly needed improving. The introduction of women's suffrage was seen as a modern invention, unnecessary in Switzerland. Moreover, in terms of private rights Swiss women were no worse off than women in other countries. This understanding of things was consolidated and almost became state doctrine during the 1930s, when the concept of "spiritual defense" was emerging as a cultural construct. (The centerpiece of a political discourse that aimed both to rally the nation and to close it off from foreign influences, "spiritual defense" defined Swiss identity as being totally at one with the institutions and traditions of the country, which are not only legitimated by history, but also intrinsically unique.) This created the idea that Switzerland was a *Sonderfall* (a special case)—an idea that predominated until at least the 1960s. One government minister, Hermann Häberlin, summarized how this conception of national identity influenced suffrage in a university lecture delivered in 1930: "If we analyze the woman's vote generally, we must insist that this civic project be understood in terms of the actual practice of male suffrage here. We cannot just copy from other nations. If we must, we should even accept the risk of not being modern."

Swiss historiography has amply demonstrated the hold of this cultural construction on Swiss mentalities and practices. At a symbolic level, Swiss women were excluded from politics. On a material level, however, their integration into the functioning of the state apparatus was historically precocious. Through this, they gained access to management and even became involved in the modalities of the political decision-making process. But as long as the definition of citizenship, which placed its emphasis on the right to vote, was not rethought, women's suffrage would continue to be regularly rebuffed by the state. In this sense, direct democracy was, in effect, an obstacle to women's suffrage in Switzerland. Direct democracy was the means through which a culturally constructed interpretation of collective references, including individual outcomes shaped by this socialization, could be articulated almost without interference from competing interpretations or new frames of reference.

Bibliography

Sources

Arbeitsgemeinschaft der schweizerischen Frauenverbände für die politischen Rechte der Frau, *[. . .im] Sinne der Gerechtigkeit in der Demokratie. . .. Orientierung über die Einführung des Frauenstimm-u. Wahlrechts in eidgenössischen Angelegenheiten*, Bern: Arbeitsgemeinschaft der schweizerischen Frauenverbände für die politischen Rechte der Frau, 1958

Bridel, Louis, *Le mouvement féministe et le droit des femmes*, Geneva: Eggimann, 1893

Confoederatio Helvetica [Switzerland], *Bulletin sténographique officiel de l'Assemblée fédérale suisse, Conseil national*, Bern

Confoederatio Helvetica [Switzerland], *Bulletin sténographique officiel de l'Assemblée fédérale suisse, Conseil des États*, Bern

Confoederatio Helvetica [Switzerland], "Message du conseil fédéral à l'Assemblée Fédérale sur l'institution du suffrage féminin en matière fédérale," *Feuille fédérale de la Confédération suisse* (1957) I

Confoederatio Helvetica [Switzerland], "Message du conseil fédéral à l'Assemblée Fédérale sur l'institution du suffrage féminin en matière fédérale," *Feuille fédérale de la Confédération suisse* (1970) I

Confoederatio Helvetica [Switzerland], "Rapport et proposition du Conseil fédéral à l'Assemblée fédérale au sujet des contributions fribourgeoises," *Feuille federale de la Confédération suisse* (1850) I

Hilty, Carl, "Frauenstimmrecht," *Politisches Jahrbuch der Schweizerischen Eidgenossenschaft* (1897)

Jenni, Léonard, *Selon l'ordre juridique existant, les droits civiques appartiennent-ils aux femmes suisses, oui ou non? Publication de documents au texte original, en partie en allemand, en partie en français, concernant la lutte pour la réalisation des droits civiques des femmes suisses au moyen d'une interprétation objective de l'ordre juridique suisse existant*, Geneva: Imprimerie Populaire, 1928; reprint, 1930

Kägi, Werner, *Der Anspruch der Schweizerfrau auf politische Gleichberechtigung*, Zurich: Polygraphischer, 1956

May Rued, Julie von, "Die Frauenfrage in der Schweiz," *Zur Bundesrevision* (12 May 1872)

Morsier, Auguste de, and D. Hamilton Smith, editors, *Why We Demand Woman Suffrage*, London: New Constitutional Society for Women's Suffrage, 1912

Roten, Iris von, *Frauen im Laufgitter: Offene Worte zur Stellung der Frau*, Bern: Hallwag, 1958; new edition, Bern: eFeF, 1996

Roten, Iris von, *Frauenstimmrechtsbrevier: Vom schweizerischen Patentmittel gegen das Frauenstimmrecht, den Mitteln gegen das Patentmittel, und wie es mit oder ohne doch noch kommt*, Basel: Frobenius, 1959

Schweizerischer Verband für das Frauenstimmrecht, *Das Frauenstimmrecht in der Schweiz: Tatsachen und Auskünfte*, N.p.: Schweizerischer Verband für das Frauenstimmrecht, 1950

Reference Works

Anteghini, Alessandra, *Parità, pace, libertà: Marie Goegg e André Léo nell'associazionismo femminile del secondo ottocento*, Genova: Name, 1998

Aregger, Jost, *Presse, Geschlecht, Politik: Gleichstellungsdiskurs in der Schweizer Presse*, Bern: Berner Texte zur Medienwissenschaft, 1998

Ballmer-Cao, Thanh-Huyen, "Suffrage, séparation des sphères et démocratie," in *Demokratie und Geschlecht: Interdisziplinäres Symposium zum 150 jährigen Jubiläum des Schweizerischen Bundesstaates; Démocratie et sexes: Symposium interdisciplinaire à l'occasion du 150ᵉ anniversaire de l'État fédéral*, edited by Birgit Christensen, Zurich: Chronos, 1999

Banaszak, Lee Ann, *Why Movements Succeed or Fail: Opportunity, Culture, and the Struggle for Woman Suffrage*, Princeton, New Jersey: Princeton University Press, 1996

Braunias, Karl, *Das parlamentarische Wahlrecht: Ein Handbuch über die Bildung der gesetzgebenden Körperschaften in Europa*, 2 vols, Berlin and Leipzig: De Gruyter, 1932; reprint, Bad Feilnbach, Germany: Schmidt Periodicals, 1999

Broda, May B., Elisabeth Joris, and Regina Müller, "Die alte und die neue Frauenbewegung," in *Dynamisierung und Umbau: Die Schweiz in den 60er und 70er Jahren*, edited by Mario König et al., Zurich: Chronos, 1998

Chiquet, Simone, "Die Diskussion um Frauenstimm: Und Frauenwahlrechte in den dreissiger und vierziger Jahren auf kantonaler Ebene: Fragen und Thesen," in *Frauen und Staat: Berichte des Schweizerischen Historikertages in Bern, Oktober 1996*, edited by Brigitte Studer, Regina Wecker, and Béatrice Ziegler, Basel: Schwabe, 1998

Delfosse, Marianne, *Emilie Kempin-Spyri (1853–1901): Das Wirken der ersten Schweizer Juristin: Unter besonderer Berücksichtigung ihres Einsatzes für die Rechte der Frau im schweizerischen und deutschen Privatrecht*, Zurich: Schulthess, 1994

Escher, Nora, "Entwicklungstendenzen der Frauenbewegung in der deutschen Schweiz, 1850–1918/19," Ph.D. diss., Universität Zurich, 1985

Fauré, Christine, "Sphère privée et espace public: (In)égalité des sexes et 150 ans de démocratie moderne," in *Demokratie und Geschlecht: Interdisziplinäres Symposium zum 150jährigen Jubiläum des Schweizerischen Bundesstaates; Démocratie et sexes: Symposium interdisciplinaire à l'occasion du 150ᵉ anniversaire de l'État fédéral*, edited by Birgit Christensen, Zurich: Chronos, 1999

Frey, Peter, *L'opinion publique et les élites face au suffrage féminin en Suisse, particulièrement dans les villes de Genève et de Zurich, 1920–1960*, Geneva: Imprimerie de la Tribune de Genève, 1970

Fussinger, Catherine, "Vie associative, vie privée: Des frontières parfois flous: Réflexions sur quelques figures du mouvement associatif féminin autour de 1900," in *Les femmes dans la société européenne; Die Frauen in der europäischen Gesellschaft*, edited by Anne-Lise Head-König and Liliane Mottu-Weber, Geneva: Droz, 2000

Hardmeier, Sibylle, *Frühe Frauenstimmrechts-Bewegung in der Schweiz (1890–1930): Argumente, Strategien, Netzwerk und Gegenbewegung*, Zurich: Chronos, 1997

Held, Thomas, and René Levy, *Die Stellung der Frau in Familie und Gesellschaft: Eine soziologische Studie am Beispiel der Schweiz*, Stuttgart and Frauenfeld, Germany: Huber, 1974; 2nd edition, Diessenhofen, Germany: Rüegger, 1983

Jaun, Rudolf, " 'Weder Frauen-Hauswehr noch Frauen-Stimmrecht': Zum Zusammenhang von Geschlecht, Stimmrecht und Wehrpflicht in der Schweiz," in *Frauen und Staat: Berichte des Schweizerischen Historikertages in Bern, Oktober 1996; Les femmes et l'état: Journée nationale des historiens suisses à Berne, octobre 1996*, edited by Brigitte Studer, Regina Wecker, and Béatrice Ziegler, Basel: Schwabe, 1998

Käppeli, Anne-Marie, *Sublime croisade: Ethique et politique du féminisme protestant, 1875–1928*, Carouge-Genève, Switzerland: Zoé, 1990

Kölz, Alfred, *Neuere schweizerische Verfassungsgeschichte: Ihre Grundlinien vom Ende der Alten Eidgenossenschaft bis 1848*, Bern: Stämpfli, 1992

Marshall, T.H., *Citizenship and Social Class*, Cambridge: Cambridge University Press, 1950

Mesmer, Beatrix, *Ausgeklammert, eingeklammert: Frauen und Frauenorganisationen in der Schweiz des 19. Jahrhunderts*, Basel and Frankfurt: Helbing und Lichtenhahn, 1988

Mesmer, Beatrix, "Pflichten erfüllen heisst Rechte begründen: Die frühe Frauenbewegung und der Staat," *Schweizerische Zeitschrift für Geschichte; Revue Suisse d'histoire; Rivista storica svizzera* 3 (1996)

Neumayer, Elisabeth, *Triebfedern und Beweggründe in der stellung des Schweizer volkes zum frauenstimmrecht*, Mannheim, Germany: Haas, 1934

Ruckstuhl, Lotti, *Frauen sprengen Fesseln: Hindernislauf zum Frauenstimmrecht in der Schweiz*, Bonstetten, Germany: Interfeminas, 1986

Schefold, Dian, *Volkssouveränität und repräsentative Demokratie in der schweizerischen Regeneration, 1830–1848*, Basel: Helbing und Lichtenhahn, 1966

Stämpfli, Regula, "Direct Democracy and Women's Suffrage: Antagonism in Switzerland," in *Women and Politics Worldwide*, edited by Barbara Nelson and Najma Chowdhury, New Haven, Connecticut: Yale University Press, 1994

Studer, Brigitte, " 'Alle Schweizer sind vor dem Gesetze gleich': Verfassung, Staatsbürgerrechte und Geschlecht," in *Herausgeforderte Verfassung: Die Schweiz im globalen Kontext*, edited by Beat Sitter-Liver, Freiburg: Universitätsverlag, 1998

Studer, Brigitte, " 'L'État c'est l'homme': Politique, citoyenneté et genre dans le débat autour du suffrage féminin après 1945," *Schweizerische Zeitschrift für Geschichte; Revue Suisse d'histoire; Rivista storica svizzera* 3 (1996)

Stump, Doris, *Sie töten uns, nicht unsere Ideen: Meta von Salis-Marschlins, 1855–1929: Schweizer Schriftstellerin und Frauenrechtskämpferin*, Thalwil/Zürich, Switzerland: Paeda Media Genossenschaftsverlag, 1986

Voegeli, Yvonne, *Zwischen Hausrat und Rathaus: Auseinandersetzung um die politische Gleichberechtigung der Frauen in der Schweiz, 1945–1971*, Zurich: Chronos, 1997

Woodtli, Susanna, *Gleichberechtigung: Der Kampf um die politischen Rechte der Frau in der Schweiz*, Frauenfeld, Germany: Huber, 1975

Ziegler, Béatrice, "Frauenstimmrechtskampf in der Schweiz: Zum Verhältnis von Frau und Staat," *Schweizerische Zeitschrift für Geschichte; Revue Suisse d'histoire; Rivista storica svizzera* 3 (1996)

WOMEN AND ISLAM IN THE WEST

DANIÈLE DJAMILA AMRANE-MINNE

AT THE END OF the 20th century—which was both abominable in its disdain for human rights and dazzling in its scientific advances—the rise in different forms of fundamentalism and the attendant violence had already destabilized a number of countries and had become a concern in the West. Early in the 21st century, this situation has escalated. Islamic fundamentalism appears as the most threatening of all: Islam is the religion of more than 600 million people worldwide and is associated with fundamentalist groups everywhere, including in Europe. Islam with a human face, lived in private, is silent and unknown. It is fundamentalist Islam—although it involves a minority group—that receives media coverage, for it brings together fanaticism, violence, and sexism, all at the same time.

The atrocities committed against women in some Muslim countries warrant an examination of women's position within Islam. While they are most frequently excluded from public life and sometimes even assassinated because they are women, some women, paradoxically, have become prime ministers, such as Benazir Bhutto in Pakistan, Tansu Ciller in Turkey, and Khaleda Zia in Bangladesh. In the West, where Islam is among the major religions, there is the question of how women of the Muslim faith reconcile their relationships to their religious beliefs with the modernity of the country in which they live.

Studies on immigration are numerous, but the issue of Islam in relation to European societies has been addressed only since the 1980s, essentially in France, while the topic has been given only secondary importance in Anglo-Saxon countries and other countries with small Muslim populations. Studies that take sexual difference into account are extremely rare. The present article, far from being exhaustive, is merely one approach to a variety of situations experienced by Muslim women in Western countries.

Muslims in the West

The Muslim presence in western Europe is the result of recent immigration that dates from the second half of the 20th century, linked to the dissolution of colonial empires and the economic boom of the 1960s. There are currently some 8.5 to 13 million Muslims living in Europe. Europeans who have converted to Islam account for an infinitesimal minority. The great majority come from the Maghrib (North Africa), Turkey, and the Indian subcontinent. Owing to the complexity of the different circumstances of this population—which includes immigrants registered as legal aliens, immigrants who have been naturalized, illegal immigrants, persons seeking asylum, and students—it is impossible to measure its precise demographics. Robert Bistolfi, in the book *Islams d'Europe* (1995; Forms of Islam in Europe) estimated the Muslim population at

> 3 to 3.5 million in France (the French minister of National Education cited a figure of 5 million, while the minister of the Interior estimated the number at 4 million; approximately 1 million Muslims were presumed to have French nationality). Between 1.6 million (official statistics) and 2.7 million Muslims have settled in Germany; more than 1 million in the United Kingdom; 550,000 in the Netherlands; 300,000 to 400,000 in Italy; 265,000 to 300,000 in Greece; 225,000 to 300,000 in Belgium; between 175,000 and 200,000 in Spain; 60,000 in Denmark; and 20,000 in Portugal.

Until the 1970s, immigration patterns focused primarily on economic motives and were often organized by agreement between states, such as Germany and Turkey, France and Algeria, Belgium and both Turkey and Morocco, and so on. Beginning in the 1980s, in addition to restrictions on the flow of migrant labor imposed by the host nations, the face of immigration changed: from the isolated worker who came for only a brief period of time, the norm changed to the settlement of families who had no wish to return to their country of origin, in part because of the wish for all family members to be reunited in one place. The proportion of women in these populations became greater and greater. In France, women accounted for 16.5 percent of the Algerian population in the 1962 census, their numbers swelling to 38.3 percent in 1982 and 44 percent in 1992. The Moroccan female population followed the same pattern and increased from 16.2 percent to 29.9 percent to 43 percent over the same time intervals. Only Spain and Italy, traditionally countries of emigration that did not become host countries until the 1980s, still have an immigrant population that is almost exclusively male. At the same time, practices and perceptions of Islam have also undergone a profound change. The children of the new generations, at least those who are practicing Muslims, are replacing the Islam of their fathers, which was basically lived in private in an almost "hidden" manner, with a much more demanding form of Islam for which they demand recognized public space. Mention must also be made of a new group of immigrants, numerically infinitesimal but made up of Muslim intellectuals who are often of high social status, who risk persecution in their own lands and have sought refuge in the West.

In North America the establishment of Islam has a different history. In Canada the Muslim community formed as the result of a relatively minor influx of immigrants and accounts for 300,000 people, 80,000 of whom have settled in Quebec. According to Canadian census figures, 98,165 people in 1981 and 253,260 people in 1991 stated they were Muslims. Religious affiliation was not among the questions on the most recent census, taken in 1996. Canada's Muslim immigrants are of very diverse origins (Indian, African, Middle Eastern, Turkish), and the community is marked by a high level of education. Among male Muslim immigrants in Canada, 26 percent hold university degrees, in comparison to 13.8 percent of other immigrants. Muslim women tend to have less education than the men, but more of them have had some university training than other immigrant women (12 percent and 8 percent, respectively).

In the United States, in contrast to other Western countries, Islam is to a great extent autochthonous, having developed primarily within the African-American community in response to exclusion, and at times taking extremist forms. The Muslim population remains a minority, between 1.2 and 3 million people.

Host countries have different attitudes that waver between the French system, which favors assimilation—implying the renunciation of all forms of cultural distinction—and the Anglo-Saxon concept, which tends to see the nation as a totality of ethnic or cultural communities. But Islam, the second largest religion of France and the third largest of Germany, has a difficult time finding its place in Western countries. Tensions and the national and religious differences between the various Muslim associations have provided a pretext for postponing recognition of Islam as an official religion, which to date has been given in only a few countries, such as Belgium and Spain.

Even in Belgium, where there is complete freedom of worship, with a privileged status for those six faiths that have become "recognized religions"—including Islam since 1974—the problem of a structure representative of all the Muslim communities has not yet been solved.

Whereas in France the Muslim past has been completely obscured, it remains alive in Spain, where coexistence was of much longer duration: seven centuries if one takes the fall of Granada in 1492 as the starting point, and nine centuries if one goes back only to 1609, the date the Moors were expelled. This may explain why Islam benefits from official recognition in Spain, even though the number of Muslims is quite small. An agreement was made in 1992 between the Islamic Commission of Spain and the Spanish government, which recognizes the secular character of Islam and acknowledges particular judicial problems, the calendar of religious holidays, and the Muslim historic patrimony.

In spite of these examples of recognition, a general ignorance or misunderstanding of Islam, intensified by the excesses of fundamentalism, makes Muslim values appear incompatible with the values of the West—notably those that concern the status of women, which it is appropriate to explain here.

Women's Status in Islam

The Koran was "revealed" in the seventh century (between 610 and 632) in a rigorously patriarchal society, governed by often-customary norms that were unfavorable to women—a situation that it attempted to remedy. Infanticide, still practiced by some tribes when female babies were born, is strictly condemned in several verses of the Koran, as shown in verses 1 to 14 of Sura 81:

> When the sun takes a new path
> When the stars grow dim
> When the mountains are made to move
> When the female camels ten months pregnant are abandoned
> When the wild beasts are gathered together
> When the boiling seas rage
> When the souls are reunited
> When the female child buried alive is asked
> What fault she committed to be put to death?
> When the scrolls are unfurled and displayed
> When heaven is dissected
> And Gehenna's fires kindled
> The Garden brought closer
> Then the soul shall know what she must say.

The stoning of an adulterous woman, a common practice in the Mediterranean world, is unlikely to occur in Muslim culture because of the requirement that four witnesses must be produced to prove adultery. Should they bear false testimony, these witnesses in turn are punishable by eighty lashes of the whip. Restrictions on polygamy tend to make it impracticable, and the repudiation of wives has been regulated. The most innovative aspect is women's right to inheritance, even though women's legacies are smaller than those men receive. In *Le harem et les cousins* (1966; *The Republic of Cousins: Women's Oppression in Mediterranean Society*), Germaine Tillion emphasizes that "At the time that the Koran was revealed, these prescripts represented the most 'feminist' legislation in the civilized world, but they constituted (and still constitute) a truly explosive bomb in a homogeneous tribe." Indeed, a woman's inheritance, in the case of a sedentary agnatic tribe, culminates in a parceling up of land and in its transfer to those foreign to the tribe—husbands or daughters' children.

However, continuing in the tradition of the monotheistic Judeo-Christian religions, Islam adopts an ambiguous attitude toward women, who are simultaneously valorized and deemed inferior. Men's supremacy is supported in several Koranic prescripts, such as in the possibility of polygamy or the fact that the testimony of at least two women is required to count as the equivalent of that of one man. This supremacy is clearly confirmed, for instance, in verse 34 of Sura 4:

Men take responsibility for women since Allah has favored them over women and since men support them from their own means. In return, good wives show their devotion and, in the absence [of their husbands], protect that which Allah holds in safeguard. Reprimand those from whom you fear insubordination, leave their bed, and chastise them. But once they have again become obedient, do not look for an excuse to punish them further. Allah is Glorious and Great.

The Koran, which contains only a few verses of a legal nature, and the "Hadith," statements and attitudes of the prophet Muhammad that were collected and interpreted after his death, constitute the essential sources of the Charia, which is the Muslim law. However, the Charia is the result of a human interpretation of Koranic prescripts rendered by Muslim jurists from the seventh through the ninth centuries. These jurists, men of their time, reestablished the patriarchy that a strict application of the Koran was threatening to undermine. They made a selection that, as Tillion explains,

> distinguished two categories in the prescripts of the Koran. First, there are the generally observed guidelines, some of which are even excessive (for example, those concerning the veil). Second, there is a whole series of peremptory commands that have been stubbornly avoided from century to century. In this latter category one basically finds the religious precepts that are aimed at granting women rights as persons.

Tillion cites the right to inheritance as an example of the latter.

Appealing to the progressive aspects of the Koran, many Muslims demand that Islam become more open to modernism. They consider it particularly important that women's emancipation can and must be accomplished on the basis of the Koranic text. By contrast, the fundamentalists actively campaign for a strict application of the Charia, as specified more than ten centuries ago, essentially where it concerns private rights, and thus the status of women. Nevertheless, the political Islamic regimes all accept as public and international law those modifications necessary to have their countries included in the process of contemporary economic development.

Thus, the status of women becomes the focus of fundamentalists' demands in Muslim countries; the issue distorts the perception of Islam in the West and often is the motivation for its rejection. For Islamists, an emancipated woman is the most obvious sign of modernity. They therefore work toward maintaining or reestablishing the patriarchal order that, by subjugating women, would slow society's evolution and perhaps even bring about a return to the mythical golden age of early Islam. In the minds of most Westerners, the aspect of Islam that is the most intolerable is women's position, and this abhorrence translates into exaggerated media attention to the struggles women wage and the atrocities committed against them, notably in the case of Algerian women.

In Islamic countries themselves, the changes are real and significant. In those countries that are attempting to shape themselves into modern nations, women, whether they are democrats or Islamists, are perfectly aware of the stakes. They are struggling to claim a public space in politics, culture, economics, and even religion. Those who are militantly Islamist want to be so as

women, and, even if they are separated from the men and covered with a veil from head to toe, they are present in large numbers in the mosques, where formerly only old women went. The democrats—most of them unveiled, others wearing a veil for personal reasons or under the pressure of their social milieu—resolutely defend the evolution toward modernism and are frequently threatened by both fundamentalists and the powers that be. One prominent example is Malika Boussouf, a journalist and the director of a highly critical political radio show widely listened to in Algeria, who has been condemned to death by the fundamentalists and banned from broadcasting by those in power. There are many other examples. Taslima Nasreen is a Pakistani writer whose novel, *La honte* (Shame), has been translated into several languages. She has been condemned to death by the fundamentalists and persecuted by the legal system of her country for blasphemy. Nawal Saadaoui, an Egyptian writer well known for her feminist battles, has been threatened by the fundamentalists and imprisoned on several occasions in her own country.

In the West, Muslim women are living in an open world, where, in theory, everything is possible for them, where they do not need to struggle for modernity, where it is given to them. How do they use this freedom?

France: Massive Integration Hidden Behind a Few Veils

France has the largest Muslim population of any European country, in terms of absolute numbers (more than 3 million) and proportionately (about 7 percent of the total population). Only foreign Muslims—assuming that every foreign national from an Islamic country is Muslim, which is generally the case culturally if not in terms of religious practice—are counted in the census. Their distribution by nationality is an indication of the origin of the whole of the French Muslim population. In the mid 1990s, they represented almost half of the foreigners living in France, in the following distribution: 795,920 Algerians, 431,120 Moroccans, 189,400 Tunisians, 123,540 Turks, and 138,080 black Africans (of whom only a percentage are Muslim). For accuracy, these figures should be augmented with figures for Muslims of French nationality who originally came from the countries listed, and a small minority of indigeneous French who have converted to Islam.

The high proportion of Muslim immigrants from the Maghrib explains why the majority of studies have been devoted to them. The focus of most studies is Algerians and French of Algerian origin because they are most numerous, and also because the Algerian War still remains a serious source of contention; this group suffers most seriously from exclusion and racism. A young man who looks Maghribi is automatically seen as a potential delinquent by a large part of the population, and frequently—in a pejorative sense—labeled as an Algerian. On the other hand, young Maghribi women tend to benefit from a certain sympathy, all the more so because they are perceived as being oppressed by Islam. This attitude can be explained by the fact that they are less visible, since they are more confined to the family circle than are the young men. It is generally assumed that young women are more easily integrated into French society . . . provided they do not wear the veil.

French Muslims' relationship to Islam, as well as the way in which French Muslims and Islam itself are perceived by the French, is culturally specific and different, for example, from the relationship the British have with Muslims in Great Britain. There, the phenomenon of fundamentalism reached public awareness at the time of the demonstrations clamoring for Salman Rushdie's condemnation to death and the public burning of his books. The seriousness of this demonstration of intolerance cast a new significance on the veil worn by some high-school girls in the assessment of the problems posed by Islam in France. Overnight, these young Muslim women, who had earlier been seen as victims, were perceived as the standard-bearers of fundamentalism. The reality of Muslim women in France is more complex than their stereotypical portrayals as the avant-garde of integration, the spearhead of fundamentalism, or the image of passive submission to a patriarchal form of Islam.

All studies distinguish between first-generation immigrant women born abroad and the young generations of women born in France or those who arrived as children. The role of Muslim mothers is essential, since it is their responsibility to pass on the cultural heritage of the home country, which is always heavily imbued with Islam, albeit in popular form. Muslim mothers are the main providers of religious examples for children (especially for girls), and they are prepared to maintain family cohesion by relying on many Islamic traditions. However, current and future developments depend above all on Muslim women of the second and third generations, many of whom were born in France and hold French nationality.

A recent inquiry, conducted in 1992–93 by the Institut National d'Études Démographiques (INED; National Institute of Demographic Studies) and the Institut National de la Statistique et Études Économiques (INSEE; National Institute of Statistics and Economic Studies), initiated and directed by Michèle Tribalat, drastically changes many earlier ideas about populations in France that are foreign or have foreign origins, particularly if they are associated with Islam. Far from being unable to assimilate, immigrants of North African origin are gradually integrating French norms. Their mother tongue is mostly French; 87 percent of the youth of Algerian origin declare that French is their first language, compared to Arabic for only 28 percent and Berber for 7 percent. Their religious practices are almost as slight as those of the average French person. Mixed marriages are on the increase. The number of those who register to vote is quite large. And, contrary to popular opinion, boys do not lag behind girls. Among the Muslim population, the only ones to withdraw into their own community are the Turks.

Discrimination is most significant in the area of employment. Unemployment rates for North Africans are higher than for foreign-born populations or those of foreign descent. The unemployment rate is 40 percent for youth of Algerian origin of both sexes between the ages of 20 to 29—twice that of their contemporaries of Spanish or Portuguese origin.

Adherence to religious beliefs and practices—which might seem to be the chief characteristics of Muslim peoples and are supposedly the major obstacle to their assimilation—is actually at low levels very close to those of the average French person. Tribalat confirms this trend, indicated earlier by the few researchers such as Bruno Étienne, who noted in his book *La France et l'Islam* (1989; France and Islam) that "in any case, there are few Muslims in France" see Étienne). Moreover, contrary to

the claims of some sociologists, women are more likely than men to be observant Muslims. Among the young people of Algerian origin, children of parents who were both born in Algeria, so often assumed to be fundamentalist, only 10 percent of the boys and 18 percent of the girls practice their religion regularly, while 30 percent of both boys and girls do not adhere to any religion.

Academic success is not any greater for young Maghribi girls than for boys. After polling seven academies, Smaïn Laacher and Alain Lenfant observed that: "If there are somewhat fewer boys than girls in the final year of secondary school, the boys are nevertheless scholastically 'better' since they are far more numerous than the girls in the most selective curricula" (see Laacher and Lenfant). Tribalat's findings indicate the same trend: although 11 percent of the girls of Algerian origin and only 9 percent of the boys acquire the *baccalauréat* diploma, it is nevertheless 14 percent of those boys who earn a university-level degree, as compared to 13 percent of the girls.

Voter registration on the part of French people of Muslim origin is an indication of their engagement in the political life of the country. The very few sociological studies that address the problems of North African youth indicate that girls are more politically aware and more "activist" than boys, which reinforces the frequently expressed notion that North African girls are better integrated into French society than their male peers. However, according to the results of the INED survey, men of all ages are somewhat more likely to register to vote than women: 80 percent of the men of Algerian descent or born in Algeria, as opposed to 69 percent of the women; 76 percent of the men of Moroccan descent or born in Morocco, as opposed to 72 percent of the women; 67 percent of the men of Turkish descent or born in Turkey, as opposed to 66 percent of the women. Among French nationals of Algerian descent, aged 20 to 29, almost 60 percent are registered to vote, without any noticeable difference between men and women.

"We should let go of the idea that there is a generation of young women of Algerian descent that stands as the avant-garde of modernity," concludes Tribalat. In fact, other than the Turkish minority, the assimilation of Muslim peoples involves both sexes and normally takes place by "osmosis." Nevertheless, there are some specifically feminine behaviors that reveal a desire to adopt secular and republican values.

Women as the Impetus for the Definitive Establishment of Islam in the West

All analysts have observed that the emigration of Muslim populations to Europe does not become definitive until it takes on a family dimension. It is interesting to note that the wish to settle in the host country essentially comes from the women.

Several studies have shown that although it is generally women who maintain the link with the country of origin—both because they are the ones who protect family traditions and also because they are often part of a more recent wave of migration and thus remain closer to their country of origin—women nevertheless do not wish to return to their homeland. Thus, in a report of surveys on "Femmes, mouvement associatif et religion dans le milieu de l'immigration à tradition musulmane"

(Women, Associations, and Religion in Muslim Immigrant Circles), Alain Mahé notes, "Among the immigrant women in our sample, not one has tried to return to her country of origin or admitted envisioning such a plan. The same thing is true for those women who were born in France" (see Mahé). In her Ph.D. dissertation, "Stratégies familiales et stratégies d'émigration des femmes algériennes" (Family Strategies and Emigration Strategies of Algerian Women), Yeza Boulahbal concludes that

> Here, too, we are far from the stereotype that claims that women only follow their husbands; on the contrary, it is often through a strategy of union, union with an emigrant or a Frenchman, that they give meaning to their choice to emigrate. Unlike their husbands perhaps, this choice is a choice of wanting to be integrated into modern society. It is not a temporary parenthesis, a stay outside of the homeland to accumulate a nest egg, while keeping the society of origin as the permanent reference point and ultimate goal. On the contrary, it is the enduring access to another lifestyle, that of consumer society, that they have come to find. (See Boulahbal.)

This feminine emigration strategy can be found again in the columns of personal classified ads that appear in certain Algerian newspapers, in which requests for marriage with an emigrant appear very frequently.

Transgression of a Taboo: Marriage with a Non-Muslim

Mixed marriages are ideal manifestations of the degree of integration of a foreign group into a given society. Whenever such marriages take place in significant numbers, they are an indicator of successful integration. "When two human groups come into contact, the exchange of women is a basic anthropological mechanism: such an exchange implies a dynamic of assimilation; its absence indicates a path of segregation," writes Emmanuel Todd, who stresses the importance of mixed marriages (see Todd). He uses these, along with fertility rates, as parameters of the process of integration or segregation of immigrants.

The number of mixed French-Maghribi marriages is on the rise. Among youth born in France of two Algerian-born parents, the proportion of mixed unions is 50 percent for men and 24 percent for women. For 32 percent of the girls and 50 percent of the boys, the first boyfriend or girlfriend is French.

For women, who must violate a formal prohibition, acceptance of a mixed marriage is more difficult. The Koran forbids marriages with polytheists in terms that are identical for both men and women. Although it authorizes Muslim men to marry women who adhere to monotheistic religions, there is no mention in the Koran of marriage between a Muslim woman and a man of a monotheistic religion. However, the taboo against this has been preserved for women by virtue of the fact that, in Muslim law, the child has the father's religion and because a woman—in principle submissive to her husband—would be compelled to renounce her faith and become apostate.

Among the Maghribi, family codes allow a man to enter into a mixed marriage, but this is formally forbidden to a woman, even in Tunisia, the most liberal Muslim country with respect to

legal codes pertaining to personal status. Because "a few Muslim women in Tunisia have knowingly decided to marry non-Muslim foreigners both within and outside of their country," a 1973 circular from the Ministry of Justice to the nation's civil servants reiterated the prohibition of celebrating such marriages and stipulated "the nullity of these marriages" and demanded that "they be officially annulled without going through a divorce." For a Muslim woman to marry a non-Muslim man is a transgression not only of Islamic law, but also of a deeply ingrained family custom. Barely 20 years ago, such a marriage entailed a complete break with the family, whereas the marriage of a son with a non-Muslim woman has always been at least tolerated. To preserve family cohesion—a major concern for women—accommodations were made to facilitate the integration of such couples. Sossie Andezian explains that "One of the strategies implemented by families facing this problem is to celebrate the marriage according to the practices established by the local Algerian community. The observance of the rituals to some degree compensates for the lack of conformity to the rule" (see Andezian). Since the organization of weddings has always been the prerogative of women, it is most likely that this approach was a woman's initiative.

In some cases, the groom agrees to a conversion, generally fictitious, that is performed in the mosque after he has received religious instruction and engaged in Islamic practice for an unspecified period of time. Traditionally, the conversion simply consists of a declaration that he is of the Muslim faith, along with compulsory circumcision. Today, the daily practices of conversion in certain mosques involve study and religious practice, as in Judeo-Christian rituals, but the process forgoes circumcision, which is often tacitly forgotten—a sign of willingness to adapt.

For women, a mixed marriage is a fundamental choice for modernity, and often it no longer provokes a break with her family, thanks to feminine "strategies." The birth control practices that are contingent upon women are another reflection of the success or failure of integration. The demographic practices of Maghribi women or of women of Maghribi descent living in France are similar to those of French women. From the 1960s to the 1980s, the fertility rate dropped from 8.5 to 3.5 children for French women of Algerian descent, from 5.9 to 3.5 for those of Moroccan descent, and from 6.3 to 4.2 for those of Tunisian descent. In the 1960s the average age at first marriage was 19.1 for French women of Algerian descent, 17.9 for those of Moroccan descent, 19.6 for those of Tunisian descent, and 22.4 for French nationals of French ancestry. In the 1980s, those ages were respectively 23.9, 21.4, 22.5, and 22.6.

Only the Turkish-born population or those of Turkish descent in France do not follow these trends. "The closed state of the Turkish minority," as Tribalat expresses it, clearly appears in demographic practices. Mixed marriages are the exception: 98 percent of Turkish immigrant girls and 94 percent of Turkish immigrant boys who are now married and who arrived in France before the age of 16 have spouses who are Turkish immigrants. The fertility rate among Turkish women, relatively low in the 1960s (4.0), has tended to increase and in the 1980s went up to 5.5, in contrast to that of Maghribi women. Only the average age at first marriage developed favorably, rising from 18.7 years in the 1960s to 20.1 in the 1980s; however, this is still younger than the average age of Maghribi women at first marriage. Yet

Turkey has older and better-structured traditions of modernity than those of the North African countries.

Todd explains this withdrawal into the community by arguing that the characteristics of the Turkish community in Germany have been transposed into France: "The Turkish immigration has brought the German attitudes toward difference within French borders." On arriving in Germany, the Turks seemed "ready to adopt anything, and in the long term to assimilate." The fertility rate among Turkish immigrants dropped early on, from 1975 to 1984, going from 4.3 to 2.5 children per woman, but later increased

> to 3.4 in 1990, that is to say, to a higher level than in the developed regions of western Turkey. . . . The exogamy rate among Turkish men supposedly was 10 percent in 1990, the same as in 1984, while among women it was 2 percent. . . . In Germany, Turkish women are defined as taboo, in the same way as African-American women in the United States.

While the Yugoslavs have been readily assimilated, the rejection of the Turkish community has led to a kind of community-centered identity that "leads directly from secularism to fundamentalism" and that includes relegating women to inferior status, according to Todd.

Great Britain: Community Withdrawal and Constraints upon Women

The total Muslim population of Great Britain is currently estimated at 1.5 million, or about 3 percent of the general population. Most Muslims living in Great Britain originally came from the Indian subcontinent, notably Pakistan and Bangladesh. The Muslim population also includes many small minorities from the Arab countries and Africa, and a few British converts.

Political authorities in Britain do not grant the Muslim population minority status because of its wide ethnic and cultural variety. At present, by virtue of the "Race Relations Act" of 1976, only Sikhs, Jews, and Gypsies are recognized as "a social or ethnic group," which gives them the benefit of legal protection against discrimination. The British state is not a secular one, and the official Anglican Church tolerates Christian churches but ignores other religions. Religious education, required in the schools, must be mainly Christian, and this principle was again confirmed in 1994. Islam has had all the more difficulty in finding its place as "English ethnic intolerance has produced a religious intolerance toward Pakistanis," explains Todd.

The first organized protests against Salman Rushdie, which condemned him for blasphemy and included the burning of his book, did not take place in Pakistan or Iran, but in Great Britain in December 1988, three months after the publication of *The Satanic Verses*. Islamists demanded that Islam be included in the law against blasphemy that protects the Anglican Church against all offenses. The Ayatollah Khomeini's death sentence against Rushdie was not issued until February 1989 in Iran.

The active militancy of Muslim fundamentalists exacerbates the rejection of the Muslim population. Communities that were once perceived as ethnic groups and designated by the name of their country of origin—Pakistan, Bangladesh—and so on, are now all identified as Islamic. Where Muslim populations are concerned, the concept of difference is no longer based on ethnic criteria but rather on religious ones, country of origin notwithstanding. When communities withdraw into themselves, their identity is shaped not by the values of the host society by instead by the cultures and the religion of origin. Women play an essential role in this process of identity formation. Their presence in the home ensures the continuity of family values, and the confirmation of Muslim identity results from the application of the Charia, which the fundamentalists in Great Britain have insisted on since 1975. More than men, women are the victims of withdrawal into the community. Their low levels of education and high fertility rate are symptomatic of their segregation.

In a study of Pakistanis of both sexes aged 16 to 29, Danièle Joly has shown the importance of the family and Islam as points of reference for a sense of identity.

> While they feel quite comfortable in England . . . Islam constitutes a very solid anchor for them that is an integral part of their identity; but they are less rigorous in their religious practice than their elders. The majority simply consider religion as an inherited fact of life, but an active minority seek to revalorize and reaffirm it.

Although young Muslim men, despite unemployment, are integrated into the workforce, young Muslim women are for the most part excluded from it. "Only a minority are allowed to study and look forward to a career, while the great majority are reduced to preparing themselves for or fulfilling their duties as mothers and wives, even if they have other aspirations and interests beyond those roles" (see Joly).

The awkwardness of immigrant women's situation is reinforced by the attitudes of the British state, which has taken restrictive measures against Muslim immigration; the first of these affects women, even though it technically involves polygamy. Werner Minski, in an essay in *Islams d'Europe: Intégration ou insertion communautaire* (1995; Forms of Islam in Europe) explains: "The explicit rejection of Muslim immigration has occurred only very recently: the immigration law, the Immigration Act of 1988, for example, includes measures that, under certain circumstances, prohibit the entry of married women under the rule of polygamy" (see Bistolfi and Zabbal). In addition, Women against Fundamentalism, a movement of left-wing British women, by offering to protect Muslim women against the excesses of Islamism, runs the risk of exacerbating the state of inferiority to which their communities try to confine them. Furthermore, among the Islamists' demands is the creation of denominational Muslim schools specifically intended to safeguard girls from the "perversions" of the West. In an article entitled "Fundamentalisme, multiculturalisme" (1991), Gita Saghal and Niza Yval-Davis show that "the majority of Muslim private schools recently opened in Great Britain are schools for girls, with the exception of two seminaries. It is their business to teach girls how to be good wives and good mothers. In the sciences, they teach the religious theory of creation, following the example of Christian fundamentalists, and they offer few opportunities for obtaining real qualifications" (see Saghal and Yval-Davis).

With little education and married at a young age, Pakistani and Bangladeshi girls have a large number of children—an average of 4.7 children for every woman in 1990. They are subjected to the pressures of their communities of origin and, simultaneously, excluded from English society by the racism that is so prevalent.

Some young women seek self-validation in Islam. They are militantly active in Islamic movements, which gives them a certain authority in their own community and allows them to better contend with racism based on the feeling of superiority derived from their certainty of following the "true way." Others become involved in various associations centered on their interests: providing English courses, information on their social or legal rights, and so forth. In a study conducted among women from Bangladesh living in Tower Hamlets in London, Catherine Neveu demonstrates the importance of such associations in awakening "self-confidence" in these women: "The names of these associations, furthermore, reveal this state of mind. 'Asha' means 'hope' in Bengali and 'Jagonari,' the name chosen for the first all-women center, means 'Women, wake up' " (see Neveu).

Canada: Fatima Houda-Pépin, First Muslim Deputy to Be Elected in the West: A Symbiosis of Islam and Western Values

The Muslim minority, made up of immigrants of diverse origins but generally highly educated, seems to have integrated itself into Canadian multiculturalism. The immigration in question is recent, since four out of five Muslims residing in Canada arrived after 1971. Two examples from Quebec illustrate the possibilities opened up by recognition and practice of cultural and religious freedoms—one in the direction of extremism, the other a model of perfect integration coupled with an affirmation of differences.

The first example concerns the so-called Islamic veil: as in all countries that accept multiculturalism, the veil is freely worn in Canada, except in Quebec, where some young girls were expelled from their schools for wearing them, despite the fact that a general position on the issue had not been taken. Anglo-Canadians perceive the issue of the veil as a manifestation of Quebecois ultranationalism, influenced by the "national drama" that the wearing of the veil in high schools had provoked in France. Franco-Canadians who are hostile to the *hidjab* see it as a symbol of fundamentalist ideology that is in opposition to Canadian values, such as equality of the sexes. In contrast, invoking the charter of rights and freedoms has pushed some Muslims to the extreme of imposing restrictions upon individual liberties. A private, subsidized Muslim school in Montreal forced three teachers of Canadian, non-Muslim origin to wear the Islamic veil at work as a condition of their employment.

The second example, which holds out some hope, is invoked in the title to this section. In France and in Great Britain, the Muslim vote is becoming increasingly important, but Muslims have still not acquired representation on the national level, and the number of their locally elected people remains small. It was in Quebec, in September 1994, that the first Muslim deputy in the Western world was elected, and that deputy was a woman: Fatima Houda-Pépin.

The two political parties, the Quebec Liberal Party and the Parti Québécois (Quebec Party), present their "ethnic" candidates at every election. At the September 1994 election, 14 "ethnic" candidates were presented. More than half of them had dedicated their lives to promoting their culture of origin by insisting upon building bridges between the ethnic groups and the French-speaking majority. But others objected to this tendency of the political parties to present candidates of foreign origin in counties with a heavy immigrant population, which they saw as a sign of "ghettoization." They declared themselves to be Quebecois and nothing else.

Fatima Houda-Pépin took full responsibility for her affiliation with the Muslim community and for having chosen to be Quebecoise. Originally from Morocco, she has lived in Quebec since 1976. Trained as a political scientist, she was for a long time president of the Centre Maghrébin de Recherche et d'Information (Center for Research and Information on the Magrib). Candidate of the Liberal Party of Quebec, she presents herself as a "woman of intercultural rapprochement and ecumenical dialogue" and thinks that "it is time to stop pointing at the differences between the Quebecois based on their ethnic origins and to get to work on defining a common identity."

The county of Pinière where Houda-Pépin was elected is predominantly French speaking (60.5 percent) and has an English-speaking community (15 percent). Its inhabitants come from 70 culturally different communities, a small minority of which are Muslim. Houda-Pépin was therefore not elected by a vote from the Muslim community. She obtained 63 percent of the votes and was elected with a majority of more than 10,000.

At the first session of the new National Assembly, Houda-Pépin was sworn in on the Koran and, in the course of her speech published in the *Journal des débats*, she specified:

> I am a Quebecoise by choice. I have become involved in politics in order to serve the best interests of Quebec. My belonging to Quebec and my pride in Quebec do not need to be demonstrated. I have worked for the promotion of the French language, because Quebec is Francophone and because of the use of French in the world. I have always identified myself as French-speaking.

The United States: Compensating for Racism

Muslims in the United States, using a high estimate of 3 million people, represent only 1.5 percent of the total population. The high proportion of American-born converts to Islam is peculiar to the United States. One third of the Muslims living in the United States are of American origin, with a small white minority: almost all American Muslims are African-American.

Muslims immigrants have come to the United States from practically everywhere in the Muslim world: Eastern Europe, the Middle East, North Africa, sub-Saharan Africa, Asia, and the Caribbean. Coming from very different cultures, they are grouped together according to ethnicity and are lost in the multitude of cultural groups that make up the population of the United States. They have not yet formed a lobby or powerful pressure group along the lines of those formed by the Jewish, Italian, or other communities. Until now, little research has been done on Muslims in the United States and very few analysts have specifically considered the feminine component of this population. Most of the interest has been directed at American converts and notably those of African origin because the converts of European origin form only a small, marginal minority.

Before the 1960s, African-Americans called for equal rights in order to allow for an integration they believed was possible. The separatist movement of the Nation of Islam founded by Elijah Muhammad, to which Malcolm X belonged, was a reaction to American racism. Since an effective recognition of equality could not be accomplished, the Black Muslims constructed a different identity for themselves through Islam. Entailing a rejection of Christianity, perceived as the religion of the white man, conversion marked the refusal of the dominant culture. Islamization of part of the African-American community reached the most disadvantaged layers of society. Prison conversions, such as that of Malcolm X, were particularly numerous. The fact that African-Americans, who represent merely 13 percent of the population in the United States, constitute 41 percent of the prison population is indicative of the exclusion with which they are faced.

Initially, these new Muslims were mostly men, but then the number of converted women became larger and larger. For women, as for men, converting to Islam is a choice that entails a break with the former culture and goes hand in hand with a transformation in everyday life: accepting dietary restrictions, following strict religious rites with a more or less exhaustive apprenticeship in Arabic, and sometimes abolishing Western-style furniture. In addition, women converts must change customs in dress, something that men are not required to do. By veiling themselves they make a visible statement of their faith and expose themselves to double ostracism, as both African-American women and Muslims. Moreover, while they are living in a country and belong to a culture in which equality between the sexes is, in theory, recognized, they now opt for a religion whose adherents openly practice sexual discrimination. They accept wearing the veil, being separated from the men in the mosque, and eating separately at communal meals during festive celebrations. Since Islam disparages unmarried women, they seek a union with a Muslim man, even if that means the marriage is arranged by the community.

This profound change provides more than a new identity and a new point of departure in life. Conversion also brings them advantages, even with respect to their status as women. They can be "real women," explains Beverly Thomas MacCloud: "Dependent and desired because of that dependency" (see MacCloud). As it does for the small minority of white American women converts, in some cases Islam seems to bring a certain stability and a possibility to flourish within the accepted limitations of the Islamic lifestyle.

Conversion to Islam is an attempt to respond to problems in American society. For African-Americans, the fundamental problem is that of racial segregation. But perhaps women, whether African-American or white, are also reacting against the difficulties of finding a place for themselves in a highly competitive society. In a sense Islam provides a sort of refuge within in a valorized family structure; it meets the need some women feel for protection, even if that means accepting inferior status.

The gains of Islam in the West are arguably a function of the number of those who are excluded from mainstream society. Muslim communities victimized by rejection turn inward and seek a new identity and renewed strength through religion. Women are the main victims of this type of withdrawal into community-oriented identity, which tends to assign them an inferior position. Nevertheless, some women, at a loss owing to the exclusion they have suffered, participate in this process, and they may view their dependence, of which the veil is one manifestation, as a form of advancement. A woman is veiled because she is desired, kept hidden and therefore protected, respected. Submission facilitates an abdication of responsibility when faced with the difficulties of everyday life. This "refuge" offered by Islam, while limiting the development of the individual in favor of codified behaviors, helps strengthen fundamentalism.

In the course of its history, Islam has adapted itself to different civilizations, from China to Africa and Mediterranean Europe, via Persia. It will therefore be possible for Islam to adapt itself to Western civilization. *Musulmanes. Une chance pour l'Islam* (Muslim Women: A Chance for Islam) is the title of a 1992 work by Florence Assouline, rendering homage to the feminine avant-garde working toward modernism in the Maghrib and in France. Islam is what its followers, men and women, make of it. In the West they benefit from a freedom that gives them the opportunity to develop a response other than that of fundamentalism: Muslims of the West, both women and men: a chance for Islam?

Bibliography

Andezian, Sossie, "Du 'religieux' dans les réseaux féminins," *Archives de sciences sociales des religions* 68, no. 1 (July–September 1989)

Assouline, Florence, *Musulmanes: Une chance pour l'Islam*, Paris: Flammarion, 1992

Bencheikh, Soheib, *Marianne et le prophète: L'Islam dans la France laïque*, Paris: Grasset, 1998

Bensalah, Nouzha, editor, *Familles turques et maghrébines aujourd'hui: Évolution dans les espaces d'origine et d'immigration*, Paris: Maisonneuve et Larose, and Louvain-la-Neuve, Belgium: Academia, 1994

Berque, Jacques, translator, *Le Coran: Essai de traduction de l'arabe annoté et suivi d'une étude exégétique*, Paris: Sindbad, 1990

Bistolfi, Robert, and François Zabbal, editors, *Islams d'Europe: Intégration ou insertion communautaire*, La Tour d'Aigues, France: Éditions de l'Aube, 1995

Boulahbal, Yeza, "Le secret des femmes: Stratégies familiales et stratégies d'émigration des femmes algériennes," Ph.D. diss., Paris: École des Hautes Études en Sciences Sociales, 1991

Boulahbal-Villac, Yeza, "Les femmes algériennes en France: Un statut négocié," *RFAS* 2 (April–June 1992)

Boussouf, Malika, *Vivre traquée*, Paris: Calmann-Lévy, 1995

Bruno, Étienne, *La France et l'Islam*, Paris: Hachette, 1989

Buijs, Gina, editor, *Migrant Women: Crossing Boundaries and Changing Identities*, Oxford and Providence, Rhode Island: Berg, 1993

Costa-Lascoux, Jacqueline, and Émile Témime, editors, *Les Algériens en France: Genèse et devenir d'une migration*, Paris: Publisud, 1983

Costa-Lascoux, Jacqueline, and Patrick Weil, editors, *Logiques d'états et immigrations*, Paris: Kimé, 1992

Della Donne, Marcella, Umberto Melloti, and Stefano Petilli, *Immigrazone in Europa solidarità e conflitto*, Rome: Centre Europeo di Scienze Sociali, 1993

Desplanques, G., "Nuptialité et fécondité des étrangères," *Économie et statistique* 179 (July–August 1985)

Gaspard, Françoise, and Farhad Khosrokhavar, *Le foulard et la République*, Paris: La Découverte, 1995

Geadah, Yolande, *Femmes voilées, intégrismes démasqués*, Montreal: VLB, 1996

Gerholm, Tomas, and Yngve Georg Lithman, editors, *The New Islamic Presence in Western Europe*, London and New York: Mansell, 1988

Gozlan, Martine, *L'Islam et la République: Des musulmans de France contre l'intégrisme*, Paris: Belfond, 1994

Haddad, Yvonne Yasbeck, and John L. Esposito, editors, *Islam, Gender, and Social Change*, Oxford and New York: Oxford University Press, 1998

Hermansen, Marcia K., "Two-Way Acculturation: Muslim Women in America between Individual Choice (Liminality) and Community Affiliation (Communitas)," in *The Muslims of America*, edited by Yvonne Yazbeck Haddad, New York: Oxford University Press, 1991

Howland, Courtney W., editor, *Religious Fundamentalisms and the Human Rights of Women*, New York: St. Martin's Press, and London: Macmillan, 1999

Institut National de la Statistique et des Études Économiques, *Recensement général de la population de 1982: Les étrangers: Sondage au 1/20: France métropolitaine*, Institut National de la Statistique et des Études Économiques (INSEE), 1984

Joly, Danièle, "Musulmans—Immigrants—Métropoles: La jeunesse Pakistanaise Musulmane de Birmingham," *Les temps modernes*, nos. 540–541 (July–August 1991)

Journal des débats 34, no. 4 (12 December 1994)

Kepel, Gilles, *Les banlieues de l'Islam: Naissance d'une religion en France*, Paris: Seuil, 1987

Knott, K., and S. Khokker, "Religions and Ethnic Identity among Young Muslim Women in Bradford," *New Community* 19, no. 4 (July 1993)

Laacher, Smaïn, and Alain Lenfant, "Où vont les jeunes filles quand elles vont à l'école? Remarques statistiques provisoires sur les élèves d'origine étrangère," *Migrants formation* 84 (March 1992)

MacCloud, Beverly Thomas, "African-American Muslim Women," in *The Muslims of America*, edited by Yvonne Yazbeck Haddad, New York: Oxford University Press, 1991

Mahé, Alain, "Femmes, mouvement associatif et religion dans le milieu de l'immigration à tradition musulmane," report edited by Fanny Colonna, CNRS (GSPM) (July 1992)

Migrants formation 84 (1991) (special issue entitled *L'intégration au féminin*)

Minces, Juliette, *La femme voilée*, Paris: Calmann-Lévy, 1990; as *Veiled: Women in Islam*, translated by S.M. Berrett, Watertown, Massachusetts: Blue Crane Books, 1994

Modood, Tarik, and Pnina Werbner, editors, *The Politics of Multiculturalism in the New Europe: Racism, Identity, and Community*, London: Zed Books, 1997

Neveu, Catherine, "Une moitié de ciel: Expériences de femmes Bangladeshis dans l'East End," *Les temps modernes*, nos. 540–541 (July–August 1991)

Noblet, Pascal, "Immigrations, minorités et politiques d'intégration aux États-Unis," *Revue française des affaires sociales* (December 1992)

Ruiz de Almodóvar y Sel, Caridad, *La mujer musulmana: Bibliografia*, 2 vols., Granada, Spain: Universidad de Granada, 1994

Sa'dawi, Nawal, *The Hidden Face of Eve: Women in the Arab World*, translated and edited by Sherif Hetata, London: Zed Books, 1980; Boston: Beacon Press, 1982

Sa'dawi, Nawal, *Qadiyat al-marah al-Misriyah al-siyasiyah wa-al-jinsiyah* (Egyptian Women: Tradition and Modernity), Cairo: Dar al-Thaqafah al-Jadidah, 1977

Saghal, Gita, and Nira Yval-Davis, "Fondamentalisme, multiculturalisme," *Les temps modernes*, nos. 540–541 (July–August 1991)

Smith, Jane I., *Islam in America*, New York: Columbia University Press, 1999

Speelman, Ge, "Muslims Women in Netherlands: Islam in Transition," *Research Papers: Muslims in Europe* 37 (March 1988)

Tillion, Germaine, *Le harem et les cousins*, Paris: Seuil, 1966; as *The Republic of Cousins: Women's Oppression in Mediterranean Society*, translated by Quintin Hoare, London: Al Saqi Books, 1983

Todd, Emmanuel, *Le destin des immigrés: Assimilation et ségrégation dans les démocraties occidentales*, Paris: Seuil, 1994

Tribalat, Michèle, *Faire France: Une enquête sur les immigrés et leurs enfants*, Paris: La Découverte, 1995

Venel, Nancy, *Musulmanes françaises: Des pratiquantes voilées à l'université*, Paris: L'Harmattan, 1999

Wahhab, Iqbal, "Muslims in Britain: Profile of a Community," *The Runnymede Trust Bulletin* (1989)

Werbner, Pnina, and Nira Yuval-Davis, editors, *Women, Citizenship, and Difference*, London and New York: Zed Books, 1999

Zehraoui, Ahsène, *L'immigration, de l'homme seul à la famille*, Paris: CIEMI, and L'Harmattan, 1994

Centers and Information Networks

Association, Développement, Relations Interculturelles (ADRI), Paris

Center for Migration Studies, Staten Island, New York

Centre d'Informations et d'Études sur les Migrations Internationales (CIEMI), Paris

Réseau d'Information sur les Migrations Internationales (REMISIS), Armelle Chervel, Centre National de Recherche Scientifique (CNRS)

TURKISH IMMIGRANT WOMEN IN EUROPE

RIVA KASTORYANO

TURKISH IMMIGRATION INTO FRANCE is a relatively recent phenomenon and is characterized by emphasis on family and community solidarity. Immigration statistics show that in 1964 there were a mere 111 Turkish workers in France, whereas in 1992 there were some 250,000. The first Turkish applicants for emigration to Europe were headed primarily for Germany. A bilateral agreement signed by the two nations in 1961 made the Federal Republic of Germany the first target of emigration; today some 1.8 million Turkish immigrants are settled in Germany. Turkish nationals are the immigrant group that is the most widely spread across Europe. Monographs on their modes of settlement in different countries attest to a degree of social insularity and community structures that limit the relationships that Turkish families maintain with the surrounding society.

Family unification is the driving force behind the growing numbers of Turks in Europe. In France in 1987, 40 percent of the Turks entering the country were motivated by the desire to reunite their families. In Germany, the influx of Turks has fallen off since the 1980s, which can be attributed both to the duration and stabilization of Turkish immigration and to more restrictive immigration policies in that country. This has not prevented an increase in Turkish immigration to other European countries, such as Belgium, the Netherlands, and Switzerland.

Women and Patterns in Turkish Immigration

Owing to the family-oriented nature of Turkish immigration, groups of Turkish nationals have tended to congregate in specific suburbs of large cities or in the center of small towns, and in Germany in particular districts. Transparency in social relations due to spatial proximity, the solidarity as well as the rivalry between families who hail from the same region or have simply found each other within the same residential area, and the pressure of social control based on values that are above all religious, are all criteria of communitarian organization. Seemingly a mat-

ter of preference in the early stages of immigration, this type of concentrated settlement appears in the long run to be the result of residency policies and the hostility of the immediate environment, as in Germany.

This social organization assigns a privileged place to women within Turkish immigration. Excluded from the workplace, woman's role and status are limited to the environment of family and reconstructed community. Far from the support of the extended family, as in the villages and often even the cities of Turkey, she alone is responsible for the task of safeguarding and passing on traditions, ensuring the education of the children by keeping them close to the culture of origin, and minimizing the "damage" caused by assimilation. It is in this manner that the "honor" of the immigrant family—of which she becomes the chief guardian—comes to be defined.

In reality, however, it is women who crystallize the contradictions peculiar to immigration. Immigration is by definition a bid for access to modernity, not only because of its economic and/or political implications, but also because of the new social relationships it engenders within the family, the community and the larger society. At the same time, immigration generates cultural resistance on the part of families, who adopt a posture of defensive traditionalism in order to develop "ethnic pride," to borrow Max Weber's expression. Directed toward both the surrounding society and other immigrant populations, this posture contradicts their wish to adopt a modern European lifestyle, the sign of upward social mobility, and is thus contrary to the goals that motivated them to emigrate in the first place. This contradiction, which distances them from the social and cultural evolution of their own country without including them in the host society, becomes apparent in the role assigned to immigrant women.

Women and Turkish Modernization

Recent studies in Turkey have debated the place of women in the political modernization of the country. In her book *Modern mahrem: Medeniyet ve örtünme* (Modern Muslim Women: The Veil and Civilization in Turkey), the sociologist Nilüfer Göle characterizes the Turkish woman as "a touchstone of westernization" (see Göle). In fact, the reforms undertaken by Mustafa Kemal Ataturk, founder of the Turkish Republic (1923), revealed an ethos of forced secularization whose objective was the destruction of the symbols of Islam in the public sphere. This was the context for the institution of the "dress code," which, following the abolition of the article of the Constitution that declared Islam the official religion of the state in April 1928, prohibited women from wearing the veil and men from wearing the fez. Although the adoption of the Swiss Civil Code in 1926 was at least as significant, if not more so, than the elimination of state religion, that change was marked by the country's apparent westernization and increased visibility for women, whose emancipation under the influence of Kemal Ataturk was part of the political project to build nationalism and secularize Turkish society. In tandem with this came equal rights for men and women in the areas of education and participation in the social and political life of the nation. It is worth recalling that Turkish women obtained both the right to vote and the right to stand for election in 1934, well before women attained those rights in France.

Of course, these reforms primarily affected the urban elite. Turkish immigrant women, the large majority of whom were of rural origin, were far removed from the modernization process in Turkey. They instead represented the traditional and religious values that had been repressed into the private sphere after the Kemalist reforms. The transition from rural to urban social organization thus constituted the first stage in their emancipation. Removed from the oppressive gaze of the mother-in-law, it was in the city that these women acquired their status within the nuclear family.

Immigration can be understood as an extension of this process. The new cultural context reinforces the woman's role within the family, in which she becomes the mediator between the society's values, introduced through the children's life at school, and those of the culture of origin. Around her, a consensus is negotiated on what is most "acceptable" in the immediate environment, both in immigrant life and in the home country. This has a particular bearing on sexual equality in education and professional training. Indeed, accepting the principle of equal opportunity constitutes the first step toward social success for girls as well as for boys and, in most cases, is experienced as a means of realizing the intention that motivated emigration and attaining modernity.

Islam in Immigrant Life

The limits of the "acceptable" are set by religion, even more decisively in a situation where immigrants constitute a minority than in their country of origin. Freed from the political taboos associated with it in Turkey, Islam becomes the hard core of Turkish national identity for the immigrant. Its importance is legitimized in the discourse on parent-child relationships, marriage, the behavior of girls, and so forth, and in the attitudes of parents, notably with regard to respecting prohibitions of certain foods and modes of dress. During the 1980s families mobilized around their consulates to request that imams be sent from Tur-

key (the bilateral accords did not include provisions for imams to be sent to Europe). The objective was to have an institutionalized support system that would ensure the religious education of children. The Turkish state, secular in its Constitution but characterized by a pervasive Muslim culture, then sent imams to its embassies in every European capital to represent the Diyanet (Bureau of Religious Affairs), under the authority of the Turkish prime minister. In doing so, Turkey certainly responded to the needs of families abroad, but its main aim, in broadening its sphere of action, was above all to remove the influence of the Islamic associations that represented different political currents, whether Turkish or international, and had become established in some areas with a strong concentration of Turkish immigrant families.

Today, despite the fact that the classrooms of Koranic schools in France, Germany, and even other European countries are filled with students, for most Turkish immigrant families Islam is preserved within the private sphere of the family and the local, reconstituted community. In effect, secularization in Turkey has transformed the social and political religion of Islam into a private and community religion—essentially a village religion. The sociologist Binnaz Toprak sees in this phenomenon the most significant achievement of Kemalist secularism—having managed to relegate Islam to a purely individual practice (see Toprak).

Once girls in immigrant families reach adulthood, they are totally excluded from the Islamic associations. In contrast to developments in Turkey, in the European countries the Islamist movement has few female adherents. On the other hand, young Turkish immigrant women are becoming more and more numerous in their participation in the activities of sociocultural associations, which are secular by definition, even when religion remains an important cultural element in the discourse.

As for the distinctive headscarf by which some Turkish immigrant women are known, in the majority of cases it represents an outward sign of "obedience" to religious values as these have been reestablished by the local community. While urban women gained "social visibility," to use Göle's expression, thanks to Mustafa Kemal Ataturk's reforms, some Turkish immigrant women in small towns or villages in Europe are thrown back on traditional rural values as a consequence of the social control exercised by the norms of the reconstituted immigrant community. In Turkey, the increasing popularity of the religious party and the reappearance of the scarf among the middle layers of society give a certain legitimacy to "the Islamic veil" as a political symbol. However, by respecting the dress code, a very large majority of immigrant women seem to be advertising their "sense of honor" and not their political affinities or membership in some religious party. Sometimes they impose the scarf upon their daughters, under pressure from neighbors, or from the imam to whom the community accords the status of political and spiritual leader. By doing so, these women express their desire for a guarantee of marriage within the group. Thus, the scarf in the context of the immigrant community seems to symbolize more the assertion of Muslim identity than women's collective political involvement, as is the case in Turkey.

Endogamy and Community Insularity

A 1995 study by the Institut National d'Études Démographiques (INED; National Institute of Demographic Studies) and the Institut National de la Statistique et Études Économiques (INSEE; National Institute of Statistics and Economic Studies) on "geographic mobility and social integration" found a high rate of endogamy among the Turkish immigrant population, with young people rarely marrying outside the community (see Tribalat). The same has tended to remain true in Germany, where the marriage rate outside the national group (sometimes even the regional group) remains quite limited. Emmanuel Todd reports that the exogamy rate for Turks in Germany in 1985 was 24 percent for men and 7 percent for women (see Todd).

Moreover, the survey in France showed that an expansion of the marriage market toward the country of origin was far greater among migrants originally from Turkey as compared to other immigrant populations. The wish to preserve their culture, to breathe new life into a national identity that has been weakened by immigration, explains this choice. In practice, marriage opens up a new road of emigration for young people who have stayed behind in the home country, through reunification with their families. The marriage of young women—who have been socialized and educated in France, sometimes have stable employment (and consequently a work permit), and in some cases have acquired French nationality—with young men living in Turkey (and no longer the opposite) and often even from the same region, shows a development in which women, often second-generation immigrants, become the main agent through which families are reunited. But more than a rethinking of the traditions in matrimonial practice and the sexual division of family roles, women's new function in the family has an effect on their status within the community (extended to Turkey) and the society.

Turkish immigrant communities in Europe live according to the rhythms of Turkey. Parabolic antennas and satellites bring the homeland back into the households in Europe, allowing the nostalgic past constructed through the experience of immigration to be updated. At the same time, caught up in a dynamic that is typical of immigration, families invent new rules of conduct and new marital traditions; they redefine roles and status so that voluntarily or involuntarily, women become the primary agents of change. In the case of families of Turkish origin, an intensified sense of religion and the closely related feelings of nationalism become markers of "difference" from the surrounding society and other populations. In France, this difference sets Turkish immigrants apart from other Muslim populations, the great majority of which are of North African origin, and creates a space for the affirmation of a Turkish Islam, its interpretations oscillating between its cultural and political conceptions. In Germany, this difference becomes a fundamental element in the demand for ethnic minority status, to be recognized on both a religious and national basis. Everything depends on the place each country grants to the immigrant or the foreigner, and to current policies of integration to which immigrant families must adapt.

Bibliography

Arat, Yesim, "The Project of Modernity and Women in Turkey," in *Rethinking Modernity and National Identity in Turkey*, edited by Sibel Bozdogan and Resat Kasaba, Seattle: University of Washington Press, 1997

Bozarslan, Hamit, "Une communauté et ses institutions: Le cas des Turcs en RFA," *Revue européenne des migrations internationales* 6, no. 6 (1990)

Bozarslan, Hamit, "État, religion, politique dans l'immigration," *Peuples méditerranéens* 60 (1992)

Collet, Beate, "Intégration et mariage: Les mariages mixtes en France et en Allemagne," Ph.D. diss., École des Hautes Études en Sciences Sociales, 1995

Gitmez, Ali, and Czarina Wilpert, "A Micro-Society or an Ethnic Community? Social Organization amongst Turkish Migrants in Berlin," in *Immigrant Associations in Europe*, edited by Wilpert, John Rex, and Danièle Joly, Aldershot, Hampshire, and Brookfield, Vermont: Gower, 1987

Gokalp, Altan, "Mariages 'à la turca': La tradition sera-t-elle de la noce?" *Archives des sciences sociales de religions* 68, no. 1 (1989)

Göle, Nilüfer, *Modern mahrem: Medeniyet ve örtünme* (Modern Muslim Women: The Veil and Civilization in Turkey), 2nd edition, Cagaloglu, Turkey: Metis Yayinlari, 1992

Kadioglu, Ayse, "Citizenship and Individuation in Turkey: The Triumph of Will over Reason," *Cahiers d'Études sur la Méditerranée orientale et le monde turco-iranien* (CEMOTI), no. 26 (July–December 1998)

Kadioglu, Ayse, "Women's Subordination in Turkey: Is Islam Really the Villain?" *Middle East Journal* 48, no. 4 (Autumn 1994)

Kandiyoti, Deniz, "End of Empire: Islam, Nationalism, and Women in Turkey," in *Islam, Women, and the State*, edited by Kandiyoti, Philadelphia, Pennsylvania: Temple University Press, and London: Macmillan, 1991

Kandiyoti, Deniz, "Gendering the Modern: On Missing Dimensions in the Study of Turkish Modernity," in *Rethinking Modernity and National Identity in Turkey*, edited by Sibel Bozdogan and Resat Kasaba, Seattle: University of Washington Press, 1997

Kanes, Thomas T., and Elisabeth Hervey Stephen, "Patterns of Intermarriage of Guestworker Populations in the Federal Republic of Germany: 1960–1985," *Zeitschrift für Bevölkerungswissenschaft* 14, no. 2 (1988)

Kastoryano, Riva, "Définitions des frontières de l'identité: Turcs musulmans," *Revue française de sciences politiques* 37, no. 6 (1987)

Kastoryano, Riva, "Les émigrés," in *Les Turcs, Orient et Occident, islam et laïcité*, edited by Stéphane Yerasimon, Paris: Autrement, 1994

Kastoryano, Riva, *Être Turc en France: Réflexions sur familles et communauté*, Paris: L'Harmattan, 1986

Kastoryano, Riva, *La France, l'Allemagne et leurs immigrés: Négocier l'identité*, Paris: Armand Colin/Masson, 1996; as *Negotiating Identities: States and Immigrants in France and Germany*, translated by Barbara Harshav, Princeton, New Jersey: Princeton University Press, 2002

Mandel, Ruth, "Sacrifice at the Bridge of Arta: Sex Roles and the Manipulation of Power," *Journal of Modern Greek Studies* 1, no. 1 (1983)

Mandel, Ruth, "Turkish Headscarves and the 'Foreigner Problem': Constructing Difference through Emblems of Identity," *New German Critique* 46, no. 1 (1989)

Mandel, Ruth, "Turkish Labor Migration to Germany: A Focus on Women," in *Mediterranean Women on the Move*, edited by Dennison Sakallariou, Athens: Mediterranean Women's Studies Institute, 1987

Mardin, Serif, "La religion dans la Turquie moderne," *Revue internationale des sciences sociales* 29, no. 2 (1977)

Tekeli, Sirin, "Les femmes, vecteur de la modernisation," in *Les Turcs, Orient et Occident, islam et laïcité*, edited by Stéphane Yerasimos, Paris: Autrement, 1994

Tekeli, Sirin, editor, *Women in Modern Turkish Society: A Reader*, London and Atlantic Heights, New Jersey: Zed Books, 1995

Todd, Emmanuel, *Le destin des immigrés: Assimilation et ségrégation dans les démocraties occidentales*, Paris: Seuil, 1994

Toprak, Binnaz, "The Religious Right," in *Turkey in Transition: New Perspectives*, edited by Irvin C. Schick and Ertugrul Ahmet Tonak, Oxford and New York: Oxford University Press, 1987

Treibel, Annette, *Migration in Modernen Gesellschaften: Soziale Folgen von Einwanderung und Gastarbeit*, Weinheim, Germany: Juventa, 1990

Tribalat, Michèle, editor, with the participation of Patrick Simon and Benoît Riandey, *De l'immigration à l'assimilation: Enquête sur les populations d'origine étrangère en France*, Paris: Découverte / Institut National d'Études Démographiques, 1996

Wilpert, Czarina, "Zukunfstorientierungen von Migrantenfamilien: Türkische Familien in Berlin," in *Gastarbeiter: Analyse und Perspektiven eines sozialen Problems*, 2nd edition, edited by Helga Reimann and Horst Reimann, Opladen, Germany: Westdeutscher, 1987

THE POLITICAL SUCCESS OF SCANDINAVIAN WOMEN

ELISABETH ELGÁN

THERE HAS BEEN A perceptible feminization of political personnel in almost all Western countries. In Germany and the Netherlands today, women make up more than 30 percent of the lower chambers of the national Parliaments. This recent feminization has been less significant in other European countries. The 1997 elections, with 18.4 percent and 10.9 percent of women in the lower chambers of the British and French Parliaments respectively, were considered victories. Since the 1970s, the Scandinavian countries have stood out as trailblazers in this area. Women accounted for 20 percent of the members of the Danish, Finnish, Norwegian, and Swedish Parliaments during the 1970s and more than 30 percent in the 1980s, and their numbers have continued to rise since then. Several hypotheses might explain this success.

Large Numbers of Women in Politics

Elected women composed 44.99 percent of the Swedish Parliament (as of September 2002), 38 percent in Denmark (as of November 2001), 36.50 percent in Finland (as of March 1999), and 35.76 percent in Norway (as of September 2001). Women's place in Swedish parliamentary work has been carefully studied by political analysts Christina Bergqvist and Lena Wängnerud. They have noted that the integration of women, initially focused on assignments and positions seen as less prestigious, now affects all of Sweden's parliamentary bodies to varying degrees (see Bergqvist et al. 1999). For example, the presidency of the Parliament of Sweden has been filled by women from 1991 to September 2001: the Conservative Ingegerd Troedsson was elected to that office in 1991; the Social-Democrat Birgitta Dahl succeeded her in 1994. In 2000, the Swedish government counted 11 women and 10 men (earlier governments have had equal representation since 1994). Finnish and Norwegian governments at the same time included 8 women out of 18 members, while the Danish government has 9 women out of 20 members.

Still, female ministers often hold less "onerous" and less prestigious offices than men. Admittedly, there have already been several female ministers of Justice, a few female ministers of Foreign Affairs and of Agriculture, and in Finland some female ministers of Defense, but few were ministers of Finance and only Norway has had a female prime minister, Gro Harlem Brundtland, who led three Social-Democratic governments (1981, 1986–89, 1990–96). Finland, which has a presidential regime, first elected a female president, Tarja Halonen, in March 2000.

Women as party leaders are also relatively rare. Out of the nine political parties represented in the Danish Parliament, two are led by women; in Sweden only one of the seven parties in Parliament has a woman at its head; in Finland and Norway there are two women leaders for seven large parties.

Nevertheless, the ongoing pattern of men occupying the most important offices shows that female authority is still accepted with difficulty. In this connection the Swedish historian Kjell Östberg wrote: "The limit to what men were able to accept in the matter of feminization is obvious: women should not have power over men—and men should not be forced to submit to women" (see Östberg). After the 1994 elections in Sweden, which were very successful for women, some of the most experienced among them called attention to the fact that their male colleagues, compelled to integrate women into their teams, had tended to choose young, relatively inexperienced women so as not to have their authority threatened.

Despite these qualifications, the success and recognition of Scandinavian women's battle to enter the world of politics are irrefutable. Women's increased presence in elected offices is not limited to national Parliaments alone, but has reached regional and local levels as well.

Four Small Countries

Both geographically and politically, Scandinavia lies at the periphery of Europe, and we should thus recall the specific institutional and historical framework for women's political success in the region. The present configuration of the the the four most important Scandinavian countries—Denmark, Finland, Norway, and Sweden—reflects the balance of European powers as it was drawn at the end of the Napoleonic Wars. In 1809 Finland, which belonged to Sweden, was incorporated into the Russian empire. Norway, which was part of Denmark, formed a union with Sweden in 1815 under the aegis of the king of Sweden.

The Scandinavian countries went through the great upheavals of the 20th century, saliently the two world wars, in different ways. Denmark, Norway and Sweden stayed out of World War I. Through its contact with the Russian Revolution, Finland experienced national enfranchisement but was affected by the civil war that broke out in the Soviet Union in 1918. During World War II, Denmark and Norway were occupied by Germany even though they were neutral. In 1939–40, Finland fought the Soviet Union in the so-called Winter War, which broke out following Soviet aggression caused by Finland's refusal to cede certain border zones. In 1941, Finland joined the German attack on the Soviet Union. Sweden did not enter World War II and was not occupied. Research on this period and on the attitudes of the Scandinavian countries in the face of Nazism is now beginning to be developed.

The Scandinavian countries have long been characterized by underdeveloped economies because of their sparse population, the barrenness of the soil in all countries except Denmark, climatic conditions so harsh that survival may be difficult, and their geographic location on Europe's periphery, isolated from contact with other continents. Finland today has 4.5 million inhabitants, Norway and Denmark about 5 million each, and Sweden almost 9 million.

It is common practice to consider the Scandinavian countries as forming a homogeneous whole. However, Scandinavian political unity, peace among the four countries, and the sense of belonging to a common culture are of recent date. There are significant economic, social, cultural, and linguistic differences. The idea of Scandinavian unity was born in the 19th century, but it was not until after World War II that true institutionalized, though limited, cooperation was established among the countries. In the area of sexual equality, however, the notion of Scandinavian unity has played a positive role, inspiring emulation among the countries. Here, while emphasizing the common traits among these countries, we shall make particular reference to Sweden, which took the leading position in the feminization of political life in the 1980s.

Recent Democracies

In comparison with other Western countries, the Scandinavian democracies are relatively young. The period that separates the introduction of general voting rights for men from the attainment of women's suffrage is relatively short, and both the advent of democracy and women's attainment of the right to vote were related to the victory of parliamentarism.

Finland was the first European country to introduce women's right to vote at the same time as male suffrage, in 1906, in the context of the struggle for the constitution of a Finnish nation. Thanks to the February 1905 events in Russia, Finland was able to institute a one-chamber national Parliament by universal male

and female suffrage. Finland gained its independence some years later, after the Russian Revolution of 1917.

Norway's move toward democracy occurred in the framework of the struggle to establish a state independent from Sweden, but here women were not involved as they had been in Finland. Norway adopted parliamentarism in 1884 and universal male suffrage in 1898; the country became independent by referendum in 1905. Norwegian women had to wait until 1913 for their right to vote to be recognized. Denmark introduced universal male suffrage in 1901 and women's right to vote in 1915. In Sweden, men obtained the right to vote in 1907, albeit with a few restrictions, which were lifted in 1919, at the same time that women's suffrage was introduced. Parliamentary democracy was definitively established rather late in Denmark and Sweden. Until the 1910s the monarchs of these two old and dominant Scandinavian states were still involved from time to time in the composition and actions of the governments.

Sixty years separate the time when women obtained the right to vote from their mass entry into political life in the Scandinavian countries. We can infer that the relative contemporaneity of male and female suffrage made the Nordic political systems more flexible than the older democracies, where political clans formed and transcended generations, their practices designed to ensure the renewal of their power.

Moreover, the political institutions of the Scandinavian countries underwent regular forms of modernization that prevented them from becoming ossified. For example, the two-chamber system, with its upper chamber, its roles, and election procedures that remained obscure to many, was abolished in Denmark in 1953 and in Sweden in 1971. With their voting system of indirect election that often favored the incumbents, it was difficult for newcomers to gain access to an upper chamber. In Sweden, the number of women in the upper chamber was always significantly lower than in the lower chamber. In Finland, where women acquired the right to vote at the same time as men, and where the two-chamber system was never instituted, the number of women in Parliament was close to 10 percent from the beginning.

In these four northern countries, the corridors of power were less closed and less selective than in the democracies with more complex, older, and tradition-laden institutions. Their respective political regimes probably offered less resistance to the true integration of women.

Social, Economic, and Historical Inequalities

The feminization of political life in the Nordic countries does not translate into economic and social equality. Women's participation in the working world, the principal source of independence and social integration, is still marked by significant inequalities, even if these have been reduced over the last 30 years, as the surveys by the economist Anita Nyberg have shown for Sweden (see Nyberg).

Among the positive aspects: in the Nordic countries women have not generally suffered a higher rate of unemployment than men, and 74 percent to 77 percent of women between the ages of 20 and 64 were employed in 1998. The corresponding rates for men varied from 80 percent to 87 percent. On the other hand, women did more part-time work that year than men, accounting for 27 percent of the part-time workforce in Sweden and 32 percent in Norway. In Denmark and Finland, part-time work is less widespread among women: only 9 percent work part time (*Women and Men in the Nordic Countries: Facts and Figures 1999*).

A division of the economy by sectors also reveals a high degree of gender segregation. Women mostly work in the service sectors, men primarily in the production of goods and in finance. Hence, about 50 percent of women have public employers, while 80 percent of men work for private employers (*Women and Men in the Nordic Countries: Facts and Figures 1999*). In executive positions, the inequality between the sexes is flagrant, despite the example of the numbers of women in political leadership positions. The proportion of women seated on boards of directors of large groups in the private sector, early in the 1990s, was around 10 percent in the Nordic countries. Women were almost absent from executive positions, although they already represented 30 percent to 40 percent of the workforce (*Women and Men in the Nordic Countries: Facts and Figures 1999*). There is no indication that this situation has seen any radical changes since then.

One of the results of this segregation is that the average income of women is far lower than that of men: Danish and Finnish women earn only about 75 percent of the average male salary and Norwegian women only about 50 percent, while the percentage for Swedish women lies somewhere between those figures (*Women and Men in the Nordic Countries: Facts and Figures 1999*).

To explain the political place of women in the Scandinavian countries, one can no more invoke historic tradition in matters of sexual equality than one can socioeconomic realities, where there are obvious weaknesses. In all of these countries, the 19th century was a long period of uncertainty and indecision about what women's status in modern society should be: their right to inheritance, the degree of their autonomy regarding the family, and their right to work. Developments throughout that period can be understood as marking the passage from a society of the old regime to a liberal society, a transition that took more than a century and began later in the Nordic countries than in the other European states. Most of the laws supporting a new status for women date only from the second half of the 19th century; the same was true for the civil rights of adult unmarried women. As for the civil rights of married women, Sweden and Finland delayed until 1921 and 1930, respectively, before granting these, while Norway and Denmark preceded them in this area by several decades.

Networks, Movements, Actions

The early 1960s saw renewed debate on the "woman question" and the arrival of a new generation of feminists, male and female. The unified actions and reasoning of this new generation of activists provide one of the main explanations for the political success of Scandinavian women.

In the 1960s, the Nordic countries were living through a period of social reforms and intense modernization on every level; the notion of sexual equality was well received and developed by activists and leaders of the Liberal and Social-Democratic political parties. There were frequent exchanges of ideas on these themes among the countries.

The debate in Sweden took flight in 1961 with the publication of an article by a young liberal journalist, Eva Moberg, who challenged the notion of the "two roles of women." That phrase was the title of a work published in 1956 by the Swedish Social-Democrat Alva Myrdal and the English sociologist Viola Klein. They argued that women should divide their lives in two: first attending to raising their children and then, when they were grown, working outside the home. In their introduction, the authors wrote:

> The emphasis has now shifted from the discussion of: "What *can* women do?" to one of "What *should* women do?" Implicit in this question is an interest both in women's individual well-being and in the welfare of society. What to do with our lives is a problem which poses itself more acutely in regard to women than to men, partly because women are relative newcomers to important sectors of the social scene, partly because their lives are more intricately linked with the existence of the family and the continuation of the race. (See Myrdal and Klein.)

They concluded that the mother should stay at home with her children until they were three years old, then work part-time until they were six.

Eva Moberg, however, asked why only women should mind the children and why they would not have the right to work and have children at the same time, as men did. Thus, in *Kvinnor och människor* (1962; Women and Human Beings), she challenged the ideal of the woman in the home, which was widely shared in every political camp at the time:

> We must stop hammering away at the concept of "women's two roles." Women like men have a principal role, that of being human. In the role of being human there is, by necessity and morality, but also through pleasure and luck, the obligation of taking good care of one's descendants. If that is not recognized, one is participating in making women's emancipation into nothing but a conditional emancipation. Woman has been emancipated only under the implicit reservation that she continue to see the raising of children as her main task. Only if she admits that therein lies her natural destiny, inscribed in some mysterious way in her character as sexual being, only then is society quite willing to see her as an individual who is wholly free to have control over herself.

The second event that catalyzed renewed debate about women was the publication of a Swedish-Norwegian book entitled *Kvinnors liv och arbete* (1962; Women's Life and Work), in which a dozen or so researchers critically analyzed "sexual roles," as they called them: the education of girls and boys, the passage into adulthood, and women's working conditions (see Dahlström). Thereafter, these books and ideas circulated through the Scandinavian countries.

Particularly important issues under discussion were married women's right to work in the same capacity as men and the need for day care centers for the very young. But the need for coeducational schooling and the need for changes in the behavior of men and fathers were also addressed. Swedish journalist Marianne Kärre, mother of five, was surprised by the absence of day care centers when she returned to Sweden after a long stay in France. She wrote a series of articles for a large daily newspaper that showed famous men, such as Prime Minister Olof Palme, as new fathers caring for their children.

Within the framework of recognizing women's right to work, the most important demand, a source of profound division among Swedish Social-Democrat women, was the end of the notion of joint tax filing for married couples or households. The joint taxation of spouses worked to the disadvantage of the married woman who worked outside the home, as it added her salary to that of her husband, leading to higher taxes under Sweden's progressive fiscal system.

This debate was initiated in Sweden mainly by somewhat militant young progressives of both sexes, whose professions were in the social, community, or media sectors and who were close to the Social-Democrats and the Liberal Party. Some of them formed a network that became influential. It would meet to debate discrimination against women, giving everyone the freedom to speak for himself or herself on matters of public opinion. The group did not indicate any specific direction or appoint a spokesperson (see Baude). The historians Christina Florin and Bengt Nilsson have done a study of the activity of the 1960s militants (see Florin and Nilsson).

Although the condition of women in the workplace and in the family lay at the heart of the debate in the 1960s, the question of abortion was not emphasized, probably for fear of causing division. In the 1930s the political federations of Swedish women had met on the issue of abortion, sometimes in collaboration with the Riksförbundet För Sexuell Upplysning (RFSU; Swedish Movement for Birth Control). At the time they demanded that abortion be made available for reasons of health or socioeconomic deprivation. Their demand was rejected. At the same time, authoritarian eugenicist policies were put into effect, mainly in Sweden, where political and medical authorities at the local and national levels were seduced by the idea of sterilizing "social cases" and persons with slight mental handicaps. Although it was in theory optional, sterilization was often the prerequisite for release from mental institutions and was mandatory after certain types of medical abortion. More than 90 percent of those affected by the sterilization policies were women. Eugenic sterilizations were an especially common practice during the 1940s. According to one estimate, some 30,000 Swedish women were sterilized, more or less against their will. This practice ceased in the 1950s. Around that time, a new conception of sexuality and the body emerged, and the struggle for the right to abortion on demand began. The Swedish historian Lena Lennerhed, who directed abortion research in the 1960s, concluded that women's attitudes toward abortion were more fearful in the 1960s than in the 1930s, although her research has not progressed sufficiently for her to suggest causes for this phenomenon (see Lennerhed 1994). The Danish historians Lau Esbensen and Bente Rosenbeck did similar research on abortion in Denmark during the same period.

In Sweden in the 1960s, it was men who were young and close to the Liberal and Social-Democratic parties who raised the issue of women's freedom to have an abortion. The feminist movements of the 1970s took up this question again, both in the Scandinavian and other Western countries, but the right to have an abortion in a hospital setting early in pregnancy was already beginning to be accepted.

In the 1960s, contraception was another theme not frequently dealt with in the debates on women's condition. In the Scandinavian countries in the 1960s, contraception seems to have been accepted gradually and without any clashes.

The book *Kvinnors liv och arbete* and the subsequent feminist renewal stimulated research in the social sciences. The Finnish-Swedish sociologist Rita Liljeström played a major role in this area. In a 1965 study intended for a general readership, she sought to counter the idea of biological destiny, analyzing the importance of social relationships in the shaping of sexual inequalities:

> When we speak of sexual roles, we do not refer to biological difference as such but to the social consequences of categorizing the human species according to the genital organs. The sex organ is the principle of selection and the exterior sign by which society determines the main division in work, as well as the apportioning of obligations and privileges, of areas of interest and possibilities offered. As a social differentiation, the importance of sex vastly surpasses the biological facts. Sexual roles have their deep roots in the preindustrial era. Through time, they have regulated the distribution of power and of the responsibilities between men and women. Consequently, sexual roles seem to form a stable structure in human relations, having received the stamp of a natural order through the length of time that this has lasted. They enjoy a kind of historical and moral legitimacy that prevents them from being questioned. (See in Fredriksson.)

Gains in Momentum during the 1970s

The reforms in favor of sexual equality developed throughout the 1960s were implemented relatively rapidly. The principle of equal pay for equal work (by then already recognized in the public sector), was recognized in the private sector in 1960 in Sweden, in 1961 in Norway, and in 1962 in Finland, but not until 1973 in Denmark. In 1960 Norway made the joint taxation of spouses' income optional. Denmark abolished that system in 1967; Sweden followed suit in 1970, and Finland, where joint taxation had previously been optional, abolished it in 1976. The right to abortion was recognized in 1973 in Denmark, in 1974 in Sweden, and in 1978 in Norway. Finland had granted abortion rights for sociomedical reasons in 1970. The implementation of this reform did not run up against any particular obstacles, as may have been the case in other countries.

The first laws forbidding discrimination based on sex were adopted during the same period: 1976 and 1978 in Denmark, 1978 in Norway, 1979 in Sweden, and 1986 in Finland. These laws essentially concerned working conditions.

In hindsight, the most innovative of these reforms seems to be the one dealing with taxation, since the others can be found in other Western countries in the same form and during the same period. Paying taxes, being seen as subject to taxes, having to complete a tax return, and being the object of individual taxation are among the most significant manifestations of citizenship. The question of the total amount of taxes was also one of the most recurrent themes in the political debate. Individualizing taxes is one of the stages toward full and complete citizenship, and, in Sweden in any case, obtaining this was clearly perceived as a victory.

The Swedish feminists who were trained in the 1960s played an important role in the concrete application of the new laws in favor of women. Some of them subsequently had long political or administrative careers. For example, Anita Gradin, who became European commissioner after serving at the ministerial level in several governments, belonged to this first generation of feminists, and who as commissioner was active in the fight against trafficking in women and human beings.

Still, until the mid 1970s the place of Scandinavian women in political life continued to be limited. Before 1974 Sweden had only had five female secretaries of state (not a ministerial position); only one held on to her position. Without the momentum gained by the new feminist movement of the 1970s, the potential of the knowledge, lines of argument, and skills accumulated during the 1960s might never have had the opportunity to become actualized.

The new feminist movement of the 1970s was an international phenomenon. In the Scandinavian countries as elsewhere, new women's groups were formed that were independent of political parties and existing structures. These groups differed from preceding movements in both their discourse and their practices. If the debate of the 1960s had caused a breach in the thinking about women's condition by introducing the social dimension of gender roles, the feminist groups of the 1970s went even further by adopting the vocabulary of antiracist and anticolonial movements and specifically identifying women as an oppressed group. Women were to become conscious of this oppression, representing the first step toward their liberation, another concept borrowed from the anticolonial movements. The second stage would consist of meeting in women's groups, without men, and of acting collectively to make women's oppression evident. The discourse of these new groups allowed for a conceptual critique of the male as the oppressor. However, the Scandinavian groups were less radical than their American or continental counterparts and were content to condemn the capitalist system and the patriarchy, mixing them together, as being responsible for their oppression. Their actions were very different from the traditional paths their predecessors had followed. Instead of petitions, articles in the press, and pressure on political parties, the new generation of feminists adopted the modes of action that other youth movements used at the time: sit-ins, street demonstrations, theater, song, exhibits, distribution of pamphlets, and disrupting electoral meetings and political events. It may be said that on a practical level these young women sought to challenge women's traditional role by the way they dressed, spoke, acted, and lived. The decade of the 1970s represented the peak of the activity of these groups, whose numbers and influence were growing. The political analyst Drude Dahlerup, author of a two-volume history entitled *Rødstrømperne* (1998; Red Stockings), after the name the Danish group adopted, has studied this movement for Denmark.

These women's groups, often close to the antiparliamentarism of the extreme Left, disrupted feminist organizations and the networks of the traditional political parties. The new feminists not only revitalized the debate on social relationships, they also restarted political action on behalf of sexual equality. Subsequently, the women's federations within the political parties adopted a more radical language, picked up by the whole organization. The Swedish Social-Democratic Party, at their congress of 1972, granted a large place to the question of sexual equality. Olof Palme, the Social-Democrat Party leader and prime minister, gave a historic speech on the subject: "We want to remove the obstacles that have always existed and still exist for women's equal rights and equal opportunities" (quoted in Florin and Bengt). That same year Palme established the first Swedish governmental office on this issue, called the Jämställdhetnämnden (National Council for Equality between Men and Women).

In the 1980s many of these women's groups were dispersed. However, individual members continued to direct their energies into areas related to specific issues: scientific research, activism to promote equality in the workplace, the protection of women against domestic violence, or the struggle against nuclear weapons.

Today, the remaining women's groups still exert pressure in Swedish political life. Before the 1994 elections, they worked to ensure that women were not left out of the electoral debate. In fact, the 1991 elections had seen the number of women in Parliament dwindle from 38.4 percent to 33.5 percent. This network threatened to establish a women's party if the traditional parties were not going to listen to women's demands. When a poll revealed that this idea would be welcomed among the voters, the Swedish Social-Democrats decided for the first time to present lists with equal representation in alternating order.

Women's Trump Cards

The feminist movement of the 1970s pushed politicians, men and women alike, to action. To this end, the women's federations within the political parties represented an important trump card. These federations existed in most of the Scandinavian political parties, which long resisted demands for better political representation of women. The women's federations had structures, budgets, and contacts already in place when the 1970s grew more radical. They were able to act more efficiently to nominate a larger number of women and have them elected; and, indeed, in Sweden the Social-Democratic women were able to enforce the principle of lists in alternating male-female order in the elections of 1994 and subsequent years.

In a comparative report on the progress of sexual quality in the Scandinavian countries entitled *Equal Democracies? Gender and Politics in the Northern Countries* (1999), the contributing authors suggest that the delay in the feminization of political life in Denmark and its relative underdevelopment in the matter of policies of sexual equality, compared to the other three Scandinavian countries, might be explained by the absence of women's federations within the parties (see Berqvist et al.). These federations had been abolished at the end of the 1960s.

Another trump card is the role of scientific research in the evolution of social relations between men and women. Significant in the 1960s during the debate on sexual roles, the research that had developed, especially in the social sciences, began to infiltrate all the traditional academic disciplines, including medicine and technology. The results were broadcast by the media and through a vigorous system of continuing education and popular training. Academic analyses sought not only to show the existence of social inequalities between the sexes, but also to understand the mechanisms through which these inequalities were perpetuated. The statistics on these inequalities presently occupy an important place in the official documents and have become an effective weapon in the struggle for women's rights (*Engendering Statistics: A Tool for Change*, 1999).

Structural Flexibility

The proportional electoral system practiced in the Scandinavian countries, in which each district each party obtains a number of elected persons corresponding to the percentage of votes, probably allowed women and other groups to be more readily integrated. With a proportional system, the choice of new types of candidates is a less risky experiment for the political parties and the struggle for endorsements less intense than under a system of majority balloting. However, it would be an exaggeration to view the proportional system as the decisive explanation of women's political success in the Scandinavian countries. This form of voting was the rule in these countries long before the massive influx of women into political life. Sweden practiced proportional voting from the time that universal suffrage was introduced, but it took 30 years after the vote was acquired before the number of women in Parliament surpassed 10 percent, and another 20 years before that figure surpassed 20 percent. The following hypothesis could be proposed: once there was a convergence of the conditions favorable to mobilization on behalf of women, the absence of majority voting meant there was one less hurdle to overcome, with positive results.

The nature of the elite and the political parties was just as important a factor as the electoral system, in terms of women's political integration. If belonging to the political elite depends upon membership in other elite groups, the efforts a group will make to reach levels of political responsibility are multiplied. In the Scandinavian countries, political offices are held less frequently than elsewhere by members of the traditional elite. The curriculum vitae of the ministers of the various governments reveal that few of them graduated from the most prestigious schools, although their educational level is higher than average. In the Swedish government in 2000, about one-fourth of the ministers have not graduated from university, while others hold university degrees but rarely beyond the master's level. Although Anna Lindh, the young Swedish minister of Foreign Affairs, has a master's degree in law, her predecessor was a secondary school teacher. The Swedish prime minister, Göran Persson, took only a few examinations in social science. Few of the ministers have a past history as high-ranking civil servants. Some of them are political professionals, but others held nonpolitical jobs before devoting themselves to politics. Marianne Jelved, the vice prime minister of Denmark and also the minister of Economy and Scandinavian Cooperation, was a teacher in the Danish in public education system for almost 20 years before she became a deputy and then a minister in 1993.

During the 1980s, at the request of the government, a survey was done in Sweden on the state of democracy. Its results showed that there are two ways to become part of the elite: one path is that of social background, going through prestigious schools and a top-ranking professional career, which is the traditional path to membership in the elite; the other path runs through community and politics (*Demokrati och makt I Sverige* [1990; Democracy in Sweden]).

Although there is often discussion of a "crisis" in party recruitment in the Scandinavian countries, approximately 10 percent of the adult population belonged to a political party at the end of the 20th century. The daily activities of members consist of meetings and continuing education. Since the 1970s the parties have attracted increasing numbers of women members. A survey done in the 1980s indicates that, at that time, there were as many women as men in the political parties of Denmark and Norway, while in Sweden and Finland women represented only about one-third of the membership. The labor unions, which offer one means of access to membership in the elite, bring together a large majority of the working population. Women belong to unions in the same numbers as men: in Sweden in 1994, 87 percent of women and 82 percent of men belonged to a labor union (see Bergqvist et al.).

The democratization and modernization of the Scandinavian countries at the turn of the the 20th century continued with the support of labor movements, Social-Democratic parties, and other popular movements. Labor movements, the global term used in the Nordic countries to refer to workers' groups and, in particular, Social-Democratic parties, have been highly significant in Scandinavian political life. These movements are based on the demand for equality between workers and the privileged sectors of society. Difference and exclusion are thus themes that have been historically present in Scandinavian political culture, and it can be conjectured that these themes facilitated the integration of feminist demands of the 1960s and 1970s, in that feminism too sought to abolish inequalities between different social groups.

In contrast to some other countries, political power in the Scandinavian countries does not seem to entail honors, privileges, or excessive respect. The relatively recent establishment of democracy, the egalitarianism of political culture, and the nature of the elite and the parties all help to explain this phenomenon. The electorate counts on the integrity of the elected, who are not expected to be able to solve every individual problem. The limits of tolerance for perceived ethical lapses are very quickly reached, as attested by some fairly recent scandals concerning often rather minor issues. In the 1990s Mona Sahlin, a minister and Swedish Social-Democratic leader, saw her career destroyed and the office of prime minister slip away from her because she had borrowed the equivalent of a few thousand euros on the ministry credit card and had delayed in repaying the charges. Later, during her tenure as secretary of state, she ran into new problems when she did not pay her parking tickets on time.

Political power in the Scandinavian countries does not encompass much pomp, nor is it the object of special reverence. This austerity makes the elective mandate less attractive and all the more accessible to determined candidates.

Bibliography

Ås, Berit, "On Female Culture," *Acta Sociologica* 18 (1975)

Baude, Annika, editor, *Visionen om jämställdhet*, Stockholm: SNS, 1992

Bergman, Solveig, "Frauen in der finnischen Politk: Auf dem weg zur Hälfte der Macht?" in *Hanbuch Politische Partizipation von*

Frauen in Europa, edited by Beate Hoecker, Komwestheim and Opladen, Germany: Leske and Budrich, 1998

Bergman, Solveig, "Women in New Social Movements," in *Equal Democracies? Gender and Politics in the Nordic Countries*, edited by Christina Bergqvist et al., Oslo: Scandinavian University Press, 1999

Bergqvist, Christina, "The Declining Corporatist State and the Political Gender Dimension in Sweden," in *Closing the Gap: Women in Nordic Politics*, edited by Lauri Karvonen and Per Selle, Aldershot, England, and Brookfield, Vermont: Dartmouth, 1995

Bergqvist, Christina, "Mäns makt och kvinnors intressen," Ph.D.diss, Uppsala University, Stockholm: Almqvist and Wiksell International, 1994

Bergqvist, Christina, et al., editors, *Equal Democracies? Gender and Politics in the Nordic Countries*, Oslo: Scandinavian University Press, 1999

Björnberg, Ulla, "Lone Mothers in Sweden: Supported Workers who Mother," in *Single Mothers in an International Context: Mothers or Workers?*, edited by Rosalind Edwards and Simon Duncan, London: UCL Press, 1997

Bruun, Niklas, "Finsk jämstdlldhetslagstiftning i stöpsleven?" in *Årsbogfor Kvinderet 1982*, edited by Jytte Lindgård and Ruth Nielsen, Copenhagen: Juristforbundets Forlag, 1982

Carlsson Wetterberg, Christina, "Equal or different? That's Not the Question: Women's Political Strategies in Historical Perspective," in *Is There a Nordic Feminism?*, edited by Drude von der Fehr, Anna G. Jónasdóttir, and Bente Rosenbeck, London and Philadelphia: UCL Press, 1998

Christensen, Anne-Dorte, "Women in the Political Parties," in *Equal Democracies? Gender and Politics in the Nordic Countries*, edited by Christina Bergqvist et al., Oslo: Scandinavian University Press, 1999

Christensen, Anne Dorte, Anna-Birte Ravn, and Iris Rittenhofer, editors, *Det kønnede samfund: Forståelser af køn og socialforandring*, Aalborg, Denmark: Aalborg Universitetsforlag, 1997

Dahlerup, Drude, "From a Small to a Large Minority: Women in Scandinavian Politics," *Scandinavian Political Studies* 11, no. 4 (1988)

Dahlerup, Drude, *Rødstrømperne: Den danske Rødstrømpebevoegelsens udvikling, nytoenkning og gennemslag 1970–1985*, 2 vols., Copenhagen: Gyldendal, 1998

Dahlström, Edmund, editor, *Kvinnors liv och arbete; Kvinners liv og arbeid: Svenska och norska studier av ett aktuellt samhällsproblem*, Stockholm: SNS, 1962

Daune-Richard, Anne-Marie, and Rianne Mahon, "La Suède: Le modèle égalitaire en danger?" in *Qui doit garder le jeune enfant? Mode d'accueil et travail des mères dans l'Europe en crise*, edited by Jane Jenson et Mariette Sineau, Paris: LGDJ, 1998.

Demokrati och makt i Sverige, Statens Offentliga Utredningar 1990:44, Stockholm: Allmänna förlaget, 1990

Elgán, Elisabeth, "Advantages and Obstacles: The Swedish Experience," in *Men and Women in European Municipalities*, Paris: Council of European Municipalities and Regions, 1999

Elgán, Elisabeth, "Genus ochpolitik: En jämförelse mellan svensk och fransk abort—och preventivmedelspolitik från sekelskiftet till andra världskriget," Ph.D. diss., Uppsala University, Stockholm: Almqvist and Wiksell International, 1994

Elgán, Elisabeth, "Qu'avaient les Suédoises de plus que les autres pour rafler presque la moitié des postes en politique?" in *Le pouvoir en force: Un colloque sur les femmes et la politique*, Brussels: Ministère de l'Emploi et du Travail et de la Politique de l'Égalité des Chances, Miet Smet, 1998

Engendering Statistics: A Tool for Change, Orebro, Sweden: Statistiska centralbyr'an (SCB), 1999

Florin, Christina, "Skatten som befriar: Hemmafruar mot yrkeskvinnor i 1960–talets sarbeskattningsdebatt," in *Kvinnor mot kvinnor: Om systerskapets svårigheter*, edited by Christina Florin, Lena Sommestad , and Ulla Wikander, Stockholm: Norstedts, 1999

Florin, Christina, and Bengt Nilsson, "Something in the Nature of a Bloodless Revolution: How New Gender Relations Became Gender Equality Policy in Sweden in the Nineteen-sixties and Seventies," in *State Policy and Gender System in the Two German States and Sweden 1945–1989*, edited by Rolf Torstendahl, Uppsala, Sweden: Uppsala University, 1999

Fredriksson, Ingrid, editor, *Könsroller: Debatt om jämställdhet*, Uppsala, Sweden: Studentföreningen Verdandi, and Stockholm: Prisma, 1965

Gonäis, Lena, and Anna Spänt, *Trends and Prospects for Women's Employment in the 1990s*, Solna, Sweden: Arbetslivsinstitutet, 1997

Gustafsson, Gunnel, Maud Eduards, and Malin Rönnblom, *Towards a New Democratic Order: Women's Organizing in Sweden in the 1990s*, Stockholm: Publica, Norstedts juridik, 1997

Haas, Linda, "Nurturing Fathers and Working Mothers: Changing Gender Roles in Sweden," in *Men, Work and Family*, edited by Jane C. Hood, Newbury Park, Calif: Sage, 1993

Haavio-Mannila, Elina, et al., editors, *Det uferdige demokratiet. Kvinner i nordiskpolitikk*, Stockholm: Liber Distribution, 1983

Haenens, Albert d', and Anders Florin, editors, *La Scandinavie*, Brussels : Éditions Artis-Historia, 1997

Hirdman, Yvonne, *Med kluven tunga: Lo och genusordningen*, Stockholm: Atlas, 1998

Holli, Anne Maria, "Why the State? Reflections on the Politics of the Finnish Equality Movement Association," in *Finnish "Undemocracy": Essays on Gender and Politics*, edited by Marja Keränen, Helsinki, Finland: Finnish Political Science Association, 1990

Karam, Azza, editor, *Women in Parliament: Beyond Numbers*, Stockholm: IDEA, 1999

Karlsson, Gunnel, "Från broderskap till systerskap: Det socialdemokratiska kvinnoförbundets kamp för inflytande och makt i SAP," Ph.D. diss., Göteborg University, Lund, Sweden: Arkiv, 1996

Karlsson, Gunnel, "Den känsliga abortfrågan: Konsten att undvika konflikt," in *Kvinnor mot kvinnor*, edited by Christina Florin, Lena Sommestad, and Ulla Wikander, Stockholm: Norstedts, 1999

Karlsson, Gunnel, "Social Democratic Women's Coup in the Swedish Parliament," in *Is there a Nordic Feminism?*, edited by Drude von der Fehr, Anna G. Jónasdóttir and Bente Rosenbeck, London and Philadelphia: UCL Press, 1998

Kärre, Marianne, "En småbamsmammas strävan—en lång historia," in *Visionen om jämställdhet*, edited by Annika Baude, Stockholm: SNS, 1992

Karvonen, Lauri, and Per Selle, editors, *Closing the Gap: Women in Nordic Politics*, Aldershot, England and Brookfield, Vermont: Dartmouth, 1995

Keränen, Marja, editor, *Essays on Gender and Politics*, Jyväskylä: Gummerus, 1990

Keränen, Marja, editor, *Gender and Politics in Finland*, Aldershot, England: Avebury, 1992

Kuusipalo, Jaana, "Finnish Women in Top-Level Politics," in *Finnish "Undemocracy": Essays on Gender and Politics*, edited by Marja Keränen, Helsinki, Finland: Finnish Political Science Association, 1990

Lennerhed, Lena, "Frihet att njuta: Sexualdebatten i Sverige på 1960-talet," Ph.D. diss., Stockholm University, Stockholm: Norstedt, 1994

Lennerhed, Lena, *Välfärdens rebeller: Sveriges liberala studentförbund och kulturradikalismen under 1960-talet*, Stockholm: Stockholm University, Avd. för idéhistoria, 1989

Liljeström, Rita, *Roles in Transition: Report of an Investigation Made for the Advisory Council on Equality between Men and Women*, Stockholm: Advisory Council to the Prime Minister on Equality between Men and Women, 1978

Liljeström, Rita, *Sex Roles in Transition: A Report on a Pilot Program in Sweden: International Women's Year 1975*, Stockholm: Advisory Council to the Prime Minister on Equality between Men and Women, 1975

Lindström, Ulf, "Politik i Norden 1889–1989: Eft socialdemokratiskt Arhundrade?" in *Norden förr och nu: Ett sekel i statistisk belysning*, Stockholm: 18e Nordiska statistikermötet, nordiskt Statistiskt samarbete 1889–1989, 1989

Lööw, Helene, "Tant Brun—män och kvinnor i vit makt världen och i de nationella leden 1930– 1992," *Historisk Tidskrift* 112, no. 4 (1992)

Moberg, Eva, "Kvinnans villkorliga frigivning," in *Unga liberaler: Nio inlägg i idédebatten*, edited by Hans Hederberg, Stockholm: A. Bonniers, 1961

Moberg, Eva, *Kvinnor och människor*, Stockholm: A. Bonniers, 1962

Myrdal, Alva, *Nation and Family: The Swedish Experiment in Democratic Family and Population Policy*, Cambridge, Massachusetts, M.I.T. Press, 1968

Myrdal, Alva, and Viola Klein, *Women's Two Roles: Home and Work*, London: Routledge and Kegan Paul, 1956

Nenno, Magnus, "Occupational Sex Segregation in Sweden 1968– 1991," *Work and Occupations* 23, no. 3 (1996)

Nyberg, Anita, *Women, Men and Incomes: Gender Equality and Economic Independence: A Report to the Committee on the Distribution of Economic Power and Economic Resources between Women and Men, Statens Offentliga Utredningar* 1997:87, Stockholm: Fritzes, 1997

Östberg, Kjell, *Efter rösträtten: Kvinnornas utrymme efter det demokratiska genombrottet*, Stockhom: Stehag, 1997

Persson, Inga, and Christina Jonung, editors, *Women's Work and Wages*, London and New York: Routledge, 1998

Peterson, Abby, "The New Women's Movement: Where Have All the Women Gone? Women and the Peace Movement in Sweden," *Women's Studies International Forum* 8, no. 6 (1985)

Peterson, Abby, "Women in Political 'Movement,'" Ph.D. diss., Göteborg University, 1987

Raaum, Nina C., "Political Citizenship: New Participants, New Values?" and "Women in Parliamentary Politics: Historical Lines of Development," in *Equal Democracies? Gender and Politics in the Nordic Countries*, edited by Christina Bergqvist et al., Oslo: Scandinavian University Press, 1999

Rosen, Sherwin, "Public Employment and the Welfare State in Sweden," *Journal of Economic Literature* 2 (1997)

Rosenbeck, Bente, "Nordic Women's Studies and Gender Research," in *Is There a Nordic Feminism?*, edited by Drude von der Fehr, Anna G. Jónasdóttir and Rosenbeck, London and Philadelphia: UCL Press, 1998

Runcis, Maija, *Sterliseringar i folkhemmet*, Stockholm: Ordfront, 1998

Skjeie, Hega, "Ending the Male Political Hegemony: The Norwegian Experience," in *Gender and Party Politics*, edited by Joni Lovenduski and Pippa Norris, London: Sage Publications, 1993

Steriliseringsfrågan i Sverige 1935–1975: Slutbetänkande av 1997 års steriliseringsutredning, Statens Offentliga Utredningar 2000:20, Stockholm: Fritzes, 2000

Streijffert, Helena, "Studier i den svenska kvinnorörelsen," Ph.D. diss., Göteborg University, 1983

Togeby, Lise, "The Disappearance of a Gender Gap: Tolerence and Liberalism in Denmark from 1971 to 1990," *Scandinavian Political Studies* 17, no. 1 (1994)

Togeby, Lise, "Feminist Attitudes in Times of Depoliticization of Women's Issues," *European Journal of Political Research* 27, no. 1 (1995)

Togeby, Lise, *Fra tilskuere til deltagere: Den kollektive politiske mobilisering af kvinder i Danmark i 1970'erne og 1980'erne*, Aarhus, Denmark: Politica, 1994

Togeby, Lise, "Political Implications of Increasing Numbers of Women in the Labour Force," *Comparative Political Studies* 27, no. 2 (1994)

Tydén, Mattias, *Från politik till praktik: De svenska steriliseringslagarna 1935–1975, Statens Offentliga Utredningar* 2000:20, Stockholm: Fritzes, 2000

Ulmanen, Petra, *Sveket mot kvinnorna och hur högern stal feminismen*, Stockholm: Atlas, 1998

Van der Ros, Janneke, "The Organisation of Equality at the Local Level: The Case of Norway," in *Sex Equality Policy in Western Europe*, edited by Frances Gardiner, London: Routledge, 1997

Wängnerud, Lena, "Ekonomisk politik: Ett manligt maktområde i riksdagen," *Styrsystem oc jämställdhet: Institutioner i förändring och könsmaktens framtid, Statens Offentliga Utredningar* 1997:114, Stockholm: Fritzes, 1997

Wängnerud, Lena, *Kvinnorepresentation: Makt och möjligheter i Sveriges riksdag*, Lund, Sweden: Studentlitteratur, 1999

Wängnerud, Lena, "Representing the Interests of Women," in *Beyond Congress and Westminister: Nordic Experiences*, edited by Peter Esaisson and Knut Heidar, Columbus: Ohio State University Press, 1999

Wikander, Ulla, "Kvinnokultur, skillnader och sociobiologi: Kvinnorörelsen från 1960– till 90– tal ur ett personligt perspektiv," in *Kvinnor mot kvinnor: Om systerskapets svårigheter*, edited by Christina Florin, Lena Sommestad, and Ulla Wikander, Stockholm: Norstedts, 1999

Women and Men in the Nordic Countries: Facts and Figures 1994, Copenhagen: Nordic Council of Ministers, 1994

Women and Men in the Nordic Countries: Facts and Figures 1999, Copenhagen: Nordic Council of Ministers, 1999

WOMEN'S REPRESENTATION IN PARLIAMENTS AND POLITICAL PARTIES IN EUROPE AND NORTH AMERICA

CHRISTINE PINTAT, INTER-PARLIAMENTARY UNION

THE EUROPEAN COUNTRIES THAT will be discussed here are those that, as of October 2002, were members of the Organization for Security and Cooperation in Europe (OSCE). With Canada and the United States, 55 countries are taken into consideration.

Voting and Being Elected

One of the symbols of democratic freedom today is the right to take part in the management of public affairs by freely expressing one's will through the election ballot or by offering one's services as a representative of that public will. Today, almost everywhere in the world, all individuals who have reached voting age and against whom no legal action is pending, whether men or women, may vote or run as candidates in a legislative election. But what seems obvious today has not always been so. In fact, the great majority of the world's population only obtained its right to vote in the course of the 20th century, once certain social and racial prejudices had been overcome. Women had to combat additional prejudices based on sex, which was the reason why, in the 55 countries considered here, they acquired electoral rights long after men did and only after a long and bitter struggle.

Women Pioneers of Electoral Rights

On 20 July 1906, the women of Finland (then still part of the Russian Empire) became the first in Europe to obtain the right to exercise their personal political choice without any restrictions. A few months later, on 16 March 1907, Finnish women were the first in the world to run as parliamentary candidates, and 19 of them were elected.

The suffragettes, such inviting targets of sarcasm even to other women, were in fact pioneers for the rights of all women and had just won the first and most symbolic round in a battle that they probably did not suspect would always remain unfinished, unrewarding, and rough: the battle for women's participation in political life in partnership with men.

In reality the stage had been set for women's suffrage much earlier, almost without women knowing it. In using the word "persons," the United States Constitution of 13 September 1788 had already implicitly recognized women's right to stand for election. However, American women had to wait for 132 years before they learned, on 26 August 1920, that the law recognized their right to place a ballot in the box. This was not the sole case in which women were entitled to run for office before they were granted the right to vote.

Elsewhere in the world, well before Finnish women, New Zealand women of European origin had been granted the right to vote on 19 September 1883, while non-aborigine Australian women became eligible to run as candidates on 12 June 1902. Nevertheless, no women in those countries were elected to that country's Parliament before 21 August 1943, 41 years later and more than 36 years after the first Finnish women had entered Finland's Parliament.

Successive Waves until the 1930s

At the beginning of the 20th century, like the character Nora in Henrik Ibsen's *Dukkenhjem* (1879; *A Doll's House*), the women of northern Europe awoke and began to close ranks to

Table 1 WOMEN IN NATIONAL PARLIAMENTS (as of 12/23/2002)

Rank	Country	Lower or single House				Upper House or Senate			
		Elections	Seats*	Women	% W	Elections	Seats*	Women	% W
1.	Sweden	09 2002	349	157	45.0	—	—	—	—
2.	Denmark	11 2001	179	68	38.0	—	—	—	—
3.	Finland	03 1999	200	73	36.5	—	—	—	—
4.	Norway	09 2001	165	60	36.4	—	—	—	—
5.	Iceland	05 1999	63	22	34.9	—	—	—	—
6.	Netherlands	05 2002	150	51	34.0	05 1999	75	20	26.7
7.	Germany	09 2002	603	194	32.2	N.A.	69	17	24.6
8.	Spain	03 2000	350	99	28.3	03 2000	259	63	24.3
9.	Bulgaria	06 2001	240	63	26.2	—	—	—	—
10.	Turkmenistan	12 1999	50	13	26.0	—	—	—	—
11.	Belgium	06 1999	150	35	23.3	06 1999	71	20	28.2
12.	Switzerland	10 1999	200	46	23.0	10 1999	46	9	19.6
13.	Monaco	02 1998	18	4	22.2	—	—	—	—
14.	Canada	11 2000	301	62	20.6	N.A.	105	34	32.4
15.	Croatia	01 2000	151	31	20.5	04 1997	65	4	6.2
16.	Poland	09 2001	460	93	20.2	09 2001	100	23	23.0
17.	Portugal	03 2002	230	44	19.1	—	—	—	—
18.	United Kingdom	06 2001	659	118	17.9	N.A.	713	117	16.4
19.	Estonia	03 1999	101	18	17.8	—	—	—	—
20.	The F.Y.R. of Macedonia	09 2002	120	21	17.5	—	—	—	—
21.	Slovakia	09 2002	150	26	17.3	—	—	—	—
22.	Czech Republic	06 2002	200	34	17.0	10 2002	81	?	?
23.	Luxembourg	06 1999	60	10	16.7	—	—	—	—
24.	San Marino	06 2001	60	10	16.7	—	—	—	—
25.	Andorra	03 2001	28	4	14.3	—	—	—	—
26.	United States of America	11 2002	435	60	13.8	11 2002	100	13	13
27.	Ireland	05 2002	166	22	13.3	07 2002	60	10	16.7
28.	Slovenia	10 2000	90	11	12.2	—	—	—	—
29.	France	06 2002	577	71	12.3	09 2001	321	35	10.9
30.	Liechtenstein	02 2001	25	3	12.0	—	—	—	—
31.	Romania	11 2000	345	37	10.7	11 2000	140	8	5.7
32.	Lithuania	10 2000	141	15	10.6	—	—	—	—
33.	Kazakhstan	10 1999	77	8	10.4	09 1999	39	5	12.8
34.	Belarus	10 2000	97	10	10.3	12 2000	61	19	31.1
35.	Italy	05 2001	630	62	9.8	05 2001	321	25	7.8
36.	Hungary	04 2002	386	35	9.1	—	—	—	—
37.	Greece	04 2000	300	26	8.7	—	—	—	—
38.	Russian Federation	12 1999	449	34	7.6	N.A.	178	6	3.4
39.	Georgia	10 1999	235	17	7.2	—	—	—	—
40.	Uzbekistan	12 1999	250	18	7.2	—	—	—	—
41.	Yugoslavia	09 2000	138	10	7.2	09 2000	40	1	2.5
42.	Albania	06 2001	140	8	5.7	—	—	—	—
43.	Armenia	05 1999	131	4	3.1	—	—	—	—
44.	Austria	11 2002	183	?	?	N.A.	62	13	21.0
45.	Bosnia and Herzegovina	10 2002	42	?	?	11 2000	15	0	0.0
46.	Turkey	11 2002	550	?	?	—	—	—	—
47.	Ukraine	03 2002	450	?	?	—	—	—	—

* Figures correspond to the number of seats currently filled in Parliament

fight for the right to vote and stand for election. Beginning in June 1913, Norwegian women were able to vote and run for office without any of the restrictions that had been imposed upon them in 1907. The women of Denmark and Iceland followed suit shortly thereafter.

The domino effect then came into play in the countries of northern and central Europe and North America. The years from 1917 to 1921 were landmark years for the women of those nations with respect to the recognition of their electoral rights.

On 29 November 1917, the women of the Netherlands won the right to run for office; they were granted the right to vote on 9 August 1919. One year later, in Georgia, women acquired both rights through a law of 22 November 1918 that was confirmed on 21 February 1921. Between February and October

1921 women of no fewer than 18 other countries obtained the same rights. Successively, the United Kingdom and Ireland, the Russian Federation, Germany, Latvia, Poland, Austria, Belarus, Ukraine, Luxembourg, Sweden, Estonia, the Czech Republic, Slovakia, Armenia, Azerbaijan, and Lithuania wrote these rights into law. The list conveys a sense of the momentum of the ideas that held sway at that time in the region.

Analogously, in North America, Canadian women who were in the armed forces or who had a spouse, father, or brother in the military acquired the right to vote at the federal level in September 1917, before that right was granted to all Canadian women in May 1918. It should be noted that at the time, the term "Canadian women" ignored the existence of Native American women; the right to vote was granted to the Native American population only in 1950 and the right to run for election in 1960–32 and 40 years after the non-native population, respectively.

The feminization of the right to vote did not begin to reach the eastern and southern parts of Europe until approximately the 1930s. On 3 April 1930, Kemal Ataturk's Turkey granted women the right to vote; they became eligible to run for Parliament a few years later, on 5 December 1934. In 1931 it was the turn of Spain and Portugal to grant women the right to vote and run for office. Uzbekistan, then one of the republics of the Soviet Union, followed in 1938. Then the build-up and eventual outbreak of World War II brought to a ten-year halt a movement that must once have seemed ineluctable.

After World War II

The war was in its final stages when French women finally acquired the right to vote and run for office on 21 April 1944. Bulgarian women were granted the same rights on 16 October of the same year. The year 1945 brought voting rights to Italian women (1 February) and to the women of Slovenia and Croatia (11 August). The pattern continued with remarkable regularity from 1946 until 1953, during which period the women of Serbia, Montenegro, Romania, Macedonia, Malta, Bosnia, Greece, and Hungary became voters as well.

A few pockets of resistance remained, among which Switzerland stood out as a symbol in the minds of many. However, between 1959 and 1984, and after much procrastination, the male citizens of Switzerland and San Marino, Cyprus, Monaco, Andorra, and Liechtenstein finally conceded that women did have a political soul.

These gains were not made without some rather strange beginnings. In Andorra, a decree of 5 November 1973 gave formal status to the general understanding that the statement "All Andorran citizens are eligible . . .," which figured in the electoral decree of 23 August 1947, in no way included women. There are thus words within words, and despite the rules of French grammar, we must concede the validity of the argument of those scrupulous feminists who demand that collective nouns that are grammatically masculine be abandoned in favor of formulations that, although more cumbersome, are explicitly inclusive with respect to sexual identity.

Conditions and Restrictions

The conditions and restrictions imposed on women before they were granted the full and complete rights to vote and run for election were far from insignificant. A closer look at those conditions and restrictions is sufficient to dispel any doubt that access to suffrage was linked historically to an elitist vision of society. Such restrictions exemplify not only a commonplace masculine resistance to the notion of sexual equality, but also forms of social and racial resistance, just as tenacious and difficult to overcome, to which some categories of men may also have been subjected.

Thus, in Norway, between 1907 and 1913, in order to become members of Parliament, women (but not men) had to have resources or personal property, good social standing, and a respectable income. In Belgium, the right to vote in legislative elections was granted on 9 May 1919, but only to widows and mothers of soldiers who had died in the war and to women political prisoners. Other women had to wait another 30 years; in fact, it was not until 27 March 1948 that all Belgian women were entitled to enjoy their full electoral rights. In Canada, too, from May 1917 on, only women who were members of the armed forces or whose father, husband, or son was in the armed forces could exercise their electoral rights, while other women would not be able to do so until several months later. There were also racial requirements of the kind already mentioned. For a man to vote in 1931 in Portugal, it was sufficient that he know to read and write, while a woman had to have completed a secondary education. In the United Kingdom and Ireland, electoral maturity was not set at the same age for men and for women, and women over the age of 30 were the first to be granted the right to vote; the voting age for women was lowered to that of men a decade later. Fortunately, such discrimination belongs to a bygone age, and all women in European countries as well as in Canada and the United States can now exercise their legal rights without hindrance. Now only their own negligence can stand in the way of them fulfilling their electoral responsibilities.

From Political Conscience to the Electoral Act

Europe and North America

For Europeans and North Americans of European origin, the beginning of an awareness that women had a part to play in politics coincided with the Age of Enlightenment. The French Revolution and the American Revolution seemed to open a new era for women, but it did not take them long to notice (as did the women engaged in the process of decolonialization in the 20th century, from the 1960s to the 1980s) that the word equality ran afoul of centuries of sexist attitudes and that the gains they made were largely illusory. Although women were a decisive force at the time of the French Revolution, they were shortchanged when the time came to share political and revolutionary responsibilities. And it was in the face of strong resistance that true feminist movements, battling for women's suffrage all the way into the streets, were born at the turn of the 20th century.

In terms of the time frame, for European and North American women the process of obtaining the rights to vote and run for office stretched from 1788 until 1984, or nearly 200 years. The process in the United States, taken separately, took some 80 years. Comparing these figures with the rest of the world, it is apparent that the native populations of many countries did not acquire electoral rights until they had rid themselves of the colonial yoke. Although the question may seem gratuitous, one may wonder whether women would have had access to political rights sooner if the colonies had never existed. The generally accepted opinion is nevertheless that European and North American women in some way opened the breach for their sisters in other countries. Since political customs were deeply rooted in their own societies, European and North American women met with enormous resistance, as do eldest children confronted with conservative parents, and these women fought long and hard. In all other regions of the world, with the exception of Latin America, the battle for women's access to electoral rights was generally fought later on and was sometimes won a good deal faster.

Latin America, Africa, Asia, and the Pacific

In Latin America and the Caribbean, the women of Santa Lucia (1924) and Ecuador (1929)—13 and 18 years, respectively after Finnish women—led the way in obtaining the right to vote. The women of Chile followed in 1931; the women of Uruguay one year later, in 1932; Cuban and Brazilian women in 1934; Bolivian women in 1938; Salvadoran women in 1939; Panamanian women in 1941; the women of Dominican Republic in 1942; Jamaican women in 1944; and the women of Guyana in 1945. Women in these last two countries won their voting rights at the same time as their counterparts in France and Italy. Then, from 1946 on, the process gathered momentum until 1961, the year in which Paraguay and the Bahamas finally granted women their electoral rights—10 years before Switzerland. In the meantime, some of the above-mentioned countries removed the conditions or restrictions they had imposed earlier, and the remaining countries amended their legislation to guarantee full electoral rights for women: Venezuela, Guatemala, and Trinidad and Tobago in 1946; Mexico and Argentina in 1947; Suriname in 1948; Costa Rica in 1949; Barbados and Haiti in 1950; Antigua and Barbuda, Dominica, Grenada, Saint Kitts and Nevis, Saint Vincent and the Grenadines in 1951; Belize and Colombia in 1954; and Honduras, Nicaragua, and Peru in 1955. In Europe, by contrast, Liechtenstein delayed another 29 years before granting women their electoral rights in 1984.

In sub-Saharan Africa, apparently to serve the interests of colonial power, the recognition of women's voting rights occurred at almost the same time as in the respective colonizing countries, or else it went hand in hand with the decolonization process and became one of its manifestations. The history of African women's electoral rights began in 1945 in Senegal, followed by Cameroon and Djibouti in 1946, and finally Niger and the Seychelles in 1948. The other 40 or so nations of the African Continent followed suit between 1952 and 1989 (the year in which Namibia gained sovereignty). The Republic of South Africa stands apart among the African nations, since three dates, symbolic of the country's social and racial evolution, marked the access of women to electoral rights: 21 May 1930 for white women, 30 March 1984 for Indian women and those of mixed race, and 14 January 1994 for blacks, both women and men.

In Asia, the women of Mongolia were the first to win suffrage, on 31 January 1924. Then there was a wait until 1931 before the women of Ceylon (since renamed Sri Lanka) became entitled to use the ballot box, followed in 1932 by the women of Thailand and the Maldives, and in 1935 by the women of Burma (since renamed Myanmar). One by one, over the course of the ensuing 30 years, the following nations granted women their electoral rights: India (1950), Pakistan (1947), Bangladesh (1972), Indonesia (1945), Japan (1945), the two Koreas of today (1948), Vietnam (1946), China (1949), Nepal (1951), Bhutan (1953), Cambodia (1955), Malaysia (1957), Laos (1958), and imperial Iran (1963). In 1965 (six years before Switzerland in 1971) Afghanistan gave women their electoral rights, thereby completing a movement that had begun 50 years earlier in that region of the world.

In the Pacific, apart from the two world pioneers mentioned above—New Zealand (19 September 1883) and Australia (12 June 1902)—it was not until the end of World War II and the acquisition of independence that the other states generally entered the picture, beginning in the 1950s to grant women the right to vote and stand for election.

In the Arab world, the women of Lebanon were the first to acquire full electoral rights in 1952. Syria granted women the right to vote in 1949, but waited until 1953 before giving them the right to run for office. In Egypt both rights became law in 1956, followed by Tunisia in 1959 and by Algeria in 1962, at the time of independence. Morocco followed suit, giving women the rights both to vote and to run for office in 1963, followed by Libya in 1964, South Yemen in 1967, North Yemen in 1970, Jordan in 1974, and Iraq in 1980.

However, as mentioned earlier, some Middle Eastern states held back. Even today, Kuwait and the United Arab Emirates continue to deny women the right to participate in politics, whether directly or through the representatives of their choice.

Rules, Procedures, and Practice

A world survey done in 1991 by the Inter-Parliamentary Union showed that modern-day procedures for voter registration are strictly the same for women and for men in all European and North American countries, and that rules about the vote being either mandatory or optional are applied to both sexes identically. This survey also showed that in those countries where voting by proxy is allowed, the law has provided for guarantees that, in principle, make any manipulation of the women's vote by men impossible.

However interesting it may be to know when women began to exercise their right to vote and the conditions under which they did so, it would be more interesting still to examine women's electoral behaviors and practices. Unfortunately, data on those issues, where it exists at all, is insufficient for in-depth comparative analysis.

Women in Parliaments

If gaining access to suffrage was a long and checkered process for women, their entry into the parliamentary chamber has hardly been any easier. Further, even when they have entered Parliament, it has not been easy for them to leave the ghetto of social committees and take on the full range of legislative and parliamentary work, thus ensuring that the positions of responsibility are not reserved for men. Indeed, who would dare claim that this has been achieved today?

An Unrealized Ideal

What is striking is the immense discrepancy in time one notices in most of the European and North American countries between four dates: the one when the parliamentary institution was established; the one when women were granted the rights to vote and run for office; the one when they entered Parliament as members and no longer as secretaries or assistants; and, finally, the date when—in some countries—a woman rose to the level of the presidency of the assembly.

The oldest Parliaments in the world are found in Europe and North America. Some form of institutional representation has existed in Iceland since the tenth century, in Hungary since the 12th century, and in the United Kingdom since the 13th century, while Poland has had a Parliament in the modern sense of that term since January 1593. In most of other countries, elected Parliaments were established from the end of the 18th century on. In France and the United States, for example, this occurred in 1789, in Spain in 1810, in Portugal in 1821, in Greece in 1844, in Belgium, Italy, and Switzerland in 1848, in Austria in 1867, in Germany in 1871, in Bulgaria in 1879, in Norway in 1884, in Finland in 1907, in Denmark in 1915, and in Ireland and Luxembourg in 1918.

But these were Parliaments in which not one woman's face was visible; they were as monotonously masculine as the canvases of Yves Klein are uniformly blue. The time period that separates the date of creating a Parliament from that of recognizing women's right to vote and run for election is to be counted in centuries or decades rather than in years. Frequently the same thing may be said about the time elapsed between granting women the right to run for office and their entry into Parliament as representatives elected by the people. Let us cite a few particularly striking examples. If the archives truly reflect reality, it took 486 years for a Swedish woman to be elected to a Parliament (in the modern sense of the word), the founding of which historians date back 1435, in a nation that is known today as the most egalitarian in the world. It took 156 years for a woman in France to be elected to a Parliament that had been established in 1789 under the revolutionary cry of "Liberty, Equality, Fraternity." In Switzerland, 123 years elapsed between the creation of a Parliament and the election of a woman. In Spain it took 121 years, in Portugal 113 years, in Greece 108 years, in Italy 98 years, in the United States 76 years, in Bulgaria 66 years, in Germany 48 years, and in Norway 37 years. On the other hand, the Parliaments of Austria, Denmark, Finland, and Luxembourg did not wait long before they heard the sound of women's voices in their midst, albeit few and far between.

1995–2002 in North America and Europe

Only seven nations in 2002 (five in 1995), all of them in northern Europe, had passed the 30 percent mark of women parliamentarians. Not a single country had yet attained parity of representation, although Sweden was approaching it, with 45 percent (up from 40 percent in 1995). Overall, parity no longer seems to be a distant dream in northern Europe: average female representation in these nations had reached 39.7 in October 2002, a significant rise from 12.5 percent in 1995.

Elsewhere, by October 2002 the proportion of women in Parliament had reached 20 to 30 percent in 10 countries (as compared to 4 countries in 1995); 15 to 20 percent in 9 countries (5 countries in 1995); 10 to 15 percent in 15 countries (11 countries in 1995); 6 to 10 percent in 8 countries (13 countries in 1995); and no countries under 6 percent (1.5–5 percent in 11 countries in 1995). For 4 additional nations, data are not available.

In this list of OSCE countries, some nations of longstanding democratic traditions occupy a surprisingly low position in rankings according to percentage of female representation. Among these are France, in 33rd place in 2002 (32nd in 1995); the United Kingdom, in 20th place in 2002 (28th in 1995), and the United States of America, in 28th place in October 2002 (25th place in 1995).

A quick comparison with the rest of the world shows that within a panel of 123 countries with statistics (and 26 countries without), the world record for women in Parliament is held by four northern European nations: Sweden with 45 percent female parliamentarians in 2002 (40.4 percent 1995), followed by Denmark with 38 percent (33.5 percent 1995), Finland with 36.5 percent (33.5 percent in 1995), and Norway with 36.4 percent (39.4 percent in 1995). Next in the rankings come Costa Rica with 35.1 percent in 2002 (up from only 14 percent in 1995) and Iceland with 34.9 percent in 2002 (25.4 percent in 1995). In the Netherlands 34 percent of the members of the Lower House of the States General were women in 2002 (31.3 percent in 1995), followed by Germany with 32.2 percent in 2002 (26.3 percent in 1995), Argentina with 30.7 percent in 2002 (21.8 percent in 1995), Mozambique with 30 percent in 2002 (25.2 percent in 1995), South Africa with 29.8 in 2002 percent (25 percent in 1995), New Zealand with 29.2 percent in 2002 (21.2 percent in 1995), Spain with 28.3 percent in 2002 (16 percent in 1995), Cuba with 27.6 percent in 2002 (22.8 percent in 1995), Vietnam with 27.3 percent in 2002 (18.5 percent in 1995), Austria with 26.8 percent in 2002 (23.5 percent in 1995), Grenada with 26.7 percent in 2002 (20 percent in 1995), Bulgaria with 26.2 percent (13.3 percent in 1995), East Timor with 26.1 percent in 2002, Turkmenistan with 26 percent in 2002 (18 percent in 1995), Rwanda with 25.7 percent in 2002 (17.1 percent in 1995), Australia with 25.3 percent in 2002 (9.5 percent in 1995), Namibia with 25 percent in 2002 (18.1 percent in 1995), and Uganda with 24.7 percent in 2002 (17.4 percent in 1995). Next in the rankings comes the Seychelles, with 23.5 percent female parliamentarians in 2002. (In 1995, with 27.3 percent female parliamentarians, this country occupied seventh place in the world for female representation in Parliament. Indeed, until the general elections of July 1993, the Seychelles had

HISTORICAL TABLE   The sovereign States covered in the table are defined in terms of their names and borders in August 1999

Country	Sovereignty after 1940	Women Presidents	Women Prime Ministers	Recognition of women's right to vote	Recognition of women's right to be elected	First legislature of the present sovereign state[2]	First woman elected (E) or nominated (N) to Parliament	Woman as presiding officer of parliament or one of its chambers
1. *Afghanistan*[1]	—	—	—	1965	1965	07.1965	07.1965 (E)	—
2. Albania	—	—	—	21.01.1920	21.01.1920	21.01.1920	12.1945 (E)	—
3. Algeria	05.07.1962	—	—	05.07.1962	05.07.1962	09.1962	09.1962 (N); 09.1964 (E)	—
4. Andorra	04.05.1993	—	—	14.04.1970	05.09.1973	12.1993	12.1993 (E)	—
5. Angola	11.11.1975	—	—	11.11.1975	11.11.1975	11.1980	11.1980 (E)	—
6. Antigua and Barbuda	01.11.1981	—	—	01.12.1951	01.12.1951	04.1984	04.1984 (N); 03.1994 (E)	1994–99 – M. Percival (Senate); 1994–99 – B. Harris (House of Representatives)
7. Argentina	—	07.1974–03.1976 Maria Estela Martínez de Perón	—	27.09.1947[3]*	27.09.1947*	01.05.1853	11.1951 (E)	12.10.1973–01.07.1974 – M.E. Martínez de Perón (Senate, *pro tempore*)
8. Armenia	21.09.1991	—	—	02.02.1921	02.02.1921	20.05.1990	05.1990 (E)	—
9. Australia	—	—	—	12.06.1902; 18.06.1962*	12.06.1902; 18.06.1962*	30.03.1901	21.08.1943 (E)	1987–90 – J. Child (House of Representatives); 1996–2002 – M. E. Reid (Senate)
10. Austria	—	—	—	19.12.1918	19.12.1918	1867	04.03.1919 (E)	1927–1928 & 1932 O. Rudel-Zeynek (Bundesrat); 1953 – J. Bayer (Bundesrat) 01.1965–30.06.1965, 01.07.1969–31.12.1969 & 01.01.1974–30.06.1974 – H. Tschitschko (Bundesrat); 01.07.1987–31.12.1987 H. Hiedensommer (Bundesrat); 01.01.1991–30.06.1991 – A.E. Haselbach (Bundesrat)
11. Azerbaijan	01.1992	—	—	19.05.1921	19.05.1921	09.1990	09.1990 (E)	—
12. Bahamas	10.07.1973	—	—	18.02.1961; 1964*	18.02.1961; 1964*	07.1973	07.1977 (N); 06.1982 (E)	1997–2002 – Rome Italia Johnson (House of Assembly)
13. *Bahrain*	15.08.1971	—	—	06.12.1973 ?	06.12.1973 ?	12.1973	No	—
14. Bangladesh	12.1971	—	03.1991–03.1996 Khaleda Zia 06.1996 – currently (08.1999) Sheikh Hasina Wajed	04.11.1972	04.11.1972	03.1973	03.1973 (E)	—
15. Barbados	30.11.1966	—	—	23.10.1950	23.10.1950	03.11.1966	03.11.1966 (N); 09.1971 (E)	—
16. Belarus	25.08.1991	—	—	04.02.1919	04.02.1919	03.1990	03.1990 (E)	—
17. Belgium	—	—	—	09.05.1919	07.02.1921	13.06.1848	27.12.1921 (N)	—
18. Belize	21.09.1981	—	—	27.03.1948*	27.03.1948*	12.1984	12.1984 (E + N)	1984–89 – D. June Garcia (Senate); 1989–93 – J. Usher (Senate); 1999 – Sylvia Flores (House of Representatives)
19. Benin	01.08.1960	—	—	1956	1956	12.1960	11.1979 (E)	—
20. Bhutan	—	—	—	1953	1953	1953	1975 (E)	1999 – Elisabeth Zabaneh (Senate)

21. Bolivia	—	11.1979–07.1980 Lydia Gueiler Tejada	—	1938 21.07.1952*	1938 21.07.1952*	10.07.1825	07.1966 (E)	1979 – L. Gueiler Tejada (Chamber of Deputies)
22. Bosnia and Herzegovina	03.1992	—	—	31.01.1949	31.01.1949	11–12.1990	12.1990 (E)	—
23. Botswana	30.09.1966	—	—	01.03.1965	01.03.1965	03.1965	10.1979 (E)	—
24. Brazil	—	—	—	16.07.1934	16.07.1934	1926	03.05.1933 (E)	—
25. *Brunei Darussalam*	01.01.1984	—	—	—	—	—	—	—
26. Bulgaria	—	—	10.1994–01.1995 Reneta Indzhova	16.10.1944	16.10.1944	17.04.1879	18.11.1945 (E)	—
27. Burkina Faso	05.08.1960	—	—	28.09.1958	28.09.1958	12.1970	04.1978 (E)	—
28. Burundi	01.07.1962	—	06.1993–02.1994 Sylvie Kinigi	17.08.1961	17.08.1961	18.09.1961	10.1982 (E)	—
29. Cambodia	09.11.1953	—	—	25.09.1955	25.09.1955	09.1955	03.1958 (E)	—
30. Cameroon	01.10.1961	—	—	10.1946	10.1946	04.1960	04.1960 (E)	—
31. Canada	—	—	06.1993–11.1993 Kim Campbel	09.1917 05.1918 1950*	07.1920 08.1960*	1867	12.1921 (E) (Commons) 02.1930 (N) (Senate)	1972–74 – M. Fergusson (Senate) 1974–1979 – R. Lapointe (Senate) 1980–1984 – J. Sauvé (House of Commons)
32. Cape Verde	05.07.1975	—	—	05.07.1975	05.07.1975	07.1975	07.1975 (E)	—
33. Central African Republic	13.08.1960	—	01.1975–04.1976 Elisabeth Domitien	1986	1986	08.1960	07.1987 (E)	—
34. Chad	11.08.1960	—	—	1958	1958	03.1962	03.1962 (E)	—
35. Chile	—	—	—	30.05.1931 15.05.1949*	30.05.1931 15.05.1949*	04.07.1811	24.04.1951 (E)	—
36. China	—	10.1968–02.1972 Song Qingling	—	01.10.1949	01.10.1949	09.1954	04.1954 (E)	—
37. Colombia	—	—	—	25.08.1954	25.08.1954	1832	25.04.1954 (N) 16.03.1958 (E)	—
38. *Comoros*	12.1975	—	—	1956	1956	12.1978	12.1993 (E)	—
39. Congo	15.08.1960	—	—	08.12.1963	08.12.1963	06.1959	12.1963 (E)	—
40. Costa Rica	—	—	—	17.11.1949	17.11.1949	16.05.1823	11.1953 (E)	1986 R.M. Karpinsky Dodero (Legislative Assembly)
41. Côte d'Ivoire	07.08.1960	—	—	1952	1952	11.1960	07.11.1965 (E)	—
42. Croatia	08.10.1991	—	—	11.08.1945	11.08.1945	08.1992	02.08.1992 (E)	1993–97 1997–2001 K. Ivanisevic (Zupanijski Dom)
43. Cuba	—	—	—	02.01.1934	02.01.1934	20.05.1902	14.07.1940 (E)	—
44. Cyprus	16.08.1960	—	—	16.08.1960	16.08.1960	07.1960	10.1963 (E)	—
45. Czech Republic	01.01.1993	—	—	1920	1920	06.1992	06.1992 (E)	12.1998–99 Libuse Benesova (Senate)
46. Dem. People's Rep. of Korea	09.09.1948	—	—	30.07.1946	30.07.1946	08.1948	08.1948 (E)	—
47. *Dem. Republic of Congo*	30.06.1960	—	—	03.05.1967	17.04.1970	06.1960	11.1970 (E)	—
48. Denmark	—	—	—	05.06.1915	05.06.1915	05.06.1849	1918 (E)	03.1950 – I. Hansen (Landsting)
49. Djibouti	27.06.1977	—	—	1946	198[??008]	05.1977	No	—
50. Dominica	03.11.1978	—	06.1980–06.1995 Mary Eugenia Charles	07.1951	07.1951	07.1980	07.1980 (E)	1980–88 – M. Davis-Pierre (House of Assembly) 1993–95 – N. Edwards (House of Assembly)
51. Dominican Republic	—	—	—	1942	1942	06.11.1844	1942 (E)	—
52. Ecuador	—	—	—	26.03.1929 1967*	26.03.1929 1967*	28.08.1830	1956 (E)	—
53. Egypt	—	—	—	23.06.1956	23.06.1956	01.1950	03.07.1957 (E)	—

(*continued*)

HISTORICAL TABLE Continued

Country	Sovereignty after 1940	Women Presidents	Women Prime Ministers	Recognition of women's right to vote	Recognition of women's right to be elected	First legislature of the present sovereign state[2]	First woman elected (E) or nominated (N) to Parliament	Woman as presiding officer of parliament or one of its chambers
54. El Salvador	—	—	—	1939	1961	09.1840	29.12.1961 (E)	1994–97 – G. Salguero Gross (Legislative Assembly)
55. Equatorial Guinea	12.10.1968	—	—	15.12.1963	15.12.1963	09.1968	09.1968 (E)	—
56. Eritrea	24.05.1993	—	—	04.11.1955	04.11.1955	02.1994	02.1994 (E)	—
57. Estonia	20.08.1991	—	—	24.11.1918	24.11.1918	29.11.1920 05.03.1990	07.04.1919 (E) 03.1990 (E)	—
58. Ethiopia	06.04.1941	—	—	04.11.1955	04.11.1955	02.11.1932	10.1957 (E)	1995–2000 – Almaz Meko (House of the Federation)
59. Fiji	10.10.1970	—	—	17.04.1963	04.05.1963	11.1970 (Senate) 05.1972 (House Rep.)	11.1970 (N) (Senate) 05.1972 (E) (House Rep.)	—
60. Finland	—	—	—	20.07.1906	20.07.1906	16.03.1907	16.03.1907 (E)	1991–95 and 1995–99 – R. Uosukainen (Parliament)
61. France	—	—	05.1991–04.1992 Edith Cresson	21.04.1944	21.04.1944	17.06.1789	10.1945 (E)	—
62. Gabon	17.08.1960	—	—	23.05.1956	23.05.1956	02.1961	12.02.61 (E)	—
63. Gambia	18.02.1965	—	—	1960	1960	05.1966	05.1982 ?(E)	—
64. Georgia	04.1991	—	—	22.11.1918* 21.02.1921*	22.11.1918* 21.02.1921*	10–11.1990	10.1992 (E)	—
65. Germany[4]	—	GDR – 05.04–02.10 1990 Sabine Bergmann-Pohl	—	12.11.1918	12.11.1918	03.03.1871	01.1919 (E)	1972–76 – A. Renger (FRG-Bundestag) 1988–94 and 94–98 – R. Süssmuth (Bundestag)
66. Ghana	06.03.1957	—	—	1954	1954	17.07.1956	08.1960 ?(N) 09.1969 (E)	—
67. Greece	—	—	—	01.01.1952	01.01.1952	1844	11.1952 (E)	—
68. Grenada	07.02.1974	—	—	08.1951	08.1951	02.1972	12.1976 (E+N)	1990–96 – M. Neckles (Senate)
69. Guatemala	—	—	—	1946	1946	?	01.03.1956 (E)	01.1991–01.1992 – A.C. Soberanis Reyes (Congress); 01.1994–01.95 – A. Castro de Camparini (Congress)
70. Guinea	02.10.1958	—	—	02.10.1958	02.10.1958	09.1963	09.1963 (E)	—
71. Guinea-Bissau	24.09.1974	—	—	1977	1977	14.10.1972	14.10.1972 (N) 31.03.1984 (E)	—
72. Guyana	26.05.1966	12.1997–12.2002 Janet Jagan	03.1997–12.1997 Janet Jagan	1953	1945	07.12.1964	12.1968 (E)	—
73. Haiti	—	03.1990–02.1991 Ertha Pascal Trouillot	11.1995–02.1996 Claudette Werleigh	25.11.1950	25.11.1950	22.04.1817	12.05.1961 (E)	—
74. Honduras	—	—	—	25.01.1955	25.01.1955	29.08.1824	1957	—
75. Hungary	—	—	—	17.05.1953	16.11.1958	12th cent. 1848	1945 (E)	—

76. Iceland	—	08.1980–08.1996 Vigdis Finnbogadottir	—	19.06.1915	19.06.1915	930–1845	08.07.1922 (E)	1974–1978 – R. Helgadottir (Lower House) 1983–1987 – S. Thorkelsdottir (Upper House) 1988–1991 – G. Helgadottir (Althingi Uni) 1991–1995 – S. Thorkelsdottir (Althingi)
77. India	15.08.1947	—	03.1966–03.1977, 01.1980–10.1984 Indira Gandhi	26.01.1950	26.01.1950	02.1952	04.1952 (E)	—
78. Indonesia	17.08.1945	—	—	17.08.1945	17.08.1945	02.1950	02.1950 (N) 07.1971 (E)	
79. Iran (Islamic Republic of)	—	—	—	06.10.1963	06.10.1963	07.10.1906	09.1963 (E+N)	—
80. Iraq	—	—	—	01.04.1980	01.04.1980	03.1920	06.1980 (E)	
81. Ireland	—	12.1990–11.1997 Mary Robinson 11.1997–11.2004 Mary McAleese	—	06.02.1918 02.07.1928*	06.02.1918 02.07.1928*	06.12.1922	14.12.1918 (E)	05.1982–02.1983 and 1987–1989 – Tras Honan (Senate)
82. Israel	15.05.1948	—	03.1969–04.1974 Golda Meir	15.05.1948	15.05.1948	25.01.1949	01.1949 (E)	—
83. Italy	—	—	—	01.02.1945	01.02.1945	1848	06.1946 (E)	1979–92 – N. Iotti (Chamber of Deputies) 1994–98 – I. Pivetti (Chamber of Deputies)
84. Jamaica	06.08.1962	—	—	20.11.1944	20.11.1944	02.1967	14.12.1944 (E)	1995–1997, 1997–2002 Violet Neilson (House of Representatives) 1997–2002 S. Marshall-Burnett (Senate)
85. Japan	—	—	—	17.12.1945 24.02.1947*	17.12.1945 24.02.1947*	01.07.1890	04.1946 (E) (Representativ es) 04.1947 (E) (Council)	1993–96 – T. Doi (House of Representatives)
86. Jordan	22.03.1946	—	—	1974	1974	1946	11.1989 (N) (Senate) 11.1993 (E) (Ch. Deputies)	—
87. Kazakhstan	16.12.1991	—	—	31.01.1924 28.01.1993*	31.01.1924 28.01.1993*	03.1990	03.1990 (E)	—
88. Kenya	12.12.1963	—	—	12.12.1963	12.12.1963	05.1963	12.1969 (E+N)	—
89. Kiribati	12.07.1979	—	—	15.11.1967	15.11.1967	02.02.1978	25.07.1990 (E)	—
90. Kuwait	19.06.1961	—	—	Right not recognized	Right not recognized	01.1962	No	—
91. Kyrghyzstan	09.1991	—	—	06.1918	06.1918	02.1990	02.1990 (E)	—
92. Lao People's Dem. Rep.	10.1953	—	—	1958	1958	25.12.1955	04.05.1958 (E)	—
93. Latvia	21.08.1991	06.1999–2002 Vaira Vike-Freiberga	—	18.11.1918	18.11.1918	03–04.1990	?	1995–1996 – Ilga Kreituse (Saeima)
94. Lebanon	22.11.1943	—	—	1952	1952	04.1947	06.1991 (N) 10.1992 (E)	—
95. Lesotho	04.10.1966	—	—	30.04.1965	30.04.1965	04.1965	04.1965 (N) 03.1993 (E)	—
96. Liberia	—	11.1996–08.1997 Ruth Perry	—	07.05.1946	07.05.1946	1889	1964 (E ?)	—

(continued)

Country	Sovereignty after 1940	Women Presidents	Women Prime Ministers	Recognition of women's right to vote	Recognition of women's right to be elected	First legislature of the present sovereign state [2]	First woman elected (E) or nominated (N) to Parliament	Woman as presiding officer of parliament or one of its chambers
97. Libyan Arab Jamahiriya	24.12.1951	—	—	1964	1964	02.1952	?	—
98. Liechtenstein	—	—	—	01.07.1984	01.07.1984	24.11.1862	02.1986 (E)	—
99. Lithuania	06.09.1991	—	03.1990–01.1991 Kazimiera Prunskiene	05.10.1921	05.10.1921	15.05.1920	15.05.1920 (N)	—
100. Luxembourg	—	—	—	15.05.1919	15.05.1919	28.07.1918	04.1919 (E)	1989–1994 and 1994–1995 – E. Hennicot-Schoepges (Chamber of Deputies)
101. Madagascar	26.06.1960	—	—	29.04.1959	29.04.1959	06.1960	08.1965 (E)	—
102. Malawi	06.07.1964	—	—	1961	1961	04.1964	04.1964 (E)	—
103. Malaysia	31.08.1957	—	—	31.08.1957	31.08.1957	08.1959	08.1959 (E) (Ch. Deputies) 05.1965 (N) (Senate)	—
104. Maldives	26.07.1965	—	—	1932	1932	11.1979	11.1979 (E)	—
105. Mali	20.06.1960	—	—	1956	1956	02.1964	02.1964 (E)	—
106. Malta	21.09.1964	02.1982–02.1997 Agatha Barbara	—	05.09.1947	05.09.1947	03.1966	28.03.1966 (E)	1996–1998 – Miriam Spiteri Debono (House of Representatives)
107. Marshall Islands	09.1991	—	—	01.05.1979	01.05.1979	11.1991	11.1991 (E)	—
108. Mauritania	28.11.1960	—	—	20.05.1961	20.05.1961	1965	10.1975 (E)	—
109. Mauritius	12.03.1968	—	—	1956	1956	12.1976	12.1976 (E)	—
110. Mexico	—	—	—	15.02.1947	17.10.1953	31.01.1824	09.1952 (N) 07.1955 (E)	1994–97 – M. Moreno Uriegas (Chamber of Deputies) 1997–2000 – Maria de los Angeles Moreno (Senate)
111. Micronesia (Fed. States of)	09.1991	—	—	03.11.1979	03.11.1979	03.1993	No	—
112. Monaco	—	—	—	17.12.1962	17.12.1962	02.1963	02.1963 (E)	—
113. Mongolia	01.1946	09.1953–07.1954 Suhbaataryn Yanjmaa	—	01.11.1924	01.11.1924	06.1951	06.1951 (E)	—
114. Morocco	02.03.1956	—	—	05.1963	05.1963	05.1963	06.1993 (E)	—
115. Mozambique	04.12.1977	—	—	25.06.1975	25.06.1975	12.1977	12.1977 (E)	—
116. *Myanmar*	—	—	—	1935	19.03.1946	04.1947	04.1947 (E)	—
117. Namibia	21.03.1990	—	—	07.11.1989	07.11.1989	11.1989	11.1989 (E)	—
118. Nauru	31.01.1968	—	—	03.01.1968	03.01.1968	31.01.1968	12.1986 (E)	—
119. Nepal	—	—	—	1951	1951	02.1959	1952 (N) 21.10.1959 (E + N)	—
120. Netherlands	—	—	—	09.08.1919	29.11.1917	1796 or 1813	07.1918 (E)	1998–2002 Jentje van Nieuwenhoven (Second-Chamber of the States-General)
121. New Zealand	—	—	12.1997 – currently (08.1999) Jenny Shipley	19.09.1893	29.10.1919	1852	13.09.1933 (E)	—
122. Nicaragua	—	04.1990–12.1996 Violeta Barrios de Chamorro	—	21.04.1955	21.04.1955	08.04.1826	02.1972 (E)	1990–1992 – M. Argüello Morales (National Assembly)
123. *Niger*	03.08.1960	—	—	1948	1948	1958	10.12.1989 (E)	—

(continued)

Country							
124. Nigeria	01.10.1960	—	1958	1958	03.1965	?	—
125. Norway	—	02–10.1981, 05.1986–10.1989, 11.1990–10.1996 Gro Harlem Brundtland	1913*	1907–1913*	1884	1911 (N)	1993–97 & 1997–2001 – K. Kolle Grondahl (Stortinget)
126. *Oman*	01.1972	—	—	—	—	—	—
127. Pakistan	—	12.1988–08.1990, 10.1993–11.1996 Benazir Bhutto	08.1947	08.1947	1973[5]	1973 (E)	—
128. Palau	01.10.1994	—	02.04.1979	02.04.1979	No	No	—
129. Panama	—	09.1999–2004 Mireya Moscoso	05.07.1941; 01.03.1946*; 15.02.1964	05.07.1941; 01.03.1946*; 27.02.1963	11.1992; 1904	1946 (E)	1994–1996 – B. Herrera Arauz (Legislative Assembly)
130. Papua New Guinea	16.09.1975	—	07.1977	07.1977	07.1977	07.1977 (E)	—
131. Paraguay	—	—	05.07.1961	05.07.1961	1811; 20.09.1822	01.04.1963 (E)	—
132. Peru	—	—	07.09.1955	07.09.1955	23.04.1946	28.07.1956 (E)	1995–1996 – Marta Chavez Cossio de Ocampo (Congress)
133. Philippines	04.07.1946	02.1986–06.1992 Corazon Aquino	30.04.1937	30.04.1937	01.1593	11.1941 (E)	—
134. Poland	—	07.1992–10.1993 Hanna Suchocka	28.11.1918	28.11.1918	27.01.1821	26.01.1919 (E) (*Sejm*); 11.03.1928 (E) (Senate)	1997–2001 – Alicja Grzeszkowiak (Senate)
135. Portugal	—	08.1979–01.1980 Maria de Lourdes Pintasilgo	05.05.1931; 16.11.1934; 02.06.1976*	05.05.1931; 16.11.1934; 02.06.1976*	—	19.11.1934 (N); 24.11.1934 (E)	—
136. *Qatar*	09.01.1971	—	—	—	—	—	—
137. Republic of Korea	15.08.1948	—	17.07.1948	17.07.1948	10.05.1948	10.05.1948 (E)	—
138. Republic of Moldova	08.1991	—	15.04.1978; 14.10.1993*	15.04.1978; 14.10.1993*	02.1990	02.1990 (E)	—
139. Romania	—	—	1929; 07.1946*; 06.1918	1929; 07.1946*; 06.1918	20.11.1919	11.1946 (E)	—
140. Russian Federation[6]	06.1990	—	—	—	12.1993	12.1993 (E)	—
141. Rwanda	01.07.1962	07.1993–04.1994 Agathe Uwilingiyimana	25.09.1961	25.09.1961	12.1965	12.1965 ?	—
142. Saint Kitts and Nevis	19.09.1983	—	1951	1951	06.1984	06.1984 (E)	—
143. Saint Lucia	22.02.1979	—	1924	1924	07.1979	07.1979 (N)	—
144. Saint Vincent and the Grenadines	27.10.1979	—	05.05.1951	05.05.1951	12.1979	12.1979 (E)	—
145. Samoa	01.01.1962	—	10.1990	10.1990	04.1964	02.1976 (N); 04.1991 (E)	—
146. San Marino	—	04–10.1984, 10.1989–04.1990 Gloriana Ranocchi; 10.1991–04.1992 Edda Ceccoli; 04–10.1984 Maria Lea Pedini-Angeli; 04–10.1992 Patricia Busignani; 04.1999–10.1999 Rosa Zafferani	29.04.1959	10.09.1973	13th cent. 1906	08.09.1974 (E)	04.1981 – M.L. Pedini Angelini (Great General Council); 04.1984 & 10.1989 – G. Ranocchini (Great General Council); 10.1991 – E. Ceccoli (Great General Council); 04.1993 – P. Busignani (Great General Council)

HISTORICAL TABLE Continued

Country	Sovereignty after 1940	Women Presidents	Women Prime Ministers	Recognition of women's right to vote	Recognition of women's right to be elected	First legislature of the present sovereign state [2]	First woman elected (E) or nominated (N) to Parliament	Woman as presiding officer of parliament or one of its chambers
147. Sao Tome and Principe	12.07.1975	—	—	12.07.1975	12.07.1975	12.1975	12.1975 (E)	05.1980–02/03.1991 – A. Graça de Espirito Santo (National Assembly)
148. Saudi Arabia	—	—	—	—	—	—	—	—
149. Senegal	04.04.1960	—	—	19.02.1945	19.02.1945	1960	12.1963 (E)	—
150. Seychelles	28.06.1976	—	—	06.08.1948	06.08.1948	01.09.1976	06.1976 (E); 09.1976 (N)	—
151. Sierra Leone	27.04.1961	—	—	27.04.1961	27.04.1961	04.1962	?	—
152. Singapore	09.08.1965	—	—	18.07.1947	18.07.1947	21.09.1963	21.09.1963 (E)	—
153. Slovakia	01.01.1993	—	—	1920	1920	06.1992	06.1992 (E)	—
154. Slovenia	08.10.1991	—	—	10.08.1945	10.08.1945	12.1992	12.1992 (E)	—
155. Solomon Islands	07.07.1978	—	—	04.1974	04.1974	08.1980	05.1993 (E)	—
156. Somalia	01.07.1960	—	—	1956	1956	02.1960	12.1979 (E)	—
157. South Africa	—	—	—	1930 – Whites; 1984 – Coloureds + Indians; 1994 – Blacks	1930 – Whites; 1984 – Coloureds + Indians; 1994 – Blacks	21.04.1933	21.04.1933 (E)	1994–99 & 1999–2004 – F.N. Ginwala (National Assembly); 1999–2004 – N. Pandore (National Council of Provinces)
158. Spain	—	—	—	09.12.1931	08.05.1931	1810	07.1931 (E)	03.1996–2000 Esperanza Aguirre y Gil de Biedma (Senate)
159. Sri Lanka	04.02.1948	11.1997–11.2003 Chandrika Kumaratunge	07.1960–03.1965, 05.1970–07.1977, 11.1994–currently (08.1999) – Sirimavo Bandaranaike; 08.1994–11.1994 Chandrika Kumaratunge	20.03.1931	20.03.1931	09.1947	09.1947 (E)	—
160. Sudan	01.01.1956	—	—	11.1964	11.1964	1954	11.1964 (E)	—
161. Suriname	25.11.1975	—	—	09.12.1948	09.12.1948	10.1975	10.1975 (E)	1996–2001 Indradevi Marijke Djawalapersad (National Assembly)
162. Swaziland	06.09.1968	—	—	06.09.1968	06.09.1968	04.1972	04.1972 (E + N)	—
163. Sweden	—	—	—	05.1919–1921	05.1919–1921	1435	09.1921 (E)	1991–94 – I. Troedsson (Riksdag); 1994–98 & 1998–2002 B. Dahl (Riksdag)
164. Switzerland	—	12.1998 – 12.1999 Ruth Dreifuss	—	07.02.1971	07.02.1971	1848	10.1971 (E)	05–11.1977 – E. Blunschy (National Council); 1982 – H. Lang (National Council); 1992 – J. Meier (Council of States); 1994 – G. Haller (National Council); 1996 – J. Stamm (National Council); 1998 & 1999 – T. Heberlein (National Council)

165. Syrian Arab Republic	17.04.1946	—	—	10.09.1949–1953*	1953	07.1947	05.1973 (E)	—
166. Tajikistan	09.09.1991	—	—	1924	1924	02.1990	02.1990 (E)	—
167. Thailand	—	—	—	1932	1932	1932	1948 (N) 1949 (E)	—
168. The Former Yugoslav Rep. of Macedonia	08.09.1991	—	—	31.12.1946	31.12.1946	11–12.1990	11–12.1990 (E)	—
169. Togo	27.04.1960	—	—	22.08.1945	22.08.1945	04.1961	09.04.1961 (E)	—
170. Tonga	04.06.1970	—	—	1960	1960	05.1975	02.1993 (E)	—
171. Trinidad and Tobago	31.08.1962	—	—	1946	1946	31.08.1962	08.1962 (E+N)	1991–96 – O. Seapaul (House of Representatives)
172. Tunisia	20.03.1956	—	—	01.06.1959	01.06.1959	04.1956	08.11.1959 (E)	—
173. Turkey	—	—	06.1993–07.1996 Tansu Çiller	03.04.1930	05.12.1934	1920	02.1935 (N) 03.1943 (E)	—
174. Turkmenistan	27.10.1991	—	—	1927	1927	01.1990	01.1990 (E)	—
175. Tuvalu	01.10.1978	—	—	01.01.1967	01.01.1967	08.1977	09.1989 (E)	—
176. Uganda	09.10.1962	—	—	1962	1962	04.1962	04.1962 (N)	—
177. Ukraine	05.12.1991	—	—	10.03.1919	10.03.1919	03.1990	03.1990 (E)	—
178. United Arab Emirates	02.12.1971	—	—	Right not recognized	Right not recognized	12.1971	No	—
179. United Kingdom	—	—	05.1979–11.1990 Margaret Thatcher	06.02.1918 02.07.1928*	06.02.1918 02.07.1928*	13th cent. 06.1886[7]	14.12.1918 (E)	1992–1997 & 1997–2002 B. Boothroyd (House of Commons)
180. United Republic of Tanzania	09.12.1961	—	—	1959	1959	09.1965	?	—
181. United States of America	—	—	—	26.08.1920	13.09.1788*	04.1789	04.03.1917 (E) (House of Rep.) 12.01.1932 (E) (Senate)	—
182. Uruguay	—	—	—	16.12.1932	16.12.1932	18.07.1830	11.1942 (E)	1963 + 1965 + 1967 – A. Roballo (Senate)
183. Uzbekistan	31.08.1991	—	—	1938	1938	02.1990	02.1990 (E)	—
184. Vanuatu	30.07.1980	—	—	11.1975 30.07.1980*	11.1975 30.07.1980*	11.1979	11.1987 (E)	—
185. Venezuela	—	—	—	28.03.1946	28.03.1946	29.04.1830	02.1948 (E)	1994–1995 – Carmen Lavria
186. Viet Nam[8]	1955 + 07.1976	—	—	06.01.1946	06.01.1946	07.1976	04.1976 (E)	—
187. Yemen[9]	30.11.1967 + 22.05.1990	—	—	1967 – (DPR of Yemen) 1970 (Arab Rep. Yemen)	1967 (DPR of Yemen) 1970 (Arab Rep. Yemen)	1967 (DPR of Yemen) 1970 (Arab Rep. Yemen)	05.1990 (E ?)	—

(continued)

HISTORICAL TABLE Continued

Country	Sovereignty after 1940	Women Presidents	Women Prime Ministers	Recognition of women's right to vote	Recognition of women's right to be elected	First legislature of the present sovereign state[2]	First woman elected (E) or nominated (N) to Parliament	Woman as presiding officer of parliament or one of its chambers
188. Yugoslavia[10]	1992	—	05.1982–05.1986 Milka Planinc	31.01.1946	31.01.1946	12.1992	29.11.1943 (E)	06.1963–05.1967 – Olga Vrabic (Chamber of Welfare and Health of the Federal Assembly of the S.F.R.Y.) 05.1967–05.1969 – Vida Tomsic (Federal Chamber and Chamber of Nationalities of the Federal Assembly) 10.1979–05.1982 – Stana Tomasevic-Amesen (Federal Chamber of the S.F.R.Y. Assembly) 05.1986–05.1987 – Milka Gligorijevic-Takeva (Federal Chamber of the S.F.R.Y) 05.1989–06.1992 – Bogdana Glumac-Levakov (Federal Chamber of the S.F.R.Y.)
189. Zambia	24.10.1964	—	—	30.10.1962	30.10.1962	01.1964	01.1964 (E+N)	—
190. Zimbabwe	18.04.1980	—	—	1957	03.1978	02.1980	02–03.1980 (E+N)	—

1. The countries where Parliament stood suspended or temporarily dissolved at the time of the study are indicated in italics. The same is applied to countries which never had a Parliament.
2. The date given is that of the first legislature of the present sovereign State. Likewise, account is taken only of the date on which a woman became a member of the first legislature after independence. For all countries which had a form of representative institution between the 10th and 13th century, this reference is given as well as the date on which a Parliament in the present day meaning of the word (i.e. having legislative and oversight powers according to internal law) was established.
3. The asterisk next to the date signifies that conditions or restrictions were attached when women were granted the right to vote and/or stand for election. Reference to several dates reflects the stages in the granting of rights.
4. Reunification of the Federal Republic of Germany and the German Democratic Republic occurred on 3 October 1990.
5. Pakistan became independent in August 1947; the dates given here are for Pakistan following the partition of Bangladesh.
6. For the USSR, see data in IPU publication *Women in Parliament: A World Statistical Survey*, Series Reports and Documents, N°23, 1995.
7. This date is that of the first elections to the House of Commons following the electoral reform of 1884, which established a uniform electoral system for the entire United Kingdom and granted adult males the right to vote and to stand for election.
8. Reunification of the Democratic Republic of Viet Nam and the Republic of Viet Nam occurred in July 1976.
9. Reunification of Yemen occurred on 22 May 1990.
10. For the SFR of Yugoslavia, see data in IPU publication *Women in Parliament: A World Statistical Survey*, Series Reports and Documents, N°23, 1995.
* Data compiled by the IPU

the highest proportion of women parliamentarians ever attained, with 45.8 percent, or almost half, of the National Assembly being women.) Only slightly lower in current rankings are Belgium with 23.3 percent in 2002 (12 percent in 1995) and Switzerland with 23 percent in 2002 (18 percent in 1995). Next come Laos with 22.9 percent in 2002 (9.4 percent in 1995), Saint-Vincent and Grenadines with 22.7 percent in 2002, (9.5 percent in 1995), Tanzania with 22.3 percent in 2002 (11.2 percent in 1995), Monaco with 22.2 percent in 2002 (up from only 5.6 percent in 1995), and China with 21.8 percent in 2002 (21 percent in 1995).

In other words, in this sort of *Guinness Book of Records* of women parliamentarians, some of the oldest democracies do not make a very good showing. Just as an example, the House of Representatives of the world's most powerful nation, the United States of America, in October 2002 barely held 59th place, with 14 percent female legislators (down from 54th place, with 10.6 percent in 1995) on the list of nations with a Parliament that includes women. The House of Commons of the United Kingdom, a venerable and much imitated institution, occupies 47th place worldwide with 17.9 percent in 2002 (a significant improvement since 1995, when it held 64th place, with 9.2 percent women parliamentarians). The National Assembly of France barely achieved 65th place in 2002 with 12.1 percent women (up from 87th place with 6.4 percent in 1995). These established democracies rank far behind South Africa, with 29.8 women parliamentarians in 2002 (25 percent in 1995), Mexico with 16 percent in 2002 (14.2 percent in 1995), Eritrea with 14.7 percent in 2002 (but 21 percent in 1995), or Angola with 15.5 percent in 2002 (9.5 percent in 1995), to name but a few.

Progress, Stagnation, or Regression

However, such comparisons would be incomplete if they were not matched to an analysis of periods in time. If one compares the postwar situation with that of the mid-1980s in some of the countries that were sovereign at the time and had a Parliament, some interesting conclusions emerge.

With regard to the Nordic countries, there is no doubt at all that progress has been made, with two clearly marked stages, the 1950s and the 1970s. For example, in 1947 the proportion of female parliamentarian in the two Danish chambers was 14.5 for the lower chamber and 5.4 percent for the upper chamber. Almost 40 years later, in 1984, 26.2 percent of the members of the by-then single-chamber Danish Parliament were women; in 1995 that figure had reached 33 percent, and in 2002 it had further risen to 38 percent. The breakthrough for Danish women came during the elections of September 1971, when the percentages jumped from 10.6 percent to 16.7 percent, and since then the climb has been fairly constant. For Norway, the rise was even more spectacular, with women moving up from 4.6 percent in 1945 to 34.4 percent in 1985, and rising again to 39.4 percent in 1995; there has since been a drop to 36.4 percent in 2002. There, too, the turning point came in the 1970s: after the general elections of September 1973, the proportion of female parliamentarians rose from 9.3 percent to 15.5 percent. In Finland, the proportion of female parliamentarians rose from 9 percent in 1945 to 30.3 percent during the general elections in March 1983; the proportion of women continued to rise, reaching 33.5

percent in 1995 and 36.5 percent in 2002. In this case, the first leap came in 1953 (from 9 percent to 15 percent), followed in March 1970 by another significant jump from 16.5 percent to 21.5 percent.

But the most spectacular progression of all unquestionably took place in Sweden, where female representation in the Riksdag jumped from 1.3 percent in the first chamber and 7.8 percent in second chamber in September 1944, to 31.5 percent in September 1985, to 40.4 percent in 1995 and to 45 percent in 2002. Between 1944 and 2002, two key steps took place, as in Finland: a first leap from 4 percent to 6.7 percent in the upper chamber and from 9.6 percent to 12.2 percent in the second chamber during the elections of September 1952; and later a second jump from 14 percent to 21.4 percent between the September 1970 elections and those of 1973 (the country switched to a unicameral Parliament in 1970). A similar two-stage process occurred in Iceland.

A true revolution took place in Spain. In 1943, the unicameral Parliament of that nation had 0.4 percent women, a proportion that continued with some slight variations until 1964 and doubled in 1971. Then, with the general elections of 1986, the proportion of female parliamentarians progressed impressively: from 5.5 percent in the Senate and 6.3 percent in the Congress of Deputies, the number of women rose to 10.6 percent and 14.6 percent respectively. In 1995, 12.6 percent of the senators and 16 percent of the deputies were women; in 2002, those figures were 24.3 and 28.3 percent, respectively.

By contrast, the situation in France leaves a lot to be desired: 6.7 percent of the Senate and 5.6 percent of the National Assembly were women in December 1946, while in 1992 those figures were 5 percent in the Senate and 6.4 percent in the National Assembly. Between these two dates, female representation was continuously low in the Senate, with a low point of 1.4 percent in 1971 and a high point of only 3.8 percent in 1948. Some fluctuation took place in the National Assembly, where the lowest proportion of women was 1.5 percent in 1955 and the highest proportions were 7.1 percent in 1981 and then 12.1 percent in 2002 (with an interim drop to 6.4 percent in 1995).

In the United States, in November 1946, there were no women in the Senate, while women made up only 2.5 percent of the House of Representatives. The figures rose during the elections of 1992 when the proportion of women elected to the Senate grew from 2 percent to 7 percent and those elected to the House from 6.4 percent to 11 percent. Continued improvement took place in both houses of Congress: women accounted for 10.9 percent of the House of Representatives in 1995 and 14 percent as of October 2002; their presence in the Senate rose from 8 percent in 1995 to 13 percent in October 2002. Still, these advances are nothing to crow about, especially not when one recalls the bitter struggle waged decades earlier by the suffragists.

With regard to the former Socialist nations, two examples will suffice to illustrate the abrupt change that has been witnessed since 1989. Romania's unicameral Parliament had 34.4 percent women in March 1983: in 1995, its two chambers included respectively 2.1 percent and 4.1 percent women, respectively, and in 2002, 7.9 and 10.7 percent. They have almost gone back to the immediate postwar situation, when the Parliament elected in November 1946 comprised 5.3 percent women. Even so, the figures of 1995 constitute a slight rise compared to those of May 1990, the date of the first multiparty elections after the fall of the Ceaucescu regime, when women elected to the Senate made up only 0.8 percent, and only 3.6 percent in the Chamber of Deputies. An almost identical conclusion is to be drawn about Hungary, where women went from 3.1 percent of the Parliament in 1945 to 17.2 percent in April 1949, then advanced to 30.1 percent in 1980, only to fall back to 20.7 percent in 1985 and drop severely to 7.3 percent in 1990. Although the elections of May 1994, coming after the first shock of a step toward pluralism, brought hope for better days, in 2002, women accounted for only 9.1 percent of Hungary's National Assembly. The same trend has prevailed in the Russian Federation and all the other republics that once constituted the Soviet Union.

What Is the Explanation?

To offer one explanation for these patterns would be a mistake, since the causes are many and varied. Where the Nordic countries are concerned, there is no doubt that a profound social dynamic is at work, accompanied by a transformation in social outlook and political attitudes, that is the key to the phenomenon of the advancement of women in Parliament.

How, then, to explain the unmistakable and disheartening stagnation noted in France, where despite the constitutional law on parity passed in 1999, levels of female representation have not greatly improved: in 2002 the Senate included only 10.9 percent women (5 percent in 1995), while the Chamber of Deputies included 12.1 percent women in 2002 (6.4 percent in 1995). To understand this phenomenon, one should undoubtedly turn to the political parties, the electoral practices of which have perhaps not changed in any fundamental way since the end of World War II. But obviously this would only be a partial explanation.

With regard to the former Socialist nations, one question inevitably arises: how is it that, in 40 years of Socialism and a perhaps artificial but in any event relatively high presence of women in the Parliaments of Eastern European countries, no female political culture was created that would guarantee the stability of their representation? The best explanation might be the one that was given to the Inter-Parliamentary Union with the Polish response to the world survey on women in politics that was conducted in 1991. It follows here, accompanied by thoughts that go beyond the analysis of the decrease in the number of female parliamentarians in the "peoples' democracies":

> The rate of women's participation in the last parliamentary (and local) elections has diminished in comparison to preceding elections. One phenomenon distinguishes the whole history of postwar Poland: in times of political or economic crisis, women's participation is less than during periods of stability. The system by which candidates to the Assembly are designated may explain this phenomenon. The political system in force in Poland until quite recently did not guarantee truly free elections. In reality, candidates were nominated by the party in power and by the political organizations close to that power. A special (key) system had been set up that ensured a certain degree of representation for each social group. What was taken into consideration was less the political activity or the candidate's abilities than his or her capacity to represent

the whole of society, of which Parliament was to reflect the characteristics. The sex of the candidate was seen as one characteristic. Women deputies, nominated on the basis of this given, were no more than an "ornament." During periods of political difficulties, however, ornaments would be forgotten. Consequently, the political activity of women can only be evaluated on the basis of their representation in Parliament during times of crisis, for the women who are then elected are those who have succeeded in beating their male opponents. (*Women and Political Power* 1992)

The European Parliament

Since European institutions are growing stronger and becoming part of the political landscape of the ordinary citizen, it is interesting to verify the proportion of women members in the European Parliament and to compare those figures with the numbers of women in the national Parliaments of the corresponding nations. Most of the nations have markedly greater female representation in the European Parliament than they have in their own national Parliaments. The exceptions are Italy and Portugal, which demonstrate great electoral constancy, with a nearly identical proportion of women in the European Parliament and the national Parliaments: women account for 12.6 of Italy's members in the European Parliament and 8 percent of Portugal's European parliamentarians, as compared to 13.7 and 8.7 percent of those nations' respective national Parliaments.

As of the elections of 1999, Finland's female representation in the European Parliament was 43.8 percent, compared to 33.5 percent of the Finnish national Parliament during the same period; in Sweden, the respective figures were 45.4 percent and 40.4 percent; in Austria the figures were 38.1 percent compared to 23.2 percent. These countries were the three most recent entrants into the European Union at that time. Since these three countries were temporarily represented in the European Parliament by delegates from their national Parliament and not by directly elected MPs, might this proportion be due to the fact that in some way men left this function to women for the time being, while they waited to take the upper hand again once direct elections took place?

Such a conclusion seems to be supported by statistics on the proportion of women among the parliamentarians directly elected. As of 2002, for Denmark the percentages were 43.8 percent in the European Parliament against 38 percent in the unicameral national Parliament; in Germany, these figures were 35.3 percent in the European Parliament compared to 32.2 percent in the Bundestag; in Luxembourg, 33.3 percent in the European Parliament compared to 16.7 percent of the national Parliament; in Spain the figures were 32.8 percent and 14.6 percent, respectively; in the Netherlands, the figures were 32.2 percent and 28.4 percent; in Belgium, 32 percent and 15.4 percent; in France, 29.9 percent and 5.94 percent; in Ireland, 26.7 percent and 12.6 percent; in the United Kingdom, 18.4 percent in the European Parliament as compared to 9.5 percent in the House of Commons; in Greece, 16 percent and 6 percent.

The question then inevitably arises as to whether men are less interested in Europe than women, and whether the latter are more dynamic and audacious than men in their vision of the future or, in some other way, see more broadly. Perhaps it is a sign that men perceive the European Parliament as having less at stake and offering less political visibility than their national Parliaments. Should one conclude that younger institutions are more supportive of women? If one compares the above data with the observation that some developing countries that have recently instituted the parliamentary system include more women parliamentarians than many an old parliamentary democracy, it is very tempting to draw such a conclusion. In truth, however, the question remains open.

Women's Role in Parliaments

Having remarked to what extent women remain minorities in Parliaments, it is appropriate to examine what they do there, starting with a look at the positions they occupy. One self-evident observation is that if there are few women to be seen in parliamentary chambers, women are downright rare (although less and less so) in positions of responsibility in Parliament, whether as speaker, deputy speaker, leader of one of the chambers, member of a standing committee, president of a special committee, and so forth.

Positions of Responsibility in Parliament

Since the European Parliament was created, on the basis of the Treaty of Rome of 25 March 1957, two women, both of them French, have presided over it: Simone Veil chaired the European Parliament from July 1979 until January 1982, and Nicole Fontaine served as chair from July 1999 to July 2002.

Women have served in top positions in many national Parliaments. For a number of years the German Bundestag has been directed by Rita Süssmuth, the second woman to hold this office in all of German parliamentary history. Since 1991, the Parliament of Finland has been under the leadership of Riitta Uosukainen, the first woman in her nation to hold this position. In Iceland, Mrs. Thorkelsdottir held the presidency for two successive legislatures between 1991 and the elections of April 1995, alternating with one of her female colleagues, who also held the position twice. In Italy, Irene Pivetti is the first woman to preside over the Chamber of Deputies, having held this position since 1994. Similarly, Erna Hennicot-Schoepges heads the Parliament of Luxembourg for the second time. Kirsti Kolle Grondahl inaugurated the female presidency of the Norwegian Parliament in 1993, and Betty Boothroyd did the same for the British House of Commons in 1992.

Other nations under consideration have had a woman as president of Parliament or of one of its chambers in the past, for a shorter or longer term. This is particularly true of Austria, where, following in the footsteps of Odile Rudel-Zeynec (who headed the Bundesrat from 1927 to 1932 and was the first woman in the world to preside over a parliamentary assembly), four other women have since held that position.

Two women in succession presided over the Canadian Senate from 1972 to 1979; similarly, two women headed Iceland's Althingi (National Assembly) from 1988 to 1995. In Ireland women have twice presided over the Senate (1982–83 and 1987–89). In San Marino, four women presided over the Grand Conseil Général between 1981 and 1991. Five Swiss women have been named to the presidency of the National Council since 1977, among them Judith Stamm. Before the break-up of the Federation, Yugoslavia on several occasions also had a woman at the head of the federal Parliament or one of its chambers. For the United States, France, Belgium or Spain, as well as the other countries considered here, having a woman take on the office of speaker or leader of the senate would truly signify some sort of revolution.

Those four countries might find some examples in the rest of the world. From 1994 to 1999, Frene Ginwala presided over the National Assembly of the first multiracial Parliament of South Africa. In Sweden, in 1994, a woman succeeded another woman, Ingegerd Troedsson, who since 1991 had occupied the presidency and was the first woman to do so in her country's history. In Belgium, Antoinette Spaak led the Parliament from 1988 and was succeeded by Anne Marie Corbisier in 1992. In Spain, Esperanza Aguirre has filled that role since February 1999.

In May 1994 and for 5 years, the same month, the two chambers of the Parliament of Antigua and Barbados, the Senate and House of Representatives, elected a female president for a five-year term. Women headed the Senate of Belize from 1984 to 1993; the upper chamber of the Sabor of Croatia in 1993; the Assembly of Dominica from 1980 to 1988; the Legislative Assembly of El Salvador from 1994 to 1997; the Senate of Grenada from 1990 to 1995; and the House of Representatives of Japan from 1993 to 1996. The same was true for the Chamber of Deputies of Mexico from 1994 to 1996; the legislative assembly of Panama from 1994 to 1996; and the House of Representatives of Trinidad and Tobago from 1991 to 1995. (*Men and Women in Politics: Democracy Still in the Making: A World Comparative Study*, Reports and Documents, no. 28, Inter-Parliamentary Union)

In 2002, there were only 25 women among the heads of the 181 extant Parliaments, 66 of which are bicameral. These countries are as follows: South Africa (National Assembly and National Council of Provinces); Antigua-and-Barbuda (House of Representatives and Senate); Australia (Senate); Bahamas (Senate); Belize (House of Representatives and Senate); Bolivia (Chamber of Senators); Chile (Chamber of Deputies); Dominica (House of Assembly); Spain (Congress of Deputies); Finland; Georgia; Hungary (National Assembly); India (Council of States); Jamaica (House of Representatives and Senate); Lesotho (National Assembly); Latvia (Parliament); Mexico (Chamber of Deputies); Republic of Moldova (Parliament); Dominican Republic (Chamber of Deputies); Trinidad and Tobago (Senate). All told, of a total of 247 positions as president of a Parliament or parliamentary chamber, only 9.7 percent were filled by women in 2002.

One may well wonder whether all these countries have overcome sexual prejudices, or, alternatively, whether they know better how to take advantage of their human resources, remembering that the population, including the political population, is made up of men and women equally qualified to assume leadership functions. It remains true that in most of the countries under consideration women are more frequently elected to the vice-presidency rather than to the presiding office of the Parliament or one of its chambers. Poland and Hungary have not yet dared go further than that, although these are countries where having a woman fulfill leadership functions is traditional. Some countries have not even gone this far.

As for parliamentary committees (the mandates and nomenclature of which vary considerably from one nation to another, thereby prohibiting any rigorous comparisons), there is no doubt that even today, most of the women are found on those committees that deal with social questions, the family, or education, and that they frequently outnumber men by far on such committees. Generally, too, it is over these committees that women preside or where they have been entrusted with the functions of secretary or reporter, rather than in defense, legal, or foreign affairs committees.

At present, there is no easy definition of the manner in which other positions of responsibility in the Parliaments under discussion are distributed among men versus women. As a general indicator, one can cite the fact that in the Swedish Parliament, with 45 percent in 2002, the positions were clearly much more evenly divided between men and women than they were in the Chamber of Deputies of France, which had only 12.1 percent women in 2002. The numerical strength of Swedish women MPs ensured that they would be taken into account when members of committees were appointed and chairpersons selected, and the inevitable diversity of their abilities made it possible for them to claim a place in every area of parliamentary activity—something a few isolated women could not do, no matter how much they might wish to.

Making a Difference

Beyond the considerations set forth above, there is one thing of particular interest to the public when it is called upon to vote: if I elect a woman, will she be able to bring something new to the position? Many voters remain undecided on this issue. For others, notably in the Nordic countries, it has already been shown that when women became involved, the order of legislative priority changed, with the parliamentary agenda opening up to the problems of the most vulnerable segments of the population, social problems, and environmental concerns. The changes to be brought about by women's presence on defense or foreign affairs committees can only be revealed by an analysis of the work of these committees in countries where women are relatively numerous, as in Canada. Unfortunately, this kind of information is not yet readily available.

Political Parties

Strong Female Participation at the Base

Everywhere in Europe and North America, many political party members and activists are women. Data from the Inter-Parliamentary Union survey carried out in 1991 support this statement. Early in the 1990s in Sweden, women represented about 51 percent of the members of the Green and Liberal parties, about 45 percent of the members of the Center Party, 43 percent of the members of the Conservative Party, 41.1 percent of the members of the Left-Wing Party, and 40 percent of the members of the Social-Democratic Party. In Romania, they represented 40 percent of the members of the National Salvation Front, 33.3 percent of the members of the Democratic Union of the Magyars of Romania, 20 percent of the members of the Social-Democratic Party, 15 percent of the members of the National Christian and Democratic Farmers' Party, and 30 percent of the Agrarian Democratic Party. In the United Kingdom, women constituted more than 50 percent of the members of the Conservative Party, about 40 percent of the members of the Labour Party, about 50 percent of the members of the Liberal Democratic Party, the Green Party and the Plaid Cymru, and finally, 30 percent of the Communist Party. In Switzerland, they represented 25 percent and 30 percent respectively of the members of the Christian-Democratic Party and the Socialist Party. In Malta, women made up 52 percent of the Nationalist Party and 47 percent of the Labor Party. In Hungary, women represented 37 percent of the members of the People's Christian-Democratic Party, 34 percent of the members of the Hungarian Socialist Party, 32.5 percent of the members of the Alliance of Young Democrats, 24 percent of the members of the Alliance of Free Democrats, and 19 percent of the Party of Small Landowners. In Spain, women comprised 21.1 percent of the members of the Socialist Party, 30 percent of the People's Party, 19.6 percent of the Christian-Democratic Socialists, and 17.6 percent of the Communist Party. Finally, in the United States, polls showed that 34 percent of women identified themselves with the Republican Party as compared to 41 percent with the Democratic Party. (*Women and Political Power*, 1992)

Women's Ascent to Leadership of Political Parties

The figures above show that women do not hesitate to become involved in political ideas and programs. Nevertheless, it has been far from easy for them to rise from the base to the top. Little by little, however, things are changing, and more recently, depending upon the nation and especially the party, one tends to see either a striking contrast between the proportion of militant women and those in positions of responsibility, or, on the contrary, a relative compatibility between these two categories. The latter case arises particularly when an obligatory quota system or even a simple electoral recommendation is in place.

In Sweden in 1991, the leadership components of all the political parties included a generally balanced proportion of men and women: from 42.3 percent to 57.1 percent women in the four principal committees of the Green Party; 50 percent of the members of the leadership committee of the Left-Wing Party, thanks to the application of a quota; 47.8 percent of the members of the principal committee of the Liberal Party; 46.4 percent of the Social-Democratic Party; 42.1 percent of the Conservative Party; and 30.7 percent of the Center Party. Similarly, in the United States, 39 percent of the members of the leadership committee of the Republican Party and 48 percent of the members of the leadership committee of the Democratic Party were women, without the existence of a quota system.

In Romania during the same period, by contrast, women seemed to have some difficulty in penetrating the parties' leadership structures: they made up 10.2 percent of the members of the principal committee of the National Salvation Front, 5 percent of the Democratic Union of the Magyars of Romania, and 4 percent of the Democratic Agrarian Party. The same was true in Poland: women constituted 9.85 percent of the members of the leadership body of the Social-Democratic Party, 12.3 percent of the Socialist Party, 14 percent of the Communist Party, and 12 percent of the Democratic-Social Center. In Belgium, the situation was comparable, with women representing 14.2 percent of the members of the main committee of the Socialist Party, 10.3 percent of the Liberal Reform Party, 10.4 percent of the Christian Social Party, and 20 percent of the Party Against Violence, thanks to the application of an obligatory quota system. It was tangibly better in Germany, with contrasts from party to party: women comprised 21.2 percent of the members of the main body of the Christian Democrat Union; 13.6 percent of the Christian Social Union; 35 percent of the Social-Democratic Party, thanks to the introduction of a quota system; 14 percent of the Free Democratic Party; and 55 percent of the Green Party, which also applies a quota system. However, these figures say nothing about the real influence exercised by these women over the decision-making process and over the overall definition of party action.

Women's Branches of Parties

Numerous political parties in European and North American countries have established a women's branch that holds more or less regular meetings. In Germany, Finland, Portugal, and the United Kingdom, every political group without exception has a women's section or organization. The exceptions to this trend are Belgium, Denmark, Norway, the Netherlands, and Sweden. Both of the two main parties in the United States, the Democratic and Republican parties, have very active national federations of women.

The extent and the nature of the activities of these branches vary in scope and their role has evolved enormously with time, if the Canadian response to the survey conducted by the Inter-Parliamentary Union on this topic in 1991 is representative. Canadian women's branches within the political parties have taken a qualitative leap in the course of the last quarter of the century:

> The nature and organization of women's management or committees in the national and provincial political parties in Canada have changed considerably over the years. At first, these components were generally dissimilar from the principal political parties or were only extensions of these. Often, the tasks women accomplished there would reflect the division of work between the sexes in society generally. Formerly, women's groups were most frequently seen as sources of inexpensive manual labor. Women were often relegated to activities such as taking care of mailings (addressing and stuffing envelopes), serving tea at the most important meetings of the party, organizing these meetings, fundraising, and so on. However, in the course of the last few years, there have been some radical changes.

In the 1970s, women's groups have tended to become more fully integrated into the federal political party to which they belonged. In the course of this period, the mandates, structure, and roles of women's organizations have become modified. A number of them have adopted plans for positive action aiming at increasing women's participation in the definition of the politics of national parties. (*Women and Political Power*)

Today, the pursuits of women's groups seem to consist above all in sensitizing women to party action and to political life in general; bringing a larger number of women to participate in all levels of decision making, including in the party itself; establishing and defending political priorities; and finally, for some, helping female representatives accomplish their missions. A thought contained in Gabon's response to the 1991 survey is worth remembering, for it is of value beyond the borders of that nation:

> [Some people] assert that having a women's branch allows women to be enclosed in a ghetto where they revel in their role as receivers of aid. In fact, there is a kind of contest of strength in the parties that women may turn to their advantage if they undergo training, become resolutely involved in the action, and play the card of solidarity.

Getting Elected, But How?

Securing a Nomination

Securing a nomination, making sure that it is for a race with a chance of success and not one that is lost in advance, obtaining the necessary moral and logistical support from the party for an electoral campaign: all of these are challenges for women. Further, women's minority presence, still too frequent, in the leadership bodies of parties has a bearing on the ways in which candidacies are decided.

Unless there is a deliberate party policy to propose equal numbers of male and female candidates (as is the case with the Greens in most Western European countries), a system for proposing women in alternation on all the lists, or an obligatory quota system, women must be persuasive and prove themselves. They have to convince the parties that they are interested in the electorate and that when they present candidates for office, at the top of the list for example, these will bring in an impressive number of votes. Then, once they are parliamentarians, it is up to them to perform in such a way that their party can aim for their reelection. Once they have cleared the obstacles on the level of the party itself, women still face those that arise from the electoral system.

The Electoral System

Even if a link of cause and effect cannot be clearly established between the electoral system and the proportion of women elected, one of the frequently advanced hypotheses to explain the scant numbers of women in Parliaments is that the electoral system, the product of a male political culture, actually works or can work to the disadvantage of women. Most political analysts would assert that proportional voting is "the" solution, or in any case the least negative one for women. This assertion deserves to be examined more closely.

According to the terse definition given by the Inter-Parliamentary Union, election on a majority basis "has as its goal the release of a force capable of shouldering the destiny of a nation," while a proportional election aims at "first guaranteeing representation on the national level of the political forces of the country and reproducing in Parliament the most faithful possible reflection of their importance in society." Mixed systems steer at combining the advantages of the previous two systems by avoiding some of their disadvantages. At first sight, the proportional electoral system would seem to be favorable to women. The Inter-Parliamentary Union survey of 1991, which polled every Parliament in the world, whatever its electoral system, was designed to give a better understanding of this issue. The question posed was hardly any simpler than the one formulated at the time of the referendums: "If the nature of the electoral system (proportional/majority; single nomination/nomination list) seems to you to have an effect—positive or negative—on the election of women to Parliament, please indicate this and, if possible, provide a thorough analysis" (*Men and Women in Politics*).

The results of the survey, about 100 answers based on national practice and sometimes on the experience of changing from one electoral system to another, were more troubling than conclusive. For example, it is somewhat disconcerting that in a country such as France the successive change from a majority electoral system to a proportional one, followed by the return to the majority system, resulted in no modification whatsoever of the gender composition of the National Assembly.

In the face of an almost equal number of responses in favor of the majority system as opposed to the proportional system, it is clearly impossible to determine which of the two systems does greater justice to women. The Inter-Parliamentary Union was forced to conclude, based on the 1991 survey, that the question remained unresolved and decided to do another, much more precise and in-depth survey on this theme in 1995. The results of that survey were reported in *Towards Partnership between Men and Women in Politics* (1997). At this point a few conjectures can be made.

The choice of electoral system is not neutral, since it corresponds to a precise objective, but what may have a positive or negative effect on the election of women is less the intrinsic nature of the system chosen than the manner in which political parties use it. For example, in a single nomination majority election, it is important to know whether the parties present women in difficult districts or, on the contrary, in districts where the parties have a strong presence, providing a solid foundation. Similarly, when this system of majority election is applied in districts with several seats, it is important to know if the parties are presenting a balanced proportion of male and female candidates. To be sure, in the context of a majority electoral system, candidates' personal talent and political charisma can significantly compensate for the disadvantages resulting from an unfavorable choice by the party, but obviously such an unfavorable choice will limit a candidate's chances of success.

In a proportional electoral system with a group list, it is obvious that the place assigned by the party to candidates on that list will be a determining factor in their election or nonelection. Being at the head of the list, among the first names, or being at the bottom of the list makes a big difference. In fact, experience has tended to show that group lists on which the names of male and female candidates alternate are the only ones that guarantee a balanced representation of the two sexes in Parliament. In the same way, if the system of proportional representation is practiced with open lists but the parties include only a negligible proportion of women, their chances of being elected are strongly reduced.

Apart from electoral mechanisms per se, many subjective criteria influence the electorate. Every party official knows that even in a system of open lists, the order in which names appear on the list significantly influences the choices made by male and female voters alike. As for the electorate, if it is called upon to make its choice from an open electoral list with the possibility of a combination of two or several lists, it can quite easily ignore or neglect women. This is all the more true for those voters who are naïve about politics or who have not been sensitized to the importance of electing women so as to have a Parliament that represents both halves of the population. It follows that the electoral system might well be merely the tip of the iceberg.

Quotas and Their Effects

The quota system was created to compensate for the various difficulties described so far as well as for the subjective attitudes of an electorate accustomed to a male political world. This system is far from being universal and, in several European countries such as France, it has been deemed unconstitutional on the basis of a conflict with the principle of sexual equality enshrined in the 1789 Déclaration des Droits de l'Homme et du Citoyen (Declaration of the Rights of Man and the Citizen). However, Article 4 (1) of the United Nations Convention on the Elimination of All Forms of Discrimination against Women (CEDAW) authorizes the temporary adoption of measures of so-called positive discrimination (the reason why Swedish and Icelandic law do not forbid such measures) in the following terms:

> Adoption by States Parties of temporary special measures aimed at accelerating de facto equality between men and women shall not be considered discrimination as defined in the present Convention, but shall in no way entail as a consequence the maintenance of unequal or separate standards; these measures shall be discontinued when the objectives of equality of opportunity and treatment have been achieved.

Without especially promoting quotas or other measures of positive action, but recognizing that they do account for a considerable number of votes, the Inter-Parliamentary Union has itself opted for a formulation that claims to be neutral:

> On a strictly interim basis, affirmative action measures may be taken. Wherever the measure chosen is a quota system, it is proposed that the quota should not target women but that, in a spirit of equity, it may be established that neither sex may occupy a proportion of seats inferior to a given percentage.

In a study published in 1992, the Inter-Parliamentary Union stated:

> It is possible to distinguish between two types of quota: (a) the quota applied to the election and therefore concerning the percentage of women candidates in relation to the total number of persons standing; and (b) the quota applied to the result of the election and hence concerning the number of seats that must be occupied by women after the vote.

Not a single European or North American country today has a provision in the constitution or the electoral law that reserves a given percentage of parliamentary seats for women, as is the case in Argentina. On the other hand, there are numerous political parties that have established a quota system. But there, too, it is appropriate to distinguish between quotas for elected seats in the party itself (the most widespread case) and quotas for seats in elected local or parliamentary bodies. Finally, it is appropriate to distinguish between formally established quotas that must be applied and instructions that indicate an objective, possibly (but not necessarily) formulated in percentages.

The Inter-Parliamentary Union's 1991 survey on quotas made it clear that both conservative and progressive parties are inclined to adopt quota systems, although it may seem that the latter are more open to the adoption of such a system. The establishment of a quota, frequently after heated debates, was often the result both of the women's conviction that this system was useful and efficient and of the weight this conviction carried among their male colleagues. Nevertheless, it is known that, in the old democracies in any case, many women consider themselves "improperly elected" if they have been elected on the basis of a quota rather than on the sole basis of their personal qualities.

One example, based on 1991 data, is furnished by Norway—a country with the second highest percentage of women in Parliament—where every political party had fixed a goal of 40 percent female candidates for the legislative elections in 1991 and 50 percent in 1997, without formally establishing a quota. In Sweden the situation was comparable, although the percentage actually managed to reach the 50 percent mark. In the United States, the Republican Party applies a 33 percent quota while the Democratic Party settled on a 50 percent quota, but neither quota is binding. In Iceland, both the Social Democratic Party and the People's Alliance set a 40 percent goal in both 1991 and 1997. In Germany, the Social Democratic Party established an approximate goal of 40 percent in 1988, while the Green Party applied a required goal of 50 percent. In Belgium, the Socialist Party and the Party Against Violence each established a 20 percent quota, the first one as a requirement and the second one as an option. In Canada, the new Democratic Party has a suggested quota of 50 percent. In Denmark, the Social Democratic Party and the Social People's Party both settled on a 40 percent quota. In Spain, only the Socialist Party and the Communist Party established quotas, 25 percent in both cases.

One could cite a great many other cases. However, these few examples are sufficient to show that the Western European and North American parties recoil from binding themselves to required quotas, but that they are, on the other hand, inclined toward establishing criteria to further the election of women.

Some 150 men and women parliamentarians from 66 nations debated the advantages and disadvantages of quotas during the symposium organized in 1989 by the Inter-Parliamentary Union. They concluded that in practice, quotas are a means of rapidly increasing the number of female candidates and that they guarantee the presence of women parliamentarians in cases where, without quotas, they would be absent or so few in number that they would hardly be able to exercise any political influence.

These positive conclusions were, however, substantially tempered by other observations. Noting that the quota system functions most efficiently in the framework of proportional representation with an electoral list, some symposium participants pointed out how easy it was to circumvent the goals of the system by placing women's names at the bottom of the list. All of them recognized that the quota should be established with a mechanism guaranteeing that women themselves, through their organizations, could propose candidates. Many stressed that the quota was too often interpreted by the parties not as a minimum guarantee but as a contract to be completed. While accepting that quotas could help them, quite a few women protested against the mechanism imposed upon them, saying they had an electorate prepared to vote for them without any need for artificial assistance.

The parliamentarians from Central and Eastern European countries were particularly hostile to quotas, emphasizing that, in explicit form or in the political system they had known so far, quotas could have a deceptive effect since they might be used to promote women with a low political profile without actually opening any real new prospects for women.

Alternative Paths: Appointments and Reserved Seats

For women as for minorities, there are two alternative paths to being elected: appointment and reserved seats. In reality, not a single example of seats reserved for women is to be found among the Parliaments of the 55 countries here under consideration. On the other hand, some Parliaments include seats for appointed members that, in principle, create openings for women.

One such opening exists in the Canadian Senate, a chamber that is made up entirely of appointed members. From the 2.1 percent proportion of women it had in 1945, it grew slowly to 15.4 percent in 1995 and then rapidly to 35 percent in 2002. As for the three Parliaments of Europe that include some appointed members, information on whether women figure among their memberships was not readily available when this essay was being written. The countries involved are Croatia, where 5 of the 68 members of the Sabor are appointed by the chief of state; the Senate of Ireland, of which 11 of the 60 members are appointed by the prime minister; and finally the Supreme Council of Kazakhstan (virtually suspended in March 1995), of which 42 of the 177 members are appointed by the chief of state. By contrast, until the May 1995 elections 50 of the 360 members of the Supreme Soviet in Belarus were representatives of public organizations, and it was their role to select a balanced proportion of men and women. Here too, however, information on the number of women among the 50 delegates was not readily available at the time this essay was written.

Women's Parties

Faced with the unwillingness of the traditional parties to grant women their rightful place and to present them as candidates for election on an equal footing with men, some women have set about organizing their own parties. The most famous case is that of Iceland's Samtök um Kvennalista (Women's Alliance), created in March 1983 after an overwhelming success in 1982 at the local level. This was a victory for a party founded in the same year. It came 74 years after a list of women candidates had been presented for election to the Municipal Council of Reykjavik in 1908 (of whom four women were elected) and 60 years after a similar experience with the Icelandic parliamentary elections in 1922, which ensured the election of the nation's first female parliamentarian.

The entrance of the Women's Alliance upon the scene in Iceland created an electoral shock wave that aided the arrival of an increased number of women in Parliament. Thus, after the local elections of 1982, the Women's Alliance gained three seats in the Althingi (the unicameral Parliament) in 1983, then six in 1987, and five in 1991. From three in 1979, women's numbers grew to nine in 1983, 13 in 1987, and 15 in 1991, a leap from 5 percent to 20.6 percent. However, this trend toward improvement was reversed during the elections of 1995, when the Women's Alliance lost two of their seats in the Althingi, reducing to 16 the total number of women parliamentarians. Proposed explanations for this electoral regression include the reproach that the presence of the Women's Alliance in the Althingi constituted a kind of gilded cage that isolated them, and the opinion that some other political parties had managed to offer a more balanced proportion than before of female and male candidates, thereby opening up new prospects for women.

The Icelandic example was followed in the Netherlands, and the attraction of an exclusively female political entity persisted in other Western European countries such as Sweden, although the idea was not actually put into effect there. Iceland's experiment has been emulated elsewhere in Europe. For example, a women's party was created in the Russian Federation under the name Women of Russia, a few months before the first multiparty elections of December 1993. Benefiting from the know-how and the vast network of contacts of the former Women's Federation of the Soviet Union, the founders and members of this new party were able to obtain 23 of the 60 seats during the elections and determined to widen their parliamentary representation in future elections.

Bibliography

United Nations

Convention on the Elimination of All Forms of Discrimination against Women, United Nations, 1979
Universal Declaration of Human Rights, United Nations, 1948

Publications of the Inter-Parliamentary Union

Declaration on Criteria for Free and Fair Elections, Inter-Parliamentary Union, 1994
Electoral Systems: A World-Wide Comparative Study, Geneva: Inter-Parliamentary Union, 1993
Free and Fair Elections: International Law and Practice, Geneva: Inter-Parliamentary Union, 1994
Goodwin-Gill, Guy S., *Codes of Conduct for Elections: A Study Prepared for the Inter-Parliamentary Union*, Geneva: Inter-Parliamentary Union, 1998.
Inter-Parliamentary Symposium on the Participation of Women in the Political and Parlementary Decision-Making Process: Geneva, 20–24.XI.1989: Reports and Conclusions, no.16, Geneva: Inter-Parliamentary Union, 1989
Men and Women in Politics: Democracy Still in the Making: A World Comparative Study, Reports and Documents, no. 28, Geneva: Inter-Parliamentary Union, 1997
Participation of Women in Political Life: An Assessment of Developments in National Parliaments, Political Parties, Governments and in the Inter-Parliamentary Union, Five Years After the Fourth World Conference on Women, Geneva: Inter-Parliamentary Union, 1999
Plan of Action to Correct Present Imbalances in the Participation of Men and Women in Political Life: Adopted by the Inter-Parliamentary Council (Paris 26 March 1994), Reports and Documents, no. 22, Geneva: Inter-Parliamentary Union, 1994
Politics: Women's Insight, Reports and Documents, no. 36, Geneva: Inter-Parliamentary Union, 2000
Systèmes électoraux. Étude comparative mondiale, Geneva: Inter-Parliamentary Union, 1993
Towards Partnership Between Men and Women in Politics, Reports and Documents, no. 29, Geneva: Inter-Parliamentary Union, 1997
Women and Political Power: Survey Carried Out among the 150 National Parliaments Existing as of 31 October 1991, Reports and Documents, no. 19, Geneva: Inter-Parliamentary Union, 1992
Women in Parliaments, 1945–1995: A World Statistical Survey, Reports and Documents, no. 23, Geneva: Inter-Parliamentary Union, 1995
Women in Politics: World Bibliography, Geneva: Inter-Parliamentary Union, 1999
Women: What the IPU Is Doing, Geneva: Inter-Parliamentary Union, 1997

BUILDING EQUALITY IN THE POLICIES OF INTERNATIONAL ORGANIZATIONS

GIOVANNA PROCACCI AND MARIAGRAZIA ROSSILLI

IN THE COURSE OF the decades of the postwar era, international organizations have played an important role in the development of equality between men and women. Indeed, apart from a few conventions of the International Labor Organization (ILO), it was only when states formed new international organizations in the wake of World War II that the international community began to concern itself with a policy on women's rights.

Among their other merits, the founders of the United Nations Organization (UN) forbade any discrimination on the basis of sex in the wording of the fundamental rights of the founding charter of the organization, approved on 26 May 1945 in San Francisco. Given the global reach of the United Nations, this beginning was of enormous historic significance in a period when patriarchal tradition and sex-based discrimination were dominant in most countries and when the process of democratization, with its counterpart in equal rights, was far from being accomplished.

Since then, the UN has exercised firm and progressive action through the elaboration of international standards for the human, civil, political, and social rights of women, through the renewal of worldwide political culture and by inspiring national constitutions and legislation. If the great majority of constitutions today guarantee the equality of men and women before the law, and if sexual discrimination is prohibited, this is partly thanks to the work of the UN. The four world conferences promoted by the UN on the themes of "Equality, Development, and Peace" in recent decades (1975 in Mexico City, 1980 in Copenhagen, 1985 in Nairobi, and 1995 in Beijing) not only laid down guidelines and essential ideas for the other international organizations and national governments, they also generated and shaped worldwide public opinion on these themes. Indeed, no other international organization has adopted such a global perspective with respect to women's rights and the prohibition of sexual discrimination—not even the European institutions, although among regional organizations they are the most progressive in these matters.

The Council of Europe, founded in 1949 by nine countries (France, Great Britain, Belgium, the Netherlands, Luxemburg, Denmark, Iceland, Italy, and Norway) with the purpose of strengthening relations among European countries, made itself the guarantor of sexual nondiscrimination in fundamental rights and civil and political rights. This was written into the Convention for the Protection of Human Rights and Fundamental Freedoms signed by the member states in 1950. The role of the Council of Europe in this field was attenuated following the achievement of formal equality of civil and political rights in all democratic Western countries. In the 1990s, however, the council gained new importance because of its enlargement to include the former Communist countries of Eastern Europe, for which the prohibition of sexual discrimination contained in the convention constitutes an effective guarantee in the realm of civil rights. The Council of Europe thus assumed a role that is now effectively pan-European. The 34 states that were members in 1995 (along with the founding nations, these now included Austria, Cyprus, Germany, Greece, Ireland, Liechtenstein, Malta, Portugal, Spain, Sweden, Switzerland, Turkey, Finland, the Republic of San Marino, Andorra, Rumania, Slovakia, the Czech Republic, Poland, Hungary, Bulgaria, Slovenia, and the three Baltic republics) will likely expand to 41 with the addition of seven ex-Communist nations applying for membership: Ukraine, Belarus, Albania, Macedonia, Croatia, Bosnia-Herzegovina, and Russia, the candidacy of which was temporarily suspended by the Parliamentary Assembly in Strasbourg because of human rights violations in the war in Chechnya.

Finally, the European Economic Community (EEC), which following the Treaty on European Union of 7 February 1992 (informally known as the Treaty of Maastricht) became the European Union (EU), has had a role and impact that have been similar and complementary, although less wide-ranging, with only 15 countries involved in 1995. In keeping with its economic mandate to create a single market, the EEC established antidiscriminatory norms in the area of the right to work, the first foundations of which were laid in its founding treaty, the Treaty Establishing the European Economic Community (informally, Treaty of Rome) signed on 25 March 1957 by France, Germany,

Italy, and the Benelux countries. Community norms shaped through progressive extensions of the principle of formal equality, beginning with the prohibition of direct sexual discrimination and moving to the prohibition of indirect forms of discrimination—that is to say, practices that disadvantage women workers even when there is no explicit reference to sex—and finally progressing to equal job opportunities as a precondition for the achievement of real equality. Taken as a whole, the actions of the three organizations, which have been both symptoms of and catalysts for the social and cultural changes produced in the postwar era, have marked crucial changes in the notion of equality.

During an initial phase that lasted until the 1970s, the central objective was that of guaranteeing formal (legal) equality, that is, women's access to all rights guaranteed to men. By the 1980s, formal equality in political rights was guaranteed in most of the countries of the world, and equality in civil rights had essentially become a reality in the democratic countries of the West, where it also began to extend into the realm of social rights. This was when the notion of equal opportunity took shape: it was based on temporary political and legislative measures promoting positive discrimination on behalf of women, making it possible for them to overcome real inequalities and extralegal disadvantages that obstructed the full exercise of equal rights. The present phase is centered on the objective of women's equal participation at all decision-making levels within the economy, society, and national and international politics.

Little by little, policies toward women have also evolved by transcending the sectorial and marginal character intrinsic to all policies aimed at underprivileged social groups. As women's contribution in all social sectors is recognized, it becomes more and more evident that women's problems concern society as a whole; policies affecting women thus take on greater and greater significance.

Despite the influence of these international institutions on national policies for promoting women's rights, there remains a considerable gap between the stated goals of international legal instruments (pacts, conventions, agreements, resolutions, recommendations, and declarations) and their actual impact within national legislation, which continues to be highly variable. This gap is basically attributable to the intrinsic limits of the action of international institutions. Governments can avoid ratifying international pacts, postpone their ratification, or ratify agreements with such qualifications that their content thereby becomes meaningless. Depending on the specific terms of national constitutions, the standards of international law may either be directly integrated into national law, or, in contrast, such standards may constitute only a source of international obligations—a circumstance that tends to weaken the very content and application of supranational guarantees.

The law of the EEC/EU differs from the normal rules of operation of international law, in that it represents a "new legal order" (to use the expression of the European Court of Justice, which recognizes that in some cases it has supremacy over national law). This means that some Community norms have a direct effect, that is to say, they immediately create individual rights in member states, independent of any action on the part of national governments. This capacity pertains not only to norms defined in treaties concerning equality between men and women workers, but also—albeit in a more limited way—to many of the dispositions contained in the Community's directives in this realm. Nevertheless, even this sphere of action of the EEC/EU has narrow limits: member states cannot be forced to apply Community directives or to not betray their spirit. They may even ignore altogether Community resolutions, recommendations, or political programs, which are legally binding to different degrees.

In this sense, the driving role that international norms have played in the promotion of women's rights has not precluded extreme diversity in national situations. In the promotion of women's rights, just as in other sectors, the relationship between, on the one hand, the establishment of international norms, and on the other, national prerogatives, has been and remains one of the great challenges of our era. The present crisis in the UN and the European institutions, following the collapse of the Soviet empire and the dissolution of the international order established in the aftermath of World War II, makes it particularly difficult to predict what the outcome of this challenge will be for the 21st century, which has already begun with a dramatic resurgence of barbarism in international relations.

The United Nations Organization

From the beginning, the UN's policy toward women has been connected both to the organization's general policy and to the vicissitudes of the women's and feminist movements. In San Francisco in 1945, representatives of women's organizations assembled under the umbrella of the Inter-American Commission on the Status of Women obtained the inclusion of the prohibition of sexual discrimination in the founding Charter of the UN. Ever since, the UN has been a reference point for many of the women's movements that have developed around the world.

The Charter incorporates the principles of Western democracies and extends equal enjoyment of basic human rights to women. Article 1 declares that the United Nations has as its goal the promotion and encouragement of respect for human rights and basic liberties for all, regardless of race, sex, language, or religion. Sexual equality is also guaranteed in other articles as well as in the preamble to the Charter.

The same principle is reaffirmed in the preamble to what remains the most important UN declaration, the Universal Declaration of Human Rights of 10 December 1948. Article 2 forbids any discrimination on grounds of race, color, sex, language, religion, opinion, or national or social origins in the enjoyment of basic rights and liberties. All rights must be guaranteed equally to women and men, from the right to life, liberty, and personal security, to the right not to be subjected to torture or inhuman or degrading punishment, to rights concerning marriage, work, and education. In the area of human rights, the Charter and the Universal Declaration of Human Rights have inspired the philosophy and principles of many international acts, constitutions, and national laws guaranteeing the prohibition of sexual discrimination—a state of affairs that represents progress of great magnitude. Even so, the prohibition of sexual discrimination stands within the framework of modern judicial tradition that defines the subject of law as an abstract, asexual subject. Consequently, sexual difference can have no legal value, since it is precisely what must be excluded from consideration. The prohibition of discrimination thus does not mean the valorization of sexual difference.

The UN's founding Charter and Universal Declaration of Human Rights guarantee a subsequent extension of women's rights to the international level, but at the price of assimilating woman into the category of an abstract universal subject and thus treating her as gender-neutral. Consequently, what is ignored here is woman's fundamental rights as a subject sexually different from man, such as the right to self-determination over her body in sexuality and procreation, a right that in fact has always been denied her, in one way or another. But since such a right is an indispensable condition for individuals' right to exercise control over their bodies, this means in reality that women's full autonomy as subjects endowed with rights has not been recognized. In this sense, the universal quality of the basic rights of the asexual subject, affirmed in the declaration of the UN, is exposed in all its limitations. Without the individual right to have free control over one's own body, it can be said that neither the right to life, nor the right to liberty, security, or respect for the dignity of one's person, has been effectively guaranteed to the female half of the human race.

It may even be said that, within the dominant conceptual perspective of the asexual subject, the problem of guaranteeing fundamental rights to the female half of the human species has hardly even been considered. This is why the word "sex" is included among the other forms of discriminations that are prohibited: that is to say, sex is treated analogously to differences in race and social condition, as if women were comparable to a racial, social, or political group rather than being a part of the entire group. One thus speaks of "women's condition," instead of speaking of the rights of half the human race—hence the name and the competencies assigned to the UN's Commission on the Status of Women (CSW).

The Commission on the Status of Women

In the interest of promoting women's rights worldwide, the women representing the Inter-American Commission had since 1946 advocated the creation of a Commission on the Status of Women, which from its inception had a more limited mandate than that of the Commission on Human Rights. It had no investigative powers regarding the respect of equal rights on the part of governments, nor did it have any power to act when violations occurred and were reported to the commission. Given these limitations in terms of power, which remain essentially the same today, over the course of 30 years of work the Commission on the Status of Women intervened only in non–legally binding ways in national policies for promoting equal rights, by means of recommendations, programs, and projects. The commission embodies the conception of women's rights that was prevalent at the time of its creation, linked to the notion of the status of women. The intrinsic ambiguities of such a conception had led the commission progressively to reduce its involvement in human rights programs, to the point of almost entirely losing its initial raison d'être when, during the 1970s, it was transferred from the UN's Human Rights division to the division of Social and Humanitarian Affairs—that is, into the realm of economic and social intervention.

From the outset, in short, efforts to promote women's rights have been less vigorous than advocacy efforts in the area of human rights. The 1966 adoption of the International Covenant on Civil and Political Rights and the International Covenant on Economic, Social and Cultural Rights (binding in 1976) transformed the moral commitments stemming from the Universal Declaration of Human Rights into obligations binding on member states, signed by France in 1984. Alongside equality between men and women in the enjoyment of all the rights cited and the prohibition of sexual discrimination among other forms of discrimination (which the two covenants have in common), Article 26 of the International Covenant on Civil and Political Rights states that all individuals are equal before the law and have the right to equal legal protection against all forms of discrimination, including sexual discrimination. This is the only standard that establishes on an international level such broad protection of equal rights, extending not only to the rights specifically named in the covenant but to all rights guaranteed by law. The relative weakness of the control mechanisms provided for in the covenants and the strength of national prerogatives of jurisdiction, in law and in fact, may explain the fact that even those states with little concern for the protection of personal rights were able to adhere to the covenants. It is revealing that the approximately 80 countries in the most disparate geographic zones that had already ratified the covenants in the mid 1980s included Socialist countries of Eastern Europe, Arab nations, and African and Latin-American states, while the United States did not ratify the Covenant on Civil and Political Rights until 1992 and still has not ratified the Covenant on Economic, Social, and Cultural Rights.

Despite these limitations, adhering to the pacts has undoubtedly prompted states to revise their constitutions and their legislation. Even before the principles of the UN's founding Declaration had been formalized into the pacts, different treaties relating to specific areas of the law had incorporated the principle of equality between men and women. The first is the Convention on the Political Rights of Women of 1953 (UNT 193.135), followed by the Convention on the Nationality of Married Women of 1957 (UNTS 309.65), and then by the Convention on Consent to Marriage, Minimum Age for Marriage, and Registration of Marriages of 1962 (UNTS 521.231).

Early in the 1960s, dissatisfaction over the low number of national ratifications of these treaties concerning specific rights prompted the revival of an initiative—already put forward, without success, in the first years of the Commission on the Status of Women—to create a tool capable of dealing again with women's rights as a whole. The countries of Eastern Europe, notably the USSR, Hungary, and Poland, led this campaign for a comprehensive measure covering all aspects of discrimination against women. The result, based on the model of the 1963 Declaration on the Elimination of All Forms of Racial Discrimination (GA Res. 1904, XVIII), was the 1967 Declaration on the Elimination of All Forms of Discrimination against Women (GA Res. 2263, XXII). The principles of the latter declaration were the basis for the similarly named Convention on the Elimination of All Forms of Discrimination against Women (CEDAW), adopted more than ten years later, in 1979, which was in fact the first international treaty to address discrimination against women specifically and separately from other types of discrimination.

The early 1970s thus marks the end of a first phase of UN policies toward women, dominated here as in other areas by the political priorities of the West, and thus by the promotion of equal rights for individuals, in contrast to the emphasis placed on social rights by Communist countries and to traditionalist opposition from Muslim and Catholic countries in the name of the patriarchal family. Subsequently, individual rights would lose their priority; notably, the battle for political rights, in particular, seemed to have run its course, since by 1970 most countries in the world had guaranteed equality to women, at least on paper, with regard to the right to vote and to stand for election (see *The World's Women, 1970–1990*).

Decolonialization and its aftermath brought new problems in terms of the needs of the great majority of Third World women. Concern with the requisite conditions for the exercise of rights became a priority. In the context of the new international economic order, policies toward women were integrated into the policies of the "Development Decades" initiated by the United Nations. A central place was given to economic and social policies, in order to encourage women's participation in development as active subjects and not merely as the beneficiaries of development—a trend that culminated in the United Nations Decade for Women (1975–85), in which 75 percent of the political actions for women aimed at their integration into socioeconomic development (E/1989/10, Population: Concise Report on the Monitoring of World Population Trends and Policies, with Special Emphasis on the Population Situation in the Least Developed Countries: Report of the Secretary General).

The Convention on the Elimination of All Forms of Discrimination Against Women (CEDAW)

The 1979 adoption of the Convention on the Elimination of All Forms of Discrimination Against Women represented a true synthesis of the policies of three decades. CEDAW called for the promotion of equality in human, civil, political, social, and economic rights and in rights to acquire, change, or retain nationality. The convention also provided for concrete commitments on the part of national governments in order to guarantee their practice (United Nations, DPI/929, 1988). A product of the encounter between the policy of equal individual rights and the more recent themes of the 1970s, the convention is often described as an international bill of rights for women; even today, it remains the highest international-level agreement concerning equal rights for women ever attained. For the first time, CEDAW defined discrimination against women:

> any distinction, exclusion or restriction made on the basis of sex which has the effect or purpose of impairing or nullifying the recognition, enjoyment or exercise by women, irrespective of their marital status, on a basis of equality of men and women, of human rights and fundamental freedoms in the political, economic, social, cultural, civil or any other field. (Art. 1)

By ratifying the convention, states commit themselves to incorporating the principle of equality between men and women into their constitution and all other legislative measures. Among other provisions, they also commit themselves to taking appropriate measures against the traffic in women and the exploitation of women, guaranteeing equality in marriage and in every aspect of family relationships, in education (Art. 10, taken from UNESCO's 1960 Convention against Discrimination in Education), in work relationships, and in social security (Art. 11). This last provision had been preceded only by certain conventions of the ILO, such as the Convention concerning Equal Remuneration for Men and Women Workers for Work of Equal Value (no. 100, 1951), the Convention concerning Discrimination in Respect of Employment and Occupation (no. 111, 1958), and by the EEC's directives of the 1970s. Women's right to equal access to, and equal opportunities in, political and public life at every level of government was also stipulated in those conventions and directives.

The Convention on the Elimination of All Forms of Discrimination against Women represented the first international compact that was not limited to merely safeguarding individual protection from discrimination, but also mandated, in Article 4.1, positive measures to promote real equality (the only precedent was a provision in a 1976 EEC directive that concerned only the workplace). In essence this meant recognizing that real inequalities constituted an obstacle to the equal exercise of individual rights. Guarantees of formal equality were no longer sufficient, since they left the real-world disparities intact: hence the necessity for special temporary measures, or "positive actions," as they were termed within the European institutions, to rebalance the conditions for the exercise of rights. The convention established the conditions of legitimacy and rules for interpretation: preferential treatment granted to an individual or a group of individuals by reason of sex would not constitute an act of discrimination and thus not contradict the general principle of sexual equality, provided that it operated in favor of women, who needed to catch up, that it was aimed at establishing real equality of opportunities and treatment, and that it was therefore understood as being an exceptional and temporary measure.

In this sense, CEDAW gave international legitimacy to positive action in all the sectors it addressed, including the institutions of political power and representation. Today, even in Europe, the convention still constitutes the only international legal basis for quota systems aimed at the advancement of women in political institutions. For the first time, an international agreement acknowledged that there is judicial value inherent in sexual difference—a premise that contradicts arguments for formal equality. Instead, sexual difference became the basis for an inequality of rights intended to overcome the real disadvantages resulting from sexual difference, creating a difficult balance with the fundamental principle of equality. Women thus came to be treated as disadvantaged group and, as such, they were included together with the young, the old, and the handicapped in the program of social development mandated for the Third Development Decade (Medium-Term Plan for the Period 1984–1989; A/37/6, 1982, chap. 21).

Ratification of CEDAW has proceeded slowly. In 1995 only 148 member states had ratified it, including the states of Central and Eastern Europe, Cuba, China, and Iraq, which had already ratified it at the end of the 1980s (*The World's Women, 1970–*

1990, Appendix II, and United Nations, *Human Development Report 1995*). The target date for its ratification by all member states was set back to 2000, but as of 2001 only 168 states had done so. The United States, which signed the convention in 1980, has still not ratified it. Furthermore, the convention remained so ineffective that at the 43rd Commission on the Status of Women, it was deemed necessary, in order to secure a means of monitoring its application, to approve a new, optional protocol for the convention. States signing the protocol agreed to recognize the commission's authority to adjudicate complaints filed by individuals or groups who had been victims of a violation of the rights guaranteed by the convention. Signatory states also agreed to take the commission's recommendations into account. For all its limitations, the convention remains the most important agreement of the Decade for Women, dedicated to the implementation of political programs adopted at the first two world conferences in Mexico City and Copenhagen.

The Conferences

Although the themes of equality, development, and peace to which the UN conferences were dedicated were not unrelated to the original and ongoing concerns of the Commission on the Status of Women, these notions were not concretized into a political program until the International Year of Women, in 1975, and with the action plan adopted by the Mexico City Conference, which was its culmination point. The two conferences insisted on the need for specific programs of positive action, to encourage women's participation as men's equal partners in the construction of socioeconomic development and peace, and the promotion of women's rights and corresponding obligations. The overall aim was to bring about an equitable sharing between the two sexes of rights and responsibilities in all areas, including the family (Declaration of Mexico on the Equality of Women and Their Contribution to Development and Peace and plans of action, United Nations, 1975; Program of Action for the Second Half of the United Nations Decade for Women, 1980).

The conferences contributed to showing the importance of women's active participation in development projects and the steadily growing recognition of the value of their labor—both paid and unpaid. Nevertheless, the theme of equality remained in a position of secondary importance in the political programs of the Decade for Women: only 8.5 percent of the measures to aid women adopted between 1975 and 1988 refer to it (E/1989/19, Cross-Organisational Program Analysis of the Activities of the United Nations System for the Advancement of Women: Report of the Secretary General).

The theme of equality was not to find its role again until the Nairobi Conference, as a part of efforts to rethink the interrelationships among equality, development, and peace. Starting with a disappointing assessment of the preceding programs, underscored by the critical contributions of political scientists and experts from the countries of the Southern Hemisphere, the final policy program outlined a development plan to be carried out through the year 2000. The plan stressed the central importance of juridical equality and achieving equality of opportunities,

both as an ultimate goal and as a tool for achieving development and peace, which can be attained only with the active participation of women (The Nairobi Forward-Looking Strategies for the Advancement of Women; AMB United Nations, 1986b). At the same time, the observation that specific programs for women, having remained marginal to the policies of the UN and the states, are only relatively effective, shifts the accent to the integration of the "women's dimension" into general policies, using the mainstreaming strategy that has been employed in the agendas of the European institutions in recent years. Finally, the Nairobi program initiated for the first time the strategy of empowerment as a premise for equality and as a fundamental condition for the success of policies on behalf of women. This strategy entailed giving power to women at every level of national and international decision making and in all public sectors, from politics to economics.

The Nairobi program marked the beginning of the present phase. The dynamics embedded in policies for equality and their potential for innovation are, in fact, far from being exhausted. This is proven by the fact that the action platform approved at the Fourth World Conference of Beijing in 1995 reconfirmed the same objectives. Due also to the contribution of feminists in these past few years (see especially the analyses of the network of women politicians and experts from the Southern Hemisphere, Development Alternatives with Women for a New Era [DAWNE]), the strategy of empowerment has even acquired a central role, to the point that the action platform approved in Beijing has become pivotal for policies to come.

The forward-looking strategies of Nairobi also have the merit of having granted, after years of decline, renewed importance to the defense of women's rights within the framework of human rights. This emphasis emerged most fully in the 1990s with the defense of human rights, undermined as never before by the calamities of war and religious fundamentalism, which at the end of the 20th century produced a new wave of violence against women (for example, wartime rapes) and, more generally, a backlash against the exercise and recognition of women's rights. This means that the problem of human rights has not only become central for women but is taking a radically new direction. The decisive moment came at the Second World Conference on Human Rights, held in Vienna in 1993.

At the Vienna Conference, it was affirmed that "the human rights of women and girls are an inalienable, integral, and indivisible part of universal human rights" (World Conference on Human Rights. The Vienna Declaration and Program of Action, June 1993, United Nations, New York, 1995). Never before had a declaration of worldwide importance recognized women's human rights as an integral part of universal human rights. Admittedly, like all such documents approved by conferences, the Vienna Declaration did not in and of itself create rights. It did, however, open the way for identifying specific rights-violations of which women are the victims, and for recognizing a new generation of sexually based human rights, namely women's sexual and reproductive rights. The declaration in effect recognized that sexual violence is incompatible with the principle of dignity of person and violates the human rights of women, and that forms of violence such as systematic rape, forced pregnancy and sexual slavery in wartime, as in the former Yugoslavia, are violations of international humanitarian laws.

The Declaration on the Elimination of Violence Against Women

The first results of this recognition have already been felt: the General Assembly of the UN adopted the Declaration on the Elimination of Violence Against Women in December 1993 (A Res. 48/104, 1993), the first universal legal instrument that specifically recognizes violence against women as a violation of human rights. This declaration, just like the Vienna Declaration—both of them products of strong pressures exerted by women's nongovernmental organizations—represents the result of a long feminist struggle to bring about recognition of all forms of sexual violence as a violation of the fundamental rights of the person. The Declaration on the Elimination of Violence against Women goes even further and extends the notion of sexual violence against women to include violence perpetrated within the family, thereby removing the issue of domestic violence from the purely private context to which it had always previously been relegated. These are first steps on the road to eliminating all forms of sexual violence against women. One must hope that from this starting point all the necessary consequences will follow in terms of civil, political, social, and cultural rights; for example, the granting of refugee status and the right to asylum to women who have fled from genital mutilation. In fact, in the final analysis, these forms of violence are born from the limited power women have over their sexual and procreative life, from their limited right to have control over their bodies, and from the consequently only partial development of their individuality. These rights continue to be denied to them and to be occulted within the context of the family unit in family-planning strategies—sometimes even with recourse to coercion—which have been the basis for the UN's demographic birth-control policies.

The Beijing World Conference on Women

Final recognition of women's sexual and reproductive rights in a political document of the UN was not to come until the 1995 World Conference on Women in Beijing. The policy program adopted at the International Conference on Population and Development held in Cairo in 1994 (United Nations, Report of the International Conference on Population and Development) had already recognized individual reproductive rights, that is, the equal right of men and women to free choice in matters of procreation; this marked a step forward from the emphasis traditionally placed on the rights of couples and family planning. But the policy platform approved in Beijing marked the first recognition that a woman's human rights include the right to control her sexuality, including sexual health and reproduction. Admittedly, the fact that legalization of abortion was left up to the discretion of each state was a strong limitation. The fact remains, however, that the right to determine one's sexuality was finally recognized as a part of women's human rights (United Nations, 1995, Art. 97). Governments that signed the platform committed themselves to recognizing politically and guaranteeing these rights, which are a basic condition for the exercise of women's rights and equal opportunities, and also demanded, to ensure these rights went into effect, as with other human rights,

that the full ramifications of women's rights be reflected in terms of civil, social, and cultural rights.

Women's rights to freedom of choice in matters of sexuality and reproduction, contraception, and abortion stand out from the universality of rights as rights specific to women. However, these rights are nevertheless the condition sine qua non for rights, such as the right to life, liberty, and respect for the dignity of the person, to be truly universal—that is, for these rights to allow women fully to realize their individuality as subjects under the law. The universality of fundamental rights guaranteed on the international level will not be achieved until it is extended to the entire human race, male and female, and until the catalogue of these rights has been extended to a new generation of human rights, centered on women's right to self-determination over their bodies as an integral part of universal human rights. The way has definitively been cleared by the Vienna Declaration and by the Beijing platform, which, through their radically new approach to human rights, emblematically synthesized the changes that occurred over half a century of international legislation.

The Council of Europe

Convention for the Protection of Human Rights and Fundamental Freedoms

In Europe it was the Council of Europe that translated the ideals of the UN's Universal Declaration of Human Rights into international institutional guarantees, through the Convention for the Protection of Human Rights and Fundamental Freedoms. Today the convention still remains the council's most important accomplishment and one of the major international legal acts in the area of human rights. In fact, it has proven to be most effective with regard to European countries' respect for the rights inscribed in the UN's Universal Declaration. This is why adhering to the convention is seen as a strict precondition for states seeking to become members of the council. In 2002, the 44 member states, including the three Baltic republics, had ratified the convention. It has thus acquired a pan-European scope.

The convention and its additional protocols guarantee civil and political rights; however, it does not contain provisions for social rights. Article 14 establishes that

[t]he enjoyment of the rights and freedoms set forth in this Convention shall be secured without discrimination on any ground such as sex, race, color, language, religion, political or other opinion, national or social origin, association with a national minority, property, birth or other status.

A product of its era, the convention forbids sexual discrimination as one among other forms discrimination, and then only with respect to the civil and political rights it guarantees. Its guarantees are therefore much more limited than the universal equality before the law ensured by Article 26 of the International Covenant on Civil and Political Rights.

By 1950, when the Convention for the Protection of Human Rights and Fundamental Freedoms was first adopted, equality of political rights had already been ensured for women of all Eastern and Western European countries, with the exceptions of only Greece, Cyprus, Switzerland, and Portugal (*The World's Women, 1970–1990*). Consequently, for the women citizens of the Western European countries that signed the convention (Belgium, Denmark, France, Federal Republic of Germany, Iceland, Ireland, Italy, Luxemburg, the Netherlands, Norway, Switzerland, Turkey, Great Britain and Northern Ireland, Greece, and Sweden), the convention actually represented only a guarantee against discriminations in civil rights, a problem that was very widespread, especially with regard to married women and in family law. Over the next two decades, as democratic constitutions were put into action, discrimination in civil rights, for the most part, gradually disappeared.

All democratic constitutions in Western Europe, including, from the 1970s on, those of the southern European countries, guarantee the general principle of equality of all citizens in the eyes of the law, reinforced by the prohibition of sexual discrimination (with the exception of the United Kingdom, which does not have a constitution in the traditional sense of the word, and of Luxemburg, whose Constitution does not mention this type of equality, although a text adopted in 1956 recognizes the equal status of men and women). In several cases (notably Greece, Ireland, Italy, Portugal, Spain, Sweden, and Turkey), constitutional measures also provided for specific guarantees of sexual nondiscrimination in economic, social, and cultural rights.

It can be said that by the 1970s, formal equality of civil and political rights had essentially been achieved for women citizens of the countries of Western Europe. It was above all only in the realm of social rights, which the convention did not touch upon, that some forms of discrimination continued to exist in the law. Consequently, the antidiscriminatory guarantees established in Article 14 became altogether insufficient. This insufficiency was aggravated by the limited number of sexual discrimination cases against the member states that the European Court of Justice was prepared to consider. Further, there was a discernible resemblance between the contents of the court's judgments and those handed down by national tribunals.

In light of the inadequacy of the protection offered by Article 14 cited above, the Council of Europe's Committee for Equality (CDEG) began in the 1980s to advocate a proposal—later made the object of a recommendation by the Parliamentary Assembly to the Ministerial Committee—of an additional protocol to the convention recognizing the principle of equal rights for men and women as a fundamental human right. This principle would be added to the list of those basic rights, ceasing to be merely a subsidiary condition of nondiscrimination in the enjoyment of rights and becoming instead the basis for equality in every area of law (Recommendation 1229, 1994).

Despite its present limitations, Article 14 of the convention and the possibility of appeal to the Court of Strasbourg serve to guarantee equality in civil rights for women of the former European Communist states (which joined the Council of Europe relatively recently) and by extension for women of the other states in that region, during the process of elaboration of the new democratic constitutions, for it is the case that the new constitutions guarantee equality for everyone before the law and forbid sexual discrimination in most cases. Nevertheless, the actual enjoyment of equality continues to be limited because of the lack of coherent standards embodying these constitutional guarantees.

The European Social Charter

In so far as guarantees against sexual discrimination in social rights are concerned, the European Social Charter (Turin, 18 November 1961) represented only a first step toward filling the gap the convention had left open. It contained only one measure: anticipated by the Convention of the International Labor Organization of 1951 and by Article 119 of the founding Treaty Establishing the European Community of 1957, it stipulated women's right to equal pay for work of equal value, thus ensuring a broader equality than the right of equal pay for the same work that was already recognized by the EEC.

Not until 1988 did the Council of Europe set forth guarantees of equality in social rights with the adoption of an additional protocol to the European Social Charter (Strasbourg, 5 May 1988)—a considerable delay relative to the norms of the EEC, to the UN Convention of 1979, already ratified by the majority of European countries, and to most national legislation. Even in May 1995, this protocol had been ratified only by five of the 34 member states: Italy, the Netherlands, Sweden, Finland, and Norway. At the end of 2002, of the 44 member states of the Council of Europe, 32 had signed the European Social Charter; of these signatories, 25 had ratified the charter and seven had not. The charter stipulated the right to equal opportunity and treatment in matters of employment and profession and the adoption of "specific measures aimed at remedying actual inequalities," but also the possibility of excluding application of the principle of equality in matters relating to social security, unemployment benefits, and benefits for senior citizens and surviving spouses. By this time, these measures had already rendered moot in the EEC countries by a stricter Community law establishing antidiscriminatory guarantees that were stronger: superior to those of the charter in that they also targeted indirect discrimination. In the former Eastern bloc countries, by contrast, the charter and protocol, once ratified, could offer better guarantees than those resulting from the ratification of the UN Convention of 1979. This might help counter the current trend in these countries, with the liberalization of the market, toward reintroducing not only indirect forms of discrimination (which had already flourished under real socialism), but also forms of direct discrimination, notably in the area of social rights.

The Council of Europe also intervened to eliminate obstacles to equality within several areas of its competence, through resolutions and recommendations of the Committee of Ministers concerning equality in work, flexibility in retirement age, and violence within the family. National governments, however, have totally disregarded their obligations arising from these decisions.

After the Nairobi Conference of 1985 in particular, the council's activity became more dynamic, directed essentially toward strategies for the year 2000. The issue of equality between men and women took on a political importance that had been unprecedented in the council's history, as the convocation of the three interministerial European conferences on this theme has shown. These conferences targeted a few main objectives: increasing women's presence at every decision-making level in elected assemblies and in the management of political power (Strasbourg, 1986); promoting positive action programs and national structures to realize effective equality and to integrate policies for women across different sectors (Vienna, 1989); and eliminating violence against women (Rome, 1993).

Political Representation and Equality: The Quota System and Parity

Since 1986 strategies for realizing equality in decision-making procedures and in political life have thus occupied a central place, in accordance with EEC initiatives in these areas. The intervention of European institutions is based on the fact that women are generally underrepresented in elected assemblies and in government bodies everywhere in Western Europe, proving the inadequacy of formal equality in political rights to bring about an equal, or at least balanced, distribution of political power.

In Western Europe, beginning in the first half of the 1980s, under strong pressure both from within the European institutions and, at the national level, from women's groups connected with the political parties (German Greens and Social-Democrats, Swedish Social-Democrats, the Socialist People's Party in Denmark, and the Democratic Party of the Left [successor party to the Italian Communist Party] in Italy) the lack of political representation by women was addressed through quota systems. In order to rebalance the conditions for exercising political rights, the European organizations recommended that governments adopt transitional positive action programs aimed at promoting women at all leadership levels in public institutions. Specifically, they recommended policies of encouragement and consciousness-raising within political parties so that they would voluntarily adopt measures (quotas, parity thresholds, or other quantitative target levels for women's representation) to support the candidacies of women in their internal structures and on their electoral lists.

In the view of women representatives in the European institutions, the transitional adoption of quotas was a means toward the strategic goal of a numerically balanced representation of both sexes in all political institutions. That was what had been conceptualized, thanks especially to the work of an expert women's group created ad hoc by the Council of Europe's Committee for Equality, through the formula of "parity democracy." Such a strategy, controversial even within the committee, which decided only in the 1980s to adopt the idea, aimed to achieve equal presence of men and women in political and administrative organizations and elected assemblies: egalitarian management of democracy through power sharing and a true partnership of the two sexes throughout the democratic process. As a precondition for the principle of equality to be integrated in every institution and every social structure, and thus to reduce the gap that existed in all European democracies between de jure and de facto equality, "parity democracy" would complete the building of "true democracy" by achieving the political representation of all citizens of both sexes, at which stage the adoption of quotas would finally lose its raison d'être.

The strategy of "parity democracy" sought to actualize women's acquisition of the right to equal representation in assemblies elected by universal suffrage. Everywhere in Europe this strategy encountered difficulties of a constitutional order, for it inevitably entailed profound changes in constitutions and in the present concept of representative democracy. Thus, the debate on parity democracy and on the means of its attainment remains open between women representing member nations and women experts of the European institutions, and several proposals for legislative and constitutional reform are presently under discussion. Some ask that the principle of "equality between men and women" be treated "as one of the constitutional elements of the political system, on the same grounds as universal suffrage, the separation of powers, etc." Others ask that the principle of parity be written into national constitutions, side by side with equal rights (European Conference on Equality and Democracy, Strasbourg, February 1995). This would mean that parity—that is, the equal sharing between the sexes of rights and responsibilities, within the family as well as in society as a whole—would constitute a positive legal principle capable of moving beyond the simple negative perspective of the prohibition of discrimination. Constructed as a legal principle, parity would provide a legal foundation for political representation, fostering the achievement of parity democracy through the practice of quotas.

It is not easy to foresee the future developments of proposals of this type, given that they remain controversial among the elected women and women experts from different nations, as was apparent at the same Conference of Strasbourg. A number of these women continue to oppose such a strategy for achieving parity political representation by law, which they see only as an objective for the future, realizable only through voluntary quota systems that parties should write into their statutes. More important still for future developments, the majority of the national governments continue to look toward the latter type of measure, which in fact constituted the only form quota systems to have been effectively implemented in continental Europe during the 1980s, and, more recently, in the Mediterranean countries.

The European organizations have played an important role in this development by sensitizing national political cultures to the contradiction between the already accomplished feminization of society, on the one hand, and its lack of political representation on the other. Even so, while balancing women's numerical political representation is without a doubt a precondition for the implementation of policies promoting women's rights, it is not enough. In the strategy of quotas and parity democracy the dominant viewpoint remains quantitative rather than qualitative. It does not contain programs that are qualitatively different in terms of the recognition and the promotion of women's rights or of overcoming the sexual division of work. In fact, there is no guarantee that elected women will not, in turn, conform to the existing idea of political representation as a neutral expression of the will of citizens, with the very concept of the citizen taken as an abstraction and emptied of sexual definition.

Moreover, these strategies do not guarantee new relationships between elected women and the people they represent. The relatively low level of women's participation in representative bodies is far from being merely the result of obstacles, a lagging behind of women, or of limitations in their taking public responsibility. It could equally well be an effect of the search for new bases of democracy and political action capable of modifying relations in the social sphere. Moreover, the fact that quotas are not sufficient for the progress of the majority of women is a lesson that might be learned from the Scandinavian experience (Sweden in the 1980s was the world leader in employment segregation).

Finally, the strategies of quotas and parity democracy are based on the idea that women are a social group with specific interests and not merely half of the human race, inevitably fissured by divergent interests within it. If women represent one interest group among other interest groups, the current demand for political power in women's and feminist movements tends, in turn, to be channeled toward a corporatist model.

The fact remains that the strategy of quotas and the debate on parity democracy will inevitably occupy a place of honor in the European institutional politics of the 21st century, supported, as they are, by a variety of pan-European pressure groups that represent the interests of women charged with responsibilities in the political and institutional apparatus and the interests of women from the privileged social classes. In the shorter term, it is necessary above all else that the additional protocol to the European Social Charter be approved, so that the Council of Europe can resume its historically central role linked to the Convention for the Protection of Human Rights and Fundamental Freedoms and to its safeguarding of equal rights for women. This is all the more important in light of the presence of the former Communist countries and the possible acceptance of the convention itself by the European Union.

The European Economic Community/ European Union

With the Treaty of Maastricht (1992), the European Union committed itself to protecting the fundamental rights guaranteed by the Convention for the Protection of Human Rights and Fundamental Freedoms. This represented enormous progress, and not only from the point of view of the protection of women's rights. Indeed, even today the Community has no standard that recognizes the equal rights of the sexes as a fundamental human right, nor one that guarantees the equality of all before the law. Thus, the right to sexual nondiscrimination as a fundamental human right has a very weak status in the legal order of the Community, being based only on the jurisprudence of the European Court of Justice (judgment rendered on 15 June 1978, *Defrenne v. Sabena*, case 149/77, Defrenne III, Belgium).

Given the absence of a general statute guaranteeing equality of the sexes, the various specific and concrete aspects of that principle have barely gained a place among the Community's legal competencies. Community norms in matters of male-female equality are limited to the right to work. But since the equality of workers is not tied to a general principle of sexual equality, Community law in this matter has developed through successive extensions to address equal pay, equal treatment, and equal opportunity. In the evolution of legislation prior to the Treaty of Maastricht, these three key principles correspond to a precise normative hierarchy.

In fact, it is the agreement on social policy annexed to the Treaty of Maastricht that recognizes equal treatment and equal opportunity, thus establishing the basis of the integration of these principles into the treaty itself. Prior to that time, the principle of equal opportunity had been legally grounded only in a vague mention in a Community directive and a nonbinding recommendation, while equal treatment had been guaranteed by directives whose application depended on corresponding legislative measures within member states. Only equal pay had been guaranteed by a provision in the founding treaty of the Community (the Treaty of Rome), which the European Court of Justice had recognized as capable of directly creating individual rights both with regard to states and to private persons, without the need for national measures to activate such rights (judgment rendered on 8 April 1976, *Defrenne v. Sabena*, case 23/75).

The Pioneering Role of the Community's Jurisprudence

The founding treaty had, indeed, established equal pay for equal work in Article 119. This was a pioneering measure, since, at the time, the pursuit of equal pay in European countries through trade unions and legal channels had only just begun. Following the liberal philosophy of the founding fathers, the treaty had been designed to prevent women's labor from impeding the workings of free competition in the common market. This article, however, remained unenforced by member states until, in the above-referenced judgment of 1976, the court recognized it as directly effective, thus delivering a true shock to governments and private enterprise in member states. In this judgment, the court stressed the principle that equal pay related not only to economic ends, but also to the goal of "equalization in progress" of living and working conditions of citizens of the member states, in accordance with an article of the treaty.

With this judgment, and to an even greater degree with the subsequent judgment of 1978, which recognized the right to sexual nondiscrimination as a fundamental human right, the Court's jurisprudence opened up a wide-ranging interpretation of Article 119, which became one of the driving forces in progress in legislation on equality. The political climate of the 1970s was favorable to this evolution: healthy economic conditions and pressure from social and women's movements made these years into a very fertile time for the Community's social policy. This became concrete in the first social action program of 1974, which produced the three principal directives on the equality of men and women in the workplace.

The Directives

A 1968 report found that the first cause of salary differences lay in the undervaluation of traditionally female forms of work and in employment segregation. On that basis, the directive of 1975 (75/117) introduced the principle of equal pay for work of equal value, taking into account the possibility of comparing radically different kinds of work and implicitly extending the prohibition of remunerative discrimination to cover forms of indirect discrimination. Thus it became illegal not only to categorize male and female work in a directly discriminatory manner, but also to draw up any list of professional staff based on criteria that appeared to be neutral but were indirectly discriminatory. Still, the Community had not yet strictly defined either criteria of evaluation and professional classification that would not be discriminatory, or the controversial notion of "work of equal value." Therefore, the only reference available was the jurisprudence of the European Court of Justice, though this was in fact very extensive (jurisprudence cited at length in the Memorandum Project on Equal Pay for Work of Equal Value of 1994, COM, 94, 6 def.).

Since equal pay without equal treatment is only effective in a very limited way, a second directive was approved in 1976 that prohibited all direct and indirect discrimination in access to and conditions of work (76/207). It permitted exceptions only in relation to maternity protection and those activities in which biological sex is a determining factor. A veritable innovation in the legal landscape of the member states was the explicit prohibition of indirect discrimination, which widened the dimension of explicit equality to include the prohibition of forms of real discrimination.

There, too, the directive provided no definitions. Ten years later, after many ambiguities, the court fixed the essential points (judgment rendered on 13 May 1986, *Billa Kaufhaus GmbH v. Karin Weber von Hartz* case 170/84, Germany). Inspired by the American notion of "disparate impact," analogous to that of indirect discrimination in English law (Sex Discrimination Act, 1975), the Court of Justice identified as indirectly discriminatory any practice that had the effect of actual disadvantage for a disproportionate number of workers of one sex. Such a practice is legitimate only if its agent can prove that his behavior derives from objectively justified factors that have nothing to do with sexual discrimination. Thus, indirect discrimination implies weighing legitimately pursued objectives against the fundamental right of not being discriminated against, a circumstance that also makes indirect discrimination difficult to prove. Depending on the weight accorded to what are considered to be legitimate justifications, the notion of indirect discrimination can be narrowed to coincide with that of direct discrimination, as the decisions of national judges often show.

The directive also forced states to revise their protective legislation, unless the reasons inspiring such laws were still considered to be justified. Restrictions of access to employment had to be abolished and, in addition, special laws relative to women's work had to be either eliminated or else extended to all workers, with the exception of protective maternity measures (Commission of European Communities, Communication, COM, 87, 105). This position was confirmed by the court in a judgment against the French government for prohibiting women from working at night (25 July 1991, case C, 345/89, Stoeckel), which opened the door to the liberalization of working hours for women in other countries of the Community (something already accomplished in England, for example).

The last directive approved in the 1970s (79/7) prohibited direct and indirect discrimination in the legal administration of social security. It was integrated into a 1986 directive that extends the same prohibition to conventional professional regulations (86/378). The two directives are valid only for the working population and permit exceptions to equal provision in family benefits and in the regulation of pension reversion, in member states' ability to set different retirement ages and benefits, and to make additional provisions for women in the regulation of pensions, old-age benefits, or disability benefits. In this way, a uniform retirement age appeared to have been postponed to an indeterminate date until the rendering of a court judgment that included, within provisions for equal pay, a specific retirement age for conventional professional regulations applying to dependent workers (17 May 1990, case 262/88, *Barber vs / Guardian*

Royal Exchange Insurance Group, England). The economic effects of this decision were so destabilizing that an ad hoc protocol to Article 199, expressly excluding retirement rights established prior to the judgment from the principle of equality, was appended to the Treaty of Maastricht.

The EEC Commission, in accordance with the court's notion of indirect discrimination, has legitimized dependent spouses' rights to benefits only to the extent of guaranteeing a minimum subsistence income for family units. But this legal justification allowed the national systems to ignore the indirect discrimination linked to the notion of the worker with a dependent spouse, given the greater economic dependence of the woman. Forms of direct discrimination (in favor of the husband) have thus been replaced by indirect equivalents, using the gender-neutral expression "worker with dependent spouse": in fact, these two directives in reality preserve traditional family roles, both by being limited to the working population and by the exceptions to equal rights they permit.

The 1980s also saw the approval of a directive on independent work (86/613), which, in rather vague terms and with many omissions, established member states' obligation to formally grant "employed" status to millions of women working in family enterprises and to provide them with maternity protection.

Impact on National Legislation

The 1980s were marked by economic difficulties and resistance to any social regulation on the part of employers' organizations, which were championed by the Conservative British government. With its veto, Britain blocked three directives proposed during those years and still not approved today, covering the regulation of part-time work, the reversal of the burden of proof of discrimination, and parental leave. Only on the last issue was a recommendation approved in 1992 (92/241), inviting member states to adopt various forms of flexible leaves, including paternity leave.

Legislative delays such as these are serious, given the spread and feminization everywhere in Europe of so-called atypical work and part-time work (women made up 83 percent of the part-time workforce in the European Community in the early 1990s). Thus, these kinds of work continue to be subject to different regulations in different nations or to be completely deregulated, as in Britain. One needs only to recall that, in most national legal systems, full participation in a social security system depends on holding a full-time job and that, even in cases of half-time work, the right to maternity protection is reduced. Part-time work represents a host of forms of indirect discrimination with respect to access to additional payments, career opportunities, and even hourly wages; it is in the process of becoming the most threatening form of employment segregation. The dramatic increase in women's share in the part-time labor market has actually reduced the percentage of women workers that is effectively covered by principles of equality; this situation, in turn, undermines the effectiveness those principles themselves.

The 1980s saw a clear global weakening of the Community's legislative initiative in matters of equality, accompanied by corresponding resistance at national levels to the implementation of EU norms, with the result that the implementation of this process has not been completed even today. Sometimes national laws were formulated in an adequate manner only after states had been negligent and had been condemned by the European Court of Justice. That situation has only added to the ambiguities of Community norms, and results in a purely formal respect for those norms, as long as the tools for their implementation are not put in place. Of course, it is impossible to evaluate the impact of the Community's legislation in the same terms in all countries, some of which already had laws governing equal pay and treatment, independently of Community norms. This is the case, for example, in the Netherlands and Ireland, where the directive on equal pay did not have a very great influence while, on the other hand, directives on social security systems had a strong impact.

Today, the laws of the member states have extended the principle of equal pay to cover work of equal value. Nevertheless, they have not adopted the same criteria concerning the definition of pay, the subjective implications of equality, the notion of equivalent work, and nondiscriminatory frameworks of professional categorization, leaving all these issues to be settled on an autonomous basis.

In continental Europe, legal actions have been rare and, for the most part, limited to issues concerning the comparability of practically identical activities. Judges have had few occasions to address the problem of equivalent work, and further, they have been reluctant to rule against indirect discrimination in pay. That is why practically all jurisprudence in these matters has stemmed from cases brought in Ireland, Britain, and to a lesser degree, Denmark and the Netherlands. But Irish and British judges have often accepted criteria so favorable to employers that they ended up undermining the very notion of indirect pay-discrimination.

Since in every country equal pay had been promoted essentially through legal and judicial channels, labor union intervention relating to collective contracts has not been able to eliminate these limitations. On the contrary, unions have frequently manifested resistance to the principle of equality, due to obsolete systems of job classification and the defense of the status quo in job hierarchies on the part of those in the strongest positions. The incorporation of the equal pay directive into national laws has led to the elimination of some forms of direct discrimination, such as the different professional classifications based on gender, and certain blatant forms of indirect discrimination, such as those linked to the classification of heavy work and light work, as was widespread in Germany until the 1970s. But forms of indirect discrimination implicit in job-classification systems have proven to be much more resistant, in terms of the distinguishing the elements chosen—flexibility, mobility, professional training, qualifications, seniority, and so forth—and the relative weight assigned to these factors. In work contracts and in legal judgments, certain so-called feminine abilities—such as dexterity, speed—are underappreciated or undervalued as compared to so-called masculine qualities such as strength or regional mobility. In fact, there are no objective parameters for measuring the equivalence of work: comparison depends on the criteria used, and is thereby necessarily sensitive to sexual prejudices. The superiority of professional categories in which men dominate in terms of union strength and the preponderance of men in negotiating structures have entailed and still entail an overvaluation of the work of men.

In that sense, it is the very notion of "work of equal value," considered to be objective by the theories of human capital, that reveals both its theoretical and practical limitations, because techniques for assessing comparable worth are very rarely applicable to forms of work that are by nature not analogous. All in all, the principle of equal value has proven to be fairly ineffective in the struggle against inequalities in pay, which are rooted in job segregation and the consequent tendencies toward forms of discrimination in treatment.

The adjustment in national laws to harmonize with the directive on equal treatment has served to put a brake on the most blatant forms of direct discrimination, such as references to sex in job advertising and descriptions, or discrimination against married or pregnant women. But indirect discrimination continues to be widespread in many forms and, in fact, excludes women from certain occupations while concentrating them in others. This persistence is due not only to the problems of verifying forms of indirect discrimination, but also to the deficiency of national laws, which in some cases have forbidden indirect discrimination only belatedly (as in Italy, where Law 125 on the "Positive actions for the realization of parity between men and women in work" dates from only 1991). In other cases, national legislation forbidding indirect discrimination did not provide an accompanying definition of forms of discrimination (as in Spain, France, and Germany), and in still other cases national laws defined indirect discrimination only in connection with civil and family status.

Thus, the revision of antidiscriminatory legislation has progressed only very slowly, resulting in dissimilar situations in different states (Commission of the European Communities, COM/87/105). Today one can consider this revision completed, at least in its main features: indisputably, it has had positive effects, but it has also been accompanied by a lowering in the level of protection for working women.

The alteration of national laws to comply with Community directives for social security, which involve significant public expenditure, has been extraordinarily slow, being implemented piecemeal through ad hoc measures except in France, Germany, Denmark, and Italy. The directive on legal regimes has had a notable effect improving national laws by attacking forms of direct discrimination in work with regard to married women and women living with a male partner outside of wedlock (for example, the automatic payment of benefits obtained by either one of the spouses to the head of the family only, or unemployment benefits that are lower for married women). With regard to forms of indirect discrimination, on the other hand, the directive has only managed to mitigate them. A trend toward reintroducing indirect discrimination has even been noted, since pressures to reduce social security benefits have provoked a tendency to refer once again to family income as the basis for allocating social benefits.

The Treaty of Amsterdam

The rise, after Maastricht, of a political culture that sacrificed social policy in order to preserve economic competitiveness, accelerated the liberal transformation of national social systems and drove women more and more toward part-time employment (85 percent of which was done by women in Europe in the mid

1990s) or positions that offered no job security. So the 1996 recommendation on the participation of women at decision-making levels, while it takes a request for parity literally, actually hides, beneath its facile rhetoric of a purely numerical parity, the stagnation of women's rights, which has a great deal to do with the unpopularity of the European Union. Women's organizations thus concentrated their efforts on the revision of the Maastricht Treaty, aiming to establish the foundations of social reform that Maastricht had denied. They took a leading role in dozens of intergovernmental conferences and meetings of all kinds that the European Union encouraged during the negotiation of the treaty. The disappointment was all the greater when it became clear that the reforms introduced were limited in scope and would thus have limited real impact.

The Treaty of Amsterdam, signed on 2 October 1997, in fact specifies in Articles 2 and 3 that the elimination of inequalities and the promotion of equality between men and women are essential tasks for Community action. However, this is a vague description of a mission, lacking clear indications either of its legal force or the actual means by which it would be carried out. It is true that the treaty entrusted to the Council of Europe the adoption of measures necessary to combat all discrimination based on sex, race, or ethnic origin, religion or beliefs, handicap, age, or sexual orientation (Art. 6). The Amsterdam treaty also granted the possibility of taking sanctions against member states responsible for such discrimination. However, it made this initiative subject to a unanimous vote, a provision that had already served to block political action in the past. It also extended Article 119, on the equality of economic treatment of the sexes in the workplace and on EU competency in this realm, by the inclusion of equal opportunity and employment. Nevertheless, the treaty neglected sectors that were quite essential, such as professional training or social protection. While there is thus cause to rejoice at having advanced beyond purely formal equality, there is also room for regret that this progress remained very limited and restricted to antidiscriminatory guarantees that are unrelated to the fundamental rights guaranteed by the treaty. The most promising aspect is the extension of the European Parliament's legislative powers with regard to social policy, which could be the starting point for a new legislative dynamics. However, we are still far from the objective of a European constitution, the source of a new citizenship and new rights.

Inadequate Individual Guarantees and Promotion of Positive Action

On the whole, the Community directives have had a catalytic effect on the laws of member states, in the sense of promoting stronger individual guarantees against forms of direct discrimination. But these individual guarantees do not touch upon indirect discrimination; they apply only to those forms of behavior that have a very visible negative impact on women's work, and not to obstacles inherent in social structures. The Community has shown itself to be aware of the inadequacy of individual guarantees. The directive on equal treatment already declared its intention not "to prejudice measures targeting the promotion of equal opportunity for men and women, notably by remedying actual disparities" (Art. 2.4). That is the first time that the promotion

of positive action was envisaged on an international level; the UN's 1979 Convention to Eliminate All Forms of Discrimination Against Women, as we have seen, was to confirm its legitimacy. But the structure outlined by the Community's norms remained rather weak on this issue: it included only another very cautious and vague recommendation (635, 13/12/1984) and was limited to suggesting the adoption of legal means of counterbalancing for women's disadvantage in the work place. It did not, however, indicate any precise model of positive action (voluntary, obligatory, or both), nor any specific system of promotion, leaving this to the discretion of the member states.

In this ambiguous situation, the most widely used concept of positive action corresponds to a justified and temporary adjustment of the fundamental right to nondiscrimination, in the sense of a measure of alleviation of actual disparities that limit women's possibilities in certain specific areas: access to professional training and work, working conditions, and social security. Positive action is conceived as a complement to antidiscriminatory measures and provisions for equal treatment (Commission of European Communities, 1988). Since it acts on negative effects produced by social structures, old discriminatory practices, or in general on various behaviors not identifiable as illegal, positive action is aimed less at providing women with jobs or careers than at rebalancing the opportunities for women workers at the outset, unlike what happens in forms of so-called reverse discrimination, such as affirmative action measures in the United States or the quota system in Sweden. Rather, the Community's positive action measures have the quality of social policy programs, of strategies for changing the organization and management of work in such a way as to eliminate the obstacles women encounter. In some states, instances of reverse discrimination even come up against specific legal prohibitions, such as the British Sex Discrimination Act, Irish law, and even, in the case of Germany, Article 3 of that nation's Constitution.

The legal framework in which positive action is situated varies from state to state. In some cases, such as Spain and Portugal, positive action measures are simply the object of political commitments. Their translation into legal acts runs up against states' reluctance to recognize the legitimacy of positive action measures that put constraints on business. The result is that the most widespread model is that of voluntary and consensual positive action measures, left up to the negotiation between social agents to whom falls the task of defining their character and means of actualization. Certain legal systems, such as those of France and Italy, also permit exceptions to the strictly voluntary character of positive action programs in the private sector by specifying that in some cases of discrimination, a court may force an employer to develop a positive action program in order to eliminate the discrimination in question. For the public sector, legal systems such as those of Italy and Belgium make positive action programs mandatory.

The inadequacy of Community norms in the area of positive action has been only partially counterbalanced by the promotion policy of the Commission of European Communities, which in the 1980s and 1990s ran three action programs setting guidelines for member states. These guidelines recommend interventions to break down structural obstacles to equal opportunity on the side of the demand for work, as well as the supply of work. The commission has also provided partial financing for a whole series of positive action programs.

With the help of networks of experts (composed of both men and women)—nine networks, including the IRIS network, which is devoted to professional training, another network dedicated to childhood issues, and still another called Positive Action in the Private Sector—the Community has directly cofinanced a group of positive action programs to combat professional segregation. These are essentially centered on professional training and requalification in traditionally male activities and sectors linked to new technologies. The emphasis on professional training in "male" work, in jointly financed programs as well as in those recommended to member states, contributes neither to revalorizing women's professional abilities nor to combating the stereotypical image of women's work, which continues to be synonymous with less qualified work. On the contrary, the Community has not encouraged positive action measures to increase valorization of women's professional competence.

In the sector of childhood services, the Community's interventions are notable only for their inadequacies. Lacking financial support, the network designed for this purpose has only been able to make states and businesses aware of the advantages of flexibility in work schedules and the rhythm of employment over a lifetime in order to better reconcile working life with child care—hence the need for parental leaves and programs for career breaks. Not until the 1990s, with the project New Opportunity for Women (NOW), did it become possible also to use structural funds for childcare resources (Commission of European Communities, 90/C327/04 and 94/C 180/10). But once again, despite its early grand ambitions and because of its meager resources (120 million euros for the 12 countries for the first three years, 1990–1993; that amount tripled for the period 1994–1999), NOW ended up in a series of rather uninspired training projects. On the whole, these jointly financed positive action programs amounted to series of pilot projects on a minimal scale that sought to identify possible multiplying effects, with the aim of offering models and financial stimuli to member states.

Also of modest overall scale were the specific action programs jointly financed by the European Social Fund (ESF), even after its reform of 1989. Here, the "women's dimension" was taken into account only within the framework of measures for disadvantaged categories such as immigrants or persons with disabilities, and then only within the setting of the struggle against long-term and youth unemployment. For this reason, until the reforms of 1993, the ESF only cofinanced specific professional training programs connected to traditionally "male" activities or work relating to new technologies: in 1990 approximately 50,000 unemployed women from the total of 12 participating countries benefited from these actions. Far greater, on the other hand, was the number of unemployed women who benefited from the mixed programs cofinanced by the ESF: in 1990, approximately 900,000 women. But these programs frequently replicated the discriminatory characteristics of the labor markets, offering women a less diversified and less qualified professional training than men and inferior guarantees of employment.

Unlike the mixed interventions of the ESF, the cofinanced positive action programs taken as a whole no doubt had a limited impact on national labor policies. On the other hand, they did provide an impetus and an institutional stimulus for national equal opportunity policies. This role was especially evident in the Mediterranean countries, where the programs have only been put into action in recent years—while other nations had already set up such policies even before the Community's intervention. Despite the disparities among member states, it may be generally said that these policies have not gone beyond fragmentary programs with specific and time-limited objectives. With the exception of Denmark, government support has been weak and has lacked a true strategy.

If, in the protected and feminized sector of public employment, positive action programs have become more developed, in the private sector the results have been fairly meager. A survey, carried out by the Community in 1990 over a sampling of 2,700 companies, received only 346 responses to the questionnaire, of which only 28.2 percent were participating in a positive action program (Commission of European Communities, 1990, V/587/91 EN). Encouragement on the part of member states has been weak, and even with financial assistance, businesses were not inclined to institute programs that would not fit into their human-resources management strategies. In substance, plans for professional development or flexible hours that presented an advantage for solving a company's problems with limited duration and objectives have been implemented, but the measures in such plans are intended to end once a company's problems have been solved (Commission of European Communities, V/1604/92 EN).

These forms of positive action did not aim to equalize access to specific occupations or, for that matter, to increase the valorization of women's professional qualities; nor did they aim, in the medium term, to modify aspects of productive organization that have a negative impact on women's labor. On the whole, national equal opportunity policies have not had any significant effect, either in terms of support for employment, given the governments' hostility to encouraging preferential recruiting, or against work segregation. All in all, equal opportunity policies have amounted to no more than a project to support women in the labor market by increasing their level of qualification and by pressing for a more flexible management of working hours and family responsibilities for women and men, with a less unfair and more modern sexual division of labor in view.

However, this modernization project, affirmed in the 1994 White Paper on social policy (Chap. 5), met with certain obstacles: a lack of willingness on the part of the governments to invest public money in the initiative, the trend toward reduced social spending, and resistance on the part of leadership groups to accepting to new restrictions on business practices. The whole of the Community's social policy is suffering from this situation. The objective of creating a base for social rights with the Community charter of fundamental social rights was defeated in 1989, when the charter was adopted only in the form of a solemn declaration unsupported by a Community social policy, which remained strictly subordinate to the demands of the market. In the context of the ever more competitive single market and under the pressure to reduce public indebtedness, this dimension of social policy has become so imperious that it sometimes even threatens to overturn the entire corpus of existing guarantees. One can read in this light the directive on the health of pregnant women at work, approved in 1992 (92/85/EEC), which likens maternity to an illness, making it subject to the same benefits. With respect to the duration of maternity leave (14 weeks, of which at least 2 weeks are obligatory), the directive was regressive compared to existing levels of protection in most of the member states. It improved conditions only for women in Portugal and Britain (for maternity leave entitlements prior to the directive, see Commission of European Communities, V/587/91 EN, Appendix II). Thus, the directive tends to homogenize the national laws toward inferior levels of protection, in open contradiction with the "equalization in progress" that is primary among the goals of the Community.

Article 6 of the agreement on social policy concluded between 11 member states of the European Community seems to be situated in a similarly retrograde perspective. This agreement is attached to the protocol on social policy, itself an annex to the treaty establishing the European Community. Each member state guarantees the application of the principle of equal pay for male and female workers for equal work (Art. 6.1), but a member state cannot be prevented from maintaining or adopting measures that that offer specific advantages designed to facilitate the practice of a professional activity by women or to prevent or compensate for disadvantages in their professional career (Art. 6.3). One wonders what was being legitimized here: the small number of positive action programs in the area of compensation, or simply discrimination against women? The measure, destined to remain obscure in its meaning until such time as the European Court of Justice gives it an interpretation, departs from explicit equality and by that very fact hints at forms of guardianship that could put the entire egalitarian legal corpus back under discussion.

In the final analysis, it may be feared that the standards of the 1990s do not give hope of positive developments in the near future. In the relentless competition of the single market, what is becoming ever clearer is the intrinsic conflict in the reasons that have guided the whole evolution of Community norms, between the need to create rules for all employers that will prevent forms of social "dumping," and, on the other hand, the promotion of equality as an integral part of the social progress that is ostensibly among the goals of the Community.

Conclusions: The Road to Equality

The world has changed since the mid 20th century. Worldwide, women have acquired unprecedented social clout, and the policies of international institutions have undergone changes of historic scope, their very evolution being the fruit of the political influence and the strength of the pressure exerted by women's and feminist organizations. From the nongovernmental organizations represented at the UN to the lobbies acting within the European institutions, a whole series of strategies has been mobilized that have had a growing influence on international policies.

The UN has played a leading role in the area of human rights: by treating these rights globally, it has helped to overcome the fragmented character of policies affecting women. In turn, that role has had repercussions on socioeconomic research, enabling a reformulation of the framework of analysis. Thus, the thinking has moved from the subject of "women and development" toward the study of the differences between the sexes as a model capable of integrating the sexual-difference factor into the presuppositions and variables of research on development. The UN's statistics have been in the vanguard in identifying the working population, as well as in work in the informal sector,

by assigning economic value to unpaid labor in agriculture and reproduction.

In contrast to the UN's global approach, the EEC has limited itself to intervening in the right to work. This limitation is due not only to the Community's prescribed competencies, but also to the understanding of social policy that has come to prevail, one that is heavily subordinated to the demands of the unification of the market. The egalitarian actions of the Community are directed only to women working full time and considered exclusively in their relation to the labor market, without taking into account at all the private work of parenting (with the exception of the recommendation on child care). The Community has above all promoted formal equality, since the norms on positive action are limited to a mention in one directive and to one not very exacting recommendation. Even the jurisprudence of the European Court of Justice has essentially been limited to the application of formal equality, although it has gradually extended the area of that application to cover work as a whole. The court has been a decisive agent in the development of Community norms to extend beyond a narrow focus on the issue of equal pay. It is through its jurisprudence, inspired by that of Strasbourg Court and the Convention on Human Rights, that the policies of the EEC opened up to the idea that sexual equality is not only an economic question but also involves the fundamental right to nondiscrimination. Through its actions to defend civil rights, the Council of Europe for its part has played a role in synergy with that of the Community; that role can be expected to further expand as the European Union is extended to include the former Communist nations.

On the whole, the action of international institutions has supported worldwide progress toward formal equality, a goal that has now been reached in a great majority of the world's nations so far as political rights are concerned, with progress being made in terms of civil rights even in the developing countries. Nevertheless, its advance remains slow and irregular: various nations have not yet accepted all of its principles, and have not ratified the UN's Convention on the Elimination of All Forms of Discrimination Against Women. There are still a great many human rights violations (of which clitoridectomy is only the best-known example) and many forms of discrimination in property rights and family law, in which women are subjugated to the head of the family. All in all, if there are still significant forms of discrimination in social rights in the industrialized nations, sometimes even reflecting a trend toward increase, formal equality in developing nations still amounts today to no more than a drop of water in the ocean of legal discrimination.

Progress in real equality has not matched progress in formal equality; numerous inequalities remain everywhere, and in all sectors. With the exception of life expectancy, all socioeconomic indicators remain less favorable for women than for men, despite the fact that the worldwide increase in literacy and paid-employment rates is proportionally higher among women (40 percent of the total in 1990; see *The World's Women*, 1970–1990). Even where formal equality is most advanced, real inequalities are not diminishing; on the contrary, they are becoming global in scope, over and above regional variations. Employment segregation is not decreasing: women are being concentrated in service-sector, office, and household jobs, a kind of "pink-collar ghetto" that is common across the spectrum of different levels of economic development. With its corollary salary gap (on the average, on the global level, women's wages remain 25 percent lower than those of men; see United Nations, *Human Development Report 1995*), job segregation reigns worldwide, equal opportunity policies notwithstanding.

Indeed, even in the United States, where they have been promoted independently of international legislation, equal opportunity policies have affected only the minority strata of women who already possess economic bargaining power, and they have been implemented only within the public employment sector; private sector support, in contrast, has been limited to promoting women's employment. Too weak to be effective for the vast majority of women workers, these policies show the difficulty of integrating international norms into national policy and ensuring their application. They show the contradiction, characteristic of the 1980s, between the appearance at the global level of an equal opportunity policy perspective, thanks to the ratification of CEDAW, and, on the other hand, the general trend toward reducing social expenditures. As a result, not only have equal opportunity policies received very meager public funding, but social policies as a whole have exacerbated inequalities in opportunities for men and women.

In the developing countries, international policies for stabilizing debt have meant a halt in development and a drastic reduction in public social spending. Their effects have weighed the most heavily on the most fragile groups of the population and therefore above all on women, the poorest of the poor. Not only has poverty increased in the world, but the gap between men and women continues to widen (see United Nations, *Report of the World Summit for Social Development*). In 1995, women represented 70 percent of the 1.3 billion people living in poverty worldwide, while the number of women working in agriculture and living in a state of poverty has practically doubled in 25 years. In rich countries, too, poverty increasingly has a woman's face: in the United States in the mid 1980s, two-thirds of the poor were women, especially those working part time. The decrease in public spending for social services has meant the perpetuation of the sexual division of labor—which has proved to be advantageous in terms of flexible labor and expansion of the informal sector of the economy, two basic aspects of the recent restructuring of the global economy. Many industrial jobs, formerly "male" and well paid, have been transferred outside the developed regions and thereby changed into underpaid and unprotected "female" jobs in developing regions (*The World's Women, 1970–1990*). This use of female labor in developing countries goes hand in hand with the increased use of illegal, temporary, or part-time labor in developed countries, mostly involving women. These new forms of illegal, part-time, or otherwise precarious women's work are the result of a general process of work deregulation; they also produce new inequalities of opportunity for men and women. Finally, these new forms of discrimination are a reaction on the part of the labor market to the extension of formal equality and the appearance of equal opportunity policies.

The present picture of the life of women is therefore marked both by some progress and by the persistence of old and new forms of inequality. The poverty of women in the developing countries visibly disproves the idea that has long inspired the strategies of the UN—that development would lead to growing equality between the sexes. On first analysis, the failures of the international policies for women undoubtedly derive from the fact that they have remained marginal and separate from mainstream socioeconomic policies. But on closer consideration, it is the very principle of equality that seems no longer to be sufficient.

The progress of formal equality in civil and political rights has meant the advancement of women as individual subjects of rights, as citizens and no longer merely members of a family. But this experience of individual emancipation has only made the intrinsic limitations of formal equality more obvious. Without the recognition of civil rights connected to her sexual specificity, such as the right to contraception and abortion, the female subject of law does not actually have control over her body, which remains caught within the family unit. She thus remains a partial individual, not autonomous in and of herself, and her enjoyment of the rights guaranteed by formal equality is undermined at its most basic level. In the area of social rights, where formal equality has made the slowest progress, it has helped foster employment and thus the economic independence of individuals. Even here, however, the framework of formal equality is open to question. If one leaves out of consideration woman's reproductive capability, maternity protection can figure in the framework of the standards on equality in work only as an exception to the principle of nondiscrimination. It is obvious that women's reproductive capability cannot be reduced to a nondiscrimination category or to the status of an exception in terms of equality with men, with the latter being taken as the norm. Women's sexual specificity, in short, necessitates stepping outside the framework of abstract equality and comparability with men workers. Female sexuality can thus become a source of discrimination (the refusal to hire or the exclusion of pregnant women from certain jobs is sometimes seen as a simple form of indirect discrimination) or, on the other hand, a source of rights. Moreover, formal equality in social rights is far from being a guarantee of progress in women's living and working conditions. It might even be the case that a lowering of the standards of living of both men and women would produce greater equality. On the other hand, since it ignores the unequal distribution of family responsibilities and disparities in levels of education, formal equality inevitably legalizes inequalities in working conditions, and may even create new ones.

The perceived deficiencies of formal equality gave rise to the paradigm of equal opportunity, which in turn does not seem able to eliminate the gap between legal equality and real equality. The premise of positive action rests upon the analogy between women and a disadvantaged social group; implicitly, this analogy makes maternal responsibilities and the related sexual division into disadvantaged situations common to half the human race. In that sense, the criticism of some feminist sectors has put its finger on the affinities between positive action and protection laws: both approaches provide "privileges" for women, taking their maternal responsibilities into account—a perspective that confirms, on the contrary, that women really do represent a disadvantage where work is concerned. The difference between the two approaches comes from the fact that protection laws sanction explicit discrimination in access to work, while positive action measures work toward the expansion of women's presence in the work place, including at the most highly qualified levels. By definition, positive action constitutes a temporary derogation in equality that can only be justified by an unbalanced female presence in some sectors. Positive action is thus incapable of satisfying the full extent of women's demands, or indeed of preventing the majority of women workers from being discriminated against because of a sexual specificity that is treated like a disadvantage in the workplace. Alongside equal opportunity policies, there is thus currently a visible trend in the industrialized countries toward a form of segregation that is extremely dangerous to women, namely the part-time job, the modern form of underemployment, which reifies the disadvantage represented by motherhood.

If, on the other hand, as the UN proposes, equal opportunity policies are extended to the point of demanding parity and the equal sharing of family responsibilities between men and women (as in the form of paternity leave), there is a risk of ratifying the idea that a woman, so as not to be at a disadvantage in her work, can be a mother only in the setting of a two-parent family. The equal sharing of family responsibilities is a crucial objective, but it threatens to confirm women's dependence in relation to the family unit. Woman as an autonomous working individual remains weak: weak because she is underprivileged in work, and weak because she is dependent on the family unit. In that light, any law that confirms unequal rights on a sexual basis ends up by reinscribing the sexual division of labor, women's disadvantages in work, and work segregation. Even legislation that protects motherhood is translated into a disadvantage as to her career, pay, and employment.

Ultimately, the need to move beyond formal equality in social rights does not seem to have a simple solution. We would need new conceptual categories, a different social agenda, and a modified concept of work that allows for thinking of women's reproductive capabilities and the sharing of family responsibilities in terms other than those of a disadvantage at work. Within the framework of the existing laws, the woman worker is pushed back into the most fragile layers of the population, if not into outright poverty, as soon as she steps outside of dependency on the family unit or state assistance. That is why, in the context of the general trend to reduce social spending, governments tend to support policies of the two-parent family. But this in turn opens up a fundamental contradiction between such a direction and the political commitment to recognizing individual reproductive rights of women, to which the Beijing women's conference subscribed.

The weak social position of the female citizen is one of the principal causes of women's underrepresentation on the political level. This cannot simply be remedied by a strategy of positive action: such action can be directed only at a minority of emancipated women for whom economic and social independence is an objective already attained. Much remains to be done to obtain the theoretical means of tackling this citizenship deficit. Unfortunately, the political climate is hardly favorable under the threats that once again weigh upon even formal equality, through the deregulation of markets and the growing power of religious fundamentalism on all sides. Among the thousands of problems that marked the end of the 20th century, the commitments to sexual and reproductive rights made in Beijing nonetheless indicate to women's movements across the world a direction to take in the struggle to have women's rights written into the human rights guaranteed by the UN.

Bibliography

Documents of the Three International Organizations

United Nations

Report of the World Conference of the International Women's Year (Mexico City, 19 June–2 July 1975), E/Conf. 66/34

Report of the World Conference of the United Nations Decade for Women: Equality, Development, and Peace (Copenhagen, 14–30 July 1980), A/Conf. 94/35

Report of the World Conference to Review and Appraise the Achievements of the United Nations Decade for Women: Equality, Development, and Peace (Nairobi, 15–26 July 1985), A/Conf./116/28/Rev. 1

Human Rights Activities of the United Nations Organization, New York: United Nations, 1986

The Nairobi Forward-Looking Strategies for the Advancement of Women, 86 44 294, May 1986

Convention on the Elimination of All Forms of Discrimination against Women, DPI/929, February 1988–8M

Population: Concise Report on the Monitoring of World Population Trends and Policies, with Special Emphasis on the Population Situation in the Least Developed Countries: Report of the Secretary General, E/1989/10

Cross-Organisational Program Analysis of the Activities of the United Nations System for the Advancement of Women: Report of the Secretary General, E/1989/19

The World's Women, 1970–1990: Trends and Statistics, New York: United Nations, 1991

Charter of the United Nations and Statute of the International Court of Justice, DPI/511, September 1993

World Conference on Human Rights: The Vienna Declaration and Programme of Action, June 1993, DPI/1394, April 1995.

Report of the International Conference on Population and Development (Cairo, 5–13 September 1994), A/Conf. 171/13/Rev. 1

Report of the World Summit for Social Development (Copenhagen, 6–12 March 1995), A/Conf. 166/9 of 19 April 1995

The Fourth World Conference of Women (Beijing, 4–15 September 1995), A/Conf. 177/19

Human Development Report 1995, New York: Oxford University Press, 1995

Multilateral Treaties Deposited with the Secretary General, Status as at 31 December 1997, ST/LEG/SER.E/16

Commission on the Status of Women: Report on the 43rd Session (1–12 March and 1 April 1999), E/1999/27-E/CN.6/1999/10

Status of the Convention on the Elimination of All Forms of Discrimination against Women: Report of the Secretary General, 13 August 1999, A/54/224

European Council

Texts adopted

Resolution (77) 1 on Women's Employment

Recommendation R (81) 18 concerning Participation at Municipal Level

Recommendation R (84) 17 on Equality between Women and Men in the Media

Recommendation R (85) 2 on Legal Protection against Sex Discrimination

Recommendation R (85) 4 on Violence in the Family

Recommendation R (89) 3 on the Flexibility of Retirement Age

Recommendation R (90) 2 on Social Measures concerning Violence within the Family

Recommendation R (90) 4 on the Elimination of Sexism from Language

The First European Ministerial Conference on Equality between Women and Men (Strasbourg, 4 March 1986): Resolution on Policy and Strategies for Achieving Equality in Political Life and in the Decision-Making Process

The Second European Ministerial Conference on Equality between Women and Men (Vienna, 4–5 July 1989): Political Strategies for the Achievement of Real Equality of Women and Men

The Third European Ministerial Conference on Equality between Women and Men (Rome, 21–22 October 1993): Strategies for the Elimination of Violence against Women in Society: The Media and Other Means, MEG–3 (93) 22

Equality and Democracy: Utopia or Challenge? European Conference on Equality and Democracy: Proceedings (Strasbourg, 9–11 February 1995), EG/DEM (95) 8

The European Economic Community/European Community

Verwilghen, Michel, editor, *Equality in Law between Men and Women in the European Community*, 2 vols., Louvain-la-Neuve, Belgium: Presses Universitaires de Louvain, 1987

Community Directives

"Council Directive 75/117/EEC of 10 February 1975 on the Approximation of the Laws of the Member States Relating to the Application of the Principle of Equal Pay for Men and Women," *Official Journal L* 45 (19 February 1975)

"Council Directive 76/207/EEC of 9 February 1976 on the Implementation of the Principle of Equal Treatment for Men and Women as Regards Access to Employment, Vocational Training and Promotion, and Working Conditions," *Official Journal L* 39 (14 February 1976)

"Council Directive 79/7/EEC of 19 December 1978 on the Progressive Implementation of the Principle of Equal Treatment for Men and Women in Matters of Social Security," *Official Journal L* 6 (10 January 1979)

"Council Directive 86/378/EEC of 24 July 1986 on the Implementation of the Principle of Equal Treatment for Men and Women in Occupational Social Security Schemes," *Official Journal L* 225 (12 August 1986)

"Council Directive 86/613/EEC of 11 December 1986 on the Application of the Principle of Equal Treatment between Men and Women Engaged in an Activity, including Agriculture, in a Self-Employed Capacity, and on the Protection of Self-Employed Women during Pregnancy and Motherhood," *Official Journal L* 359 (19 December 1986)

"Council Directive 92/85/EEC of 19 October 1992 on the Introduction of Measures to Encourage Improvements in the Safety and Health at Work of Pregnant Workers and Workers Who Have Recently Given Birth or Are Breastfeeding," *Official Journal L* 348 (28 November 1992)

Recommendations

"Council Recommendation of 13 December 1984 on the Promotion of Positive Action for Women (84/635/EEC)," *Official Journal L* 331 (19 December 1984)

"Council Recommendation of 31 March 1992 on Child Care (92/241/EEC), *Official Journal L* 123 (8 May 1992)

Resolutions

"Council Resolution of 7 June 1984 on Action to Combat Unemployment amongst Women (84/c 161/04)," *Official Journal C* 161 (21 June 1984)

"Resolution of the Council and of the Ministers for Education, Meeting within the Council, of 3 June 1985 Containing an Action Programme on Equal Opportunities for Girls and Boys in Education (85/C 166/01)," *Official Journal C* 166 (5 July 1985)

"Second Council Resolution of 24 July 1986 on the Promotion of Equal Opportunities for Women," *Official Journal C* 203 (12 August 1986)

"Council Resolution of 16 December 1988 on the Reintegration and Late Integration of Women into Working Life (88/c 333/01)," *Official Journal C* 333 (28 December 1988)

"Council Resolution of 29 May 1990 on the Protection of the Dignity of Women and Men at Work (90/C 157/02)," *Official Journal C* 157 (27 June 1990)

"Council Resolution of 21 May 1991 on the Third Medium-Term Community Action Programme on Equal Opportunities for Women and Men (1991 to 1995) (91/C 142/01)," *Official Journal C* 142 (31 May 1991)

Commission of the European Communities

"Commission Recommendation of 24 November 1987 on Vocational Training for Women (87/567/EEC)," *Official Journal L* 342 (4 December 1987)

Protective Legislation for Women in the Member States of the European Community, Communication by the Commission, COM (87) 105 final Brussels, 20 March 1987

A New Community Action Program on the Promotion of Equal Opportunities for Women, 1982–1985, COM (81) 758 final, Brussels, 9 December 1981

"Equal Opportunities for Women: Medium-Term Community Programme, 1986–90," *Bulletin of the European Communities, Supplement* 3/86

Equal Opportunities for Women and Men: The Third Medium-Term Community Action Programme, 1991–1995, COM (90) 449 final, Brussels, 6 November 1990

"NOW Initiative (90/C 327/04)," *Official Journal C* 327 (29 November 1990)

"Communication to the Member States Laying Down Guidelines for Operational Programmes or Global Grants which Member States Are Invited to Propose within the Framework of a Community Initiative on Employment and Development of Human Resources Aimed at Promoting Employment Growth Mainly through the Development of Human Resources (94/C 180/10)," *Official Journal C* 180 (1 July 1994)

Memorandum on Equal Pay for Work of Equal Value, COM (94) 6 final, Brussels, 23 June 1994

Green Paper: European Social Policy Options for the Union, COM (93) 551 final, Brussels, 17 November 1993

European Social Policy—A Way Forward for the Union: A White Paper, COM (94) 333 final, Brussels, 27 July 1994

European Parliament

Report on the Situation of Women in Europe, 3 vols., 1984

"Resolution on Women in Decision-Making Centres, A 2–169/88," *Official Journal C* 262 (10 October 1988)

"Resolution on Women in Decision-Making Bodies, A3–0035/94," *Official Journal C* 61 (28 February 1994)

Studies and Publications by the Commission of the European Communities or with Their Cooperation

Positive Action: Equal Opportunities for Women in Employment: A Guide, Luxembourg, 1988 (Directorate General Employment, Social Affairs, and Education)

An Evaluation Study of Positive Action in Favour of Women, V/ 587/91 EN, Brussels, 1990 (Directorate General Employment, Industrial Relations, and Social Affairs)

Positive Action Network: Motivating Factors, Obstacles, and Guidelines, V/1604/92, EN, 1992 (Directorate General V, Equal Opportunities Unit)

Report on the 1993 Infancy Network (Directorate General V, Equal Opportunities Unit)

Employment in Europe, 1994, COM (94) 381 final, Brussels, 1994 (Directorate General Employment, Industrial Relations, and Social Affairs)

Lanquetin, Marie-Thérèse, Christophe Pettiti, and Claire Sutter, *L'égalité juridique entre femmes et hommes dans la Communauté européenne*, Brussels: Bruylant, and Luxembourg: Office des Publications Officielles des Communautés Européennes, 1994

Moss, Peter, "Childcare and Equal Opportunity," Commission of the European Communities V/746/88, EN

Prondzynski, Ferdinand von, *Implementation of the Equality Directives*, Luxembourg: Office for Official Publications of the European Communities, 1987

Sullerot, Évelyne, *Diversification of Vocational Choices for Women*, Luxembourg: Office for Official Publications of the European Communities, 1987

Women of Europe Supplements

Davis, Melanie, *Women and the European Social Fund*, Brussels: Commission of the European Communities, Directorate-General Information, Information for Women's Organisations and Press, 1981 (*Women of Europe* Supplement 6)

Equal Opportunities for Women: Medium-Term Community Programme, 1986–1990, Brussels: Commission of the European Communities, Directorate-General Information, Communication, Culture, Women's Information Service, 1985 (*Women of Europe* Supplement 23)

Remuet-Alexandrou, Françoise, *Community Law and Women*, updated and adapted by María J. Gonzalez, Brussels: Commission of the European Communities, Directorate-General Information, Communication, Culture, Women's Information Service, 1986 (*Women of Europe* Supplement 25)

Mossuz-Lavau, Janine, *Mirroring the Course of Women's Rights in Europe*, Brussels: Commission of the European Communities, Directorate-General Information, Communication, Culture, Women's Information Service, 1988 (*Women of Europe* Supplement 27)

Moss, Peter, *Childcare in the European Community, 1985–1990*, Brussels: Commission of the European Communities, Directorate-General Information, Communication, Culture, Women's Information Service, 1990 (*Women of Europe* Supplement 31)

Maruani, Margaret, *The Position of Women on the Labour Market: Trends and Developments in the Twelve Member States of the European Community, 1983–1990*, Brussels: Commission of the European Communities, Directorate-General Audiovisual, Information, Communication, Culture, Women's Information Service, 1992 (*Women of Europe* Supplement 36)

Social Europe (journal)

"Networks for Contact, Exchange, and Action: A New Instrument of Community Policy to Promote Equal Opportunities" (January 1987)

"Equal Treatment for Men and Women in Occupational Social Security Schemes" (January 1987)

"Application of Directive 79/7/EEC—Equal Treatment for Men and Women in Matters of Social Security" (March 1987)

"The Enforcement of Community Law on Equality at the National Level" (January 1988)

"Community Initiatives on Vocational Training for Women" (January 1988)

"Application of Directive 79/7/EEC—Equal Treatment for Men and Women in Matters of Social Security" (January 1988)

Equality of Treatment for Men and Women in Social Security Matters" (February 1988)

"Business Creation by Women—Action Taken by the Commission of the European Communities" (February 1988)

"Seminar: The Industrial Challenge: The New Role of Women: Positive Actions" (February 1988)

"Positive Action for Women Taken by the Member States and the Commission to Implement the Council Recommendation of 13 December 1984" (March 1988)

(January 1989) (issue entitled "Male-Female Equality"; see especially the section "Positive Action: Equal Employment Opportunities for Women")

(January 1989) (issue entitled "Final Report on the Application of EEC Directive 79/7/EEC on the Implementation of the Principle of Equal Treatment of Men and Women in Social Security")

"IRIS—The New Community Network of Demonstration Projects on Vocational Training for Women" (February 1989)

(March 1991) (issue entitled "Equal Opportunities for Women and Men"; see especially the section by C. Alexopoulou, "Action of the European Social Fund for Women," and Chapter 4, "Examples from Some Member States")

Supplement (February 1993) (issue entitled "Evaluation of Women's Involvement in European Social Fund Cofinanced Measures in 1990")

Supplement (March 1993) (issue entitled "Occupational Segregation of Women and Men in the European Community")

Supplement (March 1993) (issue entitled "Network of Experts on the Situation of Women in the Labour Market")

Reference Works

Adinolfi, Adelina, and Roberta Bortone, "Tutela della salute delle lavoratrici madri dopo la direttiva 92/85," *Giornale del diritto del lavoro e relazioni industriali* 62 (1994)

Anderson, Malcolm, and Mary Buckley, editors, *Women, Equality, and Europe*, London: Macmillan, 1988

Barbera, Marzia, "L'evoluzione storica e normativa del problema della parità retributiva tra uomo e donna," *Lavoro e diritto* 3, no. 4 (October 1989)

Beechey, Veronica, and Tessa Perkins, *A Matter of Hours: Women, Part-Time Work, and the Labour Market*, Minneapolis: University of Minnesota Press, and Cambridge: Polity Press, 1987

Bruce, K., "Work of the United Nations Relating to the Status of Women," *Revue des droits de l'homme* 4 (1971)

Catalini, Paola, *Uguali anzi diverse: I nuovi obiettivi legislativi oltre le pari opportunità*, Rome: Ediesse, 1993

Conforti, Benedetto, *Le Nazioni Unite*, 2 vols., Padua, Italy: CEDAM, 1971; 6th edition, 2000

Cook, Rebecca J., "The International Right to Nondiscrimination on the Basis of Sex: A Bibliography," *Yale Journal of International Law* 14, no. 1 (1989)

Cox, Susan, "Equal Opportunities," in *The Social Dimension: Employment Policy in the European Community*, edited by Michael Gold, London: Macmillan, 1993

Del Re, Alisa, and Jacqueline Heinen, editors, *Quelle citoyenneté pour les femmes? La crise des États-providence et de la représentation politique en Europe*, Paris: L'Harmattan, 1996

De Salvia, Michele, *Lineamenti di diritto europeo dei diritti dell'uomo*, Padua, Italy: CEDAM, 1991

Donne legislazione europea contrattazione pari opportunita' azioni positive tra partita'a' Remplacer par parità e differenza, Milan: Angeli, 1990

Frey, Luigi, et al., *Comparable Worth e segregazione del lavoro femminile*, Milan: Angeli, 1987

Frey, Luigi, Renata Livraghi, and Tiziano Treu, *Politiche del personale e valorizzazione femminile*, Milan: Angeli, 1988

Funk, Nanette, and Magda Mueller, editors, *Gender Politics and Post-Communism: Reflections from Eastern Europe and the Former Soviet Union*, New York and London: Routledge, 1993

Gaeta, Lorenzo, and Lorenzo Zoppoli, editors, *Il diritto diseguale: La legge sulle azioni positive*, Turin, Italy: Giappichelli, 1992

Gregory, Jeanne, "Equal Pay for Work of Equal Value: The Strengths and Weaknesses of Legislation," *Work, Employment, and Society* 16, no. 3 (September 1992)

Hervey, Tamara K., "Legal Issues concerning the Barber Protocol," in *Legal Issues of the Maastricht Treaty*, edited by David O'Keeffe and Patrick M. Twomey, London and New York: Chancery Law, 1994

Hevener, Natalie Kaufman, *International Law and the Status of Women*, London and Boulder, Colorado: Westview Press, and Epping, Essex: Bowker, 1983

Hoskyns, Catherine, and Linda Luckhaus, "The European Community Directive on Equal Treatment in Social Security," *Policy and Politics* 17 (1989)

Landau, Eve C., *The Rights of Working Women in the European Community*, Brussels: Commission of the European Communities, 1985

Lanquetin, Marie-Thérèse, and Hélène Masse-Dessen, "Maastricht: Consolidation ou remise en cause des principes en matière d'égalité professionnelle," *Droit social* 4 (April 1992)

Livragthi, Renata, and Maria Rita Saulle, editors, *Uguaglianza, sviluppo e pace: Il ruolo delle donne in Italia, 1975–1985: Diece anni di profondo cambiamento*, Rome: Presidenza del Consiglio dei Ministri, 1985

Luckhaus, Linda, "The Social Security Directive: Its Impact on Part-Time Work," in *Women, Equal Opportunities, and Welfare*, edited by Margaret O'Brien, Linda Hantrais, and Steen Mangen, Birmingham, West Midlands: Cross-National Research Group, 1990

Mazey, Sonia, "European Community Action on Behalf of Women: The Limits of Legislation," *Journal of Common Market Studies* 27, no. 1 (September 1988)

McCrudden, Christopher, editor, *Women, Employment, and European Equality Law*, London: Eclipse, 1987

Meehan, Elizabeth M., *Citizenship and the European Community*, London and Newbury Park, California: Sage, 1993

Meehan, Elizabeth M., and Selma Sevenhuijsen, editors, *Equality Politics and Gender*, London and Newbury Park, California: Sage, 1991

Pari e dispari: Donne azioni positive pari opportunita' normative comunitarie sentenze della Corte di giustizia Europea, Milan: Angeli, 1993

"Positive Action for Women: The Private Sector," *European Industrial Relations Review* 167 (December 1987)

"Positive Action for Women: The Public Sector," *European Industrial Relations Review* 166 (November 1987)

Prechal, Sacha, and Noreen Burrows, *Gender Discrimination Law of the European Community*, Aldershot, Hampshire: Dartmouth, and Brookfield, Vermont: Gower, 1990

Reanda, Laura, "The Commission on the Status of Women," in *The United Nations and Human Rights: A Critical Appraisal*, edited by Philip Alston, Oxford: Clarendon Press, and New York: Oxford University Press, 1992

Rehof, Lars Adam, *Guide to the Travaux Préparatoires of the United Nations Convention on the Elimination of All Forms of Discrimination against Women* Boston and Dordrecht, The Netherlands: Nijhoff, 1993

Roccella, Massimo, and Tiziano Treu, *Diritto del lavoro della Comunita Europea*, Padua, Italy: CEDAM, 1992

Rodano, Marisa, "Il genere femminile nei sistemi politici europei," in *Il genere della rappresentanza*, edited by Maria Luisa Boccia and Isabella Peretti, Rome: Editori Riuniti Riviste, 1988

Rossilli, Mariagrazia, editor, *Gender Policies in the European Union*, New York: Peter Lang, 2000

Schmid, Günther, and Renate Weitzel, editors, *Sex Discrimination and Equal Opportunity: The Labour Market and Employment Policy*, Aldershot, Hampshire: Gower, and New York: St. Martin's Press, 1984

Szyszczak, Erika, "Social Policy: A Happy Ending or a Reworking of the Fairy Tale?" in *Legal Issues of the Maastricht Treaty*, edited by David O'Keeffe and Patrick M. Twomey, London and New York: Chancery Law, 1994

"Valutazione e classificazione dei lavori delle donne: Uno sguardo europeo," in *Appendice Il memorandum della Commissione delle Communita Europea sulla parita di retribuzione per lavori di pari valore*, Milan: Angeli, 1995

Vedovato, Giuseppe, "Impegni europei e internazionali per la parità uomo-donna e la Parte Seconda: 'Elementi di legislazione sulla condizione femminile,'" in *La condizione della donna in Europa: Atti del convegno internazionale promosso dall' Associazione degli ex parlamentari, e elementi di legislazione comparata*, Rome: Camera dei Deputati, 1991

Vogel-Polsky, Éliane, and Jean Vogel, *L'Europe sociale, 1993: Illusion, alibi ou réalité?* Brussels: Éditions de l'Université de Bruxelles, 1991

Ward, Kathryn B., editor, *Women Workers and Global Restructuring*, Ithaca, New York: ILR Press, 1990

Women's Studies International Forum 15, no. 1 (1992) (special issue entitled "A Continent in Transition: Issues for Women in Europe in the 1990s")

NOTES ON CONTRIBUTORS

SVETLANA AIVAZOVA is a state-qualified professor of history and a researcher at the Russian Academy of Sciences in Moscow, with a specialization is 19th- and 20th-century women's history. Her publications include, in French, "Le mouvement féminin en Russie: Tradition et situation actuelle," *Droit et Culture* (1995).

BARBARA ALPERN-ENGEL is a professor of history at the University of Colorado. Her publications include *Mothers and Daughters: Women of the Intelligentsia in Nineteenth Century Russia* (1983, 2000); *Between the Fields and the City: Women, Work, and Family in Russia 1861–1914* (1994); and *Women in Imperial, Soviet, and Post-Soviet Russia* (1999). She is coeditor, with Anastasia Posadskaya-Vanderbeck, of *A Revolution of Their Own: Voices of Women in Soviet History* (1998), and coauthor, with Clifford Rosenthal, of *Five Sisters: Women Against the Tsar* (1975, 1987, 1992), which was translated into Spanish (1980).

DANIÈLE DJAMILA AMRANE-MINNE is a historian and holds a doctorat-ès-État degree; she is an assistant professor at the Université de Toulouse–Le Mirail, Toulouse, France. Her publications include *Les femmes algériennes et la guerre de libération nationale en Algérie, 1954–1962* (1989); *Les femmes algériennes dans la guerre* (1991); *Femmes au combat: la guerre d'Algérie, 1954–1962* (1993) and *Des femmes dans la guerre. Entretiens* (1994). She has also written numerous articles on the Algerian War and on the transgression of norms during periods of crisis.

BONNIE S. ANDERSON is a professor of history at City University of New York. Her most recent book is *Joyous Greetings: The First International Women's Movement 1830–1860* (2000). She is also coauthor, with Judith P. Zinsser, of *A History of Their Own: Women in Europe from Prehistory to the Present* (1988, 2000), which has been translated into Spanish, Italian, and German.

FRANÇOISE BASCH is professor emerita of Anglo-American civilization in the Charles V Anglophone Studies section at l'Université de Paris VII–Denis Diderot. She is the author of *Les femmes victoriennes: Roman et société* (1972, 1979), published in English as *Relative Creatures: Victorian Women in Society and the Novel, 1837–67* (1974); and *Rebelles américaines au XIXᵉ siècle, mariage, amour libre, et politique* (1990). In addition, she is the editor of *Journal d'une gréviste par Théresa Serber Malkiel* (1980), published in English as *The Diary of a Shirtwaist Striker* (1990); and *Victor Basch, 1863–1944: Un intellectuel cosmopolite* (2000). Her book, *Victor Basch ou la passion de la justice: De l'affaire Dreyfus au crime de la Milice* (1994) was the winner of two prizes: the Prix Henri-Hertz in 1994 and the Prix du Livre Antiraciste de la Ligue Internationale contre le Racisme et l'Antisémitisme (LICRA) in 1995.

MAÏTÉ BOUYSSY is a historian and assistant professor at l'Université de Paris I–Panthéon-Sorbonne. Her Ph.D. dissertation at l'Univer-

sité de Paris I was entitled "Trente ans après: Bertrand Barère sous la Restauration ou la Rhétorique du Ténare" (1993). With publication of her study, *Réflexions sur la naissance de l'espace politique dans la France du XIXᵉ siècle* (2002), she earned her accreditation to supervise university research. Other publications include *Le Musée de Bordeaux: 1783–1789, Étude psycho-sociologique d'une société de lumières* (1973); presentation of "Jasmin" (1798–1864), in *Actes du Colloque d'Agen, 1998*, edited by Claire Torreilles et François Pic (2002); and numerous articles on cultural history and political rhetoric in the 18th and 19th centuries. She also edited *La guerre des rues et des maisons* [manuscript attributed to Maréchal Bugeaud] (1997), and coedited, with Anna Maria Rao, *Vincenzo Cuoco, Histoire de la Révolution de Naples, Ristampa anastatica della traduzione di Bertrand Barère* (2001).

HUBERT CARRIER holds a chair in classical literature at l'Université de Tours, where he heads the department of literature and political thought in the Centre d'Études Supérieures de la Renaissance. His publications include *La Fronde, contestation démocratique et misère paysanne: 52 mazarinades* (1982, 1995); and *La presse de la Fronde (1648–1653): Les Mazarinades* (1989–91), which won the Prix Araxie-Torossian of the Académie des Sciences Morales et Politiques in 1987 and the Prix Arconati-Visconti of the Chancellerie des Universités de Paris in 1988. He is also the author of *Les muses guerrières: Les mazarinades et la vie littéraire au milieu du XVIIᵉ siècle* (1996) and coeditor, with Luciano Erba, of *Complete Works of Cyrano de Bergerac, Savinien de, 1619–1655* (2000).

YOLANDE COHEN holds a chair in European history at the University of Quebec in Montreal. She is the author of *Les jeunes, le socialisme et la guerre, histoire des mouvements de jeunesse en France* (1989) and *Femmes de parole, l'histoire des cercles de fermières au Québec* (1990). She is coauthor, with Marie Berdugo-Cohen and Joseph Josy Levy, of *Les Juifs marocains à Montréal* (1987); and, with Joseph Josy Levy, of *Itinéraires sépharades, 1492–1992: Mutations d'une identité* (1992). Her essay "Du féminin au féminisme, l'exemple québecois" is included in volume 5 of *Histoire des femmes en occident*, edited by Françoise Thébaud (general editors Georges Duby and Michelle Perrot, 1992). She is the editor of two volumes of collected essays, *Femmes et politique* (1981) and *Femmes et contre-pouvoirs* (1987). Together with Claudie Weill, she coedited a special issue of the review *Mouvement social* entitled *Entre socialisme et nationalisme: les mouvements étudiants européens* (1982) and a special issue of the review *L'Homme et la Société* entitled *Générations et mémoires* (1994).

ANNE COVA is a historian and assistant professor at Aberta University, in Lisbon, Portugal. She wrote a thesis entitled "Droit des femmes et protection de la maternité en France, 1892–1939" at the European University Institute in Florence, Italy. Other publications include *Maternité et droits des femmes en France: XIXᵉ–XXᵉ siècles*

(1997); *Au service le l'Église, de la patrie et de la famille: Femmes catholiques et maternité sous la IIIᵉ République* (2000); "French Feminism and Maternity: Theories and Policies, 1890–1918," *Maternity and Gender Policies, Women and the Rise of the European Welfare States, 1880s–1950s*, edited by Gisela Bock and Pat Thane (1991); "Femmes et catholicisme social: Trois mouvements nationaux d'initiative lyonnaise," in *Cent ans de catholicisme social à Lyon et en Rhône-Alpes. La postérité de Rerum novarum*, edited by Jean-Dominique Durand et al. (Paris, 1992); and as well as several articles on women and the welfare state, including "Cécile Brunschvieg (1877–1946) et la protection de la maternité," *Actes du 113e Congrès national des Sociétés savantes* (1989); "Féminisme et natalité, Nelly Roussel (1878–1922)," *History of European Ideas* XV, nos. 4–6 (1992); "Féminismes et maternité entre les deux guerres en France. Les ambiguïtés et les divergences des féministes du passé," *Les Temps Modernes* no. 593 (1997); "Les Féministes du passé et l'apologie de la maternité," *Panoramiques* (1999); and "Généalogie d'une conquête: Maternité et droit des femmes en France, fin XIXᵉ–XXᵉ siècles," *Travail, Genre et Sociétés* 3 (2000).

CECILIA DAU-NOVELLI is a historian. Her publications include *Società, chiesa e associazionismo femminile, l'Unione fra le donne cattoliche d'Italia (1912–1919)* (1988); *Famiglia e modernizzazione in Italia tra le due guerre* (1994); *Politica e nuove identità nell'Italia del "miracolo"* (1999); and "Modelli di comportamento e ruoli familiari," in *Borghesi e imprenditori a Milano*, edited by Giorgio Fiocca (1984).

SIMONE DEBOUT-OLESZKIEWICZ is a philosopher and writer. She initiated the most recent reissue of the oeuvre of Charles Fourier, including *Préface aux oeuvres complètes de Fourier* (1966); *Préface à la "Théorie des quatre mouvements et des destinées générales, augmentée d'extraits du Nouveau monde amoureux* (1967); *Le charme composé* (1976); the previously unpublished, unabridged text of *Le nouveau monde amoureux* (1979); and *Le charme composé, inconséquence des champions de la simple nature, précédé de l'invisible actif* (1993). In addition, she is the author of *Charles Fourier* (1970); *L'utopie de Charles Fourier, illusion réelle* (1978), translated into Japanese in 1993; *Griffe au nez ou donner have ou art: Écriture inconnue de Charles Fourier* (1974); and numerous articles on Charles Fourier.

RUDOLF DEKKER is a historian and assistant professor in the Faculty of History at the Erasmus Universiteit in Rotterdam. His publications include *Uit de schaduw in't grote licht. Kinderen in egodocumenten van de gouden eeuw tot de romantiek* (1995); *Childhood, Memory and Autobiography in Holland: From the Golden Age to Romanticism* (1999); and *Humour in Dutch Culture of the Golden Age* (2001). He is coauthor, with Lotte c. Van de Pol, of *The Tradition of Female Transvestism in Early Modern Europe* (1989); with Willem Frijhoff, of *Le voyage révolutionnaire, Actes du Colloque franco-néerlandais du Bicentenaire de la Révolution française*, held in Amsterdam on 12–13 October 1989 (1991); and, with Anje Dik, of *Le journal de Magdalena van Schinne 1786–1805* (1994).

ELISABETH ELGÁN is an assistant professor of history and member of the directory board of the Institute of Contemporary History at the new University College, Södertörns högskala, south of Stockholm. Her publications include *Genus och politik: En jämförelse mellan svensk och fransk abortoch preventivmedelspolitik från sekelskiftet till andra världskriget* [Gender and politics: a comparison of Swedish and French abortion and contraceptive polities from the turn of the century to the Second World War] (1994) and "Sexualpolitikens genus i Frankrike och Sverige" [The gender of sexual politics in France and Sweden], *Kvinnovetenskaplig tidskrift* 20, no. 3 (1999).

CHRISTINE FAURÉ is a sociologist and director of research at the Centre National de la Recherche Scientifique, Centre de Recherches Politiques de la Sorbonne, Université de Paris I. Her publications include *Quatre femmes terroristes contre le Tsar* (1978); *Terre, terreur et liberté, essai sur le populisme russe* (1979); *La démocratie sans les femmes, essai sur le libéralisme en France* (1979), published in English as *Democracy without Women: Feminism and the Rise of Liberal Individualism in France* (1991); *Les Déclarations des droits de l'homme de 1789* (1988, 1992), published in Spanish as *Las declaraciones de los derechos del hombre de 1789* (1995); *Ce que déclarer des droits veut dire: Histoires*, which won the Prix Henri Tessier I of the Académie des Sciences Morales et Politiques (1997); and *Mai 68 jour et nuit* (1998). She is editor *Des manuscrits de Sièyes, 1773–1799* (1999) (with contributions from Jacques Guilhaumou and Jacques Valier); and coeditor with Tom Bishop, of *L'Amérique des Français* (1992). In 2002 she was named as a member of the Observatoire de la Parité entre les Femmes et les Hommes, an observatory body affiliated with the Ministère délégué à la Parité et à l'Égalité Professionnelle (French Ministry of Parity and Professional Equality).

DOMINIQUE FOUGEYROLLAS-SCHWEBEL is a sociologist and researcher at the Institut de Recherche et d'Information Socio-économique, Centre National de la Recherche Scientifique, Travail et Société, Université Paris–Dauphine (IRIS-TS). In 1977–78, she conducted a study entitled *Aides et relations familiales* at the Institut National de Statistique et d'Études Économiques (INSEE). She is a member of the reading committee of the *Cahiers du CEDREF* and *Cahiers du Genre* and coeditor of the collection Bibliothèque du Féminisme (Editions l'Harmattan). In 2000 she participated in a national survey, under the aegis of the Université Paris I, about acts of violence against women in France (ENVEFF). She is coauthor, with Danièle Chabaud-Rychter and Françoise Sonthonnax, of *Espace et temps du travail domestique* (1985), *Famille, travail domestique et espace-temps des femmes* (1988), and *Le travail domestique et les pratiques de déplacement des femmes et des hommes* (1988). She is the author of "De la réclusion au cloisonnement: travail domestique et salariat," in *Le partage du travail: bilan et perspectives*, edited by Hervé Defalvard and Véronique Guienne (1998); "L'essor récent de la recherche féministe en France," in *Pluralité et convergences: La recherche féministe dans la francophonie*, edited by H. Dagenais (1999); "Mouvements féministes" and "Travail domestique" in *Dictionnaire critique du féminisme*, edited by H. Hirata et al. (2000); as well as numerous articles, including: "Le contrat social entre les sexes," *Cahiers du Genre*, no. 24 (1999); "Le mouvement féministe français: Quelle force de changement," *Regards sur l'actualité*, no. 258 (2000); "La relation de service-Regards croisés," *Cahiers du Genre*, no. 28 (2000; she also guest edited this issue). She is coauthor, with Annick Houel and Maryse Jaspard, of "Approche quantitative des violences envers les femmes au travail, quelles analyses privilégier," *Travailler*, no. 4 (2000); and, with Elizabeth Brown and Maryse Jaspard, of "Les paroxysmes de la conciliation. Violence au travail et violence du conjoint," *Travail, genre et société*, no. 8 (2002).

ÉLIANE GUBIN is a professor of history at the Université Libre de Bruxelles. She is the author of *Bruxelles au XIXᵉ siècle: Berceau d'un flamingantisme démocratique* (1979). as well as a number of articles on women and citizenship in Belgium. She is editor of *Norme et marginalités: comportements féminins au 19ᵉ-20ᵉ siècles* (1991); coeditor, with Yvan Lamonde, of *Un Canadien français en Belgique au XIXᵉ siècle: Correspondance d'exil de L.A.Dessaulles (1875-1878)* (1991); with Jean-Pierre Nandrin, of *La ville et les femmes en Belgique: Histoire et sociologie, actes de la Journée d'étude organisée par les Facultés universitaires Saint-Louis et l'Université libre de Bruxelles le 12 février 1993* (1993); with Yvonne Knibiehler, of *Les femmes et la ville, un enjeu pour l'Europe: Actes du colloque organisé à Marseille en mars 1993* (1993); and with Leen Van Molle, of *Femmes et politique en Belgique* (1998).

JACQUES GUILHAUMOU is a linguist and director of research at the Centre National de la Recherche Scientifique (Telemme) at the Université de Provence. His publications include *Langage et idéologies: le discours comme objet de l'histoire* (1974); *La rhétorique du discours* (1981); *La langue politique et la Révolution française, de l'événement à la raison linguistique* (1989), published in German as *Sprache und Politik in der Französischen Revolution* (1989); *La mort de Marat 1793* (1989); *Marseille républicaine (1791-1793)* (1992); *L'avènement des porte-parole de la République (1789-1792): Essai de synthèse sur les langages de la Révolution française* (1998); and *La parole des sans: Les mouvements actuels à l'épreuve de la Révolution française* (1998). He is coeditor, with Michel Glatigny, of *Peuple et pouvoir: Études de lexicologie politique* (1981-1995); with Denise Maldidier and Régine Robin, of *Discours et archives: Expérimentations en analyse du discours* (1994); and, with Geneviève Dermenjian and Martine Lapied, of *Femmes entre ombre et lumière: Recherches sur la visibilité sociale, XVIᵉ-XXᵉ siècles* (2000).

SARAH HANLEY is a professor of history and law and a dean in the College of Liberal Arts at the University of Iowa. She is director of the Society for French Historical Studies and is a member of the executive committee of the American Historical Association, Modern European Section, and member of the U.S. International Commission for Historians. Her publications include *The Lit de Justice of the Kings of France: Constitutional Ideology in Legend, Ritual, and Discourse* (1983), which was translated into French in 1991. Her essay "Engendering the State: Family Formation and State Building in Early Modern France," *French Historical Studies* 16, no. 1 (1989) won the William Koren prize. She is the editor of *Les droits des femmes et la loi salique* (1994) and author of "The Monarchic State: Marital Regime Government and Male Right," in *Politics, Ideology, and the Law in Early Modern Europe*, edited by Adriana E. Bakos (1994). Her essay "Social Sites of Political Practice in France: Lawsuits, Civil Rights, and the Separation of Powers in Domestic and State Government, 1500-1800," *American Historical Review* 102-1 (1997) was awarded the American Political Science Association prize. Her most recent publications are "Mapping Rulership in the French Body Politic: Political Identity, Public Law and the King's One Body," *Historical Reflections* 23, no. 2 (1997) and "The Politics of Identity and Monarchic Governance

in France: The Debate over Female Exclusion," in *Women Writers and the Early Modern British Political Tradition*, edited by Hilda L. Smith (1998).

ANN HUGHES is a professor of modern history at the University of Keele, Great Britain. Her publications include *Seventeenth Century England: A Changing Culture* (1980), *Politics, Society and Civil War in Warwickshire 1620-1660* (1987), and *The Causes of the English Civil War* (1991, 1998). She is coauthor, with Richard Cust, of *Conflict in Early Stuart England: Studies in Religion and Politics, 1603-1642* (1989); and of "Gender and Politics in Leveller Literature," in *Political Culture and Cultural Politics in Early Modern England*, edited by Mark Kishlansky and Susan Amussen (1995). She is coeditor, with Richard Cust, of *The English Civil War* (1997), and, with June Hannam and Pauline Stafford, coeditor of *British Women's History, a Bibliographical Guide* (1996).

RIVA KASTORYANO is a researcher at the Centre National de la Recherche Scientifique, Centre d'Études et de Recherches Internationales (CERI), Fondation Nationale des Sciences Politiques. She is the author of *Être Turc en France. Réflexions sur familles et communauté* (1986) and *La France, l'Allemagne et leurs immigrés: Négocier l'identité* (1996), published in English as *Negotiating Identities: States and Immigrants in France and Germany* (2002), and the editor of *Quelle identité pour l'Europe?: Le multiculturalisme à l'épreuve* (1998). She has also published numerous articles on Turkish immigration, including "Paris-Berlin, politique d'immigration et modalité d'intégration des Turcs," in *Les Musulmans dans la société française*, edited by Gilles Kepel and R. Leveau (1988) and "Les émigrés," in *Les Turcs, Orient et Occident, Islam et laïcité*, edited by Stéphane Yerasimos (1994).

LINDA K. KERBER holds a May Brodbeck Liberal Arts chair and is a professor of history at the University of Iowa. She served as president of the American Studies Association in 1988-89 and as president of the Organization of American Historians in 1997-97. Her publications include *Federalists in Dissent: Imagery and Ideology in Jeffersonian America* (1970); *Women of the Republic: Intellect and Ideology in Revolutionary America* (1980-86); *History Will Do It No Justice: Women's Lives in Revolutionary America* (1987); *Toward an Intellectual History of Women: Essays* (1997); and *No Constitutional Right to be Ladies: Women and the Obligations of Citizenship* (1998). She is coeditor, with Jane De Hart-Mathews, of *Women's America: Refocusing the Past* (1982-1987-1991-1995-2000), and, with Alice Kessler-Harris and Kathryn Kish Sklar, of *U.S. History as Women's History: New Feminist Essays* (1995).

MARTINE LAPIED is a professor of modern history at the Université de Provence. Her publications include *Le Comtat et la Révolution française: Naissance des options collectives* (1996) and "Les positions politiques des femmes avignonnaises et comtadines pendant la Révolution," in vol. 1 of *Les femmes et la Révolution française*, edited by Marie-France Brive (1989). She is also coeditor, with François-Xavier Emmanuelli, of *La Provence moderne (1481-1800)* (1991) and, with Geneviève Dermenjian and Jacques Guilhaumou, of *Femmes entre ombre et lumière: Recherches sur la visibilité sociale, XVIᵉ-XXᵉ siècles* (2000). She contributed to the volume *Hommes de Dieu et Révolution en Provence*, edited by Bernard Cousin (1995).

CATHERINE LARRÈRE is a philosopher and professor at the Université Bordeaux III–Michel de Montaigne, where she specializes in moral philosophy and politics. She is the author of *L'invention de l'économie au XVIIIᵉ siècle, Du droit naturel à la physiocratie* (1992) and coauthor, with Raphaël Larrère, of *Du bon usage de la nature: Pour une philosophie de l'environnement* (1997). She has also written extensively on the political theory of the Age of Enlightenment. She is the author of *Actualités de Montesquieu* (1999); coauthor, with Christian Arnsperger and Jean Ladrière, of *Trois essais sur l'éthique économique et sociale* (2001); coeditor, with Catherine Volpilhac-Auger, of *1748, l'année de "L'esprit des lois"* (1999); and, with Jean Mondot, of *Lumières et commerce: L'exemple bordelais* (2000). A member of the Société Montesquieu, she is coeditor, with Catherine Volpilhac-Auger, et al., of a new edition of the *Œuvres complètes de Montesquieu* (2000).

JEAN-JACQUES MARIE is a historian. His publications include *Staline: 1879–1953* (1984); *Le Trotskysme* (1970), which was translated into Italian (1971), Portuguese, Spanish (1972), Swedish (1973), and published in a Brazilian edition (1990); *Trotsky, le Trotskysme et la IVᵉ Internationale* (1980); *Trotsky* (1984, 1998); *Vladimir Vissotsky* (1989); *Les dernier complots de Staline: L'affaire des blouses blanches* (1993); *Les peuples déportés d'Union soviétique* (1996); *La Russie, 1856–1956* (1997); *Staline Joseph Djougachvili* (1998); *Le Goulag* (1999) and *Staline* (2001). He is coeditor, with Carol Head, of *Les nouveaux procès de Moscou, L'Affaire Guinzbourg Galanskov* (1969), and, with Georges Haupt, of *Les Bolcheviks par eux-mêmes* (1969)

HARRIS MEMEL-FOTÊ is an anthropologist and professor emeritus at the Université d'Abidjan in the Ivory Coast. He is a member of the Académie Universelle des Cultures and in 1995–96 held the international chair in the Collège de France, where he delivered the inaugural lesson on 18 December 1995: *L'esclavage lignagier africain et l'anthropologie des droits de l'homme* (published by the Collège de France in 1996). His publications include *Le système politique de Lodjoukrou, une société lignagère à classe d'âge de la Côte d'Ivoire* (1980) and *L'esclavage dans les sociétés lignagères d'Afrique noire. Exemple de la Côte d'Ivoire précoloniale 1700–1920* (1988). He has also written many articles in the fields of social and historical anthropology, including "Les sciences sociales et la notion de civilisation de la femme. Essai sur l'inégalité social des sexes dans les sociétés africaines," in proceedings of a conference entitled *La civilisation de la femme dans la tradition africaine*, Abidjan, Ivory Coast, 1972 (1975). He is the editor of *Les représentations de la santé et de la maladie chez les Ivoiriens* (1998) and coeditor, with Bernard Contamin, of *Le modèle ivoirien en questions: Crises ajustements, recompositions* (1997). On 18 June 1991 he delivered the Marc Bloch Lecture, entitled "Des ancêtres fondateurs aux Pères de la nation," at the École des Hautes Études en Sciences Sociales in Paris.

MARY NASH holds a chair in contemporary history at the University of Barcelona, Spain. She has served as president of the Asociación Española de Investigación de Historia de la Mujeres and codirector of the journal *Arenal, Revista de Historia de las Mujeres*. Her publications include *"Mujeres libres": Espana 1936–1939* (1976) translated into French in 1977; *Mujer y movimiento obrero en España 1931–1939* (1981); *Mujer, familia y trabajo en España, 1875–1936* (1983); *Defying Male Civilization: Women in the Spanish Civil War* (1995); "Two Decades of Women's History in Spain," in *Writing Women's History: International Perspectives*, edited by Karen Offen, Ruth R. Pearson, and Jane Rendall (1991); "Identidad de género, discurso de la domesticidad y la definicion del trabajo de las mujeres en la Espana del siglo XIX" (vol. 4) and "Maternidad, maternologia y reforma eugénica en Espana" (vol. 5) in *Historia de las mujeres en Occidente*, edited by Georges Duby and Michelle Perrot (1993). With Susana Tavera, she is coauthor of *Experiencias desiguales: conflictos sociales y respuestas colectivas (Siglo XIX)* (1994). She is the editor of *Més enlla del silenci: Historia de les dones a Catalunya* (1988); coeditor, with James S. Amelang, of *Historia y género: las mujeres en la Europa moderna y contemporanea* (1990); coeditor, with M. José de la Pascua and Gloria Espigado, of *Pautas históricas de sociabilidad femenina rituales y modelos de representación: Actas del V Coloquio Internacional de la Asociación Española de Investigación Histórica de la Mujeres* (1999); and coeditor, with Diana Marre, of *Multiculturalismos y género: perspectivas interdisciplinarias* (Barcelon, 2001).

CLAUDIA OPITZ holds a doctorate in philosophy and is professor of modern history at the Universität Basle, Switzerland. Her publications include *Evatochter und Braute Christi: Weiblicher Lebenszusammenhang und Frauenkultur im Mittelalter* (1990); *Frauenaltag im Mittelalter: Biographien des 13. Un 14. Jarhunderts* (1991); and *Militarreformen zwischen Burokratisierung und Adelsreaktion: Das franzosische Kriesministerium und seine Reformen im Offizierkorps von 1760–1790* (1994). She is also the author of "Contraintes et libertés (1250–1500)," in *Le Moyen Âge*, edited by Christiane Klapisch-Zuber, vol. 2 of *Histoire des femmes en Occident*, edited by Georges Duby and Michelle Perrot (1992); "Politik und Geselligkeit der Geschlechter in Montesquieu Vom Geist der Gesetze (1748)," in *Ordnung, Politik und Gesellligkeit der Geschlechter im 18. Jahrundert*, edited by Ulricke Weckel et al. (1998); and coauthor, with Hedwig Rocklein and Dieter R. Bauer, of *Maria, Abbild oder Vorbild? Zur Sozialgeschicte mittelalterlicher Marien verehrung* (1990). She is the editor of *Weiblichkeit oder feminismus? Beiträge zur interdisziplinären Frauentagung* (1983) and coeditor, with Ilke Kleinau, of *Geschichte der Mädchen- und Frauenbildung* (1996).

CHRISTINE PINTAT, Assistant Secretary General, Inter–Parliamentary Union, Geneva, Switzerland, is also in charge of the IPU program on the promotion of Partnership between Men and Women and has been the author of, or involved in all IPU's surveys on gender issues in the last twenty years. The first multilateral political institution, the Inter-Parliamentary Union since 1889 has been the nexus for concerted political effort and parliamentary diplomacy among the legislators of political systems throughout the world. Bringing together representatives of every political orientation, the organization provides an observation post of the evolution of political thought. As of June 2000, the Parliaments of 138 sovereign states and five international parliamentary assemblies were cooperating within its structures. One of its permanent programs concerns the promotion of women's rights, with a particular emphasis on women's participation in political life. Recent Inter-Parliamentary Union publications on that topic include: *Inter-Parliamentary Symposium on the Participation of Women in the Political and Parlementary Decision-Making Process: Geneva, 20–24.XI.1989,*

Reports and Conclusions, no. 16 (1989); *Women and Political Power: Survey Carried Out among the 150 National Parliaments Existing as of 31 October 1991*, Reports and Documents, no. 19 (1992); *Plan of Action to Correct Present Imbalances in the Participation of Men and Women in Political Life: adopted by the Inter-Parliamentary Council (Paris 26 March 1994)*, Reports and Documents, no. 22 (1994); *Women in Parliaments, 1945–1995: A World Statistical Survey*, Reports and Documents no. 23 (1995); *Men and Women in Politics: Democracy Still in the Making: A World Comparative Study*, Reports and Documents, no. 28 (1997); *Towards Partnership Between Men and Women in Politics*, Reports and Documents, no. 29 (1997); *Women: What the IPU Is Doing* (1997); *Participation of Women in Political Life: An Assessment of Developments in National Parliaments, Political Parties, Governments and in the Inter-Parliamentary Union, Five Years after the Fourth World Conference on Women* (1999); *Women in Politics: World Biography* (1999); *Politics: Women's Insight*, Reports and Documents, no. 36 (2000); and *Women in Politics 1945–2000*, Reports and Documents, no. 37 (2000).

ANTONIO COSTA PINTO is a professor of contemporary history at the Instituto Superior de Ciências do Trahalho e da Emprasa (ISCTE) in Lisbon, Portugal. His publications include *The Salazar "New State" and European Fascism* (1991); *O Salazarismo e o fascismo europeu: Problemas de interpretacão nas ciencias sociais* (1992), published in English as *Salazar's Dictatorship and European Fascism: Problems and Perspectives of Interpretation* (1994); *Os camisas Azuis: Ideologia, elites e movimentos fascistas em Portugal 1914–1945* (1994), published in English as *The Blue Shirts: Portuguese fascists and the New State* (2000); *O fim do império português: a cena internacional, a guerra colonial, e a descolonização, 1961–1975* (2001). He is coauthor, with Nuno Asonso Ribeiro, of *A Accáo Escolar Vanguarda, 1933–1936: A juventude nacionalista nos primordios do Estado Novo* (1980) and with Nuno S. Teixeira, of *Southern Europe and the Making of the European Union, 1945–1980* (2002), and is the editor of *Modern Portugal* (1998).

JANET POLASKY is a professor of history at the University of New Hampshire. She is the author of *Revolution in Brussels, 1787–1793* (1987), for which she received a prize from the Académie Royale de Belgique; *The Democratic Socialism of Émile Vandervelde: Between Reform and Revolution* (1994), winner of the Prix Pierlot; and *Émile Vandervelde, Le Patron* (1995).

GIOVANNA PROCACCI is a director of research in the Department of Sociology at the University of Milan, Italy. She is the author of *Gouverner la misère: la question sociale en France (1789–1848)* (1993), published in Italian as *Governare la povertà. La società liberale e la nascita della questione sociale* (1998). She has also published numerous articles, including "Du statut de la pauvreté dans les démocraties libérales" in *Face à la pauvreté, l'Occident et les pauvres, hier et aujourd'hui*, edited by François-Xavier Merrien (1994) and "La naissance d'une rationalité moderne de la pauvreté," in *L'exclusion, l'état des savoirs*, edited by Serge Paugam (1996). She is the coeditor, with Nino Salamone, of *Mutamento sociale e identità: la sociologia di fronte alla contemporaneità* (2000).

FLORENCE ROCHEFORT is a historian and researcher at the Centre National de la Recherche Scientifique. She is coauthor, with Laur-

ence Klejman, of *L'égalité en marche: Le féminisme sous la IIIe République* (1989). She has also published numerous articles and essays on feminism and the women's suffrage movement, including "La citoyenneté interdite ou les enjeux du suffragisme," *Vingtième siècle*, no. 42 (1994); "Démocratie féministe contre démocratie exclusive," in *Démocratie et représentation*, edited by Michèle Riot-Sarcey (1995); "La prostituée et l'ouvrière, approches protestantes et catholiques du féminisme sous la IIIe République," in *Femmes et religions*, edited by Françoise Lautman (1997); "L'accès des femmes à la citoyenneté politique dans les sociétés occidentales," in *Féminismes et identités nationales: Les processus d'intégration des femmes au politique*, edited by Yolande Cohen and Françoise Thébaud (1998); "L'anti-féminisme à la Belle-Epoque, une rhétorique réactionnaire," in *Un siècle d'anti-féminisme*, edited by Christine Bard (1999); "Féminisme et protestantisme au XIXe siècle, première rencontre, 1830–1900," *Bulletin de la Société de l'histoire du protestantisme français*, no. 146–1 (2000); and "La séduction résiste-t-elle au féminisme?" in *Séduction et Société: approches historiques*, edited by Arlette Farge and Cécile Dauphin (2001).

JACQUES ROUGERIE is a historian and assistant professor at the Université de Paris I–Panthéon-Sorbonne. His publications include *Procès des Communards* (1964–78); *Paris libre, 1871* (1971); *La Commune, 1871* (1988–92) and *Paris insurgé: La Commune de 1871* (1995). He is coeditor, with Maximilien Rubel, of *La Ire Internationale* (1965), and editor, in collaboration with Tristan Haan, Georges Haupt, and Miklos Molnar, of *1871: Jalons pour une histoire de la Commune de Paris* (1973).

MARIAGRAZIA ROSSILLI is a historian and sociologist. She is the editor of *Gender Policies in the European Union* (2000) and of a special issue of *Europa Europe* (1997), entitled *Le politiche dell'Unione Europea per le donne*. She is also the author of numerous articles on women's history, including "Le sfide della storia delle donne e del genere negli Stati Uniti," *Rivista di storia contemporanea*, no. 1, (1993); and "La politica di uguaglianza dei sessi della Comunità europea: Un bilancio e qualche proposta," Europa Europe 3, nos. 27–28 (1997).

FRANÇOIS ROUQUET holds a doctorate in contemporary history and is an assistant professor at the Université de Rennes I in Rennes, France. He is the author of *Une administration française face à la deuxième Guerre mondiale: Les P. T. T.* (1990); *L'épuration dans l'Administration française, agents de l'État et collaboration ordinaire* (1993); and coeditor, with Danièle Voldman, of *Identités féminines et violences politiques: 1936–1946* (1995).

MAXIMILIEN RUBEL directed the Bibliothèque de la Pléiade edition of the works of Karl Marx: *Économie*, vol. I (1963; 6th edition, 1994); vol. II (1968; 3rd edition, 1979); *Philosophie* (1982); and *Politique*, vol. I (1994). He wrote numerous books on Marx, including *Karl Marx. Pages choisies pour une éthique socialiste* (1948); *Marx liberal* (1956); *Karl Marx, essai de biographie intellectuelle* (1957–71); *Karl Marx devant le bonapartisme* (1960; reprinted in *Karl Marx, Les luttes de classes en France*, edited by Rubel [2000]); *Marx critique du marxisme* (1974–2000); *Marx, Life and Works* (1980); and *Marx, théoricien de l'anarchisme* (1983). He was also the author of *Josef W. Stalin in Selbstzeugnissen und Bilddokumenten* (1975; 7th edition, 1994); *Guerre et paix nucléaires* (1997);

coauthor, with Margaret Manale, of *Marx without Myth: A Chronological Study of His Life and Work* (1975); and coauthor, with John Crump, of *Non-Market Socialism in the Nineteenth and Twentieth Centuries* (1987). With Jacques Rougerie, he coedited *La Iʳᵉ Internationale* (1965). Joseph O'Malley and Keith Algozin edited *Rubel on Karl Marx: Five Essays* (1981). From 1959 to 1994 Maximilien Rubel was director of Marxist studies at the *Cahiers de ISMEA* (Institut des Sciences Mathématiques, Économiques et Appliquées, Paris).

ODILE RUDELLE is a director of research at the Centre National de la Recherche Scientifique, Fondation Nationale des Sciences Politiques, in the Centre d'Étude de la Vie Politique Française (CEVIPOF). Her publications include *La République absolue. Aux origines de l'instabilité constitutionnelle de la France républicaine, 1870–1889,* (1982, 1986); *Mai 58, de Gaulle et la République* (1988); *De Gaulle pour mémoire* (1990); and "Légicentrisme républicain," in *Le siècle de l'avènement républicain* edited by François Furet and Mona Ozouf (1993). She is the editor of *La République des citoyens: Jules Ferry* (1996); coeditor, with Jacques Delarue, of *L'Attentat du Petit-Clamart: Vers la révision de la Constitution* (1990) and, with Serge Berstein, of *Le modèle républicain* (1992). She has also written numerous articles on women's suffrage, including "Le vote des femmes et la fin de l'exception française," *Vingtième siècle,* no. 42 (1994).

GORDON SCHOCHET is a professor of political science at Rutgers University. He is one of the founders of the Center for the History of British Political Thought at the Folger Shakespeare Library in Washington, D.C., and has been the editor of the center's *Proceedings* (1990–94). He is also a founding member of the Conference for the Study of Political Thought and a member of the North American Conference on British Studies. His publications include "Thomas Hobbes on the Family and the State of Nature," *Political Science Quarterly,* no. 82, (1967); *Life, Liberty, and Property, Essays on Locke's Political Ideas* (1971); *Patriarchalism in Political Thought* (1975); *The Authoritarian Family and Political Attitude in 17th Century England: Patriarchalism in Political Thought* (1988); "Intending (Political) Obligation: Hobbes on the Voluntary Basis of Society," in *Thomas Hobbes and Political Theory,* edited by Mary Dietz (1990); and "The Significant Sounds of Silence: The Absence of Women from the Political Thought of Sir Robert Filmer and John Locke (or, 'Why can't a woman be more like a man?')," in *Women Writers and the Early Modern British Political Tradition,* edited by Hilda L. Smith, (1998). He is also coeditor, with Richard W. Wilson, of *Moral Development and Politics* (1980), and, with J.G.A. Pocock and Lois G. Schwoerer, of *The Varieties of British Political Thought, 1500–1800* (1993).

BRIGITTE STUDER is a professor of contemporary history at the Universität Bern, Switzerland, and has done research on the history of Communism and Stalinism, gender and the welfare, women and work, citizenship, gender and the labor movement, and the theory of gender history. Her most recent publications include "Citizenship as Contingent National Belonging: Married Women and Foreigners in Twentieth-Century Switzerland," *Gender and History* 13, no. 3 (2001) and a study with Berthold Unfried on the formation of Stalinist party cadres in the Soviet Union, entitled *Der stalinistiche Parteikader. Identitätsstiftende Praktiken und Diskurse in der Sow-*

jetunion der dreissiger Jahre (2001). She is also coauthor, with Regina Wecker and Gaby Sutter, of *Die schutzbedürftige Frau. Zur Konstruktion von Geschlecht durch Mutterschaftsversicherung, Nachtarbeitsverbot un Sonderschutzgesetzgebung* (2001), and coeditor, with Rudolf Jaun, of *Weiblich, männlich: Geschlechterverhältnisse in der Schweiz: Rechtsprechung, diskurs, Praktiken—Féminin, masculin: rapports sociaux de sexes en Suisse: législation, discours, pratiques* (1995).

RITA THALMANN is a historian and professor emerita. She heads the Centre d'Études et de Recherche Intereuropéennes contemporaines (CERIC) at the Université de Paris VII–Denis Diderot. Her publications include *La nuit de cristal* (1972), written with Emmanuel Feinermann, which has been published in English as *Crystal Night, 9–10 November 1938* (1974) and in German as *Die Kristallnacht* (1987, 1994); *Jochen Klepper: Ein Leben Zwischen Idyllen un Katastrophen (biographie)* (1976–77–92); *Protestantisme et nationalisme en Allemagne de 1900 à 1945* (1976); *Être femme sous le IIIᵉ Reich* (1982), which has been published in German as *Frausein im Dritten Reich* (1984, 1987); *La République de Weimar* (1986, 1995), published in Portuguese (1986) and Italian (1995); and *La mise au pas: Idéologie et stratégie sécuritaire dans la France occupée* (1991), winner of the 1986 prize from the Académie des Sciences Morales et Politiques of the Institut de France. She is the editor of *Femmes et fascismes* (1986), translated into Japanese in 1990; and *Entre émancipation et nationalisme: La presse féminine d'Europe 1914–1945 (La tentation nationaliste)* (1990). In 1985 she was awarded the Prix Antiraciste Bernard Lecache for her work as a whole. Two works have been published in honor of Rita Thalmann: *Nationalismes, féminismes, exclusions: mélanges en l'honneur de Rita Thalmann,* edited by Liliane Crips (1994) and *Féminisme et nazisme: en hommage à Rita Thalmann,* edited by Liliane Kandel (1997).

ÉLÉNI VARIKAS is a historian and assistant professor of political science at the Université de Paris VIII. Her 1986 Ph.D. dissertation at the Université de Paris VIII, "La Révolte des dames. Genèse d'une conscience féministe dans la grèce au XIXᵉ siècle (1833–1908)," was published in Greek in 1987. In Greek, she has written numerous books and studies about women in 19th-century Greece, including *Me diaphoretiko prosopo: phylo, diaphora, kai oikoumenikot ēa* (2000). Other publications include "Gender and National Identity in *Fin de siècle* Greece," *Gender and History* 5, no. 2 (1993); "Les longues robes de l'esclavage: stratégies privées et publiques dans le journal d'une recluse," *Les Cahiers du CEDREF,* no. 1 (1989); "Question nationale et égalité des sexes," *Peuples méditerranéens,* no. 50 (1990); and "Légitimation de la domination et pouvoir légitime dans la théorie politique classique," in *L'invention du naturel, les sciences et la fabrication du masculin et du féminin,* edited Delphine Gardey and Ilana Lowy (2000).In French, she reedited Olympe de Gouges's piece, *L'esclavage des Noirs* (1989) and is coeditor with Françoise Collin and Evelyne Pisier, of *Les femmes, de Platon à Derrida: Anthologie critique* (2000).

JUDITH VEGA teaches social and political philosophy at the Rijkuniversiteit Groningen, the Netherlands. She is the author of *Inventing Enlightenment's Gender: The Representation of Modernity in Dispute* (1998), and has also published numerous articles on 18th-century women's history and on political philosophy during the Age of Enlightenment, including "Feminist Republicanism: Etta

Palm-Aelders on Justice, Virtue and Men," *History of European Ideas* 10, no. 3 (1989; special issue on *Women and the French Revolution*); "Luxury, Necessity, or the Morality of Men. The Republican Discourse of Etta Palm Aelders," in vol. 1 of *Les femmes et la Révolution française*, edited by Marie-France Brive (1989); "Etta Palm, une Hollandaise à Paris," in *Le voyage révolutionnaire*, edited by Willem Frijhoff and Rudolf Dekker (1991); "Feminist Discourses in the Dutch Republic at the End of the Eighteenth Century," in *Journal of Women's History* 8, no. 2 (1996); "Sade's libertijnse repiblick. Over pornografische parabels en esthetische politiek," *Jaarboek voor Vrouwengeschiedenis* 20–109 (2000); "Feminist Republicanism and the Political Perception of Gender," in *Republicanism, a Shared European Heritage*, edited by Martin Van Gelderen and Quentin Skinner (2002).

CLAUDIE WEILL is a researcher at the École des Hautes Études en Sciences Sociales (EHESS) in Paris. Her publications include *Marxistes russes et social-démocratie allemande 1898–1904* (1977);

*L'Internationale et l'autre: Les relations inter-ethniques dans la II*ᵉ *Internationale* (1987); and *Étudiants russes en Allemagne, 1900–1914, quand la Russie frappait aux portes de l'Europe* (1996). She is coauthor, with George Haupt and Michael Lowy, of *Les marxistes et la question nationale, 1848–1914* (1974); with Irène Petit and Gilbert Badia, of *Vive la lutte 1891–1914, Rosa Luxemburg* (1975); with Georges Haupt, Gilbert Badia, and Irène Petit, of *J'étais, je suis, je serai! Correspondance 1914–1919, Rosa Luxemburg* (1977); and coeditor, with Gilbert Badia, of *Rosa Luxembourg aujourd'hui, Colloque Paris, 30–31 mai 1983* (1986). With Yolande Cohen, she coedited a special issue of the journal *Mouvement social* entitled *Entre socialisme et nationalisme: Les mouvements étudiants en Europe* (1982) and a special issue of the review *L'Homme et la Société* entitled *Générations et mémoires* (1994). She has recently edited *La question nationale et l'autonomie, Rosa Luxemburg* (2001); *Rosa Luxemburg, lettres à Sophie 1916–1918* (2002); and a new edition of a volume of Rosa Luxemburg's political writings, *Sur la révolution: Écrits politiques, 1917–1918* (2002).

INDEX OF PROPER NAMES